ALSO BY AMERICA'S TEST KITCHEN

The New Essentials Cookbook

Cook's Illustrated Revolutionary Recipes

Tasting Italy: A Culinary Journey

Spiced

How to Braise Everything

How to Roast Everything

Dinner Illustrated

The Complete Diabetes Cookbook

The Complete Slow Cooker

The Complete Make-Ahead Cookbook

The Complete Mediterranean Cookbook

The Complete Vegetarian Cookbook

The Complete Cooking for Two Cookbook

Cooking at Home with Bridget and Julia

Just Add Sauce

Nutritious Delicious

What Good Cooks Know

Cook's Science

The Science of Good Cooking

The Perfect Cake

The Perfect Cookie

Bread Illustrated

Master of the Grill

Kitchen Smarts

Kitchen Hacks

100 Recipes: The Absolute Best Ways to Make the
True Essentials

The New Family Cookbook

The America's Test Kitchen Cooking School Cookbook

The Cook's Illustrated Baking Book

The Cook's Illustrated Meat Book

The Cook's Illustrated Cookbook

The America's Test Kitchen Family Baking Book

The Best of America's Test Kitchen (2007–2019 Editions)

The Complete America's Test Kitchen TV Show
Cookbook 2001–2019

Cook It in Your Dutch Oven

Air Fryer Perfection

Sous Vide for Everybody

Multicooker Perfection

Food Processor Perfection

Pressure Cooker Perfection

Vegan for Everybody

Naturally Sweet

Foolproof Preserving

Paleo Perfected

The How Can It Be Gluten-Free Cookbook: Volume 2

The How Can It Be Gluten-Free Cookbook

The Best Mexican Recipes

Slow Cooker Revolution Volume 2: The Easy-Prep Edition

Slow Cooker Revolution

The Six-Ingredient Solution

The America's Test Kitchen D.I.Y. Cookbook

The Cook's Illustrated All-Time Best Series

All-Time Best Brunch

All-Time Best Dinners for Two

All-Time Best Sunday Suppers

All-Time Best Holiday Entertaining

All-Time Best Appetizers

All-Time Best Soups

Cook's Country Titles

One-Pan Wonders

Cook It in Cast Iron

The Complete Cook's Country TV Show Cookbook

For a Full Listing of All Our Books

CooksIllustrated.com

AmericasTestKitchen.com

PRAISE FOR AMERICA'S TEST KITCHEN TITLES

"This impressive installment from America's Test Kitchen equips readers with dozens of repertoire-worthy recipes. . . . This is a must-have for beginner cooks and more experienced ones who wish to sharpen their skills."
PUBLISHERS WEEKLY (STARRED REVIEW) ON *THE NEW ESSENTIALS COOKBOOK*

"Diabetics and all health-conscious home cooks will find great information on almost every page."
BOOKLIST (STARRED REVIEW) ON *THE COMPLETE DIABETES COOKBOOK*

Selected as one of Amazon's Best Books of 2015 in the Cookbooks and Food Writing category
AMAZON ON *THE COMPLETE VEGETARIAN COOKBOOK*

Selected as the Cookbook Award Winner of 2017 in the Baking category
INTERNATIONAL ASSOCIATION OF CULINARY PROFESSIONALS (IACP) ON *BREAD ILLUSTRATED*

Selected as one of the 10 Best New Cookbooks of 2017
THE LA TIMES ON *THE PERFECT COOKIE*

"*The Perfect Cookie* . . . is, in a word, perfect. This is an important and substantial cookbook. . . . If you love cookies, but have been a tad shy to bake on your own, all your fears will be dissipated. This is one book you can use for years with magnificently happy results."
THE HUFFINGTON POST ON *THE PERFECT COOKIE*

"The book offers an impressive education for curious cake makers, new and experienced alike. A summation of 25 years of cake making at ATK, there are cakes for every taste."
THE WALL STREET JOURNAL ON *THE PERFECT CAKE*

"This book upgrades slow cooking for discriminating, 21st-century palates—that is indeed revolutionary."
THE DALLAS MORNING NEWS ON *SLOW COOKER REVOLUTION*

"Some 2,500 photos walk readers through 600 painstakingly tested recipes, leaving little room for error."
ASSOCIATED PRESS ON *THE AMERICA'S TEST KITCHEN COOKING SCHOOL COOKBOOK*

"This book is a comprehensive, no-nonsense guide . . . a well-thought-out, clearly explained primer for every aspect of home baking."
THE WALL STREET JOURNAL ON *THE COOK'S ILLUSTRATED BAKING BOOK*

"This encyclopedia of meat cookery would feel completely overwhelming if it weren't so meticulously organized and artfully designed. This is *Cook's Illustrated* at its finest."
THE KITCHN ON *THE COOK'S ILLUSTRATED MEAT BOOK*

"Some books impress by the sheer audacity of their ambition. Backed up by the magazine's famed mission to test every recipe relentlessly until it is the best it can be, this nearly 900-page volume lands with an authoritative wallop."
CHICAGO TRIBUNE ON *THE COOK'S ILLUSTRATED COOKBOOK*

"The 21st-century *Fannie Farmer Cookbook* or *The Joy of Cooking*. If you had to have one cookbook and that's all you could have, this one would do it."
CBS SAN FRANCISCO ON *THE NEW FAMILY COOKBOOK*

"The go-to gift book for newlyweds, small families, or empty nesters."
ORLANDO SENTINEL ON *THE COMPLETE COOKING FOR TWO COOKBOOK*

"The sum total of exhaustive experimentation . . . anyone interested in gluten-free cookery simply shouldn't be without it."
NIGELLA LAWSON ON *THE HOW CAN IT BE GLUTEN-FREE COOKBOOK*

"A one-volume kitchen seminar, addressing in one smart chapter after another the sometimes surprising whys behind a cook's best practices. . . . You get the myth, the theory, the science, and the proof, all rigorously interrogated as only America's Test Kitchen can do."
NPR ON *THE SCIENCE OF GOOD COOKING*

"It's all about technique and timing, and the ATK crew delivers their usual clear instructions to ensure success. . . . The thoughtful balance of practicality and imagination will inspire readers of all tastes and skill levels."
PUBLISHERS WEEKLY (STARRED REVIEW) ON *HOW TO ROAST EVERYTHING*

vegetables ILLUSTRATED

An Inspiring Guide with 700+ Kitchen-Tested Recipes

AMERICA'S TEST KITCHEN

Library of Congress Cataloging-in-Publication Data

Names: America's Test Kitchen (Firm)
Title: Vegetables illustrated : an inspiring guide with 700+ kitchen-tested recipes / America's Test Kitchen.
Description: [Boston] : America's Test Kitchen, [2019] | Includes index.
Identifiers: LCCN 2018048691 | ISBN 9781945256738 (hardcover)
Subjects: LCSH: Cooking (Vegetables) | Cookbooks.
Classification: LCC TX801 .A64 2019 | DDC 641.6/5--dc23
LC record available at https://lccn.loc.gov/2018048691

AMERICA'S
TEST KITCHEN ®

America's Test Kitchen
21 Drydock Avenue, Boston, MA 02210
Manufactured in the United States of America
10 9 8 7 6 5 4 3 2 1

Distributed by Penguin Random House Publisher Services
Tel: 800.733.3000

Pictured on front cover, clockwise from top left **Crispy Thai Eggplant Salad (page 183), Grilled Artichokes with Lemon Butter (page 6), Baguette with Radishes, Butter, and Herbs (page 368), Blistered Shishito Peppers (page 141), Beet and Carrot Noodle Salad (page 40), Vietnamese Pork Banh Mi (page 372)**

Pictured on frontispiece **Roasted Radishes with Yogurt-Tahini Sauce (page 366)**

Pictured on back cover **Teriyaki Stir-Fried Garlic Scapes with Chicken (page 230)**

Editorial Director, Books **Elizabeth Carduff**
Executive Food Editor **Dan Zuccarello**
Deputy Food Editor **Stephanie Pixley**
Project Editor **Valerie Cimino**
Senior Editor **Leah Colins**
Associate Editors **Timothy Chin and Lawman Johnson**
Test Cook **Katherine Perry**
Assistant Editor **Kelly Gauthier**
Art Director, Books **Lindsey Chandler**
Deputy Art Directors **Allison Boales and Courtney Lentz**
Associate Art Director **Katie Barranger**
Photography Director **Julie Bozzo Cote**
Photography Producer **Meredith Mulcahy**
Senior Staff Photographer **Daniel J. van Ackere**
Staff Photographers **Steve Klise and Kevin White**
Additional Photography **Keller + Keller and Carl Tremblay**
Food Styling **Catrine Kelty, Chantal Lambeth, Kendra McKnight, Marie Piraino, Elle Simone Scott, and Sally Staub**
Photoshoot Kitchen Team
    Photo Team and Special Events Manager **Timothy McQuinn**
    Lead Test Cook **Jessica Rudolph**
    Assistant Test Cooks **Sarah Ewald, Eric Haessler, and Devon Shatkin**
Illustration **John Burgoyne**
Illustration on page 89 **Jay Layman**
Senior Manager, Publishing Operations **Taylor Argenzio**
Production Manager **Christine Spanger**
Imaging Manager **Lauren Robbins**
Production and Imaging Specialists **Dennis Noble and Jessica Voas**
Copy Editor **Cheryl Redmond**
Proofreader **Patricia Jalbert-Levine**
Indexer **Elizabeth Parson**

Chief Creative Officer **Jack Bishop**
Executive Editorial Directors **Julia Collin Davison and Bridget Lancaster**

CONTENTS

List of Recipes

Welcome to America's Test Kitchen

This book has been tested, written, and edited by the folks at America's Test Kitchen. Located in Boston's Seaport District in the historic Innovation and Design Building, it features 15,000 square feet of kitchen space, including multiple photography and video studios. It is the home of *Cook's Illustrated* magazine and *Cook's Country* magazine and is the workday destination for more than 60 test cooks, editors, and cookware specialists. Our mission is to test recipes over and over again until we understand how and why they work and until we arrive at the best version.

We start the process of testing a recipe with a complete lack of preconceptions, which means that we accept no claim, no technique, and no recipe at face value. We simply assemble as many variations as possible, test a half-dozen of the most promising, and taste the results blind. We then construct our own recipe and continue to test it, varying ingredients, techniques, and cooking times until we reach a consensus. As we

like to say in the test kitchen, "We make the mistakes so you don't have to." The result, we hope, is the best version of a particular recipe, but we realize that only you can be the final judge of our success (or failure). We use the same rigorous approach when we test equipment and taste ingredients.

All of this would not be possible without a belief that good cooking, much like good music, is based on a foundation of objective technique. Some people like spicy foods and others don't, but there is a right way to sauté, there is a best way to cook a pot roast, and there are measurable scientific principles involved in producing perfectly beaten, stable egg whites. Our ultimate goal is to investigate the fundamental principles of cooking to give you the techniques, tools, and ingredients you need to become a better cook. It is as simple as that.

To see what goes on behind the scenes at America's Test Kitchen, check out our social media channels for kitchen snapshots, exclusive content, video tips, and much more. You can watch us work (in our actual test kitchen) by tuning in to *America's Test Kitchen* or *Cook's Country* on public television or on our websites. Listen in to test kitchen experts on public radio (SplendidTable.org) to hear insights that illuminate the truth about real home cooking. Want to hone your cooking skills or finally learn how to bake— with an America's Test Kitchen test cook? Enroll in one of our online cooking classes. However you choose to visit us, we welcome you into our kitchen, where you can stand by our side as we test our way to the best recipes in America.

facebook.com/AmericasTestKitchen
twitter.com/TestKitchen
youtube.com/AmericasTestKitchen
instagram.com/TestKitchen
pinterest.com/TestKitchen
google.com/+AmericasTestKitchen

AmericasTestKitchen.com
CooksIllustrated.com

Introduction

Welcome to a whole new way with vegetables. With this fresh, modern guide as your kitchen companion, you can turn any vegetable into a culinary superstar, shining the spotlight on it in every dish you make.

And that spotlight is well deserved. In addition to being delicious and healthful, so many vegetables are a treat for the eyes! There's drop-dead gorgeous radicchio, with its deep burgundy head streaked with white. Or consider romanesco, downright architectural in its fractal beauty and chartreuse color. Frisée is the wild child of the salad green family, with a profusion of feathery fronds. And don't get us started on all the shapes, sizes, and shades of heirloom tomatoes. We found so much to inspire us in the kitchen while creating this book, and we're passing everything we learned along to you.

We're always on the hunt for more interesting and tempting ways to eat our veggies, to add new and varied vegetable-based recipes to our repertoire. Everyone wants to avoid getting stuck in a rut, offering up the same old steamed broccoli or boring baked potatoes night after night. We are all seeking healthy food that is easy to prepare—and that's so delicious it will have everyone who sits down at the dinner table asking for seconds.

This comprehensive collection delivers the goods. It's jam-packed with more than 700 kitchen-tested recipes that will expand your cooking horizons in all directions. No matter your skill level, you'll find recipes here to embrace and enjoy. Even vegetables that might not be familiar to you are much more user-friendly in the kitchen than they appear at first glance—as we discovered ourselves when developing these recipes.

To make this book easy to navigate, we've organized it alphabetically by vegetable, from artichokes to zucchini. Each chapter opens with an introduction to the vegetable, along with a host of shopping and storage tips and secrets, the newest information on different veggie varieties, and the best prep techniques. Then, for the recipes, there are simple side dishes that belong in everyone's back pocket; special-occasion-worthy sides; elegant appetizers and fun party foods; snacks to suit everybody; salads both side and main; nourishing soups and stews; main courses that may (or may not) include meat, poultry, or seafood; and even some baked goods.

One of our primary goals in creating this kitchen companion was to showcase the versatility of vegetables—in both expected and unexpected ways. For instance, we went through hundreds

of ears of corn until we found the formula for perfectly plump, tender-crisp kernels, whether you prefer stovetop Foolproof Boiled Corn or smoky Husk-Grilled Corn. We made our kitchens thoroughly pink-stained and messy so that you wouldn't have to, testing until we found the very best way to prepare intensely sweet Roasted Beets. We glued the insides of our mouths together with pounds and pounds of gummy potatoes until we achieved mashed-potato perfection (both on the stovetop and in the slow cooker).

Along the way, we learned some surprising new tricks for reinvigorating our favorite vegetables. We tinkered with a typical preparation technique for meat to create perfectly seasoned Brined Grilled Carrots with Cilantro-Yogurt Sauce. We adapted a traditional Chinese preparation method to make Smashed Sichuan Cucumbers. We oven-roasted green beans until they were charred and caramelized (you'll want to eat them like French fries), and we stewed them in a garlicky Mediterranean tomato sauce until they were meltingly tender.

We also developed plenty of innovative new dishes using the ever-expanding variety of produce found at farmers' markets and specialty grocers. Teriyaki Stir-Fried Garlic Scapes with Chicken showcases the mild flavor and crisp-tender texture of garlic scapes in a superfast main course. Grilled Ramps is a foolproof way to make the most of tender seasonal wild greens. Fiddlehead Panzanella elevates baby ferns into a hearty dinner salad. And we didn't leave out sea vegetables, which are so readily available nowadays. Nori, ground to a powder, blankets our seared Nori-Crusted Salmon, for a deeply flavorful dish that tastes like the essence of the ocean.

Many of the chapters include a special feature called Vegetables Reimagined, with photographs and instructions that walk you step by step through a highlighted recipe chosen for its original technique. For example, you can transform humble parsnips into a rich, spice-infused hummus through the magic of the microwave. And you'll discover how to char avocado slices in a skillet to make a smoky, creamy relish for turkey burgers. You'll learn to oven-roast fennel wedges low and slow in seasoned olive oil for a silky-textured side dish that's perfect with a holiday roast.

We hope you'll be as inspired in your kitchen by these recipes as we were in our kitchens while creating them. Whether you already enjoy vegetables every day, or you're trying to convince your children or other family members to eat them more often, or you're seeking more tempting and delicious ways to prepare them, *Vegetables Illustrated* will be your go-to kitchen essential for years to come.

ARTICHOKES

Artichokes are beautiful and sculptural, and also somewhat mysterious and forbidding. But they are far more user-friendly in the kitchen than they may appear at first glance.

Artichokes are the immature flower buds of a perennial plant in the thistle family. These dramatic plants can grow quite large, reaching up to 6 feet in diameter and 3 to 4 feet in height. The vegetables are commonly marketed in three sizes: small (2 to 4 ounces), medium (8 to 10 ounces), and large (12 ounces or more). Curiously, different-size artichokes simultaneously bud on the same plant; those that grow on the center stalk are the largest, and the smallest grow at the juncture between the plant's leaves and the stem.

We like medium artichokes best for braising, roasting, and grilling. They are easy to prepare, and one artichoke conveniently serves one person.

We prefer to halve them for even cooking, as in our Braised Artichokes with Tomatoes and Thyme and Grilled Artichokes with Lemon Butter. We also enjoy stuffing whole artichokes, which makes for a dramatic presentation that's wonderful for entertaining. Small artichokes are perfect for frying, and in this chapter you'll find Jewish-Style Fried Artichokes, a classic Roman preparation. The small ones are also best for making tender marinated artichokes, a far more flavorful option than mushy store-bought marinated artichokes.

Ninety percent of the work that goes into preparing most artichoke dishes is cleaning the artichokes. By the time you've finished trimming away the inedible parts, it may seem like you're throwing away more of the vegetable than you're keeping! But it's well worth it to peel back those layers to discover the hidden, delicious inner edible portions.

shopping and storage

While you will see artichokes throughout most of the year, springtime is high season. Then, artichokes of all sizes are widely available. When selecting fresh artichokes, look for leaves that are tight, compact, and bright green. If you give an artichoke a squeeze, its leaves should squeak as they rub together (evidence that the artichoke still possesses much of its moisture). The leaves should also snap off cleanly. If the leaves bend rather than snap, or if they appear dried out or feathery at the edges, the artichoke is over the hill.

Because fresh artichokes are limited by seasonality, we often turn to prepared artichokes. When buying them, avoid pre-marinated versions; we prefer to control the seasonings ourselves. We also don't recommend canned hearts, which tend to taste waterlogged and have tough leaves. Smaller whole jarred artichoke hearts, labeled "baby" or "cocktail," are best. We have noted recipes in which frozen artichoke hearts are acceptable to use.

Artichokes will keep in the refrigerator for up to five days if sprinkled lightly with water and stored in a zipper-lock plastic bag.

vegetable science
Why Do Artichokes Turn Brown?
Artichokes are rich in phenolic compounds. When the cell walls of artichokes are cut or crushed, enzymes (polyphenol oxidase) in their tissues are exposed to oxygen and react with those phenols, producing unattractive black- or brown-colored pigments. Rubbing the exposed ends with acid slows the rate of browning. We found that vinegar (which is high in acetic acid) and parsley (which is high in ascorbic acid) each minimized darkening when added to cooking water. But lemon juice (which contains both citric and ascorbic acids) proved far more effective, limiting this enzymatic reaction almost completely.

anatomy of an artichoke

What's Edible and What's Not?
The entire exterior of the artichoke (including several layers of leaves), as well as the fuzzy choke and tiny pointy leaves at the center, cannot be eaten. The tender inner heart, leaves, and stem are entirely edible. The cooked heart can be eaten with a knife and fork. To eat the tough outer leaves, use your teeth to scrape the flesh from the underside of each leaf.

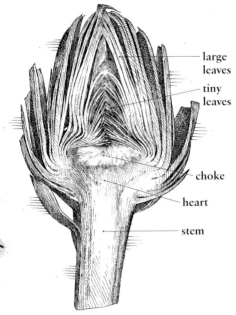

large leaves

tiny leaves

choke

heart

stem

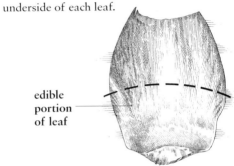

edible portion of leaf

vegetable prep

Preparing Fresh Artichokes

1. Cut off top quarter of artichoke with chef's knife.

2. Break and pull off bottom outer leaves by pulling downward on them.

3. Trim top portion of outer leaves with kitchen shears.

4. Either trim stem and base or, if called for, peel stem.

5. Cut artichoke in half lengthwise and scoop out choke using small spoon.

6. Submerge prepared artichokes in lemon water to prevent them from turning brown.

Roasted Artichokes with
Lemon Vinaigrette

ROASTED ARTICHOKES WITH LEMON VINAIGRETTE

Serves 4   Total time: 1 hour

WHY THIS RECIPE WORKS *Roasting artichokes concentrates their delicate, nutty flavor. We prepped the artichokes for the oven by trimming the leaves, halving the artichokes, and removing the fuzzy chokes. Submerging the prepped artichokes in water and lemon juice kept them from oxidizing, and tossing them with oil and roasting cut side down encouraged browning. Because they have so much surface area, artichokes can dry out and toughen in the oven, so we covered them to let them steam and tenderize in their own juice. The fresh tang of citrus pairs well with artichokes' earthy flavor, so we roasted some halved lemons alongside the artichokes and used the deeply flavorful juice in a vinaigrette. We whisked the juice with garlic and Dijon before drizzling in and emulsifying some olive oil to create a bright, intense dressing. If your artichokes are larger than 8 to 10 ounces, strip away another layer or two of the toughest outer leaves. A rasp-style grater makes quick work of turning the garlic into a paste. Serve these either warm or at room temperature.*

- 3 lemons
- 4 artichokes (8 to 10 ounces each)
- 9 tablespoons extra-virgin olive oil
     Salt and pepper
- 2 teaspoons chopped fresh parsley
- 1 small garlic clove, minced to paste
- ½ teaspoon Dijon mustard

1. Adjust oven rack to lower-middle position and heat oven to 475 degrees. Cut 1 lemon in half, squeeze halves into container filled with 2 quarts water, then add spent halves. Working with 1 artichoke at a time, trim stem to about ¾ inch and cut off top quarter of artichoke. Break off bottom 3 or 4 rows of tough outer leaves by pulling them downward. Using kitchen shears, trim off top portion of outer leaves. Using paring knife, trim outer layer of stem and base, removing any dark green parts. Cut artichoke in half lengthwise, then remove fuzzy choke and any tiny inner purple-tinged leaves using small spoon. Submerge prepped artichokes in lemon water.

2. Coat bottom of 13 by 9-inch baking dish with 1 tablespoon oil. Remove artichokes from lemon water, shaking off excess water. Toss artichokes with 2 tablespoons oil, ¾ teaspoon salt, and pinch pepper; gently rub oil and seasonings between leaves. Arrange artichokes cut side down in prepared dish. Trim ends of remaining 2 lemons, halve crosswise, and arrange cut side up next to artichokes in dish. Cover tightly with aluminum foil and roast until cut sides of artichokes begin to brown and bases and leaves are tender when poked with tip of paring knife, 25 to 30 minutes.

3. Transfer artichokes to serving platter. Let lemons cool slightly, then squeeze into fine-mesh strainer set over bowl, extracting as much juice and pulp as possible; press firmly on solids to yield 1½ tablespoons juice. Whisk parsley, garlic, mustard, and ½ teaspoon salt into juice. Whisking constantly, slowly drizzle in remaining 6 tablespoons oil until emulsified. Season with salt and pepper to taste. Serve artichokes with dressing.

ROMAN-STYLE STUFFED BRAISED ARTICHOKES

Serves 4   Total time: 1 hour 30 minutes

WHY THIS RECIPE WORKS *For this traditional Italian dish, we wanted a bright, robust stuffing, which we achieved with a blend of minced fresh parsley and mint, garlic, lemon zest, and bread crumbs moistened with extra-virgin olive oil. The stuffing infused the artichokes with flavor as they braised. Cooking the artichokes took little more than half an hour in a large Dutch oven filled with just enough water to cover the stems three-quarters of the way. (Any more liquid made for sodden stems and a gummy filling.) To prevent the uncooked filling from spilling out, we placed each artichoke stem end down into a thickly cut onion ring. For even cooking, we then rotated the artichokes at the midway point so that the stem ends were facing up. Serve each artichoke with a spoon so that diners can coax out the stuffing. If your artichokes are larger than 8 to 10 ounces, strip away another layer or two of the toughest outer leaves.*

- 1 slice hearty white sandwich bread, crust removed, cut into ½-inch pieces
- 1 lemon
- 4 artichokes (8 to 10 ounces each)
- ½ cup extra-virgin olive oil
- ¼ cup minced fresh parsley, stems reserved
- ¼ cup minced fresh mint
- 4 garlic cloves, minced
     Salt and pepper
- 1 onion, cut crosswise into ½-inch-thick slices and separated into rings

1. Pulse bread in food processor to fine crumbs, about 10 pulses; transfer to medium bowl. Grate 1 tablespoon zest from lemon and add to bowl; set aside. Cut lemon in half, squeeze halves into container filled with 2 quarts water, then add spent halves.

2. Working with 1 artichoke at a time, trim end of stem and cut off top quarter of artichoke. Break off tough outer leaves by pulling them downward until only light-colored core remains. Using kitchen shears, trim off top portion of outer leaves. Using paring knife, trim stem and base, removing any dark green parts. Spread leaves to reveal fuzzy choke at center. Using spoon, remove fuzzy choke. Rinse artichoke well, then submerge prepped artichoke in lemon water.

3. Add oil, parsley leaves, mint, garlic, and ½ teaspoon salt to bowl with bread crumbs and stir until well combined; season with pepper to taste. Using small spoon, divide filling evenly among artichokes, placing it in center of artichoke, where choke was.

4. Spread onion rings evenly over bottom of Dutch oven. Sprinkle reserved parsley stems and ¼ teaspoon salt over onion rings. Set artichokes stem ends down into onion rings. Fill pot with enough cold water so that stems are three-quarters submerged.

5. Cover and bring to boil over medium-high heat. Reduce heat to medium-low and simmer for 15 minutes. Using tongs, rotate artichokes so stem ends face up, using tongs to keep filling in place. Cover and cook until tip of paring knife is easily inserted into artichoke heart, about 15 minutes longer. Transfer artichokes to serving platter. Serve.

BRAISED ARTICHOKES WITH TOMATOES AND THYME

Serves 4   Total time: 55 minutes

WHY THIS RECIPE WORKS *Gently braising artichokes and creating a flavorful sauce at the same time keeps the focus on the flavor of these seasonal gems. We used white wine and chicken broth to impart acidity and depth of flavor. Subtle thyme complemented the artichokes' delicate flavor, and anchovies amplified the savory qualities. Canned tomatoes are common in braises, but tasters detected an unpleasant metallic note; replacing them with halved cherry tomatoes at the end of cooking preserved the brightness of the sauce and added welcome splashes of color. If your artichokes are larger than 8 to 10 ounces, strip away another layer or two of the toughest outer leaves.*

- 1   lemon, halved
- 4   artichokes (8 to 10 ounces each)
- 2   tablespoons extra-virgin olive oil
- 1   onion, chopped fine
      Salt and pepper
- 3   garlic cloves, minced
- 2   anchovy fillets, rinsed, patted dry, and minced
- 1   teaspoon minced fresh thyme or ¼ teaspoon dried
- ½   cup dry white wine
- 1   cup chicken broth
- 6   ounces cherry tomatoes, halved
- 2   tablespoons chopped fresh parsley

1. Squeeze lemon halves into container filled with 2 quarts water, then add spent halves. Working with 1 artichoke at a time, trim stem to about ¾ inch and cut off top quarter of artichoke. Break off bottom 3 or 4 rows of tough outer leaves by pulling them downward. Using kitchen shears, trim off top portion of outer leaves. Using paring knife, trim stem and base, removing any dark green parts. Cut artichoke in half lengthwise, then remove fuzzy choke and any tiny inner purple-tinged leaves using small spoon. Cut each half into 1-inch-thick wedges and submerge wedges in lemon water.

2. Heat oil in 12-inch skillet over medium heat until shimmering. Add onion, ¾ teaspoon salt, and ¼ teaspoon pepper and cook until softened and lightly browned,

5 to 7 minutes. Stir in garlic, anchovies, and thyme and cook until fragrant, about 30 seconds. Stir in wine and cook until almost evaporated, about 1 minute. Stir in broth and bring to simmer.

3. Remove artichokes from lemon water, shaking off excess water, and add to skillet. Cover, reduce heat to medium-low, and simmer until artichokes are tender, 20 to 25 minutes.

4. Stir in tomatoes, bring to simmer, and cook until tomatoes start to break down, 3 to 5 minutes. Off heat, stir in parsley and season with salt and pepper to taste. Serve.

SLOW-COOKER BRAISED ARTICHOKES WITH GARLIC BUTTER

Serves 4   Total time: 8 to 9 hours on low or 5 to 6 hours on high

WHY THIS RECIPE WORKS *A slow cooker makes impressive whole braised artichokes accessible. We simply trimmed the artichokes and placed them upright in the slow cooker (5 to 7 quarts) with a little water. Tossing them with a bit of lemon juice and olive oil beforehand helped to preserve their color. For a simple yet boldly flavored dipping sauce, we melted butter with more lemon juice and some minced garlic. If your artichokes are larger than 8 to 10 ounces, strip away another layer or two of the toughest outer leaves. These artichokes are delicious warm or at room temperature.*

- 4   artichokes (8 to 10 ounces each)
- ¼   cup lemon juice (2 lemons)
- 1   tablespoon extra-virgin olive oil
- 6   tablespoons unsalted butter
- 3   garlic cloves, minced
- ¼   teaspoon salt

1. Working with 1 artichoke at a time, cut off stem at base so artichoke sits upright, then cut off top quarter of artichoke. Using kitchen shears, trim off top portion of outer leaves. Toss artichokes with 2 tablespoons lemon juice and oil in bowl, then place right side up in slow cooker. Add ½ cup water, cover, and cook until outer leaves of

artichokes pull away easily and tip of paring knife inserted into base meets no resistance, 8 to 9 hours on low or 5 to 6 hours on high.

2. Microwave remaining 2 tablespoons lemon juice, butter, garlic, and salt in bowl until butter is melted. Whisk butter mixture to combine, then divide evenly among 4 serving bowls. Remove artichokes from slow cooker, letting any excess cooking liquid drain back into insert, and place artichokes in bowls with butter. Serve.

GRILLED ARTICHOKES WITH LEMON BUTTER

Serves 4   Total time: 1 hour 15 minutes

WHY THIS RECIPE WORKS *Grilling artichokes is a fun alternative preparation, bringing a bit of smoky char and enhancing their nutty flavor. Parboiling them in a broth with lemon juice, red pepper flakes, and salt ensured that they were completely tender and thoroughly seasoned. Tossing in extra-virgin olive oil before grilling helped develop the flavorful char marks on the grill. A simple blend of lemon zest and juice, garlic, and butter came together easily in the microwave and was perfect for dipping or drizzling. If your artichokes are larger than 8 to 10 ounces, strip away another layer or two of the toughest outer leaves.*

-     Salt and pepper
- ½   teaspoon red pepper flakes
- 2   lemons
- 4   artichokes (8 to 10 ounces each)
- 6   tablespoons unsalted butter
- 1   garlic clove, minced to paste
- 2   tablespoons extra-virgin olive oil

1. Combine 3 quarts water, 3 tablespoons salt, and pepper flakes in Dutch oven. Cut 1 lemon in half; squeeze juice into pot, then add spent halves. Bring to boil over high heat.

2. Meanwhile, working with 1 artichoke at a time, trim end of stem and cut off top quarter of artichoke. Break off bottom 3 or 4 rows of tough outer leaves by pulling them downward. Using kitchen shears, trim off top portion of outer leaves. Using paring knife, trim stem and base, removing any dark green parts.

GRILLED ARTICHOKES WITH LEMON BUTTER

Although artichokes are often braised or steamed, grilling artichokes imparts wonderfully smoky, nutty flavors. To achieve grilled artichokes that have appealing char marks on the outside and tender interiors, we jump-start the cooking process by parboiling them first. Then they become an easy side dish to finish on the grill with the rest of the meal.

1. Working with one artichoke at a time, trim the end of the stem and cut off the top quarter of the artichoke.

2. Break off the bottom three or four rows of tough outer leaves by pulling them downward. Using kitchen shears, trim off the top portion of the outer leaves.

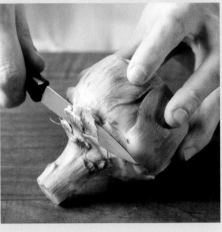

3. Using a paring knife, trim the stem and base of the artichoke, removing any dark green parts.

4. Simmer the artichokes until the tip of a paring knife inserted into the base of an artichoke meets no resistance, 25 to 28 minutes, stirring occasionally.

5. Cut the artichokes in half lengthwise. Remove the fuzzy chokes and any tiny inner purple-tinged leaves using a small spoon, leaving a small cavity in the center of each artichoke half.

6. Brush the artichokes with oil. Place the artichokes on the grill and cook until lightly charred, 2 to 4 minutes per side. Serve with the lemon butter.

3. Add artichokes to pot with boiling water mixture, cover, and reduce heat to medium-low. Simmer until tip of paring knife inserted into base of artichoke meets no resistance, 25 to 28 minutes, stirring occasionally.

4. Meanwhile, grate 2 teaspoons zest from remaining lemon; combine with butter, garlic, ½ teaspoon salt, and ¼ teaspoon pepper in bowl. Microwave at 50 percent power until butter is melted and bubbling and garlic is fragrant, about 2 minutes, stirring occasionally. Squeeze 1½ tablespoons juice from zested lemon and stir into butter. Season with salt and pepper to taste.

5. Set wire rack in rimmed baking sheet. Place artichokes stem side up on prepared rack and let drain for 10 minutes. Cut artichokes in half lengthwise. Remove fuzzy choke and any tiny inner purple-tinged leaves using small spoon, leaving small cavity in center of each half.

6a. For a charcoal grill Open bottom vent completely. Light large chimney starter filled with charcoal briquettes (6 quarts). When top coals are partially covered with ash, pour evenly over grill. Set cooking grate in place, cover, and open lid vent completely. Heat grill until hot, about 5 minutes.

6b. For a gas grill Turn all burners to high, cover, and heat grill until hot, about 15 minutes. Leave all burners on high.

7. Clean and oil cooking grate. Brush artichokes with oil. Place artichokes on grill and cook (covered if using gas) until lightly charred, 2 to 4 minutes per side. Transfer artichokes to serving platter and tent with aluminum foil. Briefly rewarm lemon butter in microwave, if necessary, and serve with artichokes.

JEWISH-STYLE FRIED ARTICHOKES

Serves 4 to 6   Total time: 40 minutes

WHY THIS RECIPE WORKS *In this classic Roman recipe, baby artichokes are pared down to their tender core and delicate inner leaves, cooked in extra-virgin olive oil until crispy and browned, and then sprinkled with sea salt and served with lemon. The cooking method was the key to success. Dropping the prepped artichokes into hot oil produced scorched, bitter leaves, while starting them in cold oil resulted in uneven browning. So we landed on an approach in the middle. We started the artichokes in extra-virgin olive oil heated to a moderate 300 degrees until the hearts were just cooked through; we then removed them while we increased the heat to 325 degrees. The artichokes required just 1 to 2 minutes in the hotter oil to develop golden, supercrisp leaves. Baby artichokes are a must here; as their tender hearts cook quickly and their soft leaves become shatteringly crisp.*

> 1 lemon, halved, plus lemon wedges for serving
> 2 pounds baby artichokes (2 to 4 ounces each)
>   Extra-virgin olive oil
>   Flake sea salt

1. Squeeze lemon halves into 4 cups cold water in large bowl; add spent halves. Working with 1 artichoke at a time, peel and trim stem to remove dark green layer, then cut off top quarter of artichoke. Break off tough outer leaves by pulling them downward until you reach delicate yellow leaves. Cut artichokes in half lengthwise and submerge in lemon water.

2. Line rimmed baking sheet with dish towel. Remove artichokes from lemon water, shaking off excess water, and transfer to prepared sheet; discard water and spent halves. Thoroughly pat artichokes dry and transfer to clean bowl.

3. Set wire rack in now-empty rimmed baking sheet and line with triple layer of paper towels. Add oil to large Dutch oven until it measures about 2 inches deep and heat over medium-high heat to 300 degrees. Carefully add artichokes to oil and cook until tender, pale green, and edges of leaves just begin to brown, 2 to 3 minutes. Using skimmer or slotted spoon, transfer artichokes to prepared baking sheet.

4. Heat oil over medium-high heat to 325 degrees. Return artichokes to oil and cook until golden and crisp, 1 to 2 minutes. Using skimmer or slotted spoon, transfer artichokes to sheet. Season with salt to taste. Serve with lemon wedges.

ROASTED ARTICHOKE DIP

Serves 8 to 10   Total time: 1 hour 30 minutes

WHY THIS RECIPE WORKS *This retro party favorite is too often overwhelmed by excess mayonnaise or sour cream or the tinny flavor of canned artichokes. This version is an irresistible crowd-pleaser, loaded with distinct artichoke flavor under a golden, crispy crust. For a simple, freshened-up take that could easily be made ahead of time, we replaced canned artichokes with frozen, which have a cleaner flavor, and we roasted them to intensify their flavor. A combination of mayonnaise and cream cheese for our base gave the dip a creamy, rich texture, and sprinkling on a Parmesan–bread crumb topping made for a crunchy, savory finishing touch. We prefer frozen artichoke hearts for this recipe, and don't recommend substituting jarred. Do not thaw the frozen artichoke hearts. This dip is best served warm. Serve with crackers or a thinly sliced baguette.*

TOPPING
> 2 slices hearty white sandwich bread, torn into quarters
> 2 tablespoons grated Parmesan cheese
> 1 tablespoon unsalted butter, melted

DIP
> 18 ounces frozen artichoke hearts
> 2 tablespoons extra-virgin olive oil
>   Salt and pepper
> 1 onion, chopped fine
> 2 garlic cloves, minced
> 1 cup mayonnaise
> 4 ounces cream cheese, softened
> 1 ounce Parmesan cheese, grated (½ cup)
> 2 tablespoons lemon juice
> 1 tablespoon minced fresh thyme
>   Pinch cayenne pepper

Jewish-Style Fried Artichokes

1. For the topping Pulse bread in food processor until coarsely ground, about 12 pulses. Toss bread crumbs with Parmesan and melted butter; set aside.

2. For the dip Adjust oven rack to middle position and heat oven to 450 degrees. Line rimmed baking sheet with aluminum foil. Toss artichokes with 1 tablespoon oil, ½ teaspoon salt, and ¼ teaspoon pepper on prepared sheet. Roast artichokes, stirring occasionally, until browned at edges, about 25 minutes. When cool enough to handle, chop artichokes coarse. Reduce oven temperature to 400 degrees.

3. Meanwhile, heat remaining 1 tablespoon oil in 10-inch skillet over medium-high heat until just shimmering. Add onion and cook until softened, about 5 minutes. Stir in garlic and cook until fragrant, about 30 seconds. Transfer onion mixture to large bowl.

4. Stir mayonnaise, cream cheese, Parmesan, lemon juice, thyme, and cayenne into onion mixture until well combined and smooth. Gently fold in artichokes and season with salt and pepper to taste. Transfer mixture to 1-quart baking dish and smooth top. Sprinkle topping evenly over dip. (Dip can be covered tightly in plastic wrap and refrigerated for up to 3 days.)

5. Bake dip until hot throughout and topping is golden, 20 to 25 minutes. Let dip cool for 5 minutes before serving.

～

MARINATED ARTICHOKES

Serves 6 to 8   Total time: 1 hour 15 minutes
WHY THIS RECIPE WORKS *Marinated artichokes have so many uses that they should be considered a pantry staple; they're perfect for everything from topping pizzas to tossing into a salad or pasta to arranging on an antipasto platter. But store-bought versions tend to be mushy and bland—and expensive. We set out to make our own recipe for easy, inexpensive, and boldly flavorful marinated artichokes. To get the best tender-yet-meaty texture and sweet, nutty flavor, we started with fresh baby artichokes, simmering them gently in olive oil with lemon zest, garlic,*

red pepper flakes, and thyme. Then they rested off the heat until perfectly fork-tender and infused with the aromatic marinade. We stirred fresh lemon juice, more zest, and minced garlic into the mixture before transferring the artichokes to a bowl and sprinkling them with fresh mint.

    2 lemons
  2½ cups extra-virgin olive oil
    3 pounds baby artichokes
       (2 to 4 ounces each)
    8 garlic cloves, peeled (6 smashed,
       2 minced)
    2 sprigs fresh thyme
   ¼ teaspoon red pepper flakes
       Salt and pepper
    2 tablespoons minced fresh mint

1. Using vegetable peeler, remove three 2-inch strips zest from 1 lemon. Grate ½ teaspoon zest from second lemon and set aside. Halve and juice lemons to yield ¼ cup juice, reserving spent lemon halves and setting aside juice. Combine oil and lemon zest strips in large saucepan.

2. Working with 1 artichoke at a time, peel and trim stem to remove dark green layer, then cut off top quarter of artichoke. Break off tough outer leaves by pulling them downward until you reach delicate yellow leaves. Cut artichokes in half lengthwise (quarter if large). Rub each artichoke half with spent lemon half and place in saucepan.

3. Add smashed garlic, thyme sprigs, pepper flakes, 1 teaspoon salt, and ¼ teaspoon pepper to saucepan and bring to rapid simmer over high heat. Reduce heat to medium-low and simmer, stirring occasionally to submerge all artichokes, until artichokes can be pierced with fork but are still firm, about 5 minutes. Off heat, let sit, covered, until artichokes are fork-tender and fully cooked, about 20 minutes.

4. Gently stir in ½ teaspoon reserved grated lemon zest, ¼ cup reserved lemon juice, and minced garlic. Transfer artichokes and oil to serving bowl and let cool to room temperature. Season with salt to taste and sprinkle with mint. Serve. (Artichokes and oil can be refrigerated for up to 4 days.)

BRUSCHETTA WITH ARTICHOKE HEARTS AND PARMESAN

Serves 8 to 10   Total time: 25 minutes
WHY THIS RECIPE WORKS *We wanted punchy, concentrated flavors for our artichoke bruschetta, a favorite hors d'oeuvre, so we turned to jarred artichoke hearts and sharp Parmesan cheese. We also wanted to be able to eat it without making a mess, so we pulsed some of the topping ingredients in a food processor until they formed a coarse paste. Spread on the toasted bread, it provided a stable anchor for the shaved Parmesan and drizzled oil. Toast the bread just before assembling the bruschetta. While we prefer the flavor and texture of jarred whole baby artichoke hearts in this recipe, you can substitute 6 ounces frozen artichoke hearts, thawed and patted dry, for the jarred.*

    1 (10 by 5-inch) loaf rustic bread,
       ends discarded, sliced crosswise into
       ¾-inch-thick pieces
    2 garlic cloves, peeled (1 whole, 1 minced)
   ¼ cup extra-virgin olive oil, plus extra
       for serving
       Salt and pepper
    1 cup jarred whole baby artichoke hearts
       packed in water, rinsed and patted dry
    2 tablespoons chopped fresh basil
    2 teaspoons lemon juice
    2 ounces Parmesan cheese (1 ounce
       grated [½ cup], 1 ounce shaved)

1. Adjust oven rack 4 inches from broiler element and heat broiler. Place bread on aluminum foil–lined rimmed baking sheet. Broil until bread is deep golden and toasted on both sides, 1 to 2 minutes per side. Lightly rub 1 side of each toast with whole garlic clove (you will not use all of garlic). Brush rubbed side with 2 tablespoons oil and season with salt to taste.

2. Pulse artichoke hearts, basil, lemon juice, minced garlic, remaining 2 tablespoons oil, ¼ teaspoon salt, and ¼ teaspoon pepper in food processor until coarsely ground, about 6 pulses, scraping down sides of bowl as needed. Add grated Parmesan and pulse to combine, about 2 pulses. Spread artichoke mixture evenly over toasts and top with shaved Parmesan. Season with pepper and drizzle with extra oil to taste. Serve.

ARTICHOKE SOUP À LA BARIGOULE

Serves 4 to 6   Total time: 1 hour 15 minutes

WHY THIS RECIPE WORKS *This classic Provençal-style recipe uses easy jarred artichokes. We seared them to intensify their subtle taste. Cooking the mushrooms covered and then uncovered evaporated excess moisture before browning, and simmering the parsnips brought out their sweetness. Umami-rich anchovy fillets and garlic supplied depth, and leek contributed further sweetness and body. White wine and white wine vinegar brightened up the dish. A little cream brought it all together. We prefer jarred whole baby artichokes here, but you can substitute 18 ounces frozen artichoke hearts, thawed and patted dry.*

- 3 tablespoons extra-virgin olive oil
- 3 cups jarred whole baby artichoke hearts packed in water, quartered, rinsed, and patted dry
- 12 ounces white mushrooms, trimmed and sliced thin
- 1 leek, white and light green parts only, halved lengthwise, sliced ¼ inch thick, and washed thoroughly
- 4 garlic cloves, minced
- 2 anchovy fillets, rinsed, patted dry, and minced
- 1 teaspoon minced fresh thyme or ¼ teaspoon dried
- 3 tablespoons all-purpose flour
- ¼ cup dry white wine
- 3 cups chicken broth
- 3 cups vegetable broth
- 6 ounces parsnips, peeled and cut into ½-inch pieces
- 2 bay leaves
- ¼ cup heavy cream
- 2 tablespoons minced fresh tarragon
- 1 teaspoon white wine vinegar, plus extra for seasoning
  Salt and pepper

1. Heat 1 tablespoon oil in Dutch oven over medium heat until shimmering. Add artichokes and cook until browned, 8 to 10 minutes. Transfer to cutting board, let cool slightly, then chop coarse. Set aside.

2. Heat 1 tablespoon oil in now-empty pot over medium heat until shimmering. Add mushrooms, cover, and cook, stirring occasionally, until mushrooms have released their liquid, 8 to 10 minutes. Uncover and continue to cook until mushrooms are dry, about 5 minutes.

3. Stir in leek and remaining 1 tablespoon oil and cook until leek is softened and mushrooms are browned, 8 to 10 minutes. Stir in garlic, anchovies, and thyme and cook until fragrant, about 30 seconds. Stir in flour and cook for 1 minute. Stir in wine, scraping up any browned bits, and cook until nearly evaporated, about 1 minute.

4. Slowly whisk in chicken broth and vegetable broth, smoothing out any lumps. Stir in artichokes, parsnips, and bay leaves and bring to simmer. Cover, reduce heat to medium-low, and simmer gently until parsnips are tender, 15 to 20 minutes. Off heat, discard bay leaves. Stir in cream, tarragon, and vinegar. Season with salt, pepper, and extra vinegar to taste. Serve.

TAGLIATELLE WITH ARTICHOKES AND PARMESAN

Serves 4 to 6   Total time: 1 hour 15 minutes

WHY THIS RECIPE WORKS *Artichokes and pasta come together in an elegant and ultra-flavorful Italian-inspired dish. We trimmed the leaves from the hearts and then gave them a quick soak in water. Drying the hearts promoted deep, nutty browning. Garlic and oregano combined with white wine, olive oil, and Parmesan made a flavorful sauce. Parsley and lemon zest kept the pasta bright without overshadowing the artichoke flavor, and a simple bread-crumb and Parmesan topping gave the dish savory crunch.*

TOPPING

- 2 slices hearty white sandwich bread
- 2 tablespoons extra-virgin olive oil
- ¼ cup grated Parmesan cheese
  Salt and pepper

PASTA

- 4 cups jarred whole baby artichoke hearts packed in water
- ¼ cup extra-virgin olive oil, plus extra for serving
  Salt and pepper
- 4 garlic cloves, minced
- 2 anchovy fillets, rinsed, patted dry, and minced
- 1 tablespoon minced fresh oregano or 1 teaspoon dried
- ⅛ teaspoon red pepper flakes
- ½ cup dry white wine
- 1 pound tagliatelle
- 1 ounce Parmesan cheese, grated (½ cup), plus extra for serving
- ¼ cup minced fresh parsley
- 1½ teaspoons grated lemon zest

1. For the topping Pulse bread in food processor until finely ground, 10 to 15 pulses. Heat oil in 12-inch nonstick skillet over medium heat until shimmering. Add bread crumbs and cook, stirring constantly, until crumbs begin to brown, 3 to 5 minutes. Add Parmesan and continue to cook, stirring constantly, until crumbs are golden, 1 to 2 minutes. Transfer crumbs to bowl and season with salt and pepper to taste.

2. For the pasta Cut leaves from artichoke hearts and place in bowl. Cut hearts in half and pat dry with paper towels. Cover artichoke leaves in bowl with water and let sit for 15 minutes. Drain well.

3. Heat 1 tablespoon oil in 12-inch nonstick skillet over medium-high heat until shimmering. Add artichoke hearts and ⅛ teaspoon salt and cook, stirring frequently, until spotty brown, 7 to 9 minutes. Stir in garlic, anchovies, oregano, and pepper flakes and cook, stirring constantly, until fragrant, about 30 seconds. Stir in wine and bring to simmer. Off heat, stir in artichoke leaves.

4. Meanwhile, bring 4 quarts water to boil in large pot. Add pasta and 1 tablespoon salt and cook, stirring often, until al dente. Reserve 1½ cups cooking water, then drain pasta and return it to pot. Add 1 cup reserved cooking water, artichoke mixture, Parmesan, parsley, lemon zest, and remaining 3 tablespoons oil and toss to combine. Season with salt and pepper to taste and adjust consistency with remaining ½ cup reserved cooking water as needed. Serve, sprinkling individual portions with bread crumbs and extra Parmesan and drizzling with extra oil.

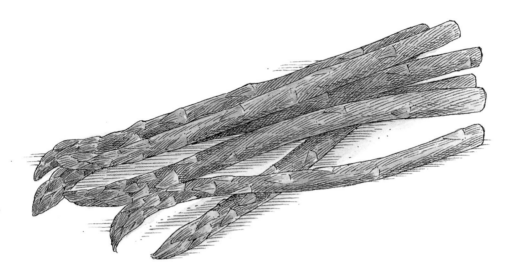

ASPARAGUS

Asparagus has serious staying power: The spears are the aboveground plant shoots of an underground crown that produces for up to 20 years—something to keep in mind if you decide to plant asparagus in your home garden!

In the market, you will see a pretty purple variety in addition to the traditional green type. These purple spears turn green when cooked. Less-common white asparagus lacks color because it is grown without sunlight. Although white asparagus is sweeter and more buttery in flavor than traditional green asparagus, it is also considerably more expensive, and its more delicate flavor doesn't typically survive long-distance shipping.

You might assume that thinner spears are younger and more tender than thicker ones. However, the thickness of an asparagus spear has nothing to do with its age—a thin spear will not mature into a thick spear. Instead, the diameter is determined by the age of the entire plant (younger crowns produce more slender stalks) and its variety. Thick or thin, asparagus is sweet, nutty, and grassy, with a pleasing texture.

Since both thick and thin spears are good bets, choose the size that best suits the cooking method. We have noted in the recipes when you should choose a particular size. Thicker stalks are better for recipes like Roasted Asparagus with Mint-Orange Gremolata and Grilled Asparagus with Chili-Lime Butter because they will stand up to the intense dry heat that would shrivel skinnier spears. Thin spears are good candidates for soups and stir-fries, such as our emerald-hued Creamy Asparagus Soup and Stir-Fried Asparagus with Shiitake Mushrooms, as well as for topping our buttery Asparagus–Goat Cheese Tart.

shopping and storage

Once a seasonal springtime treat, asparagus is now available year-round. No matter what thickness you buy, look for spears with the top tightly closed and the bottom still moist. (You may see asparagus sold upright in shallow tubs of water for this reason.) Spears with the tops flowering open and dry bottoms are past their prime. Thicker spears (½ to ¾ inch) are the most versatile and we found that they worked best in many recipes, since thinner spears can easily overcook. Purchase thinner spears (½ inch or thinner), which are less fibrous, for recipes where the asparagus is raw or for recipes where it is pureed. Pencil-thin spears often command a high price at the market.

To store asparagus in the refrigerator, trim off the ends and stand the spears up in a glass or jar filled with 1 inch of water. Cover with plastic wrap. If you haven't stored your asparagus this way and it has wilted, you can also perk it up by leaving it in the water-filled glass overnight.

to peel or not to peel?

Pencil-thin asparagus spears need only a quick trim at the base and they are good to go. But thicker stalks have woodier bases that need to be dealt with before you cook with them. Oftentimes recipes simply instruct you to snap off the bottom portion of each stalk at its natural breaking point. But is it worth the fuss to instead trim off a smaller amount and then peel the lower part of the asparagus spears? Yes, it really is. We discovered that spears snapped off at their natural breaking point lost an average of half their weight. You lose a lot of tasty asparagus that way! If you trim the bottom 1 inch from the base of each spear and then peel the lower half of each stalk to remove its woody exterior, you will end up with much less waste, not to mention long, elegant-looking, tender spears that cook evenly every time.

vegetable science
Shades of Asparagus

We only eat young asparagus—the new shoots of the plant crown. Much of the flavor and prized texture of asparagus resides in the tips, which are comprised of leaf-like cladodes, or stems. As mature asparagus begins to bud out, the stems become woody and nearly inedible. This is particularly true of green asparagus, the most common variety. White asparagus, which is more common in Europe, is more tender. It is an artificially cultivated crop: The shoots are covered in soil as they grow, shielding them from sunlight and preventing the photosynthesis that would turn them green from chlorophyll. They remain white but continue to grow—a process called blanching. Purple asparagus, a cultivar of green asparagus, gets its violet color from anthocyanins, a beneficial type of antioxidant.

vegetable prep

Trimming Asparagus

1. Trim bottom 1 inch from each spear (whether asparagus spears are thick or thin).

2. For thicker asparagus, peel bottom half of each stalk using vegetable peeler to remove woody exterior and expose tender inner flesh.

Cutting Asparagus on Bias

After trimming asparagus, if recipe specifies, cut on bias.

PAN-ROASTED ASPARAGUS

Serves 4 to 6   Total time: 20 minutes

WHY THIS RECIPE WORKS *Pan roasting delivers crisp, evenly browned asparagus spears without the need to turn on the oven. We decided on thicker spears because thin ones overcooked before they browned. To help the asparagus release moisture, which encourages caramelization and better flavor, we parcooked it, covered, with oil and water before browning it. The evaporating water helped to steam the asparagus, producing bright green, crisp-tender spears. At this point, we removed the lid and cranked up the heat until the spears were evenly browned on the bottom. There is no need to brown the asparagus all over; tasters preferred the flavor of spears browned on only one side, and, as a bonus, the partially browned spears never had a chance to go limp. Look for asparagus spears between ½ and ¾ inch in diameter. You can use white or green asparagus here; if using white, peel just the outermost layer of the bottom halves of the spears. You will need a 12-inch nonstick skillet with a tight-fitting lid for this recipe.*

    2 pounds thick asparagus
    1 tablespoon extra-virgin olive oil
    1 teaspoon water
       Salt and pepper
       Lemon wedges

1. Trim bottom inch of asparagus spears and discard. Peel bottom halves of spears until white flesh is exposed. Heat oil in 12-inch nonstick skillet over medium-high heat until shimmering. Add half of asparagus with tips pointed in 1 direction and remaining asparagus with tips pointed in opposite direction. Shake skillet gently to help distribute spears evenly (they will not quite fit in single layer). Add water, cover, and cook until asparagus is bright green but still crisp, about 5 minutes.

2. Uncover, season with salt and pepper to taste, increase heat to high, and cook until asparagus is well browned on one side and tip of paring knife inserted at base of largest spear meets little resistance, 5 to 7 minutes. Transfer asparagus to serving dish and serve with lemon wedges.

VARIATIONS

Pan-Roasted Asparagus with Red Onion and Bacon

Before cooking asparagus, cook 4 chopped bacon slices in 12-inch nonstick skillet over medium heat until crisp, 7 to 10 minutes; transfer to paper towel–lined plate. Pour off all but 1 tablespoon fat left in pan, add 1 thinly sliced red onion, and cook over medium-high heat until slightly softened, about 3 minutes. Add 2 tablespoons balsamic vinegar and 1 tablespoon maple syrup and cook until onions are well glazed, about 2 minutes; transfer to bowl. Rinse and dry skillet, then cook asparagus as directed. Before serving, top asparagus with onions and bacon.

Pan-Roasted Asparagus with Cherry Tomatoes and Kalamata Olives

Before cooking asparagus, cook 2 minced garlic cloves with 1 tablespoon extra-virgin olive oil in 12-inch nonstick skillet over medium heat until just golden, 2 to 3 minutes. Stir in 2 cups halved cherry tomatoes and ½ cup pitted, chopped kalamata olives and cook until tomatoes begin to break down, 1 to 2 minutes; transfer mixture to bowl. Rinse and dry skillet, then cook asparagus as directed. Before serving, top asparagus with tomato mixture, ¼ cup chopped fresh basil, and ½ cup grated Parmesan cheese.

ROASTED ASPARAGUS WITH MINT-ORANGE GREMOLATA

Serves 4 to 6   Total time: 25 minutes

WHY THIS RECIPE WORKS *Oven roasting can bring out the best in seasonal vegetables. But when it comes to delicate asparagus, simply tossing the spears with oil, salt, and pepper and spreading them on a baking sheet doesn't always produce reliably crisp-tender spears. After a few tests, we discovered that thicker asparagus (½ to ¾ inch in diameter) held up better to roasting. To ensure a hard sear on our spears, we preheated the baking sheet and resisted the urge to give it a shake during roasting. The result? Intense, flavorful browning on one side of the asparagus and vibrant green on the other. For complementary seasoning, we took our cue from Italian cuisine and prepared a bright garnish of minced fresh herbs called a gremolata. All of our versions reinforced the stalks' vibrant flavor and gave this simple side a more distinct presence. You can use white or green asparagus in this recipe; if using white, peel just the outermost layer of the bottom halves of the spears.*

    2 tablespoons minced fresh mint
    2 tablespoons minced fresh parsley
    2 teaspoons grated orange zest
    1 garlic clove, minced
       Pinch cayenne pepper
    2 pounds thick asparagus
    2 tablespoons plus 2 teaspoons
       extra-virgin olive oil
    ½ teaspoon salt
    ¼ teaspoon pepper

1. Adjust oven rack to lowest position, place rimmed baking sheet on rack, and heat oven to 500 degrees. Combine mint, parsley, orange zest, garlic, and cayenne in bowl; set aside.

2. Trim bottom inch of asparagus spears and discard. Peel bottom halves of spears until white flesh is exposed. Place asparagus in large baking pan and toss with 2 tablespoons oil, salt, and pepper.

3. Transfer asparagus to preheated sheet and spread into even layer. Roast, without moving asparagus, until undersides of spears are browned, tops are vibrant green, and tip of paring knife inserted at base of largest spear meets little resistance, 8 to 10 minutes. Transfer asparagus to serving platter, drizzle with remaining 2 teaspoons oil, sprinkle with gremolata, and serve immediately.

VARIATIONS

Roasted Asparagus with Cilantro-Lime Gremolata

Omit mint and cayenne. Substitute ¼ cup minced fresh cilantro for parsley and lime zest for orange zest.

Roasted Asparagus with Tarragon-Lemon Gremolata

Omit cayenne. Substitute tarragon for mint and lemon zest for orange zest.

ROASTED ASPARAGUS WITH MINT-ORANGE GREMOLATA

Our roasting method for asparagus results in one side of the stalk becoming beautifully browned, with all of the accompanying rich roasted flavors, and the other side remaining bright green, for a vibrant presentation. Thicker asparagus stalks (½ to ¾ inch) hold up better to the intense dry heat of roasting, and peeling the bottom halves of the stalks results in a silky finished texture in the roasted spears.

1. Place a rimmed baking sheet on the lowest rack of the oven and heat the oven to 500 degrees.

2. Trim the bottom 1 inch from each asparagus spear. This ensures less waste than breaking off the spears where they bend.

3. Peel the bottom halves of the asparagus spears using a vegetable peeler to expose the tender white flesh.

4. Toss the asparagus with the oil and seasonings and arrange the spears in an even layer on the preheated baking sheet.

5. Roast the asparagus without moving it. This creates flavorful browning on one side of the spears and leaves vibrant green color on the other side.

6. Transfer the roasted asparagus to a serving platter, sprinkle the bright, citrusy gremolata over the top, and serve.

Parmesan-Crusted Asparagus

PARMESAN-CRUSTED ASPARAGUS

Serves 4 to 6   Total time: 50 minutes

WHY THIS RECIPE WORKS *A cheesy, light-and-crisp coating makes asparagus irresistible, so naturally you want it to stay put when you're eating the asparagus. So, we first salted the spears to rid them of excess moisture. Then we whipped a combination of honey and egg whites to soft peaks, dipped the asparagus spears in the clingy mixture, and coated them with a mixture of bread crumbs and Parmesan. We sprinkled the spears with more cheese at the end of roasting. Look for asparagus spears between ½ and ¾ inch in diameter. Work quickly when tossing the asparagus with the egg whites, as the salt on the asparagus will rapidly begin to deflate the whites.*

- 2 pounds thick asparagus, trimmed
  Salt and pepper
- 3 ounces Parmesan cheese, grated (1½ cups)
- ¾ cup panko bread crumbs
- 1 tablespoon unsalted butter, melted and cooled
  Pinch cayenne pepper
- 2 large egg whites
- 1 teaspoon honey

1. Adjust oven rack to middle position and heat oven to 450 degrees. Line rimmed baking sheet with aluminum foil and spray with vegetable oil spray. Using fork, poke holes up and down asparagus spears. Toss asparagus with ½ teaspoon salt and let sit for 30 minutes on paper towel–lined baking sheet.

2. Meanwhile, combine 1 cup Parmesan, panko, melted butter, ¼ teaspoon salt, ⅛ teaspoon pepper, and cayenne in bowl. Transfer half of panko mixture to shallow dish; set aside remaining panko mixture. Using stand mixer fitted with whisk attachment, whip egg whites and honey on medium-low speed until foamy, about 1 minute. Increase speed to medium-high and whip until soft peaks form, 2 to 3 minutes. Scrape into 13 by 9-inch baking dish and toss asparagus in mixture. Working with 1 spear at a time, dredge half of asparagus in panko and transfer to prepared sheet. Refill shallow dish with remaining panko mixture and repeat with remaining half of asparagus.

3. Bake asparagus until just beginning to brown, 6 to 8 minutes. Sprinkle with remaining ½ cup Parmesan and continue to bake until cheese is melted, panko is golden brown, and tip of paring knife inserted at base of largest spear meets little resistance, 6 to 8 minutes. Transfer to platter. Serve.

BRAISED ASPARAGUS, PEAS, AND RADISHES WITH TARRAGON

Serves 4 to 6   Total time: 30 minutes

WHY THIS RECIPE WORKS *Braising asparagus is an unexpected but delightful way to capitalize on its tender springtime freshness. To turn our early-season asparagus into a side dish, we started by softening minced shallot in olive oil with additional aromatics. To build a flavorful braising liquid, we poured in water and lemon and orange zest and dropped in a bay leaf. Adding the vegetables in stages ensured that each cooked at its own rate and maintained a crisp texture. Peppery radishes, which turned soft and sweet with cooking, nicely complemented the greener notes of asparagus and peas (frozen peas were reliably sweet, and adding them off the heat prevented overcooking). In no time at all, we had a simple, warm dish of radiant vegetables in an invigorating, complex broth, proof positive that braising can bring out the best in even the most delicate flavors. The addition of chopped fresh tarragon was a final nod to spring. Look for asparagus spears no thicker than ½ inch.*

- ¼ cup extra-virgin olive oil
- 1 shallot, sliced into thin rounds
- 2 garlic cloves, sliced thin
- 3 fresh thyme sprigs
  Pinch red pepper flakes
- 10 radishes, trimmed and quartered
- 1¼ cups water
- 2 teaspoons grated lemon zest
- 2 teaspoons grated orange zest
- 1 bay leaf
  Salt and pepper
- 1 pound thin asparagus, trimmed and cut into 2-inch lengths
- 2 cups frozen peas
- 4 teaspoons chopped fresh tarragon

1. Cook oil, shallot, garlic, thyme sprigs, and pepper flakes in Dutch oven over medium heat until shallot is just softened, about 2 minutes. Stir in radishes, water, lemon zest, orange zest, bay leaf, and 1 teaspoon salt and bring to simmer. Reduce heat to medium-low, cover, and cook until radishes can be easily pierced with tip of paring knife, 3 to 5 minutes. Stir in asparagus, cover, and cook until tender, 3 to 5 minutes.

2. Off heat, stir in peas, cover, and let sit until heated through, about 5 minutes. Discard thyme sprigs and bay leaf. Stir in tarragon and season with salt and pepper to taste. Serve.

GRILLED ASPARAGUS

Serves 4   Total time: 35 minutes

WHY THIS RECIPE WORKS *The main challenge with grilling delicate asparagus is protecting it from overcooking while still developing a good char. For great grilled asparagus, we opted for thicker spears, which combined maximum browning potential with a meaty, crisp-tender texture. A simple medium-hot fire worked best—the spears were on and off the grill in less than 10 minutes. Brushing the spears with butter rather than oil before grilling gave us crispy, nutty asparagus. We tried infusing flavor with zesty marinades, but because asparagus has a naturally tough outer skin, most of the seasonings were left behind in the bowl. Instead, we decided to add flavorings directly to the butter we were brushing on the asparagus, which worked perfectly. Look for asparagus spears between ½ and ¾ inch in diameter. You can use white or green asparagus in this recipe; if using white, peel just the outermost layer of the bottom halves of the spears.*

- 1½ pounds thick asparagus
- 3 tablespoons unsalted butter, melted
  Salt and pepper

1. Trim bottom inch of asparagus spears and discard. Peel bottom halves of spears until white flesh is exposed. Brush asparagus with melted butter and season with salt and pepper.

2a. For a charcoal grill Open bottom vent completely. Light large chimney starter three-quarters filled with charcoal briquettes (4½ quarts). When top coals are partially covered with ash, pour evenly over grill. Set cooking grate in place, cover, and open lid vent completely. Heat grill until hot, about 5 minutes.

2b. For a gas grill Turn all burners to high, cover, and heat grill until hot, about 15 minutes. Turn all burners to medium-high.

3. Clean and oil cooking grate. Place asparagus in even layer on grill and cook until browned and tip of paring knife inserted at base of largest spear meets little resistance, 4 to 10 minutes, turning halfway through cooking. Transfer asparagus to platter and serve.

VARIATIONS

Grilled Asparagus with Chili-Lime Butter
Add 1 teaspoon grated lime zest, ½ teaspoon chili powder, ¼ teaspoon cayenne pepper, and ⅛ teaspoon red pepper flakes to butter before brushing asparagus in step 1.

Grilled Asparagus with Orange-Thyme Butter
Add 1 teaspoon grated orange zest and 1 teaspoon minced fresh thyme to butter before brushing asparagus in step 1.

ASPARAGUS SALAD WITH RADISHES, PECORINO ROMANO, AND CROUTONS

Serves 4 to 6   Total time: 30 minutes
WHY THIS RECIPE WORKS *Raw asparagus is just as delicious as cooked; it's mildly sweet and nutty, with a delicate crunch and none of the sulfurous flavors that cooked asparagus sometimes has. Many recipes call for cut-up lengths of raw asparagus, but even when we peeled the spears, they were too fibrous. As long as we chose the right spears (bright green, firm, and crisp, with tightly closed tips) and sliced them very thin on the bias, we could avoid woodiness but still keep things crunchy. This technique worked best with thicker spears, a welcome discovery because they're available year-round. To complement*

the fresh asparagus, we wanted an herby dressing, and turned to mint and basil. A high ratio of herbs to oil created a pesto-style dressing potent enough to enhance but not mask the flavor of the asparagus. A food processor made it easy to chop the herbs together with Pecorino Romano cheese, garlic, lemon, and seasonings before stirring in extra-virgin olive oil. A few radishes, more Pecorino, and buttery croutons rounded out the salad. Look for asparagus spears between ½ and ¾ inch in diameter. Parmesan can be substituted for the Pecorino Romano. Grate the cheese for the dressing with a rasp-style grater or use the small holes of a box grater; shave the cheese for the salad with a vegetable peeler.

CROUTONS
  2 tablespoons unsalted butter
  1 tablespoon extra-virgin olive oil
  2 slices hearty white sandwich bread, crusts discarded, cut into ½-inch pieces (1⅓ cups)
  Salt and pepper

PESTO DRESSING
  2 cups fresh mint leaves
  ¼ cup fresh basil leaves
  ¼ cup grated Pecorino Romano cheese
  1 teaspoon grated lemon zest plus 2 teaspoons juice
  1 garlic clove, minced
  Salt and pepper
  ½ cup extra-virgin olive oil

SALAD
  2 pounds thick asparagus, trimmed
  5 radishes, trimmed and sliced thin
  2 ounces Pecorino Romano cheese, shaved (¾ cup)
  Salt and pepper

1. For the croutons Heat butter and oil in 12-inch nonstick skillet over medium heat until butter is melted. Add bread pieces and ⅛ teaspoon salt and cook, stirring frequently, until golden brown, 7 to 10 minutes. Season with salt and pepper to taste and set aside.

2. For the pesto dressing Process mint, basil, Pecorino, lemon zest and juice, garlic, and ¾ teaspoon salt in food processor until smooth, about 20 seconds, scraping down sides of bowl as needed. With processor

running, slowly add oil until incorporated; transfer to large bowl and season with salt and pepper to taste.

3. For the salad Cut asparagus tips from spears into ¾-inch-long pieces. Slice asparagus spears ⅛ inch thick on bias. Add asparagus tips and spears, radishes, and Pecorino to dressing and toss to combine. Season with salt and pepper to taste. Transfer salad to serving platter and top with croutons. Serve.

VARIATIONS

Asparagus Salad with Oranges, Feta, and Hazelnuts
Omit croutons and radishes. Substitute 4 ounces crumbled feta cheese for Pecorino in the salad. Cut away peel and pith from 2 oranges. Holding fruit over bowl, use paring knife to slice between membranes to release segments. Add to salad in step 3. Add ¾ cup toasted, skinned, and chopped hazelnuts to salad in step 3.

Asparagus Salad with Grapes, Goat Cheese, and Almonds
Omit croutons. Substitute 6 ounces thinly sliced grapes for radishes and 4 ounces crumbled goat cheese for Pecorino in the salad. Add ¾ cup toasted and chopped almonds to salad in step 3.

TORTELLINI SALAD WITH ASPARAGUS AND FRESH BASIL DRESSING

Serves 8 to 10   Total time: 55 minutes
WHY THIS RECIPE WORKS *For a supereasy pasta salad that would impress any picnic crowd, we paired convenient store-bought cheese tortellini with crisp asparagus and a dressing inspired by the flavors of classic pesto. First, we blanched the asparagus in the same water we later used to cook the tortellini, which imbued the pasta with the asparagus's delicate flavor. Once the tortellini were cooked, we marinated them briefly with bright, juicy cherry tomatoes in a bold dressing of extra-virgin olive oil, basil, lemon juice, shallot, and garlic. To finish the salad, we tossed in some grated Parmesan and toasted pine nuts along with the*

blanched asparagus just before serving. Cooking the pasta until it is completely tender and leaving it slightly wet after rinsing are important for the texture of the finished salad. Be sure to set up the ice water bath before cooking the asparagus; plunging the pieces into the cold water immediately after blanching retains their bright green color and ensures that they don't overcook.

    1 pound asparagus, trimmed and
       cut into 1-inch pieces
       Salt and pepper
    1 pound dried cheese tortellini
    6 tablespoons extra-virgin olive oil
    3 tablespoons lemon juice
    1 shallot, minced
    1 garlic clove, minced
   12 ounces cherry tomatoes, halved
   ½ cup chopped fresh basil
    1 ounce Parmesan cheese, grated (½ cup)
   ¼ cup pine nuts, toasted

1. Bring 4 quarts water to boil in large pot. Fill large bowl halfway with ice and water. Add asparagus and 1 tablespoon salt to boiling water and cook until crisp-tender, about 2 minutes. Using slotted spoon, transfer asparagus to ice water, and let sit until cool, about 2 minutes. Transfer asparagus to baking sheet lined with triple layer of paper towels and dry well.

2. Return pot of water to boil. Add tortellini and cook, stirring often, until tender. Drain tortellini, rinse with cold water, and drain again, leaving tortellini slightly wet.

3. Whisk oil, lemon juice, shallot, garlic, ½ teaspoon salt, and ½ teaspoon pepper in large bowl until combined. Add tortellini and tomatoes and toss to combine. Cover and let sit for 15 minutes. Stir in asparagus, basil, Parmesan, and pine nuts and season with salt and pepper to taste before serving.

CREAMY ASPARAGUS SOUP

Serves 6   Total time: 45 minutes

WHY THIS RECIPE WORKS *Cream of asparagus soup should be bright green, bursting with asparagus flavor, and flawlessly smooth, but often the butter and cream stirred in before serving make the soup heavy. To eke out maximum asparagus flavor, we tried sautéing the spears, but ended up with a dark, bitter soup. Broiling the asparagus yielded similar results. Lowering the heat and cooking the asparagus spears gently to slowly coax out their flavor worked. (Tasters agreed that the richness of butter was a must here.) We learned the hard way not to overcook the asparagus; to retain their fresh flavor, the pieces must be just tender enough to puree. To achieve more creaminess without adding more cream, leeks, which are great for adding sweet silkiness without muddling flavors, came to mind. For a beautiful emerald hue, we stirred a handful of peas into the pot just before pureeing. They added further sweetness and body, thanks to their starch. A bit of Parmesan lent a nuttiness that echoed that of the asparagus, while lemon juice brightened the dish. Look for asparagus spears no thicker than ½ inch.*

    2 pounds thin asparagus, trimmed
    3 tablespoons unsalted butter
    1 pound leeks, white and light green
       parts only, halved lengthwise, sliced
       thin, and washed thoroughly
       Salt and pepper
   3½ cups chicken broth
   ½ cup frozen peas
    2 tablespoons grated Parmesan cheese
   ¼ cup heavy cream
   ½ teaspoon lemon juice

1. Cut tips off asparagus spears and reserve. Cut spears into ½-inch pieces. Melt 1½ tablespoons butter in Dutch oven over medium-high heat. Add asparagus tips and cook, stirring occasionally, until just tender, about 2 minutes; transfer to bowl and set aside.

2. Add remaining 1½ tablespoons butter, asparagus spears, leeks, ½ teaspoon salt, and ⅛ teaspoon pepper to now-empty pot and cook over medium-low heat, stirring occasionally, until vegetables are softened, about 10 minutes.

3. Add broth to pot and bring to boil over medium-high heat. Reduce heat to medium-low and simmer until vegetables are tender, about 5 minutes. Stir in peas and Parmesan.

Working in batches, process soup in blender until smooth, about 1 minute; transfer to clean pot. Stir in cream, lemon juice, and asparagus tips and cook over medium-low heat until warmed through, about 2 minutes. Season with salt and pepper to taste. Serve.

ASPARAGUS–GOAT CHEESE TART

Serves 4   Total time: 55 minutes

WHY THIS RECIPE WORKS *This beautiful tart takes just minutes to assemble and makes for an impressive brunch dish, appetizer, or even a simple light lunch or dinner. We experimented with several different crusts, trying a pie shell, a tart shell, and parbaked puff pastry. The buttery, flaky puff pastry was absolutely irresistible, and so easy to prep. For a fresh, light filling, we simply scattered the asparagus and other toppings over the pastry base. Cutting the asparagus spears into thin 1-inch pieces made the tart easier to eat and ensured that the asparagus didn't need precooking. We tossed the pieces with olive oil, plus garlic, lemon zest, scallions, and olives. For a creamy base to anchor the toppings, tangy, soft goat cheese nicely complemented the bright, grassy asparagus. Blending in a bit of olive oil made it easier to spread. We dolloped more cheese on top of the asparagus and baked the tart to golden perfection. To thaw frozen puff pastry, let it sit either in the refrigerator for 24 hours or on the counter for 30 minutes to 1 hour. Look for asparagus spears no thicker than ½ inch.*

- 6 ounces thin asparagus, trimmed and cut ¼ inch thick on bias (1 cup)
- 2 scallions, sliced thin
- 3 tablespoons extra-virgin olive oil
- 2 tablespoons chopped pitted kalamata olives
- 1 garlic clove, minced
- ¼ teaspoon grated lemon zest
- ¼ teaspoon salt
- ¼ teaspoon pepper
- 4 ounces (1 cup) goat cheese, softened
- 1 (9½ by 9-inch) sheet puff pastry, thawed

1. Adjust oven rack to upper-middle position and heat oven to 425 degrees. Line rimmed baking sheet with parchment paper. Combine asparagus, scallions, 1 tablespoon oil, olives, garlic, zest, salt, and pepper in bowl. In separate bowl, mix ¾ cup goat cheese and 1 tablespoon oil until smooth; set aside.

2. Unfold pastry onto lightly floured counter and roll into 10-inch square; transfer to prepared sheet. Lightly brush outer ½ inch of pastry square with water to create border, then fold border toward center, pressing gently to seal.

3. Spread goat cheese mixture in even layer over center of pastry, avoiding folded border. Scatter asparagus mixture over goat cheese, then crumble remaining ¼ cup goat cheese over top of asparagus mixture.

4. Bake until pastry is puffed and golden and asparagus is crisp-tender, 15 to 20 minutes. Let cool for 15 minutes. Drizzle with remaining 1 tablespoon oil, cut into 4 equal pieces, and serve.

STIR-FRIED ASPARAGUS WITH SHIITAKE MUSHROOMS

Serves 4   Total time: 20 minutes

WHY THIS RECIPE WORKS *Asparagus, like many vegetables, is a natural candidate for stir-frying because it cooks in a flash. The intense heat beautifully caramelizes it, while the short cooking time ensures that its crisp-tender bite is preserved. Starting with a hot skillet and then stirring the asparagus only occasionally during cooking allowed the asparagus to char before it overcooked, creating a natural sweetness that paired perfectly with the potent Asian-inspired sauce. Thinly sliced shiitake mushrooms complemented the fresh-flavored asparagus and added some heft. To ensure that the asparagus and mushrooms cooked evenly, we added a bit of water, creating a small amount of steam that cooked the vegetables through before evaporating and leaving behind a flavorful, clingy glaze. Look for asparagus spears no thicker than ½ inch. Serve as a side dish, or over rice.*

- 2 tablespoons water
- 1 tablespoon soy sauce
- 1 tablespoon dry sherry
- 2 teaspoons packed brown sugar
- 2 teaspoons grated fresh ginger
- 1 teaspoon toasted sesame oil
- 1 tablespoon vegetable oil
- 1 pound thin asparagus, trimmed and cut on bias into 2-inch lengths
- 4 ounces shiitake mushrooms, stemmed and sliced thin
- 2 scallions, green parts only, sliced thin on bias

1. Combine water, soy sauce, sherry, sugar, ginger, and sesame oil in bowl.

2. Heat vegetable oil in 12-inch nonstick skillet over high heat until smoking. Add asparagus and mushrooms and cook, stirring occasionally, until asparagus is spotty brown, 3 to 4 minutes. Add soy sauce mixture and cook, stirring twice, until asparagus is crisp-tender, 1 to 2 minutes. Transfer to serving platter, sprinkle with scallion greens, and serve.

VARIATION

Stir-Fried Asparagus with Red Bell Pepper
Omit soy sauce, sherry, brown sugar, ginger, and sesame oil. Reduce water to 1 tablespoon. Whisk 1 tablespoon orange juice, 1 tablespoon rice vinegar, 1 tablespoon granulated sugar, 1 teaspoon ketchup, and ½ teaspoon salt into water. Substitute 1 stemmed and seeded red bell pepper cut into 2-inch-long matchsticks for shiitakes.

Asparagus–Goat Cheese Tart

AVOCADOS

Although the avocado is technically a fruit, in the kitchen we think of it and treat it like a vegetable. While it can be used in desserts, such as ice cream, its culinary uses fall more clearly into the savory category. However, avocados are most often not cooked. They are nearly always used raw, in smoothies, salads—and, of course, guacamole. That said, we have developed a delicious burger recipe using skillet-charred avocados.

There are hundreds of varieties of avocado, but the most common is Hass, grown mainly in California and Mexico; it is small and rough-skinned, with a buttery, meaty texture that was preferred by our tasters. You will also see Fuerte avocados, grown primarily in Florida, which are larger, bright green, and smooth-skinned. These don't handle the demands of shipping as well as Hass avocados. Our tasters found this variety sweeter, fruitier in flavor, and more watery than the Hass.

You may see Florida avocados marketed under the brand name SlimCado. This is not a new variety, but rather a marketing angle. Florida avocados are slightly lower in fat than Hass, due to their higher water content, but this makes them less suited for classic uses such as guacamole and dressings. All avocados are relatively high in heart-healthy mono-unsaturated fat. This buttery richness is why they are so adaptable in the kitchen for use in dips, spreads, and dressings. What's more, avocados have the highest protein content of any fruit.

In this chapter, we've included several fun versions of guacamole for all your party desires, as well as lots of fresh salad combinations, a California-style grain bowl, and a Hawaiian tuna poke bowl. And certainly no collection of avocado recipes would be complete without at least one great recipe for avocado toast.

shopping and storage

Thanks to Mexico's long growing season, avocados are available year-round. Regardless of the variety, supermarket avocados are typically sold rock-hard and unripe. That's fine, because avocados ripen off the tree; in two to five days, your avocados should be ready to eat. The skin of Hass avocados turns from deep green to dark purply black as it ripens, and the fruit yields to gentle pressure. Once you get them home, storage couldn't be easier: Just add them to the fruit bowl on your counter. Or, to speed ripening, store them in a paper bag. Once softened and ripe, they can be refrigerated for several days to extend their shelf life.

is it ripe?

A soft avocado is sometimes just bruised rather than truly ripe. To determine whether it is ripe, remove the small stem with your fingers. If you see green underneath it, the avocado is ripe. But if the stem does not come off easily or you see brown underneath, the avocado is not ripe. Conversely, if your avocado is soft like a tomato, or it feels like there's a gap between the skin and the flesh underneath, your avocado is overripe.

it isn't easy being green

A cut avocado seems to turn brown almost instantaneously. Storing it cut side down in water with a few squeezes of lemon juice keeps it green for a couple of days. Vacuum sealing will preserve its green color for a week. Or try one of the avocado "huggers" now available.

vegetable prep

Pitting an Avocado

1. Slice around pit and through both ends with chef's knife.

2. With your hands, twist avocado to separate halves. Strike blade of chef's knife sharply into pit. Lift knife, twisting blade to loosen and remove pit.

3. Do not pull pit off knife with your hands. Instead, use large wooden spoon to pry pit safely off knife.

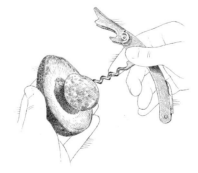

Alternatively, use waiter's corkscrew to remove pit. Hook it securely into pit, and simply pull pit out of avocado half.

Dicing an Avocado

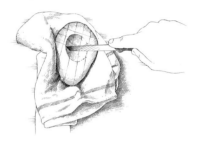

1. Use dish towel to hold avocado steady. Make ½-inch crosshatch incisions in flesh of each avocado half with butter knife, cutting down to but not through avocado skin.

2. Separate diced flesh from avocado skin using spoon inserted between skin and flesh, gently scooping out avocado cubes.

POWER SMOOTHIE

Serves 2   Total time: 10 minutes

WHY THIS RECIPE WORKS *Rich and subtly sweet, avocado is a natural choice for blending into smoothies. This feel-good "green" power smoothie, with kale, avocado, pineapple, and banana, tastes great while also making you feel virtuous. And it's filling enough to call it breakfast. We turned to a surprising source for protein for this smoothie: hemp seed hearts. They packed a nutritional punch, and their neutral flavor didn't overwhelm the produce in the drink. In fact, hemp seed hearts can handle just about any smoothie flavor combination you throw at them. The hulled center of the hemp seed, a soft, almost waxy nugget, blended beautifully into our drink, leaving just a trace of pleasantly grassy, sweet flavor. You can use 2 tablespoons almond butter or ¼ cup wheat germ instead, if you prefer. Do not use frozen chopped kale for this recipe.*

- 1 cup baby kale
- 1 cup frozen pineapple chunks
- 1 cup water
- 1 ripe banana, peeled and halved lengthwise
- ½ cup pineapple juice
- ½ ripe avocado, cut into quarters
- 2 tablespoons hemp seed hearts
- ⅛ teaspoon salt

Combine all ingredients in blender. Process on low speed until mixture is combined but still coarse in texture, about 10 seconds. Increase speed to high and puree until completely smooth, about 1 minute. Serve.

SUPER GUACAMOLE

Makes about 2 cups   Total time: 20 minutes

WHY THIS RECIPE WORKS *No party is complete without a bowl (or two) of guacamole. And now that avocado is such a food celebrity, this tried-and-true standby has become even more adored. Our super guac is all about bold flavor and great texture. First, we chopped the avocados into small pieces. Next, we minced our supercharged seasonings of onion, chile, and lime together to ensure that these strong flavors would be evenly distributed. Mashing everything together with a whisk and then gently folding in the tomato and cilantro made the guac cohesive but still chunky. The variations on our classic offer smoky crunch (with chipotles and pepitas), bright, fruity hotness (with habanero and mango), and creamy, peppery flavor (with feta and arugula). Naturally, all of these can be served with pita chips; the feta and arugula version would also be great with toasted pita wedges.*

- 2 tablespoons finely chopped onion
- 1 serrano chile, stemmed, seeded, and chopped fine
- ¼ teaspoon grated lime zest plus 1½ tablespoons juice Kosher salt
- 3 ripe avocados, halved, pitted, and cut into ½-inch pieces
- 1 plum tomato, cored, seeded, and minced
- 2 tablespoons chopped fresh cilantro

Chop and mash onion, chile, and lime zest with 1 teaspoon salt until very finely minced and homogeneous. Transfer to medium serving bowl and stir in lime juice. Add avocados and, using sturdy whisk, mash and stir mixture until well combined with some ¼- to ½-inch chunks remaining. Fold in tomato and cilantro and season with salt to taste. Serve.

VARIATIONS

Chipotle and Pepita Guacamole
Substitute 1 tablespoon minced canned chipotle chile in adobo sauce for serrano and ¼ cup toasted pepitas for tomato.

Habanero and Mango Guacamole
Substitute 1 stemmed, seeded, and minced habanero chile for serrano and ½ mango, peeled and cut into ¼-inch pieces, for tomato.

Feta and Arugula Guacamole
Substitute ½ cup chopped baby arugula for tomato. Add 1 cup crumbled feta cheese with cilantro.

BEAN AND BEEF TAQUITOS WITH AVOCADO SAUCE

Makes 12 taquitos

Total time: 1 hour 30 minutes

WHY THIS RECIPE WORKS *The unctuous texture of avocados lends itself well to simple, creamy uncooked sauces that perfectly complement crispy, spicy foods. Taquito means "little taco," but these filled and fried party-food bites have outsize appeal. Traditional versions can be work-intensive so we streamlined things for an easy at-home method. Spiced ground beef replaced long-braised chuck. Mashed pinto beans thickened the filling and kept it from falling out of the ends. A quick egg wash helped seal the taquitos. Switching from deep frying to shallow frying in a mere cup of oil allowed us to start cooking the taquitos with the seam side in contact with the bottom of the pan, guaranteeing that they didn't unroll as they cooked. This preparation method also meant they absorbed a minimum of oil during frying. Serve with Mexican crema or your favorite dipping sauce—or make extra avocado sauce.*

TAQUITOS

- 1 cup plus 4 teaspoons vegetable oil
- 8 ounces 90 percent lean ground beef
- 1 cup canned pinto beans, rinsed
- 1 onion, halved and sliced thin
- 2 jalapeño chiles, stemmed, seeded, and minced
- 3 garlic cloves, minced
- 1 teaspoon ground cumin
- 1 teaspoon chili powder
- 1 (8-ounce) can tomato sauce
- ½ cup water
- 3 tablespoons minced fresh cilantro Salt and pepper
- 12 (6-inch) corn tortillas
- 1 large egg, lightly beaten

AVOCADO SAUCE

- 2 ripe avocados, halved, pitted, and chopped
- ½ cup sour cream
- ¼ cup water
- 3 tablespoons lime juice (2 limes)
- 2 tablespoons minced fresh cilantro Salt and pepper

Super Guacamole

1. **For the taquitos** Heat 1 teaspoon oil in 12-inch nonstick skillet over medium-high heat until just smoking. Add beef and cook, breaking up meat with wooden spoon, until no longer pink, about 5 minutes. Drain beef in colander. Mash beans to paste with potato masher.

2. Heat 1 tablespoon oil in now-empty skillet over medium heat until shimmering. Add onion and cook until beginning to brown, 5 to 7 minutes. Stir in jalapeños, garlic, cumin, and chili powder and cook until fragrant, about 30 seconds. Stir in drained beef, mashed beans, tomato sauce, water, cilantro, ½ teaspoon salt, and ½ teaspoon pepper and cook, stirring occasionally, until thickened and beginning to sizzle, about 10 minutes. Season with salt and pepper to taste. Transfer to bowl and let cool, about 20 minutes.

3. Line rimmed baking sheet with parchment paper. Set wire rack inside second rimmed baking sheet. Place 6 tortillas on plate, cover with clean, damp dish towel, and microwave until hot and pliable, about 90 seconds. Working with 1 tortilla at a time, brush edges of top half with egg. Place row of 3 level tablespoons filling across lower half of tortilla. Fold bottom of tortilla up over filling, then pull back on tortilla to tighten it around filling. Roll tightly and place seam side down on lined sheet. Cover with second clean, damp towel. Microwave remaining 6 tortillas and repeat with remaining filling. (Taquitos can be refrigerated, covered with damp towel and wrapped tightly in plastic, for up to 24 hours.)

4. Adjust oven rack to middle position and heat oven to 200 degrees. Heat remaining 1 cup oil in 12-inch nonstick skillet over medium-high heat until shimmering. Using tongs, place 6 taquitos, seam side down, in oil and fry until golden, about 5 minutes. Flip and fry until second side is golden, about 3 minutes. Transfer to wire rack and place sheet in oven to keep warm. Repeat with remaining 6 taquitos.

5. **For the avocado sauce** Combine avocados, sour cream, water, lime juice, and cilantro in bowl and mash with potato masher (or fork) until smooth. Season with salt and pepper to taste. Serve taquitos with sauce.

AVOCADO SALAD WITH TOMATOES AND RADISHES

Serves 6   Total time: 45 minutes

WHY THIS RECIPE WORKS *In salad, buttery avocados demand an acidic dressing to cut their richness. Using a little mayonnaise as an emulsifier allowed us to make a creamy dressing with equal parts vinegar and olive oil. To add flavor and textural contrast, we steered clear of leafy greens and relied on crunchier vegetables like fennel and radishes and sweet, juicy fruits like cherry tomatoes and mango. A garnish of salty cheese was the perfect finishing touch to complement the creamy avocado. Arranging the dressed avocado chunks below the other ingredients maximized visual appeal by preventing the avocado from turning the salad a murky army green. Crumbled feta cheese can be substituted for the ricotta salata. Don't skip the step of soaking the shallot—the ice water helps tame its oniony bite.*

1   large shallot, sliced thin
3   tablespoons red wine vinegar
1   garlic clove, minced
½   teaspoon mayonnaise
     Salt and pepper
3   tablespoons extra-virgin olive oil
3   avocados, halved, pitted, and
     cut into ¾-inch pieces
12   ounces cherry tomatoes, quartered
3   radishes, trimmed and sliced thin
½   cup chopped fresh basil
3   ounces ricotta salata, shaved thin

1. Place shallot in 2 cups ice water and let stand for 30 minutes; drain and pat dry.

2. Whisk vinegar, garlic, mayonnaise, ¼ teaspoon salt, and ¼ teaspoon pepper together in medium bowl. Whisking constantly, drizzle in oil. Gently toss avocados with 2 tablespoons dressing and ½ teaspoon

salt in separate bowl, then transfer to serving platter. Toss shallot, tomatoes, radishes, and basil in bowl with remaining dressing and spoon over avocados. Sprinkle with ricotta salata and serve.

VARIATIONS

Avocado Salad with Oranges and Fennel
Omit pepper. Substitute sherry vinegar for red wine vinegar and ½ teaspoon hot paprika for garlic in dressing. Substitute 1 fennel bulb, cored and sliced thin for tomatoes, ⅓ cup toasted slivered almonds for radishes, ¼ cup chopped fresh parsley for basil, and ¼ cup sliced green olives for ricotta salata. Add 1 teaspoon grated orange zest to dressing in step 2. Cut away peel and pith from 3 oranges, quarter each orange, then slice crosswise into ¼-inch-thick pieces and add to shallot mixture in step 2.

Avocado Salad with Mangos and Jícama
Reduce shallot to 1 tablespoon, minced, and skip step 1. Substitute pinch cayenne for garlic and ½ teaspoon lemon zest plus 3 tablespoons lemon juice for red wine vinegar in dressing. Substitute 2 mangos, peeled, pitted, and cut into ½-inch pieces for tomatoes; 2 cups peeled jícama cut into 2-inch-long matchsticks for radishes; and feta cheese for ricotta salata. Reduce basil to ¼ cup and add ¼ cup chopped fresh mint to shallot mixture in step 2.

COBB SALAD WITH CREAMY AVOCADO DRESSING

Serves 6 to 8   Total time: 50 minutes

WHY THIS RECIPE WORKS *This is a show-stopper of a salad, a celebration of avocado's unctuous texture and a welcome update for an American classic. Cobb salad generally features everything but the kitchen sink: chopped salad greens, chicken breast, hard-boiled eggs, bacon, avocado, tomatoes, blue cheese, and a litany of other ingredients. Stories vary as to its origin, but popular belief is that Robert Howard Cobb, owner of the Hollywood Brown Derby restaurant, needed a late-night fix, so he mixed together whatever he could find in the kitchen. In our* *version, we wanted to bring the avocado into the limelight in a more untraditional way. Instead of using the expected chunks of avocado, we capitalized on the creamy texture of this fruit to make a smooth, velvety dressing that coated every piece of lettuce. To give our dressing some zing, we pulsed in lemon and garlic. To complement this tangy dressing, there's plenty of romaine for sturdy, refreshing crunch and also pieces of radicchio for their slightly bitter notes. We drizzled extra avocado dressing over the top, creating a striking vibrant green contrast against all the other colorful elements of this dish.*

DRESSING

- 1 ripe avocado, halved, pitted, and cut into 2-inch pieces
- 2 tablespoons extra-virgin olive oil
- 1 teaspoon grated lemon zest plus 3 tablespoons juice
- 1 garlic clove, minced
  Salt and pepper

SALAD

- 6 large eggs
- 1½ pounds boneless, skinless chicken breasts, trimmed and cut into ½-inch pieces
  Salt and pepper
- 8 slices bacon, chopped
- 3 romaine lettuce hearts (18 ounces), torn into bite-size pieces
- ½ small head radicchio (3 ounces), cored and cut into ½-inch pieces
- 10 ounces cherry tomatoes, halved
- 2 ounces blue cheese, crumbled (½ cup)
- 2 tablespoons minced fresh chives

1. For the dressing Process avocado, oil, lemon zest and juice, garlic, ¾ teaspoon salt, and ¼ teaspoon pepper in food processor until smooth, about 30 seconds, scraping down sides of bowl as needed. Transfer to large bowl and adjust consistency with up to ¼ cup water as needed. Season with salt and pepper to taste, cover, and refrigerate until needed.

2. For the salad Bring 1 inch water to rolling boil in medium saucepan over high heat. Place eggs in steamer basket, then transfer basket to saucepan. Cover, reduce heat to medium-low, and cook eggs for 13 minutes. When eggs are almost finished cooking, fill medium bowl halfway with ice and water. Using tongs or spoon, transfer eggs to ice bath; let sit for 15 minutes. Peel and quarter eggs, and set aside.

3. Meanwhile, pat chicken dry with paper towels and season with salt and pepper. Cook bacon in 12-inch skillet over medium heat until crisp, 5 to 7 minutes. Using slotted spoon, transfer bacon to paper towel–lined plate; set aside. Pour off all but 1 tablespoon fat from skillet, add chicken, and cook over medium-high heat, stirring occasionally, until cooked through, 4 to 6 minutes. Transfer to plate and let cool slightly.

4. Toss romaine, radicchio, and ½ cup dressing together in large bowl. Transfer to serving platter and mound in even layer. Arrange eggs and tomatoes in single, even rows over greens, leaving space at either end. Arrange half of chicken in each open space at ends of platter. Sprinkle bacon and blue cheese over top of salad. Drizzle remaining dressing over salad and sprinkle with chives. Serve immediately.

~~~

SHRIMP SALAD WITH AVOCADO AND ORANGE

Serves 4   Total time: 40 minutes

WHY THIS RECIPE WORKS *The buttery richness of avocado pairs beautifully with sweet shrimp in this fresh take on a classic deli salad. For firm yet tender shrimp, we started the shrimp in cold court bouillon, heating the shrimp and liquid together to just a near-simmer. For a perfect deli-style dressing that wouldn't mask the flavor of the salad ingredients, we kept the traditional mayonnaise, but limited the amount to ¼ cup per pound of shrimp. Radishes added a hit of peppery flavor, the orange contributed a bright citrusy punch, and the mint lent a cool herbal note. The avocado adds velvety texture along with its creamy flavor. This recipe can also be prepared with large shrimp (26 to 30 per pound); the cooking time will be 1 to 2 minutes less. The shrimp can be cooked up to 24 hours in advance, but hold off on dressing the salad until ready to serve. The recipe can be easily doubled; cook the shrimp in a 7-quart Dutch oven and increase the cooking time to 12 to 14 minutes. Serve the salad on a bed of greens, on a buttered and grilled bun, or in a hollowed-out avocado half.*

- 1 pound extra-large shrimp (21 to 25 per pound), peeled, deveined, and tails removed
- 5 tablespoons lemon juice, spent halves reserved (2 lemons)
- 5 sprigs fresh parsley
- 1 teaspoon black peppercorns
- 1 tablespoon sugar
  Salt and pepper
- ¼ cup mayonnaise
- 1 small shallot, minced
- 2 teaspoons minced fresh mint
- 4 radishes, halved and thinly sliced
- 1 orange, peeled and cut into ½-inch pieces
- ½ avocado, cut into ½-inch pieces

1. Fill large bowl halfway with ice and water; set aside. Combine 2 cups cold water, shrimp, ¼ cup lemon juice, reserved lemon halves, parsley sprigs, peppercorns, sugar, and 1 teaspoon salt in medium saucepan. Place saucepan over medium heat and cook shrimp, stirring several times, until opaque throughout, 8 to 10 minutes (water should be just bubbling around edge of pan and register 165 degrees). Off heat, cover, and let shrimp stand in broth for 2 minutes.

2. Using slotted spoon, transfer shrimp to ice water, and let sit until cool, about 3 minutes. Transfer shrimp to triple layer of paper towels and dry well. Cut shrimp in half lengthwise, then cut each half crosswise into thirds.

3. Whisk mayonnaise, shallot, mint, and remaining 1 tablespoon lemon juice together in serving bowl. Add shrimp, radishes, orange, and avocado to mayonnaise mixture and toss to combine. Season with salt and pepper to taste, and serve.

CRISPY SKILLET TURKEY BURGERS WITH CHARRED AVOCADO RELISH

Sure, you can simply mash up an avocado for a quick burger topping, but charring sliced avocados in a skillet takes things to a whole new level. The char amps up the normally mild-tasting fruit with a punch of smokiness. Chopping the charred avocado shows off the black and green color contrast, and tossing it in the vinaigrette brightens the flavors. It's a versatile addition to your burger repertoire.

1. Halve and pit the avocados, using one of the methods described on page 23.

2. Cut each avocado half lengthwise into ½-inch-thick slices.

3. Heat the oil in a 12-inch nonstick skillet and cook the avocado slices until well charred on both sides, flipping them carefully.

4. Cut the charred avocado slices into ¼-inch pieces to highlight the contrast between the char marks and the green color.

5. Toss the avocado pieces with the vinaigrette to brighten their flavor and retain their color.

6. Spread half of the avocado relish over the bun bottoms; top with the lettuce, tomato, and burgers; and then top the burgers with the remaining relish and the alfalfa sprouts.

CRISPY SKILLET TURKEY BURGERS WITH CHARRED AVOCADO RELISH

Serves 4   Total time: 45 minutes

WHY THIS RECIPE WORKS *Sliced or mashed avocado is a great addition to burgers and sandwiches, but it's usually more about richness than flavor. We wanted to develop an intensely flavored avocado topping that offered more than just textural contrast. Grilling or charring avocados produces robust, smoky flavors that linger and cut through the vegetable's fattiness. We started by charring avocado slices in a skillet and mashing them in a simple vinaigrette of garlic and smoked paprika. Although the mashed avocados boasted an intense smokiness, we wanted to improve the look of our topping. So instead, we chopped the avocados, which showed the contrast between black and green and made it a beautiful, spoonable relish. Be sure to use ground turkey, not ground turkey breast (also labeled 99 percent fat-free) in this recipe. A rasp-style grater makes quick work of turning the garlic into a paste.*

RELISH

- 3 tablespoons extra-virgin olive oil
- 1 tablespoon minced fresh chives
- 1 teaspoon sherry vinegar
- 1 small garlic clove, minced to paste
- ¼ teaspoon smoked paprika
  Salt and pepper
- 2 avocados, halved, pitted, and sliced lengthwise ½ inch thick

BURGERS

- 1 cup panko bread crumbs
- 2 ounces Monterey Jack cheese, shredded (½ cup)
- ¼ cup mayonnaise
  Salt and pepper
- 1 pound ground turkey
- 1 tablespoon extra-virgin olive oil
- 4 hamburger buns, toasted
- 1 tomato, cored and sliced thin
- ½ head Bibb lettuce (4 ounces), leaves separated
- 2 ounces (2 cups) alfalfa sprouts

1. For the relish Whisk 2 tablespoons oil, chives, vinegar, garlic, paprika, ¼ teaspoon salt, and ¼ teaspoon pepper in bowl until combined. Heat remaining 1 tablespoon oil in 12-inch nonstick skillet over medium-high heat until just smoking. Add avocados in single layer and cook without moving until charred on both sides, 1 to 2 minutes per side. Transfer avocados to cutting board and cut into ¼-inch pieces. Add avocados to bowl with vinaigrette and toss gently to combine; set aside until ready to serve.

2. For the burgers Combine panko, Monterey Jack, mayonnaise, ½ teaspoon salt, and ½ teaspoon pepper in bowl. Add ground turkey and knead with your hands until combined. Using your hands, pat turkey mixture into four ¾-inch-thick patties, about 4 inches in diameter. Season patties with salt and pepper.

3. Heat oil in now-empty skillet over medium heat until shimmering. Add patties and cook until well browned and burgers register 160 degrees, about 5 minutes per side. Spread half of relish evenly over bun bottoms and top with tomato and lettuce. Place burgers on lettuce; top with remaining relish, sprouts, and bun tops. Serve.

TUNA POKE WITH AVOCADO

Serves 4   Total time: 1 hour 15 minutes (plus 18 hours refrigeration time)

WHY THIS RECIPE WORKS *Hawaiian fishermen would save the trimmings from their daily catch to season and serve raw, with colorful vegetable toppings. Their humble working-class dish has now exploded onto the fast-casual dining scene. Avocado is a common addition to poke, so we wanted to highlight it by dialing the amount way up. Its richness is offset by the pungent ginger and mirin in the soy-sesame dressing. To pack more tuna flavor into every bite, we wrapped the tuna in kombu (the Japanese kelp used to make dashi broth) and cured it overnight—a simple Japanese technique called kobu-jime. This treatment drew out moisture from the fish, firming up the flesh, and gave it an umami boost. The success of this dish depends on using fresh, high-quality tuna. If you can't find one large tuna steak, purchase two ½-inch-thick 6-ounce steaks. Hijiki seaweed is milder than kombu or wakame (the leafy green seaweed swimming in your miso soup) and adds an understated vegetal sea flavor without being briny. It can be purchased at well-stocked grocery stores or online. You can substitute wakame for hijiki; just be sure to roughly chop wakame after soaking in step 3.*

- 1¾ ounces dried kombu
- 1 (12-ounce) tuna steak, 1 inch thick
- 2 teaspoons kosher salt
- ⅛ ounce dried hijiki
- ½ Vidalia or Walla Walla onion, chopped fine
- 4 teaspoons soy sauce
- 1½ teaspoons toasted sesame oil
- 1 teaspoon mirin
- 1 teaspoon corn syrup
- ¼ teaspoon grated fresh ginger
- 2 avocados, halved, pitted, and cut in ¾-inch pieces
- ¼ cup salted dry-roasted macadamia nuts, chopped coarse
- 6 scallions, sliced thin on bias
- 2 teaspoons sesame seeds, toasted

1. Soak kombu in container filled with 1 quart water until slightly softened and pliable, about 10 minutes. Drain kombu and pat dry with paper towels.

2. Slice tuna horizontally into two ½-inch-thick steaks and sprinkle evenly with salt. Lay half of kombu strips in single layer on counter to make a 7-inch square. Place 1 tuna steak in center of kombu square. Fold edges of kombu up around tuna and top with additional pieces of kombu as needed to completely encase. Wrap tightly with plastic wrap and transfer to plate. Repeat with remaining kombu and second tuna steak; transfer to plate. Refrigerate kombu-wrapped tuna steaks for at least 18 hours or up to 24 hours.

3. Soak hijiki in 1 quart water until softened and plumped, at least 20 minutes or up to 1 hour. Place onion in 2 cups ice water and let sit for 30 minutes.

4. Whisk soy sauce, oil, mirin, corn syrup, and ginger together in large bowl. Unwrap tuna, discard kombu, and pat tuna dry with paper towels. Cut tuna into ½-inch pieces and transfer to bowl with dressing. Drain hijiki and onion in fine-mesh strainer, pressing to extract as much liquid as possible. Pat dry with paper towels and add to bowl with tuna. Add avocados and nuts and gently toss to combine. Divide poke among individual serving bowls and sprinkle with scallions and sesame seeds. Serve immediately.

AVOCADO TOAST

Serves 4   Total time: 15 minutes

WHY THIS RECIPE WORKS *Some dishes are so simple that they are not even worth talking about. But avocado toast is definitely worth a discussion. Avocado toast is here to stay: It's healthy, delicious, satisfying, and one of the simplest things to make for a quick breakfast or lunch. We took ours up a notch by whisking together a lemony vinaigrette and mixing it in as we mashed one of the avocados, giving our dish a distinct citrusy punch. Smeared on toasted rustic country bread, topped with sliced avocado, then sprinkled with a little coarse sea salt and red pepper flakes, our version of avocado toast is spectacularly tasty. Topping it with fried eggs just takes it over the top.*

2 tablespoons extra-virgin olive oil
1 teaspoon grated lemon zest plus
   1 tablespoon juice
   Coarse sea salt or kosher salt
   and pepper
2 ripe avocados
4 (½-inch-thick) slices crusty bread
¼ teaspoon red pepper flakes (optional)

1. Whisk oil, lemon zest and juice, ¼ teaspoon salt, and ⅛ teaspoon pepper together in small bowl. Halve and pit 1 avocado. Carefully make ½-inch crosshatch incisions in flesh with butter knife, cutting down to but not through skin. Insert spoon between skin and flesh, gently scoop out avocado cubes, and add to bowl with oil mixture. Mash avocado into vinaigrette with potato masher (or fork). Halve remaining avocado, remove pit and peel, and slice thin; set aside.

2. Adjust oven rack 4 inches from broiler element and heat broiler. Place bread on aluminum foil–lined rimmed baking sheet. Broil until bread is deep golden on both sides, 1 to 2 minutes per side.

3. Spread mashed avocado mixture evenly on toasts. Arrange avocado slices evenly over top. Sprinkle with ¼ teaspoon salt and pepper flakes, if using, and serve.

VARIATION
Avocado Toast with Fried Eggs
Crack 4 eggs into 2 small bowls (2 eggs per bowl) and season with salt and pepper. Heat 2 teaspoons vegetable oil in 12-inch nonstick skillet over medium-high heat until shimmering. Pour 1 bowl of eggs into 1 side of pan and second bowl into other side. Cover and cook for 1 minute. Remove skillet from heat and let sit, covered, for 15 to 45 seconds for runny yolks (white around edge of yolk will be barely opaque), 45 to 60 seconds for soft but set yolks, or about 2 minutes for medium-set yolks. Top avocado toasts with fried eggs and serve.

CALIFORNIA BARLEY BOWLS WITH AVOCADO, SNOW PEAS, AND LEMON-MINT YOGURT SAUCE

Serves 4   Total time: 50 minutes

WHY THIS RECIPE WORKS *For a fresh, California-style take on wildly popular rice bowls, we swapped the rice for hearty barley and paired it with snow peas, chunks of ripe avocado, and toasted spiced sunflower seeds. While the barley cooked, we sautéed the snow peas with some coriander and toasted the sunflower seeds with lots of warm spices. Last, we mixed together a quick lemon-mint yogurt sauce to drizzle over the top. We tossed the barley with the peas, topped it with the chunks of avocado and the sunflower seeds, and drizzled it all with the sauce. Do not substitute hulled or hull-less barley in this recipe. If using quick-cooking or presteamed barley (read the ingredient list on the package carefully to determine this), you will need to alter the barley cooking time in step 1.*

1 cup plain yogurt
2 teaspoons grated lemon zest
   plus 3 tablespoons juice
2 tablespoons minced fresh mint
   Salt and pepper
1 cup pearl barley
¼ cup extra-virgin olive oil

8 ounces snow peas, strings removed
   and halved lengthwise
1 teaspoon ground coriander
¾ cup sunflower seeds
½ teaspoon ground cumin
⅛ teaspoon ground cardamom
2 avocados, halved, pitted, and
   cut into ½-inch pieces

1. Whisk yogurt, 1 teaspoon lemon zest and 2 tablespoons juice, 1 tablespoon mint, ½ teaspoon salt, and ¼ teaspoon pepper together in small bowl; cover and refrigerate until ready to serve.

2. Bring 4 quarts water to boil in large pot. Add barley and 1 tablespoon salt and cook until tender, 20 to 25 minutes. Drain barley. Meanwhile, whisk 3 tablespoons oil, remaining 1 teaspoon lemon zest and 1 tablespoon juice, and remaining 1 tablespoon mint together in large bowl and season with salt and pepper to taste. Stir in barley and toss to coat. Cover to keep warm.

3. While barley cooks, heat 1½ teaspoons oil in 12-inch skillet over medium-high heat until just smoking. Add snow peas and ½ teaspoon coriander and cook until peas are spotty brown, about 3 minutes; add to bowl with barley and toss to combine.

4. Add remaining 1½ teaspoons oil to now-empty skillet and heat over medium heat until shimmering. Stir in sunflower seeds, cumin, cardamom, remaining ½ teaspoon coriander, and ½ teaspoon salt. Cook, stirring constantly, until seeds are toasted, about 2 minutes; let cool slightly off heat.

5. Portion barley into individual serving bowls, top with avocados and spiced sunflower seeds, and drizzle with yogurt sauce. Serve.

Avocado Toast

BEETS

The beets many of us remember from childhood were likely canned, with a tinny flavor and mushy texture, or pickled in sharp, acrid white vinegar. In contrast, what a revelation freshly cooked beets are, with their juicy, firm texture and sweetly earthy flavor.

And what a treat for the eyes they are! All of the varieties available these days are show-stoppingly gorgeous. Red beets are the most commonly available and probably the first image that comes to mind when we think of beets. These are the messiest to prepare thanks to their pigment, which stains everything pink. Golden beets are a bit mellower in flavor than red beets and have a beautiful carroty hue. They are great in mixed vegetable dishes because they don't bleed their pigment into other ingredients. Chioggia beets are an Italian heirloom variety; they are also called candy cane beets because of their interior red-and-white rings.

You may also find Chioggia beets with a yellow-and-white striped interior. White beets look like turnips and are less sweet than other varieties. Harvested small, they are table beets. Large white beets are grown for animal feed and for making sugar.

The recipes in this chapter are surprisingly varied. We made our kitchens messy so that you wouldn't have to while experimenting with the best method for roasting beets. We also teach you how to braise beets and use the flavorful leftover cooking liquid to make three tasty finishing glazes.

We modernized the old standbys of pickled beets and borscht, created a better baked beet chip for snacking, spiralized them into noodles, and incorporated them into a Middle Eastern dip. Our Beet and Barley Risotto features the mild-tasting but often-overlooked beet greens, as does the Sautéed Beet Greens with Raisins and Almonds.

shopping and storage

Beets, both with and without their greens, are available year-round. Beet greens are at their most tender in the springtime. Small beets are more tender than large ones, but they are also more labor-intensive to peel and prep. Very large beets can be woody. Choose medium-size beets for the best return on investment. And don't forget those beet greens! When they are attached to the beetroots, it's a sign of freshness for the whole vegetable. For storage, separate the roots from the greens and store the greens loosely wrapped in paper towels in a plastic produce bag in the refrigerator for a few days. Store the roots in an open plastic produce bag in the refrigerator, where they will keep for at least a month.

vegetable science
Beets' Survival Strategy
Beets are one of the sweetest vegetables in existence. In terms of the amount of sugar per 100 grams, they are sweeter than several fruits! This hallmark sweetness is actually the result of the plant's cold-weather defense mechanism. The natural sugars in beets act like antifreeze, lowering the freezing point of water in the plant and thus helping prevent that water from freezing and forming destructive ice crystals that would rupture the cell walls. And those startlingly bright colors that dye your skin and kitchen tools so prettily but so persistently? They come from water-soluble pigments called betalains, which have antioxidant and anti-inflammatory properties.

removing beet stains from hands

Although beets have a beautiful hue, they easily stain your hands with their pigment. There are several effective ways to remove beet stains from your hands.

Sprinkle with salt, then scrub with soap.

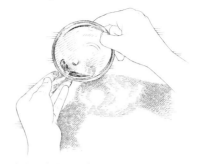

Rub hand that will be holding beets with ½ teaspoon vegetable oil, keeping hand that will be holding knife dry. Afterward, wash with hot, soapy water.

Rub a dab of whitening toothpaste with peroxide on hands, then wash with hot, soapy water.

Or, to prevent stains to begin with, wear disposable food handling gloves when working with beets.

vegetable prep

Grating Raw Beets

After trimming and peeling beets, grate on large holes of box grater or use shredding disk of food processor.

Peeling Cooked Beets

To avoid stained hands when peeling cooked beets, when cool enough to handle, cradle beets in paper towel and gently rub off skin.

SAUTÉED BEET GREENS WITH RAISINS AND ALMONDS

Serves 2 or 3   Total time: 20 minutes

WHY THIS RECIPE WORKS *If you find beet greens attached to the beets at your market, please bring them home with you—they are mild and delicious. Among blanching, steaming, microwaving, and wilting, we found the simplest, most straightforward recipe for these tender greens to be wilting on the stovetop. We simply tossed the leaves, still wet from washing, into a heated sauté pan, covered it, and cooked them, stirring occasionally, until the greens wilted via the steam from their own liquid. We then found that we got even better results when combining this technique with sautéing—we heated oil in a sauté pan, added the wet greens, covered and steamed them until wilted, and then uncovered the pan and cooked on high until all the liquid had evaporated. Sweet golden raisins and crunchy almonds gave the greens Mediterranean flavors. For the variation, onion, fresh ginger and jalapeño, and curry, along with a finishing touch of cream, moved the greens east to India.*

- 2 pounds beet greens, stemmed and chopped
- 3 tablespoons extra-virgin olive oil
- 2 garlic cloves, minced
- ¼ teaspoon red pepper flakes
- ¼ cup golden raisins, chopped
- ½ teaspoon grated lemon zest
- 3 tablespoons slivered almonds, toasted
  Salt and pepper

1. Wash and drain beet greens, leaving greens slightly wet. Heat oil in Dutch oven over medium-high heat until shimmering. Add garlic and pepper flakes and cook until golden, about 30 seconds. Add raisins and wet greens. Cover and cook, stirring occasionally, until greens are wilted but still bright green, about 3 minutes.

2. Stir in lemon zest. Increase heat to high and cook, uncovered, until liquid evaporates, 2 to 3 minutes. Stir in almonds and season with salt and pepper to taste. Serve.

VARIATION

Sautéed Beet Greens with Indian Spices
Omit olive oil, pepper flakes, raisins, lemon zest, and almonds. Before cooking greens in step 1, heat 2 teaspoons vegetable oil in Dutch oven over medium-high heat until shimmering. Add 1 small onion, chopped fine, and cook until softened, about 5 minutes. Add garlic; 1 teaspoon minced fresh ginger; ½ jalapeño chile, stemmed, seeded, and minced; 2 teaspoons curry powder; and ½ teaspoon ground cumin and cook until fragrant, about 1 minute. After evaporating liquid in pan in step 2, add ¼ cup heavy cream and 2 teaspoons packed brown sugar and cook until cream thickens, about 2 minutes. Serve.

ROASTED BEETS

Serves 4   Total time: 1 hour 15 minutes

WHY THIS RECIPE WORKS *The flavor of roasted fresh beets is head-and-shoulders above that of the canned version. They are intensely sweet and firm, rather than tinny, tangy, and mushy. So how, exactly, do you roast a beet? We tried several different methods. The first approach simply blasted untrimmed beets in a hot oven. While they possessed an intense flavor, they took hours, shrank to a fraction of their size, and the skins dried to desiccated husks that required a razor-sharp paring knife to remove. Another method involved roasting the beets in a covered baking dish partially filled with water. The beets cooked faster, but in terms of flavor, they might as well have been boiled. A third approach roasted the beets in a covered dish with no water. This made an unholy mess as exuded beet juices stuck fast to the pan bottom. For our fourth method, we wrapped each unpeeled beet tightly in foil and roasted them on a baking sheet. The results tasted every bit as sweet and intense as those roasted uncovered, but they cooked in half the time and peeled easily.*

- 1 pound beets, trimmed
- 2 tablespoons extra-virgin olive oil
  Salt and pepper

1. Adjust oven rack to middle position and heat oven to 400 degrees. Wrap beets individually in aluminum foil and place on rimmed baking sheet. Roast until beets can be easily pierced with paring knife, 45 minutes to 1 hour, removing beets individually from oven as they finish cooking.

2. Open foil packets to allow steam to escape and let cool slightly. Once beets are cool enough to handle, rub off skins with paper towels. Slice beets ¼ inch thick and place in medium bowl.

3. Add oil, season with salt and pepper to taste, and toss to combine. Serve warm or at room temperature.

VARIATIONS

Roasted Beets with Dill-Walnut Vinaigrette
Increase oil to 6 tablespoons. While beets cool in step 2, whisk oil, 1 minced shallot, 1½ tablespoons minced fresh dill, 1 tablespoon red wine vinegar, and 2 teaspoons lemon juice together in medium bowl. Add cooled, sliced beets and ½ cup toasted, chopped walnuts to bowl with vinaigrette and toss gently to combine.

Roasted Beets with Ginger Butter and Chives
Omit oil. While beets cool in step 2, melt 4 tablespoons unsalted butter in 8-inch skillet over medium heat. Add one 1-inch piece fresh ginger, peeled and cut into matchsticks, to skillet and cook until fragrant and crispy, 3 to 4 minutes. Off heat, add 1 tablespoon minced fresh chives and stir to combine. Add butter mixture to bowl with beets in step 3.

Roasted Beets

BRAISED BEETS WITH LEMON AND ALMONDS

Serves 4 to 6   Total time: 1 hour 15 minutes
WHY THIS RECIPE WORKS *We sought a streamlined stovetop recipe for beets that maximized their sweet, earthy flavor—with minimal mess. Braising worked perfectly. We partially submerged the beets in just 1¼ cups of water so that they partially simmered and partially steamed. Halving the beets cut down our cooking time. In just 45 minutes, the beets were tender and their skins slipped off easily. We reduced the braising liquid and added brown sugar and vinegar to make a glossy glaze. Shallot, toasted almonds, fresh mint and thyme, and a little lemon zest finished the dish. Look for beets that are 2 to 3 inches in diameter. You can use an 11-inch straight-sided sauté pan in place of the Dutch oven in this recipe. The beets can be served warm or at room temperature. If serving at room temperature, add the nuts (or seeds, if making the variation with lime and pepitas) and fresh herbs right before serving.*

1½	pounds beets, trimmed and halved horizontally
1¼	cups water
	Salt and pepper
3	tablespoons distilled white vinegar
1	tablespoon packed light brown sugar
1	shallot, sliced thin
1	teaspoon grated lemon zest
½	cup whole almonds, toasted and chopped
2	tablespoons chopped fresh mint
1	teaspoon chopped fresh thyme

1. Place beets, cut side down, in single layer in Dutch oven. Add water and ¼ teaspoon salt and bring to simmer over high heat. Reduce heat to low, cover, and simmer until beets are tender and can be easily pierced with paring knife, 45 to 50 minutes.

2. Transfer beets to cutting board to cool slightly. Meanwhile, increase heat to medium-high and reduce cooking liquid, stirring occasionally, until pan is almost dry, 5 to 6 minutes. Add vinegar and sugar, return to boil, and cook, stirring constantly with heat-resistant spatula, until spatula leaves wide trail when dragged through glaze, 1 to 2 minutes. Remove pan from heat.

3. Once beets are cool enough to handle, rub off skins with paper towels and cut into ½-inch wedges. Add beets, shallot, lemon zest, ½ teaspoon salt, and ¼ teaspoon pepper to glaze and toss to coat. Transfer to serving platter, sprinkle with almonds, mint, and thyme, and serve.

VARIATIONS
Braised Beets with Lime and Pepitas
Omit thyme. Substitute lime zest for lemon zest, toasted pepitas for almonds, and cilantro for mint.

Braised Beets with Orange and Walnuts
Substitute orange zest for lemon zest, walnuts for almonds, and parsley for mint.

PICKLED BEETS

Makes four 1-pint jars   Total time: 2 hours
WHY THIS RECIPE WORKS *To create a recipe that had nothing in common with the one-dimensional, mushy, cloying pickled beets that line supermarket shelves, we started by briefly roasting our beets in the oven to concentrate their flavor and make them just tender enough to peel. Cutting them into ⅓-inch-thick slices helped the beets stay firm. Fruity cider vinegar was the right base for the brine, and sugar softened its acidity. Ginger and star anise added a clean spice flavor to balance the earthy beets. Heating the jars with hot water and then draining them before adding the hot brine ensured that the jars wouldn't crack from the abrupt temperature change. Choose beets that are uniform in size; for added charm, try golden or Chioggia varieties. You can easily double this recipe; simply use a larger pot (or two pots) when making the brine and cooking the beets. The pickled beets can be refrigerated for up to three months.*

3	pounds beets, trimmed
3	cups cider vinegar
1	cup sugar
1	(3-inch) piece fresh ginger, peeled and sliced thin
3	star anise pods
1	teaspoon kosher salt
1	teaspoon black peppercorns

1. Adjust oven rack to middle position and heat oven to 400 degrees. Wrap beets individually in aluminum foil and place on rimmed baking sheet. Roast until paring knife inserted into beets meets some resistance, 30 to 45 minutes; remove beets individually from oven as they reach appropriate doneness. Open foil packets to allow steam to escape and let cool slightly. Once beets are cool enough to handle, rub off skins with paper towels. Quarter beets, then cut crosswise into ⅓-inch-thick slices.

2. Bring vinegar, 2 cups water, sugar, ginger, star anise, salt, and peppercorns to boil in Dutch oven over medium-high heat. Remove from heat, cover, and let steep for 30 minutes. Strain brine through fine-mesh strainer, return it to pot, and bring to boil. Add beets and return to brief boil, then immediately remove from heat.

3. Meanwhile, fill four 1-pint jars with hot water to warm. Drain jars, then using slotted spoon, pack beets into jars. Using funnel and ladle, pour hot brine over beets to cover. Let jars cool completely, cover with lids, and refrigerate for at least 1 week before serving.

BEET MUHAMMARA

Makes about 2 cups   Total time: 30 minutes
WHY THIS RECIPE WORKS *Traditional muhammara is a sweet-smoky blend of roasted red peppers, toasted walnuts, pomegranate molasses, and Turkish or Syrian spices. It makes a delicious dip for crudités or pita, a spread for sandwiches, or a sauce for meat and fish. Ours incorporates beets, which gives it a splendid color and deeper flavor. For optimal creaminess, we found that microwaving grated beets softened them just enough to blend into the mixture. Jarred roasted peppers added smokiness without any hassle. Pomegranate molasses gave the dip its hallmark sweet yet slightly bitter flavor. It can be found in the international aisle of supermarkets; or substitute 1 tablespoon lemon juice plus 1 tablespoon mild molasses for the 2 tablespoons of pomegranate molasses. You can use the large holes of a box grater or a food processor fitted with a shredding disk to shred the beets.*

BRAISED BEETS WITH LEMON AND ALMONDS

Don't dump that beet-braising water down the sink! Using a small amount of water to braise beets on the stovetop both cooks them in a way that minimizes color-staining mess and leaves you with a flavorful infused liquid that can be reduced and used in a simple, versatile glaze or vinaigrette.

1. Trim the beets and then, to cut down on the cooking time, halve them horizontally.

2. Place the beets, cut side down, in a single layer in a Dutch oven and add the water and salt.

3. Simmer the beets until they are tender and can be easily pierced with a paring knife, 45 to 50 minutes. Transfer them to a cutting board to cool before rubbing off the skins.

4. Reduce the braising liquid in the pot, then add the vinegar and sugar and reduce the liquid again until a spatula leaves a trail when dragged through the glaze.

5. Cut the beet halves into ½-inch wedges, then add them to the pan with the glaze and toss with the flavorings to combine.

6. Transfer the beets to a serving platter, sprinkle with the nuts and herbs, and serve warm.

Beet Chips

8 ounces beets, trimmed, peeled,
   and shredded
1 cup jarred roasted red peppers,
   rinsed and patted dry
1 cup walnuts, toasted
1 scallion, sliced thin
2 tablespoons extra-virgin olive oil,
   plus extra for drizzling
2 tablespoons pomegranate molasses
2 teaspoons lemon juice
   Salt
½ teaspoon ground cumin
⅛ teaspoon cayenne pepper
2 tablespoons minced fresh parsley

1. Microwave beets in covered bowl, stirring often, until tender, about 4 minutes. Transfer beets to fine-mesh strainer set over bowl and let drain for 10 minutes.

2. Process drained beets, peppers, walnuts, scallion, oil, pomegranate molasses, lemon juice, ¾ teaspoon salt, cumin, and cayenne in food processor until smooth, about 1 minute, scraping down sides of bowl as needed.

3. Transfer mixture to serving bowl and season with salt to taste. Drizzle with extra oil to taste, and sprinkle with parsley before serving.

BEET CHIPS

Serves 2   Total time: 2 hours 45 minutes
WHY THIS RECIPE WORKS *A snackable chip made from beets has become a popular and more healthful alternative to potato chips. Beet chips sounded delightful, but we were skeptical about getting truly crisp results without any special equipment. Indeed, many of the recipes we tested produced chips that were leathery and floppy, or overcooked and bitter. Crispness depended on extracting as much moisture as possible from the beets. To do this without overcooking the chips, we lightly salted them to draw out some water—almost 2 tablespoons! Microwaving is a popular alternative to frying, but the process was inconsistent at best; the difference between perfection and burnt was mere seconds. So we took a cue from our kale chip method and slow-baked our beets in a 200-degree oven. It took a couple of hours but produced chips with*

a concentrated beet flavor, light crunch, and deep color. Be careful to not let the beet chips turn brown, as they will become bitter. Thinly sliced beets are key to crispy beet chips—use a mandoline, V-slicer, or the slicing disk on a food processor.

1 pound beets, trimmed, peeled,
   and sliced 1/16 inch thick
½ teaspoon salt

1. Adjust oven racks to upper-middle and lower-middle positions and heat oven to 200 degrees. Set wire racks in 2 rimmed baking sheets and spray with vegetable oil spray. Combine beets and salt in colander set over bowl and let drain for 25 minutes. Pat beets dry with paper towels.

2. Arrange beet slices on prepared racks, making sure slices overlap as little as possible. Bake beets until shrunken slightly and crisp throughout, 2 to 3 hours, switching and rotating sheets halfway through baking. Let beet chips cool completely before serving (beets will continue to crisp as they cool).

MARINATED BEET SALAD WITH ORANGES AND PECORINO

Serves 4   Total time: 2 hours 15 minutes
WHY THIS RECIPE WORKS *For this sweet and savory salad, we enlisted our preferred roasting technique, but with a twist, wrapping the beets together in aluminum foil rather than individually. We then roasted them until they were soft and tender and their skins were ready to slip away. Peeling, cutting into wedges, and tossing the roasted beets in the marinade while they were still warm helped them absorb the potent dressing. Orange segments, shaved Pecorino Romano cheese, and toasted walnuts arranged over the top added layers of complex flavors. To ensure even cooking, look for beets of similar size—2 to 3 inches in diameter. Red or golden beets work equally well in this recipe. Peel the cooked beets over the leftover foil packet to minimize mess. This recipe requires you to refrigerate the marinated beets for at least 30 minutes or up to 24 hours.*

1 pound beets, trimmed
½ cup water
¼ cup sherry vinegar
2 tablespoons extra-virgin olive oil,
   plus extra for drizzling
1 teaspoon fresh thyme leaves
   Salt and pepper
2 oranges
4 ounces (4 cups) baby arugula
2 ounces Pecorino Romano cheese, shaved
½ cup walnuts, toasted and chopped

1. Adjust oven rack to middle position and heat oven to 400 degrees. Place 16 by 12-inch piece of aluminum foil on rimmed baking sheet. Arrange beets in center of foil and lift sides of foil to form bowl. Add water to beets and crimp foil tightly to seal. Roast until beets can be easily pierced with paring knife, 1¼ to 1½ hours. Open foil packet to allow steam to escape and let cool slightly.

2. Whisk vinegar, oil, thyme, ½ teaspoon salt, and ¼ teaspoon pepper together in large bowl. Once beets are cool enough to handle, rub off skins with paper towels. Halve each beet vertically, then cut into ½-inch-thick wedges and add to bowl with vinaigrette. Cover and refrigerate for at least 30 minutes or up to 24 hours.

3. Cut away peel and pith from oranges. Holding fruit over small bowl to catch juice and fruit, use paring knife to slice between membranes to release segments. Arrange arugula on serving platter. Spoon beets over arugula and drizzle with remaining dressing from bowl. Arrange orange segments over salad and top with Pecorino and walnuts. Season with salt and pepper to taste. Drizzle with extra oil and serve.

VARIATIONS
Marinated Beet Salad with Pear and Feta
Substitute 1 halved, cored, and thinly sliced pear for oranges; ¾ cup crumbled feta cheese for Pecorino; and 2 tablespoons toasted pistachios for walnuts.

Marinated Beet Salad with Raspberries and Blue Cheese
Substitute ⅔ cup raspberries for oranges, ¾ cup crumbled blue cheese for Pecorino, and skinned toasted hazelnuts for walnuts.

CHARRED BEET SALAD

Serves 4 to 6   Total time: 1 hour 45 minutes

WHY THIS RECIPE WORKS *This charred salad reinvents and reinvigorates the pairing of creamy, salty goat cheese and earthy, sweet beets. After roasting foil-wrapped beets, we sliced and quickly charred them on the stovetop. This step essentially burned some of the sugar, adding pleasantly complementary bitterness. We amplified that with crisp radicchio and tossed it all with a dressing made from the beet cooking liquid. A simple spread of feta and Greek yogurt replaced the goat cheese. A final flourish of tart pomegranate seeds provided pops of bright acidity (and stayed on message with the ruby color scheme). Be sure to scrub the beets clean before roasting, as the roasting liquid forms the basis of the dressing.*

    4 ounces feta cheese, crumbled (1 cup)
    ½ cup plain Greek yogurt
    1½ pounds beets, trimmed
    3 tablespoons extra-virgin olive oil
    2 tablespoons water
    2 tablespoons sherry vinegar
      Salt and pepper
    1 tablespoon vegetable oil
    4 ounces radicchio, cut into 2-inch pieces
    ½ cup pomegranate seeds
    1 tablespoon roughly chopped fresh dill
    1 tablespoon roughly chopped fresh tarragon

1. Adjust oven rack to middle position and heat oven to 375 degrees. Set wire rack in rimmed baking sheet. Combine feta and ¼ cup yogurt in small bowl and mash to form coarse spread; refrigerate until ready to serve.

2. Toss beets, olive oil, water, vinegar, 1½ teaspoons salt, and 1 teaspoon pepper in bowl to combine. Stack two 16 by 12-inch pieces of aluminum foil on prepared rack. Arrange beets in center of foil and lift sides of foil to form bowl. Pour liquid over top and crimp foil tightly to seal.

3. Bake until beets can be easily pierced with paring knife, 1 to 1½ hours for small beets and 1½ to 2½ hours for medium to large beets. Open foil packet and set beets aside, then pour cooking liquid into large bowl (you

should have about ½ cup). Whisk remaining ¼ cup yogurt into beet cooking liquid until smooth; set aside. Once beets are cool enough to handle, rub off skins with paper towels and cut into ½-inch-thick rounds.

4. Heat vegetable oil in 12-inch skillet over medium-high heat until just smoking. Arrange beets in skillet in single layer and cook until both sides are well charred, about 3 minutes per side. Transfer to cutting board and cut into 1½-inch pieces, then add to bowl with yogurt-beet dressing.

5. Add radicchio to bowl with beets and toss to combine. Season with salt and pepper to taste. Spread yogurt-feta mixture in even layer on large serving plate. Arrange beets and radicchio over top, then sprinkle with pomegranate seeds, dill, and tarragon. Serve.

BEET AND CARROT NOODLE SALAD

Serves 6   Total time: 25 minutes

WHY THIS RECIPE WORKS *With their dense texture, beets are an excellent candidate for spiralizing into vegetable "noodles." Adding carrots made this salad even more visually stunning. The noodles' crisp-tender texture was a perfect foil for the creamy, nutty, sweet-and-savory dressing. Tasters loved the contrast of flavors and textures. For the best noodles, use beets at least 1½ inches in diameter and carrots at least ¾ inch across at the thinnest end and 1½ inches across at the thickest end. We prefer to spiralize our own vegetables, but you can substitute store-bought spiralized raw beets and carrots, though they tend to be drier and less flavorful. You can use smooth or chunky almond or peanut butter in this recipe.*

DRESSING
    ¼ cup almond or peanut butter
    3 tablespoons tahini
    3 tablespoons lime juice (2 limes)
    1 tablespoon soy sauce
    1 tablespoon honey
    1 tablespoon grated fresh ginger
    2 garlic cloves, minced
    ½ teaspoon toasted sesame oil
    ½ cup hot water

NOODLES
    1 pound beets, trimmed and peeled
    1 pound carrots, peeled
    5 scallions, sliced thin on bias
    ¼ cup fresh cilantro leaves
    1 tablespoon sesame seeds, toasted
      Lime wedges

1. **For the dressing** Whisk almond butter, tahini, lime juice, soy sauce, honey, ginger garlic, and oil together in large bowl until well combined. Whisking constantly, add water, 1 tablespoon at a time, until dressing has consistency of heavy cream (you may not need all of water). Set aside.

2. **For the noodles** Using spiralizer, cut beets and carrots into ⅛-inch-thick noodles; then cut beet and carrot noodles into 6-inch lengths.

3. Add beet and carrot noodles and scallions to dressing and toss well to combine. Sprinkle with cilantro and sesame seeds. Serve with lime wedges.

BEET AND WHEAT BERRY SOUP WITH DILL CREAM

Serves 6   Total time: 1 hour 30 minutes

WHY THIS RECIPE WORKS *For a lighter, fresher version of too-often-heavy borscht, a version that truly focused on the beets, we used vegetable broth and swapped out starchy potatoes for wheat berries. Toasting the wheat berries gave them a rich, nutty flavor and a pleasant chewy consistency in the soup. To build a flavorful backbone, we sautéed onion, garlic, thyme, and tomato paste before stirring in the broth. Red wine vinegar, red cabbage, and a pinch of cayenne helped to round out the flavor of the beets as well. A dollop of dill-flecked sour cream to finish added tang. You can use the large holes of a box grater or a food processor fitted with a shredding disk to shred the beets and carrot. Do not use presteamed or quick-cooking wheat berries here, as they have a much shorter cooking time; be prepared to read the package carefully to determine what kind of wheat berries you are using.*

Beet and Carrot Noodle Salad

DILL CREAM

½ cup sour cream
¼ cup minced fresh dill
½ teaspoon salt

SOUP

⅔ cup wheat berries, rinsed
3 tablespoons vegetable oil
2 onions, chopped fine
2 tablespoons tomato paste
4 garlic cloves, minced
1 teaspoon minced fresh thyme
 or ½ teaspoon dried
¼ teaspoon cayenne pepper
8 cups vegetable broth
3 cups water
1½ cups thinly sliced red cabbage
1 pound beets, trimmed, peeled,
 and shredded
1 small carrot, peeled and shredded
1 bay leaf
 Salt and pepper
1 tablespoon red wine vinegar

1. For the dill cream Combine all ingredients in bowl; set aside until ready to serve.

2. For the soup Toast wheat berries in Dutch oven over medium heat, stirring often, until fragrant and beginning to darken, about 5 minutes; transfer to bowl.

3. Heat oil in now-empty pot over medium heat until shimmering. Add onions and cook until softened, about 5 minutes. Stir in tomato paste, garlic, thyme, and cayenne and cook until fragrant and darkened slightly, about 2 minutes.

4. Stir in toasted wheat berries, broth, water, cabbage, beets, carrot, bay leaf, and ¾ teaspoon pepper, scraping up any browned bits, and bring to boil. Reduce heat to low and simmer until wheat berries are tender but still chewy and vegetables are tender, 45 minutes to 1¼ hours.

5. Off heat, discard bay leaf and stir in vinegar and 1 teaspoon salt. Season with additional salt and pepper to taste. Serve, passing dill cream separately.

PINTO BEAN–BEET BURGERS

Serves 8   Total time: 1 hour

WHY THIS RECIPE WORKS *Vegetarian or vegan burgers are often bean-based, but why not include beets? They bring both a lighter texture and a sweet-earthy flavor to the pinto beans. We added heft with bulgur and used ground nuts to provide meaty richness. Garlic and mustard deepened the savory flavors. While the bulgur cooked, we pulsed the other ingredients in the food processor. To bind the burgers, we found a surprising ingredient: carrot baby food. This added the necessary tackiness, and its subtle sweetness heightened that of the shredded beets; plus, it was already conveniently pureed. Panko bread crumbs further bound the mixture and helped the patties sear up with a crisp crust. When shopping, don't confuse bulgur with cracked wheat, which has a much longer cooking time and will not work here. Use the large holes of a box grater or a food processor fitted with a shredding disk to shred the beets. Serve with your favorite burger fixings.*

 Salt and pepper
⅔ cup medium-grind bulgur, rinsed
1 large beet (9 ounces), trimmed,
 peeled, and shredded
¾ cup walnuts
½ cup fresh basil leaves
2 garlic cloves, minced
1 (15-ounce) can pinto beans, rinsed
1 (4-ounce) jar carrot baby food
1 tablespoon whole-grain mustard
1½ cups panko bread crumbs
6 tablespoons vegetable oil, plus extra
 as needed
8 burger buns

1. Bring 1½ cups water and ½ teaspoon salt to boil in small saucepan. Off heat, stir in bulgur, cover, and let stand until tender, 15 to 20 minutes. Drain bulgur, spread onto rimmed baking sheet, and let cool slightly.

2. Meanwhile, pulse beet, walnuts, basil, and garlic in food processor until finely chopped, about 12 pulses, scraping down sides of bowl as needed. Add beans, baby food, 2 tablespoons water, mustard, 1½ teaspoons salt, and ½ teaspoon pepper and pulse until well combined, about 8 pulses. Transfer mixture to large bowl and stir in panko and cooled bulgur.

3. Adjust oven rack to middle position and heat oven to 200 degrees. Divide beet mixture into 8 equal portions and pack into 3½-inch-diameter patties.

4. Heat 3 tablespoons oil in 12-inch nonstick skillet over medium-high heat until shimmering. Gently lay 4 patties in skillet and cook until crisp and well browned on both sides, about 4 minutes per side, adding extra oil if skillet looks dry.

5. Transfer burgers to wire rack set in rimmed baking sheet and place in oven to keep warm. Wipe out skillet with paper towels and repeat with remaining 3 tablespoons oil and remaining 4 patties. Transfer to buns and serve.

BEET AND BARLEY RISOTTO

Serves 6   Total time: 1 hour 15 minutes

WHY THIS RECIPE WORKS *Hearty pearl barley holds its own against the sweet earthiness of beets and their sturdy greens. Pearl barley has had its outer husk removed, exposing the starchy interior, which helps create a velvety sauce when simmered. We stirred raw grated beets into the barley—half at the beginning for a base of flavor, and half at the end for freshness and color. Do not substitute hulled, hull-less, quick-cooking, or presteamed barley for the pearl barley. You can use the large holes of a box grater or a food processor fitted with a shredding disk to shred the beets.*

3 cups vegetable broth
3 cups water
2 tablespoons extra-virgin olive oil
1 pound beets with greens attached, beets trimmed, peeled, and shredded, greens stemmed and cut into 1-inch pieces (2 cups)
1 onion, chopped
   Salt and pepper
1½ cups pearl barley, rinsed
4 garlic cloves, minced
1 teaspoon minced fresh thyme or ¼ teaspoon dried
1 cup dry white wine
1 ounce Parmesan cheese, grated (½ cup)
2 tablespoons chopped fresh parsley

1. Bring broth and water to simmer in medium saucepan. Reduce heat to lowest setting and cover to keep warm.

2. Heat oil in large saucepan over medium heat until shimmering. Add half of grated beets, onion, and ¾ teaspoon salt and cook until vegetables are softened, 5 to 7 minutes. Stir in barley and cook, stirring often, until fragrant, about 4 minutes. Stir in garlic and thyme and cook until fragrant, about 30 seconds. Stir in wine and cook until fully absorbed, about 2 minutes.

3. Stir in 3 cups warm broth. Simmer, stirring occasionally, until liquid is absorbed and bottom of pan is dry, 22 to 25 minutes. Stir in 2 cups warm broth and simmer, stirring occasionally, until liquid is absorbed and bottom of pan is dry, 15 to 18 minutes.

4. Add beet greens and continue to cook, stirring often and adding remaining broth as needed to prevent pan bottom from becoming dry, until greens are softened and barley is cooked through but still somewhat firm in center, 5 to 10 minutes. Off heat, stir in remaining grated beets and Parmesan. Season with salt and pepper to taste and sprinkle with parsley. Serve.

RED FLANNEL HASH

Serves 4   Total time: 45 minutes

WHY THIS RECIPE WORKS *Red flannel hash gets its name from the beets that are included; this version adds sweet potatoes to the usual russets to amplify the sweetness of the beets. To speed things up, we parcooked the potatoes and beets in the microwave until tender and then moved them to the skillet to brown and crisp. Onion, garlic, chili powder, and a dash of hot sauce gave the hash backbone, and heavy cream brought richness. To make this a hearty meal, we poached eight eggs right in the hash. If you notice that the potato-beet mixture isn't getting brown in step 3, turn up the heat (but don't let it burn). Note that the beets will not brown like the potatoes; they will burn if the pan gets too dry. You will need a 12-inch nonstick skillet with a tight-fitting lid for this recipe.*

8 ounces russet potatoes, peeled and cut into ¼-inch pieces
8 ounces sweet potatoes, peeled and cut into ¼-inch pieces
8 ounces beets, peeled and cut into ¼-inch pieces
2 tablespoons vegetable oil
   Salt and pepper
1 onion, chopped fine
2 garlic cloves, minced
½ teaspoon minced fresh thyme or ¼ teaspoon dried
½ teaspoon chili powder
⅓ cup heavy cream
¼ teaspoon Worcestershire sauce
¼ teaspoon hot sauce
8 large eggs

1. Microwave russets, sweet potatoes, beets, 1 tablespoon oil, ½ teaspoon salt, and ¼ teaspoon pepper in covered bowl until potatoes are translucent around edges, 5 to 8 minutes, stirring halfway through microwaving.

2. Meanwhile, heat remaining 1 tablespoon oil in 12-inch nonstick skillet over medium-high heat until shimmering. Add onion and cook until softened and lightly browned, 5 to 7 minutes.

3. Stir in garlic, thyme, and chili powder and cook until fragrant, about 30 seconds. Stir in hot potato mixture, cream, Worcestershire, and hot sauce. Using back of spatula, gently pack beet-potato mixture into pan and cook undisturbed for 2 minutes. Flip hash, 1 portion at a time, and lightly repack into pan. Repeat flipping process every few minutes until mixture is nicely browned, 6 to 8 minutes.

4. Off heat, make 4 shallow indentations (about 2 inches wide) in surface of hash using back of spoon. Crack 2 eggs into each indentation and season eggs with salt and pepper. Cover and cook over medium-low heat until egg whites are just set and yolks are still runny, 5 to 10 minutes. Serve.

BROCCOLI

Although broccoli might seem like the ultimate all-American vegetable, it only became widely available in the United States in the 1920s and '30s, thanks to Italian immigrants. Both its popularity and its consumption have skyrocketed since the 1960s. We think it couldn't have happened to a better vegetable.

Broccolini, with its long, svelte stalks and smaller, loose florets, looks like a baby version of broccoli, but it's not. It's a hybrid of regular broccoli and Chinese broccoli that was developed by a Japanese seed company in the 1990s. You might see it labeled with the rather odd name Asparation in supermarkets. Broccolini cooks quickly and has a sweet, nutty, altogether delicious flavor. If anyone in your family claims to dislike broccoli, try serving broccolini as a "starter broc."

Broccoli rabe, though it looks like a hippie cousin to broccolini, is actually closely related to the turnip. In fact, in Puglia, the heel of the Italian boot, where it is beloved, it's called *cime di rapa*, or "turnip tops." Broccoli rabe is also sometimes called rapini or broccoli raab. Its flavor is pungent, bold, and aggressive, and it can be bitter and tough if not cooked properly. The wildly generous leaves as well as the stems and florets are edible.

Our creative everyday ways with broccoli include Pan-Roasted Broccoli with Lemon Browned Butter and Broccolini with Pancetta and Parmesan. Our Beef and Chinese Broccoli Stir-Fry is leaps and bounds better than takeout. And Cheesy Broccoli Calzones, made with either homemade or store-bought dough, are a surefire crowd-pleaser.

shopping and storage

All of the varieties of broccoli are available year-round and generally hold up well both in the supermarket and at home in the refrigerator. Store all of these types of broccoli wrapped in paper towels in a loosely closed plastic produce bag for up to a week.

BROCCOLI Choose heads with firm florets that are tightly closed and are dark green or purplish-green. Avoid broccoli heads where the green buds are starting to turn yellow or tiny flowers are emerging; this is a sign it's past its prime and will be bitter.

BROCCOLINI Slender, sweet, and crunchy broccolini tends to come at a premium price as compared to broccoli, but its sweeter, milder flavor might just make it worth it to you. Unlike with regular broccoli, the tiny yellow flowers that often appear on broccolini are tasty and perfectly edible.

BROCCOLI RABE This sturdy, strongly flavored variety is widely available in supermarkets, even in the dead of winter. As with regular broccoli, avoid bunches with yellowing leaves and flowers in favor of dark green foliage and florets.

vegetable science

A Good Reason Not to Overcook Broccoli

When broccoli cells are destroyed (as through cutting, chopping, or chewing), enzymatic reactions result in the formation of sulforaphane. This potent phytochemical is formed in all cruciferous vegetables, but broccoli is one of the richest sources of this antioxidant. If broccoli is overcooked, chemical changes cause the chlorophyll to begin to break down, while the acids leach out. This intensifies as cooking continues, and the broccoli will begin to fade in color. Other, non-beneficial sulfur compounds are formed instead of sulforaphane—which is why overcooked broccoli smells and tastes so unpleasant.

vegetable prep

Prepping Broccoli for Roasting

1. Cut crown from stalk and slice crown in half or into wedges, as directed.

2. Trim florets into small pieces, if directed.

3. Trim tough outer peel from stalk with chef's knife (or vegetable peeler).

4. Trim stalk into oblong coins or planks, as recipe directs.

Trimming Broccolini

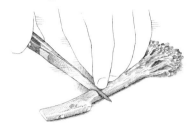

1. Trim bottom ends of stems.

2. If stalk measures more than ¼ inch at base, split stalk in half lengthwise for even cooking.

Trimming Broccoli Rabe

1. Trim off tough ends of broccoli rabe.

2. If recipe directs, cut rabe into 1-inch to 2-inch pieces.

STEAMED BROCCOLI WITH LIME-CUMIN DRESSING

Serves 4   Total time: 20 minutes

WHY THIS RECIPE WORKS *To meet the challenge of adding flavor without fuss to simple cooked broccoli, we experimented with tossing uncooked dressings and sauces with steamed broccoli. We found that potent flavorings like citrus juices, garlic and onions, chiles, and spices, all of which are assertive enough to stand up to the strong flavor of broccoli, worked best in our basic broccoli recipes. You will need a collapsible steamer basket for this recipe.*

DRESSING
¼ cup finely chopped red onion
3 tablespoons extra-virgin olive oil
1 teaspoon grated lime zest plus
  1 tablespoon juice
½ teaspoon ground cumin
⅛ teaspoon hot sauce, plus extra
  for serving

BROCCOLI
1½ pounds broccoli, florets cut into
  1-inch pieces, stalks peeled and
  sliced ¼ inch thick
  Salt

1. For the dressing Whisk all ingredients together in large bowl; set aside for serving.

2. For the broccoli Bring 1 inch water to boil in Dutch oven. Place broccoli in collapsible steamer basket, then transfer basket to pot. Cover and cook until broccoli is tender and bright green, about 5 minutes.

3. Transfer broccoli to bowl with dressing and gently toss to combine. Season with salt and extra hot sauce to taste. Serve warm or at room temperature.

VARIATION
Steamed Broccoli with Spicy Balsamic Dressing and Black Olives
Whisk ¼ cup chopped pitted kalamata olives, ¼ cup extra-virgin olive oil, 2 teaspoons balsamic vinegar, 2 teaspoons red wine vinegar, 1 minced garlic clove, ½ teaspoon red pepper flakes, and ¼ teaspoon salt together in bowl. Substitute for lime-cumin dressing.

PAN-ROASTED BROCCOLI WITH LEMON BROWNED BUTTER

Serves 6   Total time: 25 minutes

WHY THIS RECIPE WORKS *The first step to perfecting our pan-roasted broccoli recipe was to transform a head of broccoli into pieces that would cook evenly. First, we trimmed the florets into small pieces and the stalks into oblong coins. Then we layered the stalks evenly in a hot, lightly oiled skillet, and once they began to brown we added the florets along with seasoned water and allowed the mixture to steam until nearly tender. A lemony browned butter was the finishing touch. You will need a 12-inch skillet with a tight-fitting lid for this recipe. When prepping the broccoli, keep the stalks and florets separate.*

BROCCOLI
¼ teaspoon salt
⅛ teaspoon pepper
2 tablespoons vegetable oil
1¾ pounds broccoli, florets cut into
  1½-inch pieces, stalks peeled and
  sliced ¼ inch thick on bias

LEMON BROWNED BUTTER
4 tablespoons unsalted butter,
  cut into 4 pieces
1 small shallot, minced
2 garlic cloves, minced
¼ teaspoon salt
⅛ teaspoon pepper
1½ teaspoons lemon juice
½ teaspoon minced fresh thyme

1. For the broccoli Stir 3 tablespoons water, salt, and pepper together in small bowl until salt dissolves. Heat oil in 12-inch non-stick skillet over medium-high heat until just smoking. Add broccoli stalks in even layer and cook, without stirring, until browned on bottoms, about 2 minutes. Add florets and toss to combine. Cook, without stirring, until bottoms of florets just begin to brown, 1 to 2 minutes.

2. Add water mixture and immediately cover skillet. Cook until broccoli is bright green but still crisp, about 2 minutes. Uncover and continue to cook until water has evaporated, broccoli stalks are tender, and florets are tender-crisp, about 2 minutes; transfer to bowl.

3. For the lemon browned butter Melt butter in now-empty skillet over medium-high heat and continue to cook, swirling occasionally, until butter is browned and releases nutty aroma, about 1½ minutes. Off heat, add shallot, garlic, salt, and pepper, and stir constantly until garlic and shallot are fragrant, about 1 minute. Stir in lemon juice and thyme. Return broccoli to skillet and toss to coat with browned butter. Serve.

VARIATION
Pan-Roasted Broccoli with Creamy Gruyère Sauce
In step 3, melt 1 tablespoon unsalted butter in empty skillet over medium heat. Add 1 thinly sliced shallot and cook until softened, about 2 minutes. Stir in ½ cup heavy cream, ½ teaspoon Dijon mustard, ½ teaspoon dry sherry, ⅛ teaspoon salt, and pinch cayenne pepper. Increase heat to medium-high and cook until mixture bubbles and thickens, about 1 minute. Off heat, stir in 3 tablespoons finely grated Gruyère cheese and 1 teaspoon lemon juice until cheese is melted. Substitute for lemon browned butter. Sprinkle broccoli with 1 tablespoon finely grated Gruyère before serving.

ROASTED BROCCOLI

Serves 6   Total time: 30 minutes

WHY THIS RECIPE WORKS *Oven roasting is a great way to deepen the flavor of vegetables, but broccoli can be tricky to roast given its awkward shape; dense, woody stalks; and shrubby florets. We wanted a roasted broccoli recipe that would give us evenly cooked broccoli—both stalks and florets—and add concentrated flavor and dappled browning. The way we prepared the broccoli was the key. We sliced the crown in half and then cut each half into uniform wedges. We cut the stalks into rectangular pieces slightly smaller than the more delicate wedges. This promoted even cooking and great browning by maximizing contact with the hot baking sheet. Preheating the baking sheet on the*

ROASTED BROCCOLI

The dry heat of a hot oven works magic on broccoli, creating all sorts of roasty, caramelized flavors while rendering the stems tender and the florets crispy. And it's really no harder than steaming it. Don't skip the ½ teaspoon sugar—it helps promote browning and tames any bitterness. Besides being a great simple side, roasted broccoli can be used to fill frittatas or to top pizzas.

1. Cut the broccoli stalks from the crowns horizontally across the base of the broccoli crowns.

2. Cut the broccoli crowns into either four or six wedges, depending on the size of the crowns.

3. Trim or peel the tough outer skin from the stalks, then cut the stalks into ½-inch-thick planks 2 to 3 inches long.

4. Toss the broccoli crowns and stalks in a bowl with the oil, sugar, salt, and pepper.

5. Working quickly, arrange the broccoli pieces in a single layer, cut side down, on the preheated baking sheet.

6. Transfer the roasted broccoli to a serving platter and serve with the lemon wedges.

lowest rack of the oven gave us even better browning. Tossing a scant ½ teaspoon of sugar over the broccoli along with salt, pepper, and a splash of olive oil gave us crisp-tipped florets and blistered and browned stalks that were sweet and full-flavored.

1 ¾ pounds broccoli
3 tablespoons extra-virgin olive oil
½ teaspoon sugar
½ teaspoon salt
    Pinch pepper
    Lemon wedges

1. Adjust oven rack to lowest position, place rimmed baking sheet on rack, and heat oven to 500 degrees. Cut broccoli horizontally at juncture of crowns and stalks. Cut crowns into 4 wedges if 3 to 4 inches in diameter or 6 wedges if 4 to 5 inches in diameter. Trim tough outer peel from stalks, then cut into ½-inch-thick planks 2 to 3 inches long.

2. Toss broccoli with oil, sugar, salt, and pepper in bowl. Working quickly, lay broccoli in single layer, flat sides down, on hot sheet. Roast until stalks are well browned and tender and florets are lightly browned, 9 to 11 minutes. Transfer to serving platter and serve with lemon wedges.

VARIATIONS
Roasted Broccoli with Garlic
Stir 1 tablespoon minced garlic into oil before tossing it with raw broccoli.

Roasted Broccoli with Shallots and Fennel Seeds
While broccoli roasts, heat 1 tablespoon extra-virgin olive oil in 8-inch skillet over medium heat until shimmering. Add 3 thinly sliced shallots and cook until softened and lightly browned, 5 to 6 minutes. Stir in 1 teaspoon cracked fennel seeds and cook until shallots are golden brown, 1 to 2 minutes; remove from heat. Toss roasted broccoli with shallot mixture before serving.

GRILLED BROCCOLI WITH LEMON AND PARMESAN
Serves 6 to 8   Total time: 50 minutes
WHY THIS RECIPE WORKS *For vivid green broccoli florets with flavorful char, there's no beating the grill. To avoid toughness, we peeled the stalks with a vegetable peeler and cut the head into spears small enough to cook quickly but large enough to grill easily. Since grilling alone would yield dry broccoli, we tossed the spears in olive oil and water and steamed them in sealed foil packets on the grill. As soon as the stalks and florets were evenly cooked, we placed them directly on the grill to give them plenty of char. A squeeze of grilled lemon and a sprinkling of Parmesan sealed the deal. To keep the packs from tearing, use heavy-duty aluminum foil. Use the large holes of a box grater to shred the Parmesan.*

¼ cup extra-virgin olive oil, plus
    extra for drizzling
1 tablespoon water
    Salt and pepper
2 pounds broccoli
1 lemon, halved
¼ cup shredded Parmesan cheese

1. Cut two 26 by 12-inch sheets of heavy-duty aluminum foil. Whisk oil, water, ¾ teaspoon salt, and ½ teaspoon pepper together in large bowl.

2. Trim stalks so each entire head of broccoli measures 6 to 7 inches long. Trim tough outer peel from stalks, then cut heads in half lengthwise into spears (stems should be ½ to ¾ inch thick and florets 3 to 4 inches wide). Add broccoli to oil mixture and toss well to coat.

3. Divide broccoli between sheets of foil, cut side down and alternating direction of florets and stalks. Bring short sides of foil together and crimp tightly. Crimp long ends to seal packs tightly.

4a. **For a charcoal grill** Open bottom vent completely. Light large chimney starter filled with charcoal briquettes (6 quarts). When top coals are partially covered with ash, pour evenly over half of grill. Set cooking grate in place, cover, and open lid vent completely. Heat grill until hot, about 5 minutes.

4b. **For a gas grill** Turn all burners to high, cover, and heat grill until hot, about 15 minutes. Turn all burners to medium-high. (Adjust burners as needed to maintain grill temperature around 400 degrees.)

5. Clean and oil cooking grate. Arrange packets evenly on grill (over coals if using charcoal), cover, and cook for 8 minutes, flipping packets halfway through cooking.

6. Transfer packets to rimmed baking sheet and, using scissors, carefully cut open, allowing steam to escape away from you. (Broccoli should be bright green and fork inserted into stalks should meet some resistance.)

7. Discard foil and place broccoli and lemon halves cut side down on grill (over coals if using charcoal). Grill (covered if using gas), turning broccoli about every 2 minutes, until stalks are fork-tender and well charred on all sides, 6 to 8 minutes. Transfer broccoli to now-empty sheet as it finishes cooking. Grill lemon halves until well charred on cut side, 6 to 8 minutes.

8. Transfer broccoli to cutting board and cut into 2-inch pieces. Transfer to serving platter and season with salt and pepper to taste. Squeeze lemon over broccoli to taste, sprinkle with Parmesan, and drizzle with extra oil. Serve.

VARIATIONS
Grilled Broccoli with Anchovy-Garlic Butter
Omit lemon and Parmesan cheese. Whisk 4 tablespoons melted unsalted butter, 3 rinsed and minced anchovy fillets, 1 minced garlic clove, 1 teaspoon lemon juice, ½ teaspoon salt, ¼ teaspoon red pepper flakes, and ⅛ teaspoon pepper together in bowl. Drizzle butter mixture over broccoli before serving.

Grilled Broccoli with Sweet Chili Sauce
Omit lemon and Parmesan cheese. Whisk 4 teaspoons toasted sesame oil, 2 ½ teaspoons sugar, 2 teaspoons Asian chili-garlic sauce, 1 teaspoon distilled white vinegar, and ¼ teaspoon salt together in bowl. Drizzle oil mixture over broccoli before serving.

Grilled Broccoli with Lemon and Parmesan

BROCCOLINI WITH PANCETTA AND PARMESAN

Serves 4   Total time: 30 minutes

WHY THIS RECIPE WORKS *Meaty pancetta, sharp Parmesan cheese, and a pinch of red pepper flakes lend a bold Italian twist to mild, sweet broccolini. Using a Dutch oven instead of a skillet gave us enough room to render the pancetta and steam-sauté the broccolini with water all in the same pot. Splitting the thicker stalks, which can sometimes be tough and woody, allowed them to cook evenly. Don't split the broccolini stalks if they are already very thin (¼ inch or less). If you can't find pancetta, use bacon.*

1	pound broccolini, trimmed
3	ounces pancetta, cut into ½-inch pieces
1½	tablespoons extra-virgin olive oil
2	garlic cloves, minced
¼	teaspoon red pepper flakes
2	teaspoons balsamic vinegar
	Salt and pepper
1	ounce Parmesan cheese, grated (½ cup)

1. Cut broccolini stalks measuring more than ½ inch in diameter at base in half lengthwise. Cut stalks measuring ¼ to ½ inch in diameter at base in half lengthwise, starting below where florets begin and keeping florets intact. Leave stalks measuring less than ¼ inch in diameter at base whole.

2. Cook pancetta in Dutch oven over medium heat until crisp, 6 to 8 minutes. Using slotted spoon, transfer pancetta to paper towel–lined plate; set aside.

3. Add 1 tablespoon oil, garlic, and pepper flakes to fat left in pot and cook over medium heat until fragrant, about 30 seconds. Add broccolini and cook, stirring frequently, until bright green, about 5 minutes. Add ¾ cup water, cover, and cook until broccolini is tender, about 5 minutes.

4. Uncover and continue to cook until liquid has evaporated, about 1 minute. Off heat, stir in pancetta, vinegar, and remaining 1½ teaspoons oil. Season with salt and pepper to taste. Transfer to serving platter and sprinkle with Parmesan. Serve.

PAN-STEAMED BROCCOLINI WITH SHALLOT

Serves 4   Total time: 25 minutes

WHY THIS RECIPE WORKS *This simple and speedy one-pan broccolini side dish is gently flavored with shallot, lemon zest, and thyme. We split the thicker broccolini stalks down the middle so that they were the same size as the thinner ones in the bunch, ensuring even cooking. There's no need to split stalks that are ¼ inch or thinner. You will need a 12-inch skillet with a tight-fitting lid for this recipe.*

1	pound broccolini, trimmed
½	teaspoon salt
2	tablespoons unsalted butter
2	teaspoons minced shallot
1	teaspoon grated lemon zest
1	teaspoon minced fresh thyme
¼	teaspoon pepper

1. Cut broccolini stalks measuring more than ½ inch in diameter at base in half lengthwise. Cut stalks measuring ¼ to ½ inch in diameter at base in half lengthwise, starting below where florets begin and keeping florets intact. Leave stalks measuring less than ¼ inch in diameter at base whole.

2. Bring ⅓ cup water to boil in 12-inch skillet. Add broccolini and sprinkle with salt. Cover, reduce heat to medium-low, and cook for 3 minutes. Uncover and gently toss broccolini with tongs. Cover and continue to cook until broccolini is bright green and crisp-tender, 3 to 5 minutes. Uncover and continue to cook until any remaining liquid has evaporated, about 30 seconds.

3. Off heat, push broccolini to one side of skillet. Add butter, shallot, lemon zest, thyme, and pepper to cleared side of skillet and stir to combine. Using tongs, toss broccolini with butter mixture until evenly-coated. Serve.

VARIATION

Pan-Steamed Broccolini with Ginger
Reduce lemon zest to ½ teaspoon. Substitute 2 teaspoons grated fresh ginger and ¼ teaspoon honey for shallot and thyme.

SAUTÉED BROCCOLI RABE WITH ROASTED RED PEPPERS

Serves 6 to 8   Total time: 30 minutes

WHY THIS RECIPE WORKS Assertive, peppery broccoli rabe is extremely appealing when combined with roasted sweet red bell peppers in this Italian-inspired side dish. We chose store-bought jarred roasted peppers for maximum convenience without sacrificing flavor. Chopping the broccoli rabe into small pieces and quickly blanching it in a large amount of salted water is a way to tame its bitterness while retaining its round, deep flavor. This is a quick, dependable, and versatile side dish for any night of the week.

- 2 pounds broccoli rabe, trimmed and cut into 1-inch pieces
  Salt and pepper
- 3 tablespoons extra-virgin olive oil
- 2 garlic cloves, minced
- ½ cup jarred roasted red peppers, patted dry and chopped fine

1. Bring 3 quarts water to boil in Dutch oven. Fill large bowl halfway with ice and water. Add broccoli rabe and 2 teaspoons salt to boiling water and cook until wilted and tender, about 2 minutes. Drain broccoli rabe, then transfer bowl of ice water and let sit until chilled. Drain again and thoroughly pat dry.

2. Cook 2 tablespoons oil and garlic in now-empty Dutch oven over medium heat, stirring often, until garlic begins to sizzle, about 2 minutes. Increase heat to medium-high, add broccoli rabe, red peppers, and ½ teaspoon salt and cook, stirring to coat with oil, until heated through, about 1 minute. Season with salt and pepper to taste. Transfer to serving platter and drizzle with remaining 1 tablespoon oil. Serve.

VARIATION

Sautéed Broccoli Rabe with Sun-Dried Tomatoes and Pine Nuts

Omit red peppers. Add ¼ cup oil-packed sun-dried tomatoes, cut into thin strips, and ¼ teaspoon red pepper flakes to pot with garlic. Sprinkle broccoli rabe with 3 tablespoons toasted pine nuts before serving.

BROILED BROCCOLI RABE

Serves 4   Total time: 20 minutes

WHY THIS RECIPE WORKS Broiling broccoli rabe is a simple, superfast way to create deep caramelization, adding just a touch of contrasting sweetness to this bitter green vegetable. And it takes mere minutes, requiring nothing more than a rimmed baking sheet. To keep things streamlined, we skipped the usual blanching step and simply cut the tops (the leaves and florets) from the stalks, but did no further chopping. Toss the pieces with the garlicky oil and they're ready for the oven.

- 3 tablespoons extra-virgin olive oil
- 1 pound broccoli rabe, trimmed
- 1 garlic clove, minced
- ¾ teaspoon kosher salt
- ¼ teaspoon red pepper flakes
  Lemon wedges

1. Adjust oven rack 4 inches from broiler element and heat broiler. Brush rimmed baking sheet with 1 tablespoon oil.

2. Cut tops (leaves and florets) of broccoli rabe from stalks, keeping tops whole, then cut stalks into 1-inch pieces. Transfer to prepared sheet.

3. Combine remaining 2 tablespoons oil, garlic, salt, and pepper flakes in small bowl. Pour oil mixture over broccoli rabe and toss to combine.

4. Broil until exposed half of leaves are well browned, 2 to 2½ minutes. Using tongs, toss to expose unbrowned leaves. Return sheet to oven and continue to broil until most leaves are lightly charred and stalks are crisp-tender, 2 to 2½ minutes. Serve with lemon wedges.

BROCCOLI RABE AND SPICY TOMATO SAUCE

Serves 6 to 8   Total time: 45 minutes

WHY THIS RECIPE WORKS This guest-worthy braised broccoli rabe delivers rustic robust flavor with less bitterness. We blanched it in a large amount of salted water to tame its bitterness. Then we braised it in a sauce that complemented its strong flavor. To replicate the long-simmered flavors of traditional arrabbiata sauce, we started by sautéing onions—finely diced for more surface area—in extra-virgin olive oil. Dried herbs and garlic completed the base flavors, while a generous amount of red pepper flakes brought the heat. Canned crushed tomatoes, which require no chopping or pureeing, made up the bulk of the sauce. We added grated Parmesan for nutty richness and chopped parsley for a bright, fresh finish. Be sure to set up the ice water bath before cooking the broccoli rabe, as plunging it into the cold water immediately after blanching retains its bright green color and ensures that it doesn't overcook.

- 2 pounds broccoli rabe, trimmed
  Salt and pepper
- 1 tablespoon extra-virgin olive oil, plus extra for serving
- 1 small onion, chopped fine
- 4 garlic cloves, minced
- ¾ teaspoon red pepper flakes
- ¼ teaspoon dried oregano
- 1 (28-ounce) can crushed tomatoes
- ¼ teaspoon sugar
- 1 ounce Parmesan cheese, grated (½ cup)
- 2 tablespoons chopped fresh basil or parsley

1. Bring 4 quarts water to boil in Dutch oven. Fill large bowl halfway with ice and water. Cut tops (leaves and florets) of broccoli rabe from stalks and separate. Add broccoli rabe stalks and 1 tablespoon salt to boiling water and cook for 1 minute. Add broccoli rabe tops and cook until tops are just tender and wilted, about 1 minute. Drain broccoli rabe, then transfer to bowl of ice water and let sit until chilled. Drain again and thoroughly pat dry.

2. Heat oil in now-empty pot over medium heat until shimmering. Add onion and ½ teaspoon salt and cook until softened, about 5 minutes. Stir in garlic, pepper flakes, and oregano and cook until fragrant, about 30 seconds.

3. Stir in tomatoes and sugar and bring to simmer. Stir in broccoli rabe and cook until sauce is thickened slightly and broccoli rabe is tender, about 10 minutes. Season with salt and pepper to taste. Transfer to serving platter, drizzle with extra oil, and sprinkle with Parmesan and basil. Serve.

BROCCOLI RABE WITH WHITE BEANS

Serves 4 to 6   Total time: 20 minutes
WHY THIS RECIPE WORKS *We wanted to showcase the bold flavor of broccoli rabe alongside creamy white beans, a classic pairing in Italian cooking. Cutting the broccoli rabe into 1-inch pieces meant that the pieces cooked evenly when quickly sautéed. Canned beans were the obvious choice to make this an easy weeknight side dish or light dinner. Adding the beans early in the cooking process gave them time to absorb the flavors of the garlic-infused olive oil. A shot of savory chicken broth rounded out the dish.*

- ¼ cup extra-virgin olive oil
- 3 garlic cloves, sliced thin
- ¼ teaspoon red pepper flakes
- 1 pound broccoli rabe, trimmed and cut into 1-inch pieces
- 1 (15-ounce) can cannellini beans, rinsed
- ¼ cup chicken or vegetable broth
   Salt and pepper
   Grated Parmesan cheese
   Lemon wedges

Cook 2 tablespoons oil, garlic, and pepper flakes in Dutch oven over medium heat until garlic is golden brown, 2 to 4 minutes. Stir in broccoli rabe, beans, broth, and ½ teaspoon salt and cook, stirring occasionally, until broccoli rabe is tender, 4 to 6 minutes. Off heat, stir in remaining 2 tablespoons oil and season with salt and pepper to taste. Serve, passing Parmesan and lemon wedges separately.

BROCCOLI SALAD WITH RAISINS AND WALNUTS

Serves 4 to 6   Total time: 30 minutes
WHY THIS RECIPE WORKS *Most recipes for this potluck and picnic classic leave the broccoli raw, but we found that cooking it briefly in boiling water improved both its flavor and its appearance. Adding the hardier stalks to the cooking water before the florets leveled the playing field, so both became tender at the same time. Drying the broccoli in a salad spinner rid it of excess moisture after cooking, so the dressing—a tangy mayo-and-vinegar mixture—didn't get watered down. Toasted walnuts and golden raisins brought crunch and salty-sweet balance to this salad. You can substitute currants or dried cranberries for the raisins. When prepping the broccoli, keep the stalks and florets separate.*

- ½ cup golden raisins
- 1½ pounds broccoli, florets cut into 1-inch pieces, stalks peeled and sliced ¼ inch thick
- ½ cup mayonnaise
- 1 tablespoon balsamic vinegar
   Salt and pepper
- ½ cup walnuts, toasted and chopped
- 1 shallot, minced

1. Bring 3 quarts water to boil in Dutch oven. Meanwhile, fill large bowl halfway with ice and water. Combine ½ cup boiling water and raisins in small bowl, cover, and let sit for 5 minutes; drain.

2. Add broccoli stalks to remaining boiling water and cook for 1 minute. Add florets and cook until slightly tender, about 1 minute. Drain broccoli, then transfer to bowl of ice water and let sit until chilled. Drain again and then spin broccoli in a salad spinner to remove moisture (or thoroughly pat dry).

3. Whisk mayonnaise, vinegar, ½ teaspoon salt, and ¼ teaspoon pepper together in large bowl. Add broccoli, raisins, walnuts, and shallot and toss to combine. Season with salt and pepper to taste. Serve. (Salad can be refrigerated for up to 6 hours.)

BROCCOLI-CHEESE SOUP

Serves 6 to 8   Total time: 50 minutes
WHY THIS RECIPE WORKS *Overcooking— yes, overcooking—the broccoli for our soup recipe coaxed all the flavor out of it. Adding a bit of baking soda to the cooking water sped up the cooking process, and pureeing fresh baby spinach along with the other ingredients intensified the soup's bright green color and enhanced its green vegetable flavor. Finally, a duo of cheddar and Parmesan gave our soup adequate cheesy flavor without making it heavy.*

- 2 tablespoons unsalted butter
- 2 pounds broccoli, florets cut into 1-inch pieces, stalks peeled and sliced ¼-inch-thick
- 1 onion, chopped
- 2 garlic cloves, minced
- 1½ teaspoons dry mustard powder
   Salt and pepper
   Pinch cayenne pepper
- 3 cups water
- ¼ teaspoon baking soda
- 2 cups chicken or vegetable broth, plus extra as needed
- 2 ounces (2 cups) baby spinach
- 3 ounces sharp cheddar cheese, shredded (¾ cup)
- 1½ ounces Parmesan cheese, grated (¾ cup), plus extra for serving

1. Melt butter in Dutch oven over medium-high heat. Add broccoli, onion, garlic, mustard powder, 1 teaspoon salt, and cayenne. Cook, stirring frequently, until fragrant, about 6 minutes. Stir in 1 cup water and baking soda and bring to simmer. Cover, reduce heat to medium, and cook until broccoli is very soft, about 20 minutes, stirring once halfway through cooking.

2. Stir in broth and remaining 2 cups water and bring to simmer. Stir in spinach and cook until wilted, about 1 minute.

3. Working in batches, process soup, cheddar, and Parmesan in blender until smooth, 1 to 2 minutes. Return soup to now-empty pot and bring to brief simmer over medium heat. Season with salt and pepper to taste. Adjust consistency with extra hot broth. Serve, passing extra Parmesan separately.

Broccoli Rabe with White Beans

3. **For the topping** Meanwhile, cook oil, sun-dried tomatoes, garlic, pepper flakes, and ½ teaspoon salt in 12-inch nonstick skillet over medium-high heat until garlic is fragrant and slightly toasted, about 1½ minutes. Add broccoli rabe and broth, cover, and cook until broccoli rabe turns bright green, about 2 minutes. Uncover and continue to cook, stirring frequently, until most of broth has evaporated and broccoli rabe is just tender, 2 to 3 minutes. Season with salt to taste.

4. Remove polenta from heat, stir in Parmesan and butter, and season with salt and pepper to taste. Let sit, covered, for 5 minutes. Spoon topping over individual portions of polenta and sprinkle with Parmesan and pine nuts. Serve, passing extra Parmesan separately.

FARRO AND BROCCOLI RABE GRATIN

Serves 4 to 6   Total time: 1 hour

WHY THIS RECIPE WORKS *This is a whole new kind of casserole, featuring a hearty whole grain, creamy white beans, and robust broccoli rabe. Toasting the farro in the aromatics and oil gave it extra nuttiness and ensured even cooking. White beans added creaminess and protein. Blanching the rabe in salted water tamed its bitterness. We sautéed the blanched rabe with garlic and pepper flakes for extra flavor. Sun-dried tomatoes gave another flavor pop. All that was left was to combine everything in a casserole dish and run it under the broiler to brown the Parmesan dusted over the top. We prefer the flavor and texture of whole farro; pearled farro can be used, but the texture may be softer. Do not substitute quick-cooking or presteamed farro; read the package carefully to determine this.*

- 2 tablespoons extra-virgin olive oil
- 1 onion, minced
- 1½ cups whole farro, rinsed
- 2 cups chicken or vegetable broth
- 1½ cups water
- 4 ounces Parmesan cheese, grated (2 cups)
   Salt and pepper
- 1 pound broccoli rabe, trimmed and cut into 2-inch pieces

PARMESAN POLENTA WITH BROCCOLI RABE, SUN-DRIED TOMATOES, AND PINE NUTS

Serves 4   Total time: 1 hour

WHY THIS RECIPE WORKS *Broccoli rabe, sun-dried tomatoes, garlic, and red pepper flakes combine to make a savory, intensely flavored topping for sweet, nutty polenta. We reduced the polenta's usual long cooking time by adding baking soda, which softened the outer layer of the grains. The baking soda also encouraged the polenta to release its starch uniformly, creating a creamy consistency and soft texture with minimal stirring. Parmesan cheese and butter stirred in at the last minute, along with toasted pine nuts sprinkled on top, finished the dish in a satisfyingly rich way. You will need a 12-inch nonstick skillet with a tight-fitting lid for this recipe. If the polenta bubbles or sputters even slightly after the first 10 minutes, lower the heat.*

POLENTA

- 7½ cups water
   Salt and pepper
   Pinch baking soda
- 1½ cups coarse-ground cornmeal
- 4 ounces Parmesan cheese, grated (2 cups)
- 2 tablespoons unsalted butter

TOPPING

- 3 tablespoons extra-virgin olive oil
- ½ cup oil-packed sun-dried tomatoes, chopped coarse
- 6 garlic cloves, minced
- ½ teaspoon red pepper flakes
   Salt
- 1 pound broccoli rabe, trimmed and cut into 1½-inch pieces
- ¼ cup chicken or vegetable broth
- ¼ cup grated Parmesan cheese, plus extra for serving
- 3 tablespoons pine nuts, toasted

1. **For the polenta** Bring water to boil in large saucepan. Stir in 1½ teaspoons salt and baking soda. While whisking constantly, slowly pour cornmeal into water; bring to boil. Reduce heat to lowest setting and cover.

2. After 5 minutes, whisk polenta to smooth out any lumps that may have formed, about 15 seconds. (Make sure to scrape down sides and bottom of pan.) Cover and continue to cook, without stirring, until polenta grains are tender but slightly al dente, about 25 minutes. (Polenta should be loose and barely hold its shape; it will continue to thicken as it cools.)

6 garlic cloves, minced
⅛ teaspoon red pepper flakes
1 (15-ounce) can small white beans or navy beans, rinsed
½ cup oil-packed sun-dried tomatoes, chopped

1. Heat 1 tablespoon oil in large saucepan over medium heat until shimmering. Add onion and cook until softened and lightly browned, 5 to 7 minutes. Stir in farro and cook until lightly toasted, about 2 minutes. Stir in broth and water, bring to simmer, and cook, stirring often, until farro is just tender and remaining liquid has thickened into creamy sauce, 20 to 25 minutes. Off heat, stir in 1 cup Parmesan and season with salt and pepper to taste.

2. Meanwhile, bring 4 quarts water to boil in Dutch oven. Add broccoli rabe and 1 tablespoon salt and cook until just tender, about 2 minutes. Drain broccoli rabe and transfer to bowl.

3. Cook remaining 1 tablespoon oil, garlic, and pepper flakes in now-empty pot over medium heat until fragrant and sizzling, 1 to 2 minutes. Stir in broccoli rabe and cook until hot and well coated, about 2 minutes. Off heat, stir in beans, sun-dried tomatoes, and farro mixture. Season with salt and pepper to taste.

4. Position oven rack 6 inches from broiler element and heat broiler. Pour bean-farro mixture into 3-quart broiler-safe casserole dish and sprinkle with remaining 1 cup Parmesan. Broil until lightly browned and hot, 3 to 5 minutes. Let cool for 5 minutes before serving.

THAI-STYLE STIR-FRIED NOODLES WITH CHICKEN AND BROCCOLINI

Serves 4   Total time: 1 hour

WHY THIS RECIPE WORKS *We wanted to create a version of* pad see ew—*the traditional Thai dish of chewy, lightly charred rice noodles with chicken, crisp broccoli, and moist egg, bound with a sweet-and-salty soy-based sauce—that would work in the American home kitchen. Finding the ingredients wasn't a problem; the real challenge was simulating the high heat of a restaurant wok burner on a home stovetop. Since we were already using maximum heat, we increased the surface area by using a skillet instead of a wok, and we cooked in batches, combining all of the components just before serving. Most important, we found that eliminating much of the stirring in our stir-fry helped achieve the all-important char that characterizes this dish. The flat pad thai–style rice noodles used in this recipe can be found in the Asian section of most supermarkets. You can substitute an equal amount of conventional broccoli, but be sure to trim and peel the stalks before cutting. You will need a 12-inch nonstick skillet with a tight-fitting lid for this recipe.*

CHILE VINEGAR
⅓ cup distilled white vinegar
1 serrano chile, stemmed and sliced into thin rings

STIR-FRY
8 ounces (¼-inch-wide) rice noodles
¼ cup vegetable oil
12 ounces boneless, skinless chicken breasts, trimmed and sliced crosswise ¼ inch thick
1 teaspoon baking soda
¼ cup oyster sauce
1 tablespoon plus 2 teaspoons soy sauce
2 tablespoons packed dark brown sugar
1 tablespoon distilled white vinegar
1 teaspoon molasses
1 teaspoon fish sauce
3 garlic cloves, sliced thin
3 large eggs
10 ounces broccolini, trimmed, florets cut into 1-inch pieces, stalks cut ½ inch thick on bias

1. For the chile vinegar Combine vinegar and serrano in bowl. Let sit at room temperature for at least 15 minutes.

2. For the stir-fry Bring 6 cups water to boil. Place noodles in large bowl. Pour boiling water over noodles. Stir, then soak until noodles are almost tender, about 8 minutes, stirring once halfway through soaking. Drain and rinse with cold water. Drain well, then toss with 2 teaspoons oil in now-empty bowl; set aside.

3. Combine chicken with 2 tablespoons water and baking soda in bowl. Let sit at room temperature for 15 minutes. Rinse chicken in cold water and drain well.

4. Whisk oyster sauce, soy sauce, sugar, vinegar, molasses, and fish sauce together in bowl.

5. Heat 2 teaspoons oil and garlic in 12-inch nonstick skillet over high heat, stirring occasionally, until garlic is deep golden brown, 1 to 2 minutes. Add chicken and 2 tablespoons sauce mixture, toss to coat, and spread chicken into even layer. Cook, without stirring, until chicken begins to brown, 1 to 1½ minutes. Flip chicken and cook, without stirring, until second side begins to brown, 1 to 1½ minutes. Push chicken to one side of skillet. Add 2 teaspoons oil to cleared side of skillet. Add eggs to cleared side. Using rubber spatula, stir eggs gently and cook until set but still wet. Stir eggs into chicken and continue to cook, breaking up large pieces of egg, until eggs are fully cooked, 30 to 60 seconds. Transfer chicken mixture to bowl.

6. Heat 2 teaspoons oil in now-empty skillet over high heat until just smoking. Add broccolini and 2 tablespoons sauce and toss to coat. Cover and cook for 2 minutes, stirring once halfway through cooking. Uncover and continue to cook until broccolini is crisp and very brown in spots, 2 to 3 minutes, stirring once halfway through cooking. Transfer to bowl with chicken mixture.

7. Heat 2 teaspoons oil in again-empty skillet over high heat until just smoking. Add half of noodles and 2 tablespoons sauce and toss to coat. Cook until noodles are starting to brown in spots, about 2 minutes, stirring halfway through cooking. Transfer to bowl with chicken mixture. Repeat with remaining 2 teaspoons oil, noodles, and sauce. When second batch of noodles is cooked, add contents of bowl back to skillet and toss to combine. Cook, without stirring, until everything is heated through, 1 to 1½ minutes. Serve immediately, passing chile vinegar separately.

BEEF AND CHINESE BROCCOLI STIR-FRY

Serves 4   Total time: 45 minutes

WHY THIS RECIPE WORKS *Here's a modern take on a popular but tired take-out favorite. We chose Chinese broccoli for greater authenticity. One of the parents of broccolini, and available in Asian supermarkets, Chinese broccoli has long, slender stems, small florets, and a slightly bitter flavor. To keep the broccoli beautifully green and crisp-tender, we simply browned the beef for about 4 minutes, added the supersavory sauce, topped the whole thing with the broccoli florets, and covered the skillet to just steam them through. In only 10 minutes of cooking, we had a better version of the take-out classic. Stir-frying in a regular nonstick skillet makes cleanup a breeze. You will need a 12-inch nonstick skillet with a tight-fitting lid for this recipe. The skillet will be very full when you add the broccoli, but it will quickly wilt down once covered.*

1½ pounds flank steak, trimmed
¼ cup oyster sauce
1½ tablespoons cornstarch
1 tablespoon water
¼ teaspoon baking soda
3 scallions, white and green parts separated and sliced thin
3 tablespoons vegetable oil
6 garlic cloves, minced
2 teaspoons grated fresh ginger
¼ cup chicken broth
2 tablespoons soy sauce
1 tablespoon sugar
1 pound Chinese broccoli, trimmed

1. Cut steak into thirds with grain, then slice each third thin against grain. Whisk 1 tablespoon oyster sauce, 1 tablespoon cornstarch, water, and baking soda together in medium bowl. Add beef, stir to coat, and let sit at room temperature for 15 to 30 minutes.

2. Combine scallion whites, 2 tablespoons oil, garlic, and ginger in second bowl. Whisk broth, soy sauce, sugar, remaining 3 tablespoons oyster sauce, and remaining 1½ teaspoons cornstarch together in third bowl. Set bowls aside.

3. Cut tops (leaves and florets) of broccoli from stalks, then cut tops into 1½-inch pieces. Cut broccoli stalks measuring more than ¼ inch in diameter at base in half lengthwise, then cut all stalks crosswise into 1½-inch pieces.

4. Heat remaining 1 tablespoon oil in 12-inch nonstick skillet over high heat until just smoking. Add beef and separate pieces with tongs. Cook, without stirring, until beef is browned on one side, about 2 minutes. Stir and continue to cook until beef is spotty brown and no longer pink, about 2 minutes.

5. Push beef to sides of skillet. Add scallion mixture to center of skillet and cook, mashing mixture into skillet, until fragrant, about 1 minute. Stir mixture into beef. Whisk broth mixture to recombine, then stir into skillet. Fold in broccoli, cover, and cook until crisp-tender, about 3 minutes. Off heat, stir in scallion greens. Serve.

PHILADELPHIA ROAST PORK SANDWICHES WITH BROCCOLI RABE

Serves 4   Total time: 1 hour 15 minutes

WHY THIS RECIPE WORKS *The underdog rival for the title of Philly's best sandwich loads up a hoagie (aka Italian sub) roll with juicy pork, garlicky broccoli rabe, provolone, and vinegary hot peppers: a feast in a bun. Sandwich shops prepare each component separately hours in advance, but for a streamlined home version, we roasted the meat, greens, and peppers side by side on a sheet pan. We skipped the standard roasted large pork shoulder in favor of smaller, quick-cooking pork tenderloin, seasoning it heavily with rosemary and fennel seeds and roasting it until just cooked through. Shaving it as thinly as possible mimicked the usual shreds of long-cooked pork shoulder. Finally, tossing it with oil and vinegar punched up the flavor and kept it moist. The vegetables roasted alongside the tenderloin: assertive broccoli rabe with lots of garlic and pepper flakes, and sweet red bell pepper to complement the bitter greens. While the meat rested, we used our sheet pan to toast the rolls; slices of provolone melted over the buns gave the extra richness we needed to make these sandwiches perfect.*

1 (1-pound) pork tenderloin, trimmed
6 tablespoons extra-virgin olive oil
Salt and pepper
1 tablespoon minced fresh rosemary
1 tablespoon fennel seeds
1 pound broccoli rabe, trimmed and cut into 1-inch pieces
4 garlic cloves, minced
1 teaspoon red pepper flakes
2 red bell peppers, stemmed, seeded, and sliced thin
4 (6-inch) Italian sub rolls, split lengthwise
6 ounces sliced provolone cheese
2 tablespoons red wine vinegar

1. Adjust oven rack to middle position and heat oven to 450 degrees. Rub tenderloin with 2 tablespoons oil, season with salt and pepper, and sprinkle with rosemary and fennel seeds. Place on one side of rimmed baking sheet and roast for 10 minutes.

2. Toss broccoli rabe with 2 tablespoons oil, garlic, and pepper flakes in bowl. In separate bowl, toss bell peppers with 1 tablespoon oil and season with salt and pepper. Remove sheet from oven and flip pork. Spread broccoli rabe and bell peppers on hot sheet next to pork. Roast until pork reaches 145 degrees and broccoli rabe and bell peppers are browned, about 20 minutes.

3. Remove sheet from oven. Transfer pork to cutting board, tent with aluminum foil, and let rest for 5 minutes. Transfer vegetables to bowl and cover with foil to keep warm. Wipe sheet clean with paper towels, lay split rolls open on sheet, and top with provolone. Bake rolls until bread is lightly toasted and cheese is melted, about 5 minutes.

4. Slice pork as thin as possible, transfer to clean bowl, and toss with vinegar and remaining 1 tablespoon oil. Nestle pork, broccoli rabe, and bell peppers into warm rolls and serve.

Beef and Chinese Broccoli Stir-Fry

ORECCHIETTE WITH BROCCOLI RABE AND SAUSAGE

Serves 4 to 6   Total time: 40 minutes

WHY THIS RECIPE WORKS *Orecchiette is a small, bowl-shaped pasta that's perfect for catching and holding a variety of sauce types. (The name translates as "little ears.") Orecchiette is also ideal for cradling chunky ingredients, like the broccoli rabe and sausage in this preparation. This hearty, subtly spicy pasta is an iconic southern Italian dish. We cooked the pasta in the water used for cooking the broccoli rabe, as is traditional—and it's also quite convenient. The garlicky pork's richness mingled beautifully with the vegetal bitterness of the greens. Tossing the sausage, rabe, and pasta with Pecorino and a bit of cooking water brought a touch of creamy texture to the finished dish.*

2 tablespoons extra-virgin olive oil
8 ounces hot or sweet Italian sausage, casings removed
6 garlic cloves, minced
¼ teaspoon red pepper flakes
1 pound broccoli rabe, trimmed and cut into 1½-inch pieces
   Salt and pepper

1 pound orecchiette
2 ounces Pecorino Romano cheese, grated (1 cup)

1. Heat oil in 12-inch nonstick skillet over medium-high heat until just smoking. Add sausage and cook, breaking up meat into rough ½-inch pieces with wooden spoon, until lightly browned, about 5 minutes. Stir in garlic and pepper flakes and cook until fragrant, about 30 seconds.

2. Meanwhile, bring 4 quarts water to boil in large pot. Add broccoli rabe and 1 tablespoon salt and cook, stirring often, until crisp-tender, about 2 minutes. Using slotted spoon, transfer broccoli rabe to skillet with sausage mixture.

3. Return water to boil, add pasta, and cook, stirring often, until al dente. Reserve 1 cup cooking water, then drain pasta and return it to pot. Add sausage–broccoli rabe mixture, Pecorino, and ⅓ cup reserved cooking water and toss to combine. Adjust consistency with remaining ⅔ cup reserved cooking water as needed. Season with salt and pepper to taste. Serve.

ROASTED SALMON AND BROCCOLI RABE WITH PISTACHIO GREMOLATA

Serves 4   Total time: 30 minutes

WHY THIS RECIPE WORKS *This fast one-pan dinner combines rich oven-roasted salmon with flavorful broccoli rabe. To accent their flavors, we topped the dish with a quick gremolata, an Italian condiment made with parsley, lemon zest, garlic, and in this case, pistachios. Roasting the broccoli rabe tempered its characteristic bitterness into something richer and more well-rounded. Using only one pan and the oven streamlined this dish for an ideal (and healthy) weeknight dinner. To ensure uniform pieces of fish that cooked at the same rate, we found it best to buy a whole center-cut fillet and cut it into four pieces ourselves.*

¼ cup shelled pistachios, toasted and chopped fine
2 tablespoons minced fresh parsley
1 teaspoon grated lemon zest
2 garlic cloves, minced
1 pound broccoli rabe, trimmed and cut into 1½-inch pieces
2 tablespoons plus 2 teaspoons extra-virgin olive oil
   Salt and pepper
   Pinch red pepper flakes
1 (2-pound) skinless salmon fillet, 1 to 1½ inches thick

1. Adjust oven rack to middle position and heat oven to 450 degrees. Combine pistachios, parsley, lemon zest, and half of garlic in small bowl; set gremolata aside.

2. Toss broccoli rabe with 2 tablespoons oil, ¼ teaspoon salt, ¼ teaspoon pepper, pepper flakes, and remaining garlic in bowl. Arrange on one half of rimmed baking sheet. Cut salmon crosswise into 4 fillets. Pat salmon dry with paper towels, then rub with remaining 2 teaspoons oil and season with salt and pepper. Arrange salmon on empty half of sheet, skinned side down.

3. Roast until salmon registers 125 degrees (for medium-rare) and broccoli rabe is tender, about 10 minutes. Sprinkle individual portions with gremolata before serving.

CHEESY BROCCOLI CALZONES

Serves 4 **Total time: 1 hour (plus rising time)**

WHY THIS RECIPE WORKS *The best calzone recipe should offer a satisfying balance of crisp, chewy crust and flavorful filling. Our easy-to-make filling features broccoli, mozzarella, and ricotta, with feta, Parmesan, and olive oil for richness and an egg yolk to thicken the mixture. We spread the filling onto the bottom halves of two rolled-out pizza rounds and brushed egg wash over the edges before folding the top halves over to seal. The calzones needed only 15 minutes in a very hot oven and a few minutes to cool. We like to make our own pizza dough; you can substitute 1 pound of store-bought pizza dough. Let the dough sit at room temperature while preparing the remaining ingredients and heating the oven, or it will be difficult to stretch. Serve with your favorite marinara or tomato pasta sauce.*

DOUGH

- 2 cups (11 ounces) plus 2 tablespoons bread flour, plus extra as needed
- 1⅛ teaspoons instant or rapid-rise yeast
- ¾ teaspoon salt
- 1 tablespoon extra-virgin olive oil
- ¾ cup warm water (110 degrees)

FILLING

- 10 ounces broccoli florets, chopped
- 6 ounces mozzarella cheese, shredded (1½ cups)
- 4 ounces (½ cup) whole-milk ricotta cheese
- 2 ounces feta cheese, crumbled (½ cup)
- 1 ounce Parmesan cheese, grated (½ cup)
- 1 tablespoon extra-virgin olive oil
- 1 large egg yolk, plus 1 large egg lightly beaten with 2 tablespoons water
- 2 garlic cloves, minced
- 1½ teaspoons minced fresh oregano
- ⅛ teaspoon red pepper flakes

1. For the dough Pulse flour, yeast, and salt in food processor to combine, about 5 pulses. With processor running, add oil, then water, and process until rough ball forms, 30 to 40 seconds. Let dough rest for 2 minutes, then process for 30 seconds longer. (If after 30 seconds dough is very sticky and clings to blade, add extra flour as needed.)

2. Transfer dough to lightly floured counter and knead by hand to form smooth, round ball, about 1 minute. Place dough in large, lightly greased bowl, cover tightly with greased plastic wrap, and let rise until doubled in size, 1 to 1½ hours. (Alternatively, dough can be refrigerated for at least 8 hours or up to 16 hours.)

3. For the filling Adjust oven rack to lower-middle position and heat oven to 500 degrees. Cut two 9-inch square pieces of parchment paper.

4. Microwave broccoli and 2 tablespoons water in large covered bowl until bright green and crisp-tender, about 5 minutes; drain well. Combine broccoli, mozzarella, ricotta, feta, Parmesan, oil, egg yolk, garlic, oregano, and pepper flakes in now-empty bowl.

5. Press down on dough to deflate. Transfer to lightly floured counter, divide in half, and cover loosely with greased plastic wrap. Press and roll 1 piece of dough (keep remaining piece covered) into 9-inch round of even thickness. Transfer to parchment square and reshape as needed. Repeat with remaining piece of dough.

6. Spread half of filling evenly over bottom half of each dough round, leaving 1-inch border at edge. Brush edges with egg wash. Fold top half of dough over filling, leaving ½-inch border of bottom half uncovered.

7. Press edges of dough together, pressing out any air pockets in calzones. Starting at 1 end of calzone, place your index finger diagonally across edge and pull bottom layer of dough over tip of your finger and press to seal.

8. Using sharp knife or single-edge razor blade, cut 5 steam vents, about 1½ inches long, in top of calzones. Brush tops with remaining egg wash. Transfer calzones (still on parchment) to rimmed baking sheet, trimming parchment as needed to fit. Bake until golden brown, about 15 minutes, rotating sheet halfway through baking. Transfer calzones to wire rack and discard parchment. Let cool for 10 minutes before serving.

assembling calzones

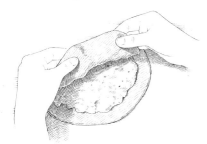

1. Fold top half of dough over filling, leaving ½-inch border of bottom half uncovered.

2. Press edges of dough together, pressing out any air pockets in calzones.

3. Starting at 1 end of calzone, place your index finger diagonally across edge and pull bottom layer of dough over tip of your finger; press to seal.

4. Using sharp knife or single-edge razor blade, cut 5 steam vents, about 1½ inches long, in top of calzones.

BRUSSELS SPROUTS

Not so long ago, Brussels sprouts were a veritable vegetable pariah, something that parents threatened their children with if they didn't behave. Usually prepared by being boiled to near-death, these miniature cabbages—as most people seemed to think of them—were a prime example of healthy food that no one actually wanted to eat.

Nowadays, though, these vibrant little green bundles have become culinary superstars. You can't avoid them on the menus of trendy restaurants, where they are often combined with bacon to tempt pork-obsessed diners. Or they are left raw and shaved thinly, tossed with olive oil, and scattered over wood oven–fired pizza. They're even deep-fried and served Buffalo-style.

Home cooks have come to love them, too. No Thanksgiving dinner, for example, seems complete these days without Brussels sprouts. And that's the time of year when you're most likely to see them sold still attached to their long stalks, a dramatic and festive sight in the market.

We think this is a very positive development, a good demonstration of how our collective palate has expanded in recent years. Plus, we have to admit that we love Brussels sprouts. Our recipes in this chapter would make any other vegetable green with envy. We've prepared them every which way—glazed with maple syrup, braised with mustard-herb butter, shredded in a Southeast Asian slaw, fried with a lemony mayo dipping sauce—and, yes, caramelized with bacon.

vegetable science

Does X Mark the Spot?

The idea behind the technique of laboriously cutting a small X in the stem end of each Brussels sprout when trimming them is that this will result in more even cooking by allowing moisture from cooking to penetrate the stem end. Through multiple test-kitchen experiments, however, we learned that, once cooking was completed, it was impossible to tell the difference in the cooking evenness or tenderness of Brussels sprouts that had been cut versus those that had not been cut. In other words, the notorious X appears to be a bit of kitchen "wisdom" based on myth. Cutting an X into the stem end of a Brussels sprout has no effect on producing evenly cooked results.

avoiding the bull's-eye

When there isn't enough oil in the skillet or pan, Brussels sprouts will brown (or even burn) only at the center, rather than browning evenly across the cut sides. So for perfectly and evenly browned sprouts, please don't skimp on the oil when cooking them.

eat 'em raw

Part of Brussels sprouts' surge in popularity includes serving them raw—which isn't as weird as it might sound. They are very much like miniature cabbages in both taste and texture, so why not treat them that way? Thinly sliced or shredded raw sprouts lend themselves beautifully to slaw-like salads with other strongly flavored ingredients and bright dressings. Since sprouts are so sturdy, you can also make these types of salads well ahead of serving time.

shopping and storage

Although they are available for most of the year, Brussels sprouts' traditional season is from late fall through the end of winter. They are at their sweetest when harvested after the first frost of the growing season—which makes their traditional season the best time to cook with them, especially if you know they have been grown in an area that experiences cold weather.

They are sometimes sold still attached to their long stalks, which from a practical perspective helps them keep longer once you bring them home. More often, they are sold loose in bins or packaged in pint containers or mesh bags. Look for Brussels sprouts that are similar in size, with small, tight heads that are no more than 1½ inches in diameter, as smaller sprouts are likely to be sweeter and more tender than larger sprouts. More and more we are seeing tiny Brussels sprouts being sold, often labeled "baby" Brussels sprouts. They are delicious, although trimming all those stems is a bit fussy. Very large sprouts often have a woody center and pronounced cabbage-y flavor. All sprouts should be tightly closed, with dark green leaves; avoid those with yellowing leaves.

Store Brussels sprouts still on the stalk loosely wrapped in paper towels in the refrigerator. Keep loose sprouts in an open plastic produce bag in the refrigerator for up to a week.

vegetable prep

Trimming and Halving Brussels Sprouts

1. If you choose to wash your sprouts before cooking, do so before trimming and halving. To keep sprouts' leaves intact and attached to cores, trim just a small amount from stems.

2. Pull off outer leaves if you like, but this is not necessary. For Brussels sprouts larger than 1½ inches in diameter, recipes will often direct you to halve or quarter them.

Thinly Slicing Brussels Sprouts

A. Use sharp chef's knife to slice Brussels sprouts as thin as possible.

B. For larger amounts, use slicing disk of food processor to shred Brussels sprouts.

SAUTÉED SLICED BRUSSELS SPROUTS

Serves 4 to 6   **Total time: 20 minutes**

WHY THIS RECIPE WORKS *Thinly slicing and quickly cooking Brussels sprouts is the ideal way to get sweet, crisp-tender results. A quick soak in cold water before cooking provided extra moisture and helped keep the sprouts from burning as we sautéed them over relatively high heat; do not skip this step. Allowing the sprouts to cook undisturbed for a few minutes encouraged browning, which added some sweetness, and the addition of lemon juice and parsley at the end of cooking provided a shot of brightness and freshness. For a variation, we turned to the classic pairing of Brussels sprouts with the smoky, salty crunch of bacon. Slice the sprouts as thin as possible; if available, you can use the slicing disk of a food processor to slice the Brussels sprouts. You will need a 12-inch nonstick skillet with a tight-fitting lid for this recipe.*

1½ pounds Brussels sprouts, trimmed
       and sliced thin
  1 tablespoon vegetable oil
       Salt and pepper
  2 tablespoons chopped fresh parsley
  1 tablespoon lemon juice

1. Place Brussels sprouts in large bowl, cover with cold water, and let sit for 3 minutes. Drain well and set aside.

2. Heat oil in 12-inch nonstick skillet over medium heat until shimmering. Add Brussels sprouts, 1 teaspoon salt, and ¼ teaspoon pepper. Cover and cook, without stirring, until Brussels sprouts are wilted and lightly browned on bottom, about 4 minutes.

3. Stir and continue to cook, uncovered, until Brussels sprouts are crisp-tender, about 3 minutes, stirring once halfway through cooking. Off heat, stir in parsley and lemon juice. Season with salt and pepper to taste. Serve.

VARIATION

Sautéed Sliced Brussels Sprouts with Bacon
Before cooking Brussels sprouts, cook 4 slices bacon, chopped, in 12-inch nonstick skillet over medium heat until crisp, 7 to 10 minutes. Transfer bacon to paper towel–lined bowl and pour off all but 1 tablespoon fat from skillet. Cook sprouts as directed, substituting fat left in skillet for oil. Substitute cider vinegar for lemon juice and sprinkle sprouts with bacon before serving.

PAN-ROASTED BRUSSELS SPROUTS WITH LEMON AND PECORINO ROMANO

Serves 4   **Total time: 15 minutes**

WHY THIS RECIPE WORKS *To create stovetop Brussels sprouts that were deeply browned on the cut sides while still bright green on the uncut sides and crisp-tender within, we started the sprouts in a cold skillet with plenty of oil and cooked them covered. This gently heated the sprouts and created a steamy environment that cooked them through without adding any extra moisture. We then removed the lid and continued to cook the sprouts cut sides down so they had time to develop a substantial, caramelized crust. Using enough oil to completely coat the skillet ensured that all the sprouts made full contact with the fat to brown evenly from edge to edge. Parmesan cheese can be substituted for the Pecorino, if desired. You will need a 12-inch nonstick skillet with a tight-fitting lid for this recipe.*

  1 pound Brussels sprouts, trimmed
       and halved
  5 tablespoons extra-virgin olive oil
  1 tablespoon lemon juice
       Salt and pepper
  ¼ cup shredded Pecorino Romano cheese

1. Arrange Brussels sprouts in single layer, cut sides down, in 12-inch nonstick skillet. Drizzle oil evenly over sprouts. Cover skillet, place over medium-high heat, and cook until sprouts are bright green and cut sides have started to brown, about 5 minutes.

2. Uncover and continue to cook until cut sides of sprouts are deeply and evenly browned and paring knife meets little to no resistance, 2 to 3 minutes, adjusting heat and moving sprouts as needed to prevent them from overbrowning. While sprouts cook, combine lemon juice and ¼ teaspoon salt in small bowl.

3. Off heat, add lemon juice mixture to skillet and stir to evenly coat sprouts. Season with salt and pepper to taste. Transfer to serving platter, sprinkle with Pecorino, and serve.

VARIATIONS

Pan-Roasted Brussels Sprouts with Pomegranate and Pistachios
Omit pepper. Substitute 1 tablespoon pomegranate molasses and ½ teaspoon ground cumin for lemon juice. Substitute ¼ cup shelled pistachios, toasted and chopped fine, and 2 tablespoons pomegranate seeds for Pecorino.

Pan-Roasted Brussels Sprouts with Mustard and Brown Sugar
Omit pepper and Pecorino. Substitute 1 tablespoon Dijon mustard, 1 tablespoon packed brown sugar, 2 teaspoons white wine vinegar, and ⅛ teaspoon cayenne pepper for lemon juice.

Pan-Roasted Brussels Sprouts with Gochujang and Sesame Seeds
Gochujang is a savory Korean red chili paste that can be found in Asian markets or large supermarkets.

Omit pepper. Substitute 1 tablespoon gochujang and 1 tablespoon rice vinegar for lemon juice and 2 teaspoons toasted sesame seeds for Pecorino.

ROASTED BRUSSELS SPROUTS

Serves 6 to 8   **Total time: 40 minutes**

WHY THIS RECIPE WORKS *Oven roasting is a simple and quick way to produce Brussels sprouts that are well caramelized on the outside and tender on the inside. To ensure that we achieved this balance, we started out roasting the "tiny cabbages," covered, with a little bit of water. This created a steamy environment, which cooked the vegetable through. We then removed the foil and allowed the exterior to dry out and caramelize. If you can find only large sprouts (greater than 1½ inches in diameter), quarter them instead of halving them.*

Pan-Roasted Brussels Sprouts with
Gochujang and Sesame Seeds

Fried Brussels Sprouts with
Sriracha Dipping Sauce

2¼ pounds Brussels sprouts, trimmed
and halved
3 tablespoons extra-virgin olive oil
Salt and pepper

1. Adjust oven rack to upper-middle position and heat oven to 500 degrees. Toss Brussels sprouts with oil, 1 tablespoon water, ¾ teaspoon salt, and ¼ teaspoon pepper in large bowl. Arrange Brussels sprouts in single layer, cut sides down, on rimmed baking sheet.

2. Cover sheet tightly with aluminum foil and roast for 10 minutes. Remove foil and continue to roast until Brussels sprouts are well browned and tender, 10 to 12 minutes. Season with salt and pepper to taste. Serve.

VARIATION

Roasted Brussels Sprouts with Garlic, Red Pepper Flakes, and Parmesan
While Brussels sprouts roast, cook 3 tablespoons extra-virgin olive oil, 2 minced garlic cloves, and ½ teaspoon red pepper flakes in 8-inch skillet over medium heat until garlic is golden and fragrant, about 1 minute. Remove from heat. Toss roasted Brussels sprouts with garlic oil and sprinkle with ¼ cup grated Parmesan cheese before serving.

BRAISED BRUSSELS SPROUTS WITH MUSTARD-HERB BUTTER

Serves 4   Total time: 20 minutes
WHY THIS RECIPE WORKS *Braising is one of the best and simplest ways to produce tender, not-too-bitter, attractively green-colored Brussels sprouts with little fuss. You could braise these in low-sodium chicken or vegetable broth instead of water; if you try that, adjust the amount of salt you add accordingly. If you can find only large sprouts (greater than 1½ inches in diameter), halve them. You will need a 12-inch skillet with a tight-fitting lid for this recipe.*

1 pound Brussels sprouts, trimmed
Salt and pepper
4 tablespoons unsalted butter, melted
1 tablespoon Dijon mustard
1 tablespoon minced fresh chives, parsley, or tarragon
Lemon wedges

1. Bring sprouts, ½ cup water, and ½ teaspoon salt to simmer in 12-inch skillet over medium-high heat. Cover, reduce heat to medium-low, and cook until sprouts are tender, 8 to 10 minutes, shaking skillet halfway through cooking to redistribute sprouts. Drain well.

2. Combine melted butter, mustard, and chives in large bowl. Add Brussels sprouts and gently toss to coat. Season with salt and pepper to taste. Serve with lemon wedges.

MAPLE-GLAZED BRUSSELS SPROUTS

Serves 6 to 8   Total time: 30 minutes
WHY THIS RECIPE WORKS *Maple syrup and cider vinegar combine to create a sweet-sour New England–style glaze for stovetop Brussels sprouts. Halving the sprouts through the stem end ensured that they cooked through evenly and stayed together in the skillet. We mimicked the caramelized edges achieved through oven roasting by sautéing the sprouts in butter for several minutes before adding the broth. Be sure to use pure maple syrup, not pancake syrup. You will need a 12-inch skillet with a tight-fitting lid for this recipe.*

4 tablespoons unsalted butter
2 pounds Brussels sprouts, trimmed and halved
½ cup chicken or vegetable broth
2 tablespoons maple syrup
1 teaspoon minced fresh thyme or ¼ teaspoon dried
⅛ teaspoon cayenne pepper
4 teaspoons cider vinegar
Salt and pepper

1. Melt 2 tablespoons butter in 12-inch skillet over medium-high heat. Add Brussels sprouts and cook, stirring occasionally, until browned, 6 to 8 minutes. Stir in broth,

1 tablespoon maple syrup, thyme, and cayenne. Cover, reduce heat to medium-low, and cook until sprouts are nearly tender, 6 to 8 minutes.

2. Uncover, increase heat to medium-high, and cook until liquid has nearly evaporated, about 5 minutes. Off heat, stir in remaining 2 tablespoons butter, remaining 1 tablespoon maple syrup, and vinegar until combined. Season with salt and pepper to taste. Serve.

FRIED BRUSSELS SPROUTS WITH LEMON-CHIVE DIPPING SAUCE

Serves 6 to 8   Total time: 40 minutes
WHY THIS RECIPE WORKS *Fried Brussels sprouts at restaurants can be delightfully crispy, nutty, and salty. Yet when we tried making them at home, the Brussels sprouts splattered every time they hit the hot oil. Instead, we tried submerging the sprouts in cold oil and heating the oil and the sprouts together over high heat. As long as we cooked the Brussels sprouts until they were deep brown, this method produced beautifully crisped sprouts. An easy stir-together lemon-chive sauce offered a vibrant creamy counterpoint, perfect for dipping. Stir gently and not too often in step 2; excessive stirring will cause the leaves to separate from the sprouts.*

DIPPING SAUCE
½ cup mayonnaise
2 tablespoons minced fresh chives
1 teaspoon grated lemon zest plus 1 tablespoon juice
1 teaspoon Worcestershire sauce
1 teaspoon Dijon mustard
¼ teaspoon garlic powder

BRUSSELS SPROUTS
2 pounds Brussels sprouts, trimmed and halved
1 quart peanut or vegetable oil
Kosher salt

1. **For the dipping sauce** Whisk all ingredients together in bowl. Cover and refrigerate until ready to serve. (Sauce can be refrigerated for up to 3 days.)

2. For the Brussels sprouts Line rimmed baking sheet with triple layer of paper towels. Combine Brussels sprouts and oil in Dutch oven. Cook over high heat, gently stirring occasionally, until dark brown throughout and crispy, 20 to 25 minutes.

3. Using wire strainer or slotted spoon, transfer Brussels sprouts to prepared sheet. Roll gently so paper towels absorb excess oil. Season with salt to taste. Serve immediately with sauce.

VARIATION
Fried Brussels Sprouts with Sriracha Dipping Sauce
Whisk ½ cup mayonnaise, 1½ tablespoons Sriracha sauce, 2 teaspoons lime juice, and ¼ teaspoon garlic powder together in bowl. Substitute for lemon-chive dipping sauce.

BRUSSELS SPROUT SALAD WITH PECORINO AND PINE NUTS

Serves 6 to 8   Total time: 45 minutes
WHY THIS RECIPE WORKS *Slicing raw Brussels sprouts very thin and then marinating them in a lemony, mustardy vinaigrette really makes them shine in this salad. We gave them a 30-minute soak in the acidic dressing, which softened and seasoned the sprouts, tempering their flavor. Adding toasted pine nuts and shredded Pecorino Romano just before serving brought a layer of crunch and nutty richness. Slice the Brussels sprouts as thin as possible; if you have a food processor with a slicing disk, you can use that for the job. Use the large holes of a box grater to shred the Pecorino Romano.*

- 3 tablespoons lemon juice
- 2 tablespoons Dijon mustard
- 1 small shallot, minced
- 1 garlic clove, minced
  Salt and pepper
- 6 tablespoons extra-virgin olive oil
- 2 pounds Brussels sprouts, trimmed, halved, and sliced thin
- 3 ounces Pecorino Romano cheese, shredded (1 cup)
- ½ cup pine nuts, toasted

1. Whisk lemon juice, mustard, shallot, garlic, and ½ teaspoon salt together in large bowl. While whisking constantly, drizzle in oil until combined. Add Brussels sprouts and toss to combine. Cover and let sit at room temperature for at least 30 minutes or up to 2 hours.

2. Stir in Pecorino and pine nuts. Season with salt and pepper to taste. Serve.

VARIATIONS
Brussels Sprout Salad with Cheddar, Hazelnuts, and Apple
Substitute 1 cup shredded sharp cheddar for Pecorino and ½ cup hazelnuts, toasted, skinned, and chopped, for pine nuts. Add 1 Granny Smith apple, cored and cut into ½-inch pieces, with cheese and nuts.

Brussels Sprout Salad with Smoked Gouda, Pecans, and Dried Cherries
Substitute 1 cup shredded smoked gouda for Pecorino and ½ cup pecans, toasted and chopped, for pine nuts. Add ½ cup chopped dried cherries with cheese and nuts.

BRUSSELS SPROUT AND KALE SLAW WITH HERBS AND PEANUTS

Serves 4 to 6   Total time: 45 minutes
WHY THIS RECIPE WORKS *Brussels sprouts and kale leaves may sound like an odd combination for a salad, but these two vegetables are perfect together; since the uncooked leaves hold up well for hours, they're ideal for picnics and making ahead. To keep our slaw crisp and light, we left the Brussels sprouts raw and marinated them in the dressing to soften them just slightly. A vigorous massage tenderized the kale leaves in just a minute. A simple cider and coriander vinaigrette, fresh cilantro and mint, chopped peanuts, plus a squeeze of lime juice gave this slaw a refreshing Southeast Asian profile. Tuscan kale (also known as dinosaur or Lacinato kale) is more tender than curly-leaf and red kale; if using curly-leaf or red kale, increase the massaging time to 5 minutes. Do not use baby kale. Slice the sprouts as thin as possible; if you have a food processor with a slicing disk, you can use that for the job.*

- ⅓ cup cider vinegar
- 3 tablespoons sugar
- ½ teaspoon ground coriander
  Salt and pepper
- 2 tablespoons extra-virgin olive oil
- 1 pound Brussels sprouts, trimmed, halved, and sliced thin
- 8 ounces Tuscan kale, stemmed and sliced ¼ inch thick (4½ cups)
- ¼ cup salted dry-roasted peanuts, chopped coarse
- 1 tablespoon chopped fresh cilantro
- 1 tablespoon chopped fresh mint
  Lime juice

1. Whisk vinegar, sugar, coriander, ½ teaspoon salt, and ¼ teaspoon pepper together in large bowl. While whisking constantly, drizzle in oil until combined. Add Brussels sprouts and toss to combine. Cover and let sit at room temperature for at least 30 minutes or up to 2 hours.

2. Vigorously squeeze and massage kale with your hands until leaves are uniformly darkened and slightly wilted, about 1 minute. Add kale, peanuts, cilantro, and mint to bowl with Brussels sprouts and toss to combine. Season with salt and lime juice to taste. Serve.

SKILLET BRATWURST WITH BRUSSELS SPROUTS AND APPLES

Serves 4   Total time: 40 minutes
WHY THIS RECIPE WORKS *Sausages with cabbage and apples are a classic combination. We freshened it up and added more texture and flavor by using Brussels sprouts instead of cabbage. And we turned it into a speedy supper by adding a cup of water to the skillet with the bratwurst. The water hastened the cooking of the sausages and onions and helped the onions caramelize evenly. Honeycrisp, Granny Smith, or Braeburn apples will also work in this recipe. If you can find only large Brussels sprouts (greater than 1½ inches in diameter), quarter them. You will need a 12-inch nonstick skillet with a tight-fitting lid for this recipe.*

2 pounds bratwurst
2 onions, halved and sliced thin
1 cup water
¼ cup extra-virgin olive oil
2 tablespoons honey
  Salt and pepper
1 pound Brussels sprouts, trimmed and halved
3 Gala apples, cored and quartered
⅓ cup dried cranberries
1 tablespoon cider vinegar
1 tablespoon Dijon mustard

1. Combine bratwurst, onions, water, 1 tablespoon oil, 1 tablespoon honey, ½ teaspoon salt, and ¼ teaspoon pepper in 12-inch nonstick skillet. Cover and cook over medium-high heat until bratwurst is nearly cooked through, about 10 minutes, flipping bratwurst halfway through cooking. Uncover and continue to cook, stirring frequently, until water has evaporated and bratwurst and onions are well browned, 7 to 10 minutes. Transfer to serving platter and tent with aluminum foil.

2. Wipe skillet clean with paper towels. Heat remaining 3 tablespoons oil in now-empty skillet over medium-high heat until just smoking. Add Brussels sprouts, ¼ teaspoon salt, and ¼ teaspoon pepper and cook, covered, until browned, about 4 minutes, stirring often. Stir in apples, cranberries, vinegar, mustard, and remaining 1 table-spoon honey and cook until apples are browned and Brussels sprouts are tender, about 5 minutes. Serve bratwurst and onions with Brussels sprouts and apples.

SEARED TROUT WITH BRUSSELS SPROUTS AND BACON

Serves 4   Total time: 45 minutes

WHY THIS RECIPE WORKS *Pairing caramelized Brussels sprouts and crispy bacon with seared trout fit the bill for a simple but satisfying fish-and-veggies dinner that could go from stovetop to table in 45 minutes. First, we quickly pan-roasted the Brussels sprouts until they were deeply browned. Crisp bacon added meaty flavor to the sprouts, and we took advantage of the flavorful bacon fat to sear the trout. We kept the sprouts warm in a low oven while we quickly cooked our trout in batches. Nixing the flour or cornstarch often used to dredge the thin fish before searing, we turned to a spice mixture of coriander and dry mustard powder to help with browning and give our trout a crisp crust. Lemon wedges provided a bright counterpoint to the fish and rich Brussels sprouts. You will need a 12-inch nonstick skillet with a tight-fitting lid for this recipe.*

1 pound Brussels sprouts, trimmed and halved
¼ cup extra-virgin olive oil
2 garlic cloves, minced
½ teaspoon minced fresh thyme or ⅛ teaspoon dried
  Salt and pepper
3 slices bacon, cut into ½-inch pieces
1 teaspoon ground coriander
½ teaspoon dry mustard
4 (6- to 8-ounce) boneless, butterflied whole trout
  Lemon wedges

1. Adjust oven rack to middle position and heat oven to 200 degrees. Arrange Brussels sprouts in single layer, cut sides down, in 12-inch nonstick skillet. Drizzle oil evenly over sprouts. Cover skillet, place over medium-high heat, and cook until sprouts are bright green and cut sides have started to brown, about 5 minutes.

2. Uncover and continue to cook until cut sides of sprouts are deeply and evenly browned and paring knife slides in with little to no resistance, 2 to 3 minutes, adjusting heat and moving sprouts as necessary to prevent them from overbrowning. Stir in garlic, thyme, ¼ teaspoon salt, and ⅛ tea-spoon pepper and cook until fragrant, about 30 seconds. Transfer sprouts to large heat-proof bowl, cover loosely with aluminum foil, and keep warm in oven.

3. Cook bacon in now-empty skillet over medium-high heat until crispy, 5 to 7 minutes. Using slotted spoon, transfer bacon to paper towel–lined plate. Pour off and reserve 2 tablespoons fat from skillet. (If necessary, add extra oil to equal 2 tablespoons.)

4. Combine coriander, mustard, 1 teaspoon salt, and ½ teaspoon pepper in bowl. Pat trout dry with paper towels and sprinkle with spice mixture. Heat 1 tablespoon reserved fat in again-empty skillet over medium-high heat until shimmering. Place 2 fillets flesh side down in skillet and cook until browned and trout flakes apart when gently prodded with paring knife, about 3 minutes per side. Transfer to serving platter and keep warm in oven. Repeat with remaining 1 tablespoon reserved fat and remaining 2 fillets; transfer to platter.

5. Gently fold bacon into Brussels sprouts and season with salt and pepper to taste. Serve trout with Brussels sprouts and lemon wedges.

WHOLE-WHEAT ROTINI WITH BRUSSELS SPROUTS

Serves 4 to 6   Total time: 35 minutes

WHY THIS RECIPE WORKS *The combination of earthy Brussels sprouts and nutty whole-wheat pasta makes a uniquely satisfying pasta dish. To ensure even cooking, we sliced the Brussels sprouts and then sautéed them along with some sliced shallots before simmering them in a combination of chicken broth and heavy cream. Parmesan imparted a tangy note and gave the sauce some body, while toasted walnuts provided further rich flavor and an appealing crunch. Frozen sweet peas were an easy addition that paired nicely with the Brussels sprouts; we added them at the end to preserve their texture and color. Slice the sprouts as thin as possible; if you have a food processor with a slicing disk, you can use that for the job.*

3 tablespoons extra-virgin olive oil
1 pound Brussels sprouts, trimmed and sliced thin
2 shallots, sliced thin
  Salt and pepper
1 cup chicken or vegetable broth
1 cup heavy cream
¾ cup frozen peas, thawed
1 pound whole-wheat rotini
2 ounces Parmesan cheese, grated (1 cup), plus extra for serving
½ cup walnuts, toasted and chopped

1. Heat oil in 12-inch skillet over medium-high heat until shimmering. Add Brussels sprouts, shallots, ½ teaspoon salt, and ¼ teaspoon pepper and cook until sprouts begin to soften, 3 to 5 minutes. Stir in broth and cream, cover, and simmer until sprouts are tender, about 3 minutes. Off heat, stir in peas, cover, and let sit until heated through, about 2 minutes.

2. Meanwhile, bring 4 quarts water to boil in large pot. Add pasta and 1 tablespoon salt and cook, stirring often, until al dente. Reserve ½ cup cooking water, then drain pasta and return it to pot.

3. Stir in Brussels sprouts mixture, Parmesan, and walnuts, and toss to combine. Adjust consistency with reserved cooking water as needed. Season with salt and pepper to taste. Serve with extra Parmesan.

BRUSSELS SPROUT AND POTATO HASH

Serves 4   Total time: 40 minutes

WHY THIS RECIPE WORKS *This hearty hash combines potatoes with earthy Brussels sprouts and sweet carrots. But hashing together different vegetables presented a challenge: The potatoes and carrots took longer than the Brussels sprouts to soften. Microwaving them for 5 minutes solved the problem. Meanwhile, we cooked the sprouts (cut into wedges) in the skillet to get good browning. We tried slicing the sprouts, but smaller pieces tended to steam rather than brown. Next, we added the microwaved carrots and potatoes along with onion, garlic, thyme, and a little water to help the Brussels sprouts cook through. Finally, we gently poached eggs right in the flavorful hash. If you can find only large sprouts (greater than 1½ inches in diameter), halve them and cut each half into thirds.*

- 1 pound red potatoes, unpeeled, cut into ½-inch pieces
- 2 carrots, peeled and cut into ½-inch pieces
- 3 tablespoons extra-virgin olive oil
   Salt and pepper
- 1 pound Brussels sprouts, trimmed and quartered

- 1 onion, chopped fine
- 1 tablespoon minced fresh thyme or 1 teaspoon dried
- 1 garlic clove, minced
- 1 tablespoon unsalted butter
- 8 large eggs
- 2 scallions, sliced thin

1. Toss potatoes and carrots with 1 tablespoon oil, ½ teaspoon salt, and ¼ teaspoon pepper together in large bowl. Microwave, covered, until vegetables are tender, 5 to 7 minutes, stirring halfway through microwaving.

2. Heat 1 tablespoon oil in 12-inch nonstick skillet over medium-high heat until shimmering. Add Brussels sprouts and cook, stirring occasionally, until browned, 6 to 8 minutes. Add potato-carrot mixture, onion, 2 tablespoons water, thyme, garlic, ¾ teaspoon salt, ¼ teaspoon pepper, and remaining 1 tablespoon oil. Reduce heat to medium, cover, and cook until Brussels sprouts are just tender, 5 to 7 minutes, stirring halfway through cooking.

3. Off heat, stir in butter and season with salt and pepper to taste. Make 4 shallow indentations (about 2 inches wide) in surface of hash using back of spoon. Crack 2 eggs into each indentation and season eggs with salt and pepper. Cover and cook over medium-low heat until egg whites are just set and yolks are still runny, 5 to 10 minutes. Sprinkle with scallions and serve immediately.

BRUSSELS SPROUT GRATIN

Serves 6 to 8   Total time: 1 hour 15 minutes

WHY THIS RECIPE WORKS *In developing a Brussels sprout gratin, we wanted to make a dish that highlighted the earthy flavor of Brussels sprouts. Preroasting the sprouts made them rich and nutty, not cabbage-y. We made a quick, creamy Mornay sauce, using a combination of Gruyère and Parmesan cheeses, to bind the gratin. To add crunch, we topped the gratin with toasted panko bread crumbs and more nutty Gruyère. If you can find only large Brussels sprouts (greater than 1½ inches in diameter), quarter them.*

- 2½ pounds Brussels sprouts, trimmed and halved
- 1 tablespoon vegetable oil
   Salt and pepper
- 3 tablespoons unsalted butter
- ¼ cup panko bread crumbs
- 1 shallot, minced
- 1 garlic clove, minced
- 1 tablespoon all-purpose flour
- 1¼ cups heavy cream
- ¾ cup chicken or vegetable broth
- 2 ounces Gruyère cheese, shredded (½ cup)
- 1 ounce Parmesan cheese, grated (½ cup)
   Pinch ground nutmeg
   Pinch cayenne pepper

1. Adjust oven rack to middle position and heat oven to 450 degrees. Grease 13 by 9-inch baking dish. Toss Brussels sprouts with oil, ½ teaspoon salt, and ¼ teaspoon pepper in prepared dish. Bake until sprouts are well browned and tender, 30 to 35 minutes. Transfer to wire rack and set aside to cool for at least 5 minutes or up to 30 minutes.

2. Melt 1 tablespoon butter in medium saucepan over medium heat. Add panko and cook, stirring frequently, until golden brown, about 3 minutes. Transfer to bowl and stir in ¼ teaspoon salt and ¼ teaspoon pepper; set aside. Wipe saucepan clean with paper towels.

3. Melt remaining 2 tablespoons butter in now-empty saucepan over medium heat. Add shallot and garlic and cook until just softened, about 1 minute. Stir in flour and cook for 1 minute. Slowly whisk in cream and broth and bring to boil over medium-high heat. Once boiling, remove from heat and whisk in ¼ cup Gruyère, Parmesan, nutmeg, cayenne, ¼ teaspoon pepper, and ⅛ teaspoon salt until smooth.

4. Pour cream mixture over Brussels sprouts in dish and stir to combine. Sprinkle evenly with panko mixture and remaining ¼ cup Gruyère. Bake until bubbling around edges and golden brown on top, 5 to 7 minutes. Let cool for 10 minutes before serving.

Brussels Sprout Gratin

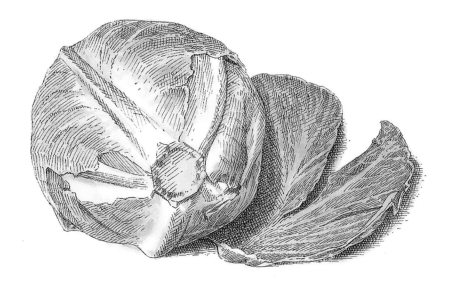

CABBAGES

Cabbage is an underappreciated vegetable—except for identifying it with coleslaw, few people seem to give it much thought. But, like superstar cauliflower, it's cruciferous, which means it's superhealthy. It's also a real kitchen workhorse, offering crunchy refreshment when used raw, meltingly soft sweetness when braised, and pleasing sourness when fermented into sauerkraut. In addition to providing you with classic recipes for slaws and stuffed cabbage rolls, we wanted to look for new ways to use this underdog of the vegetable world. And we sure found them.

There are lots of cabbages to choose from. Green cabbage's mild flavor makes it extremely versatile in recipes, whether raw or cooked. Red cabbage, the sweetest of the cabbages, looks beautiful incorporated raw into salads. It's also often prepared in a sweet-sour preparation: Our

Braised Red Cabbage includes red wine, brown sugar, and green apple. Soft-leaved savoy cabbage has a sweet, nutty flavor that becomes even more pronounced when cooked. Delicate napa cabbage is leafy, refreshing, and mild—a great choice for our Napa Cabbage Slaw with Apples and Walnuts. And bok choy lends a peppery flavor and crisp-tender texture to Stir-Fried Bok Choy with Soy Sauce and Ginger.

Since cabbage works so well with bold and unconventional flavor combinations, we've given you several versatile coleslaw recipes that take advantage of this, from classic Creamy Buttermilk Coleslaw to mustardy Memphis Chopped Coleslaw. And for a unique recipe that may change your whole outlook on cabbage, try the Savoy Cabbage "Soup" with Ham, Rye Bread, and Fontina, a casserole beloved by skiers in the Italian Alps.

shopping and storage

All cabbages are available year-round, although you will likely see the greatest variety and highest quality from the end of summer through the end of winter. No matter what variety you are purchasing, look for bright color: Dulled or washed-out color means the cabbage has been sitting around for a while. Most cabbages are quite hardy and will keep for more than a week in the refrigerator. If the outer leaves start to dry out, simply peel them off before using the cabbage. The exceptions to this storage rule are napa cabbage and bok choy, which, with their more open and looser leaves, are more perishable and will wilt faster.

hard versus soft

HARD-HEADED CABBAGES These are the most commonly found cabbages, with firm, compact heads that are heavy for their size and smooth leaves attached to a dense core. They are sometimes called Dutch head cabbage. Standard green and red cabbages fall under this rubric.

SOFT-HEADED CABBAGES This category contains those that look more like lettuce and can often be treated like lettuce, with looser, open heads and crinkly leaves. Savoy cabbage (sometimes called curly cabbage) and napa cabbage (often referred to as Chinese cabbage) are included here. Bok choy (or pak choi) is a type of Chinese cabbage that has distinct stalks and leaves attached to a base, without any central core.

salting cabbage for perfect slaw

Although it's tempting to toss freshly cut cabbage with dressing, resist the urge, or your flavorful cole slaw will become a watery puddle. Because cabbage contains so much water, it's important to remove some of it. If the recipe directs you, toss cut cabbage and salt in a colander set over a bowl, let sit for an hour, then rinse and blot dry.

vegetable prep

Shredding Cabbage

1. Cut cabbage into quarters and slice away hard piece of core attached to each quarter.

2. Separate cored cabbage quarter into stacks of leaves that flatten when pressed lightly.

3a. Use chef's knife to slice each stack into very thin shreds.

3b. Or roll stacked leaves crosswise and fit into feed tube of food processor fitted with shredding disk.

Preparing Baby Bok Choy

Simply slice heads in half lengthwise.

Preparing Mature Bok Choy

1. Cut stalks from greens, and halve stalks lengthwise.

2. Cut halved stalks crosswise into ½-inch pieces.

3. Slice greens into ½-inch-thick pieces.

SAUTÉED BABY BOK CHOY WITH MISO SAUCE

Serves 4   Total time: 25 minutes

WHY THIS RECIPE WORKS *Part of the allure of cooking with baby bok choy is showing off its diminutive size. But if you leave it whole, it's difficult to clean properly. Cutting the bok choy in half lengthwise provided access to the areas where most of the dirt and grit typically hide so we could thoroughly clean them. Cutting them in half also helped them cook more evenly, so the stalks became perfectly tender-crisp before the leaves went limp. We spun the bok choy dry in a salad spinner after washing in order to avoid adding too much water to the skillet. An initial stint of steaming gave the stems the head start they needed to soften slightly before sautéing. A mixture of miso, mirin, and sugar formed the base of a salty-sweet sauce. If using heads larger than 2 ounces each, quarter them instead of halving. You will need a 12-inch nonstick skillet with a tight-fitting lid for this recipe.*

- 4 teaspoons vegetable oil
- 1 teaspoon grated fresh ginger
- 1 garlic clove, minced
- 2 tablespoons white miso
- 1 tablespoon mirin
- 2 teaspoons sugar
- ½ teaspoon cornstarch
- 8 small heads baby bok choy (1½ to 2 ounces each), halved, washed thoroughly, and spun dry

1. Combine 1 teaspoon oil, ginger, and garlic in small bowl. Whisk miso, mirin, sugar, and cornstarch together in second small bowl.

2. Heat remaining 1 tablespoon oil in 12-inch nonstick skillet over medium heat until shimmering. Add bok choy and 2 tablespoons water and immediately cover. Cook, covered, shaking skillet occasionally, for 2 minutes. Uncover, toss bok choy, and then push bok choy to sides of skillet. Add ginger-garlic mixture to center and cook, stirring constantly, until fragrant, about 20 seconds. Stir ginger-garlic mixture into bok choy and continue to cook, stirring constantly, until all water has evaporated, stems are crisp-tender, and leaves are wilted, 1 to 2 minutes. Add miso mixture and cook, stirring constantly, until sauce is thickened and coats bok choy, about 15 seconds. Serve.

VARIATIONS

Sautéed Baby Bok Choy with Chili-Garlic Sauce
Omit ginger. Substitute 1 tablespoon soy sauce for miso and chili-garlic sauce for mirin. Increase garlic to 2 cloves and decrease sugar to 1 teaspoon.

Sautéed Baby Bok Choy with Shallot and Fish Sauce
Omit ginger. Substitute 1 tablespoon fish sauce for miso, water for mirin, and brown sugar for white sugar. Increase cornstarch to 1 teaspoon. Add 2 tablespoons minced shallot to garlic mixture and ¼ teaspoon red pepper flakes to fish sauce mixture in step 1.

STIR-FRIED BOK CHOY WITH SOY SAUCE AND GINGER

Serves 4 to 6   Total time: 20 minutes

WHY THIS RECIPE WORKS *Stir-frying nicely preserves the crisp-tender texture of bok choy stalks. We sliced the bok choy heads and started the stalks first in the skillet, then added the greens later. This way, both stalks and greens ended up perfectly cooked. Be sure to add the ginger, and then the soy sauce mixture, just as the edges of the stalks turn translucent; otherwise, the stalks won't retain their bite.*

- 2 tablespoons soy sauce
- 1 teaspoon sugar
- 2 tablespoons vegetable oil
- 1½ pounds bok choy, stalks halved lengthwise then cut crosswise into ½-inch pieces, greens sliced into ½-inch-thick pieces
- 1 tablespoon grated fresh ginger

1. Whisk soy sauce and sugar in small bowl until sugar has dissolved.

2. Heat oil in 12-inch nonstick skillet over high heat until just smoking. Add bok choy stalks and cook, stirring constantly, until edges begin to turn translucent, about 5 minutes. Stir in ginger and cook until fragrant, about 30 seconds. Add bok choy greens and soy sauce mixture and cook, stirring frequently, until greens are wilted and tender, about 1 minute. Serve.

VARIATION

Stir-Fried Bok Choy with Oyster Sauce and Garlic
Substitute 2 tablespoons oyster sauce (or substitute hoisin sauce, if desired) and 1 tablespoon rice vinegar for soy sauce. Add 2 minced garlic cloves with ginger.

BRAISED BOK CHOY WITH GARLIC

Serves 4 to 6   Total time: 25 minutes

WHY THIS RECIPE WORKS *Bok choy takes well to being braised in a covered pan with some seasoned liquid, as you might with kale or another sturdy green. We first stir-fried the stalks to give them some light color and then added the greens and some stock and let the bok choy simmer away. After a few minutes, the stalks were soft but not mushy, their texture creamy and delicious, the leaves completely tender. This dish is fairly brothy, making it an excellent accompaniment to seared pork chops, sautéed chicken breasts, or a firm fish like cod. You will need a 12-inch nonstick skillet with a tight-fitting lid for this recipe.*

- 2 tablespoons vegetable oil
- 1½ pounds bok choy, stalks halved lengthwise then cut crosswise into ½-inch pieces, greens sliced into ½-inch-thick pieces
- 4 garlic cloves, minced
- ½ cup chicken or vegetable broth
- 1 teaspoon rice vinegar
  Salt and pepper

1. Heat oil in 12-inch nonstick skillet over high heat until just smoking. Add bok choy stalks and cook, stirring constantly, until edges begin to turn translucent, about 5 minutes. Stir in garlic and cook until fragrant, about 30 seconds. Add broth and bok choy greens. Cover, reduce heat to medium-low, and cook, stirring occasionally, until bok choy is just tender, about 4 minutes.

Sautéed Baby Bok Choy with
Chili-Garlic Sauce

2. Uncover, increase heat to medium-high, and cook for 2 minutes. Stir in vinegar and season with salt and pepper to taste. Serve.

VARIATION

Braised Bok Choy with Shiitake Mushrooms
Microwave 1 cup water and ¼ ounce dried shiitake mushrooms, covered, until steaming, about 1 minute. Let sit until softened, about 5 minutes. Drain mushrooms in fine-mesh strainer lined with coffee filter, reserve ½ cup strained liquid, and slice mushrooms ¼ inch thick. Substitute 1 tablespoon grated fresh ginger for 2 garlic cloves and substitute mushroom liquid and mushrooms for chicken broth.

SAUTÉED CABBAGE WITH PARSLEY AND LEMON

Serves 4 to 6   Total time: 35 minutes
WHY THIS RECIPE WORKS *This simple, anytime preparation for green cabbage brings out the vegetable's natural sweetness while maintaining its crisp-tender texture. We decided to pan-steam and sauté the cabbage over relatively high heat to cook it quickly and add an extra layer of flavor from browning. A precooking step of soaking the cabbage reduced any bitterness while providing extra moisture to help the cabbage steam. Cooked onion helped reinforce sweetness, and lemon juice provided punch. Fresh parsley offered a bright finish. You will need a 12-inch nonstick skillet with a tight-fitting lid for this recipe.*

- 1   **small head green cabbage (1¼ pounds), cored and sliced thin**
- 2   **tablespoons vegetable oil**
- 1   **onion, halved and sliced thin**
   Salt and pepper
- ¼   **cup chopped fresh parsley**
- 1½ **teaspoons lemon juice**

1. Place cabbage in large bowl and cover with cold water; let stand for 3 minutes. Drain well.

2. Heat 1 tablespoon oil in 12-inch nonstick skillet over medium-high heat until shimmering. Add onion and ¼ teaspoon salt

and cook, stirring occasionally, until softened and lightly browned, 5 to 7 minutes; transfer to bowl.

3. Heat remaining 1 tablespoon oil in now-empty skillet over medium-high heat until shimmering. Add cabbage and sprinkle with ½ teaspoon salt and ¼ teaspoon pepper. Cover and cook, without stirring, until cabbage is wilted and lightly browned on bottom, about 3 minutes. Stir and continue to cook, uncovered, until cabbage is crisp-tender and lightly browned in places, about 4 minutes, stirring once halfway through cooking. Off heat, stir in onion, parsley, and lemon juice. Season with salt and pepper to taste, and serve.

VARIATIONS

Sautéed Cabbage with Bacon and Caraway Seeds
Substitute red cabbage for green. Whisk 1 tablespoon cider vinegar and 2 teaspoons packed brown sugar together in medium bowl. Omit oil. Cook 4 slices chopped bacon in skillet over medium-high heat until crisp, 5 to 7 minutes. Transfer bacon to paper towel–lined plate and pour off all but 1 tablespoon fat into bowl (reserve fat).

Substitute red onion for onion and cook in fat in skillet until softened, about 5 minutes. Add 1 teaspoon caraway seeds and cook for 1 minute; transfer to bowl with vinegar mixture. Cook cabbage in 1 tablespoon reserved fat. Stir bacon into cabbage with onion mixture before serving.

Sautéed Cabbage with Chile and Peanuts
Substitute red onion for onion. Cook 1 thinly sliced jalapeño, seeds reserved (optional), with onion in step 2. Once onion is crisp-tender, about 4 minutes, add 2 garlic cloves, minced to paste, and cook until fragrant, about 30 seconds. Substitute 4 teaspoons fish sauce and 2 teaspoons packed brown sugar for salt and pepper in step 3. Substitute ½ cup chopped fresh cilantro for parsley and 1 tablespoon lime juice for lemon juice. Add reserved jalapeño seeds, if desired. Sprinkle cabbage with 2 tablespoons chopped unsalted dry-roasted peanuts before serving.

Sautéed Cabbage with Fennel and Garlic
Substitute savoy cabbage for green. Substitute extra-virgin olive oil for vegetable oil and 1 cored and thinly sliced fennel bulb for

onion. Cook fennel bulb until softened, 8 to 10 minutes, then add 2 garlic cloves, minced to paste, and ¼ teaspoon red pepper flakes and continue to cook until fragrant, about 30 seconds. Omit pepper. Substitute fennel fronds for parsley and increase lemon juice to 2 teaspoons. Drizzle cabbage with 1 tablespoon extra-virgin olive oil and sprinkle with 2 tablespoons grated Parmesan before serving.

PAN-ROASTED CABBAGE

Serves 6   Total time: 40 minutes

WHY THIS RECIPE WORKS *Here's a stovetop recipe that mimics the melt-in- your-mouth caramelized flavors of oven-roasted cabbage. A small head of cabbage cut into six wedges fit comfortably in a 12-inch skillet. Adding some water to the skillet steamed the wedges, helping them cook through evenly. A simple mix of butter, caraway seeds, basil, and lemon juice finished this satisfying side dish. When slicing the cabbage into wedges, be sure to leave the core intact so the wedges don't fall apart when flipped in step 2. Avoid heads of cabbage that weigh more than 2 pounds, because the larger wedges will not fit in the skillet. You will need a 12-inch nonstick skillet with a tight-fitting lid for this recipe.*

 ¼ cup water
 2 tablespoons vegetable oil
 1 head green cabbage (2 pounds), cut into 6 wedges through core
  Salt and pepper
 4 tablespoons unsalted butter, cut into 4 pieces
 3 tablespoons chopped fresh basil
 ½ teaspoon caraway seeds
 1 tablespoon lemon juice

1. Combine water and oil in 12-inch nonstick skillet. Arrange cabbage wedges cut side down in single layer in skillet. Sprinkle with 1 teaspoon salt and cook over medium heat, uncovered, until water has evaporated and wedges are well browned, 16 to 20 minutes.

2. Flip wedges to second cut side, and add 2 tablespoons water to skillet. Cover and cook until wedges are tender and second side is well browned, 4 to 6 minutes.

3. Scatter butter among wedges and cook, uncovered, until butter is melted and bubbling, about 1 minute. Sprinkle with basil, caraway seeds, and ½ teaspoon pepper and continue to cook, using large spoon halfway through cooking to baste wedges with melted butter (tilting skillet so butter pools at low point and can be easily scooped into spoon), until fragrant, about 1 minute.

4. Transfer wedges to serving platter. Off heat, stir lemon juice into any remaining butter in skillet, then spoon over wedges. Season with salt and pepper to taste. Serve.

SIMPLE CREAM-BRAISED CABBAGE

Serves 4   Total time: 25 minutes

WHY THIS RECIPE WORKS *The French have been cooking the simple but elegant dish of cabbage in cream for ages, and when we tried it, tasters loved the sophisticated blend of flavors, complemented by the slight residual crunch of the cabbage. To cut the richness of the cream, we incorporated lemon juice (for its acidity) and shallot (for its subtle, sweet onion flavor). The cabbage needed only minutes to braise in the skillet before it was ready to serve. You will need a 12-inch skillet with a tight-fitting lid for this recipe.*

 ¼ cup heavy cream
 1 shallot, minced
 1 teaspoon lemon juice
 ½ head green cabbage, cored and sliced thin (4 cups)
  Salt and pepper

Bring cream, shallot, and lemon juice to simmer in 12-inch skillet over medium heat. Add cabbage and toss to coat. Cover and cook, stirring occasionally, until cabbage is wilted but still bright green, 7 to 9 minutes. Season with salt and pepper to taste. Serve.

BRAISED RED CABBAGE

Serves 6 to 8   Total time: 1 hour 45 minutes

WHY THIS RECIPE WORKS *This German-American dish, traditionally served with sausages, is all about balancing sweet and sour flavors. In order to achieve this, we braised the red cabbage in orange juice concentrate, red wine, and brown sugar. Removing the lid partway through cooking allowed the braising liquid to reduce to a thick, syrupy glaze. Finishing the dish with a tart Granny Smith apple, butter, and chopped parsley brought everything into harmony. We developed this recipe with inexpensive Cabernet Sauvignon, but any dry red wine will work.*

 3 tablespoons unsalted butter
 1 onion, halved and sliced thin
 1 head red cabbage (2 pounds), cored and sliced ½ inch thick
 1 cup dry red wine
 ½ cup frozen orange juice concentrate
 1½ tablespoons packed brown sugar
  Salt and pepper
 1 Granny Smith apple, peeled, cored, and cut into ¼-inch pieces
 3 tablespoons minced fresh parsley

1. Melt 2 tablespoons butter in Dutch oven over medium heat. Add onion and cook until softened and golden, 7 to 9 minutes. Stir in cabbage, wine, orange juice concentrate, sugar, 1¼ teaspoons salt, and ½ teaspoon pepper and bring to simmer. Cover, reduce heat to low, and cook for 45 minutes.

2. Stir in apple. Increase heat to medium-low and cook, uncovered, until cabbage is tender and liquid is syrupy, 25 to 30 minutes. Off heat, stir in parsley and remaining 1 tablespoon butter. Season with salt and pepper to taste. Serve.

GRILLED CABBAGE

Grilling cabbage wedges over a live fire elevates this humble, rustic vegetable to a versatile and attractive, deliciously smoky-sweet side dish. For even cooking on the grill, we borrow a technique from making coleslaw: Salting the cabbage draws out moisture so that the interior cooks through properly before the exterior gets too charred.

1. Cut the cabbage head into wedges, being careful to keep the core intact. This will keep the wedges from breaking apart on the grill.

2. Sprinkle 1 teaspoon salt evenly over the cabbage wedges and let them sit for 45 minutes to draw out moisture.

3. Set up a single-level fire in your charcoal or gas grill.

4. Pat the moisture from the cabbage wedges. Brush one cut side of the cabbage wedges with the lemon vinaigrette and grill, brushed side down, until well browned.

5. Brush the second cut side with the vinaigrette, flip the wedges, and grill until they are browned and fork-tender.

6. Transfer the cabbage wedges to a serving platter, drizzle with the reserved vinaigrette, and serve.

GRILLED CABBAGE

Serves 6 to 8   Total time: 1 hour 15 minutes

WHY THIS RECIPE WORKS *The fire of a hot grill tames the crunch of cabbage, resulting in a tender, sweet, deliciously smoky dish. Slicing the head into thick wedges that kept the core intact prevented it from falling apart on the grill. High heat helped develop browning, which created more sweetness. We also wanted to make sure the interior softened before the exterior overcooked. In the test kitchen, we prevent soggy coleslaw by salting chopped cabbage. The salt draws out moisture, which we drain off before dressing the coleslaw. Following that principle, we salted our cabbage wedges so the moisture would turn to steam on the grill. The steam then helped the interior of the wedges cook through. Brushing a simple lemon-herb vinaigrette on the cabbage both before and after grilling added bright flavor.*

　　　Salt and pepper
　1　head green cabbage (2 pounds), cut into 8 wedges through core
　6　tablespoons extra-virgin olive oil
　1　tablespoon minced fresh thyme
　2　teaspoons minced shallot
　2　teaspoons honey
　1　teaspoon Dijon mustard
　½　teaspoon grated lemon zest plus 2 tablespoons juice

1. Sprinkle 1 teaspoon salt evenly over cabbage wedges and let sit for 45 minutes. Whisk oil, thyme, shallot, honey, mustard, lemon zest and juice, and ¼ teaspoon pepper together in bowl. Measure out and reserve ¼ cup vinaigrette for serving.

2a. For a charcoal grill Open bottom vent completely. Light large chimney starter half-filled with charcoal briquettes (3 quarts). When top coals are partially covered with ash, pour evenly over grill. Set cooking grate in place, cover, and open lid vent completely. Heat grill until hot, about 5 minutes.

2b. For a gas grill Turn all burners to high, cover, and heat grill until hot, about 15 minutes. Turn all burners to medium.

3. Clean and oil cooking grate. Pat cabbage wedges dry, then brush 1 cut side of wedges with half of remaining vinaigrette. Place cabbage on grill, vinaigrette side down, and cook (covered if using gas) until well browned, 7 to 10 minutes. Brush top cut side of wedges with remaining vinaigrette. Flip and cook (covered if using gas) until second side is well browned and fork-tender, 7 to 10 minutes. Transfer cabbage to serving platter and drizzle with reserved vinaigrette. Season with salt and pepper to taste. Serve.

SAUERKRAUT

Makes about 1½ quarts

Total time: 25 minutes (plus at least 6 days fermenting time)

WHY THIS RECIPE WORKS *Sauerkraut delivers a huge flavor punch when paired with bratwurst, hot dogs, Reuben sandwiches, and more. It's complex, and seems complicated, yet it's nothing more than shredded cabbage and salt left to ferment. Naturally occurring bacteria do all the work: They devour sugars in the cabbage, producing lactic acid. This acidity and the flavor compounds they produce lend sauerkraut its trademark flavor. The kosher salt keeps bad bacteria at bay, so don't skimp on it. On the flip side, too much salt halted the fermentation; this meant that our sauerkraut didn't become acidic enough and bad bacteria took over. The same principle applied to the temperature range, since temperature can encourage certain types of bacteria to either flourish or go dormant. A fermentation temperature of about 65 degrees was best; too cool and the cabbage didn't ferment, too hot and the sauerkraut was mushy and overly funky. To keep the cabbage submerged, we placed a bag of brine on top. We like to use brine rather than water, because if the bag breaks it won't ruin the careful balance of salinity inside the jar (something we learned the hard way).*

　2½　pounds green cabbage (1 head), quartered, cored, and sliced ⅛ inch thick (7 cups)
　2　tablespoons kosher salt
　1½　teaspoons juniper berries
　2　cups water

1. Cut out parchment paper round to match diameter of ½-gallon widemouthed jar. Toss cabbage with 4 teaspoons salt in large bowl. Using your hands, forcefully knead salt into cabbage until cabbage has softened and begins to release moisture, about 3 minutes. Stir in juniper berries.

2. Tightly pack cabbage mixture and any accumulated liquid into jar, pressing down firmly with your fist to eliminate air pockets as you pack. Press parchment round flush against surface of cabbage.

3. Dissolve remaining 2 teaspoons salt in water and transfer to 1-quart zipper-lock plastic bag; squeeze out air and seal bag well. Place bag of brine on top of parchment and gently press down. Cover jar with triple layer of cheesecloth and secure with rubber band.

4. Place jar in 50- to 70-degree location away from direct sunlight and let ferment for 6 days; check jar daily, skimming residue from surface and pressing to keep cabbage submerged. After 6 days, taste sauerkraut daily until it has reached desired flavor (this may take up to 7 days longer; sauerkraut should be pale and translucent, with a tart and floral flavor).

5. When sauerkraut has reached desired flavor, discard cheesecloth, bag of brine, and parchment; skim off any residue. Serve. (Sauerkraut and accumulated juices can be transferred to clean jar, covered, and refrigerated for up to 6 weeks; once refrigerated, flavor of sauerkraut will continue to mature).

CREAMY BUTTERMILK COLESLAW

Serves 4   Total time: 1 hour 45 minutes

WHY THIS RECIPE WORKS *Cabbage has a high water content, and this water leaching out of the vegetable is typically the culprit when you end up with a watery coleslaw. The simple step of salting and then draining the cabbage first draws out this excess moisture. That technique allowed our creamy coleslaw recipe to produce crisp, evenly cut pieces of cabbage lightly coated with a flavorful buttermilk dressing that clung to the cabbage instead of collecting in the bottom of the bowl. The combination of* buttermilk, mayonnaise, and sour cream was ideal for the creamy, hefty dressing. This recipe can be easily doubled to serve a crowd or bring to a potluck.

½ head red or green cabbage, cored and shredded (6 cups)
Salt and pepper
1 carrot, peeled and shredded
½ cup buttermilk
2 tablespoons mayonnaise
2 tablespoons sour cream
2 tablespoons minced fresh parsley
1 small shallot, minced
½ teaspoon cider vinegar
½ teaspoon sugar
¼ teaspoon Dijon mustard

1. Toss shredded cabbage with 1 teaspoon salt in colander set over large bowl and let sit until wilted, at least 1 hour or up to 4 hours. Rinse cabbage under cold running water. Press, but do not squeeze, to drain, and blot dry with paper towels.

2. Discard liquid and wipe bowl clean with paper towels. Combine cabbage and carrot in now-empty bowl. In separate bowl, whisk together buttermilk, mayonnaise, sour cream, parsley, shallot, vinegar, sugar, mustard, ¼ teaspoon salt, and ⅛ teaspoon pepper. Pour dressing over cabbage and toss to combine. Cover and refrigerate until chilled, at least 30 minutes or up to 1 day. Season with salt and pepper to taste. Toss to recombine before serving.

VARIATIONS

Creamy Buttermilk Coleslaw with Scallions and Cilantro
Omit Dijon mustard. Substitute 2 thinly sliced scallions and 1 tablespoon minced fresh cilantro for parsley and 1 teaspoon lime juice for cider vinegar.

Lemony Buttermilk Coleslaw
Substitute 1 teaspoon lemon juice for cider vinegar. Add 1 teaspoon minced fresh thyme and 1 tablespoon minced fresh chives to dressing.

HONEY-MUSTARD COLESLAW

Serves 6 to 8   Total time: 1 hour 45 minutes

WHY THIS RECIPE WORKS *A sweet and pungent honey-mustard dressing is a welcome addition to an otherwise classic slaw. We first tossed the cabbage in a colander with a mixture of salt and sugar to soften it and pull out a bit of its liquid. Adding sugar enhanced the cabbage's flavor and kept the saltiness from dominating. This step also allowed us to simply stir in the sauce ingredients without having to rinse and dry the cabbage. For sharp, bold mustard flavor tamed with just the right amount of sweetness, we used twice as much mustard as honey here; tasters preferred spicy brown mustard to yellow mustard for its complexity. For a bit of welcome creaminess, we added a small amount of mayonnaise.*

1 head green or red cabbage (2 pounds), cored and sliced thin (12 cups)
Salt and pepper
1½ teaspoons sugar
½ cup spicy brown mustard
¼ cup honey
3 tablespoons minced fresh chives
2 tablespoons mayonnaise

1. Toss cabbage with 1½ teaspoons salt and sugar in colander set over large bowl. Let sit until cabbage has wilted and released about 2 tablespoons water, at least 1 hour or up to 4 hours, stirring and pressing on cabbage occasionally with rubber spatula.

2. Discard liquid and wipe bowl clean with paper towels. Whisk mustard, honey, chives, mayonnaise, ½ teaspoon pepper, and ⅛ teaspoon salt in now-empty bowl until combined. Add cabbage and toss to combine. Cover and refrigerate until chilled, at least 30 minutes or up to 2 days. Season with salt and pepper to taste. Toss to recombine before serving.

MEMPHIS CHOPPED COLESLAW

Serves 6 to 8   Total time: 1 hour 45 minutes

WHY THIS RECIPE WORKS *Memphis chopped coleslaw is traditionally studded with celery seeds and crunchy green peppers and tossed with an unapologetically sugary mustard dressing that's balanced by a bracing hit of vinegar. To ensure that our slaw boasted brash—but balanced—flavor, we quickly cooked the spicy dressing to meld the flavors tougher, and then tossed the hot dressing with the cabbage. We found that employing our usual trick of salting and then draining the cabbage removed excess water and wilted it to a perfect pickle-crisp texture. The salted cabbage absorbed the dressing, becoming thoroughly and evenly seasoned. Use the large holes of a box grater to shred the carrot and onion.*

1 head green cabbage (2 pounds), cored and chopped fine (12 cups)
1 jalapeño chile, stemmed, seeded, and minced
1 carrot, peeled and shredded
1 small onion, peeled and shredded
Salt and pepper
¼ cup yellow mustard
¼ cup chili sauce
¼ cup mayonnaise
¼ cup sour cream
¼ cup cider vinegar
1 teaspoon celery seeds
⅔ cup packed light brown sugar

1. Toss cabbage with jalapeño, carrot, onion, and 2 teaspoons salt in colander set over large bowl. Let sit until cabbage has wilted and released about 2 tablespoons water, at least 1 hour or up to 4 hours. Rinse cabbage under cold running water. Press, but do not squeeze, to drain, and blot dry with paper towels.

2. Discard liquid and wipe bowl clean with paper towels. Bring mustard, chili sauce, mayonnaise, sour cream, vinegar, celery seeds, and sugar to boil in saucepan over medium heat; stir to blend. Combine cabbage and hot dressing in now-empty bowl. Cover and refrigerate until chilled, at least 30 minutes or up to 1 day. Season with salt and pepper to taste. Toss to recombine before serving.

NAPA CABBAGE SLAW WITH CARROTS AND SESAME

Serves 6 to 8   Total time: 35 minutes

WHY THIS RECIPE WORKS *For a slaw with a more tender, delicate texture and sweeter flavor than usual, we traded traditional green cabbage for napa cabbage. But napa cabbage's more delicate structure means that it leaches even more water than regular cabbage. Our solution to avoid a soggy slaw? We made a potent dressing with a high ratio of vinegar to oil, and we also cooked down the dressing's vinegar to offset the diluting power of the cabbage's water. After we tossed the cabbage with the dressing and let it sit for about 5 minutes, the slaw achieved the perfect level of bright acidity. Adding crunchy carrots, some colorful herbs, and a handful of sesame seeds gave the slaw additional layers of flavor and texture. Use the large holes of a box grater to shred the carrots. This slaw is best served within an hour of being dressed.*

⅓ cup white wine vinegar
2 teaspoons toasted sesame oil
2 teaspoons vegetable oil
1 tablespoon rice vinegar
1 tablespoon soy sauce
1 tablespoon sugar
1 teaspoon grated fresh ginger
¼ teaspoon salt
1 small head napa cabbage (1½ pounds), cored and sliced thin (8¼ cups)
2 carrots, peeled and shredded
4 scallions, sliced thin on bias
¼ cup sesame seeds, toasted

1. Bring white wine vinegar to simmer in small saucepan over medium heat and cook until reduced to 2 tablespoons, 4 to 6 minutes. Transfer vinegar reduction to large bowl and let cool completely, about 10 minutes. Whisk in sesame oil, vegetable oil, rice vinegar, soy sauce, sugar, ginger, and salt.

2. Add cabbage and carrots to dressing and toss to coat. Let sit for 5 minutes. Add scallions and sesame seeds and toss to combine. Serve.

VARIATIONS

Napa Cabbage Slaw with Apple and Walnuts
Omit sesame oil and increase vegetable oil to 4 teaspoons. Omit soy sauce and ginger. Substitute cider vinegar for rice vinegar. Decrease sugar to 2 teaspoons and increase salt to ¾ teaspoon. Substitute 2 celery ribs, sliced thin on bias, and 1 grated Fuji apple for carrots. Substitute 3 tablespoons minced fresh chives for scallions and ½ cup walnuts, toasted and chopped fine, for sesame seeds.

Napa Cabbage Slaw with Jícama and Pepitas
Omit sesame oil and increase vegetable oil to 4 teaspoons. Omit soy sauce. Substitute lime juice for rice vinegar, honey for sugar, and ½ teaspoon ground coriander for ginger. Increase salt to ¾ teaspoon. Add 1 seeded and minced jalapeño. Substitute 6 ounces jícama, peeled and grated, for carrots. Substitute ¼ cup coarsely chopped fresh cilantro for scallions and ½ cup roasted and salted pepitas, chopped fine, for sesame seeds.

CHINESE CHICKEN SALAD

Serves 6   Total time: 1 hour

WHY THIS RECIPE WORKS *Chinese chicken salad is a chain-restaurant classic, but we wanted to give it a seriously fresh makeover—so we started by nixing anything from a can. The salad bar pile-ons (chow mein noodles, sprouts, snow peas, fried wonton strips, and water chestnuts) also got the ax, and instead, we chose to highlight crisp napa cabbage and romaine lettuce, bell peppers, fresh cilantro, and scallions. To keep the title ingredient from tasting like an afterthought, we eschewed rotisserie chicken, instead poaching boneless, skinless chicken breasts in a flavorful mixture of soy sauce, orange juice, rice vinegar, and ginger. Whisking more of the same mixture with sesame and vegetable oils made a bold dressing for our salad. The whole shebang was finished with orange segments—fresh, of course— and crunchy roasted peanuts.*

2 oranges
¼ cup rice vinegar
¼ cup soy sauce
3 tablespoons grated fresh ginger
3 tablespoons sugar
1 tablespoon Asian chili-garlic sauce
2 pounds boneless, skinless chicken breasts, trimmed
3 tablespoons vegetable oil
2 tablespoons toasted sesame oil

Kimchi Beef and Tofu Soup

½ head napa cabbage, cored and sliced thin (5½ cups)
2 romaine lettuce hearts (12 ounces), sliced thin
2 red bell peppers, stemmed, seeded, and cut into 2-inch-long matchsticks
1 cup fresh cilantro leaves
1 cup salted dry-roasted peanuts, chopped
6 scallions, sliced thin on bias

1. Cut away peel and pith from oranges. Holding fruit over large bowl to catch juice, use paring knife to slice between membranes to release segments; set segments aside for serving. Squeeze juice from membrane into bowl (juice should measure ¼ cup). Whisk in vinegar, soy sauce, ginger, sugar, and chili-garlic sauce.

2. Transfer ½ cup orange juice mixture to 12-inch skillet and bring to simmer over medium-high heat; set aside remaining orange juice mixture. Add chicken to skillet, cover, and reduce heat to medium-low. Cook until chicken registers 160 degrees, 10 to 15 minutes, flipping chicken halfway through cooking.

3. Transfer chicken to cutting board, let cool slightly, then shred into bite-size pieces using 2 forks.

4. Bring pan juices to boil and cook until reduced to ¼ cup, 1 to 3 minutes. Off heat, stir in chicken and any accumulated juices and let sit for 10 minutes.

5. Slowly whisk vegetable oil and sesame oil into reserved orange juice mixture. Add cabbage, romaine, bell peppers, cilantro, peanuts, and scallions and toss to combine. Transfer to serving platter and top with chicken and reserved orange segments. Serve.

KIMCHI BEEF AND TOFU SOUP

Serves 4 to 6   Total time: 1 hour

WHY THIS RECIPE WORKS *This warming and traditional Korean soup gets tons of tangy flavor from kimchi, a spicy fermented vegetable condiment that uses cabbage as its base. There's also a double dose of hearty protein from both beef and tofu. Make sure to save the kimchi brine when draining and measuring the kimchi; we used the brine to add extra zing to our broth. Note that the flavor and spiciness of kimchi can vary from brand to brand, and this will slightly affect the flavor of the soup. Sirloin steak tips, also known as flap meat, can be sold as whole steaks, cubes, or strips. To ensure uniform pieces for our soup, we prefer to buy whole steaks and cut them ourselves. For supple, tender bites of tofu, we chose firm tofu. You can also use extra-firm tofu.*

8 ounces firm tofu, cut into ½-inch pieces
1 pound sirloin steak tips, trimmed and cut into ½-inch pieces
Salt and pepper
1 tablespoon vegetable oil
1 tablespoon grated fresh ginger
½ cup mirin
3 cups water
2 cups beef broth
3 cups cabbage kimchi, drained and chopped, 1 cup kimchi brine reserved
4 scallions, sliced thin on bias
1 tablespoon soy sauce
1 tablespoon toasted sesame oil

1. Spread tofu on paper towel–lined baking sheet and let drain for 20 minutes. Pat beef dry with paper towels and season with salt and pepper. Heat oil in Dutch oven over medium-high heat until just smoking. Brown beef well on all sides, 8 to 10 minutes.

2. Stir in ginger and cook until fragrant, about 30 seconds. Slowly stir in mirin, scraping up any browned bits. Stir in water, broth, kimchi, and kimchi brine and bring to simmer. Cover, reduce heat to low, and cook until meat is tender, 25 to 30 minutes.

3. Off heat, stir tofu, scallions, soy sauce, and sesame oil into soup. Season with salt and pepper to taste. Serve.

SAVOY CABBAGE "SOUP" WITH HAM, RYE BREAD, AND FONTINA

Serves 6 to 8   Total time: 1 hour 45 minutes

WHY THIS RECIPE WORKS *This decadent combination of rich beef broth, cabbage, rye bread, pancetta, and nutty fontina cheese comes from Italian ski country, high in the Alps. Although it's called a soup, this dish is heartier than that—reminiscent of the cheesy top layer of French onion soup. Savoy cabbage is the regional favorite, and its subtly sweet flavor worked beautifully with the earthy rye bread that we cubed and dried at a low temperature in the oven. We built flavor and tenderized the cabbage by first braising it with pancetta, onion, bay leaf, and beef broth before layering it in a casserole dish with the toasted bread. The casserole received a blanket of cheese, which turned bubbly under the broiler. Any type of hearty rye bread will work well here. You will need a 13 by 9-inch broiler-safe baking dish for this recipe.*

12 ounces hearty rye bread, cut into 1½-inch pieces
3 tablespoons extra-virgin olive oil
1 tablespoon unsalted butter
4 ounces pancetta, chopped fine
1 onion, halved and sliced thin
½ teaspoon salt
3 garlic cloves, minced
1 head savoy cabbage (1½ pounds), cored and cut into 1-inch pieces
4 cups beef broth
2 bay leaves
4 ounces fontina cheese, shredded (1 cup)
1 tablespoon chopped fresh parsley

1. Adjust oven rack to middle position and heat oven to 400 degrees. Toss bread with 2 tablespoons oil and spread into even layer on rimmed baking sheet. Bake, stirring occasionally, until golden brown and crisp, 10 to 12 minutes; let cool to room temperature.

2. Heat butter and remaining 1 tablespoon oil in Dutch oven over medium-low heat until butter is melted. Add pancetta and cook until browned and rendered, about 8 minutes. Stir in onion and salt and cook over medium heat until softened and lightly browned, 5 to 7 minutes. Stir in garlic and cook until fragrant, about 30 seconds.

3. Stir in cabbage, broth, and bay leaves and bring to boil. Cover, reduce heat to low, and simmer until cabbage is tender, about 45 minutes.

4. Adjust oven rack to 6 inches from broiler element and heat broiler. Discard bay leaves. Spread half of cabbage mixture evenly in bottom of 13 by 9-inch broiler-safe baking dish, then top with half of croutons. Repeat with remaining cabbage mixture and croutons. Gently press down on croutons with rubber spatula until thoroughly saturated. Sprinkle fontina over top and broil until melted and spotty brown, about 4 minutes. Sprinkle with parsley and serve.

STIR-FRIED CHICKEN WITH BOK CHOY AND CRISPY NOODLE CAKE

Serves 4   Total time: 1 hour 15 minutes

WHY THIS RECIPE WORKS *Chicken, bok choy, and red bell pepper make a colorful stir-fry. A quick soak in a simple marinade brightened up our chicken, and a savory stir-fry sauce with soy sauce and oyster sauce tied everything together. A pan-fried noodle cake—crispy and crunchy on the outside and tender and chewy inside— offered a fun change of pace from the usual white rice. We had the most success with fresh Chinese egg noodles, which made for a cohesive cake. A nonstick skillet was crucial, as it kept the cake from sticking and falling apart and allowed us to use less oil so the cake wasn't greasy. Fresh Chinese noodles are often found in the produce section of larger supermarkets.*

SAUCE
- ¼ cup chicken broth
- 2 tablespoons soy sauce
- 1 tablespoon dry sherry
- 1 tablespoon oyster sauce
- 1 teaspoon sugar
- 1 teaspoon cornstarch
- ¼ teaspoon red pepper flakes

NOODLE CAKE
- 1 (9-ounce) package fresh Chinese noodles
- 1 teaspoon salt
- 2 scallions, sliced thin
- ¼ cup vegetable oil

CHICKEN STIR-FRY
- 1 pound boneless, skinless chicken breasts, trimmed and sliced thin
- 1 tablespoon soy sauce
- 1 tablespoon dry sherry
- 2 tablespoons toasted sesame oil
- 1 tablespoon cornstarch
- 1 tablespoon all-purpose flour
- 2 tablespoons plus 2 teaspoons vegetable oil
- 1 tablespoon grated fresh ginger
- 1 garlic clove, minced
- 1 pound bok choy, stalks sliced ¼ inch thick on bias, greens sliced ½ inch thick
- 1 small red bell pepper, stemmed, seeded, and cut into ¼-inch-wide strips

1. For the sauce Whisk all ingredients together in small bowl; set aside.

2. For the noodle cake Bring 6 quarts water to boil in large pot. Add noodles and salt and cook, stirring often, until almost tender, 2 to 3 minutes. Drain noodles, then toss with scallions.

3. Heat 2 tablespoons oil in 12-inch nonstick skillet over medium heat until shimmering. Spread noodles evenly across bottom of skillet and press with spatula to flatten. Cook until bottom of cake is crispy and golden brown, 5 to 8 minutes.

4. Slide noodle cake onto large plate. Add remaining 2 tablespoons oil to skillet and swirl to coat. Invert noodle cake onto second plate and slide, browned side up, back into skillet. Cook until golden brown on second side, 5 to 8 minutes.

5. Slide noodle cake onto cutting board and let sit for at least 5 minutes before slicing into wedges. (Noodle cake can be transferred to wire rack set in rimmed baking sheet and kept warm in 200 degree oven for up to 20 minutes.) Wipe skillet clean with paper towels.

6. For the chicken stir-fry While noodles boil, toss chicken with soy sauce and sherry in large bowl and let sit for at least 10 minutes or up to 1 hour. Whisk sesame oil, cornstarch, and flour together in large bowl. Combine 1 teaspoon vegetable oil, ginger, and garlic in small bowl; set aside.

7. Transfer chicken to cornstarch mixture. Heat 2 teaspoons vegetable oil in now-empty skillet over high heat until just smoking. Add half of chicken, breaking up any clumps, and cook without stirring until meat is browned around edges, about 1 minute. Stir chicken and continue to cook until cooked through, about 1 minute longer. Transfer chicken to clean, dry large bowl and cover with aluminum foil. Repeat with 2 teaspoons vegetable oil and remaining chicken.

8. Heat remaining 1 tablespoon vegetable oil in again-empty skillet over high heat until just smoking. Add bok choy stalks and bell pepper and cook until lightly browned, 2 to 3 minutes.

9. Push vegetables to sides of skillet. Add ginger mixture to center and cook, mashing mixture into skillet, until fragrant, about 30 seconds. Stir mixture into vegetables. Add bok choy greens and cook until beginning to wilt, about 30 seconds.

10. Add chicken with any accumulated juices. Whisk sauce to recombine, then add to skillet and cook, tossing constantly, until sauce is thickened, about 30 seconds. Transfer to serving platter and serve with noodle cake.

STUFFED CABBAGE ROLLS

Serves 4   Total time: 2 hours
WHY THIS RECIPE WORKS *Cabbage rolls stuffed with a seasoned beef filling and bathed in a light tomato sauce are serious comfort food. Sautéed onions and garlic provided a savory foundation for both sauce and filling, and ground ginger,* *cinnamon, and nutmeg added a warm spice flavor to the sauce. Tasters preferred brown sugar to white for its more complex flavor, and red wine vinegar to white for its mellow bite. We supplemented the beef filling with bratwurst, a mild German sausage, to boost the meaty flavor. A panade (paste) of milk and bread helped keep the filling soft and moist. If the tops of the cabbage rolls appear dry after the foil is removed in step 5, spoon some of the sauce over them before returning to the oven.*

1 head green cabbage (2 pounds), cored
1 tablespoon vegetable oil
1 onion, chopped fine
3 garlic cloves, minced
1 teaspoon ground ginger
½ teaspoon ground cinnamon
¼ teaspoon ground nutmeg
1 (28-ounce) can tomato sauce
¼ cup packed light brown sugar
3 tablespoons red wine vinegar
Salt and pepper
2 slices hearty white sandwich bread, torn into pieces
½ cup milk
12 ounces 85 percent lean ground beef
12 ounces bratwurst, casings removed

1. Adjust oven rack to middle position and heat oven to 375 degrees. Microwave cabbage in covered bowl until outer leaves are pliable and translucent, 3 to 6 minutes. Using tongs, carefully remove wilted outer leaves; set aside. Cover and repeat until you have 15 to 17 large, intact leaves.

2. Heat oil in Dutch oven over medium heat until shimmering. Add onion and cook until softened, about 5 minutes. Stir in garlic, ginger, cinnamon, and nutmeg and cook until fragrant, about 30 seconds. Transfer half of onion mixture to small bowl; set aside. Off heat, stir tomato sauce, sugar, vinegar, ½ teaspoon salt, and ¼ teaspoon pepper into pot with remaining onion mixture until sugar has dissolved.

3. Process bread and milk in food processor until smooth, about 30 seconds. Add reserved onion mixture, beef, bratwurst, ½ teaspoon salt, and ¼ teaspoon pepper and pulse until well combined, about 10 pulses.

4. Working with 1 cabbage leaf at a time, cut along both sides of rib at base of leaf to form narrow triangle; remove rib. Continue cutting up center of leaf about 1 inch above triangle, then slightly overlap cut ends of cabbage. Place 2 heaping tablespoons of meat mixture on each leaf, about ½ inch from bottom of where cut ends overlap. Fold bottom of leaf over filling and fold in sides. Roll leaf tightly around filling. Repeat with remaining leaves and remaining filling. Arrange rolls, seam side down, in 13 by 9-inch baking dish. (Unbaked rolls can be refrigerated for up to 24 hours.)

5. Pour sauce over cabbage rolls, cover with aluminum foil, and bake until sauce is bubbling and rolls are heated through, about 45 minutes. Remove foil and bake, uncovered, until sauce is slightly thickened and cabbage is tender, about 15 minutes. Serve.

assembling stuffed cabbage

1. Cut along both sides of rib at base of leaf to form narrow triangle. Continue cutting up center of leaf about 1 inch above triangle, then slightly overlap cut ends of cabbage.

2. Place 2 heaping tablespoons of meat mixture on each leaf about ½ inch from bottom of where cut ends overlap.

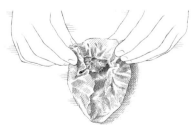

3. Fold bottom of leaf over filling and fold in sides. Roll leaf tightly around filling.

C A R R O T S

Carrots are so ubiquitous that it's easy to take them for granted. And not just here in America—this root vegetable is eaten around the world. Originally grown for the leaves and seeds rather than its root (the part we eat), today's domesticated carrot has been bred for large, sweet, durable, crunchy-textured roots.

Raw carrots, with their sweetly satisfying crisp crunchability, are one of the greatest vegetable snacks out there, beloved by young and old alike. Next to beets, they're nature's sweetest vegetable. But there's so much more you can do with carrots in the kitchen. (Plus, cooking them releases more of their healthy beta-carotene.)

Getting carrots to taste good is easy. The trick is cooking them to the proper texture. Undercooked carrots are better suited for rabbits; overcooked carrots will remind you of baby food. In our test kitchen, we perfected plenty of recipes using different varieties and sizes—chopped, sliced, spiralized, and even left whole, for a dramatic presentation.

Next time you entertain, break out our recipe for Carrot-Habanero Dip, rich and redolent with Moroccan spices. Glazed Carrots with Orange and Cranberries adds a burst of colors and flavors to any holiday spread. Warm up a cold evening with quick, easy, silky-smooth Carrot-Ginger soup. We also show you a few neat tricks for cooking carrots whole: how to grill them, with an herbal yogurt sauce, and how to slowly cook them to melting tenderness on the stovetop, with a trio of flavorful relishes. With their long shape, carrots are a natural choice for spiralizing, and we make things even more interesting by roasting our carrot "noodles" with honey and thyme.

taste the rainbow

Until recently, you probably thought carrots were orange, and that was that. But commercially cultivated carrots as we know them—with their bright orange color and crispy-juicy texture—represent just a few of the types, or cultivars, of carrots that exist in the world. Before we domesticated them for a food crop, wild carrots were anything but orange: They originated in ancient Persia and had a deep purple color. The first cultivated carrots, grown in Afghanistan in roughly 900 AD, were purple and white. Purple, white, and red cultivars eventually spread to central and north Asia, and Japan. These became known as Eastern carrots.

The orange carrots we know and love today were developed in the Netherlands in the 17th century. They quickly became predominant in Europe and then America, and became known as Western carrots.

Eastern and Western cultivars are not just different in color—they're also a little different in taste and texture. White carrots are sweet, with a crisp, apple-like texture. Purple carrots have a slight peppery flavor and a woodier, less-juicy texture than orange carrots. They're also high in anthocyanins—the same pigments that make red onions red and blueberries blue. Red carrots are high in lycopene, the same beneficial phytonutrient found in tomatoes.

Orange carrots, more and more grown the world over, have been bred and grown specially for their size, juiciness, and appealing-to-all-ages crunch and sweetness.

vegetable prep

Slicing Carrots on the Bias

For braising and glazing, slice carrots ¼ thick on bias.

Cutting Carrots Lengthwise

For evenly roasted carrots, trim ends, peel carrots, and slice in half lengthwise. If ends are very thick, slice lengthwise into quarters to get pieces of about the same size.

Shredding Carrots

When shredding carrots for slaws or salads, do so on the large holes of a box grater rather than pulling out a food processor.

shopping and storage

Carrots are readily available year-round. Small to medium-size carrots are best; larger carrots typically have tough, woody, tasteless cores. The quality of prebagged carrots is usually very high. Perky-looking greens still attached to carrots is a sign of freshness, so snatch them up if you find them. At home, twist off the greens and store them separately from the carrots.

So-called baby carrots are actually full-grown carrots that are too cosmetically ugly to sell. They were created in the 1980s by a California carrot farmer and have been a smash hit ever since. Full-size carrots are mechanically cut into smaller pieces, sculpted into small rounded batons, washed, and bagged. They may seem convenient, but they are drier and less flavorful than regular carrots.

Rainbow carrots have become fashionable in both farmers' markets and supermarkets. They make a strikingly beautiful substitution for regular orange carrots in any recipe. Something to keep in mind: Purple carrots, like beets, can stain other vegetables, and they also turn nearly black when roasted. It's very dramatic-looking, but maybe not everyone's cup of tea.

Carrots keep for a least a week in an open plastic produce bag in the refrigerator. Often prebagged carrots have moisture inside them from getting sprayed by the vegetable mister in the market; to keep them from turning slimy, pat them dry and transfer them to a dry plastic produce bag.

BOILED CARROTS WITH CUMIN, LIME, AND CILANTRO

Serves 4   Total time: 25 minutes

WHY THIS RECIPE WORKS *Boiling is the quickest, simplest way to produce tender, well-seasoned carrots. We cut 1 pound of carrots into 1½- to 2-inch lengths and then halved or quartered them lengthwise, depending on thickness, so that they all cooked at the same rate. Well-salted water not only added seasoning but also helped the carrots retain some of their natural sugars as well as helped them cook faster. After draining, we added olive oil for richness and some citrus juice or vinegar for brightness. A bit of spice and some fresh herbs completed this simple side dish. For even cooking, the carrot pieces should be of similar size. Choose carrots that are between 1 and 1½ inches in diameter.*

    1 pound carrots, peeled
    2 teaspoons salt
    1 tablespoon extra-virgin olive oil
    1 tablespoon chopped fresh cilantro
    ½ teaspoon lime zest plus 1 teaspoon
       juice, plus extra juice for seasoning
    ½ teaspoon cumin seeds, crushed

1. Cut carrots into 1½- to 2-inch lengths. Leave thin pieces whole, halve medium pieces lengthwise, and quarter thick pieces lengthwise.

2. Bring 2 cups water to boil in medium saucepan over high heat. Add carrots and salt, cover, and cook until tender, about 6 minutes.

3. Drain carrots, then return to saucepan. Stir in oil, cilantro, lime zest and juice, and cumin seeds and stir to coat. Season with extra lime juice to taste, and serve.

VARIATIONS

Boiled Carrots with Fennel Seeds and Citrus
Substitute ½ teaspoon orange zest for lime zest. Substitute ½ teaspoon fennel seeds, crushed, for cumin, and parsley for cilantro.

Boiled Carrots with Mint and Paprika
Omit lime zest. Substitute sherry vinegar for lime juice, ½ teaspoon paprika for cumin, and mint for cilantro.

ROASTED CARROTS AND SHALLOTS WITH CHERMOULA

Serves 4   Total time: 35 minutes

WHY THIS RECIPE WORKS *We discovered that there are two keys to good browning when roasting carrots: butter and oven position. Melting the butter first helps coat the carrots evenly before they go onto the baking sheet. The butter itself helps brown the vegetables while also keeping them from sticking. Roasting the buttered carrots lower in the oven also helps promote browning. The closer the heat source is to the baking sheet, the better the browning. The resulting carrots are tender, sweet, and almost caramel-like on the roasted sides. To spice up this simple preparation, we served our carrots with an intense, spicy green chermoula and plenty of toasted pine nuts. Choose carrots that are about 1½ inches in diameter at the thicker end. If your carrots are smaller, leave them whole; if they're larger, extend the roasting time slightly.*

CARROTS

    1½ pounds carrots, peeled and halved
        lengthwise
     4 large shallots, peeled and halved
        through root end
     2 tablespoons unsalted butter, melted
        Salt and pepper
     2 tablespoons toasted and coarsely
        chopped pine nuts

CHERMOULA

    ¾ cup fresh cilantro leaves
    2 tablespoons lemon juice
    4 garlic cloves, minced
    1 serrano chile, stemmed, seeded,
       and minced
    ½ teaspoon ground cumin
    ½ teaspoon salt
    ⅛ teaspoon cayenne pepper
    ¼ cup extra-virgin olive oil

1. For the carrots Adjust oven rack to lowest position and heat oven to 450 degrees. Toss carrots, shallots, melted butter, ½ teaspoon salt, and ¼ teaspoon pepper together in bowl to coat. Spread carrot-shallot mixture in even layer on rimmed baking sheet, cut sides down. Roast until tender and cut sides are well browned, 15 to 25 minutes.

2. For the chermoula Process cilantro, lemon juice, garlic, serrano, cumin, salt, and cayenne in food processor until finely chopped, about 1 minute, scraping down sides of bowl as needed. With processor running, slowly add oil until incorporated. Transfer to small bowl.

3. Transfer carrots and shallots to serving platter and season with salt to taste. Drizzle with chermoula and sprinkle with pine nuts. Serve.

ROASTED CARROT NOODLES

Serves 4 to 6   Total time: 45 minutes

WHY THIS RECIPE WORKS *We set out to create a simple and versatile carrot side that would work with a wide range of dishes. Roasting carrots draws out their natural sugars and intensifies their flavor—but high heat can cause them to become dry, shriveled, and jerky-like. Using a spiralizer to cut the carrots into uniform ⅛-inch noodles ensured that the carrots cooked evenly, and cooking them covered for half the roasting time steamed them slightly and prevented them from drying out. We then uncovered the baking sheet and returned it to the oven to allow the noodles' surface moisture to evaporate, encouraging light caramelization and creating perfectly tender noodles. We kept the flavorings simple to allow the carrots' flavor to shine—just a handful of fresh thyme for earthy notes and a spoonful of honey to accent the carrots' natural sweetness. Choose carrots that are at least 1½ inches in diameter for this recipe.*

    2 pounds carrots, peeled
    2 tablespoons extra-virgin olive oil
    2 teaspoons minced fresh thyme or
       ½ teaspoon dried
    1 teaspoon honey
       Salt and pepper

1. Adjust oven rack to middle position and heat oven to 375 degrees. Using spiralizer, cut carrots into ⅛-inch-thick noodles, then cut noodles into 12-inch lengths. Toss carrots with 1 tablespoon oil, thyme, honey, ½ teaspoon salt, and ½ teaspoon pepper on rimmed baking sheet. Cover carrots tightly

Roasted Carrots and Shallots
with Chermoula

WHOLE CARROTS WITH RED PEPPER AND ALMOND RELISH

To achieve whole cooked carrots that are perfectly tender—but not at all mushy—from end to end, it's well worth the small amount of effort to make a cartouche from parchment paper, a circle of parchment that sits directly on the cooking carrots. This traps the steam on top of the carrots, so that the tops cook at the same rate as the bottoms. The end result? A restaurant-worthy side dish.

1. Make the relish first and set it aside to let the flavors blend while you cook the carrots.

2. Bring the water, butter, and salt to a simmer in a 12-inch skillet and lay the carrots in a single layer in the simmering liquid.

3. Place the parchment cartouche directly on top of the carrots, cover the skillet, remove it from the heat, and let the carrots stand in the hot liquid for 20 minutes.

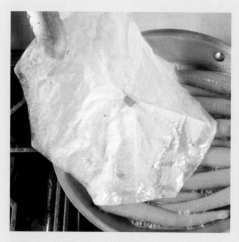

4. Remove the lid and simmer the carrots with just the parchment cartouche on top for about 45 minutes. This allows the carrots to cook through evenly, while also evaporating the cooking liquid. Remove and discard the cartouche.

5. Increase the heat and cook the carrots, shaking the pan frequently, until all the water has evaporated and the carrots are cloaked in the rich, flavorful glaze.

6. Arrange the carrots on a serving platter, top with the red pepper and almond relish, and serve.

with aluminum foil and roast for 15 minutes. Remove foil and continue to roast until carrots are tender, 10 to 15 minutes.

2. Transfer carrots to serving platter, drizzle with remaining 1 tablespoon oil, and season with salt and pepper to taste. Serve.

VARIATIONS

Roasted Carrot Noodles with Garlic, Red Pepper Flakes, and Basil

Substitute 2 thinly sliced garlic cloves and ½ teaspoon red pepper flakes for thyme. Toss roasted carrots with oil and 1 table-spoon chopped fresh basil before serving.

Roasted Carrot Noodles with Shallot, Dill, and Orange

Substitute 1 thinly sliced shallot for thyme. Toss roasted carrots with oil, 1 tablespoon minced fresh dill, 1 teaspoon orange zest, and 1 tablespoon orange juice before serving.

BRAISED CARROTS WITH APPLE

Serves 6 to 8   Total time: 30 minutes

WHY THIS RECIPE WORKS *The cooking liquid becomes your sauce when braising, so the trick to making a great braised vegetable side dish is to create a sauce that coats the vegetables well and infuses them with flavor but also stands on its own. Colorful, sweet carrots served as the anchor here. Slicing the carrots ¼ inch thick ensured that they cooked through evenly and quickly. We found that a mixture of chicken broth and apple cider gave us a sauce base with depth and sweetness that complemented the carrots. Reducing the cooking liquid slightly before the carrots were added and finishing with butter and Dijon mustard gave the sauce a silky texture and some body. Apple and fresh marjoram lent color and bright, fresh flavors.*

- 3 tablespoons unsalted butter, cut into ½-inch pieces
- 1 shallot, minced
- 1 cup chicken or vegetable broth
- 1 cup apple cider
- 6 sprigs fresh thyme
- 2 bay leaves
  Salt and pepper

- 2 pounds carrots, peeled and sliced ¼ inch thick on bias
- 1 Fuji or Honeycrisp apple, cored and cut into ¼-inch pieces
- 1 tablespoon Dijon mustard
- 1 teaspoon minced fresh marjoram or parsley

1. Melt 1 tablespoon butter in Dutch oven over high heat. Add shallot and cook, stirring frequently, until softened and just beginning to brown, about 3 minutes. Add broth, cider, thyme sprigs, bay leaves, 1½ teaspoons salt, and ½ teaspoon pepper; bring to simmer and cook to reduce slightly for 5 minutes. Add carrots, stir to combine, and return to simmer. Reduce heat to medium-low, cover, and cook, stirring occasionally, until tender, 10 to 14 minutes.

2. Off heat, discard thyme sprigs and bay leaves and stir in apple. Push carrots to sides of pot. Add mustard and remaining 2 table-spoons butter to center and whisk into cooking liquid. Stir to coat vegetable mixture with sauce, transfer to serving platter, sprinkle with marjoram, and serve.

WHOLE CARROTS WITH RED PEPPER AND ALMOND RELISH

Serves 4 to 6   Total time: 1 hour 45 minutes

WHY THIS RECIPE WORKS *Here's a technique for cooking whole carrots that yields a sweet and meltingly tender vegetable from one end to the other without the carrots becoming mushy or waterlogged. Gently "steeping" the carrots in warm water before cooking them firmed up the vegetable's cell walls so that they could be cooked for a long time without falling apart. We also topped the carrots with a cartouche (a circle of parchment that sits directly on the food) during cooking to ensure that the moisture in the pan cooked the carrots evenly. Finishing cooking at a simmer evaporated the liquid and concentrated the carrots' flavor so that they tasted great when served with the flavorful relish. Choose carrots that are between ¾ to 1¼ inches in diameter. You can use rainbow carrots in this recipe, if desired. You will need a skillet with a tight-fitting lid for this recipe.*

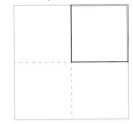

making a parchment lid (cartouche)

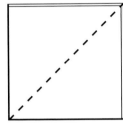

1. Fold 12-inch square of parchment into quarters to create 6-inch square.

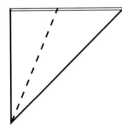

2. With openings at top and right sides, fold bottom right corner of square to top left corner.

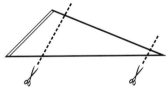

3. Fold triangle again, right side over left, to create narrow triangle.

4. Cut off ¼ inch of tip to create hole. Cut base of triangle straight across where it measures 5 inches from hole.

RED PEPPER AND ALMOND RELISH

- ½ cup finely chopped jarred roasted red peppers
- ¼ cup slivered almonds, toasted and chopped coarse
- 2 tablespoons extra-virgin olive oil
- 2 tablespoons minced fresh parsley
- 1 tablespoon white wine vinegar
- 1 teaspoon minced fresh oregano
- ¼ teaspoon salt

CARROTS

    3 cups water
    1 tablespoon unsalted butter
    ½ teaspoon salt
   12 carrots (1½ to 1¾ pounds), peeled

1. **For the relish** Combine all ingredients in bowl; set aside for serving.

2. **For the carrots** Make the cartouche (see previous page). Bring water, butter, and salt to simmer in 12-inch skillet over high heat. Remove pan from heat, add carrots in single layer, and place parchment round on top of carrots. Cover skillet and let stand for 20 minutes.

3. Remove lid from skillet, leaving parchment round in place, and bring to simmer over high heat. Reduce heat to medium-low and simmer until almost all water has evaporated and carrots are very tender, about 45 minutes. Discard parchment round, increase heat to medium-high, and continue to cook carrots, shaking pan frequently, until lightly glazed and all water has evaporated, 2 to 4 minutes. Transfer carrots to serving platter, top with relish, and serve.

VARIATIONS

Whole Carrots with Green Olive and Golden Raisin Relish
Omit red pepper relish. Microwave ⅓ cup raisins and 1 tablespoon water in medium bowl until hot, about 1 minute; let stand for 5 minutes. Stir in ½ cup chopped green olives, 1 minced shallot, 2 tablespoons extra-virgin olive oil, 1 tablespoon red wine vinegar, 1 tablespoon minced fresh parsley, ½ teaspoon ground fennel, and ¼ teaspoon salt. Spoon relish over carrots before serving.

Whole Carrots with Onion-Balsamic Relish with Mint
Omit red pepper relish. Heat 3 tablespoons extra-virgin olive oil in medium saucepan over medium heat until shimmering. Add 1 finely chopped red onion and ¼ teaspoon salt and cook until soft and well browned, about 15 minutes. Stir in 2 minced garlic cloves and cook until fragrant, about 30 seconds. Stir in 2 tablespoons balsamic vinegar and cook for 1 minute. Let cool for 15 minutes. Stir in 2 tablespoons minced fresh mint. Spoon relish over carrots before serving.

GLAZED CARROTS WITH ORANGE AND CRANBERRIES

Serves 4   Total time: 30 minutes

WHY THIS RECIPE WORKS *Glazing is probably the most popular way to prepare carrots, but they often turn out saccharine, with a limp and soggy or undercooked and fibrous texture. We wanted fully tender, well-seasoned carrots with a glossy and clingy—yet modest—glaze. Peeling regular bagged carrots and cutting them on the bias yielded uniform ovals that cooked evenly. We cooked and glazed the carrots in one single operation, starting by cooking the sliced carrots in a covered skillet with chicken broth, salt, sugar, and orange juice. After the carrots were cooked until almost tender, we removed the lid and turned up the heat to reduce the liquid. Finally, a little butter and a bit more sugar added to the skillet resulted in a pale amber glaze with lightly caramelized flavor.*

    1 pound carrots, peeled and sliced
       ¼ inch thick on bias
    ¼ cup dried cranberries
    ¼ cup chicken or vegetable broth
    2 tablespoons sugar
    ¼ teaspoon grated orange zest plus
       ¼ cup juice
       Salt and pepper
    1 tablespoon unsalted butter, cut into
       4 pieces

1. Bring carrots, cranberries, broth, 1 tablespoon sugar, orange zest and juice, and ½ teaspoon salt to boil, covered, in 12-inch nonstick skillet over medium-high heat; reduce heat to medium and simmer, stirring occasionally, until carrots are almost tender, about 5 minutes. Uncover, increase heat to high, and simmer rapidly, stirring occasionally, until liquid is reduced to 2 tablespoons, 1 to 2 minutes.

2. Add butter and remaining 1 tablespoon sugar to skillet. Toss carrots to coat and cook, stirring frequently, until carrots are completely tender and glaze is light golden, about 3 minutes. Transfer carrots to serving platter, scraping glaze from pan onto platter. Season with salt and pepper to taste and serve immediately.

VARIATIONS

Glazed Carrots with Ginger and Rosemary
Omit cranberries, orange zest, and orange juice. Increase broth to ½ cup. Add 1-inch piece of fresh ginger, sliced ¼ inch thick with carrots in step 1. Add an additional 1 tablespoon sugar as well as 1 teaspoon minced fresh rosemary with butter in step 2. Stir 2 teaspoons lemon juice into skillet before serving.

Honey-Glazed Carrots with Lemon and Thyme
Omit cranberries, orange zest, and orange juice. Increase broth to ½ cup. Substitute 3 tablespoons honey for sugar, and add honey in step 1. Add ½ teaspoon minced fresh thyme and ½ teaspoon grated lemon zest with butter in step 2. Stir 2 teaspoons lemon juice into skillet before serving.

BRINED GRILLED CARROTS WITH CILANTRO-YOGURT SAUCE

Serves 4   Total time: 1 hour

WHY THIS RECIPE WORKS *We all know that brining can transform lean, easy-to-overcook cuts of meat and poultry into juicy, well-seasoned showstoppers. Now it's time to brine your vegetables. Seriously. We love grilling whole carrots, but let's face it: They are tricky to season evenly. Dusting raw carrots with salt is like throwing a tennis ball at a wall—it just bounces right off. But 45 minutes in a salty bath changes the game, infusing the carrots evenly. Whereas we brine meat to increase tenderness and season, our goal here was primarily seasoning (though the carrots did soften slightly in the brine). We grilled them quickly over a hot fire to develop char and smoky flavor without sacrificing crunch. Drizzled with a piquant cilantro-yogurt sauce and sprinkled with peanuts and fresh herbs, these carrots might just become your new favorite side dish during grilling season. Young carrots are immature carrots, harvested early in their growing cycle. Look for carrots that are 3 to 5 inches long and ½ to 1 inch in diameter. Peeled carrots will absorb salt more rapidly, so we don't recommend peeling them for this recipe. If you can't find*

5. Drizzle yogurt sauce over carrots, then sprinkle with remaining ¼ cup cilantro, remaining ¼ cup carrot greens, and remaining 1 tablespoon peanuts. Serve.

CARROT-HABANERO DIP

Makes 2 ½ cups
Total time: 1 hour 15 minutes
WHY THIS RECIPE WORKS *To really bring out the fruity-earthy flavor qualities of carrots, a little spicy heat works wonders. This highly seasoned dip is full of vibrant carrot flavor. Cooking the carrots over an initial blast of heat quickly broke down cell walls and released their sugars. To maintain their brilliant color, we avoided browning and instead added water after the initial cooking, simmering the carrots until perfectly tender. We threw in some Moroccan-inspired spices that stood up well to the intense sweet carrot flavor, and added habanero chile for a surprise kick (use one or two depending on your preference). Processing the mixture at the end produced a smooth, spreadable dip that reminded us of hummus. With a healthy drizzle of olive oil and some crunchy pepitas on top, this is a simple dip that's sure to be a crowd-pleaser.*

  3 tablespoons extra-virgin olive oil, plus extra for serving
  2 pounds carrots, peeled and sliced ¼ inch thick
      Salt and pepper
1 or 2 habanero chiles, seeded and minced
  2 garlic cloves, minced
  ¾ teaspoon ground coriander
  ¾ teaspoon ground cumin
  ¾ teaspoon ground ginger
  ⅛ teaspoon chili powder
  ⅛ teaspoon ground cinnamon
  ⅓ cup water
  1 tablespoon white wine vinegar
  1 tablespoon roasted, salted pepitas
  1 tablespoon minced fresh cilantro

1. Heat 1 tablespoon oil in large saucepan over medium-high heat until shimmering. Add carrots and ½ teaspoon salt and cook until carrots begin to soften, 5 to 6 minutes. Stir in habanero, garlic, coriander, cumin, ginger, chili powder, and cinnamon and cook until fragrant, about 30 seconds. Add

---

carrots with their tops attached or the greens aren't in good shape, use thin carrots and 2 cups cilantro.

1½ pounds young carrots with greens attached, carrots unpeeled, greens chopped (1¼ cups)
    Salt
1¼ cups coarsely chopped fresh cilantro leaves and stems
  ½ cup plain Greek yogurt
  ¼ cup dry-roasted peanuts, chopped
  1 jalapeño chile, stemmed, seeds reserved, and minced
  1 ice cube
  1 teaspoon grated fresh ginger
  1 garlic clove, minced
  ¼ teaspoon ground coriander

1. Rinse and scrub carrots to remove any dirt. Whisk 1 quart water and ¼ cup salt in large bowl until salt is dissolved. Submerge carrots in brine and let sit at room temperature for at least 45 minutes or up to 1 hour. (Carrots brined with this salt concentration will start to taste too salty if brined longer than 1 hour. Brined carrots can be removed from brine, patted dry, and refrigerated for up to 3 hours before cooking.) Transfer carrots to paper towel–lined plate and pat dry. Discard brine.

2. Meanwhile, process 1 cup cilantro, 1 cup carrot greens, yogurt, 3 tablespoons peanuts, jalapeño, ice cube, ginger, garlic, and coriander in blender on high speed until smooth and creamy, about 2 minutes, scraping down sides of blender jar halfway through processing. Taste for spiciness; if desired, add more spice by blending in reserved jalapeño seeds. Season with salt to taste. Transfer yogurt sauce to small bowl, cover, and refrigerate until ready to serve.

3a. For a charcoal grill Open bottom vent completely. Light large chimney starter filled with charcoal briquettes (6 quarts). When top coals are partially covered with ash, pour evenly over half of grill. Set cooking grate in place, cover, and open lid vent completely. Heat grill until hot, about 5 minutes.

3b. For a gas grill Turn all burners to high, cover, and heat grill until hot, about 15 minutes. Leave all burners on high.

4. Clean and oil cooking grate. Place carrots on grill (directly over coals if using charcoal) and cook, turning occasionally, until carrots are well charred on all sides and exteriors are just beginning to soften, 3 to 5 minutes for very small carrots or 5 to 7 minutes for larger ones. Transfer to serving platter.

Chopped Carrot Salad with Mint, Pistachios, and Pomegranate Seeds

water and bring to simmer. Cover, reduce heat to low, and cook, stirring occasionally, until carrots are tender, 15 to 20 minutes.

2. Transfer carrots to bowl of food processor, add vinegar, and process until smooth, scraping down sides of bowl as needed, 1 to 2 minutes. With processor running, slowly add remaining 2 tablespoons oil until incorporated. Transfer to serving bowl, cover, and refrigerate until chilled, 30 minutes to 1 hour. Season with salt and pepper to taste. Sprinkle with pepitas and cilantro, and drizzle with extra oil. Serve.

CHOPPED CARROT SALAD WITH MINT, PISTACHIOS, AND POMEGRANATE SEEDS

Serves 4 to 6   Total time: 20 minutes
WHY THIS RECIPE WORKS *Carrots chopped in the food processor create a delicately crunchy, light-textured base for our carrot salad. It's a lovely change of pace from the more typical shredded, slaw-style cut that is often called for in carrot-based salads. The food processor broke down the carrots in seconds. We added contrasting flavor and texture to the carrots with lots of fresh mint (chopped by hand to avoid overprocessing the leaves in the food processor), pomegranate seeds, and toasted pistachios. A bright dressing bound it all together. We prefer the convenience and the hint of bitterness that leaving the carrots unpeeled lends to this salad; just be sure to scrub the carrots well before using them.*

¾ cup shelled pistachios, toasted
¼ cup extra-virgin olive oil
3 tablespoons lemon juice
1 tablespoon honey
   Salt and pepper
½ teaspoon smoked paprika
⅛ teaspoon cayenne pepper
1 pound carrots, unpeeled and cut into 1-inch pieces
1 cup pomegranate seeds
½ cup minced fresh mint

1. Pulse pistachios in food processor until coarsely chopped, 10 to 12 pulses; transfer to small bowl. Whisk oil, lemon juice, honey, 1 teaspoon salt, ½ teaspoon pepper, paprika, and cayenne in large bowl until combined.

2. Process carrots in now-empty processor until finely chopped, 10 to 20 seconds, scraping down sides of bowl as needed. Transfer carrots to bowl with dressing. Add ½ cup pomegranate seeds, mint, and half of pistachios and toss to combine. Season with salt to taste. Transfer to serving platter, sprinkle with remaining pomegranate seeds and pistachios, and serve.

VARIATIONS

Chopped Carrot Salad with Fennel, Orange, and Hazelnuts
Substitute toasted and skinned hazelnuts for pistachios. Omit paprika, cayenne, and pomegranate seeds. Substitute ¼ teaspoon grated orange zest plus ⅓ cup juice and 2 tablespoons white wine vinegar for lemon juice. Substitute chives for mint, saving ¼ cup to use as garnish. Before processing carrots, pulse 1 fennel bulb, cored and cut into 1-inch pieces, in food processor until coarsely chopped, 10 to 12 pulses, then add to dressing.

Chopped Carrot Salad with Radishes and Sesame Seeds
Omit pistachios. Substitute 3 tablespoons vegetable oil and 2 teaspoons toasted sesame oil for olive oil. Substitute rice vinegar for lemon juice and 1½ teaspoons Korean red pepper flakes (gochugaru) for paprika, cayenne, and pepper. Increase honey to 2 tablespoons and salt to 1¼ teaspoons. Before processing carrots, pulse 8 ounces radishes, trimmed and halved, in food processor until coarsely but evenly chopped, 10 to 12 pulses; add to dressing. Substitute ¼ cup toasted sesame seeds for pomegranate seeds and cilantro for mint.

BROWN RICE BOWLS WITH ROASTED CARROTS, KALE, AND FRIED EGGS

Serves 4   Total time: 1 hour 15 minutes
WHY THIS RECIPE WORKS *Carrots, kale, and fried eggs over brown rice make for a colorful, healthy, and hearty anytime-of-day meal. We tossed carrot batons with za'atar, a bold Middle Eastern spice blend, and roasted them until they were tender and spotty brown. When we uncovered the carrots to finish their roasting, we spread some chopped kale over the top. Briefly roasting the kale gave it great flavor and a crispiness that provided the dish with nice textural contrast. Taking advantage of the time the vegetables spent in the oven, we baked the rice right alongside, a conveniently hands-off method that produced great results. For the crowning touch, we topped each bowl with a fried egg, adding another layer of richness to the dish. Medium-grain or short-grain brown rice can be substituted for the long-grain rice.*

2 cups boiling water
1 cup long-grain brown rice, rinsed
   Salt and pepper
5 carrots, peeled and cut into 2-inch lengths, thin pieces halved lengthwise, thick pieces quartered lengthwise
⅓ cup extra-virgin olive oil
2 teaspoons za'atar
8 ounces kale, stemmed and cut into 1-inch strips
2 tablespoons red wine vinegar
1 small shallot, minced
4 large eggs

1. Adjust oven racks to upper-middle and lower-middle positions and heat oven to 375 degrees. Combine boiling water, rice, and ¾ teaspoon salt in 8-inch square baking dish and cover tightly with 2 layers of aluminum foil. Bake rice on lower rack until tender, 45 to 50 minutes. Remove rice from oven, uncover, and fluff with fork. Cover with dish towel and let sit for 5 minutes.

2. Meanwhile, toss carrots, 1 tablespoon oil, za'atar, ¼ teaspoon salt, and ⅛ teaspoon pepper together in bowl. Spread carrots onto parchment paper–lined rimmed baking sheet, cover with foil, and roast on upper rack for 20 minutes.

3. Toss kale, 1 tablespoon oil, ¼ teaspoon salt, and ⅛ teaspoon pepper together in bowl. Remove foil from sheet and arrange kale over top of carrots. Return sheet to oven and roast uncovered until carrots are spotty brown and tender and kale is crisp and edges are lightly browned, about 15 minutes.

4. Portion brown rice into individual bowls and top with roasted vegetables. Whisk vinegar, shallot, and 3 tablespoons oil together in bowl and season with salt and pepper to taste. Drizzle vinaigrette over rice and vegetables; cover to keep warm.

5. Crack eggs into 2 small bowls (2 eggs per bowl) and season with salt and pepper. Heat remaining 1 teaspoon oil in 12-inch nonstick skillet over medium-high heat until shimmering. Pour 1 bowl of eggs into 1 side of pan and second bowl into other side. Cover and cook for 1 minute. Remove skillet from heat and let sit, covered, for 15 to 45 seconds for runny yolks (white around edge of yolk will be barely opaque), 45 to 60 seconds for soft but set yolks, or about 2 minutes for medium-set yolks. Top each bowl with fried egg, and serve.

BULGUR SALAD WITH CARROTS AND ALMONDS

Serves 4 to 6   Total time: 1 hour 30 minutes
WHY THIS RECIPE WORKS *Sweet carrots nicely accent rich, nutty bulgur in this Mediterranean-inspired salad. Bulgur is a staple ingredient for grain-based salads, prized for its texture and versatility and acting as a nutritious, hearty medium for delivering big, bold flavors. We started by softening the bulgur in a mixture of water, lemon juice, and salt for an hour and a half until it had the perfect chew and was thoroughly seasoned. Fresh mint, cilantro, and scallions made our salad crisp and bright, and cumin and cayenne added depth of flavor to our simple lemon vinaigrette. Toasted almonds provided complementary crunch. When shopping, do not confuse bulgur with cracked wheat, which has a much longer cooking time and will not work in this recipe. Use the large holes of a box grater to shred the carrots.*

1½ cups medium-grind bulgur, rinsed
1 cup water
6 tablespoons lemon juice (2 lemons)
    Salt and pepper
⅓ cup extra-virgin olive oil
½ teaspoon ground cumin
⅛ teaspoon cayenne pepper
4 carrots, peeled and shredded
3 scallions, sliced thin
½ cup sliced almonds, toasted
⅓ cup chopped fresh mint
⅓ cup chopped fresh cilantro

1. Combine bulgur, water, ¼ cup lemon juice, and ¼ teaspoon salt in bowl. Cover and let sit at room temperature until grains are softened and liquid is fully absorbed, about 1½ hours.

2. Whisk remaining 2 tablespoons lemon juice, oil, cumin, cayenne, and ½ teaspoon salt together in large serving bowl. Add bulgur, carrots, scallions, almonds, mint, and cilantro and gently toss to combine. Season with salt and pepper to taste. Serve.

CHICKPEA SALAD WITH CARROTS, ARUGULA, AND OLIVES

Serves 6   Total time: 40 minutes
WHY THIS RECIPE WORKS *For a flavorful and easy side salad or light lunch, we combined nutty chickpeas and carrots with the Mediterranean flavors of arugula and olives. But simply tossing the ingredients with a lemon vinaigrette resulted in a lackluster salad with a pool of dressing at the bottom of the bowl. We wanted the seasoning to go beyond the surface of the chickpeas and fully infuse each one with big, bold flavor. The key was to warm the chickpeas before mixing them with the dressing ingredients: The seed coats that cover the chickpeas are rich in pectin, which breaks down when exposed to heat and moisture, creating a more porous inner surface that our dressing could easily penetrate. Letting the dressed chickpeas rest for 30 minutes put the flavor over the top and also allowed the chickpeas to cool. Use the large holes of a box grater to shred the carrots.*

2 (15-ounce) cans chickpeas, rinsed
¼ cup extra-virgin olive oil
2 tablespoons lemon juice
    Salt and pepper
    Pinch cayenne pepper
3 carrots, peeled and shredded
1 cup baby arugula, chopped
½ cup pitted kalamata olives, chopped

1. Microwave chickpeas in medium bowl until hot, about 2 minutes. Stir in oil, lemon juice, ¾ teaspoon salt, ½ teaspoon pepper, and cayenne and let stand for 30 minutes.

2. Add carrots, arugula, and olives to chickpea mixture and toss to combine. Season with salt and pepper to taste. Serve.

CARROT-GINGER SOUP

Serves 6   Total time: 1 hour
WHY THIS RECIPE WORKS *Sometimes the simplest recipes get overcomplicated as more and more versions appear. Case in point: carrot-ginger soup, whose flavors often get elbowed out with the addition of other vegetables, fruits, or dairy. For a fresh, clean-tasting soup, we decided to go back to the basics. With a combination of cooked carrots and carrot juice, we were able to get well-rounded, fresh carrot flavor. Using a mixture of grated fresh ginger and crystallized ginger gave us bright, refreshing ginger flavor with a moderate kick of heat. Finally, for a silky-smooth texture, we added a touch of baking soda to help break down the carrots and ginger, producing a perfectly creamy soup. We finished with some simple garnishes of sour cream, chopped chives, and croutons to provide tang, texture, and crunch.*

CROUTONS
3 tablespoons unsalted butter
1 tablespoon extra-virgin olive oil
3 slices hearty sandwich bread, cut into ½-inch pieces
    Salt

SOUP

- 2 tablespoons unsalted butter
- 2 onions, chopped fine
- ¼ cup minced crystallized ginger
- 1 tablespoon grated fresh ginger
- 2 garlic cloves, peeled and smashed
  Salt and pepper
- 1 teaspoon sugar
- 2 pounds carrots, peeled and sliced
  ¼ inch thick
- 4 cups water
- 1½ cups carrot juice
- 2 sprigs fresh thyme
- ½ teaspoon baking soda
- 1 tablespoon cider vinegar
  Chopped chives
  Sour cream

1. For the croutons Heat butter and oil in 12-inch skillet over medium heat until butter is melted. Add bread and cook, stirring frequently, until golden brown, about 10 minutes. Transfer croutons to paper towel–lined plate and season with salt to taste. Set aside until ready to serve.

2. For the soup Melt butter in large saucepan over medium heat. Stir in onions, crystallized ginger, fresh ginger, garlic, 2 teaspoons salt, and sugar and cook until onions are softened but not browned, 5 to 7 minutes.

3. Add carrots, water, ¾ cup carrot juice, thyme sprigs, and baking soda and bring to simmer over high heat. Cover, reduce heat to medium-low, and simmer until carrots are very tender, 20 to 25 minutes.

4. Discard thyme sprigs. Working in batches, process soup in blender until smooth, 1 to 2 minutes. Return soup to clean pot and stir in vinegar and remaining ¾ cup carrot juice. Return to simmer over medium heat and season with salt and pepper to taste. Serve with sprinkle of chives, dollop of sour cream, and croutons.

ONE-PAN CHICKEN WITH COUSCOUS AND CARROTS

Serves 4   Total time: 1 hour 15 minutes
WHY THIS RECIPE WORKS *This aromatic one-skillet meal takes its flavor cues from North Africa. First we browned the chicken pieces in the skillet and transferred them to a plate. Next, carrots and onions went into the skillet along with fragrant spices, and then chickpeas and couscous. We nestled the browned chicken in among it all, and baked the dish until everything was tender and the flavors melded together. Before serving, we fluffed up the couscous, adding fresh lemon juice and fresh parsley to brighten up the savory dish. The chicken will crowd the skillet in step 2 but, if left undisturbed, will still brown well. You will need a 12-inch oven-safe skillet with a tight-fitting lid for this recipe.*

- 8 (5- to 7-ounce) bone-in chicken thighs, trimmed
  Salt and pepper
- 1 teaspoon vegetable oil
- 1 pound carrots, peeled and cut into 2-inch lengths, thin pieces halved lengthwise, thick pieces quartered lengthwise
- 1 onion, chopped
- 4 garlic cloves, minced
- 1 teaspoon paprika
- ½ teaspoon ground cumin
- 1 (15-ounce) can chickpeas, rinsed
- ¾ cup water
- 1 cup couscous
- ⅓ cup minced fresh parsley
- 2 tablespoons lemon juice, plus lemon wedges for serving

1. Adjust oven rack to middle position and heat oven to 450 degrees. Pat chicken dry with paper towels and season with salt and pepper.

2. Heat oil in 12-inch ovensafe skillet over medium-high heat until just smoking. Add chicken, skin side down, and cook until skin is crispy and golden, 7 to 9 minutes. Flip chicken and continue to cook until golden on second side, 7 to 9 minutes. Transfer chicken to large plate, skin side up.

3. Pour off all but 1 tablespoon fat from skillet, then heat over medium heat until shimmering. Add carrots, onion, 1 teaspoon salt, and ½ teaspoon pepper and cook until onions are softened, about 5 minutes. Add garlic, paprika, and cumin and cook until fragrant, about 30 seconds. Stir in chickpeas and water and bring to boil, scraping up any browned bits.

4. Stir in couscous and nestle chicken, skin side up, along with any accumulated juices, into couscous mixture. Cover, transfer skillet to oven, and bake until chicken registers 175 degrees, about 18 minutes.

5. Transfer chicken to serving platter and let rest for 5 to 10 minutes. Add parsley and lemon juice to couscous mixture and fluff with fork. Season with salt and pepper to taste. Serve chicken and couscous with lemon wedges.

CARROT LAYER CAKE

Serves 12 to 16   Total time: 1 hour 15 minutes (plus 1 hour chilling time)

WHY THIS RECIPE WORKS *What's a collection of great carrot recipes without a carrot cake? This one is a showpiece: a sleek, stacked, dressed-up version of carrot cake with thin layers of light cake and a tangy cream cheese filling and frosting. We baked our cake in a rimmed baking sheet, sliced it into four pieces, and stacked them. The thin cake baked in only about 15 minutes. Using buttermilk powder in the cream cheese frosting both provided the desired tang and thickened the frosting to just the right consistency to hold the impressively towering creation together. To ensure the proper consistency for the frosting, use cold cream cheese. Shred the carrots on the large holes of a box grater or in a food processor fitted with the shredding disk. If your baked cake is of an uneven thickness, which can happen when baking a cake this way, adjust the orientation of the layers as you stack them to produce a level cake. Assembling this cake on a cardboard cake rectangle trimmed to 8 by 6 inches makes it easy to pick it up and press the pecans onto the sides.*

CAKE

- 1¾ cups (8¾ ounces) all-purpose flour
- 2 teaspoons baking powder
- 1 teaspoon baking soda
- 1½ teaspoons ground cinnamon
- ¾ teaspoon ground nutmeg
- ½ teaspoon salt
- ¼ teaspoon ground cloves
- 1¼ cups packed (8¾ ounces) light brown sugar
- ¾ cup vegetable oil
- 3 large eggs
- 1 teaspoon vanilla extract
- 2⅔ cups shredded carrots (4 carrots)
- ⅔ cup dried currants

FROSTING AND NUTS

- 16 tablespoons unsalted butter, softened
- 3 cups (12 ounces) confectioners' sugar
- ⅓ cup (1 ounce) buttermilk powder
- 2 teaspoons vanilla extract
- ¼ teaspoon salt
- 12 ounces cream cheese, cut into 12 equal pieces and chilled
- 2 cups pecans, toasted and chopped coarse

1. **For the cake** Adjust oven rack to middle position and heat oven to 350 degrees. Grease 18 by 13-inch rimmed baking sheet, line with parchment paper, and grease parchment.

2. Whisk flour, baking powder, baking soda, cinnamon, nutmeg, salt, and cloves together in large bowl. Whisk sugar, oil, eggs, and vanilla in second large bowl until mixture is smooth. Stir in carrots and currants. Add flour mixture and fold with rubber spatula until mixture is just combined.

3. Transfer batter to prepared sheet and smooth top with offset spatula. Bake until center is firm to touch, 15 to 18 minutes, rotating sheet halfway through baking. Let cake cool in pan on wire rack for 5 minutes. Invert cake onto rack (do not remove parchment), then reinvert onto second rack. Let cake cool completely, about 30 minutes.

4. **For the frosting and nuts** Using stand mixer fitted with paddle, beat butter, sugar, buttermilk powder, vanilla, and salt on low speed until smooth, about 2 minutes, scraping down bowl as needed. Increase speed to medium-low, add cream cheese, 1 piece at a time, and mix until smooth, about 2 minutes.

5. Transfer cooled cake to cutting board, parchment side down. Using sharp chef's knife, cut cake and parchment in half crosswise, then lengthwise, making 4 equal rectangles, about 8 by 6 inches each.

6. Place 1 cake layer, parchment side up, on 8 by 6-inch cardboard rectangle and carefully remove parchment. Spread ⅔ cup frosting evenly over top, right to edge of cake. Repeat with 2 more cake layers, pressing lightly to adhere and spreading ⅔ cup frosting evenly over each layer. Top with remaining cake layer and spread 1 cup frosting evenly over top. Spread remaining frosting evenly over sides of cake. (It's fine if some crumbs show through frosting on sides, but if you go back to smooth top of cake, be sure that spatula is free of crumbs.)

7. Hold cake with your hand and gently press pecans onto sides with your other hand. Refrigerate for at least 1 hour. Transfer cake to platter and serve. (Cake can be refrigerated for up to 24 hours; bring to room temperature before serving.)

making carrot layer cake

1. Smooth batter in baking sheet to create thin, level cake.

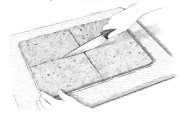

2. Slice cooled sheet cake into 4 equal rectangles.

3. Spread frosting over rectangular layer placed on cardboard; repeat with remaining layers.

4. Press chopped pecans onto sides of cake to hide any imperfections and add crunch.

Carrot Layer Cake

CAULIFLOWER

With its tightly knit milky florets and the sculptural green base that entwines them, a head of cauliflower is a truly beautiful thing. And its versatility in the kitchen has caught on for keeps, inspiring chefs everywhere to experiment with new ways of cooking it.

Here in the test kitchen, we've developed plenty of recipes that put this vegetable at center stage, whether as a side dish or a main course. When you discover our Roasted Cauliflower with Paprika and Chorizo or our Baja-Style Cauliflower Tacos, you'll begin to see it in a brand-new light.

Mild-tasting, adaptable cauliflower is positively irresistible when paired with bold, strong flavors, particularly in Whole Pot-Roasted Cauliflower with Tomatoes and Olives, roasted Cauliflower Steaks with Salsa Verde, and Thai Red Curry with Cauliflower. You can also magically blitz it into "rice" to serve as a simple side or a bed for any number of main-course toppings.

In farmers' markets and some supermarkets, you will often find deep orange or purple cauliflower. Both of these varieties can be substituted for regular white cauliflower. The orange variety has 25 times more vitamin A than white cauliflower, and the purple variety is high in antioxidants.

Romanesco is a beautiful cousin: Key-lime green in hue, and so fractal in appearance that it has even been studied by architects for new models of building design. Our recipe for broiled whole romanesco dusted with the Ethiopian spice blend berbere and served with a tangy yogurt-tahini sauce is a showstopper of a dish that comes together in a flash.

shopping and storage

Cauliflower is readily available year-round, though it's at its best in the fall and winter. Look for fresh, firm, bright white or deeply colored heads of cauliflower that are free of discolored brown spots and soft spots and that feel heavy for their size, with tightly packed florets and firm leaves without any fading; florets are more likely to separate from older heads of cauliflower. Romanesco should be a bright chartreuse color and similarly free of blemishes.

You can store cauliflower and romanesco in the packaging they come in, but for longer life, transfer them to a loosely closed plastic produce bag in the refrigerator with paper towels wrapped around them. They should keep for a week or longer.

vegetable science
The Silky Side of Cauliflower
All vegetables contain both soluble and insoluble fiber. The first kind breaks down fully during cooking, but the second does not. Cauliflower is very low in fiber overall, and only half of that fiber is insoluble. This meant that we could easily puree cauliflower into a silky-smooth sauce for our modern gratin and make a creamy soup and an Alfredo sauce for pasta without the cream.

vegetable prep

Cutting Cauliflower into Florets

1. Trim outer leaves of cauliflower and cut stem flush with bottom florets, trimming and reserving stem if needed.

2. Place cauliflower head stem side down and cut head into ¾-inch-thick slabs.

3. Working with 1 slab at a time, cut around core to separate florets, reserving core if needed.

4. Cut florets into desired size.

Cutting Cauliflower into Wedges

1. After trimming outer leaves of cauliflower and cutting stem flush with bottom florets, halve cauliflower lengthwise through core.

2. Cut into desired number of wedges by cutting through core into equal-sized wedges, keeping core and florets intact.

Cutting Cauliflower into Steaks

1. After trimming outer leaves of cauliflower and cutting stem flush with bottom florets, halve cauliflower lengthwise through core.

2. Cut one 1½-inch-thick slab from each cauliflower half. Reserve remaining cauliflower for another use.

PAN-ROASTED CAULIFLOWER WITH GARLIC AND LEMON

Serves 4 to 6   Total time: 40 minutes

WHY THIS RECIPE WORKS *Roasting cauliflower is a great way to caramelize its sugars and transform this mild vegetable into something sweet and nutty-tasting. We wanted to create a stovetop method that would deliver oven results in a faster time frame. Heating oil and adding florets resulted in the craggy exteriors browning before the interiors softened. Adding water to the pan to soften the florets resulted in anemic, bland cauliflower. But starting the oil and cauliflower together in a cold pan, first covered, then uncovered, resulted in caramelized, tender florets. A combination of sautéed garlic and lemon zest, plus fresh chopped parsley, perked up the flavors. With a sprinkle of crunchy toasted bread crumbs, our newfangled skillet-roasted cauliflower was complete. You will need a 12-inch nonstick skillet with a tight-fitting lid for this recipe.*

- 1 slice hearty white sandwich bread, torn into 1-inch pieces
- 5 tablespoons extra-virgin olive oil
  Salt and pepper
- 1 head cauliflower (2 pounds), cut into 1½-inch florets
- 1 garlic clove, minced
- 1 teaspoon grated lemon zest, plus lemon wedges for serving
- ¼ cup chopped fresh parsley

1. Pulse bread in food processor to coarse crumbs, about 10 pulses. Heat bread crumbs, 1 tablespoon oil, pinch salt, and pinch pepper in 12-inch nonstick skillet over medium heat, stirring frequently, until bread crumbs are golden brown, 3 to 5 minutes. Transfer crumbs to bowl and wipe out skillet.

2. Combine 2 tablespoons oil and cauliflower florets in now-empty skillet and sprinkle with 1 teaspoon salt and ½ teaspoon pepper. Cover skillet and cook over medium-high heat until florets start to brown and edges just start to become translucent (do not lift lid during this time), about 5 minutes.

3. Uncover and continue to cook, stirring occasionally, until golden, about 12 minutes.

4. Push florets to edges of skillet. Add remaining 2 tablespoons oil, garlic, and lemon zest to center and cook, stirring with rubber spatula, until fragrant, about 30 seconds. Stir garlic mixture into florets and continue to cook, stirring occasionally, until florets are tender but still firm, about 3 minutes.

5. Remove skillet from heat and stir in parsley. Transfer florets to serving platter and sprinkle with bread crumbs. Serve, passing lemon wedges separately.

VARIATIONS

Pan-Roasted Cauliflower with Capers and Pine Nuts

Omit bread and reduce oil to ¼ cup. Reduce salt in step 2 to ¾ teaspoon. Substitute 2 tablespoons capers, rinsed and minced, for garlic. Substitute 2 tablespoons minced fresh chives for parsley and stir in ¼ cup toasted pine nuts with chives in step 5.

Pan-Roasted Cauliflower with Cumin and Pistachios

Omit bread and reduce oil to ¼ cup. Heat 1 teaspoon cumin seeds and 1 teaspoon coriander seeds in 12-inch nonstick skillet over medium heat, stirring frequently, until lightly toasted and fragrant, 2 to 3 minutes. Transfer to spice grinder or mortar and pestle and coarsely grind. Wipe out skillet. Substitute ground cumin-coriander mixture, ½ teaspoon paprika, and pinch cayenne pepper for garlic; lime zest for lemon zest; and 3 tablespoons chopped fresh mint for parsley. Sprinkle with ¼ cup pistachios, toasted and chopped, before serving with lime wedges.

~

ROASTED CAULIFLOWER

Serves 4 to 6   Total time: 1 hour

WHY THIS RECIPE WORKS *Recipes for roasting cauliflower typically call for tossing the florets with oil and roasting them on a baking sheet in a very hot oven. But because of their shape, the florets don't always brown evenly. Our solution was twofold: First, instead of slicing florets, we cut a head of cauliflower into eight wedges, which gave us more—and flatter— surface area for browning. A bonus? There were fewer pieces to flip partway through roasting. Next, we arranged the wedges on a baking sheet, covered them tightly with foil, and set them in a 475-degree oven so that the cauliflower could begin to steam in its own moisture. After we removed the foil, the cauliflower had enough time to caramelize on both sides but not dry out. Paired with smoked paprika and chorizo in one variation, and bacon and scallions in another, the cauliflower tastes so substantial it could almost be a meal. Combined with curry, cilantro, and cashews, it shows its exotic side.*

- 1 head cauliflower (2 pounds), cut into 8 equal wedges
- ¼ cup extra-virgin olive oil
  Salt and pepper

1. Adjust oven rack to lowest position and heat oven to 475 degrees. Place cauliflower wedges cut side down on parchment paper–lined rimmed baking sheet. Drizzle with 2 tablespoons oil and season with salt and pepper to taste; rub gently to distribute oil and seasonings.

2. Cover sheet tightly with aluminum foil and cook for 10 minutes. Remove foil and continue to roast until bottoms of cauliflower wedges are golden, about 15 minutes. Remove sheet from oven and, using spatula, carefully flip wedges. Return sheet to oven and continue to roast until cauliflower is golden all over, about 15 minutes. Season with salt and pepper to taste, transfer to serving platter, drizzle with remaining 2 tablespoons oil, and serve.

VARIATIONS

Roasted Cauliflower with Bacon and Scallions

In step 1, combine 2 tablespoons oil and 4 minced garlic cloves in small bowl before drizzling over cauliflower. Distribute 6 slices bacon, cut into ½-inch pieces, and ½ onion, cut into ½-inch-thick slices, on baking sheet around cauliflower before roasting. In step 2, whisk remaining 2 tablespoons oil with 2 teaspoons cider vinegar in large bowl. Toss roasted cauliflower mixture with oil-vinegar mixture. Season with salt and pepper to taste, transfer to serving platter, and sprinkle with 2 thinly sliced scallions.

Pan-Roasted Cauliflower with
Capers and Pine Nuts

Roasted Cauliflower with Curry and Lime

In step 1, combine 2 tablespoons oil and 1½ teaspoons curry powder in small bowl before drizzling over cauliflower. Distribute ½ onion, cut into ½-inch-thick slices, on baking sheet around cauliflower before roasting. In step 2, whisk remaining 2 tablespoons oil with 2 teaspoons lime juice in large bowl. Toss roasted cauliflower with oil–lime juice mixture. Season with salt and pepper to taste; transfer to serving platter; and sprinkle with ¼ cup toasted and chopped cashews and 2 tablespoons chopped fresh cilantro.

Roasted Cauliflower with Paprika and Chorizo

In step 1, combine 2 tablespoons oil and 1½ teaspoons smoked paprika in small bowl before drizzling over cauliflower. Distribute ½ red onion, cut into ½-inch-thick slices, on baking sheet around cauliflower before roasting. In step 2, after removing aluminum foil, distribute 6 ounces chorizo sausage, halved lengthwise and sliced ½ inch thick, on sheet with cauliflower. Whisk remaining 2 tablespoons oil with 2 teaspoons sherry vinegar in large bowl. Toss roasted cauliflower mixture with oil-vinegar mixture. Season with salt and pepper to taste, transfer to serving platter, and sprinkle with 2 tablespoons chopped fresh parsley.

BRAISED CAULIFLOWER WITH GARLIC AND WHITE WINE

Serves 4 to 6   Total time: 25 minutes

WHY THIS RECIPE WORKS *When properly cooked and imaginatively flavored, braised cauliflower can be nutty and slightly sweet, with a pleasing texture. However, it's easy to overcook braised cauliflower. To avoid this, we needed to quickly braise the florets. We cut them into 1½-inch pieces to reduce the total cooking time. Sautéing the pieces in olive oil imparted nuttiness. Because we wanted the cauliflower to braise for only a short amount of time, we maximized its impact by creating an ultraflavorful broth that the vegetable could absorb. White wine and broth made for a complexly flavored base, and a generous amount of garlic along with a pinch of red*

pepper flakes added punch and deeper flavor. For the best texture and taste, make sure to brown the cauliflower well in step 1. You will need a skillet with a tight-fitting lid for this recipe.

3 tablespoons plus 1 teaspoon extra-virgin olive oil
3 garlic cloves, minced
⅛ teaspoon red pepper flakes
1 head cauliflower (2 pounds), cut into 1½-inch florets
 Salt and pepper
⅓ cup chicken or vegetable broth
⅓ cup dry white wine
2 tablespoons minced fresh parsley

1. Combine 1 teaspoon oil, garlic, and pepper flakes in small bowl. Heat remaining 3 tablespoons oil in 12-inch skillet over medium-high heat until shimmering. Add cauliflower florets and ¼ teaspoon salt and cook, stirring occasionally, until florets are golden, 7 to 9 minutes.

2. Push florets to sides of skillet. Add garlic mixture to center and cook, mashing mixture into skillet, until fragrant, about 30 seconds. Stir garlic mixture into florets.

3. Stir in broth and wine and bring to simmer. Reduce heat to medium-low, cover, and cook until florets are crisp-tender, 4 to 6 minutes. Off heat, stir in parsley and season with salt and pepper to taste. Serve.

VARIATIONS

Braised Cauliflower with Capers and Anchovies

Add 2 anchovy fillets, rinsed and minced, and 1 tablespoon rinsed and minced capers to oil mixture in step 1. Stir 1 tablespoon lemon juice into cauliflower with parsley in step 3.

Braised Cauliflower with Sumac and Mint

Omit wine. Substitute 2 teaspoons ground sumac for pepper flakes and increase broth to ½ cup. In step 3, once cauliflower is crisp-tender, uncover and continue to cook until liquid is almost evaporated, about 1 minute. Substitute 2 tablespoons chopped fresh mint for parsley and stir ¼ cup plain yogurt into cauliflower with mint.

WHOLE POT-ROASTED CAULIFLOWER WITH TOMATOES AND OLIVES

Serves 4 to 6   Total time: 1 hour 15 minutes

WHY THIS RECIPE WORKS *Pot-roasted cauliflower has taken the internet by storm. As a hearty side or light vegetarian main, cauliflower braised in an aromatic tomato sauce is making its way into blogs, magazines, and restaurant menus alike. The recipes we came across all started by searing the cumbersome cauliflower first in hopes of browning the exterior. But we found this task unwieldy, with the cauliflower slipping from our tongs and the hot oil spitting at our forearms. After all was said and done, browning was spotty at best. And, once it was coated in a piquant sauce of chunky tomatoes, golden raisins, and salty capers and olives, we couldn't taste or see the difference between browned and unbrowned cauliflower. So we skipped the hassle. To ensure all of the rich flavors penetrated the dense vegetable, we started by cooking it upside down and spooned some of the sauce into the crevices between the stalk and florets. Then we flipped it right side up, spooned more sauce over the top, and left the pot uncovered to finish cooking. The sauce thickened but remained plentiful and the flavors intensified as the cauliflower became fork-tender.*

2 (28-ounce) cans whole peeled tomatoes
2 tablespoons extra-virgin olive oil, plus extra for serving
6 anchovy fillets, rinsed and minced
6 garlic cloves, minced
¼ teaspoon red pepper flakes
¼ teaspoon salt
1 head cauliflower (2 pounds)
¼ cup golden raisins
¼ cup pitted kalamata olives, chopped coarse
3 tablespoons capers, rinsed
1 ounce Parmesan cheese, grated (½ cup)
¼ cup minced fresh parsley

1. Adjust oven rack to middle position and heat oven to 450 degrees. Pulse tomatoes and their juice in food processor until coarsely chopped, 6 to 8 pulses.

2. Cook oil, anchovies, garlic, and pepper flakes in Dutch oven over medium heat, stirring constantly, until fragrant, about 2 minutes. Stir in tomatoes and salt, bring to simmer, and cook until slightly thickened, about 10 minutes.

3. Meanwhile, trim outer leaves of cauliflower and cut stem flush with bottom florets. Stir raisins, olives, and capers into tomatoes in pot, then nestle cauliflower, stem side up, into sauce. Spoon some of sauce over top, cover, transfer pot to oven, and roast until cauliflower is just tender (paring knife slips in and out of core with some resistance), 30 to 35 minutes.

4. Uncover pot and using tongs, flip cauliflower stem side down. Spoon some of sauce over cauliflower, then scrape down sides of pot. Continue to roast, uncovered, until cauliflower is tender, 10 to 15 minutes.

5. Remove pot from oven. Sprinkle cauliflower with Parmesan and parsley and drizzle with extra oil. Cut cauliflower into wedges and serve, spooning sauce over individual portions.

WHOLE ROMANESCO WITH BERBERE AND YOGURT-TAHINI SAUCE

Serves 4 Total time: 30 minutes

WHY THIS RECIPE WORKS *This beautiful, fractal-looking vegetable is perfect for cooking whole, as we do in this showstopper of a dish. For a tender interior and nicely charred exterior, we started with the microwave, partially cooking the romanesco. Then we brushed melted butter over the romanesco and transferred it to the oven to finish cooking and develop some browning. We basted the broiled romanesco with more butter and berbere, a warmly aromatic and highly flavorful Ethiopian spice blend. A bright, cooling yogurt sauce and crunchy pine nuts finished it off. Berbere is available in large supermarkets and by mail-order. If you can't find a 2-pound head of romanesco, purchase two 1-pound heads, and reduce the microwaving time in step 2 to 5 to 7 minutes. You can substitute cauliflower for the romanesco.*

YOGURT-TAHINI SAUCE

- ½ cup whole-milk yogurt
- 2 tablespoons tahini
- ½ teaspoon grated lemon zest plus 1 tablespoon juice
- 1 garlic clove, minced
  Salt and pepper

ROMANESCO

- 1 head romanesco or cauliflower (2 pounds)
- 6 tablespoons unsalted butter, cut into 6 pieces
  Salt and pepper
- ½ teaspoon paprika
- ¼ teaspoon cayenne pepper
- ¼ teaspoon ground coriander
- ⅛ teaspoon ground allspice
- ⅛ teaspoon ground cardamom
- ⅛ teaspoon ground cumin
- 2 tablespoons toasted and coarsely chopped pine nuts
- 1 tablespoon minced fresh cilantro

1. For the sauce Whisk all ingredients in bowl until combined. Season with salt and pepper to taste and set aside until ready to serve.

2. For the romanesco Adjust oven rack 6 inches from broiler element and heat broiler. Trim outer leaves of romanesco and cut stem flush with bottom florets. Microwave romanesco and 3 tablespoons butter in large, covered bowl until paring knife slips easily in and out of core, 8 to 12 minutes.

3. Transfer romanesco, stem side down, to 12-inch ovensafe skillet. Brush romanesco evenly with melted butter from bowl and sprinkle with ¼ teaspoon salt. Transfer skillet to oven and broil until top of romanesco is spotty brown, 8 to 10 minutes. Meanwhile, microwave remaining 3 tablespoons butter, paprika, cayenne, coriander, allspice, cardamom, cumin, and ⅛ teaspoon pepper in now-empty bowl, stirring occasionally, until fragrant and bubbling, 1 to 2 minutes.

4. Using pot holder, remove skillet from oven and transfer to wire rack. Being careful of hot skillet handle, gently tilt skillet so butter pools to one side. Using spoon, baste romanesco until butter is absorbed, about 30 seconds.

5. Cut romanesco into wedges and transfer to serving platter. Season with salt to taste and sprinkle pine nuts and cilantro over top. Serve with sauce.

Grilled Cauliflower

GRILLED CAULIFLOWER

Serves 4 to 6   Total time: 35 minutes

WHY THIS RECIPE WORKS *To make grilled cauliflower with a tender interior and a flavorful, nicely browned exterior, we first microwaved it until it was cooked through and then briefly grilled it to pick up color and flavor. To ensure that the cauliflower held up on the grill without falling through the grate and to provide sufficient surface area for browning, we cut the head into wedges. Dunking the cauliflower in a salt and sugar solution before microwaving seasoned it all over, even in the nooks and crannies. Look for cauliflower with densely packed florets that feels heavy for its size. Using tongs or a thin metal spatula to gently flip the wedges helps keep them intact. This dish stands well on its own, but to dress it up, serve it sprinkled with 1 tablespoon of Pistachio Dukkah or Almond, Raisin, and Caper Relish (recipes follow).*

- ¼ cup salt
- 2 tablespoons sugar
- 1 head cauliflower (2 pounds), cut into 6 equal wedges
- 2 tablespoons extra-virgin olive oil
- 1 tablespoon minced fresh chives
- 1 tablespoon topping (recipes follow) Lemon wedges

1. Whisk 2 cups water, salt, and sugar in medium bowl until salt and sugar dissolve. Holding wedges by core, gently dunk in salt-sugar mixture until evenly moistened (do not dry—residual water will help cauliflower steam). Transfer wedges, rounded side down, to large plate and cover with inverted large bowl. Microwave until cauliflower is translucent and tender and paring knife slips easily in and out of thickest stem of florets (not core), 14 to 16 minutes.

2. Carefully (bowl and cauliflower will be very hot) transfer cauliflower to paper towel–lined plate and pat dry with paper towels. Brush cut sides of wedges with 1 tablespoon oil.

3a. For a charcoal grill Open bottom vent completely. Light large chimney starter three-quarters filled with charcoal briquettes (4½ quarts). When top coals are partially covered with ash, pour evenly over grill. Set cooking grate in place, cover, and open lid vent completely. Heat grill until hot, about 5 minutes.

3b. For a gas grill Turn all burners to high, cover, and heat grill until hot, about 15 minutes. Turn all burners to medium-high.

4. Clean and oil cooking grate. Place cauliflower, cut side down, on grill and cook, covered, until well browned with spots of charring, 3 to 4 minutes. Using tongs or thin metal spatula, flip cauliflower and cook second cut side until well browned with spots of charring, 3 to 4 minutes. Flip again so cauliflower is sitting on rounded edge and cook until browned, 1 to 2 minutes.

5. Transfer cauliflower to serving platter. Drizzle with remaining 1 tablespoon oil, sprinkle with chives and topping, and serve with lemon wedges.

Pistachio Dukkah

Makes about ⅓ cup

WHY THIS RECIPE WORKS *The combination of toasted spices, nuts, and seeds makes for a fragrant and crunchy garnish for our grilled cauliflower. This Middle Eastern spice blend also can be sprinkled on a plate of extra-virgin olive oil and served as a dip for bread or sprinkled over soups, grain dishes, or bean salads. If you do not own a spice grinder, you can process the spices in a mini food processor.*

- 1½ tablespoons sesame seeds, toasted
- 1½ teaspoons coriander seeds, toasted
- ¾ teaspoon cumin seeds, toasted
- ½ teaspoon fennel seeds, toasted
- 2 tablespoons shelled pistachios, toasted and chopped fine
- ½ teaspoon salt
- ½ teaspoon pepper

Process sesame seeds in spice grinder or mortar and pestle until coarsely ground; transfer to bowl. Process coriander seeds, cumin seeds, and fennel seeds in now-empty grinder until finely ground. Transfer to bowl with sesame seeds. Stir pistachios, salt, and pepper into sesame mixture until combined. (Dukkah can be refrigerated in airtight container for up to 1 month.)

Almond, Raisin, and Caper Relish

Makes about ½ cup

WHY THIS RECIPE WORKS *Golden raisins plus briny capers, crunchy almonds, and white wine vinegar make for a sweet, salty, and tangy topping. Champagne vinegar can be used in place of white wine vinegar and regular raisins in place of golden raisins, if desired.*

- 2 tablespoons golden raisins
- 1 teaspoon white wine vinegar
- ¼ cup sliced almonds, toasted and chopped fine
- 1 tablespoon capers, rinsed and chopped fine
- 1 teaspoon minced fresh parsley Pinch red pepper flakes
- 3–4 tablespoons extra-virgin olive oil Salt and pepper

Combine raisins and 2 tablespoons hot water in small bowl and let stand for 5 minutes. Drain raisins and chop fine. Toss raisins and vinegar in bowl, then stir in almonds, capers, parsley, and pepper flakes. Stir in 3 tablespoons oil; mixture should be well moistened. If still dry, add remaining 1 tablespoon oil. Season with salt and pepper to taste.

CAULIFLOWER RICE

Serves 4 to 6   Total time: 35 minutes

WHY THIS RECIPE WORKS *This shape-shifter of a vegetable approximates cooked white rice surprisingly well, providing a neutral-flavored but more nutrient-dense companion to all sorts of dishes. The key was to blitz the florets in a food processor until transformed into perfect rice-size granules. To make our cauliflower rice foolproof, we worked in batches, making sure all the florets broke down evenly. Next, shallot and a small amount of broth boosted the flavor. To ensure that the cauliflower was tender but still maintained a rice-like chew, we first steamed the "rice" in a covered pot, then finished cooking it uncovered to evaporate any remaining moisture. The faux rice cooked up pleasantly fluffy, making it the perfect accompaniment to any meal.*

1 head cauliflower (2 pounds), cut into 1-inch florets (6 cups)
1 tablespoon extra-virgin olive oil
1 shallot, minced
½ cup chicken or vegetable broth
   Salt and pepper
2 tablespoons minced fresh parsley

1. Working in 2 batches, pulse cauliflower florets in food processor until finely ground into ¼- to ⅛-inch pieces, 6 to 8 pulses, scraping down sides of bowl as needed; transfer to bowl.

2. Heat oil in large saucepan over medium-low heat until shimmering. Add shallot and cook until softened, about 3 minutes. Stir in cauliflower, broth, and ¾ teaspoon salt. Cover and cook, stirring occasionally, until cauliflower is tender, 12 to 15 minutes.

3. Uncover and continue to cook, stirring occasionally, until cauliflower rice is almost completely dry, about 3 minutes. Off heat, stir in parsley and season with salt and pepper to taste. Serve.

VARIATIONS

Tex-Mex Cauliflower Rice
Add 1 minced garlic clove, 1 teaspoon ground cumin, and 1 teaspoon ground coriander to saucepan with shallot in step 2. Substitute 2 tablespoons minced fresh cilantro for parsley and stir 1 teaspoon lime juice into cauliflower rice with cilantro.

Curried Cauliflower Rice
Add ¼ teaspoon ground cardamom, ¼ teaspoon ground cinnamon, and ¼ teaspoon ground turmeric to saucepan with shallot. Substitute 1 tablespoon minced fresh mint for parsley and stir ¼ cup toasted sliced almonds into cauliflower rice with mint.

CAULIFLOWER BUFFALO BITES

Serves 4 to 6   Total time: 40 minutes

WHY THIS RECIPE WORKS *These crunchy, tangy, spicy, and just plain addictive cauliflower bites will be the new star of your game day table. The key was to come up with a flavorful, crunchy coating that would hold up under the Buffalo sauce. A mixture of cornstarch and cornmeal gave us an ultracrisp exterior. But because cauliflower is not naturally moist (like chicken), the mixture didn't stick; so first we dunked the florets in canned coconut milk, which had just the right viscosity. We got decent results when we baked our bites, but we absolutely flipped over the crackly crust and tender interior we achieved through frying. An herby ranch dressing was a cooling foil to the kick of the bites. We used Frank's RedHot Original Cayenne Pepper Sauce, but other hot sauces can be used. Use a Dutch oven that holds 6 quarts or more for this recipe. When you open the can of coconut milk, you may notice that it's separated— there may be a more solid mass above the watery liquid. If so, be sure to mix it together before measuring.*

RANCH DRESSING
½ cup mayonnaise
2 tablespoons plain yogurt
1 teaspoon white wine vinegar
1½ teaspoons minced fresh chives
1½ teaspoons minced fresh dill
¼ teaspoon garlic powder
⅛ teaspoon salt
⅛ teaspoon pepper

BUFFALO SAUCE
4 tablespoons unsalted butter, cut into 4 pieces
½ cup hot sauce
1 tablespoon packed dark brown sugar
2 teaspoons cider vinegar

CAULIFLOWER
1–2 quarts peanut or vegetable oil
¾ cup cornstarch
¼ cup cornmeal
   Salt and pepper
⅔ cup canned coconut milk
1 tablespoon hot sauce
1 pound cauliflower florets, cut into 1½-inch pieces

1. **For the ranch dressing** Whisk all ingredients in bowl until smooth. Refrigerate until serving. (Dressing can be refrigerated for up to 4 days.)

2. **For the buffalo sauce** Melt butter in small saucepan over low heat. Whisk in hot sauce, brown sugar, and vinegar until combined. Remove from heat and cover to keep warm; set aside.

3. **For the cauliflower** Line platter with triple layer of paper towels. Add oil to large Dutch oven until it measures about 1½ inches deep and heat over medium-high heat to 400 degrees. While oil heats, combine cornstarch, cornmeal, ½ teaspoon salt, and ¼ teaspoon pepper in small bowl. Whisk coconut milk and hot sauce together in large bowl. Add cauliflower; toss to coat well. Sprinkle cornstarch mixture over cauliflower; fold with rubber spatula until thoroughly coated.

4. Fry half of cauliflower, adding 1 or 2 pieces to oil at a time, until golden and crisp, gently stirring as needed to prevent pieces from sticking together, about 3 minutes. Using slotted spoon, transfer fried cauliflower to prepared platter.

5. Return oil to 400 degrees and repeat with remaining cauliflower. Transfer ½ cup sauce to clean large bowl, add fried cauliflower and gently toss to coat. Serve immediately with ranch dressing and remaining sauce.

NORTH AFRICAN CAULIFLOWER SALAD WITH CHERMOULA

Serves 4 to 6   Total time: 45 minutes

WHY THIS RECIPE WORKS *Chermoula is a traditional Moroccan mixture made with hefty amounts of cilantro, lemon, and garlic. While it's traditionally used as a marinade for meat or fish, we decided to make it the flavor base for this zippy cauliflower salad. We focused first on the cooking method of the starring vegetable. Roasting was the best choice to add deep flavor to the cauliflower and balance the bright chermoula. To keep the cauliflower from overbrowning on the exterior before the interior was cooked, we*

CAULIFLOWER BUFFALO BITES

Buffalo-spiced vegetables are being seen more and more often on restaurant menus, and in particular, Buffalo cauliflower has become an uber-popular choice. This makes perfect sense, since cauliflower has so many nooks and crannies to highlight the crunch factor of the batter and trap pockets of the deliciously spicy sauce. It's easy and fun to create an even better version of this addictively poppable favorite at home.

1. Cut the cauliflower into bite-size florets, about 1½ inches. Discard the tougher core, since those pieces would lend an unappealing woody texture.

2. Combine the cornstarch and cornmeal in a bowl. This dry mixture ensures a very crisp coating that will hold up to both frying and sauce-dunking.

3. Stir together the canned coconut milk and hot sauce in a bowl. Add the cauliflower and stir to coat all the pieces evenly.

4. Sprinkle the cornstarch-cornmeal mixture over the cauliflower–coconut milk mixture and fold everything together with a rubber spatula until thoroughly coated.

5. Fry the cauliflower in the hot oil in batches. Keeping the oil at 400 degrees ensures that every piece will be well browned and supercrispy.

6. It wouldn't be buffalo cauliflower without the final coating in hot sauce! Serve the hot bites with the cooling ranch dressing.

started it covered and let it steam until barely tender. Then we removed the foil, added sliced onions, and returned it to the oven to let both the onions and cauliflower caramelize. Adding the onions to the same pan eased their preparation and ensured that they would finish cooking at the same time. To highlight the natural sweetness of the cooked vegetables, we added shredded carrot and raisins, two traditional North African ingredients. The result was a warm and flavorful salad sure to spice up any meal. Use the large holes of a box grater to shred the carrot.

SALAD

- 1 head cauliflower (2 pounds), cut into 2-inch florets
- 2 tablespoons extra-virgin olive oil Salt and pepper
- ½ red onion, sliced thin
- 1 cup shredded carrot
- ½ cup raisins
- 2 tablespoons chopped fresh cilantro
- 2 tablespoons toasted sliced almonds

CHERMOULA

- ¾ cup fresh cilantro leaves
- ¼ cup extra-virgin olive oil
- 2 tablespoons lemon juice
- 4 garlic cloves, minced
- ½ teaspoon ground cumin
- ½ teaspoon paprika
- ¼ teaspoon salt
- ⅛ teaspoon cayenne pepper

1. **For the salad** Adjust oven rack to lowest position and heat oven to 475 degrees. Toss cauliflower florets with oil and season with salt and pepper. Arrange florets in single layer in parchment paper–lined rimmed baking sheet. Cover tightly with aluminum foil and roast until softened, 5 to 7 minutes. Remove foil and spread onion evenly in sheet. Roast until vegetables are tender, florets are deep golden, and onion slices are charred at edges, 10 to 15 minutes, stirring halfway through roasting. Let cool slightly, about 5 minutes.

2. **For the chermoula** Process all ingredients in food processor until smooth, about 1 minute, scraping down sides of bowl as needed. Transfer to large bowl.

3. Gently toss cauliflower-onion mixture, carrot, raisins, and cilantro with chermoula until coated. Transfer to serving platter and sprinkle with almonds. Serve warm or at room temperature.

CAULIFLOWER SOUP

Serves 4 to 6   Total time: 1 hour 15 minutes
WHY THIS RECIPE WORKS *For a creamy cauliflower soup without cream, we relied on cauliflower's low insoluble fiber content to produce a velvety smooth puree. To ensure that the cauliflower flavor remained at the forefront, we cooked the cauliflower in seasoned water (instead of broth), skipped the spice rack entirely, and bolstered the soup with sautéed onion and leek. We added the cauliflower to the simmering water in two stages so that we got the grassy flavor of just-cooked cauliflower and the sweeter, nuttier flavor of long-cooked cauliflower. Finally, we fried florets in butter until both browned and used each as a separate, richly flavored garnish. White wine vinegar may be substituted for the sherry vinegar. Be sure to thoroughly trim the cauliflower's core of green leaves and leaf stems, which can be fibrous and contribute to a grainy texture in the soup.*

- 8 tablespoons unsalted butter, cut into 8 pieces
- 1 leek, white and light green parts only, halved lengthwise, sliced thin, and washed thoroughly
- 1 small onion, halved and sliced thin Salt and pepper
- 4½–5 cups water
- 1 head cauliflower (2 pounds), cut into 1 cup ½-inch florets, remaining head sliced into ½-inch-thick slabs, core sliced thin
- ½ teaspoon sherry vinegar
- 3 tablespoons minced fresh chives

1. Melt 3 tablespoons butter in large saucepan over medium-low heat. Add leek, onion, and 1½ teaspoons salt; cook, stirring frequently, until leek and onion are softened but not browned, about 7 minutes.

2. Increase heat to medium-high; add 4½ cups water, sliced cauliflower core, and half of cauliflower slabs; and bring to simmer. Reduce heat to medium-low and simmer gently for 15 minutes. Add remaining cauliflower slabs, return to simmer, and continue to cook until cauliflower is tender and crumbles easily, 15 to 20 minutes.

3. While soup simmers, melt remaining 5 tablespoons butter in 8-inch skillet over medium heat. Add cauliflower florets and cook, stirring frequently, until florets are golden and butter is browned and imparts nutty aroma, 6 to 8 minutes. Off heat, use slotted spoon to transfer florets to small bowl. Toss florets with vinegar and season with salt to taste. Set browned butter in skillet aside for garnishing.

4. Process soup in blender until smooth, about 45 seconds. Rinse out saucepan. Return pureed soup to saucepan and return to simmer over medium heat, adjusting consistency with remaining water as needed and seasoning with salt and pepper to taste. Serve, garnishing individual serving bowls with browned florets, drizzle of browned butter, and chives.

CAULIFLOWER STEAKS WITH SALSA VERDE

Serves 4   Total time: 40 minutes
WHY THIS RECIPE WORKS *When you cook thick slabs of cauliflower as vegetarian "steaks," they develop a substantial, meaty texture and become nutty, sweet, and caramelized. Recipes for cauliflower steaks abound, but many involve fussy transitions between stovetop and oven. To find a simple way to produce four perfectly cooked cauliflower steaks simultaneously, we opted for a rimmed baking sheet and a scorching oven. Steaming the cauliflower briefly by covering the baking sheet with foil, followed by high-heat uncovered roasting on the lowest oven rack, produced dramatic-looking, caramelized seared steaks with tender interiors. To elevate the cauliflower to centerpiece status, we paired it with a vibrant Italian-style salsa verde—a blend of parsley, mint, capers, olive oil, and white wine vinegar. Brushing the hot steaks with the salsa verde ensured they'd soak up all of its robust flavor.*

1½ cups fresh parsley leaves
½ cup fresh mint leaves
½ cup extra-virgin olive oil
2 tablespoons water
1½ tablespoons white wine vinegar
1 tablespoon capers, rinsed
1 garlic clove, minced
Salt and pepper
2 heads cauliflower (2 pounds each),
cut into four 1½-inch-thick slabs
Lemon wedges

1. Adjust oven rack to lowest position and heat oven to 500 degrees. Pulse parsley, mint, ¼ cup oil, water, vinegar, capers, garlic, and ⅛ teaspoon salt in food processor until mixture is finely chopped but not smooth, about 10 pulses, scraping down sides of bowl as needed. Transfer salsa verde to small bowl and set aside until ready to serve.

2. Place slabs on rimmed baking sheet and drizzle with 2 tablespoons oil. Sprinkle with ¼ teaspoon salt and ⅛ teaspoon pepper and rub to distribute. Flip slabs and repeat.

3. Cover baking sheet tightly with aluminum foil and roast for 5 minutes. Remove foil and roast until bottoms of steaks are well browned, 8 to 10 minutes. Gently flip steaks and continue to roast until tender and second sides are well browned, 6 to 8 minutes.

4. Transfer steaks to platter and brush evenly with ¼ cup salsa verde. Serve with lemon wedges, passing remaining salsa verde separately.

THAI RED CURRY WITH CAULIFLOWER

Serves 4   Total time: 30 minutes
WHY THIS RECIPE WORKS *Cauliflower is a good candidate for a vegetable curry because it's hearty and filling. Thai red curries feature big, eye-opening flavors, so we needed to develop the cauliflower's deep, nutty flavor so it could shine. Typically we turn to oven roasting, but this felt like an unnecessary step for a quick curry dish. So we confined ourselves to the skillet. First we cooked the cauliflower with water in a covered skillet for about 5 minutes, steaming it until it was*

just tender. Then we uncovered the skillet to finish the cooking. This uncovered cooking time drove off any remaining water, tenderized the cauliflower further, and allowed it to brown without charring. It took just a few minutes in the skillet at the very end of cooking for the red curry sauce to thicken and for its flavors to bloom. You can use regular basil if you can't find Thai basil. You will need a 12-inch nonstick skillet with a tight-fitting lid for this recipe. Serve over rice.

1 (13.5-ounce) can coconut milk
3 tablespoons fish sauce
1 tablespoon packed light brown sugar
2 teaspoons Thai red curry paste
1 teaspoon grated lime zest plus
1 tablespoon juice
⅛ teaspoon red pepper flakes
2 tablespoons plus 1 teaspoon
vegetable oil
2 garlic cloves, minced
1 teaspoon grated fresh ginger
1 large head cauliflower (3 pounds),
cut into ¾-inch florets
¼ cup water
⅛ teaspoon salt
¼ cup fresh Thai basil leaves, torn

1. Whisk coconut milk, fish sauce, sugar, curry paste, lime zest and juice, and pepper flakes together in bowl. Combine 1 teaspoon oil, garlic, and ginger in second bowl.

2. Combine remaining 2 tablespoons oil, cauliflower florets, water, and salt in 12-inch nonstick skillet. Cover skillet and cook over high heat until florets start to brown and edges just start to become translucent (do not lift lid), about 5 minutes. Uncover and continue to cook, stirring occasionally, until florets are tender and well browned, 8 to 10 minutes.

3. Push florets to sides of skillet. Add garlic mixture to center and cook, mashing mixture into pan, until fragrant, about 30 seconds. Stir garlic mixture into florets and reduce heat to medium-high. Whisk coconut milk mixture to recombine, then add to skillet and simmer until slightly thickened, about 4 minutes. Off heat, stir in basil and serve.

INDIAN-STYLE MIXED VEGETABLE CURRY

Serves 4 to 6   Total time: 55 minutes
WHY THIS RECIPE WORKS *This is possibly the ultimate Indian vegetable curry, with its wide variety of perfectly cooked vegetables and deeply flavorful (but weeknight- friendly) curry sauce. Toasting store-bought curry powder in a skillet made it a flavor powerhouse, and garam masala added even more spice flavor. We also used a generous amount of sautéed onion, garlic, ginger, and fresh chile, as well as tomato paste for sweetness. For the vegetables, we chose potatoes, cauliflower, and peas, plus convenient canned chickpeas. Sautéing the spices and main ingredients together enhanced and melded the flavors. Finally, we rounded out the sauce with pureed canned tomatoes, water, and a splash of coconut milk. For more heat, include the chile seeds and ribs when mincing. We prefer the richer flavor of regular coconut milk here; however, light coconut milk can be substituted. Serve over rice or with naan.*

1 (14.5-ounce) can diced tomatoes
3 tablespoons vegetable oil
1 tablespoon plus 1 teaspoon curry
powder
1½ teaspoons garam masala
2 onions, chopped fine
12 ounces red potatoes, unpeeled,
cut into ½-inch pieces
Salt and pepper
3 garlic cloves, minced
1 serrano chile, stemmed, seeded,
and minced
1 tablespoon grated fresh ginger
1 tablespoon tomato paste
½ head cauliflower (1 pound), cut
into 1-inch florets
1½ cups water
1 (15-ounce) can chickpeas, rinsed
1½ cups frozen peas
½ cup canned coconut milk
¼ cup minced fresh cilantro

1. Pulse diced tomatoes with their juice in food processor until nearly smooth, with some ¼-inch pieces visible, about 3 pulses.

2. Heat oil in Dutch oven over medium-high heat until shimmering. Add curry powder and garam masala and cook until fragrant, about 10 seconds. Stir in onions, potatoes,

and ¼ teaspoon salt and cook, stirring occasionally, until onions are browned and potatoes are golden at edges, about 10 minutes.

3. Reduce heat to medium. Stir in garlic, chile, ginger, and tomato paste and cook until fragrant, about 30 seconds. Add cauliflower florets and cook, stirring constantly, until florets are coated with spices, about 2 minutes.

4. Gradually stir in water, scraping up any browned bits. Stir in chickpeas and processed tomatoes and bring to simmer. Cover, reduce heat to medium-low, and gently simmer until vegetables are tender, 20 to 25 minutes.

5. Uncover, stir in frozen peas and coconut milk, and continue to cook until peas are heated through, 1 to 2 minutes. Off heat, stir in cilantro, season with salt and pepper to taste, and serve.

VEGAN FETTUCCINE ALFREDO

Serves 4 to 6   Total time: 50 minutes
WHY THIS RECIPE WORKS *Classic fettuccine Alfredo is a special-occasion meal, since it's so luxuriously loaded with cream, Parmesan cheese, and butter. This vegan version replicates the creamy deliciousness of the original in a far healthier way so that you can enjoy this pasta dish more often. The sauce has a silky base of pureed cauliflower and cashews, with almond milk, coconut oil, and miso paste added to achieve the richness of a savory cream sauce. Just like with classic fettuccine Alfredo, the texture of this sauce changes dramatically after the dish stands for several minutes; serving the pasta in warmed bowls helps ensure that it retains its creamy texture. While we prefer the flavor and texture of almond milk in this recipe, you can substitute coconut milk or soy milk (the sauce will be slightly thicker if made with soy milk).*

- 2½   cups unsweetened almond milk
- ⅓   cup coconut oil
- 3   tablespoons white miso
    Salt and pepper

- 10   ounces cauliflower florets, cut into ½-inch pieces (3 cups)
- ¾   cup raw cashews, chopped
- 1   pound fettuccine
    Pinch ground nutmeg
- 2   tablespoons chopped fresh parsley

1. Combine almond milk, oil, miso, and 1 teaspoon salt in large saucepan and bring to simmer over medium-high heat, whisking to dissolve miso. Stir in cauliflower and cashews, reduce heat to medium-low, and cook, partially covered, until cauliflower is very soft and falls apart easily when poked with fork, about 20 minutes.

2. Process cauliflower mixture and ½ cup water in blender until smooth, about 2 minutes, scraping down sides as needed. Strain through fine-mesh strainer set over bowl, pressing on solids to extract as much puree as possible; discard solids.

3. Meanwhile, bring 4 quarts water to boil in large pot. Add pasta and 1 tablespoon salt and cook, stirring often, until nearly tender. Reserve ½ cup cooking water, then drain pasta and set aside in colander.

4. Transfer pureed cauliflower mixture to now-empty pot. Whisk in nutmeg and bring to gentle simmer over medium-low heat. Add drained pasta and cook, stirring constantly, until warmed through and sauce is slightly thickened, about 3 minutes. Adjust consistency with reserved cooking water as needed. Season with salt and pepper to taste. Sprinkle individual portions with parsley, and serve immediately.

CAMPANELLE WITH ROASTED CAULIFLOWER, GARLIC, AND WALNUTS

Serves 4 to 6   Total time: 1 hour 15 minutes
WHY THIS RECIPE WORKS *Bold, rustic flavors and hearty textures make this an exceptional pasta meal. The high-heat roasting transformed the cauliflower from a mild-mannered vegetable into an intensely flavored, sweetly nutty foil for the campanelle, a ruffled cone-shaped pasta that looks a little like a flower. For golden cauliflower, we sliced the head into wedges to create maximum surface area while leaving the core and florets intact. Tossing the cauliflower with a little sugar jump-started the browning; preheating the baking sheet also helped to develop lots of flavor. For the sauce, we focused on a simple lemon–roasted garlic combination, rounded out with fresh parsley and Parmesan. We topped each serving with a handful of pleasingly crunchy toasted walnuts. If campanelle is unavailable, farfalle or fusilli makes a good substitute.*

- 2   garlic heads
- 6   tablespoons plus 1 teaspoon extra-virgin olive oil
- 1   head cauliflower (2 pounds), cut into 8 equal wedges
    Salt and pepper
- ¼   teaspoon sugar
- 2   tablespoons lemon juice, plus extra for seasoning
- ¼   teaspoon red pepper flakes
- 1   pound campanelle
- 1   ounce Parmesan cheese, grated (½ cup), plus extra for serving
- 1   tablespoon chopped fresh parsley
- ¼   cup walnuts, toasted and chopped coarse

1. Adjust oven rack to middle position, place large rimmed baking sheet on rack, and heat oven to 500 degrees. Cut ½ inch off top of each garlic head to expose most of tops of garlic cloves. Place garlic heads, cut side up, in center of 12-inch square of aluminum foil. Drizzle each with ½ teaspoon oil and gather foil tightly around garlic to form packet. Place packet on oven rack next to baking sheet and roast until garlic is very tender, about 40 minutes.

2. While garlic roasts, drizzle cauliflower wedges with 2 tablespoons oil and sprinkle with 1 teaspoon salt, ¼ teaspoon pepper, and sugar in bowl; rub gently to distribute oil and seasonings. Remove baking sheet from oven. Carefully lay cauliflower wedges cut side down on hot baking sheet. Roast cauliflower until well browned and tender, 20 to 25 minutes.

3. Transfer cauliflower and garlic packet to cutting board and let cool slightly, about 10 minutes. Once cool enough to handle, cut cauliflower into ½-inch pieces and

unwrap garlic. Gently squeeze garlic cloves from skin into small bowl, and mash smooth with fork. Stir in lemon juice and pepper flakes, then slowly whisk in remaining ¼ cup oil.

4. Meanwhile, bring 4 quarts water to boil in large pot. Add pasta and 1 tablespoon salt and cook, stirring often, until al dente. Reserve 1 cup cooking water, then drain pasta and return it to pot. Add chopped cauliflower, garlic sauce, Parmesan, parsley, and ¼ cup reserved cooking water, and toss to combine. Season with salt, pepper, and extra lemon juice to taste. Adjust consistency with remaining reserved cooking water as needed. Sprinkle individual portions with walnuts and serve with extra Parmesan.

LAVASH PIZZAS WITH CAULIFLOWER, FENNEL, AND CORIANDER

Makes two 12 by 9-inch flatbreads, serving 4 to 6   Total time: 30 minutes

WHY THIS RECIPE WORKS *The Middle Eastern flatbread known as lavash has a crisp, cracker-like texture that makes a great base for a quick and easy vegetarian dinner. Store-bought lavash tasted great and kept the recipe streamlined, and to make sure the flatbreads were crisp enough to support the toppings, we brushed them with oil and toasted them quickly in the oven. A combination of cauliflower, fennel, and fragrant coriander made for a simple yet flavorful topping. Two types of cheese, mildly nutty fontina and full-flavored Parmesan, gave our lavash more complex flavor; sprinkling the Parmesan on top and allowing it to brown slightly in the hot oven offered an appealing finish. You will need a 12-inch skillet with a tight-fitting lid for this recipe.*

- ¼ cup extra-virgin olive oil
- 2 cups chopped cauliflower florets
- 1 fennel bulb, stalks discarded, bulb halved, cored, and chopped
- 3 garlic cloves, minced
- 3 tablespoons water
- 1 teaspoon ground coriander
  Salt and pepper
- 4 ounces whole-milk mozzarella cheese, shredded (1 cup)

- ¼ teaspoon red pepper flakes
- 2 (12 by 9-inch) lavash breads
- 2 ounces goat cheese, crumbled (½ cup)
- 1 scallion, sliced thin

1. Adjust oven racks to upper-middle and lower-middle positions and heat oven to 475 degrees. Heat 2 tablespoons oil in 12-inch skillet over medium heat until shimmering. Add cauliflower florets, fennel, garlic, water, coriander, and ½ teaspoon salt. Cover and cook, stirring occasionally, until tender, 6 to 8 minutes; let cool slightly. Stir in mozzarella and pepper flakes.

2. Brush both sides of lavash with remaining 2 tablespoons oil, lay on 2 baking sheets, and bake until golden brown, about 4 minutes, flipping lavash halfway through baking. Spread cauliflower mixture evenly on each lavash and sprinkle with goat cheese. Bake until cheese is melted and spotty brown, 6 to 8 minutes, switching and rotating sheets halfway through baking. Sprinkle with scallion and season with salt and pepper to taste. Slice and serve.

BAJA-STYLE CAULIFLOWER TACOS

Serves 4 to 6   Total time: 45 minutes

WHY THIS RECIPE WORKS *A true Baja California experience requires sunny, breezy patios, a plate of tacos, and cold beer. We aimed to re-create the feel of Baja-style fish tacos at home, instead bringing veggies to the forefront. Battered cauliflower, drizzled with a cool, creamy sauce, was the perfect stand-in for the fish. To avoid the mess of deep-frying, we cut the cauliflower into large florets and roasted them after dunking the pieces in coconut milk seasoned with garlic and spices and then rolling them in a mixture of panko bread crumbs and shredded coconut. Not only did this add richness and the flavors of a cabana-shaded getaway, but it also mimicked the crisp crust of batter-fried fish. A crunchy slaw with juicy mango and spicy jalapeño provided a balance of sweetness and heat. For a creamy topping, we blended equal parts mayonnaise and sour cream, plus cilantro and lime zest. For a spicier slaw, add the jalapeño ribs and seeds.*

TACOS
- 3 cups (7½ ounces) coleslaw mix
- ½ mango, peeled and cut into ¼-inch pieces (¾ cup)
- 2 tablespoons lime juice, plus lime wedges for serving
- 1 tablespoon chopped fresh cilantro
- 1 tablespoon minced jalapeño
  Salt and pepper
- 1 cup unsweetened shredded coconut
- 1 cup panko bread crumbs
- 1 cup canned coconut milk
- 1 teaspoon garlic powder
- 1 teaspoon ground cumin
- ¼ teaspoon cayenne pepper
- ½ head cauliflower (1 pound), cut into 1-inch florets
- 8–12 (6-inch) corn tortillas, warmed

CILANTRO SAUCE
- ¼ cup mayonnaise
- ¼ cup sour cream
- 3 tablespoons water
- 3 tablespoons minced fresh cilantro
- ¼ teaspoon salt

1. **For the tacos** Adjust oven rack to middle position and heat oven to 450 degrees. Combine coleslaw mix, mango, lime juice, cilantro, jalapeño, and ¼ teaspoon salt in bowl, cover, and refrigerate until ready to serve.

2. Spray rimmed baking sheet with vegetable oil spray. Combine coconut and panko in shallow dish. Whisk coconut milk, garlic powder, cumin, cayenne, and 1 teaspoon salt together in bowl. Add cauliflower florets to coconut milk mixture and toss to coat well. Working with 1 floret at a time, remove from coconut milk, letting excess drip back into bowl, then coat well with coconut-panko mixture, pressing gently to adhere; transfer to prepared sheet.

3. Bake until florets are tender, golden, and crisp, 20 to 25 minutes, flipping florets and rotating sheet halfway through baking.

4. **For the cilantro sauce** Meanwhile, combine all ingredients in bowl; set aside until ready to serve.

5. Divide slaw evenly among warm tortillas and top with florets. Drizzle with cilantro sauce and serve with lime wedges.

CAULIFLOWER CAKES

Serves 4   Total time: 1 hour 30 minutes
WHY THIS RECIPE WORKS *Vegetable cakes are a unique, creative addition to the dinner table. These cauliflower cakes have creamy interiors, crunchy browned exteriors, and complex flavors. To ensure that the flavor of the cauliflower didn't get lost and to drive off excess moisture that would make our cakes fall apart, we cut the cauliflower into florets and roasted them until they were well browned and tender. Tossing the florets with warm spices like turmeric, coriander, and ground ginger gave the cakes an aromatic backbone. Next we needed a binder to hold the shaped cakes together. Egg and flour are standard additions, but we also added some goat cheese to provide extra binding, creaminess, and tangy flavor. Though these cakes held together, they were very soft and tricky to flip in the pan. Refrigerating the cakes for 30 minutes before cooking them proved to be the best solution. The chilled cakes transferred from baking sheet to skillet without a problem and were much sturdier when it came time to flip them.*

YOGURT-HERB SAUCE
    1   cup plain yogurt
    2   tablespoons minced fresh cilantro
    2   tablespoons minced fresh mint
    1   garlic clove, minced
        Salt and pepper

CAULIFLOWER CAKES
    1   head cauliflower (2 pounds),
        cut into 1-inch florets
    ¼   cup extra-virgin olive oil
    1   teaspoon ground turmeric
    1   teaspoon ground coriander
    1   teaspoon salt
    ½   teaspoon ground ginger
    ¼   teaspoon pepper
    4   ounces goat cheese, softened
    2   scallions, sliced thin
    1   large egg, lightly beaten
    2   garlic cloves, minced
    1   teaspoon grated lemon or lime zest,
        plus lemon or lime wedges for serving
    ¼   cup all-purpose flour

1. For the yogurt-herb sauce Whisk yogurt, cilantro, mint, and garlic together in bowl until combined and season with salt and pepper to taste. Cover and refrigerate until ready to serve, at least 30 minutes.

2. For the cauliflower cakes Adjust oven rack to middle position and heat oven to 450 degrees. Toss cauliflower florets with 1 tablespoon oil, turmeric, coriander, salt, ginger, and pepper. Transfer to aluminum foil–lined rimmed baking sheet and spread into single layer. Roast until florets are well browned and tender, about 25 minutes. Let cool slightly, then transfer to large bowl.

3. Line clean rimmed baking sheet with parchment paper. Mash florets coarsely with potato masher. Stir in goat cheese, scallions, egg, garlic, and lemon zest until well combined. Sprinkle flour over cauliflower mixture and stir to incorporate. Using wet hands, divide mixture into 4 equal portions, pack gently into ¾-inch-thick cakes about 3½ inches in diameter, and place on prepared sheet. Refrigerate cakes until chilled and firm, about 30 minutes.

4. Line large plate with paper towels. Heat remaining 3 tablespoons oil in 12-inch nonstick skillet over medium heat until shimmering. Gently lay cakes in skillet and cook until deep golden brown and crisp, 5 to 7 minutes per side. Drain cakes briefly on prepared plate. Serve with yogurt sauce and lemon wedges.

MODERN CAULIFLOWER GRATIN

Serves 8 to 10   Total time: 1 hour 30 minutes
WHY THIS RECIPE WORKS *To create a rich and flavorful but not heavy cauliflower gratin, we relied on cauliflower's natural ability to become an ultracreamy puree, using it as the sauce to bind the florets together. For a streamlined cooking setup, we placed the cores and stems in water in the bottom of a Dutch oven and set a steamer basket with florets right on top. Butter and Parmesan gave the sauce a rich flavor and texture, and a few pantry spices lent some complexity. Topping the gratin with Parmesan and panko gave it savory crunch, and minced chives added color. When buying cauliflower for this recipe, look for heads without many leaves. If your cauliflower does have a lot of leaves, buy slightly larger heads—about 2¼ pounds*

Modern Cauliflower Gratin

each. This recipe can be halved to serve four to six; cook the cauliflower in a large saucepan and bake the gratin in an 8-inch square baking dish.

- 8 tablespoons unsalted butter
- ½ cup panko bread crumbs
- 2 ounces Parmesan cheese, grated (1 cup)
- 2 heads cauliflower (2 pounds each), cut into 1½-inch florets, stems halved lengthwise then sliced thin crosswise, cores sliced thin (12 cups florets and 3 cups stems and cores)
  Salt and pepper
- ½ teaspoon dry mustard
- ⅛ teaspoon ground nutmeg
  Pinch cayenne pepper
- 1 teaspoon cornstarch
- 1 tablespoon minced fresh chives

1. Adjust oven rack to middle position and heat oven to 400 degrees. Melt 2 tablespoons butter in 10-inch skillet over medium heat. Add panko and cook, stirring frequently, until golden brown, 3 to 5 minutes. Transfer to bowl and let cool. Once cool, add ½ cup Parmesan and toss to combine; set aside.

2. Combine sliced cauliflower stems and cores, 2 cups florets, 3 cups water, and remaining 6 tablespoons butter in Dutch oven and bring to boil over high heat. Place remaining florets in steamer basket. Once mixture is boiling, place steamer basket in pot, cover, and reduce heat to medium. Steam florets in basket until translucent and paring knife slips easily in and out of stem ends, 10 to 12 minutes. Remove steamer basket and set aside florets to drain. Re-cover pot, reduce heat to low, and continue to cook stem mixture until very soft, about 10 minutes. Transfer drained florets to 13 by 9-inch baking dish.

3. Transfer stem mixture and cooking liquid to blender and add 2 teaspoons salt, ½ teaspoon pepper, dry mustard, nutmeg, cayenne, and remaining ½ cup Parmesan. Process until smooth and velvety, about 1 minute (puree should be pourable; adjust consistency with additional water as needed). Combine cornstarch and 1 teaspoon water in small bowl, whisking with fork to dissolve; then, with blender running, add cornstarch slurry to blender. Season cauliflower puree with salt and pepper to taste. Pour puree over cauliflower florets in dish and toss gently to coat (it will be quite loose), then smooth top with spatula.

4. Scatter panko mixture evenly over top. Transfer dish to oven and bake until sauce bubbles around edges, 13 to 15 minutes. Let stand for 20 to 25 minutes. Sprinkle with chives and serve.

~

ROAST CHICKEN WITH CAULIFLOWER AND TOMATOES
Serves 4   Total time: 1 hour
WHY THIS RECIPE WORKS *Chicken leg quarters are the cauliflower of the poultry world: Both are woefully underused. But why? Chicken leg quarters are cheap, easy to work with, flavorful, and hard to overcook. We wanted to roast them simultaneously with the cauliflower for an easy weeknight dinner with great flavor and minimal cleanup. We whisked lemon, garlic, and chopped sage into olive oil and brushed it onto the chicken. Arranging the vegetables in the middle of the baking sheet and positioning the chicken legs around the edge ensured that everything cooked at the same rate. Tossing a handful of grape tomatoes into the pan and blasting the pan under the broiler at the end made for crispy chicken skin, browned cauliflower, and blistered tomatoes. Some leg quarters are sold with the backbone attached. Remove it before cooking to make serving easier. If you substitute cherry tomatoes, cut them in half before adding them to the baking sheet.*

- 1 head cauliflower (2 pounds), cut into 8 equal wedges
- 6 shallots, peeled and halved
- ¼ cup extra-virgin olive oil
- 2 tablespoons chopped fresh sage or 2 teaspoons dried
  Salt and pepper
- 4 (10-ounce) chicken leg quarters, trimmed

- 2 garlic cloves, minced
- 1 teaspoon grated lemon zest, plus lemon wedges for serving
- 8 ounces grape tomatoes
- 1 tablespoon chopped fresh parsley

1. Adjust 1 oven rack to lower-middle position and second rack 6 inches from broiler element. Heat oven to 475 degrees. Gently toss cauliflower wedges, shallots, 2 tablespoons oil, 1 teaspoon sage, ½ teaspoon salt, and ½ teaspoon pepper together on rimmed baking sheet to combine. Position vegetables cut sides down in single layer in center of sheet.

2. Pat chicken dry with paper towels. Leaving drumsticks and thighs attached, make 4 parallel diagonal slashes in chicken: one across drumsticks, one across leg joints, and two across thighs (each slash should reach bone). Season chicken with salt and pepper. Place 1 piece of chicken, skin side up, in each corner of sheet (chicken should rest directly on sheet, not on vegetables).

3. Whisk garlic, lemon zest, remaining 2 tablespoons oil, and remaining 1 tablespoon sage together in bowl, then brush all over skin side of chicken. Transfer sheet to lower rack and bake until cauliflower is browned, shallots tender, and chicken registers 175 degrees, 25 to 30 minutes.

4. Remove sheet from oven and heat broiler. Scatter tomatoes over vegetables and place sheet on upper rack. Broil until chicken skin is browned and crisp and tomatoes have started to wilt, 3 to 5 minutes.

5. Transfer sheet to wire rack and let rest for 5 minutes. Sprinkle with parsley and serve with lemon wedges.

CELERY

Celery is one of those vegetables that most people who cook regularly probably have at the bottom of their crisper drawer. Often we cut it into sticks for crudité platters or for quick snacking. If we remember it's there, we slice it up for salads, or soups, or stir-fries. And if celery gets really lucky, we use it to garnish brunchtime bloody Marys. But generally, in today's world of fashionable vegetables, celery is about as hip as bingo night.

But as this chapter proves, celery has so much more to offer. Raw, its supercrisp texture and mildly peppery flavor play a starring role in Shaved Celery Salad with Pomegranate-Honey Vinaigrette. When cooked (as it often is in European cuisine) in Braised Celery with Vermouth-Butter Glaze, it makes a perfect side dish for nearly any seafood.

Celery root, or celeriac, on the other hand, probably isn't something most of us have in our crisper drawer, but that's a situation worth remedying. This knobby tuber is a variety of celery cultivated for its root rather than its stems. It's not much to look at—in fact, it's one of the least-promising-looking vegetables out there. But peel away its brown, bumpy skin to reveal crisp white flesh that tastes like celery ribs crossed with parsley, with a hint of anise for good measure.

Cooked celery root comes alive with earthy sweetness. Roast it to yield a crispy brown crust and a tender interior. Or puree it to velvety smoothness with miso or horseradish, to serve like mashed potatoes. Or simmer up a batch of brightly flavored Celery Root, Fennel, and Apple Chowder. However you choose to cook it, let's give this ugly duckling the love it deserves.

shopping and storage

You often have three choices when buying celery: loose heads topped with their bushy leaves, bagged heads with the leaves trimmed down, and packages labeled as celery hearts, with two or three dwarfed and cropped heads inside. In general, the loose heads tend to be the freshest-tasting. Do purchase celery with the leafy greens still attached, if possible. The leaves should be darker green than the ribs and perky-looking. Make sure there is no browning or bruising on the celery ribs or excessive moisture accumulating around the base of the celery head. The best way to store celery is to wrap it snugly, but not tightly, in aluminum foil. It seals in moisture but lets the ripening ethylene gas escape. Celery stored this way will stay fresh and crisp for several weeks.

Celery roots should feel heavy for their size; that's a sign that the flesh will be dense and creamy after cooking. Extremely large celery roots may be fibrous or tough, so select medium-size when available. Since it's a root vegetable, celery root keeps extremely well. In a loose plastic produce bag in the refrigerator, it will stay fresh for two weeks, and probably longer.

use those celery leaves

Many recipes that call for chopped celery make no mention of the leaves; most people seem to just throw them out. But these soft leaves have loads of herby celery flavor. Reserve trimmed leaves in a plastic produce bag in the fridge and add them to salads, like the Shaved Celery Salad with Pomegranate-Honey Vinaigrette or the Rhubarb, Celery, and Radish Salad with Feta and Cilantro.

vegetable prep

Removing Strings from Celery Ribs

For cooked preparations, such as braised celery, strings can be distracting in the finished dish. But they are easy to remove: Simply run vegetable peeler along outside edge of each rib to remove stringy fibers.

Chopping Celery Quickly

If recipe calls for chopped celery, rather than breaking off one or more ribs, chop entire bunch across the top. It's easier to get just the amount needed, and the bunch gets shorter and easier to store.

what about celery seeds?

Celery seeds, which come from a close relative of the celery we use in cooking, pack a powerfully concentrated celery flavor punch. These seeds are easily found in the spice section of any supermarket, and they are most often used in pickling spice blends, to add celery flavor without having to use the vegetable itself. But, similar to poppy seeds, they also work great in slaws or added to salad dressings. And they can boost celery flavor in a cooked celery dish—we employ them this way in our classic Braised Celery with Vermouth-Butter Glaze.

Trimming and Peeling Celery Root

1. Using chef's knife, cut ½ inch from both root end and opposite end of celery root.

2a. Turn celery root so 1 cut side rests on cutting board. To peel, cut from top to bottom, rotating celery root while removing wide strips of skin.

2b. Alternatively, use sturdy vegetable peeler to remove skin.

reviving limp celery

Just because celery ribs go limp doesn't mean you should toss them out. Revive limp stalks by cutting off about 1 inch from both ends and submerging stalks in bowl of ice water for 30 minutes.

BRAISED CELERY WITH VERMOUTH-BUTTER GLAZE

Serves 4 to 6   Total time: 30 minutes

WHY THIS RECIPE WORKS *Celery's flavor becomes even more delicate when braised, making for a lovely light side dish. Sprinkling celery seeds into the braising liquid added an aromatic punch, while a bit of dry vermouth contributed acidity and an herbal sweetness. Peeling the strings from the celery ribs might seem fussy, but it didn't take long and it really improved both the texture and the color of this dish (unpeeled cooked celery ended up like a mouthful of string). Peeling also stripped away the surface green color, so that the resulting hue of the braised celery was a pretty sea-washed bottle green. This glazed celery's pure flavor is a wonderful complement to sautéed fish. You can substitute ¼ cup fresh parsley leaves for the celery leaves. You will need a 12-inch skillet with a tight-fitting lid for this recipe.*

- 1 head celery (1½ pounds), plus ¼ cup leaves, minced
- 1 cup water
- ½ cup dry vermouth
- 3 tablespoons unsalted butter
- ¼ teaspoon celery seeds
  Salt and pepper

1. Using sharp vegetable peeler, remove fibrous threads from outside of celery stalks. Halve stalks lengthwise, then slice on bias into 2-inch lengths.

2. Bring celery, water, vermouth, butter, celery seeds, ¼ teaspoon salt, and ⅛ teaspoon pepper to simmer in 12-inch skillet over medium-high heat. Cover, reduce heat to medium-low, and cook, stirring occasionally, until celery is tender, 15 to 20 minutes.

3. Uncover and continue to simmer, stirring occasionally, until cooking liquid is reduced to thin glaze and begins to coat celery, 5 to 7 minutes. Season with salt and pepper to taste. Sprinkle with celery leaves and serve.

SAGE–BROWN BUTTER CELERY ROOT PUREE

Serves 6 to 8   Total time: 1 hour 15 minutes

WHY THIS RECIPE WORKS *The velvety texture and pleasantly mild flavor of celery root pureed in the food processor is a more refined, lighter alternative to classic mashed potatoes. To develop creaminess and character in this puree similar to that of mashed potatoes, we lightly sautéed the celery root in butter, which concentrated its flavor and added richness. To bring out even deeper flavor, we simmered it in garlic-infused chicken broth. Next, it went into the food processor along with all of that rich, aromatic broth. Although starchy potatoes can turn gluey when whipped in a food processor, the celery root broke down beautifully into a smooth, luscious puree. We bloomed fresh sage in browned butter to give the celery root a nutty, savory profile. For a different take on this puree, we blended in white miso; its subtly sweet, floral flavor complemented the celery root's earthiness. The second variation punches things up with prepared horseradish and scallions.*

- 8 tablespoons unsalted butter
- 4 pounds celery root, trimmed, peeled, and cut into 1-inch pieces
- 4 garlic cloves, peeled and smashed
- ½ cup chicken or vegetable broth, plus extra as needed
  Salt and pepper
- 1 tablespoon minced fresh sage
- 1½ teaspoons lemon juice

1. Melt 4 tablespoons butter in large saucepan over medium heat. Add celery root and garlic and cook, stirring occasionally, until celery root is softened and lightly browned, 10 to 12 minutes. (If after 4 minutes celery root has not started to brown, increase heat to medium-high.)

2. Stir in broth, 1 teaspoon salt, and ¼ teaspoon pepper and bring to simmer over medium heat. Cover, reduce heat to low, and cook, stirring occasionally, until celery root is very tender and breaks apart when poked with fork, about 40 minutes; let cool slightly.

3. Melt remaining 4 tablespoons butter in 12-inch skillet over medium-high heat, swirling occasionally, until butter is browned and releases nutty aroma, about 1½ minutes. Off heat, stir in sage and cook, using residual heat of skillet, until fragrant, about 1 minute. Stir in lemon juice.

4. Working in batches, process celery root in food processor until smooth, about 2 minutes, scraping down sides of bowl as needed. Return puree to now-empty pot and adjust consistency with extra hot broth as needed. Stir in browned butter mixture and season with salt and pepper to taste. Serve.

VARIATIONS

Miso Celery Root Puree

Omit sage and lemon juice. Increase garlic to 8 cloves. Decrease butter to 4 tablespoons and omit step 3. Stir ¼ cup white miso into celery root puree in saucepan in step 4.

Horseradish Celery Root Puree with Scallions

Omit sage and lemon juice. Increase garlic to 6 cloves. Decrease butter to 4 tablespoons and omit step 3. Stir 2 tablespoons prepared horseradish and 4 thinly sliced scallions into celery root puree in saucepan in step 4.

ROASTED CELERY ROOT WITH YOGURT AND SESAME SEEDS

Serves 6 to 8   Total time: 1 hour

WHY THIS RECIPE WORKS *Roasting is a terrific method for unlocking the herbal flavor and creamy texture of celery root. By cooking celery root slices on the bottom oven rack at a high temperature, we were able to caramelize the exteriors and concentrate the flavors. Tangy yogurt, with reinforced brightness from both lemon juice and zest, complemented the rich and savory celery root. To finish, we sprinkled an aromatic combination of toasted sesame seeds, coriander, and dried thyme over the top before adding a fresh pop of whole cilantro leaves.*

Roasted Celery Root with
Yogurt and Sesame Seeds

¼ cup plain yogurt

¼ teaspoon grated lemon zest plus
   1 teaspoon juice
   Salt and pepper

1 teaspoon sesame seeds, toasted

1 teaspoon coriander seeds, toasted
   and crushed

¼ teaspoon dried thyme

2½ pounds celery root, trimmed, peeled,
   halved, and sliced ½ inch thick

3 tablespoons extra-virgin olive oil

¼ cup fresh cilantro leaves

1. Adjust oven rack to lowest position and heat oven to 425 degrees. Whisk yogurt, lemon zest and juice, and pinch salt together in bowl. In separate bowl, combine sesame seeds, coriander seeds, thyme, and pinch salt. Set both aside until ready to serve.

2. Toss celery root with oil, ½ teaspoon salt, and ¼ teaspoon pepper and arrange on rimmed baking sheet in single layer. Roast celery root until bottom sides toward back of oven are well browned, 25 to 30 minutes. Rotate baking sheet and continue to roast until bottom sides toward back of oven are well browned, 6 to 10 minutes.

3. Use metal spatula to flip each piece and continue to roast until celery root is very tender and other sides are browned, 10 to 15 minutes. Transfer celery root to serving platter. Drizzle celery root with yogurt sauce and sprinkle with seed mixture and cilantro. Serve.

ROASTED CELERY ROOT BITES WITH CHIMICHURRI

Serves 6 to 8   Total time: 1 hour 45 minutes

WHY THIS RECIPE WORKS *An innovative but easy two-step oven-roasting and pan-roasting method creates a rustic, satisfying side dish that highlights the flavor and texture of celery root. We started by scrubbing and halving the root—no peeling required. We wrapped both halves in tightly sealed foil packets along with butter, water, salt, and pepper. With heat and time, the rough, tough exterior of the vegetable*

broke down, and after a little over an hour of roasting in a 400-degree oven, the entire root was rendered creamy, tender, and aromatic. After removing them from the foil packets, we broke the halves apart by hand into random, jagged chunks, providing greater surface area for crisping up during the final stovetop step. For the chimichurri, we anchored bright red wine vinegar and fresh herbs in a rich and fruity extra-virgin olive oil, and spooned a generous amount over the tops of the roasted pieces.

1 large celery root (2 pounds), trimmed
   and halved
   Salt and pepper

2 tablespoons unsalted butter

6 tablespoons hot water

2 teaspoons dried oregano

1⅓ cups fresh parsley leaves

⅔ cup fresh cilantro leaves

6 garlic cloves, minced

½ teaspoon red pepper flakes

¼ cup red wine vinegar

½ cup plus 3 tablespoons extra-virgin
   olive oil

1. Adjust oven rack to middle position and heat oven to 400 degrees. Stack two 16- by 12-inch sheets of aluminum foil. Season 1 celery root half with salt and pepper, place cut side down in center of foil, and drizzle with 1 tablespoon butter and 1 tablespoon water. Crimp foil tightly around celery root to seal; transfer to rimmed baking sheet. Repeat with 2 sheets of foil, remaining celery root, remaining 1 tablespoon butter, and 1 tablespoon water.

2. Roast celery root until tender and skewer inserted into center meets little resistance (you will need to unwrap foil to test), 1 hour to 1 hour 20 minutes, rotating sheet halfway through roasting.

3. Meanwhile, combine remaining ¼ cup hot water, oregano, and 1 teaspoon salt in small bowl; let sit for 5 minutes to soften oregano. Pulse parsley, cilantro, garlic, and pepper flakes in food processor until coarsely chopped, about 10 pulses. Add water mixture and vinegar and pulse until

combined. Transfer to bowl and slowly whisk in ½ cup oil until incorporated. Set chimichurri aside until ready to serve.

4. Carefully open foil packets to allow steam to escape and let sit until cool enough to touch, about 15 minutes. Using your hands, break celery root into rough 1-inch chunks. Heat 1½ tablespoons oil in 12-inch nonstick skillet over high heat until shimmering. Add half of celery root chunks and cook, turning occasionally, until well browned on all sides, 6 to 8 minutes. Transfer celery root to serving platter and tent with foil to keep warm. Repeat with remaining 1½ tablespoons oil and celery root; transfer to platter. Drizzle with chimichurri. Serve.

SHAVED CELERY SALAD WITH POMEGRANATE-HONEY VINAIGRETTE

Serves 4 to 6   Total time: 30 minutes

WHY THIS RECIPE WORKS *This fresh, light salad employs both celery ribs and celery root. Our tasters especially loved how the combination of sweet-tart pomegranate seeds and rich, salty Pecorino Romano cheese boosted the flavors and textures of the celery. Shaving the celery root thin using a vegetable peeler eliminated any need to cook the root. Chopped frisée gave the salad more substance, and toasted walnuts added another nice crunch. For the dressing, we echoed the use of pomegranate seeds by starting with pomegranate molasses, along with red wine vinegar, honey, and shallot. Pomegranate molasses can be found in the international aisle of well-stocked grocery stores. You can substitute 1 to 2 tablespoons chopped fresh parsley for the celery leaves. Use the large holes of a box grater to shred the Pecorino Romano. A mandoline or V-slicer can also be used to shave the celery root in step 2.*

ROASTED CELERY ROOT BITES WITH CHIMICHURRI

Celery root is delicious in all of its classical uses, such as salads, slaws, and soups. But here's a more modern way to highlight the flavors and textures of this homely-looking vegetable. The two-step oven-roasting and pan-roasting treatment we developed is simple, and it results in creamy, delicate interiors and a crunchy, cragged, perfectly browned crust. The garlicky, herbal, bright green chimichurri sauce will have you scooping up anything left on your plate with bits of the roasted root.

1. Cradle the seasoned celery root in aluminum foil "bowls," and add the butter and water. Place on a baking sheet and steam-roast in the oven until creamy and tender.

2. To gauge whether the celery root is fully tender, unwrap the foil bowl and pierce the celery root with a wooden skewer. The skewer should meet little resistance.

3. For the chimichurri, pulse the parsley, cilantro, garlic, and pepper flakes in the food processor, then add the water mixture and vinegar and pulse to combine. Transfer to a bowl and whisk in the olive oil.

4. After the celery root has cooled slightly, break it up into irregular 1-inch pieces with your hands. This provides great visual appeal and also ensures great browning in the skillet.

5. Heat the oil in a 12-inch nonstick skillet and sear the celery root pieces, turning occasionally, until they are browned on all sides. Searing in two batches ensures good browning by not overcrowding the skillet.

6. Arrange the celery root on a platter, sprinkle with salt, and drizzle the colorful chimichurri sauce over the top.

2 tablespoons pomegranate molasses
1 tablespoon red wine vinegar
2 teaspoons honey
1 small shallot, minced
  Salt and pepper
2 tablespoons extra-virgin olive oil
14 ounces celery root, trimmed, peeled, and quartered
4 celery ribs, sliced thin on bias, plus ½ cup celery leaves
1 head frisée (6 ounces), trimmed and cut into 1-inch pieces
1½ ounces Pecorino Romano cheese, shredded (½ cup)
¼ cup pomegranate seeds
½ cup walnuts, toasted and chopped coarse

1. Whisk pomegranate molasses, vinegar, honey, shallot, ¼ teaspoon salt, and pinch pepper together in large bowl. While whisking constantly, slowly drizzle in oil until combined.

2. Using sharp vegetable peeler, shave celery root into thin ribbons. Add celery root, celery ribs and leaves, frisée, Pecorino, and 2 tablespoons pomegranate seeds to bowl with dressing and gently toss to coat. Season with salt and pepper to taste. Sprinkle with walnuts and remaining 2 tablespoons pomegranate seeds. Serve.

RHUBARB, CELERY, AND RADISH SALAD WITH FETA AND CILANTRO

Serves 4 to 6   Total time: 30 minutes

WHY THIS RECIPE WORKS *For a refreshing side salad with plenty of crunch that bursts with mouthwatering tart-spicy flavor, look no further. Rhubarb's sharp acidity, celery's herbal spiciness, and radishes' peppery element all play off each other to create a colorful slaw-type salad with a uniquely bright flavor profile. Allowing the vinaigrette to sit for a while lets the salt work its magic on drawing out liquid from the finely chopped rhubarb. The vinaigrette gets even more of a flavor boost from jalapeño and lime. The only thing this salad is missing is a platter of fried chicken, or maybe a summer barbecue spread. You can substitute ½ cup fresh parsley leaves for the celery leaves.*

VINAIGRETTE
1 rhubarb stalk, cut into ½-inch pieces
1 jalapeño chile, stemmed, seeded, and cut into ½-inch pieces
1 tablespoon grated lime zest plus 2 tablespoons juice
1 small shallot, sliced thin
¼ teaspoon salt
½ teaspoon pepper
¼ cup extra-virgin olive oil

SALAD
2 rhubarb stalks, sliced ¼ inch thick on bias
1 celery rib, sliced thin on bias, plus ½ cup celery leaves
5 radishes, trimmed and cut into ¼-inch wedges
1 teaspoon extra-virgin olive oil
⅛ teaspoon salt
⅛ teaspoon chipotle chile powder
2 ounces feta cheese, crumbled (½ cup)
½ cup fresh cilantro leaves

1. For the vinaigrette Pulse rhubarb, jalapeño, lime zest and juice, shallot, salt, and pepper in food processor until finely chopped, about 10 pulses. Transfer to bowl and let sit until rhubarb releases its juice, 20 to 25 minutes. Stir in oil and set aside.

2. For the salad Toss rhubarb, celery, radishes, oil, salt, and chile powder together in bowl. Transfer to serving bowl and sprinkle with feta. Spoon ½ cup vinaigrette over salad and sprinkle with celery leaves and cilantro leaves. Serve, passing remaining vinaigrette separately.

CELERY ROOT SALAD WITH APPLE AND PARSLEY

Serves 4   Total time: 15 minutes

WHY THIS RECIPE WORKS *Celery root maintains its pristine white appearance, its crunchy, coleslaw-like texture, and (maybe most important) its refreshing herbal flavor in this crisp salad. For easy peeling, we removed the top and bottom from the celery root and then used a paring knife to remove the outer layer of flesh. For thin pieces of celery root that would retain their crunch, we grated it coarse. Tart Granny Smith apple complemented the celery root, and we freshened it up with sliced scallions and a combination of fresh parsley and tarragon. A dressing with lemon, mustard, and sour cream lent the salad a tangy, creamy richness. You can use the large holes of a box grater or the shredding disk of a food processor to shred the celery root and apple. Add a teaspoon or so more oil to the dressed salad if it seems a bit dry.*

3 tablespoons sour cream
2 tablespoons lemon juice
1½ tablespoons Dijon mustard
1 teaspoon honey
  Salt and pepper
3 tablespoons vegetable oil
14 ounces celery root, trimmed,
  peeled, and shredded
½ Granny Smith apple, peeled, cored,
  and shredded
2 scallions, sliced thin
2 teaspoons minced fresh parsley
2 teaspoons minced fresh tarragon

1. Whisk sour cream, lemon juice, mustard, honey, and ½ teaspoon salt together in medium bowl. While whisking constantly, slowly drizzle in oil until combined.

2. Stir celery root, apple, scallions, parsley, and tarragon into dressing and season with salt and pepper to taste. Cover and refrigerate salad for at least 30 minutes or up to 24 hours before serving.

VARIATION

Celery Root Salad with Red Onion, Mint, Orange, and Fennel Seeds
Add ½ teaspoon grated orange zest and 1 teaspoon fennel seeds to dressing. Substitute 2 tablespoons finely chopped red onion for scallions and mint for tarragon.

CELERY ROOT, CELERY, AND APPLE SLAW

Serves 4 to 6   Total time: 35 minutes
WHY THIS RECIPE WORKS *With so much texture and flavor, this is a slaw you'll want to have on your dinner table all year long. Many root vegetables, including celery root, stay just as crisp as cabbage once shredded and dressed in a slaw. Here we complemented celery root's distinctive flavor with the addition of its aboveground celery ribs and sweet apples. A vinaigrette made with cider vinegar (to echo the apples) and plenty of Dijon mustard was a fresher, more flavorful alternative to the common mayonnaise-based slaw dressing. To save time, we recommend shredding and treating the celery root with the sugar and salt before*

prepping the remaining ingredients. You can use the large holes of a box grater or the shredding disk of a food processor to shred the celery root.

1½ pounds celery root, trimmed,
  peeled, and shredded
¼ cup sugar, plus extra for seasoning
  Salt and pepper
3 tablespoons cider vinegar, plus
  extra for seasoning
2 tablespoons Dijon mustard
½ cup extra-virgin olive oil
5 celery ribs, sliced thin on bias
2 Honeycrisp or Fuji apples, peeled, cored,
  and cut into 2-inch-long matchsticks
½ cup chopped fresh parsley

1. Toss celery root, sugar, and 1 teaspoon salt together in large bowl and let sit until partially wilted and reduced in volume by one-third, about 15 minutes.

2. Meanwhile, whisk vinegar, mustard, ½ teaspoon salt, and ½ teaspoon pepper together in large bowl. While whisking constantly, slowly drizzle in oil until combined.

3. Transfer celery root to salad spinner and spin until excess water is removed, 10 to 20 seconds. Transfer celery root to bowl with dressing. Add celery, apples, and parsley to bowl with celery root and toss to combine. Season with salt, pepper, extra sugar, and extra vinegar to taste. Serve immediately.

CREAM OF CELERY SOUP

Serves 6 to 8   Total time: 1 hour
WHY THIS RECIPE WORKS *Canned cream of celery soup, which seems most often to be used in casseroles, bears scant evidence of its namesake vegetable. To make a flavorful homemade version worthy of its name that we'd be proud to serve on its own, we used a generous 12 ribs of celery. We employed butter, flour, and cooked potatoes to add thickness and body, and sage, bay leaf, and a possibly surprising but definitely effective bit of sugar to round out the flavors. A judicious amount of cream stirred in at the end made it oh-so rich.*

4 tablespoons unsalted butter
12 celery ribs, chopped
1 pound russet potatoes, peeled,
  quartered, and sliced thin
2 onions, chopped
2 tablespoons sugar
2 teaspoons dried sage
  Salt and pepper
2 tablespoons all-purpose flour
6 cups chicken or vegetable broth
1 bay leaf
½ cup heavy cream

1. Melt butter in Dutch oven over medium-low heat. Add celery, potatoes, onions, sugar, sage, ½ teaspoon salt, and ½ teaspoon pepper and cook, covered, until celery and onions are softened, about 15 minutes.

2. Stir in flour and cook for 1 minute. Stir in broth and bay leaf, bring to simmer, and cook, uncovered, until potatoes are tender, about 20 minutes.

3. Discard bay leaf. Working in batches, process soup in blender until smooth, 1 to 2 minutes. Return soup to clean pot, stir in cream, and bring to brief simmer over medium heat. Season with salt and pepper to taste. Serve.

CELERY ROOT, FENNEL, AND APPLE CHOWDER

Serves 6   Total time: 1 hour 30 minutes
WHY THIS RECIPE WORKS *Celery root's creamy-but-not-starchy texture makes it a wonderful choice for a hearty vegetable chowder. To enhance the anise aspect of its flavor profile, we sautéed a chopped fennel bulb along with big pieces of onion. Chunks of tender red potatoes bulked up the chowder, and grated apple and a strip of orange zest contributed a sweetly fruity counterpoint. To get the perfect amount of smooth body, we pureed 2 cups of the chowder with a modest amount of cream and then stirred the puree back into the pot. Last, but not least, we stirred in minced fresh fennel fronds to brighten the finished soup.*

2 tablespoons unsalted butter

1 onion, chopped

1 fennel bulb, 1 tablespoon fronds minced and reserved, stalks discarded, bulb halved, cored, and cut into ½-inch pieces

Salt and pepper

6 garlic cloves, minced

2 teaspoons minced fresh thyme or ¾ teaspoon dried

2 tablespoons all-purpose flour

½ cup dry white wine

4 cups vegetable broth

1½ cups water

14 ounces celery root, trimmed, peeled, and cut into ½-inch pieces

12 ounces red potatoes, unpeeled, cut into ½-inch pieces

1 Golden Delicious apple, peeled and shredded

1 bay leaf

1 (3-inch) strip orange zest

¼ cup heavy cream

1. Melt butter in Dutch oven over medium heat. Add onion, fennel, and 1½ teaspoons salt and cook until vegetables are softened, 5 to 7 minutes. Stir in garlic and thyme and cook until fragrant, about 30 seconds. Stir in flour and cook for 1 minute. Stir in wine, scraping up any browned bits and smoothing out any lumps, and cook until nearly evaporated, about 1 minute.

2. Stir in broth, water, celery root, potatoes, apple, bay leaf, and orange zest and bring to boil. Reduce heat to low, partially cover, and simmer gently until stew is thickened and vegetables are tender, 35 to 40 minutes.

3. Off heat, discard bay leaf and orange zest. Puree 2 cups chowder and cream in blender until smooth, about 1 minute, then return to pot. Stir in reserved fennel fronds, season with salt and pepper to taste, and serve.

CELERY ROOT AND POTATO ROESTI WITH LEMON-PARSLEY CRÈME FRAÎCHE

Serves 2 or 3   Total time: 1 hour 30 minutes

WHY THIS RECIPE WORKS *Roesti has its origins in Switzerland as a large golden-brown pancake of simply seasoned grated potatoes fried in butter. Wanting to prepare pan-fried cakes with plenty of heartiness but a decidedly fresh flavor, we swapped out nearly half of the potatoes for celery root, which gave this roesti a brighter taste and texture. To achieve a tender, creamy interior, we eliminated excess moisture by salting the vegetables and then wringing them dry in a dish towel. A small amount of cornstarch ensured that the roesti held together to create a crunchy, crisp exterior. Preparing a rich but bright sauce to accompany it was as simple as combining tangy crème fraîche with parsley and lemon zest and juice. Use the large holes of a box grater to shred the potatoes and celery root. You will need a 10-inch nonstick skillet with a tight-fitting lid for this recipe.*

1 pound russet potatoes, peeled and shredded

14 ounces celery root, trimmed, peeled, and shredded

Salt and pepper

¼ cup crème fraîche

3 tablespoons minced fresh parsley

2½ teaspoons grated lemon zest plus ½ teaspoon juice

2 teaspoons cornstarch

4 tablespoons unsalted butter

1. Toss potatoes and celery root with ¾ teaspoon salt, then let drain in colander for 30 minutes. Meanwhile, whisk crème fraîche, 1 tablespoon parsley, ½ teaspoon lemon zest, lemon juice, and ⅛ teaspoon salt together in bowl. Cover and refrigerate until ready to serve.

2. Working in 3 batches, wrap potato mixture in clean dish towel and wring tightly to squeeze out as much liquid as possible; transfer to large bowl. Add remaining 2 tablespoons parsley, remaining 2 teaspoons lemon zest, cornstarch, and ¼ teaspoon pepper, and toss to combine.

3. Melt 2 tablespoons butter in 10-inch nonstick skillet over medium-low heat. Add potato mixture and spread into even layer. Cover and cook for 5 minutes. Uncover and, using greased spatula, gently press potato mixture to form compact, round cake.

Cook, pressing on cake occasionally, until bottom is deep golden brown, about 10 minutes.

4. Run spatula around edge of pan and shake pan to loosen roesti; slide onto large plate. Melt remaining 2 tablespoons butter in now-empty skillet. Invert roesti onto second plate, then slide it, browned side up, back into skillet. Cook, pressing on cake occasionally, until bottom is well browned, about 15 minutes. Transfer roesti to wire rack and let cool for 5 minutes. Cut into wedges and serve with crème fraîche sauce.

SHRIMP SALAD WITH CELERY AND SHALLOT

Serves 4   Total time: 50 minutes

WHY THIS RECIPE WORKS *Sweet, tender shrimp pairs beautifully with the herbal, grassy flavor of celery and fresh herbs and the mild bite of minced shallot in this pretty pink-and-green salad. The classic deli-style dressing, made with mayo and lemon juice, enhances the flavor of all the ingredients. We added the raw shrimp to cold court bouillon (seasoned poaching broth) and then heated the mixture to a near-simmer to cook the shrimp gently. This recipe can also be prepared with large shrimp (26 to 30 per pound); the cooking time will be 1 to 2 minutes less. The recipe can be easily doubled; cook the shrimp in a 7-quart Dutch oven and increase the cooking time to 12 to 14 minutes. Serve this salad over greens or on toasted, buttered buns.*

- 1 pound extra-large shrimp (21 to 25 per pound), peeled, deveined, and tails removed
- 5 tablespoons lemon juice (2 lemons), spent halves reserved
- 5 sprigs fresh parsley plus 1 teaspoon minced
- 3 sprigs fresh tarragon plus 1 teaspoon minced
- 1 tablespoon sugar
- 1 teaspoon black peppercorns
  Salt and pepper
- ¼ cup mayonnaise
- 1 celery rib, minced
- 1 small shallot, minced

1. Combine shrimp, 2 cups cold water, ¼ cup lemon juice, reserved lemon halves, parsley sprigs, tarragon sprigs, sugar, peppercorns, and 1 teaspoon salt in medium saucepan. Cook over medium heat, stirring often, until shrimp are pink and firm to touch, and centers are no longer translucent, 8 to 10 minutes (water should be just bubbling around edge of saucepan and should register 165 degrees). Meanwhile, fill bowl halfway with ice and water.

2. Remove saucepan from heat, cover, and let shrimp sit in broth for 2 minutes. Drain shrimp, discarding lemon halves, herbs, and peppercorns, and transfer to ice water to cool, about 3 minutes. Transfer shrimp to triple layer of paper towels and dry well.

3. Whisk mayonnaise, celery, shallot, remaining 1 tablespoon lemon juice, minced parsley, and minced tarragon together in medium serving bowl. Cut shrimp in half lengthwise and then cut each half into thirds. Add shrimp to mayonnaise mixture and toss to combine. Season with salt and pepper to taste. Serve.

SALMON EN COCOTTE WITH CELERY AND ORANGE

Serves 4   Total time: 45 minutes

WHY THIS RECIPE WORKS *Here's an easy but elegant dinner, made entirely in a Dutch oven, to serve on any night of the week. The French term* en cocotte *simply means to bake something at a very low temperature in a covered vessel; in this recipe, the trapped moisture in the Dutch oven produces supremely tender salmon. Leeks and celery are often used as aromatic accessories when cooking fish, but here they play a prominent role as the main vegetables. After cooking the salmon on top of leeks, celery, thyme, and garlic in the covered pot, we removed the fish, added a healthy dose of white wine to the vegetables, and simmered the mixture until it had reduced slightly. We then whisked in some butter for richness. For uniform pieces of fish that cook at the same rate, we prefer to buy a whole center-cut fillet and cut it into individual fillets. If you can only find skin-on salmon, remove the skin before cooking or the dish will be greasy; you can have the fishmonger do this for you. If using wild salmon, which contains less fat than farmed salmon, cook the fillets until they register 120 degrees (for medium-rare).*

- 1 (2-pound) skinless salmon fillet, 1 to 1½ inches thick
  Salt and pepper
- 2 tablespoons extra-virgin olive oil
- 1 pound leeks, white and light green parts only, halved lengthwise, sliced thin, and washed thoroughly
- 2 celery ribs, sliced thin
- 2 oranges, 1 whole, 1 grated to yield 1 teaspoon zest and juiced to yield ½ cup juice
- 2 sprigs fresh thyme
- 2 garlic cloves, minced
- 2 tablespoons unsalted butter, cut into 2 pieces

1. Adjust oven rack to lowest position and heat oven to 250 degrees. Cut salmon crosswise into 4 fillets. Pat salmon dry with paper towels and season with salt and pepper.

2. Heat oil in Dutch oven over medium-low heat until shimmering. Add leeks, celery, orange zest, thyme, and pinch salt, cover, and cook until softened, 8 to 10 minutes. Stir in garlic and cook until fragrant, about 30 seconds.

3. Off heat, lay salmon, skinned side down, on top of leeks. Place large sheet of foil over pot and press to seal, then cover tightly with lid. Transfer pot to oven and cook until salmon flakes apart when gently prodded with paring knife and registers 125 degrees (for medium-rare), 25 to 30 minutes.

4. Meanwhile, cut away peel and pith from whole orange. Holding fruit over bowl, use paring knife to slice between membranes to release segments.

5. Transfer salmon to serving platter and tent with aluminum foil. Stir orange juice into leeks and simmer over medium-high heat until slightly thickened, about 2 minutes. Off heat, stir in butter until combined, then stir in orange segments. Season with salt and pepper to taste. Spoon sauce over salmon and serve.

CHICORIES

Bittersweet and beautiful, these multicolored lettuce cousins are finally having their time in the sun. Since they're so drop-dead gorgeous, it should come as no surprise that chicories belong to the sunflower family of plants. Whether curly-leafed or flat-leafed, these "greens" are begging to be seasoned with intense flavors.

BELGIAN ENDIVE has a petite torpedo-shaped head of cream-colored leaves with pale green edges. Individual leaves are perfect elegant little cups for holding all sorts of creative appetizer bites. Endive is lovely in salads, like our Endive, Beet, and Pear Slaw, and it's also wonderful gently braised, as we show you with white wine and herbs.

ESCAROLE looks like a giant, pale green, leafier head of Boston lettuce, with broad, white-spined, curly-topped leaves that are pale at the base and darken to green at the tips. Escarole and Orange Salad with Green Olive Vinaigrette is a classic fresh Southern Italian preparation. Or to warm up a cold day, simmer a pot of Lentil-Escarole Soup.

FRISÉE has a wildly feathery, fern-like pale green and yellow-green head. (In French, *frisée* means "curly.") Use it as a salad green in our Bistro Salad, made unctuous with bacon and fried eggs, or in the Bitter Greens Salad—the best Greek salad you'll ever eat.

RADICCHIO'S rich burgundy-colored head can be round, like a mini cabbage, or oblong, like a small romaine head. Make the most of its strong flavor by grilling it to lightly smoky, slightly crispy perfection with our recipe for Grilled Radicchio with Garlic and Rosemary-Infused Oil. On the flip side, you can temper its bold assertiveness with sweet counterpoints, as in Braised Radicchio with Apple and Cream.

shopping and storage

Most chicories are available year-round, although fall through spring is generally the traditional season for all of them. Endive and radicchio should have firm, closed heads that feel heavy for their size. Choose endive with unblemished outer leaves, and make sure the stem end is white with no browning—which is a sign the endive is past its prime. Choose radicchio heads with bright outer leaves that haven't darkened or gone limp. Both endive and radicchio are sturdier chicories and can be stored in an open plastic produce bag in the refrigerator for about a week. Escarole and frisée should be brightly colored with perky leaves, with no browning or excessive moisture on them. With their more delicate leaves, escarole and frisée will stay fresh wrapped in paper towels in a plastic produce bag for a few days.

vegetable science
Some Like It Bitter
Chicories have a bitter edge to their flavor that can be quite polarizing. Some people love it, while others consider it totally unpalatable. Two naturally occurring substances are responsible for this bitterness: lactucin and lactucopicrin. Both of these very bitter substances have traditional uses as analgesics and sedatives. For instance, they are components in a milky fluid called lactucarium that is secreted from the base of lettuce stems. Known as "lettuce opium," this fluid was first used in ancient Egypt as a sedative. When dried and smoked, it produced feelings of mild euphoria. There is some evidence to suggest that preference for bitter foods such as chicories comes down to genetic variation: Differences in taste-receptor genes seem to affect how people perceive the taste of bitter foods, ranging from mildly bitter to downright inedible.

a chicory by any other name

ESCAROLE This gently bitter green, popular in Italian cooking in particular, has a similar level of crunch to Boston lettuce but a very different, more assertive flavor. It's great raw in salads and stands up well to cooking in soups or quick braises.

ENDIVE Also called Belgian endive or, less commonly, witloof endive, this is grown either underground or indoors, without sunlight, to prevent the leaves from turning green. Red Belgian endive, which is actually a small radicchio, can be used just like green endive.

FRISÉE Otherwise known as curly endive, frisée is the most delicate of the chicories and is best used raw in recipes, like a salad green.

RADICCHIO Most commonly available is the Chioggia variety, which looks like a smaller, more delicate head of red cabbage, and that is what we used in the recipes in this chapter. It takes well to braising, grilling, roasting, and using raw. Treviso and Tardivo are less common, oblong varieties that can be used in the same way. Castelfranco is a cream-colored leafy head splashed with wine-red speckles that is best used as a salad green.

what is chicory coffee?

You often hear about the famous coffee of New Orleans, made with chicory root. The root of the common blue-flowered chicory plant is dried, ground, and blended into dark roasted coffee, adding an almost chocolaty flavor note. Supposedly chicory was first added to coffee during the Union Army blockade of New Orleans during the Civil War, as a way to stretch the scarce supply of coffee. Over the years, the tradition took hold.

vegetable prep
Preparing Endive for Braising

1. Remove and discard any wilted or bruised leaves.

2. Shave off very thin slice from root ends, then cut each head in half through core.

Cutting Radicchio into Wedges

1. Cut radicchio in half through core.

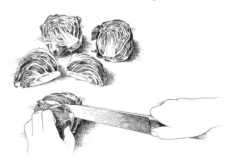

2. Cut each half again through core so that quarters stay intact.

BRAISED BELGIAN ENDIVE

Serves 4   Total time: 35 minutes

WHY THIS RECIPE WORKS *Braising endive transforms it into a side dish of uncommonly complex flavor—at once mellow, sweet, and rich, yet still with that faint natural bitter bite. We browned the endive halves in butter and sugar for maximum richness and sweetness, then braised them quickly in white wine and chicken broth for a deep yet brightly flavored vegetable side. To avoid discoloration, don't cut the endive far in advance of cooking. Delicate endive can fall apart easily if not handled gently, so move the halved endive in the pan by grasping the curved sides gingerly with tongs and supporting the cut sides with a spatula while lifting and turning. You will need a 12-inch skillet with a tight-fitting lid for this recipe.*

- 3 tablespoons unsalted butter
- ½ teaspoon sugar
- Salt and pepper
- 4 heads Belgian endive (4 ounces each), halved lengthwise
- ¼ cup dry white wine
- ¼ cup chicken or vegetable broth
- ½ teaspoon minced fresh thyme
- 1 tablespoon minced fresh parsley
- 1 teaspoon lemon juice

1. Melt 2 tablespoons butter in 12-inch skillet over medium-high heat. Sprinkle sugar and ¼ teaspoon salt evenly in skillet and set endive, cut sides down, in single layer. Cook, shaking skillet occasionally to prevent sticking, until golden brown, about 5 minutes (reduce heat if endives brown too quickly). Flip endive and cook until curved sides are golden brown, about 3 minutes.

2. Flip endive cut sides down, then add wine, broth, and thyme to skillet. Cover, reduce heat to low, and simmer until leaves open up slightly and endive are tender when poked with tip of paring knife, 13 to 15 minutes (add 2 tablespoons water during cooking if pan appears dry). Transfer endive to serving platter and cover with aluminum foil to keep warm.

3. Increase heat to medium-high and bring liquid in skillet to boil; reduce heat and simmer until reduced to syrupy consistency, 1 to 2 minutes. Off heat, whisk in remaining 1 tablespoon butter, parsley, and lemon juice. Season with salt and pepper to taste, spoon sauce over endive, and serve.

VARIATION

Braised Belgian Endive with Bacon and Cream

Omit butter and lemon juice. Before cooking endive, cook 3 slices bacon, cut into ¼-inch pieces, in 12-inch skillet over medium heat until crisp, 5 to 7 minutes. Transfer bacon to paper towel–lined plate and set aside. Pour off all but 2 tablespoons fat from skillet and continue with step 1. Add 2 tablespoons heavy cream to skillet with parsley in step 3. Sprinkle crisped bacon over endive before serving.

UTICA GREENS

Serves 6   Total time: 40 minutes

WHY THIS RECIPE WORKS *This robust Italian-American treatment of escarole originated in the 1980s in Utica, New York, where it's often served with "riggies," a spicy chicken and rigatoni dish. The escarole is braised on the stovetop with capicola, garlic, and cherry peppers until tender, then tossed with Pecorino Romano cheese and bread crumbs. Capicola (also called coppa), one of the main flavor accents here, is an Italian dry-cured cold cut made from pork shoulder and neck meat. Both hot and sweet varieties of capicola worked great. Browning the meat first helped build a savory flavor base. Bread crumbs stirred into the cooked greens absorbed excess moisture and gave the dish some crunch. For greater texture, we sprinkled more toasted crumbs over the greens just before serving. Tasters overwhelmingly preferred freshly made, toasted bread crumbs to store-bought dry crumbs—and who wouldn't? Whether you choose sweet or hot capicola, buy a ½-inch-thick slice; avoid the prepackaged thin slices, since you'll want hearty cubes of meat for this dish.*

- 1 slice hearty white sandwich bread, torn into pieces
- 3 tablespoons extra-virgin olive oil
- 4 ounces thick-cut capicola, cut into ½-inch pieces
- 1 onion, chopped
- ¼ cup jarred sliced hot cherry peppers, chopped fine
- 4 garlic cloves, minced
- 2 large heads escarole (2½ pounds), trimmed and chopped
- ½ cup chicken broth
- ¾ teaspoon salt
- ½ teaspoon pepper
- 1 ounce Pecorino Romano cheese, grated (½ cup)

1. Pulse bread and 1 tablespoon oil in food processor until coarsely ground, about 10 pulses. Toast bread crumbs in Dutch oven over medium heat, stirring occasionally, until golden brown, about 5 minutes. Transfer crumbs to medium bowl and set aside. Wipe out pot with paper towels.

2. Add remaining 2 tablespoons oil and capicola to now-empty pot and cook, stirring occasionally, until capicola begins to brown, 3 to 5 minutes. Stir in onion and cook until onion is softened and capicola is browned and crisp, about 5 minutes. Add cherry peppers and garlic and cook until fragrant, about 30 seconds.

3. Stir in half of escarole, broth, salt, and pepper and cook until beginning to wilt, about 1 minute. Stir in remaining escarole, cover, reduce heat to medium-low, and cook, stirring occasionally, until greens are tender, about 10 minutes.

4. Off heat, stir in Pecorino and ⅓ cup bread crumbs. Transfer to serving platter and top with remaining bread crumbs. Serve.

SESAME-HOISIN BRAISED ESCAROLE

Serves 4   Total time: 30 minutes

WHY THIS RECIPE WORKS *A savory Asian flavor profile enlivens this quick and easy take on braised greens. We started with a generous 2 pounds of leafy, slightly bitter escarole. To fit everything in the pot, we sautéed half of the greens before adding the rest. We then removed the lid to allow most of the remaining liquid to evaporate as the escarole finished cooking. Chopped onions, browned to bring out their sweetness, served as a simple flavor foundation. For seasoning, we combined hoisin sauce, soy sauce, rice vinegar, and sesame oil, along with pepper flakes, which added some welcome heat. Adding the sauce during the last few minutes ensured the sauce would have enough time to season the greens without over-reducing. Toasted sesame seeds sprinkled over the top gave this dish a little textural contrast and more sesame flavor.*

 2 tablespoons extra-virgin olive oil
 1 onion, chopped fine
 1 garlic clove, minced
 ¼ teaspoon red pepper flakes
 2 heads escarole (2 pounds), trimmed and sliced ½ inch thick
    Salt and pepper
 1 tablespoon hoisin sauce
 1 tablespoon rice vinegar
 1 tablespoon toasted sesame oil
 2 teaspoons soy sauce
 2 tablespoons sesame seeds, toasted

1. Heat olive oil in Dutch oven over medium heat until shimmering. Add onion and cook until softened and lightly browned, 5 to 7 minutes. Stir in garlic and pepper flakes and cook until fragrant, about 30 seconds. Stir in half of escarole and cook until beginning to wilt, about 2 minutes. Stir in remaining escarole and ¼ teaspoon salt. Cover, reduce heat to medium-low, and cook, stirring occasionally, until greens are tender, about 10 minutes.

2. Uncover and increase heat to medium. Stir in hoisin, rice vinegar, sesame oil, and soy sauce. Cook until most of liquid has evaporated, about 3 minutes. Season with salt and pepper to taste. Sprinkle with sesame seeds and serve.

BRAISED RADICCHIO WITH APPLE AND CREAM

Serves 4   Total time: 25 minutes

WHY THIS RECIPE WORKS *Chioggia radicchio might look like red cabbage, but it has more in common with Belgian endive. Both have that enjoyably bitter flavor that mellows with cooking. And, as with endive, braising is an easy and delicious way to cook radicchio. Slicing the heads into thin strips ensured a short cooking time. Cream proved to be a great braising liquid, considerably tempering the vegetable's assertiveness. After just 5 minutes in a covered pan, the radicchio was wilted and tender. We then removed the cover and allowed the excess liquid to evaporate as the radicchio continued to simmer for another minute or so. Don't be alarmed if the cream turns a lovely shade of purple! This dish is especially good with pork.*

 2 tablespoons unsalted butter
 1 onion, chopped fine
 1 Granny Smith apple, peeled, cored, and cut into ½-inch pieces
 2 heads radicchio (1¼ pounds), halved, cored, and sliced ½ inch thick
 ½ cup heavy cream
 1 tablespoon sugar
 1 tablespoon cider vinegar
    Salt and pepper

Melt butter in Dutch oven over medium-high heat. Add onion and apple and cook, stirring occasionally, until golden, 5 to 6 minutes. Stir in radicchio, cream, and sugar, cover, and cook until radicchio is tender, about 5 minutes. Uncover and simmer until liquid is reduced slightly, about 1 minute. Stir in vinegar and season with salt and pepper to taste. Serve.

LEMONY ROASTED RADICCHIO, FENNEL, AND ROOT VEGETABLES

Serves 4 to 6   Total time: 45 minutes

WHY THIS RECIPE WORKS *A medley of radicchio, fennel, potatoes, parsnips, and shallots creates an intriguing balance of flavors and textures in this hearty winter vegetable salad. To ensure that the* vegetables would roast evenly, we cut them into comparably sized pieces. Arranging the radicchio in the center of the baking sheet, with the other vegetables around the perimeter, kept the more delicate radicchio from charring in the hot oven. Before roasting, we tossed the veggies with olive oil, garlic, thyme, rosemary, and a little sugar (to promote browning). Then, once all of the vegetables were perfectly tender and caramelized, we tossed the whole shebang with a bright-tasting lemony dressing.

2 fennel bulbs, halved, cored, and sliced into ½-inch wedges
1 pound red potatoes, unpeeled, cut into 1-inch pieces
1 head radicchio (10 ounces), halved, cored, and cut into 2-inch wedges
8 ounces parsnips, peeled and cut into 2-inch pieces
8 shallots, peeled and halved
3 tablespoons extra-virgin olive oil
6 garlic cloves, peeled
2 teaspoons minced fresh thyme or ½ teaspoon dried
1 teaspoon minced fresh rosemary or ¼ teaspoon dried
1 teaspoon sugar
  Salt and pepper
2 tablespoons chopped fresh basil
2 tablespoons minced fresh chives
1 tablespoon lemon juice, plus extra for seasoning

1. Adjust oven rack to middle position and heat oven to 450 degrees. Toss fennel, potatoes, radicchio, parsnips, shallots, 1 tablespoon oil, garlic, thyme, rosemary, sugar, ¾ teaspoon salt, and ¼ teaspoon pepper to coat.

2. Spread vegetables into single layer in rimmed baking sheet, arranging radicchio in center of sheet. Roast until vegetables are tender and golden brown, 30 to 35 minutes, rotating sheet halfway through roasting.

3. Whisk basil, chives, lemon juice, and remaining 2 tablespoons oil together in large serving bowl. Add roasted vegetables and toss to combine. Season with salt, pepper, and extra lemon juice to taste. Serve.

GRILLED RADICCHIO WITH GARLIC- AND ROSEMARY-INFUSED OIL

Serves 4 to 6   Total time: 30 minutes

WHY THIS RECIPE WORKS When grilled, the beautiful red-purple leaves of radicchio become lightly crisp and smoky-tasting. To keep the fragile radicchio from falling apart on the grill, we cut it through the core end into thick wedges. And for leaves that were smoky but not singed, we found it was necessary to coat the leaves liberally with olive oil; we infused that oil with extra flavor by microwaving it with garlic and rosemary before brushing it on the radicchio wedges. For optimal browning, we flipped each wedge of radicchio so that the two cut sides of the wedges could rest directly against the grill grate. This simple side is great with grilled steaks.

6 tablespoons extra-virgin olive oil
1 garlic clove, minced
1 teaspoon minced fresh rosemary or ¼ teaspoon dried
3 heads radicchio (10 ounces each), quartered
  Salt and pepper

1. Microwave oil, garlic, and rosemary in bowl until bubbling, about 1 minute; let mixture steep for 1 minute. Brush radicchio with ¼ cup oil mixture and season with salt and pepper.

2a. For a charcoal grill Open bottom vent completely. Light large chimney starter half filled with charcoal briquettes (3 quarts). When top coals are partially covered with ash, pour evenly over grill. Set cooking grate in place, cover, and open lid vent completely. Heat grill until hot, about 5 minutes.

2b. For a gas grill Turn all burners to high, cover, and heat grill until hot, about 15 minutes. Turn all burners to medium.

3. Clean and oil cooking grate. Place radicchio on grill. Cook (covered if using gas), flipping as needed, until radicchio is softened and lightly charred, 3 to 5 minutes. Transfer to serving platter and drizzle with remaining oil mixture. Serve.

WHEAT BERRY AND ENDIVE SALAD WITH BLUEBERRIES AND GOAT CHEESE

Serves 4 to 6   Total time: 1 hour 15 minutes

WHY THIS RECIPE WORKS Endive makes lovely light salads, but it's also a great choice for a substantial summer dinner salad. Here it's paired with nutty, chewy wheat berries, creamy goat cheese, and sweet fresh blueberries. We cooked the wheat berries like pasta, simply simmering them in a large pot of water until they were tender but still had some nice chew. A bright vinaigrette made with champagne vinegar, shallot, chives, and mustard brought all the ingredients together harmoniously. If using quick-cooking or presteamed wheat berries (read the package carefully to determine this), you will need to adjust the wheat berry cooking time downward in step 1.

1½ cups wheat berries
  Salt and pepper
2 tablespoons champagne vinegar
1 tablespoon minced shallot
1 tablespoon minced fresh chives
1 teaspoon Dijon mustard
6 tablespoons extra-virgin olive oil
2 heads Belgian endive (4 ounces each), halved, cored, and sliced crosswise ¼ inch thick
7½ ounces (1½ cups) blueberries
¾ cup pecans, toasted and chopped
4 ounces goat cheese, crumbled (1 cup)

1. Bring 4 quarts water to boil in large pot. Add wheat berries and ¼ teaspoon salt, partially cover, and cook, stirring often, until wheat berries are tender but still chewy, 50 minutes to 1 hour 10 minutes. Drain and rinse under cold running water until cool; drain well.

2. Whisk vinegar, shallot, chives, mustard, ½ teaspoon salt, and ¼ teaspoon pepper together in large bowl. While whisking constantly, slowly drizzle in oil until combined. Add drained wheat berries, endive, blueberries, and pecans and toss to combine. Season with salt and pepper to taste, sprinkle with goat cheese, and serve.

Wheat Berry and Endive Salad with
Blueberries and Goat Cheese

ENDIVE, BEET, AND PEAR SLAW

Serves 4 to 6   Total time: 30 minutes

WHY THIS RECIPE WORKS *You'll forget that cabbage is supposed to be the traditional choice for slaw after tasting this delicious and unique salad. It combines the natural mild bitterness and light texture of endive with the dense, earthy sweetness of beets and the floral fruitiness of pears. Tossing the beets with a combination of sugar and salt and then spinning them in a salad spinner extracts some of their water, which otherwise would make for a watery slaw. Let them sit in the sugar and salt while you prep the remaining ingredients and mix up the sherry-Dijon vinaigrette. Loaded with so much texture, flavor, and alluring color, this salad will be welcome on your table throughout the year. To save time, we recommend shredding and treating the beets before prepping the remaining ingredients. Shred the beets on the large holes of a box grater or with the shredding disk of a food processor.*

1½ pounds beets, trimmed, peeled, and shredded
¼ cup sugar, plus extra for seasoning
    Salt and pepper
3 tablespoons sherry vinegar, plus extra for seasoning
2 tablespoons Dijon mustard
½ cup extra-virgin olive oil
2 heads Belgian endive (4 ounces each), halved, cored and sliced thin on bias
2 pears, peeled, halved, cored, and cut into ⅛-inch matchsticks
1 cup fresh cilantro leaves

1. Toss beets with sugar and 1 teaspoon salt in large bowl and let sit until partially wilted and reduced in volume by one-third, about 15 minutes.

2. Meanwhile, whisk vinegar, mustard, ½ teaspoon salt, and ½ teaspoon pepper together in large serving bowl. While whisking constantly, slowly drizzle in oil until combined.

3. Transfer beets to salad spinner and spin until excess water is removed, 10 to 20 seconds. Transfer beets to bowl with dressing. Add endive, pears, and cilantro to bowl with beets and toss to combine. Season with salt, pepper, extra sugar, and extra vinegar to taste. Serve immediately.

ESCAROLE AND ORANGE SALAD WITH GREEN OLIVE VINAIGRETTE

Serves 4 to 6   Total time: 15 minutes

WHY THIS RECIPE WORKS *This escarole salad especially brightens up a winter table, but it's delicious anytime. Surprisingly, citrus fruits have a natural affinity for olive oil, salt, and pepper, and oranges treated this way on top of sturdy chicory is a traditional Sicilian preparation. The green olives add a briny, meaty element. For an escarole and oranges salad that boasts lots of citrusy flavor, we used orange zest to boost the vinaigrette and we cut the oranges into sections instead of larger rounds, so they were more evenly and abundantly distributed throughout the salad. That said, when arranging the orange segments on the escarole, leave behind any juice that is released; it will dilute the dressing.*

½ cup chopped brine-cured green olives
⅓ cup extra-virgin olive oil
3 shallots, minced
2 tablespoons sherry vinegar
1 garlic clove, minced
2 oranges (1 zested to yield 1 teaspoon)
    Salt and pepper
1 head escarole (1 pound), trimmed and chopped
½ cup slivered almonds, toasted

1. Whisk olives, oil, shallots, vinegar, garlic, and orange zest in large bowl until combined. Add escarole and toss to coat. Season with salt and pepper to taste.

2. Cut away peel and pith from oranges. Holding knife over separate bowl, use paring knife to slice between membranes to release segments. Divide dressed greens among individual serving plates, top with orange segments, and sprinkle with almonds. Serve.

BISTRO SALAD

Serves 4   Total time: 20 minutes

WHY THIS RECIPE WORKS *If you ever thought to categorize frisée, you'd probably think of it as a lettuce, especially since it's often included in mesclun mixes. But this wildly curly chicory is sturdier than your typical salad green, so it stands up nicely to warm ingredients without wilting, as it does in this French bistro classic. Thick-cut bacon and fried eggs add unctuous flavor and substance to the frisée and romaine, which are dressed with a rich Dijon vinaigrette. Open up a crisp white wine and voilà: A quick salad is turned into supper.*

8 slices thick-cut bacon, cut into 1-inch pieces
4 large eggs
    Salt and pepper
1 tablespoon red wine vinegar
1½ teaspoons minced shallot
½ teaspoon mayonnaise
½ teaspoon Dijon mustard
3 tablespoons extra-virgin olive oil
1 head frisée (6 ounces), trimmed and cut into 1-inch pieces
1 romaine lettuce heart (6 ounces), trimmed and cut into 1-inch pieces

1. Cook bacon in 12-inch nonstick skillet over medium heat until crisp, 5 to 7 minutes. Using slotted spoon, transfer bacon to paper towel–lined plate. Pour off all but 1 tablespoon fat from skillet.

2. Crack eggs into 2 small bowls (2 eggs per bowl) and season with salt and pepper. Heat fat left in skillet over medium-high heat until shimmering. Pour 1 bowl of eggs in 1 side of skillet and second bowl in other side. Cover and cook for 1 minute. Remove skillet from heat and let sit, covered, for 15 to 45 seconds for runny yolks (white around edge of yolk will be barely opaque), or 45 to 60 seconds for soft but set yolks.

3. Meanwhile, whisk vinegar, shallot, mayonnaise, mustard, ⅛ teaspoon salt, and ⅛ teaspoon pepper together in bowl. While whisking constantly, slowly drizzle in oil until combined. Add frisée and romaine and toss to coat. Divide salad among individual

RADICCHIO SALAD WITH APPLE, ARUGULA, AND PARMESAN

Serves 4   Total time: 30 minutes

WHY THIS RECIPE WORKS *We often cook radicchio to mellow out the sharp, pleasantly bitter flavor of this vibrant red-and-white sphere, but it's also a welcome raw addition to many dishes, including this simple textured salad. Here it's paired with a bright honey-mustard vinaigrette, peppery arugula, sweet sliced apple, nutty Parmesan cheese, and toasted almonds. To soften the lightly fibrous texture of the radicchio, let it sit in the dressing for 15 minutes before tossing it with the rest of the ingredients. The easiest way make thin Parmesan shavings is with a sharp vegetable peeler.*

3 tablespoons honey
2 tablespoons white wine vinegar
1 teaspoon Dijon mustard
  Salt and pepper
5 tablespoons extra-virgin olive oil
1 head radicchio (10 ounces), halved, cored, and cut into 1-inch pieces
1 apple, cored, halved, and sliced thin
2 ounces (2 cups) baby arugula
2 ounces Parmesan cheese, shaved
¼ cup almonds, toasted and chopped

1. Whisk honey, vinegar, mustard, 1 teaspoon salt, and ½ teaspoon pepper together in large bowl. While whisking constantly, slowly whisk in oil until combined. Fold in radicchio and let sit until slightly softened, about 15 minutes.

2. Add apple, arugula, and Parmesan to radicchio mixture and toss to combine. Season with salt and pepper to taste. Transfer to serving platter, sprinkle with almonds, and serve.

VARIATION

Radicchio Salad with Pear, Parsley, and Blue Cheese

Substitute balsamic vinegar for white wine vinegar, 1 ripe pear for apple, 1 cup fresh parsley leaves for baby arugula, ½ cup crumbled blue cheese for Parmesan, and chopped toasted pistachios for almonds.

serving bowls, then top each bowl with 1 fried egg and sprinkle with bacon. Season with salt and pepper to taste. Serve.

~

BITTER GREENS SALAD

Serves 4 to 6   Total time: 15 minutes

WHY THIS RECIPE WORKS *Here's an authentic Greek salad that's a far cry from the neighborhood pizza shop version of a Greek salad. In America, Greek salads are typically made for timid palates: bland iceberg lettuce, a few thin slices of green pepper, a couple of cherry tomatoes and canned olives, and feta. If you're very lucky, you'll get a pepperoncini on top. But this version, with escarole and frisée starring as the peppery, crisp salad greens, is one of the authentic salads traditionally eaten in Greece. Dill is a classic component of many bitter greens salads, and we enjoyed it so much that we ended up adding a generous amount to allow its clean, slightly sweet flavor to really shine. We then accented the greens with a bright lemon vinaigrette, a mix of briny feta cheese and kalamata olives, and tangy, spicy pepperoncini peppers. If you prefer more heat, do not seed the pepperoncini.*

⅓ cup chopped fresh dill
3 tablespoons extra-virgin olive oil
2 tablespoons lemon juice
1 garlic clove, minced
  Salt and pepper
1 head escarole (1 pound), trimmed and cut into 1-inch pieces
1 small head frisée (4 ounces), trimmed and torn into 1-inch pieces
½ cup pitted kalamata olives, halved
2 ounces feta cheese, crumbled (½ cup)
⅓ cup pepperoncini, seeded and cut into ¼-inch-thick strips

Whisk dill, oil, lemon juice, garlic, ¼ teaspoon salt, and ⅛ teaspoon pepper in large serving bowl until combined. Add escarole, frisée, olives, feta, and pepperoncini and toss gently to coat. Season with salt and pepper to taste, and serve.

Citrus-Radicchio Salad with Dates and Smoked Almonds

CITRUS-RADICCHIO SALAD WITH DATES AND SMOKED ALMONDS

Serves 4 to 6   Total time: 30 minutes

WHY THIS RECIPE WORKS *Bring the sunny Mediterranean right to your dinner table with this colorful salad. In a reversal of what you might expect, we used sliced grapefruits and oranges as the base, topping them with the thinly sliced radicchio. To tame the bitterness of the grapefruit and prevent its ample juice from overwhelming the other components, we treated the grapefruit (and the oranges) with sugar and salt and let them sit for 15 minutes. Draining the seasoned fruit enabled us to preemptively remove the excess juice, and reserving some to use in the simple mustard and shallot vinaigrette for the greens helped to make the salad more cohesive. Salty smoked almonds added mellow richness, and chopped dates contributed sweetness. We prefer to use navel oranges, tangelos, or Cara Caras here.*

- 2 red grapefruits
- 3 oranges
- 1 teaspoon sugar
  Salt and pepper
- 3 tablespoons extra-virgin olive oil
- 1 small shallot, minced
- 1 teaspoon Dijon mustard
- 1 small head radicchio (6 ounces), halved, cored, and sliced thin
- ⅔ cup chopped pitted dates
- ½ cup smoked almonds, chopped

1. Cut away peel and pith from grapefruits and oranges. Cut each fruit in half from pole to pole, then slice crosswise ¼ inch thick. Transfer to bowl, toss with sugar and ½ teaspoon salt, and let sit for 15 minutes.

2. Drain fruit in fine-mesh strainer set over bowl, reserving 2 tablespoons juice. Arrange fruit in even layer on serving platter and drizzle with oil. Whisk reserved citrus juice, shallot, and mustard together in medium bowl. Add radicchio, ⅓ cup dates, and ¼ cup almonds and gently toss to coat. Season with salt and pepper to taste. Arrange radicchio mixture over fruit, leaving 1-inch border of fruit around edges. Sprinkle with remaining ⅓ cup dates and remaining ¼ cup almonds. Serve.

ORZO SALAD WITH RADICCHIO, CHICKPEAS, AND PECORINO

Serves 4 to 6   Total time: 1 hour 15 minutes

WHY THIS RECIPE WORKS *Radicchio contributes its gorgeous hue and welcome assertive chicory flavor to this flavor-packed pasta salad. Orzo, a tiny rice-shaped pasta, performed its role here beautifully, providing enough bulk to make the salad satisfying but not so much that it became too heavy and starchy. Chickpeas provided protein and a nice textural contrast. Pecorino Romano cheese has a stronger taste than Parmesan and so held up very well against the other strong flavors here. Basil added a fresh herbal note. And last but not least, the strong vinaigrette, with its high proportion of vinegar to oil and two garlic cloves, really made everything zingy.*

- 1¼ cups orzo
  Salt and pepper
- 6 tablespoons extra-virgin olive oil, plus extra for serving
- ¼ cup balsamic vinegar
- 2 garlic cloves, minced
- 1 (15-ounce) can chickpeas, rinsed
- ½ small head radicchio (3 ounces), cored and chopped fine
- 2 ounces Pecorino Romano cheese, grated (1 cup)
- ½ cup chopped fresh basil

1. Bring 2 quarts water to boil in large saucepan. Add orzo and 1½ teaspoons salt and cook, stirring often, until al dente. Drain orzo and transfer to rimmed baking sheet. Toss with 1 tablespoon oil and let cool completely, about 15 minutes.

2. Whisk remaining 5 tablespoons oil, vinegar, garlic, ½ teaspoon salt, and ½ teaspoon pepper in large bowl until combined. Add chickpeas, radicchio, Pecorino, basil, and cooled orzo to dressing and toss to coat. Season with salt and pepper to taste.

3. Let salad sit at room temperature for 30 minutes to allow flavors to meld. Serve, drizzling with extra oil to taste.

LENTIL-ESCAROLE SOUP

Serves 6   Total time: 55 minutes

WHY THIS RECIPE WORKS *The escarole in this warming, comforting lentil soup is a revelation. While it's common as a soup ingredient, many recipes call for a long simmering time after it's added. Here we stirred it in toward the end of cooking so that the leaves retained much of their sturdy chicory character and flavor. We prefer French green lentils or brown lentils for this soup; black will also work, but don't use red or yellow (note that cooking times may vary).*

- ¼ cup extra-virgin olive oil, plus extra for serving
- 1 onion, chopped fine
- 1 carrot, peeled and chopped fine
- 1 celery rib, chopped fine
  Salt and pepper
- 6 garlic cloves, sliced thin
- 2 tablespoons minced fresh parsley
- 4 cups chicken or vegetable broth, plus extra as needed
- 3 cups water
- 8 ounces (1¼ cups) lentilles du Puy or brown lentils, picked over and rinsed
- 1 (14.5-ounce) can diced tomatoes
- 1 Parmesan cheese rind (optional), plus grated Parmesan for serving
- 2 bay leaves
- ½ head escarole (8 ounces), trimmed and cut into ½-inch pieces

1. Heat oil in Dutch oven over medium heat until shimmering. Add onion, carrot, celery, and ½ teaspoon salt and cook until softened and lightly browned, 8 to 10 minutes. Stir in garlic and parsley and cook until fragrant, about 30 seconds. Stir in broth; water; lentils; tomatoes and their juice; Parmesan rind, if using; and bay leaves and bring to simmer. Cover, leaving lid slightly ajar, reduce heat to medium-low and simmer until lentils are tender, 25 to 30 minutes.

2. Discard Parmesan rind, if using, and bay leaves. Stir in escarole, 1 handful at a time, and cook until wilted, about 5 minutes. Adjust consistency with extra hot broth as needed. Season with salt and pepper to taste. Drizzle individual portions with extra oil and serve, passing grated Parmesan separately.

Tuscan White Bean and Escarole Soup

TUSCAN WHITE BEAN AND ESCAROLE SOUP

Serves 8 to 10   Total time: 1 hour

WHY THIS RECIPE WORKS *Our version of* acquacotta, *one of Italy's traditional soups, features creamy cannellini beans, faintly bitter escarole, tender fennel, and chopped tomatoes. Though* acquacotta *translates as "cooked water," we used chicken broth and amped up the flavor with a* soffritto, *a mixture of sautéed onion, celery, and garlic. We thickened the broth with the bean canning liquid and egg yolks and ladled our finished soup over toasted bread, turning a humble vegetable soup into a hearty one-bowl meal. We prefer Pecorino Romano here, but Parmesan can be substituted, if desired. If your cheese has a rind, slice it off the wedge and add it to the pot with the broth in step 3.*

SOUP

- 1 large onion, chopped
- 2 celery ribs, chopped
- 4 garlic cloves, peeled
- 1 (28-ounce) can whole peeled tomatoes
- ½ cup extra-virgin olive oil
  Salt and pepper
- ⅛ teaspoon red pepper flakes
- 8 cups chicken or vegetable broth
- 1 fennel bulb, 2 tablespoons fronds minced, stalks discarded, bulb halved, cored, and cut into ½-inch pieces
- 2 (15-ounce) cans cannellini beans, drained with liquid reserved, beans rinsed
- 1 small head escarole (10 ounces), trimmed and cut into ½-inch pieces
- 2 large egg yolks
- ½ cup chopped fresh parsley
- 1 tablespoon minced fresh oregano
  Grated Pecorino Romano cheese
  Lemon wedges

TOAST

- 10 (½-inch-thick) slices thick-crusted country bread
- ¼ cup extra-virgin olive oil
  Salt and pepper

1. For the soup Pulse onion, celery, and garlic in food processor until very finely chopped, 15 to 20 pulses, scraping down sides of bowl as needed. Transfer onion mixture to Dutch oven. Add tomatoes and their juice to now-empty processor and pulse until tomatoes are finely chopped, 10 to 12 pulses; set aside.

2. Stir oil, ¾ teaspoon salt, and pepper flakes into onion mixture. Cook over medium-high heat, stirring occasionally, until light brown fond begins to form on bottom of pot, 12 to 15 minutes. Stir in tomatoes, increase heat to high, and cook, stirring frequently, until mixture is very thick and rubber spatula leaves distinct trail when dragged across bottom of pot, 9 to 12 minutes.

3. Add broth and fennel bulb to pot and bring to simmer. Reduce heat to medium-low and simmer until fennel begins to soften, 5 to 7 minutes. Stir in beans and escarole and cook until fennel is tender, about 10 minutes.

4. Whisk egg yolks and reserved bean liquid together in bowl, then stir into soup. Stir in parsley, oregano, and fennel fronds. Season with salt and pepper to taste.

5. For the toast Adjust oven rack 5 inches from broiler element and heat broiler. Place bread on aluminum foil–lined rimmed baking sheet, drizzle with oil, and season with salt and pepper. Broil until bread is deep golden brown.

6. Place 1 slice bread in bottom of each individual serving bowl. Ladle soup over toasted bread. Serve, passing Pecorino and lemon wedges separately.

WHOLE-WHEAT PASTA WITH LENTILS, ESCAROLE, AND PANCETTA

Serves 6   Total time: 1 hour

WHY THIS RECIPE WORKS *"Greens and beans" is an endlessly adaptable recipe template. Our favored greens here are escarole, paired with lentils, nutty whole-wheat pasta, and savory pancetta, for a soul-satisfying meal. Carrots added a touch of sweetness, and white wine provided a bright punch of acidity. French green lentils, or* lentilles du Puy, *were our first choice for this recipe, since they retained their firm yet tender texture, but brown, black, or regular green lentils work (note that cooking times will vary depending on the type used).*

- ¼ cup extra-virgin olive oil
- 4 ounces pancetta, cut into ¼-inch pieces
- 1 onion, chopped fine
- 2 carrots, peeled, halved lengthwise, and sliced ¼-inch-thick
- 2 garlic cloves, minced
- 2 cups chicken broth
- 1½ cups water
- ¾ cup lentilles du Puy, picked over and rinsed
- ¼ cup dry white wine
- 1 head escarole (1 pound), trimmed and sliced ½-inch-thick
- 1 pound whole-wheat spaghetti
  Salt and pepper
- ¼ cup chopped fresh parsley
  Grated Parmesan cheese

1. Heat 2 tablespoons oil in large saucepan over medium heat until shimmering. Add pancetta and cook, stirring occasionally, until beginning to brown, 3 to 5 minutes. Add onion and carrots and cook until softened, 5 to 7 minutes. Stir in garlic and cook until fragrant, about 30 seconds. Stir in broth, water, and lentils and bring to simmer. Cover, reduce heat to medium-low, and simmer until lentils are fully cooked and tender, 30 to 40 minutes.

2. Stir in wine and simmer, uncovered, for 2 minutes. Stir in escarole, 1 handful at a time, and cook until wilted, about 5 minutes.

3. Meanwhile, bring 4 quarts water to boil in large pot. Add pasta and 1 tablespoon salt and cook, stirring often, until al dente. Reserve ¾ cup cooking water, then drain pasta and return it to pot. Add ½ cup reserved cooking water, lentil mixture, parsley, and remaining 2 tablespoons oil to pasta in pot and toss to combine. Season with salt and pepper to taste and adjust consistency with remaining ¼ cup reserved cooking water as needed. Serve with Parmesan.

CHILES

The world of chiles is so vast that entire books have been devoted to them. Chile peppers have a uniquely broad flavor profile in the vegetable world, from mild and fresh to acidic and spicy to rich and toasty. Some are used mainly for their heat, while others are deployed to bring complex flavors to sauces, chilis, noodle dishes, curries, and much more. Regardless, chileheads everywhere are passionate about the endorphins that result from eating fiery peppers.

Unlike other vegetables, chiles are just as likely to be used dried as they are fresh. Each category has its best uses, but there is some wiggle room to mix, match, and substitute. Generally, fresh chiles have vegetal or grassy flavors and clean, punchy heat. Dried chiles have deeper, earthier flavors, with fruity, nutty, or smoky undertones.

Chile peppers usually bring to mind Mexican food, and that's where they originated. About half of the 200 varieties in existence today come from Mexico. However, food cultures all over the world use them in cooking, particularly those countries nearest to the equator, where they have learned that the fiery heat of chile peppers actually creates a cooling effect on the body.

To warm things up here, we start on the milder side, with Blistered Shishito Peppers, an addictively poppable snack using Japanese chiles; Pickled Jalapeños are the next step up in terms of heat. Of course, there are chilis and tacos to please everyone. For a change of pace, try Stir-Fried Thai-Style Beef with Chiles and Shallots. And Italy gets in on the action too, with a fiery pasta dish of bucatini with smoky, spicy crushed Calabrian peperoncini.

shopping and storage

We use the most common American names for chiles, but confusingly, the same chile can sometimes go by different names in different parts of the country. (For example, Anaheim chiles are sometimes called California chiles.) If you can't find a particular variety, odds are that a good substitute will be available.

When shopping for fresh chiles, use the same principles you'd use for bell peppers: Look for those with bright colors and firm, unblemished skin. As with bell peppers, store them in an open plastic produce bag in the refrigerator for a week or so.

Dried chiles should still be pliable; they shouldn't be crisp and shatter like crackers. If you have the opportunity to smell them, they should be fragrant, in a somewhat raisiny way. Oftentimes, dried chiles are sold prepackaged in cellophane bags. Store dried chiles in an airtight container at room temperature; for extended storage, freeze them in an airtight container.

can't take the heat?

Chiles get their heat from a group of chemical compounds called capsaicinoids, the best known of which is capsaicin. It's present mostly in the inner whitish pith (or ribs), with progressively smaller amounts in the seeds and flesh. Capsaicin activates our sensory receptors that are associated with pain and touch, creating a burning sensation when we eat them.

To tamp down the fire, remove the ribs and seeds before adding the chiles to a dish. You can always reserve the seeds to add them later to the finished dish.

There are many folk remedies for cooling the fiery heat from eating chiles. The casein proteins found in dairy products like milk, yogurt, or sour cream really do help soothe your burning mouth. Capsaicin is also alcohol-soluble, so it's not your imagination that an ice-cold beer makes you feel better. Starchy grains like rice and corn tortillas also work quite well. One thing that definitely doesn't work at all? Water.

pantry chile products

CAYENNE Contrary to its name, cayenne pepper usually contains a variety of ground dried chiles, not just the dried red cayenne chile. A little of this fiery spice goes a long way. But, as with other dried chiles and dried spices in general, be sure to replace cayenne pepper every few months, as its volatile oils will lose their potency.

RED PEPPER FLAKES Made from a blend of various roasted, dried, crushed chiles, these flakes pack a clean, hot punch. As with cayenne pepper, freshness is important, so replace your red pepper flakes every few months.

CHILI POWDER Different brands vary, but most chili powder is a blend of roasted dried chiles, garlic powder, oregano, ground cumin, and sometimes salt. For a purer chile flavor with no distractions, experiment with making your own custom blend by grinding dried chiles in a spice grinder. (To clean your spice grinder afterward, add some raw white rice to the grinder and pulverize it to a powder. The rice will absorb the chile oils left behind.)

vegetable prep

Working with Fresh Chiles

Always wear food-handling gloves when working with fresh chiles, or put your hands into plastic bags. Avoid touching your mouth or eyes, and always wash utensils afterward in hot, very soapy water.

An Easy Way to Seed Fresh Chiles

Use chef's knife to cut down 1 side, using edge of chile's crown as guide for where to position knife. Place chile on cut side and repeat on remaining sides to create 4 planks. Discard stem and core, reserving seeds if specified in recipe.

Cleaning Dried Chiles

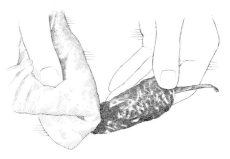

Dried chiles may look ready to use directly out of the packaging, but they're often coated in a residue of some sort. We're not sure whether it's ground chile residue left from processing or whether it's actually dust or dirt, but we'd rather not take the chance. Simply wipe chiles with dish towel before using.

HOW HOT DO YOU WANT IT?

The spice level of both fresh and dried chile peppers ranges from extremely mild to unbelievably, searingly hot. And everyone's taste buds are different, so one person can enjoy Scotch bonnets while another can't even go near jalapeños. Here's a quick guide to fresh and dried chiles, with substitution suggestions.

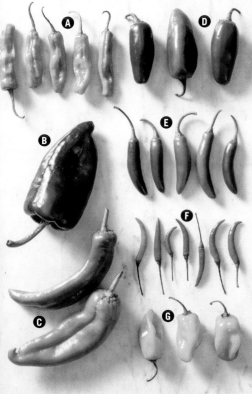

FRESH

A Shishitos

Shishitos are very mild medium-size Japanese chiles that are long, skinny, and shiny bright green, with a grassy, citrusy flavor. Substitute Padrón chiles.
Heat: ◐○○○

B Poblanos

Poblanos are mild, large, triangular chiles that are green to red-brown in color, with a crisp, vegetal flavor. Substitute Anaheim chiles.
Heat: ●○○○

C Anaheims

Anaheims are mild to medium-hot large chiles that are long and skinny, yellow-green to red, and mildly tangy and vegetal. Substitute poblanos.
Heat: ●●○○

D Jalapeños

Jalapeños are medium-hot small green or red chiles that are smooth and shiny, with a bright, grassy flavor. Substitute serranos.
Heat: ●●○○

E Serranos

Serranos are medium-hot, small dark green chiles with a bright, citrusy flavor. Substitute jalapeños.
Heat: ●●●○

F Thai chiles

Thai chiles are hot, bright red or green, narrow, and petite, with a clean flavor similar to black peppercorns. Substitute a half-dose of habaneros.
Heat: ●●●◐

G Habaneros

Habaneros are very hot, bulbous, bright orange to red, deeply floral, and fruity. Substitute a double dose of Thai chiles.
Heat: ●●●●

DRIED

H Guajillos

Guajillos are mild to medium-hot, with a fruity flavor and subtle natural smokiness. Substitute anchos or pasillas.
Heat: ●○○○

I Anchos

Anchos are mild to medium-hot. These dried poblanos have deep, earthy flavors that evoke chocolate, coffee, raisins, and licorice. Substitute mulatos or pasillas.
Heat: ●○○○

J Chipotles

Chipotles are medium-hot. These dried, smoked jalapeños have charred wood, tobacco, and barbecue flavors balanced by subtle sweetness. Substitute anchos. Chipotles are also available canned in tangy red adobo sauce.
Heat: ●●○○

K New Mexican chiles

New Mexican chiles are medium-hot, with a sweet, earthy flavor reminiscent of roasted red peppers, tomatoes, and cherries. Substitute guajillos or cascabels.
Heat: ●●○○

L Calabrian peperoncini

Calabrian peperoncini are hot, tiny, and a bit smoky, with a mildly fruity flavor. They are available as flakes and whole. Arbol chiles are a better substitute than regular red pepper flakes.
Heat: ●●●○

BLISTERED SHISHITO PEPPERS

Serves 4 to 6   Total time: 10 minutes

WHY THIS RECIPE WORKS *Fried blistered little chile peppers that you pick up by the stems and pop into your mouth whole are much-desired menu items wherever trendy bar snacks are sold. Shishitos are what you usually find at Asian-style restaurants; they are the Japanese cousin to Spain's Padrón chiles, which are prevalent at tapas restaurants. These bright-tasting, citrusy, mild green chiles are thin-skinned and crisp-textured and altogether addictive. Restaurants often deep-fry the whole shishitos, but we have found that cooking them in a small amount of oil works just as well. The larger granules of kosher salt sprinkled on top add a wonderful crunch, but you can use regular table salt instead, if you prefer. It's said that only one in ten shishito peppers is truly spicy, so happy hunting!*

    2 tablespoons vegetable oil
    8 ounces shishito peppers
       Kosher salt

Heat oil in 12-inch skillet over medium-high heat until just smoking. Add shishito peppers and cook, without stirring, until skins are blistered, 3 to 5 minutes. Using tongs, flip peppers and continue to cook until blistered on second side, 3 to 5 minutes. Transfer to serving bowl, season with salt to taste, and serve.

PICKLED JALAPEÑOS

Makes about 1½ cups
Total time: 40 minutes

WHY THIS RECIPE WORKS *What jarred pickled jalapeños offer in convenience, they lack in flavor and texture. Here's a simple recipe that you can make in half an hour that boasts fresh green chile flavor, crisp texture, and subtle heat. Distilled white vinegar provided the best tang to complement the chiles. We brought the vinegar, sugar, and salt to a boil over medium heat until the sugar dissolved before pouring the mixture over the prepped chiles and letting them sit for 30 minutes until the quick pickle cooled off. If using a glass jar in this recipe, be sure to fill the jar with hot water to warm it, then drain the jar before filling it with jalapeños and hot brine. This process ensures that the jar won't crack from the sudden temperature change. These pickled jalapeños can be refrigerated for up to one week.*

    4 jalapeño chiles, stemmed and sliced thin
    1 cup distilled white vinegar
    ⅓ cup sugar
    ¼ teaspoon kosher salt

Place jalapeños in small jar or bowl. Bring vinegar, sugar, and salt to simmer in small saucepan over medium-high heat, stirring occasionally, until sugar dissolves. Pour vinegar mixture over jalapeños. Set aside to cool completely, about 30 minutes. Serve.

HABANERO AND PEACH CHUTNEY

Makes 2 cups   Total time: 25 minutes

WHY THIS RECIPE WORKS *This sweet and fiery chutney pairs height-of-season peaches with super-spicy habanero chiles, along with red onion, warm spices, brown sugar, wine vinegar, and fresh mint. Not only is it beautiful and very quick to prepare, but its fruity-spicy flavor combo also makes it hugely appealing. Remember that habanero chiles are extremely spicy: This chutney needed only half a habanero to really bring the heat. If you would like an even spicier chutney, add the minced ribs and seeds from the chile. We recommend wearing gloves when working with habanero chiles. This chutney will keep in the refrigerator for up to one week. Serve this with grilled chicken, duck, or salmon.*

    1½ tablespoons vegetable oil
     1 red onion, chopped fine
     2 ripe but firm peaches, halved, pitted, and chopped
     ½ habanero chile, stemmed, seeded, and minced
     ¼ teaspoon ground ginger
        Pinch ground allspice
        Pinch ground cloves
     ¼ cup packed light brown sugar
     ¼ cup red wine vinegar
     1 tablespoon shredded fresh mint

Heat oil in medium saucepan over medium heat until shimmering. Add onion and cook until softened, about 5 minutes. Stir in peaches and cook until softened but still intact, about 4 minutes. Stir in habanero, ginger, allspice, and cloves and cook until

Stuffed Jalapeños

fragrant, about 1 minute. Stir in sugar and vinegar, bring to simmer, and cook until liquid is very thick and syrupy, about 9 minutes. Transfer to serving bowl and let cool to room temperature. Stir in mint and serve.

STUFFED JALAPEÑOS

Serves 6 to 8   Total time: 45 minutes

WHY THIS RECIPE WORKS *These Tex-Mex appetizers are a party favorite and a little sibling to traditional Mexican chiles rellenos (stuffed green chiles). While the stuffed poppers are often breaded and deep fried, our baked version is faster and fresher, eliminating the heavy, greasy outer coating to better highlight the green heat of the jalapeños. We cut the chiles in half, scooped out the ribs and seeds, and parcooked them in a hot oven to soften them before stuffing with a mixture of three cheeses, bread crumbs, bacon, cilantro, scallions, lime juice, and cumin. Once stuffed, these jalapeños needed only about 10 more minutes in the oven before they were ready for our tasters. They all agreed that this was a perfect snack as they reached for more.*

 6 slices bacon, chopped fine
 12 jalapeño chiles, halved lengthwise with stems left intact, seeds and ribs removed
    Salt
 4 ounces mild cheddar cheese, shredded (1 cup)
 4 ounces Monterey Jack cheese, shredded (1 cup)
 4 ounces cream cheese, softened
 2 scallions, sliced thin
 3 tablespoons minced fresh cilantro
 2 tablespoons panko bread crumbs
 1 large egg yolk
 2 teaspoons lime juice
 1 teaspoon ground cumin

1. Adjust oven rack to upper-middle position and heat oven to 500 degrees. Set wire rack in rimmed baking sheet. Cook bacon in 12-inch nonstick skillet over medium heat until crispy, 7 to 9 minutes. Using slotted spoon, transfer bacon to paper towel–lined plate; set aside.

2. Season jalapeños with salt and place cut side down on prepared rack. Bake until just beginning to soften, about 5 minutes. Remove jalapeños from oven and reduce oven temperature to 450 degrees. Flip jalapeños cut side up.

3. Mix cheddar, Monterey Jack, cream cheese, scallions, cilantro, panko, egg yolk, lime juice, cumin, and bacon in bowl until thoroughly combined. Divide cheese mixture among jalapeños, pressing into cavities to fill. (Filled jalapeños can be covered and refrigerated for up to 24 hours.)

4. Bake jalapeños until tender and filling is lightly browned, 9 to 14 minutes. Let cool for 5 minutes. Serve.

SPICY PINTO BEAN SOUP

Serves 6   Total time: 1 hour 30 minutes (plus 8 hours soaking time)

WHY THIS RECIPE WORKS *Sopa tarasca, as this silky bean soup is called in its southwest Mexico home, features deep chile flavor from three different varieties. Ancho chiles provide subtle sweetness, canned chipotle chiles in adobo sauce contribute smoky, spicy flavor with a bit of acidity, and a fresh jalapeño offers bright vegetal notes. Pureeing the chiles with tomatoes, onion, garlic, and oregano in a blender created a vibrant puree, which we cooked in hot oil to concentrate its flavor. Adding the broth to this rich base allowed us to scrape up the flavorful browned bits on the bottom of the pot, and cooking the beans in that aromatic broth infused them with flavor. Serve with toasted pepitas, chopped fresh cilantro, and Mexican crema or sour cream. If you are pressed for time you can "quick-brine" your beans. In step 1, combine the salt, water, and beans in a large Dutch oven and bring to a boil over high heat. Remove the pot from the heat, cover, and let stand for 1 hour. Drain and rinse the beans and proceed with the recipe.*

    Salt and pepper
 8 ounces (1¼ cups) dried pinto beans, picked over and rinsed
 1½ ounces (3 or 4) dried ancho chiles, stemmed, seeded, and torn into 1-inch pieces (¾ cup)
 2 tomatoes, cored and quartered
 1 onion, quartered
 3 garlic cloves, peeled
 1 jalapeño chile, stemmed, halved, and seeded
 1 tablespoon minced canned chipotle chile in adobo sauce
 1 tablespoon dried oregano
 3 tablespoons vegetable oil
 7 cups chicken or vegetable broth, plus extra as needed
 2 bay leaves

1. Dissolve 1½ tablespoons salt in 2 quarts cold water in large container. Add beans and soak at room temperature for at least 8 hours or up to 24 hours. Drain and rinse well.

2. Toast anchos in Dutch oven over medium-high heat, stirring frequently, until fragrant, 2 to 6 minutes. Transfer to blender and let cool slightly, about 5 minutes. Add tomatoes, onion, garlic, jalapeño, chipotle, and oregano and process until smooth, about 30 seconds.

3. Heat oil in now-empty pot over medium-high heat until shimmering. Add ancho-tomato mixture and 1 teaspoon salt and cook, stirring frequently, until mixture has darkened in color and liquid has evaporated, about 10 minutes. Stir in broth, beans, and bay leaves, scraping up any browned bits, and bring to simmer. Cover, reduce heat to low, and simmer gently until beans are tender, 1 to 1½ hours.

4. Discard bay leaves. Working in batches, process soup in clean, dry blender until smooth, 1 to 2 minutes. Return soup to again-empty pot, adjust consistency with extra broth as needed, and season with salt and pepper to taste. Serve.

PORK POSOLE ROJO

Serves 8 to 10   Total time: 2 hours 45 minutes

WHY THIS RECIPE WORKS *This hearty Mexican stew of hominy (degerminated corn kernels), pork, chiles, and vegetables dates all the way back to the Aztecs. Today, no Mexican family celebration would be complete without posole. It's infinitely customizable, but rojo, or red, posole gets its color from tomatoes and chiles. Traditionally it includes bones from a pig's head, neck, shank, and feet, supplemented with shoulder or loin meat. We simplified this to make at home by using a bone-in pork butt roast split into small chunks. We loved the rich, slightly sweet flavor of dried ancho chiles, which we soaked and pureed into a thick paste. We mixed most of the puree into the stew, saving a bit to add later for those who wanted extra heat. Pork butt roast is often labeled Boston butt in the supermarket. For an accurate measurement of boiling water, bring a full kettle of water to a boil and then measure out the desired amount. Serve this as they do in modern-day Mexico, with lime wedges, diced avocado, shredded cabbage, and/or sliced radishes.*

- 1 (5-pound) bone-in pork butt roast, trimmed and pulled apart at seams, bones reserved
  Salt and pepper
- 2 tablespoons vegetable oil
- 2 large onions, chopped
- 5 garlic cloves, minced
- 6 cups chicken broth
- 1 (14.5-ounce) can diced tomatoes
- 1 tablespoon minced fresh oregano or 1 teaspoon dried
- 1½ ounces (3 or 4) ancho chiles, stemmed and seeded
- 1½ cups boiling water
- 3 (15-ounce) cans white or yellow hominy, rinsed

1. Adjust oven rack to lower-middle position and heat oven to 300 degrees. Season pork with salt and pepper. Heat oil in Dutch oven over medium heat until shimmering. Add onions and ¼ teaspoon salt and cook until softened, 8 to 10 minutes. Stir in garlic and cook until fragrant, about 30 seconds. Add pork and bones and cook, stirring often, until exterior of pork is no longer pink, about 8 minutes.

2. Stir in broth, tomatoes and their juice, oregano, and ½ teaspoon salt and bring to simmer, skimming foam from surface as needed. Cover, place pot in oven, and cook until pork is tender, about 2 hours.

3. Meanwhile, soak anchos in boiling water until softened, about 20 minutes. Process anchos and soaking liquid in blender until smooth, about 30 seconds. Drain in fine-mesh strainer set over bowl, pressing with rubber spatula to help pass ancho mixture through strainer. Measure out and reserve ¼ cup strained ancho mixture for serving.

4. Remove pot from oven, transfer pork to cutting board, and let cool; discard bones. Meanwhile, stir hominy and ancho mixture into pot and bring to simmer over medium heat. Cover, reduce heat to low, and simmer gently until flavors meld, about 30 minutes.

5. Once pork is cool enough to handle, shred into bite-size pieces using 2 forks. Stir shredded pork into stew and cook until warmed through, about 2 minutes. Season with reserved ancho mixture, salt, and pepper to taste. Serve.

BEST GROUND BEEF CHILI

Serves 8 to 10

Total time: 2 hours 30 minutes

WHY THIS RECIPE WORKS *Most ground beef chiles are all about quick convenience, relying on jarred chili powders. This thick, spicy, ultrabeefy chili ratchets things up a notch with a homemade chili powder mixture combining smoky ancho chiles with ground tortilla chips, garlic powder, and potent, earthy spices. For even more smoky chile flavor, we added chipotle chiles in adobo to the beef as it cooked. We also made sure to stir in any orange fat that collected on the top of the cooked chili before serving it, since this fat contained so much of the flavor from the fat-soluble spices in the chili powder. Serve up this chili at your next TV game-day gathering along with your favorite chili toppings. Diced avocado, sour cream, and shredded Monterey Jack or cheddar cheese are great choices.*

- 2 pounds 85 percent lean ground beef
- 2 tablespoons plus 2 cups water
  Salt and pepper
- ¾ teaspoon baking soda
- 3 ounces (6 to 8) ancho chiles, stemmed, seeded, and torn into 1-inch pieces (1½ cups)
- 1 ounce tortilla chips, crushed (¼ cup)

2 tablespoons ground cumin
1 tablespoon paprika
1 tablespoon garlic powder
1 tablespoon ground coriander
2 teaspoons dried oregano
½ teaspoon dried thyme
1 (14.5-ounce) can whole peeled
   tomatoes
1 tablespoon vegetable oil
1 onion, chopped fine
3 garlic cloves, minced
1–2 teaspoons minced canned chipotle
   chile in adobo sauce
1 (15-ounce) can pinto beans
2 teaspoons sugar
2 tablespoons cider vinegar
   Lime wedges
   Coarsely chopped cilantro
   Chopped red onion

1. Adjust oven rack to lower-middle position and heat oven to 275 degrees. Toss beef with 2 tablespoons water, 1½ teaspoons salt, and baking soda in bowl until thoroughly combined. Set aside for 20 minutes.

2. Meanwhile, toast anchos in Dutch oven over medium-high heat, stirring frequently, until fragrant, 2 to 6 minutes. Transfer to food processor and let cool slightly, about 5 minutes. Add tortilla chips, cumin, paprika, garlic powder, coriander, oregano, thyme, and 2 teaspoons pepper and process until finely ground, about 2 minutes; transfer to bowl. Process tomatoes and their juice in now-empty work bowl until smooth, about 30 seconds.

3. Heat oil in now-empty pot over medium-high heat until shimmering. Stir in onion and cook until softened, about 5 minutes. Add garlic and cook until fragrant, about 30 seconds. Add beef and cook, breaking up meat with wooden spoon into pieces no larger than ¼ inch, until beef is browned and fond begins to form on bottom of pot, 12 to 14 minutes. Add ancho mixture and chipotle and cook, stirring frequently, until fragrant, 1 to 2 minutes.

4. Add remaining 2 cups water, beans and their liquid, sugar, and processed tomatoes. Bring to boil, scraping bottom of pot to loosen any browned bits. Cover, place in

oven, and cook until meat is tender and chili is slightly thickened, 1½ to 2 hours, stirring occasionally to prevent sticking.

5. Remove chili from oven and let sit, uncovered, for 10 minutes. Stir in vinegar and season with salt to taste. Serve, passing lime wedges, cilantro, and chopped onion separately.

THREE-CHILE WHITE BEAN CHILI

Serves 4 to 6   Total time: 1 hour 45 minutes

WHY THIS RECIPE WORKS *White bean chili is a fresher version of the thicker red chili with tomatoes that most Americans know and love. The fresh chiles take center stage, and we had fun choosing them: Banana peppers and Italian peppers weren't inspiring enough. Serranos were too hot even for the chileheads among us. The trio of poblanos, Anaheims, and jalapeños provided the right level of complex, modest heat. We broiled the poblanos and Anaheims to develop depth and smokiness. To keep the flavor of the jalapeños bright, we chopped them in the food processor with onions and then sautéed the mixture. Broiled fresh corn added to the chili just before serving gave it a sweet quality. To thicken the chili, we processed some of the broiled peppers with a portion of the beans and broth. Serve with sour cream, tortilla chips, and lime wedges.*

5 poblano chiles, halved lengthwise,
   stemmed, and seeded
3 Anaheim chiles, halved lengthwise,
   stemmed, and seeded
3 tablespoons vegetable oil
3 ears corn, kernels cut from cobs
   and cobs reserved
2 onions, cut into large pieces
2 jalapeño chiles, stemmed, seeded,
   and chopped
2 (15-ounce) cans cannellini beans,
   rinsed
4 cups vegetable broth
6 garlic cloves, minced
1 tablespoon tomato paste
1 tablespoon ground cumin
1½ teaspoons ground coriander
   Salt and pepper

1 (15-ounce) can pinto beans, rinsed
4 scallions, green parts only, sliced thin
¼ cup minced fresh cilantro
1 tablespoon lime juice

1. Adjust oven rack 6 inches from broiler element and heat broiler. Toss poblanos and Anaheims with 1 tablespoon oil and arrange skin side up on aluminum foil–lined rimmed baking sheet. Broil until poblanos and Anaheims begin to blacken and soften, about 10 minutes, rotating sheet halfway through broiling. Transfer broiled poblanos and Anaheims to bowl, cover with plastic wrap, and let steam until skins peel off easily, 10 to 15 minutes. Peel poblanos and Anaheims, then cut into ½-inch pieces, reserving any accumulated juices.

2. Meanwhile, toss corn kernels with 1 tablespoon oil, spread evenly over second foil-lined rimmed baking sheet, and broil, stirring occasionally, until beginning to brown, 5 to 10 minutes; let cool on sheet.

3. Pulse onions and jalapeños in food processor until coarsely ground, 6 to 8 pulses; transfer to bowl. In now-empty processor, process 1 cup cannellini beans, 1 cup broth, and ½ cup poblano-Anaheim mixture and any accumulated juices until smooth, about 45 seconds.

4. Heat remaining 1 tablespoon oil in Dutch oven over medium heat until shimmering. Add onion-jalapeño mixture and cook until softened, 5 to 7 minutes. Stir in garlic, tomato paste, cumin, coriander, and ½ teaspoon salt and cook until tomato paste begins to darken, about 2 minutes. Stir in remaining 3 cups broth, scraping up any browned bits. Stir in pureed bean mixture, remaining poblano-Anaheim mixture, remaining cannellini beans, pinto beans, and corn cobs. Bring to simmer, then reduce heat to low and simmer gently until chili is thickened and flavorful, about 40 minutes.

5. Discard corn cobs. Stir in broiled corn kernels and cook until warmed through, about 1 minute. Off heat, stir in scallions, cilantro, and lime juice and season with salt and pepper to taste. Serve.

ULTIMATE VEGETARIAN CHILI

Serves 6 to 8   Total time: 4 hours (plus 8 hours soaking time)

WHY THIS RECIPE WORKS *This vegetarian version of classic chili is so flavorful and satisfying that even meat lovers will go back for seconds. For the chiles, we chose a combination of dried ancho and New Mexican chiles, toasted them in the oven until fragrant, and then ground them. Two kinds of beans plus bulgur gave it a substantial, hearty texture. A combination of umami-rich ingredients—tomatoes, mushrooms, and (surprisingly) soy sauce—added deep, savory flavor. Ground walnuts stirred in contributed even more savoriness, plus richness and body. We recommend a mix of at least two types of beans, one creamy (such as cannellini or navy) and one earthy (such as pinto, black, or red kidney). You will need to soak the beans for at least 8 hours or up to 24 hours. Serve the chili with lime wedges, sour cream, diced avocado, chopped red onion, and/or shredded Monterey Jack or cheddar cheese, as desired.*

Salt
1 pound (2½ cups) assorted dried beans, picked over and rinsed
1 ounce (about 2) ancho chiles
½ ounce (about 2) New Mexican chiles
½ ounce dried shiitake mushrooms, chopped coarse
4 teaspoons dried oregano
½ cup walnuts, toasted
1 (28-ounce) can diced tomatoes, drained with juice reserved
3 tablespoons tomato paste
3 tablespoons soy sauce
1 or 2 jalapeño chiles, stemmed and chopped coarse
6 garlic cloves, minced
¼ cup vegetable oil
2 pounds onions, chopped fine
1 tablespoon ground cumin
⅔ cup medium-grind bulgur
¼ cup minced fresh cilantro

1. Dissolve 3 tablespoons salt in 4 quarts cold water in large container. Add beans and soak at room temperature for at least 8 hours or up to 24 hours. Drain and rinse well.

2. Adjust oven rack to middle position and heat oven to 300 degrees. Arrange ancho and New Mexican chiles on rimmed baking sheet and toast until fragrant and puffed, about 8 minutes. Transfer to plate, let cool for 5 minutes, then remove stems and seeds. Working in batches, grind toasted chiles, mushrooms, and oregano in spice grinder until finely ground.

3. Process walnuts in food processor until finely ground, about 30 seconds; transfer to bowl. Process drained tomatoes, tomato paste, soy sauce, jalapeño, and garlic in food processor until tomatoes are finely chopped, about 45 seconds.

4. Heat oil in Dutch oven over medium-high heat until shimmering. Add onions and 1¼ teaspoons salt and cook, stirring occasionally, until onions begin to brown, 8 to 10 minutes. Reduce heat to medium, add ground chile mixture and cumin, and cook, stirring constantly, until fragrant, about 1 minute. Stir in beans and 7 cups water and bring to boil. Cover pot, transfer to oven, and cook for 45 minutes.

5. Stir in bulgur, ground walnuts, tomato mixture, and reserved tomato juice and continue to cook in oven, covered, until beans are fully tender, about 2 hours. Remove pot from oven, stir well, and let stand, uncovered, for 20 minutes. Stir in cilantro and season with salt to taste before serving.

～

MACCHERONI DI FUOCO

Serves 6 to 8   Total time: 55 minutes

WHY THIS RECIPE WORKS *"Pasta of fire" is truly an apt name for this deceptively simple southern Italian dish. A potent chile-garlic oil made from spicy, mildly fruity Calabrian peperoncini flakes dresses bucatini pasta both inside and out, allowing the pasta's hollow strands to fully absorb the delicious oil. Since the essential oils in chiles are oil-soluble, we bloomed the chile flakes in hot olive oil to produce complexly spicy flavor. We gently cooked whole cloves of garlic in the oil as well before mincing them. This allowed their flavor to become sweeter and rounder than if we had minced them before cooking. Allowing the oil to steep while we toasted bread crumbs (for a little crunch) and cooked our pasta boosted its intensity even more. Calabrian peperoncini flakes are available at most Italian markets; use more or less of them according to your heat tolerance. If you can't find them, about 1½ teaspoons of ground dried arbol chile is the best substitute. You can substitute spaghetti or linguini for the bucatini.*

½ cup plus 1 tablespoon extra-virgin olive oil
4 garlic cloves, peeled
2–4 teaspoons Calabrian peperoncini flakes
½ cup panko bread crumbs
Salt and pepper
1 pound bucatini
2 tablespoons chopped fresh parsley
Grated Parmesan cheese

1. Cook ¼ cup oil and garlic in 8-inch skillet over medium-low heat, stirring occasionally, until garlic begins to brown, 5 to 7 minutes. Stir in peperoncini flakes and cook until slightly darkened in color, about 45 seconds. Immediately transfer oil mixture to bowl and let cool for 5 minutes. Transfer garlic to cutting board, mince to paste, then return to oil mixture. Let stand until flavors meld, about 20 minutes.

2. Wipe skillet clean with paper towels. Cook panko, 1 tablespoon oil, and ⅛ teaspoon salt in now-empty skillet over medium heat, stirring often, until lightly toasted, 3 to 5 minutes. Transfer to clean bowl and set aside for serving.

3. Meanwhile, bring 4 quarts water to boil in large pot. Add pasta and 1 tablespoon salt and cook, stirring often, until al dente. Reserve ½ cup cooking water, then drain pasta and return it to pot. Add oil mixture, ¼ cup reserved cooking water, parsley, ½ teaspoon salt, and remaining ¼ cup oil and toss to combine. Adjust consistency with remaining reserved cooking water as needed. Season with salt and pepper to taste. Sprinkle individual portions with bread crumbs and Parmesan before serving.

assembling chiles rellenos

1. Cut 3-inch vertical slit in poblano, then cut out seed bulb with scissors.

2. Place 2 cubes of cheese inside each poblano.

3. Overlap opening and thread with skewer to seal.

4. Dredge poblano in flour, shaking gently to remove excess.

5. Holding poblano by stem, dunk in batter to coat and transfer to hot oil.

CHILES RELLENOS

Serves 4 to 6   Total time: 1 hour 15 minutes

WHY THIS RECIPE WORKS *Chiles rellenos (cheese-stuffed poblano chiles) are on the menu at virtually every Mexican restaurant. They always sound so good but in reality are often soggy and bland. This version comes to the rescue with a delicate and crispy coating for the poblanos, a deeply flavorful sauce, and plenty of comforting cheesiness. Broiling the chiles on a baking sheet for a few minutes was the best route to getting peppers just soft enough to stuff and fry without being mushy. Our tasters voted for mild, soft Muenster cheese in the filling. The beer batter coated the peppers just enough, creating a light, crispy, coating that enhanced what was inside. For the sauce, a mixture of tomato sauce, chicken broth, and spices, bolstered with the smoky, rich sauce from chipotles in adobo, was just right. Use a Dutch oven that holds 6 quarts or more. We prefer a mild lager for this recipe; nonalcoholic lagers will also work.*

SAUCE

- 1 tablespoon vegetable oil
- 1 teaspoon chili powder
- ½ teaspoon onion powder
- ¼ teaspoon garlic powder
- 1½ cups chicken broth
- 1 (15-ounce) can tomato sauce
- 1 teaspoon adobo sauce from canned chipotle chiles in adobo sauce
- 1 bay leaf
- 1 tablespoon lime juice
  Salt and pepper

CHILES

- 6 (4- to 5-ounce) poblano chiles
- 8 ounces Muenster cheese cut into 12 (1-inch) cubes
- 6 (4-inch) wooden skewers
- 1½ cups all-purpose flour
- 1¼ cups (5 ounces) cornstarch
- 2 teaspoons baking powder
  Salt
- 1½ cups beer
- 3 quarts peanut or vegetable oil

1. For the sauce Heat oil in medium saucepan over medium-high heat until shimmering. Add chili powder, onion powder, and garlic powder and cook until fragrant, about 30 seconds. Stir in broth, tomato sauce, adobo sauce, and bay leaf and bring to boil. Reduce heat to medium and cook at vigorous simmer until reduced to 2 cups, 12 to 15 minutes. Discard bay leaf, stir in lime juice, and season with salt and pepper to taste. Remove from heat and cover to keep warm.

2. **For the chiles** Meanwhile, adjust oven rack 6 inches from broiler element and heat broiler. Line rimmed baking sheet with aluminum foil. Evenly space poblanos on sheet and broil until skins just begin to blister on first side, 3 to 5 minutes. Flip poblanos and continue to broil until skins just begin to blister on second side, about 3 minutes. Set poblanos aside until cool enough to handle, about 10 minutes. Adjust oven temperature to 200 degrees.

3. Peel off any loose skin from poblanos, if desired. Working with 1 poblano at a time, leaving stem intact and starting at stem end of pepper, make 3-inch-long vertical incision down 1 side of chile. Use kitchen shears to cut away interior seed bulb, then use spoon to scoop out and discard bulb and seeds. (Some tearing may occur, and it's OK if you don't remove all of the seeds.)

4. Place 2 cubes Muenster inside each poblano. Overlap poblano opening and thread with skewer to seal. (Use 1 additional skewer per chile if necessary.) Allow top of skewer to remain exposed by at least ½ inch for easy removal.

5. Place ½ cup flour in shallow dish. Combine remaining 1 cup flour, cornstarch, baking powder, and 1 teaspoon salt in medium bowl. Whisk beer into flour mixture until smooth.

6. Set wire rack in rimmed baking sheet and line rack with triple layer of paper towels. Add oil to large Dutch oven until it measures 2 inches deep and heat over medium-high heat to 375 degrees.

7. Working with 3 poblanos at a time, dredge poblanos in flour, shaking gently to remove excess. Holding each poblano by its stem, dunk in batter to evenly coat and then transfer to hot oil. Fry until golden and crispy, 4 to 5 minutes, turning frequently for even cooking. Adjust burner, if necessary, to maintain oil temperature between 350 and 375 degrees.

8. Transfer fried poblanos to prepared rack and let drain for 30 seconds. Season poblanos with salt, remove skewers, and transfer sheet to oven to keep warm. Return oil to 375 degrees and repeat with remaining poblanos and batter. Serve with sauce.

THAI GREEN CURRY WITH CHICKEN, BROCCOLI, AND MUSHROOMS

Serves 4   Total time: 50 minutes

WHY THIS RECIPE WORKS *Thai curries embrace a delicate balance of tastes, textures, and colors that come together to create a harmonious whole. This authentic green curry is perfumed with green chiles, lemon grass, and coconut milk. A food processor made quick work of blending together the curry paste, made with Thai chiles, shallots, lemongrass, cilantro, garlic, ginger, coriander, and cumin. To approximate the flavor of traditional makrut lime leaves, we added grated lime zest. We then cooked coconut milk with the curry paste to make the silky, intensely rich sauce. With the inclusion of chicken, broccoli, mushrooms, and bell pepper, all you need is some white rice to accompany it. If you can't find Thai chiles, substitute serranos or jalapeños.*

GREEN CURRY PASTE

- ⅓ cup water
- 12 green Thai chiles, stemmed, seeded, and chopped
- 8 garlic cloves, peeled
- 3 shallots, quartered
- 2 lemon grass stalks, trimmed to bottom 6 inches, and sliced thin
- 2 tablespoons grated lime zest (3 limes)
- 2 tablespoons vegetable oil
- 2 tablespoons minced fresh cilantro stems
- 1 tablespoon grated fresh ginger
- 2 teaspoons ground coriander
- 1 teaspoon ground cumin
- 1 teaspoon salt

CURRY

- 2 (14-ounce) cans coconut milk, not shaken
- 2 tablespoons fish sauce
- 2 tablespoons packed brown sugar
- 1½ pounds boneless, skinless chicken breasts, trimmed and sliced thin
  Salt
- 8 ounces broccoli florets, cut into 1-inch pieces
- 4 ounces white mushrooms, trimmed and quartered
- 1 red bell pepper, stemmed, seeded, and cut into ¼-inch-wide strips
- 1 green Thai chile, stemmed, seeded, and quartered lengthwise
- ½ cup fresh basil leaves
- ½ cup fresh mint leaves
- 1 tablespoon lime juice

1. **For the green curry paste** Process all ingredients in food processor to smooth paste, about 3 minutes, scraping down sides of bowl as needed; set aside.

2. **For the curry** Spoon off 1 cup of top layer of cream from one can of coconut milk. Whisk coconut cream and green curry paste in Dutch oven until combined. Bring to simmer over high heat and cook until nearly all liquid is evaporated, 5 to 7 minutes. Reduce heat to medium-high and continue to cook, whisking constantly, until cream mixture is separated and curry paste is very aromatic, 4 to 10 minutes.

3. Whisk remaining coconut milk, fish sauce, and sugar into sauce in pot, return to simmer, and cook until sauce thickens, about 5 minutes. Season chicken with salt. Stir chicken, broccoli, and mushrooms into sauce and cook until vegetables are nearly tender, about 5 minutes. Stir in bell pepper and Thai chile, and cook until bell pepper is crisp-tender, about 2 minutes. Off heat, stir in basil, mint, and lime juice. Serve.

JERK CHICKEN

Serves 4   Total time: 1 hour 45 minutes

WHY THIS RECIPE WORKS *Spicy, smoky Jamaican jerk is one of the world's great barbecue traditions. Meat (traditionally chicken or pork) is rubbed with an intensely flavored liquidy paste made from fiery Scotch bonnet chiles, allspice berries, herbs, and spices, and then it is smoked over pimento wood. Our jerk marinade has plenty of bold ingredients, including habanero chiles (in place of the Scotch bonnets), scallions, garlic, lime zest, and mustard for zingy brightness, and brown sugar, nutmeg, and ginger for warm sweetness. It's potent enough to infuse the chicken in just*

Jerk Chicken

30 minutes. We substituted easy-to-find hickory chips for the traditional pimento wood, and we smoked allspice berries, thyme, and rosemary along with the wood chips to give our chicken a great authentic flavor that mimicked pimento's sweet, herbal smoke.

JERK MARINADE
- 1½ tablespoons coriander seeds
- 1 tablespoon allspice berries
- 1 tablespoon black peppercorns
- 1–3 habanero chiles, stemmed, seeded, and quartered
- 8 scallions, chopped
- 6 garlic cloves, peeled
- 3 tablespoons vegetable oil
- 2 tablespoons soy sauce
- 2 tablespoons grated lime zest (3 limes), plus lime wedges for serving
- 2 tablespoons yellow mustard
- 1 tablespoon dried thyme
- 1 tablespoon ground ginger
- 1 tablespoon packed brown sugar
- 2¼ teaspoons salt
- 2 teaspoons dried basil
- ½ teaspoon dried rosemary
- ½ teaspoon ground nutmeg

CHICKEN
- 3 pounds bone-in chicken pieces (split breasts cut in half crosswise, drumsticks, and/or thighs), trimmed
- 2 tablespoons allspice berries
- 2 tablespoons dried thyme
- 2 tablespoons dried rosemary
- 2 tablespoons water
- 1 cup wood chips (preferably hickory), soaked in water for 15 minutes and drained

1. For the jerk marinade Grind coriander seeds, allspice berries, and peppercorns in spice grinder or mortar and pestle until coarsely ground. Transfer spices to blender jar. Add remaining ingredients and process to smooth paste, 1 to 3 minutes, scraping down sides of blender jar as necessary. Transfer marinade to 1-gallon zipper-lock bag.

2. For the chicken Add chicken pieces to bag with marinade and toss to coat; press out air and seal bag. Let sit at room

temperature for at least 30 minutes while preparing grill, flipping bag after 15 minutes. (Marinated chicken can be refrigerated for up to 24 hours.)

3. Combine allspice berries, thyme, rosemary, and water in bowl and set aside for 15 minutes, until moistened. Using large piece of heavy-duty aluminum foil, wrap soaked chips and moistened allspice mixture in 8 by 4½-inch foil packet. (Make sure chips do not poke holes in sides or bottom of packet.) Cut 2 evenly spaced 2-inch slits in top of packet.

4a. For a charcoal grill Open bottom vent halfway. Arrange 1 quart unlit charcoal briquettes in single layer over half of grill. Light large chimney starter one-third filled with charcoal briquettes (2 quarts). When top coals are partially covered with ash, pour on top of unlit charcoal, keeping coals arranged over half of grill. Place wood chip packet on coals. Set cooking grate in place, cover, and open lid vent halfway. Heat grill until hot and wood chips are smoking, about 5 minutes.

4b. For a gas grill Remove cooking grate and place wood chip packet directly on primary burner. Set grate in place, turn all burners to high, cover, and heat grill until hot and wood chips are smoking, 15 to 25 minutes. Turn primary burner to medium and turn off other burner(s).

5. Clean and oil cooking grate. Place chicken skin side up on cooler side of grill, as far away from fire as possible, with thighs closest to heat and breasts farthest away. Cover (positioning lid vent over chicken if using charcoal) and cook for 30 minutes.

6. Move chicken skin side down to hotter side of grill. Cook until browned and skin renders, 3 to 6 minutes. Using tongs, flip chicken pieces and cook until browned on second side and breasts register 160 degrees and thighs and drumsticks register 175 degrees, 5 to 12 minutes.

7. Transfer chicken to serving platter, tent with foil, and let rest for 5 to 10 minutes. Serve warm or at room temperature with lime wedges.

CHICKEN MOLE POBLANO
Serves 6 to 8   Total time: 1 hour 45 minutes
WHY THIS RECIPE WORKS *Although "mole" is used to describe a wide variety of Mexican sauces, the most famous is mole poblano, a dark, complex, aromatic sauce typically served with chicken or turkey. Traditionally, it relies on several types of chiles for its deep spiciness, counterbalanced by the bittersweet richness of chocolate and thickened by ground almonds. For simplicity, we pared our recipe down to ancho chiles, for a robust base, and chipotles, for smoky, intense flavor. We also added warmth and a touch of sweetness with cayenne, cinnamon, cloves, and raisins. Our preference is to cook the chicken with the skin on, but it can be removed before cooking, if desired. Serve with white rice and/or corn tortillas.*

- 3 ounces (6 to 8) ancho chiles, stemmed, seeded, and torn into 1-inch pieces (1½ cups)
- 3½ cups chicken broth
- ½ cup raisins
- 1 onion, chopped
- ¼ cup vegetable oil
- 2 tablespoons tomato paste
- 4 garlic cloves, peeled
- 1 tablespoon minced canned chipotle chile in adobo sauce
- ¾ cup sliced almonds
- 1 slice hearty white sandwich bread, torn into 1-inch pieces
- 3 tablespoons sesame seeds
- 2 teaspoons salt
- 1–2 teaspoons cayenne pepper
- 1 teaspoon dried oregano
- ½ teaspoon dried thyme
- ½ teaspoon ground cinnamon
- ½ teaspoon ground cumin
- ½ teaspoon ground coriander
- ½ teaspoon pepper
- 2 ounces unsweetened chocolate, chopped
- 4 pounds bone-in chicken pieces (split breasts cut in half, drumsticks, and/or thighs), trimmed

1. Adjust oven rack to middle position and heat oven to 325 degrees. Place anchos on rimmed baking sheet and toast until fragrant and pliable, about 5 minutes. Combine toasted anchos, 2 cups broth, and raisins in bowl, cover, and microwave until steaming,

about 2 minutes. Let sit until softened, about 5 minutes. Drain mixture in fine-mesh strainer set over bowl, reserving liquid.

2. Process onion, 2 tablespoons oil, tomato paste, garlic, chipotle, and ancho-raisin mixture in food processor until smooth, about 5 minutes, scraping down sides of bowl as needed. Add almonds, bread, 2 tablespoons sesame seeds, salt, cayenne, oregano, thyme, cinnamon, cumin, coriander, pepper, and ¼ cup reserved ancho soaking liquid and continue to process to smooth paste, about 3 minutes, scraping down sides of bowl as needed and adding additional soaking liquid if necessary.

3. Heat remaining 2 tablespoons oil in Dutch oven over medium-high heat until shimmering. Add mole paste and cook, stirring frequently, until steaming, about 3 minutes. Stir in chocolate, transfer pot to oven, and cook, uncovered, for 30 minutes, stirring twice. (Paste will darken during cooking.) (Paste can be refrigerated for up to 1 week or frozen for up to 1 month.)

4. Place pot over medium-high heat and whisk remaining reserved soaking liquid and remaining 1½ cups broth into mole paste until smooth. Arrange chicken pieces in even

layer in pot, cover, reduce heat to low, and cook until breasts register 160 degrees and thighs and drumsticks register 175 degrees, 25 to 30 minutes, stirring halfway through cooking. Transfer chicken pieces to serving platter as they finish cooking. Pour sauce over chicken, garnish with remaining 1 tablespoon sesame seeds, and serve.

STIR-FRIED THAI-STYLE BEEF WITH CHILES AND SHALLOTS

Serves 4   Total time: 50 minutes

WHY THIS RECIPE WORKS *Two types of chiles bring the heat to this sophisticated Thai stir-fry: a generous amount of sliced serrano chiles, plus Asian chili-garlic paste, a versatile, easily controllable heat source. First we marinated the sliced steak in a flavorful blend of fish sauce, white pepper, citrusy coriander, and a little light brown sugar; the beef needed only 15 minutes to develop full flavor. Then we browned the beef, stir-fried the serranos and shallots, and combined everything with the stir-fry sauce. Fresh herbs stirred in at the end added brightness, and peanuts made for a crunchy garnish. White pepper lends this stir-fry a unique flavor; black pepper is not a good substitute. Serve with steamed jasmine rice.*

BEEF STIR-FRY

- 1 tablespoon fish sauce
- 1 teaspoon packed light brown sugar
- ¾ teaspoon ground coriander
- ⅛ teaspoon ground white pepper
- 2 pounds beef blade steaks, trimmed and sliced crosswise ¼ inch thick

SAUCE AND GARNISH

- 2 tablespoons fish sauce
- 2 tablespoons rice vinegar
- 2 tablespoons water
- 1 tablespoon packed light brown sugar
- 1 tablespoon Asian chili-garlic sauce
- 3 garlic cloves, minced
- 3 tablespoons vegetable oil
- 3 serrano chiles, stemmed, seeded, and sliced thin
- 3 shallots, peeled, quartered, and layers separated
- ½ cup fresh mint leaves, torn
- ½ cup fresh cilantro leaves
- ⅓ cup dry-roasted peanuts, chopped
  Lime wedges

1. For the stir-fry Combine fish sauce, sugar, coriander, and white pepper in large bowl. Add beef, toss well to coat, and let sit for 15 minutes.

2. For the sauce and garnish Whisk fish sauce, vinegar, water, sugar, and chili-garlic sauce in small bowl until sugar dissolves; set aside. In second small bowl, combine garlic and 1 teaspoon oil; set aside.

3. Heat 2 teaspoons oil in 12-inch nonstick skillet over high heat until just smoking. Add one-third of beef in single layer and cook, without stirring, for 2 minutes. Stir beef and continue to cook until browned, about 30 seconds; transfer to bowl. Repeat with 4 teaspoons oil and remaining beef in 2 batches; transfer to bowl.

4. Heat remaining 2 teaspoons oil in now-empty skillet over medium heat until shimmering. Add serranos and shallots and cook, stirring frequently, until beginning to soften, 3 to 4 minutes. Push chile mixture to sides of skillet. Add garlic mixture to center and cook, mashing mixture into pan, until fragrant, about 30 seconds. Stir mixture into chile mixture.

Ground Beef and Cheese Enchiladas

5. Return beef and any accumulated juices to skillet and toss to combine. Add fish sauce mixture, increase heat to high, and cook, stirring constantly, until thickened and slightly reduced, about 30 seconds. Off heat, stir in half of mint and cilantro. Serve with lime wedges and sprinkle individual portions with peanuts and remaining herbs.

GROUND BEEF AND CHEESE ENCHILADAS

Serves 4 to 6   Total time: 1 hour 15 minutes

WHY THIS RECIPE WORKS *The combination of dried ancho chiles and chipotles in adobo in the enchilada sauce brought an authentic, deeper, smokier flavor to this classic Tex-Mex dish than what could be achieved using commercial chili powder. The spices added to the beef, along with the rich sauce and melted cheese, elevated the filling to a higher level. Brushing the tortillas lightly with oil and briefly baking them helped to waterproof them so that they didn't get soggy when baked. Fresh herbs and a spritz of lime brightened the dish and provided balance for the rich, cheesy filling. Don't use ground beef that's fattier than 90 percent lean or the dish will be greasy.*

SAUCE

1½ ounces (3 or 4) dried ancho chiles, stemmed, seeded, and torn into 1-inch pieces (¾ cup)
2 cups beef broth
1 tablespoon minced canned chipotle chile in adobo sauce
2 tablespoons vegetable oil
2 onions, chopped fine
6 garlic cloves, minced
¼ cup tomato paste
1 teaspoon ground cumin
Salt

ENCHILADAS

3 tablespoons vegetable oil
1 pound 90 percent lean ground beef
1 teaspoon ground cumin
1 teaspoon ground coriander
Salt
8 ounces Monterey Jack cheese, shredded (2 cups)
¼ cup minced fresh cilantro

12 (6-inch) corn tortillas
2 scallions, sliced thin on bias
Sour cream
Lime wedges

1. For the sauce Adjust oven rack to middle position and heat oven to 400 degrees. Heat anchos in 12-inch nonstick skillet over medium-high heat, stirring frequently, until fragrant, 2 to 3 minutes. Combine anchos and broth in bowl, cover, and microwave until steaming, about 2 minutes. Let sit until softened, about 5 minutes. Transfer anchos and broth to blender and add chipotle.

2. Heat oil in now-empty skillet over medium heat until shimmering. Add onions and cook, stirring occasionally, until translucent, about 5 minutes. Add garlic and cook until fragrant, about 1 minute. Transfer half of onion mixture to large bowl and set aside. Return skillet with remaining onion mixture to medium heat and add tomato paste and cumin. Cook, stirring frequently, until tomato paste begins to darken, 3 to 5 minutes. Transfer onion mixture in skillet to blender with ancho mixture and process until smooth, about 1 minute. Season sauce with salt to taste and wipe skillet clean with paper towels.

3. For the enchiladas Heat 1 tablespoon oil in now-empty skillet over medium heat until shimmering. Add beef, cumin, coriander, and ½ teaspoon salt and cook for 2 minutes, breaking meat into ¼-inch pieces with wooden spoon. Add reserved onion mixture (do not wash bowl) and continue to cook until beef is no longer pink, 3 to 4 minutes. Return beef mixture to bowl; add 1½ cups Monterey Jack, 2 tablespoons cilantro, and ¼ cup sauce and stir to combine. Season with salt to taste.

4. Spread ½ cup sauce over bottom of 13 by 9-inch baking dish. Brush both sides of tortillas with remaining 2 tablespoons oil. Arrange tortillas on rimmed baking sheet, overlapping as needed, and bake until warm and pliable, about 5 minutes. Spread ¼ cup filling down center of each tortilla. Roll each tortilla tightly around filling and place seam side down in dish, arranging enchiladas in 2 rows across width of dish.

5. Spread remaining sauce over top of enchiladas. Sprinkle with remaining ½ cup Monterey Jack. Bake until cheese is lightly browned and sauce is bubbling at edges, about 15 minutes. Let cool for 10 minutes. Sprinkle with scallions and remaining 2 tablespoons cilantro. Serve with sour cream and lime wedges.

SHREDDED BEEF TACOS WITH CABBAGE-CARROT SLAW

Serves 6 to 8   Total time: 3 hours

WHY THIS RECIPE WORKS *The aromas of a fragrant shredded beef taco filling that has been braised until meltingly tender along with just the right mix of chiles and spices will transport you to Mexico. To achieve flavorful browning without having to sear the short ribs, we raised the beef up out of the braising liquid by resting it on onion rounds. Next, we created an ancho chile–spiked braising liquid that would infuse the beef and act as the sauce base. Beer provided depth, and the smoky-sweet anchos gave the sauce a rounded, gently spicy kick. Cumin, cinnamon, cloves, oregano, and bay leaves added warmth and complexity. A bright, tangy slaw with the green heat of jalapeños provided a punchy counterbalance to the rich, ancho-smoky meat. Use a full-bodied lager or ale here. Warm the tortillas in the microwave for 60 to 90 seconds, covered with a damp dish towel.*

BEEF

1½ cups beer
½ cup cider vinegar
2 ounces (4 to 6) dried ancho chiles, stemmed, seeded, and torn into 1-inch pieces (1 cup)
2 tablespoons tomato paste
6 garlic cloves, lightly crushed and peeled
3 bay leaves
2 teaspoons ground cumin
2 teaspoons dried oregano
Salt and pepper
½ teaspoon ground cloves
½ teaspoon ground cinnamon
1 large onion, sliced into ½-inch-thick rounds
3 pounds boneless beef short ribs, trimmed and cut into 2-inch pieces

CABBAGE-CARROT SLAW

- 1 cup cider vinegar
- ½ cup water
- 1 tablespoon sugar
- 1½ teaspoons salt
- ½ head green cabbage, cored and sliced thin (6 cups)
- 1 onion, sliced thin
- 1 carrot, peeled and shredded
- 1 jalapeño chile, stemmed, seeded, and minced
- 1 teaspoon dried oregano
- 1 cup chopped fresh cilantro

- 18 (6-inch) corn tortillas, warmed
- 4 ounces queso fresco, crumbled (1 cup)
  Lime wedges

1. **For the beef** Adjust oven rack to lower-middle position and heat oven to 325 degrees. Combine beer, vinegar, anchos, tomato paste, garlic, bay leaves, cumin, oregano, 2 teaspoons salt, ½ teaspoon pepper, cloves, and cinnamon in Dutch oven. Arrange onion rounds in single layer on bottom of pot, then place beef on top of onion rounds in single layer. Cover, transfer to oven, and cook until meat is well browned and tender, 2½ to 3 hours.

2. **For the cabbage-carrot slaw** While beef cooks, whisk vinegar, water, sugar, and salt in large bowl until sugar and salt are dissolved. Add cabbage, onion, carrot, jalapeño, and oregano and toss to combine. Cover and refrigerate for at least 1 hour or up to 24 hours. Drain slaw and stir in cilantro just before serving.

3. Remove pot from oven. Using slotted spoon, transfer beef to large bowl, cover loosely with aluminum foil, and set aside. Strain cooking liquid into fat separator and let sit for 5 minutes (do not wash pot). Discard onion rounds and bay leaves. Transfer remaining solids to blender. Pour 1 cup defatted liquid into blender (adding water as needed to equal 1 cup), along with reserved solids, and blend until smooth, about 2 minutes. Transfer sauce to now-empty pot.

4. Using 2 forks, shred beef into bite-size pieces. Bring sauce to simmer over medium heat. Add shredded beef and stir to coat. Season with salt to taste.

5. Spoon small amount of beef into each warm tortilla and serve, passing slaw, queso fresco, and lime wedges separately.

TACOS AL PASTOR

Serves 6 to 8   Total time: 3 hours
WHY THIS RECIPE WORKS *The traditional filling for "shepherd-style tacos" is made from slices of chile-marinated pork shoulder that are tightly packed onto a vertical spit and roasted. The pork is often topped with a whole pineapple, the juices of which drip down and help caramelize the meat. Thin shavings of the roasted pork and pineapple are carved off into warm tortillas and topped with raw onion, avocado, cilantro, and a squeeze of fresh lime. Since most home cooks don't own a vertical rotisserie, here is our translation for your home kitchen (you're welcome). To infuse the richly marbled pork and complement the pineapple, we chose flavorful fruity-smoky dried guajillo chiles for the tomato-based marinade. To replicate the crisp, browned exterior of authentic versions, we grilled the pork slabs and pineapple rounds over a hot fire. Boneless pork butt roast is often labeled Boston butt in the supermarket.*

- 1¾ ounces (12 to 14) dried guajillo chiles, stemmed, seeded and torn into ½-inch pieces (1½ cups)
- 1½ cups water
- 1¼ pounds plum tomatoes, cored and quartered
- 8 garlic cloves, peeled
- 4 bay leaves
  Salt and pepper
- ¾ teaspoon sugar
- ½ teaspoon ground cumin
- ⅛ teaspoon ground cloves
- 3 pounds boneless pork butt roast, fat cap trimmed to ¼ inch thick, pork sliced against grain into ½-inch-thick slabs
- 1½ teaspoons lime juice, plus lime wedges for serving
- ½ pineapple, peeled, cored, and cut into ½-inch-thick rings
  Vegetable oil
- 18 (6-inch) corn tortillas
- ½ cup chopped fresh cilantro

1. Toast guajillos in Dutch oven over medium heat, stirring frequently, until fragrant, 2 to 6 minutes. Stir in water, tomatoes, garlic, bay leaves, 2 teaspoons salt, ½ teaspoon pepper, sugar, cumin, and cloves and bring to simmer over medium-high heat. Cover, reduce heat to low, and simmer, stirring occasionally, until guajillos are softened and tomatoes mash easily, about 20 minutes.

2. Transfer guajillo mixture to blender and process until smooth, about 1 minute. Strain puree through fine-mesh strainer set over bowl, pressing on solids to extract as much liquid as possible; discard solids and return puree to pot.

3. Submerge pork in sauce and bring to simmer over medium heat. Partially cover, reduce heat to medium-low, and gently simmer until pork is tender but not falling apart, about 1½ hours, flipping and rearranging pork halfway through cooking. (Pork and sauce can be refrigerated for up to 2 days.)

4. Transfer pork to large plate, season both sides with salt, and cover tightly with aluminum foil. Whisk sauce to recombine and transfer ½ cup to bowl for grilling. Pour off all but ½ cup sauce left in pot (reserve excess sauce for another use). Stir lime juice into sauce in pot and season with salt to taste. Brush pineapple with oil and season with salt.

5a. For a charcoal grill Open bottom vent completely. Light large chimney starter filled with charcoal briquettes (6 quarts). When top coals are partially covered with ash, pour evenly over grill. Set cooking grate in place, cover, and open lid vent completely. Heat grill until hot, about 5 minutes.

5b. For a gas grill Turn all burners to high, cover, and heat grill until hot, about 15 minutes. Turn all burners to medium.

6. Clean and oil cooking grate. Place pineapple on grill and cook, turning as needed, until softened and caramelized, 10 to 15 minutes; transfer to cutting board. Meanwhile, brush 1 side of pork with ¼ cup reserved sauce, then place on grill, sauce side down. Cook until well browned and crisp, 5 to 7 minutes. Repeat with second side using remaining ¼ cup reserved sauce; transfer to cutting board and tent with foil.

7. Working in batches, grill tortillas, turning as needed, until warm and spotty brown, about 30 seconds; wrap tightly in foil to keep warm.

8. Chop pineapple and transfer to serving bowl. Cut pork crosswise into ⅛-inch pieces. Bring sauce in pot to simmer over medium heat. Off heat, stir in sliced pork. Spoon small amount of pork into each tortilla and serve, passing cilantro, pineapple, and lime wedges separately.

CARNE ADOVADA

Serves 6   Total time: 3 hours 30 minutes

WHY THIS RECIPE WORKS *Carne adovada is a classic New Mexican dish made from chunks of pork stewed in a thick red chile sauce. It's saucy enough to be served over rice or in a bowl with some accompanying toasted corn tortillas, but the meat can also be used as a filling for tacos and burritos. Although it takes a little while in the oven, it's a very easy dish to prepare, and it will give you the basis for several delicious meals. If you can't find New Mexican chiles, you can substitute dried California chiles. We suggest using Mexican oregano if you have it, though Mediterranean oregano is a suitable substitute. Boneless pork butt roast is often labeled Boston butt in the supermarket. Serve this with rice and beans, crispy roasted potatoes, or flour tortillas with shredded lettuce, chopped tomato, and sliced avocado.*

1 (3½-to 4-pound) boneless pork butt roast, trimmed and cut into 1½-inch pieces
  Salt
4 ounces (14 to 16) dried New Mexican chiles, stemmed, seeded, and torn into 1-inch pieces (3 cups)
2 tablespoons honey
2 tablespoons distilled white vinegar
5 garlic cloves, peeled
2 teaspoons dried Mexican oregano
2 teaspoons ground cumin
½ teaspoon cayenne pepper
⅛ teaspoon ground cloves
  Lime wedges

1. Toss pork and 1½ teaspoons salt together in bowl; refrigerate for 1 hour. Combine New Mexican chiles and 4 cups boiling water in medium bowl. Cover and let sit until chiles are softened, about 30 minutes. Adjust oven rack to lower-middle position and heat oven to 325 degrees.

2. Drain chiles, reserving 2 cups soaking liquid. Process chiles, honey, vinegar, garlic, oregano, cumin, cayenne, cloves, and ½ teaspoon salt in blender to thick paste, about 30 seconds. With blender running, slowly add reserved soaking liquid and blend until smooth, about 3 minutes.

3. Combine pork and chile sauce in Dutch oven, stirring to coat, then bring to boil over high heat. Cover pot, transfer to oven, and cook until pork is tender and fork inserted into pork meets little resistance, 2 to 2½ hours.

4. Using wooden spoon or rubber spatula, scrape any browned bits from sides of pot and stir into pork until sauce is smooth and homogeneous. Let stand, uncovered, for 10 minutes. Season with salt to taste. Serve with lime wedges.

CORN

In American history, corn is inextricably linked to pre-Colonial days and the tribes of Indians who used easy-to-grow and long-keeping corn as both sustenance and trading currency. The history of corn in the Americas is so long and storied that entire books have been written about the path it forged through our farmlands and economy.

These days, most of the corn we eat has been crossbred for sweeter, plumper ears that keep hold of their fresh flavor and tender texture. But when those first ears of corn start appearing in farmers' markets and local supermarkets, most of us in the test kitchen turn giddy with excitement, especially since here in the Northeast, we often have to wait until late July or August for true local corn. And then the season is practically over by Labor Day. Not so in the South and the Midwest, where corn season happily stretches across the entire summer. Regardless of where you live, when fresh corn is

piled high, it's time to get creative. We love perfect boiled or grilled corn (check out our foolproof methods for both), but it's great prepared so many other ways, too. Corn has a natural affinity for fat and dairy, so it's no surprise that in Mexico they love to slather it with a spicy mayo mixture after grilling it (see page 160). It makes a rich, creamy Roasted Corn and Poblano Chowder, as well as a transcendent sauce for a summer pasta dish in Creamy Corn Bucatini with Ricotta and Basil. And there's a reason why creamed corn goes back hundreds of years—all you need is water, fresh corn, and cream to turn out a decadent side dish. This is Yankee thrift at its best.

From salsa and relish to fritters and spoonbread to shrimp boil and succotash, there is so much regional history behind the dishes that put corn front and center, and you will find them all here.

shopping and storage

Regardless of variety, look for plump ears with green, pliable husks that are closely wrapped around the ear and clean, pale golden or white silk extending from the tops (the more silk, the better, since it is an indicator of the number of kernels). Don't peel back the husk and silk (which makes ears less desirable for other shoppers). Instead, gently press on the kernels through the husk; they should feel tightly packed, plump, and firm, with no spots where it feels like there's an absence of kernels.

To store corn (for up to a few days), wrap it in a wet paper bag and then in a plastic produce bag and refrigerate it. If you want to keep your fresh summer corn sweet all year round, you can freeze it. Blanch the husked ears in boiling water for 5 minutes to deactivate the enzyme that causes the sugar to convert to starch, and then immediately place the ears in a bowl of ice water to halt the cooking. Spread the cooled corn on a clean kitchen towel to dry. Place the dry ears in a zipper-lock freezer bag, squeeze out the air, seal, and freeze for up to six months. The corn may lose some of its crisp texture, but the kernels fare well in cooked recipes.

how sweet it is

It used to be that when you purchased fresh corn, there was a mad dash to bring it home and cook it pronto, before the sugars inside the kernels converted to starch. But those are bygone days. Most corn varieties sold in supermarkets today—whether yellow, white, or bicolor—are classified as "supersweet" and often have sugar contents approaching 35 percent, which is nearly three times higher than the corn of decades ago. This means that the conversion from sugar to starch occurs much more slowly, making it a myth that fresh corn only tastes good the day it is picked. But, if you are buying true local corn, from a small farmer, you may be purchasing a "standard" or heirloom variety, which will start the conversion from sugar to starch more quickly. If shopping at a farmers' market, be sure to ask the vendor for advice.

vegetable prep

Cutting Corn Kernels from the Cob

To cut kernels off an ear of corn, hold ear on its end inside large, wide bowl and use paring knife to cut off kernels. Depending on size of corn, you will get between ½ cup and ¾ cup of kernels per ear.

Milking Corn

Corn "milk" is the term for the sweet pulp and juices that are left behind when kernels are stripped from the cob. Many recipes call for capturing this flavorful thickening liquid to add to dishes such as soups and chowders, risotto, or polenta.

After removing corn kernels from cob, firmly scrape each cob with back of butter knife to remove milk and pulp.

Dish Rack–Drained Corn

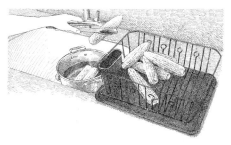

A clean, empty dish rack accommodates many more ears of corn than a colander. Put the ears into the dish rack as you remove them from the pot.

pantry corn products

The United States produces 42 percent of the world's corn—three times as much as any other nation. Much of that is produced for livestock feed and processed foods. Even so, with all that corn, it's little wonder that we use it in so many ways other than just as a vegetable.

POPCORN Kernels of popping corn consist of a moist, starchy center sealed inside a tough, dried hull. Heating the kernels softens the starch and turns the moisture into steam, which increases pressure inside until the hull pops into a "flake."

CORNMEAL Corn kernels are dried and then ground into cornmeal. Stone-ground cornmeal is coarse-textured; finely ground cornmeal is made using steel rollers. Polenta and grits are both types of cornmeal.

CORNSTARCH This thickener is made from the dried ground corn endosperm (which contains starch and protein). It's often used to thicken sauces, gravies, pie fillings, and other liquids.

CORN SYRUP Corn syrup is made from cornstarch, a complicated process that results in a sweet food syrup. It is about 45 percent as sweet as sugar, is very thick, and doesn't crystallize. The corn syrup in the baking aisle at the supermarket is not the same as the high-fructose corn syrup used in processed foods.

CORN OIL A relatively modern invention, corn oil was refined for cooking in 1910. The oil is bleached and deodorized; only some trace amounts of flavor compounds remain.

save the cobs for corn stock

Stripped corn cobs will produce a flavorful stock that can enrich polenta, cornbread, and vegetable soups. Cut 8 corn cobs into quarters. Place in large saucepan with 2 quarts water, bring to simmer, and cook for 15 minutes. Strain liquid through fine-mesh strainer. Makes about 7½ cups.

Foolproof Boiled Corn
with Chili-Lime Salt

FOOLPROOF BOILED CORN WITH CHILI-LIME SALT

Serves 4 to 6   Total time: 30 minutes

WHY THIS RECIPE WORKS *You might think that you don't need a recipe for boiled corn, but who hasn't pulled out the ears too early only to reveal underdone, starchy kernels or let them sit in the cooling water too long, turning mushy and shriveled? Corn season is so fleeting that we wanted a foolproof method for perfect corn every time. There are two key variables at play: starches and pectin. As corn heats, the starches in the kernels absorb water, swell, and gelatinize, and the corn "milk" becomes smoother, silkier, and more translucent. Simultaneously, the pectin (essentially the glue holding together the cell walls inside each kernel) dissolves, so the corn softens. The more pectin that dissolves, the mushier the corn becomes. To produce perfectly done, juicy corn every time, we learned that the ideal doneness range is 150 to 170 degrees—when the starches have gelatinized but a minimum amount of the pectin has dissolved. Here's how you get there: bringing a measured amount of water to a boil, shutting off the heat, dropping in six ears of corn, and letting the corn stand for at least 10 minutes. Even better, the method is flexible: It can accommodate six to eight ears of different sizes, and the ears can sit in the water for up to 30 minutes without overcooking.*

CORN
- 6 ears corn, husks and silk removed
- Unsalted butter, softened
- Salt

CHILI-LIME SALT
- 2 tablespoons kosher salt
- 4 teaspoons chili powder
- ¾ teaspoon grated lime zest

1. **For the corn** Bring 4 quarts water to boil in Dutch oven over high heat. Off heat, add corn, cover, and let sit for at least 10 minutes or up to 30 minutes.

2. **For the chili-lime salt** Combine all ingredients in bowl; set aside.

3. Transfer corn to serving platter and serve immediately, passing softened butter and chili-lime salt separately.

GARDEN-FRESH CORN WITH ZUCCHINI AND HERBS

Serves 4   Total time: 30 minutes

WHY THIS RECIPE WORKS *We love fresh corn on the cob during its all-too-brief season, and we're always on the search for new corn inspiration to jazz up this summer favorite. In this side dish, a variety of fresh garden herbs and a light touch with the cooking are the keys. To capture all of the fresh corn's natural sweetness, we "milked" the cob by scraping it with the back of a knife. We then briefly sautéed the corn to bring out its summery flavors, and combined it with zucchini (another summertime must-have vegetable), a variety of soft herbs, and the corn "milk."*

- 5 ears corn, kernels cut from cobs (about 5 cups), cobs reserved
- 1 tablespoon vegetable oil
- 2 zucchini, chopped fine
- 3 garlic cloves, minced
- 2 tablespoons minced fresh basil
- 1 tablespoon minced fresh chives
- 1 tablespoon minced fresh parsley
- 1½ teaspoons lemon juice
- Salt and pepper

1. Working over bowl, run back of knife down each corn cob to scrape away milk, reserving milk. Heat oil in 12-inch skillet over medium-high heat until shimmering. Add zucchini and cook until softened and browned at edges, about 3 minutes.

2. Add corn kernels and cook until deep yellow and softened, about 2 minutes. Add garlic and cook until fragrant, about 30 seconds. Off heat, stir in corn milk, basil, chives, parsley, and lemon juice. Season with salt and pepper to taste. Serve.

VARIATIONS
Garden-Fresh Corn with Sausage and Sage
Omit garlic. Substitute 5 ounces crumbled breakfast sausage for zucchini. Substitute 1 teaspoon chopped fresh sage and 1 tablespoon chopped fresh thyme for basil, chives, and parsley. Add 1 finely chopped red bell pepper to skillet after cooking breakfast sausage in step 1, and cook until softened, about 1 minute. Stir in 2 tablespoons maple syrup with herbs before serving.

Garden-Fresh Southwestern Corn
Omit garlic. Substitute 1 finely chopped red onion for zucchini. Substitute 3 tablespoons minced fresh cilantro for basil, chives, and parsley. Substitute 2 teaspoons lime juice for lemon juice. Add 1 finely chopped red bell pepper to skillet after cooking red onion in step 1, and cook until softened, about 1 minute. Stir 1 teaspoon minced canned chipotle chiles in adobo sauce in with cilantro before serving.

CREAMED CORN

Serves 4 to 6   Total time: 40 minutes

WHY THIS RECIPE WORKS *Corn and cream make a fantastic combination; their sweet flavors mingle to bring out the best in each other. Those who dread creamed corn have probably had only the canned version, which contains no cream at all—only water, thickeners, sugar, and who-knows-what else suspended in a gelatinous, gloppy goo. We set out to rescue this dish and return it to its rightful place at the summertime table. To start, we stripped plump, yellow kernels from a stack of husked corn cobs and simmered the kernels gently in water, to deactivate the natural enzymes that might cause the cream to curdle. This cooking liquid turned into a flavorful, concentrated corn broth. To thicken this broth, we blended a portion of the kernels with ¼ cup of cream until smooth and then added this puree back to the rest of the corn in the saucepan, which gave us the perfect texture. Do not substitute frozen corn for fresh.*

- 7 ears corn, kernels cut from cobs (about 7 cups)
- 1¼ cups water
- ¼ cup heavy cream
- Salt and pepper

1. Combine corn and water in large saucepan and bring to boil over high heat. Cover, reduce heat to low, and cook, stirring occasionally, until corn is crisp-tender, about 20 minutes.

2. Remove saucepan from heat and transfer 1½ cups corn mixture to blender. Add cream, 1⅛ teaspoons salt, and ¼ teaspoon pepper and process until smooth, about

1 minute. Stir pureed corn mixture into corn mixture in saucepan and season with salt and pepper to taste. Serve. (If creamed corn looks thin, return to low heat and cook gently until thickened slightly, about 3 minutes.)

VARIATIONS

Creamed Corn with Bacon and Scallions
Cook 2 slices chopped bacon in 10-inch skillet over medium-high heat until crispy, 5 to 7 minutes; transfer to paper towel–lined plate. Stir crisped bacon and 2 minced scallions into saucepan with pureed corn before serving.

Creamed Corn with Chipotle and Cilantro
Add 2 teaspoons minced canned chipotle chiles in adobo sauce to blender with corn. Stir 2 tablespoons minced fresh cilantro into saucepan with pureed corn before serving.

HUSK-GRILLED CORN

Serves 6   Total time: 50 minutes

WHY THIS RECIPE WORKS *Corn is the perfect vegetable to grill because its sweet flavor loves a smoky accent and it's large enough that you never have to worry about it falling through the grate. Our goal here was to achieve a classic char while preventing the corn kernels from drying out on the fire. We found that initially cooking the ears with their husks on worked best. We then shucked the hot corn, rolled the ears in seasoned butter, and returned them to the grill to caramelize. This way, the kernels achieved a great char but weren't on the grill long enough to dry out. One last roll in the butter and our corn was ready. The flavored butters can be made ahead and refrigerated for up to three days; bring to room temperature before using. Set up a cutting board and knife next to your grill to avoid traveling back and forth between kitchen and grill.*

- 6 ears corn (unshucked)
- 6 tablespoons unsalted butter, softened
- ½ teaspoon salt
- ½ teaspoon pepper

1. Cut and remove silk protruding from top of each ear of corn. Combine butter, salt, and pepper in bowl. Fold one 14 by 12-inch

piece heavy-duty aluminum foil in half to create 7 by 12-inch rectangle; then crimp into boat shape long and wide enough to accommodate 1 ear of corn. Transfer butter mixture to prepared foil boat.

2a. For a charcoal grill Open bottom vent completely. Light large chimney starter mounded with charcoal briquettes (7 quarts). When top coals are partially covered with ash, pour evenly over half of grill. Set cooking grate in place, cover, and open lid vent completely. Heat grill until hot, about 5 minutes.

2b. For a gas grill Turn all burners to high, cover, and heat grill until hot, about 15 minutes.

3. Clean and oil grate. Place corn on grill (over coals, with stem ends facing cooler side of grill, for charcoal). Cover and cook, turning corn every 3 minutes, until husks have blackened all over, 12 to 15 minutes. (To check for doneness, carefully peel down small portion of husk. If corn is steaming and bright yellow, it is ready.) Transfer corn to cutting board. Using chef's knife, cut base from corn. Using dish towel to hold corn, peel away and discard husk and silk with tongs.

4. Roll each ear of corn in butter mixture to coat lightly and return to grill (over coals for charcoal). Cook, turning as needed to char corn lightly on each side, about 5 minutes total. Remove corn from grill and roll each ear again in butter mixture. Transfer corn to platter. Serve, passing any remaining butter mixture.

VARIATIONS

Husk-Grilled Corn with Rosemary-Pepper Butter
Increase pepper to 1 teaspoon. Stir 1 tablespoon minced fresh rosemary and 1 minced small garlic clove into butter mixture in step 1.

Husk-Grilled Corn with Mustard-Paprika Butter
Stir 2 tablespoons spicy brown mustard and 1 teaspoon smoked paprika into butter mixture in step 1.

Husk-Grilled Corn with Cilantro-Lime Butter
Stir ¼ cup minced fresh cilantro, 2 teaspoons grated lime zest plus 1 tablespoon juice, and 1 minced small garlic clove into butter mixture in step 1.

Husk-Grilled Corn with Brown Sugar–Cayenne Butter
Stir 2 tablespoons packed brown sugar and ¼ teaspoon cayenne pepper into butter mixture in step 1.

MEXICAN-STYLE GRILLED CORN

Serves 6   Total time: 35 minutes

WHY THIS RECIPE WORKS *In Mexico, street vendors add kick to grilled corn by slathering it with a creamy, spicy, cheesy sauce. The corn takes on an irresistibly sweet, smoky, charred flavor, which is heightened by the lime juice and chili powder in the sauce. For our own rendition of this south-of-the-border street fare, we ditched the husks, coated the ears with oil to prevent sticking, and grilled them directly on the grate over a hot fire so the corn could develop plenty of char. The traditional base for the sauce is crema, a thick, soured Mexican cream. But given its limited availability in supermarkets, we replaced the crema with a combination of mayonnaise (for richness) and sour cream (for tanginess). If you can find queso fresco or cotija, use either in place of the Pecorino Romano.*

- 1½ ounces Pecorino Romano cheese, grated (¾ cup)
- ¼ cup mayonnaise
- 3 tablespoons sour cream
- 3 tablespoons minced fresh cilantro
- 4 teaspoons lime juice
- 1 garlic clove, minced
- ¾ teaspoon chili powder
- ¼ teaspoon pepper
- ¼ teaspoon cayenne pepper
- 4 teaspoons vegetable oil
- ¼ teaspoon salt
- 6 ears corn, husks and silk removed

1. Combine Pecorino, mayonnaise, sour cream, cilantro, lime juice, garlic, ¼ teaspoon chili powder, pepper, and cayenne in large bowl; set aside. In second large bowl, combine oil, salt, and remaining ½ teaspoon chili powder. Add corn to oil mixture and toss to coat.

2a. **For a charcoal grill** Open bottom vent completely. Light large chimney starter filled with charcoal briquettes (6 quarts). When top coals are partially covered with ash, pour evenly over half of grill. Set cooking grate in place, cover, and open lid vent completely. Heat grill until hot, about 5 minutes.

2b. **For a gas grill** Turn all burners to high, cover, and heat grill until hot, about 15 minutes. Leave all burners on high.

3. Clean and oil cooking grate. Place corn on grill (on hotter side if using charcoal) and cook (covered if using gas), turning as needed, until lightly charred on all sides, 7 to 12 minutes. Transfer corn to bowl with cheese mixture and toss to coat. Serve.

CORN RELISH
Makes four 1-cup jars
Total time: 30 minutes (plus cooling time)
WHY THIS RECIPE WORKS *This bright condiment adds a summery flair to hot dogs, burgers, and sandwiches. Several recipes we tried called for cooking the kernels before packing them into jars. However, we found that this method produced overcooked, rubbery corn. To maintain the crispness of the corn, we used raw corn and let the warm pickling brine do its work in the jar. We stripped the kernels from the cobs, simmered our aromatics in vinegar until softened and stirred in the corn off the heat. We added poblano and red jalapeño chiles for a hint of punchy heat and bright color. Cumin seeds and ground coriander added the right spice without overpowering the mild corn, and some sugar enhanced the natural sweetness of the corn and balanced the tangy vinegar. Heating the jars with hot water and then draining them before adding the hot relish ensures that the jars won't crack from the abrupt temperature change. The relish can be refrigerated for up to one month; its flavor will deepen over time.*

1¼ cups cider vinegar
¼ cup sugar
2½ teaspoons salt
¾ teaspoon cumin seeds
¼ teaspoon ground coriander
2 poblano chiles, stemmed, seeded, and cut into ¼-inch pieces
2 red jalapeño or Fresno chiles, stemmed, seeded, and chopped fine
1 small onion, chopped fine
4 ears corn, kernels cut from cobs (about 4 cups)

1. Bring vinegar, ¼ cup water, sugar, salt, cumin seeds, and coriander to boil in Dutch oven over high heat. Add poblanos, jalapeños, and onion; reduce heat to medium and simmer until softened, about 5 minutes. Off heat, stir in corn.

2. Fill four 1-cup jars with hot water to warm. Drain jars, then, using ladle, portion relish into jars. Let relish cool completely. Cover and refrigerate before serving.

FRESH CORN SALSA WITH TOMATO
Makes 3 cups   Total time: 40 minutes
WHY THIS RECIPE WORKS *Of all of summer's produce, corn just might be our favorite as a central ingredient for fresh, vibrant salsas: Its juicy, crisp texture lights up simply prepared chicken or fish and is equally terrific with chips. Plus, corn's natural sweetness makes it an exemplary foil for salsa's signature spicy chiles and tart citrus juice. The key was how to handle the corn. Grilled corn was impractical and raw corn was too chewy. We found that if we added the kernels to boiling water and then let them sit off the heat for 10 minutes they acquired just the right texture. A little baking soda added to the water softened their hulls so that the kernels burst with crisp sweetness. For the other ingredients, fruits that were sweet but with a hint of acidity (like tomato, pineapple, and peach) worked well. An avocado variation made a nice change of pace. Herbs and chiles were essential additions, as was finely minced*

shallot. We whisked a tablespoon of vegetable oil and a tiny bit of honey into lime juice for a tangy dressing with enough body to cling to the vegetables. Do not substitute frozen corn for fresh.

- 2 ears corn, kernels cut from cobs (about 2 cups)
- ¼ teaspoon baking soda
  Salt and pepper
- 2 tablespoons lime juice
- 1 tablespoon vegetable oil
- ½ teaspoon honey
- 1 tomato, cored, seeded, and cut into ¼-inch pieces
- 1 shallot, minced
- 1 jalapeño chile, stemmed, seeded, and minced
- ¼ cup chopped fresh cilantro

1. Bring 2 cups water to boil in small saucepan over high heat. Stir in corn, baking soda, and ¼ teaspoon salt, then let sit off heat for 10 minutes. Drain corn and let cool slightly, about 10 minutes.

2. Whisk lime juice, oil, honey, and ⅛ teaspoon salt together in bowl. Add drained corn, tomato, shallot, jalapeño, and cilantro and toss to combine. Let sit for 10 minutes. Season with salt and pepper to taste. Serve.

VARIATIONS

Fresh Corn Salsa with Avocado and Toasted Cumin
Add ½ teaspoon toasted cumin seeds and ⅛ teaspoon cayenne pepper to lime juice mixture in step 2. Substitute 1 avocado cut into ¼-inch pieces and 3 thinly sliced scallions for tomato.

Fresh Corn Salsa with Jícama and Pineapple
Substitute ¾ cup pineapple, cut into ¼-inch pieces, and ½ cup jícama, cut into ¼-inch pieces, for tomato. Substitute 1 minced serrano chile for jalapeño.

Fresh Corn Salsa with Peaches and Radishes
Substitute 1 peeled and pitted peach, cut into ¼-inch pieces, and 4 thinly sliced radishes for tomato. Substitute 1 minced habanero chile for jalapeño, and basil for cilantro.

CORN FRITTERS WITH CHIPOTLE-MAPLE MAYONNAISE
Makes 12 fritters   Total time: 45 minutes
WHY THIS RECIPE WORKS *A Southern favorite, corn fritters are an irresistible side at a barbecue but also make a delicious appetizer, especially when served with a sweet-and-spicy mayo. The ideal fritter is amazingly crisp and golden brown on the outside, creamy and bursting with sweet corn flavor on the inside. For light—not leaden—fritters, we minimized the number of added fillers, processing some of the kernels to use as a thickener rather than more flour or cornmeal. This also helped the fresh corn flavor shine through. Browning the corn puree in a skillet drove off excess moisture and deepened the flavor even more. Cayenne, nutty Parmesan, and oniony chives balanced the natural sweetness of the corn, and a touch of cornstarch crisped the exteriors and helped provide a wonderful textural contrast with the light and creamy interior.*

CHIPOTLE-MAPLE MAYONNAISE
- ½ cup mayonnaise
- 1 tablespoon maple syrup
- 1 tablespoon minced canned chipotle chile in adobo sauce
- ½ teaspoon Dijon mustard

FRITTERS
- 3 ears corn, kernels cut from cobs (about 3 cups)
- 1 teaspoon plus ½ cup vegetable oil
  Salt and pepper
- ¼ cup all-purpose flour
- ¼ cup minced fresh chives
- 2 tablespoons grated Parmesan cheese
- 1 tablespoon cornstarch
  Pinch cayenne pepper
- 1 large egg, lightly beaten

1. **For the mayonnaise** Whisk all ingredients in bowl until smooth; set aside for serving.

2. **For the fritters** Process 1½ cups corn in food processor to uniform coarse puree, 15 to 20 seconds, scraping down sides of bowl halfway through processing; set aside.

3. Heat 1 teaspoon oil in 12-inch nonstick skillet over medium-high heat until shimmering. Add remaining 1½ cups corn and

⅛ teaspoon salt and cook, stirring frequently, until light golden, 3 to 4 minutes. Transfer to large bowl.

4. Return skillet to medium heat, add corn puree, and cook, stirring frequently, until puree is consistency of thick oatmeal (puree should cling to spatula rather than dripping off), about 5 minutes. Stir puree into corn in bowl. Rinse skillet and wipe dry with paper towels.

5. Stir flour, 3 tablespoons chives, Parmesan, cornstarch, cayenne, ¼ teaspoon salt, and ⅛ teaspoon pepper into corn mixture until well combined. Gently stir in egg until incorporated.

6. Line rimmed baking sheet with paper towels. Heat remaining ½ cup oil in now-empty skillet over medium heat until shimmering. Drop six 2-tablespoon portions batter into skillet, then flatten with spatula into 2½-inch disks. Fry until deep golden brown on both sides, 2 to 3 minutes per side. Transfer fritters to prepared sheet. Repeat with remaining batter.

7. Transfer fritters to serving platter and sprinkle with remaining 1 tablespoon chives. Serve immediately with chipotle-maple mayonnaise.

FRESH CORN SALAD
Serves 4 to 6   Total time: 1 hour 15 minutes
WHY THIS RECIPE WORKS *It's not hard to find recipes for corn salad, but it's surprisingly hard to find a good recipe. The standard preparation method—stripping kernels off the cob, adding vegetables (usually tomatoes, onions, and/or peppers), and tossing with dressing—produced salads that were not up to snuff. Instead, browning the kernels lightly in a skillet for a few minutes gave even inferior, out-of-season corn a complex, nutty dimension. As for the dressing, it took equal parts oil and vinegar to create a dressing that balanced the sugary corn. Don't add the tomatoes to the toasted corn until it is cool, as otherwise the heat from the corn will partially cook them.*

Fresh Corn Salad

2 tomatoes, cored and cut into
½-inch pieces
Salt and pepper
2½ tablespoons extra-virgin olive oil
5 ears corn, kernels cut from cobs
(about 5 cups)
2 scallions, sliced thin
1½ tablespoons white wine vinegar
¼ cup minced fresh parsley

1. Toss tomatoes with ½ teaspoon salt in bowl, then transfer to colander. Set colander over bowl and let drain for 30 minutes.

2. Meanwhile, heat 1 tablespoon oil in 12-inch nonstick skillet over medium-high heat until shimmering. Add corn and cook, stirring occasionally, until spotty brown, 5 to 7 minutes. Transfer to large bowl and stir in scallions, vinegar, remaining 1½ tablespoons oil, ¾ teaspoon salt, and ½ teaspoon pepper; let cool to room temperature, about 20 minutes.

3. Stir in drained tomatoes and parsley. Let sit until flavors meld, about 30 minutes. Season with salt and pepper to taste. Serve.

VARIATIONS

Watermelon-Feta Fresh Corn Salad
Replace tomatoes with 2 cups watermelon, cut into ½-inch pieces, and 2 cucumbers, peeled, quartered lengthwise, seeded, and cut into ½-inch pieces. Stir 1 cup crumbled feta cheese into cooked and cooled corn. Replace parsley with ¼ cup minced fresh mint.

Arugula–Goat Cheese Fresh Corn Salad
Omit parsley. Replace white wine vinegar with 1½ tablespoons lemon juice. Stir in 2 cups chopped baby arugula and 1 cup crumbled goat cheese with tomatoes.

Tuscan Fresh Corn Salad
Replace white wine vinegar with 1½ tablespoons red wine vinegar. Toss 1 (15-ounce) can rinsed cannellini beans with vinaigrette and hot corn. Replace parsley with 2 tablespoons chopped fresh basil.

ROASTED CORN AND POBLANO CHOWDER

Serves 6 to 8   Total time: 1 hour 15 minutes
WHY THIS RECIPE WORKS *In this appealing and hearty chowder, the sweet flavor of corn is a great counterpoint to the slightly spicy poblano chiles. After stripping the corn kernels from the cob, we tossed them with oil, salt, and pepper, spread them over a baking sheet with halved poblanos on the side, and set the whole thing to broil. In just 10 minutes, we had beautiful charred vegetables with caramelized flavor. Turning to the chowder, we rendered some bacon in the pot and used its fat to cook the onion and garlic; we then added the potatoes, corn, broth, and half-and-half. We whirred a few ladles of the simmered soup in the blender and stirred this puree back into the pot to thicken it (adding some fried tortilla pieces to the blender gave the soup body and deepened the corn flavor). To finish, we added the chopped poblanos, lime juice for acidity, and fresh cilantro for an herbal pop. An array of crunchy and creamy garnishes made this chowder irresistible. Do not substitute frozen corn for fresh.*

FRIED CORN TORTILLA PIECES
¾ cup vegetable oil
4 (6-inch) corn tortillas, cut into
½-inch pieces
Salt

CHOWDER
2 poblano chiles, stemmed, halved
lengthwise, and seeded
1 tablespoon vegetable oil
5¼ cups fresh corn kernels (about 6 ears)
Salt and pepper
4 slices bacon, chopped fine
1 onion, chopped fine
2 garlic cloves, minced
7 cups chicken broth
1 pound red potatoes, unpeeled,
cut into ½-inch pieces
¼ cup half-and-half
2 (6-inch) corn tortillas, torn into
1-inch pieces
1 tablespoon minced fresh cilantro,
plus leaves for serving
1 tablespoon lime juice, plus lime wedges
for serving
Sour cream
Crumbled queso fresco

1. **For the fried tortilla pieces** Heat oil in 10-inch skillet over medium-high heat until shimmering. Add tortillas and cook, stirring occasionally, until golden brown, 3 to 5 minutes. Using slotted spoon, transfer tortillas to paper towel–lined plate. Season with salt and set aside for serving; discard oil.

2. **For the chowder** Adjust oven rack 6 inches from broiler element and heat broiler. Line rimmed baking sheet with aluminum foil. Toss poblanos with 1 teaspoon oil in bowl. Arrange poblanos cut side down in single column flush against short side of sheet.

3. Toss corn, remaining 2 teaspoons oil, ½ teaspoon salt, and ½ teaspoon pepper together in now-empty bowl. Spread corn in even layer over empty portion of sheet next to poblanos. Broil until poblanos are mostly blackened and corn is well browned and tender, 10 to 15 minutes, flipping poblanos and stirring corn halfway through broiling.

4. Place poblanos in bowl, cover with plastic wrap, and let cool for 5 minutes. Peel skins, then chop poblanos into ½-inch pieces; set aside.

5. Meanwhile, cook bacon in Dutch oven over medium heat until crispy, 5 to 7 minutes. Using slotted spoon, transfer bacon to paper towel–lined plate. Add onion and ¼ teaspoon salt to fat left in pot and cook until onion is softened and beginning to brown, 5 to 7 minutes. Add garlic and cook until fragrant, about 30 seconds.

6. Add broth, potatoes, browned corn, and ½ teaspoon salt to Dutch oven and bring to simmer, scraping up any browned bits. Cook at vigorous simmer until potatoes are tender, 15 to 20 minutes. Off heat, stir in half-and-half.

7. Transfer 2 cups chowder to blender. Add tortillas and process until smooth, about 1 minute. Return pureed chowder to pot and stir in chopped poblanos. Return to simmer over medium heat. Stir in minced cilantro, lime juice, ¾ teaspoon salt, and ¾ teaspoon pepper. Serve, passing fried tortilla pieces, bacon, cilantro leaves, lime wedges, sour cream, and queso fresco separately.

CRISPY PORK CHOPS WITH SUCCOTASH

Serves 4   Total time: 55 minutes

WHY THIS RECIPE WORKS *This one-dish supper features crispy, cornflake-crusted pork chops and a classic succotash with an abundance of fresh corn. For a flavorful and crisp breading for the pork chops, we started with buttermilk for a light texture and tangy flavor, plus garlic and mustard. Crushed cornflakes added a desirable cragginess. To ensure that the breading adhered to the chops, we lightly scored the meat before breading and gave it a short rest before adding the chops to the pan. For the succotash, we chose the classic American vegetable blend of lima beans, corn, and bell pepper, with zucchini for an extra layer of freshness. You can substitute ¾ cup of store-bought cornflake crumbs for the whole cornflakes. If using store-bought crumbs, omit the processing step and mix the crumbs with the cornstarch, salt, and pepper. You can substitute frozen corn, thawed and patted dry, for fresh. We prefer to use a well-seasoned cast-iron skillet in this recipe, but a 12-inch nonstick skillet can be used in its place. Serve with lemon wedges.*

- 3 cups (3 ounces) cornflakes
- ⅔ cup cornstarch
- 1 teaspoon minced fresh thyme
  Salt and pepper
- ¼ teaspoon cayenne pepper
- 1 cup buttermilk
- 2 tablespoons Dijon mustard
- 2 garlic cloves, minced
- 4 (6- to 8-ounce) boneless pork chops, ¾ to 1 inch thick
- ½ cup vegetable oil
- 2 tablespoons unsalted butter
- 1 zucchini, cut into ½-inch pieces
- 1 red bell pepper, stemmed, seeded, and cut into ½-inch pieces
- 1 small onion, chopped fine
- 1½ cups frozen baby lima beans, thawed
- 2 ears corn, kernels cut from cobs (about 2 cups)
- 1 tablespoon minced fresh tarragon

1. Process cornflakes, ⅓ cup cornstarch, thyme, ½ teaspoon salt, ½ teaspoon pepper, and cayenne in food processor until cornflakes are finely ground, about 10 seconds; transfer to shallow dish. Spread remaining ⅓ cup cornstarch in second shallow dish. Whisk buttermilk, mustard, and half of minced garlic together in third shallow dish.

2. Adjust oven rack to middle position and heat oven to 200 degrees. Using sharp knife, cut ¹⁄₁₆-inch-deep slits on both sides of chops, spaced ½ inch apart, in crosshatch pattern. Season chops with salt and pepper. Working with 1 chop at a time, dredge chops in cornstarch, dip in buttermilk mixture, then coat with cornflake mixture, pressing gently to adhere. Transfer coated chops to plate and let sit for 10 minutes.

3. Set wire rack in rimmed baking sheet and line with triple layer of paper towels. Heat oil in 12-inch cast-iron skillet over medium heat until shimmering. Place chops in skillet and cook until golden brown and crisp on first side, about 5 minutes. Carefully flip chops, reduce heat to medium-low, and continue to cook until golden brown and crisp on second side and pork registers 145 degrees, about 5 minutes. Transfer chops to prepared rack and keep warm in oven.

4. Discard oil and wipe skillet clean with paper towels. Melt 1 tablespoon butter in now-empty skillet over medium heat. Add zucchini, bell pepper, onion, ½ teaspoon salt, and ¼ teaspoon pepper and cook until softened, about 5 minutes. Stir in lima beans, corn, and remaining garlic and cook until heated through, about 5 minutes. Off heat, stir in remaining 1 tablespoon butter and tarragon and season with salt and pepper to taste. Serve chops with succotash.

SOUTH CAROLINA SHRIMP BOIL

Serve 8   Total time: 55 minutes

WHY THIS RECIPE WORKS *Just about every coastal hamlet features a clam, crab, or shrimp "bake" or "boil," and while the particulars vary in terms of combos of ingredients, one remains a constant: the corn. South Carolina is famous for its shrimp boil, which is inspired by Frogmore stew, made by simmering local shell-on shrimp, smoked sausage, corn on the cob, and potatoes in a broth seasoned with Old Bay. We wanted perfectly cooked meat,*

CREAMY CORN BUCATINI WITH RICOTTA AND BASIL

During the height of summer, when fresh corn is plentiful and perfect, this pasta dish is an inventive way to use it. In fact, here the corn is transformed into a luscious sauce for the pasta. When topped with ricotta and fresh basil leaves, it becomes the essence of summer.

1. Cut the corn kernels from the cobs, positioning the ears in a bowl to catch all the kernels and liquid.

2. Add the corn kernels and milk to a 12-inch skillet and cook over medium heat until simmering, about 4 minutes. This activates the starch in the corn to thicken the mixture and intensifies the corn flavor.

3. Transfer the corn-milk mixture to the blender and let cool just slightly. Then carefully process it until smooth, about 3 minutes, scraping down the sides of the blender as needed.

4. Strain the corn-milk mixture through a fine-mesh strainer into the empty skillet. Meanwhile, cook the pasta in boiling water until just flexible, about 5 minutes. (It will finish cooking in the skillet with the corn sauce.)

5. Add the partially cooked pasta to the corn sauce in the skillet, add 1½ cups reserved cooking water, and cook until the pasta is cooked and well coated with the sauce, 2 to 4 minutes.

6. Turn the pasta out onto a serving platter, dollop with the ricotta, sprinkle with the basil, and serve immediately.

seafood, and vegetables that were flavored by—but not overwhelmed by—the Old Bay. We began by browning the smoky, spicy andouille sausage to render fat and boost flavor. We replaced some of the cooking liquid (water, in this case) with clam juice, which reinforced the taste of the sea and amped up the flavor. (You don't eat the broth in this boil, but if it has no flavor, the stuff you do eat won't either.) We used only enough liquid to barely cover the ingredients. We staggered the ingredients' cooking times, starting with the potatoes and corn first until the potatoes were almost tender, then adding the sausage and shrimp. This ensured intact potatoes, plump corn, and nicely cooked sausage and shrimp. This dish is always made with shell-on shrimp, and we think peeling them is half the fun of eating this. Use small red potatoes measuring 1 to 2 inches in diameter. You will need a collapsible steamer basket for this recipe.

1½ pounds andouille sausage, cut into 2-inch lengths
2 teaspoons vegetable oil
4 cups water
1½ pounds small red potatoes, unpeeled, halved
4 ears corn, husks and silks removed, cut into 2-inch lengths
1 (14.5-ounce) can diced tomatoes, drained
1 (8-ounce) bottle clam juice
5 teaspoons Old Bay seasoning
1 bay leaf
2 pounds extra-large shrimp (21 to 25 per pound)

1. Cook sausage and oil in Dutch oven over medium-high heat until sausage is browned, about 5 minutes. Using slotted spoon, transfer sausage to large plate.

2. Bring water, potatoes, corn, tomatoes, clam juice, 1 tablespoon Old Bay, and bay leaf to boil in now-empty pot. Reduce heat to medium-low, cover, and simmer until potatoes are just tender, about 10 minutes.

3. Nestle browned sausage into pot and place steamer basket over top. Toss shrimp with remaining 2 teaspoons Old Bay and

transfer to steamer basket. Cook, covered, stirring shrimp occasionally, until cooked through, about 10 minutes. Transfer shrimp to serving platter. Drain stew, discarding bay leaf and liquid, and transfer to platter with shrimp. Serve.

CREAMY CORN BUCATINI WITH RICOTTA AND BASIL

Serves 4 to 6   Total time: 45 minutes
WHY THIS RECIPE WORKS *In this ingenious summer recipe, corn serves as the base for a simple, creamy pasta sauce that comes together in a flash. We started by bringing corn and milk to a simmer before blending the mixture to a smooth puree. Corn kernels naturally contain cornstarch, which thickens into a pasta-coating sauce if heated above 150 degrees. Heating also intensifies the characteristic aroma of corn, which is largely due to a compound that is also prominent in the aroma of milk. That means that our puree tasted more like corn, and it also tasted more like milk. Simmering our pasta in this sauce further thickened the sauce to a velvety consistency while ensuring a perfect al dente texture for the pasta. We even added a touch of red pepper flakes for a subtle kick. Finished with dollops of creamy ricotta and fresh basil, this is a satisfying dish that's great any day of the week. You can substitute 18 ounces frozen corn for fresh. You can also use spaghetti in place of bucatini.*

4 ears corn, kernels cut from cobs (about 4 cups)
1 cup whole milk
1 pound bucatini
Salt and pepper
¼ teaspoon red pepper flakes
6 ounces (¾ cup) whole-milk ricotta
¼ cup fresh basil leaves, torn

1. Bring corn and milk to simmer in 12-inch skillet over medium heat. Carefully transfer corn and milk to blender and let cool slightly, about 5 minutes. Process until smooth, about 3 minutes, scraping down sides of blender jar as needed. Strain corn

mixture through fine-mesh strainer into now-empty skillet, pressing on solids to extract as much liquid as possible.

2. Meanwhile, bring 4 quarts water to boil in large pot. Add pasta and 1 tablespoon salt and cook, stirring often, until pasta is flexible but still firm, about 5 minutes. Reserve 2 cups cooking water, then drain pasta.

3. Stir pasta, 1½ cups reserved cooking water, ¼ teaspoon salt, and pepper flakes into corn mixture in skillet. Cook over medium-high heat, stirring constantly, until pasta is al dente and well coated with sauce, 2 to 4 minutes. Adjust consistency with remaining reserved cooking water. Season with salt and pepper to taste.

4. Transfer pasta to serving dish, dollop with ricotta, and sprinkle with basil. Serve.

FRESH CORN CORNBREAD

Serves 6 to 8   Total time: 1 hour
WHY THIS RECIPE WORKS *Cornbread falls into two main styles: the sweet, cakey Northern type and the crusty, savory kind more often found in Southern kitchens. Each has its die-hard fans, but—let's face the facts—neither tastes much like corn. This is because most cornbreads are made with cornmeal alone, and no fresh corn at all. Furthermore, the so-called "field" or "dent" corn used to make cornmeal is far starchier (read: less flavorful) than the sweet corn grown to eat off the cob. So what would it take to get real corn flavor in cornbread? It wouldn't be as simple as just tossing some fresh-cut kernels into the batter. We found that we needed to add at least 2 whole cups of kernels for the corn flavor to really shine, and that created a slew of problems. Since fresh kernels are full of moisture, the crumb of the cornbread became riddled with unpleasant gummy pockets. What's more, the kernels turned chewy and tough as the bread baked. So we turned our attention first to the base of the cornbread, using slightly more cornmeal than flour and abandoning fine-ground cornmeal in favor*

of the stone-ground type, which contains both the hull and the oil-rich germ of the corn kernel. The upshot: a more rustic texture and fuller flavor. For sweetness, honey, maple syrup, and brown sugar all masked the fresh corn taste, but 2 tablespoons of regular granulated sugar fell neatly in line. For the liquid component, traditional tangy buttermilk could not be beat. Turning back to the issue of the corn, we decided to try making a "corn butter" by pureeing fresh kernels and then reducing the mixture on the stove until thick. Using just three ears of corn, we found that the puree thickened and turned deep yellow in minutes, transforming into a "butter" packed with concentrated corn flavor. Added to the batter, this puree turned the tide: For the first time, the cornbread tasted like real corn—and without any distracting chewiness or gumminess. We prefer to use a well-seasoned cast-iron skillet in this recipe, but an ovensafe 10-inch skillet can be used in its place. Alternatively, in step 4, you can add 1 tablespoon of butter to a 9-inch cake pan and place it in the oven until the butter melts, about 3 minutes.

1⅓ cups (6⅔ ounces) stone-ground
    cornmeal
  1 cup (5 ounces) all-purpose flour
  2 tablespoons sugar
1½ teaspoons baking powder
  ¼ teaspoon baking soda
1¼ teaspoons salt
  2 ears corn, kernels cut from cobs
    (about 2 cups)
  6 tablespoons unsalted butter, cut
    into 6 pieces
  1 cup buttermilk
  2 large eggs plus 1 large yolk

1. Adjust oven rack to middle position and heat oven to 400 degrees. Whisk cornmeal, flour, sugar, baking powder, baking soda, and salt together in large bowl; set aside.

2. Process corn in blender until very smooth, about 2 minutes. Transfer to medium saucepan (you should have about 1½ cups). Cook puree over medium heat, stirring constantly, until very thick and deep yellow and reduced to ¾ cup, 5 to 8 minutes.

3. Off heat, whisk in 5 tablespoons butter until melted. Whisk in buttermilk until incorporated. Whisk in eggs and yolk until incorporated. Transfer to bowl with cornmeal mixture and, using rubber spatula, fold until just combined.

4. Melt remaining 1 tablespoon butter in 10-inch cast-iron skillet over medium heat. Scrape batter into skillet and spread into even layer. Transfer skillet to oven and bake until cornbread is golden brown and toothpick inserted in center comes out clean, 23 to 28 minutes.

5. Remove skillet from oven and transfer to wire rack. Let cornbread cool in skillet for 5 minutes. Remove cornbread from skillet and let cool for 20 minutes before cutting into wedges. Serve.

SWEET CORN SPOONBREAD

Serves 6   Total time: 2 hours

WHY THIS RECIPE WORKS *Spoonbread is a Southern specialty made from a combination of fresh corn and cornmeal, with a texture somewhere on the line between a rich cornbread and a true soufflé. We wanted a fluffy, soufflé-style sweet corn spoonbread with deep corn flavor, one that was light and soft, so we focused first on corn flavor, then on texture. Sautéing the corn in butter, before steeping it in milk and pureeing it, ensured that the sweet corn flavor permeated our spoonbread. To make sure the cornmeal didn't impart a gritty texture, we soaked it in the milk beforehand to soften it. And to guarantee a stable egg foam and an impressive rise, we beat the egg whites with a bit of cream of tartar. You can substitute frozen corn, thawed and patted dry, for fresh.*

  1 cup cornmeal
2¾ cups whole milk
  4 tablespoons unsalted butter
  2 ears corn, kernels cut from cobs
    (about 2 cups)
  1 teaspoon sugar
  1 teaspoon salt
  ⅛ teaspoon cayenne pepper
  3 large eggs, separated
  ¼ teaspoon cream of tartar

1. Adjust oven rack to middle position and heat oven to 400 degrees. Grease 1½-quart soufflé dish or 8-inch baking dish. Whisk cornmeal and ¾ cup milk together in bowl; set aside.

2. Melt butter in Dutch oven over medium-high heat. Add corn and cook until beginning to brown, about 3 minutes. Stir in sugar, salt, cayenne, and remaining 2 cups milk and bring to boil. Cover pot and let sit, off heat, for 15 minutes.

3. Transfer warm corn mixture to blender and process until smooth, about 2 minutes. Return to now-empty pot and bring to boil over medium-high heat. Reduce heat to low, add cornmeal mixture, and cook, whisking constantly, until thickened, 2 to 3 minutes; transfer to large bowl and let cool to room temperature, about 20 minutes. Once mixture is cool, whisk in egg yolks until combined.

4. Using stand mixer fitted with whisk attachment, whip egg whites and cream of tartar on medium-low speed until foamy, about 1 minute. Increase speed to medium-high and whip until stiff peaks form, 3 to 4 minutes. Whisk one-third of whites into cooled corn mixture, then gently fold in remaining whites until combined. Scrape batter into prepared dish and transfer to oven. Reduce oven temperature to 350 degrees and bake until spoonbread is golden brown and has risen above rim of dish, about 45 minutes. Serve immediately.

Fresh Corn Cornbread

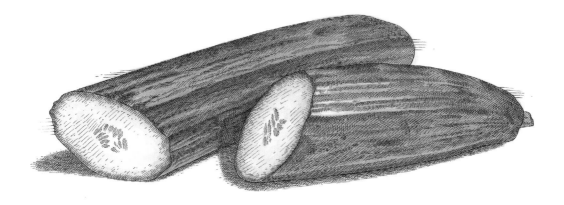

CUCUMBERS

Cucumbers, which are native to India, are thought to have been cultivated more than 3,000 years ago. Given their high water content (about 96 percent), they were used to quench thirst in ancient times, and even today, we continue to enjoy this refreshing quality in salads. And while they add a nice substance and crunch to a simple green salad, they can also be the main attraction in a salad, and we believe everyone should have a few of these dishes in their repertoire; for example, the Country-Style Greek Salad and the Parsley-Cucumber Salad with Feta, Walnuts, and Pomegranate.

The simple keys to working with cucumbers are how you cut them, whether or not or when you peel them, and how you ensure that they remain crunchy. We are not dogmatic about the methods and have found them to be very recipe-specific.

Cucumbers have a subtle and appealing vegetal flavor that can be coaxed out in simple preparations like Chilled Cucumber and Yogurt Soup. And certainly no one would debate the fact that fresh, height-of-season cucumbers are great sliced and drizzled with a lively vinaigrette as an accompaniment to grilled or barbecued foods. They also make a great foil to spicy foods—witness our Grilled Thai Beef Salad with Cucumbers, where the bed of sliced English cucumbers catches the spicy marinade. And then there is a whole culinary legacy of cucumber-based dishes worth replicating at home, like Smashed Sichuan Cucumbers and the Tzatziki Sauce with our lamb pitas.

In truth, the mild-mannered cucumber has many wonderful attributes that can put it squarely at center stage given the right technique and recipe. Here are our favorites, both classic and inventive.

shopping and storage

In general, most of the mainstream varieties of cucumbers are readily available year-round. Pickling cucumbers, also called Kirby cucumbers, are more typically available from summer through late fall than at other times of year. Look for specialty cukes like lemon cucumbers at farmers' markets in the summertime.

When buying cucumbers, look for ones that are firm and solid and don't have any shriveling skin, soft spots, or yellowing spots. Smaller cucumbers of any variety tend to have fewer seeds and thus less waste. All cucumbers should feel heavy for their size. If you can buy cucumbers that have not been waxed, do so. They are probably fresher than cucumbers that have been coated with wax. If you do buy waxed (regular slicing cucumbers often are sold this way), when you get them home, wrap them in plastic and store them in the crisper drawer of the refrigerator, which will keep them fresh for up to 10 days. Unwaxed cucumbers are more delicate, so they should be stored in a loosely closed plastic produce bag in the refrigerator, where they will keep for up to a week.

vegetable prep

Seeding Cucumbers
The seeds are watery and add little to finished dishes, so it is best to remove them.

Peel cucumber and halve lengthwise. Run small spoon inside each half to scoop out seeds and any surrounding excess liquid.

The Neatest Way to Smash Cucumbers
For Smashed Sichuan Cucumbers, smashing the cucumbers breaks them up to expose more surface area for the vinaigrette to adhere to.

Cut cucumbers into thirds and place them in zipper-lock bag before gently pounding them with small skillet or rolling pin.

Dicing Cucumbers

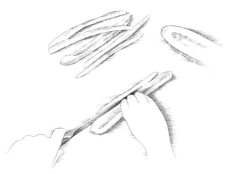

1. Cut ¾-inch section off both ends of cucumbers. Halve cucumbers lengthwise and scoop out seeds with dinner spoon. Cut each seeded half lengthwise into ¼-inch strips.

2. Turn strips 90 degrees and cut into even ¼-inch pieces.

cucumber varieties

There are dozens of cucumber varieties available, very broadly divided into the categories of "slicing cucumbers" and "pickling cucumbers."

AMERICAN CUCUMBERS Also called garden cucumbers, these slicing cucumbers have thick, somewhat bitter dark-green skin and large, plentiful seeds. They are often sold waxed, which keeps them fresher longer but renders their skin unpleasant. American cucumbers have a crisp texture and mild flavor.

ENGLISH CUCUMBERS Also called seedless or hothouse cucumbers, these slicing cukes are long and slim with thin skins and a medium-crunchy texture that is less watery than that of American cucumbers. They are not actually seedless, but their seeds are tiny. Their flavor is slightly sweet and melony. Seedless cucumbers are often sold shrink-wrapped.

KIRBY CUCUMBERS The most common type of pickling cucumbers, these are small and squat, with dense, crunchy flesh and bumpy skins that can be tough (but not as much as slicing cucumbers). These are our favorite pickling cukes, and they are great in salads as well.

MINI CUCUMBERS Also called Persian cucumbers, these small, slim cucumbers have thin skins, few seeds, and a medium-crunchy texture. Their mild flavor is similar to that of English cucumbers, but they are much smaller in size. They tend to be the most expensive variety.

LEMON CUCUMBERS Still primarily in the domain of farmers' markets, these petite round cucumbers are starting to become more available at some supermarkets. They have thin golden-colored skins and have a crisp texture and delicate, sweet flavor.

SMASHED SICHUAN CUCUMBERS

Serves 4   Total time: 30 minutes

WHY THIS RECIPE WORKS *Smashed cucumbers, or pai huang gua, is a Sichuan dish that is typically served with rich, spicy food. We started with English cucumbers, which are nearly seedless and have thin, crisp skins. Placing them in a zipper-lock bag and smashing them into large, irregular pieces sped up a salting step that helped expel excess water. The craggy pieces also did a better job of holding on to the dressing. Using black vinegar, an aged rice-based vinegar, added a mellow complexity to the soy and sesame dressing. We prefer the complex flavor of Chinese Chinkiang (or Zhenjiang) black vinegar in this dish, but if you can't find it, you can substitute 2 teaspoons of rice vinegar and 1 teaspoon of balsamic vinegar. A rasp-style grater makes quick work of turning the garlic into a paste. We like to drizzle the cucumbers with Sichuan chili oil when serving them with milder dishes such as grilled fish or chicken.*

2 (14-ounce) English cucumbers, ends trimmed
1½ teaspoons kosher salt
4 teaspoons Chinese black vinegar
1 teaspoon garlic, minced to paste
1 tablespoon soy sauce
2 teaspoons toasted sesame oil
1 teaspoon sugar
1 teaspoon sesame seeds, toasted

1. Cut each cucumber crosswise into 3 equal lengths and place in zipper-lock bag. Seal bag. Using small skillet or rolling pin, firmly but gently smash cucumbers until flattened and split lengthwise into 3 to 4 spears each. Tear spears into rough 1-inch pieces and transfer to colander set in large bowl. Toss cucumbers with salt and let sit for at least 15 minutes and up to 30 minutes.

2. Meanwhile, whisk vinegar and garlic together in medium bowl; let sit for at least 5 minutes or up to 15 minutes.

3. Whisk soy sauce, oil, and sugar into vinegar mixture to dissolve sugar. Add cucumbers, discarding any extracted liquid, and sesame seeds to bowl with dressing and toss to combine. Serve immediately.

QUICK PICKLE CHIPS

Makes one 1-pint jar

Total time: 45 minutes (plus 2½ hours chilling time)

WHY THIS RECIPE WORKS *A snap to make, these quick-pickled cucumber slices are ready to jump in on short notice to brighten up a picnic, barbecue, or weeknight meal. They're a great fuss-free pickle for a novice and a super go-to recipe for anyone looking to satisfy a craving without the effort involved in larger pickling projects. These chips get a hint of warm pickle spice from black peppercorns, mustard seeds, and turmeric. Fresh dill sprigs add their flavor, as befitting a classic hamburger pickle. To streamline preparation, we chose seasoned rice vinegar—with vinegar, sugar, and salt—and eliminated the work of separately measuring three ingredients. We sliced the cukes into ¼-inch chips using a chef's knife, though a mandoline or a cutter for making crinkle cuts can also be used for added flair. After 3 hours, these pickles were thoroughly suffused with a lively combination of sweet, sour, and aromatic tones. For guaranteed crunch, choose the freshest, firmest pickling cucumbers (we like Kirby cucumbers) available. Heating the jar with hot water and then draining it before adding the hot brine ensures that the jar won't crack from the abrupt temperature change. These pickles can be refrigerated for up to six weeks.*

¾ cup seasoned rice vinegar
1 garlic clove, peeled and halved
¼ teaspoon ground turmeric
⅛ teaspoon black peppercorns
⅛ teaspoon yellow mustard seeds
8 ounces pickling cucumbers, trimmed, sliced crosswise ¼ inch thick
2 sprigs fresh dill

1. Bring ¼ cup water, vinegar, garlic, turmeric, peppercorns, and mustard seeds to boil in medium saucepan over medium-high heat.

2. Fill one 1-pint jar with hot water to warm. Drain jar, then pack cucumbers and dill sprigs into jar. Using funnel and ladle, pour hot brine over cucumbers to cover. Let jar cool completely, about 30 minutes.

3. Cover jar with lid and refrigerate for at least 2½ hours before serving.

BREAD-AND-BUTTER PICKLES

Makes four 1-pint jars

Total time: 45 minutes (plus 1 day chilling time)

WHY THIS RECIPE WORKS *These bread-and-butter pickles feature a lively balance of sweet and sour flavors, just as they should. Using pickling cucumbers (we prefer Kirbys) and salting them beforehand ensures a crisp texture. Most recipes for these types of pickles call for combining cucumbers and onions in a syrupy spiced brine; we cut back on the sugar and added red bell pepper for its fresh flavor and color. Heating the jars with hot water and then draining them before adding the hot brine ensures that the jars won't crack from the abrupt temperature change. These pickles can be refrigerated for up to three months; their flavor will continue to mature over time. You can easily double this recipe; just be sure to use a larger pot when making the brine.*

2 pounds pickling cucumbers, trimmed and sliced ¼ inch thick crosswise
1 onion, quartered and sliced thin
1 red bell pepper, stemmed, seeded, and cut into 1½-inch matchsticks
2 tablespoons kosher salt
3 cups cider vinegar
2 cups sugar
1 tablespoon yellow mustard seeds
¾ teaspoon ground turmeric
½ teaspoon celery seeds
¼ teaspoon ground cloves

1. Toss cucumbers, onion, and bell pepper with salt in large bowl and refrigerate for 3 hours. Drain vegetables in colander (do not rinse), then pat dry with paper towels.

2. Bring 1 cup water, vinegar, sugar, mustard seeds, turmeric, celery seeds, and cloves to boil in large saucepan over medium-high heat; remove from heat.

3. Fill four 1-pint jars with hot water to warm. Drain jars, then pack tightly with vegetables. Using funnel and ladle, pour hot brine over vegetables to cover, distributing spices evenly. Let jars cool completely, about 30 minutes.

4. Cover jars with lids and refrigerate for at least 1 day before serving.

Quick Pickle Chips

PARSLEY-CUCUMBER SALAD WITH FETA, WALNUTS, AND POMEGRANATE

Serves 4 to 6   Total time: 20 minutes

WHY THIS RECIPE WORKS *Sweet, crisp, nearly seedless English cucumber pairs well with fresh parsley in terms of both flavor and texture in this pretty salad. A surprising but welcome quantity of fresh parsley leaves—3 whole cups—serves as the salad greens in this dish, which makes a crisp, refreshing accompaniment to rich grilled meats. The bracing vinaigrette, made from olive oil, sweet-tart pomegranate molasses, and red wine vinegar, brought layers of flavor, while adding a pinch of cayenne pepper to the dressing gave it a bit of heat. For a beautiful finishing touch and some richness, we topped the salad with thinly sliced feta cheese, chopped toasted walnuts, and juicy, jewel-like pomegranate seeds. Use flat-leaf parsley (also called Italian parsley) rather than curly parsley for this salad.*

- 3 tablespoons extra-virgin olive oil
- 1 tablespoon pomegranate molasses
- 1 tablespoon red wine vinegar
  Salt and pepper
  Pinch cayenne pepper
- 3 cups fresh parsley leaves
- 1 English cucumber, halved lengthwise and sliced thin
- 1 cup walnuts, toasted and chopped coarse
- ½ cup pomegranate seeds
- 4 ounces feta cheese, sliced thin

Whisk oil, molasses, vinegar, ¼ teaspoon salt, ⅛ teaspoon pepper, and cayenne in large bowl until fully incorporated. Add parsley and cucumber and toss to coat. Add half of walnuts and half of pomegranate seeds and toss to combine. Season with salt and pepper to taste. Transfer to serving platter and top with feta, remaining walnuts, and remaining pomegranate seeds. Serve.

CREAMY CUCUMBER SALAD WITH RADISHES, LEMON, AND MINT

Serves 4 to 6   Total time: 35 minutes

WHY THIS RECIPE WORKS *Cucumbers and red onions are a great salad combo: The cucumber gives the salad some heft and juicy crunch, while the bite of red onion serves as a great foil to the cucumber's subtle flavor. In this recipe, we added peppery sliced radishes and brought everything together with a creamy, lemony dressing. All too often, creamy cucumber salads suffer from limp, flimsy slices of cucumber swimming in a diluted dressing. Here we found that laying the sliced cucumbers on a paper towel–lined baking sheet, instead of the more typical step of salting them, dried them out sufficiently while keeping them crisp. Marinating the onions in vinegar before we added them to the salad tamed their raw strength, and the thick, sour cream–based dressing resulted in a creamy—never watery—cucumber salad.*

- 3 cucumbers, peeled, halved lengthwise, seeded, and sliced thin crosswise
- ½ cup thinly sliced red onion
- 3 tablespoons cider vinegar
- ½ cup sour cream
- 3 tablespoons chopped fresh mint
- 1 teaspoon grated lemon zest
- ½ teaspoon sugar
  Salt and pepper
- 6 radishes, trimmed and sliced thin

1. Spread cucumber slices in single layer on paper towel–lined baking sheet and refrigerate for 20 minutes. Meanwhile, combine onion and vinegar in bowl and let stand for 20 minutes.

2. Whisk sour cream, mint, lemon zest, sugar, and ½ teaspoon salt together in large bowl. Add cucumbers, radishes, and onion-vinegar mixture and toss to combine. Season with salt and pepper to taste. Serve.

COUNTRY-STYLE GREEK SALAD

Serves 6 to 8   Total time: 35 minutes

WHY THIS RECIPE WORKS *Most versions of Greek salad consist of iceberg lettuce, a few bits of green pepper, and a couple of pale tomato wedges, sparsely dotted with cubes of feta and garnished with one forlorn olive of questionable heritage and a few rounds of cucumber thrown in for good measure. For our Greek salad, we left out the lettuce altogether in favor of a "country style" salad that is popular throughout Greece. Naturally, it features an abundance of crisp, thinly sliced cucumbers. For the bright-tasting dressing, we used a combination of lemon juice and red wine vinegar and added fresh oregano, olive oil, and a small amount of garlic. Briefly marinating the cucumbers and onion in the vinaigrette both flavored the cucumber and tamed the onion's harshness. We then added ripe tomatoes, roasted red peppers, kalamata olives, and fresh mint and parsley, and topped it all with a generous amount of crumbled feta.*

- 6 tablespoons extra-virgin olive oil
- 1½ tablespoons red wine vinegar
- 2 teaspoons minced fresh oregano
- 1 teaspoon lemon juice
- 1 garlic clove, minced
  Salt and pepper
- 2 English cucumbers, halved lengthwise and sliced thin
- ½ red onion, sliced thin
- 6 large ripe tomatoes, cored, seeded, and cut into ½-inch-thick wedges
- 1 cup jarred roasted red peppers, rinsed, patted dry, and cut into ½-inch strips
- ½ cup pitted kalamata olives, quartered
- ¼ cup chopped fresh parsley
- ¼ cup chopped fresh mint
- 5 ounces feta cheese, crumbled (1¼ cups)

1. Whisk oil, vinegar, oregano, lemon juice, garlic, ½ teaspoon salt, and ⅛ teaspoon pepper together in large bowl. Add cucumbers and onion, toss to coat, and let sit for 20 minutes.

2. Add tomatoes, red peppers, olives, parsley, and mint to bowl with cucumber-onion mixture and toss to combine. Season with salt and pepper to taste. Transfer to serving dish and sprinkle with feta. Serve.

3. Break pitas into ½-inch pieces and place in large bowl. Add tomatoes, cucumber, arugula, cilantro, mint, and scallions. Drizzle dressing over top and gently toss to coat. Season with salt and pepper to taste. Serve, sprinkling individual portions with extra sumac if desired.

ORZO SALAD WITH CUCUMBER, RED ONION, AND MINT

Serves 4 to 6   Total time: 1 hour 15 minutes
WHY THIS RECIPE WORKS *Cucumber really shines when paired with rice-shaped orzo in this pasta salad. An assertive lemony dressing and a few supporting players that always pair nicely with cucumber—namely red onion, feta, and mint—ensured an appealingly bright and flavorful side dish or light lunch. To start, we cooked the orzo in salted water, stirring frequently to keep all the pieces separate; when it was al dente, we drained it and tossed it with a tablespoon of oil to further ensure that it wouldn't clump. For our dressing, a combo of 5 tablespoons extra-virgin olive oil and a full ¼ cup of lemon juice plus minced garlic ensured there would be enough dressing to coat the orzo and all the mix-ins and also deliver the requisite punch of lively flavor.*

- 1¼ cups orzo
    Salt and pepper
- 6 tablespoons extra-virgin olive oil, plus extra for drizzling
- ¼ cup lemon juice (2 lemons)
- 2 garlic cloves, minced
- ½ English cucumber, halved lengthwise and sliced thin
- 2 ounces feta cheese, crumbled (½ cup)
- ½ cup finely chopped red onion
- ½ cup chopped fresh mint
- ¼ cup thinly sliced scallions

1. Bring 2 quarts water to boil in large saucepan. Add orzo and 1½ teaspoons salt and cook, stirring often, until al dente. Drain orzo and transfer to rimmed baking sheet. Toss with 1 tablespoon oil and let cool completely, about 15 minutes.

PITA BREAD SALAD WITH TOMATOES AND CUCUMBER (FATTOUSH)

Serves 4   Total time: 35 minutes
WHY THIS RECIPE WORKS *The eastern Mediterranean salad fattoush puts cucumbers and tomatoes at center stage along with herbs, toasted pita bread, and bright, tangy sumac. We opted to use an ample amount of ground sumac in the dressing to intensify the flavor, as well as use it as a garnish for the finished salad. Many recipes call for eliminating excess moisture from the salad by taking the time-consuming step of seeding and salting the cucumbers and tomatoes. We skipped this in order to preserve the crisp texture of the cucumber and the flavorful seeds and juice of the tomatoes. Instead, we made the pita pieces more resilient by brushing them with plenty of olive oil before baking, which prevented them from becoming soggy in the dressing. The success of this recipe depends on ripe, in-season tomatoes. Tart, lemony sumac can be found in the spice aisle of larger supermarkets.*

- 2 (8-inch) pita breads
- 7 tablespoons extra-virgin olive oil
    Salt and pepper
- 3 tablespoons lemon juice
- 4 teaspoons ground sumac, plus extra for sprinkling (optional)
- ¼ teaspoon minced garlic
- 1 pound ripe tomatoes, cored and cut into ¾-inch pieces
- 1 English cucumber, sliced ⅛ inch thick
- 1 cup arugula, chopped coarse
- ½ cup chopped fresh cilantro
- ½ cup chopped fresh mint
- 4 scallions, sliced thin

1. Adjust oven rack to middle position and heat oven to 375 degrees. Using kitchen shears, cut around perimeter of each pita and separate into 2 thin rounds. Cut each round in half. Place pitas smooth side down on wire rack set in rimmed baking sheet. Brush 3 tablespoons oil over surface of pitas. (Pitas do not need to be uniformly coated. Oil will spread during baking.) Season with salt and pepper. Bake until pitas are crisp and pale golden brown, 10 to 14 minutes. Let cool to room temperature.

2. Whisk lemon juice; sumac, if using; garlic; and ¼ teaspoon salt together in small bowl and let sit for 10 minutes. While whisking constantly, slowly drizzle in remaining ¼ cup oil.

2. Whisk remaining 5 tablespoons oil, lemon juice, garlic, ½ teaspoon salt, and ½ teaspoon pepper in large bowl until combined. Add cucumber, feta, onion, mint, scallions, and cooled orzo and toss to coat. Season with salt and pepper to taste.

3. Let salad sit at room temperature for 30 minutes to allow flavors to meld. Serve, drizzling with extra oil.

CHILLED CUCUMBER AND YOGURT SOUP

Serves 6   Total time: 20 minutes
(plus 1 hour chilling time)
WHY THIS RECIPE WORKS *Both refreshing and elegant, this chilled soup is the perfect antidote for a swelteringly hot summer's evening. But because it has so few ingredients, we knew that balance and finesse would be key, especially if the subtle vegetal flavor of the cucumbers was to shine through. A food processor turned our soup mushy, and hand chopping all of the cucumber gave us something watery and inconsistent. We found that blending some of the cucumbers and reserving a final chopped handful as a garnish gave us the smooth consistency we wanted with texture to boot. Peeling and seeding the cucumbers removed any unpleasantly bitter flavors. We tried garlic, shallots, red onion, and scallions in the soup, but they were all too astringent; it was only after we left in just the scallion greens that we found the right balance. Tasters preferred dill and mint to other herb combinations, as they brought out the freshest aspect of this appealing soup.*

- 5   pounds cucumbers, peeled and seeded (1 cucumber cut into ½-inch pieces, remaining cucumbers cut into 2-inch pieces)
- 4   scallions, green parts only, chopped coarse
- 2   cups water
- 2   cups plain Greek yogurt
- 1   tablespoon lemon juice
      Salt and pepper
- ¼   teaspoon sugar
- 1½ tablespoons minced fresh dill
- 1½ tablespoons minced fresh mint
      Extra-virgin olive oil

1. Toss 2-inch pieces of cucumber with scallions. Working in 2 batches, process cucumber-scallion mixture in blender with water until completely smooth, about 2 minutes; transfer to large bowl. Whisk in yogurt, lemon juice, 1½ teaspoons salt, sugar, and pinch pepper. Cover and refrigerate to blend flavors, at least 1 hour or up to 12 hours.

2. Stir in dill and mint and season with salt and pepper to taste. Serve, topping individual portions with remaining ½-inch pieces of cucumber and drizzling with oil.

GREEK-STYLE LAMB PITA SANDWICHES WITH TZATZIKI SAUCE

Serves 4   Total time: 1 hour 15 minutes
WHY THIS RECIPE WORKS *Tzatziki sauce, with its trademark combination of cucumbers and yogurt laced with salt, garlic, lemon, and mint, is the crowning glory of lamb pita sandwiches. These classic Greek gyros feature seasoned, marinated lamb; the traditional method for cooking the meat employs an electric vertical rotisserie on which layers of sliced and marinated leg of lamb are stacked.*

After cooking for hours, the meat is shaved with a long slicing knife, creating pieces with crisp exteriors and moist interiors infused with garlic and oregano. We wanted to translate this recipe for the home kitchen. Surprisingly, using ground lamb—which we formed into patties—was easy and came close to reproducing the texture of rotisserie lamb. A modified panade, or wet binder, of pita bread crumbs, lemon juice, and garlic gave our patties a sturdier structure and fuller, more savory flavor. Although we prefer the richness of plain whole-milk yogurt for the sauce, low-fat yogurt can be substituted. If using pocketless pitas, do not cut off the tops in step 4; instead, use a portion of a fifth pita to create crumbs. The skillet may appear crowded when you begin cooking the patties, but they will shrink slightly as they cook.

TZATZIKI SAUCE

- 1   cup plain whole-milk yogurt
- ½   cucumber, peeled, seeded, and cut into ¼-inch pieces (½ cup)
- 1   tablespoon lemon juice
      Salt
- 1   tablespoon minced fresh mint or dill
- 1   small garlic clove, minced

SANDWICHES

- 4 (8-inch) pita breads
- ½ onion, chopped coarse
- 4 teaspoons fresh lemon juice
- 1 tablespoon minced fresh oregano or 1 teaspoon dried
- 2 garlic cloves, minced
- ½ teaspoon salt
- ¼ teaspoon ground black pepper
- 1 pound ground lamb
- 2 teaspoons vegetable oil
- 1 large tomato, sliced thin
- 2 cups shredded iceberg lettuce
- 2 ounces feta cheese, crumbled (½ cup)

1. For the tzatziki sauce Line fine-mesh strainer set over deep container or bowl with 3 paper coffee filters or triple layer of paper towels. Spoon yogurt into lined strainer, cover, and refrigerate for 30 minutes.

2. Meanwhile, combine cucumber, lemon juice, and ⅛ teaspoon salt in colander set over bowl and let sit for 30 minutes.

3. Discard drained yogurt liquid. Combine yogurt, cucumber, mint, garlic, and ⅛ teaspoon salt in clean bowl.

4. For the sandwiches Adjust oven rack to middle position and heat oven to 350 degrees. Cut top quarter off each pita bread. Tear quarters into 1-inch pieces. (You should have ¾ cup pita pieces.) Stack pitas and tightly wrap with aluminum foil. Process onion, lemon juice, oregano, garlic, salt, pepper, and pita bread pieces in food processor until smooth paste forms, about 30 seconds. Transfer onion mixture to large bowl; add lamb and gently mix with your hands until thoroughly combined. Divide mixture into 12 equal pieces and roll into balls. Gently flatten balls into round disks, about ½ inch thick and 2½ inches in diameter.

5. Place foil-wrapped pitas directly on oven rack and heat for 10 minutes. Meanwhile, heat oil in 12-inch nonstick skillet over medium-high heat until just smoking. Add patties and cook until well browned and crust forms, 3 to 4 minutes. Flip patties, reduce heat to medium, and cook until well browned and crust forms on second side, about 5 minutes longer. Transfer patties to paper towel–lined plate.

6. Using spoon, spread ¼ cup tzatziki sauce inside each pita. Divide patties evenly among pitas; top each sandwich with tomato slices, ½ cup shredded lettuce, and 2 tablespoons feta. Serve immediately.

GRILLED THAI BEEF SALAD WITH CUCUMBERS
Serves 4 to 6   Total time: 1 hour

WHY THIS RECIPE WORKS *In this light and refreshing yet satisfying dish, perfectly grilled flank steak is tossed in an aromatic mixture of fish sauce, lime juice, and spices; topped with a chile, herb, and shallot combo; and then arranged over a bed of crisp, cool English cucumber. The flavor elements of Thai cooking—hot, sour, salty, sweet, and bitter—come into harmony here. To grill the beef, we used the test kitchen's standard half-grill fire, starting the meat over high heat to sear the exterior and then moving it to the cooler side to finish cooking for a perfect medium-rare steak with a nicely charred crust. The dressing for this dish should have a good balance between hot, sour, salty, and sweet to provide a counterpoint to the subtle bitter char of the meat. Fish sauce, lime juice, sugar, and a mix of hot spices provided these elements and the final addition—toasted rice powder made in a food processor—added extra body to the dressing. Don't skip the toasted rice; it's integral to the texture and flavor of the dish. Toasted rice powder (kao kua) can also be found in many Asian markets; substitute 1 tablespoon rice powder for the white rice. If fresh Thai chiles are unavailable, substitute ½ serrano chile.*

- 1 teaspoon paprika
- 1 teaspoon cayenne pepper
- 1 tablespoon white rice
- 3 tablespoons lime juice (2 limes)
- 2 tablespoons fish sauce
- 2 tablespoons water
- ½ teaspoon sugar
- 1 (1½-pound) flank steak, trimmed
  Salt and coarsely ground white pepper
- 1 English cucumber, sliced ¼ inch thick on bias
- 4 shallots, sliced thin
- 1½ cups fresh mint leaves, torn
- 1½ cups fresh cilantro leaves
- 1 Thai chile, stemmed, seeded, and sliced thin into rounds

1. Heat paprika and cayenne in 8-inch skillet over medium heat; cook, shaking pan, until fragrant, about 1 minute. Transfer to small bowl. Return skillet to medium-high heat, add rice and toast, stirring constantly, until deep golden brown, about 5 minutes. Transfer to small bowl and let cool for 5 minutes. Grind rice with spice grinder, mini food processor, or mortar and pestle until it resembles fine meal, 10 to 30 seconds (you should have about 1 tablespoon rice powder).

2. Whisk lime juice, fish sauce, water, sugar, and ¼ teaspoon toasted paprika mixture in large bowl and set aside.

3a. For a charcoal grill Open bottom vent completely. Light large chimney starter filled with charcoal briquettes (6 quarts). When top coals are partially covered with ash, pour in even layer over half of grill. Set cooking grate in place, cover, and open lid vent completely. Heat grill until hot, about 5 minutes.

3b. For a gas grill Turn all burners to high, cover, and heat grill until hot, about 15 minutes. Leave primary burner on high and turn off other burner(s).

4. Clean and oil cooking grate. Pat steak dry and season with salt and white pepper. Place steak on hotter part of grill and cook until beginning to char and beads of moisture appear on outer edges of meat, 5 to 6 minutes. Flip steak and continue to cook on second side until meat registers 120 to 125 degrees (for medium-rare), about 5 minutes longer. Transfer to carving board, tent with aluminum foil, and let rest for 10 minutes (or up to 1 hour).

5. Line large platter with cucumber slices. Slice steak ¼ inch thick against grain on bias. Transfer sliced steak to bowl with fish sauce mixture. Add shallots, mint, cilantro, Thai chile, and half of rice powder, and toss to combine. Arrange steak over cucumber-lined platter. Serve, passing remaining rice powder and remaining toasted paprika mixture separately.

EGGPLANT

With their often dark, luminous skin and beautiful shapes, eggplants are an alluring but somewhat mysterious vegetable. Technically a fruit and a member of the nightshade family, eggplants were first cultivated in China, but they have culinary roots across the Mediterranean, the Middle East, and India.

The beauty of eggplants is that they can be prepared in so many ways: They are, in essence, a bit of a chameleon, as they easily take on the flavors of other ingredients or sauces that surround them, as in baba ghanoush or caponata. Their flesh turns creamy and silky when roasted and appealingly tender when sautéed and browned. But they are full of moisture, so the key when cooking with eggplants is to know when and how to salt them to draw out the excess water before cooking to avoid insipid flavors and a mushy texture. Here in the test kitchen, we have learned that there is no hard and fast answer to this question. Oftentimes salting is necessary, but sometimes it is not—for example, there is no need to do so when grilling or stir-frying, as you'll learn here.

In this chapter, you will find some classic and inventive recipes starring eggplant. Our Walkaway Ratatouille simplifies this usually time-consuming dish, and you will want to make it again and again when farmers' markets are brimming with eggplants of all shapes and sizes. Three company-worthy Italian dishes are also here, including our authentic yet refined Eggplant Parmesan (no breading or frying required). Our Stuffed Eggplant couldn't be easier: Simply roast the eggplant, push the soft, creamy flesh to the sides, and add the fragrant stuffing. And since eggplants are happy to absorb pungent spices and chiles, you'll find two super-flavorful stir-fries using slender Japanese eggplant.

shopping and storage

There are many varieties of eggplant, but generally in the supermarket you will find the larger deep purple globe eggplants or the smaller Italian eggplants, as well as sometimes Japanese or Chinese eggplants or specialty eggplants like Thai or Indian. Buy all-purpose globe eggplants unless a recipe specifies a specific type of eggplant. Look for eggplants that are firm, glossy, and without blemishes. The purple varieties should be a deep, rich color, and other varieties should be bright in whatever color they happen to be. A ripe eggplant will feel heavy for its size. Larger eggplants tend to be more bitter and have more seeds than smaller specimens.

The refrigerator is not the best place to store eggplants. It's preferable to store eggplants uncovered on your kitchen counter away from direct sunlight. But since they are fairly perishable, plan to use them within a few days of purchasing them.

a cure for what ails eggplant

To rid eggplant of excess moisture and collapse the air pockets that make it soak up oil like a sponge, we came up with a novel solution: salting it and then heating it in the microwave. The salt pulls out liquid at the same time the microwave causes the eggplant to steam and compress, making it less spongy. We set it on a layer of coffee filters to soak up the released liquid. By absorbing all of that liquid, the filters also helped to maintain a high salt concentration on the exterior of the eggplant, which drew out even more unwanted moisture.

eggplant varieties

There are countless eggplant varieties, ranging from 2 to 12 inches long, from round to oblong, and from dark purple to striped to white. Here are some of the most common varieties you'll find in the market.

GLOBE The most common type in the United States, the bulbous globe eggplant has a mild flavor and tender texture that work well in most cooked applications. It not only contains far fewer seeds than smaller varieties like Italian and Chinese, but its firm flesh also retains its shape even after cooking. It is a true multitasker and can be sautéed, broiled, grilled, and pureed. Because of its high water content, it's often best to salt and drain it before cooking.

ITALIAN Also called baby eggplant, Italian eggplant looks like a smaller version of a globe eggplant. It is a bit more tender than the globe eggplant, with moderately moist flesh, lots of seeds, and a distinct spicy flavor. It can be sautéed, broiled, grilled, and more.

JAPANESE AND CHINESE Both of these types are long and slender, with Japanese having a deep purple hue and Chinese being lighter in color, sometimes almost lavender. Both are thin skinned and have few seeds and creamy flesh. They are perfect for use in grilling or stir-frying.

THAI These eggplants are small and apple shaped and usually have a greenish-white hue. They are becoming increasingly easier to find in large supermarkets. They are notable for tasting bright and grassy, and are appealing even simply eaten raw. They are terrific roasted with pungent spices or used in Thai curries.

INDIAN Also sometimes called baby eggplant, these are smaller and more squat than Italian eggplants, with a dark reddish-purple color. They make a pretty presentation halved and stuffed, and they are great cooked and mashed into dips.

vegetable prep

Cutting Up an Eggplant

1. To cut eggplant into tidy cubes, first cut eggplant crosswise into 1-inch-thick rounds.

2. Cut rounds into even 1-inch cubes.

Preparing Eggplant for Stuffing

Using 2 forks, gently push cooked flesh to sides of each eggplant half to make room in center for filling.

Sicilian Eggplant Relish (Caponata)

BROILED EGGPLANT WITH BASIL

Serves 4 to 6   Total time: 40 minutes

WHY THIS RECIPE WORKS *When you want to enjoy eggplant as a simple side dish, broiling it is a great way to do so; while you can jazz it up with a simple glaze if you want, all you really need is a sprinkling of fresh herbs. That said, if you try to simply slice and broil eggplant, it will steam in its own juices rather than brown. So to get broiled eggplant with great color and texture, we started by salting it to draw out its moisture. After 30 minutes, we patted the slices dry, moved them to a baking sheet (lined with aluminum foil for easy cleanup), and brushed them with oil. With the excess moisture taken care of, all the eggplant required was a few minutes per side under the blazing-hot broiler to turn a beautiful mahogany color. With its concentrated roasted flavor, the only accent needed was a sprinkling of fresh basil. Make sure to slice the eggplant thin so that the slices will cook through by the time the exterior is browned.*

- 1½ pounds eggplant, sliced into ¼-inch- thick rounds
  Salt and pepper
- 3 tablespoons extra-virgin olive oil
- 2 tablespoons chopped fresh basil

1. Spread eggplant over rimmed baking sheet lined with paper towels, sprinkle both sides with 1½ teaspoons salt (¾ teaspoon per side), and let sit for 30 minutes.

2. Adjust oven rack 4 inches from broiler element and heat broiler. Thoroughly pat eggplant dry, arrange in single layer on aluminum foil–lined baking sheet, and brush both sides with oil. Broil eggplant until tops are mahogany brown, 3 to 4 minutes. Flip eggplant and broil until second side is brown, 3 to 4 minutes.

3. Transfer eggplant to serving platter, season with pepper to taste, and sprinkle with basil. Serve.

VARIATION

Broiled Eggplant with Sesame-Miso Glaze
Any type of miso will work well here. Mirin is a sweet Japanese cooking wine; sherry can be substituted for the mirin if necessary.

Substitute vegetable oil for olive oil and 1 sliced scallion for basil. Whisk 1 tablespoon miso, 3 tablespoons mirin, and 1 tablespoon tahini together in bowl. After browning second side, brush with miso mixture, sprinkle with 1 tablespoon sesame seeds, and continue to broil until miso and seeds are browned, about 2 minutes.

GRILLED EGGPLANT WITH CHERRY TOMATOES AND CILANTRO VINAIGRETTE

Serves 4 to 6   Total time: 35 minutes

WHY THIS RECIPE WORKS *When grilled, the skin of the eggplant turns beautifully brown and becomes crisp in spots. And the great advantage of grilling is that there is no need to salt the eggplant in advance because the moisture vaporizes or drips harmlessly through the cooking grate into the hot fire. In our tests, we found that thinner slices can fall apart on the cooking grate. Thicker pieces, ideally ¾-inch-thick rounds, can better withstand the rigors of grilling. To impart flavor to the eggplant while we grilled it, we whisked together a mixture of olive oil and minced garlic, brushing it on liberally. Our pungent vinaigrette included shallot, lime juice, and a little cayenne pepper, with quartered cherry tomatoes added for their bright flavor. We spooned this over the grilled eggplant slices for a simple but superflavorful side dish.*

- ½ cup plus 1 tablespoon extra-virgin olive oil
- 1 shallot, minced
- 2 tablespoons minced fresh cilantro
- 2 tablespoons lime juice
  Salt and pepper
  Pinch cayenne pepper
- 6 ounces cherry tomatoes, quartered
- 2 garlic cloves, minced
- 1½ pounds eggplant, sliced into ¾-inch- thick rounds

1. Whisk 6 tablespoons oil, shallot, cilantro, lime juice, ¼ teaspoon salt, and cayenne together in medium bowl. Add tomatoes and toss to coat; set aside.

2. Whisk garlic and remaining 3 tablespoons oil together in small bowl and season with salt and pepper to taste. Brush eggplant with oil mixture.

3a. **For a charcoal grill** Open bottom vent completely. Light large chimney starter filled with charcoal briquettes (6 quarts). When top coals are partially covered with ash, pour evenly over grill. Set cooking grate in place, cover, and open lid vent completely. Heat grill until hot, about 5 minutes.

3b. **For a gas grill** Turn all burners to high, cover, and heat grill until hot, about 15 minutes. Leave all burners on high.

4. Clean and oil cooking grate. Grill eggplant (covered if using gas) until browned and tender, 4 to 5 minutes per side. Transfer to serving platter. Spoon vinaigrette over eggplant. Serve immediately.

SICILIAN EGGPLANT RELISH (CAPONATA)

Makes about 3 cups   Total time: 40 minutes

WHY THIS RECIPE WORKS *Sicilian caponata distinguishes itself with boldly flavored eggplant and a sweet-and-sour finish. To make sure the eggplant didn't turn to oil-soaked mush, we salted and microwaved it to eliminate excess moisture. We used V8 juice to deliver bright tomato flavor. Brown sugar and red wine vinegar enhanced the traditional sweet-and-sour profile. A scoopful of raisins brought additional sweetness, minced anchovies added a rich umami boost, and briny black olives offered balance. Simmering everything together for just a few minutes allowed the mixture to thicken and the flavors to meld. Although we prefer the complex flavor of V8 juice, tomato juice can be substituted. If coffee filters are not available, food-safe, undyed paper towels can be substituted when microwaving the eggplant. Be sure to remove the eggplant from the microwave immediately so that the steam can escape. Serve caponata with slices of toasted baguette or with grilled meat or fish.*

1½ pounds eggplant, cut into ½-inch pieces
½ teaspoon salt
¾ cup V8 juice
¼ cup red wine vinegar, plus extra for seasoning
2 tablespoons packed brown sugar
¼ cup chopped fresh parsley
3 anchovy fillets, rinsed and minced
1 large tomato, cored, seeded, and chopped
¼ cup raisins
2 tablespoons minced black olives
2 tablespoons extra-virgin olive oil
1 celery rib, chopped fine
1 red bell pepper, stemmed, seeded, and chopped fine
1 small onion, chopped fine
¼ cup pine nuts, toasted

1. Toss eggplant with salt in bowl. Line entire surface of large plate with double layer of coffee filters and lightly spray with vegetable oil spray. Spread eggplant in even layer on coffee filters. Microwave until eggplant is dry and shriveled to one-third of its original size, 8 to 15 minutes (eggplant should not brown). Transfer eggplant immediately to paper towel–lined plate.

2. Whisk V8 juice, vinegar, sugar, parsley, and anchovies together in medium bowl. Stir in tomato, raisins, and olives.

3. Heat 1 tablespoon oil in 12-inch nonstick skillet over medium-high heat until shimmering. Add eggplant and cook, stirring occasionally, until edges are browned, 4 to 8 minutes, adding 1 teaspoon more oil if pan appears dry; transfer to bowl.

4. Add remaining oil to now-empty skillet and heat over medium-high heat until shimmering. Add celery, bell pepper, and onion and cook, stirring occasionally, until softened and edges are spotty brown, 6 to 8 minutes.

5. Reduce heat to medium-low and stir in eggplant and juice mixture. Bring to simmer and cook until juice is thickened and coats vegetables, 4 to 7 minutes. Transfer to serving bowl and let cool to room temperature. Season with extra vinegar to taste and sprinkle with pine nuts before serving. (Caponata can be refrigerated for up to 1 week; bring to room temperature before serving.)

WALKAWAY RATATOUILLE

Serves 6 to 8   Total time: 1 hour 45 minutes

WHY THIS RECIPE WORKS *Most ratatouille recipes call for labor- and time-intensive treatments like salting and/or pressing to remove excess moisture from the vegetables. We started our streamlined recipe by sautéing onions and aromatics and then added chunks of eggplant and tomatoes before transferring the pot to the oven, where the dry, ambient heat would thoroughly evaporate moisture, concentrate flavors, and caramelize some of the vegetables. After 45 minutes, the tomatoes and eggplant became meltingly soft and could be mashed into a thick, silky sauce. Zucchini and bell peppers went into the pot last so that they retained some texture. Finishing the dish with fresh herbs, sherry vinegar, and extra-virgin olive oil tiedeverything together. This dish is best prepared using ripe, in-season tomatoes. If good tomatoes are not available, substitute one 28-ounce can of whole peeled tomatoes that have been drained and chopped. Ratatouille can be served warm, at room temperature, or chilled, as an accompaniment to meat or fish, topped with an egg, over pasta, or on its own with crusty bread.*

⅓ cup plus 1 tablespoon extra-virgin olive oil
2 large onions, cut into 1-inch pieces
8 large garlic cloves, peeled and smashed
Salt and pepper
1½ teaspoons herbes de Provence
¼ teaspoon red pepper flakes
1 bay leaf
2 pounds plum tomatoes, peeled, cored, and chopped coarse
1½ pounds eggplant, peeled and cut into 1-inch pieces
2 small zucchini, halved lengthwise and cut into 1-inch pieces
1 red bell pepper, stemmed, seeded, and cut into 1-inch pieces
1 yellow bell pepper, stemmed, seeded, and cut into 1-inch pieces
2 tablespoons chopped fresh basil
1 tablespoon minced fresh parsley
1 tablespoon sherry vinegar

1. Adjust oven rack to middle position and heat oven to 400 degrees. Heat ⅓ cup oil in Dutch oven over medium-high heat until shimmering. Add onions, garlic, 1 teaspoon salt, and ¼ teaspoon pepper and cook, stirring occasionally, until onions are translucent and starting to soften, about 10 minutes. Stir in herbes de Provence, pepper flakes, and bay leaf and cook until fragrant, about 1 minute. Stir in tomatoes, eggplant, ½ teaspoon salt, and ¼ teaspoon pepper.

2. Transfer pot to oven and cook, uncovered, until vegetables are very tender and spotty brown, 40 to 45 minutes.

3. Remove pot from oven and, using potato masher, mash eggplant mixture to coarse puree. Stir in zucchini, bell peppers, ¼ teaspoon salt, and ¼ teaspoon pepper and return to oven. Cook, uncovered, until zucchini and bell peppers are just tender, 20 to 25 minutes.

4. Remove pot from oven, cover, and let stand until zucchini is translucent and easily pierced with tip of paring knife, 10 to 15 minutes. Using wooden spoon, scrape any browned bits from sides of pot and stir back into ratatouille. Discard bay leaf.

5. Stir in 1 tablespoon basil, parsley, and vinegar. Season with salt and pepper to taste. Transfer to large platter, drizzle with remaining 1 tablespoon oil, sprinkle with remaining 1 tablespoon basil, and serve.

BABA GHANOUSH

Makes about 2 cups   Total time: 1 hour 15 minutes (plus 1 hour chilling time)

WHY THIS RECIPE WORKS *When roasted, eggplant flesh becomes concentrated and turns creamy and soft, making the perfect base for baba ghanoush. Before roasting the eggplants, we pricked their skin to encourage moisture to evaporate during cooking, then roasted them whole in a very hot oven until the flesh was very soft and tender. To avoid a watery texture in the finished dish, we scooped the hot pulp into a colander to drain before processing it. We kept the flavorings simple, processing the eggplant with lemon juice, olive oil, garlic, and tahini. Look for eggplants with an even shape for this recipe, as bulbous eggplants won't cook evenly. We prefer to serve baba ghanoush only lightly chilled; if cold, let it stand at room temperature for about 20 minutes before serving. Serve with fresh warm pita or raw vegetables for dipping. You will need to refrigerate the dip for at least 1 hour or up to 24 hours.*

- 2 eggplants (1 pound each), pricked all over with fork
- 2 tablespoons tahini
- 2 tablespoons extra-virgin olive oil, plus extra for serving
- 4 teaspoons lemon juice
- 1 small garlic clove, minced
  Salt and pepper
- 2 teaspoons chopped fresh parsley

1. Adjust oven rack to middle position and heat oven to 500 degrees. Place eggplants on aluminum foil–lined rimmed baking sheet and roast, turning eggplants every 15 minutes, until uniformly soft when pressed with tongs, 40 minutes to 1 hour. Let eggplants cool for 5 minutes on sheet.

2. Set colander over bowl. Trim top and bottom ¼ inch of eggplants, then slice eggplants lengthwise. Using spoon, scoop hot pulp into colander (you should have about 2 cups pulp); discard skins. Let pulp drain for 3 minutes.

3. Transfer drained eggplant to food processor. Add tahini, oil, lemon juice, garlic, ¾ teaspoon salt, and ¼ teaspoon pepper. Pulse mixture to coarse puree, about 8 pulses. Season with salt and pepper to taste.

4. Transfer to serving bowl, cover tightly with plastic wrap, and refrigerate until chilled, about 1 hour. Season with salt and pepper to taste, drizzle with extra oil to taste, and sprinkle with parsley before serving. (Dip can be refrigerated for up to 24 hours; bring to room temperature before serving.)

CRISPY THAI EGGPLANT SALAD

Serves 2 or 3   Total time: 45 minutes

WHY THIS RECIPE WORKS *For this recipe, we took elements from Sicilian caponata—eggplant, tomatoes, herbs, and vinegary notes—and married them with intense Thai flavors. We used the same microwave dehydrating method from our Charred Sichuan-Style Eggplant (page 190) and then shallow-fried the eggplant before marinating it in nam prik—a bright Thai condiment made with lime juice, fish sauce, rice vinegar, ginger, garlic, and chiles. We tossed in juicy cherry tomatoes, a healthy amount of fresh herbs, and crispy fried shallots for a dish that delivered all of the five tastes and as many different textures. Japanese eggplant was our unanimous favorite when we tested this recipe, but globe or Italian eggplant can be substituted if necessary. Traditional Genovese basil is a fine substitute for the Thai basil. Depending on the size of your microwave, you may need to microwave the eggplant in two batches. Be sure to remove the eggplant from the microwave immediately so that the steam can escape. Serve this salad with sticky rice, grilled steak, or both.*

- ¼ cup fish sauce
- ¼ cup unseasoned rice vinegar
- ¼ cup plus 1 teaspoon lime juice (3 limes)
- ¼ cup packed light brown sugar
- 1 (2-inch piece) ginger, peeled and chopped
- 4 garlic cloves, chopped
- 1 red Thai chile, seeded and sliced thin
- 6 ounces cherry tomatoes, halved
- 2 large Japanese eggplants, halved lengthwise, then sliced crosswise 1½ inches thick
- ½ teaspoon salt
- 2 cups vegetable oil
- ½ cup fresh cilantro leaves
- ½ cup fresh mint leaves
- ½ cup fresh Thai basil leaves
- ½ cup dry-roasted peanuts, chopped

1. Process fish sauce, vinegar, ¼ cup lime juice, sugar, ginger, garlic, and chile in blender until dressing is mostly smooth, about 1 minute. Transfer to large serving bowl and stir in tomatoes; set aside.

2. Toss eggplant with salt in medium bowl. Line entire surface of large plate with double layer of coffee filters and lightly spray

with vegetable oil spray. Spread eggplant in even layer on coffee filters. Microwave until eggplant is dry and shriveled to one-third of its original size, about 10 minutes, flipping halfway through to dry sides evenly (eggplant should not brown). Transfer eggplant immediately to paper towel–lined plate.

3. Heat oil in large Dutch oven over medium-high heat to 375 degrees. Add eggplant to oil and cook until flesh is deep golden brown and edges are crispy, 5 to 7 minutes. Using skimmer or slotted spoon, transfer to paper towel–lined plate and blot to remove excess oil. Transfer to bowl with dressing.

4. Toss cilantro, mint, basil, and remaining 1 teaspoon lime juice together in small bowl. Add half of herb mixture to bowl with eggplant, tossing to combine, then sprinkle remaining herb mixture and peanuts over top. Serve.

HASSELBACK EGGPLANT WITH GARLIC-YOGURT SAUCE

Serves 4 as an appetizer or 2 as a main dish
Total time: 1 hour 30 minutes
WHY THIS RECIPE WORKS *We wanted to create a roasted eggplant dish that featured some of the smoky eggplant goodness that we love in baba ghanoush—but with more textural variety and structural integrity. To achieve a creamy interior and crispy edges, we borrowed the technique used for Hasselback potatoes: By making slices every ¼ inch crosswise down the length of the eggplant, stopping just short of slicing through, we opened up a whole new world of eggplant possibilities. This technique allowed steam to escape during cooking so the eggplant became tender without bursting and turning to mush. More importantly, we could pack the spaces between the slices with a sweet and spicy Middle Eastern paste made from jarred piquillo peppers, walnuts, bread crumbs, and pomegranate molasses. Finally, we balanced the rich spiciness and mild bitterness of the roasted eggplant with a creamy garlic-yogurt sauce. To ensure you don't cut through the eggplant halves in step 2, you can create a guard by placing a chopstick on either side of the eggplant.*

EGGPLANT

- 1 large eggplant (1½ pounds)
  Salt
- 1 cup jarred piquillo peppers, patted dry and chopped
- 1 cup walnuts, toasted
- 1 cup panko bread crumbs
- 7 scallions, cut into 1-inch pieces
- 3 tablespoons pomegranate molasses
- 2 tablespoons ground dried Aleppo pepper
- 1 tablespoon lemon juice
- 1 teaspoon ground cumin
- 6 tablespoons extra-virgin olive oil
- 2 tablespoons chopped fresh mint

GARLIC-YOGURT SAUCE

- 1 cup plain Greek yogurt
- 1 tablespoon lemon juice
- 1 tablespoon chopped fresh mint
- 1 garlic clove, minced
- ½ teaspoon salt

1. **For the eggplant** Adjust oven rack to upper-middle position and heat oven to 400 degrees. Line rimmed baking sheet with aluminum foil and place wire rack in sheet.

2. Trim stem and bottom ¼ inch of eggplant, then halve lengthwise. Working with 1 half at a time, place eggplant cut side down on cutting board and slice crosswise at ¼-inch intervals, leaving bottom ¼ inch intact. Sprinkle eggplant fans evenly with 1 teaspoon salt, making sure to get salt in between slices, and let sit for 15 minutes.

3. Process piquillos, walnuts, 6 tablespoons panko, scallions, pomegranate molasses, Aleppo pepper, lemon juice, cumin, and 1 teaspoon salt in food processor to coarse paste, about 30 seconds, scraping down sides of bowl as needed. With processor running, slowly add ¼ cup oil until incorporated.

4. Pat eggplant dry with paper towels. Spread 1½ cups pepper paste over eggplant, being sure to spread paste between cut sides of eggplant. Transfer eggplant, fanned side up, to prepared rack and roast until eggplant can be easily pierced with tip of paring knife and edges are crispy and golden brown, 40 minutes to 1 hour.

5. Remove eggplant from oven and heat broiler. Combine remaining 10 tablespoons panko, remaining 2 tablespoons oil, and 2 tablespoons pepper paste in bowl. (Set aside remaining pepper paste for another use.) Spread panko mixture evenly over top of eggplant and broil until topping is crisp and golden brown, 1 to 3 minutes.

6. **For garlic-yogurt sauce** Whisk all ingredients in bowl until combined. Transfer eggplant to serving platter and sprinkle with mint. Serve with yogurt sauce.

ROASTED EGGPLANT AND TOMATO SOUP

Serves 4 to 6   Total time: 55 minutes
WHY THIS RECIPE WORKS *Eggplants and tomatoes are found together throughout the eastern Mediterranean in countless dishes, especially soups. For a wonderfully creamy and satisfying soup, we began by dicing and roasting eggplant and found that by doing this, we could skip the task of salting, rinsing, and drying it. We left the skin on for deeper eggplant flavor and broiled it to develop a flavorful char. To build our soup, we started with the usual aromatics—onion and garlic—and added the flavorful North African spice blend* ras el hanout *plus some extra cumin, which gave the soup complex flavor. We added subtle sweetness with raisins, which, once pureed, also gave our soup body. Canned tomatoes were easy and offered rich tomato flavor. We reserved some eggplant to add to the pureed soup for a pleasantly chunky texture. Lemon juice provided brightness, almonds gave a nice crunch, and cilantro added freshness. You can find* ras el hanout *in the spice aisle of most well-stocked supermarkets.*

- 2 pounds eggplant, cut into ½-inch pieces
- 6 tablespoons extra-virgin olive oil, plus extra for serving
- 1 onion, chopped
  Salt and pepper
- 2 garlic cloves, minced
- 1½ teaspoons ras el hanout
- ½ teaspoon ground cumin
- 4 cups chicken or vegetable broth, plus extra as needed

1 (14.5-ounce) can diced tomatoes, drained
¼ cup raisins
1 bay leaf
2 teaspoons lemon juice
2 tablespoons slivered almonds, toasted
2 tablespoons minced fresh cilantro

1. Adjust oven rack 4 inches from broiler element and heat broiler. Toss eggplant with 5 tablespoons oil, then spread in aluminum foil–lined rimmed baking sheet. Broil eggplant until mahogany brown, 5 to 7 minutes, stirring once halfway through. Set aside 2 cups eggplant.

2. Heat remaining 1 tablespoon oil in large saucepan over medium heat until shimmering. Add onion, ¾ teaspoon salt, and ¼ teaspoon pepper and cook until softened and lightly browned, 5 to 7 minutes. Stir in garlic, ras el hanout, and cumin and cook until fragrant, about 30 seconds. Stir in broth, tomatoes, raisins, bay leaf, and remaining eggplant and bring to simmer. Cover, reduce heat to low, and simmer gently until eggplant is softened, about 20 minutes.

3. Discard bay leaf. Working in batches, process soup in blender until smooth, about 2 minutes. Return soup to clean saucepan and stir in reserved eggplant. Heat soup gently over low heat until warmed through (do not boil), and adjust consistency with extra hot broth as needed. Stir in lemon juice and season with salt and pepper to taste. Serve, sprinkling individual portions with almonds and cilantro and drizzling with extra oil.

STUFFED EGGPLANT

Serves 4   Total time: 1 hour 15 minutes

WHY THIS RECIPE WORKS *Stuffed eggplant is terrifically appealing and can be made in myriad ways. This recipe is a study in simplicity, requiring very little prep work, and the best part is that the flavor of the eggplant itself shines through. We selected Italian eggplant as the best variety for stuffing—one half made a perfect side-dish portion, and two halves were ideal as a main dish. Next, we worked on the best way to cook the eggplant before stuffing, cutting the eggplants in half before cooking and baking them on a preheated baking sheet covered with foil until tender, in just under an hour. We chose to stuff our eggplants with a mixture of sautéed onion, garlic, and tomatoes combined with Pecorino Romano cheese and pine nuts for a nice blend of tastes and textures. If you can't find Italian eggplants, substitute small globe eggplants.*

4 Italian eggplants (10 ounces each), halved lengthwise
¼ cup extra-virgin olive oil
Salt and pepper
1 onion, chopped fine
3 garlic cloves, minced
2 teaspoons minced fresh oregano or ½ teaspoon dried
¼ teaspoon ground cinnamon
⅛ teaspoon cayenne pepper
1 pound plum tomatoes, cored, seeded, and chopped
2 ounces Pecorino Romano cheese, grated (1 cup)
¼ cup pine nuts, toasted
1 tablespoon red wine vinegar
2 tablespoons minced fresh parsley

1. Adjust oven racks to upper-middle and lowest positions, place parchment paper–lined rimmed baking sheet on lower rack, and heat oven to 400 degrees.

2. Brush cut sides of eggplant with 2 tablespoons oil and season with salt and pepper. Place eggplant cut side down on preheated sheet and carefully cover with aluminum foil. Roast until eggplant is golden brown and tender, 50 to 55 minutes. Transfer eggplant, cut side down, to paper towel–lined baking sheet and let drain.

3. Meanwhile, heat remaining 2 tablespoons oil in 12-inch skillet over medium heat until shimmering. Add onion and ½ teaspoon salt and cook until softened and browned, about 10 minutes. Stir in garlic, oregano, cinnamon, and cayenne and cook until fragrant, about 30 seconds. Stir in tomatoes, ¾ cup Pecorino, pine nuts, and vinegar and cook until warmed through, about 1 minute. Season with salt and pepper to taste.

4. Return eggplant, cut side up, to sheet. Using 2 forks, gently push eggplant flesh to sides to make room in center for filling. Mound ¼ cup filling into eggplant halves and sprinkle with remaining ¼ cup Pecorino. Roast on upper rack until cheese is melted, 5 to 10 minutes. Sprinkle with parsley. Serve.

EGGPLANT INVOLTINI

Serves 4 to 6   Total time: 1 hour 30 minutes

WHY THIS RECIPE WORKS *Eggplant involtini ("little bundles" in Italian) can be so complicated and messy that it makes you wonder whether these cheese-filled eggplant bundles are worth it. But trust us: They are. Still, we wanted to come up with a version of involtini that would emphasize the eggplant and minimize the fuss. Generally this recipe calls for frying, but in order to fry eggplant, you must first get rid of the excess water or the eggplant will turn mushy and oily. Salting can fix this problem, but we opted for a lighter and more hands-off option: baking. We brushed the eggplant planks with oil, seasoned them with salt and pepper, and then baked them for 30 minutes. They emerged light brown and tender, with a compact texture that was neither mushy nor sodden. To lighten up the filling, we replaced part of the ricotta with more flavorful Pecorino Romano cheese, and brightened it with a squeeze of lemon juice. We added bread crumbs to the mixture to lighten it further. We made a simple tomato sauce while the eggplant baked, then added the eggplant rolls directly to the sauce. Using a skillet meant that we could easily transfer the whole operation to the oven. We crowned the skillet with an additional dusting of Pecorino and a sprinkling of basil before serving. Select shorter, wider eggplants for this recipe. Part-skim ricotta may be used, but do not use fat-free.*

- 2 large eggplants (1½ pounds each), peeled
- 6 tablespoons vegetable oil
  Salt and pepper
- 2 garlic cloves, minced
- ¼ teaspoon dried oregano
  Pinch red pepper flakes
- 1 (28-ounce) can whole peeled tomatoes, drained with juice reserved, chopped
- 1 slice hearty white sandwich bread, torn into 1-inch pieces
- 8 ounces (1 cup) whole-milk ricotta cheese
- 1½ ounces Pecorino Romano cheese, grated (¾ cup)
- ¼ cup plus 1 tablespoon chopped fresh basil
- 1 tablespoon lemon juice

1. Slice each eggplant lengthwise into ½-inch thick planks (you should have 12 planks). Trim rounded surface from each end piece so it lies flat.

2. Adjust 1 oven rack to lower-middle position and second rack 8 inches from broiler element. Heat oven to 375 degrees. Line 2 rimmed baking sheets with parchment paper and spray with vegetable oil spray.

3. Arrange eggplant slices in single layer on prepared sheets. Brush 1 side of eggplant slices with 2½ tablespoons oil and sprinkle with ¼ teaspoon salt and ¼ teaspoon pepper. Flip eggplant slices and brush with 2½ tablespoons oil and sprinkle with ¼ teaspoon salt and ¼ teaspoon pepper. Bake until tender and lightly browned, 30 to 35 minutes, switching and rotating sheets halfway through baking. Let cool for 5 minutes. Using thin spatula, flip each slice. Heat broiler.

4. While eggplant cooks, heat remaining 1 tablespoon oil in 12-inch broiler-safe skillet over medium-low heat until just shimmering. Add garlic, oregano, pepper flakes, and ¼ teaspoon salt and cook, stirring occasionally, until fragrant, about 30 seconds. Stir in tomatoes and their juice. Increase heat to high and bring to simmer. Reduce heat to medium-low and simmer until thickened, about 15 minutes. Cover and set aside.

5. Pulse bread in food processor until finely ground, 10 to 15 pulses. Combine bread crumbs, ricotta, ½ cup Pecorino, ¼ cup basil, lemon juice, and ¼ teaspoon salt in bowl. With widest ends of eggplant slices facing you, evenly distribute ricotta mixture on bottom third of each slice. Gently roll up each eggplant slice and place seam side down in tomato sauce.

6. Bring sauce to simmer over medium heat. Simmer for 5 minutes. Transfer skillet to oven and broil until eggplant is well browned and cheese is warmed through, 5 to 10 minutes. Sprinkle with remaining ¼ cup Pecorino and let stand for 5 minutes. Sprinkle with remaining 1 tablespoon basil and serve.

EGGPLANT PARMESAN

Serves 8   Total time: 1 hour 45 minutes

WHY THIS RECIPE WORKS *Perhaps the most iconic of eggplant dishes, eggplant Parmesan takes many forms, sometimes breaded, sometimes not, but almost always layered with so much mozzarella that the flavor of the eggplant is totally lost. This authentic version is a more refined and delicate affair where the flavor of the eggplant is front and center. Here, thin, silky, unbreaded eggplant slices are layered with fresh mozzarella and tomato sauce, and topped with Parmesan. We wanted to skip the time-consuming step of salting the eggplant, so we tested numerous methods of salting, frying, and roasting and found that we could get creamy, tender eggplant slices simply by roasting them. The dry heat drove off unwanted moisture, making salting unnecessary, and with just a thin brush of olive oil the slices maintained a creamy, delicate interior and golden, roasted exterior. Be careful when opening the oven in step 3, as the eggplant will release steam. Fresh mozzarella is the key to success here; do not substitute low-moisture mozzarella. If using fresh mozzarella packed in water, press the slices between layers of paper towels to remove excess moisture before using. If you can't find Italian eggplants, substitute 4 pounds of small globe eggplants.*

TOMATO SAUCE
- 1 (28-ounce) can crushed tomatoes
- 1 tablespoon extra-virgin olive oil
- 2 garlic cloves, minced
- ⅛ teaspoon red pepper flakes
- ¼ teaspoon salt
- 2 tablespoons chopped fresh basil

EGGPLANT
- ½ cup extra-virgin olive oil
- 4½ pounds Italian eggplant, sliced lengthwise into ¼-inch-thick planks
  Salt and pepper
- 8 ounces fresh mozzarella, sliced thin
- 7 tablespoons grated Parmesan cheese
- ¼ cup torn fresh basil

EGGPLANT INVOLTINI

These delicious bundles of eggplant wrapped around a rich but light ricotta filling and nestled in a homemade tomato sauce are irresistible. They are old school made new again. And while there are a few steps to this recipe, none are difficult and the eggplant planks are baked rather than fried, giving you time to make the simple tomato sauce and ricotta filling while the eggplant planks are in the oven.

1. To make thin planks that can be rolled around the cheese filling, lay each eggplant on its side and slice it lengthwise into ½-inch-thick slices.

2. Arrange the eggplant slices on two parchment-lined baking sheets and brush with oil. Bake for about 30 minutes, switching and rotating the sheets halfway through baking.

3. Meanwhile, make the tomato sauce on the stovetop: Sauté the garlic, oregano, red pepper flakes, and salt briefly, then add the tomatoes and their juice and cook until thickened, about 15 minutes.

4. For the filling, make the homemade bread crumbs in a food processor and then combine them with the ricotta, Pecorino Romano, basil, and lemon juice.

5. With the widest ends of the eggplant slices facing you, evenly distribute the filling on the bottom third of each slice. Gently roll up each eggplant slice and place seam side down in the tomato sauce.

6. Simmer the involtini in the sauce for 5 minutes. Transfer the skillet to the oven and broil until the eggplant is browned and the cheese is warmed through, 5 to 10 minutes. Sprinkle with the remaining Pecorino and let stand for 5 minutes. Sprinkle with the remaining basil and serve.

Pasta alla Norma

1. **For the tomato sauce** Pulse tomatoes in food processor until smooth, about 10 pulses, scraping down sides of bowl as needed. Cook oil and garlic in large saucepan over medium heat, stirring occasionally, until fragrant, about 2 minutes. Stir in pepper flakes and cook until fragrant, about 30 seconds. Stir in tomatoes and salt, bring to simmer, and cook until thickened slightly, about 10 minutes. Off heat, stir in basil.

2. **For the eggplant** Adjust oven racks to upper-middle and lower-middle positions and heat oven to 450 degrees. Line 2 rimmed baking sheets with aluminum foil and brush each sheet with 1 tablespoon oil. Arrange half of eggplant in single layer on prepared sheets. Brush tops of eggplant planks with 2 tablespoons oil and sprinkle with ½ teaspoon salt.

3. Roast eggplant until tender and lightly browned, 15 to 20 minutes, switching and rotating sheets halfway through baking. Let eggplant cool slightly on sheets, then transfer, still on foil, to wire racks to cool completely. Line now-empty sheets with additional foil and brush each sheet with 1 tablespoon oil. Repeat brushing, seasoning, and roasting remaining eggplant; transfer to wire racks.

4. Reduce oven temperature to 375 degrees. Spread ½ cup tomato sauce in bottom of 13 by 9-inch baking dish. Layer one-quarter of eggplant over sauce, overlapping planks as needed. Spread ¼ cup sauce over eggplant, then top with one-third of mozzarella and 1 tablespoon Parmesan. Repeat layering of eggplant, tomato sauce, mozzarella, and Parmesan 2 more times.

5. Layer remaining eggplant in dish, spread remaining tomato sauce over top, and sprinkle with remaining ¼ cup Parmesan. Bake until bubbling around edges, about 25 minutes. Let cool for 10 minutes before sprinkling with basil. Serve.

PASTA ALLA NORMA

Serves 4 to 6   Total time: 50 minutes

WHY THIS RECIPE WORKS *Eggplant is the star of this Sicilian pasta, which also features a robust tomato sauce. The cooked eggplant and sauce are mixed with al dente pasta and finished with shreds of salty, milky ricotta salata. The dish gets its name from the epic opera* Norma, *which was composed by Vincenzo Bellini, a native of Catania. We salted and microwaved the eggplant to quickly draw out its moisture so that it wouldn't absorb too much oil. Then we sautéed it in just a tablespoon of oil until it was perfectly browned, and built a simple but pungent tomato sauce in the same skillet. We found that it was best to wait until the last minute to combine the eggplant and sauce; this prevented the eggplant from soaking up too much tomato and becoming soggy. If coffee filters are not available, food-safe, undyed paper towels can be substituted when microwaving the eggplant. Be sure to remove the eggplant from the microwave immediately so that the steam can escape.*

1½	pounds eggplant, cut into ½-inch pieces
	Salt
¼	cup extra-virgin olive oil
4	garlic cloves, minced
2	anchovy fillets, minced
¼–½	teaspoon red pepper flakes
1	(28-ounce) can crushed tomatoes
6	tablespoons chopped fresh basil
1	pound ziti, rigatoni, or penne
3	ounces ricotta salata, shredded (1 cup)

1. Toss eggplant with ½ teaspoon salt in bowl. Line entire surface of large plate with double layer of coffee filters and lightly spray with vegetable oil spray. Spread eggplant in even layer on coffee filters; wipe out and reserve bowl. Microwave until eggplant is dry and shriveled to one-third of its original size, 8 to 15 minutes (eggplant should not brown). Transfer eggplant immediately to paper towel–lined plate. Let cool slightly.

2. Transfer eggplant to now-empty bowl, add 1 tablespoon oil, and toss gently to coat. Heat 1 tablespoon oil in 12-inch nonstick skillet over medium-high heat until shimmering. Add eggplant and cook, stirring occasionally, until well browned and tender, about 10 minutes. Remove skillet from heat and transfer eggplant to plate.

3. Add 1 tablespoon oil, garlic, anchovies, and pepper flakes to now-empty skillet and cook using residual heat, stirring constantly, until fragrant and garlic becomes pale golden, about 1 minute (if skillet is too cool, set over medium heat). Add tomatoes and bring to simmer over medium-high heat. Cook, stirring occasionally, until thickened slightly, 8 to 10 minutes.

4. Gently stir in eggplant and cook until warmed through and flavors meld, 3 to 5 minutes. Stir in basil and remaining 1 tablespoon oil. Season with salt to taste.

5. Meanwhile, bring 4 quarts water to boil in large pot. Add pasta and 1 tablespoon salt and cook, stirring often, until al dente. Reserve ½ cup cooking water, then drain pasta and return it to pot. Add sauce and toss to combine. Adjust consistency with reserved cooking water as needed. Serve, passing ricotta salata separately.

STIR-FRIED JAPANESE EGGPLANT

Serves 4 to 6   Total time: 25 minutes

WHY THIS RECIPE WORKS *Eggplant is something of a blank canvas. It is neutral in flavor, but it sucks up whatever flavors you cook it with. That quality makes eggplant ideal for stir-fries, which feature deeply savory sauces that cling to each vegetable. Cooking the eggplant over high heat in a shallow skillet allowed the eggplant's excess moisture to evaporate quickly, leaving the eggplant browned and tender. For our sauce, we opted for classic stir-fry flavors: soy sauce, Chinese rice wine, and, for umami depth, hoisin sauce. Just a teaspoon of cornstarch was enough to thicken it to the glossy consistency characteristic of restaurant-style stir-fries. Scallions and fresh cilantro lent the dish some herbaceous notes that played nicely off the savory sauce. This recipe works equally well with Italian or globe eggplants. You can substitute dry sherry for the Chinese rice wine.*

SAUCE

- ½ cup chicken or vegetable broth
- ¼ cup Chinese rice wine
- 3 tablespoons hoisin sauce
- 1 tablespoon soy sauce
- 1 teaspoon cornstarch
- 1 teaspoon toasted sesame oil

EGGPLANT

- 6 garlic cloves, minced
- 2 tablespoons plus 1 teaspoon vegetable oil
- 1 tablespoon grated fresh ginger
- 1½ pounds Japanese eggplant, cut into ¾-inch pieces
- 2 scallions, sliced thin on bias
- ½ cup fresh cilantro sprigs, cut into 2-inch pieces
- 1 tablespoon sesame seeds, toasted

1. For the sauce Whisk all ingredients together in bowl; set aside.

2. For the eggplant Combine garlic, 1 teaspoon oil, and ginger in small bowl. Heat 1 tablespoon oil in 12-inch nonstick skillet over high heat until just smoking. Add half of eggplant and cook, stirring frequently, until browned and tender, 4 to 5 minutes; transfer to bowl. Repeat with remaining 1 tablespoon oil and eggplant.

3. Return first batch of eggplant and any accumulated juices to skillet and push to sides. Add garlic-ginger mixture to center and cook, mashing mixture into skillet, until fragrant, about 30 seconds. Stir garlic-ginger mixture into eggplant. Whisk sauce to recombine, then add to skillet and cook until eggplant is well coated and sauce is thickened, about 30 seconds. Off heat, stir in scallions and cilantro and sprinkle with sesame seeds. Serve.

VARIATIONS

Sesame-Basil Stir-Fried Japanese Eggplant
Substitute 2 tablespoons fish sauce, 2 tablespoons packed brown sugar, and 1 tablespoon rice wine vinegar for hoisin sauce. Substitute ½ cup torn fresh basil leaves for cilantro.

Sweet Chili-Garlic Stir-Fried Japanese Eggplant
Substitute 3 tablespoons chili-garlic sauce and 2 tablespoons packed brown sugar for hoisin sauce.

CHARRED SICHUAN-STYLE EGGPLANT

Serves 2 to 3   Total time: 55 minutes

WHY THIS RECIPE WORKS *In this eggplant stir-fry, we take advantage of the fact that eggplant can absorb serious quantities of oil by providing the eggplant with a seriously tasty, spicy Sichuan-style chili oil to soak up. To speed cooking and get great char on the eggplant, we used the microwave to slightly dehydrate it before putting it in a smoking-hot pan. Some green bell pepper, scallions, and fresh cilantro sprigs provided a fresh and cooling reprieve to the rest of the dish. But let's be clear here: You want to serve this dish with plenty of steamed white rice to tame the heat. Bird chiles are dried red Thai chiles. Fermented black beans are actually soybeans that have been packed in salt and fermented; they can be found in the Asian section of most well-stocked supermarkets, in Asian specialty markets, and online. You can substitute dry sherry for the Chinese rice wine and 1½ pounds globe or Italian eggplants for the Japanese eggplants in this recipe. Use a spice grinder to grind the chiles. Be sure to remove the eggplant from the microwave immediately so that the steam can escape.*

- ⅓ cup plus 3 tablespoons vegetable oil
- 2 garlic cloves, sliced thin
- 15 bird chiles, ground fine (1½ tablespoons)
- 1 (½-inch) piece fresh ginger, peeled and sliced thin
- 1 star anise pod
- ¼ cup hoisin sauce
- ½ cup fermented black beans
- 6 tablespoons Chinese rice wine
- 1 tablespoon sugar
- 1½ pounds Japanese eggplant, halved lengthwise, then cut crosswise into 1½-inch pieces
- ½ teaspoon salt
- 1 green bell pepper, stemmed, seeded, and cut into 1-inch pieces
- ¼ cup water
- 6 scallions, green parts cut into 1-inch pieces, white parts sliced thin
- ½ cup fresh cilantro sprigs, cut into 2-inch pieces

1. Heat ⅓ cup oil, garlic, bird chiles, ginger, and star anise in small saucepan over medium-high heat until sizzling. Reduce heat to low and gently simmer until garlic and ginger are soft but not browned, about 5 minutes. Let cool off heat for 5 minutes. Stir in hoisin, black beans, 2 tablespoons rice wine, and sugar until combined; set aside.

2. Toss eggplant with salt in bowl. Line entire surface of large plate with double layer of coffee filters and lightly spray with vegetable oil spray. Spread eggplant in even layer on coffee filters. Microwave until eggplant is dry and shriveled to one-third of its original size, about 10 minutes, flipping halfway through to dry sides evenly (eggplant should not brown). Transfer eggplant immediately to paper towel–lined plate.

3. Heat 2 tablespoons oil in 12-inch skillet over high heat until just smoking. Add eggplant in even layer and cook, stirring occasionally, until charred on most sides, 5 to 7 minutes. Push eggplant to sides of skillet and add remaining 1 tablespoon oil and bell pepper to center. Cook, without stirring, until bell pepper is lightly charred, about 3 minutes.

4. Reduce heat to medium, add water and remaining ¼ cup rice wine, scraping up any browned bits, and cook until liquid is reduced by half, about 15 seconds. Stir in scallion greens and cook until just wilted, about 15 seconds. Off heat, stir in garlic–black bean sauce. Transfer to serving platter and top with scallion whites and cilantro. Serve immediately.

Charred Sichuan-Style Eggplant

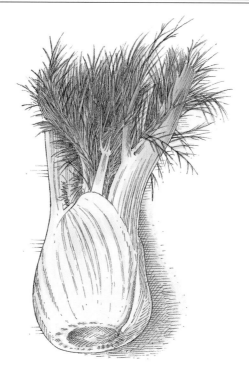

FENNEL

Although it's widely available in nearly all markets these days, many of us are not really sure what to do with fennel. Perhaps it's because it's somewhat funny-looking and appears patched together, with its bulbous white base narrowing into several thick light green stems, all topped with feathery dark green fronds. A member of the parsley family, fennel is native to the Mediterranean. Most of the fennel we see in the United States comes from California.

Often used only in a minor role, as a supporting aromatic, fennel fully deserves its chance in the limelight, since it shines in dishes that highlight its wonderful qualities in a leading role. If you don't know fresh fennel, you're in for a treat. Raw fennel is crisp and crunchy, similar to celery in texture but a bit less watery, with a stronger, cleaner flavor with a strong hint of anise. Served chilled, it is extremely refreshing. A great way to get to know this underused (at least in the United States) vegetable is thinly sliced in a salad, as in our Algerian-Style Fennel Salad with Oranges and Olives.

While raw fennel's bright, licorice-forward flavor is often tempered through combining it with other ingredients, cooked fennel takes on a very different character. When braised, roasted, or sautéed, it is transformed into a slightly sweet, subtly caramelized rich treat with a faint hint of licorice aroma. And, unlike celery, it is not at all fibrous or stringy when cooked. We offer two braising recipes—one on the stovetop and another in the slow cooker. Whole-Wheat Pasta with Italian Sausage and Fennel takes advantage of fennel's natural affinity for pork sausage. And both Roasted Fennel with Rye Crumble and Fennel Confit are showstopper dishes that are still simple and treat this vegetable in a fresh new way.

shopping and storage

Fennel is available year-round, though traditionally it's considered a winter vegetable, with its season from fall through spring. When shopping for fennel (sometimes labeled as "fresh anise" in the supermarket), look for bulbs that are firm and creamy white, with as little discoloration or brownish spots as possible. (Some of this discoloration is to be expected even on the freshest fennel; just like with onions, the toughest outer layers should be removed.) The fennel stalks should be crisp and firm, and the fronds should be feathery and bright green. Although the stalks are not generally eaten, they can be used to add flavor to broth. However, the fronds can be used just like an herb, making a delicious garnish, so leave the vegetable whole until you're ready to cook with it. Store fennel in an open plastic produce bag in the fridge for up to a week.

fennel seeds or anise seeds?

Many cooks assume that fennel and anise are simply different names for the same seeds, but that is not the case. Fennel seeds, which are a key component of the flavor profile of Italian sausage, come from a perennial flowering herb plant called common fennel (also referred to as herb, sweet, or wild fennel), which has no vegetable bulb. Anise seeds, which have a more pronounced and sweeter licorice flavor than fennel seeds, come from a different species. These two seeds often can be substituted for one another, but in general it's better to purchase the specific type that the recipe calls for.

vegetable prep

Trimming and Coring Fennel

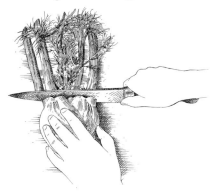

1. Cut off stalks and feathery fronds, reserving fronds if desired or recipe instructs.

2. Trim thin slice from base and remove tough or blemished outer layers.

3. Halve fennel lengthwise through core.

4. Use sharp knife to remove pyramid-shaped core.

Cutting Fennel into Strips

After cutting off stalks and fronds, trimming base, and removing core, slice bulb halves lengthwise into desired thickness.

Cutting Fennel into Wedges

After cutting off stalks and fronds and trimming base, halve bulb through core. Remove core if specified in recipe. Cut bulb halves into wedges of desired thickness.

Cutting Fennel into Slabs

After cutting off stalks and fronds and trimming base, cut fennel lengthwise through core into slabs of desired thickness. (Do not core fennel for slabs.)

Roasted Fennel with Rye Crumble

BRAISED FENNEL WITH RADICCHIO AND PARMESAN

Serves 4   Total time: 45 minutes

WHY THIS RECIPE WORKS *This richly flavored braised dish works equally well as a side dish as it does served over polenta for a main course. First, we cut the fennel into thick slabs and braised them with wine and aromatics. Leaving the fennel in the skillet even after the braising liquid had evaporated developed a deep golden, caramelized crust on the fennel and some serious flavor-boosting fond in the pan. To take advantage of these browned bits, and to balance the sweetness of the fennel, we stirred in a whole head of radicchio, cooking it briefly with water, honey, and butter to tame its harsh edge and create a richly flavored pan sauce. All this dish needed was a sprinkle of Parmesan cheese and toasted pine nuts for added richness and crunch, and some of the minced fennel fronds for a bright finish. You will need a 12-inch skillet with a tight-fitting lid for this recipe. Don't core the fennel bulb before cutting it into slabs; the core will help hold the layers of fennel together during cooking.*

- 4 tablespoons unsalted butter
- 3 fennel bulbs, 2 tablespoons fronds minced, stalks discarded, bulbs cut lengthwise into ½-inch-thick slabs
- ½ cup dry white wine
- ½ teaspoon grated lemon zest plus 2 teaspoons juice
  Salt and pepper
- 1 head radicchio (10 ounces), halved, cored, and sliced thin
- ¼ cup water
- 2 teaspoons honey
- 2 tablespoons pine nuts, toasted and chopped
  Shaved Parmesan cheese

1. Melt 3 tablespoons butter in 12-inch skillet over medium heat. Arrange fennel in single layer over bottom of skillet, then drizzle with wine and sprinkle with lemon zest, ½ teaspoon salt, and ¼ teaspoon pepper. Cover, reduce heat to medium-low, and cook for 15 minutes. (Skillet will be crowded at first, but fennel will shrink as it cooks.)

2. Flip fennel. Continue to cook, covered, until fennel is tender and well browned, about 7 minutes per side. Transfer fennel to serving platter and tent with aluminum foil.

3. Add radicchio, water, and honey to skillet and cook over low heat, scraping up any browned bits, until wilted, 3 to 5 minutes. Off heat, stir in lemon juice and remaining 1 tablespoon butter until melted and thickened slightly. Season with salt and pepper to taste. Pour radicchio and sauce over fennel, then sprinkle with pine nuts, minced fennel fronds, and shaved Parmesan. Serve.

SLOW-COOKER BRAISED FENNEL WITH ORANGE-TARRAGON DRESSING

Serves 4 to 6   Total time: 8 to 9 hours on low or 5 to 6 hours on high

WHY THIS RECIPE WORKS *Braising fennel in the slow cooker is a hands-off way to infuse it with deep, savory flavor and give it a melting texture. Cutting the fennel into wedges turned out to be the key to evenly slow-cooked fennel, and we made sure to braise it long enough to deliver uniformly tender but not mushy results. A combination of water, garlic, thyme, and juniper berries provided the seasoning base for this appealing side dish, and we finished it off with a simple orange-tarragon dressing. Don't core the fennel bulb before cutting it into wedges; the core will help hold the layers of fennel together during cooking. You will need a 5- to 7-quart oval slow cooker for this recipe.*

- 2 garlic cloves, peeled and smashed
- 2 sprigs fresh thyme
- 1 teaspoon juniper berries
  Salt and pepper
- 2 fennel bulbs, stalks discarded, bulbs halved and cut into 1-inch wedges
- 2 tablespoons extra-virgin olive oil
- 2 teaspoons grated orange zest plus 1 tablespoon juice
- 1 teaspoon minced fresh tarragon

1. Combine 1 cup water, garlic, thyme sprigs, juniper berries, and ½ teaspoon salt in slow cooker. Place fennel wedges cut side down in

slow cooker (wedges may overlap). Cover and cook until fennel is tender, 8 to 9 hours on low or 5 to 6 hours on high.

2. Whisk oil, orange zest and juice, and tarragon together in bowl. Season with salt and pepper to taste. Using slotted spoon, transfer fennel to serving platter, discarding any garlic cloves, thyme sprigs, and juniper berries that stick to fennel. Drizzle fennel with dressing. Serve.

ROASTED FENNEL WITH RYE CRUMBLE

Serves 4 to 6   Total time: 1 hour

WHY THIS RECIPE WORKS *These subtly caramelized wedges of perfectly roasted fennel make an elegant tableside presentation. To start, we cut the fennel bulbs into 1-inch-thick wedges through the core before tossing them in a mixture of butter, lemon juice, and thyme and shingling them evenly into a baking dish. Covering the dish with aluminum foil for the first half-hour of roasting ensured that the edges didn't dry out. With the fennel in the oven, we used the time to make a simple crumb topping in the food processor. After testing different flavor combinations, we decided upon hearty rye bread, earthy caraway seeds, and nutty Parmesan cheese, which combined to beautifully complement the flavor of the roasted fennel. Once the fennel wedges were nearly tender, we uncovered the dish and sprinkled this mixture evenly over the top, baking until the crumble was crisped and deep golden brown and the fennel perfectly tender. Don't core the fennel bulb before cutting it into wedges; the core will help hold the layers of fennel together during cooking.*

- 6 tablespoons unsalted butter, melted
- 1 tablespoon lemon juice
  Salt and pepper
- ½ teaspoon minced fresh thyme or ¼ teaspoon dried
- 2 fennel bulbs, stalks discarded, bulbs halved and cut into 1-inch wedges
- 3 ounces rye bread, cut into 1-inch pieces (3 cups)
- 1 ounce Parmesan cheese, grated (½ cup)
- 1 teaspoon caraway seeds

1. Adjust oven rack to middle position and heat oven to 425 degrees. Whisk 3 tablespoons melted butter, lemon juice, 1 teaspoon salt, thyme, and ¼ teaspoon pepper together in large bowl. Add fennel and toss to coat. Arrange fennel cut side down in single layer in 13 by 9-inch baking dish. Cover dish with aluminum foil and bake until fennel is nearly tender, 25 to 30 minutes.

2. Meanwhile, pulse bread, Parmesan, caraway seeds, ¼ teaspoon salt, ⅛ teaspoon pepper, and remaining 3 tablespoons melted butter in food processor to coarse crumbs, about 20 pulses; set aside.

3. Remove foil from dish and sprinkle fennel with bread crumb mixture. Continue to bake, uncovered, until fennel is tender and topping is browned and crisp, 15 to 20 minutes. Let cool for 5 minutes before serving.

FENNEL CONFIT

Serves 6 to 8   Total time: 2 hours 15 minutes
WHY THIS RECIPE WORKS *The confit technique is most often used with duck, but it's also a versatile way of transforming vegetables ("confit" simply means to preserve something, with either fat or sugar). Fennel is a perfect candidate, since long cooking times coax out its hidden flavors and turn it luxuriously creamy. We wanted to confit enough fennel to serve as a side dish for a group, but most recipes called for up to 2 quarts of olive oil—an amount that would drain a home pantry. We found that two layers of fennel slabs arranged in the bottom of a large Dutch oven allowed us to use just 3 cups of oil. The oil didn't fully cover the fennel, but the fennel shrank and released liquid during cooking, causing it to sink. We flavored the oil with lemon zest, garlic and complementary fennel seeds and caraway seeds. The oven was perfect for our purpose: It provided even heat for the 2-hour cooking time and was completely hands-off. The fennel emerged buttery and aromatic, and pieces that remained above the oil became golden and caramelized, which tasters loved. We finished with a scattering of fronds, for a unique and unforgettable fennel dish. Don't core the fennel before cutting it into slabs; the core will help hold the slabs*

together during cooking. This recipe will yield extra oil that can be strained, cooled, and stored for up to two weeks. The infused oil is great as a base for salad dressings or for dipping bread.

    3   fennel bulbs, 2 tablespoons fronds
        minced, stalks discarded, bulbs cut
        lengthwise into ½-inch-thick slabs
        Salt
    3   garlic cloves, lightly crushed and peeled
    3   (2-inch) strips lemon zest, plus lemon
        wedges for serving
    1   teaspoon caraway seeds
    1   teaspoon fennel seeds
    3   cups extra-virgin olive oil
        Flake sea salt

1. Adjust oven rack to middle position and heat oven to 300 degrees. Arrange half of fennel, cut side down, in single layer in Dutch oven. Sprinkle with ⅛ teaspoon salt. Repeat with remaining fennel and additional ⅛ teaspoon salt. Scatter garlic, lemon zest, caraway seeds, and fennel seeds over top, then add oil (fennel may not be completely submerged).

2. Cover pot, transfer to oven, and cook until fennel is very tender and is easily pierced with tip of paring knife, about 2 hours.

3. Remove pot from oven. Using slotted spoon, transfer fennel to serving platter, brushing off any garlic, lemon zest, caraway seeds, or fennel seeds that stick to fennel. Drizzle ¼ cup cooking oil over fennel, sprinkle with fennel fronds, and sprinkle with sea salt to taste. Serve with lemon wedges.

QUICK PICKLED FENNEL

Makes one 1-pint jar   Total time: 20 minutes
(plus at least 3 hours cooling time)
WHY THIS RECIPE WORKS *These quick fennel pickles offer a crunchy burst of sweet anise and fresh citrus flavors to accompany a surprising range of dishes. As welcome as a garnish for roasted or smoked fish as they are alongside a rich braised lamb shoulder, these bright pickles, when drizzled with a bit of extra-virgin olive oil, can even hold their own as the base of a vibrant salad. We chose seasoned rice vinegar as the base of our brine,*

because it added more depth to the pickling liquid than unseasoned vinegar. To that we added orange zest, a classic complement to the warm licorice tones of fennel, as our primary aromatic. Garlic, black peppercorns, and mustard seeds added just a touch of savory heat. We sliced the fennel ¼ inch thick—thin enough to take on a slightly supple texture in the brine but thick enough to remain satisfyingly crisp. Heating the jars with hot water and then draining them before adding the hot brine ensured that the jars wouldn't crack from the abrupt temperature change. You can easily double this recipe.

    ¾   cup seasoned rice vinegar
    ¼   cup water
    1   garlic clove, peeled and halved
    1   (1-inch) strip orange zest
    ¼   teaspoon fennel seeds
    ⅛   teaspoon black peppercorns
    ⅛   teaspoon yellow mustard seeds
    1   fennel bulb, stalks discarded,
        bulb halved, cored, and sliced
        ¼ inch thick

1. Bring vinegar, water, garlic, orange zest, fennel seeds, peppercorns, and mustard seeds to boil in medium saucepan.

2. Fill one 1-pint jar with hot water to warm. Drain jar, then pack fennel into jar. Using funnel and ladle, pour hot brine over fennel to cover. Let jar cool completely, cover with lid, and refrigerate for at least 2½ hours before serving. (The fennel can be refrigerated for up to 6 weeks; the fennel will soften significantly after that.)

FENNEL SALAD

Serves 4 to 6   Total time: 45 minutes
WHY THIS RECIPE WORKS *This salad, a mix of bright colors, lively flavors, and contrasting textures, is an edible advertisement for fennel. Since fennel is a classic Mediterranean ingredient, we decided to create an assertively flavored Mediterranean-style salad, with a balance of sweet, salty, slightly sour, and bitter flavors. For sweetness, we tossed a handful of raisins into a salad bowl, and for the salty component, we chose capers. Thinly sliced red onion contributed pungency, while Italian*

FENNEL CONFIT

This oven recipe for fennel confit results in a silky-textured, super-flavorful vegetable that is absolutely delicious as a side dish for seafood or chicken, a sandwich or pizza topping, or a part of an antipasto platter. And as a bonus, you'll be left with a flavorful and aromatic oil that you can use for anything from vinaigrettes to brushing on grilled seafood to simply dipping crusty bread.

1. After trimming the fennel bulb, mincing 2 tablespoons of the fronds, and discarding the stalks, cut the bulb into ½-inch-thick slabs.

2. Arrange half of the fennel in a single layer, cut side down, in a large Dutch oven. Sprinkle the fennel with ⅛ teaspoon salt. Repeat with the remaining fennel and another ⅛ teaspoon salt.

3. Scatter the garlic, lemon zest strips, caraway seeds, and fennel seeds over the top of the fennel, then pour in the oil. The fennel may not be completely submerged.

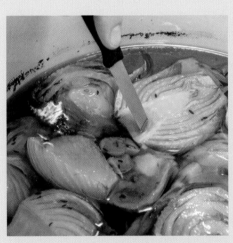

4. Cover the Dutch oven, transfer to the oven, and cook until the fennel is very tender and is easily pierced with the tip of a paring knife, about 2 hours.

5. Using a slotted spoon, transfer the fennel to a serving platter, brushing off any garlic, lemon zest, caraway seeds, or fennel seeds that stick to the fennel.

6. Drizzle ¼ cup of the fennel cooking oil over the fennel, sprinkle with the reserved fennel fronds, and season with flake sea salt to taste.

flat-leaf parsley added an herbal note—especially when treated more like a vegetable by tossing in whole leaves rather than mincing it. For the vinaigrette, olive oil was a given, and we liked bright, fresh lemon juice balanced with a little honey. Dijon mustard helped emulsify the vinaigrette and added its mustardy bite. Letting the fennel and onion slices macerate briefly with some vinaigrette for 30 minutes seasoned the fennel nicely and softened the onion's raw bite. Just before serving, we stirred in the parsley and some toasted almonds.

3 tablespoons lemon juice
2 teaspoons Dijon mustard
2 teaspoons honey
   Salt and pepper
¼ cup extra-virgin olive oil
2 fennel bulbs, stalks discarded, bulbs halved, cored, and sliced thin
½ red onion, halved through root end and sliced thin
½ cup golden raisins, chopped
3 tablespoons capers, rinsed and minced
½ cup fresh parsley leaves
½ cup sliced almonds, toasted

1. Whisk lemon juice, mustard, honey, 1 teaspoon salt, and 1 teaspoon pepper in large serving bowl until combined. While whisking constantly, slowly drizzle in oil until combined. Add fennel, onion, raisins, and capers and toss to coat. Cover and refrigerate for 30 minutes.

2. Stir in parsley and almonds and season with salt and pepper to taste. Serve.

⚬

ALGERIAN-STYLE FENNEL SALAD WITH ORANGES AND OLIVES

Serves 4 to 6   Total time: 15 minutes
WHY THIS RECIPE WORKS In Algeria and Tunisia, raw fennel is often used to make distinctive crisp, light salads. We liked the fennel best in this salad when it was sliced very thin, for the most tender texture. Sweet, juicy oranges were an excellent flavor match for the crisp fennel. To ensure that they were evenly distributed in the salad, we cut the oranges into bite-size pieces and tossed the salad gently

to keep the segments from falling apart. To finish it off, we added some oil-cured black olives, which are ubiquitous in the region's dishes, plus some fresh mint, lemon juice, extra-virgin olive oil, salt, and pepper. Because this dish is so simple, using high-quality ingredients is essential. Blood oranges are traditional in this dish; navel oranges, tangelos, or Cara Caras can be substituted, but since they are larger, you'll need just three of them.

¼ cup extra-virgin olive oil
2 tablespoons lemon juice
   Salt and pepper
4 blood oranges
2 fennel bulbs, stalks discarded, bulbs halved, cored, and sliced thin
½ cup pitted oil-cured black olives, sliced thin
¼ cup chopped fresh mint

1. Whisk oil, lemon juice, ¼ teaspoon salt, and ⅛ teaspoon pepper in large serving bowl until combined; set aside.

2. Cut away peel and pith from oranges. Quarter oranges, then slice crosswise into ¼-inch-thick pieces. Add oranges, fennel, olives, and mint to bowl with dressing and toss gently to coat. Season with salt and pepper to taste. Serve.

⚬

FENNEL, OLIVE, AND GOAT CHEESE TARTS

Serves 4   Total time: 45 minutes
WHY THIS RECIPE WORKS These easy yet elegant rectangular tarts are so beautiful and perfect for entertaining, whether as a snack with cocktails or as an al fresco main course with a big salad on a summer night. We kept things simple by using convenient store-bought puff pastry for the tart crust. Fresh anise-flavored fennel and briny cured olives made a light but bold filling combination. Tangy goat cheese, thinned with olive oil and brightened with fresh basil, contrasted nicely with the rich, flaky pastry and helped anchor the vegetables to the pastry crust. Parbaking the pastry without the weight of the filling allowed it to puff up nicely. To keep the filling firmly in place, we cut a border around the edges of the baked crusts and

lightly pressed down on the centers to make neat beds for the cheese and vegetables. Just 5 minutes more in the oven heated the filling through and browned the crusts beautifully. To thaw frozen puff pastry, let it sit either in the refrigerator for 24 hours or on the counter for 30 minutes to 1 hour.

1 (9½ by 9-inch) sheet puff pastry, thawed and halved
3 tablespoons extra-virgin olive oil
1 large fennel bulb, stalks discarded, bulb halved, cored, and sliced thin
3 garlic cloves, minced
½ cup dry white wine
½ cup pitted oil-cured black olives, chopped
1 teaspoon grated lemon zest plus 1 tablespoon juice
   Salt and pepper
8 ounces goat cheese, softened
5 tablespoons chopped fresh basil

1. Adjust oven rack to middle position and heat oven to 425 degrees. Arrange puff pastry halves spaced evenly apart on parchment paper–lined rimmed baking sheet and poke pastry all over with fork. Bake pastry until puffed and golden brown, about 15 minutes, rotating sheet halfway through baking. Using tip of paring knife, cut ½-inch-wide border around top edge of each pastry, then press centers down with your fingertips.

2. While pastry bakes, heat 1 tablespoon oil in 12-inch skillet over medium-high heat until shimmering. Add fennel and cook until softened and browned, about 10 minutes. Stir in garlic and cook until fragrant, about 30 seconds. Add wine, cover, and cook for 5 minutes. Uncover and cook until liquid has evaporated and fennel is very soft, 3 to 5 minutes. Off heat, stir in olives and lemon juice and season with salt and pepper to taste.

3. Mix goat cheese, ¼ cup basil, remaining 2 tablespoons oil, lemon zest, and ¼ teaspoon pepper together in bowl, then spread evenly over center of pastry shells. Spoon fennel mixture over top.

4. Bake tarts until cheese is warmed through and crust is deep golden, 5 to 7 minutes. Sprinkle with remaining 1 tablespoon basil and serve.

Fennel, Olive, and Goat Cheese Tarts

WHOLE-WHEAT PASTA WITH ITALIAN SAUSAGE AND FENNEL

Serves 4 to 6   Total time: 35 minutes

WHY THIS RECIPE WORKS *Fennel is a traditional and classic flavoring for Italian sausage, usually in the form of fennel seeds in the sausage mixture. Here, we upped the ante by sautéing fresh fennel slices, plenty of garlic, and a not-shy amount of red pepper flakes in the fat left in the pan from cooking the sweet sausage. The sauce had such bold flavor that we decided to put it over whole-wheat pasta, which has a distinctively full, nutty flavor and a firmer texture than regular spaghetti. Starch from the pasta cooking water thickened the sauce nicely and helped it cling to the spaghetti. Pine nuts contributed nutty crunch to the dish, and a sprinkling of freshly grated Pecorino Romano at the end added a salty tang to this hearty pasta dish that's quick enough for any weeknight.*

- 8 ounces sweet Italian sausage, casings removed
- 1 fennel bulb, stalks discarded, bulb halved, cored, and sliced thin
  Salt
- ¼ cup extra-virgin olive oil
- 6 garlic cloves, minced
- ½ teaspoon red pepper flakes
- ½ cup pine nuts, toasted and chopped
- ½ cup chopped fresh basil
- 2 tablespoons lemon juice
- 1 pound whole-wheat spaghetti
  Pecorino Romano cheese

1. Cook sausage in 12-inch nonstick skillet over medium-high heat, breaking up any large pieces with wooden spoon, until well browned, about 5 minutes. Using slotted spoon, transfer sausage to paper towel–lined plate.

2. Add fennel and ¼ teaspoon salt to fat left in skillet and cook over medium heat until softened, about 5 minutes. Add oil, garlic, pepper flakes, and ½ teaspoon salt to skillet and cook until fragrant, about 30 seconds. Off heat, stir in pine nuts, basil, lemon juice, and browned sausage.

3. Meanwhile, bring 4 quarts water to boil in large pot. Add pasta and 1 tablespoon salt and cook, stirring often, until tender.

Reserve ¾ cup cooking water, then drain pasta and return it to pot. Add sausage mixture and reserved cooking water and toss to combine. Season with salt to taste. Serve with Pecorino.

SPICE-RUBBED PORK TENDERLOIN WITH FENNEL, TOMATOES, ARTICHOKES, AND OLIVES

Serves 4   Total time: 1 hour 15 minutes

WHY THIS RECIPE WORKS *Be transported to Provence with this dinner that's low on fuss but high on flavor. Plenty of sweet, herbal fennel, supplemented with artichokes, olives, and cherry tomatoes, serves as the bed for pork tenderloin. The mild flavor of the pork lends itself well to bold seasonings, so we used a dry rub here, which added both flavor and color to our tenderloins without having to brown them before roasting. Herbes de Provence lent a distinct flavor profile; a little of this spice goes a long way, so just 2 teaspoons were sufficient. After jump-starting the fennel in the microwave, we cooked the tenderloins on top of the bed of vegetables in a roasting pan. While we prefer the flavor and texture of jarred whole baby artichoke hearts in this recipe, you can substitute 12 ounces frozen artichoke hearts, thawed and patted dry, for the jarred. To ensure that the tenderloins don't curl during cooking, remove the silverskin from the meat.*

- 2 large fennel bulbs, stalks discarded, bulbs halved, cored, and sliced ½ inch thick
- 2 cups jarred whole baby artichokes packed in water, quartered, rinsed, and patted dry
- ½ cup pitted kalamata olives, halved
- 3 tablespoons extra-virgin olive oil
- 2 (12- to 16-ounce) pork tenderloins, trimmed
- 2 teaspoons herbes de Provence
  Salt and pepper
- 1 pound cherry tomatoes, halved
- 1 tablespoon grated lemon zest
- 2 tablespoons minced fresh parsley

1. Adjust oven rack to lower-middle position and heat oven to 450 degrees. Microwave fennel and 2 tablespoons water in covered bowl until softened, about 5 minutes. Drain fennel, then toss with artichokes, olives, and oil.

2. Pat tenderloins dry with paper towels. Sprinkle with herbes de Provence and season with salt and pepper. Spread fennel mixture evenly in large roasting pan, then place tenderloins over top. Roast until pork registers 145 degrees, 25 to 30 minutes, turning tenderloins over halfway through roasting.

3. Remove roasting pan from oven and transfer tenderloins to carving board. Tent with aluminum foil and let rest for 10 minutes. Meanwhile, stir tomatoes and lemon zest into fennel mixture in pan and return to oven. Roast until fennel is tender and tomatoes have softened, about 10 minutes. Stir in parsley and season with salt and pepper to taste. Slice pork ½ inch thick and serve with vegetables.

STEAMED MUSSELS WITH FENNEL, WHITE WINE, AND TARRAGON

Serves 4   Total time: 30 minutes

WHY THIS RECIPE WORKS *Belgians are particularly enamored of mussels and have developed many different flavor combinations for cooking them. This highly aromatic version, with white wine and fennel, is one of the most popular and classic offerings. Simmering the broth for a few minutes before adding the mussels allowed the fennel both to soften and to flavor the broth. The garlic in the broth balanced and enriched the flavor of the mollusks, and simmering the broth for a few minutes before adding the mussels concentrated its flavor. A toasted baguette was perfect for soaking up the richly flavorful liquid. When cleaning the mussels, discard any with cracked or broken shells or a shell that won't close when lightly tapped.*

- 8 tablespoons unsalted butter, softened
- 6 garlic cloves, minced
- ¼ cup minced fresh tarragon
  Salt and pepper
- 1 (12-inch) baguette, cut on bias into 12 (1-inch-thick) slices
- 1 fennel bulb, stalks discarded, bulb quartered, cored, and chopped
- 1½ cups dry white wine
- 4 pounds mussels, scrubbed and debearded

1. Adjust oven rack 4 inches from broiler element and heat broiler. Combine butter, garlic, 2 tablespoons tarragon, ½ teaspoon salt, and ½ teaspoon pepper in bowl. Spread 5 tablespoons butter mixture on 1 side of baguette slices. Place slices, buttered side up, on rimmed baking sheet. Set aside.

2. Melt 1 tablespoon butter mixture in Dutch oven over medium heat and cook until garlic is fragrant, about 30 seconds. Add fennel, cover, and cook until softened, about 2 minutes. Stir in wine and ½ teaspoon salt, bring to simmer, and cook, uncovered, for 3 minutes. Add mussels, cover, and cook, stirring occasionally, until mussels open, 4 to 6 minutes. Off heat, transfer mussels to individual serving bowls using slotted spoon, leaving remaining broth in pot; discard any mussels that refuse to open.

3. Broil baguette slices until lightly browned, about 1 minute per side. Whisk remaining 2 tablespoons butter mixture and remaining 2 tablespoons tarragon into broth in pot until melted and season with salt and pepper to taste. Pour broth over mussels and serve with toasted baguette slices.

COD BAKED IN FOIL WITH FENNEL AND SHALLOTS

Serves 4   Total time: 45 minutes

WHY THIS RECIPE WORKS *For a rich and aromatic foil-baked seafood-and-vegetables dish where all the components mingle in perfect harmony, the selection of both fish and vegetables is equally important. We chose mild cod over more assertive salmon or tuna, which can overpower other ingredients. Fennel and shallots created the tender yet firm vegetable bed. Placing the packets on the lower-middle rack of the oven close to the heat source concentrated and deepened the flavors of the exuded liquid, which we made even better by adding a citrusy compound butter to the packets. For a bright finishing touch, we spooned fresh orange segments over the top after the packets came out of the oven. Other flaky white fish, such as haddock, red snapper, halibut, or sea bass, can be substituted. Open each packet promptly after baking to prevent overcooking, being careful to open them away from you to avoid the hot steam.*

1 large fennel bulb, stalks discarded, halved, cored, and sliced into ¼-inch strips
2 large shallots, sliced thin
4 tablespoons unsalted butter, softened
2 teaspoons minced fresh tarragon
1 garlic clove, minced
¼ teaspoon grated orange zest plus 2 oranges, peeled, quartered, and sliced into ¼-inch-thick pieces
Salt and pepper
4 (6-ounce) skinless cod fillets, 1 to 1¼ inches thick
¼ cup dry white wine

1. Microwave fennel and shallots in tightly covered large bowl until fennel has started to wilt, 3 to 4 minutes, stirring once halfway through cooking. Combine butter, 1 teaspoon tarragon, garlic, orange zest, ¼ teaspoon salt, and ⅛ teaspoon pepper in small bowl. Combine orange pieces and remaining 1 teaspoon tarragon in second small bowl; set aside.

2. Adjust oven rack to lower-middle position and heat oven to 450 degrees. Pat fish dry with paper towels and season with salt and pepper. Cut eight 12-inch-long sheets of aluminum foil. Arrange 4 pieces foil flat on counter. Divide fennel-shallot mixture among arranged foil pieces, mounding vegetables in center of each piece. Drizzle 1 tablespoon wine over each vegetable mound, then place 1 fillet on top of each vegetable mound. Divide butter mixture evenly among fillets, spreading over top of each piece. Place second square of foil on top of fish and fold edges of foil until packet is well sealed and measures about 7 inches square. Place packets on rimmed baking sheet, overlapping as needed.

3. Bake until cod registers 140 degrees, about 15 minutes. (To check temperature, poke thermometer through foil of 1 packet and into cod). Remove sheet from oven and carefully open packets, allowing steam to escape away from you. Using thin metal spatula, gently slide fish and vegetables onto plate, along with any accumulated juices. Spoon orange and tarragon mixture over fish. Serve immediately.

FORAGED GREENS

Most of us will likely never forage in the wild for our food. But the vegetables here certainly can be harvested in this way, and there's an undeniable romance to that, evoking Ralph Waldo Emerson's themes of self-reliance. Still, if you prefer to do your foraging at farmers' markets, you're in luck. Many greens that traditionally have only been available as wild foraged plants are now seen in farmers' markets and supermarkets. Some of them have even been transformed from foraged to cultivated status, like dandelions.

DANDELIONS are, in fact, the most commonly seen foraged green. While it may seem like they have transformed rapidly from despised weed to farmers' market darling, their culinary history is long and rich everywhere from Italy to the American South. The next most commonly seen foraged green is probably **PURSLANE**—perhaps not in markets, but definitely in the wild, since it grows easily and prolifically.

FIDDLEHEADS are the most beautiful of the foraged greens. These tightly coiled ferns are so-named for their resemblance to the scroll of a violin. For many, their brief annual appearance signals the true beginning of spring, and fiddlehead lovers frenzy to get their yearly haul. We offer two creative recipes that go beyond the usual simple sauté. **RAMPS** also have a short season, so grab them by the handful at the farmers' market and pickle them for year-round eating.

Though prickly, **NETTLES** are easy to work with, and we show you how to make a comforting soup as well as a guest-worthy galette. Last, but not least, **SORREL** brings its unique lemony flavor to a bright sauce to top crispy smashed potatoes.

shopping and storage

DANDELIONS Mature dandelions are cultivated and readily available in supermarkets much of the year; look for baby dandelion greens in the springtime at farmers' markets. Avoid any bunches with yellow or wilted leaves or woody stems. Wrap them in paper towels inside a plastic produce bag and refrigerate for up to several days.

FIDDLEHEADS Find these coiled greens at farmers' markets and, increasingly, supermarkets. The season is very short: two to three weeks in any given area. Look for fiddleheads that are tightly coiled and bright green with no browning, with bits of their brown, papery sheath clinging to them. Store them in a plastic produce bag in the refrigerator for just a few days.

NETTLES Nettles appear at farmers' markets in the early spring. They are sometimes sold with their stalks or thick stems still attached; if so, be sure to remove them before using. Store them wrapped in paper towels in a plastic produce bag in the refrigerator for up to several days.

PURSLANE Farmers' markets are likely to feature purslane from early to mid-summer. The small, oar-shaped leaves should be smooth and dark green, with a slight sheen. Store in a plastic produce bag in the refrigerator for up to a week.

RAMPS Ramps can be found at farmers' markets and some upscale supermarkets in mid-spring. Look for small white bulbs with long, bright green, narrow leaves attached; the root ends are likely to still be attached. Wrap the root ends in paper towels and store the ramps in the refrigerator for up to several days.

SORREL Look for sorrel at farmers' markets from late spring through midsummer. Its leaves, which resemble spinach, range from pale to dark green; avoid bunches with wilted or browning leaves or stalks. Store wrapped in paper towels in the refrigerator for up to a week.

foraged greens by any other name

DANDELIONS You will most often see mature dandelion greens, 12 inches or longer in length, in supermarkets; similar to other hearty greens, these are best sautéed or quickly braised. Farmers' markets (and your local foraging spot) are more likely to have baby dandelions, which are smaller and more tender and barely need cooking; they are great as part of a salad mix or very quickly wilted, as in our Orecchiette with Baby Dandelion Greens in Lemony Cream Sauce.

FIDDLEHEADS These beautifully coiled fronds of the ostrich fern (or sometimes, in the Pacific Northwest, the lady fern) have an ephemeral harvesting window, and those who forage for them jealously guard the location of their picking spots. Never eat raw fiddleheads; they should always be blanched first before using them in any recipe.

NETTLES This perennial flowering plant has been used medicinally since ancient Greek times; you may have seen nettle tea with the herbal tea selection in the market. The fresh leaves can be cooked and treated much like spinach, with one caveat: When raw, they have very fine prickly hairs, a natural defense mechanism that can cause redness or itching when you handle them. Fortunately, cooking eliminates this issue.

PURSLANE The succulent, moisture-rich, bite-size leaves of this ubiquitous and easy-to-forage plant have a crisp, crunchy texture and tart, peppery flavor. Purslane also happens to have the highest omega-3 fatty acid content of any plant. It grows prolifically in the manner of a weed in gardens, at the edges of lawns, in planters—you name it. It makes a wonderful salad green, as in our Purslane and Watermelon Salad.

RAMPS Also called wild leeks, ramps may be a lesser-known wild-growing member of the onion family that appear only briefly in the spring, but don't let that discourage you from grabbing a few handfuls of this beautiful and aromatic green vegetable at your local farmers' market. They are great either quickly grilled or pickled, and we do both in this chapter.

SORREL Technically an herb, sorrel grows enthusiastically as a foraged weed and is not cultivated for wide commercial availability like other herbs. In the Middle Ages, before citrus fruit reached Europe, cooks used sorrel to bring a lemony flavor to foods. It adds an unexpected herbal tartness to salads and sauces thanks to its oxalic acid (the same compound found in black tea and spinach).

vegetable prep

Trimming Ramps

Slip off thin outer layer of skin from the ramps (similar to scallions) and then cut off root ends. Submerge trimmed ramps in bowl of water and swish them around thoroughly to rid them of dirt and sand.

Handling Nettles

Always wear food-handling gloves (we recommend a double layer), and wash your hands well with warm soapy water afterward. If any of the little hairs cling to your skin, remove them with duct tape.

HORTA

Serves 6 to 8   Total time: 25 minutes

WHY THIS RECIPE WORKS *In Greece, where this recipe hails from,* horta *simply means any wild green, and they are prepared simply: either boiled or steamed and then drizzled with plenty of good olive oil, sprinkled with salt, and served with lemon. Dandelion greens—nutritious, easily accessible, and unabashedly bitter—are especially popular prepared in this manner. Tasters preferred the boiled version to the steamed version, noting that the former was brighter green in color and less muddy-tasting than the steamed version. Then we looked at possible additions: olives, feta cheese, tomatoes, and herbs. But, in the end, tradition prevailed: Tasters wanted their horta both perfectly cooked and free of distracting adjunct flavors. Olive oil, salt, and lemon were all they desired to get the best flavor from the greens. This dish can be served warm, room temperature, or chilled. Use mature dandelion greens for this recipe; do not use baby dandelion greens.*

- 2 pounds dandelion greens, trimmed and cut into 2-inch lengths
  Salt
- ¼ cup extra-virgin olive oil
  Flake sea salt
  Lemon wedges

1. Bring 4 quarts water to boil in large pot over high heat. Add dandelion greens and 1 tablespoon salt and cook until thickest stems are just tender, 4 to 7 minutes. Drain greens in colander and, using rubber spatula, gently press greens to release excess liquid.

2. Transfer greens to serving platter, drizzle with oil, and season with sea salt to taste. Serve with lemon wedges.

FRIED FIDDLEHEADS WITH LEMON-CHIVE DIPPING SAUCE

Serves 6 to 8   Total time: 50 minutes (plus 30 minutes chilling time)

WHY THIS RECIPE WORKS *You might not immediately think of fiddleheads as finger food, but when we looked at these bite-size coiled ferns, we saw a frying opportunity we couldn't pass up. Our goal was clear: deep-fried fiddleheads with a coating that was both delicious and didn't completely obscure their signature shape. Beer batter was tasty, but the flavor was too strong and the batter completely cloaked the fiddleheads. Tasters liked the flavor and look of lacy tempura batter, but didn't like the way it stuck the fiddleheads together, fusing them into large clumps. A simple panko crust was too tough and disguised the fiddleheads' shape. When we tried a cornmeal coating, tasters were finally satisfied. The cornmeal brought a faint sweetness and great crunch, while cornstarch kept the crust crisp and flour gave it structure—and it was light enough for us to still see the beautiful coils. We blanched the fiddleheads before coating and frying them, so they were cooked through by the time the crust turned golden brown. Served with a bright lemon-chive dipping sauce, these were delicious fiddleheads we could see—but unlike we'd ever seen before. Use a Dutch oven that holds 6 quarts or more for this recipe. Be sure to set up the ice water bath before cooking the fiddleheads; plunging them into the cold water immediately after blanching retains their bright green color and ensures that they don't overcook.*

LEMON-CHIVE DIPPING SAUCE

- ½ cup mayonnaise
- 2 tablespoons minced fresh chives
- 1 teaspoon grated lemon zest plus 1 tablespoon juice
- 1 teaspoon Worcestershire sauce
- 1 teaspoon Dijon mustard
- ¼ teaspoon garlic powder

FIDDLEHEADS

- 1 pound fiddleheads, trimmed and cleaned (see right)
  Salt and pepper
- ⅔ cup buttermilk
- 1 large egg
- ¾ cup cornmeal
- ½ cup cornstarch
- ¼ cup all-purpose flour
- ½ teaspoon garlic powder
- ¼ teaspoon cayenne pepper
- 3 quarts peanut or vegetable oil

1. For the lemon-chive dipping sauce Whisk all ingredients together in bowl. Cover and refrigerate until ready to serve.

2. For the fiddleheads Bring 4 quarts water to boil in large Dutch oven. Fill large bowl halfway with ice and water. Add fiddleheads and 1 tablespoon salt to boiling water and cook for 2 minutes. Using slotted spoon, transfer fiddleheads to ice water, and let sit until cool, about 2 minutes. Drain, transfer fiddleheads to platter lined with triple layer of paper towels, and dry well.

3. Meanwhile, adjust oven rack to middle position and heat oven to 200 degrees. Line rimmed baking sheet with parchment paper. Set wire rack in second rimmed baking sheet and line with triple layer of paper towels. Whisk buttermilk and egg together in shallow dish. Whisk cornmeal, cornstarch, flour, garlic powder, cayenne, 1 teaspoon salt, and ¼ teaspoon pepper together in second shallow dish. Working in batches, dip fiddleheads in buttermilk mixture, letting excess drip back into dish, then dredge in cornmeal mixture, pressing firmly to adhere. Transfer fiddleheads to parchment-lined sheet. Refrigerate, uncovered, for at least 30 minutes or up to 4 hours.

4. Add oil to clean, dry Dutch oven until it measures 2 inches deep and heat over medium-high heat to 375 degrees. Carefully add half of fiddleheads to hot oil and cook, stirring as needed to prevent sticking, until fiddleheads are golden and crisp, 2 to 4 minutes. Adjust burner, if necessary, to maintain oil temperature between 350 and 375 degrees. Using wire skimmer or slotted spoon, transfer fiddleheads to prepared rack. Season with salt and transfer to oven to keep warm.

5. Return oil to 375 degrees and repeat with remaining fiddleheads. Serve immediately with lemon-chive dipping sauce.

FRIED FIDDLEHEADS WITH LEMON-CHIVE DIPPING SAUCE

Fried fiddleheads are a highly addictive way to enjoy this fleeting seasonal vegetable; they disappeared like French fries in our test kitchen. The cornmeal batter provides textural crunch and lightly sweet corn flavor, and it seems altogether in keeping with this foraged green's New England roots. The simple lemony aïoli-style dipping sauce, with chives, Worcestershire, and mustard, is creamy and bright-tasting and will have you dipping, and dipping, and dipping again.

1. Trim the stems of the fiddleheads so they are no longer than 1 inch in length.

2. Clean the fiddleheads by submerging them in water and agitating them to release the dirt and brown husks. Gently rub the fiddleheads to remove any remaining debris. Repeat this step until the fiddleheads are completely clean and then drain in a colander and rinse with running water.

3. Blanch the fiddleheads in the salted boiling water for 2 minutes. Then transfer them to the ice-water bath and let sit until cool, about 2 minutes. Drain and dry well with paper towels.

4. Working in batches, dip the fiddleheads into the buttermilk mixture, letting the excess drip back into the bowl. Dredge the fiddleheads in the cornmeal mixture, pressing firmly to adhere.

5. Transfer the battered fiddleheads to a parchment-lined baking sheet and refrigerate, uncovered, for at least 30 minutes or up to 4 hours.

6. Fry the fiddleheads in the hot oil for 2 to 4 minutes, then transfer to the prepared rack to drain. Serve the fried fiddleheads sprinkled with salt, with the lemon-chive dipping sauce.

Grilled Ramps

GRILLED RAMPS

Serves 4   Total time: 35 minutes

WHY THIS RECIPE WORKS *A foolproof and easy way to celebrate the distinctive fresh onion flavor and short window of availability of ramps is by simply grilling them. To ensure that the thicker white bulbous ends of the ramps cooked through without the more delicate green ends of the ramps burning, we made sure to cook the white ramp bulbs over the high heat of the grill, arranging the green ends of the ramps over the cooler side of the grill. A simple toss of oil, salt, and pepper was all the flavor boost our ramps needed. Grilled lemon quarters made for a beautiful presentation and a welcomed tart finish of flavor for this beautiful side dish. The ramp greens will blister and char quickly, so make sure to watch them carefully. Serve with grilled steak, chicken, or fish, or chop them up and add to vegetable or grain salads.*

- 5 ounces ramps, trimmed
- 1 tablespoon extra-virgin olive oil
- 1 lemon, quartered
  Salt and pepper

1a. For a charcoal grill Open bottom vent completely. Light large chimney starter filled with charcoal briquettes (6 quarts). When top coals are partially covered with ash, pour evenly over half of grill. Set cooking grate in place, cover, and open lid vent completely. Heat grill until hot, about 5 minutes.

1b. For a gas grill Turn all burners to high, cover, and heat grill until hot, about 15 minutes. Leave primary burner on high and turn off other burner(s).

2. Clean and oil cooking grate. Toss ramps with oil. Arrange ramps on grill, perpendicular to grate bars, with whites over hotter side of grill and greens over cooler side. Place lemon quarters over hotter side of grill. Grill ramps until whites are softened and lightly charred and lemons are well charred, turning ramps as needed, about 5 minutes.

3. Flip ramps so that greens are over hotter side of grill and cook, turning as needed, until greens are blistered and charred, about 15 seconds. Transfer ramps and lemon quarters to serving platter and season with salt and pepper to taste. Serve.

PICKLED RAMPS

Makes one 1-quart jar
Total time: 45 minutes
(plus 24 hours chilling time)

WHY THIS RECIPE WORKS *Preserving ramps is a great way to enjoy their flavor past their short growing season, and pickling is our preferred preservation choice. A snap to make, these aromatic, zesty pickled ramps are ready to jump in on short notice to brighten up and add flavor to any salad or cheese plate; they're even great as a burger topping. Through testing, we found that cutting the ramps in half to separate the white bulbs from the greens was important for even pickling. We poured the hot pickle brine over the thick white bulbous ends of the ramps first, and let this cool to room temperature before adding the ramp greens to the jar. This ensured both that the sharp oniony bite of the bulbs was properly mellowed and that the delicate texture and bright color of the greens were preserved. Heating the jars with hot water and then draining them before adding the hot brine ensured that the jars wouldn't crack from the abrupt temperature change. Be sure to submerge the ramps completely in the brine and refrigerate for a full 24 hours to ensure a balanced sweet-and-sour flavor.*

- 1½ cups unseasoned rice vinegar
- ¼ cup sugar
- 1 teaspoon salt
- 2 bay leaves
- 1 teaspoon yellow mustard seeds
- ⅛ teaspoon black peppercorns
- 8 ounces ramps, trimmed, white and green parts separated

1. Bring vinegar, ½ cup water, sugar, salt, bay leaves, mustard seeds, and peppercorns to boil in medium saucepan over medium-high heat.

2. Fill one 1-quart jar with hot water to warm. Drain jar, then, using tongs, pack ramp whites into jar. Using funnel and ladle, pour hot brine over ramp whites to cover, and let cool to room temperature, about 30 minutes.

3. Using tongs, pack ramp greens into jar, being sure to submerge completely. Refrigerate, covered, for at least 24 hours before serving. (Pickled ramps can be refrigerated for up to 3 weeks; the greens will soften significantly after 3 weeks.)

VARIATION

Thai Pickled Ramps

Omit bay leaves and mustard seeds. Add 1 (3-inch) piece fresh ginger, peeled and sliced thin, 4 teaspoons fish sauce, 2 thinly sliced Thai chiles, and 1 teaspoon lime zest to vinegar mixture in step 1. Add 3 sprigs fresh Thai basil to jar with ramp greens.

NETTLE SOUP

Serves 4 to 6   Total time: 1 hour 15 minutes

WHY THIS RECIPE WORKS *Cream of nettle soup is often the first recipe a new nettle forager (or farmers' market explorer) will try out. Many available recipes end up muting the nettles' delicate flavor and vibrant color. We wanted to create a soup that coaxed out and highlighted the unique, subtle character of the nettles. Recipes that called for simmering them along with the other ingredients, sometimes for as long as half an hour, produced soups that looked and tasted muddy. Those that simply blanched the nettles resulted in the loss of much of their vivid color. So we went with a tried-and-true method for the greenest greens: We blanched the nettles quickly and shocked them in ice water. Next, for the base and thickener, it turned out that less was more: Too much broth distracted, water alone lacked depth, and cream dramatically dulled the nettle flavor. We landed on a mixture of broth and water, which we infused with nettle flavor by using it as our blanching liquid. Potatoes are a commonly used thickener for nettle soup, but their flavor was so overwhelming that tasters called the result "Green Potato Soup." We hit on a clever trick: A small amount of Arborio rice, cooked in the broth, thickened the soup but had a neutral flavor. Tasters loved the delicacy of the soup but had one qualm: Some swore the soup was "stinging" them. After some research, we found that while the stinging chemicals were completely deactivated, the sharp hairs had avoided full pulverization and were irritating some mouths; this was easily fixed by straining the soup after we pureed it. We drizzled a bit of rich, tangy crème fraîche over the top, sprinkled on nutty, crunchy pepitas, and ended up with a beautiful green soup with the essence of nettles. Always use thick kitchen gloves when handling fresh nettles to avoid being pricked by their fine hairs. Be sure to set up the ice water bath before cooking the nettles; plunging them into the water after blanching ensures a brightly colored soup.*

- 6 tablespoons crème fraîche
- 4 cups chicken or vegetable broth
- 6 ounces (12 packed cups) stinging nettles leaves
- 4 tablespoons unsalted butter
- 3 shallots, chopped
  Salt and pepper
- ⅓ cup Arborio rice
- 3 sprigs fresh thyme
- 1 bay leaf
- 1½ tablespoons lemon juice
- ⅓ cup roasted, salted pepitas

1. Combine crème fraîche and 1 tablespoon water in bowl; set aside until ready to serve. Bring broth and 3 cups water to boil in Dutch oven over high heat. Meanwhile, fill large bowl halfway with ice and water.

2. Add nettles to boiling broth mixture and cook until nettles are wilted and tender, about 3 minutes. Drain nettles in fine-mesh strainer set over large bowl. Using rubber spatula, press nettles to release excess liquid; reserve blanching liquid. Transfer nettles to ice water, and let sit until cool, about 3 minutes. Drain nettles and set aside.

3. Melt butter in now-empty pot over medium heat. Add shallots and ¼ teaspoon salt and cook, stirring occasionally, until shallots are softened, about 3 minutes. Stir in reserved blanching liquid, rice, thyme sprigs, and bay leaf and bring to simmer. Cover, reduce heat to low, and cook until rice is very soft, about 30 minutes.

4. Discard thyme sprigs and bay leaf. Working in batches, process broth mixture and nettles in blender until smooth, about 2 minutes. Strain soup through fine-mesh strainer into clean pot and bring soup to simmer over

medium heat. Adjust consistency of soup with additional water as needed. Stir in lemon juice and season with salt and pepper to taste. Drizzle individual portions with crème fraîche mixture and sprinkle with pepitas before serving.

PURSLANE AND WATERMELON SALAD

Serves 4 to 6   Total time: 45 minutes

WHY THIS RECIPE WORKS *In the height of summer, you have probably seen purslane growing all around—in open fields, in sidewalk cracks, maybe even in your backyard— without realizing that this common foraged green is not only edible but also delicious. Its crisp, juicy stems and leaves and slightly tart, tangy flavor make it a special ingredient perfect for highlighting in a fresh salad. Since purslane is available only in the summer, we created a salad that celebrates a pairing of two fresh, summery ingredients. To start, we cubed watermelon into 1-inch hunks, tossed them with sugar, and let them drain of any excess liquid. This ensured that we wouldn't have a soupy mess on our hands.*

To gently balance the melon's sweetness and the purslane's tangy bite, we added thinly sliced shallot for delicate onion flavor. Tearing the fresh purslane into 2-inch pieces ensured that every bite would have purslane flavor. Fresh basil lent brightness, torn bits of fresh mozzarella added creamy substance, and a simple vinaigrette of olive oil, cider vinegar, and lemon brought everything together. This salad benefits from a liberal sprinkling of salt and pepper, so don't be shy when seasoning the mozzarella.

- 4 cups watermelon cut into 1-inch pieces
- 2 teaspoons sugar
- 2 tablespoons extra-virgin olive oil, plus extra for drizzling
- 1 tablespoon cider vinegar
- ½ teaspoon grated lemon zest plus 1 tablespoon juice
  Salt and pepper
- 6 ounces purslane, trimmed and torn into 1½-inch pieces (6 cups)
- ¼ cup fresh basil leaves, torn
- 1 shallot, sliced thin
- 6 ounces fresh mozzarella cheese, torn into 1-inch pieces

1. Toss watermelon with sugar in colander set over bowl; set aside for 30 minutes.

2. Whisk oil, vinegar, lemon zest and juice, ½ teaspoon salt, and ¼ teaspoon pepper together in large bowl. Add purslane, basil, shallot, and drained watermelon and toss gently to combine. Transfer to serving platter and scatter mozzarella over top. Drizzle with extra oil and season with salt and pepper to taste. Serve.

FIDDLEHEAD PANZANELLA

Serves 6   Total time: 45 minutes
WHY THIS RECIPE WORKS *While fiddleheads are often prepared in a simple sauté or pickled, we wanted to create a more complex dish that would both showcase the fiddlehead's showstopping appearance and highlight its unique flavor and texture. We envisioned a bread salad, or panzanella, abundant with bright green fiddleheads and studded with complementary vibrant flavors and colors. We knew from our initial testing that tasters thought fiddleheads were at their best when they were blanched before any further preparation. Blanching ensured that they were fully clean and also turned the fiddleheads a vivid green. We tried sautéing them with aromatics after blanching, but that sauté turned our fiddleheads an unappealing shade of brown-green, and the aromatics masked their fresh asparagus-like flavor. So we returned to a simple blanching; tasters loved the color and unadulterated flavor. We tossed them with rich, chewy-crispy croutons, sweet grape tomatoes, and a simple vinaigrette. Fresh basil and creamy goat cheese finished the dish, for a beautiful salad that showed off the foraged ferns' best side. You can substitute 6 ounces cherry tomatoes for the grape tomatoes. A rasp-style grater makes quick work of turning the garlic into a paste. Be sure to set up the ice water bath before cooking the fiddleheads; plunging them into the cold water immediately after blanching retains their bright green color and ensures that they don't overcook.*

1 pound fiddleheads, trimmed and cleaned
   Salt and pepper
6 ounces ciabatta or sourdough bread, cut into ¾-inch pieces (4 cups)
½ cup extra-virgin olive oil
1 garlic clove, minced to paste
¼ cup red wine vinegar
5 ounces grape tomatoes, halved
2 ounces goat cheese, crumbled (½ cup)
¼ cup chopped fresh basil

1. Bring 4 quarts water to boil in large pot. Fill large bowl halfway with ice and water. Add fiddleheads and 1 tablespoon salt to boiling water and cook until crisp-tender, about 5 minutes. Using slotted spoon, transfer fiddleheads to ice water and let sit until cool, about 2 minutes. Transfer fiddleheads to platter lined with triple layer of paper towels and dry well.

2. Toss bread, 3 tablespoons water, and ¼ teaspoon salt together in large bowl, squeezing bread gently until water is absorbed. Cook bread mixture and ¼ cup oil in 12-inch nonstick skillet over medium-high heat, stirring often, until browned and crisp, 7 to 10 minutes.

3. Off heat, push bread to sides of skillet. Add 1 tablespoon oil, garlic, and ¼ teaspoon pepper, and cook using residual heat of skillet, mashing mixture into skillet, until fragrant, about 10 seconds. Stir bread into garlic mixture, then transfer croutons to bowl to cool slightly, about 5 minutes.

4. Whisk remaining 3 tablespoons oil, vinegar, ¼ teaspoon salt, and ¼ teaspoon pepper together in large bowl until combined. Add fiddleheads, croutons, and tomatoes and toss gently to coat. Season with salt and pepper to taste. Transfer to serving platter and sprinkle with goat cheese and basil. Serve.

SMASHED POTATOES WITH SORREL-ALMOND SAUCE

Serves 6 to 8   Total time: 1 hour 30 minutes
WHY THIS RECIPE WORKS *Sorrel is unique among herbs in the common herb garden—or forager's sack. There's nothing that can quite mimic its lemony tartness, and we wanted to capture that quality in a fresh sauce, which would thus allow us to add sorrel's essence to a range of dishes. Many recipes for sorrel sauces or pestos cut the sorrel with another herb, like parsley, basil, or mint. While these were delicious, we found that the subtler flavors of the sorrel were completely lost, reducing it to simply a lemon juice substitute. Once we decided sorrel would be our sole herb, we knew we had to carefully balance our sauce, or it would come out too sour and astringent. Toasted almonds brought depth, and a touch of honey tempered the acidity. Mild toasted garlic and some red pepper flakes provided an aromatic background with a hint of heat. Now we had a bright sauce that showcased sorrel's best qualities, and we decided to pair it with decadent crispy smashed potatoes. It was a perfect match— the fat, salt, and starch of the potatoes cried out for a tangy topping. While this sauce is excellent on many roasted or grilled vegetables, it also pairs wonderfully with fish and rich cuts of meat. Use small red potatoes measuring 1 to 2 inches in diameter. It is important to thoroughly cook the potatoes so that they will smash easily. Remove the potatoes from the baking sheet as soon as they are done browning—they will toughen if left in the oven too long.*

POTATOES
2 pounds small red potatoes, unpeeled
6 tablespoons extra-virgin olive oil
   Salt and pepper

SORREL-ALMOND SAUCE
1 garlic clove, unpeeled
3 ounces (3 cups) sorrel leaves, trimmed and torn into 2-inch pieces
¼ cup extra-virgin olive oil
2 tablespoons chopped toasted almonds
¼ teaspoon honey
⅛ teaspoon red pepper flakes
   Salt

1. **For the potatoes** Adjust oven racks to top and lowest positions and heat oven to 500 degrees. Place potatoes on rimmed baking sheet, pour ¾ cup water into sheet, and wrap tightly with aluminum foil. Place sheet on lower rack and roast until paring knife slips in and out of potatoes easily (to check potatoes for doneness, poke knife through foil), 25 to 30 minutes. Remove foil and cool slightly, about 10 minutes. Wipe sheet dry with paper towels.

2. Drizzle 3 tablespoons oil over potatoes on sheet and roll to coat. Space potatoes evenly over baking sheet and place second baking sheet on top. Press top sheet down firmly, flattening potatoes to ⅓- to ½-inch thickness. Season generously with salt and pepper and drizzle evenly with remaining 3 tablespoons oil. Roast potatoes on upper rack for 15 minutes. Transfer potatoes to lower rack and continue to roast until well browned, 20 to 30 minutes longer.

3. **For the sorrel-almond sauce** Meanwhile, toast garlic in 8-inch skillet over medium heat, stirring occasionally, until fragrant and skin is spotty brown, about 7 minutes. When cool enough to handle, peel garlic. Pulse sorrel, oil, almonds, peeled garlic, honey, pepper flakes, and ¼ teaspoon salt in food processor until coarsely chopped, scraping down sides of bowl as needed, about 10 pulses. Add 2 tablespoons water and process until combined. Adjust consistency of sauce with extra water as needed. Season with salt and pepper to taste.

4. Transfer potatoes to serving platter, dollop evenly with sorrel-almond sauce, and serve.

◝

ORECCHIETTE WITH BABY DANDELION GREENS IN LEMONY CREAM SAUCE

Serves 4 to 6   Total time: 40 minutes
WHY THIS RECIPE WORKS *Like their mature incarnation, baby dandelion greens pack strong, grassy flavors and a bitter punch. But unlike their grownup selves, the babies are very tender and require minimal cooking, making them the perfect addition to a range of dishes that cry out for wilted greens. We wanted to create a pasta dish in which baby dandelion greens were the main event but weren't too strongly bitter. Initially thinking a light and fresh dish would be appropriate for an early spring green, we started out with a wine and butter sauce. But tasters found that the acidic wine only compounded the greens' bitterness. So we switched direction and made a rich, creamy Parmesan sauce instead. This sauce beautifully tamed the greens without overshadowing them, and the addition of fresh lemon juice and zest and basil finished the dish on a bright note. If you can't find baby dandelion greens, you can substitute 12 ounces of arugula. We chose orecchiette for its talent for scooping up pockets of sauce, but farfalle can be substituted.*

1   pound orecchiette
     Salt and pepper
2   tablespoons extra-virgin olive oil
1   shallot, halved and sliced thin
2   garlic cloves, minced
¼   teaspoon red pepper flakes
8   ounces baby dandelion greens, cut into 1-inch pieces
1   cup heavy cream
2   tablespoons unsalted butter
2½   ounces Parmesan cheese, grated (1¼ cups)
½   teaspoon lemon zest plus 1 tablespoon lemon juice
¼   cup chopped fresh basil

1. Bring 4 quarts water to boil in large pot. Add pasta and 1 tablespoon salt and cook, stirring occasionally, until al dente. Reserve 1 cup cooking water, then drain pasta and return it to pot.

2. Meanwhile, heat oil in 12-inch skillet over medium heat until shimmering. Add shallot, ¼ teaspoon salt, and ¼ teaspoon pepper and cook until softened, about 3 minutes. Stir in garlic and pepper flakes and cook until fragrant, about 30 seconds. Add dandelion greens 1 handful at a time, and cook until greens are just wilted, 2 to 3 minutes; transfer to pot with pasta. Wipe skillet clean with paper towels.

3. Bring cream and butter to simmer in now-empty skillet over medium-high heat. Reduce heat to medium-low and simmer gently until reduced to ¾ cup, about 3 minutes. Reduce heat to low, whisk in ¾ cup Parmesan, lemon zest and juice, and ½ teaspoon salt, and cook until Parmesan is fully incorporated and sauce is smooth, about 1 minute.

4. Add sauce and basil to pot with pasta and toss to combine. Adjust consistency with reserved cooking water as needed. Season with salt and pepper to taste. Serve, passing remaining ½ cup Parmesan separately.

◝

NETTLE AND MUSHROOM GALETTE

Serves 4 to 6   Total time: 1 hour 45 minutes (plus 1 hour 30 minutes chilling time)
WHY THIS RECIPE WORKS *Despite their name, stinging nettles aren't really a pain to prepare. Once the leaves are off, the hard part is over, and you can use nettles pretty much the way you would any other tender green. Because of their ephemeral and dramatic nature, we wanted to elevate our nettles with a special-occasion preparation. For that, nothing beats a showstopping savory galette. For the filling, we chose rich cremini mushrooms to pair with our greens. We treated the vegetables simply, sautéing them with garlic and pairing them with rich, potent binders like Parmesan, crème fraîche, and Dijon mustard. To increase the flavor of the crust and keep it tender yet sturdy, we swapped out part of the white flour for nutty whole wheat and used butter rather than shortening. To punch up its flaky texture and introduce more structure, we gave the crust a series of folds to create numerous interlocking layers. Baking the galette on a preheated pizza stone resulted in an extra-crisp crust (though this is not essential). Poking a few small holes in the dough circle prevented it from lifting off the pan and "doming" as it baked. Finished with a sprinkle of tarragon on top of the golden cheese for a fresh herbal flavor, our galette was a dinner party–worthy dish made with a special secret ingredient. Always use food-handling gloves when preparing fresh nettles to avoid being pricked by their fine hairs.*

Nettle and Mushroom Galette

folding galette dough

1. Place dough on lightly floured counter and roll into 11 by 8-inch rectangle with short side parallel to edge of counter.

2. Using bench scraper, fold bottom third of dough away from you.

3. Using bench scraper, fold upper third of dough toward you into 8 by 4-inch rectangle.

4. Turn dough 90 degrees counterclockwise. Repeat steps 1 to 3. Turn dough 90 degrees and repeat steps 1 to 3 again.

5. After third roll-and-fold, fold dough rectangle in half to create 4-inch square, pressing gently to seal.

DOUGH

- 1¼ cups (6¼ ounces) all-purpose flour
- ½ cup (2¾ ounces) whole-wheat flour
- 1 tablespoon sugar
- ¾ teaspoon salt
- 10 tablespoons unsalted butter, cut into ½-inch pieces and chilled
- 7 tablespoons ice water
- 1 teaspoon distilled white vinegar

FILLING

- ¼ cup extra-virgin olive oil
- 8 ounces cremini mushrooms, trimmed and sliced thin
  Salt and pepper
- 1 garlic clove, minced
- 6 ounces (12 cups) stinging nettle leaves
- 2 ounces Parmesan cheese, grated (1 cup)
- 2 tablespoons crème fraîche
- 1 tablespoon Dijon mustard
- 1 large egg, lightly beaten
- 1 tablespoon minced fresh tarragon

1. **For the dough** Process all-purpose flour, whole-wheat flour, sugar, and salt in food processor until combined. Scatter chilled butter over top and pulse until butter is pea-sized, about 10 pulses; transfer to medium bowl.

2. Sprinkle ice water and vinegar over flour mixture. Using rubber spatula, fold mixture until loose, shaggy mass forms with some dry flour remaining (do not overwork). Transfer to center of large sheet of plastic wrap, press gently into rough 4-inch square, and wrap tightly. Refrigerate for 45 minutes.

3. Transfer dough to lightly floured counter and roll into 11 by 8-inch rectangle with short side parallel to edge of counter. Using bench scraper, fold bottom third of dough away from you, then fold upper third toward you (as for business letter) into 8 by 4-inch rectangle. Turn dough 90 degrees counterclockwise. Repeat rolling dough into 11 by 8-inch rectangle and folding into thirds. Turn dough 90 degrees counterclockwise and repeat rolling and folding into thirds. After third set of folds, fold dough in half to create 4-inch square. Press top of dough gently to seal. Wrap with plastic and refrigerate for at least 45 minutes or up to 2 days.

4. **For the filling** Heat 1 tablespoon oil in 12-inch skillet over medium heat until shimmering. Add mushrooms and ¼ teaspoon salt, cover, and cook, stirring occasionally, until mushrooms have released their liquid, 3 to 5 minutes. Stir in 2 tablespoons oil and garlic and cook, uncovered, until fragrant, about 30 seconds. Add nettles, 1 handful at a time, and cook, stirring occasionally, until mushrooms begin to brown and nettles are tender, 5 to 7 minutes. Transfer to bowl and stir in ¾ cup Parmesan, crème fraîche, and mustard. Season with salt and pepper to taste; set aside.

5. Adjust oven rack to lower-middle position, set baking stone on rack, and heat oven to 400 degrees. Line rimmed baking sheet with parchment paper. Remove dough from refrigerator and let sit at room temperature for 15 to 20 minutes. Roll dough into 14-inch circle about ⅛ inch thick on well-floured counter. (Trim edges as needed to form rough circle.) Transfer dough to prepared sheet. Using straw or tip of paring knife, poke five ¼-inch circles in dough (one at center and four evenly spaced halfway from center to edge of dough). Brush top of dough with 1 teaspoon oil.

6. Spread filling evenly over dough, leaving 2-inch border around edge. Drizzle remaining 2 teaspoons oil over filling, then sprinkle with remaining ¼ cup Parmesan. Grasp 1 edge of dough and fold outer 2 inches over filling. Repeat around circumference of tart, overlapping dough every 2 to 3 inches; gently pinch pleated dough to secure, but do not press dough into filling. Brush dough with egg wash.

7. Reduce oven temperature to 375 degrees. Set sheet on stone and bake until crust is deep golden brown and filling is well browned, 35 to 45 minutes. Let tart cool on sheet on wire rack for 10 minutes. Using offset spatula or wide metal spatula, loosen tart from parchment and carefully slide tart onto cutting board. Sprinkle tarragon over filling and cut tart into wedges. Serve.

CRISPY PAN-SEARED SEA BASS WITH RAMP PESTO

Serves 4   Total time: 1 hour 15 minutes

WHY THIS RECIPE WORKS *The distinctively pungent flavor of ramps makes for a deliciously bright and aromatic pesto. To create an elegant meal with a simple presentation, we paired a zesty ramp pesto with easy pan-seared crispy-skinned sea bass fillets. Scoring and brining the white fish with a salt-sugar mixture ensured a perfectly seasoned fillet once cooked. To tame the ramps' raw oniony bite in our pesto, we first sautéed the sliced ramp bulbs in a 12-inch skillet until softened; we then added most of the ramp greens (reserving ¼ cup fresh greens for later) and cooked until the greens were just wilted but still maintained their bright color. Processing the cooked ramps along with the reserved fresh ramps in a food processor created a pesto that had balanced, fresh flavor without an overwhelming allium quality. Pistachios, lemon juice, and Parmesan rounded out the flavor of the pesto and complemented the crispy fish fillets. If sea bass is unavailable, any skin-on white fish fillets may be substituted. This recipe will make about 1 cup of the ramp pesto. The remaining ½ cup can be refrigerated for up to three days; try tossing it with pasta or spreading it on flatbread or bruschetta.*

Salt and pepper
1½ teaspoons sugar
4 (6- to 8-ounce) skin-on sea bass fish fillets, 1 to 1½ inches thick
½ cup extra-virgin olive oil
6 ounces ramps, white parts sliced thin, green parts cut into 1-inch pieces
3 tablespoons chopped toasted pistachios
1 tablespoon lemon juice, plus lemon wedges for serving
¼ cup grated Parmesan cheese

1. Combine 1½ teaspoons salt and sugar in small bowl. Using sharp knife, make 3 or 4 shallow slashes, about ½ inch apart, lengthwise in skin side of each fillet, being careful not to cut into flesh and stopping ½ inch from top and bottom edge of skin. Season flesh side of fillets evenly with salt mixture and place skin side up on wire rack set in rimmed baking sheet. Sprinkle skin side with ¼ teaspoon salt. Refrigerate for 45 minutes.

2. Meanwhile, measure out ¼ cup greens and set aside. Heat 2 tablespoons oil in 12-inch nonstick skillet over medium heat until shimmering. Add ramp whites and cook until softened, about 2 minutes. Stir in remaining ramp greens and cook until just wilted, about 1 minute. Transfer to food processor and let cool slightly, about 10 minutes.

3. Add pistachios, 2 tablespoons water, lemon juice, ¼ teaspoon salt, reserved ramp greens, and ¼ cup oil to food processor and process until smooth, about 30 seconds, scraping down sides of bowl as needed. Transfer to bowl and stir in Parmesan. Adjust consistency with additional water as needed; set aside until ready to serve.

4. Pat fillets dry with paper towels. Heat remaining 2 tablespoons oil in now-empty skillet over high heat until just smoking. Place fillets skin side down in skillet. Immediately reduce heat to medium-low and, using fish spatula, firmly press fillets for 20 to 30 seconds to ensure contact between skin and skillet. Continue to cook until skin is well browned and flesh is opaque except for top ¼ inch, 8 to 14 minutes. (If at any time during searing, oil starts to smoke or sides of fish start to brown, reduce heat so that oil is sizzling but not smoking.)

5. Off heat, flip fish and continue to cook using residual heat of skillet until fish registers 125 degrees, about 30 seconds longer. Transfer fish skin side up to large plate. Serve fish with pesto and lemon wedges.

FRESH LEGUMES

The umbrella term "legumes" refers to both the dried seeds, like kidney beans and lentils, and the fresh pods, such as green beans and peas. The latter two merit their own chapters in this book, while here we highlight some of the other fresh favorites in this category.

PEANUTS originated in South America, traveled to Africa with Portuguese explorers, and then came to North America on slave-carrying British ships. Today the United States is one of the top three producers worldwide—thanks mostly to our collective love of peanut butter. But the protein-packed peanut shines in recipes both savory and sweet, as in our Kung Pao Shrimp and our Peanut Granola.

A highlight of spring, **FAVA BEANS** are nutty and buttery, nestled in a wonderfully fuzzy green pod. Boil or roast whole pods to pop open, or try the Fava Bean Crostini with Manchego and Pine Nuts.

EDAMAME are young soybeans. Although we tend to associate soybeans with their processed forms, like tofu and soy milk, fresh young soybeans have a savory, nutty flavor and firm, dense texture. Boiled and salted whole pods are a familiar starter in sushi restaurants everywhere, meant to be popped open with the fingers so the beans inside can be eaten. We also love the beans stir-fried with ginger or in Edamame and Spicy Peanut Noodle Bowl.

In addition to the legumes themselves, we can also eat their **BEAN SPROUTS**. The Chinese have cultivated bean sprouts for thousands of years; in the States they gained popularity during the health-food craze of the 1970s. They add snappy crunch to stir-fries like our easy Fried Rice with Bean Sprouts and Peas. In our Sizzling Saigon Crêpes, they serve as the filling for savory Vietnamese rice-flour pancakes.

shopping and storage

BEAN SPROUTS Bean sprouts are available year-round. Purchase bean sprouts with white roots and yellow or light green leaves. Don't buy any bean sprouts that have dark roots or any off-odor or sliminess. They are extremely perishable; wrap them loosely in paper towels and store in an open plastic produce bag in the refrigerator for only a couple of days.

EDAMAME Edamame were once only available in the frozen-food section of the supermarket, both in their pods and pre-shelled. However, they are now far more readily available fresh, in their pods, in the produce section. Look for fresh edamame in late summer and early fall. Pods should be emerald green, plump, and somewhat velvety-looking. We prefer fresh edamame, but frozen are generally an acceptable substitute (preshelled frozen edamame are especially convenient if you are using larger quantities in a recipe). Fresh edamame will keep in an open plastic produce bag in the refrigerator for up to a week.

FAVA BEANS Fava beans are in season from mid- to late spring. These sturdy bright light green pods are napped with velvety fuzz. The smaller pods will have tender, sweet beans; avoid any with brown spots or overly large beans bulging the pods too much (those favas will be tough and woody). Store fresh favas in an open plastic produce bag in the refrigerator for a week or longer. Frozen favas are available (both in the pod and shucked) and can be a good substitute for the seasonal fresh version. We don't suggest the bottled favas that are often seen in supermarkets, because they have tough skins and are high in sodium.

PEANUTS Peanuts are available year-round, in both raw and dry-roasted form ("raw" peanuts have actually been air-dried to remove some of their moisture for long-term storage). The recipes here use both raw and dry-roasted peanuts. Store peanuts in an air-tight container in a cool, dry cupboard or the freezer for up to six months.

fresh legumes by any other name

BEAN SPROUTS Although any type of bean can be sprouted, the plump white bean sprouts we see most frequently in the market come from the small, bright green mung bean. Soybeans are another common source of bean sprouts. (Seeds can also be sprouted; for example, alfalfa sprouts are the thin filaments that are often used as sandwich toppings.)

EDAMAME Though the terms "edamame" and "soybeans" are often used interchangeably, there is a slight difference: Soybeans are the mature beans, whereas edamame are the immature beans, harvested while they are still green and young. All soybeans are noteworthy due to their high concentration of phytonutrients called isoflavones, plant hormones that may help prevent certain types of cancer. They are also the only beans that contain all of the essential amino acids.

FAVA BEANS Also called broad beans or field beans, these members of the pea family have been a staple of Mediterranean and Middle Eastern cuisines for centuries. They somewhat resemble lima beans. After removing fava beans from their outer, inedible pod, you must then remove the waxy sheath that covers each bean; blanching is the best way to make this process easier.

PEANUTS Although "nut" is in the name, peanuts are indeed legumes, edible seeds that grow in pods (their shells). Unlike tree nuts, such as almonds and walnuts, peanuts grow below the surface of the soil. True fresh peanuts, called "green" peanuts, straight from the plant, are highly perishable and need to be eaten within a few days. For this reason, they are not usually found outside their growing regions.

vegetable prep

Preparing Fava Beans for Cooking

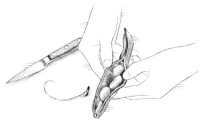

1. Use paring knife to snip off tip of pod. Pull apart sides of pod to release beans.

2. Blanch beans in boiling water for 1 minute, then plunge into ice water for 2 minutes to cool. Pat dry with paper towels.

3. Using paring knife, make small cut along edge of each bean through waxy sheath, then gently squeeze sheath to release bean; discard sheath.

BOILED PEANUTS

Makes about 16 cups
Total time: 8 hours 15 minutes

WHY THIS RECIPE WORKS *Boiled peanuts are a beloved snack in the southern United States, where they are sold in small paper bags from roadside stands. If you live outside the South, you may never have tasted this treat, but it's a delicious snack and nutritious alternative to shell-on roasted peanuts. For our recipe, we found that the typical method of boiling raw, shell-on (not roasted) peanuts in heavily seasoned water was the most common cooking method for good reason: It worked best. Cooking the peanuts covered for 5 to 6 hours and letting them cool in the cooking water for another 2 hours ensured that they were perfectly tender. They should have the texture and consistency of a cooked dried bean. If you're using fresh green peanuts, which are available in late summer and early fall, reduce the cooking time to about 2 hours.*

    2 pounds raw, shell-on peanuts
    1 cup salt

Combine peanuts, 2 gallons water, and salt in 12-quart stockpot. Bring to boil over high heat. Reduce heat to low, cover, and simmer until peanuts are tender, about 6 hours, stirring occasionally. Remove from heat and let peanuts cool completely in water, about 2 hours. Strain and serve.

PEANUT GRANOLA

Makes about 9 cups
Total time: 1 hour (plus 1 hour cooling time)

WHY THIS RECIPE WORKS *Store-bought granola is convenient but too often chock-full of pale, dried-out oats and stale-tasting nuts. It provides texture but not a whole lot of flavor. This homemade granola focuses simply on roasted peanuts and oats; it has an ideal crispy, crunchy texture, and you can break it up into whatever size pieces you like. We found that the secret to perfect crunchiness was to firmly pack the granola mixture into a rimmed baking sheet before baking. Once it was baked, we had a granola "bark" that we could break into crunchy clumps of any size. Caramel sauce, maple syrup, and salt added a welcome buttery*

flavor and an ideal salty-sweet balance—and we didn't skimp on the amounts. This would be as delicious sprinkled over ice cream as it would be with yogurt for breakfast. Do not use quick oats in this recipe.

    ¾ cup caramel sauce
    ½ cup vegetable oil
    ⅓ cup maple syrup
    4 teaspoons vanilla extract
    1½ teaspoons salt
    5 cups (15 ounces) old-fashioned
       rolled oats
    2 cups (10 ounces) unsalted dry-roasted
       peanuts, chopped

1. Adjust oven rack to upper-middle position and heat oven to 325 degrees. Line rimmed baking sheet with parchment paper. Spray parchment with vegetable oil spray. Whisk caramel, oil, maple syrup, vanilla, and salt together in large bowl. Stir in oats and peanuts until thoroughly combined.

2. Transfer oat mixture to prepared sheet and spread in even layer. Using stiff metal spatula, press down firmly on oat mixture until very compact. Bake until lightly browned, 35 to 40 minutes, rotating sheet halfway through baking.

3. Transfer sheet to wire rack and let granola cool completely in sheet, about 1 hour. Break cooled granola into pieces of desired size. Serve. (Granola can be stored in airtight container for up to 2 weeks.)

GINGERY STIR-FRIED EDAMAME

Serves 4   Total time: 15 minutes

WHY THIS RECIPE WORKS *Superfast and superflavorful, this quick side dish makes for a great weeknight accompaniment to practically any protein. The toasted sesame oil amplified the nuttiness of the edamame, and a generous amount of fresh ginger gave the fresh legumes an aromatic, spicy punch. Soy sauce stirred in at the end tied all the flavors together. You can substitute frozen, thawed, and patted dry edamame beans for fresh here. You will need a 12-inch nonstick skillet with a tight-fitting lid for this recipe.*

    12 ounces shelled edamame beans (2 cups)
    ½ cup water
    1 tablespoon toasted sesame oil
    1 scallion, minced
    1 tablespoon grated fresh ginger
    1 tablespoon soy sauce

1. Cook edamame and water in 12-inch nonstick skillet, covered, until edamame are nearly tender, about 7 minutes. Uncover and cook until water evaporates and edamame are tender, about 2 minutes longer.

2. Push edamame to sides of skillet. Add sesame oil, scallion, and ginger to center and cook, mashing mixture into pan, until fragrant, about 30 seconds. Stir mixture into edamame, then stir in soy sauce. Serve.

FAVA BEAN CROSTINI WITH MANCHEGO AND PINE NUTS

Serves 8 to 10   Total time: 1 hour 30 minutes

WHY THIS RECIPE WORKS *Showcasing the rich flavor and buttery texture of fava beans, this sophisticated hors d'oeuvre is a surefire crowd-pleaser. Although fresh favas do require some prep work, the results are well worth the effort. The beans must first be removed from their tough outer pod, and then the translucent waxy sheath covering each bean should also be removed. To preserve the creamy-tangy flavor of the beans, we simmered them with aromatic shallot, garlic, and cumin. Once the beans were softened and most of the water evaporated, we used a potato masher to turn them into a smooth, creamy topping. Stirring in lemon juice and parsley added a final fresh flavor punch. We spread the fava puree onto crispy thin toasted baguette slices and garnished them with Manchego cheese shavings and toasted pine nuts. This recipe works best with fresh fava beans, but if you can't find them, you can substitute 1 pound (3 cups) frozen shucked fava beans, thawed. Skip step 2 if using frozen favas. Be sure to set up the ice water bath before cooking the fava beans, as plunging them immediately in the cold water after blanching retains their bright green color and ensures that they don't overcook.*

24 (¼-inch thick) slices baguette
   (1 baguette)
5 tablespoons extra-virgin olive oil,
   plus extra for serving
   Salt and pepper
3 pounds fava beans, shelled (3 cups)
1 shallot, minced
1 garlic clove, minced
½ teaspoon ground cumin
3 tablespoons minced fresh parsley
1 tablespoon lemon juice
1 ounce Manchego cheese, shaved
2 tablespoons pine nuts, toasted

1. Adjust oven rack to middle position and heat oven to 400 degrees. Place baguette slices in single layer on rimmed baking sheet. Bake until golden and crisp, 8 to 10 minutes, flipping slices halfway through baking. Brush bread with 1 tablespoon oil and season with salt. Let cool completely on sheet, about 30 minutes.

2. Meanwhile, bring 4 quarts water to boil in large pot. Fill large bowl halfway with ice and water. Add fava beans to boiling water and cook for 1 minute. Using slotted spoon, transfer fava beans to ice water and let cool, about 2 minutes. Transfer fava beans to triple layer of paper towels and dry well. Using paring knife, make small cut along edge of each bean through waxy sheath, then gently squeeze sheath to release bean; discard sheath.

3. Heat remaining ¼ cup oil in medium saucepan over medium heat until shimmering. Add shallot and cook until softened, about 3 minutes. Stir in garlic and cumin and cook until fragrant, about 30 seconds. Stir in fava beans, 1 cup water, and ½ teaspoon salt and bring to simmer. Cook until fava beans are softened and most of liquid has evaporated, 12 to 15 minutes.

4. Off heat, using potato masher, mash bean mixture until mostly smooth. Stir in parsley and lemon juice and let cool to room temperature, about 20 minutes.

5. Spread fava bean mixture evenly over toasted baguette slices and top with Manchego and pine nuts. Drizzle with extra oil to taste. Serve.

FAVA BEAN AND RADISH SALAD

Serves 4 to 6   Total time: 40 minutes

WHY THIS RECIPE WORKS   *This vibrant, flavorful salad featuring fava beans, radishes, and pea shoots celebrates springtime in every bite. Since it takes a bit of time to prepare fresh favas, we wanted to make sure this salad was interesting enough to be worth the effort. The fresh pea shoots supplied a layer of texture and a bit of natural sweetness. We added thin half-moons of peppery radishes to provide a nice crunchy, spicy bite as well as flecks of contrasting red-and-white color to our otherwise green salad. Basil and a lemony vinaigrette were the final additions. This recipe works best with fresh fava beans, but if you can't find them, you can substitute 1 pound (3 cups) frozen shucked fava beans, thawed. Skip step 1 if using frozen favas. Be sure to set up the ice water bath before cooking the fava beans, as plunging them immediately in the cold water after blanching retains their bright green color and ensures that they don't overcook.*

3 pounds fava beans, shelled (3 cups)
¼ cup extra-virgin olive oil
3 tablespoons lemon juice
2 garlic cloves, minced
½ teaspoon salt
¼ teaspoon pepper
¼ teaspoon ground coriander
10 radishes, trimmed, halved, and
   sliced thin
1½ ounces (1½ cups) pea shoots
¼ cup chopped fresh basil

1. Bring 4 quarts water to boil in large pot over high heat. Fill large bowl halfway with ice and water. Add fava beans to boiling water and cook for 1 minute. Using slotted spoon, transfer fava beans to ice water and let cool, about 2 minutes. Transfer fava beans to triple layer of paper towels and dry well. Using paring knife, make small cut along edge of each bean through waxy sheath, then gently squeeze sheath to release bean; discard sheath.

2. Whisk oil, lemon juice, garlic, salt, pepper, and coriander together in large bowl until combined. Add fava beans, radishes, pea shoots, and basil and gently toss to coat. Serve immediately.

Edamame and Spicy Peanut Noodle Bowls

EDAMAME SALAD

Serves 4   Total time: 30 minutes

WHY THIS RECIPE WORKS *Edamame are a great base for salads because their bright, fresh flavor and satisfying pop of texture pair perfectly with leafy greens and a variety of vegetables. However, keeping the focus on the edamame was a challenge, as tart vinaigrettes or bold-flavored vegetables easily overpowered the beans' mildness. Baby arugula worked well as a flavor and texture complement, thanks to its subtle peppery flavor and delicate, tender leaves. Lots of mint and basil helped to bring a light, summery flavor to the salad. Thinly sliced shallot added mild onion flavor, and just a couple of radishes added crunch and color. For the vinaigrette, we chose to use rice vinegar for its mild acidity, incorporating a little honey for sweetness and to help emulsify the dressing. One small clove of garlic added its flavor without taking over the dish. The finishing touch was a sprinkling of roasted sunflower seeds, which added nuttiness and depth to this bright salad. You can substitute frozen edamame beans that have been thawed and patted dry for the fresh edamame in this recipe.*

- 2 tablespoons unseasoned rice vinegar
- 1 tablespoon honey
- 1 small garlic clove, minced
  Salt and pepper
- 3 tablespoons extra-virgin olive oil
- 18 ounces shelled edamame beans (3 cups)
- 2 ounces (2 cups) baby arugula
- ½ cup shredded fresh basil
- ½ cup chopped fresh mint
- 2 radishes, trimmed, halved, and sliced thin
- 1 shallot, halved and sliced thin
- ¼ cup roasted sunflower seeds

Whisk vinegar, honey, garlic, and 1 teaspoon salt together in large bowl. While whisking constantly, slowly whisk in oil until combined. Add edamame, arugula, basil, mint, radishes, and shallot and toss to combine. Sprinkle with sunflower seeds and season with salt and pepper to taste. Serve.

BUTTERNUT SQUASH AND PEANUT CHILI WITH QUINOA

Serves 6   Total time: 1 hour 30 minutes

WHY THIS RECIPE WORKS *Stews and soups made with peanuts are staples of African cuisines. This stick-to-your-ribs African-style vegetable chili is aromatic and boldly flavored with coconut milk, garlic, and ginger. It gets its silky body from a combination of blended dry-roasted salted peanuts and squash, which we roasted with chopped onions until both the squash and the onions started to char around the edges, giving the dish an incredible backbone of flavor. Pureeing a portion of the roasted vegetables with the peanuts created a rich, smooth base. We sautéed sweet bell pepper and spicy jalapeño and briefly bloomed the warm spices before adding the liquid. A combination of diced tomatoes and coconut milk made a creamy but bright broth, and nutty quinoa added heartiness and textural interest. If you buy unwashed quinoa (or if you are unsure whether it's washed), be sure to rinse it before cooking to remove its bitter protective coating (called saponin). Serve with hot sauce.*

- 3 pounds butternut squash, peeled, seeded, and cut into ½-inch pieces (9 cups)
- 2 onions, chopped
- 6 tablespoons vegetable oil
  Salt and pepper
- 5 cups water, plus extra as needed
- ¾ cup dry-roasted salted peanuts, chopped
- 1 large red bell pepper, stemmed, seeded, and cut into ½-inch pieces
- 1 jalapeño chile, stemmed, seeded, and minced
- 3 garlic cloves, minced
- 2 tablespoons grated fresh ginger
- ¾ teaspoon ground cinnamon
- ¾ teaspoon ground coriander
- ½ teaspoon cayenne pepper
- 1 (14.5-ounce) can diced tomatoes
- 1 (14-ounce) can coconut milk
- 1 cup prewashed white quinoa
- ¼ cup minced fresh cilantro or parsley

1. Adjust oven racks to upper-middle and lower-middle positions and heat oven to 450 degrees. Toss squash, onions, ¼ cup oil, 1 teaspoon salt, and ½ teaspoon pepper together in bowl to coat. Arrange vegetables in even layer over 2 rimmed baking sheets. Roast vegetables, stirring occasionally, until tender, 45 to 50 minutes, switching and rotating sheets halfway through roasting.

2. Process ½ cup roasted vegetables, 2 cups water, and ¼ cup peanuts in food processor until smooth, about 1 minute.

3. Heat remaining 2 tablespoons oil in Dutch oven over medium-high heat until shimmering. Add bell pepper, jalapeño, and 2 teaspoons salt and cook until peppers begin to soften, about 5 minutes. Stir in garlic, ginger, cinnamon, coriander, cayenne, and ¾ teaspoon pepper, and cook until fragrant, about 30 seconds.

4. Stir in remaining 3 cups water, tomatoes and their juice, coconut milk, and quinoa and bring to boil. Reduce heat to low and simmer, stirring occasionally, until quinoa is tender, about 15 minutes.

5. Stir in pureed vegetable mixture and remaining roasted vegetables and cook until warmed through, about 3 minutes. Season with salt and pepper to taste. Adjust consistency with additional hot water as needed. Serve, sprinkling individual portions with cilantro and remaining ½ cup peanuts.

EDAMAME AND SPICY PEANUT NOODLE BOWLS

Serves 4 to 6   Total time: 45 minutes

WHY THIS RECIPE WORKS *Inspired by the sweet, savory, and spicy flavors of Southeast Asia, this noodle bowl is a real stunner, boasting a colorful medley of simple but texturally interesting toppings. We combined tender rice noodles with savory edamame, tangy lightly pickled carrots, and crunchy cabbage, and we draped it all with a rich peanut sauce that's a little spicy, a little sweet, and enlivened with a hint of curry powder for aromatic appeal. Instead of taking the time to pickle our carrots in advance of making the dish, we simply added seasoned rice vinegar to shredded carrots and let them sit while the rice noodles soaked and softened. After the 20-minute soaking period, we started the cooking process by first quickly sautéing the edamame just until they were speckled brown but still maintained a tender-crisp texture and fresh flavor. After removing the edamame from the skillet, we finished cooking the noodles in the same pan with half the sauce and some water until the noodles were perfectly tender and chewy. After topping our bowls with the veggies, we added plenty of garnishes—chopped peanuts, fragrant Thai basil, lime wedges, and a drizzle of additional sauce. If you can't find Thai basil, you can substitute regular basil. You can substitute frozen shelled edamame beans for fresh in this recipe. We prefer the flavor of seasoned rice vinegar in this recipe.*

PEANUT SAUCE

- 1 tablespoon vegetable oil
- 2 Thai, serrano, or jalapeño chiles, stemmed, seeded, and minced
- 3 garlic cloves, minced
- 1 tablespoon grated fresh ginger
- 1½ teaspoons curry powder
- ½ cup water, plus extra as needed
- ⅓ cup creamy peanut butter
- 3 tablespoons seasoned rice vinegar
- 2 tablespoons soy sauce
- 1 tablespoon sugar

NOODLES

- 1 cup shredded carrots
- 2 tablespoons seasoned rice vinegar
- 12 ounces (¼-inch-wide) rice noodles
- 3 tablespoons vegetable oil
- 6 ounces shelled edamame beans (1 cup)
- 1 cup shredded red cabbage
- ⅓ cup dry-roasted peanuts, chopped
- 2 tablespoons torn fresh Thai basil
  Lime wedges

1. For the peanut sauce Heat oil in medium saucepan over medium heat until shimmering. Add Thai chiles, garlic, ginger, and curry powder and cook until fragrant, about 30 seconds. Stir in water, peanut butter, vinegar, soy sauce, and sugar and bring to simmer. Cook, stirring occasionally, until thickened slightly and flavors meld, about 2 minutes. Adjust consistency as needed with additional water; set aside off heat.

2. For the noodles Combine carrots and vinegar in small bowl; set aside. Cover noodles with very hot water in large bowl and stir to separate. Let noodles soak until softened, pliable, and limp but not fully tender, about 20 minutes. Drain noodles.

3. Heat 1 tablespoon oil in 12-inch nonstick skillet over medium-high heat until just smoking. Add edamame and cook until spotty brown but still bright green, about 2 minutes. Transfer to bowl. In now-empty skillet, heat remaining 2 tablespoons oil over medium heat until shimmering, add drained noodles, 1¼ cups water, and ½ cup peanut sauce and cook until sauce has thickened slightly and noodles are well coated and tender, about 1 minute.

4. Divide noodles among individual serving bowls, then top with carrots, edamame, and cabbage. Drizzle with remaining peanut sauce, sprinkle with peanuts and basil, and serve with lime wedges.

～

FRIED RICE WITH BEAN SPROUTS AND PEAS

Serves 4 to 6   Total time: 1 hour 15 minutes
WHY THIS RECIPE WORKS *This simple fried rice transforms a handful of basic ingredients into a restaurant-worthy dish that's faster and far tastier than takeout. Sweet baby green peas, crunchy-juicy bean sprouts, and pungent scallions add the vegetable interest here. Using chilled cooked rice is key to achieving the best texture in any fried rice, but we rarely have leftover rice on hand. To get freshly cooked rice to act like leftover rice, we used a three-pronged approach: First we sautéed the rice in oil to keep the grains separate; then we cooked it in less water than usual, making it drier from the start; and finally, we encouraged the rice to cool quickly by spreading it on a baking sheet and refrigerating it for 20 minutes. To make sure the eggs didn't overcook, we scrambled them lightly and then removed them from the pan while we combined the sauce and the rice. The tender peas and bean sprouts didn't need much cooking, so we added them at the end so they could just warm through. We prefer baby peas in this recipe, but regular peas can be substituted.*

RICE

- 2 tablespoons vegetable oil
- 2 cups jasmine rice or long-grain white rice, rinsed
- 2⅔ cups water

STIR-FRY

- 4 teaspoons vegetable oil
- 2 large eggs, lightly beaten
- ¼ cup oyster sauce
- 2 tablespoons soy sauce
- 2 tablespoons unseasoned rice vinegar
- 2 garlic cloves, minced
- 1 cup frozen baby peas, thawed
- 2 ounces (1 cup) bean sprouts
- 5 scallions, sliced thin

1. For the rice Heat oil in large saucepan over medium heat until shimmering. Add rice and stir to coat. Stir in water and bring to boil. Reduce heat to low, cover, and simmer until rice is tender and water is absorbed, 16 to 18 minutes. Off heat, lay clean folded dish towel underneath lid and let sit for 10 minutes. Spread rice onto rimmed baking sheet and let cool for 10 minutes. Transfer to refrigerator and chill for 20 minutes. (Chilled rice can be covered and refrigerated for up to 1 day.)

2. For the stir-fry Heat 1 teaspoon oil in 12-inch nonstick skillet over medium heat until shimmering. Add eggs and cook, without stirring, until just beginning to set, about 20 seconds. Continue to cook, stirring constantly with rubber spatula and breaking curds into small pieces, until eggs are cooked through but not browned, about 30 seconds; transfer to bowl.

3. Whisk oyster sauce, soy sauce, vinegar, and garlic in bowl until combined; set aside. Break up any large clumps of rice with your fingers. Heat remaining 1 tablespoon oil in now-empty skillet over medium heat until shimmering. Add rice and cook until beginning to sizzle and pop loudly, about 3 minutes. Add sauce and cook, stirring and folding constantly, until rice is heated through and evenly coated with sauce, about 3 minutes. Stir in eggs, peas, bean sprouts, and scallions and cook until heated through, about 2 minutes. Serve.

ALMOST HANDS-FREE RISOTTO WITH FAVA BEANS, PEAS, AND ARUGULA

Serves 6   Total time: 1 hour

WHY THIS RECIPE WORKS *Celebrate the flavors of springtime with a green-and-white risotto showcasing fresh legumes. The texture of the nutty, buttery fresh fava beans works well with the firm yet tender rice, and the green peas and arugula add serious vegetal punch. To minimize the constant stirring associated with classic risotto, we chose to cook this in a Dutch oven rather than a saucepan. A Dutch oven's thick, heavy bottom, deep sides, and tight-fitting lid are made to trap and distribute heat as evenly as possible. Also, we added most of the broth at once, rather than in small increments. Then we covered the pan and simmered the rice until almost all the broth had been absorbed, stirring just twice. After adding the second and final addition of broth, we stirred the pot for a few minutes to make sure the bottom didn't cook more quickly than the top and then turned off the heat. The rice turned out perfectly creamy, velvety, and just barely chewy. To finish, we stirred in butter, a squeeze of lemon juice, and some chopped arugula to brighten the flavors. This more hands-off method does require precise timing, so we strongly recommend using a timer. This recipe works best with fresh fava beans, but if you can't find them, you can substitute 5 ounces (1 cup) frozen shucked fava beans, thawed. The consistency of risotto is largely a matter of personal taste, so if you prefer a brothy risotto, add extra broth in step 4.*

- 5 cups chicken or vegetable broth
- 1½ cups water
- 4 tablespoons unsalted butter
- 1 large onion, chopped fine
  Salt and pepper
- 1 garlic clove, minced
- 2 cups Arborio rice
- 1 cup dry white wine
- 1 pound fava beans, shelled (1 cup)
- 1 cup frozen peas, thawed
- 2 ounces Parmesan cheese, grated (1 cup)
- 2 ounces (2 cups) baby arugula, chopped
- 1 teaspoon lemon juice

1. Bring broth and water to boil in large saucepan over high heat. Cover and reduce heat to medium-low to maintain gentle simmer.

2. Melt 2 tablespoons butter in Dutch oven over medium heat. Add onion and ¾ teaspoon salt and cook until onion is softened, about 5 minutes. Stir in garlic and cook until fragrant, about 30 seconds. Stir in rice and cook, stirring often, until grain edges begin to turn translucent, about 3 minutes.

3. Stir in wine and cook, stirring constantly, until fully absorbed, 2 to 3 minutes. Stir in 5 cups hot broth mixture. Reduce heat to medium-low, cover, and simmer until almost all liquid has been absorbed and rice is just al dente, 16 to 19 minutes, stirring twice during cooking.

4. Add ¾ cup hot broth mixture and stir gently and constantly until risotto becomes creamy, about 3 minutes. Stir in fava beans, peas, and Parmesan. Remove pot from heat, cover, and let stand for 5 minutes. Stir in arugula, lemon juice, and remaining 2 tablespoons butter. Season with salt and pepper to taste. Before serving, stir in remaining hot broth mixture as needed to loosen consistency of risotto.

SIZZLING SAIGON CRÊPES

Serves 8 (makes 9 crêpes)

Total time: 1 hour 30 minutes

WHY THIS RECIPE WORKS *Named for the sound these crêpes make when the batter hits a hot wok, sizzling Saigon crêpes are best described as paper-thin Vietnamese pancakes. These crispy, yellow, rice-flour crêpes are wrapped with lettuce and fresh herbs and dipped into a sweet-tart dipping sauce. Though pork and shrimp are often used for the stuffing, we created this lighter vegetable-based version with a simple filling of bean sprouts, shredded carrots, and sliced onions. The batter for the crêpes is simple: just water, rice flour, and coconut milk. To give them a subtle savory flavor, we added scallions and turmeric. To make the flipping and folding of these delicate crêpes easier, we cooked them in a 10-inch nonstick skillet instead of a traditional wok. For the dipping sauce, we combined fish sauce with lime juice, sugar, minced fresh chiles, and garlic. You can find rice flour in the baking aisle of most well-stocked supermarkets; you cannot substitute regular flour or cornstarch for the rice flour. If you can't find Thai basil, you can substitute regular basil. To allow for trial and error (just in case), the recipe yields nine crêpes.*

DIPPING SAUCE AND GARNISH

- ⅓ cup fish sauce
- ¼ cup warm water
- 3 tablespoons lime juice (2 limes)
- 2 tablespoons sugar
- 2 Thai, serrano, or jalapeño chiles, stemmed, seeded, and minced
- 1 garlic clove, minced
- 2 heads red or green leaf lettuce, leaves separated
- 1 cup fresh Thai basil leaves
- 1 cup fresh cilantro leaves

CRÊPES

- 2¾ cups water
- 1¾ cups rice flour
- ½ cup coconut milk
- 4 scallions, sliced thin
  Salt
- 1 teaspoon ground turmeric
- ¼ cup vegetable oil
- 1 onion, halved and sliced thin
- 1 pound carrots, peeled and shredded
- 6 ounces (3 cups) bean sprouts

1. For the dipping sauce and garnish
Whisk fish sauce, warm water, lime juice, sugar, chiles, and garlic in bowl until sugar dissolves. Divide dipping sauce among 8 small dipping bowls. Arrange lettuce, basil, and cilantro on serving platter.

2. For the crêpes Adjust oven rack to middle position and heat oven to 200 degrees. Set wire rack in rimmed baking sheet. Whisk water, flour, coconut milk, scallions, 1 teaspoon salt, and turmeric in bowl until combined.

3. Heat 1 tablespoon oil in 10-inch nonstick skillet over medium-high heat until shimmering. Add onion and ½ teaspoon salt and cook until onion is softened, 5 to 7 minutes. Transfer to bowl. Add carrots to skillet and cook until tender, about 2 minutes. Transfer to bowl with onions and let cool slightly. Stir in bean sprouts and set vegetable mixture aside.

4. Wipe out skillet with paper towels. Heat 1 teaspoon oil in now-empty skillet over medium-high heat until just smoking. Whisk batter to recombine, then pour ½ cup batter into skillet while swirling pan gently to

distribute it evenly over pan bottom. Reduce heat to medium and cook crêpe until edges pull away from sides and are deep golden, 3 to 5 minutes.

5. Gently slide spatula underneath edge of crêpe, grasp edge with your fingertips, and flip crêpe. Cook until spotty brown on second side, 2 to 3 minutes. Slide crêpe out of skillet and onto prepared wire rack and transfer to oven to keep warm. Repeat with remaining oil and remaining batter.

6. Divide vegetable mixture evenly among crêpes and fold crêpes in half. Serve crêpes with dipping sauce, passing garnish platter separately. (To eat, slice off wedge of crêpe, nestle basil and cilantro in lettuce leaf, wrap wedge in lettuce, and dip into sauce.)

KUNG PAO SHRIMP

Serves 4   Total time: 35 minutes

WHY THIS RECIPE WORKS *Sweet, spicy, and iconic, kung pao is a classic Sichuan preparation that is distinguished by its use of peanuts, vegetables, and chile peppers. Chicken is the most typically used protein in the dish, but for our version we decided to infuse delicate shrimp with the bold flavor of the kung pao sauce. The dry-roasted peanuts, stirred in at the end of the shrimp's cooking time, added plenty of crunchy texture and nutty flavor. For the vegetables, we kept it simple, focusing on sweet peppers and scallions; we sautéed the red bell peppers to give them a touch of char, and stirred in the scallions at the end to retain their oniony punch. The sauce thickened just a bit as it cooked, giving the dish the requisite silky consistency. You can substitute 1 teaspoon of dried red pepper flakes for the arbol chiles. Do not eat the whole chiles in the finished dish. Serve with rice.*

SAUCE

- ¾ cup chicken or vegetable broth
- 1 tablespoon oyster sauce
- 1 tablespoon hoisin sauce
- 2 teaspoons Chinese black vinegar or plain rice vinegar
- 2 teaspoons toasted sesame oil
- 1½ teaspoons cornstarch

SHRIMP

- 1 pound extra-large shrimp (21 to 25 per pound), peeled and deveined
- 1 tablespoon Chinese rice wine or dry sherry
- 2 teaspoons soy sauce
- 3 tablespoons vegetable oil
- 3 garlic cloves, minced
- 2 teaspoons grated fresh ginger
- ½ cup dry-roasted peanuts
- 6 arbol chiles
- 1 red bell pepper, stemmed, seeded, and cut into ½-inch pieces
- 3 scallions, sliced thin

1. For the sauce Whisk all ingredients together in bowl; set aside.

2. For the shrimp Toss shrimp with rice wine and soy sauce in bowl and let stand for 10 minutes. Meanwhile, combine 1 tablespoon oil, garlic, and ginger in small bowl; set aside. Combine peanuts and chiles in second small bowl; set aside.

3. Heat 1 tablespoon oil in 12-inch skillet over high heat until just smoking. Add shrimp and cook, stirring every 10 seconds, until barely opaque, 30 to 40 seconds. Add peanut mixture and continue to cook until shrimp are almost completely opaque and peanuts have darkened slightly, 30 to 40 seconds. Transfer mixture to clean bowl.

4. Heat remaining 1 tablespoon oil in now-empty skillet over high heat until just smoking. Add bell pepper and cook, stirring occasionally, until slightly softened, about 45 seconds. Push bell pepper to sides of skillet. Add garlic mixture to center and cook, mashing mixture into pan, until fragrant, about 30 seconds. Stir mixture into bell pepper. Stir shrimp mixture and any accumulated juices into bell pepper mixture in skillet. Whisk sauce to recombine, add to skillet, and cook, stirring constantly and scraping up any browned bits, until sauce has thickened to syrupy consistency, about 45 seconds. Stir in scallions and serve immediately.

Kung Pao Shrimp

GARLIC

Garlic holds a time-honored place not just in the kitchen, but also throughout the history of humankind. It belongs to the allium genus, which also includes onions and chives. The word "allium" derives from the Greek "to avoid"—and for a very long time, that's exactly what people did with garlic.

But the ancient Greeks eventually embraced garlic as a food, leading the way for Roman soldiers to consume it before battle, with the aim of gaining courage. Throughout the centuries, European folklore held that garlic warded off the "evil eye," and as such it was to be used against vampires, werewolves, and just plain bad luck. Furthermore, garlic has been used for antibiotic purposes for thousands of years in China, India, and Egypt, and its healing properties continue to be studied today in both Eastern and Western medicine.

All of this is to our ongoing benefit. Pungent and aromatic garlic is used in countless ways in nearly every cuisine. Its flavor in any given dish is influenced, interestingly, by the way it is cut. This is because when garlic is cut, a flavor and aroma compound called allicin (a powerful antioxidant) forms. The more you manhandle a garlic clove, the more allicin is released. So slicing versus chopping versus mincing matters. Success in cooking with garlic lies in knowing how to harness its flavor—whether that means aiding and abetting its pungency or tempering and mellowing it.

Often the best way to achieve the garlicky goal is to use it in two ways, as in our Garlic-Potato Soup, the Garlicky Spaghetti with Lemon and Pine Nuts, and our crisp, buttery, golden Garlic Bread. And our Garlic Fried Chicken and Sunday Best Garlic Roast Beef each deploy a trifecta of garlicky perfection.

shopping and storage

Garlic does actually have a season—it's the summer. But because it stores so well, it's readily available year-round. Look for garlic heads with no signs of black spots or sprouting, and not much garlic aroma. Squeeze the head in your hand. It should be firm and solid; if you feel hollow skins where cloves should be or if the head feels spongy or rubbery, pass it up.

Garlic is highly sensitive to temperature extremes and sunlight. For long-term commercial storage, garlic is normally stored in a nitrogen atmosphere to keep it from sprouting. At home, store it away from direct sunlight in a dry environment for a few weeks. Don't store it in the refrigerator, as the combination of low temperature and moisture will hasten spoilage.

Garlic scapes are in season a month or two before the bulbs, so they are found at farmers' markets and specialty grocers from late spring to early summer. They can be stored wrapped in paper towels in a plastic produce bag in the refrigerator for up to three weeks.

garlic types

Garlic falls into two primary categories: soft-neck and hard-neck. Because soft-neck garlic is prolific, more heat-tolerant, and stores well, it has become the favored commercially available garlic. But hard-neck garlic, which is the original cultivated type, is considered superior in flavor. You are more likely to find it at a farmers' market than a supermarket.

Elephant garlic is actually a different species, even though it's still part of the same allium genus as conventional garlic. Its flavor is much weaker than true garlic. We don't recommend elephant garlic; if you want a milder garlic flavor in your food, just use less of the genuine article.

pantry garlic products

The spice rack standbys of granulated garlic and garlic powder may seem artificial, but they're actually not. Granulated garlic is made from fresh garlic that is minced and then dehydrated and packaged. Garlic powder is simply dehydrated garlic that's been ground to a powder. Are they acceptable substitutes for fresh? When garlic is a predominant flavor in a recipe, nothing comes close to the taste of fresh. In recipes where garlic is a more of a background flavor, such as in salad dressings, in a pinch you can use granulated or ground, substituting ¼ teaspoon for each fresh clove. Rehydrating these dried products in an equal amount of water for a couple of minutes before using them "wakes up" their flavor.

garlic scapes

Garlic scapes are the long, slim flower stems that grow from the tops of hard-neck garlic. Farmers have long known that removing them encourages the plant to direct its energy toward growing a plump underground bulb, and in recent years this agricultural by-product has become the darling of springtime farmers' markets.

Raw garlic scapes have a milder garlic flavor that's grassier and less fiery than that of raw cloves. They can be pureed raw with olive oil, Parmesan cheese, and pine nuts to make a flavorful pesto.

They are also delicious grilled or stir-fried. Tasters noted that their garlic flavor became more muted and sweet when cooked—more like roasted garlic than raw—and the texture was impressively dense and meaty. For the simplest preparation, toss the scapes with oil, salt, and pepper and cook them on the grill over medium-high heat until they are softened and lightly charred. We also found that they worked very well in a stir-fry like the Teriyaki Stir-Fried —Garlic Scapes with Chicken, as their mellow garlic flavor complemented the heat.

The stem ends and the flower pods can be quite fibrous even when cooked, so we recommend trimming them before use.

vegetable prep

Peeling Garlic

Lay cloves flat on cutting board and press flat side of chef's knife against them to slightly crush them and loosen skins.

Grating Garlic

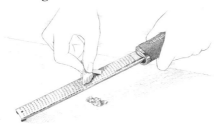

Garlic grated to a paste (rather than minced or crushed) is ideal for garlic bread. Cut unpeeled clove of garlic in half crosswise, then use skin as "handle" while you grate clove using rasp-style grater.

Slicing Garlic Thin

Pick flattest side of peeled clove and hold it face down against cutting board. Then carefully slice garlic thin, holding clove securely. Use tip of paring knife to pull out green stem, if present, in middle of clove.

ROASTED GARLIC

Makes about ½ cup
Total time: 1 hour 45 minutes

WHY THIS RECIPE WORKS *Perhaps no other vegetable is transformed by the roasting process quite as dramatically as garlic. Roasting turns it from intensely pungent and sharp to nutty, sweet, and spreadably soft with minimal work. For an easy, foolproof method, we simply trimmed off the top of each head of garlic, exposing the tops of the cloves, and drizzled them with olive oil. Sealed tightly into an aluminum foil packet, the cloves turned buttery soft in a 425-degree oven; opening up the packet for the last 20 minutes allowed the tops of the cloves to caramelize. The softened cloves are perfect for spreading onto bread; they also add rich flavor to simple condiments and sauces. This recipe can be adjusted for as many or as few garlic heads as you want.*

4 large garlic heads
2 teaspoons extra-virgin olive oil
Salt

1. Adjust oven rack to middle position and heat oven to 425 degrees. Cut ½ inch off top of each garlic head to expose most of tops of garlic cloves. Place garlic heads, cut side up, in center of large piece of aluminum foil. Drizzle each with ½ teaspoon oil, season with salt, and gather foil tightly around garlic to form packet.

2. Place packet directly on oven rack and roast garlic for 45 minutes. Carefully open just top of foil to expose garlic and continue to roast until garlic is soft and golden brown, about 20 minutes.

3. Remove garlic from oven and let cool for 20 minutes. When cool, squeeze garlic from skins into bowl. (Roasted garlic can be refrigerated for up to 1 week.)

ROASTED GARLIC VINAIGRETTE

Makes ½ cup   Total time: 5 minutes

WHY THIS RECIPE WORKS *This versatile vinaigrette has big, bold flavors that will stand up to hearty greens, roasted vegetables, or grilled chicken or fish. A generous amount of mashed roasted garlic defines the flavor profile with its sweet, pungent, lingering flavor, so the other ingredients needed to be assertive enough to complement the garlic without competing with it. The Dijon mustard offered a soft heat, the balsamic vinegar brought caramelized sweetness, and regular olive oil (as opposed to extra-virgin) lent the dressing simple, pure flavor. Fresh thyme gave everything an herbal lift. The couple of tablespoons of water whisked into the vinegar mixture countered the thickening effect of the roasted garlic without having to use more vinegar. We prefer to use our Roasted Garlic (see preceding recipe) for this vinaigrette.*

2 tablespoons roasted garlic cloves
2 tablespoons hot water
1 tablespoon balsamic vinegar
2 teaspoons Dijon mustard
½ teaspoon minced fresh thyme
Salt and pepper
¼ cup extra-virgin olive oil

Using fork, mash roasted garlic cloves to paste in large bowl. Whisk in water, vinegar, mustard, thyme, ¼ teaspoon salt, and ⅛ teaspoon pepper. While whisking constantly, slowly drizzle in oil until combined. Season with salt and pepper to taste. (Vinaigrette can be refrigerated for up to 1 week; return to room temperature and whisk to recombine before using.)

ROASTED GARLIC HUMMUS

Makes about 2 cups   Total time: 50 minutes

WHY THIS RECIPE WORKS *Store-bought hummus is undeniably convenient, but we like our hummus silky-smooth and rich, with plenty of roasted garlicky flavor. To achieve that, nothing beats homemade. We did start with convenient canned chickpeas,* since we didn't want to spend hours dealing with dried chickpeas. Creating an emulsion in the food processor with the chickpeas and roasted garlic, water, and lemon juice, then blending in tahini and garlic-infused olive oil, resulted in a lush, flavorful puree with a light, creamy texture. Earthy cumin, a pinch of cayenne, and a sprinkling of fresh herbs balanced the flavors, and a few fried garlic slices were the perfect garnish. We prefer to use our Roasted Garlic (see left) in this recipe.*

2 tablespoons extra-virgin olive oil, plus extra for drizzling
2 garlic cloves, sliced thin lengthwise
Salt
¼ cup water
3 tablespoons lemon juice
6 tablespoons tahini
1 (15-ounce) can chickpeas, rinsed
¼ cup roasted garlic cloves
Pinch cayenne pepper
2 teaspoons minced fresh parsley

1. Heat oil and sliced garlic in 8-inch nonstick skillet over medium-low heat. Cook, stirring occasionally, until garlic is golden brown, about 15 minutes. Using slotted spoon, transfer garlic to paper towel–lined plate and season with salt to taste; set aside for serving. Reserve garlic oil.

2. Combine water and lemon juice in small bowl. In separate bowl, whisk together tahini and reserved garlic oil.

3. Process chickpeas, roasted garlic cloves, cayenne, and ½ teaspoon salt in food processor until almost fully ground, about 15 seconds, scraping down sides of bowl as needed. With processor running, add lemon juice mixture in steady stream and process for 1 minute. With processor running, add tahini mixture in steady stream and process until hummus is smooth and creamy, about 15 seconds. Season with salt to taste.

4. Transfer hummus to serving bowl, cover with plastic wrap, and let sit at room temperature until flavors meld, about 30 minutes. Sprinkle with parsley and reserved garlic chips and drizzle with extra oil before serving.

GARLIC-POTATO SOUP

Serves 6 Total time: 1 hour 30 minutes

WHY THIS RECIPE WORKS *For this creamy, textural soup, getting just the right garlic flavor was not as much about quantity as it was about cooking technique. First, we sautéed three garlic cloves and a chopped leek before adding the chicken broth, and then we simmered two whole heads of garlic in the broth. Once they were completely tender, we squeezed out the softened cloves, mashed them, and added them back to the soup. Choosing the right potatoes was also important. We liked starchy russets for the way they broke down and thickened the broth, and we found that adding red potatoes to the mix ramped up the flavor even more. Topping the soup with crispy garlic chips made for just the right garnish, creating a trinity of garlic flavor. We prefer this soup made with chicken broth, but vegetable broth can be substituted.*

GARLIC CHIPS

- 3 tablespoons extra-virgin olive oil
- 6 garlic cloves, sliced thin lengthwise
  Salt

SOUP

- 3 tablespoons unsalted butter
- 1 leek, white and light green parts only, halved lengthwise, finely chopped, and washed thoroughly
- 3 garlic cloves, minced, plus 2 whole heads garlic, outer papery skins removed and top third of heads cut off and discarded
- 6 cups chicken broth, plus extra as needed
- 2 bay leaves
  Salt and pepper
- 1½ pounds russet potatoes, peeled and cut into ½-inch pieces
- 1 pound red potatoes, unpeeled, cut into ½-inch pieces
- ½ cup heavy cream
- 1½ teaspoons minced fresh thyme
- ¼ cup minced fresh chives

1. For the garlic chips Heat oil and garlic in 10-inch nonstick skillet over medium-low heat. Cook, stirring occasionally, until garlic is golden brown, about 15 minutes. Using slotted spoon, transfer garlic to paper towel–lined plate and season with salt to taste; set aside for serving. Discard garlic oil or save for another use.

2. For the soup Melt butter in Dutch oven over medium heat. Add leek and cook until softened, 5 to 8 minutes. Stir in minced garlic and cook until fragrant, about 1 minute. Add garlic heads, broth, bay leaves, and ¾ teaspoon salt and bring to simmer. Partially cover pot, reduce heat to medium-low, and cook until garlic is very tender when pierced with tip of knife, 30 to 40 minutes. Stir in potatoes and continue to cook, partially covered, until potatoes are tender, 15 to 20 minutes.

3. Discard bay leaves. Remove garlic heads and squeeze cooked garlic from skins into bowl. Mash garlic to smooth paste with fork.

4. Stir cream, thyme, and half of mashed garlic into soup and let sit until heated through, about 2 minutes. Taste soup; add remaining garlic paste if desired. Transfer 1½ cups potatoes and 1 cup broth to blender and process until smooth. (Process more potatoes for thicker consistency.) Return puree to pot and adjust consistency with extra broth as needed. Season with salt and pepper to taste. Serve, sprinkling individual portions with chives and garlic chips.

GARLICKY SPAGHETTI WITH LEMON AND PINE NUTS

Serves 4 Total time: 40 minutes

WHY THIS RECIPE WORKS *The late-night spaghetti monster will be tamed with this flavor-packed pasta that comes together quickly from pantry ingredients. The key here is making the most of the garlic. We toasted a whopping 2 tablespoons of minced garlic in extra-virgin olive oil over low heat just until it cooked to a sweet and buttery pale golden brown. (Be careful not to let it go any darker or it will be harsh.) Also, we cooked the spaghetti in just 2 quarts of salted water to ensure that the cooking water ended up loaded with starch; adding some of that starchy water back to the finished spaghetti gave our simple pantry sauce lots of body and texture. Finally, adding a little minced raw garlic right at the end of the cooking time created a garlicky duality between the buttery sweetness of the toasted garlic and the fire of the raw garlic. This is endlessly adaptable, depending on what you have in your pantry. (No Parmesan? Toast up some bread crumbs instead. No basil? Try parsley, or leave it out. If you're really hungry, add a can of tuna at the end. And don't forget about the variations that follow.)*

¼ cup extra-virgin olive oil

2 tablespoons plus ½ teaspoon minced garlic

¼ teaspoon red pepper flakes

1 pound spaghetti
Salt and pepper

2 teaspoons grated lemon zest plus 2 tablespoons juice

1 cup chopped fresh basil

1 ounce Parmesan, grated (½ cup), plus extra for serving

½ cup pine nuts, toasted

1. Combine oil and 2 tablespoons garlic in 8-inch nonstick skillet. Cook over low heat, stirring occasionally, until garlic is pale golden brown, 9 to 12 minutes. Off heat, stir in pepper flakes; set aside.

2. Bring 2 quarts water to boil in large pot. Add pasta and 2 teaspoons salt and cook, stirring frequently, until al dente. Reserve 1 cup cooking water, then drain pasta and return it to pot. Add remaining ½ teaspoon garlic, lemon zest and juice, reserved garlic-oil mixture, and reserved cooking water to pasta in pot. Stir until pasta is well coated with oil and no water remains in bottom of pot. Add basil, Parmesan, and pine nuts and toss to combine. Season with salt and pepper to taste. Serve, passing extra Parmesan separately.

VARIATIONS

Garlicky Spaghetti with Capers and Currants
Omit lemon zest, basil, and pine nuts. Reduce lemon juice to 1 tablespoon. Stir 3 tablespoons capers, rinsed and minced; 3 tablespoons currants, minced; and 2 anchovy fillets, rinsed, patted dry, and minced, into pasta with lemon juice.

Garlicky Spaghetti with Green Olives and Almonds
Omit lemon zest and reduce lemon juice to 1 tablespoon. Stir 1 cup green olives, chopped fine, into pasta with lemon juice. Substitute Pecorino Romano for Parmesan and toasted sliced almonds for pine nuts.

Garlicky Spaghetti with Clams
Omit lemon zest and pine nuts. Reduce lemon juice to 2 teaspoons. Stir 2 (6½-ounce) cans whole clams, drained and chopped, and 4 anchovy fillets, rinsed, patted dry, and

minced, into pasta with lemon juice. Increase Parmesan to ¾ cup and substitute 2 tablespoons chopped fresh parsley for basil.

SPANISH TORTILLA WITH GARLIC AÏOLI

Serves 4 to 6   Total time: 50 minutes

WHY THIS RECIPE WORKS *Boasting meltingly tender potatoes in a dense, creamy omelet, a Spanish tortilla is an immensely appealing tapas bar favorite. But it's very easy to make at home. Garlic is often included in the omelet, but we liked the idea of topping the tortilla with a garlicky aïoli instead, the creaminess of which beautifully complemented the potatoes and eggs. We upped the flavor ante of the tortilla even further by adding green peas and roasted red peppers. To flip the omelet, we slid it onto a plate, put another plate on top, flipped the setup, and then slid it back into the skillet—a potentially messy task made foolproof. Spanish tortillas are often served as a snack, but this would work just as well alongside a salad as a light entrée. You will need a 10-inch nonstick skillet with a tight-fitting lid for this recipe. Since the egg yolks in the aïoli are not cooked, ¼ cup Egg Beaters may be substituted, if you prefer.*

AÏOLI

2 large egg yolks

2 garlic cloves, peeled and smashed

4 teaspoons lemon juice

1 tablespoon water, plus extra as needed

¼ teaspoon Dijon mustard

⅛ teaspoon sugar
Salt and pepper

¾ cup vegetable oil

TORTILLA

6 tablespoons plus 1 teaspoon extra-virgin olive oil

1½ pounds Yukon Gold potatoes, peeled, quartered, and cut into ⅛-inch-thick slices

1 small onion, halved and sliced thin
Salt and pepper

8 large eggs

½ cup jarred roasted red peppers, rinsed, patted dry, and cut into ½-inch pieces

½ cup frozen peas, thawed

1. For the aïoli Process egg yolks, garlic, lemon juice, water, mustard, sugar, and ¼ teaspoon salt in blender until combined, about 10 seconds, scraping down sides of blender jar as needed. With blender running, slowly add oil and process until mayonnaise is emulsified, about 2 minutes. Adjust

consistency with extra water as needed. Season with salt and pepper to taste. (Aïoli can be refrigerated for up to 3 days.)

2. For the tortilla Toss ¼ cup oil, potatoes, onion, ½ teaspoon salt, and ¼ teaspoon pepper together in bowl. Heat 2 tablespoons oil in 10-inch nonstick skillet over medium-high heat until shimmering. Add potato mixture to skillet and reduce heat to medium-low. Cover and cook, stirring every 5 minutes, until potatoes are tender, about 25 minutes.

3. Whisk eggs and ½ teaspoon salt together in now-empty bowl, then gently fold in cooked potato mixture, red peppers, and peas. Make sure to scrape all of potato mixture out of skillet.

4. Heat remaining 1 teaspoon oil in now-empty skillet over medium-high heat until just smoking. Add egg mixture and cook, shaking skillet and folding mixture constantly for 15 seconds. Smooth top of egg mixture, reduce heat to medium, cover, and cook, gently shaking skillet every 30 seconds, until bottom is golden brown and top is lightly set, about 2 minutes.

5. Off heat, run heatproof rubber spatula around edge of skillet and shake skillet gently to loosen tortilla; it should slide around freely in skillet. Slide tortilla onto large plate, then invert onto second large plate and slide back into skillet browned side up. Tuck edges of tortilla into skillet with rubber spatula. Continue to cook over medium heat, gently shaking skillet every 30 seconds, until second side is golden brown, about 2 minutes. Slide tortilla onto cutting board and let cool slightly. Serve warm or at room temperature with aïoli.

CHICKEN WITH 40 CLOVES OF GARLIC

Serves 4   Total time: 50 minutes

WHY THIS RECIPE WORKS *The iconic James Beard revolutionized the American kitchen in so many ways, and here's just one of them. When he first published his recipe for chicken with 40 cloves of garlic in the 1970s, he reassured home cooks about the "wonderful, buttery paste perfumed with garlic" that would result from this recipe. Luckily for us today, they believed him. This rustic but fancy-sounding dish is very easy to make and yields huge flavor dividends. We gave the garlic a head start on cooking in the microwave to soften and start to mellow it. The small amount of sugar added also helped it brown more quickly when it went into the skillet. Chicken broth, heavy cream, dry sherry, and fresh thyme combined to make the luscious sauce, and mashing half of the garlic cloves into the sauce ensured sweet garlic flavor in every bite. You will need three or four heads of garlic to yield 40 cloves. You can substitute four bone-in, skin-on chicken breasts (halved crosswise) for the thighs, but reduce the cooking time in step 3 to 15 to 20 minutes. Serve this with plenty of crusty bread to scoop up the rich, garlicky sauce.*

- 40 **garlic cloves, peeled**
- 2 **teaspoons vegetable oil**
- ½ **teaspoon sugar**
- 8 **(5- to 7-ounce) bone-in chicken thighs, trimmed**
-   **Salt and pepper**
- ½ **cup dry sherry**
- ¾ **cup chicken broth**
- ½ **cup heavy cream**
- 2 **teaspoons cornstarch dissolved in 1 tablespoon water**
- 2 **sprigs fresh thyme**
- 1 **bay leaf**

1. Adjust oven rack to upper-middle position and heat oven to 450 degrees. Toss garlic in bowl with 1 teaspoon oil and sugar. Microwave garlic until slightly softened, with light brown spotting, about 4 minutes, stirring halfway through microwaving.

2. Pat chicken dry with paper towels and season with salt and pepper. Heat remaining 1 teaspoon oil in 12-inch oven-safe skillet over medium-high heat until just smoking. Place chicken skin side down in skillet and cook until skin is well browned, 7 to 10 minutes. Transfer to plate, skin side up. Pour off all but 1 tablespoon fat from skillet. Reduce heat to medium-low, add garlic, and cook until evenly browned, about 1 minute.

3. Off heat, add sherry to skillet. Return skillet to medium heat and bring sherry to simmer, scraping up any browned bits. Cook until sherry coats garlic and pan is nearly dry, about 4 minutes. Stir in broth, cream, cornstarch mixture, thyme sprigs, and bay leaf and simmer until slightly thickened, about 3 minutes. Return chicken skin side up to skillet along with any accumulated juices. Transfer skillet to oven and roast until chicken registers 175 degrees, 18 to 22 minutes.

4. Using potholder (skillet handle will be hot), remove skillet from oven. Transfer chicken and half of garlic to serving platter. Discard thyme sprig and bay leaf. Using potato masher, mash remaining garlic into sauce, and season with salt and pepper to taste. Pour half of sauce around chicken. Serve, passing remaining sauce separately.

GARLIC FRIED CHICKEN

Serves 4   Total time: 1 hour 15 minutes (plus 1 hour marinating time)

WHY THIS RECIPE WORKS *A garlic trifecta deeply infuses this fried chicken with pungent flavor and aroma. First, we marinated bone-in chicken pieces in a mixture of extra-virgin olive oil, minced fresh garlic, and granulated garlic for at least an hour. Then, the pieces got a dip in egg whites and a dredge in flour seasoned with granulated garlic, salt, and pepper. To up the ante in terms of both spicy garlic flavor and unctuous texture, we made a quick butter sauce with a generous amount of sautéed minced garlic and parsley and drizzled that over the hot fried chicken. We found that a garlic press created very strong garlic taste in the butter sauce, so we preferred to mince the cloves with a knife in this case, for the ideal balance of flavors. Use a Dutch oven that holds 6 quarts or more for frying. Serve this decadent chicken with plenty of napkins!*

CHICKEN

- 3 tablespoons extra-virgin olive oil
- 2 tablespoons granulated garlic
- 5 garlic cloves, minced
  Kosher salt and pepper
- 3 pounds bone-in chicken pieces (split breasts cut in half crosswise, drumsticks, thighs, and/or wings), trimmed
- 2 cups all-purpose flour
- 4 large egg whites
- 3 quarts peanut or vegetable oil

GARLIC BUTTER

- 8 tablespoons unsalted butter, softened
- 2 tablespoons minced fresh parsley
- ¼ teaspoon kosher salt
- ¼ teaspoon pepper
- 8 garlic cloves, minced
- 1 tablespoon water

1. For the chicken Combine olive oil, 1 tablespoon granulated garlic, minced garlic, 2 teaspoons salt, and 2 teaspoons pepper in large bowl. Add chicken and toss to thoroughly coat with garlic mixture. Cover with plastic wrap and refrigerate for at least 1 hour or up to 24 hours.

2. Set wire rack in rimmed baking sheet. Whisk flour, remaining 1 tablespoon granulated garlic, 2 teaspoons salt, and 2 teaspoons pepper together in separate bowl. Lightly beat egg whites together in shallow dish.

3. Remove chicken from marinade and brush away any solidified clumps of oil with paper towels. Working with 1 piece at a time, dip chicken into egg whites to thoroughly coat, letting excess drip back into dish. Dredge in flour mixture, pressing firmly to adhere. Transfer chicken to prepared wire rack and refrigerate, uncovered, for at least 30 minutes or up to 2 hours.

4. Set second wire rack in second rimmed baking sheet and line with triple layer of paper towels. Add peanut oil to Dutch oven until it measures about 2 inches deep and heat over medium-high heat to 325 degrees. Add half of chicken to hot oil and fry until breasts register 160 degrees and drumsticks/thighs register 175 degrees, 13 to 16 minutes. Adjust burner, if necessary, to maintain oil temperature between 300 and 325 degrees.

Transfer to paper towel–lined rack, return oil to 325 degrees, and repeat with remaining chicken.

5. For the garlic butter While chicken rests, combine 7 tablespoons butter, parsley, salt, and pepper in bowl; set aside. Melt remaining 1 tablespoon butter in 8-inch nonstick skillet over medium heat. Add garlic and water and cook, stirring frequently, until garlic is softened and fragrant, 1 to 2 minutes. Add hot garlic mixture to butter-parsley mixture and whisk until well combined. Transfer chicken to serving platter and spoon garlic butter over top. Serve.

~~~

TERIYAKI STIR-FRIED GARLIC SCAPES WITH CHICKEN

Serves 4   Total time: 30 minutes

WHY THIS RECIPE WORKS *This speedy, simple, and deliciously savory stir-fry showcases garlic scapes, highlighting their grassy, mild garlic flavor and crisp-tender texture. Chicken and earthy cremini mushrooms are a great pairing with the scapes, and our teriyaki stir-fry sauce ties everything together. For a sauce with the right balance of sweet, savory, and acidic notes, we combined soy sauce, oyster sauce, dry sherry, and sugar, with red pepper flakes for some subtle heat. The simple technique of "velveting" the chicken with a mixture of cornstarch, flour, toasted sesame oil, and soy sauce encouraged the flavorful sauce to cling to the chicken. We skipped the wok in favor of a large nonstick skillet, whose wide, broad cooking surface promoted good browning. To further promote browning, we sautéed the chicken in batches. Then we gave the mushrooms a head start in the pan before adding the scapes, allowing them to develop some char before adding a healthy amount of aromatic fresh ginger. Finally, we added everything back to the skillet and poured in our sauce, allowing it to thicken and evenly cloak the vegetables and chicken.*

SAUCE

- ⅓ cup water
- ¼ cup chicken broth
- 1 tablespoon soy sauce
- 1 tablespoon dry sherry
- 1 tablespoon oyster sauce
- 1 teaspoon sugar
- 1 teaspoon cornstarch
- ¼ teaspoon red pepper flakes

STIR-FRY

- 2 tablespoons toasted sesame oil
- 1 tablespoon cornstarch
- 1 tablespoon all-purpose flour
- 1 tablespoon soy sauce
- 1 pound boneless, skinless chicken breasts, trimmed, halved lengthwise, and sliced ¼ inch thick
- 2 tablespoons plus 1 teaspoon vegetable oil
- 1 tablespoon grated fresh ginger
- 8 ounces cremini mushrooms, trimmed and sliced thin
- 12 ounces garlic scapes, trimmed and cut into 2-inch lengths
- 2 tablespoons chopped fresh basil

1. For the sauce Whisk all ingredients together in bowl; set aside.

2. For the stir-fry Whisk sesame oil, cornstarch, flour, and soy sauce together in medium bowl until smooth, then stir in chicken. In separate bowl, combine 1 teaspoon vegetable oil and ginger.

3. Heat 2 teaspoons vegetable oil in 12-inch nonstick skillet over high heat until just smoking. Add half of chicken mixture, breaking up any clumps, and cook, without stirring, for 1 minute. Stir chicken and continue to cook until lightly browned, about 30 seconds; transfer to clean bowl. Repeat with 2 teaspoons vegetable oil and remaining chicken mixture; transfer to bowl.

4. Heat remaining 2 teaspoons vegetable oil in now-empty skillet over high heat until just smoking. Add mushrooms and cook, stirring frequently, until tender and well browned, about 5 minutes. Add garlic scapes and cook until well charred, 2 to 4 minutes.

5. Push vegetables to sides of skillet. Add ginger-oil mixture to center and cook, mashing mixture into skillet, until fragrant, about 30 seconds. Stir ginger-oil mixture into vegetables.

Teriyaki Stir-Fried Garlic Scapes
with Chicken

Garlicky Broiled Shrimp with
Cilantro and Lime

6. Return chicken and any accumulated juices to skillet and toss to combine. Add sauce and cook, stirring constantly, until chicken and vegetables are evenly coated and sauce is thickened, about 30 seconds. Off heat, sprinkle with basil. Serve.

SUNDAY BEST GARLIC ROAST BEEF

Serves 8 Total time: 2 hours 15 minutes (plus 1 hour marinating time)

WHY THIS RECIPE WORKS *Every bite of this beefy top sirloin roast is thoroughly infused with complex, sweet-savory garlic flavor. Achieving this garlicky goal called for a multipronged approach, so first we studded the beef with nutty toasted garlic, rubbed it with minced raw garlic, and let it infuse before roasting. We then rubbed it with garlic oil before it went into the oven and, finally, coated it with a garlic paste partway through cooking. We skipped a stovetop sear for the roast, but naturally we still wanted a well-browned exterior. To accomplish this goal, we started it at a high temperature in a preheated roasting pan and then reduced the heat for the majority of the cooking time—which also resulted in a perfectly medium-rare interior. Look for a top sirloin roast that has a thick, substantial fat cap attached, because the cap's rendered fat will help to keep the roast moist.*

BEEF
- 11 garlic cloves (8 whole and unpeeled, 3 minced)
- 1 (4-pound) center-cut boneless top sirloin roast, fat trimmed to ¼ inch and tied at 1½-inch intervals
- 1 teaspoon dried thyme
  Kosher salt and pepper

GARLIC PASTE
- ½ cup extra-virgin olive oil
- 12 garlic cloves, peeled and cut in half lengthwise
- 2 sprigs fresh thyme
- 2 bay leaves
- 1 teaspoon kosher salt

JUS
- 1½ cups beef broth
- 1½ cups chicken broth

1. For the beef Toast unpeeled garlic cloves in 8-inch skillet over medium-high heat, tossing frequently, until spotty brown, about 8 minutes; set aside. When cool enough to handle, peel and cut into ¼-inch slivers. Using paring knife, make 1-inch-deep slits all over roast and insert toasted garlic slivers into slits.

2. Combine minced garlic, thyme, and 1 teaspoon salt in small bowl and rub all over roast. Refrigerate, uncovered, for at least 1 hour or up to 24 hours.

3. For the garlic paste Heat oil, garlic, thyme sprigs, bay leaves, and salt in small saucepan over medium-high heat until bubbles start to rise to surface. Reduce heat to low and cook until garlic is soft, about 30 minutes. Let cool completely, then strain, reserving oil. Discard herbs and transfer garlic to small bowl. Mash garlic with 1 tablespoon garlic oil until paste forms. Cover and refrigerate paste until ready to use. Cover and reserve remaining garlic oil.

4. Adjust oven rack to middle position, place large roasting pan on rack, and heat oven to 450 degrees. Using paper towels, wipe garlic-salt rub off roast. Rub with 2 tablespoons reserved garlic oil and season with pepper. Transfer roast, fat side down, to preheated pan and roast, turning as needed until browned on all sides, 10 to 15 minutes.

5. Reduce oven temperature to 300 degrees. Remove pan from oven, turn roast fat side up, and coat top with garlic paste. Roast until beef registers 120 to 125 degrees (for medium-rare), 50 minutes to 1 hour 10 minutes. Transfer to carving board and let rest for 20 minutes.

6. For the jus Pour off fat from pan and place pan over high heat. Add broths and bring to boil, scraping up any browned bits. Simmer, stirring occasionally, until reduced to 2 cups, about 5 minutes. Taste, and, if desired, add accumulated meat juices and cook for 1 minute. Pour through fine-mesh strainer into bowl; set aside for serving.

7. Remove twine from roast and slice ¼ inch thick. Serve with jus.

GARLICKY BROILED SHRIMP WITH PARSLEY AND ANISE

Serves 4 to 6 Total time: 30 minutes

WHY THIS RECIPE WORKS *For a shrimp dish that's bursting with garlic flavor, we found that a simple mixture of butter and olive oil combined with a healthy amount of potent minced garlic, plus anise seeds and red pepper flakes, delivered loads of aromatic, complex flavor to sweet jumbo shrimp that we roasted under the high heat of the broiler. To keep the shrimp plump and moist, we brined them briefly in salt water. To further protect them as they cooked and to produce a more roasted flavor, we left their shells on. The shells browned quickly in the heat of the oven and transferred that flavor to the shrimp itself. Leaving the shells on also allowed the garlic butter to get under them and really permeate the shrimp. The parsley and lemon provided assertive fresh flavors that complemented the rich garlic butter. Don't be tempted to use smaller shrimp with this cooking technique, as they will likely end up overseasoned and overcooked.*

- ¼ cup salt
- 2 pounds shell-on jumbo shrimp (16 to 20 per pound)
- 4 tablespoons unsalted butter, melted
- ¼ cup extra-virgin olive oil
- 6 garlic cloves, minced
- 1 teaspoon anise seeds
- ½ teaspoon red pepper flakes
- ¼ teaspoon pepper
- 2 tablespoons minced fresh parsley
  Lemon wedges

1. Dissolve salt in 1 quart cold water in large container. Using kitchen shears or sharp paring knife, cut through shell of shrimp and devein but do not remove shell. Using paring knife, continue to cut shrimp ½ inch deep, taking care not to cut in half completely. Submerge shrimp in brine, cover, and refrigerate for 15 minutes.

2. Adjust oven rack 4 inches from broiler element and heat broiler. Combine melted butter, oil, garlic, anise seeds, pepper flakes, and pepper in large bowl. Remove shrimp from brine and pat dry with paper towels. Add shrimp and parsley to butter mixture;

toss well, making sure butter mixture gets into interior of shrimp. Arrange shrimp in single layer on wire rack set in rimmed baking sheet.

3. Broil shrimp until opaque and shells are beginning to brown, 2 to 4 minutes, rotating sheet halfway through broiling. Flip shrimp and continue to broil until second side is opaque and shells are beginning to brown, 2 to 4 minutes longer, rotating sheet halfway through broiling. Transfer shrimp to serving dish and serve with lemon wedges.

VARIATIONS
Garlicky Broiled Shrimp with Cilantro and Lime

Annatto powder, also called achiote, can be found with the Latin American foods at your supermarket. An equal amount of paprika can be substituted.
Omit butter and increase oil to ½ cup. Omit anise seeds and pepper. Add 2 teaspoons lightly crushed coriander seeds, 2 teaspoons grated lime zest, and 1 teaspoon annatto powder to oil mixture in step 2. Substitute ¼ cup minced fresh cilantro for parsley and lime wedges for lemon wedges.

Garlicky Broiled Shrimp with Sesame, Ginger, and Cumin

Omit butter and increase oil to ½ cup. Decrease garlic to 2 cloves and omit anise seeds and pepper. Add 2 teaspoons toasted sesame oil, 1½ teaspoons grated fresh ginger, and 1 teaspoon cumin seeds to oil mixture in step 2. Substitute 2 thinly sliced scallion greens for parsley and omit lemon wedges.

GARLIC BREAD

Serves 8   Total time: 30 minutes
WHY THIS RECIPE WORKS *Garlic bread might seem like such a simple thing to make—why do you even need a recipe? The answer is, because more often than not, this Italian American classic ends up being a disappointment to eat. There's either too much or not enough garlic flavor, or the garlic tastes acrid and harsh, or the bread is soggy or pale. For a perfectly toasted version with garlic flavor that was prominent, sweet, and roasty, but not harsh, we microwaved fresh garlic (grated to a paste with a*

rasp-style grater) and butter and combined it with garlic powder. We then combined this melted garlic butter with solid butter and just a bit of cayenne and salt to make a spreadable paste that could be smeared evenly onto the bread. We baked the buttered bread cut side up on a baking sheet and then flipped it and compressed it with a second baking sheet. The panini-style setup pressed the buttered side onto the hot sheet so that it evenly crisped and browned while also compressing the bread for a better balance of crust to crumb. The amount of time needed to brown the bread after flipping it depends on the color of your baking sheet. If using a dark-colored sheet, the browning time will be on the shorter end of the range. In true Italian American style, a 12 by 5-inch loaf of supermarket Italian bread, with its soft, thin crust and fine crumb, works best here. Do not use a crusty or rustic artisan-style loaf.

- 1 teaspoon garlic powder
- 1 teaspoon water
- 8 tablespoons unsalted butter
- ½ teaspoon salt
- ⅛ teaspoon cayenne pepper
- 4 or 5 garlic cloves, grated to paste
- 1 (1-pound) loaf soft Italian bread, halved horizontally

1. Adjust oven rack to lower-middle position and heat oven to 450 degrees. Combine garlic powder and water in medium bowl. Add 4 tablespoons butter, salt, and cayenne to bowl; set aside.

2. Place remaining 4 tablespoons butter in small bowl and microwave, covered, until melted, about 30 seconds. Stir in garlic and continue to microwave, covered, until mixture is bubbling around edges, about 1 minute, stirring halfway through microwaving. Transfer melted butter mixture to bowl with garlic powder–butter mixture and whisk until homogeneous loose paste forms. (If mixture melts, set aside and let solidify before using.)

3. Spread cut sides of bread evenly with butter mixture. Transfer bread, cut sides up, to rimmed baking sheet. Bake until butter mixture has melted and seeped into bread, 3 to 4 minutes. Remove sheet from oven.

Flip bread cut sides down, place second rimmed baking sheet on top, and gently press. Return sheet to oven, leaving second sheet on top of bread, and continue to bake until cut sides are golden brown and crisp, 4 to 12 minutes, rotating sheet halfway through baking. Transfer bread to cutting board. Using serrated knife, cut each half into 8 slices. Serve immediately.

GARLIC KNOTS

Makes 12 knots   Total time: 1 hour 15 minutes (plus 2 hours rising time)
WHY THIS RECIPE WORKS *Buttery, supremely garlicky garlic knots are a pizzeria classic made from leftover pizza dough. Now you can bring them home without the help of a pizza delivery driver. These irresistible garlic knots have a texture somewhere in between chewy pizza crust and fluffy dinner rolls. To give our knots potent garlic flavor, we sautéed minced garlic—nine cloves of it—in butter. We stirred some of this butter and its toasty garlic solids into the dough itself. Then, to further satisfy our garlic cravings, we brushed the knots with the garlic butter during baking and again just after taking them out of the oven. The knots can be stored in a zipper-lock bag at room temperature for up to three days. Wrapped in aluminum foil before being placed in the bag, the knots can be frozen for up to one month. To reheat, wrap the knots (thawed if frozen) in foil, place them on a baking sheet, and bake in a 350-degree oven for 10 minutes.*

- 9 garlic cloves, minced
- 6 tablespoons unsalted butter
- 1 teaspoon plus ¾ cup (6 ounces) water
- 2 cups (10 ounces) all-purpose flour
- 1½ teaspoons instant or rapid-rise yeast
- 1 teaspoon salt
- Coarse sea salt

1. Cook garlic, 1 tablespoon butter, and 1 teaspoon water in 8-inch nonstick skillet over low heat, stirring occasionally, until garlic is pale golden brown, 9 to 12 minutes. Stir in remaining butter until melted. Strain into bowl, reserving garlic solids.

2. Whisk flour, yeast, and salt together in bowl of stand mixer. Whisk remaining ¾ cup water, 1 tablespoon garlic butter, and garlic solids together in 4-cup liquid measuring cup. Using dough hook on low speed, slowly add water mixture to flour mixture and mix until cohesive dough starts to form and no dry flour remains, about 2 minutes, scraping down bowl as needed. Increase speed to medium-low and knead until dough is smooth and elastic and clears sides of bowl but sticks to bottom, about 8 minutes.

3. Transfer dough to lightly floured counter and knead by hand to form smooth, round ball, about 30 seconds. Place dough seam side down in lightly greased large bowl or container, cover tightly with plastic wrap, and let rise until doubled in size, 1 to 1½ hours.

4. Line rimmed baking sheet with parchment paper. Press down on dough to deflate. Transfer dough to clean counter. Press and stretch dough into 12 by 6-inch rectangle, with long side parallel to counter edge. Using pizza cutter or chef's knife, cut dough vertically into 12 (6 by 1-inch) strips, and cover loosely with greased plastic.

5. Working with 1 piece of dough at a time (keep remaining pieces covered), stretch and roll into 14-inch rope. Shape rope into U with 2-inch-wide bottom curve. Tie ends into single overhand knot, with 1½-inch open loop at bottom. Wrap 1 tail over loop and press through opening from top. Wrap other tail under loop and through opening from bottom. Pinch ends together to seal.

6. Arrange knots pinched side down on prepared sheet, spaced about 1 inch apart. Cover loosely with greased plastic and let rise until nearly doubled in size and dough springs back minimally when poked gently with your knuckle, 1 to 1½ hours. (Unrisen garlic knots can be refrigerated for up to 16 hours; let garlic knots sit at room temperature for 1 hour before baking.)

7. Adjust oven rack to middle position and heat oven to 500 degrees. Bake knots until set, about 5 minutes. Brush with 2 tablespoons garlic butter, rotate sheet, and bake until knots are golden brown, about 5 minutes.

8. Transfer knots to wire rack. Brush with remaining garlic butter, sprinkle with sea salt, and let cool for 15 minutes. Serve warm.

forming garlic knots

1. Cut dough rectangle vertically into twelve 6 by 1-inch strips.

2. Working with 1 piece of dough at a time, stretch and roll into 14-inch rope.

3. Shape rope into U with 2-inch-wide bottom curve.

4. Tie ends into single overhand knot, with 1½-inch open loop at bottom.

5. Wrap 1 tail over loop and press through opening from top. Wrap other tail under loop and through opening from bottom. Pinch ends together to seal.

GREEN BEANS

Green beans have long been a favorite choice among home vegetable gardeners, because they're easy to grow and they usually offer abundant and frequent harvests. They're also among the first vegetables that most children are exposed to in a practical, hands-on sort of way in the kitchen—many of us probably have an early memory of being put to work, snapping the tips and tails from a giant pile of green beans and maybe snacking on a few crunchy raw beans in the process.

Green beans are legumes, which are plants that produce a pod with edible seeds inside. They are related to fresh shell beans (like lima beans and chickpeas) and dried beans (like kidney beans and cannellini beans). But unlike those types of beans, green beans are grown and eaten for their pods rather than for what's inside them. Different varieties—yellow wax, purple, romano, haricots verts—may vary in texture, color, and size, but all have a sweet, grassy flavor and crisp texture.

These sturdy vegetables adapt amiably to a variety of preparation methods (except for haricots verts, which are so tender and sweet that they barely need cooking). We especially like to cook green beans in one of two ways: fast or slow. They're terrific after a quick roast in the oven, as in our Roasted Green Beans with Goat Cheese and Hazelnuts, or a speedy blanch-and-shock treatment on the stove-top, as in the Blanched Green Beans with Bistro Mustard Vinaigrette. They also hold up wonder-fully to long braises, without turning to mush like other green vegetables. Enjoy their silky yet stable texture in our tomato-saucy Mediterranean Braised Green Beans and in the Thanksgiving classic Extra-Crunchy Green Bean Casserole.

shopping and storage

All types of green beans are generally grown for commercial availability year-round, though the traditional garden season for them runs from midsummer through fall.

When shopping, select thinner beans if possible, since those will be crisper and sweeter. Avoid really thick beans that are bulging with seeds, because they are more likely to be mealy in texture. If the green beans are loose in a bin, snap one in half—it should truly snap, rather than bend. If the beans are packaged, they should look bright in color, fresh, and firm (not limp). The one exception to this rule is Chinese long beans, which will be a bit droopy and flexible even when fresh.

Across the board, green beans are fairly perishable, losing both texture and flavor quickly. Store them wrapped in paper towels in an open plastic produce bag in the refrigerator for no more than a few days.

bean varieties

"Green beans," "snap beans," and "string beans" are general terms that cover many different varieties of beans. The most commonly available variety sold in markets is Blue Lake. Though they are often still called string beans, the tough string that ran down the seam was bred out of green beans a long time ago. As they age, regular green beans can become tough and start to develop a stronger, slightly bitter flavor edge. Several purple varieties are also available; they're very pretty when raw but turn plain old green when cooked.

HARICOTS VERTS Haricots verts, also called French beans, are a thinner, shorter variety. They have a more delicate texture than regular green beans and a fresh, lightly sweet flavor. They cook much more quickly than regular green beans and are even tender enough to eat raw.

WAX BEANS Wax beans, like green beans, encompass many varieties. They are pale yellow snap beans with a flavor that's similar to green beans but slightly milder and sweeter. Wax beans have been cultivated to have none of the chlorophyll pigment that makes green beans green. You might also sometimes see yellow wax beans with vivid purple streaks. Wax beans can be substituted for green beans in any dish.

ROMANO BEANS Romano beans, also called Italian flat beans or Italian pole beans, are flatter and broader than regular green beans and have a crisp texture and sweet flavor. Like regular green beans, they also come in yellow wax and purple varieties. They can be used similarly to regular green beans.

CHINESE LONG BEANS Chinese long beans, also called yard-long beans, asparagus beans, or snake beans, can grow up to nearly 3 feet in length (and can grow several inches in a single day!). They have a flavor that's a little more mellow than regular green beans and a softer, chewier texture, which is best highlighted by stir-frying or deep frying.

vegetable science

Team Green or Team Yellow?

Green beans get their color from chlorophyll, whereas yellow wax beans are simply green beans that have been bred to contain none of this pigment. So the questions are: Does chlorophyll contribute to the flavor of green beans? And will you miss it if it's not there?

We tasted green beans and wax beans two ways: steamed until crisp-tender, and braised in our Mediterranean Braised Green Beans recipe. In both applications, tasters were hard-pressed to discern that much difference between the flavors and textures of the two beans, calling both sweet and grassy. But wax beans did demonstrate one noticeable advantage over green beans. Because they have little color to lose during prolonged braising, their appearance changes less than that of green beans, which tend to turn a drab olive shade. So if you're making a long-cooked bean dish and are picky about aesthetics, go for the gold.

vegetable prep

Trimming Green Beans

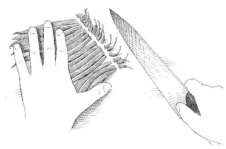

To trim green beans quickly, line up several so stem ends are even and then cut off stems with one swipe of the knife.

BLANCHED GREEN BEANS WITH BISTRO MUSTARD VINAIGRETTE

Serves 4   Total time: 30 minutes

WHY THIS RECIPE WORKS *Green beans are excellent candidates for the classic, simple cooking technique of blanching. Cooked quickly in rapidly boiling salted water and then chilled in ice water to cool them and stop their cooking instantly, green beans hold their fresh flavor, bright color, and crisp-tender texture beautifully. The rustic, slightly sharp mustard vinaigrette here brought out the best in the beans without overshadowing their mild flavor. Be sure to set up the ice water bath before cooking the green beans, as plunging them in the cold water immediately after blanching both retains their bright green color and ensures that they don't overcook. The beans are delicious at room temperature, slightly chilled, or briefly rewarmed in the microwave.*

- 1 pound green beans, trimmed
  Salt and pepper
- ¼ cup extra-virgin olive oil
- 1 tablespoon whole-grain mustard
- 1½ teaspoons red wine vinegar
- 1 small shallot, minced
- 1 small garlic clove, minced
- ½ teaspoon minced fresh thyme

1. Bring 4 quarts water to boil in large pot. Fill large bowl halfway with ice and water. Add green beans and 1 tablespoon salt to boiling water and cook until crisp-tender, 2 to 4 minutes. Drain beans, then transfer immediately to ice water. Let beans cool completely, about 5 minutes, then drain again and pat dry with paper towels.

2. Whisk oil, mustard, vinegar, shallot, garlic, thyme, ¼ teaspoon salt, and ⅛ teaspoon pepper together in bowl. Add green beans and toss to combine. Season with salt and pepper to taste. Serve.

SAUTÉED GREEN BEANS WITH GARLIC AND HERBS

Serves 4   Total time: 20 minutes

WHY THIS RECIPE WORKS *For tender and lightly browned green beans using just one pan, look to sautéing. We discovered that simply sautéing the raw beans in hot oil resulted in blackened exteriors and under-cooked interiors. So, for the best results, we sautéed the beans until spotty brown, then added a little water to the pan and covered it so the beans could cook through. Once the beans were bright green but still crisp, we lifted the lid to evaporate the water and promote browning. A little butter added to the pan at this stage lent richness and encouraged even more browning. A few additional ingredients—garlic, herbs, and lemon—added flavor without overcomplicating things. This recipe yields crisp-tender beans. If you prefer a slightly more tender texture, increase the water by 1 tablespoon and increase the covered cooking time by 1 minute. You will need a 12-inch nonstick skillet with a tight-fitting lid for this recipe.*

- 4 teaspoons extra-virgin olive oil
- 1 pound green beans, trimmed and
  cut into 2-inch lengths
  Salt and pepper
- ¼ cup water
- 1 tablespoon unsalted butter, softened
- 3 garlic cloves, minced
- 1 teaspoon minced fresh thyme
- 2 teaspoons lemon juice

1. Heat oil in 12-inch nonstick skillet over medium-high heat until just smoking. Add beans, ¼ teaspoon salt, and ⅛ teaspoon pepper and cook, stirring occasionally, until spotty brown, 4 to 6 minutes. Add water, cover, and cook until beans are bright green and still crisp, about 2 minutes.

2. Uncover, increase heat to high, and continue to cook until liquid evaporates, about 3 minutes. Add butter, garlic, and thyme and cook, stirring often, until beans are crisp-tender, lightly browned, and beginning to wrinkle, 1 to 3 minutes. Off heat, stir in lemon juice and season with salt and pepper to taste. Serve.

VARIATIONS

Sautéed Green Beans with Roasted Red Peppers and Basil
Substitute extra-virgin olive oil for butter, 1 minced shallot for garlic, and ⅛ teaspoon red pepper flakes for thyme. Add ⅓ cup chopped jarred roasted red peppers to skillet with shallot. Substitute 1 teaspoon red wine vinegar for lemon juice. Stir in 2 tablespoons chopped fresh basil with vinegar.

Sautéed Green Beans with Ginger and Sesame
Omit lemon juice. Substitute 1 teaspoon toasted sesame oil for butter, 1 teaspoon grated fresh ginger for garlic, and 1 tablespoon Asian chili-garlic paste for thyme. Sprinkle green beans with 2 teaspoons toasted sesame seeds before serving.

GREEN BEANS AMANDINE

Serves 4 to 6   Total time: 25 minutes

WHY THIS RECIPE WORKS *The simple French preparation of green beans tossed in a light sauce of butter, shallots, and lemon, topped with toasted sliced almonds, is refined yet not at all intimidating. Unfortunately, over the years it has descended into a cliché, made with frozen green beans tossed with a bag of sliced blanched almonds and loads of butter. We've reclaimed this side dish with crisp-tender fresh beans, crunchy toasted almonds, and a balanced lemon butter sauce. To achieve a more elegant feel, we replaced regular green beans with thin haricots verts. For maximum flavor, we first toasted the almonds, then added a little butter to the skillet and allowed it to brown for further nuttiness. Adding lemon juice off the heat brightened the sauce. After steaming the haricots verts in a little water in a covered skillet until crisp-tender, we tossed them with the sauce. You will need a 12-inch skillet with a tight-fitting lid for this recipe. If using regular green beans, increase the covered cooking time in step 2 to 8 to 10 minutes.*

⅓ cup sliced almonds

3 tablespoons unsalted butter, cut into 3 pieces

1 shallot, minced

1 garlic clove, minced

2 teaspoons lemon juice

1½ pounds haricots verts or green beans, trimmed

¼ cup water

Salt

1. Toast almonds in 12-inch skillet over medium-low heat, stirring often, until just golden, about 6 minutes. Add butter, shallot, and garlic and cook, stirring constantly, until shallot softens and butter is golden brown and has nutty aroma, about 3 minutes. Transfer almond mixture to small bowl and stir in lemon juice.

2. Add haricots verts, water, and ½ teaspoon salt to now-empty skillet. Cover and cook over medium-high heat, occasionally tossing with tongs to redistribute, until beans are bright green and still crisp, 4 to 6 minutes. Uncover, increase heat to high, and cook until liquid evaporates, about 3 minutes. Off heat, add almond mixture and toss to combine. Season with salt to taste. Serve.

ROASTED GREEN BEANS WITH GOAT CHEESE AND HAZELNUTS

Serves 4 to 6   Total time: 45 minutes

WHY THIS RECIPE WORKS *This technique for roasting green beans has a lot going for it: It's supersimple, it frees up your stovetop, and it gives mature supermarket green beans a flavor comparable to sweet fresh-picked beans. We knew the quick-cooking beans could only handle a short stay in the oven before they overcooked, so we ensured plenty of flavor-boosting color by tossing them with a touch of sugar along with olive oil, salt, and pepper. Spreading them on a baking sheet and sealing them under aluminum foil allowed them to steam gently in the oven. Uncovering the beans for the final 10 minutes let the sugar caramelize, turning the beans an appealing blistered, speckled brown. To lift the flavorful beans to another level entirely, we tossed them with a warm orange vinaigrette and fresh chives and topped them with goat cheese and hazelnuts.*

1½ pounds green beans, trimmed

6 tablespoons extra-virgin olive oil

¾ teaspoon sugar

Kosher salt and pepper

2 garlic cloves, minced

1 teaspoon grated orange zest plus 2 teaspoons juice

2 teaspoons lemon juice

1 teaspoon Dijon mustard

2 tablespoons minced fresh chives

2 ounces goat cheese, crumbled (½ cup)

¼ cup hazelnuts, toasted, skinned, and chopped

1. Adjust oven rack to lowest position and heat oven to 475 degrees. Toss green beans with 2 tablespoons oil, sugar, ¾ teaspoon salt, and ½ teaspoon pepper in bowl. Evenly distribute green beans on rimmed baking sheet.

2. Cover sheet tightly with aluminum foil and roast for 10 minutes. Remove foil and continue to roast until green beans are spotty brown, about 10 minutes, stirring halfway through roasting.

3. Meanwhile, combine garlic, orange zest, and remaining ¼ cup oil in large bowl and microwave until bubbling, about 1 minute; let steep for 1 minute. Whisk in orange juice,

lemon juice, mustard, ¼ teaspoon salt, and ¼ teaspoon pepper. Add green beans and chives and toss to combine. Transfer to serving platter and sprinkle with goat cheese and hazelnuts. Serve.

VARIATION

Roasted Green Beans with Pecorino and Pine Nuts

Substitute 1 teaspoon grated lemon zest for orange zest, 4 teaspoons lemon juice for orange juice and lemon juice, chopped fresh basil for chives, ½ cup shredded Pecorino Romano cheese for goat cheese, and ¼ cup toasted pine nuts for hazelnuts.

MEDITERRANEAN BRAISED GREEN BEANS

Serves 4 to 6   Total time: 1 hour 15 minutes

WHY THIS RECIPE WORKS *In the crisp-tender craze of recent years, a lesser-known but time-honored approach to cooking green beans has become overlooked and underappreciated. A slow braise turns green beans into something silky-smooth and altogether different. This Mediterranean version calls for sautéing the aromatics on the stovetop in a Dutch oven, then adding the green beans and tomatoes and transferring the pot*

MEDITERRANEAN BRAISED GREEN BEANS

Lightly crisp green beans are so commonplace that many cooks assume that's the only way you're supposed to prepare them. But there is another way—a velvety soft and silky way. Because the natural pectin found in the beans makes them slow to break down in the acidic tomato sauce, we added a small amount of baking soda to lower the acidity and get this braise on the table more quickly. This is a good thing, because these are great served with simply grilled or roasted chicken. Or make like an Italian nonna and serve them on their own in a bowl, with a hunk of crusty bread alongside.

1. Trim the ends from the green beans and cut them into 2- to 3-inch lengths.

2. In a Dutch oven, sauté the onion in the olive oil until it's softened, 3 to 5 minutes, then add the garlic and cayenne and cook until fragrant, about 30 seconds.

3. Add the water, baking soda, and green beans to the Dutch oven, bring to a simmer, and then reduce the heat and cook for 10 minutes.

4. Stir in the chopped tomatoes with their juice and the tomato paste.

5. Cover the Dutch oven, transfer to the oven, and cook until the sauce is thickened and the green beans can easily be cut with the side of a fork, 40 to 50 minutes.

6. Drizzle the braised beans with more olive oil and serve either warm or at room temperature.

to the oven for hands-off simmering until the sauce is thickened and the beans become infused with the tomato and garlic. The best part is the velvety texture of the beans: The slow cooking renders them so meltingly tender that they're almost creamy.

- 5 tablespoons extra-virgin olive oil
- 1 onion, chopped fine
- 4 garlic cloves, minced
  Pinch cayenne pepper
- 1½ cups water
- ½ teaspoon baking soda
- 1½ pounds green beans, trimmed and cut into 2- to 3-inch lengths
- 1 (14.5-ounce) can diced tomatoes, drained with juice reserved, chopped coarse
- 1 tablespoon tomato paste
- 1 teaspoon salt
- ¼ teaspoon pepper
- ¼ cup chopped fresh parsley
  Red wine vinegar

1. Adjust oven rack to lower-middle position and heat oven to 275 degrees. Heat 3 tablespoons oil in Dutch oven over medium heat until shimmering. Add onion and cook, stirring occasionally, until softened, 3 to 5 minutes. Add garlic and cayenne and cook until fragrant, about 30 seconds. Add water, baking soda, and green beans and bring to simmer. Reduce heat to medium-low and cook, stirring occasionally, for 10 minutes. Stir in tomatoes and their juice, tomato paste, salt, and pepper.

2. Cover pot, transfer to oven, and cook until sauce is slightly thickened and green beans can be easily cut with side of fork, 40 to 50 minutes. Stir in parsley and season with vinegar to taste. Drizzle with remaining 2 tablespoons oil and serve warm or at room temperature.

VARIATIONS

Mediterranean Braised Green Beans with Potatoes and Basil
Substitute 2 teaspoons oregano for cayenne, 3 tablespoons chopped fresh basil for parsley, and 2 teaspoons lemon juice for red wine vinegar. In step 1, add 1 pound peeled Yukon Gold potatoes, cut into 2- to 3-inch pieces, to pot with green beans and increase salt to 2 teaspoons.

Mediterranean Braised Green Beans with Mint and Feta
Add ¾ teaspoon ground allspice with garlic and cayenne. Substitute 2 tablespoons chopped fresh mint for parsley. Omit 2 tablespoons oil in step 2. Sprinkle green beans with ½ cup crumbled feta cheese before serving.

GREEN BEAN SALAD WITH CILANTRO SAUCE

Serves 6 to 8   Total time: 35 minutes

WHY THIS RECIPE WORKS *In this picnic-perfect green bean salad, the sweet, grassy flavors of the green beans and cilantro really shine through. For a creative variation on pesto sauce, we swapped the traditional basil for bright, herbal cilantro and traded the pine nuts for walnuts. Last but not least, a touch of lemon juice balanced out the richer flavors and helped to loosen the sauce to just the right dressing-like consistency. We blanched and shocked the beans to set their vibrant green color and ensure that they were evenly cooked. Be sure to set up the ice water bath before cooking the green beans, as plunging them in the cold water immediately after blanching retains their bright green color and ensures that they don't overcook. Don't worry about drying the beans before tossing them with the sauce; any water that clings to the beans will help to thin out the sauce. Serve this at room temperature.*

- 2 pounds green beans, trimmed
  Salt and pepper
- ¼ cup walnuts
- 2 garlic cloves, unpeeled
- 2½ cups fresh cilantro leaves and stems, tough stem ends trimmed (about 2 bunches)
- ½ cup extra-virgin olive oil
- 4 teaspoons lemon juice
- 1 scallion, sliced thin

1. Bring 4 quarts water to boil in large pot over high heat. Fill large bowl halfway with ice and water. Add green beans and 1 tablespoon salt to boiling water and cook until crisp-tender, 2 to 4 minutes. Drain beans,

then transfer immediately to ice water. Let beans cool completely, about 5 minutes, then drain again and return to now-empty bowl.

2. Meanwhile, cook walnuts and garlic in dry 8-inch skillet over medium heat, stirring often, until toasted and fragrant, 5 to 7 minutes; transfer to bowl. Let garlic cool slightly, then peel and chop coarse.

3. Process walnuts, garlic, cilantro, oil, lemon juice, scallion, ½ teaspoon salt, and ⅛ teaspoon pepper in food processor until smooth, about 1 minute, scraping down sides of bowl as needed. Season with salt and pepper to taste. Add cilantro sauce to green beans and toss to coat. Season with salt and pepper to taste, and serve.

TARRAGON-MUSTARD BEAN SALAD

Serves 4 to 6   Total time: 25 minutes
(plus 30 minutes chilling time)

WHY THIS RECIPE WORKS *String bean salad is a terrific side dish for any summertime gathering—especially if it can be made ahead of time, as this one can. We combined green beans and yellow wax beans with a potent vinaigrette while still warm, and then refrigerated the salad until chilled. The honey and Dijon mustard are a classic pairing that thickened the vinaigrette enough for it to coat the beans nicely, with the bite of the mustard and touch of cayenne pepper intensifying the overall flavor and pairing nicely with the fresh tarragon. Skipping the typical step of plunging the beans into ice water after cooking worked to this salad's advantage. Tossing the beans with the dressing immediately after boiling and draining them caused the warm beans to soak up some of the flavorful vinaigrette, resulting in a tender, not-too-crunchy texture. The salad tasted even better after the short chilling time in the refrigerator let the flavors mingle.*

- 3 tablespoons extra-virgin olive oil
- 1½ tablespoons white wine vinegar
- 1½ tablespoons Dijon mustard
- 1 tablespoon lemon juice
- 2 teaspoons honey

2 teaspoons minced fresh tarragon,
   dill, or parsley
   Salt and pepper
⅛ teaspoon cayenne pepper
12 ounces green beans, trimmed
12 ounces yellow wax beans, trimmed

1. Whisk oil, vinegar, mustard, lemon juice, honey, tarragon, ¼ teaspoon pepper, and cayenne together in large bowl; set aside.

2. Bring 4 quarts water to boil in large pot. Add beans and 2 teaspoons salt and cook until beans are crisp-tender, about 5 minutes. Drain beans, add to bowl with dressing, and toss to combine. Refrigerate for at least 30 minutes or up to 3 days. Season with salt and pepper to taste. Serve cold or at room temperature.

THREE-BEAN SALAD
Serves 4 to 6   Total time: 30 minutes
WHY THIS RECIPE WORKS *Store-bought three-bean salad may be convenient, but it's also mushy and sugary. Here's our simple, superior take on this summertime classic. First we steamed fresh romano beans and yellow wax beans to crisp-tender perfection. To avoid the need to soak and simmer dried beans for hours, canned kidney beans rounded out our trio. Letting the garlic and onion sit in the vinaigrette while preparing the beans tamed the garlic and quick-pickled the onions. A touch of honey in the bright dressing added the appropriate hint of sweetness to recall the classic formula, and a generous amount of parsley folded in just before serving contributed a lively finish. Be sure to set up the ice water bath before cooking the green beans, as plunging them in the cold water immediately after blanching retains their bright green color and ensures that they don't overcook.*

¼ cup cider vinegar
3 tablespoons extra-virgin olive oil
1 tablespoon honey
1 garlic clove, minced
   Salt and pepper
½ small red onion, sliced thin
8 ounces yellow wax beans, trimmed
   and halved on bias

8 ounces romano beans, trimmed
   and halved on bias
1 (15-ounce) can red kidney beans, rinsed
¼ cup minced fresh parsley

1. Whisk vinegar, oil, honey, garlic, ½ teaspoon salt, and ⅛ teaspoon pepper together in large bowl. Stir in onion and set aside.

2. Bring 4 quarts water to boil in large pot over high heat. Fill large bowl halfway with ice and water. Add wax beans, romano beans, and 1 tablespoon salt to boiling water and cook until crisp-tender, 3 to 5 minutes. Drain beans, then transfer immediately to ice water. Let beans cool completely, about 5 minutes, then drain again and pat dry with paper towels.

3. Add drained wax and romano beans, kidney beans, and parsley to vinaigrette and toss to coat. Season with salt and pepper to taste. Serve.

EXTRA-CRUNCHY GREEN BEAN CASSEROLE
Serves 6 to 8   Total time: 1 hour
WHY THIS RECIPE WORKS *The original "green bean casserole" was created by the Campbell Soup Company in 1955 to showcase one of its star products: canned cream of mushroom soup. The recipe also called for frozen green beans. For our modern remake of this beloved Thanksgiving favorite, naturally we wanted fresh green beans and mushrooms, along with the richness that comes from fresh heavy cream. We jump-started the cooking of the green beans in the microwave, which took just a few minutes. For the sauce, we browned the mushrooms to drive off moisture (to avoid a watery sauce) and develop deep flavor. And for the topping? Absolutely nothing we tried in our test kitchen got a better response with tasters than the traditional canned fried onions. However, adding some panko bread crumbs to the onions did give the topping even more crunch and saved us from having to bake the casserole further after topping it. You can substitute white mushrooms for the cremini, if desired.*

TOPPING
½ cup panko bread crumbs
1 tablespoon unsalted butter, melted
2½ cups canned fried onions

CASSEROLE
2 pounds green beans, trimmed and
   cut into 1-inch lengths
3 tablespoons unsalted butter
1 pound cremini mushrooms, trimmed
   and sliced thin
1 tablespoon minced fresh thyme
2 garlic cloves, minced
1½ teaspoons salt
½ teaspoon pepper
¼ cup all-purpose flour
1½ cups chicken broth
1½ cups heavy cream
½ cup dry white wine

1. For the topping Combine panko and melted butter in bowl. Microwave, stirring occasionally, until panko is golden brown, about 2 minutes. Let cool completely, then stir in fried onions; set aside.

2. For the casserole Adjust oven rack to middle position and heat oven to 400 degrees. Combine green beans and ½ cup water in large bowl. Cover and microwave until green beans are just tender, about 8 minutes, stirring halfway through microwaving. Drain green beans in colander; set aside.

3. Melt butter in 12-inch nonstick skillet over medium-high heat. Add mushrooms, thyme, garlic, salt, and pepper and cook until liquid is nearly evaporated, 6 to 8 minutes.

4. Stir in flour and cook for 1 minute. Slowly whisk in broth, cream, and wine and bring to boil, scraping up any browned bits and smoothing out any lumps. Cook, stirring occasionally, until sauce has thickened, 4 to 6 minutes. Transfer green beans to 13 by 9-inch baking dish. Pour sauce over green beans and toss to combine.

5. Bake until bubbling and green beans are completely tender, about 25 minutes. Remove from oven, top with fried-onion mixture, and let cool for 10 minutes. Serve.

Extra-Crunchy Green Bean Casserole

ONE-PAN PORK TENDERLOIN WITH GREEN BEANS AND POTATOES

Serves 4   Total time: 50 minutes

WHY THIS RECIPE WORKS *Pairing green beans and potatoes with quick-cooking pork tenderloin makes a hearty meat-and-veg dinner that's quick enough for any night. We started with a base of green beans and halved fingerling potatoes on a rimmed baking sheet and then perched two tenderloins right on top of the vegetables. Keeping the tenderloins up off the metal pan helped protect the lean meat from drying out while at the same time the vegetables developed great browning. Brushing a layer of salty-sweet-spicy hoisin sauce over the meat before roasting gave it a complex flavor boost and an appealing caramelized layer. After just 20 minutes of roasting, we took the tenderloins out to rest and gave the vegetables a little extra time in the oven to pick up more color. An easy garlic-chive butter, melted over the resting pork and tossed with the vegetables, made for a rich, flavorful finish. To ensure that the tenderloins don't curl during cooking, remove the silverskin. A rasp-style grater makes quick work of turning the garlic into a paste.*

- 4 tablespoons unsalted butter, softened
- 2 tablespoons minced fresh chives
- 1 garlic clove, minced to paste
  Salt and pepper
- 1 pound green beans, trimmed
- 3 tablespoons extra-virgin olive oil
- 1½ pounds fingerling potatoes, unpeeled, halved lengthwise
- 2 (12- to 16-ounce) pork tenderloins, trimmed
- ¼ cup hoisin sauce

1. Adjust oven rack to lower-middle position and heat oven to 450 degrees. Combine butter, chives, garlic, ¼ teaspoon salt, and ¼ teaspoon pepper in bowl; set aside.

2. Toss green beans with 1 tablespoon oil, ¼ teaspoon salt, and ¼ teaspoon pepper in separate bowl. Arrange beans crosswise down center of rimmed baking sheet, leaving room on both sides for potatoes. Toss potatoes with remaining 2 tablespoons oil, ¼ teaspoon salt, and ¼ teaspoon pepper in now-empty bowl. Place potatoes, cut side down, on either side of green beans.

3. Pat tenderloins dry with paper towels, season with salt and pepper, and brush thoroughly with hoisin. Lay tenderloins lengthwise, without touching, on top of green beans. Roast until pork registers 145 degrees, 20 to 25 minutes.

4. Remove sheet from oven and transfer tenderloins to carving board. Dot each tenderloin with 1 tablespoon chive butter and let rest while vegetables finish cooking. Gently stir vegetables on sheet to combine and continue to roast until tender and golden, 5 to 10 minutes.

5. Remove sheet from oven, add remaining 2 tablespoons butter to vegetables, and toss to coat. Slice pork ½ inch thick and serve with vegetables.

~

STIR-FRIED SICHUAN GREEN BEANS

Serves 4   Total time: 30 minutes

WHY THIS RECIPE WORKS *The flavors of Sichuan green beans are addictive: wrinkled, sweet beans tossed with morsels of flavorful pork and coated in a pungent sauce. The dish is spicy, aromatic, and tangy all at the same time. In Chinese restaurants, the beans are usually deep-fried in a wok filled with oil, which produces their wrinkled appearance, slightly chewy texture, and intense flavor. To make this at home, we opted instead to stir-fry the beans until the skins began to shrivel. The time spent in the pan produced spotty charring, which resulted in a nice chewy texture and a deeper flavor that more than compensated for their not being deep-fried. For the sauce, to achieve the desired characteristic tanginess and modest heat, we used dry mustard and sherry for their subtle tang and red pepper flakes and white pepper for their aromatic warmth and complex muskiness. The ground pork, already stir-fried with lots of garlic and ginger, absorbed the sauce perfectly, adding meaty richness. Some chopped scallions and a drizzle of sesame oil were the perfect finishing touches.*

- 2 tablespoons soy sauce
- 2 tablespoons water
- 1 tablespoon dry sherry
- 1 teaspoon sugar
- ½ teaspoon cornstarch
- ¼ teaspoon white pepper
- ¼ teaspoon red pepper flakes
- ¼ teaspoon dry mustard
- 2 tablespoons vegetable oil
- 1 pound green beans, trimmed and cut into 2-inch lengths
- 4 ounces ground pork
- 3 garlic cloves, minced
- 1 tablespoon grated fresh ginger
- 3 scallions, white and light green parts only, sliced thin
- 1 teaspoon toasted sesame oil

1. Whisk soy sauce, water, sherry, sugar, cornstarch, pepper, pepper flakes, and mustard in small bowl until sugar dissolves.

2. Heat vegetable oil in 12-inch nonstick skillet over high heat until just smoking. Add green beans and cook, stirring frequently, until crisp-tender and skins are shriveled and blackened in spots, 5 to 8 minutes (reduce heat to medium-high if green beans begin to darken too quickly). Transfer green beans to large plate and cover loosely with aluminum foil to keep warm.

3. Reduce heat to medium-high and add pork to now-empty skillet. Cook, breaking pork into small pieces with wooden spoon, until no longer pink, about 2 minutes. Push pork to sides of skillet. Add garlic and ginger to center and cook, mashing mixture into skillet, until fragrant, 30 seconds. Stir mixture into pork; transfer to platter.

4. Whisk sauce to recombine, then add to again-empty skillet. Cook over high heat until sauce is thickened and reduced slightly, about 15 seconds. Return green beans and pork to skillet and gently toss to coat with sauce. Off heat, stir in scallions and sesame oil. Serve immediately.

STIR-FRIED SHRIMP AND LONG BEANS

Serves 4   Total time: 40 minutes

WHY THIS RECIPE WORKS *Chinese long beans make a dramatic and exotic presentation alongside sweet pink shrimp in this light stir-fry. Traditional Chinese recipes for these serpentine beans employ a double-cooking technique of deep frying followed by stir-frying, which renders them tender and juicy. We wanted to nod toward this tradition, but without the hassle of deep frying. Since long beans can be a couple of feet in length, cooking them by any method wasn't without challenges. Fitting the beans into the typical home cook's 12-inch skillet was our first hurdle. We decided to cut them in half—however, they were still very long beans. Microwaving the beans jump-started the cooking process and also made them more pliable for getting them into the skillet. Stir-frying the beans in batches allowed for the desired charring and blistering. We then cooked the shrimp with fresh ginger and garlic and built the finishing sauce with chicken broth, oyster sauce, sherry, sesame oil, and rice vinegar. The savory sauce thickened to just the right consistency to lightly glaze the shrimp and beans.*

¾ cup chicken broth
3 tablespoons oyster sauce
2 tablespoons dry sherry
1 tablespoon toasted sesame oil
1 tablespoon rice vinegar
1½ teaspoons cornstarch
¼ teaspoon white pepper
¼ cup vegetable oil
1½ tablespoons grated fresh ginger
2 garlic cloves, minced
1½ pounds long beans, trimmed and halved
1 pound large shrimp (26 to 30 per pound), peeled, deveined, and tails removed

1. Whisk broth, oyster sauce, sherry, sesame oil, vinegar, cornstarch and white pepper together in bowl. Combine 1 tablespoon vegetable oil, ginger, and garlic in small bowl; set aside.

2. Combine long beans and ¼ cup water in large bowl. Cover and microwave until beans are pliable, 7 to 9 minutes, stirring halfway through microwaving. Drain beans, transfer to paper towel–lined plate, and pat dry.

3. Heat 1 tablespoon vegetable oil in 12-inch nonstick skillet over high heat until just smoking. Add half of long beans in single layer and cook, without stirring, until beans begin to blister and char, about 3 minutes. Stir and continue to cook, stirring occasionally, until beans are just softened and well charred, about 3 minutes. Transfer beans to serving platter and cover loosely with aluminum foil to keep warm. Repeat with 1 tablespoon vegetable oil and remaining beans; transfer to platter.

4. Heat remaining 1 tablespoon vegetable oil in now-empty skillet over high heat until just smoking. Add shrimp in single layer and cook, without stirring, until shrimp turn opaque and brown around edges, about 1 minute. Push shrimp to sides of skillet. Add ginger-garlic mixture to center and cook, mashing mixture into skillet, until fragrant, about 30 seconds. Stir mixture into shrimp; transfer to platter.

5. Whisk broth mixture to recombine, then add to again-empty skillet. Cook over high heat, stirring occasionally, until sauce is thickened and reduced slightly, about 1 minute. Return beans and shrimp to skillet and gently toss to coat with sauce. Serve.

HEARTY GREENS

Hearty greens, also called winter greens, are sturdy green-leaved vegetables, related to cabbage, that are at their best in the colder months. What's included in this category could be open to some debate, but here we've focused on kale (both curly and Lacinato), collard greens, and mustard greens. While escarole can be considered a winter green, we've included it in the chicory chapter—and we've devoted an entire chapter to Swiss chard.

COLLARDS are a staple of Southern cooking, and many Southern cooks insist that the only proper preparation involves long, slow cooking and plenty of cured pork. Thanks to their earthy, naturally slightly smoky flavor, they're swooningly good cooked this way, as in the Southern Braised Collard Greens. But they're also delicious cooked quickly, with simple flavors, as in our Quick Collard Greens.

KALE'S wild popularity, which exploded in the first decade of this century, shows no sign of subsiding. People even wear "Eat More Kale" T-shirts, and farmers are having trouble keeping up with demand. Not bad for a vegetable that was considered a useless garnish not so long ago. Ruffled dark green kale has a pleasant rich cabbagey flavor that's never bitter or spicy. Its underlying sweetness comes to the forefront when cooked. We show you how to braise it quickly, and also slowly, and turn it into three different kinds of kale chips, and how to massage raw leaves for our superfood-packed Kale Salad with Sweet Potatoes and Pomegranate Vinaigrette.

Aptly named **MUSTARD GREENS** bring the spice to this trio, and really do taste a bit reminiscent of prepared mustard. We especially love them with Asian flavors, as in the Udon Noodles with Mustard Greens and Shiitake-Ginger Sauce.

shopping and storage

Fall and winter are the traditional seasons for hearty, cold-resistant greens, although they are often available in supermarkets year-round. Darker-colored greens like collards and kale should have rich, deep green color and very firm, stiff leaves. Mustard greens should be a brilliant lighter green, with crisp leaves. Across the board, the leaves should not have any yellowing, browning, or wilting. If you have a choice, purchase bunches with thinner rather than thicker stems; the leaves will be more tender. To store any hearty green, wrap in paper towels inside an open plastic produce bag in the refrigerator for several days.

hearty greens by any other name

COLLARD GREENS Collard greens have large, broad, flat, very stiff leaves—almost like fans—with firm veins running through them. They have a mild flavor and taste and feel a bit like cabbage, which won't be surprising once you know that this green is technically a cabbage.

CURLY KALE Curly kale (also called green kale) has broad, dark green, wonderfully curly and frilly leaves. It has an earthy, grassy flavor that takes on nutty notes when cooked. It's a true powerhouse of vitamin A, with double the amount typically found in other leafy greens.

LACINATO KALE Lacinato kale (also called Tuscan kale, dinosaur kale, or black kale) has long, slender, very dark green leaves. It has a sweet, mineral-y flavor and a tender texture when eaten raw, and it becomes robust and rich when braised.

MUSTARD GREENS "Mustard greens" actually encompasses several varieties. Most commonly you'll see narrow, bright green frilly leaves with a leafier, less leathery texture than other hearty greens. Mustard greens can also have a purplish tinge, and the leaves can also be flat. They're peppery and pleasantly sharp-hot in flavor.

vegetable prep

Preparing Hearty Greens For Cooking

Hearty greens have very tough stems that need to be cut away from the leaves and discarded before using the leaves in a recipe.

1. Cut away leafy portion from either side of stalk or stem using chef's knife.

2. Stack several leaves and cut according to recipe directions, whether halved, sliced crosswise, or otherwise cut into pieces.

3. Place leaves in large bowl and cover with water. Swish with your hand to remove grit. Repeat with fresh water, as needed, until grit no longer appears in bottom of bowl. Dry cut leaves using salad spinner.

QUICK COLLARD GREENS

Serves 4 to 6   Total time: 35 minutes

WHY THIS RECIPE WORKS *Our quick blanch-and-sauté recipe for tough collard greens will give you the same tender results as long braising. Stemming the greens was a necessary first step, and blanching the leaves in salt water tenderized them quickly and neutralized their bitter qualities. To remove excess water left from blanching, we used a spatula to press on the drained greens, and then rolled them up in a dish towel to dry them further. We chopped the compressed collards into thin slices perfect for quickly sautéing with pungent, aromatic garlic and spicy red pepper flakes, which provided immediate potent seasoning. You can substitute mustard or turnip greens for the collards; reduce their boiling time to 2 minutes.*

    Salt and pepper
2½ pounds collard greens, stemmed and halved lengthwise
  3 tablespoons extra-virgin olive oil
  2 garlic cloves, minced
  ¼ teaspoon red pepper flakes

1. Bring 4 quarts water to boil in large pot over high heat. Stir in 1 tablespoon salt, then add collard greens, 1 handful at a time. Cook until tender, 4 to 5 minutes. Drain and rinse with cold water until greens are cool, about 1 minute. Press greens with rubber spatula to release excess liquid. Place greens on dish towel and compress into 10-inch log. Roll up towel tightly, then remove greens from towel. Cut greens crosswise into ¼-inch slices.

2. Heat oil in 12-inch nonstick skillet over medium-high heat until just smoking. Scatter greens in skillet and cook, stirring frequently, until just beginning to brown, 3 to 4 minutes. Stir in garlic and pepper flakes and cook until greens are spotty brown, 1 to 2 minutes. Season with salt and pepper to taste, and serve.

COLLARD GREENS WITH RAISINS AND ALMONDS

Serves 4 to 6   Total time: 30 minutes

WHY THIS RECIPE WORKS *For a fresh take on collard greens and a different spin on the preceding Quick Collard Greens, we decided to steam and then sauté them. Cutting the greens into 2-inch pieces helped them soften quickly but left greater texture than thinner slices, while draining and pressing the excess water from the steamed collards kept them from getting waterlogged. A generous dose of extra-virgin olive oil for sautéing the collards, along with sweet raisins, delicate shallots, toasted almonds, and umami-rich grated Parmesan, elevated these humble collards into an elegant side. You can substitute kale for the collards. Leave the collards slightly wet after washing; the moisture helps them to steam properly in step 1.*

  2 pounds collard greens, stemmed and cut into 2-inch pieces
    Salt and pepper
  6 tablespoons extra-virgin olive oil
  ½ cup golden raisins
  2 shallots, sliced thin
  4 garlic cloves, sliced thin
  ⅛ teaspoon red pepper flakes
  ¼ cup grated Parmesan cheese, plus extra for serving
  ¼ cup sliced almonds, toasted
    Lemon wedges for serving

1. Add collard greens, 1 teaspoon salt, and ½ teaspoon pepper to Dutch oven. Cover and cook over medium-high heat until tender, 14 to 17 minutes, stirring occasionally. (If pot becomes dry, add ¼ cup water so collards continue to steam.) Drain greens in colander, pressing with rubber spatula to release excess liquid. Wipe pot clean with paper towels.

2. Heat ¼ cup oil in now-empty pot over medium heat until shimmering. Add raisins, shallots, garlic, and pepper flakes and cook until just beginning to brown, 2 to 4 minutes. Add greens, ½ teaspoon salt, and ¼ teaspoon pepper and cook until heated through, about 3 minutes. Off heat, stir in Parmesan and season with salt and pepper to taste.

3. Transfer greens to serving platter. Drizzle with remaining 2 tablespoons oil and sprinkle with almonds. Serve with lemon wedges and extra Parmesan.

SOUTHERN BRAISED COLLARD GREENS

Serves 4 to 6   Total time: 1 hour 30 minutes

WHY THIS RECIPE WORKS *Long braising with smoky cured pork is the Southern method for preparing collards. And it's definitely true that slowly cooking these greens in a sweet, smoky broth goes a long way toward tempering their assertive bitterness and adding rich, savory flavors. Cooking the greens in a Dutch oven in the oven rather than on the stovetop made it easy to maintain a constant temperature, resulting in tender but not mushy collards, and it also made this dish relatively hands-off. The leftover cooking liquid, traditionally called pot "liquor" (or "likker"), can be sopped up with cornbread or biscuits, or used to cook a second batch of collard greens, as is traditionally done in the South. Serve with hot sauce or vinegar, if desired.*

  4 slices bacon, chopped
  1 onion, chopped fine
    Salt and pepper
  3 garlic cloves, minced
  6 cups chicken broth
  2 pounds collard greens, stemmed and cut into 2-inch pieces

1. Adjust oven rack to lower-middle position and heat oven to 350 degrees. Cook bacon in Dutch oven over medium heat until fat begins to render, about 2 minutes. Stir in onion and ¼ teaspoon salt and cook until softened, about 5 minutes. Stir in garlic and cook until fragrant, about 30 seconds. Stir in broth and bring to simmer.

2. Stir in collard greens, 1 handful at a time, and cook until beginning to wilt, about 5 minutes. Cover, transfer pot to oven, and cook until greens are tender and broth is flavorful, about 45 minutes, stirring halfway through cooking. Remove pot from oven and season with salt and pepper to taste. Serve.

Southern Braised Collard Greens

BLACK-EYED PEAS AND COLLARD GREENS

Serves 6 to 8   Total time: 1 hour

WHY THIS RECIPE WORKS *Southern tradition holds that if, on New Year's Day, you eat a plate of collards and black-eyed peas all stewed up with tomatoes, spices, and a hambone, you will experience greater wealth and prosperity in the coming year. To get a jump on acquiring said prosperity, we decided to speed up this one-pot dish a little bit. We swapped the more time-consuming dried legumes for a couple of convenient cans of black-eyed peas, and gave the collards a 15-minute head start on the stove before adding the peas. We also relied on smoky bacon and savory chicken broth to quickly build a meaty backbone of flavor. For maximum good luck, be careful not to crush those black-eyed peas—stir them gently.*

    6 slices bacon, cut into ½-inch pieces
    1 onion, halved and sliced thin
1¼ teaspoons salt
    4 garlic cloves, minced
    ½ teaspoon ground cumin
    ½ teaspoon pepper
    ¼ teaspoon red pepper flakes
1½ cups chicken broth
    1 (14.5-ounce) can diced tomatoes
    1 pound collard greens, stemmed and cut into 2-inch pieces
    2 (15-ounce) cans black-eyed peas, rinsed
    1 tablespoon cider vinegar
    1 teaspoon sugar

1. Cook bacon in Dutch oven over medium heat until crisp, 5 to 7 minutes. Using slotted spoon, transfer bacon to paper towel–lined plate; set aside.

2. Pour off all but 2 tablespoons fat from pot. Add onion and salt and cook over medium heat, stirring frequently, until golden brown, about 10 minutes. Stir in garlic, cumin, pepper, and pepper flakes and cook until fragrant, about 30 seconds.

3. Stir in broth and tomatoes and their juice and bring to boil. Add collard greens, cover, and reduce heat to medium-low. Simmer until greens are tender, about 15 minutes.

4. Add black-eyed peas and cook, covered, stirring occasionally, until greens are silky and completely tender, about 15 minutes. Uncover, increase heat to medium-high, and cook until liquid is reduced by one-quarter, about 5 minutes. Stir in vinegar, sugar, and reserved bacon. Serve.

GARLICKY BRAISED KALE

Serves 4 to 6   Total time: 55 minutes

WHY THIS RECIPE WORKS *This straightforward one-pot approach turns kale tender without taking hours or leaving it awash in excess liquid, but this technique will work equally well with any of the sturdy winter greens, such as collards or mustard greens. Adding the greens one handful at a time to the seasoned cooking liquid and letting them wilt briefly before adding more allowed us to fit the large volume of leaves into the pot more easily. When the kale had almost the finished tender texture we wanted, we removed the lid to allow the liquid to cook off. Garlic, lemon, and red pepper is a classic flavor combo, but this cooking method lends itself nicely to different flavors, as in the two variations that follow.*

    3 tablespoons extra-virgin olive oil
    1 onion, chopped fine
    5 garlic cloves, minced
    ⅛ teaspoon red pepper flakes
    1 cup chicken broth
    1 cup water
       Salt and pepper
    2 pounds kale, stemmed and cut into 2-inch pieces
    2 teaspoons lemon juice, plus extra for seasoning

1. Heat 2 tablespoons oil in Dutch oven over medium heat until shimmering. Add onion and cook until softened and lightly browned, 5 to 7 minutes. Stir in garlic and pepper flakes and cook until fragrant, about 30 seconds. Stir in broth, water, and ¼ teaspoon salt and bring to simmer.

2. Stir in kale, 1 handful at a time, and cook until beginning to wilt, about 5 minutes. Cover, reduce heat to medium-low, and simmer, stirring occasionally, until kale is tender, 25 to 35 minutes.

3. Uncover and increase heat to medium-high. Cook, stirring occasionally, until most of liquid has evaporated (bottom of pot will be almost dry and kale will begin to sizzle), 8 to 12 minutes. Off heat, stir in lemon juice and remaining 1 tablespoon oil. Season with salt, pepper, and extra lemon juice to taste. Serve.

VARIATIONS

Garlicky Braised Kale with Bacon and Onion
Cook 6 slices bacon, cut into ¼-inch pieces, over medium heat until crisp, 5 to 7 minutes. Using slotted spoon, transfer bacon to paper towel–lined plate, then pour off all but 2 tablespoons fat. Substitute rendered fat for 2 tablespoons oil; 1 red onion, halved and sliced thin, for chopped onion; and cider vinegar for lemon juice. Stir reserved bacon into kale before serving.

Garlicky Braised Kale with Coconut and Curry
Substitute 2 teaspoons grated fresh ginger and 1 teaspoon curry powder for red pepper flakes and 1 (14-ounce) can coconut milk for water. Substitute lime juice for lemon juice and sprinkle kale with ⅓ cup toasted chopped cashews before serving.

SLOW-COOKER BRAISED KALE WITH GARLIC AND CHORIZO

Serves 4 to 6   Total time: 7 to 8 hours on low or 4 to 5 hours on high

WHY THIS RECIPE WORKS *A long cooking time helps to turn kale and other hearty greens meltingly tender, gentling their strong flavors, so taking advantage of the slow cooker seemed like a no-brainer. Spanish-style chorizo (the cured, smoked type of chorizo) and garlic brought a meaty, spicy kick to these simple greens and ensured things didn't get too toned down, though. This would be delicious served as a bed for over-easy eggs, and it could also be served over rice for a light main course. You will need a 5- to 7-quart slow cooker for this recipe.*

8 ounces Spanish-style chorizo sausage, halved lengthwise and sliced ½ inch thick
1 tablespoon extra-virgin olive oil
2 garlic cloves, minced
1½ cups chicken broth
  Salt and pepper
2 pounds kale, stemmed and cut into 2-inch pieces

1. Lightly coat slow cooker with vegetable oil spray. Microwave chorizo, oil, and garlic in bowl, stirring occasionally, until fragrant, about 1 minute. Transfer to prepared slow cooker. Stir in broth and ¼ teaspoon salt.

2. Microwave half of kale in covered bowl until slightly wilted, about 5 minutes, and transfer to slow cooker. Stir in remaining kale, cover, and cook until kale is tender, 7 to 8 hours on low or 4 to 5 hours on high. Season with salt and pepper to taste. Serve.

KALE CHIPS

Serves 4   Total time: 1 hour

WHY THIS RECIPE WORKS *Kale chips were originally conceived as a nutritious alternative to potato chips. But the store-bought versions that came on the scene to take advantage of the kale chip craze are often deep-fried and loaded with salt. We wanted a light-as-air, earthy kale chip that would remain crispy from cooking right through consumption. We discovered three keys to getting them to the perfect texture. First, we started with completely dry leaves, blotted between dish towels to make sure no water was left clinging. Next, we baked the kale on wire racks to allow the oven air to circulate above and beneath the leaves. Finally, we lengthened the cooking time and lowered the oven temperature to mimic the drying effects of a food dehydrator. Tossed with olive oil and seasoned lightly with crunchy kosher salt, these ultracrisp kale chips were a super-satisfying snack. We prefer to use Lacinato kale in this recipe, but curly leaf kale can be substituted; chips made with curly leaf kale will taste a bit chewy at the edges and won't keep as well. We prefer the larger crystal size of kosher salt here; if using table salt, reduce the amount by half.*

12 ounces Lacinato kale, stemmed and torn into 3-inch pieces
1 tablespoon extra-virgin olive oil
½ teaspoon kosher salt

1. Adjust oven racks to upper-middle and lower-middle positions and heat oven to 200 degrees. Set wire racks in 2 rimmed baking sheets. Dry kale thoroughly between dish towels, transfer to large bowl, and toss with oil and salt.

2. Arrange kale on prepared racks, making sure leaves overlap as little as possible. Bake kale until very crisp, 45 minutes to 1 hour, switching and rotating sheets halfway through baking. Let kale chips cool completely before serving. (Kale chips can be stored in paper towel–lined airtight container for up to 1 day.)

VARIATIONS

Ranch-Style Kale Chips
Combine 2 teaspoons dried dill, 1 teaspoon garlic powder, and 1 teaspoon onion powder with salt before sprinkling over kale.

Spicy Sesame-Ginger Kale Chips
Substitute 1 tablespoon sesame oil for olive oil. Combine 2 teaspoons toasted sesame seeds, 1 teaspoon ground ginger, and ¼ teaspoon cayenne pepper with salt before sprinkling over kale.

KALE SALAD WITH SWEET POTATOES AND POMEGRANATE VINAIGRETTE

Serves 4   Total time: 1 hour

WHY THIS RECIPE WORKS *We love the earthy vegetal flavor of raw kale, but its chewy texture can be a little tough to take. Many recipes call for tossing it with dressing and letting it marinate in the fridge overnight to tenderize. But this method didn't deliver the tender leaves we were after. Luckily, we found another technique that worked better: massage. Squeezing and massaging the kale leaves broke down their cell walls in much the same way that heat would, darkening the leaves and turning them silky. Roasted sweet potatoes, shredded radicchio, crunchy pecans, a sprinkling of Parmesan cheese, and a sweet*

KALE SALAD WITH SWEET POTATOES AND POMEGRANATE VINAIGRETTE

Kale is quickly becoming the number-one salad green of choice—if it isn't already there. But raw kale, even when mixed into a salad with other ingredients, can take a lot of jaw power to chew through. Letting it marinate overnight in dressing is neither convenient nor effective. We discovered that a vigorous massage softens the strips of kale leaves nicely; it has a similar effect on breaking down the cell walls as the heat of cooking does, rendering the sturdy, chewy leaves softer and silkier in no time.

1. Roast the sweet potato pieces on a rimmed baking sheet until the bottom edges are browned on both sides. While they cool for 20 minutes, prep the kale.

2. Slice the stemmed kale leaves into ½-inch-wide strips.

3. Using your (clean) hands, vigorously squeeze and massage the kale strips until the leaves are uniformly darker in color and slightly wilted, about 1 minute. They should end up looking almost like they were cooked.

4. Whisk together the ingredients for the sweet-tart pomegranate vinaigrette in the bottom of a large bowl.

5. Add the roasted potatoes, massaged kale, and sliced radicchio to the bowl with the vinaigrette and toss gently to combine everything.

6. Sprinkle the salad with the chopped pecans and shaved Parmesan, and serve.

pomegranate vinaigrette turned our salad into a meal with a medley of flavors and textures. Pomegranate molasses can be found in the international aisle of large supermarkets; if you can't find it, substitute 2 tablespoons of lemon juice, 2 teaspoons of mild molasses, and 1 teaspoon of honey. We prefer to use Lacinato kale in this recipe, but curly-leaf kale can be substituted; if using curly-leaf kale, increase the massaging time to 5 minutes. Do not use baby kale.

SALAD

1½ pounds sweet potatoes, peeled, quartered lengthwise, and cut crosswise into ½-inch pieces
1 tablespoon extra-virgin olive oil
   Salt and pepper
12 ounces Lacinato kale, stemmed and sliced crosswise into ½-inch-wide strips
½ head radicchio (5 ounces), cored and sliced thin
½ cup pecans, toasted and chopped
   Shaved Parmesan cheese

VINAIGRETTE

2 tablespoons water
1½ tablespoons pomegranate molasses
1 small shallot, minced
1 tablespoon honey
1 tablespoon cider vinegar
¼ teaspoon salt
¼ teaspoon pepper
⅓ cup extra-virgin olive oil

1. For the salad Adjust oven rack to middle position and heat oven to 400 degrees. Toss sweet potatoes with oil and season with salt and pepper. Lay potatoes in single layer on rimmed baking sheet and roast until bottom edges are browned on both sides, 25 to 30 minutes, flipping potatoes halfway through roasting time. Transfer potatoes to plate and let cool for 20 minutes.

2. Meanwhile, vigorously squeeze and massage kale with your clean hands until leaves are uniformly darkened and slightly wilted, about 1 minute.

3. For the vinaigrette Whisk water, pomegranate molasses, shallot, honey, vinegar, salt, and pepper together in large bowl. Whisking constantly, drizzle in oil.

4. Add roasted potatoes, kale, and radicchio to vinaigrette and toss gently to coat. Sprinkle with pecans and shaved Parmesan to taste. Serve.

EASY CHICKPEA AND KALE SOUP

Serves 4   Total time: 45 minutes

WHY THIS RECIPE WORKS *Many cuisines have an iteration of kale soup, from the famous Portuguese kale and linguica soup to Italian versions made with white beans and sausage. We took our inspiration from those, with Mediterranean flavors, but left out the sausage component. Sautéing onion and fennel built a strong foundation of flavor, which we enhanced with garlic and red pepper flakes. Once the soup base was ready, we added convenient canned chickpeas along with chopped kale. After just 15 minutes of simmering, the kale was tender and the rich flavors had all melded together into a satisfyingly hearty and warming soup.*

2 tablespoons extra-virgin olive oil
1 onion, chopped
1 fennel bulb, stalks discarded, bulb halved, cored, and chopped
   Salt and pepper
3 garlic cloves, minced
¼ teaspoon red pepper flakes
4 cups chicken broth
1 (15-ounce) can chickpeas, rinsed
6 ounces kale, stemmed and chopped
   Grated Pecorino Romano cheese

1. Heat oil in Dutch oven over medium-high heat until shimmering. Add onion, fennel, ½ teaspoon salt, and ½ teaspoon pepper and cook until vegetables have softened and are starting to brown, about 8 minutes. Stir in garlic and pepper flakes and cook until fragrant, about 30 seconds.

2. Stir in broth, chickpeas, and kale and bring to simmer. Cover, reduce heat to medium-low, and cook until kale is tender, about 15 minutes. Season with salt and pepper to taste. Serve, passing Pecorino separately.

CALDO VERDE

Serves 6 to 8   Total time: 1 hour

WHY THIS RECIPE WORKS *Everything about caldo verde, the classic Portuguese soup of smoky sausage, potatoes, and sturdy greens, is hearty and satisfying. Its intentionally thin broth is usually made with just water, but for our version we wanted something with a little more body. We used chicken broth for deeper flavor, and also realized that we could nicely thicken the broth by pureeing some of the softened potatoes with a few tablespoons of olive oil. Using plenty of potatoes and garlicky chorizo turned this simple soup into a filling meal; we chose Yukon Golds because they held their shape better than russets. We prefer collard greens here for their delicate sweetness and meatier bite, but kale can be substituted. Serve this soup with hearty bread and a final drizzle of extra-virgin olive oil.*

¼ cup extra-virgin olive oil
12 ounces Spanish-style chorizo sausage, cut into ½-inch pieces
1 onion, chopped fine
4 garlic cloves, minced
   Salt and pepper
¼ teaspoon red pepper flakes
2 pounds Yukon Gold potatoes, peeled and cut into ¾-inch pieces
4 cups chicken broth
4 cups water
1 pound collard greens, stemmed and cut into 1-inch pieces
2 teaspoons white wine vinegar

1. Heat 1 tablespoon oil in Dutch oven over medium-high heat until shimmering. Add chorizo and cook, stirring occasionally, until lightly browned, 4 to 5 minutes. Using slotted spoon, transfer chorizo to bowl; set aside.

2. Add onion, garlic, 1¼ teaspoons salt, and pepper flakes to fat left in pot and cook over medium heat, stirring frequently, until onion is softened, about 5 minutes. Stir in potatoes, broth, and water, bring to simmer, and cook until potatoes are just tender, 8 to 10 minutes.

3. Transfer ¾ cup solids and ¾ cup broth to blender. Stir collard greens into pot, return to simmer, and cook for 10 minutes. Stir in chorizo and cook until greens are tender, 8 to 10 minutes.

4. Add remaining 3 tablespoons oil to soup in blender and process until smooth, about 1 minute. Off heat, stir pureed soup mixture and vinegar into soup. Season with salt and pepper to taste. Serve.

UDON NOODLES WITH MUSTARD GREENS AND SHIITAKE-GINGER SAUCE

Serves 4 to 6   Total time: 35 minutes

WHY THIS RECIPE WORKS *The spicy flavor of mustard greens lends itself to Asian flavor combinations, and since noodles and greens are a common pairing in Asia, we decided to create a recipe that married the pungent bite of mustard greens with earthy, chewy udon noodles. We made a quick but highly aromatic and boldly flavorful broth using both fresh and dried shiitake mushrooms, along with mirin, rice vinegar, soy sauce, garlic, fresh ginger, and chili-garlic sauce. Letting this mixture reduce resulted in a brothy sauce perfect for pairing with the cooked noodles and greens. Because fresh noodles cook so quickly, we made sure to add the greens to the pot before the noodles. Do not substitute other types of noodles for the udon noodles here.*

    1 tablespoon vegetable oil
    8 ounces shiitake mushrooms, stemmed
       and sliced thin
    ¼ cup mirin
    3 tablespoons rice vinegar
    3 tablespoons soy sauce
    2 garlic cloves, smashed and peeled
    1 (1-inch) piece ginger, peeled, halved,
       and smashed
    ½ ounce dried shiitake mushrooms,
       rinsed and minced
    1 teaspoon toasted sesame oil
    1 teaspoon Asian chili-garlic sauce
    1 pound mustard greens, stemmed and
       cut into 2-inch pieces
       Salt and pepper
    1 pound fresh udon noodles

1. Heat vegetable oil in Dutch oven over medium-high heat until shimmering. Add fresh mushrooms and cook, stirring occasionally, until softened and lightly browned, about 5 minutes. Stir in 2 cups water, mirin, vinegar, soy sauce, garlic, ginger, dried mushrooms, sesame oil, and chili-garlic sauce. Bring to simmer and cook until liquid has reduced by half, 8 to 10 minutes. Off heat, discard garlic and ginger. Cover pot to keep warm; set aside.

2. Meanwhile, bring 4 quarts water to boil in large pot. Add mustard greens and 1 tablespoon salt and cook until almost tender, 4 to 5 minutes. Add noodles and cook until greens and noodles are both tender, about 2 minutes. Reserve ⅓ cup cooking water, drain noodles and greens, and return them to pot. Add sauce and reserved cooking water, and toss to combine. Cook over medium-low heat, tossing constantly, until sauce clings to noodles, about 1 minute. Season with salt and pepper to taste. Serve.

SALMON TACOS WITH COLLARD SLAW

Serves 6   Total time: 35 minutes

WHY THIS RECIPE WORKS *It seems like seafood tacos these days can include practically any kind of fish, prepared in any number of ways, whereas the slaw and creamy sauce are still typically made using cabbage and sour cream. We wanted a slaw with more texture and flavor oomph to stand up to our rich spice-rubbed salmon— and collard greens were just the ticket. Thinly sliced, they required no cooking. Combined with crunchy radishes, cooling jícama, red onion, cilantro, and lime, they perfectly complemented the fish. For a bright crema, we pureed avocado with lime juice, yogurt, and cilantro. It all added up to a flavor-supercharged take on fish tacos. To ensure uniform pieces of fish that cooked at the same rate and didn't fall apart, we found it best to buy a whole skin-on center-cut fillet and cut it into four pieces ourselves.*

AVOCADO CREMA
    ½ avocado, pitted and chopped
    ¼ cup chopped fresh cilantro
    3 tablespoons water

    1 tablespoon lime juice
    1 tablespoon plain low-fat yogurt
       Salt and pepper

TACOS
    ¼ teaspoon grated lime zest plus
       2 tablespoons juice
       Salt and pepper
    4 ounces collard greens, stemmed and
       sliced very thin (2 cups)
    4 ounces jícama, peeled and cut into
       2-inch-long matchsticks
    4 radishes, trimmed and cut into
       1-inch-long matchsticks
    ½ small red onion, halved and sliced thin
    ¼ cup fresh cilantro leaves
    1½ teaspoons chili powder
    1 (2-pound) skin-on salmon fillet,
       1 inch thick
    1 tablespoon canola oil
    12 (6-inch) corn tortillas, warmed
       Hot sauce

1. For the avocado crema Process all ingredients in food processor until completely smooth, about 1 minute, scraping down sides of bowl as needed. Season with salt and pepper to taste. Transfer crema to bowl and refrigerate until ready to serve.

2. For the tacos Whisk lime zest and juice and ¼ teaspoon salt together in large bowl. Add collard greens, jícama, radishes, onion, and cilantro and toss to combine; set aside.

3. Combine chili powder, ¾ teaspoon salt, and ¼ teaspoon pepper in small bowl. Cut salmon crosswise into 4 fillets. Pat salmon dry with paper towels and sprinkle evenly with spice mixture. Heat oil in 12-inch nonstick skillet over medium-high heat until shimmering. Cook salmon skin side up until well browned, 3 to 5 minutes. Flip and continue to cook until salmon is still translucent when checked with tip of paring knife and registers 120 to 125 degrees (for medium-rare), 3 to 5 minutes. Transfer salmon to plate and let cool slightly, about 2 minutes. Using 2 forks, flake fish into 2-inch pieces; discard skin.

4. Divide fish, collard slaw, and avocado crema evenly among tortillas, and drizzle with hot sauce to taste. Serve.

SAUSAGE AND WHITE BEANS WITH MUSTARD GREENS

Serves 4 to 6   Total time: 1 hour 15 minutes

WHY THIS RECIPE WORKS *Hearty, sturdy greens are great to use in stewy dishes, since they become tender while holding their texture. Our inspiration for this stick-to-your-ribs Dutch oven dish came from the south of France, where rich stews that combine meaty sausage, creamy white beans, and hearty greens are signature country-style offerings. Since the authentic garlic sausage used there was difficult to find, we subbed flavorful Italian sausage instead—use hot or sweet, depending on your preference. The clean, peppery spice of mustard greens was a great counterpoint to the unctuous sausage and the creaminess of the white beans. Using canned cannellini beans was untraditional, but it brought greater ease of preparation without sacrificing any flavor. To finish, a sprinkle of cheesy bread crumbs and parsley added crunch and freshness. You can substitute kale for the mustard greens.*

PARMESAN BREAD CRUMBS

- 2   slices hearty white sandwich bread
- 2   tablespoons extra-virgin olive oil
- ¼   cup Parmesan cheese
     Salt and pepper

STEW

- 1   pound hot or sweet Italian sausages
- 2   tablespoons extra-virgin olive oil
- 1   onion, chopped fine
     Salt and pepper
- 2   tablespoons minced fresh thyme or 2 teaspoons dried
- 6   garlic cloves, minced
- ½   cup dry white wine
- 1   (14.5-ounce) can diced tomatoes, drained with juice reserved
- 1½ cups chicken broth
- 1   (15-ounce) can cannellini beans, rinsed
- 12 ounces mustard greens, stemmed and cut into 2-inch pieces
- 2   tablespoons minced fresh parsley

1. For the Parmesan bread crumbs Pulse bread in food processor until finely ground, 10 to 15 pulses. Heat oil in 12-inch nonstick skillet over medium heat until shimmering. Add bread crumbs and cook, stirring constantly, until crumbs begin to brown, 3 to 5 minutes. Add Parmesan and continue to cook, stirring constantly, until crumbs are golden brown, 1 to 2 minutes. Transfer crumbs to bowl and season with salt and pepper to taste; set aside.

2. For the stew Prick sausages with fork in several places. Heat 1 tablespoon oil in Dutch oven over medium-high heat until just smoking. Brown sausages well on all sides, about 8 minutes, then transfer to plate.

3. Heat remaining 1 tablespoon oil in now-empty pot over medium heat until shimmering. Add onion and ¼ teaspoon salt and cook until softened and lightly browned, 5 to 7 minutes. Stir in thyme and garlic and cook until fragrant, about 30 seconds. Stir in wine and reserved tomato juice, scraping up any browned bits, and cook until nearly evaporated, about 5 minutes. Stir in broth, beans, and tomatoes and bring to simmer.

4. Stir in mustard greens and cook until slightly wilted, about 1 minute. Place sausages on top of greens. Cover, reduce heat to low, and cook until greens are wilted and reduced in volume by about half, about 10 minutes.

5. Uncover, increase heat to medium-low, and continue to cook, stirring occasionally, until sausages are cooked through and greens are tender, about 15 minutes. Off heat, using back of spoon, mash portion of beans against side of pot to thicken sauce. Serve, sprinkling individual portions with bread crumbs and parsley.

SMOKED TROUT HASH WITH EGGS

Serves 4   Total time: 45 minutes

WHY THIS RECIPE WORKS *Deliciously oily smoked fish is often paired with mustard or horseradish, pleasantly sharp flavors that cut through and counterbalance the richness of the seafood. So based on that line of reasoning, we thought that mustard greens, with their clean, spicy bite and leafy chew, would pair well with smoked trout—and we were right. This creative hash is just as much at home on a dinner table as it is on a lazy Sunday morning. To give the hash the requisite saucy element, we cooked four eggs nestled right in the top once it finished browning—because what's a hash without eggs on top? Dill and a squeeze of lemon added brightness to the finished hash. You will need a 12-inch nonstick skillet with a tight-fitting lid for this recipe.*

- 1   pound russet potatoes, peeled and cut into ¼-inch pieces
- 2   tablespoons extra-virgin olive oil
     Salt and pepper
- 1½ pounds mustard greens, stemmed and cut into 1-inch pieces
- 1   onion, chopped fine
- 1   garlic clove, minced
- 6   ounces smoked trout, flaked
- 4   large eggs
- 1   tablespoon minced fresh dill
     Lemon wedges

1. Microwave potatoes, 1 tablespoon oil, ½ teaspoon salt, and ¼ teaspoon pepper in covered bowl until potatoes are translucent around edges, 5 to 8 minutes, stirring halfway through microwaving.

2. Microwave mustard greens in second covered bowl until wilted, 8 to 10 minutes, stirring halfway through microwaving. Transfer to colander, drain well, then add to bowl with potatoes; set aside.

3. Heat remaining 1 tablespoon oil in 12-inch nonstick skillet over medium-high heat until shimmering. Add onion and cook until softened and lightly browned, 5 to 7 minutes.

Whole-Wheat Pizza with Kale and
Sunflower Seed Pesto

4. Stir in garlic and cook until fragrant, about 30 seconds. Stir in potatoes and mustard greens, breaking up any clumps. Using back of spatula, firmly pack potato mixture into skillet and cook undisturbed for 2 minutes. Flip hash, 1 portion at a time, and repack into skillet. Repeat flipping process every few minutes until potatoes are well browned and greens are tender, 6 to 8 minutes.

5. Off heat, sprinkle trout evenly over hash. Make 4 shallow indentations (about 2 inches wide) in surface of hash using back of spoon. Crack 1 egg into each indentation and season eggs with salt and pepper. Cover and cook over medium-low heat until egg whites are just set and yolks are still runny, 4 to 6 minutes. Sprinkle with dill and serve immediately with lemon wedges.

~~~

WHOLE-WHEAT PIZZA WITH KALE AND SUNFLOWER SEED PESTO

Makes two 12-inch pizzas
Total time: 1 hour 45 minutes (plus 18 hours for proofing the dough)
WHY THIS RECIPE WORKS *Loaded with healthy kale, this is a nutritional powerhouse of a pizza that's also delicious. "Healthy" pizzas often seem to taste like cardboard, but this one is guaranteed to satisfy all your pizza cravings. We used whole-wheat flour along with a smaller amount of bread flour for the crust, which required making an extra-wet dough for optimal chew. Our Kale and Sunflower Seed Pesto topped the dough, and cherry tomatoes on top provided bursts of sweetness and acidity to balance the earthy pesto underneath. We topped the pizza with even more kale, which crisped up nicely in the oven. A few shavings of Parmesan completed the picture. The pizza dough needs to proof for at least 18 hours or up to 2 days before baking, and the superhot oven is key to getting a crisp, chewy, not-at-all-cardboardy crust. If you do not have a baking stone, you can use a preheated rimless (or inverted rimmed) baking sheet, though the crust will be less crisp. Shape the second dough ball while the first pizza bakes, but don't top the pizza until right before you bake it. We prefer to use our whole-wheat pizza dough, but you can substitute 2 pounds store-bought whole-wheat pizza dough.*

DOUGH
1½ cups (8¼ ounces) whole-wheat flour
1 cup (5½ ounces) bread flour
2 teaspoons honey
¾ teaspoon instant or rapid-rise yeast
1¼ cups ice water
2 tablespoons extra-virgin olive oil
1¾ teaspoons salt

KALE AND SUNFLOWER SEED PESTO
2½ ounces kale, stemmed and chopped (1½ cups)
1 cup fresh basil leaves
1 cup baby spinach
⅓ cup roasted sunflower seeds
3 tablespoons water
3 garlic cloves, minced
Salt and pepper
½ cup extra-virgin olive oil
1 ounce grated Parmesan cheese (½ cup)

TOPPINGS
5½ ounces kale, stemmed and cut into 1½-inch pieces (3½ cups)
1 tablespoon extra-virgin olive oil, plus extra for drizzling
Salt and pepper
6 ounces cherry tomatoes, quartered
1 ounce Parmesan cheese, shaved

1. For the dough Process whole-wheat flour, bread flour, honey, and yeast in food processor until combined, about 2 seconds. With processor running, add ice water and process until dough is just combined and no dry flour remains, about 10 seconds. Let dough sit for 10 minutes.

2. Add oil and salt to dough and process until it forms satiny, sticky ball that clears sides of bowl, 45 to 60 seconds. Remove from bowl and knead on oiled counter until smooth, about 1 minute. Divide dough in half, shape each half into a tight ball, and place each in lightly oiled bowl. Cover tightly with plastic wrap and refrigerate for at least 18 hours or up to 2 days.

3. One hour before baking pizza, adjust oven rack to middle position, set pizza stone on rack, and heat oven to 500 degrees. Remove dough from refrigerator and let sit until dough springs back minimally when poked gently with your knuckle, at least 1 hour.

4. For the pesto Process kale, basil, spinach, sunflower seeds, water, garlic, and ¼ teaspoon salt in food processor until smooth, about 30 seconds, scraping down bowl as needed. With processor running, slowly add oil until incorporated. Transfer mixture to bowl, stir in Parmesan, and season with salt and pepper to taste. Set aside 1 cup for recipe; reserve ½ cup for another use.

5. For the toppings Combine kale, oil, and ¼ teaspoon salt in bowl and massage lightly to coat leaves evenly. Heat broiler for 10 minutes. Meanwhile, coat 1 ball of dough generously with flour and place on well-floured counter. Using your fingertips, gently flatten into 8-inch disk, leaving 1 inch of outer edge slightly thicker than center. Lift edge of dough and, using back of your hands and knuckles, gently stretch disk into 12-inch round, working along edges and giving disk quarter turns as you stretch. Transfer dough to well-floured pizza peel and stretch into 13-inch round.

6. Spread ½ cup pesto over surface of dough, leaving ½-inch border around edge. Scatter half of tomatoes and half of kale mixture over pizza. Slide pizza carefully onto stone, return oven to 500 degrees, and bake until crust is well browned and edges of kale leaves are crisp and brown, 8 to 10 minutes. Remove pizza, place on wire rack, and let pizza rest for 5 minutes. Drizzle with additional oil to taste and sprinkle with half of Parmesan. Slice pizza into 8 slices and serve.

7. Heat broiler for 10 minutes. Repeat process of stretching, topping, and baking with remaining dough and toppings, returning oven to 500 degrees when pizza is placed on stone.

HERBS

You may be asking yourself whether herbs qualify as vegetables. It all comes down to how they are used. Often, you might think they don't, since we frequently use herbs in small quantities to enhance dishes, rather than as the star component of a dish. But when basil is crushed in large quantities to make a pesto, we embrace the fact that it's being used as a vegetable. Likewise, in Thai-Style Chicken with Basil, in which a full 2 cups of fresh basil leaves are used in three different ways to flavor the chopped chicken, it's difficult to dispute basil's function as a vegetable.

The recipes here all put fresh herbs firmly front and center in dishes in which they act as integral vegetable ingredients. We offer a number of pestos, both classic and inventive, that showcase the bright freshness of herbs. In addition to our Classic Pesto (with basil), we include versions with oregano and parsley, as well as our Cilantro-Mint Chutney. Herbs are also the star in other sauces, including our Chimichurri, which we pair with grilled steaks, and our Mint-Almond Relish, which is a new way to apply the classic mint flavor profile to rack of lamb. And a fragrant herb-packed butter flavors a succulent brined roast chicken that starts on the stovetop and finishes in the oven for perfect crispy browned skin.

Beyond meat and seafood, fresh herbs also lift and brighten the earthy flavor of grains. Although you may think of tabbouleh as a grain-based dish, its original version features parsley first and fore-most, and our recipe honors that tradition. And earthy, musky sage pairs well with floral thyme in our Classic Bread Stuffing with Sage and Thyme.

shopping and storage

Fresh herbs are readily available year-round. Generally, herbs sold in loose bunches are a better bet than those in plastic clamshell packaging, which can be of inconsistent quality and tend to get slimy quickly. Look for fresh herb bunches with perky, vibrantly colored leaves; avoid any bunches with bruised, wilting, or yellowing leaves.

The best way to store delicate fresh herbs—basil, parsley, cilantro, mint, dill, and tarragon—is stems down in water, with the leaves covered by a plastic bag. If using them within a day or two, store them at room temperature. Refrigerating them will prolong their life, but even so, delicate herbs don't keep well for more than a few days. For herbs with sturdier leaves and woodier stems—oregano, sage, rosemary, thyme, and marjoram—wrap them in damp paper towels, place in a sealed zipper-lock bag, and store in the crisper drawer of the refrigerator for about a week.

vegetable science
Does Cilantro Taste Soapy to You?

There is no herb more divisive among home cooks than cilantro. Some people have a visceral reaction against it, describing the flavor as soapy, or like metallic pennies or moldy shoes! Though some aversion could be cultural, there is also a possible genetic reason. The personal genomics company 23andMe found that variations in a single-nucleotide polymorphism (or SNP, part of our DNA building blocks) are strongly associated with the perception of a soapy taste in cilantro. This SNP lies within a cluster of olfactory genes—and aroma is strongly associated with our perception of taste. Among these olfactory genes is the OR6A2 gene, a receptor that binds many of the compounds associated with cilantro's unique smell. Still, this SNP shows relatively low heritability, making it an uncommon trait.

vegetable prep

Easier Herb Washing

Use a salad spinner to wash herbs. Swish loose sprigs around in cold water and, once herbs are clean, lift basket with herbs out of water, discard water, fit basket back into its base, and spin herbs dry.

DIY Dried Herbs in a Flash

Try this quick, easy way to dry and store a plethora of fresh herbs.

1. Place washed and dried herbs on paper towel and microwave for 30 to 40 seconds.

2. Crumble dried herbs and store in airtight container for up to 3 months.

using dried herbs

We all have dried herbs in our pantry and sometimes need to use those instead of fresh. We recommend avoiding dried forms of delicate, leafy herbs like basil, parsley, chives, mint, and cilantro, which are vastly inferior in flavor. Heartier herbs, such as oregano, sage, and thyme, dry well and can be good substitutes for fresh, especially in recipes where the herbs will cook in liquid (such as soups and sauces). Use only about one-third the amount, and add them at the same time as you would fresh.

Freezing Fresh Herbs

Often, home cooks buy a bunch of herbs only to end up using just a small fraction, leaving the rest to go bad. Luckily, there's a good way to keep leftover herbs usable indefinitely.

1. Chop leftover fresh herbs by hand or in food processor, transfer spoonfuls into ice cube trays, and top with water to cover. For standard ice cube tray, place 2 tablespoons chopped herbs and approximately 1 tablespoon water in each cube.

2. Once cubes are frozen, transfer them to zipper-lock bag and seal. Store until you want to add them to sauces, soups, or stews.

flat-leaf or curly?

Flat-leaf parsley (also called Italian parsley) is the strong favorite over curly parsley in the test kitchen. Flat-leaf parsley is much more fragrant, and it has a sweet, bright flavor that we prefer to the more bitter, grassier notes of curly-leaf parsley.

Classic Pesto

HERB-GARLIC COMPOUND BUTTER

Makes about 1 cup   Total time: 15 minutes

WHY THIS RECIPE WORKS *It's handy to have a compound butter packed with herbs in your freezer to pull out at the last minute to top a grilled steak, roast fish, potatoes, and more. It instantly takes just about any dish to a higher level with bright herb flavor. We started with a stick of softened butter and mashed it with a mixture of minced fresh herbs, minced garlic, and salt and pepper. You can use it right away or shape it into a log, wrap it in plastic wrap, and store it in your freezer for up to two months.*

- 8 tablespoons unsalted butter, softened
- 2 tablespoons minced fresh sage or 1½ teaspoons dried
- 1 tablespoon minced fresh parsley
- 1 tablespoon minced fresh thyme or ¾ teaspoon dried
- 2 garlic cloves, minced
- ¼ teaspoon salt
- ¼ teaspoon pepper

Combine all ingredients in bowl. Cover with plastic wrap and let sit to blend flavors, about 10 minutes, or roll into log, wrap in plastic wrap, and refrigerate or freeze.

CLASSIC PESTO

Makes about 1½ cups; enough for 2 pounds pasta   Total time: 25 minutes

WHY THIS RECIPE WORKS *There are a few basic rules for a great pesto: Use high-quality extra-virgin olive oil (its flavor will really shine through), toast the garlic (to help tame its fiery flavor), pound the herbs to bring out their flavorful oils, and add some type of nuts or seeds (for richness and body). Classic pesto includes fresh basil, pine nuts, garlic, and Parmesan. When you're tossing the pesto with cooked pasta, it is important to add some pasta cooking water to achieve the proper sauce consistency. Or try any of the following pairings for a new spin: as a spread on a sandwich, in place of tomato sauce on pizza, dolloped onto soups and stews before serving, brushed onto fish or chicken after cooking, thinned with lemon juice to make a vinaigrette, or stirred into mashed potatoes.*

- 6 garlic cloves, unpeeled
- ½ cup pine nuts
- 4 cups fresh basil leaves
- ¼ cup fresh parsley leaves
- 1 cup extra-virgin olive oil
- 1 ounce Parmesan cheese, grated (½ cup)
  Salt and pepper

1. Toast garlic in 8-inch skillet over medium heat, shaking skillet occasionally, until softened and spotty brown, about 8 minutes. When garlic is cool enough to handle, discard skins and chop coarse. Meanwhile, toast pine nuts in now-empty skillet over medium heat, stirring often, until golden and fragrant, 4 to 5 minutes.

2. Place basil and parsley in 1-gallon zipper-lock bag. Pound bag with flat side of meat pounder or with rolling pin until all leaves are bruised.

3. Process garlic, pine nuts, and herbs in food processor until finely chopped, about 1 minute, scraping down sides of bowl as needed. With processor running, slowly add oil until incorporated. Transfer pesto to bowl, stir in Parmesan, and season with salt and pepper to taste. (Pesto can be refrigerated for up to 3 days or frozen for up to 3 months. To prevent browning, press plastic wrap flush to surface or top with thin layer of olive oil. Bring to room temperature before using.)

PARSLEY AND PECAN PESTO

Makes about ¾ cup; enough for 1 pound pasta   Total time: 25 minutes

WHY THIS RECIPE WORKS *Once you go beyond the classic version, pesto can actually be prepared with a variety of ingredients— other herbs and greens like parsley or arugula, or even potent ingredients like sun-dried tomatoes or olives. For this delicious variation, we chose parsley as the star. To balance out the flavor of the parsley, which is grassier and heartier than the traditional basil, we found it necessary to ramp up the nut flavor profile. Pecans have a more pronounced flavor than pine nuts, so we decided to use those here. You can substitute*

walnuts, blanched almonds, skinned hazelnuts, or any combination of these three for the pecans. Stir this into rice or a bowl of steamed or sautéed green beans.

- 2 garlic cloves, unpeeled
- ½ cup pecans
- 2 tablespoons fresh parsley leaves
- 3½ tablespoons extra-virgin olive oil
- 2 tablespoons grated Parmesan cheese
  Salt and pepper

1. Toast garlic in 8-inch skillet over medium heat, shaking skillet occasionally, until softened and spotty brown, about 8 minutes. When garlic is cool enough to handle, discard skins and chop coarse. Meanwhile, toast pecans in now-empty skillet over medium heat, stirring often, until golden and fragrant, 4 to 5 minutes.

2. Place parsley in 1-quart zipper-lock bag. Pound bag with flat side of meat pounder or with rolling pin until all leaves are bruised.

3. Process garlic, pecans, and parsley in food processor until finely chopped, about 1 minute, scraping down sides of bowl as needed. With processor running, slowly add oil until incorporated. Transfer pesto to bowl, stir in Parmesan, and season with salt and pepper to taste. (Pesto can be refrigerated for up to 3 days or frozen for up to 3 months. To prevent browning, press plastic wrap flush to surface or top with thin layer of olive oil. Bring to room temperature before using.)

OREGANO, LEMON, AND FETA PESTO

Makes about ¾ cup; enough for 1 pound pasta   Total time: 25 minutes

WHY THIS RECIPE WORKS *For a pesto with a definitively Greek bent, we added fresh, fragrant oregano, crumbled feta cheese, and lemon zest and juice to the traditional ingredients—basil, pine nuts, and garlic. Fresh oregano is crucial here; do not substitute dried oregano. This pesto is delicious combined with pasta or roasted potatoes, or dollop it on top of grilled zucchini or yellow summer squash.*

3 garlic cloves, unpeeled
¼ cup pine nuts
1¾ cups packed fresh basil leaves
¼ cup packed fresh oregano leaves
½ teaspoon grated lemon zest plus
2 tablespoons juice
7 tablespoons extra-virgin olive oil
1 ounce feta cheese, crumbled (¼ cup)
Salt and pepper

1. Toast garlic in 8-inch skillet over medium heat, shaking skillet occasionally, until softened and spotty brown, about 8 minutes. When garlic is cool enough to handle, discard skins and chop coarse. Meanwhile, toast pine nuts in now-empty skillet over medium heat, stirring often, until golden and fragrant, 4 to 5 minutes.

2. Place basil and oregano in 1-gallon zipper-lock bag. Pound bag with flat side of meat pounder or with rolling pin until all leaves are bruised.

3. Process garlic, pine nuts, herbs, and lemon zest and juice in food processor until finely chopped, about 1 minute, scraping down sides of bowl as needed. With processor running, slowly add oil until incorporated. Transfer pesto to bowl, stir in feta, and season with salt and pepper to taste. (Pesto can be refrigerated for up to 3 days or frozen for up to 3 months. To prevent browning, press plastic wrap flush to surface or top with thin layer of olive oil. Bring to room temperature before using.)

CILANTRO-MINT CHUTNEY

Makes about 1 cup   Total time: 10 minutes
WHY THIS RECIPE WORKS *This herb-based chutney comes together in a flash in the food processor, with no need to chop the herbs in advance. We used a 2:1 ratio of grassy cilantro leaves to sweet mint leaves for the herbal flavor here, and chose whole-milk yogurt for a creamy base. A little sugar added balance, while the onion and cumin delivered a savory punch. We prefer to use whole-milk yogurt here but low-fat yogurt can be substituted; do not use nonfat yogurt. Dollop this chutney on grilled chicken or spread it on flatbread or naan.*

2 cups fresh cilantro leaves
1 cup fresh mint leaves
⅓ cup plain whole-milk yogurt
¼ cup finely chopped onion
1 tablespoon lime juice
1½ teaspoons sugar
½ teaspoon ground cumin
¼ teaspoon salt

Process all ingredients in food processor until smooth, about 20 seconds, scraping down sides of bowl as needed. (Chutney can be refrigerated for up to 2 days.)

GREEN GODDESS DIP

Makes about 1¾ cups
Total time: 10 minutes (plus 1 hour chilling time)
WHY THIS RECIPE WORKS *Green goddess dip is all about the fresh herbs, and here we use a trio of them: parsley, chives, and tarragon. For our base, we tested mayonnaise, sour cream, yogurt, buttermilk, heavy cream, cottage cheese, and cream cheese—in all possible combinations. It turned out that a combo of mayonnaise and sour cream made the strongest pairing with the herbs. The mayonnaise contributed the body, richness, and velvety texture we wanted in a creamy dip, while the sour cream heightened the tanginess. The flavor of this dip will continue to develop over the chilling and storage time. This is great with all manner of crudités, and it can even be thinned with a little water to use as a salad dressing.*

¾ cup mayonnaise
¾ cup sour cream
¼ cup minced fresh parsley
¼ cup minced fresh chives
2 tablespoons minced fresh tarragon
1 tablespoon lemon juice
2 garlic cloves, minced
⅛ teaspoon salt
⅛ teaspoon pepper

Whisk all ingredients together in serving bowl until smooth and creamy. Cover with plastic wrap and refrigerate until flavors are blended, at least 1 hour. (Dip can be refrigerated for up to 2 days.)

TABBOULEH

Serves 4 to 6   Total time: 40 minutes (plus 1 hour resting time)
WHY THIS RECIPE WORKS *Tabbouleh is a signature Levantine salad from the Eastern Mediterranean that puts parsley front and center, along with bulgur, tomatoes, and onion, all steeped in a penetrating mint and lemon dressing. We started by salting the tomatoes to rid them of excess moisture that otherwise would have made our salad soggy. Soaking the bulgur in lemon juice and some of the drained tomato liquid, rather than in water, allowed it to absorb lots of flavor as it softened. Chopped onion overwhelmed the salad, but a couple of mild scallions added just the right amount of oniony flavor. Fresh mint and a bit of cayenne pepper rounded out the dish. Adding the herbs and vegetables while the bulgur was still soaking gave the components time to mingle, resulting in a cohesive dish. Don't confuse bulgur with cracked wheat, which has a much longer cooking time and will not work in this recipe.*

3 tomatoes, cored and cut into ½-inch pieces
Salt and pepper
½ cup medium-grind bulgur, rinsed
¼ cup lemon juice (2 lemons)
6 tablespoons extra-virgin olive oil
⅛ teaspoon cayenne pepper
1½ cups minced fresh parsley
½ cup minced fresh mint
2 scallions, sliced thin

1. Toss tomatoes with ¼ teaspoon salt in fine-mesh strainer set over bowl and let drain, tossing occasionally, for 30 minutes; reserve 2 tablespoons drained tomato juice. Toss bulgur with 2 tablespoons lemon juice and reserved tomato juice in bowl and let sit until grains begin to soften, 30 to 40 minutes.

2. Whisk remaining 2 tablespoons lemon juice, oil, cayenne, and ¼ teaspoon salt together in large serving bowl. Add tomatoes, bulgur, parsley, mint, and scallions and toss gently to combine. Cover and let sit at room temperature until flavors have blended and bulgur is tender, about 1 hour. Toss salad to recombine and season with salt and pepper to taste. Serve.

VARIATION

Spiced Tabbouleh

Add ¼ teaspoon ground cinnamon and ¼ teaspoon ground allspice to dressing with cayenne.

HERBED ROAST CHICKEN

Serves 6   Total time: 1 hour 45 minutes (plus 1 hour chilling time)

WHY THIS RECIPE WORKS *One of our favorite ways to roast a chicken is to pack it with lots of fresh herb flavor. But the reality is that this is one of the hardest culinary tasks to get right, since the heat of the oven tends to destroy the flavor of fresh herbs. The most common approach—spreading herb butter under the skin of the breast— flavors the chicken weakly at best. After much testing with herb pastes (and lots of torn chicken skin), we decided to butterfly the chicken. This simple step made it far easier both to spread the paste and to get the crisp skin we were after. After brining, we made shallow cuts in the dark meat, which not only helped the skin render but also created pockets to trap the flavorful herbs. We carefully rubbed part of our herb paste under the skin on the breast meat and then browned the chicken in a large skillet before transferring the skillet to the oven. Halfway through cooking, we slathered on more of the herb paste. Just to make sure that every bite of chicken was bursting with herby flavor, we made a quick pan sauce using the drippings in the skillet, finishing it off with a couple of tablespoons of extra herb butter and a few drops of lemon juice. You can substitute an equal amount of basil for the tarragon and replace the thyme with rosemary, oregano, or sage. If using a kosher chicken, do not brine in step 1. The chicken may slightly overhang the skillet at first, but once browned it will fit.*

CHICKEN

- 1 (5-pound) whole chicken, trimmed, giblets discarded
  Salt and pepper
- 6 tablespoons unsalted butter, softened
- 6 scallions, green parts only, minced
- ¼ cup minced fresh tarragon
- 1 tablespoon minced fresh thyme
- 1 garlic clove, minced
- 1 tablespoon vegetable oil

SAUCE

- 1–1½ cups chicken broth
- 2 teaspoons all-purpose flour
- 1 teaspoon lemon juice
  Salt and pepper

1. For the chicken With chicken breast side down, use kitchen shears to cut through bones on either side of backbone and discard backbone. Flip chicken over and press on breastbone to flatten. Using sharp knife, cut 2 slashes, ⅛ inch deep, into skin of thighs and legs, about ¾ inch apart. Dissolve ½ cup salt in 2 quarts cold water in large container. Submerge chicken in brine, cover, and refrigerate for 1 hour.

2. Meanwhile, adjust oven rack to middle position and heat oven to 450 degrees. Combine softened butter, scallions, tarragon, thyme, garlic, ¼ teaspoon salt, and ¼ teaspoon pepper in bowl. Transfer 2 tablespoons herb butter to small bowl and refrigerate; set remaining herb butter aside.

3. Remove chicken from brine and pat dry with paper towels. Using your fingers or handle of spoon, gently loosen center portion of skin covering each side of breast. Using spoon, place 1 tablespoon room-temperature herb butter underneath skin over center of each side of breast. Gently press on skin to distribute butter over meat. Season chicken with pepper.

4. Heat oil in 12-inch ovensafe skillet over medium-high heat until just smoking. Add chicken skin side down and reduce heat to medium. Cook until lightly browned, 8 to 10 minutes. Transfer skillet to oven and roast chicken for 25 minutes.

5. Using pot holder, remove chicken from oven. Using 2 large wads of paper towels, flip chicken skin side up. Using spoon or spatula, evenly coat chicken skin with remaining room-temperature herb butter and return to oven. Roast chicken until skin is golden brown, breast registers 160 degrees, and thighs register 175 degrees, 15 to 20 minutes. Transfer chicken to cutting board and let rest for 20 minutes.

6. For the sauce While chicken rests, pour pan juices into fat separator. Let liquid settle for 5 minutes, then pour juices into 2-cup liquid measuring cup. Add enough broth to measure 1½ cups. Heat 2 teaspoons fat from fat separator in now-empty skillet over medium heat until shimmering. Add flour and cook, stirring constantly, until golden, about 1 minute. Slowly whisk in broth mixture, scraping up any browned bits. Bring to rapid simmer and cook until reduced to 1 cup, 5 to 7 minutes. Stir in any accumulated chicken juices, return to simmer, and cook for 30 seconds. Off heat, whisk in lemon juice and reserved cold herb butter. Season with salt and pepper to taste. Carve chicken and serve, passing sauce separately.

THAI-STYLE CHICKEN WITH BASIL

Serves 4   Total time: 40 minutes

WHY THIS RECIPE WORKS *This traditional Thai street food features the bright flavor of basil in three ways. First, we ground a cup of basil leaves in the food processor with garlic and Thai chiles for a stir-fry base for the chicken. We removed a tablespoon of that base mixture to make a pungent sauce with ingredients including fish sauce and oyster sauce, which we added toward the end of cooking as a finishing sauce. Finally, we stirred another cup of fresh basil leaves into the dish right before serving, for a big pop of herbal flavor. This dish, called* gai pad krapow, *is normally very spicy; we halved the amount of chiles, cutting the amount of sugar by half as well to keep the flavors balanced. If fresh Thai chiles are unavailable, substitute two serranos or one medium jalapeño. In Thailand, red pepper flakes and sugar are passed at the table, along with extra fish sauce and white vinegar, so that the dish can be adjusted to suit individual tastes. Serve with steamed rice and vegetables, if desired.*

- 2 cups fresh basil leaves
- 3 garlic cloves, peeled
- 6 green or red Thai chiles, stemmed
- 2 tablespoons fish sauce, plus extra for serving
- 1 tablespoon oyster sauce
- 1 tablespoon sugar, plus extra for serving
- 1 teaspoon distilled white vinegar, plus extra for serving
- 1 pound boneless, skinless chicken breasts, trimmed and cut into 2-inch pieces
- 3 shallots, sliced thin
- 2 tablespoons vegetable oil
  Red pepper flakes

1. Pulse 1 cup basil, garlic, and Thai chiles in food processor until finely chopped, 6 to 10 pulses, scraping down sides of bowl as needed. Transfer 1 tablespoon basil mixture to small bowl and stir in 1 tablespoon fish sauce, oyster sauce, sugar, and vinegar; set aside. Transfer remaining basil mixture to 12-inch nonstick skillet.

2. Pulse chicken and remaining 1 tablespoon fish sauce in now-empty food processor until meat is chopped into approximately ¼-inch pieces, 6 to 8 pulses. Transfer to bowl and refrigerate for 15 minutes.

3. Stir shallots and oil into basil mixture in skillet. Heat over medium-low heat (mixture should start to sizzle after about 1½ minutes; if it doesn't, adjust heat accordingly), stirring constantly, until garlic and shallots are golden brown, 5 to 8 minutes.

4. Add chicken, increase heat to medium, and cook, stirring and breaking up chicken with rubber spatula, until only traces of pink remain, 2 to 4 minutes. Add reserved basil–fish sauce mixture and continue to cook, stirring constantly, until chicken is no longer pink, about 1 minute. Stir in remaining 1 cup basil and cook, stirring constantly, until basil is wilted, 30 seconds to 1 minute. Serve immediately, passing extra fish sauce, sugar, vinegar, and pepper flakes separately.

GRILLED ARGENTINE STEAKS WITH CHIMICHURRI SAUCE

Serves 6 to 8   Total time: 1 hour 30 minutes (plus 30 minutes salting time)

WHY THIS RECIPE WORKS *A fresh, herb-packed chimichurri sauce complementing rich, smoky grilled steaks is an Argentine favorite. We think it's a perfect meal for summer evenings outside with friends and family. To translate the Argentine grilling method to our smaller American steaks, we rubbed the boneless strip steaks with salt and used the freezer as a dehydrator to evaporate the surface moisture; this, along with rubbing the steaks with cornstarch, helped them develop a substantial browned exterior on the grill. Covering the grill for the initial cooking jump-started the flavoring process.*

CHIMICHURRI SAUCE
- ¼ cup hot water
- 2 teaspoons dried oregano
- 1 teaspoon salt
- 1⅓ cups fresh parsley leaves
- ⅔ cup fresh cilantro leaves
- 6 garlic cloves, minced
- ½ teaspoon red pepper flakes
- ¼ cup red wine vinegar
- ½ cup extra-virgin olive oil

STEAKS
- 1 tablespoon cornstarch
  Salt and pepper
- 4 (1-pound) boneless strip steaks, 1½ inches thick, trimmed
- 4 medium wood chunks, unsoaked
- 1 (9-inch) disposable aluminum pie plate (if using gas)

1. For the chimichurri sauce Combine water, oregano, and salt in small bowl and let sit until oregano is softened, about 15 minutes. Pulse parsley, cilantro, garlic, and pepper flakes in food processor until coarsely chopped, about 10 pulses. Add water mixture and vinegar and pulse to combine. Transfer mixture to bowl and slowly whisk in oil until combined. Cover and let sit at room temperature for 1 hour. (Chimichurri sauce can be refrigerated for up to 3 days.)

2. For the steaks Meanwhile, combine cornstarch and 1½ teaspoons salt in bowl. Pat steaks dry with paper towels and place on wire rack set in rimmed baking sheet. Rub entire surface of steaks with cornstarch mixture and place steaks in freezer, uncovered, until very firm, about 30 minutes.

3a. For a charcoal grill Open bottom vent halfway. Light large chimney starter filled with charcoal briquettes (6 quarts). When top coals are partially covered with ash, pour evenly over grill. Using tongs, place wood chunks directly on top of coals, spacing them evenly around perimeter of grill. Set cooking grate in place, cover, and open lid vent halfway. Heat grill until hot and wood chunks are smoking, about 5 minutes.

3b. For a gas grill Turn all burners to high, cover, and heat grill until hot, about 15 minutes. Leave all burners on high. Place wood

Grilled Argentine Steaks with
Chimichurri Sauce

chunks in disposable aluminum pie plate and set on cooking grate. Close lid and heat until wood chunks begin to smoke, about 5 minutes.

4. Clean and oil cooking grate. Season steaks with pepper. Place steaks on grill, cover, and cook until beginning to brown, 2 to 3 minutes per side.

5. Flip steaks and cook, uncovered, until well browned on first side, 2 to 4 minutes. Flip steaks and continue to cook until meat registers 115 to 120 degrees (for rare) or 120 to 125 degrees (for medium-rare), 2 to 6 minutes longer.

6. Transfer steaks to carving board, tent with aluminum foil, and let rest for 5 to 10 minutes. Slice each steak ¼ inch thick. Serve, passing chimichurri sauce separately.

RACK OF LAMB WITH MINT-ALMOND RELISH

Serves 4 to 6   Total time: 2 hours 15 minutes

WHY THIS RECIPE WORKS *Mint and lamb are a venerable flavor pairing—some might even say a bit old-fashioned—so we wanted to reinvigorate this classic in a new way. The simple stir-together mint relish, loaded with bright flavors, and the anise-spiced salt achieved this simply but effectively. To make this a company-worthy dish, we decided on rack of lamb. To prepare the racks, we frenched them (cleaned the rib bones of meat and fat) and also discovered that we needed to remove a second layer of fat to avoid a greasy finished dish. We slowly roasted the lamb in a low oven to ensure a uniformly rosy, juicy interior. To brown and crisp the exterior, we quickly seared the racks after roasting. We prefer the milder taste and bigger size of domestic lamb, but you may substitute imported lamb from New Zealand and Australia. Since imported racks are generally smaller, in step 1, season each rack with ½ teaspoon of the salt mixture and reduce the cooking time to 50 minutes to 1 hour 10 minutes. You can substitute ground fennel for the ground anise if you prefer.*

LAMB

- 2 (1¾- to 2-pound) racks of lamb, fat trimmed to ⅛ to ¼ inch and rib bones frenched
  Kosher salt
- 1 teaspoon ground anise
- 1 teaspoon vegetable oil

MINT-ALMOND RELISH

- ½ cup minced fresh mint
- ¼ cup sliced almonds, toasted and chopped fine
- ¼ cup extra-virgin olive oil
- 2 tablespoons red currant jelly
- 4 teaspoons red wine vinegar
- 2 teaspoons Dijon mustard
  Salt and pepper

1. **For the lamb** Adjust oven rack to middle position and heat oven to 250 degrees. Using sharp knife, cut slits ½ inch apart in cross-hatch pattern in fat cap of lamb, being careful not to cut into meat. Combine 2 tablespoons salt and anise in bowl. Rub ¾ teaspoon salt mixture over entire surface of each rack and into slits. Reserve remaining salt mixture. Place racks, bone side down, on wire rack set in rimmed baking sheet. Roast until lamb registers 130 to 135 degrees (for medium), about 1 hour 25 minutes.

2. **For the mint-almond relish** Meanwhile, combine all ingredients in bowl, seasoning with salt and pepper to taste. Let sit at room temperature for 1 hour.

3. Heat oil in 12-inch skillet over high heat until just smoking. Place 1 rack, bone side up, in skillet and cook until well browned, 1 to 2 minutes. Transfer to carving board. Pour off all but 1 teaspoon fat from skillet and repeat browning with second rack. Tent racks with aluminum foil and let rest for 20 minutes. Cut between ribs to separate chops and sprinkle cut side of chops with ½ teaspoon salt mixture. Serve, passing mint-almond relish and remaining salt mixture separately.

GRAVLAX

Serves 8 to 10   Total time: 25 minutes (plus 3 days curing time)

WHY THIS RECIPE WORKS *Gravlax, salmon that's cured with sugar and salt and infused with sweet, slightly citrusy fresh dill, is a favorite throughout Scandinavia. Homemade gravlax sounds like it would require an extravagant time commitment and specialty tools and ingredients, but in fact it's a supereasy and fun project that is an impressive make-ahead choice for a weekend brunch. For gravlax that was evenly moist, tender, and consistently seasoned, we drizzled the fish with brandy, coated it in brown sugar, salt, and dill, and then pressed and refrigerated it. The salt drew liquid from the fish and cured it, while the brown sugar counterbalanced the salt and added deep flavor. The brandy helped the rub adhere and also added flavor. We basted the fish once a day to keep it moist. Once it was finished, all we had to do was slice the salmon as thin as possible. This homemade gravlax is ready when the fish is no longer translucent and its flesh is firm, with no give.*

- ⅓ cup packed light brown sugar
- ¼ cup kosher salt
- 1 (1-pound) skin-on center-cut salmon fillet
- 3 tablespoons brandy
- 1 cup coarsely chopped fresh dill

1. Combine sugar and salt in bowl. Place salmon, skin side down, in 13 by 9-inch glass baking dish. Drizzle with brandy, making sure to cover entire surface. Rub salmon evenly with sugar mixture, pressing firmly to adhere. Sprinkle dill over top, pressing firmly to adhere.

2. Cover salmon loosely with plastic wrap, top with square baking dish, and weight with several large, heavy cans. Refrigerate until salmon feels firm, about 3 days, basting salmon with liquid released into baking dish once a day.

3. Scrape dill off salmon. Remove fillet from dish and pat dry with paper towels. Slice salmon crosswise on bias into very thin pieces and serve. (Unsliced gravlax can be wrapped tightly in plastic wrap and refrigerated for up to 1 week.)

ALMOST HANDS-FREE RISOTTO WITH HERBS AND PARMESAN

Serves 6   Total time: 50 minutes

WHY THIS RECIPE WORKS *Risotto with fresh mixed herbs, butter, and cheese is a wonderful side dish for all manner of braised meats. We love the combination of parsley and chives here to brighten the richness of the dish. However, classic risotto can demand half an hour of stovetop stirring tedium. We set out to create a version that would free the cook to prepare the other parts of the meal while the risotto cooked. We chose to cook our risotto in a Dutch oven rather than a saucepan, because the former's thick, heavy bottom, deep sides, and tight-fitting lid are made to trap and distribute heat as evenly as possible. We also added most of the broth at once, instead of in small increments as is typical. Then we covered the pan and simmered the rice until almost all the broth had been absorbed, stirring just twice. After adding the final addition of broth, we stirred the pot for a few minutes and then took it off the heat. The rice turned out thickened, velvety, and just barely chewy. Stirring in the herbs at the end kept their flavors assertive. This more hands-off method does require precise timing, so we strongly recommend using a timer. The consistency of risotto is largely a matter of personal taste, so if you prefer a brothy risotto, add extra broth in step 4.*

   5 cups chicken or vegetable broth
1½ cups water
   4 tablespoons unsalted butter
   1 large onion, chopped fine
      Salt and pepper
   1 garlic clove, minced
   2 cups Arborio rice
   1 cup dry white wine
   2 ounces Parmesan cheese, grated (1 cup)
   1 teaspoon lemon juice
   2 tablespoons chopped fresh parsley
   2 tablespoons chopped fresh chives

1. Bring broth and water to boil in large saucepan over high heat. Cover and reduce heat to medium-low to maintain gentle simmer.

2. Melt 2 tablespoons butter in Dutch oven over medium heat. Add onion and ¾ teaspoon salt and cook until onion is softened, about 5 minutes. Stir in garlic and cook until fragrant, about 30 seconds. Stir in rice and cook, stirring often, until grain edges begin to turn translucent, about 3 minutes.

3. Stir in wine and cook, stirring constantly, until fully absorbed, 2 to 3 minutes. Stir in 5 cups hot broth mixture. Reduce heat to medium-low, cover, and simmer until almost all liquid has been absorbed and rice is just al dente, 16 to 19 minutes, stirring twice during cooking.

4. Add ¾ cup hot broth mixture and stir gently and constantly until risotto becomes creamy, about 3 minutes. Stir in Parmesan. Remove pot from heat, cover, and let stand for 5 minutes. Stir in remaining 2 tablespoons butter, lemon juice, parsley, and chives. Season with salt and pepper to taste. Before serving, stir in remaining hot broth mixture as needed to loosen consistency of risotto.

SUMMER ROLLS WITH BASIL AND SPICY ALMOND BUTTER SAUCE

Makes 12 rolls; serves 4
Total time: 30 minutes (plus 1 hour marinating time)

WHY THIS RECIPE WORKS *Vietnamese-style summer rolls can be made from a variety of fresh ingredients, including shrimp or chicken and several choices of vegetable. One hallmark and constant, however, is their generous use of fresh herbs. Though you can use a combination of herbs, for our rolls we decided to give sweet basil the starring role. We gathered up a rainbow of healthful veggies—red cabbage, red bell pepper, cucumber, and carrots—to give our rice paper packages color and crunch. Strips of marinated tofu made the rolls hearty enough for lunch. Instead of a thin soy dipping sauce, we whisked up a more satisfying sriracha-spiked almond butter sauce. Thick and rich, it clung easily to our rolls, taking the dish to a new level. You can use smooth or chunky almond or peanut butter for the sauce. Be sure to make one roll at a time to keep the wrappers moist and pliable. Brands of rice paper wrappers vary in the time it takes to soak and become pliable.*

SAUCE

   3 tablespoons almond or peanut butter
   3 tablespoons water
   1 tablespoon rice vinegar
   1 tablespoon soy sauce
   2 teaspoons grated fresh ginger
   1 teaspoon sriracha
   1 garlic clove, minced

ROLLS

   6 tablespoons rice wine vinegar
   1 tablespoon soy sauce
   2 teaspoons sriracha
   2 scallions, sliced thin on bias
   ½ (14-ounce) package extra-firm tofu, cut into 3-inch-long by ½-inch-thick strips
   ½ small head red cabbage, halved, cored, and sliced thin (3½ cups)
  12 (8-inch) round rice paper wrappers
   1 cup fresh basil leaves
   1 red bell pepper, stemmed, seeded, and cut into 2-inch-long matchsticks
   ½ seedless English cucumber, cut into 3-inch matchsticks
   2 carrots, peeled and shredded

1. For the sauce Whisk all ingredients in bowl until well combined; set aside.

2. For the rolls Whisk 2 tablespoons vinegar, soy sauce, sriracha, and scallions in shallow dish until combined. Add tofu and let sit for 1 hour. Toss cabbage with remaining ¼ cup vinegar and let sit for 1 hour. Drain cabbage in fine-mesh strainer, pressing gently with back of spatula to remove as much liquid as possible. Transfer to large plate and pat dry with paper towels.

3. Spread clean, damp dish towel on work surface. Fill 9-inch pie plate with 1 inch room-temperature water. Working with 1 wrapper at a time, submerge in water until just pliable, 10 seconds to 2 minutes; lay softened wrapper on towel. Scatter 3 basil leaves over wrapper. Arrange 5 matchsticks each of bell pepper and cucumber horizontally on wrapper, leaving 2-inch border at bottom. Top with 1 tablespoon carrots, then arrange 2 tablespoons cabbage on top of carrots. Place 1 strip tofu horizontally on top of vegetables, being sure to shake off excess marinade.

Rosemary and Parmesan Drop Biscuits

4. Fold bottom of wrapper over filling, pulling back on it firmly to tighten it around filling, then fold sides of wrapper in and continue to roll tightly into spring roll. Transfer to platter and cover with second damp dish towel.

5. Repeat with remaining wrappers and filling. Serve with almond butter sauce. (Spring rolls are best eaten immediately but can be covered with a clean, damp dish towel and refrigerated for up to 4 hours.)

ROSEMARY AND PARMESAN DROP BISCUITS

Makes 12 biscuits   Total time: 35 minutes

WHY THIS RECIPE WORKS *Fresh, piney rosemary and Parmesan cheese make these savory biscuits perfect to accompany simply prepared meats, stews, or soups. We wanted a biscuit that could be easily broken apart and enjoyed piece by buttery piece; too many drop biscuits are dense, gummy, and doughy, or else too lean and dry. While oil-based biscuits are easy to work with, they lack flavor, so butter was a must. Using buttermilk instead of milk gave the biscuits a rich tang and made them crisper on the exterior and fluffier on the interior. For the leavening, we needed a substantial amount, but too much baking powder left a metallic aftertaste. Replacing some of the baking powder with baking soda gave the biscuits the rise they needed without that metallic bitterness. Then we were left with only one problem: Properly combining the butter and buttermilk required that both ingredients be at just the right temperature; if they weren't, the melted butter clumped in the buttermilk. Since we wanted this to be an easy recipe, we tried making a batch with the lumpy buttermilk. The result was a surprisingly better biscuit, slightly higher and with better texture. The water in the lumps of butter turned to steam in the oven, helping create the additional height.*

      2 cups (10 ounces) all-purpose flour
  1 ½ ounces Parmesan cheese, grated (¾ cup)
      2 teaspoons baking powder
      ½ teaspoon baking soda
      1 teaspoon sugar
      ¾ teaspoon salt

      ½ teaspoon minced fresh rosemary
      1 cup buttermilk, chilled
     10 tablespoons unsalted butter, melted

1. Adjust oven rack to middle position and heat oven to 475 degrees. Line rimmed baking sheet with parchment paper.

2. Whisk flour, Parmesan, baking powder, baking soda, sugar, salt, and rosemary together in large bowl. In separate bowl, stir chilled buttermilk and 8 tablespoons melted butter together until butter forms small clumps. Stir buttermilk mixture into flour mixture until just incorporated and dough pulls away from sides of bowl.

3. Using greased ¼-cup measure, scoop out scant ¼ cup dough and drop onto prepared sheet, spacing dough mounds about 1 ½ inches apart (you should have 12 mounds). Bake until tops are golden brown and crisp, 12 to 14 minutes, rotating sheet halfway through baking.

4. Brush baked biscuits with remaining 2 tablespoons melted butter, transfer to wire rack, and let cool slightly before serving.

VARIATION

Cheddar and Scallion Drop Biscuits
Substitute ½ cup shredded cheddar cheese for Parmesan and 2 thinly sliced scallions for rosemary.

CLASSIC BREAD STUFFING WITH SAGE AND THYME

Serves 8 to 10   Total time: 2 hours 45 minutes

WHY THIS RECIPE WORKS *We usually prefer to cook our stuffing outside the turkey, since a stuffed bird takes longer and often results in overcooked meat by the time the stuffing has reached a safe temperature. For this recipe, we used fresh parsley, sage, thyme, and marjoram to create an herby stuffing with a great balance of flavors and textures. Half-inch cubes of bread made the stuffing pleasantly chunky and allowed the other ingredients to be distributed evenly throughout. Tasters preferred chicken broth to other liquid ingredients, since it gave the stuffing clean, savory flavor; a couple of eggs offered richness,*

moisture, and structure. The celery and onion boosted the herbs to give the stuffing a traditional flavor profile. Covering the stuffing for only part of the baking time ensured that it was moist throughout, with a crispy, crunchy top. Instead of oven drying in step 1, you can let bread stale overnight at room temperature. This recipe can be doubled and baked in a 15 by 10-inch baking dish for a larger crowd.

  1 ½ pounds hearty white sandwich bread, cut into ½-inch pieces
      6 tablespoons unsalted butter
      2 celery ribs, minced
      1 onion, chopped fine
      ¼ cup minced fresh parsley
  1 ½ tablespoons minced fresh sage or 1 teaspoon dried
  1 ½ tablespoons minced fresh thyme or ½ teaspoon dried
  1 ½ teaspoons minced fresh marjoram or ½ teaspoon dried
  2 ½ cups chicken broth
      2 large eggs, lightly beaten
      1 teaspoon salt
      1 teaspoon pepper

1. Adjust oven rack to middle position and heat oven to 300 degrees. Grease 13 by 9-inch baking dish. Spread bread onto rimmed baking sheet and bake, stirring occasionally, until bread is dry, 45 minutes to 1 hour. Let bread cool completely on sheet, about 30 minutes.

2. Increase oven temperature to 400 degrees. Melt butter in 12-inch skillet over medium-high heat. Add celery and onion and cook until softened, about 10 minutes. Stir in parsley, sage, thyme, and marjoram and cook until fragrant, about 1 minute. Transfer to very large bowl.

3. Add dried cooled bread, broth, eggs, salt, and pepper to vegetable mixture and toss to combine. Transfer to prepared baking dish.

4. Cover with aluminum foil and bake for 25 minutes. Remove foil and continue to bake until golden, about 30 minutes longer. Let cool for 10 minutes. Serve.

KOHLRABI, RUTABAGAS, AND TURNIPS

Visually striking **KOHLRABI** is hard to overlook, with round, pale green or lavender bulbs anchoring antenna-like stalks and leafy greens. It looks a bit like an alien life form, but rest assured, kohlrabi has a firmly earthbound culinary tradition, particularly in Eastern Europe. Although kohlrabi may not be a staple in American kitchens, its delicate, slightly sweet flavor and versatility should make it a household favorite. Raw kohlrabi has a refreshing, crisp texture and flavor similar to jicama or even apple; it's a marvelous addition to salads, as highlighted in our Kohlrabi, Radicchio, and Apple Slaw. It's also great quickly roasted with seasonings and makes a decadent yet healthful soup.

RUTABAGAS, often labeled "yellow turnips" (or sometimes "Swedes") in the market, are related to turnips, and preparation and cooking methods are often the same. Yet they are definitely a different vegetable, thought to be a cross between wild cabbages and turnips. Rutabagas are large, starchy, dense, and creamy. They can be cut into matchsticks and used raw in salads, but their true strength is their mellow sweetness when cooked. They're a highlight in our Root Vegetable Gratin as well as Cornish Pasties, a traditional use for this vegetable.

TURNIPS are smaller than rutabagas and have a more peppery bite. They have the ability to absorb added flavors well while still retaining their own character, which makes them versatile. Raw and sliced thin, turnips add crunch to salads, and they make a great pickle, as in our Pink Pickled Turnips. Cooked, they have a mildly spicy flavor and a dense, creamy flesh similar to potatoes, but with less starch. Turnips transform wonderfully into smooth, light purees, as in our Simple Glazed Pork Tenderloins with Creamy Turnip Puree.

shopping and storage

KOHLRABI is generally available from summer through early fall. Look for smaller bulbs, about the size of an orange; grapefruit-size kohlrabi is likely to be spongy or woody. Whether green or purple, the color should be pale but vibrant and free of blemishes. If you purchase kohlrabi with the stalks and leaves attached, separate them before storing them both in loosely closed plastic produce bags in the refrigerator. Bulbs will stay fresh for a week or longer; the greens will keep for several days.

RUTABAGAS are found in the market from fall through spring. They are usually yellowish, with purple coloring near the stem end, and very large, a pound or heavier. They are typically covered with a wax coating to prevent loss of moisture. If you do find ones without wax, choose those. Avoid rutabagas with cracks or any shriveling. Store them in the refrigerator in a loosely closed plastic bag for a couple of weeks (for waxed rutabagas) or a week (for unwaxed).

TURNIPS taste best when sweet and young, which is generally between November and February. As they mature, their texture gets more fibrous and woodier, and they lose their sweetness. In general, smaller turnips will be sweeter and more tender than larger ones. The greens are also edible and can be sautéed just like any other hearty greens. Turnips should be white, with purple coloring near the stem end, with unblemished skins; if the greens are attached, they should look crisp and fresh. Store turnips and their greens (separately) in the refrigerator in a loosely closed plastic produce bag for a week or longer.

vegetable prep

Peeling Kohlrabi

After trimming the stalks and leaves, peel the thick skin from the bulbs. A paring knife (rather than a vegetable peeler) is the best tool for this task. Make sure to remove the outer ⅛ inch of the vegetable, so that both the skin and the fibrous green parts underneath the skin are removed and only the white flesh remains.

Peeling Rutabagas

Peel the thick, waxy skin using a paring knife. Also peel away the thin layer of greenish-white flesh right under the skin to expose the yellowish-orange flesh beneath.

Peeling Turnips

Most turnips have thin enough skin that it can be removed with a vegetable peeler. For very large turnips, you may need to use a paring knife. There may also be some fibrous parts right under the skin, which you can trim away with a knife.

Slicing Kohlrabi, Rutabagas, and Turnips

A mandoline or V-slicer is a good way to get uniform, thin slices of kohlrabi, rutabagas, and turnips, as is needed in our recipe for Root Vegetable Gratin.

Cutting Turnips into Long Pieces

Our recipe for Pink Pickled Turnips calls for cutting turnips into 2 by ½-inch pieces.

1. Cut peeled turnips into slabs.

2. Cut slabs into ½-inch batons.

ROASTED KOHLRABI WITH CRUNCHY SEEDS

Serves 4   Total time: 35 minutes

WHY THIS RECIPE WORKS A simple, quick roast with a trio of flavorful seeds is an excellent and crowd-pleasing way to bring mild-tasting kohlrabi to the dinner table. A hot oven (450 degrees) browned the kohlrabi beautifully, and the ¾-inch pieces cooked in just 20 minutes. Usually seeds are toasted before being included in a dish, but here the high heat of the oven rendered that extra step unnecessary. Lining the baking sheet with foil prevented the kohlrabi from sticking to the pan. (We initially tried using more oil, rather than foil, but that just made the kohlrabi greasy.) As the kohlrabi roasts, make sure to shake the pan once or twice to encourage even browning.

- 2 tablespoons extra-virgin olive oil
- 2 teaspoons sesame seeds
- 1 teaspoon poppy seeds
- ½ teaspoon fennel seeds, cracked
  Salt and pepper
- 2 pounds kohlrabi, trimmed, peeled, and cut into ¾-inch pieces

1. Adjust oven rack to middle position and heat oven to 450 degrees. Combine oil, sesame seeds, poppy seeds, fennel seeds, ½ teaspoon salt, and ¼ teaspoon pepper in large bowl. Add kohlrabi and toss to coat.

2. Spread kohlrabi onto foil-lined rimmed baking sheet and roast, stirring occasionally, until browned and tender, about 20 minutes. Season with salt and pepper to taste. Serve.

SPICY TURNIPS WITH CHICKPEAS

Serves 4 to 6   Total time: 50 minutes

WHY THIS RECIPE WORKS This spicy dish featuring turnips and chickpeas can be enjoyed as a side dish but is also hearty enough to serve on its own, as an entrée. It hails from Tunisia, in North Africa, where turnips are often incorporated into dishes. Tunisian food is also known for being quite hot and spicy. In Tunisia, fresh Baklouti chiles are the main source of heat, but here we opted for the readily available jalapeño pepper, which has a similar heat level. We added some extra punch with cayenne pepper. Once the aromatic foundation for this dish was in place, we added the turnips (cut into bite-size pieces so they would cook quickly and evenly) and chickpeas (canned, for streamlined convenience). Including the starchy chickpea liquid from the cans gave our sauce good flavor and body. A final touch of lemon juice was all this zesty dish needed before serving.

- 2 tablespoons extra-virgin olive oil
- 2 onions, chopped
- 2 red bell peppers, stemmed, seeded, and chopped
  Salt and pepper
- ¼ cup tomato paste
- 1 jalapeño chile, stemmed, seeded, and minced
- 5 garlic cloves, minced
- ¾ teaspoon ground cumin
- ¼ teaspoon cayenne pepper
- 2 (15-ounce) cans chickpeas
- 12 ounces turnips, peeled and cut into ½-inch pieces
- ¾ cup water, plus extra as needed
- ¼ cup chopped fresh parsley
- 2 tablespoons lemon juice, plus extra for seasoning

1. Heat oil in Dutch oven over medium heat until shimmering. Add onions, bell peppers, ½ teaspoon salt, and ¼ teaspoon pepper and cook until softened and lightly browned, 5 to 7 minutes. Stir in tomato paste, jalapeño, garlic, cumin, and cayenne and cook until fragrant, about 30 seconds.

2. Stir in chickpeas and their liquid, turnips, and water. Bring to simmer and cook until turnips are tender and sauce has thickened, 25 to 35 minutes.

3. Stir in parsley and lemon juice. Season with salt, pepper, and extra lemon juice to taste. Adjust consistency with extra hot water as needed. Serve.

PINK PICKLED TURNIPS

Makes 4 cups   Total time: 30 minutes (plus 2 days refrigeration time)

WHY THIS RECIPE WORKS Refreshing and crunchy, pink pickled turnips are a staple in Middle Eastern cuisine. Because they are traditionally served with robust foods like falafel and shawarma, we chose to keep them mild, with just a bit of garlic, allspice, and black peppercorns. Pink pickled turnips get their whimsically fuchsia color from beets. Betacyanin, the pigment responsible for beetroot's deep red color, brightens into a vibrant pink when in contact with acid, so our vinegar brine was the perfect medium. We tried boiling pieces of raw peeled beet in the brine along with the aromatics, but this made for a dull pinkish-brown brine and pickles that took on an overwhelming beet flavor. So instead, we mixed pieces of beets with the turnips in the jar and poured the hot brine over them. This coaxed a beautiful hot-pink color from the beets, and the turnips kept their flavor. The turnips need to be refrigerated for two days before serving. The beets will eventually become pickled and make for a tasty treat. If using a glass storage container, be sure to fill it with hot water to warm, then drain it before packing with the vegetables.

- 1 pound turnips, peeled and cut into 2 by ½-inch pieces
- 1 small beet, peeled and cut into 1-inch pieces
- 1¼ cups white wine vinegar
- 1¼ cups water
- 2½ tablespoons sugar
- 1½ tablespoons kosher salt
- 3 garlic cloves, smashed and peeled
- ¾ teaspoon whole allspice berries
- ¾ teaspoon black peppercorns

1. Pack turnips and beet into 1-quart airtight container, leaving ½ inch headspace. Bring vinegar, water, sugar, salt, garlic, allspice, and peppercorns to boil in medium saucepan. Cover, remove from heat, and let steep for 10 minutes.

2. Strain hot brine over vegetables and let cool to room temperature. Cover and refrigerate for at least 2 days before serving. (Pickled turnips can be refrigerated for up to 1 month; turnips will soften over time.)

Pink Pickled Turnips

CREAMY KOHLRABI SOUP

This comforting, nourishing, and deeply satisfying soup uses just about every part of the vegetable, for a harmonious blend of flavors and textures. Because kohlrabi is low in fiber, it blends up easily with the added milk into a creamy, velvet-textured soup. The kohlrabi greens bring a pop of bright color and a fresh flavor to the sweet earthiness of the cooked kohlrabi bulb.

1. Trim and peel the kohlrabi bulbs and cut them into ½-inch pieces. Trim the tough stems from the leaves and cut the leaves into 1-inch pieces.

2. Cook the onions in the butter until softened and then stir in the kohlrabi pieces, water, and milk. Simmer until the kohlrabi is tender, 10 to 12 minutes.

3. Remove and set aside 1½ cups of the kohlrabi pieces to add back to the finished soup. Continue to cook the soup until the remaining kohlrabi in the pot easily breaks apart when poked with a paring knife. Then stir in the dry mustard.

4. Working in batches, process the soup in the blender until smooth, about 1 minute. Return the soup to the pot and bring back to a simmer.

5. Add the sliced kohlrabi leaves and cook until they are tender and vibrant green in color, about 5 minutes. Remove the soup from the heat and stir in the reserved cooked kohlrabi pieces.

6. Sprinkle individual servings with the macadamia nuts and chives.

KOHLRABI, RADICCHIO, AND APPLE SLAW

Serves 4 to 6   Total time: 30 minutes

WHY THIS RECIPE WORKS *For a fresh and flavorful take on coleslaw, we traded out everyday cabbage for crisp, juicy kohlrabi, supplementing it with sliced Granny Smith apples and radicchio to lend contrasting sweet, tart, assertive flavor and texture and bright color to this year-round side dish. We used a box grater (or you could use the shredding disk attachment of a food processor) to quickly turn the hard kohlrabi into tender shreds. To avoid a waterlogged slaw, we tossed the shredded kohlrabi with salt and sugar to soften it slightly and draw out moisture, and then spun it in a salad spinner to dry before combining it with the other ingredients. A generous amount of fresh mint and a bright Dijon mustard–based vinaigrette tied everything together.*

- 1½ pounds kohlrabi, trimmed, peeled, and shredded
- ¼ cup sugar, plus extra for seasoning
   Salt and pepper
- ½ cup extra-virgin olive oil
- 3 tablespoons white wine vinegar, plus extra for seasoning
- 2 tablespoons Dijon mustard
- 2 Granny Smith apples, peeled, cored, and cut into matchsticks
- 1 small head radicchio (6 ounces), halved, cored, and sliced ½ inch thick
- ½ cup fresh mint, chopped

1. Toss kohlrabi with sugar and 1 teaspoon salt in large bowl and let sit until partially wilted and reduced in volume by one-third, about 15 minutes. Transfer kohlrabi to salad spinner and spin until excess water is removed, 10 to 20 seconds.

2. Whisk oil, vinegar, mustard, ½ teaspoon salt, and ½ teaspoon pepper in large bowl until combined. Add kohlrabi, apples, radicchio, and mint and toss to combine. Season with salt, pepper, extra sugar, and extra vinegar to taste. Serve immediately.

CREAMY KOHLRABI SOUP

Serves 4 to 6   Total time: 1 hour

WHY THIS RECIPE WORKS *Here's a simple, deeply satisfying soup that utilizes nearly every part of the vegetable—root to leaf, so to speak. Similar to cauliflower, kohlrabi is particularly low in overall fiber, so it tends to blend up perfectly into smooth soups and purees. Here we wanted to highlight the delicate flavor of this brassica in a creamy, velvety soup. We started by cooking kohlrabi in an aromatic base of butter, onions, and vegetable stock and then blending it all up. Tasters loved the smooth texture of this soup, but wanted more kohlrabi flavor. Switching from broth to water helped to highlight the delicate flavor of the vegetable, but to really amplify the brassica flavor, we added a bit of dry mustard. (Brassicas like kohlrabi belong to the mustard family and share the same aromatic compounds that give mustard its characteristic zing.) To give more richness and body to the soup, we added a bit of milk to this base. For textural variation, we even cooked the kohlrabi greens in the soup at the end, which added a welcome element of contrast. Macadamia nuts and chives sprinkled on top made a crunchy garnish. You can substitute 4 ounces kale, stemmed and cut into 1-inch pieces, for the kohlrabi leaves.*

- 4 tablespoons unsalted butter
- 1 onion, chopped
   Salt
- 4 pounds kohlrabi with their leaves, kohlrabi trimmed, peeled, and cut into ½-inch pieces (6 cups), leaves stemmed and cut into 1-inch pieces (2 cups)
- 2 cups water, plus extra as needed
- 1 cup whole milk
- 1½ teaspoons dry mustard
- ⅓ cup salted dry-roasted macadamia nuts, chopped coarse
- 1 tablespoon minced fresh chives

1. Melt butter in Dutch oven over medium heat. Add onions and 1¼ teaspoons salt and cook, stirring occasionally, until softened, about 5 minutes. Stir in kohlrabi pieces, water, and milk, and bring to simmer. Cover, reduce heat to medium-low, and cook, stirring occasionally, until kohlrabi is tender (paring knife should slip easily in and out of pieces), 10 to 12 minutes.

2. Using slotted spoon, transfer 1½ cups kohlrabi to bowl. Continue to cook soup, covered, until remaining kohlrabi is very tender and easily breaks apart when poked with paring knife, 6 to 8 minutes. Stir in mustard.

3. Working in batches, process soup in blender until smooth, about 1 minute. Return soup to now-empty pot and bring to simmer over medium-low heat. Add kohlrabi leaves and cook, stirring occasionally, until tender and vibrant green, about 5 minutes. Off heat, stir in reserved cooked kohlrabi. Adjust consistency with extra hot water as needed. Season with salt to taste. Sprinkle individual portions with macadamia nuts and chives before serving.

IRISH STEW WITH TURNIPS AND CARROTS

Serves 6   Total time: 2 hours 45 minutes

WHY THIS RECIPE WORKS *Hearty Irish stew is made from meat and root vegetables in a richly flavored base. The recipe can vary from town to town and household to household, though the traditional meat is lamb. Some versions use only potatoes for the vegetable component, but we think that's a shame and prefer our Irish stew to also incorporate peppery turnips, pungent onions, and sweet carrots. We chose lamb shoulder chops for the meat, because we found that slicing the meat off the bone from a lamb shoulder chop, browning it, and adding the bones and meat to the stewing liquid gave us a great stew with a rich-tasting broth and the velvety texture that only marrow-rich bones can contribute. If possible, try to buy the shoulder chops from a butcher. In most supermarkets, lamb shoulder chops are sold too thin, often only about ½ inch thick. Though we prefer chops cut 1½ inches thick, 1-inch-thick chops will suffice.*

- 4½ pounds lamb shoulder chops (blade or round bone), 1 to 1½ inches thick, trimmed, meat removed from bones and cut into 1½-inch pieces, bones reserved
   Salt and pepper
- 3 tablespoons vegetable oil
- 2½ pounds onions, chopped
- ¼ cup all-purpose flour
- 3 cups water, plus extra as needed

1 teaspoon dried thyme
3 carrots, peeled and sliced ¼ inch thick
8 ounces turnips, peeled and cut into
1-inch pieces
¼ cup minced fresh parsley

1. Adjust oven rack to lower-middle position and heat oven to 300 degrees. Pat lamb dry with paper towels and season with salt and pepper. Heat 1 tablespoon oil in Dutch oven over medium-high heat until just smoking. Brown half of lamb on all sides, about 8 minutes; transfer to bowl. Repeat with 1 tablespoon oil and remaining lamb; transfer to bowl.

2. Add remaining 1 tablespoon oil, onions, and ¼ teaspoon salt to fat left in pot and cook over medium heat until onions are softened and lightly browned, about 8 minutes. Stir in flour and cook until onions are evenly coated, about 1 minute.

3. Stir in 1½ cups water, scraping up any browned bits and smoothing out any lumps. Gradually add remaining 1½ cups water, stirring constantly. Stir in thyme and 1 teaspoon salt and bring to simmer. Add reserved bones and lamb along with any accumulated juices and return to simmer. Cover, transfer pot to oven, and cook for 1 hour.

4. Remove pot from oven and place carrots and turnips on top of lamb and bones. Cover, return pot to oven, and cook until lamb is tender, about 1 hour.

5. Remove pot from oven and discard bones. Stir carrots and turnips into stew. Using large spoon, skim excess fat from surface of stew. Adjust consistency with extra hot water as needed. Stir in parsley and season with salt and pepper to taste. Serve.

VEGETABLE POT PIE

Serves 4 to 6   Total time: 1 hour 30 minutes (plus 1 hour chilling time)

WHY THIS RECIPE WORKS *The best vegetable pot pie should feature a rich, flavorful gravy; a flaky, golden crust; and a hearty combination of sturdy vegetables that can handle the baking time without turning to mush. We chose a combination of mushrooms, sweet potatoes, turnips, and Swiss chard. So that each vegetable came out cooked just right, we sautéed the mushrooms, sweet potato, and turnip before stirring in the chard. Since those vegetables left behind a good amount of fond in the pot, this also helped us to create a flavorful gravy. When we whisked in the broth, the fond was incorporated into the gravy, lending it deep, complex flavor. We prefer our homemade pie dough, but you can substitute store-bought pie dough in this recipe. If using store-bought dough, you will still need to roll the dough into a 10-inch circle.*

PIE DOUGH
1¼ cups (6¼ ounces) **all-purpose flour**
1 tablespoon sugar
½ teaspoon salt

4 tablespoons vegetable shortening, cut into ¼-inch pieces and chilled
6 tablespoons unsalted butter, cut into ¼-inch pieces and chilled
3–4 tablespoons ice water

POT PIE
4 tablespoons unsalted butter
1 onion, chopped fine
8 ounces cremini mushrooms, trimmed and quartered if large or halved if small
Salt and pepper
1 sweet potato (12 ounces), peeled and cut into ½-inch pieces
8 ounces turnips, peeled and cut into ½-inch pieces
3 garlic cloves, minced
½ teaspoon grated lemon zest plus 1 tablespoon juice
8 ounces Swiss chard, stemmed and cut into 1-inch pieces
2 tablespoons all-purpose flour
2 cups vegetable broth
1 ounce Parmesan cheese, grated (½ cup)
2 tablespoons minced fresh parsley
1 large egg
1 teaspoon water

1. **For the pie dough** Process flour, sugar, and salt in food processor until combined, about 5 seconds. Scatter shortening over top and process until mixture resembles coarse cornmeal, about 10 seconds. Scatter butter over top and pulse until mixture resembles coarse crumbs, about 10 pulses. Transfer to bowl.

making a pot pie crust

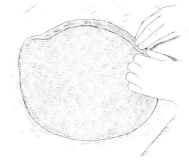

1. After rolling dough into 10-inch circle, fold over outer ½-inch edge of dough.

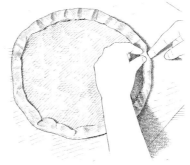

2. Crimp edge into tidy fluted edge using your fingers.

3. Using paring knife, cut four 2-inch oval-shaped vents in center.

2. Sprinkle 3 tablespoons water over flour mixture. Using rubber spatula, stir and press dough until it sticks together. If dough does not come together, add remaining 1 tablespoon water. Form dough into 4-inch disk, wrap tightly in plastic wrap, and refrigerate for 1 hour. (Dough can be refrigerated for up to 2 days or frozen for up to 1 month; if frozen, thaw completely at room temperature before rolling.)

3. Let chilled dough soften slightly on counter for 10 minutes. Roll dough between 2 large sheets parchment paper into 10-inch circle, flouring as needed. Remove parchment on top of dough. Fold over outer ½-inch edge of dough, then crimp into tidy fluted edge using your fingers. Using paring knife, cut four 2-inch oval-shaped vents in center. Slide parchment paper with crust onto baking sheet and refrigerate until needed.

4. **For the pot pie** Adjust oven rack to middle position and heat oven to 400 degrees. Melt 2 tablespoons butter in Dutch oven over medium heat. Stir in onion, mushrooms, and ½ teaspoon salt and cook until mushrooms have released their liquid, about 5 minutes.

5. Stir in sweet potato and turnips. Reduce heat to medium-low, cover, and cook, stirring occasionally, until potato and turnips begin to soften around edges, 7 to 9 minutes. Stir in garlic and lemon zest and cook until fragrant, about 30 seconds. Stir in chard and cook until wilted, about 2 minutes, and transfer to bowl.

6. Melt remaining 2 tablespoons butter in now-empty pot over medium-high heat. Stir in flour and cook for 1 minute. Gradually whisk in broth, scraping up any browned bits and smoothing out any lumps. Bring to simmer and cook until sauce thickens slightly, about 1 minute. Off heat, whisk in Parmesan, parsley, lemon juice, and ½ teaspoon salt. Stir in cooked vegetables, along with any accumulated juices, and season with salt and pepper to taste.

7. Transfer filling to 9½-inch deep-dish pie plate set on aluminum foil–lined rimmed baking sheet. Place chilled crust on top. Lightly beat egg, water, and pinch salt together in bowl, then brush over crust.

Bake until crust is golden brown and filling is bubbling, about 30 minutes. Let cool for 10 minutes before serving.

ROOT VEGETABLE GRATIN

Serves 6 to 8   Total time: 1 hour 45 minutes (plus 25 minutes resting time)

WHY THIS RECIPE WORKS *Sweet rutabaga and herbal celery root complement the earthiness of potatoes in our root vegetable gratin. We allowed all these flavors to come to the forefront by adding just a few aromatics: onion, garlic, thyme, and Dijon mustard. We added white wine to the gratin mixture because the wine's acidity strengthens the pectin in the potatoes, ensuring they remain intact while the denser, less-starchy rutabaga and celery root cook through; the wine also brightens the flavor of the vegetables. To help the top layers of the gratin cook through at the same rate as the bottom layers, we covered the dish for the first portion of the cooking time. A layer of Parmesan-enhanced panko bread crumbs, added after removing the foil, toasted to a golden brown while the gratin finished cooking, resulting in a crispy, nutty, cheesy crust. Uniform thin slices of rutabaga, celery root, and potatoes are key to even cooking—use a mandoline, a V-slicer, or the slicing disk on a food processor.*

  1   tablespoon plus 1½ cups water
  2   teaspoons all-purpose flour
1½   teaspoons Dijon mustard
       Salt and pepper
  ⅔   cup dry white wine
  ½   cup heavy cream
  ½   onion, chopped fine
1¼   teaspoons minced fresh thyme
  1   garlic clove, minced
  2   pounds large Yukon Gold potatoes, peeled and sliced ⅛ inch thick
  1   pound rutabaga, trimmed, peeled, quartered, and sliced ⅛ inch thick
  1   pound celery root, trimmed, peeled, quartered, and sliced ⅛ inch thick
  ¾   cup panko bread crumbs
1½   ounces Parmesan cheese, grated (¾ cup)
  4   tablespoons unsalted butter, melted and cooled

1. Adjust oven rack to middle position and heat oven to 375 degrees. Grease 13 by 9-inch baking dish. Whisk 1 tablespoon water, flour, mustard, and 1½ teaspoons salt in bowl until smooth. Add wine, cream, and remaining 1½ cups water, whisking to combine. Combine onion, thyme, garlic, and ¼ teaspoon pepper in separate bowl.

2. Layer half of potatoes in prepared dish, arranging so they form even thickness. Sprinkle half of onion mixture evenly over potatoes. Arrange rutabaga and celery root slices in even layer over onions. Sprinkle remaining onion mixture over rutabaga and celery root. Layer remaining potatoes over onions. Slowly pour water mixture over — vegetables. Using rubber spatula, gently press down on vegetables to create even, compact layer. Cover tightly with aluminum foil and bake for 50 minutes. Remove foil and continue to bake until knife inserted into center of gratin meets no resistance, 20 to 25 minutes.

3. Meanwhile, combine panko, Parmesan, and butter in bowl and season with salt and pepper. Remove gratin from oven and sprinkle evenly with panko mixture. Continue to bake until panko is golden brown, 15 to 20 minutes. Remove gratin from oven and let sit for 25 minutes. Serve.

SIMPLE GLAZED PORK TENDERLOINS WITH CREAMY TURNIP PUREE

Serves 4 to 6   Total time: 45 minutes

WHY THIS RECIPE WORKS *A creamy, buttery turnip puree elevates quick-cooking pork tenderloins to make a satisfying winter meal that's as great for company as it is for a family weeknight. Making the puree couldn't be easier: After microwaving the turnip pieces, we pureed them in the food processor with butter and cream while the pork cooked on the stovetop. For the mild tenderloins, we opted for a sweet-tart glaze with the bright flavor of cherries and the warmth of port, with rosemary to add just the right herbal depth. By adding the glaze ingredients to the pan after browning the pork, we thickened the glaze, plumped the cherries, and gently cooked the pork through all at once.*

Cornish Pasties

2 pounds turnips, trimmed, peeled, and cut into ½-inch pieces
½ cup heavy cream
4 tablespoons unsalted butter
Salt and pepper
2 (12- to 16-ounce) pork tenderloins, trimmed
1 tablespoon vegetable oil
1 cup ruby port
1 cup chicken broth
1 cup dried cherries
1 sprig fresh rosemary

1. Place turnips in bowl and microwave, covered, until tender, 7 to 9 minutes, stirring halfway through microwaving. Bring cream and butter to simmer in small saucepan over medium heat. Process turnips and butter mixture in food processor until smooth and creamy, about 30 seconds. Transfer puree to bowl and season with salt and pepper to taste. Cover to keep warm.

2. Pat pork dry with paper towels and season with salt and pepper. Heat oil in 12-inch skillet over medium-high heat until just smoking. Cook tenderloins until well browned on all sides, 5 to 8 minutes. Add port, broth, cherries, and rosemary and cook, turning pork occasionally, until mixture is slightly thickened and pork registers 145 degrees, about 10 minutes. Transfer pork to carving board, tent with aluminum foil, and let rest for 5 minutes.

3. Continue to cook sauce mixture over medium-high heat until thick and syrupy, about 3 minutes. Discard rosemary and season with salt and pepper to taste. Slice pork ½ inch thick and serve with sauce and turnip puree.

CORNISH PASTIES
Serves 6   Total time: 2 hours
WHY THIS RECIPE WORKS *These handheld savory turnovers, traditionally eaten as quick but hearty lunches in England, should be rich, flaky, and moist. They can vary a bit in their filling components, but they nearly always include rutabagas or turnips. For the best version, we tossed the uncooked meat (skirt steak) and vegetables (onion, rutabaga, and potato) with a little flour before wrapping the filling tightly in our dough rounds. The flour combined with the filling's exuded juices as the pasties baked to create the flavorful gravy right inside the crust. We didn't want to stray very far from the pasties' roots, but we did add some garlic and fresh thyme to punch up the flavor of the filling. To ensure easy dough assembly, we used sour cream to make it both pliable and rip-resistant. If you can't find skirt steak, you can use 1½ pounds of blade steak; the extra ¼ pound accounts for the trimming required with the blade cut. The pasties fit best on the baking sheet when placed crosswise in two rows of three.*

CRUST
⅔ cup sour cream, chilled
1 large egg, lightly beaten
3 cups (15 ounces) all-purpose flour
1¾ teaspoons salt
16 tablespoons unsalted butter, cut into ½-inch pieces and chilled

FILLING
1 tablespoon unsalted butter
1 onion, chopped fine
Salt and pepper
1 tablespoon minced fresh thyme
2 garlic cloves, minced
1¼ pounds skirt steak, trimmed and cut into ½-inch pieces
10 ounces rutabaga, trimmed, peeled, and cut into ½-inch pieces
10 ounces russet potatoes, peeled and cut into ½-inch pieces
¼ cup all-purpose flour
1 large egg

1. For the crust Whisk sour cream and egg together in small bowl. Process flour and salt in food processor until combined, about 3 seconds. Add butter and pulse until only pea-size pieces remain, about 10 pulses. Add half of sour cream mixture and pulse until combined, about 5 pulses. Add remaining sour cream mixture and pulse until dough begins to form, about 15 pulses.

2. Transfer mixture to lightly floured counter and knead briefly until dough comes together. Form dough into 6-inch disk, wrap tightly in plastic wrap, and refrigerate for 30 minutes. (Dough can be refrigerated for up to 24 hours; let chilled dough sit on counter for 15 minutes to soften before rolling.)

3. For the filling Melt butter in 10-inch skillet over medium heat. Add onion and ¼ teaspoon salt and cook until softened, about 5 minutes. Stir in thyme and garlic and cook until fragrant, about 30 seconds. Let cool slightly, about 5 minutes. Combine cooled onion mixture, steak, rutabaga, potatoes, 2 teaspoons salt, and ¾ teaspoon pepper in bowl. Add flour and toss to coat.

4. Adjust oven rack to upper-middle position and heat oven to 375 degrees. Line rimmed baking sheet with parchment paper. Remove dough from refrigerator, cut into 6 equal pieces (about 5 ounces each), and cover with plastic wrap. Divide filling into 6 equal portions, about 1 heaping cup each.

5. Working with 1 piece of dough at a time, roll into 10 by 8-inch oval (about ⅛ inch thick) on lightly floured counter. Place 1 portion filling in center of dough. Moisten edges of dough with water, then fold narrow end of oval over filling to form half-moon shape. Press dough around filling to adhere.

6. Trim any ragged edges, then crimp edges with fork to seal and transfer to prepared sheet. (For more decorative edge, trim any ragged edges and, starting at 1 end, pinch and slightly twist dough diagonally across seam between your thumb and index finger. Continue pinching and twisting dough around seam.) Repeat with remaining dough and filling.

7. Using paring knife, cut 1-inch vent hole on top of each pasty. Whisk egg and 2 teaspoons water together in bowl. Brush pasties with egg wash. Bake until crust is golden brown and filling is bubbling up through vent hole, about 45 minutes, rotating sheet halfway through baking. Transfer pasties to wire rack and let cool for 10 minutes before serving.

LETTUCES AND LEAFY GREENS

ettuces and similar soft leafy greens are
among the most widely eaten vegetables in
America today—as witnessed by the dizzying
array of these greens available at supermarkets and
farmers' markets alike. Luckily, all of these greens
are extremely easy to work with, most typically
being served raw as the base of a salad (but not
always, as you'll see here). Given the wide variety
you have to choose from, we think it's smart to
know how to mix and match them properly to
build all sorts of interesting salads with different
textures, flavors, and colors.

More delicate lettuces like **BOSTON**, **BIBB**, and red
and green **LEAF LETTUCE** usually work best with
simple, mild flavor combinations, so that the subtle
greens are highlighted rather than overpowered.
Stronger-flavored leafy greens like **ARUGULA** and
WATERCRESS can easily stand up to bigger flavors.

And ever-popular **ROMAINE** lettuce may well be
the culinary bridge between these two categories,
because it goes so well with all sorts of flavors.

Since lettuces and leafy greens are most classically
used in salads, we offer several distinct side salads,
ranging from our couldn't-be-easier Simplest Salad
to a classic steakhouse-style Wedge Salad to our
bold, beautifully charred Grilled Caesar Salad. But
salads can also be a satisfyingly substantial main
course, as you'll see in the Arugula Salad with
Steak Tips and Gorgonzola. We also use Bibb
lettuce leaves as wraps in our Chinese Chicken
Lettuce Wraps. And tender but peppery baby
arugula is an integral and flavorful component
of Spaghetti al Vino Bianco, a unique dish in
which pasta is cooked, risotto-style, in white
wine to infuse it with rich flavor.

shopping and storage

A vast array of lettuces and leafy greens are available year-round. Not only that, but the same greens are available in multiple options: as prewashed full heads in a bag, as prewashed full heads or chopped heads in a clamshell, prewashed and chopped in a bag, and loose (and not prewashed) in bulk bins. How do you decide?

Whole lettuce heads, prewashed or not, are always better choices than bags or clamshells of chopped lettuce that you can otherwise buy as whole heads, like romaine, Bibb, or red leaf. Precut lettuce will be inferior in quality because the leaves begin to spoil once they are cut.

Crisp lettuce, like romaine, is fine to buy prewashed, since it will keep well for up to a week. For tender lettuce, like Bibb, the best choice is the non-prewashed heads in bulk bins. Leafy greens like arugula, mâche, and watercress are often sold prewashed in cellophane bags. They offer great convenience, but be sure to turn the bags over and inspect the greens closely. If you see moisture trapped in the bag or hints of blackened leaf edges, move on. If you purchase these greens in bunches (sometimes the roots will be attached), wash them well before using, as they can be sandy.

To store crisp lettuce, such as iceberg or romaine, core the lettuce, wrap it in paper towels, and refrigerate it in a partially open plastic produce bag.

To store tender lettuce, such as Boston or Bibb, if the lettuce comes with the roots attached, leave them attached and store in the original plastic container or an open plastic produce bag. If the lettuce is without roots, wrap it in paper towels and refrigerate in an open plastic produce bag.

To store leafy greens, such as arugula, mesclun, and watercress, refrigerate in the original plastic container or bag if prewashed. If not prewashed, lightly roll in paper towels and store in an open plastic produce bag in the refrigerator.

pairing salad greens with vinaigrettes

Most salad greens fall into one of two categories: mellow or assertive. When you're making a green salad, it's important to choose your vinaigrette recipe carefully to complement the greens you're using.

Milder Boston, Bibb, iceberg, mâche, mesclun, red and green leaf, and romaine lettuces are best highlighted by a simple dressing such as a classic red wine or lemony vinaigrette.

Assertive, spicier greens like arugula, watercress, and escarole can easily stand up to strong flavors like mustard, shallots, and balsamic vinegar and can also be paired with a slightly sweet or creamy vinaigrette.

vegetable prep

Perfectly Dry Salad Greens

To make sure salad greens are as dry as possible before dressing them, add paper towels to the salad spinner with the greens and spin them together, or toss spun greens in a large bowl with a few sheets of torn paper towels. The paper towels will wick away any last traces of moisture. In either case, be sure to pick out all of the towel pieces before dressing the salad!

all about salad greens

ARUGULA Also called rocket, these delicate dark green leaves have a peppery bite. Serve them alone for a full-flavored salad, or combine them with milder greens like Belgian endive.

BIBB These small, compact heads have pale- to medium-green leaves; they are soft and buttery outside and crunchier inside, with a sweet, mild flavor. Combine Bibb with watercress, endive, or romaine.

BOSTON The loose, fluffy heads range in color from pale green to red-tipped. Boston lettuce is similar in texture and flavor to Bibb, but with softer leaves. Combine them with watercress, endive, or romaine.

ICEBERG Large, round, tightly packed very pale green heads are very crisp and crunchy, with minimal flavor. Toss chunks with Bibb, Boston, or loose-leaf lettuce.

LOOSE-LEAF LETTUCES Green leaf and red leaf lettuces have ruffled leaves in big, loose, heads; the leaves have a soft yet crunchy texture. Pair either with watercress, arugula, radicchio, or romaine.

MÂCHE Also called lamb's lettuce or lamb's tongue, these small heads of deep green leaves are very delicate and sweet. Combine mâche with arugula or watercress.

MESCLUN Also called spring mix or field greens, this blend can contain up to 14 different types of baby greens, so its flavors can range from mild to more assertive and slightly bitter depending on the specific mix. Mesclun is great for multi-textured and -flavored salads.

ROMAINE Long, full heads are made up of deep green leaves that are crisp and crunchy, with a mild flavor. The tough outer leaves should be discarded from full heads. Hearts of romaine are also sold in bags of three. This all-purpose lettuce is great alone or mixed with any others.

WATERCRESS The delicate, dark green leaves have tough, bitter stems that should be trimmed; the leaves have a refreshing spicy flavor similar to arugula. Mix with milder greens like Bibb or Boston to add punch and texture.

SIMPLEST SALAD

Serves 4   Total time: 15 minutes

WHY THIS RECIPE WORKS *This utterly minimalist way to make a simple green salad requires no measuring, no whisking, and (virtually) no thought. It's an elegant pairing with just about any dish. And you need only the bare minimum of ingredients: salad greens of your choice, extra-virgin olive oil, vinegar, a garlic clove, and salt and pepper. We like to rub the bowl with the peeled and halved garlic clove to impart just a hint of flavor. Because of the pure simplicity of this salad, it's vital to use high-quality ingredients— there are no bells and whistles to let you get away with camouflaging wilted lettuce, flavorless oil, or too-harsh vinegar. Be sure to use interesting and flavorful leafy greens, such as mesclun, arugula, or Bibb lettuce, rather than those with a very neutral flavor, like iceberg lettuce.*

½ garlic clove, peeled
8 ounces (8 cups) lettuce, torn into
    bite-size pieces if necessary
    Extra-virgin olive oil
    Vinegar
    Salt and pepper

Rub inside of salad bowl with garlic. Add lettuce. Slowly drizzle oil over lettuce, tossing greens very gently, until greens are lightly coated and just glistening. Season with vinegar, salt, and pepper to taste, and toss gently to coat. Serve.

BIBB LETTUCE, ORANGE, AND JÍCAMA SALAD WITH HONEY-MUSTARD VINAIGRETTE

Serves 4 to 6   Total time: 20 minutes

WHY THIS RECIPE WORKS *Oranges and lettuce greens are a classic salad combination that makes for a refreshing side dish all year long. Soft-textured, mild-tasting Bibb lettuce is a perfect canvas for citrusy flavors, so we decided to create a version with more orange flavor than usual. We discovered two tricks to get us there: First, adding orange zest intensified the orange flavor of the vinaigrette, which also included honey and mustard.*

Second, cutting the oranges into sections, rather than the more usual route of slicing them into rounds, ensured that we got rid of the bitter membranes and also that the sweet citrus pieces were more evenly and abundantly distributed throughout the salad. To complement the soft Bibb, jícama added its juicy crunch.

2 oranges, plus 2 teaspoons grated
    orange zest
2 tablespoons red wine vinegar
3 shallots, minced
1 tablespoon Dijon mustard
2 teaspoons honey
    Salt and pepper
¼ cup extra-virgin olive oil
2 heads Bibb lettuce (1 pound),
    leaves separated and torn into
    bite-size pieces (9 cups)
8 ounces jícama, peeled and sliced
    into ¼-inch matchsticks

1. Cut away peel and pith from oranges. Holding fruit over bowl, use paring knife to slice between membranes to release segments; set aside.

2. Whisk vinegar, shallots, mustard, honey, ½ teaspoon salt, ¼ teaspoon pepper, and orange zest together in medium bowl. While whisking constantly, slowly drizzle in oil until combined.

3. Pour all but 2 tablespoons dressing over greens in large bowl and toss to coat. Add jícama to bowl with remaining dressing and toss to coat. Season with salt and pepper to taste. Divide dressed greens among individual plates, then top with jícama and orange segments. Serve immediately.

WEDGE SALAD

Serves 6   Total time: 25 minutes

WHY THIS RECIPE WORKS *A crisp, chilled wedge salad is an ideal accompaniment to a steakhouse-style dinner: cool, crunchy iceberg lettuce, rings of red onion, a slice or two of beefsteak tomato, and creamy blue cheese dressing. A sprinkling of diced bacon is the pièce de résistance. But trying to replicate the*

wedge salad at home isn't as straightforward as it sounds. Many blue cheese dressing recipes yield gloppy dressings that sit like a gluey paste on the lettuce, or thin dressings that slide right off the lettuce wedge, or mass-market cheese. Here we used lots of crumbled Stilton—there's a reason the British call it the "king of cheeses." For balanced creaminess and tang, we included both mayonnaise and sour cream. A little milk thinned it to just the right consistency to nap the iceberg wedge. To assemble the salad, we decided on shallots rather than red onions, soaked briefly in vinegar to tame their flavor (and we used that vinegar in the dressing). Cherry tomatoes were a more flavorful year-round choice than beefsteak tomatoes. And, oh yes—the bacon. This wedge salad is so good that you barely need that T-bone.

1 large shallot, sliced into thin rings
¼ cup red wine vinegar
4 slices bacon
4 ounces Stilton blue cheese,
    crumbled (1 cup)
⅓ cup mayonnaise
¼ cup sour cream
3 tablespoons milk
1 garlic clove, minced
¼ teaspoon salt
¼ teaspoon pepper
1 head iceberg lettuce (2 pounds),
    cored and cut into 6 wedges
12 ounces cherry tomatoes, halved

1. Combine shallot and vinegar in bowl and let sit for 20 minutes. Meanwhile, cook bacon in 10-inch nonstick skillet over medium heat until crispy, 5 to 7 minutes. Using slotted spoon, transfer bacon to paper towel–lined plate; set aside.

2. Using fork, remove shallot from vinegar and set aside. Whisk 2 tablespoons vinegar, 3 ounces Stilton, mayonnaise, sour cream, milk, garlic, salt, and pepper in bowl until combined.

3. Arrange lettuce wedges on platter, drizzle with dressing, and top with reserved shallot and tomatoes. Crumble bacon over top and sprinkle with remaining 1 ounce Stilton. Serve.

KILLED SALAD

Serves 4   Total time: 20 minutes

WHY THIS RECIPE WORKS *Far from being "killed," this favorite side dish hailing from the mountains of Appalachia is vibrant and lively. At its simplest, killed salad (also called "kilt" salad, wilted salad, or smothered lettuce) is made by pouring hot bacon grease over torn fresh lettuce and chopped onions to warm and barely wilt the leafy greens. Recipes range from bare bones to more elaborate, and we found that the best approach fell somewhere in between. Using six slices of bacon with one head of greens (about 12 cups) allowed the bacon to enhance the lettuce rather than overwhelm it. Scallions provided a more harmonious flavor than onions. Apple cider vinegar, the traditional choice for the dressing, was also our favorite, packing a tangy punch with a bit of fruity sweetness. We used ½ cup to cut the richness of the bacon fat, and added a bit of sugar to temper the vinegar's acidity. Pouring the hot dressing over the lettuce and watching it wilt proved to be a remarkably satisfying sight. Firm greens work best for this salad—tasters especially liked green leaf lettuce, followed closely by romaine.*

- 1 head green leaf lettuce (12 ounces), torn into bite-size pieces
- 4 scallions, sliced thin
- 6 slices bacon, cut into ½-inch pieces
   Vegetable oil
- ½ cup cider vinegar
- 3 tablespoons sugar
   Salt and pepper

1. Combine lettuce and scallions in large serving bowl. Cook bacon in 10-inch non-stick skillet over medium heat until crispy, 5 to 7 minutes. Using slotted spoon, transfer bacon to paper towel–lined plate; set aside. Pour off all but 3 tablespoons fat from skillet (if you don't have 3 tablespoons, supplement with vegetable oil).

2. Whisk vinegar, sugar, 1 teaspoon salt, and ½ teaspoon pepper into skillet with fat and bring to boil.

3. Once boiling, immediately pour hot dressing over lettuce-scallion mixture and toss to combine. Season with salt and pepper to taste. Sprinkle with bacon and serve.

GRILLED CAESAR SALAD

Serves 6   Total time: 30 minutes

WHY THIS RECIPE WORKS *The smoky char of the grill brings a whole new dimension to plain old Caesar salad. To develop good char and maintain crisp lettuce without ending up with scorched, wilted, even slimy leaves, we used sturdy, compact romaine hearts, which withstood the heat of the grill better than whole heads. Halving them lengthwise and grilling on just one side gave them plenty of surface area for charring without turning limp. A hot fire meant that the heat didn't have time to penetrate and wilt the crunchy inner leaves before the exterior developed grill marks. Our boldly seasoned Caesar dressing replaced the raw egg with mayonnaise. It was so good that we got the idea to brush it on the cut side of the uncooked lettuce instead of olive oil, allowing the dressing to pick up a mildly smoky flavor on the grill along with the lettuce. For the croutons, we brushed baguette slices with olive oil, toasted them over the coals, and then rubbed them with a garlic clove. We combined the lettuce and croutons, drizzled on extra dressing, dusted everything with Parmesan, and called tasters. The salad disappeared. With apologies to Shakespeare: It's not that we love Caesar less, but that we love grilled Caesar more.*

DRESSING

- 1 tablespoon lemon juice
- 1 garlic clove, minced
- ½ cup mayonnaise
- ¼ cup grated Parmesan cheese
- 1 tablespoon white wine vinegar
- 1 tablespoon Worcestershire sauce
- 1 tablespoon Dijon mustard
- 2 anchovy fillets, rinsed
- ½ teaspoon salt
- ½ teaspoon pepper
- ¼ cup extra-virgin olive oil

SALAD

- 1 (12-inch) baguette, sliced ½ inch thick on bias
- 3 tablespoons extra-virgin olive oil
- 1 garlic clove, peeled
- 3 romaine lettuce hearts (18 ounces), halved lengthwise through cores
- ¼ cup grated Parmesan cheese

1. For the dressing Combine lemon juice and garlic in bowl and let stand for 10 minutes. Process lemon-garlic mixture, mayonnaise, Parmesan, vinegar, Worcestershire, mustard, anchovies, salt, and pepper in blender until smooth, about 30 seconds. With blender running, slowly add oil until incorporated. Measure out and reserve 6 tablespoons dressing for brushing romaine.

Chinese Chicken Lettuce Wraps

2a. For a charcoal grill Open bottom vent completely. Light large chimney starter filled with charcoal briquettes (6 quarts). When top coals are partially covered with ash, pour evenly over half of grill. Set cooking grate in place, cover, and open lid vent completely. Heat grill until hot, about 5 minutes.

2b. For a gas grill Turn all burners to high, cover, and heat grill until hot, about 15 minutes. Leave all burners on high.

3. For the salad Clean and oil cooking grate. Brush bread with oil and grill (over coals if using charcoal), uncovered, until browned, about 1 minute per side. Transfer to serving platter and rub with garlic clove. Brush cut sides of lettuce with half of reserved dressing. Place half of lettuce, cut side down, on grill (over coals if using charcoal). Grill, uncovered, until lightly charred, 1 to 2 minutes. Transfer to platter with bread. Repeat with remaining reserved dressing and lettuce. Drizzle lettuce with remaining dressing. Sprinkle with Parmesan. Serve.

ROAST CHICKEN AND WARM BREAD SALAD WITH ARUGULA

Serves 4 to 6   Total time: 1 hour 30 minutes (plus 24 hours refrigeration time)

WHY THIS RECIPE WORKS *San Francisco's famed Zuni Café serves a perfect roast chicken over a chewy-crisp, warm bread-and-greens salad that has a cultlike following. We pay homage with this simplified take, which is much more streamlined but still hits all the right notes: salty, savory, sweet, fresh, and bright. To preserve the soft texture of the arugula and highlight the way its pepperiness offsets the moist chicken and unctuous bread, we served the salad on the side. Salting and refrigerating the chicken drew moisture from the flesh, forming a brine that was eventually reabsorbed, seasoning the meat and keeping it juicy. The salt also made the skin crisp up better when roasted. This recipe was developed using Diamond Crystal Kosher Salt. If you have Morton Kosher Salt, which is denser, use only ½ teaspoon in the chicken cavity. For the bread, we prefer a round rustic loaf with a chewy, open crumb and a sturdy crust.*

1 (4-pound) whole chicken, giblets discarded
Kosher salt and pepper
4 (1-inch-thick) slices crusty bread (8 ounces), bottom crust removed, cut into ¾- to 1-inch pieces (5 cups)
¼ cup chicken broth
6 tablespoons plus 2 teaspoons extra-virgin olive oil
2 tablespoons champagne vinegar
1 teaspoon Dijon mustard
3 scallions, sliced thin
2 tablespoons dried currants
5 ounces (5 cups) baby arugula

1. With chicken breast side down, use kitchen shears to cut through bones on either side of backbone and discard backbone. Do not trim any excess fat or skin. Flip chicken over and press on breastbone to flatten.

2. Using your fingers, gently loosen center portion of skin covering each side of breast and legs. Rub ½ teaspoon salt under skin of each side of breast, ½ teaspoon salt under skin of each leg, and 1 teaspoon salt into bird's cavity. Tuck wingtips behind back and turn legs so drumsticks face inward toward breasts. Place chicken on large plate and refrigerate, uncovered, for 24 hours.

3. Adjust oven rack to middle position and heat oven to 475 degrees. Spray 12-inch skillet with vegetable oil spray. Toss bread with broth and 2 tablespoons oil until pieces are evenly moistened. Arrange bread in skillet in single layer, with majority of crusted pieces near center, crust side up.

4. Pat chicken dry with paper towels and place, skin side up, on top of bread, centered over crusted pieces. Brush 2 teaspoons oil over chicken skin and sprinkle with ¼ teaspoon salt and ¼ teaspoon pepper. Roast chicken until skin is deep golden brown and thickest part of breast registers 160 degrees and thighs register 175 degrees, 45 to 50 minutes, rotating skillet halfway through roasting. (Bread should be mix of softened, golden-brown, and crunchy pieces.)

5. While chicken roasts, whisk vinegar, mustard, ¼ teaspoon salt, and ¼ teaspoon pepper together in large bowl. While whisking constantly, slowly drizzle in remaining ¼ cup oil until combined. Stir in scallions and currants and set aside.

6. Transfer chicken to carving board and let rest, uncovered, for 15 minutes. Carve chicken and whisk any accumulated juices into vinaigrette. Add bread and arugula to vinaigrette and toss to coat. Transfer salad to serving platter and serve with chicken.

CHINESE CHICKEN LETTUCE WRAPS

Serves 4   Total time: 50 minutes

WHY THIS RECIPE WORKS *Tender Bibb lettuce leaves are soft enough to cradle other ingredients yet sturdy enough to hold together, and their naturally cupped shape begs you to fill them with something savory. Chinese chicken—tender morsels of chicken and crunchy vegetables stir-fried in a deeply flavored sauce—is a favorite choice. Boneless chicken thighs brought far more flavor than ground chicken. Freezing them briefly and then pulsing them in a food processor and tossing them in a soy sauce–rice wine mixture achieved juicy texture. Tasters agreed that including both water chestnuts and celery was ideal. We also added shiitake mushrooms, garlic, and scallions. The stir-fry was as bold and complex as it was light, and it all came together in less than an hour. We suggest serving the Bibb lettuce leaves on the side, for fun tableside assembly. Salty-sweet hoisin sauce is the perfect accompaniment. You can substitute dry sherry for the Chinese rice wine.*

CHICKEN

1 pound boneless, skinless chicken thighs, trimmed and cut into 1-inch pieces
2 teaspoons Chinese rice wine
2 teaspoons soy sauce
2 teaspoons toasted sesame oil
2 teaspoons cornstarch

SAUCE

3 tablespoons oyster sauce
1 tablespoon Chinese rice wine
2 teaspoons soy sauce
2 teaspoons toasted sesame oil
½ teaspoon sugar
¼ teaspoon red pepper flakes

STIR-FRY

- 2 tablespoons vegetable oil
- 2 celery ribs, cut into ¼-inch pieces
- 6 ounces shiitake mushrooms, stemmed and sliced thin
- ½ cup water chestnuts, cut into ¼-inch pieces
- 2 scallions, white parts minced, green parts sliced thin
- 2 garlic cloves, minced
- 1 head Bibb lettuce (8 ounces), leaves separated
  Hoisin sauce

1. For the chicken Place chicken on large plate in single layer and freeze until firm and beginning to harden around edges, about 20 minutes.

2. Whisk rice wine, soy sauce, oil, and cornstarch together in bowl. Pulse half of chicken in food processor until chopped into approximate ¼-inch pieces, about 10 pulses. Transfer to bowl with rice wine mixture and repeat with remaining chicken. Toss chicken to coat and refrigerate for 15 minutes.

3. For the sauce Whisk all ingredients together in bowl; set aside.

4. For the stir-fry Heat 1 tablespoon oil in 12-inch nonstick skillet over high heat until smoking. Add chicken and cook, stirring constantly, until opaque, 3 to 4 minutes. Transfer to bowl and wipe out skillet.

5. Heat remaining 1 tablespoon oil in now-empty skillet over high heat until smoking. Add celery and mushrooms and cook, stirring constantly, until mushrooms have reduced in size by half and celery is crisp-tender, 3 to 4 minutes. Add water chestnuts, scallion whites, and garlic and cook, stirring constantly, until fragrant, about 1 minute. Whisk sauce to recombine. Return chicken to skillet and add sauce, tossing to combine. Transfer to serving platter and sprinkle with scallion greens. Serve with lettuce leaves and hoisin sauce.

ARUGULA SALAD WITH STEAK TIPS AND GORGONZOLA

Serves 4   Total time: 30 minutes

WHY THIS RECIPE WORKS *Dressing peppery arugula with a simple vinaigrette and fortifying it with tender steak tips and blue cheese makes for a quick and elegant dinner salad. The vinaigrette has Dijon mustard to amp up the spiciness of the arugula, along with cider vinegar and honey to add a complementary fruity, sweet touch to the assertive greens. Sirloin steak tips, also known as flap meat, can be sold as whole steaks, cubes, and strips. To ensure uniform pieces, we prefer to purchase whole steaks and cut them ourselves after cooking. For optimal tenderness, make sure to slice the cooked steak against the grain (perpendicular to the fibers). You can substitute any blue cheese for the Gorgonzola.*

- 1 pound sirloin steak tips, trimmed
  Salt and pepper
- 6 tablespoons extra-virgin olive oil
- 1 shallot, minced
- 2 tablespoons cider vinegar
- 2 garlic cloves, minced
- 1 teaspoon Dijon mustard
- 1 teaspoon honey
- 12 ounces (12 cups) baby arugula
- 6 ounces Gorgonzola cheese, crumbled (1½ cups)

1. Pat steak dry with paper towels and season with salt and pepper. Heat 2 tablespoons oil in 12-inch nonstick skillet over medium-high heat until just smoking. Add steak and cook until well browned all over and beef registers 125 degrees, 8 to 10 minutes. Transfer to plate, tent with aluminum foil, and let rest for 5 to 10 minutes.

2. Whisk shallot, vinegar, garlic, mustard, honey, ¼ teaspoon salt, and ¼ teaspoon pepper together in large bowl. While whisking constantly, slowly drizzle in remaining ¼ cup oil until combined. Add arugula and Gorgonzola to vinaigrette and toss to combine. Season with salt and pepper to taste. Slice steak against grain ¼ inch thick. Divide salad among individual plates and top with sliced steak. Serve.

SALMON, AVOCADO, GRAPEFRUIT, AND WATERCRESS SALAD

Serves 4   Total time: 45 minutes

WHY THIS RECIPE WORKS *A composed salad layered on a platter should present an appealing mix of contrasting flavors, textures, and colors. The best examples can also be the simplest, as is the case with this beautiful pink-and-green salad. Watercress has a slight, pleasant bitterness and a peppery flavor punch, and a sturdy enough texture to act as the perfect bed for the rich toppings here. We roasted the salmon only until just translucent before flaking it into large chunks. Thick slices of buttery avocado added creaminess and more richness. For a bright, light contrast, we cut up two sweet-tart red grapefruits; the segments mimicked the shape of the avocado. We reserved some of the grapefruit juice to whisk up a simple vinaigrette. Finally, we added a sprinkle of crunchy toasted hazelnuts and torn mint leaves to take our composed salad over the top. To ensure uniform pieces of fish that cooked at the same rate, we found it best to buy a whole center-cut fillet and cut it into four pieces ourselves.*

- 1 (2-pound) skin-on center-cut salmon fillet, 1 inch thick
- 3 tablespoons plus 1 teaspoon extra-virgin olive oil
  Salt and pepper
- 2 red grapefruits
- 1 tablespoon minced shallot
- 1 teaspoon white wine vinegar
- 1 teaspoon Dijon mustard
- 4 ounces (4 cups) watercress, torn into bite-size pieces
- 1 ripe avocado, halved, pitted, and sliced ¼ inch thick
- ¼ cup fresh mint leaves, torn
- ¼ cup blanched hazelnuts, toasted and chopped

1. Adjust oven rack to lowest position, place foil-lined rimmed baking sheet on rack, and heat oven to 500 degrees.

2. Cut salmon crosswise into 4 fillets. Pat salmon dry with paper towels, rub with 1 teaspoon oil, and season with salt and pepper. Reduce oven to 275 degrees. Carefully place salmon skin side down on prepared

sheet. Roast until center is still translucent when checked with tip of paring knife and registers 120 degrees (for medium-rare), 6 to 8 minutes. Let salmon cool to room temperature, about 20 minutes. Flake salmon into 2-inch pieces.

3. Cut away peel and pith from grapefruits. Holding fruit over bowl, use paring knife to slice between membranes to release segments. Measure out 2 tablespoons grapefruit juice and transfer to medium bowl.

4. Whisk shallot, vinegar, mustard, and ½ teaspoon salt into grapefruit juice in bowl. While whisking constantly, slowly drizzle in remaining 3 tablespoons oil until combined. Arrange watercress in even layer on platter. Arrange salmon pieces, grapefruit segments, and avocado on top of watercress. Drizzle dressing over top, then sprinkle with mint and hazelnuts. Serve.

SPAGHETTI AL VINO BIANCO

Serves 4 to 6   Total time: 35 minutes

WHY THIS RECIPE WORKS *A plate of al dente pasta with peppery arugula, rich pancetta, toasted pine nuts, and salty Pecorino Romano sounds like a perfect dish to pair with a glass of white wine. Well, in this case, we actually cooked the pasta in the wine, exploiting this natural affinity to its fullest. The concept is not without precedent. There's an Italian dish called* spaghetti al vino rosso, *made with red wine. And stirring rice in a wine-spiked broth as it cooks transforms it from a blank slate into a complex and wonderful risotto. So, we reduced about a third of a bottle of white wine to a glaze in a skillet while the spaghetti parcooked in a pot of boiling water. Then we introduced the spaghetti to the delicate glaze and added the remainder of the bottle gradually, stirring as the spaghetti finished cooking. Stirring in assertive arugula, a bit of the pasta-cooking water, and some cream created our simple, satisfying sauce. Pancetta, pine nuts, and grated Pecorino sprinkled over the pasta before serving were shoo-ins. For this dish, use a good-quality dry white wine that's not heavily oaked.*

4 ounces pancetta, cut into ¼-inch pieces
1 tablespoon extra-virgin olive oil
2 garlic cloves, minced
  Pinch red pepper flakes
1 bottle (750 ml) dry white wine
  Salt and pepper
  Sugar
1 pound spaghetti
5 ounces (5 cups) baby arugula
⅓ cup heavy cream
1 ounce Pecorino Romano, grated
  (½ cup), plus extra for serving
¼ cup pine nuts, toasted and chopped

1. Cook pancetta and oil in 12-inch skillet over medium-high heat until pancetta is browned and crisp, 4 to 5 minutes. Using slotted spoon, transfer pancetta to paper towel–lined plate. Pour off all but 2 tablespoons fat from skillet.

2. Reduce heat to medium-low, stir in garlic and pepper flakes, and cook, stirring frequently, until garlic begins to turn golden, 1 to 2 minutes. Carefully add 1½ cups wine and increase heat to medium-high. Cook until wine is reduced to ½ cup, 8 to 10 minutes. Add ½ teaspoon salt and season with sugar to taste (add sugar as needed in 1-teaspoon increments).

3. Bring 4 quarts water to boil in large pot. Add pasta and 1 tablespoon salt and cook, stirring often, until pasta is flexible but not fully cooked, about 4 minutes. Reserve 2 cups pasta water, then drain pasta.

4. Transfer pasta to skillet with reduced white wine and add ½ cup unreduced wine. Cook over medium heat, tossing pasta constantly, until wine is fully absorbed. Add remaining wine, ½ cup at a time, tossing pasta constantly, until pasta is al dente, about 8 minutes. (If wine is absorbed before spaghetti is fully cooked, add ½ cup reserved pasta water at a time to skillet and continue to cook.)

5. Off heat, top spaghetti with arugula. Pour ¼ cup reserved pasta water over arugula, cover, and let stand for 1 minute. Add cream and ¼ cup Pecorino Romano, tossing until pasta is lightly coated with sauce and arugula is evenly distributed. Season with salt and pepper to taste. Transfer to serving platter and sprinkle with pancetta, remaining ¼ cup Pecorino Romano, and pine nuts. Serve immediately, passing extra Pecorino Romano separately.

MUSHROOMS

With more than 300 edible mushroom varieties, it's surprising that until relatively recently, most markets carried just one type of fresh mushroom consistently: the white button mushroom. The primary reason? Availability. But happily, those days are gone for good. Cremini and portobello were the first to make inroads on the white mushroom's domain, and nowadays stores display up to a dozen varieties. Also, many mushrooms that were once truly wild and seasonal, like oyster and shiitake mushrooms, are now farmed year-round.

Until the turn of the 20th century, even the white mushroom was considered rare and exotic. The French were the first to discover how to cultivate mushrooms, when 17th-century Parisian melon growers discovered that compost from their crops provided a favorable growing medium for white mushrooms. Soon mushrooms grown in specially prepared caves dotted the city, earning them the moniker *champignon de Paris*. In the United States, late-19th-century florists in Pennsylvania were the first to successfully cultivate mushrooms, using the dark spaces under their greenhouse shelves. These efforts were followed in the 20th century with "mushroom houses," which made cultivation easier through their controlled environments.

Today the United States leads the world in mushroom consumption. In this chapter, we enjoy them sautéed (with sesame and ginger), roasted (with garlic and smoky paprika, or Parmesan and pine nuts), marinated (for a new take, check out our Brioche Toasts with Mushroom Conserva and Ricotta), and grilled (portobellos make a mean burger). They also add their unique umami qualities to stir-fries, stews, and sauces, as in our Stir-Fried Portobellos with Soy-Maple Sauce and our Mushroom Ragu.

shopping and storage

We prefer loose rather than prepackaged mushrooms, since you can more closely inspect their condition. Look for large, intact caps; avoid those with discoloration or dry patches. The mushrooms should feel faintly damp but never moist or slimy, and their texture should be springy, not spongy. Aroma is another indicator of quality and intensity—the stronger the sweet, earthy scent, the more flavorful the mushrooms. Don't buy mushrooms that smell sour, and look for those with minimal stems, since those are often discarded.

Fresh mushrooms are extremely perishable, thanks to their high moisture content. To keep them fresh for as long as possible, store loose mushrooms in a partially open zipper-lock bag, which maximizes air circulation without drying them out. If you purchase prepackaged mushrooms, keep them in their original containers, which are designed to breathe. If you open a sealed box but don't use all the mushrooms, simply rewrap the container with plastic wrap. Don't store mushrooms in a paper bag or cover them with damp paper towels (two often suggested techniques); both will speed rather than slow deterioration.

Dried mushrooms are typically sold in cellophane packages. Look for packages without a lot of dust or crumbled bits inside; also, those labeled "wild mushroom mix" are often of lesser quality. Dried mushrooms should smell earthy, not musty or stale. Store them in an airtight container in a dry place for up to a year.

rehydrating dried mushrooms

If a recipe calls for rehydrating dried mushrooms before use, place them in a bowl, cover with water, and let soak as directed, allowing sand and dirt to fall to the bottom of the bowl. Use a fork to gently lift the mushrooms from the water without stirring up the sand. For a flavorful cooking liquid, strain the soaking water through a small strainer lined with a coffee filter.

commonly available fresh and dried varieties

WHITE Also called button mushrooms, these are the highly adaptable blank canvas of the mushroom world. They have a soft texture and extremely mild flavor.

CREMINI Cremini mushrooms are firmer in texture and more flavorful than white mushrooms. These are our favorite all-purpose mushrooms.

PORTOBELLO These giant oversized creminis have a meaty texture and strong, earthy flavor. Portobellos are often grilled or broiled whole, which makes a dramatic presentation.

SHIITAKE (FRESH AND DRIED) These Asian mushrooms have umbrella-shaped brown caps that add a meaty texture and delicious flavor when cooked. Discard the tough stems before cooking.

OYSTER Ranging from pale to dark gray in color, with a fluted cap resembling their namesake, oyster mushrooms are chewy yet delicate in texture, with a slight anise flavor.

KING TRUMPET Also called king oyster, this is a different species from regular oyster mushrooms. The large, thick white stem is topped by a stout brown cap. They have a firm texture and meaty flavor.

CHANTERELLE Golden wavy caps with ruffled gills make chanterelle mushrooms look a little like flowers. They have a dense texture and nutty flavor.

MAITAKE Also called hen of the woods or sheepshead, these large clustered mushrooms somewhat resemble those alternate names. They have a soft texture and earthy, gamy flavor.

DRIED PORCINI The fresh version of this aromatic mushroom is wildly popular in Italy and France (where they are called cèpes). In America, we usually only see the dried version. They have a smooth texture and woodsy flavor.

vegetable prep

Cleaning Fresh Mushrooms

Although many sources advise against washing mushrooms (to avoid their soaking up any additional moisture), once we learned that mushrooms are over 80 percent water, we began to question their ability to absorb more liquid. To find out, we rinsed a batch in cold water, weighing them before and after their wash. Six ounces of mushrooms gained only about a quarter ounce of water, and most of this was beaded on the surface. So wash whole mushrooms just before cooking with them.

We like to use a salad spinner:

1. Place mushrooms in salad spinner basket and spray with water until clean.

2. Quickly fit basket into salad spinner and spin mushrooms dry.

Washing does cause discoloration, so if you're serving mushrooms raw, as in salad, clean them with a dry toothbrush for the prettiest presentation.

SAUTÉED MUSHROOMS WITH SHALLOTS AND THYME

Serves 4   Total time: 30 minutes

WHY THIS RECIPE WORKS *Simply sautéed mushrooms make a delicious and versatile side dish. But white mushrooms tend to shrink quite a bit when sautéed, so what looks like plenty when raw seems to shrivel away to nothing when cooked. We wanted to develop a quick sauté method that resulted in a big enough quantity to make an ample side dish. We discovered that overloading the skillet and extending the cooking time allowed the mushrooms to give up just enough liquid to eventually fit in a single layer and cook properly without shrinking away to nothing. They browned very nicely after we added a little butter to the skillet, and from there it was easy to enhance the dish with shallot, thyme, and Marsala—a classic flavor combination for complementing mushrooms. Halve small (under 1-inch) mushrooms, or quarter medium (1- to 2-inch) or large (more than 2-inch) ones.*

- 1 tablespoon vegetable oil
- 1½ pounds white mushrooms, trimmed and halved if small or quartered if medium or large
- 1 tablespoon unsalted butter
- 1 shallot, minced
- 1 tablespoon minced fresh thyme or 1 teaspoon dried
- ¼ cup dry Marsala
  Salt and pepper

1. Heat oil in 12-inch nonstick skillet over medium-high heat until shimmering. Add mushrooms and cook, stirring occasionally, until they release their liquid, about 5 minutes. Increase heat to high and cook, stirring occasionally, until liquid has evaporated, about 8 minutes.

2. Stir in butter, reduce heat to medium, and cook, stirring often, until mushrooms are dark brown, about 8 minutes.

3. Stir in shallot and thyme and cook until shallot is softened, about 3 minutes. Add Marsala and cook until evaporated, about 2 minutes. Season with salt and pepper to taste, and transfer to platter. Serve.

VARIATION

Sautéed Mushrooms with Sesame and Ginger

Substitute 1 tablespoon vegetable oil for butter and 2 tablespoons mirin and 2 tablespoons soy sauce for Marsala. Omit shallot and thyme. After browning mushrooms in step 2, stir in 1 tablespoon toasted sesame seeds and 1 tablespoon grated fresh ginger and cook until fragrant, about 30 seconds. Stir in 1 teaspoon toasted sesame oil and sprinkle with 2 thinly sliced scallions after seasoning with salt and pepper to taste in step 3.

ROASTED KING TRUMPET MUSHROOMS

Serves 4   Total time: 45 minutes

WHY THIS RECIPE WORKS *The king trumpet mushroom (or king oyster mushroom) is a popular variety native to the Mediterranean, the Middle East, North Africa, and many parts of Asia. These large, stumpy mushrooms have little aroma or flavor when raw. But cooking transforms them: They become deeply savory, with the meaty texture of squid or tender octopus. We wanted to highlight this special quality by preparing these mushrooms almost like a piece of meat. We started by halving and crosshatching each mushroom, creating attractive "fillets," and then salting them and letting them sit briefly. Roasting the mushrooms cut side down in a hot oven resulted in plump and juicy well-seasoned mushrooms with a nicely browned exterior crust. These mushrooms are delicious on their own, with just a squeeze of lemon. But to gild the lily, we also developed two potent sauces (which follow). Look for trumpet mushrooms that are 3 to 4 ounces in size.*

- 1¾ pounds king trumpet mushrooms
  Salt and pepper
- 4 tablespoons unsalted butter, melted
  Lemon wedges

1. Adjust oven rack to lowest position and heat oven to 500 degrees. Trim bottom ½ inch of mushroom stems, then halve mushrooms lengthwise. Cut ¹⁄₁₆-inch-deep slits on cut side of mushrooms, spaced ½ inch apart, in crosshatch pattern. Sprinkle cut side of mushrooms with ½ teaspoon salt and let sit for 15 minutes.

2. Brush mushrooms evenly with melted butter, season with pepper to taste, and arrange cut side down on rimmed baking sheet. Roast until mushrooms are browned on cut side, 20 to 24 minutes. Transfer to serving platter. Serve with lemon wedges.

SAUCES

Red Wine–Miso Sauce

Bring 1 cup dry red wine, 1 cup vegetable broth, 2 teaspoons sugar, and ½ teaspoon soy sauce to simmer in 10-inch skillet over medium heat and cook until reduced to ⅓ cup, 20 to 25 minutes. Off heat, whisk in 1 tablespoon unsalted butter and 5 teaspoons miso until smooth. Serve with mushrooms.

Brown Butter–Lemon Vinaigrette

Melt 4 tablespoons unsalted butter in 10-inch skillet over medium heat. Cook, swirling constantly, until butter is dark golden brown and has nutty aroma, 3 to 5 minutes. Off heat, whisk in 2 tablespoons lemon juice, 1 teaspoon Dijon mustard, 1 teaspoon maple syrup, ¼ teaspoon salt, and ⅛ teaspoon pepper. Serve with mushrooms.

ROASTED MUSHROOMS WITH PARMESAN AND PINE NUTS

Serves 4   Total time: 55 minutes

WHY THIS RECIPE WORKS *This rich, woodsy blend of cremini and shiitake mushrooms shows that roasting is a fantastic—and largely hands-off—way to cook mushrooms. The unusual step of brining the mushrooms first turned out to be the key to flavorful, moist roasted mushrooms. This quick process seasoned the mushrooms evenly and allowed them to absorb moisture through their gills and cut surfaces, which improved the texture of the drier shiitakes in particular. After spreading them on a rimmed baking sheet, we roasted the brined mushrooms for just under an hour, until they were darkly browned. To give the savory mushrooms a rich finish, we coated them in melted butter and lemon juice and tossed in Parmesan, parsley, and toasted pine nuts.*

Roasted King Trumpet Mushrooms
with Red Wine–Miso Sauce

Salt and pepper

1½ pounds cremini mushrooms, trimmed and left whole if small, halved if medium, or quartered if large

1 pound shiitake mushrooms, stemmed, caps larger than 3 inches halved

2 tablespoons extra-virgin olive oil

1 ounce Parmesan cheese, grated (½ cup)

2 tablespoons pine nuts, toasted

2 tablespoons chopped fresh parsley

2 tablespoons unsalted butter, melted

1 teaspoon lemon juice

1. Adjust oven rack to lowest position and heat oven to 450 degrees. Whisk 5 teaspoons salt into 2 quarts water in large container until dissolved. Add cremini mushrooms and shiitake mushrooms, cover with plate or bowl to submerge, and let sit for 10 minutes.

2. Drain mushrooms, then pat dry with paper towels. Transfer mushrooms to rimmed baking sheet and toss with oil to coat. Roast until liquid has completely evaporated, 35 to 45 minutes.

3. Carefully stir mushrooms and continue to roast until mushrooms are deeply browned, 5 to 10 minutes.

4. Transfer mushrooms to large serving bowl and toss with Parmesan, pine nuts, parsley, melted butter, and lemon juice. Season with salt and pepper to taste. Serve immediately.

VARIATIONS

Roasted Mushrooms with Harissa and Mint
Omit Parmesan and pine nuts and increase lemon juice to 2 teaspoons. Substitute 2 tablespoons mint for parsley. Add 1 minced garlic clove, 2 teaspoons harissa, ¼ teaspoon ground cumin, and ¼ teaspoon salt to mushroom mixture in step 4.

Roasted Mushrooms with Roasted Garlic and Smoked Paprika
Add 3 unpeeled garlic cloves to sheet with mushrooms in step 2. Remove garlic from sheet in step 3 when stirring mushrooms. When garlic is cool to touch, peel and mash. Omit Parmesan and pine nuts and substitute 2 teaspoons sherry vinegar for lemon juice. Add mashed garlic, ½ teaspoon smoked paprika, and ¼ teaspoon salt to mushroom mixture in step 4.

MARINATED MUSHROOMS

Makes about 4 cups   Total time: 45 minutes (plus 1 hour chilling time)

WHY THIS RECIPE WORKS *Tangy and flavorful, marinated mushrooms are great as a side dish or part of an antipasto platter, on salads and sandwiches, in pasta or egg dishes, and more. We found that recipes calling for raw mushrooms tended to become watery and flabby, because the raw mushrooms released a lot of liquid as they broke down in the dressing. So we first cooked the mushrooms in a skillet, covered to encourage them to release their liquid, and then uncovered so the liquid could evaporate. Adding shallot, garlic, oregano, and pepper flakes, along with vinegar, water, oil, and mustard, created an aromatic vinaigrette that the mushrooms soaked in as they cooled. The garlicky vinaigrette perfectly accented the meaty savoriness of the tender mushrooms. Use small mushrooms that are less than 1 inch in diameter. If you can't find small mushrooms, halve medium (1- to 2-inch) mushrooms or quarter large (more than 2-inch) ones before cooking.*

½ cup extra-virgin olive oil

2 pounds small white mushrooms, trimmed
Salt and pepper

1 large shallot, sliced thin

3 garlic cloves, crushed and peeled

1 teaspoon dried oregano

¼ teaspoon red pepper flakes

¾ cup red wine vinegar

½ cup water

1 tablespoon Dijon mustard

2 tablespoons minced fresh parsley

1. Heat 1 tablespoon oil in 12-inch nonstick skillet over medium heat until shimmering. Add mushrooms and ½ teaspoon salt, cover, and cook, stirring occasionally, until mushrooms have released their liquid, 8 to 10 minutes. Uncover, stir in 1 tablespoon oil, and cook until mushrooms are deep golden brown and tender, 10 to 12 minutes.

2. Stir in shallot, garlic, oregano, and pepper flakes and cook until fragrant, about 1 minute. Stir in vinegar and water and bring to boil. Cook until liquid is reduced by half, about 5 minutes.

3. Whisk remaining 6 tablespoons oil, mustard, ¼ teaspoon salt, and ¼ teaspoon pepper together in medium bowl. Add mushroom mixture and stir to combine. Let cool completely, then stir in parsley. Cover and refrigerate until chilled, at least 1 hour. Season with salt and pepper to taste. Serve.

BRIOCHE TOASTS WITH MUSHROOM CONSERVA AND RICOTTA

Serves 8   Total time: 1 hour

WHY THIS RECIPE WORKS *Falling somewhere between a marinade and a quick pickle, a conserva is a type of preserves that can be made with vegetables or fruits. It's a versatile pantry product to keep on hand for the holiday season or anytime you are planning to entertain. We started by cooking the mushrooms to drive off nearly all their moisture, first covering them to draw out their liquid and then uncovering them to cook it off, leaving behind perfect, umami- packed mushrooms. We stirred in a bright, tangy mixture of oil, vinegar, and herbs and gently processed the mixture until roughly chopped. Letting the mixture infuse for at least 30 minutes before serving was integral to developing flavor (and over more time, the conserva got even better). To serve this delicious condiment, we spread creamy, rich ricotta over toasted brioche slices and topped them with a generous portion of the mushrooms. We prefer the soft texture and rich flavor of brioche here, but any rustic bread will work.*

MUSHROOM CONSERVA

6 tablespoons extra-virgin olive oil

1 pound cremini mushrooms, halved

½ teaspoon salt

¼ teaspoon pepper

¼ cup white wine vinegar

1 teaspoon chopped fresh rosemary

1 teaspoon chopped fresh thyme

TOASTS

8 (½-inch-thick) slices brioche bread

1 garlic clove, peeled and halved
Extra-virgin olive oil

½ pound (1 cup) whole-milk ricotta
Flake sea salt

1 tablespoon minced fresh chives

1. **For the mushroom conserva** Heat 2 tablespoons oil in 12-inch nonstick skillet over medium-high heat until shimmering. Add mushrooms, salt, and pepper, cover, and cook until mushrooms have released their liquid, about 5 minutes. Uncover, increase heat to high, and cook, stirring occasionally, until mushrooms begin to brown, about 8 minutes. Stir in remaining ¼ cup oil, vinegar, rosemary, and thyme and bring to brief simmer. Remove from heat and let cool slightly, about 5 minutes.

2. Transfer mushroom mixture to food processor and pulse until coarsely chopped, about 5 pulses. Transfer conserva to bowl and set aside to cool to room temperature, about 30 minutes. (Conserva can be refrigerated for up to 2 weeks.)

3. **For the toasts** Adjust oven rack to middle position and heat oven to 400 degrees. Place bread slices in single layer on rimmed baking sheet. Bake until dry and crisp, about 10 minutes, flipping slices halfway through baking. While still warm, rub 1 side of each slice with garlic and drizzle with oil. Spread 2 tablespoons ricotta evenly over each slice of bread, followed by 2 tablespoons conserva. Drizzle toasts with extra oil, season with salt, and sprinkle with chives. Cut slices in half on diagonal. Serve.

SHAVED MUSHROOM AND CELERY SALAD

Serves 6   Total time: 25 minutes

WHY THIS RECIPE WORKS *Mushrooms and celery seem to have a natural flavor affinity, so we combined them in pursuit of salad perfection. To start, we chose earthy, full-flavored cremini mushrooms, slicing them very thin and marinating them in a bright lemon vinaigrette. This 10-minute soak in the acidic dressing softened and seasoned them, bringing out and balancing their flavor. Fresh celery gave our salad a much-desired crunch. Additional greenery came by way of parsley, for its clean taste, and tarragon, which supplied a pleasant bittersweetness with a hint of anise. Shaved Parmesan tossed in just before serving added nutty, salty richness. If your celery came without its leaves, you can substitute an extra 1 to 2 tablespoons chopped fresh parsley. Slice the mushrooms and celery as thinly as possible; this keeps the texture cohesive and allows the dressing to be absorbed more easily. Make sure not to marinate the mushrooms for longer than 10 minutes, or the salad will be too watery.*

8 ounces cremini mushrooms, trimmed and sliced thin
¼ cup extra-virgin olive oil
1 shallot, halved and sliced thin
1½ tablespoons lemon juice
   Salt and pepper
4 celery ribs, sliced thin, plus ½ cup celery leaves
2 ounces Parmesan cheese, shaved
½ cup fresh parsley leaves
2 tablespoons chopped fresh tarragon

1. Combine mushrooms, oil, shallot, lemon juice, and ¼ teaspoon salt in large bowl. Toss to coat, then let sit for 10 minutes.

2. Add celery ribs and leaves, Parmesan, parsley, and tarragon to mushroom-shallot mixture and toss to combine. Season with salt and pepper to taste. Serve.

WILD RICE AND MUSHROOM SOUP

Serves 6 to 8   Total time: 1 hour 45 minutes

WHY THIS RECIPE WORKS *Supremely comforting, this substantial and hearty—but not heavy—creamy soup is full of earthy, nutty, umami-rich depth from two kinds of mushrooms. Chewy, nutty wild rice is classically complemented by fresh cremini mushrooms and, for a dose of potent mushroom flavor, dried shiitakes. Grinding the shiitakes to a powder ensured that their flavor completely permeated the broth. Simmering the wild rice with baking soda decreased its cooking time and brought out more of its robust flavor. We used the rice simmering liquid as our broth, thus infusing the entire soup with wild rice flavor. Some cream stirred in at the end gave our soup a velvety texture. We finished the soup with chives and lemon zest for brightness. We used a spice grinder to process the dried shiitakes, but a blender also works.*

¼ ounce dried shiitake mushrooms, rinsed
5 garlic cloves, peeled (1 whole, 4 minced)
1 sprig fresh thyme
1 bay leaf

Salt and pepper

¼ teaspoon baking soda
1 cup wild rice
4 tablespoons unsalted butter
1 pound cremini mushrooms, trimmed and sliced ¼ inch thick
1 onion, chopped fine
1 teaspoon tomato paste
⅔ cup dry sherry
4 cups chicken or vegetable broth
1 tablespoon soy sauce
¼ cup cornstarch
½ cup heavy cream
¼ cup minced fresh chives
¼ teaspoon grated lemon zest

1. Adjust oven rack to middle position and heat oven to 375 degrees. Grind shiitake mushrooms in spice grinder until finely ground (you want about 3 tablespoons).

2. Bring 4 cups water, whole garlic clove, thyme, bay leaf, ¾ teaspoon salt, and baking soda to boil in medium saucepan over high heat. Add rice and return to boil. Cover, transfer to oven, and bake until rice is tender, 35 to 50 minutes. Strain rice through fine-mesh strainer set in 4-cup liquid measuring cup. Discard garlic, thyme, and bay leaf and set aside rice. Add enough water to reserved cooking liquid to measure 3 cups.

3. Melt butter in Dutch oven over high heat. Add cremini mushrooms, onion, tomato paste, minced garlic, ¾ teaspoon salt, and 1 teaspoon pepper. Cook, stirring occasionally, until vegetables are browned and dark fond develops on bottom of pot, about 15 minutes. Stir in sherry, scraping up any browned bits, and cook until pot is almost dry, about 2 minutes. Stir in ground shiitake mushrooms, reserved rice cooking liquid, broth, and soy sauce and bring to boil. Reduce heat to low and simmer, covered, until onion and mushrooms are tender, about 20 minutes.

4. Whisk cornstarch and ¼ cup water in small bowl until cornstarch is dissolved. Stir cornstarch mixture into soup, return to simmer, and cook until thickened, about 2 minutes. Off heat, stir in cooked rice, cream, chives, and lemon zest. Cover and let stand for 20 minutes. Season with salt and pepper to taste. Serve.

STIR-FRIED PORTOBELLOS WITH SOY-MAPLE SAUCE

Serves 4   Total time: 40 minutes

WHY THIS RECIPE WORKS *Hefty, meaty portobello mushrooms, in conjunction with snow peas and carrots, make for a super-satisfying vegetable stir-fry that's great as is or over rice. Cooking the mushrooms in two batches kept them from steaming in their own juices, guaranteeing even cooking and good browning, and adding a quick glaze at the end gave the mushrooms a strong sweet-salty flavor boost. We then stir-fried the snow peas and carrots in the same skillet until crisp-tender, added garlic and ginger and cooked until they were just fragrant, and stirred in the mushrooms and sauce to coat everything with its glossy goodness.*

GLAZE

3 tablespoons maple syrup
2 tablespoons mirin
1 tablespoon soy sauce

SAUCE

½ cup chicken or vegetable broth
2 tablespoons soy sauce
1½ tablespoons mirin
2 teaspoons rice vinegar
2 teaspoons cornstarch
2 teaspoons toasted sesame oil

VEGETABLES

3 tablespoons vegetable oil
2 garlic cloves, minced
2 teaspoons grated fresh ginger
¼ teaspoon red pepper flakes
2 pounds portobello mushroom caps, gills removed, cut into 2-inch wedges
8 ounces snow peas, strings removed and sliced ¼ inch thick on bias
2 carrots, peeled and cut into 2-inch-long matchsticks

1. For the glaze Whisk all ingredients together in bowl.

2. For the sauce Whisk all ingredients together in bowl.

3. For the vegetables Combine 1 teaspoon oil, garlic, ginger, and pepper flakes in bowl. Heat 1 tablespoon oil in 12-inch nonstick skillet over high heat until shimmering. Add half of mushrooms and cook, without stirring,

until browned on one side, 2 to 3 minutes. Flip mushrooms, reduce heat to medium, and cook until second side is browned and mushrooms are tender, about 5 minutes. Transfer to second bowl. Repeat with 1 tablespoon oil and remaining mushrooms.

4. Return all mushrooms to pan, add glaze, and cook over medium-high heat, stirring frequently, until glaze is thickened and mushrooms are coated, 1 to 2 minutes. Transfer mushrooms to bowl.

5. Wipe now-empty skillet clean with paper towels. Heat remaining 2 teaspoons oil in clean skillet over high heat until shimmering. Add snow peas and carrots and cook, stirring occasionally, until vegetables are crisp-tender, about 5 minutes. Clear center of skillet, add garlic mixture, and cook, mashing mixture into skillet, until fragrant, about 30 seconds. Stir garlic mixture into vegetables.

6. Return mushrooms to skillet. Whisk sauce to recombine, then add to skillet. Cook, stirring constantly, until sauce is thickened, 1 to 2 minutes. Transfer to serving platter. Serve.

GRILLED PORTOBELLO BURGERS

Serves 4   Total time: 50 minutes

WHY THIS RECIPE WORKS *Portobello mushroom burgers are no longer just a sad substitute for beef burgers; they are legitimately delicious choices on their own. For charry grilled portobellos that wouldn't leak moisture and make the buns soggy, we decided to try scoring them, a technique that works well with oven-roasted mushrooms. It worked like a charm on the grill. We lightly scored the mushrooms on the smooth, non-gill side in a crosshatch pattern. This helped expedite the release of moisture, which dripped out and evaporated on the grill, ensuring intense mushroom flavor and toasty, non-soggy buns. The crosshatching also allowed the mushrooms to absorb more marinade—a flavorful mix of olive oil, red wine vinegar, and garlic. Once they were cooked, we filled the portobello caps with a savory mixture of feta, sun-dried tomatoes, and roasted red peppers before stacking them on grilled buns with basil mayo, baby*

Flip mushrooms and onions and continue to cook (covered if using gas) until mushrooms are charred on second side, 3 to 5 minutes.

5. Transfer onions to platter and discard toothpicks. Transfer mushrooms to platter, gill side up, and divide feta mixture evenly among caps, packing down mixture. Return mushrooms to grill, feta side up, and cook, covered, until heated through, about 3 minutes.

6. Return mushrooms to platter and tent with aluminum foil. Spread basil mayonnaise evenly over roll bottoms and top each with 1 mushroom and 1 onion slice. Divide arugula evenly among burgers, then cap with roll tops. Serve.

MUSHROOM RAGU

Serves 4   Total time: 40 minutes

WHY THIS RECIPE WORKS *A treasure trove of fresh and dried mushrooms offers a bounty of flavors and textures in this saucy dish, which is ideal for topping pasta or polenta. Dried porcini delivered rich depth, while a combination of chanterelles— the very best wild mushrooms available in America—and portobellos provided deep, nutty flavor and meaty texture, respectively. To jump-start the process of developing fond (those flavorful brown bits that cling to the bottom of a pot), we microwaved the fresh mushrooms until they were tender and releasing some of their juice. We then added them to the Dutch oven with the dried porcini, along with red wine and tomatoes, and simmered everything until all the flavors melded. You can substitute any wild mushrooms for the chanterelles.*

18 ounces chanterelle mushrooms, trimmed and halved if small or quartered if large
1 pound portobello mushroom caps, gills removed, halved and sliced ½ inch thick
2 tablespoons unsalted butter
1 onion, chopped fine
½ ounce dried porcini mushrooms, rinsed and minced

arugula, and sweet grilled onions. If your mushrooms are larger or smaller than 4 to 5 inches, you may need to adjust the cooking time accordingly. If the mushrooms absorb all the marinade, simply brush the onions with olive oil before grilling in step 4.

4 portobello mushroom caps (4 to 5 inches in diameter), gills removed
½ cup extra-virgin olive oil
3 tablespoons red wine vinegar
1 garlic clove, minced
1 teaspoon salt
½ teaspoon pepper
4 ounces feta cheese, crumbled (1 cup)
½ cup jarred roasted red peppers, patted dry and chopped
½ cup oil-packed sun-dried tomatoes, patted dry and chopped
½ cup mayonnaise
½ cup chopped fresh basil
4 (½-inch-thick) slices red onion
4 kaiser rolls, split and toasted
1 ounce (1 cup) baby arugula

1. Cut ¹⁄₁₆-inch-deep slits on top of mushroom caps, spaced ½ inch apart, in crosshatch pattern. Combine mushrooms, oil, vinegar, garlic, salt, and pepper in

1-gallon zipper-lock bag, seal bag, and turn to coat. Let sit for at least 30 minutes or up to 1 hour.

2. Combine feta, red peppers, and sun-dried tomatoes in bowl. Whisk mayonnaise and basil together in separate bowl. Push 1 toothpick horizontally through each onion slice to keep rings intact while grilling.

3a. For a charcoal grill Open bottom vent completely. Light large chimney starter filled with charcoal briquettes (6 quarts). When top coals are partially covered with ash, pour evenly over grill. Set cooking grate in place, cover, and open lid vent completely. Heat grill until hot, about 5 minutes.

3b. For a gas grill Turn all burners to high, cover, and heat grill until hot, about 15 minutes. Turn all burners to medium-high.

4. Clean and oil cooking grate. Remove mushrooms from marinade, and brush onions all over with remaining mushroom marinade. Place onions and mushrooms, gill side up, on grill. Cook (covered if using gas) until mushrooms have released their liquid and are charred on first side, 4 to 6 minutes.

Salt and pepper

3 garlic cloves, minced

1 teaspoon minced fresh thyme or
¼ teaspoon dried

½ cup dry red wine

1 (14.5-ounce) can diced tomatoes,
drained with juice reserved, chopped

2 tablespoons minced fresh parsley

1. Microwave chanterelle mushrooms and portobello mushrooms in covered bowl, stirring occasionally, until tender and mushrooms have released their liquid, 6 to 8 minutes. Transfer mushrooms to colander set in bowl and let drain, reserving liquid.

2. Melt butter in Dutch oven over medium heat. Add onion, porcini mushrooms, and ½ teaspoon salt and cook until softened and lightly browned, 5 to 7 minutes. Add portobello and chanterelle mushrooms and cook, stirring often, until dry and lightly browned, about 5 minutes. Stir in garlic and thyme and cook until fragrant, about 30 seconds.

3. Stir in wine and reserved mushroom liquid, scraping up any browned bits. Stir in tomatoes and their juice, bring to simmer, and cook until ragu is slightly thickened, about 8 minutes. Off heat, stir in parsley and season with salt and pepper to taste. Serve.

MUSHROOM BOLOGNESE

Serves 4 to 6   Total time: 1 hour

WHY THIS RECIPE WORKS *Traditional Bolognese sauce gets its rich flavor from a combination of several types of meat. Since mushrooms are used so frequently, with great success, as a meat alternative, we wanted to develop a mushroom version of this classic Italian sauce that would have long-cooked flavor and hearty texture. We turned to two types of mushrooms to replicate that complexity: Dried porcini delivered depth of flavor, while a whopping 2 pounds of fresh cremini gave the sauce a satisfying, substantial texture. To further round out the sauce's savory qualities, we added two more umami-rich ingredients: soy sauce and tomato paste. To make prep easy, we used the food processor both to chop the cremini roughly and then to finely*

chop the onion and carrot. Pulsing whole canned tomatoes in the food processor gave us just the right texture. We also used red wine to bring richness and depth and a little sugar for some balancing sweetness. A dash of heavy cream (a traditional ingredient in Bolognese sauce) stirred in at the end gave it decadent silkiness.

2 pounds cremini mushrooms, trimmed and quartered

1 carrot, peeled and chopped

1 small onion, chopped

1 (28-ounce) can whole peeled tomatoes

3 tablespoons unsalted butter

½ ounce dried porcini mushrooms, rinsed and minced

3 garlic cloves, minced

1 teaspoon sugar

2 tablespoons tomato paste

1 cup dry red wine

½ cup vegetable broth

1 tablespoon soy sauce
Salt and pepper

3 tablespoons heavy cream

1 pound fettuccine or linguine
Grated Parmesan cheese

1. Working in batches, pulse cremini mushrooms in food processor until pieces are no larger than ½ inch, 5 to 7 pulses; transfer to large bowl. Pulse carrot and onion in now-empty processor until finely chopped, 5 to 7 pulses; transfer to bowl with mushrooms. Pulse tomatoes and their juice in now-empty processor until finely chopped, 6 to 8 pulses; set aside separately.

2. Melt butter in Dutch oven over medium heat. Add processed vegetables and porcini mushrooms, cover, and cook, stirring occasionally, until they release their liquid, about 5 minutes. Uncover, increase heat to medium-high, and cook until vegetables begin to brown, 12 to 15 minutes.

3. Stir in garlic and sugar and cook until fragrant, about 30 seconds. Stir in tomato paste and cook for 1 minute. Stir in wine and simmer until nearly evaporated, about 5 minutes.

4. Stir in processed tomatoes, broth, soy sauce, ½ teaspoon salt, and ¼ teaspoon pepper, and bring to simmer. Reduce heat

to medium-low and simmer until sauce has thickened but is still moist, 8 to 10 minutes. Off heat, stir in cream.

5. Meanwhile, bring 4 quarts water to boil in large pot. Add pasta and 1 tablespoon salt and cook, stirring often, until al dente. Reserve ½ cup cooking water, then drain pasta and return it to pot. Add sauce and toss to combine. Season with salt and pepper to taste and adjust consistency with reserved cooking water as needed. Serve with Parmesan.

MUSHROOM BOURGUIGNON

Serves 8   Total time: 1 hour 45 minutes

WHY THIS RECIPE WORKS *Chunks of portobello mushrooms napped in a silky, luscious sauce with pearl onions, carrots, garlic, and red wine will make you forget that traditional French bourguignon has boeuf (beef). Dried porcini mushrooms and anchovy paste helped "beef up" the flavor in this stew with their umami qualities. To achieve the body that would normally come from the collagen in the meat breaking down into the sauce, we simply stirred in a bit of powdered gelatin (giving us a smooth, unctuous sauce and cutting the cooking time to boot). Use a good-quality medium-bodied red wine, such as a Burgundy or other Pinot Noir, for this stew. If the pearl onions have a papery outer coating, remove by rinsing the onions in warm water and gently squeezing individual onions between your fingertips. Serve this over pasta, grains, or polenta.*

½ cup extra-virgin olive oil

5 pounds portobello mushroom caps, quartered

1½ cups frozen pearl onions, thawed
Salt and pepper

⅓ cup all-purpose flour

4 cups chicken or vegetable broth

1 (750-ml) bottle red wine

2 tablespoons unflavored gelatin

2 tablespoons tomato paste

1 tablespoon anchovy paste

2 onions, chopped

2 carrots, peeled and chopped

1 garlic head, cloves separated (unpeeled) and smashed

MUSHROOM BOURGUIGNON

It's with excellent reason that firm, "meaty" portobello mushrooms are often used in place of meat in vegetarian recipes. Here we set out to create a mushroom-based version of classic French beef bourguignon that had all the rich flavor and silky texture of the original dish. We think you'll agree that this is, at the least, equally delicious and impressive (and as a side bonus, it's so much faster).

1. Without removing the gills, cut the portobello mushroom caps into quarters.

2. After heating the oil to shimmering in a Dutch oven, add half of the portobello mushrooms, half of the pearl onions, and the salt and pepper.

3. After cooking the mushrooms and onions covered for 8 to 10 minutes to extract the mushroom liquid, uncover and continue to cook them for 12 to 15 minutes longer to drive off their moisture and concentrate their flavor. Repeat this with the remaining mushrooms.

4. Stir the aromatics into the broth mixture and simmer until the liquid is thickened and the onions are softened.

5. After extracting as much flavor as possible from the aromatics, strain the liquid through a fine-mesh strainer, pressing to extract as much liquid as possible. Discard the solids.

6. Stir in the remaining wine and cook to thicken the sauce. Stir the portobello-onion mixture into the sauce and cook until heated through, 3 to 5 minutes. Serve over polenta, pasta, or grains.

Chicken Marsala

1 ounce dried porcini mushrooms, rinsed
10 sprigs fresh parsley, plus 3 tablespoons minced
6 sprigs fresh thyme
2 bay leaves
½ teaspoon black peppercorns

1. Heat 3 tablespoons oil in Dutch oven over medium-high heat until shimmering. Add half of portobello mushrooms, half of pearl onions, ¼ teaspoon salt, and ⅛ teaspoon pepper, cover, and cook, stirring occasionally, until mushrooms have released their liquid, 8 to 10 minutes.

2. Uncover and continue to cook, stirring occasionally and scraping bottom of pot, until mushrooms are tender and pan is dry, 12 to 15 minutes. Transfer vegetables to bowl, cover, and set aside. Repeat with 3 tablespoons oil, remaining portobello mushrooms, remaining pearl onions, ¼ teaspoon salt, and ⅛ teaspoon pepper.

3. Add remaining 2 tablespoons oil and flour to now-empty pot and whisk until no dry flour remains. Whisk in broth, 2 cups wine, gelatin, tomato paste, and anchovy paste until combined, scraping up any browned bits and smoothing out any lumps. Stir in chopped onions, carrots, garlic, porcini mushrooms, parsley sprigs, thyme sprigs, bay leaves, and peppercorns. Bring to boil and cook, stirring occasionally, until liquid is slightly thickened and onions are translucent and softened, about 15 minutes.

4. Strain liquid through fine-mesh strainer set over large bowl, pressing on solids to extract as much liquid as possible; discard solids. Return liquid to now-empty pot and stir in remaining wine.

5. Bring mixture to boil over medium-high heat. Cook, stirring occasionally, until sauce has thickened to consistency of heavy cream, 5 to 7 minutes. Reduce heat to medium-low, stir in reserved portobello-onion mixture, and cook until just heated through, 3 to 5 minutes. Stir in minced parsley and serve.

CHICKEN MARSALA

Serves 4 to 6   Total time: 1 hour 30 minutes

WHY THIS RECIPE WORKS *Beloved for its silky, winey, mushroomy sauce, chicken Marsala is an Italian-American restaurant favorite that we wanted to make more approachable—and more delicious—for the home cook. White mushrooms are often used in restaurants, but here we use more flavorful cremini, along with even more intensely flavored dried porcini. To make identically sized pieces of chicken that could easily be pounded into cutlets, we first cut each chicken breast in half crosswise. Then, we cut the thicker half in half horizontally to make three pieces. We salted the cutlets briefly and then dredged them in flour, which helped accelerate browning and prevented the meat from overcooking. For the sauce, we used reduced dry Marsala and chicken broth for rich flavor and a little powdered gelatin to create a silky, full-bodied texture. Use a good-quality dry Marsala for this recipe.*

2¼ cups dry Marsala
4 teaspoons unflavored gelatin
1 ounce dried porcini mushrooms, rinsed
4 (6- to 8-ounce) boneless, skinless chicken breasts, trimmed
Salt and pepper
2 cups chicken broth
¾ cup all-purpose flour
¼ cup plus 1 teaspoon vegetable oil
3 ounces pancetta, cut into ½-inch pieces
1 pound cremini mushrooms, trimmed and sliced thin
1 shallot, minced
1 tablespoon tomato paste
1 garlic clove, minced
2 teaspoons lemon juice
1 teaspoon minced fresh oregano
3 tablespoons unsalted butter, cut into 6 pieces
2 teaspoons minced fresh parsley

1. Bring 2 cups Marsala, gelatin, and porcini mushrooms to boil in medium saucepan, then reduce heat to medium-high and simmer vigorously until reduced by half, 6 to 8 minutes.

2. Meanwhile, cut each chicken breast in half crosswise, then cut thick end in half horizontally, creating 3 cutlets per breast of about same thickness. Pound cutlets between 2 sheets of plastic wrap to uniform ½-inch thickness. Toss cutlets with 1 teaspoon salt and ½ teaspoon pepper in bowl and set aside for 15 minutes.

3. Strain Marsala reduction through fine-mesh strainer, pressing on solids to extract as much liquid as possible; discard solids. Return Marsala reduction to saucepan, add broth, and return to boil. Reduce heat to medium-high and simmer until reduced to 1½ cups, 10 to 12 minutes; set aside.

4. Spread flour in shallow dish. Working with 1 cutlet at a time, dredge in flour, shaking gently to remove excess, then place on wire rack set in rimmed baking sheet. Heat 2 tablespoons oil in 12-inch skillet over medium-high heat until just smoking. Place 6 cutlets in skillet and reduce heat to medium. Cook until golden brown, 2 to 3 minutes per side. Return cutlets to wire rack. Repeat with 2 tablespoons oil and remaining 6 cutlets.

5. Cook pancetta in now-empty skillet over medium-low heat, stirring and scraping pan bottom to loosen any browned bits, until brown and crisp, about 4 minutes. Stir in cremini mushrooms, increase heat to medium-high, and cook until mushrooms begin to brown, about 8 minutes. Using slotted spoon, transfer cremini mushrooms and pancetta to bowl. Add remaining 1 teaspoon oil and shallot to fat left in pan and cook until softened, 1 minute. Add tomato paste and garlic and cook until fragrant, 30 seconds. Stir in lemon juice, oregano, reduced Marsala mixture, and remaining ¼ cup Marsala and bring to simmer.

6. Nestle cutlets into sauce and simmer for 3 minutes, flipping halfway through simmering. Transfer cutlets to serving platter. Off heat, whisk butter into sauce in skillet. Stir in parsley and cremini mushroom mixture and season with salt and pepper to taste. Spoon sauce over chicken and serve.

OKRA

Okra is a quintessential vegetable of the American South, where, evocatively, it is also sometimes called "ladies' fingers." It's the edible seedpod of a plant in the same family as hibiscus and cotton, two other plants that thrive in the South. Okra's fresh green vegetal flavor and delicate crunch is something like a cross between green beans and zucchini. However, for many people, its most memorable characteristic is its unique texture. It has a rich, moist quality, but if cooked improperly, it can become, for lack of a more appetizing description, downright slimy.

Southerners have a long history with okra (the plant came to America from Africa in the days of slavery) and know how to treat it right. They fry, pickle, smother, and bake their okra. But its most famous use, and the reason it is probably most known outside the South, is its role as a thickener in Cajun dishes like gumbos and étouffées. This thickening quality is thanks to the viscous liquid, called mucilage, inside the pods—similar to that found in the aloe vera plant. In other recipes, the goal is generally to minimize rather than empha-size this unique gelatinous characteristic.

Fresh okra, with its crisp-tender texture and bright flavor, shines in recipes like Roasted Okra with Fennel and Oregano and Charred Sichuan-Style Okra. There are times when convenient and always available frozen okra works as well as fresh, includ-ing in our irresistibly poppable Deep-Fried Okra, and recipes that involve stew-type cooking methods, like Caribbean Okra Pepper Pot, Greek Stewed Okra with Tomatoes, and—of course—our gumbo.

shopping and storage

Okra is becoming more and more available throughout the country, not just in the South, but its best season is summer and into the fall. When shopping for okra, size is the most important consideration. Look for firm, unblemished fresh okra pods that are no longer than 3 inches in length. Pods larger than that will often be tough, and no cooking method will prevent them from becoming slimy. Okra is more perishable than most vegetables; store the fresh pods in a paper bag in the refrigerator for just a day or two.

frozen is a-ok

It might seem slightly off-kilter to suggest using frozen veggies in a book that's all about the bounty of fresh vegetables. And although we typically prefer fresh okra to frozen, there are certain times when using frozen okra provides higher convenience and greater accessibility without sacrificing anything in the way of flavor. Namely, if you are making stewy types of dishes, like our Gumbo, Red Beans and Rice with Okra and Tomatoes, or Caribbean Okra Pepper Pot, frozen works just as well as fresh. For okra cooked using dry, high heat, such as Sautéed Okra, fresh is still best.

vegetable prep

Trimming Okra

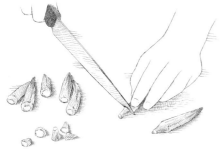

Trim tough, woody stems from okra pods before cooking. If using pods whole, be sure to leave top "cap" just below stem intact. This will prevent whole okra from turning gooey during cooking.

salting okra to minimize sliminess

The texture of okra can be highly dependent on the cooking method you employ and whether you use the okra pods whole or cut them into pieces. Texture also depends on whether you are using fresh or frozen okra.

When cooking fresh whole okra pods using a dry-heat, high-heat method, such as oven roasting or quick sautéing, usually you can simply trim the stems and be ready to go without worrying about excessive mucilage. And in our Deep-Fried Okra recipe, for example, which uses cut okra, the interior mucilage is blasted away when the cut pieces hit the hot frying oil. And then there are certain traditional classic southern dishes, such as gumbo, where that mucilaginous quality is actually desired because it adds a valuable thickening quality to the finished dish.

However, for most instances where you are cooking fresh whole okra slowly in a stew-type dish, a simple precooking treatment with salt is necessary to achieve a pleasing moist but non-slimy texture. To minimize sliminess, toss the whole okra pods with salt (use 1 teaspoon salt per 1 pound of okra) in a colander and let sit for 1 hour, tossing again halfway through. Rinse the okra well and pat dry before using.

We have found that, for some reason, frozen okra is less slimy than fresh okra. Although we generally prefer using fresh, we do skip the salting step if using frozen.

vegetable science
Why Does Okra Turn Slimy?

Okra contains a substance called mucilage, which is a naturally occurring pectin-like substance also found in seaweeds, aloe and other cacti, and flaxseed. It's made up of chains of sugar molecules secreted outside the okra pod's cells (called exopolysaccharrides) and glycoproteins. Just like other food gels we're more familiar with, like gelatin or cornstarch slurry, okra's starches need both heat and water to fully form a gel. The molecules are loosened by the heat, and they then form a microscopic network that retains the water. This is why okra's mucilage viscosity increases with exposure to heat and water—in other words, this is why cooked okra is sometimes unpalatably slimy.

Dry heat above 190°F damages the sugar-molecule chains so that they're less able to turn viscous. For this reason, many okra recipes call for dry, high heat (like the Deep-Fried Okra and the Roasted Okra with Fennel and Oregano), which keeps the okra as crisp as possible with minimal sliminess.

For recipes that slowly cook fresh okra in a moist environment, as in Greek Stewed Okra with Tomatoes, we've found it's best to pretreat the okra with salt, letting the pods sit for an hour before rinsing them. Why does this help? The salt treatment draws out the slightly viscous, starchy liquid from the pods, leaving less of it behind in the finished dish.

Roasted Okra with Fennel and Oregano

SAUTÉED OKRA

Serves 4   Total time: 15 minutes

WHY THIS RECIPE WORKS As okra is boiled or braised, the inside can become gelatinous (or, to put it another way, slimy). That's obviously a deal breaker, whether in our test kitchen or in your kitchen at home. We wanted to develop a simple stovetop okra recipe that was as crisp-tender as any other green vegetable. We found that quickly sautéing whole pods over medium-high heat was a great way to minimize their slipperiness and maximize their fresh flavor and crisp texture. This side dish makes a perfect accompaniment to chicken or fish, such as halibut or catfish. Do not substitute frozen okra here.

2 tablespoons plus 1 teaspoon extra-virgin olive oil
1 pound okra, stemmed
1 garlic clove, minced
Salt and pepper
Lemon wedges

1. Heat 2 tablespoons oil in 12-inch skillet over medium-high heat until just smoking. Add okra and cook, stirring occasionally, until crisp-tender and well browned on most sides, 5 to 7 minutes.

2. Push okra to sides of skillet. Add garlic and remaining 1 teaspoon oil to center and cook, mashing mixture into pan, until fragrant, about 30 seconds. Stir mixture into okra, season with salt and pepper to taste, and serve immediately with lemon wedges.

ROASTED OKRA WITH FENNEL AND OREGANO

Serves 4 to 6   Total time: 35 minutes

WHY THIS RECIPE WORKS This easy high-heat roasting technique is a simple, delicious way to bring out the best qualities of whole okra pods. The very hot oven, with its dry environment, keeps the okra from becoming too gelatinous. In fact, the hotter the oven, the better. A 500-degree oven produced okra with pleasant texture inside and a beautifully browned outside. To speed things along, we preheated the baking sheet on the lowest rack. We took our first seasoning combination in a Mediterranean direction, tossing the okra with cracked fennel and dried oregano, along with a fair amount of oil, which gave us a good sear on the okra and helped the spices to toast and bloom. Sesame and cumin proved to be another delicious combination, as was a smoky paprika and cayenne mix. All that the okra needed was a squeeze of citrus to add brightness, and we had a simple, delicious dish that had okra skeptics asking for seconds. Do not substitute frozen okra here.

1½ pounds okra, stemmed
3 tablespoons extra-virgin olive oil
2 teaspoons dried oregano
2 teaspoons fennel seeds, cracked
Salt and pepper
Lemon wedges

1. Adjust oven rack to lowest position, place rimmed baking sheet on rack, and heat oven to 500 degrees. Toss okra with oil, oregano, fennel, and ¼ teaspoon salt in bowl.

2. Working quickly, carefully transfer okra to hot baking sheet and spread into single layer. Roast until okra is crisp-tender and well browned on most sides, 20 to 25 minutes, stirring occasionally to ensure even browning. Season with salt and pepper to taste. Serve with lemon wedges.

VARIATIONS

Roasted Okra with Sesame and Cumin
Substitute 1 tablespoon sesame seeds for oregano, 2 teaspoons cracked cumin seeds for fennel seeds, and lime wedges for lemon. Toss cooked okra with 1 teaspoon toasted sesame oil after roasting in step 2.

Roasted Okra with Smoked Paprika and Cayenne
Substitute 1 tablespoon smoked paprika for oregano and ⅛ teaspoon cayenne pepper for fennel seeds.

GREEK STEWED OKRA WITH TOMATOES

Serves 6 to 8   Total time: 1 hour 30 minutes

WHY THIS RECIPE WORKS The bright-tasting but warmly spiced tomato sauce that envelops whole okra pods in this recipe allows the vegetal green freshness of the okra to shine through. Greek-style tomato sauce is often seasoned with cinnamon, allspice, and other warm baking spices. This version also includes onion, garlic, and lemon juice, for a sweet-savory balance. We found that salting the okra pods before stewing them minimized their slippery qualities. While we prefer the flavor and texture of fresh okra in this recipe, you can substitute frozen whole okra, thawed, for fresh.

2 pounds okra, stemmed
Salt and pepper
2 (28-ounce) cans whole peeled tomatoes, drained
½ cup extra-virgin olive oil
1 onion, chopped fine
5 garlic cloves, sliced thin
½ teaspoon ground allspice
¼ teaspoon ground cinnamon
2 tablespoons lemon juice
¼ cup minced fresh parsley

1. Toss okra with 2 teaspoons salt in colander and let sit for 1 hour, tossing again halfway through. Rinse well and set aside.

2. Process tomatoes in food processor until smooth, about 1 minute. Heat oil in Dutch oven over medium heat until shimmering. Add onion and cook until softened and lightly browned, 5 to 7 minutes. Stir in garlic, allspice, cinnamon, ¾ teaspoon salt, and ¼ teaspoon pepper and cook until fragrant, about 30 seconds. Stir in tomatoes and lemon juice and bring to simmer. Cook, stirring occasionally, until thickened slightly, about 10 minutes.

3. Stir in okra and return to simmer. Reduce heat to medium-low, cover, and cook, stirring occasionally, until okra is just tender, 20 to 25 minutes. Season with salt and pepper to taste. Sprinkle with parsley and serve.

CHARRED SICHUAN-STYLE OKRA

Serves 4   Total time: 30 minutes

WHY THIS RECIPE WORKS *Since okra stands up so well to the heat and punch of Creole cuisine, it makes sense that it would also pair well with a spicy Sichuan flavor profile. We started by making a concentrated chile oil, with the tingle-inducing flavor of Sichuan peppercorns. Broad bean chili paste gave the sauce heat and the distinct umami of fermented beans. Hoisin sauce and rice wine brought sweetness, acidity, and body to the sauce. Last but not least, scallions provided fresh balance. Charring the okra pods whole before cloaking them with the sauce lent a beautiful sear to the exterior and kept good texture on the inside. Altogether, this is a sumptuous showstopper of a dish. If you can't find dried bird chiles (Thai red chiles), you can substitute ground red pepper flakes. Asian broad bean chili paste (or sauce) is readily available online; our favorite brand is Pixian. Lee Kum Kee brand is a good supermarket option. Use a spice grinder to grind the bird chiles and Sichuan peppercorns. Do not substitute frozen okra here.*

⅓ cup plus 2 tablespoons vegetable oil
2 garlic cloves, sliced thin
1 (½-inch) piece fresh ginger, peeled and sliced into thin rounds
5 dried bird chiles, ground fine (1½ teaspoons)
1 teaspoon Sichuan peppercorns, ground fine (½ teaspoon)
1 star anise pod
6 tablespoons Chinese rice wine or dry sherry
¼ cup hoisin sauce
3 tablespoons Asian broad bean chili paste
1 pound okra, stemmed
¼ cup water
6 scallions, white parts sliced thin on bias, green parts cut into 1-inch pieces
12 sprigs fresh cilantro, chopped coarse

1. Combine ⅓ cup oil, garlic, ginger, ground chiles, ground Sichuan peppercorns, and star anise in small saucepan and cook over medium-high heat until sizzling, 1 to 2 minutes. Reduce heat to low and gently simmer until garlic and ginger are softened but not browned, about 5 minutes. Let cool off heat for 5 minutes, then stir in 2 tablespoons rice wine, hoisin, and chili paste until combined; set aside.

2. Heat remaining 2 tablespoons oil in 12-inch skillet over medium-high heat until just smoking. Add okra and cook, stirring occasionally, until okra is crisp-tender and well browned on most sides, 5 to 7 minutes.

3. Stir remaining ¼ cup rice wine, water, and scallion greens and whites into skillet with okra, reduce heat to medium, and cook until liquid is reduced by half and scallion greens are just wilted, about 15 seconds. Off heat, stir in garlic-hoisin mixture until combined. Discard star anise and sprinkle with cilantro. Serve immediately.

DEEP-FRIED OKRA

Serves 4 to 6   Total time: 30 minutes (plus 30 minutes chilling time)

WHY THIS RECIPE WORKS *Hailed as a southern staple, fried okra is an indulgent treat that, for many, is simply the only way to eat okra. For the ultimate crunchy bite, we cut the pods into pieces so that the interior mucilage would evaporate when it hit the hot oil. For a light and crispy fried exterior that wouldn't crumble and fall off the okra when we bit into it, we made a "glue" of buttermilk and egg in which to dip the pieces before dredging. The ratio of cornmeal to cornstarch to all-purpose flour was key in creating a crunchy outer fried shell that adhered well. The cornmeal was crucial for the classic southern fried flavor profile, the cornstarch added a light crispy effect, and the flour added the glutinous structure needed to ensure that the coating stayed put. We added a final flavorful stir-in of garlic powder and cayenne to the blend before dredging and frying. While we prefer the flavor and texture of fresh okra in this recipe, you can substitute frozen cut okra, thawed and thoroughly patted dry, for fresh. We recommend frying in three batches if using frozen okra.*

⅔ cup buttermilk
1 large egg
¾ cup cornmeal
½ cup cornstarch
¼ cup all-purpose flour
1 teaspoon garlic powder
½ teaspoon cayenne pepper
  Salt and pepper
1 pound okra, stemmed and cut into 1-inch pieces
3 quarts peanut or vegetable oil
  Lemon wedges
  Hot sauce

1. Adjust oven rack to middle position and heat oven to 200 degrees. Line rimmed baking sheet with parchment paper. Set wire rack in second rimmed baking sheet and line with triple layer of paper towels.

2. Whisk buttermilk and egg together in shallow dish. Whisk cornmeal, cornstarch, flour, garlic powder, cayenne, 1½ teaspoons salt, and ¼ teaspoon pepper together in second shallow dish. Working in batches, dip okra in buttermilk mixture, letting excess drip back into dish. Dredge in cornmeal mixture, pressing firmly to adhere; transfer to parchment-lined sheet. Refrigerate, uncovered, for at least 30 minutes or up to 4 hours.

3. Add oil to large Dutch oven until it measures about 2 inches deep and heat over medium-high heat to 375 degrees. Carefully add half of okra to oil and fry, stirring as needed to prevent sticking, until okra is golden and crisp, 2 to 4 minutes. Adjust burner if necessary to maintain oil temperature between 350 and 375 degrees. Using wire skimmer or slotted spoon, transfer okra to prepared rack. Season with salt and transfer to oven to keep warm.

4. Return oil to 375 degrees and repeat with remaining okra. Serve immediately with lemon wedges and hot sauce.

CHARRED SICHUAN-STYLE OKRA

Okra is usually thought of in terms of Cajun or Creole recipes, or you might see it on the menu at Indian restaurants. Since it's such a natural pairing with the bold flavor profiles of those cuisines, why not use it in a spicy Chinese-inspired dish? Our version has ground dried red chiles, tongue-tingling Sichuan peppercorns, and broad bean chili paste for a trinity of flavorings that really bring the heat.

1. Trim the stems from the okra pods, making sure to leave the top "cap" on each okra pod intact. This will prevent the okra from becoming gooey as it cooks.

2. Use a spice grinder (or a mortar and pestle) to grind the dried bird chiles and the Sichuan peppercorns for the spicy simmered sauce mixture.

3. Cook the whole okra in the hot oil over medium-high heat, stirring occasionally, until the pods are well browned on most sides and still crisp-tender.

4. Add the rice wine, water, and scallions to the okra, lower the heat, and cook until the liquid is reduced by half and the scallion greens are wilted.

5. Remove the skillet from the heat and stir the Sichuan sauce into the okra. Don't forget to remove the star anise pod.

6. Transfer the spicy charred okra to a serving platter, sprinkle with the chopped cilantro sprigs, and serve.

CAJUN PICKLED OKRA

Makes two 1-pint jars
Total time: 30 minutes

WHY THIS RECIPE WORKS *For an okra pickle packed with punchy Cajun flavor, you need a spicy, aromatic brine. This one includes a hefty dose of cayenne pepper and smoked paprika for both bright fiery heat and some slightly sweet smoky flavor. Oregano adds a nice roundness to these red spices. Spooning raw minced garlic straight into the jars alongside the okra (rather than steeping it in the brine first) built the sharp, peppery backbone needed to make these pickles the ultimate Cajun treat. This pickle needs one week for the brine to fully penetrate the okra and for the flavors to develop, but it will continue to get crisper as it sits in the refrigerator. Do not substitute frozen okra here.*

1½ cups white wine vinegar
1 cup water
2 tablespoons sugar
2 tablespoons kosher salt
1 teaspoon smoked paprika
1 teaspoon dried oregano
½ teaspoon cayenne pepper
6 garlic cloves, minced
14 ounces okra, stemmed

1. Bring vinegar, water, sugar, salt, paprika, oregano, and cayenne to boil in medium saucepan over medium-high heat; cover and remove from heat.

2. Fill two 1-pint jars with hot water to warm. Drain jars, then portion garlic into warm jars. Tightly pack okra vertically into jars, alternating the pods upside down and right side up for best fit.

3. Return brine to brief boil. Using funnel and ladle, pour hot brine over okra to cover. Let jars cool to room temperature, cover with lids, and refrigerate for 1 week before serving. (Pickled okra can be refrigerated for at least 6 months; okra will become crisper and flavor will mature over time.)

CARIBBEAN OKRA PEPPER POT

Serves 6 to 8   Total time: 1 hour 15 minutes

WHY THIS RECIPE WORKS *A Caribbean pepper pot is a classic island dish traditionally made with beef, mutton, or pork and aggressively flavored with hot peppers. Okra and cassava are typical vegetable additions. We used skinless, boneless chicken thighs for a lighter dinner option, and the combination of okra, collards, and sweet potatoes (a more convenient alternative to cassava) made this a flavorful and colorful one-pot meal. One Scotch bonnet pepper was all it took to give this dish its characteristic heat, while allspice and thyme lent Caribbean authenticity. While we prefer the flavor and texture of fresh okra in this recipe, you can substitute frozen cut okra, thawed and thoroughly patted dry, for fresh. Skip step 1 if using frozen okra.*

1 pound okra, stemmed
    Salt and pepper
1½ pounds boneless, skinless chicken thighs, trimmed and cut into 1-inch pieces
2 tablespoons vegetable oil
1 onion, chopped fine
6 garlic cloves, minced
2 tablespoons tomato paste
1 teaspoon dried thyme
½ teaspoon ground allspice
4 cups chicken broth
1 Scotch bonnet chile, stemmed, seeded, and minced
2¼ pounds sweet potatoes, peeled and cut into 1-inch pieces
1 pound collard greens, stemmed and chopped
    Lime wedges

1. Toss okra with 1 teaspoon salt in colander and let sit for 1 hour, tossing again halfway through. Rinse well, cut into 1-inch pieces, and set aside.

2. Pat chicken dry with paper towels and season with salt and pepper. Heat oil in Dutch oven over medium-high heat until just smoking. Add chicken and cook, stirring occasionally, until golden, 8 to 10 minutes. Transfer to bowl.

3. Reduce heat to medium-low, add onion to now-empty pot, and cook until softened, about 5 minutes. Add garlic, tomato paste, thyme, and allspice and cook until fragrant, about 30 seconds. Add chicken broth, chile, sweet potatoes, collard greens, and chicken along with any accumulated juices and bring to simmer over medium-high heat. Cook until chicken and sweet potatoes are almost tender, 15 to 20 minutes. Add okra and cook until chicken and potatoes are completely tender, about 5 minutes. Season with salt and pepper to taste, and serve with lime wedges.

GUMBO

Serves 6 to 8   Total time: 2 hours 15 minutes

WHY THIS RECIPE WORKS *Since traditional gumbo relies on the thickening power of okra, for this recipe there is no need to salt the whole okra pods to draw out their excess mucilage. We also engineered this recipe for efficiency, with an oven roux instead of a stovetop roux. Get the roux in the oven and then prep the remaining ingredients. A heavy cast-iron Dutch oven yields the fastest oven roux. If a lightweight pot is all you've got, increase the oven time by 10 minutes. The chicken broth must be at room temperature to prevent lumps from forming. The fish sauce, which is sold in most grocery stores in the Asian section, is untraditional but lends an essential savory quality. Since the salt content varies among brands, taste the finished gumbo before seasoning with salt. Look for firm, unblemished okra pods that are smaller than 3 inches. While we prefer the flavor and texture of fresh okra in this recipe, you can substitute 2 cups frozen cut okra, thawed and thoroughly patted dry, for fresh.*

¾ cup plus 1 tablespoon all-purpose flour
½ cup vegetable oil
1 onion, chopped fine
1 green bell pepper, stemmed, seeded, and chopped
1 celery rib, chopped fine
5 garlic cloves, minced
1 teaspoon minced fresh thyme or ¼ teaspoon dried
¼ teaspoon cayenne pepper

Gumbo

1 (14.5-ounce) can diced tomatoes,
　 drained
3¾ cups chicken broth
¼ cup fish sauce
2 pounds bone-in chicken thighs,
　 trimmed, skin removed
　 Salt and pepper
2 pounds extra-large shrimp (21 to
　 25 per pound), peeled and deveined
8 ounces andouille sausage, halved
　 lengthwise and sliced thin
6 ounces okra, stemmed and cut into
　 1-inch pieces

1. Adjust oven rack to lowest position and heat oven to 350 degrees. Toast ¾ cup flour in Dutch oven on stovetop over medium heat, stirring constantly, until just beginning to brown, about 5 minutes. Off heat, whisk in oil until smooth. Cover, transfer pot to oven, and cook until mixture is deep brown and fragrant, about 45 minutes. (Roux can be refrigerated in airtight container for 1 week. To use, heat in Dutch oven over medium-high heat, whisking constantly, until just smoking, and continue with step 2.)

2. Transfer Dutch oven to stovetop and whisk cooked roux to combine. Stir in onion, bell pepper, and celery and cook over medium heat until softened, about 10 minutes. Stir in remaining 1 tablespoon flour, garlic, thyme, and cayenne and cook until fragrant, about 1 minute. Add tomatoes and cook until dry, about 1 minute. Slowly whisk in broth and fish sauce, scraping up any browned bits and smoothing out any lumps. Season chicken with pepper, then add to pot and bring to boil.

3. Reduce heat to medium-low and simmer, covered, until chicken registers 175 degrees, about 30 minutes. Using large spoon, skim fat from surface, then transfer chicken to large plate. When chicken is cool enough to handle, shred into bite-size pieces using 2 forks and return to pot; discard bones.

4. Stir in shrimp, sausage, and okra and simmer until shrimp is opaque throughout and sausage and okra are warmed through, about 5 minutes. Season with salt and pepper to taste. Serve.

RED BEANS AND RICE WITH OKRA AND TOMATOES

Serves 6 to 8   Total time: 1 hour 45 minutes (plus 8 hours soaking time)

WHY THIS RECIPE WORKS *Staying close to home with okra's Cajun roots, we boosted the flavor profile of classic New Orleans red beans and rice by adding okra and tomatoes to create a hearty, vegetable-packed meal. To replicate this traditional dish using ingredients more easily found in supermarkets, we made some simple substitutions: small red beans for Camellia-brand dried red beans and bacon for hard-to-find tasso ham. Fine-tuning the proportions of sautéed green peppers, onions, and celery gave this dish balance. To ensure the stewed okra keeps some crunchy bite, toss the whole okra pods in salt and let sit for an hour before rinsing, cutting, and adding them to the beans for the final half hour of cooking. If you are pressed for time, you can "quick-brine" your beans. In step 1, combine the salt, water, and beans in a large Dutch oven and bring to a boil over high heat. Remove the pot from the heat, cover, and let stand for 1 hour. Drain and rinse the beans; they can be refrigerated for up to two days before proceeding with the recipe. While* *we prefer the flavor and texture of fresh okra in this recipe, you can substitute frozen cut okra, thawed and thoroughly patted dry, for fresh. If using frozen, skip step 2.*

RED BEANS
　 Salt and pepper
1 pound small red beans (2 cups),
　 picked over and rinsed
1 pound okra, stemmed
4 slices bacon, chopped fine
1 onion, chopped fine
1 green bell pepper, stemmed, seeded,
　 and chopped fine
1 celery rib, minced
3 garlic cloves, minced
1 teaspoon minced fresh thyme or
　 ¼ teaspoon dried
1 teaspoon paprika
2 bay leaves
¼ teaspoon cayenne pepper
3 cups chicken broth
5 cups water
2 (14.5-ounce) cans diced tomatoes,
　 drained
1 tablespoon red wine vinegar,
　 plus extra for seasoning
3 scallions, sliced thin
　 Hot sauce

RICE

- 1 tablespoon unsalted butter
- 2 cups long-grain white rice, rinsed
- 3 cups water
- 1 teaspoon salt

1. For the red beans Dissolve 3 tablespoons salt in 4 quarts cold water in large bowl or container. Add beans and soak at room temperature for at least 8 hours or up to 24 hours. Drain and rinse well; set aside.

2. Toss okra with 1 teaspoon salt, and let sit for 1 hour, stirring halfway through. Rinse well, then cut into 1-inch pieces; set aside.

3. Cook bacon in Dutch oven over medium heat, stirring occasionally, until crispy, 5 to 7 minutes. Add onion, bell pepper, and celery and cook until vegetables are softened, 5 to 7 minutes. Stir in garlic, thyme, paprika, bay leaves, cayenne, and ¼ teaspoon pepper and cook until fragrant, about 30 seconds.

4. Stir in beans, broth, and water and bring to boil over high heat. Reduce to vigorous simmer and cook, stirring occasionally, until beans are just softened and liquid begins to thicken, 45 minutes to 1 hour.

5. Stir in okra, tomatoes, and vinegar and cook until liquid is thickened and beans are fully tender and creamy, about 30 minutes.

6. For the rice Meanwhile, melt butter in large saucepan over medium heat. Add rice and cook, stirring often, until edges begin to turn translucent, about 2 minutes. Stir in water and salt and bring to boil. Cover, reduce heat to low, and simmer until liquid is absorbed and rice is tender, about 20 minutes. Remove pot from heat, lay clean folded dish towel underneath lid, and let rice sit for 10 minutes. Fluff rice with fork.

7. Discard bay leaves from beans. Season with salt, pepper, and extra vinegar to taste. Top individual portions of rice with beans and sprinkle with scallions. Serve with hot sauce.

MADRAS OKRA CURRY

Serves 4 to 6   Total time: 50 minutes

WHY THIS RECIPE WORKS *In Indian cuisine, okra has a long and varied history. We wanted our Madras-style okra curry to have a plentiful, rich sauce, with okra that retained some of its fresh bite. We made a pantry-friendly sauce with the classic flavors of onion, ginger, garlic, and coconut milk. Searing the okra whole—and not letting it stew in the sauce—kept it crisp-tender, with an appealing texture. Fresh cilantro sprigs and bright lime wedges balanced out our rich curry. We prefer the spicier flavor of Madras curry powder here, but you can substitute regular curry powder. Do not substitute frozen okra here. Serve with rice.*

- 6 tablespoons vegetable oil
- 1½ pounds okra, stemmed
- 1 small onion, chopped fine
- 3 garlic cloves, minced
- 1 tablespoon grated fresh ginger
- 1 tablespoon Madras curry powder
- 2½ cups chicken or vegetable broth
- 1 cup canned coconut milk
- 2 teaspoons honey
- 1 teaspoon cornstarch
  Salt and pepper
- 10 sprigs fresh cilantro, chopped coarse
  Lime wedges

1. Heat 2 tablespoons oil in 12-inch skillet over medium-high heat until just smoking. Add half of okra to skillet and cook, stirring occasionally, until crisp-tender and well browned on most sides, 5 to 7 minutes; transfer to bowl. Repeat with 2 tablespoons oil and remaining okra; transfer to bowl. Let skillet cool slightly.

2. Heat remaining 2 tablespoons oil in now-empty skillet over medium heat until shimmering. Add onion and cook until softened, about 5 minutes. Stir in garlic, ginger, and curry powder and cook until fragrant, about 1 minute. Stir in broth, scraping up any browned bits, and bring to simmer. Cook, stirring occasionally, until reduced to 1¼ cups, 15 to 20 minutes.

3. Whisk coconut milk, honey, and cornstarch together in bowl to dissolve cornstarch, then whisk mixture into skillet. Bring to simmer and cook until slightly thickened, about 30 seconds. Stir in okra and any accumulated juices and ¼ teaspoon salt and return to brief simmer to warm through. Season with salt and pepper to taste. Sprinkle with cilantro and serve with lime wedges.

O N I O N S

Onions are often thought of as a supporting player rather than a star ingredient. They provide aromatic seasoning to countless dishes in nearly every cuisine around the world. But since there always seems to be a bunch of onions lurking around, even when the crisper drawer is empty, it makes good kitchen sense to have a repertoire of great recipes for onions as both legitimate side dish and main course.

The onion is the most widely cultivated member of the allium family, which also includes leeks, scallions, shallots, garlic, and chives. The more often you chop onions, the less likely you are to suffer from that stinging sensation in the eyes that comes from the volatile sulfuric gases released by a cut onion. So let's peel back the layers and get cooking!

Our side dishes show you how to caramelize, glaze, grill, roast, braise, pickle, and beer-batter onions. The Roasted Cipollini and Escarole Salad (with prosciutto and blue cheese!) makes an elegant yet satisfying appetizer or light main course. And Oklahoma Fried Onion Cheeseburgers is a dish that was born out of necessity but now holds a hallowed place in America's foodways.

Like onions, leeks are often used as a seasoning component. However, braised leeks are an easy and elegant side dish, and we show you how to perfectly braise leeks in two different ways: on the stovetop and in the slow cooker. Leeks are also incorporated into our Creamy Leek and Potato Soup and used in the gorgeous-looking Smoked Salmon and Leek Tart.

shopping and storage

Onions are available year-round. Purchase rock-hard onions covered with smooth, papery skin. Avoid any with soft spots, dark powdery spots, or green sprouts. Stored in a cool, well-ventilated spot, onions will keep for several weeks. Don't refrigerate onions, since their odors will permeate other foods.

Leeks and scallions are traditionally in season from spring through fall, but nowadays they, too, are available year-round. Look for firm stalks, with crisp dark green leaves and healthy-looking attached roots. Avoid leeks that have had their greens trimmed. Refrigerate them in an open plastic produce bag for a week.

the allium family

YELLOW ONIONS These all-purpose gold standards of the onion world are sweet and rich when cooked. Spanish onions are a larger, milder, firmer variety.

RED ONIONS Crisply pungent when raw (they're great in salads), red onions are jammier than yellow onions when cooked.

WHITE ONIONS White onions have a simpler, less complex flavor than yellow onions and break down more quickly when cooked.

SWEET ONIONS Vidalia, Maui, Walla Walla, and other sweet onions are best when they are the star of the dish.

PEARL ONIONS Pearl onions and flying saucer–shaped Italian cipollini onions are intensely sweet when cooked.

SHALLOTS Like garlic, shallots comprise a head with multiple cloves. Raw or cooked, they have a mellow oniony-garlicky flavor.

SCALLIONS The earthy flavor and delicate crunch of scallions work well in dishes that involve little or no cooking.

LEEKS The edible portions of leeks are found in their long, leafy stalks; there is no bulb. Their flavor is the mildest of all.

vegetable prep

Dicing Onions and Shallots

Onions and shallots can be diced using the same technique.

1. Halve onion through root end, then peel onion and trim top. Make several horizontal cuts from 1 end to the other, but don't cut all way through root end.

2. Make several lengthwise cuts.

3. Rotate onion so that root end is in back, behind your hand, and slice onion thin across previous cuts. As you slice, onion will fall apart into chopped pieces.

Slicing Onions

Slice lengthwise through root end to preserve structure and maintain shape while cooking—perfect for French onion soup or caramelized onions.

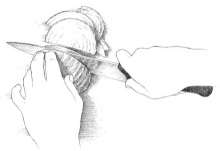

Slice crosswise across layers to separate them into pieces that soften when cooked—ideal for pureeing into a smooth soup or sauce.

don't cry over cut onions

When an onion is cut, a volatile compound called thiopropanal sulfoxide forms. When thiopropanal sulfoxide evaporates in the air, it irritates the eyes, causing us to cry. Ideas for reducing tears range from the commonsensible (work underneath an exhaust fan or freeze onions for 30 minutes before slicing) to the comical (wear ski goggles or hold a toothpick in your teeth). After putting more than 20 methods to the test, we learned that it worked best to protect our eyes by covering them with goggles or contact lenses or to introduce a flame (a candle or gas burner) near the cut onions. The flame changes the activity of the thiopropanal sulfoxide by completing its oxidization. Contact lenses and goggles form a physical barrier that the thiopropanal cannot penetrate. So if you want to keep tears at bay when handling onions, light a candle or gas burner or put on some ski goggles.

CARAMELIZED ONIONS

Makes about 2 cups   Total time: 35 minutes

WHY THIS RECIPE WORKS *Caramelized onions are, quite simply, fantastic. And super-versatile: Add them to an omelet or frittata. Top grilled cheese sandwiches or burgers with them. Toss some into pasta dishes or green salads. Sprinkle them over pizza or mashed potatoes. Or use them in our tangy Caramelized Onion Dip (page 315). Starting the onions in a covered nonstick skillet over high heat with water helped the onions quickly soften. Then we removed the lid, lowered the heat, and pressed the softened onions into the bottom and sides of the skillet to allow for maximum contact with the hot pan. We prefer yellow or Spanish onions here for their complex flavor. Slicing the onions through their root end prevents them from breaking down too much during cooking. The tiny bit of baking soda converts flavorless inulin (a polysaccharide present in onions) to sweet fructose. These will keep refrigerated for up to three days or frozen for up to one month.*

- 3 pounds onions, halved and sliced through root end into ¼-inch-thick pieces
- ¾ cup plus 1 tablespoon water
- 2 tablespoons vegetable oil
- ¾ teaspoon salt
- ⅛ teaspoon baking soda

1. Bring onions, ¾ cup water, oil, and salt to boil in 12-inch nonstick skillet over high heat. Cover and cook until water has evaporated and onions start to sizzle, about 10 minutes.

2. Uncover, reduce heat to medium-high, and use rubber spatula to gently press onions into sides and bottom of skillet. Cook, without stirring, for 30 seconds. Stir onions, scraping fond from skillet, then gently press onions into sides and bottom of skillet again. Repeat pressing, cooking, and stirring until onions are softened, well browned, and slightly sticky, 15 to 20 minutes.

3. Combine baking soda and remaining 1 tablespoon water in bowl. Stir baking soda solution into onions and cook, stirring constantly, until solution has evaporated, about 1 minute. Transfer onions to bowl. Serve.

GLAZED PEARL ONIONS

Serves 4   Total time: 1 hour

WHY THIS RECIPE WORKS *Glazed whole pearl onions are a beautiful and natural addition to any holiday table, since they complement just about any type of roast. For sweet, flavorful pearl onions, we found that they were best served by a dual cooking approach of browning followed by braising. Browning the onions in olive oil and butter helped to enhance their natural sweetness. Braising them in chicken broth added savoriness. Brown sugar and rosemary were welcome additions. When trimming the root ends of the blanched onions, shave off the thinnest slice possible. If too much is taken off, the onion will fall apart. You can substitute frozen pearl onions for the fresh onions in this recipe; frozen pearl onions come already peeled, so skip step 1.*

- 1 pound pearl onions
- 1 tablespoon unsalted butter
- 1 tablespoon extra-virgin olive oil
- ½ cup chicken or vegetable broth
- 1½ tablespoons packed brown sugar
- ½ teaspoon minced fresh rosemary
  Salt and pepper

1. Bring 2 quarts water to boil in large saucepan. Add onions and cook for 1 minute. Drain in colander and run under cold water until cool to touch, about 1 minute. Transfer onions to paper towel–lined plate and pat dry. Trim root and stem ends, then peel onion skins.

2. Melt butter with oil in 12-inch skillet over medium heat. Add onions and cook, stirring occasionally, until onions are lightly browned, 7 to 9 minutes.

3. Add broth, sugar, and rosemary and bring to boil. Cover, reduce heat to medium-low, and simmer until onions are tender, about 12 minutes. Uncover, increase heat to medium-high, and simmer until liquid is reduced to syrupy glaze, 4 to 5 minutes. Season with salt and pepper to taste and serve immediately.

BALSAMIC GLAZED CIPOLLINI ONIONS

Serves 6 to 8   Total time: 1 hour

WHY THIS RECIPE WORKS *Cipolline in agrodolce is a traditional country-style Italian dish featuring small, flat cipollini onions braised and bathed in a sweet-and-sour vinegar-and-sugar glaze. But within this simple formula, there are many possibilities: balsamic or wine vinegar? White or brown sugar? Butter or olive oil? With the goal of keeping the cipollinis' sweet, buttery flavor front and center, we kept the ingredient list short and focused on delivering a big payout of flavor. Tasters chose balsamic vinegar for its rich, distinctive flavor and inherent sweetness, and granulated sugar over brown sugar for its cleaner flavor. To finish, all the dish needed was a bit of extra butter swirled in for enrichment and a sprinkle of fresh, fragrant basil. You can use frozen cipollini onions in this recipe; they are already peeled, so skip step 1.*

- 2 pounds cipollini onions
- 3 tablespoons unsalted butter, cut into 3 pieces
- 2½ tablespoons sugar
- ¾ teaspoon salt
- ⅛ teaspoon red pepper flakes
- ⅓ cup balsamic vinegar
- 2 tablespoons chopped fresh basil

1. Bring 2 quarts water to boil in large saucepan. Add onions and cook for 30 seconds. Drain in colander and run under cold water until cool to touch, about 1 minute. Transfer onions to paper towel–lined plate and pat dry. Trim root and stem ends, then peel and discard onion skins.

2. Bring onions, ½ cup water, 1 tablespoon butter, 1½ teaspoons sugar, salt, and pepper flakes to boil over medium-high heat in 12-inch nonstick skillet. Cover and cook until water is nearly evaporated, about 10 minutes, stirring halfway through cooking.

3. Uncover skillet and reduce heat to medium. Cook onions, flipping as needed, until well-browned on both sides, 4 to 7 minutes.

4. Reduce heat to medium-low, and stir in vinegar, 1 tablespoon water, and remaining 2 tablespoons sugar. Simmer until liquid is reduced to syrupy glaze, 3 to 5 minutes. Off heat, stir in remaining 2 tablespoons butter. Sprinkle with basil and serve.

VARIATION
White Balsamic Glazed Cipollini Onions with Tarragon
Substitute white balsamic vinegar for balsamic vinegar and 1 tablespoon minced fresh tarragon for basil.

BRAISED LEEKS

Serves 4 to 6   Total time: 50 minutes

WHY THIS RECIPE WORKS *Braised leeks make a gently aromatic, meltingly tender side dish for chicken or fish. Browning the leeks before adding the braising liquid to the skillet yielded deep flavor. A simple dressing of white wine vinegar, Dijon mustard, garlic, and olive oil enhanced this depth of flavor. We also found that adding some of the leek braising liquid gave the dressing even more complexity. A sprinkling of tarragon at the end brightened the dish. We prefer to use leeks measuring 1 inch or less in diameter here, because they're more tender than larger leeks. If you have larger leeks, discard their first two outer layers because they tend to be fibrous. Orienting the leeks in one direction makes them easier to transfer in and out of the skillet. When trimming the leeks, be careful to leave the root ends intact so that the layers stay together when the leeks are halved.*

3 **pounds small leeks, white and light green parts only**
   Salt and pepper
6 **tablespoons extra-virgin olive oil**
1 **cup chicken or vegetable broth**
1 **tablespoon white wine vinegar**
1 **teaspoon Dijon mustard**
1 **small garlic clove, minced**
1 **tablespoon chopped fresh tarragon**

1. Trim roots from leeks, leaving ends intact so layers stay together when halved. Halve leeks lengthwise, wash thoroughly between layers to remove any dirt, and pat dry with paper towels. Season cut sides with salt and pepper.

2. Heat 1 tablespoon oil in 12-inch nonstick skillet over medium-high heat until shimmering. Add half of leeks to skillet, with root ends pointed in same direction, and cook until browned, about 2 minutes per side. Transfer to plate. Repeat with 1 tablespoon oil and remaining leeks.

3. Return all leeks to skillet, facing same direction. Add broth and bring to boil. Cover, reduce heat to medium-low, and simmer until leeks are tender when poked with tip of paring knife, 10 to 12 minutes. Using slotted spatula, transfer leeks to shallow serving platter, leaving braising liquid in skillet.

4. Increase heat to medium-high and bring braising liquid to boil; cook until reduced to about 2 tablespoons, 2 to 4 minutes. Transfer braising liquid to small jar (or bowl) and add vinegar, mustard, garlic, remaining ¼ cup oil, ¼ teaspoon salt, and ¼ teaspoon pepper. Affix lid and shake jar vigorously until vinaigrette is emulsified, about 15 seconds (or whisk in the bowl). Spoon vinaigrette over leeks. Sprinkle with tarragon and serve.

SLOW-COOKER BRAISED LEEKS

Serves 4 to 6   Total time: 3 to 4 hours on low or 2 to 3 hours on high

WHY THIS RECIPE WORKS *Braising leeks in the slow cooker is a hands-off way to a delicious side dish for a holiday meal, leaving your oven and stovetop free for other dishes. The slow cooker's relatively low heat and slow cooking time helped to coax out their delicate flavor. We jump-started the leeks in the microwave, along with garlic and thyme, to build even more complex flavor. A generous amount of cream ensured a rich, velvety texture, while a splash of wine added acidity. Pecorino stirred in at the end of cooking enriched the dish further and provided an even creamier texture. Because heavy cream, unlike milk or half-and-half, can be simmered without curdling, it is essential here. You will need a 5- to 7-quart slow cooker for this recipe.*

3 **pounds leeks, white and light green parts only, halved lengthwise, sliced thin, washed thoroughly, and drained**
1 **tablespoon vegetable oil**
2 **garlic cloves, minced**
2 **teaspoons minced fresh thyme or ½ teaspoon dried**

Salt and pepper
1 cup heavy cream
½ cup dry white wine
¼ cup grated Pecorino Romano cheese

1. Microwave leeks, oil, garlic, thyme, 1 teaspoon salt, and ¼ teaspoon pepper in bowl, stirring occasionally, until leeks are softened, 8 to 10 minutes; transfer to slow cooker. Stir in cream and wine, cover, and cook until leeks are tender but not mushy, 3 to 4 hours on low or 2 to 3 hours on high.

2. Stir Pecorino into leek mixture and season with salt and pepper to taste. Let sit for 5 minutes, until slightly thickened. Serve. (Leeks can be held on warm or low setting for up to 2 hours; adjust consistency with hot water as needed before serving.)

GRILLED ONIONS WITH BALSAMIC VINAIGRETTE

Serves 4   Total time: 55 minutes

WHY THIS RECIPE WORKS *Grilled onions aren't just a great burger topping—they also stand on their own as a side dish. Grilling halved onions cut side down directly over the flame until very dark ensured that they developed sufficient chargrilled flavor; we then transferred them to a covered disposable pan to finish cut side up so they would cook through evenly, turning buttery soft. Leaving the skins on kept the bottoms of the onions from burning but still allowed for plenty of caramelization. The simple balsamic vinaigrette complemented their sweetness and lent a burst of acidity. In step 3, be sure to err on the side of achieving darker charring, as the steaming step will soften the char's appearance and flavor.*

½ cup extra-virgin olive oil
3 tablespoons balsamic vinegar
Salt and pepper
4 onions (8 ounces each)
1 (13 x 9-inch) disposable aluminum pan
1 tablespoon minced fresh chives

1. Whisk 6 tablespoons oil, vinegar, ½ teaspoon salt, and ¼ teaspoon pepper together in bowl; set aside. Trim stem end of onions and halve onions from root end to stem end, leaving skin intact. (Root end can be trimmed, but don't remove it or the onions will fall apart.) Brush cut sides of onions with remaining 2 tablespoons oil and sprinkle each half with ⅛ teaspoon salt.

2a. For a charcoal grill Open bottom vent completely. Light large chimney starter three-quarters filled with charcoal briquettes (4½ quarts). When top coals are partially covered with ash, pour evenly over grill. Set cooking grate in place, cover, and open lid vent completely. Heat grill until hot, about 5 minutes.

2b. For a gas grill Turn all burners to high, cover, and heat grill until hot, about 15 minutes. Turn all burners to medium.

3. Clean and oil cooking grate. Place onions cut side down on grill and cook (covered if using gas) until well charred, 10 to 15 minutes, moving onions as needed to ensure even cooking. Flip onions and cook cut side up until lightly charred on skin side, about 5 minutes.

4. Transfer onions cut side up to disposable pan and cover tightly with aluminum foil. Return disposable pan to grill and cook over medium heat (covered if using gas) until onions are tender and easily pierced with paring knife, 10 to 15 minutes. Set aside to cool slightly, about 10 minutes.

5. When onions are cool enough to handle, remove and discard charred outer skin; arrange onions cut side up on serving platter. Whisk vinaigrette to recombine and drizzle evenly over onions. Sprinkle with chives, season with salt and pepper to taste, and serve.

QUICK SWEET AND SPICY PICKLED RED ONIONS

Makes 1 cup   Total time: 1 hour 15 minutes

WHY THIS RECIPE WORKS *Sweet and spicy pickled onions are an absolute breeze to make—just a few minutes of hands-on preparation plus a 30-minute briny bath transformed simple slices of red onion and jalapeño chile into a vibrant topping for tacos, sandwiches, and burgers alike. Red wine vinegar offered a clean and fruity background for the brine, accentuating the delicate pungency of the onion; plus, its rosy color complemented the purple-tinged slices. To balance the acidity and bring out the onion's natural sweetness, we added a good measure of sugar. A bit of ground chipotle or cumin would have given the mixture a decidedly south-of-the-border profile, but we preferred the clean, grassy heat of jalapeño. Look for a firm, dry onion with thin, shiny skin and a deep purple color. When working with jalapeños, it's a good idea to wear gloves and wash your knife and cutting board with hot, soapy water as soon as you're done. These pickled onions cannot be processed for long-term storage.*

1 red onion, halved and sliced thin through root end
1 cup red wine vinegar
⅓ cup sugar
¼ teaspoon kosher salt
2 jalapeño chiles, stemmed, seeded, and sliced into thin rings

1. Place onion in medium bowl. In small saucepan, bring vinegar, sugar, salt, and jalapeños to simmer over medium-high heat, stirring occasionally, until sugar dissolves.

2. Pour vinegar mixture over onion, cover, and let cool to room temperature, about 1 hour.

3. When cool, drain vegetables in colander and serve. (Pickled onions can be refrigerated for up to 1 week; onions will turn soft and harsh after 1 week.)

a time, until batter falls from whisk in steady stream and leaves faint trail across surface of batter.

3. Drain onions and pat dry with paper towels. Separate into rings. Transfer one-third of rings to batter. Carefully transfer battered rings to oil. Fry until rings are golden brown and crisp, about 5 minutes, flipping halfway through frying. Drain rings on prepared baking sheet, season with salt and pepper to taste, and transfer to oven to keep warm. Return oil to 350 degrees and repeat 2 more times with remaining onion rings and batter. Serve.

CARAMELIZED ONION DIP

Makes 2 cups
Total time: 1 hour 15 minutes
WHY THIS RECIPE WORKS *Once you taste this creamy, tangy, oniony dip, you'll wonder why you ever bothered with the powdered soup-mix version. We showcased the savory-sweet flavor of caramelized onions, accented by fresh chives, in this homemade version of the party classic. The minced chives offered a burst of oniony freshness to counterbalance the sweetness of the caramelized onions, and the combination of sour cream and yogurt gave the dip its tangy depth without being too rich. The dip should be refrigerated for at least 1 hour before serving to let the flavors meld. It can be refrigerated for up to 24 hours before serving. Serve this with potato chips, naturally.*

> 1 cup sour cream
> ⅔ cup caramelized onions, chopped fine (page 312)
> ⅓ cup plain yogurt
> 2 tablespoons minced fresh chives
> ¾ teaspoon white vinegar
> Salt and pepper

Combine sour cream, onions, yogurt, chives, vinegar, ½ teaspoon salt, and ⅛ teaspoon pepper in serving bowl. Refrigerate dip for at least 1 hour. Season with salt and pepper to taste. Serve.

BEER-BATTERED ONION RINGS

Serves 4 to 6   Total time: 50 minutes
WHY THIS RECIPE WORKS *For tender, flavor-filled onion rings, sweet onions like Vidalia, Maui, or Walla Walla are the way to go—although ordinary yellow onions will also produce quite acceptable onion rings. After testing many different batters in a quest to find just the right consistency, we settled on one with beer, flour, salt, pepper, baking powder, and cornstarch. The beer gave the coating flavor, and its carbonation provided lift to the batter. The baking powder contributed to a coating that was thick and substantial, yet light, while cornstarch added crunch. Before frying our onion rings, we soaked the onions in a mixture of beer, malt vinegar, and salt to soften them and build flavor. We like full-bodied beers in this recipe. Cider vinegar can be used in place of malt vinegar. In step 1, do not soak the onion rounds longer than 2 hours or they will turn soft and become too saturated to crisp up properly. You will need a 6-quart or larger Dutch oven for this recipe.*

> 2 Vidalia onions, sliced into ½-inch- thick rounds
> 3 cups beer
> 2 teaspoons malt vinegar
> Salt and pepper
> 2 quarts peanut or vegetable oil
> ¾ cup all-purpose flour
> ¾ cup cornstarch
> 1 teaspoon baking powder

1. Combine onion rounds, 2 cups beer, vinegar, ½ teaspoon salt, and ½ teaspoon pepper in large bowl, cover, and refrigerate for at least 30 minutes or up to 2 hours.

2. Line rimmed baking sheet with triple layer of paper towels. Adjust oven rack to middle position and heat oven to 200 degrees. Add oil to Dutch oven until it measures about 1½ inches deep and heat over medium-high heat to 350 degrees. While oil heats, combine flour, cornstarch, baking powder, ½ teaspoon salt, and ¼ teaspoon pepper in second large bowl. Slowly whisk in ¾ cup beer until just combined (some lumps will remain). Whisk in remaining beer as needed, 1 tablespoon at

ROASTED CIPOLLINI AND ESCAROLE SALAD

Italian cipollini onions are no longer a rare gourmet treat, so keep your eyes peeled for them in your supermarket. We developed an easier way to peel the thin skins by blanching them, as well as a simple roasting method that guarantees evenly browned and meltingly soft cipollinis every time. The sweet onions paired with the slightly bitter salad greens, salty-crispy prosciutto, and pungent blue cheese make a fantastic lunch or light dinner.

1. Blanch the whole cipollini onions in boiling water for 30 seconds, then drain them, run them under cold water to cool, and pat the onions dry.

2. Trim both the root and stem ends of the cipollini onions, peel them, and cut them in half through their root end.

3. After tossing them with olive oil, roast the cipollini onions on a parchment-lined baking sheet until softened and well browned, rotating the baking sheet halfway through roasting for even browning.

4. Lay the prosciutto slices on a paper towel–lined plate and crisp them up in the microwave. Let cool, then crumble the prosciutto into ½-inch pieces.

5. Whisk the tangy, sweet-and-savory vinaigrette together right in the serving bowl.

6. Add the salad greens, roasted cipollini onions, and prosciutto to the serving bowl, toss together, sprinkle with the blue cheese, and serve.

ROASTED CIPOLLINI AND ESCAROLE SALAD

Serves 4 to 6   Total time: 1 hour 15 minutes

WHY THIS RECIPE WORKS *Cipollini onions have more residual sugar than regular yellow or white onions; they have more in common with Vidalia onions in that way. When roasted, those additional sugars caramelize beautifully, creating a melt-in-your-mouth texture. We wanted to develop a foolproof roasting method to ensure perfectly caramelized cipollini onions every time—plus a great recipe to use them in. Halving the cipollinis and roasting on the middle oven rack ensured that they cooked through until buttery and tender at the same rate as they browned and caramelized. With the goal of keeping this sweet, buttery flavor front and center, we kept this salad complementary to its northern Italian roots. Crisp and slightly bitter escarole and frisée paired well with the onions' roasted sweetness. Crunchy prosciutto and creamy blue cheese made it a meal. A tangy cracked caraway seed dressing added the final flavor balance. You can use prepeeled cipollini onions in this recipe; simply halve them through the root end and proceed with step 2.*

- 1½ pounds cipollini onions
- 6 tablespoons extra-virgin olive oil
  Salt and pepper
- 4 ounces thin-sliced prosciutto
- 2 tablespoons apple cider vinegar
- 2 teaspoons Dijon mustard
- 1½ teaspoons caraway seeds, toasted and cracked
- 1 teaspoon honey
- 1 head escarole (1 pound), trimmed and cut into 1-inch pieces
- ½ head frisée (3 ounces), trimmed and cut into 1-inch pieces
- 2 ounces blue cheese, crumbled (½ cup)

1. Adjust oven rack to middle position and heat oven to 400 degrees. Bring 2 quarts water to boil in large saucepan. Add onions and cook for 30 seconds. Drain in colander and run under cold water until onions are cool enough to handle, about 1 minute. Transfer onions to paper towel–lined plate and pat dry. Trim root and stem ends, then peel and discard onion skins. Halve onions through root end and transfer to bowl.

2. Add 3 tablespoons oil, ¼ teaspoon salt, and ⅛ teaspoon pepper to bowl with onions and toss to coat. Arrange onions, cut side down, on parchment paper–lined rimmed baking sheet and roast until well browned and softened, 35 to 40 minutes, rotating sheet halfway through roasting. Let cool slightly, about 10 minutes.

3. Line plate with double layer of paper towels. Lay prosciutto slices in single layer on prepared plate and microwave until rendered and beginning to crisp, 2 to 4 minutes. Set aside until cool enough to handle, then crumble into ½-inch pieces.

4. Whisk vinegar, mustard, caraway seeds, honey, and ¼ teaspoon salt together in large bowl. While whisking constantly, slowly drizzle in remaining 3 tablespoons oil until combined. Add escarole, frisée, onions, and prosciutto and gently toss to combine. Season with salt and pepper to taste. Transfer to serving platter, and sprinkle with blue cheese. Serve.

CREAMY LEEK AND POTATO SOUP

Serves 4 to 6   Total time: 1 hour 30 minutes

WHY THIS RECIPE WORKS *Julia Child thought so highly of potato-leek soup that she made it her very first recipe in* Mastering the Art of French Cooking. *The satiny texture of her soup is due in no small part to the fact that it calls for a food mill rather than a blender to puree it. But most of us don't own a food mill, so how do we achieve a simple, delicious soup that doesn't turn gluey in the blender from the potato starch? Some recipes try to compensate by adding lots of cream, but this dulls the leek flavor. In the test kitchen, we tried using waxy potatoes, which have less starch than russets, but their flavor and texture were too distinct. That starch that can turn gluey is also what thickens the soup, so one russet potato worked best. To avoid adding cream, we turned to the thickening power of bread. Voilà: Like Julia's recipe, this soup "smelled good, tasted good, and was simplicity itself to make." Don't fill the blender more than two-thirds with hot soup; if necessary, process in batches. Or use an immersion blender to process the soup directly in the pot. Use the lowest setting on your toaster to dry out the bread without overbrowning it. Garnish this soup with crisp bacon bits, a dollop of sour cream, chopped fresh chives, or croutons.*

- 2 pounds leeks, white and light green parts halved lengthwise, sliced thin, and washed thoroughly; dark green parts halved, cut into 2-inch pieces, and washed thoroughly
- 2 cups chicken or vegetable broth
- 2 cups water
- 4 tablespoons unsalted butter
- 1 onion, chopped
  Salt and pepper
- 1 small russet potato (6 ounces), peeled, halved lengthwise, and cut into ¼-inch-thick slices
- 1 bay leaf
- 1 sprig fresh thyme or tarragon
- 1 slice hearty white sandwich bread, lightly toasted and torn into ½-inch pieces

1. Bring dark green leek pieces, broth, and water to boil in large saucepan over high heat. Reduce heat to low, cover, and simmer 20 minutes. Strain broth through fine-mesh strainer into medium bowl, pressing on solids to extract as much liquid as possible; set aside. Discard solids in strainer and rinse out saucepan.

2. Melt butter in now-empty saucepan over medium-low heat. Stir in sliced white and light green leeks, onion, and 1 teaspoon salt. Reduce heat to low and cook, stirring frequently, until vegetables are softened, about 10 minutes.

3. Increase heat to high, stir in reserved broth, potato, bay leaf, and herb sprig and bring to boil. Reduce heat to low and simmer until potato is tender, about 10 minutes. Add bread and simmer until bread is completely saturated and starts to break down, about 5 minutes.

4. Discard bay leaf and herb sprig. Working in batches, process soup in blender until smooth, 1 to 2 minutes. Return soup to clean saucepan and bring to simmer; season with salt and pepper to taste. Serve.

Best French Onion Soup

BEST FRENCH ONION SOUP

Serves 6   Total time: 4 hours 30 minutes

WHY THIS RECIPE WORKS *The ideal French onion soup combines a rich broth redolent of sweet caramelized onions with a slice of toasted baguette topped with perfectly melted cheese. The secret to a deeply flavored broth was to caramelize the onions fully, traditionally a laborious, hands-on process. By cooking the onions covered in a hot oven for 2½ hours, we only needed to deglaze the onions on the stovetop a few times. Just one type of onion (yellow) was sufficient, while both chicken broth and beef broth added maximum flavor. We toasted the baguette slices to ward off sogginess, and we added only a modest sprinkling of nutty Gruyère so the broth wasn't overpowered. Use a Dutch oven that holds 7 quarts or more for this recipe. Sweet onions, such as Vidalia or Walla Walla, will make this recipe overly sweet. Use broiler-safe crocks and keep the rims of the bowls 4 to 5 inches from the heating element to obtain a proper gratin of melted, bubbly cheese. If using ordinary soup bowls, sprinkle the toasted bread slices with Gruyère, return them to the broiler until the cheese melts, and then float them on top of the soup to serve.*

SOUP

- 4 pounds onions, halved and sliced through root end into ¼-inch-thick pieces
- 3 tablespoons unsalted butter, cut into 3 pieces
  Salt and pepper
- 2¾–3 cups water
- ½ cup dry sherry
- 4 cups chicken broth
- 2 cups beef broth
- 6 sprigs fresh thyme, tied with kitchen twine
- 1 bay leaf

CHEESE CROUTONS

- 1 (12-inch) baguette, cut into ½-inch-thick slices
- 8 ounces Gruyère cheese, shredded (2 cups)

1. For the soup Adjust oven rack to lower-middle position and heat oven to 400 degrees. Generously spray inside of Dutch oven with vegetable oil spray. Add onions, butter, and 1 teaspoon salt. Cover, transfer pot to oven, and cook for 1 hour (onions will be moist and slightly reduced in volume). Remove pot from oven and stir onions, scraping bottom and sides of pot. Return pot to oven with lid slightly ajar and continue to cook until onions are very soft and golden brown, 1½ to 1¾ hours longer, stirring onions and scraping bottom and sides of pot after 1 hour.

2. Carefully remove pot from oven (leave oven on) and place over medium-high heat. Cook onions, stirring frequently and scraping bottom and sides of pot, until liquid evaporates and onions brown, 15 to 20 minutes (reduce heat to medium if onions brown too quickly). Continue to cook, stirring frequently, until bottom of pot is coated with dark crust, 6 to 8 minutes, adjusting heat as necessary. (Scrape any browned bits that collect on spoon back into onions.) Stir in ¼ cup water, scraping pot bottom to loosen crust, and cook until water evaporates and pot bottom has formed another dark crust, 6 to 8 minutes. Repeat process of deglazing 2 or 3 more times, until onions are very dark brown. Stir in sherry and cook, stirring frequently, until sherry evaporates, about 5 minutes.

3. Stir in 2 cups water, chicken broth, beef broth, thyme sprigs, bay leaf, and ½ teaspoon salt, scraping up any browned bits on bottom and sides of pot. Increase heat to high and bring to simmer. Cover, reduce heat to low, and simmer for 30 minutes. Discard thyme sprigs and bay leaf and season with salt and pepper to taste.

4. For the cheese croutons While soup simmers, arrange baguette slices in single layer on rimmed baking sheet and bake until bread is dry, crisp, and golden at edges, about 10 minutes. Set aside.

5. Adjust oven rack 8 inches from broiler element and heat broiler. Set 6 broiler-safe crocks on rimmed baking sheet and fill each with about 1¾ cups soup. Top each bowl with 1 or 2 baguette slices (do not overlap slices) and sprinkle evenly with Gruyère. Broil until cheese is melted and bubbly around edges, 3 to 5 minutes. Let cool for 5 minutes before serving.

MUJADDARA

Serves 4 to 6   Total time: 1 hour 45 minutes

WHY THIS RECIPE WORKS *Essentially the "rice and beans" of the Middle East, this is a spectacular example of how a few humble ingredients can add up to a complex, savory, and deeply satisfying dish. Though each household and restaurant differs in its approach, mujaddara is simple to throw together: Boil basmati rice and lentils together until tender, then work in warm spices such as coriander, cumin, cinnamon, allspice, and pepper, as well as minced garlic. In every version, the real showpiece is the onions—either fried or caramelized—that get stirred into and also sprinkled over the pilaf just before serving. Their flavor is as deep as their mahogany color suggests. Finished with a bracing, garlicky yogurt sauce, this is comfort food at its best. Large green or brown lentils both work well in this recipe; do not use French green lentils. Long-grain white, jasmine, or Texmati rice can be substituted for the basmati. It is crucial to thoroughly dry the microwaved onions after rinsing. The remaining oil from the onions may be refrigerated for up to four weeks in an airtight container and used for cooking.*

YOGURT SAUCE

- 1 cup plain whole-milk yogurt
- 2 tablespoons lemon juice
- ½ teaspoon minced garlic
- ½ teaspoon salt

CRISPY ONIONS

- 2 pounds onions, halved and sliced crosswise ¼-inch-thick
- 2 teaspoons salt
- 1½ cups vegetable oil

RICE AND LENTILS

- 8¾ ounces (1¼ cups) green or brown lentils, picked over and rinsed
  Salt and pepper
- 1¼ cups basmati rice
- 3 garlic cloves, minced
- 1 teaspoon ground coriander
- 1 teaspoon ground cumin
- ½ teaspoon ground cinnamon
- ½ teaspoon ground allspice
- ⅛ teaspoon cayenne pepper
- 1 teaspoon sugar
- 3 tablespoons minced fresh cilantro

1. **For the yogurt sauce** Whisk all ingredients together in bowl. Refrigerate until ready to serve.

2. **For the onions** Toss onions and salt together in large bowl. Microwave for 5 minutes. Rinse thoroughly, transfer to paper towel–lined baking sheet, and dry well.

3. Cook onions in oil in Dutch oven over high heat, stirring frequently, until onions are golden brown, 25 to 30 minutes. Drain onions in colander set in large bowl. Transfer onions to paper towel–lined baking sheet to drain. Reserve 3 tablespoons oil.

4. **For the rice and lentils** Bring lentils, 4 cups water, and 1 teaspoon salt to boil in medium saucepan over high heat. Reduce heat to low and cook until lentils are tender, 15 to 17 minutes. Drain and set aside. While lentils cook, place rice in medium bowl and cover by 2 inches with hot water; let stand for 15 minutes.

5. Using your hands, gently swish rice grains to release excess starch. Carefully pour off water, leaving rice in bowl. Add cold water to rice and pour off water. Repeat adding and pouring off cold water 4 or 5 times, until water runs almost clear. Drain rice in fine-mesh strainer.

6. Heat reserved onion oil, garlic, coriander, cumin, cinnamon, allspice, cayenne, and ¼ teaspoon pepper in now-empty Dutch oven over medium heat until fragrant, about 2 minutes. Add rice and cook, stirring occasionally, until edges of rice begin to turn translucent, about 3 minutes. Add 2¼ cups water, sugar, and 1 teaspoon salt and bring to boil. Stir in lentils, reduce heat to low, cover, and cook until all liquid is absorbed, about 12 minutes.

7. Off heat, remove lid, fold dish towel in half, and place over pot; replace lid. Let stand for 10 minutes. Fluff rice and lentils with fork and stir in cilantro and half of crispy onions. Transfer to serving platter, top with remaining crispy onions, and serve, passing yogurt sauce separately.

LEEK AND GOAT CHEESE QUICHE

Serves 6 to 8   Total time: 3 hours 15 minutes (plus 1 hour cooling time)
WHY THIS RECIPE WORKS *In this appealing quiche, the tender, buttery pastry crust embraces an eggy custard that's rich with sweet leeks and tangy goat cheese. To prevent a soggy crust, we parbaked it before adding the filling. To avoid spillage, we set the parbaked crust in the oven before pouring the custard into the pastry. Baking temperature was important: 350 degrees was low enough to set the custard gently, yet hot enough to brown the top without drying out the filling. For perfectly baked quiche every time, pull it out of the oven when it is still slightly soft, which allows it to set up properly as it cools. Be sure to add the custard to the parbaked crust while the crust is still warm so that the quiche will bake evenly. You can substitute thyme, parsley, or marjoram for the chives. You can also substitute store-bought pie dough.*

DOUGH
1¼ cups (6¼ ounces) **all-purpose flour**
1 tablespoon **sugar**
½ teaspoon **salt**
4 tablespoons **vegetable shortening, cut into ¼-inch pieces and chilled**
6 tablespoons **unsalted butter, cut into ¼-inch pieces and chilled**
3–4 tablespoons **ice water**

FILLING
2 tablespoons **unsalted butter**
1 pound **leeks, white and light green parts only, chopped fine, and washed thoroughly**
5 large **eggs**
2 cups **half-and-half**
¼ teaspoon **salt**
¼ teaspoon **pepper**
4 ounces **goat cheese, crumbled (1 cup)**
1 tablespoon **minced fresh chives**

1. **For the dough** Process flour, sugar, and salt in food processor until combined, about 5 seconds. Scatter shortening pieces over top and process until mixture resembles coarse cornmeal, about 10 seconds. Scatter butter pieces over top and pulse until mixture resembles coarse crumbs, about 10 pulses. Transfer to bowl.

2. Sprinkle 3 tablespoons water over flour mixture. Using rubber spatula, stir and press dough until it sticks together. If dough does not come together, add remaining 1 tablespoon water.

3. Turn dough onto sheet of plastic wrap and flatten into 4-inch disk. Wrap tightly and refrigerate for 1 hour.

4. Let dough sit on counter to soften slightly, about 10 minutes. Roll dough into 12-inch circle on well-floured counter. Loosely roll dough around rolling pin and gently unroll it onto 9-inch pie plate, letting excess dough hang over edge. Ease dough into plate by gently lifting edge of dough with your hand while pressing into plate bottom with your other hand. Trim overhang to ½ inch. Tuck overhang under itself; folded edge should be flush with edge of plate. Crimp dough evenly around edge of plate using your fingers. Wrap dough-lined plate loosely in plastic and refrigerate until dough is firm, about 30 minutes.

5. Adjust oven rack to middle position and heat oven to 400 degrees. Line chilled pie crust with double layer of aluminum foil, covering edges to prevent burning, and fill with pie weights. Bake until pie dough looks dry and is pale in color, 25 to 30 minutes.

6. **For the filling** Adjust oven rack to lower-middle position and reduce oven temperature to 350 degrees. Melt butter in 10-inch skillet over medium-high heat. Add leeks and cook until softened, about 6 minutes; transfer to bowl. Whisk eggs, half-and-half, salt, and pepper into bowl with leeks. Stir in goat cheese.

7. Place warm pie shell on rimmed baking sheet and place in oven. Carefully pour egg mixture into warm shell until it reaches about ½ inch from top edge of crust (you may have extra egg mixture).

8. Bake quiche until top is lightly browned, center is set but soft, and knife inserted about 1 inch from edge comes out clean, 40 to 50 minutes. Let quiche cool for at least 1 hour. Sprinkle with chives and serve warm.

ROASTED CHICKEN THIGHS WITH CREAMED SHALLOTS AND BACON

Serves 4 Total time: 45 minutes

WHY THIS RECIPE WORKS *Less assertive than onions, with a mild garlicky flavor, shallots are a delicious way to lend oniony flavor to dishes without adding the pungency and texture of a regular onion. Here, we brought their delicate onion profile to a quick, hearty chicken dinner. Browning the chicken thighs in a skillet on the stovetop and then finishing them on a baking sheet in the oven left the skillet free for cooking the bacon and then caramelizing the shallots in the bacon fat, which deepened their flavor. You will need a 12-inch skillet with a tight-fitting lid for this recipe.*

- 8 (5- to 7-ounce) bone-in chicken thighs, trimmed
- Salt and pepper
- 1 tablespoon vegetable oil
- 4 slices bacon, cut into 1-inch pieces
- 8 shallots, peeled and halved lengthwise
- ½ cup brandy
- ¼ cup water
- ½ cup heavy cream
- 1 tablespoon minced fresh thyme

1. Adjust oven rack to upper-middle position and heat oven to 450 degrees. Line rimmed baking sheet with aluminum foil. Pat chicken dry with paper towels and season with salt and pepper. Heat oil in 12-inch skillet over medium-high heat until just smoking. Cook chicken, skin side down, until well browned, about 8 minutes. Transfer chicken to prepared sheet, skin side up, and roast until chicken registers 175 degrees, 15 to 20 minutes.

2. Meanwhile, pour off fat from skillet. Add bacon and cook over medium heat until crisp, 6 to 8 minutes. Using slotted spoon, transfer bacon to paper towel–lined plate, leaving fat in pan. Add shallots to skillet, cut side down. Cover and cook until well browned, about 3 minutes. Off heat, add brandy and water. Return skillet to heat and cook, covered, until shallots are tender, about 5 minutes.

3. Stir in cream and thyme and simmer, uncovered, until thickened, about 3 minutes. Season with salt and pepper to taste. Transfer creamed shallots to serving platter, arrange chicken on top, and sprinkle with bacon. Serve.

OKLAHOMA FRIED ONION CHEESEBURGERS

Serves 4 Total time: 50 minutes

WHY THIS RECIPE WORKS *During the Depression, enterprising cooks in Oklahoma discovered that they could mash thinly sliced onions into ground beef patties as a way to use less meat without reducing portion size. This trick not only bulked up the patties, but it also created a delicious layer of caramelized onions on the outside that infused the meat with richness. What started out of necessity became a tradition. Our version focuses on flavor, not thrift. We sliced an onion as thin as possible and salted the slices to draw out moisture so they'd caramelize fully, squeezing the salted onion in a dish towel to dry them further. We then formed the patties by making a small mound of onion, placing a loosely formed ball of ground beef on top, and pressing the beef into the onion. We cooked the patties, onion side down, over gentle heat until the onion layer developed a deep golden-brown color and began to crisp. Layering the finished burgers on top of—rather than beneath—the cheese kept the onions crisp.*

- 1 onion, halved and sliced thin
- 1 teaspoon salt
- ½ teaspoon pepper
- 12 ounces 85 percent lean ground beef
- 1 tablespoon unsalted butter
- 1 teaspoon vegetable oil
- 4 slices American cheese (4 ounces)
- 4 hamburger buns, toasted

1. Combine onion and salt in colander and let sit for 30 minutes, tossing occasionally. Transfer to clean dish towel, gather edges, and squeeze onion dry.

2. Spread onion on rimmed baking sheet, sprinkle with pepper, and toss to combine. Divide onion mixture into four 2-inch-wide mounds. Divide beef into 4 lightly packed balls. Place balls on top of onion mounds and flatten balls firmly so onion adheres and patties measure 4 inches in diameter.

3. Melt butter with oil in 12-inch nonstick skillet over medium heat. Using spatula, place patties onion side down in skillet and cook until onion is deep golden brown and beginning to crisp around edges, 6 to 8 minutes.

4. Flip patties, increase heat to high, and continue to cook until well browned on second side, about 2 minutes. Place 1 slice American cheese on each bun bottom and top each with burger and bun top. Serve.

SOUTHERN-STYLE SMOTHERED PORK CHOPS

Serves 4   Total time: 2 hours 15 minutes

WHY THIS RECIPE WORKS *Pork chops smothered in a rich onion pan gravy and then oven-braised until tender are a Southern specialty. We stirred up a seasoning mixture of Lawry's Seasoned Salt, onion powder, granulated garlic, paprika, and pepper, and used this mixture in three places: on the chops, in the flour dredge that the chops are coated in, and in the gravy. We first browned the coated chops well and then built the gravy in the same skillet using vegetable oil and flour. We cooked the roux until it was the color of peanut butter, stirred in onions and water, and poured the mixture over the chops. After cooking for about 1½ hours, the pork chops were supertender and flavorful from the thickened gravy. Try to find chops of the same thickness for even cooking; for the most tender and moist chops, start with ¾- to 1-inch-thick bone-in blade chops. For proper sauce consistency, it's important to measure the amount of fat left in the skillet before making the roux.*

- 2 tablespoons Lawry's Seasoned Salt
- 1 tablespoon onion powder
- 1 teaspoon garlic powder
- 1 teaspoon paprika
  Pepper
- 4 (8- to 10-ounce) bone-in pork blade-cut chops, ¾ to 1 inch thick, trimmed
- 1 cup all-purpose flour
- ½ cup vegetable oil

- 2 onions, quartered through root end and sliced thin crosswise
- 3 cups water
- 1 tablespoon cider vinegar

1. Adjust oven rack to middle position and heat oven to 350 degrees. Set wire rack in rimmed baking sheet. Combine seasoned salt, onion powder, garlic powder, paprika, and 1 teaspoon pepper in bowl. Pat chops dry with paper towels and sprinkle each chop with 1 teaspoon spice mixture (½ teaspoon per side).

2. Combine ½ cup flour and 4 teaspoons spice mixture in shallow dish. Dredge chops lightly in seasoned flour, shake off excess, and transfer to prepared rack.

3. Heat oil in 12-inch skillet over medium-high heat until just smoking. Add 2 chops to skillet and fry until deep golden brown, 3 to 5 minutes per side. Let excess oil drip from chops, then return chops to rack. Repeat with remaining 2 chops.

4. Transfer fat left in skillet to liquid measuring cup. Return ¼ cup fat to skillet and stir in remaining ½ cup flour. Cook over medium heat, stirring constantly, until roux is color of peanut butter, 3 to 5 minutes. Add onions and remaining 4 teaspoons spice mixture and cook, stirring constantly, until onions begin to soften slightly, about 2 minutes.

5. Slowly stir water into roux mixture until gravy is smooth and free of lumps. Bring to simmer and cook until gravy begins to thicken, about 2 minutes. Pour half of gravy into 13 by 9-inch baking dish. Nestle browned chops in dish, overlapping slightly as needed. Pour remaining gravy over chops and cover dish tightly with aluminum foil. Bake until chops are fully tender, about 1½ hours.

6. Carefully transfer chops to serving platter. (Chops will be delicate and may fall apart.) Use wide spoon to skim fat from surface of gravy. Add vinegar to gravy and season with pepper to taste. Pour gravy over chops. Serve.

BRAISED HALIBUT WITH LEEKS AND MUSTARD

Serves 4   Total time: 35 minutes

WHY THIS RECIPE WORKS *Cooking mild, sweet, meaty halibut fillets on a generous pile of sliced leeks in butter and white wine creates an irresistible fusion of flavors. Finishing this fast and easy-to-prepare but elegant dish with a quick lemony mustard pan sauce sealed the deal. The gentle, moist heat of braising resulted in perfectly silky-textured fish fillets. Halibut has a delicate flavor and firm texture that we prefer in this recipe, but another similar firm-fleshed white fish such as striped bass or sea bass that is between ¾ and 1 inch thick can be substituted. To ensure that your fish cooks evenly, purchase fillets that are similarly shaped and uniformly thick.*

- 4 (6- to 8-ounce) skinless halibut fillets, ¾ to 1 inch thick
  Salt and pepper
- 6 tablespoons unsalted butter
- 1 pound leeks, white and light green parts only, halved lengthwise, sliced thin, and washed thoroughly
- 1 teaspoon Dijon mustard
- ¾ cup dry white wine
- 1 teaspoon lemon juice, plus lemon wedges for serving
- 1 tablespoon minced fresh parsley

1. Sprinkle fish with ½ teaspoon salt. Melt butter in 12-inch skillet over low heat. Place fish in skillet, skinned side up, increase heat to medium, and cook, shaking pan occasionally, until butter begins to brown (fish should not brown), 3 to 4 minutes. Using spatula, carefully transfer fish to large plate, raw side down.

2. Add leeks, mustard, and ½ teaspoon salt to skillet and cook, stirring frequently, until leeks begin to soften, 2 to 4 minutes. Add wine and bring to gentle simmer. Place fish, raw side down, on top of leeks. Cover skillet and cook, adjusting heat to maintain gentle simmer, until fish registers 135 to 140 degrees, 10 to 14 minutes. Remove skillet from heat and, using 2 spatulas, transfer fish and leeks to serving platter or individual plates. Tent with aluminum foil.

½ cup pitted niçoise olives, chopped coarse

8 anchovy fillets, rinsed, patted dry, and chopped coarse, plus 12 fillets for garnish (optional)

2 teaspoons minced fresh thyme

1 teaspoon fennel seeds

½ teaspoon pepper

2 tablespoons minced fresh parsley

1. For the dough Pulse flour, sugar, and yeast in food processor until combined, about 5 pulses. With processor running, slowly add ice water and process until dough is just combined and no dry flour remains, about 10 seconds. Let dough rest for 10 minutes.

2. Add oil and salt to dough and process until dough forms satiny, sticky ball that clears sides of bowl, 30 to 60 seconds. Transfer dough to lightly floured counter and knead by hand to form smooth, round ball, about 30 seconds. Place dough seam side down in lightly greased large bowl or container, cover tightly with plastic wrap, and refrigerate for at least 24 hours or up to 3 days.

3. For the toppings Heat 2 tablespoons oil in 12-inch nonstick skillet over medium heat until shimmering. Stir in onions, sugar, and salt. Cover and cook, stirring occasionally, until onions are softened and have released their juice, about 10 minutes. Remove lid and continue to cook, stirring often, until onions are golden brown, 10 to 15 minutes. Transfer onions to bowl, stir in water, and let cool completely before using.

4. One hour before baking, adjust oven rack 4 inches from broiler element, set baking stone on rack, and heat oven to 500 degrees. Press down on dough to deflate. Transfer dough to clean counter, divide in half, and cover loosely with greased plastic. Pat 1 piece of dough (keep remaining piece covered) into 4-inch round. Working around circumference of dough, fold edges toward center until ball forms.

5. Flip ball seam side down and, using your cupped hands, drag in small circles on counter until dough feels taut and round and all seams are secured on underside. (If dough sticks to your hands, lightly dust top

---

3. Return skillet to high heat and simmer briskly until sauce is thickened, 2 to 3 minutes. Off heat, stir in lemon juice and season with salt and pepper to taste. Spoon sauce over fish and sprinkle with parsley. Serve immediately with lemon wedges.

PISSALADIÈRE

Makes two 14 by 8-inch tarts, serving 4 to 6
Total time: 2 hours 45 minutes (plus 24 hours refrigeration time)

WHY THIS RECIPE WORKS *Pissaladière is a savory Provençal tart that is prized for its flavor and texture contrasts: salty black olives and anchovies on a backdrop of sweet caramelized onions and earthy fresh thyme, all laid over a wheaty crust that is part chewy pizza and part crisp cracker. The tart is easy to prepare, provided each ingredient is handled carefully. We made the dough in a food processor and kneaded it just enough so that it had the structure to stand up to the toppings. To keep our crust thin and prevent it from bubbling, we poked it all over with the tines of a fork. Starting the onions covered and then uncovering them to finish left them perfectly browned and caramelized, with no burning.*

A bit of water stirred in at the end of cooking kept them from clumping when spread over the crust. To protect the black olives and thyme from burning in the oven, we spread them on the dough first and then covered them with the onions. Finally, we chopped the anchovies to keep them from overpowering the other flavors (though some fish-loving tasters opted to add more whole fillets on top). Some baking stones can crack under the intense heat of the broiler; be sure to check the manufacturer's website. You must refrigerate the dough for at least 24 hours or up to three days.

DOUGH

3 cups (16½ ounces) bread flour

2 teaspoons sugar

½ teaspoon instant or rapid-rise yeast

1⅓ cups ice water

1 tablespoon extra-virgin olive oil

1½ teaspoons salt

TOPPINGS

¼ cup extra-virgin olive oil

2 pounds onions, halved and sliced ¼-inch-thick

1 teaspoon packed brown sugar

½ teaspoon salt

1 tablespoon water

Smoked Salmon and Leek Tart

of dough with flour.) Repeat with remaining piece of dough. Space dough balls 3 inches apart, cover loosely with greased plastic, and let rest for 1 hour.

6. Heat broiler for 10 minutes. Meanwhile, generously coat 1 dough ball with flour and place on well-floured counter. Press and roll into 14 by 8-inch oval. Transfer oval to well-floured pizza peel and reshape as needed. (If dough resists stretching, let it relax for 10 to 20 minutes before trying to stretch it again.) Using fork, poke entire surface of oval 10 to 15 times.

7. Brush dough oval with 1 tablespoon oil, then sprinkle evenly with ¼ cup olives, half of chopped anchovies, 1 teaspoon thyme, ½ teaspoon fennel seeds, and ¼ teaspoon pepper, leaving ½-inch border around edge. Arrange half of onions on top, followed by 6 whole anchovies, if using.

8. Slide flatbread carefully onto baking stone and return oven to 500 degrees. Bake until bottom crust is evenly browned and edges are crisp, 13 to 15 minutes, rotating flatbread halfway through baking. Transfer flatbread to wire rack and let cool for 5 minutes. Sprinkle with 1 tablespoon parsley.

9. Heat broiler for 10 minutes. Repeat with remaining dough, oil, and toppings, returning oven to 500 degrees when flatbread is placed on stone. Slice and serve.

SMOKED SALMON AND LEEK TART

Serves 8   Total time: 2 hours (plus 2 hours cooling time)

WHY THIS RECIPE WORKS *Unexpected and elegant, this savory tart makes a stunning presentation as either a brunch dish or a holiday starter. It features a trio of flavors and textures in every bite: flaky pastry; creamy, leek-filled custard; and briny, smoky salmon.*

The pink salmon and green leeks blanketing the pale custard created a beautiful color contrast. Using half-and-half in the leek and custard filling added flavor and richness. Chopping up the salmon, rather than layering it on in slices, made the tart easier to both slice and eat. You will need a 9-inch fluted tart pan with a removable bottom for this recipe. Buy smoked salmon that looks bright and glossy and avoid salmon that looks milky and dry. Serve either at room temperature or chilled, with lemon wedges if you like.

DOUGH

1¼ cups (6¼ ounces) all-purpose flour
1 tablespoon sugar
½ teaspoon salt
8 tablespoons unsalted butter, cut into ½-inch cubes and chilled
2–4 tablespoons ice water

FILLING

1 tablespoon unsalted butter
1 pound leeks, white and light green parts only, halved lengthwise, sliced thin, and washed thoroughly
Salt and pepper
2 large eggs
½ cup half-and-half
1 tablespoon minced fresh dill
6 ounces thinly sliced smoked salmon, cut into ¼-inch pieces
1 tablespoon extra-virgin olive oil
1 tablespoon minced fresh chives

1. For the dough Spray 9-inch tart pan with removable bottom with vegetable oil spray. Pulse flour, sugar, and salt in food processor until combined, about 4 pulses. Scatter butter pieces over top and pulse until mixture resembles coarse sand, about 15 pulses. Add 2 tablespoons ice water and continue to process until clumps of dough just begin to form and no powdery bits remain, about 5 seconds. If dough doesn't clump, add remaining ice water, 1 tablespoon at a time, and pulse to incorporate, about 4 pulses.

2. Press two-thirds of dough into bottom of prepared pan. Press remaining one-third of dough into fluted sides of pan. Lay plastic wrap over dough and smooth out any bumps or shallow areas using your fingertips. Place pan on plate and freeze dough until firm, about 30 minutes. Meanwhile, adjust oven rack to middle position and heat oven to 375 degrees.

3. Place frozen tart shell on rimmed baking sheet. Gently press piece of greased aluminum foil against dough and over edges of tart pan. Fill tart pan with pie weights and bake until top edge of dough just starts to color and surface of dough no longer looks wet, about 30 minutes.

4. Remove sheet from oven and carefully remove foil and weights. Return sheet to oven and continue to bake until tart shell is golden brown, 5 to 10 minutes. Set sheet with tart shell on wire rack and let cool.

5. For the filling Melt butter in 10-inch skillet over medium heat. Add leeks and ½ teaspoon salt and cook, covered, stirring occasionally, until leeks are softened, about 10 minutes. Remove pan from heat and let leeks cool, uncovered, for 5 minutes.

6. Whisk eggs, half-and-half, dill, and ¼ teaspoon pepper together in bowl. Stir in leeks until just incorporated. Place cooled tart shell on rimmed baking sheet and place in oven. Carefully pour egg mixture into cooled shell and bake until filling has set and center feels firm to touch, 20 to 25 minutes. Transfer sheet to wire rack and let tart cool completely, at least 2 hours.

7. Just before serving, toss salmon, oil, and chives together in bowl and season with salt and pepper to taste before sprinkling evenly over cooled tart. Slice and serve.

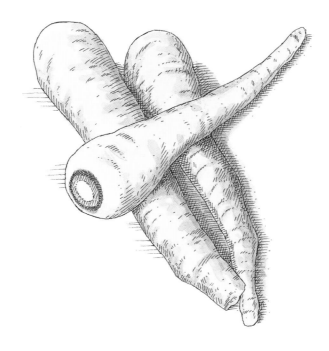

PARSNIPS

Parsnips look a lot like bulbous albino carrots. Home cooks often pass them by in the market, unsure about how to approach this pale, primitive-looking relative of both carrot and parsley. That's a shame, since parsnips are easy to cook by almost any method. They're simultaneously sweeter and earthier than carrots, with more complex and subtle floral notes, but they are just as versatile in the kitchen. Their flavor, along with their satisfyingly hearty texture, means they can shine in a wide variety of preparations.

Parsnips have been cultivated since ancient times in Europe and Asia, and made their way to America in the 1600s. At least since the Roman era they have been a ubiquitous staple food for everyday people, because they are hardy and easy to grow, they store well, and they offer vitamins and minerals, including plenty of potassium, as well as starch and sugar. In fact, before sugar became widely available in modern times, parsnips were used to sweeten items such as cakes. Their tragic decline in popularity coincided with the rise in popularity of potatoes and the availability of white sugar.

Parsnips do differ from carrots in that they are typically eaten cooked, not raw. Whether oven-roasted or pan-roasted, sautéed, pureed, glazed, or braised, they make for a perfect fuss-free side dish. They can even be cooked in the same skillet as your protein for a quick dinner, as in our recipe for Roasted Chicken with Honey-Glazed Parsnips. Braised Parsnips with Cranberries is a simple but festive stovetop side that begs to be included on your Thanksgiving table. And Sautéed Parsnips with Ginger, Maple, and Fennel Seeds will forever change the way you think about this humble root vegetable.

shopping and storage

The peak season for parsnips is fall through winter, although they are available year-round. They should be rock hard, just like carrots; if they bend, they are past their prime. When shopping, if you find medium-size parsnips—with the bases no larger than 1 inch in diameter at their thickest point—these will be the most tender and do not need to be cored. Larger parsnips (up to about 2½ inches in diameter at their thickest point) are still tasty and sweet, but they need to be cored before cooking. Parsnips larger than that are too tough, even after cooking, and are best avoided. Store parsnips just as you would carrots: wrapped loosely in a paper towel in a plastic produce bag in the refrigerator for up to two weeks. As with carrots, if your parsnips come with their greens attached, remove them before storage. This will likely only happen if you purchase your parsnips from a farmers' market, since, unlike carrot greens, parsnip greens aren't edible.

acidulate your parsnips

Similar to artichokes and apples, parsnips will oxidize and turn brown very quickly after you peel and cut them. So if you aren't planning to cook parsnips right away after prepping them, submerge them in a bowl of water with a little lemon juice or vinegar. The acid in the juice or vinegar will slow down the browning.

vegetable prep

With their thick bulbous stem and thin tapered end, cutting parsnips into even pieces can stump even the most skilled cook. To get more evenly sized pieces, we often like to cut parsnips on the bias or into matchsticks.

Cutting Parsnips on Bias

1. Cut thin tapered end from bulbous part of parsnip, then quarter bulbous end lengthwise.

2. Holding knife at 45-degree angle to parsnips, cut each piece into desired thickness on bias.

Cutting Parsnips into Matchsticks

1. Cut parsnip crosswise into desired lengths.

2. Cut each piece lengthwise into planks of desired thickness.

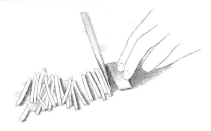

3. Cut each plank lengthwise into matchsticks of desired thickness.

Coring Parsnips

1. If parsnips are large, cut them lengthwise into quarters.

2. Lay parsnip quarter flat-side down on cutting board and trim woody core that runs along interior of piece.

Sautéed Parsnips with Ginger, Maple, and Fennel Seeds

SAUTÉED PARSNIPS WITH GINGER, MAPLE, AND FENNEL SEEDS

Serves 4   Total time: 20 minutes

WHY THIS RECIPE WORKS *This delicious and dead-easy one-pan side dish will definitely linger in your mind. It's simple enough to serve any night of the week but sophisticated enough for company. Cooking the parsnips was a short project: Cutting them into uniform sticks, a smoking-hot pan, and minimal stirring charred, caramelized, and cooked through those parsnips in just minutes. Since parsnips have warm spice and licorice-like notes, we chose glaze ingredients, including fennel seeds and ginger, that would bring out those unique qualities. The glaze achieved the perfect sweet, salty, and tart balance using maple syrup, soy sauce, and balsamic vinegar. You can substitute anise seeds for fennel. Look for parsnips with tops no larger than 1 inch in diameter for this recipe. If yours are larger, remove their fibrous cores before cooking.*

- 2 tablespoons soy sauce
- 2 tablespoons balsamic vinegar
- 1 tablespoon maple syrup
- 1½ teaspoons fennel seeds
- 2 tablespoons minced fresh ginger
- 2 tablespoons plus 1 teaspoon vegetable oil
- 1½ pounds parsnips, peeled and cut into 2-inch-long by ½-inch-wide matchsticks

1. Stir soy sauce, vinegar, maple syrup, and fennel seeds together in bowl; set aside. Combine ginger and 1 teaspoon oil in separate bowl; set aside.

2. Heat remaining 2 tablespoons oil in 12-inch skillet over medium-high heat until just smoking. Add parsnips and cook, stirring occasionally, until well charred and crisp-tender, 5 to 7 minutes.

3. Push parsnips to sides of skillet. Add ginger mixture to center and cook, mashing mixture into pan, until fragrant, about 30 seconds. Stir ginger into parsnips. Add soy mixture and toss to coat parsnips; cook until liquid is reduced to syrupy glaze, about 15 seconds. Serve immediately.

PAN-ROASTED PARSNIPS

Serves 6 to 8   Total time: 25 minutes

WHY THIS RECIPE WORKS *Here, the sweet caramelized flavor of oven-roasted parsnips is replicated on the stovetop, a streamlined technique that provides great roasted flavor and allows you to use your oven for other dishes. After browning the parsnips in vegetable oil, we added water to the pan before covering—this created a gentle steaming effect that guaranteed perfectly cooked parsnips every time, coaxing out the best flavor and texture. We cut the parsnips into ½-inch-thick pieces on the bias to assure even browning and cooking, as well as an attractive presentation. Look for parsnips no wider than 1 inch at their base, or you may need to discard their fibrous cores. You will need a 12-inch skillet with a tight-fitting lid for this recipe.*

- 2 tablespoons vegetable oil
- 2 pounds parsnips, peeled and cut ½ inch thick on bias
- ½ cup water
  Salt and pepper
- 1 tablespoon minced fresh parsley
  Lemon wedges

1. Heat oil in 12-inch skillet over medium-high heat until shimmering. Add parsnips and cook, stirring occasionally, until golden, 8 to 10 minutes.

2. Add water and ¾ teaspoon salt and bring to simmer. Cover, reduce heat to medium-low, and cook, stirring occasionally, until vegetables are tender and liquid has evaporated, 8 to 10 minutes. Stir in parsley and season with salt and pepper to taste. Serve with lemon wedges.

VARIATIONS

Pan-Roasted Cilantro-Lime Parsnips
Add 1 teaspoon chili powder to skillet with parsnips in step 1. Substitute 2 tablespoons cilantro for parsley. Add ¾ teaspoon lime zest plus 1 tablespoon lime juice to parsnips with cilantro in step 2. Serve with lime wedges.

Pan-Roasted Orange Parsnips
Substitute 1 teaspoon fresh minced thyme for parsley. Add ¾ teaspoon orange zest to parsnips with thyme in step 2. Serve with orange wedges.

SIMPLE PUREED PARSNIPS

Serves 4   Total time: 30 minutes

WHY THIS RECIPE WORKS *For a change of pace from mashed potatoes, try this quick and simple puree. Its flavor is pure, sweet, and intense, thanks to the fact that the parsnips are steamed rather than boiled before pureeing. Because parsnips are not as high in starch as potatoes, you can puree them in a food processor without turning them into a gummy mess—unlike potatoes. If you don't want to take out your food processor, you can puree the parsnips using any of the tools you might use to mash potatoes, though you will get a more rustic consistency.*

- 1½ pounds parsnips, peeled, cut into 2½-inch lengths, and thick ends halved lengthwise
- 1½ tablespoons unsalted butter, softened
  Salt and pepper

1. Bring 1 inch water to boil in covered Dutch oven over medium-high heat (water should not touch bottom of steamer basket).

2. Arrange parsnips in steamer basket. Set steamer basket inside Dutch oven, cover, and cook until they can be easily pierced with paring knife, about 10 minutes. Reserve cooking liquid.

3. Puree parsnips in food processor until smooth, about 1 minute, adding reserved cooking liquid as needed to achieve desired consistency. Return puree to now-empty Dutch oven and reheat over medium low-heat, stirring in butter. Season to taste with salt and pepper. Serve immediately. (Puree can be refrigerated for up to 3 days or frozen in airtight container for up to 1 month.)

VARIATION

Creamy Parsnip Puree with Shallots
While parsnips are cooking, melt butter in 12-inch skillet over medium heat. Add 3 chopped shallots and cook until golden, 2 to 3 minutes. Substitute ¼ cup chicken broth and ¼ cup milk for reserved cooking liquid, adding more milk as needed to achieve desired consistency. Top puree with shallots and serve.

BRAISED PARSNIPS WITH CRANBERRIES

Serves 4 to 6   Total time: 35 minutes

WHY THIS RECIPE WORKS *The cooking liquid becomes your sauce when braising, so the trick to making a great braised vegetable side dish is to create a sauce that coats the vegetables well and infuses them with flavor without overwhelming them. Parsnips, with their slightly licorice-y sweetness, can stand up to rich sauces—but if not correctly balanced, the finished dish can come off as cloying. For our braising liquid, we found that a mixture of vegetable broth and apple cider gave us a base with depth, fruitiness, and a touch of acidity that complemented the parsnips perfectly. Reducing the cooking liquid slightly before adding the parsnips and finishing with Dijon mustard and butter gave the sauce extra bite, plus silky texture and body. Dried cranberries brought a contrasting tartness, and fresh parsley lent color and bright flavor, bringing this dish into perfect balance. Look for parsnips with bases no larger than 1 inch in diameter for this recipe.*

- 3 tablespoons unsalted butter, 2 tablespoons cut into ½-inch pieces
- 1 shallot, minced
- 1 cup chicken or vegetable broth
- 1 cup apple cider
- 6 sprigs fresh thyme
- 2 bay leaves
  Salt and pepper
- 2 pound parsnips, peeled and cut ¼ inch thick on bias
- ½ cup dried cranberries
- 1 tablespoon Dijon mustard
- 2 tablespoons minced fresh parsley

1. Melt 1 tablespoon butter in large Dutch oven over high heat. Add shallot and cook, stirring frequently, until softened and just beginning to brown, about 1 minute. Add broth, cider, thyme sprigs, bay leaves, 1½ teaspoons salt, and ½ teaspoon pepper; bring to simmer and cook for 5 minutes. Add parsnips, stir to combine, and return to simmer. Reduce heat to medium-low, cover, and cook, stirring occasionally, until vegetables are tender, 10 to 14 minutes.

2. Remove pot from heat. Discard thyme sprigs and bay leaves and stir in cranberries. Push vegetable mixture to sides of pot. Add mustard and remaining 2 tablespoons butter to center and whisk into cooking liquid. Stir to coat vegetable mixture with sauce, transfer to serving dish, sprinkle with parsley, and serve.

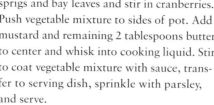

GLAZED PARSNIPS AND CELERY

Serves 4   Total time: 25 minutes

WHY THIS RECIPE WORKS *Parsnips and celery have complementary flavors but contrasting textures, making for an unusual side dish that will keep you coming back bite after bite. To ensure that the parsnips and celery cooked evenly, we cut them into pieces of equal size, ½ inch thick on the bias. Browning the vegetables without stirring created nice caramelization and roasted flavors. Then, to get the parsnips and celery to a tender-but-not-mushy state, we simmered them, covered, in a mixture of broth and seasonings. Once the vegetables were tender, it was easy to create a lightly sweet glaze from the remaining liquid in the skillet. Choose parsnips with bases no larger than 1 inch in diameter for this recipe. If your parsnips are larger, cut away their fibrous cores before cooking. You will need a 12-inch skillet with a tight-fitting lid for this recipe.*

- 3 tablespoons unsalted butter
- 1 pound parsnips, peeled and cut ½ inch thick on bias
- 3 celery ribs, sliced ½ inch thick on bias, leaves reserved
- 1 cup chicken or vegetable broth
- 1 tablespoon white wine vinegar
- 1 tablespoon sugar
- ¼ teaspoon red pepper flakes
  Salt and pepper

1. Melt 1 tablespoon butter in 12-inch nonstick skillet over medium-high heat; swirl to coat skillet. Add parsnips in even layer and cook, without stirring, until browned, 2 to 4 minutes. Stir in celery and cook, stirring occasionally, until well browned, 2 to 4 minutes.

2. Add broth, vinegar, sugar, pepper flakes, ½ teaspoon salt, and ¼ teaspoon pepper. Cover, reduce heat to medium-low, and simmer until vegetables are just tender, 6 to 8 minutes.

3. Uncover, increase heat to high, and cook, stirring frequently, until liquid reduces to syrupy glaze, about 1 minute. Off heat, stir in remaining 2 tablespoons butter until melted and parsnips are well coated. Sprinkle with celery leaves, season with salt and pepper to taste, and serve.

PARSNIP HUMMUS

Makes about 2 cups   Total time: 50 minutes

WHY THIS RECIPE WORKS *Hummus is supposed to be all about the chickpeas—right? Well, this version turns that notion on its head, keeping the typical flavorings (tahini, olive oil, garlic, and lemon juice) but losing the legumes in favor of earthy, floral parsnips. The ideal cooking method for this recipe turned out to be microwaving, which was easy and resulted in flavor nearly as intense as roasting. Just ¼ cup of tahini was enough to stand up to the parsnips without overwhelming the hummus. To round out the flavors, we added warm spices: paprika, coriander, and cumin. Chipotle chile powder and garlic tempered the sweetness of the parsnips, while lemon juice brought the flavors into focus. Look for tender, thin parsnips for this hummus, as large parsnips can turn bitter. Serve with crackers, chips, or crudités.*

- 1 pound parsnips, peeled, cut into 1-inch lengths, and thick ends halved lengthwise
- ¼ cup tahini
- 3 tablespoons extra-virgin olive oil, plus extra for drizzling
- ¾ cup water
- 2 tablespoons lemon juice
  Salt and pepper
- 1 garlic clove, minced
- 1 teaspoon paprika
- ½ teaspoon ground coriander
- ¼ teaspoon ground cumin
- ¼ teaspoon chipotle chile powder
- 1 tablespoon toasted sesame seeds

PARSNIP HUMMUS

Hummus versions abound, but they are almost entirely based on chickpeas. Our new take on this tried-and-true standard uses parsnips instead. We kept the traditional tahini, garlic, and olive oil, and countered the sweetness of the cooked parsnips with warm, savory spices including cumin and chipotle chiles and the acidic punch of lemon juice. Just like its legume-based parent, it's great as a dip with crackers, but it also works as a salad topping or alongside roasted chicken.

1. Peel the parsnips and cut the thick ends in half lengthwise. Cut the parsnips into 1-inch lengths of even thickness.

2. Place the parsnips in a bowl, cover, and microwave them until they are very tender, about 10 minutes.

3. Meanwhile, combine the tahini and olive oil in a small bowl.

4. Add the parsnips, water, lemon juice, and spices to the food processor and process until the mixture is completely smooth, scraping down the sides of the bowl as needed.

5. With the food processor running, add the tahini-oil mixture in a steady stream and process until the hummus is completely smooth and creamy.

6. Drizzle the parsnip hummus generously with olive oil, sprinkle it with sesame seeds, and serve.

1. Microwave parsnips in covered bowl until tender, about 10 minutes. Combine tahini and oil in small bowl.

2. Process parsnips, water, lemon juice, ¾ teaspoon salt, garlic, paprika, coriander, cumin, and chile powder in food processor until completely smooth, about 1 minute, scraping down sides of bowl as needed. With processor running, add tahini mixture in steady stream and process until hummus is smooth and creamy, about 15 seconds, scraping down bowl as needed. Season with salt and pepper to taste.

3. Transfer hummus to bowl, cover with plastic wrap, and let sit at room temperature until flavors meld, about 30 minutes. Drizzle with extra oil and sprinkle with sesame seeds. Serve. (Hummus can be refrigerated for up to 5 days; stir in 1 tablespoon warm water to loosen if necessary before serving.)

CREAMY ROOT VEGETABLE SOUP

Serves 4 to 6   Total time: 45 minutes

WHY THIS RECIPE WORKS *Classic creamy soups like potato-leek or carrot-ginger tend to focus on a single vegetable or two, letting one root shine. For this recipe, we wanted a mélange of mellow, sweet, earthy root vegetables, while still highlighting one as a standout flavor. So we started with the usual suspects—potatoes, carrots, and celery—but then added parsnips for a gentle, haunting sweetness. For browning the vegetables, tasters definitely preferred the nutty flavor of butter, rather than oil. And, of course, cream is a must in a creamy soup, but too much dairy muted and obscured the vegetable flavors. We settled on ½ cup of heavy cream, supplemented with leeks to add sweet silkiness. A bay leaf added just the right herbal note. This pureed soup is silky smooth, sweetly earthy, and intensely flavorful.*

    4 tablespoons unsalted butter
    6 ounces parsnips, peeled and chopped
    2 carrots, peeled and chopped
    1 leek, white and light green parts only, halved lengthwise, sliced thin, and washed thoroughly
    1 celery rib, chopped
    1 garlic clove, peeled and smashed
       Salt and pepper
   12 ounces russet potatoes, peeled and cut into ½-inch pieces
  4¼ cups chicken or vegetable broth
    1 bay leaf
    ½ cup heavy cream

1. Melt butter in Dutch oven over medium-high heat. Add parsnips, carrots, leek, celery, garlic, and ½ teaspoon salt and cook until browned, 6 to 8 minutes. Stir in potatoes and cook, stirring constantly, until starch begins to release and vegetables begin to stick together, about 2 minutes. Add broth and bay leaf and bring to boil.

2. Reduce heat to low and simmer, stirring occasionally, until vegetables are tender, 15 to 20 minutes. Discard bay leaf. Working in batches, process soup in blender until smooth, 1 to 2 minutes. Return soup to clean pot and stir in cream. Season with salt and pepper to taste. Serve. (Soup can be refrigerated for up to 2 days.)

ROASTED CHICKEN WITH HONEY-GLAZED PARSNIPS

Serves 4   Total time: 45 minutes

WHY THIS RECIPE WORKS *Using quick-cooking bone-in, skin-on split chicken breasts for this roasted chicken and parsnips dish, rather than a whole chicken, turned a typically time-intensive preparation into a one-skillet meal that's quick enough for any night of the week. We started the chicken in a skillet on the stovetop to brown the skin; we then transferred the skillet to the oven to finish cooking the chicken. Roasting the parsnips right in the skillet with the chicken concentrated their flavor, and they also picked up some of the juices released by the chicken. The 20 minutes it took to roast the chicken pieces was the same amount of time it took to almost fully cook the parsnips. Once the chicken was roasted and beautifully bronzed, we set it aside so we could make the glaze on the stovetop and finish cooking the parsnips. The honey and rosemary glaze perfectly complemented the parsnips' earthy sweetness.*

4 (10- to 12-ounce) bone-in split chicken breasts, trimmed and halved crosswise
Salt and pepper
2 tablespoons vegetable oil
2 pounds parsnips, peeled and cut into 3-inch-long by ¾-inch-wide matchsticks
3 tablespoons honey
1 tablespoon minced fresh rosemary

1. Adjust oven rack to middle position and heat oven to 450 degrees. Pat breasts dry with paper towels and season with salt and pepper. Heat oil in 12-inch oven-safe skillet over medium-high heat until just smoking. Add breasts skin side down and cook until skin is crispy and golden, about 4 minutes. Transfer breasts to plate.

2. Add parsnips to now-empty skillet and cook until lightly browned, about 3 minutes. Nestle breasts skin side up among parsnips in skillet. Transfer skillet to oven and roast until chicken registers 160 degrees and parsnips are almost tender, about 20 minutes.

3. Using potholder (skillet handle will be hot), remove skillet from oven. Transfer breasts to serving platter and tent with aluminum foil. Being careful of hot skillet handle, add honey and rosemary to parsnips, and cook over medium heat until liquid has thickened to glaze, about 3 minutes. Transfer glazed parsnips to platter with chicken, drizzle with remaining glaze, and serve.

RED WINE–BRAISED SHORT RIBS WITH BACON, PARSNIPS, AND PEARL ONIONS

Serves 6   Total time: 4 hours 15 minutes (plus 2 hours cooling time and 8 hours refrigeration time)

WHY THIS RECIPE WORKS *Bone-in braised short ribs are so impressive and a terrific make-ahead option when cooking for company, since it's best to rest them overnight (at least) before serving. This version tops the stew with parsnips and pearl onions cooked in bacon fat until golden brown—yes, please! We wanted a straightforward option for browning the short ribs, so we browned them all at once in the oven, allowing the ribs to spend more time in the heat and maximizing the amount of fat rendered. We added lots of savory aromatics—garlic, red wine, rosemary, thyme, and tomato paste. Plenty of fat still came out in the braise, so we let the braised ribs rest to allow the fat to separate out and solidify, making it easy to scoop off the top. If you're braising and serving the ribs on the same day, bypass cooling the ribs in the braising liquid; instead, remove them from the pot straight out of the oven, strain the liquid, then let it settle so that the fat separates to the top. With a wide shallow spoon, skim off as much fat as possible and continue with the recipe. We recommend a full-bodied red wine, such as a Cabernet Sauvignon. You will need to refrigerate the ribs and liquid separately for at least 8 hours or up to three days.*

STEW
6 pounds bone-in English-style beef short ribs, trimmed
Salt and pepper
3 cups red wine
3 onions, chopped
2 carrots, chopped
1 celery rib, chopped
9 garlic cloves, chopped
¼ cup all-purpose flour
4 cups chicken broth
1 (14.5-ounce) can diced tomatoes, drained
1½ tablespoons minced fresh rosemary
1 tablespoon minced fresh thyme
3 bay leaves
1 teaspoon tomato paste

GARNISH
6 slices bacon, cut into ¼-inch pieces
10 ounces parsnips, peeled and cut ¾ inch thick on bias
1 cup frozen pearl onions, thawed
¼ teaspoon granulated sugar
¼ teaspoon salt
6 tablespoons chopped fresh parsley

1. For the stew Adjust oven rack to lower-middle position and heat oven to 450 degrees. Arrange short ribs bone side down in single layer in large roasting pan; season with salt and pepper. Roast until meat begins to brown, about 45 minutes; drain off all liquid. Return pan to oven and continue to cook until meat is well browned, 15 to 20 minutes. Transfer ribs to large plate; set aside. Drain off and reserve fat. Reduce oven temperature to 300 degrees. Heat roasting pan on 2 stove-top burners over medium heat; add wine and bring to simmer, scraping up browned bits. Set pan with wine aside.

2. Heat 2 tablespoons reserved fat in Dutch oven over medium-high heat; add onions, carrots, and celery and cook, stirring occasionally, until vegetables soften, about 12 minutes. Add garlic and cook until fragrant, about 30 seconds. Stir in flour until combined, about 45 seconds. Stir in wine from roasting pan, broth, tomatoes, rosemary, thyme, bay leaves, tomato paste, and salt and pepper to taste. Bring to boil and add ribs, completely submerging meat in liquid; return to boil, cover, transfer to oven, and simmer until ribs are tender, 2 to 2½ hours. Transfer pot to wire rack and cool, partially covered, until warm, about 2 hours.

3. Transfer ribs to large plate and discard loose bones. Strain braising liquid into medium bowl, pressing out liquid from solids; discard solids. Cover ribs and liquid separately and refrigerate overnight (or for at least 8 hours). (Ribs and liquid can be refrigerated for up to 3 days.)

4. For the garnish In Dutch oven, cook bacon over medium heat until crispy, 8 to 10 minutes. Using slotted spoon, transfer to paper towel–lined plate. Add parsnips, pearl onions, sugar, and salt to now-empty pot and cook over high heat, stirring occasionally, until browned, about 5 minutes. Spoon off and discard solidified fat from reserved braising liquid. Add defatted liquid and bring to simmer, stirring occasionally; season with salt and pepper to taste. Submerge ribs in liquid, return to simmer. Reduce heat to medium and cook, partially covered, until ribs are heated through and vegetables are tender, about 5 minutes; gently stir in bacon. Divide ribs and sauce among individual bowls, sprinkle each with 1 tablespoon parsley, and serve.

PEAS

Plump and sweet, fresh **ENGLISH PEAS**—the green garden peas we're all familiar with—are a quintessential vegetable of late spring and early summer. Freshly picked peas are as sweet as candy, so snap them up when you can. However, fresh peas turn starchy and lose their nutrients quickly, so we think that peas are one of those rare vegetables where frozen is as good as—or often better than—fresh. Highlight them in Quick Buttered Peas, a versatile side dish everyone should master. Or create an easy, pretty finger food with our Ricotta Crostini with Peas and Mint.

Supermarkets seldom carry whole English peapods, both because they're a bit of work to shell and because the pods are too tough to eat. But there are two edible peapods you will readily find: snow peas and sugar snap peas.

SNOW PEAS are recognizable for their flat, almost translucent pods in which no peas (or tiny peas) have developed. They cook in a flash, so they're ideal for quickly sautéing with bold flavors for simple side dishes, as in our Sautéed Snow Peas with Lemon and Parsley.

SUGAR SNAP PEAS are a hybrid of English peas and snow peas, and they combine the best of both worlds—crunchy, juicy pods with plump, sweet peas inside. Stir-fry them with beef and orange for a Sichuan-style meal, or nestle them into a bed of black rice in a room-temperature grain salad.

Flavorful **PEA GREENS** in their various growth stages are increasingly seen in specialty markets and farmers' markets. Our altogether delicious Pea Green Salad with Warm Apricot-Pistachio Vinaigrette celebrates the best of spring with delicate greens, peas, and a fruity, nutty dressing.

shopping and storage

PEAS Look for fresh peas at farmers' markets in the springtime and early summer, and don't hesitate to ask the vendor when they were picked and if you can taste before you buy. Once you get them home, use them as soon as possible. Fresh peas in the supermarket are often at least several days old, so the peas are likely to be some degree of starchy or even mealy. That's when we typically head to the frozen-foods aisle.

SNOW PEAS AND SUGAR SNAP PEAS Both are available year-round, although spring through summer is the best season. Pods should be a vibrant emerald green. To check freshness for snow peas, bend a snow peapod until it breaks—fresh snow peas will snap cleanly in half. Sugar snap peas should be firm and plump. Both snow and sugar snap peas will keep in an open plastic produce bag in the refrigerator for several days.

PEA GREENS If you find pea greens in any form in the spring or summer, they should look fresh and vibrant, with no signs of wilting, browning, or yellowing. They are extremely perishable, so wrap them loosely in paper towels and store them in the refrigerator for only a day or two.

all about pea greens

Although the term "pea greens" is used generically to indicate any growth from the pea plant, there are actually three distinct stages and forms that you might be able to find.

PEA SHOOTS Pea shoots are the first growth of the plant and are extremely delicate; they are sometimes shelved and labeled as "pea sprouts" in markets. They are sweet and mild and are great used raw as a topping for salads and sandwiches.

PEA TENDRILS Pea tendrils are the next stage of growth. Tender leaves have developed, and long, thin coils (the tendrils) spring out in every direction, all the better to capture sunlight for growth. Pea tendrils are more intense in flavor than pea shoots and are great in stir-fries.

PEA GREENS Pea greens are the third stage of growth. The rounded, bright green leaves are grassy and faintly bitter, tasting of fresh peas but without the sweetness. They are excellent salad greens, and they also can be used instead of basil or other herbs to make a pesto.

vegetable prep

Trimming Snow and Sugar Snap Peas

The tough strings should be removed from these peapods before using them in a recipe.

1. Use paring knife to slice off stem end of peapod.

2. Use your thumb to pull stem end along flat side of pod to remove string.

frozen is a-ok

We've always been big fans of frozen peas. Shucked from the pod, quick-blanched, and individually frozen within hours of being harvested, they are often sweeter and fresher-tasting than the shuck-'em-yourself "fresh" peas that may have spent many days in storage. We've seen two varieties in the freezer aisle: regular frozen peas and bags labeled "petite peas" (or sometimes "petit pois" or "baby sweet peas"). To see if there is a difference, we tasted each type with butter. Tasters unanimously favored the smaller peas for their sweeter flavor and creamier texture. Regular peas were by no means unacceptable, but they did have tougher skins and mealier interiors than the smaller ones. Since both varieties are available for the same price, we favor the smaller ones.

QUICK BUTTERED PEAS

Serves 4   Total time: 15 minutes

WHY THIS RECIPE WORKS *When it comes to making a quick, delicious, crowd-pleasing side dish to go with all manner of meals, buttered peas are hard to beat. Because frozen peas have already been blanched, the keys to cooking with them are to avoid overcooking the peas and to pair the peas with other ingredients that don't require much preparation. We found that after sautéing shallot, thyme, and garlic in butter, we could simply add the peas and let them cook through for a few minutes for a fresh and bright-tasting side dish. Using a skillet instead of a saucepan allowed the peas to heat more quickly and evenly over the larger surface, and covering the skillet sped up the cooking time. Adding a bit of sugar to the skillet helped to highlight the peas' sweet, refreshing flavor. Do not thaw the peas before adding them to the skillet. You will need a 12-inch nonstick skillet with a tight-fitting lid for this recipe.*

  2 tablespoons unsalted butter
  1 shallot, minced
  1 teaspoon minced fresh thyme
  1 garlic clove, minced
  1 pound frozen peas
  2 teaspoons sugar
    Salt and pepper

Melt butter in 12-inch nonstick skillet over medium-high heat. Add shallot, thyme, and garlic and cook until softened and fragrant, about 2 minutes. Add peas and sugar, cover, and cook, stirring occasionally, until peas are heated through, about 4 minutes. Season with salt and pepper to taste. Serve.

SMASHED MINTY PEAS

Serves 4 to 6   Total time: 20 minutes

WHY THIS RECIPE WORKS *Most cooks boil peas until tender in salted water. However, this method doesn't really add anything in the way of flavor to the peas. When developing this recipe, we wanted to find a method for cooking and flavoring the peas at the same time, and we found that simply simmering the peas right in a sauce allowed them to quickly absorb the sauce's flavor. To intensify the sweetness of the*

peas, we added a small amount of sugar. Pulsing the cooked peas, lettuce, and mint in a food processor until coarsely mashed produced a delicious dish with a pleasing texture. Do not thaw the peas before adding them to the saucepan. Be careful not to overprocess the peas; they can quickly go from smashed to pureed.

  1 pound frozen peas
  2 cups chopped Boston or Bibb lettuce
  ½ cup chicken broth
  2 tablespoons chopped fresh mint
  4 tablespoons unsalted butter
  ½ teaspoon sugar
    Salt and pepper

1. Bring peas, lettuce, broth, mint, butter, and sugar to simmer in medium saucepan over medium-high heat. Cover and cook until peas are tender, 8 to 10 minutes.

2. Transfer mixture to food processor and pulse until coarsely mashed, about 10 pulses, scraping down sides of bowl as needed. Season with salt and pepper to taste. Serve.

SAUTÉED SNOW PEAS WITH LEMON AND PARSLEY

Serves 4   Total time: 20 minutes

WHY THIS RECIPE WORKS *Sweet, grassy snow peas are the star component in this superspeedy side. We knew we wanted to caramelize them a bit to highlight and amplify their delicate flavor. First we tried a traditional stir-fry technique, but the constant stirring left us with greasy, overcooked pods without any browning. Adding a sprinkle of sugar and cooking the peas without stirring for a short time helped to achieve the flavorful sear we were after, and then we continued to cook them, stirring constantly, until they were just crisp-tender. To boost flavor, we cleared the center of the pan and quickly sautéed a mixture of minced shallot, oil, and lemon zest before stirring everything together. A squeeze of lemon juice and a sprinkling of parsley just before serving kept this dish fresh and bright. Chives, tarragon, cilantro, or basil can be substituted for the parsley.*

  1 tablespoon vegetable oil
  1 small shallot, minced
  1 teaspoon finely grated lemon zest
    plus 1 teaspoon juice
    Salt and pepper
  ⅛ teaspoon sugar
  12 ounces snow peas, strings removed
  1 tablespoon minced fresh parsley

1. Combine 1 teaspoon oil, shallot, and lemon zest in bowl. In separate bowl, combine ¼ teaspoon salt, ⅛ teaspoon pepper, and sugar.

2. Heat remaining 2 teaspoons oil in 12-inch nonstick skillet over high heat until just smoking. Add snow peas, sprinkle with salt mixture, and cook, without stirring, for 30 seconds. Stir briefly, then cook, without stirring, for 30 seconds. Continue to cook, stirring constantly, until peas are crisp-tender, 1 to 2 minutes.

3. Push peas to sides of skillet. Add shallot mixture to center and cook, mashing mixture into skillet, until fragrant, about 30 seconds. Stir shallot mixture into peas. Stir in lemon juice and parsley and season with salt and pepper to taste. Serve.

VARIATIONS

Sautéed Snow Peas with Garlic, Cumin, and Cilantro

Add 2 minced garlic cloves and ½ teaspoon toasted and cracked cumin seeds to shallot mixture in step 1. Substitute ½ teaspoon lime zest for lemon zest, lime juice for lemon juice, and cilantro for parsley.

Sautéed Snow Peas with Shallot, Lemon Grass, and Basil

Substitute 2 teaspoons minced fresh lemon grass for lemon zest, lime juice for lemon juice, and basil for parsley.

SUGAR SNAP PEAS WITH PINE NUTS, FENNEL, AND LEMON ZEST

Serves 4   Total time: 20 minutes

WHY THIS RECIPE WORKS *A quick sauté is an excellent way to cook these sweet, crisp pods with their small, juicy peas inside. To ensure that the pods and the peas inside cooked through at the same rate, we used a hybrid method to steam the sugar snap peas briefly before sautéing them; the trapped steam transferred heat more efficiently than air, so the peas cooked through more quickly. Cutting the sugar snap peas in half further reduced the cooking time, so the pods retained more of their snap, and as a bonus, the pockets captured the seasonings rather than letting them slide to the bottom of the platter. Sprinkling the snap peas with dukkah—an Egyptian condiment made from finely chopped nuts, seeds, and seasonings—dressed up this simple preparation with distinct (but not overwhelming) flavor and crunch. Do not substitute ground fennel for the fennel seeds in this recipe. You will need a 12-inch skillet with a tight-fitting lid for this recipe.*

- 3 tablespoons pine nuts
- 1 teaspoon fennel seeds
- ½ teaspoon grated lemon zest
- ½ teaspoon kosher salt
- ⅛ teaspoon red pepper flakes
- 2 teaspoons vegetable oil
- 12 ounces sugar snap peas, strings removed, halved crosswise on bias
- 2 tablespoons water
- 1 garlic clove, minced
- 3 tablespoons chopped fresh basil

1. Toast pine nuts in 12-inch skillet over medium heat, stirring frequently, until just starting to brown, about 3 minutes. Add fennel seeds and continue to toast, stirring constantly, until pine nuts are lightly browned and fennel is fragrant, about 1 minute. Transfer pine nut mixture to cutting board. Sprinkle lemon zest, salt, and pepper flakes over pine nut mixture. Chop mixture until finely minced and well combined. Transfer to bowl and reserve for serving.

2. Heat oil in now-empty skillet over medium heat until shimmering. Add snap peas and water, immediately cover, and cook for 2 minutes. Uncover, add garlic, and continue to cook, stirring frequently, until moisture has evaporated and snap peas are crisp-tender, about 2 minutes. Off heat, stir in basil and three-quarters of pine nut mixture. Transfer snap peas to serving platter and sprinkle with remaining pine nut mixture. Serve.

VARIATION

Sugar Snap Peas with Almonds, Coriander, and Orange Zest
Omit pepper flakes. Substitute sliced almonds for pine nuts, coriander seeds for fennel seeds, ¼ teaspoon orange zest for lemon zest, and cilantro for basil.

RICOTTA CROSTINI WITH PEAS AND MINT

Makes 24 crostini   Total time: 25 minutes (plus 30 minutes cooling time)

WHY THIS RECIPE WORKS *We wanted these attractive, rustic crostini to be as easy to make as they were to enjoy, so we broke down the recipe into three simple steps. We started by slicing a baguette thin and baking the slices until they were crispy. We then made a silky-smooth ricotta topping in the food processor, using a combination of ricotta cheese, extra-virgin olive oil, salt, and pepper. We topped the ricotta with vibrant peas, a bit of minced shallot, and refreshing mint leaves. We prefer to use day-old bread for this recipe because it is easier to slice. The crostini are best topped shortly before serving. A 12-inch demi-baguette will easily yield the 24 slices needed for this recipe.*

- 24 (¼-inch-thick) slices baguette
- 6 tablespoons extra-virgin olive oil
- 1 cup frozen peas, thawed
- 1 small shallot, minced
- 2 teaspoons red wine vinegar
  Salt and pepper
- 6 ounces (¾ cup) whole-milk ricotta cheese
- ¼ cup fresh mint leaves, torn

1. Adjust oven rack to middle position and heat oven to 400 degrees. Arrange baguette slices in single layer on rimmed baking sheet. Brush tops of slices with 2 tablespoons oil. Bake until golden brown and crispy, 8 to 10 minutes. Let cool completely on sheet, about 30 minutes.

2. Combine peas, shallot, vinegar, ¼ teaspoon salt, ¼ teaspoon pepper, and 2 tablespoons oil in bowl; set aside.

3. Process ricotta, ¼ teaspoon salt, and ¼ teaspoon pepper in food processor until smooth, about 10 seconds. With processor running, slowly add remaining 2 tablespoons oil until incorporated. Spread ricotta mixture evenly on toasted baguette slices. Spoon pea mixture over ricotta and sprinkle with mint. Serve.

PEA GREEN SALAD WITH WARM APRICOT-PISTACHIO VINAIGRETTE

Serves 4 to 6   Total time: 40 minutes

WHY THIS RECIPE WORKS *A delicate tangle of grassy pea greens forms the basis of this salad, complemented by fresh peas, endive, and a warm, fruity vinaigrette that both offsets the faintly bitter quality of the pea greens and lightly wilts them. To boost our salad with sweet springtime flavor, we steamed the fresh peas in a skillet until just tender before adding them. In the same skillet we used to cook our peas, we toasted pistachios to build our warmed vinaigrette. Then we added a microwaved mixture of shallots, apricots, mustard, and white wine vinegar to the hot oil. We made sure to add the apricot mixture to the oil off the heat, as the hot oil was likely to sizzle. The last step was simply tossing the warmed vinaigrette with the pea greens, cooked peas, and a bit of Belgian endive for welcome crunch. You can substitute frozen, thawed peas for the fresh peas; if using frozen peas, skip step 1.*

- 1 pound fresh peas, shelled (1¼ cups)
- 3 tablespoons white wine vinegar
- 2 teaspoons whole-grain mustard
- ½ teaspoon sugar
  Salt and pepper
- 1 small shallot, halved and sliced thin
- ½ cup dried apricots, chopped
- 3 tablespoons vegetable oil
- ⅓ cup shelled pistachios, chopped
- 8 ounces (8 cups) pea greens
- 2 heads Belgian endive (8 ounces), trimmed, halved lengthwise, and sliced ¼ inch thick

1. Bring peas and ¼ cup water to simmer in 10-inch skillet over medium-high heat. Cover, reduce heat to medium-low, and cook, stirring occasionally, until peas are tender, 5 to 7 minutes. Drain peas and set aside. Wipe skillet clean with paper towels.

2. Whisk vinegar, mustard, sugar, and ¼ teaspoon salt together in medium bowl. Add shallot and apricots, cover, and microwave until steaming, 30 seconds to 1 minute. Stir to submerge shallot, then let cool to room temperature, about 15 minutes.

3. Heat oil in now-empty skillet over medium heat until shimmering. Add pistachios and cook, stirring frequently, until toasted and fragrant, 1 to 2 minutes. Off heat, stir in shallot mixture and let sit until heated through, about 30 seconds.

4. Gently toss pea greens, endive, and peas with warm vinaigrette in large bowl until evenly coated and wilted slightly. Season with salt and pepper to taste. Serve.

BLACK RICE SALAD WITH SUGAR SNAP PEAS AND GINGER-SESAME VINAIGRETTE

Serves 4 to 6   Total time: 1 hour

WHY THIS RECIPE WORKS *Asian flavors and ingredients combine beautifully in this colorful rice salad. The emerald green snap peas, red-and-white radishes, and red bell peppers are like jewels against the black rice. Also known as purple or forbidden rice, black rice is an ancient grain that was once reserved for the emperors of China. It has a deliciously roasted, nutty taste and can be used in anything from salads to dessert puddings. Its only drawback is that it is easy to overcook, so our major obstacle was finding the right method. We discovered that the best approach was to cook it like pasta, in lots of boiling water, giving it space to move around. Once it was done, we drained it, drizzled it with a little vinegar for a flavor boost, and let it cool completely on a baking sheet. This ensured perfectly cooked grains that had the expected chew of black rice without any mushiness. We mixed up an Asian vinaigrette with sesame oil, ginger, chili-garlic sauce, and honey, and stirred in some cilantro, and our simple salad was complete.*

- 1½ cups black rice
  Salt and pepper
- 3 tablespoons plus 1 teaspoon rice vinegar
- ¼ cup extra-virgin olive oil
- 1 tablespoon toasted sesame oil
- 2 teaspoons minced shallot
- 2 teaspoons honey
- 2 teaspoons Asian chili-garlic sauce
- 1 teaspoon grated fresh ginger
- 6 ounces sugar snap peas, strings removed, halved
- 5 radishes, trimmed, halved, and sliced thin
- 1 red bell pepper, stemmed, seeded, and chopped fine
- ¼ cup minced fresh cilantro

1. Bring 4 quarts water to boil in Dutch oven over medium-high heat. Add rice and 1 teaspoon salt and cook until rice is tender, 20 to 25 minutes. Drain rice, spread onto rimmed baking sheet, and drizzle with 1 teaspoon vinegar. Let rice cool completely, about 15 minutes.

2. Whisk remaining 3 tablespoons vinegar, olive oil, sesame oil, shallot, honey, chili-garlic sauce, ginger, ¼ teaspoon salt, and ⅛ teaspoon pepper in large bowl until combined. Add rice, snap peas, radishes, bell pepper, and cilantro and toss to combine. Season with salt and pepper to taste. Serve.

CREAMY PEA SOUP

Serves 8   Total time: 30 minutes

WHY THIS RECIPE WORKS *This streamlined recipe couldn't be simpler, and it results in a velvety, creamy, yet vibrant-tasting pea soup that's as appropriate to serve for a springtime holiday meal as it is to serve in the dead of winter. Although pea soups often have ham, we left out that meaty element so that the sweet green pea flavor could really shine through. Slowly whisking the chicken broth into the flour and onion mixture avoided floury lumps, the half-and-half added richness without heaviness, and the mint garnish gave our Creamy Pea Soup a fresh herbal finish. You can use tarragon in place of the mint if you like.*

PEA GREEN SALAD WITH WARM APRICOT-PISTACHIO VINAIGRETTE

This warm, slightly wilted salad celebrates both the essence of springtime and the essence of green pea goodness with seasonal pea greens and fresh shelled garden peas. It is visually stunning, with several shades of green from the pea greens, peas, endive, and pistachios offset by the color of the chopped apricots, making it an impressive choice for entertaining.

1. Shell the peas, slice the shallots, chop the apricots and pistachios, and slice the endive.

2. Cook the fresh peas in a skillet in ¼ cup of simmering water until they are tender, 5 to 7 minutes. Drain the peas and set them aside.

3. Whisk the vinegar, mustard, sugar, and salt together in a bowl. Add the shallots and apricots, cover, and microwave until they are steaming, 30 seconds to 1 minute.

4. Heat the oil in the skillet and cook the pistachios until they are toasty and smell delicious, 1 to 2 minutes.

5. Remove the skillet from the heat and stir in the warm shallot mixture.

6. Toss the pea greens, endive, and fresh peas with the warm vinaigrette until the vegetables are coated and just slightly wilted.

Tagliatelle with Prosciutto and Peas

2 tablespoons unsalted butter
1 onion, chopped fine
  Salt and pepper
2 tablespoons all-purpose flour
4 cups chicken broth, plus extra
  as needed
1½ pounds frozen peas, thawed
½ cup half-and-half
2 tablespoons minced fresh mint

1. Melt butter in Dutch oven over medium heat. Add onion and ½ teaspoon salt and cook until softened, about 5 minutes. Stir in flour and cook for 1 minute. Slowly whisk in broth, scraping up any browned bits and smoothing out any lumps. Bring to simmer and cook until slightly thickened, about 5 minutes. Stir in peas and cook until tender, 7 to 10 minutes.

2. Working in batches, process soup in blender until smooth, 1 to 2 minutes. Return soup to clean pot and stir in half-and-half. Adjust consistency with extra hot broth as needed. Bring soup to brief simmer over medium heat. Season with salt and pepper to taste. Sprinkle individual portions with mint before serving.

RISI E BISI

Serves 4 to 6   Total time: 45 minutes
WHY THIS RECIPE WORKS *Somewhere in between a risotto and a soup in consistency, this rice-and-peas dish is traditional to the Veneto region of Italy, where peas are celebrated as a springtime crop and rice is an important grain year-round. For our version, we decided to streamline preparation by cooking the dish more like a soup than a risotto. After the dish cooked hands-off for most of the time, a vigorous whisking of the rice at the end of cooking liberated enough of its starch to thicken the broth, providing the dish with a satisfying consistency. By using thawed frozen baby peas and adding them just at the end of cooking to warm through, we mimicked the sweetness and texture of the fresh spring peas that are the hallmark of this* dish. *Balancing the peas' sweetness with judicious amounts of Parmesan and pancetta created savory complexity without heaviness. We use frozen petite peas here, but regular frozen peas can be substituted, if desired. For the proper consistency, make sure to cook the rice at a gentle boil.*

4 cups chicken broth
1½ cups water
3 tablespoons extra-virgin olive oil
2 ounces pancetta, chopped fine
1 onion, chopped fine
2 garlic cloves, minced
1 cup Arborio rice
2 cups frozen petite peas, thawed
1 ounce Parmesan cheese, grated
  (½ cup), plus extra for serving
3 tablespoons minced fresh parsley
1 teaspoon lemon juice, plus lemon
  wedges for serving
  Salt and pepper

1. Bring broth and water to boil in large saucepan over high heat. Remove from heat and cover to keep warm.

2. Cook oil and pancetta in Dutch oven over medium-low heat until pancetta is browned and fat is rendered, 5 to 7 minutes. Add onion and cook until softened, about 5 minutes. Stir in garlic and cook until fragrant, about 30 seconds. Add rice and stir to coat, about 1 minute.

3. Add 5 cups broth mixture, increase heat to high, and bring to boil. Cover, reduce heat to medium-low, and simmer until rice is tender but not mushy, about 15 minutes, stirring every 5 minutes to ensure that rice is gently boiling.

4. Remove pot from heat and whisk rice vigorously until broth has thickened slightly, 15 seconds. Stir in peas, Parmesan, parsley, and lemon juice. Adjust consistency with remaining ½ cup broth mixture as needed. Season with salt and pepper to taste. Serve, passing extra Parmesan and lemon wedges separately.

TAGLIATELLE WITH PROSCIUTTO AND PEAS

Serves 4 to 6   Total time: 30 minutes
WHY THIS RECIPE WORKS *Simplicity and high-quality ingredients are at the heart of all Italian cooking, so for our version of the classic dish of tagliatelle with peas, we chose our ingredients through careful testing. Opting for a dried Italian-made egg pasta over traditional dried pasta got us very close to the texture of labor-intensive fresh pasta. Frozen peas, which are picked and frozen at peak ripeness, offered the most consistently sweet results. To make the most of the full flavor of pricey imported prosciutto di Parma, we used it in two ways: minced and cooked with the cream, and also sliced into strips and tossed with the pasta right before serving. If using sliced-to-order prosciutto, ask for it to be sliced 1/16 inch thick. Look for a hard Gruyère that is aged for at least 10 months and use a rasp-style grater or the small holes of box grater to grate it. If you cannot find tagliatelle, substitute pappardelle.*

6 ounces thinly sliced prosciutto
1 tablespoon unsalted butter
1 shallot, minced
  Salt and pepper
1 cup heavy cream
1 pound tagliatelle
1½ cups frozen petite peas, thawed
1 ounce Parmesan cheese, grated (½ cup)
1 ounce Gruyère cheese, grated (½ cup)

1. Slice 5 ounces prosciutto crosswise into ¼-inch-wide strips; set aside. Mince remaining 1 ounce prosciutto. Melt butter in 10-inch skillet over medium-low heat. Add shallot and ¼ teaspoon salt and cook until softened, about 2 minutes. Stir in cream and minced prosciutto and bring to simmer. Cook, stirring occasionally, until cream mixture measures 1 cup, 5 to 7 minutes. Remove skillet from heat and cover to keep warm.

2. Meanwhile, bring 4 quarts water to boil in large pot. Add pasta and 1 tablespoon salt and cook, stirring often, until al dente.

Reserve 2 cups cooking water, then drain pasta and return it to pot. Add 1 cup reserved cooking water, cream mixture, prosciutto strips, peas, Parmesan, Gruyère, and 1 teaspoon pepper and gently toss until well coated. Adjust consistency with remaining reserved cooking water as needed. Serve immediately.

EASY SICHUAN-STYLE ORANGE BEEF WITH SUGAR SNAP PEAS

Serves 4   Total time: 35 minutes

WHY THIS RECIPE WORKS *Delicately sweet and crunchy sugar snap peas perfectly complement rich flank steak in this Sichuan-style favorite that is quick enough to prepare any night of the week. Although Sichuan cuisine is often quite spicy, this dish has more of a bright, citrusy flavor profile, with just a touch of warmth from the red pepper flakes. Cooking the beef right in the sauce thoroughly flavors the meat, while the honey in the sauce aids in browning and caramelization. You will need a 12-inch nonstick skillet with a tight-fitting lid for this recipe. Serve with rice.*

1½ pounds flank steak, trimmed
¼   cup soy sauce
2   tablespoons toasted sesame oil
1   tablespoon honey
2   teaspoons grated orange zest plus
    ½ cup juice
2   garlic cloves, minced
¼   teaspoon red pepper flakes
8   ounces sugar snap peas, strings removed
2   scallions, sliced thin

1. Cut steak into thirds with grain, then slice each third thin against grain. Combine soy sauce, oil, honey, orange zest and juice, garlic, and pepper flakes in bowl. Cook beef and ⅓ cup orange juice mixture in 12-inch nonstick skillet over medium-high heat, stirring occasionally, until liquid has evaporated and beef is caramelized, about 15 minutes. Transfer beef to plate and tent with aluminum foil.

2. Add remaining orange juice mixture and snap peas to now-empty skillet and cook, covered, over medium heat, until snap peas are bright green, about 2 minutes. Uncover and continue to cook, stirring occasionally, until sauce thickens and snap peas are tender, about 1 minute. Return beef to skillet and toss with snap peas to combine. Sprinkle with scallions and serve.

PAN-SEARED SCALLOPS WITH SUGAR SNAP PEA SLAW

Serves 4   Total time: 25 minutes

WHY THIS RECIPE WORKS *For a new take on vegetable slaw, we thinly sliced sweet snap peas, juicy English cucumbers, and peppery radishes for a fresh, crunchy accompaniment to skillet-seared sea scallops. We brightened up the mayonnaise-based slaw dressing with plenty of fresh chives and lemon zest and juice. A quick sear on the scallops deliciously caramelized the exterior while keeping the inside tender. Blotting the scallops on a baking sheet with a clean kitchen towel dried them so that they could quickly develop a flavorful crust without overcooking. We recommend buying "dry" scallops, which don't have chemical additives and taste better than "wet." Dry scallops will look ivory or pinkish; wet scallops are bright white.*

1½ pounds large sea scallops, tendons removed
¼   cup mayonnaise
2   tablespoons chopped fresh chives
¼   teaspoon grated lemon zest plus
    2 tablespoons juice
    Salt and pepper
8   ounces sugar snap peas, strings removed, sliced thin on bias
1   English cucumber, halved lengthwise and sliced thin
6   radishes, trimmed, halved lengthwise, and sliced thin
2   tablespoons vegetable oil

1. Place scallops in rimmed baking sheet lined with clean kitchen towel. Place second clean kitchen towel on top of scallops and press gently on towel to blot liquid. Let scallops sit at room temperature, covered with towel, for 10 minutes.

2. Whisk mayonnaise, chives, lemon zest and juice, and ¼ teaspoon salt together in large bowl. Add snap peas, cucumber, and radishes and toss to combine; set aside for serving.

3. Heat 1 tablespoon oil in 12-inch nonstick skillet over medium-high heat until just smoking. Add half of scallops to skillet in single layer and cook, without moving them, until well browned on first side, about 1½ minutes. Flip scallops and continue to cook, without moving them, until well browned on second side, about 1½ minutes. Transfer scallops to serving platter and tent with aluminum foil. Repeat with remaining 1 tablespoon oil and remaining scallops. Serve scallops with slaw.

Pan-Seared Scallops with
Sugar Snap Pea Slaw

POTATOES

Potatoes are America's most frequently eaten vegetable (perhaps to the dismay of some parents with small children). Whether you bake, braise, mash, roast, fry, stew, or steam them, there's hardly any way you can cook potatoes without achieving delicious results.

Despite its enormous popularity, the potato is actually the second-most important vegetable crop worldwide (after corn). Native to the Americas and domesticated by the Incas and other Andean peoples, potatoes were brought to Europe in the early 16th century, during the age of European explorers. It was there, thanks to the 18th-century efforts of Antoine-Augustin Parmentier—the Johnny Appleseed of potatoes—that potatoes eventually became cultivated on a huge scale, thus putting an end to famine in that part of the world in the 18th and 19th centuries (with the notable exception of the Irish Potato Famine). It's not an overstatement to say that the potato fueled the rise of the West and led to the development of modern agriculture.

In the 21st century, we take them for granted, but we shouldn't. The possibilities for side dishes are vast. We love Buttermilk Mashed Potatoes with Leeks and Chives, and Slow-Cooker Mashed Potatoes with sour cream. We roast them with garlic and rosemary and turn them into creative potato salads. We grill them on skewers with oregano and lemon. Of course, we adore frying them into French fries, hash browns, latkes, and homemade kettle chips.

But potatoes aren't just sides. Irish cooks know their potatoes, and few dishes prove that better than Shepherd's Pie. And Potato and Chorizo Tacos, a favorite Mexican preparation, take us back near to where the colorful story of the potato began.

shopping and storage

Potatoes are available year-round. Look for firm specimens that are free of green spots, sprouts, cracks, and other blemishes. We generally prefer to buy loose potatoes, so that we can see what we are getting. Stay away from potatoes sold in plastic bags, as those storage conditions can cause them to sprout and rot.

Keep potatoes in a cool, dark, dry place and away from onions, which give off gases that will hasten sprouting. Baking and all-purpose varieties will keep for several months. Boiling potatoes will keep for about one month. To further extend shelf life, we tried storing them in a cool, dark place with an apple—a common old wives' tale. To our surprise, the apple did indeed boost storage time, by almost two weeks. The ethylene gas emitted by the apple suppresses the elongation of the potatoes' cells, which is what causes the sprouts to form.

vegetable science
Stress-Free Spud Storage

Since potatoes seem almost indestructible, you might not give much thought to their storage. But it matters. For four weeks, we stored all-purpose potatoes in five environments: a cool (50 to 60 degrees), dark place; the refrigerator; a basket near a sunny window; a warm (70 to 80 degrees), dark place; and a drawer with some onions at room temperature.

The potatoes stored in the cool, dark place and in the refrigerator were firm, sprout-free, and crisp and moist. We could not discern any noticeable difference in quality between these methods. The other three tests produced poor results: The potatoes in the basket became gray and mottled, and the potatoes stored both in a warm place and with the onions softened and sprouted. All of the stressed potatoes ended up with greenish tinges, the result of a naturally occurring toxin called solanine, which is not destroyed by cooking.

all about potatoes

To make sense of the many varieties, it is helpful to group potatoes into three major categories based on texture.

BAKING POTATOES These floury potatoes contain more total starch (20 to 22 percent) than the others, giving these varieties a drier texture. Because of that, these potatoes are excellent candidates when baking and frying. They are also wonderful for mashing because they can drink up the butter and cream. They work well when you want to thicken a stew or soup, but not when you want distinct chunks of potatoes in the finished stew. Common varieties include russet, Russet Burbank, Idaho, and White Creamer.

ALL-PURPOSE POTATOES These potatoes contain less total starch (18 to 20 percent) than baking potatoes but more than the total starch in boiling potatoes. Although they are considered "in-between" potatoes, they are closer in texture to baking potatoes than to boiling potatoes. So they are also great choices for baking, frying, and mashing. You can also use them in salads and soups, but they won't be quite as firm as boiling potatoes. Common varieties include Yukon Gold, Yellow Finn, Purple Peruvian, Kennebec, and Katahdin.

BOILING POTATOES These potatoes contain a relatively low amount of total starch (16 to 18 percent), giving them a firm, smooth, waxy texture and a higher moisture content than those in other categories. They are often called "new" because they are less-mature potatoes harvested in late spring and summer. They are less starchy than "old" potatoes because they haven't had the longer storage time to convert their sugar to starch. They also have thinner skins than the others. Boiling potatoes are perfect when you want the pieces to hold their shape, as with potato salad, or when roasting. Common varieties include Red Bliss, French Fingerling, Red Creamer, Red Pontiac, and White Rose.

vegetable prep
Cutting Potatoes for French Fries

1. Halve potatoes lengthwise and turn halves cut sides down on cutting board. Trim thin slice from both long sides of each potato half, discarding trimmings.

2. Slice potatoes lengthwise into ⅓- to ½-inch-thick planks. Potatoes are ready for making Thick-Cut Oven Fries.

3. If cutting into thinner fries, as for Easier French Fries, slice each plank into ¼-inch-thick fries.

X Marks the Spot

For fluffy—not dense—baked potatoes, cut X in top of baked potato and gently squeeze with your fingers so steam can escape.

BUTTERMILK MASHED POTATOES

Serves 4   Total time: 45 minutes

WHY THIS RECIPE WORKS *Buttermilk mashed potatoes should be both rich and tangy, like a baked potato drenched in butter and sour cream. But simply stirring buttermilk into boiled and mashed potatoes didn't yield the flavorful results we were after. The key to having the potatoes soak up the buttermilk flavor turned out to be cooking the potatoes directly in the buttermilk, which we thinned with a little water. Buttermilk is acidic, which slows cooking, but a pinch of baking soda balanced the acid so that the potatoes cooked through in a reasonable amount of time. Because simmering the buttermilk dulled its flavor slightly, we added a little reserved buttermilk at the end to revive the tanginess. Don't be alarmed if the buttermilk looks separated. Once you mash the potatoes into it, the puree comes together.*

    2 pounds Yukon Gold potatoes, peeled,
       quartered, and cut into ½-inch pieces
    1 cup buttermilk
    6 tablespoons water
    6 tablespoons unsalted butter,
       cut into 6 pieces
  ⅛ teaspoon baking soda
       Salt and pepper

1. Combine potatoes, ¾ cup buttermilk, water, 2 tablespoons butter, baking soda, and ½ teaspoon salt in Dutch oven. Bring to boil over medium-high heat. Cover, reduce heat to low, and simmer, stirring occasionally, until potatoes are tender and paring knife can be slipped in and out of potatoes with no resistance, 20 to 25 minutes.

2. Uncover and cook over medium heat until liquid has nearly evaporated, about 3 minutes. Off heat, add remaining 4 tablespoons butter and mash potatoes smooth with potato masher. Using rubber spatula, fold in remaining ¼ cup buttermilk until absorbed. Season with salt and pepper to taste, and serve.

VARIATIONS

Buttermilk Mashed Potatoes with Leeks and Chives

While potatoes are cooking, melt 1 tablespoon unsalted butter in 8-inch nonstick skillet over medium heat. Add 1 leek, white and light green parts only, halved lengthwise, sliced ¼ inch thick, and washed thoroughly. Cook, stirring occasionally, until lightly browned, about 8 minutes. Add leek and 3 tablespoons minced fresh chives to potatoes with buttermilk in step 2.

Buttermilk Ranch Mashed Potatoes

Add ⅓ cup sour cream, 3 very thinly sliced scallions, 2 tablespoons minced fresh parsley, and 1 minced garlic clove along with buttermilk in step 2.

FRENCH-STYLE MASHED POTATOES (POMMES PURÉE)

Serves 8   Total time: 1 hour

WHY THIS RECIPE WORKS *Chef Joël Robuchon's indulgent recipe for ultrasilky and buttery mashed potatoes is amazingly decadent and a perfect side for dinner parties. However, it poses a number of challenges for the home cook, including peeling piping-hot whole boiled potatoes, laboriously beating a full pound of cold butter into the potatoes, and passing the puree multiple times through a special restaurant sieve called a tamis. Our recipe eliminates all those challenges. Instead of using water, we cooked peeled, diced potatoes directly in the milk and butter that would be incorporated into the mash. This approach eliminated the need to laboriously beat in the butter after the fact and also captured the potato starch released during cooking, which is key to producing an emulsified texture in which the butter doesn't separate out. You will need a food mill or potato ricer for this recipe. When serving, keep the richness in mind: A small dollop on each plate should suffice.*

    2 pounds Yukon Gold potatoes, peeled
       and cut into 1-inch pieces
  20 tablespoons (2½ sticks) unsalted butter
  1⅓ cups whole milk
       Salt and white pepper

1. Place potatoes in fine-mesh strainer and rinse under cold running water until water runs clear; set aside to drain.

2. Heat butter, milk, and 1 teaspoon salt in large saucepan over low heat until butter has melted. Add potatoes, increase heat to medium-low, and cook until liquid just starts to boil. Reduce heat to low, partially cover, and gently simmer until potatoes are tender and paring knife can be slipped in and out of potatoes with no resistance, 30 to 40 minutes, stirring every 10 minutes.

3. Drain potatoes in fine-mesh strainer set over large bowl, reserving cooking liquid. Wipe saucepan clean with paper towels. Return cooking liquid to now-empty saucepan and place over low heat.

4. Set food mill or ricer fitted with finest disk over saucepan. Working in batches, transfer potatoes to hopper and process. Using whisk, recombine potatoes and cooking liquid until smooth, 10 to 15 seconds (potatoes should almost be pourable). Season with salt and pepper to taste. Serve immediately.

SLOW-COOKER MASHED POTATOES

Serves 10 to 12   Total time: 5 to 6 hours on low or 3 to 4 hours on high

WHY THIS RECIPE WORKS *For perfectly moist, fluffy, and smooth mashed potatoes in the slow cooker, we used a small amount of water and a parchment shield to create a moist, steamy environment. Thinly sliced potatoes cooked more evenly than chunks, and boiling the water first jump-started the cooking process. We brushed the top layer of potatoes with melted butter to help prevent discoloration, and mashed in the rest of the butter about 4 hours later, when the potatoes were tender. (The top layer of potatoes may discolor slightly, but this won't be noticeable upon mashing.) We mashed the potatoes right in the cooking liquid, rather than draining them. Along with the added butter, the cooking liquid easily created a nice smooth texture when incorporated. You will need a 5- to 7-quart slow cooker for this recipe.*

5 pounds russet potatoes, peeled and sliced ¼ inch thick
2¾ cups boiling water, plus extra as needed
Salt and pepper
12 tablespoons unsalted butter, melted
½ cup sour cream
3 tablespoons minced fresh chives

1. Combine potatoes, boiling water, and 2 teaspoons salt in slow cooker. Brush top layer with 3 tablespoons melted butter. Press 16 by 12-inch sheet of parchment paper firmly onto potatoes, folding down edges as needed. Cover and cook until potatoes are tender and paring knife can be slipped in and out of potatoes with no resistance, 5 to 6 hours on low or 3 to 4 hours on high.

2. Discard parchment. Mash potatoes with potato masher until smooth. Stir in sour cream, chives, and remaining 9 tablespoons melted butter until combined. Season with salt and pepper to taste. Serve.

BRAISED RED POTATOES WITH LEMON AND CHIVES

Serves 4 to 6   Total time: 50 minutes

WHY THIS RECIPE WORKS *What if you could achieve red potatoes with the creamy interiors created by steaming and the crispy browned exteriors produced by roasting— without doing either? That's the result often promised by recipes for braised red potatoes, but they rarely deliver. To make good on that promise, we combined halved small red potatoes, butter, and salted water (plus thyme for flavoring) in a 12-inch skillet and simmered the spuds until their interiors were perfectly creamy and the water was fully evaporated. Then we let the potatoes continue to cook in the now-dry skillet until their cut sides browned in the butter, developing the rich flavor and crispy edges of roasted potatoes. These potatoes were so good that they needed only a minimum of seasoning: We simply tossed them with some minced garlic (softened in the simmering water along with the potatoes), lemon juice, chives, and pepper. Use small red potatoes measuring 1 to 2 inches in diameter. You will need a 12-inch nonstick skillet with a tight-fitting lid for this recipe.*

1½ pounds small red potatoes, unpeeled, halved
2 cups water
3 tablespoons unsalted butter
3 garlic cloves, peeled
3 sprigs fresh thyme
¾ teaspoon salt
1 teaspoon lemon juice
¼ teaspoon pepper
2 tablespoons minced fresh chives

1. Arrange potatoes in single layer, cut side down, in 12-inch nonstick skillet. Add water, butter, garlic, thyme sprigs, and salt and bring to simmer over medium-high heat. Reduce heat to medium, cover, and simmer until potatoes are just tender, about 15 minutes.

2. Remove lid and use slotted spoon to transfer garlic to cutting board; discard thyme sprigs. Increase heat to medium-high and simmer vigorously, swirling skillet occasionally, until water evaporates and butter starts to sizzle, 15 to 20 minutes. When cool enough to handle, mince garlic to paste. Transfer paste to bowl and stir in lemon juice and pepper.

3. Continue to cook potatoes, swirling skillet frequently, until butter browns and cut sides of potatoes turn spotty brown, 4 to 6 minutes. Off heat, add chives and garlic mixture and toss to coat thoroughly. Serve.

VARIATIONS

Braised Red Potatoes with Dijon and Tarragon
Substitute 2 teaspoons Dijon mustard for lemon juice and 1 tablespoon minced fresh tarragon for chives.

Braised Red Potatoes with Miso and Scallions
Reduce salt to ½ teaspoon. Substitute 1 tablespoon red miso paste for lemon juice and 3 thinly sliced scallions for chives.

Best Baked Potatoes

BEST BAKED POTATOES

Serves 4   Total time: 1 hour 15 minutes

WHY THIS RECIPE WORKS *Baked potatoes are one of those dishes most home cooks think they don't need a recipe for, but following our precise roasting technique guarantees a perfect potato—with a fluffy interior, crispy skin, and even seasoning—every time. For starters, our testing pointed us to an ideal doneness temperature: 205 degrees. Baking russet potatoes in a hot oven propped up on a wire rack prevented a leathery ring from forming beneath the peel, and taking the potato's temperature with an instant-read thermometer ensured we hit the 205-degree sweet spot every time. Coating the potatoes in salty water before baking was all the effort required to season the skin; brushing on vegetable oil once the potatoes were cooked through and then baking the potatoes for an additional 10 minutes promised the crispest exterior possible. Potatoes this good deserve an accompaniment, so we came up with some simple but sophisticated toppings to serve with them. Open up the potatoes immediately after removal from the oven in step 3 so steam can escape. Top the potatoes as desired, or with one of our flavorful toppings.*

    Salt and pepper
4   small russet potatoes (8 ounces each), unpeeled, each lightly pricked with fork in 6 places
1   tablespoon vegetable oil

1. Adjust oven rack to middle position and heat oven to 450 degrees. Dissolve 2 tablespoons salt in ½ cup water in large bowl. Place potatoes in bowl and toss so exteriors of potatoes are evenly moistened. Transfer potatoes to wire rack set in rimmed baking sheet and bake until center of largest potato registers 205 degrees, 45 minutes to 1 hour.

2. Remove potatoes from oven and brush tops and sides with oil. Return potatoes to oven and bake for 10 minutes.

3. Remove potatoes from oven and, using paring knife, make 2 slits, forming X, in each potato. Using clean dish towel, hold ends and squeeze slightly to push flesh up and out. Season with salt and pepper to taste. Serve immediately.

VARIATIONS

Best Baked Potatoes with Herbed Goat Cheese

Mash 4 ounces softened goat cheese with fork. Stir in 2 tablespoons extra-virgin olive oil, 2 tablespoons minced fresh parsley, 1 tablespoon minced shallot, and ½ teaspoon lemon zest. Season with salt and pepper to taste, and dollop on potatoes before serving.

Best Baked Potatoes with Creamy Egg Topping

Stir 3 chopped hard-cooked eggs, ¼ cup sour cream, 1½ tablespoons minced cornichons, 1 tablespoon minced fresh parsley, 1 tablespoon Dijon mustard, 1 tablespoon minced capers, and 1 tablespoon minced shallot together in bowl. Season with salt and pepper to taste, and dollop over potatoes before serving.

TWICE-BAKED POTATOES WITH BACON, CHEDDAR, AND SCALLIONS

Serves 8   Total time: 1 hour 45 minutes

WHY THIS RECIPE WORKS *Twice-baked potatoes—essentially baked russet potatoes whose flesh has been removed from the shells, mashed with dairy products and seasonings, mounded back into the shells, and baked again—offer a variety of textures and flavors in a single bite. Done well, the skin is chewy and substantial without being tough, with just a hint of crispness to play off the smooth, creamy filling. In the course of developing our perfect rendition, tests revealed that tasters preferred a combination of sharp cheddar and sour cream enriched with 4 tablespoons of butter. To this, we added bacon, sautéed onion, and a final sprinkling of fresh scallions. Be sure to leave a layer of potato inside the potato skins; it helps them retain their shape when stuffed and baked.*

4   small russet potatoes (8 ounces each), unpeeled, rubbed lightly with vegetable oil, each lightly pricked with fork in 6 places
4   slices bacon, chopped fine
1   onion, chopped fine

6   ounces sharp cheddar cheese, shredded (1½ cups)
1   cup sour cream
4   tablespoons unsalted butter, softened
    Salt and pepper
2   scallions, sliced thin

1. Adjust oven rack to upper-middle position and heat oven to 400 degrees. Place potatoes directly on hot oven rack and bake until skins are crisp and deep brown and paring knife easily pierces flesh, about 1 hour, flipping potatoes halfway through baking. Transfer potatoes to wire rack and let cool slightly, about 10 minutes. Increase oven temperature to 500 degrees.

2. Meanwhile, cook bacon in 10-inch nonstick skillet over medium-high heat until crisp, 5 to 7 minutes. Using slotted spoon, transfer bacon to paper towel. Add onion to fat left in skillet and cook over medium heat until softened and lightly browned, 5 to 7 minutes; set aside. Line rimmed baking sheet with aluminum foil and set wire rack in sheet.

3. Using oven mitt to handle hot potato, cut each potato in half lengthwise. Using soupspoon, scoop flesh from each half into medium bowl, leaving ¼- to ½-inch thickness of flesh in each shell. Transfer potato shells to prepared rack.

4. Mash potato flesh with fork until smooth. Stir in 1 cup cheddar, sour cream, butter, and sautéed onion, and season with salt and pepper to taste. Spoon mixture into potato shells, mounding slightly at center. Sprinkle with remaining ½ cup cheddar and crisp bacon.

5. Bake until shells are crisp and filling is heated through, 10 to 15 minutes. Sprinkle with scallions and serve.

VARIATIONS

Twice-Baked Potatoes with Bacon, Blue Cheese, and Caramelized Onions

For more caramelized onion flavor, add an extra onion.

Substitute ½ cup crumbled blue cheese for cheddar. Add 1 tablespoon brown sugar to onion in step 2; cook until onion is very soft and deeply browned, about 20 minutes.

Southwestern Twice-Baked Potatoes
Substitute 1½ cups shredded pepper Jack cheese for cheddar. Add 3 minced garlic cloves to onion during final minute of cooking in step 2. Add 1 teaspoon minced chipotle chile in adobo sauce to mashed potato mixture in step 4.

───

ROASTED SMASHED POTATOES

Serves 4   Total time: 1 hour 30 minutes

WHY THIS RECIPE WORKS *Yes, you can savor the creamy, smooth texture of mashed potatoes and the satisfying crunch of deep-fried spuds in one foolproof recipe. Success started with choosing the right potato; only small red potatoes, with their moist texture and thin skin, fit the bill. Before we could begin smashing, we needed to soften them, so we parcooked them, covered, on a baking sheet. Unlike boiling, which washed out flavor, this steaming approach kept the potatoes earthy and sweet. After a short rest (very hot potatoes crumbled apart when smashed), we drizzled them with olive oil and smashed them all at once by placing a second baking sheet on top and pushing down evenly and firmly. After adding chopped fresh thyme and more olive oil, and another stint in the oven, we ended up with browned, crisped potatoes that were super-creamy inside. Use small red potatoes measuring 1 to 2 inches in diameter. Remove the potatoes from the baking sheet as soon as they are done browning—they will toughen if left for too long.*

- 2 pounds small red potatoes, unpeeled
- 6 tablespoons extra-virgin olive oil
- 1 teaspoon chopped fresh thyme
  Salt and pepper

1. Adjust oven racks to top and lowest positions and heat oven to 500 degrees. Arrange potatoes on rimmed baking sheet, pour ¾ cup water into sheet, and wrap tightly with aluminum foil. Cook on lower rack until paring knife can be slipped into and out of center of potatoes with very little resistance (poke through foil to test), 25 to 30 minutes. Remove foil and let cool for 10 minutes. If any water remains on sheet, blot dry with paper towel.

2. Drizzle 3 tablespoons oil over potatoes and roll to coat. Space potatoes evenly on sheet and place second baking sheet on top. Press down firmly on second sheet, flattening potatoes until ⅓ to ½ inch thick. Sprinkle with thyme, season with salt and pepper, and drizzle evenly with remaining 3 tablespoons oil. Roast potatoes on upper rack for 15 minutes, then transfer potatoes to bottom rack and roast until well browned, 20 to 30 minutes. Serve immediately.

───

CRISP ROASTED FINGERLING POTATOES

Serves 4 to 6   Total time: 1 hour

WHY THIS RECIPE WORKS *For this different take on roasted potatoes, we chose creamy, dense fingerling potatoes, halved them, and boiled them in a mixture of salt and baking soda. The salt made these boiling potatoes nice and fluffy, and the baking soda brought the potatoes' starch to the surface. After boiling them, we let the potatoes cool to vent steam and then arranged them, cut side down, on a hot baking sheet so that the now starch-covered potatoes would become crispy in the oven. Look for fingerling potatoes measuring approximately 3 inches long and 1 inch in diameter.*

- 2 pounds fingerling potatoes, unpeeled, halved lengthwise
- ½ cup salt
- ½ teaspoon baking soda
- 2 tablespoons extra-virgin olive oil
- ¼ teaspoon pepper

1. Adjust oven rack to lowest position, place rimmed baking sheet on rack, and heat oven to 500 degrees. Bring 2 quarts water to boil in large saucepan. Add potatoes, salt, and baking soda, return to simmer, and cook until potatoes are tender but centers offer slight resistance when pierced with paring knife, 7 to 10 minutes. Drain potatoes in colander and shake vigorously to roughen edges. Transfer potatoes to large platter lined with kitchen towel and arrange cut side up. Let sit until no longer steaming and surface is tacky, about 5 minutes.

2. Transfer potatoes to large bowl and toss with 1 tablespoon oil and pepper. Working quickly, remove sheet from oven and drizzle remaining 1 tablespoon oil over surface. Arrange potatoes cut side down on sheet in even layer. Roast until cut sides are crisp and skins spotty brown, 20 to 25 minutes, rotating sheet halfway through roasting. Flip potatoes cut side up and let cool on sheet for 5 minutes. Serve.

───

SALT-CRUSTED FINGERLING POTATOES

Serves 4 to 6   Total time: 45 minutes

WHY THIS RECIPE WORKS *We started developing this recipe with a nontraditional ingredient: seawater. In our research in the test kitchen, we found a number of older recipes that called for it, so we wanted to try cooking our potatoes in a saline solution to see if we could develop a salty crust and an interesting minerally flavor. The potatoes we tested were creamy and tender and had a unique briny flavor profile. But was this a practical way to cook potatoes? To mimic the effect without having to trek to the beach, we boiled fingerling potatoes in a skillet with 1 teaspoon of salt and enough water to cover them. Covering the skillet for the first 15 minutes of cooking ensured that the potatoes cooked through and were fluffy and tender. Removing the lid for the second half of the cooking time allowed the water to evaporate, giving the potatoes a crackly, salty sheen. Look for fingerling potatoes measuring approximately 3 inches long and 1 inch in diameter. These potatoes can be served with melted butter, if desired.*

- 4 cups water
- 1 teaspoon salt
- 2 pounds fingerling potatoes, unpeeled
- 2 sprigs fresh rosemary

1. Whisk water and salt in 12-inch skillet until salt is dissolved, about 15 seconds. Add potatoes and rosemary sprigs (potatoes may not be fully submerged) and bring to simmer over medium-high heat. Reduce heat to medium-low, cover, and cook until potatoes are nearly tender, about 15 minutes.

Crisp Roasted Fingerling Potatoes

2. Uncover and increase heat to medium-high. Simmer vigorously until all water has evaporated and potatoes are fully tender, 15 to 20 minutes. Discard rosemary sprigs. Serve.

SLOW-COOKER LEMON-HERB FINGERLING POTATOES

Serves 4 to 6   Total time: 5 to 6 hours on low or 3 to 4 hours on high
WHY THIS RECIPE WORKS *Cooking small whole potatoes in the slow cooker requires no prep work, frees up your stove, and turns out perfectly tender little spuds. For this supereasy and attractive side dish, we turned to fingerlings. We could put them into the slow cooker without any liquid whatsoever, and they retained their delicate sweetness without a hint of mushiness. To enhance their flavor, we added some olive oil, garlic, and scallions. Unlike with some other slow-cooker potato dishes, they cooked through properly without our having to cover them first with a sheet of parchment paper. Look for fingerling potatoes about 3 inches long and 1 inch in diameter. You will need a 5- to 7-quart slow cooker for this recipe. This recipe can easily be doubled in a 7-quart slow cooker, but you will need to increase the cooking time range by 1 hour.*

2   pounds fingerling potatoes, unpeeled
2   tablespoons extra-virgin olive oil
2   scallions, white parts minced, green parts sliced thin
3   garlic cloves, minced
     Salt and pepper
1   tablespoon chopped fresh parsley
1   teaspoon grated lemon zest plus 1 tablespoon juice

1. Combine potatoes, 1 tablespoon oil, scallion whites, garlic, 1 teaspoon salt, and ¼ teaspoon pepper in slow cooker. Cover and cook until potatoes are tender, 5 to 6 hours on low or 3 to 4 hours on high.

2. Stir in parsley, lemon zest and juice, scallion greens, and remaining 1 tablespoon oil. Season with salt and pepper to taste. Serve.

POTATO GALETTE

Serves 6 to 8   Total time: 1 hour 15 minutes
WHY THIS RECIPE WORKS *With its crispy exterior crust and beautifully layered presentation, a potato galette is a simple but sophisticated side or brunch dish. For even cooking and great browning, we began our galette recipe on the stovetop and then slid the pan onto the bottom rack of a hot oven. Using an ovensafe nonstick skillet averted the risk that our potato galette would stick to the pan's bottom. To keep the potatoes from sliding away from one another when we sliced our galette, we included cornstarch in the butter that we were using to coat the potatoes and compressed the galette using a cake pan filled with pie weights for the first half of cooking. Slicing the potatoes ⅛ inch thick is crucial for the success of this dish; use a mandoline, a V-slicer, or a food processor fitted with a ⅛-inch-thick slicing blade. You will need a 10-inch ovensafe nonstick skillet for this recipe. A pound of dried beans or rice can be substituted for the pie weights.*

2½   pounds Yukon Gold potatoes, unpeeled, sliced ⅛ inch thick
5   tablespoons unsalted butter, melted
1   tablespoon cornstarch
1½   teaspoons chopped fresh rosemary
1   teaspoon salt
½   teaspoon pepper

1. Adjust oven rack to lowest position and heat oven to 450 degrees. Place potatoes in large bowl and fill with cold water. Swirl to remove excess starch, then drain in colander. Spread potatoes on towels and dry thoroughly.

2. Whisk 4 tablespoons melted butter, cornstarch, rosemary, salt, and pepper together in large bowl. Add potatoes and toss until thoroughly coated. Add remaining 1 tablespoon melted butter to 10-inch ovensafe nonstick skillet and swirl to coat. Place 1 potato slice in center of skillet, then overlap slices in circle around center slice, followed by outer circle of overlapping slices. Gently place remaining sliced potatoes on top of first layer, arranging so they form even thickness.

3. Place skillet over medium-high heat and cook until potatoes are sizzling and slices around edge of cake start to turn translucent, about 5 minutes. Spray 12-inch square of aluminum foil with vegetable oil spray. Place foil, sprayed side down, on top of potatoes. Place 9-inch round cake pan on top of foil and fill with 2 cups pie weights. Firmly press down on cake pan to compress potatoes. Transfer skillet to oven and bake for 20 minutes.

4. Remove cake pan and foil from skillet. Continue to cook until paring knife can be inserted in center of cake with no resistance, 20 to 25 minutes. Being careful of hot skillet handle, return skillet to medium heat on stovetop and cook, gently shaking pan (skillet handle will be hot), until galette releases from sides of skillet, 2 to 3 minutes. Carefully slide galette onto large plate, place cutting board over galette, and gently invert plate and cutting board together, then remove plate. Using serrated knife, gently cut galette into wedges and serve immediately.

CLASSIC POTATO GRATIN

Serves 4 to 6   Total time: 1 hour 45 minutes
WHY THIS RECIPE WORKS *A bubbling, creamy potato gratin is the ultimate in comfort food and is as much at home on a weeknight table as it as at holiday time. For our classic recipe, we found that the potato variety mattered less than having evenly sliced potatoes. Uniformly thin slices (easily obtained using a mandoline) yielded a gratin with distinct slices of potato bathed in a velvety sauce. As for the choice of dairy, we tried making gratins with milk, half-and-half, and heavy cream, and our favorite turned out to be half-and-half. Baked at 350 degrees for about an hour, gratins made this way had just the right balance of saturated potato and saucy liquid, without the sauce overwhelming the taste of the potato. For a more pronounced crust, sprinkle 3 tablespoons of heavy cream or grated Gruyère cheese on top of the potatoes after 45 minutes of baking. Slicing the potatoes ⅛ inch thick is crucial for the success of this dish; use a mandoline, a V-slicer, or a food processor fitted with a ⅛-inch-thick slicing blade.*

1 garlic clove, peeled and smashed
1 tablespoon unsalted butter, softened
2 pounds potatoes, peeled and sliced
  ⅛ inch thick
2¼ cups half-and-half
1¼ teaspoons salt
  ⅛ teaspoon pepper
  Pinch ground nutmeg
  Pinch cayenne pepper (optional)

1. Adjust oven rack to middle position and heat oven to 350 degrees. Rub bottom and sides of 1½-quart gratin dish or shallow baking dish with half garlic clove. Mince remaining garlic and set aside. Once garlic in dish has dried, about 2 minutes, spread dish with ½ tablespoon butter.

2. Bring potatoes; half-and-half; salt; pepper; nutmeg; cayenne, if using; and reserved minced garlic to boil in medium saucepan over medium-high heat, stirring occasionally (liquid will just barely cover potatoes). Reduce to simmer and cook until liquid thickens, about 2 minutes.

3. Pour potato mixture into prepared dish. Shake dish or use fork to distribute potatoes evenly. Gently press down potatoes until submerged in liquid. Cut remaining ½ tablespoon butter into small pieces and scatter over potatoes.

4. Bake until top is golden brown, about 1¼ hours, basting once or twice during first 45 minutes. Let rest for 5 minutes, and serve.

KETTLE CHIPS

Serves 6 to 8   Total time: 1 hour

WHY THIS RECIPE WORKS *Whether thick-cut, crinkle-cut, plain, or flavored, potato chips are one of America's most beloved snack foods. Our favorites are small-batch kettle-style chips, which cook up thicker and sturdier than regular chips, with a distinctive caramelized flavor. Store-bought versions tend to be greasy and oversalted, but making a perfect batch at home is actually pretty simple. The first trick is getting the potatoes to the perfect thickness. Thicker chips never get properly crisp, while those that are too thin fry up as light as confetti. We found the sweet spot at ¹⁄₁₆ inch for substantial, crisp chips. Frying at too low a temperature made the chips soggy, but when we increased the heat, they burned. Realizing that the potatoes' starch was the source of our troubles, we landed on a method of rinsing, parboiling, and then frying. Rinsing washed away the exterior starch, while parboiling jump-started the cooking and further reduced the amount of starch. It was a bit of work, but the reward of fresh, golden chips was well worth it. Slicing the potatoes ¹⁄₁₆ inch thick is crucial for success; use a mandoline or a V-slicer. Use a Dutch oven that holds 6 quarts or more for this recipe. These chips are best enjoyed the day they are made.*

1 pound Yukon Gold potatoes, unpeeled, sliced ¹⁄₁₆ inch thick
2 quarts peanut or vegetable oil
  Fine sea salt

1. Line rimmed baking sheet with clean dish towel. Set wire rack in second rimmed baking sheet and line with triple layer of paper towels; set both sheets aside. Place potato slices in large bowl and cover with cold water. Gently swirl potatoes to release starch. Drain potatoes and return to bowl. Repeat rinsing step until water no longer turns cloudy, about 5 rinses.

2. Bring 2 quarts water to boil in large saucepan over high heat. Add potatoes, return to gentle boil, and cook until just beginning to soften, 2 to 3 minutes. Drain potatoes in colander. Spread potatoes on towels and dry thoroughly.

3. Meanwhile, add oil to large Dutch oven until it measures about 1½ inches deep and heat over medium-high heat to 325 degrees. Carefully place one-quarter of potato slices in hot oil. Fry, stirring frequently with wire skimmer or slotted spoon, until oil stops bubbling and chips turn golden and crisp, 3 to 4 minutes. Adjust burner, if necessary, to maintain oil temperature around 325 degrees. As soon as chips finish frying (some chips may cook slightly faster than others), transfer to prepared wire rack using skimmer or slotted spoon. Season with salt to taste.

4. Return oil to 325 degrees and repeat with remaining potato slices in 3 more batches. Let cool to room temperature before serving.

THICK-CUT OVEN FRIES

Serves 4 to 6   Total time: 55 minutes

WHY THIS RECIPE WORKS *When traditional French fries are fried, water is rapidly driven out of the starch cells at the surface of the potato, leaving behind tiny cavities. These cavities create the delicate, crispy crust on a French fry. Since oven fries don't heat fast enough for air pockets to form, they usually don't develop that type of crust. Here, we coated the potatoes in a cornstarch slurry that crisped up just like a deep-fried fry. We arranged the potatoes on a baking sheet coated with both vegetable oil spray and vegetable oil; the former contains a surfactant called lecithin, which prevented the oil from pooling and the potatoes from sticking. Using the spray also allowed us to use only 3 tablespoons of oil. Covering the baking sheet with aluminum foil for the first half of cooking ensured that the potatoes were fully tender by the time they were browned. Choose potatoes that are 4 to 6 inches in length to ensure well-proportioned fries. This recipe's success is dependent on a heavy-duty rimmed baking sheet that will not warp in the heat of the oven. Trimming thin slices from the ends of the potatoes in step 2 ensures that each fry has two flat surfaces for even browning.*

3 tablespoons vegetable oil
2 pounds Yukon gold potatoes, unpeeled
¾ cup water
3 tablespoons cornstarch
Salt

1. Adjust oven rack to lowest position and heat oven to 425 degrees. Generously spray rimmed baking sheet with vegetable oil spray. Pour oil into prepared sheet and tilt sheet until surface is evenly coated with oil.

2. Halve potatoes lengthwise and turn halves cut sides down on cutting board. Trim thin slice from both long sides of each potato half, discarding trimmings. Slice potatoes lengthwise into ⅓- to ½-inch-thick planks.

3. Combine water and cornstarch in large bowl, making sure no lumps of cornstarch remain on bottom of bowl. Microwave, stirring every 20 seconds, until mixture begins to thicken, 1 to 3 minutes. Remove from microwave and continue to stir until mixture

thickens to pudding-like consistency. (If necessary, add up to 2 tablespoons water to achieve correct consistency.)

4. Transfer potatoes to bowl with cornstarch mixture and toss until each plank is evenly coated. Arrange planks on prepared sheet, leaving small gaps between planks. (Some cornstarch mixture will remain in bowl.) Cover sheet tightly with lightly greased aluminum foil and bake for 12 minutes.

5. Remove foil and bake until bottom of each fry is golden brown, 10 to 18 minutes. Remove sheet from oven and, using thin metal spatula, carefully flip each fry. Return sheet to oven and continue to bake until second sides are golden brown, 10 to 18 minutes. Sprinkle fries with ½ teaspoon salt. Using spatula, carefully toss fries to distribute salt. Transfer fries to paper towel–lined plate and season with salt to taste. Serve.

EASIER FRENCH FRIES

Serves 4 to 6   Total time: 40 minutes

WHY THIS RECIPE WORKS *Traditional methods of making French fries involve rinsing, soaking, double-frying, and then draining and salting them—not an easy process. We wanted a recipe for crispy fries with a tender interior and lots of potato flavor, but without all of that fuss. The key was to submerge the potatoes in room-temperature oil before frying them over high heat until browned. This gave the potatoes' interiors an opportunity to soften and cook through before the exteriors started to crisp. We tried starchy russets, but they turned leathery with the longer cooking time. With lower-starch Yukon Golds, however, the result was a crisp exterior and a creamy interior. The fries stuck to the bottom of the pot at first, but letting the potatoes cook in the oil for 20 minutes before stirring gave them enough time to form a crust that would protect them. Thinner fries were also less likely to stick. This recipe will not work with sweet potatoes or russets. Use a Dutch oven that holds 6 quarts or more for this recipe.*

2½ pounds Yukon Gold potatoes, unpeeled
6 cups peanut or vegetable oil
Kosher salt

1. Using chef's knife, square off sides of potatoes. Cut potatoes lengthwise into ¼-inch planks, then slice each plank into ¼-inch-thick fries. Combine potatoes and oil in large Dutch oven. Cook over high heat until oil has reached rolling boil, about 5 minutes.

2. Once boiling, continue to cook, without stirring, until potatoes are limp but exteriors are beginning to firm, about 15 minutes.

3. Using tongs, stir potatoes, gently scraping up any that stick, and continue to cook, stirring occasionally, until golden and crisp, 5 to 10 minutes. Using wire skimmer or slotted spoon, transfer fries to paper towel–lined baking sheet. Season with salt and serve.

PATATAS BRAVAS

Serves 4 to 6   Total time: 1 hour

WHY THIS RECIPE WORKS *The best versions of patatas bravas, a favorite Spanish tapas preparation, showcase crispy, well-browned potato pieces served with a smoky, spicy tomato-based sauce. To create an ultracrispy crust without double frying, we parboiled russet potatoes with baking soda, which triggers a chain reaction that causes the pectin on the exteriors of the potatoes to release a layer of starch that, when fried, develops into a thick crust. We tossed the parcooked potatoes with kosher salt, which roughs up the surfaces of the potatoes, creating nooks and crannies through which steam can escape. The nooks and crannies also trap oil, helping to make an even more substantial crunchy crust. For our sauce, we cooked tomato paste, cayenne, sweet smoked paprika, garlic, and water, finishing with sherry vinegar. Finally, adding mayonnaise allowed us to combine the bravas sauce and another common accompaniment, aïoli, into a single sauce. Bittersweet or hot smoked paprika can be used in place of sweet, if desired. If you make this substitution, be sure to taste the sauce before deciding how much cayenne to add, if any. A rasp-style grater makes quick work of turning the garlic into a paste. Use a Dutch oven that holds 6 quarts or more for this recipe.*

CRISPY POTATO LATKES

Makes 10 latkes   Total time: 50 minutes

WHY THIS RECIPE WORKS *Latkes come in all shapes and sizes, but the textural goal is always the same: delicate and light throughout, with a creamy, buttery, soft interior surrounded by a shatteringly crispy outer shell. Unfortunately, many recipes produce latkes that soak up oil like sponges, leaving them greasy and soft. Others are crispy outside but gluey inside or are simply undercooked and tough. To achieve latkes that were light and not greasy, with flavorful, tender interiors and a pleasingly crisp outer shell, we needed to do two things: First, we removed as much water as possible from the potato shreds by wringing them out in a dish towel. Then, we briefly microwaved them. This caused the starches in the potatoes to form a gel that held on to the potatoes' moisture so it didn't leach out during cooking. With the water taken care of, the latkes crisped up quickly and absorbed minimal oil. We prefer using the shredding disk of a food processor to shred the potatoes, but you can use the large holes of a box grater if you prefer. Top with applesauce and sour cream and serve with a green salad.*

- 2 pounds russet potatoes, unpeeled, shredded
- ½ cup grated onion
  Salt and pepper
- 2 large eggs, lightly beaten
- 2 teaspoons minced fresh parsley
  Vegetable oil

1. Adjust oven rack to middle position, place rimmed baking sheet on rack, and heat oven to 200 degrees. Toss potatoes, onion, and 1 teaspoon salt together in bowl. Working in 2 batches, wrap potato mixture in clean dish towel and wring tightly to squeeze out as much liquid as possible into measuring cup, reserving drained liquid. Let liquid sit until starch settles to bottom, 5 to 10 minutes.

2. Return potato mixture to bowl, cover, and microwave until just warmed through but not hot, 1 to 2 minutes, stirring mixture with fork every 30 seconds. Spread potato mixture evenly over second rimmed baking sheet and let cool for 10 minutes.

SAUCE

- 1 tablespoon vegetable oil
- 2 teaspoons garlic, minced to paste
- 1 teaspoon sweet smoked paprika
- ½ teaspoon kosher salt
- ½–¾ teaspoon cayenne pepper
  Pinch red pepper flakes
- ¼ cup tomato paste
- ½ cup water
- 2 teaspoons sherry vinegar
- ¼ cup mayonnaise

POTATOES

- 2¼ pounds russet potatoes, peeled and cut into 1-inch pieces
- ½ teaspoon baking soda
  Kosher salt
- 3 cups vegetable oil

1. For the sauce Heat oil in small saucepan over medium-low heat until shimmering. Add garlic, paprika, salt, cayenne, and pepper flakes and cook until fragrant, about 30 seconds. Add tomato paste and cook for 30 seconds. Whisk in water and bring to boil over high heat. Reduce heat to medium-low and simmer until slightly thickened, 4 to 5 minutes. Transfer sauce to bowl, stir in vinegar, and let cool completely, about 20 minutes. Once cool, whisk in mayonnaise.

2. For the potatoes Bring 2 quarts water to boil in large saucepan over high heat. Add potatoes and baking soda. Return to boil and cook for 1 minute. Drain potatoes.

3. Return potatoes to now-empty saucepan and place over low heat. Cook, shaking saucepan occasionally, until any surface moisture has evaporated, 30 seconds to 1 minute. Remove from heat. Add 1½ teaspoons salt and stir with rubber spatula until potatoes are coated with thick, starchy paste, about 30 seconds. Transfer potatoes to rimmed baking sheet in single layer to cool.

4. Set wire rack in second rimmed baking sheet and line with triple layer of paper towels. Heat oil in large Dutch oven to 375 degrees over high heat. Add all potatoes (they should just be submerged in oil) and cook, stirring occasionally with wire skimmer or slotted spoon, until deep golden brown and crispy, 20 to 25 minutes.

5. Using skimmer or slotted spoon, transfer potatoes to prepared rack. Season with salt to taste. Spoon ½ cup sauce onto bottom of serving platter or 1½ tablespoons sauce onto individual plates. Arrange potatoes over sauce and serve immediately, passing remaining sauce separately.

3. Pour off water from reserved potato liquid, leaving potato starch in measuring cup. Whisk in eggs until smooth. Return cooled potato mixture to bowl. Add parsley, ¼ teaspoon pepper, and potato starch mixture and toss to combine.

4. Set wire rack in clean rimmed baking sheet and line with triple layer of paper towels. Add oil to 12-inch skillet until it measures ¼ inch deep and heat over medium-high heat until shimmering. Place ¼-cup mound of potato mixture in oil and press with nonstick spatula into ⅓-inch-thick disk. Repeat until 5 latkes are in skillet.

5. Cook, adjusting heat so oil bubbles around latke edges, until golden brown on both sides, about 6 minutes. Let latkes drain briefly on paper towels, then transfer to sheet in oven. Repeat with remaining potato mixture, adding oil between batches as needed to maintain ¼-inch depth. Season with salt and pepper to taste. Serve.

BETTER HASH BROWNS

Serves 4 to 6   Total time: 1 hour 15 minutes
WHY THIS RECIPE WORKS *This breakfast and brunch favorite can be more difficult than you might expect: The potatoes discolor, the potato cake falls apart when you try to flip it, and the exterior often burns before the interior is fully cooked. For our better hash browns, we prevented discoloration by rinsing the grated potatoes in salted water. This seasoned the potatoes and lowered the gelatinization temperature of the potato starch, which helped the shreds stick together. After squeezing excess water out of the potatoes, we parcooked them in the microwave, which removed moisture and jump-started the gelatinization process so that the potatoes were cohesive even before they went into the skillet. Molding the hash browns in a cake pan meant we didn't have to fiddle with sticky potatoes in a pan of hot oil. It also made a smoother potato cake that was less likely to stick to the pan. We prefer using the shredding disk of a food processor to shred the potatoes, but you can use the large holes of a box grater if you prefer.*

4 teaspoons salt
2½ pounds Yukon Gold potatoes, peeled and shredded
¼ teaspoon pepper
¼ cup vegetable oil

1. Spray 8-inch round cake pan with vegetable oil spray. Whisk 2 cups water and salt in large bowl until salt dissolves. Transfer potatoes to salt water and toss briefly to coat. Immediately drain in colander. Place 2½ cups potatoes in center of clean dish towel. Gather ends together and twist tightly to wring out excess moisture. Toss dried potatoes with pepper in large bowl. Microwave until very hot and slightly softened, about 5 minutes. Place remaining potatoes in towel and wring out excess moisture. Add to microwaved potatoes and toss with 2 forks until mostly combined (potatoes will not combine completely). Continue to microwave until potatoes are hot and form cohesive mass when pressed with spatula, about 6 minutes, stirring halfway through microwaving.

2. Transfer potatoes to prepared pan and let cool until no longer steaming, about 5 minutes. Using your lightly greased hands, press potatoes firmly into pan to form smooth disk. Refrigerate until cool, at least 20 minutes or up to 24 hours (if refrigerating longer than 30 minutes, wrap pan with plastic wrap once potatoes are cool).

3. Heat 2 tablespoons oil in 10-inch skillet over medium heat until shimmering. Invert potato cake onto plate and carefully slide cake into skillet. Cook, swirling skillet occasionally to distribute oil evenly and prevent cake from sticking, until bottom of cake is brown and crispy, 6 to 8 minutes. (If not browning after 3 minutes, turn heat up slightly. If browning too quickly, reduce heat.) Slide cake onto large plate. Invert onto second large plate. Heat remaining 2 tablespoons oil until shimmering. Carefully slide cake, browned side up, back into skillet. Cook, swirling skillet occasionally, until bottom of cake is brown and crispy, 5 to 6 minutes. Carefully slide cake onto plate and invert onto serving plate. Cut into wedges and serve.

ALL-AMERICAN POTATO SALAD

Serves 4 to 6   Total time: 1 hour 15 minutes (plus 30 minutes chilling time)
WHY THIS RECIPE WORKS *For flavorful, potluck-perfect potato salad, we used firm-textured Yukon Gold potatoes because they hold their shape after cooking. Our recipe benefited from the sweetness of an unexpected ingredient: pickle juice. We drizzled the warm potatoes with a mixture of pickle juice and mustard. The potatoes easily absorbed the acidic seasoning liquid right through to the middle. Mayonnaise and sour cream formed the base of our creamy dressing, seasoned with celery seeds, celery, and red onion. Chopped hard-cooked eggs stirred in at the end completed our all-American potato salad; you can omit them if you prefer. Make sure not to overcook the potatoes or the salad will be sloppy. Keep the water at a gentle simmer and use the tip of a paring knife to judge their doneness. If the knife inserts easily, they are done.*

2 hard-cooked large eggs, peeled and chopped coarse (optional)
Salt
2 pounds Yukon Gold potatoes, peeled and cut into ¾-inch pieces
3 tablespoons dill pickle juice, plus ¼ cup finely chopped dill pickles
1 tablespoon yellow mustard
½ teaspoon celery seeds
¼ teaspoon pepper
½ cup mayonnaise
¼ cup sour cream
1 celery rib, chopped fine
½ small red onion, chopped fine

1. Place potatoes and 1 teaspoon salt in large saucepan and add water to cover by 1 inch. Bring to boil over high heat, reduce heat to medium-low, and simmer until potatoes are just tender and paring knife can be slipped in and out of potatoes with little resistance, 10 to 15 minutes.

2. Drain potatoes thoroughly, then spread out on rimmed baking sheet. Mix 2 tablespoons pickle juice and mustard together in small bowl, drizzle pickle juice mixture over hot potatoes, and toss until evenly coated. Refrigerate until cooled, about 30 minutes.

3. Mix remaining 1 tablespoon pickle juice, chopped pickles, celery seeds, ½ teaspoon salt, pepper, mayonnaise, sour cream, celery, and red onion in large bowl. Add cooled potatoes and gently toss to coat. Cover and refrigerate until chilled, about 30 minutes. (Salad can be refrigerated for up to 2 days.) Gently stir in eggs just before serving.

FRENCH POTATO SALAD WITH DIJON AND FINES HERBES

Serves 4 to 6   Total time: 45 minutes

WHY THIS RECIPE WORKS *Fresh green herbs and a vinaigrette dressing are the hallmarks of a French potato salad, making the dish pleasing not only to the eye but also to the palate. Small red potatoes are the traditional choice, and they should be tender but not mushy, with the flavor of the vinaigrette fully permeating the mild potatoes. To eliminate torn skins and broken slices, a common side effect of boiling skin-on red potatoes, we sliced the spuds before boiling. To evenly infuse the potatoes with the garlicky mustard vinaigrette, we spread the warm potatoes on a baking sheet and poured the vinaigrette over the top. Gently folding in the minced fresh herbs just before serving helped keep the potatoes intact. If fresh chervil isn't available, substitute an additional ½ tablespoon of minced parsley and an additional ½ teaspoon of tarragon. Use small red potatoes measuring 1 to 2 inches in diameter.*

- 2 **pounds small red potatoes, unpeeled, sliced ¼ inch thick**
- 2 **tablespoons salt**
- 1 **garlic clove, peeled and threaded on skewer**
- ¼ **cup extra-virgin olive oil**
- 1½ **tablespoons champagne vinegar or white wine vinegar**
- 2 **teaspoons Dijon mustard**
- ½ **teaspoon pepper**
- 1 **small shallot, minced**
- 1 **tablespoon minced fresh chervil**
- 1 **tablespoon minced fresh parsley**
- 1 **tablespoon minced fresh chives**
- 1 **teaspoon minced fresh tarragon**

1. Place potatoes and salt in large saucepan and add water to cover by 1 inch. Bring to boil over high heat, reduce heat to medium-low, and simmer until potatoes are just tender and paring knife can be slipped in and out of potatoes with little resistance, 5 to 6 minutes.

2. While potatoes are cooking, lower skewered garlic into simmering water and blanch for 45 seconds. Run garlic under cold running water, then remove from skewer and mince.

3. Drain potatoes, reserving ¼ cup cooking water. Arrange hot potatoes close together in single layer on rimmed baking sheet. Whisk oil, minced garlic, vinegar, mustard, pepper, and reserved potato cooking water together in bowl, then drizzle evenly over potatoes. Let potatoes sit at room temperature until flavors meld, about 10 minutes.

4. Transfer potatoes to large bowl. Combine shallot and herbs in small bowl, then sprinkle over potatoes and combine gently. Serve.

VARIATION

French Potato Salad with Fennel, Tomato, and Olives

If desired, chop 1 tablespoon of the fennel fronds and add it to the salad with the parsley. Omit chervil, chives, and tarragon. Increase parsley to 3 tablespoons. Add ½ bulb thinly sliced fennel, 1 cored and chopped tomato, and ¼ cup pitted oil-cured black olives, quartered, to salad with shallots and parsley.

POTATO GNOCCHI WITH SAGE BROWN BUTTER

Serves 4   Total time: 1 hour 15 minutes

WHY THIS RECIPE WORKS *Potato gnocchi are a culinary paradox: airy, pillow-like dumplings created from dense, starchy ingredients. The method is simple: Knead mashed potatoes into a dough; shape; and boil for a minute. And yet the potential pitfalls are numerous (lumpy mashed potatoes, too much or too little flour, a heavy hand when kneading). We wanted a foolproof recipe for impossibly light gnocchi with unmistakable potato flavor. Microwaving and then baking russets was an excellent start to our gnocchi base. To avoid lumps, which can cause gnocchi to break apart, we turned to a ricer for a smooth, supple mash. While many recipes offer a range of*

Potato Gnocchi with Sage Brown Butter

the quantity of flour, we used an exact amount based on the ratio of potato to flour so that our gnocchi dough was mixed as little as possible. And we found that an egg, while not traditional, tenderized our gnocchi further, delivering delicate potato pillows. For the most accurate measurements, weigh the potatoes and flour. After processing, you may have slightly more than the 3 cups (16 ounces) of potatoes required for this recipe. Discard any extra or set it aside for another use.

GNOCCHI

- 2 **pounds russet potatoes, unpeeled**
- 1 **large egg, lightly beaten**
- ¾ **cup plus 1 tablespoon (4 ounces) all-purpose flour, plus extra for counter**
- 1 **tablespoon plus 1 teaspoon salt**

SAUCE

- 4 **tablespoons unsalted butter, cut into 4 pieces**
- 1 **small shallot, minced**
- 1 **teaspoon minced fresh sage**
- 1½ **teaspoons lemon juice**
- ¼ **teaspoon salt**

1. For the gnocchi Adjust oven rack to middle position and heat oven to 450 degrees. Poke each potato 8 times with paring knife. Microwave potatoes until slightly softened at ends, about 10 minutes, flipping potatoes halfway through cooking. Transfer potatoes directly to oven rack and bake until skewer glides easily through flesh and potatoes yield to gentle pressure, 18 to 20 minutes.

2. Holding potatoes with dish towel, peel with paring knife. Process potatoes through ricer or food mill onto rimmed baking sheet. Gently spread potatoes into even layer and let cool for 5 minutes.

3. Transfer 3 cups (16 ounces) warm potatoes to bowl. Using fork, gently stir in egg until just combined. Sprinkle flour and 1 teaspoon salt over top and gently combine using fork until no pockets of dry flour remain. Press mixture into rough ball, transfer to lightly floured counter, and gently knead until smooth but slightly sticky, about 1 minute, lightly dusting counter with flour as needed to prevent sticking.

4. Line 2 clean rimmed baking sheets with parchment paper and dust liberally with flour. Divide dough into 8 equal pieces. Lightly dust counter with flour. Gently roll 1 piece of dough into ½-inch-thick rope, dusting with flour to prevent sticking. Cut rope into ¾-inch lengths.

5. Holding fork with tines upside down in your hand, press each dough piece cut side down against tines with thumb of your other hand to create indentation. Roll dough down tines to form ridges on sides. If dough sticks, dust thumb and/or fork with flour. Transfer formed gnocchi to prepared sheets and repeat with remaining dough.

6. For the sauce Melt butter in 12-inch skillet over medium-high heat, swirling occasionally, until butter is browned and releases nutty aroma, about 1½ minutes. Off heat, add shallot and sage, stirring until shallot is fragrant, about 1 minute. Stir in lemon juice and salt and cover to keep warm.

7. Bring 4 quarts water to boil in large pot. Add 1 tablespoon salt. Using parchment paper as sling, add half of gnocchi and cook until firm and just cooked through, about 90 seconds (gnocchi should float to surface after about 1 minute). Remove gnocchi with slotted spoon, transfer to skillet with sauce, and cover to keep warm. Repeat with remaining gnocchi. Gently toss gnocchi with sauce to combine and serve.

VARIATION

Potato Gnocchi with Parmesan, Pancetta, and Walnut Sauce
Whisk ½ cup chicken broth, ½ cup grated Parmesan, ¼ cup heavy cream, 2 large egg yolks, and ⅛ teaspoon pepper in bowl until smooth. Heat 2 teaspoons extra-virgin olive oil in 12-inch skillet over medium heat until shimmering. Add 3 ounces finely chopped pancetta and cook until crisp, 5 to 7 minutes. Stir in ½ cup chopped walnuts and cook until golden and fragrant, about 1 minute. Off heat, gradually add broth mixture, whisking constantly. Return skillet to medium heat and cook, stirring often, until sauce is thickened slightly, 2 to 4 minutes. Season with salt to taste. Remove from heat and cover to keep warm. Substitute Parmesan sauce for brown butter sauce.

SKILLET-ROASTED CHICKEN AND POTATOES

Serves 4   Total time: 1 hour 45 minutes
WHY THIS RECIPE WORKS *What's more delicious and satisfying than a whole chicken, roasted to perfection, atop a bed of perfectly browned and tender potatoes? To achieve this ideal, universally loved dish, we started by choosing a skillet instead of a roasting pan. To fit a full 2 pounds of potatoes into a 12-inch skillet, we cut them into thick rounds and gave them a jump-start on the stovetop to get a crust started. For a full-flavored bird, we carefully separated the skin from the breast and thighs and applied a fragrant blend of fresh thyme, smoked paprika, and lemon zest. Keeping the potatoes in the skillet and roasting the chicken on top of them not only elevated the bird for greater exposure to the oven's heat, but also allowed the potatoes to soak up the chicken's tasty drippings. Once the chicken was fully cooked, we let it rest while we covered the potatoes and returned them to the oven. By the time the chicken was ready to be served, the potatoes were perfectly tender. Use uniform, medium potatoes. You will need a 12-inch ovensafe nonstick skillet with a tight-fitting lid for this recipe.*

- 3 **tablespoons vegetable oil**
- 2 **teaspoons minced fresh thyme**
- 1½ **teaspoons smoked paprika**
- 1½ **teaspoons grated lemon zest, plus lemon wedges for serving Salt and pepper**
- 1 **(3½- to 4-pound) whole chicken, giblets discarded**
- 2 **pounds Yukon Gold potatoes, peeled, ends squared off, and sliced into 1-inch-thick rounds**

1. Adjust oven rack to lower-middle position and heat oven to 400 degrees. Combine 2 tablespoons oil, thyme, paprika, lemon zest, 1 teaspoon salt, and ½ teaspoon pepper in bowl. Pat chicken dry with paper towels. Using your fingers or handle of spoon, gently loosen skin from breast and thighs. Rub oil mixture all over chicken and underneath skin of breast, directly onto meat. Tie legs together with kitchen twine and tuck wingtips behind back.

2. Toss potatoes with 1½ teaspoons salt, ½ teaspoon pepper, and remaining 1 tablespoon oil. Arrange potatoes, flat sides down, in single layer in 12-inch ovensafe nonstick skillet. Place skillet over medium heat and cook potatoes, without moving them, until brown on bottom, 7 to 9 minutes (do not flip).

3. Place chicken, breast side up, on top of potatoes and transfer skillet to oven. Roast until breast registers 160 degrees and thighs register 175 degrees, 1 to 1¼ hours. Remove skillet from oven. Transfer chicken to carving board and let rest while finishing potatoes.

4. Meanwhile, being careful of hot skillet handle, cover skillet, return potatoes to oven, and roast until tender, about 20 minutes. Carve chicken and serve with potatoes and lemon wedges.

SHEPHERD'S PIE

Serves 4 to 6   Total time: 1 hour 30 minutes

WHY THIS RECIPE WORKS *Shepherd's pie, a robust casserole of meat, gravy, and vegetables all topped with a blanket of mashed potatoes, can take the better part of a day to prepare. And while the dish is indeed satisfying, traditional versions are simply too rich for most people. We wanted to both scale back its preparation time and lighten the dish to fit in better with modern eating sensibilities. Per other modern recipes, we chose ground beef as our filling over ground lamb. To prevent the beef from turning dry and crumbly, we tossed it with a little baking soda (diluted in water) before browning it. This unusual step raises the pH level of the beef, resulting in more tender meat. An onion and mushroom gravy, spiked with Worcestershire sauce, complemented the beef filling. For the mashed potatoes, we took our cue from an Irish dish called champ and cut way back on the dairy in favor of fresh scallions, which made for a lighter, more flavorful topping for the hearty meat filling underneath. Don't use ground beef that's fattier than 93 percent or the dish will be greasy. You will need a 10-inch broiler-safe skillet for this recipe.*

1½   pounds 93 percent lean ground beef
       Salt and pepper
½   teaspoon baking soda
2½   pounds russet potatoes, peeled and
       cut into 1-inch pieces
4   tablespoons unsalted butter, melted
½   cup milk
1   large egg yolk
8   scallions, green parts only, sliced thin
2   teaspoons vegetable oil
1   onion, chopped
4   ounces white mushrooms, trimmed
       and chopped
1   tablespoon tomato paste
2   garlic cloves, minced
2   tablespoons Madeira or ruby port
2   tablespoons all-purpose flour
1¼   cups beef broth
2   carrots, peeled and chopped
2   teaspoons Worcestershire sauce
2   sprigs fresh thyme
1   bay leaf
2   teaspoons cornstarch

1. Toss beef with 2 tablespoons water, 1 teaspoon salt, ¼ teaspoon pepper, and baking soda in bowl until thoroughly combined. Set aside for 20 minutes.

2. Place potatoes and 1 tablespoon salt in medium saucepan and add water to cover by 1 inch. Bring to boil over high heat, reduce heat to medium-low, and simmer until potatoes are tender and paring knife can be slipped in and out of potatoes with no resistance, 8 to 10 minutes. Drain potatoes and return to saucepan. Return saucepan to low heat and cook, shaking saucepan occasionally, until any surface moisture on potatoes has evaporated, about 1 minute. Off heat, mash potatoes or press potatoes through ricer set over saucepan. Stir in melted butter. Whisk milk and egg yolk together in small bowl, then stir into potatoes. Stir in scallion greens and season with salt and pepper to taste. Cover and set aside.

3. Heat oil in 10-inch broiler-safe skillet over medium heat until shimmering. Add onion, mushrooms, ½ teaspoon salt, and ¼ teaspoon pepper and cook, stirring occasionally, until vegetables are just starting to soften and dark bits form on bottom of skillet, 4 to 6 minutes.

4. Stir in tomato paste and garlic and cook until bottom of skillet is dark brown, about 2 minutes. Stir in Madeira and cook, scraping up any browned bits, until evaporated, about 1 minute. Stir in flour and cook for 1 minute. Stir in broth, carrots, Worcestershire, thyme sprigs, and bay leaf and bring to boil, scraping up any browned bits.

5. Reduce heat to medium-low, add beef in 2-inch chunks to broth, and bring to gentle simmer. Cover and cook until beef is cooked through, 10 to 12 minutes, stirring and breaking up meat chunks with 2 forks halfway through cooking. Stir cornstarch and 2 teaspoons water together in bowl. Stir cornstarch mixture into filling and continue to simmer for 30 seconds. Discard thyme sprigs and bay leaf. Season with salt and pepper to taste.

6. Adjust oven rack 5 inches from broiler element and heat broiler. Place mashed potatoes in large zipper-lock bag and snip off 1 corner to create 1-inch opening. Pipe potatoes in even layer over filling, making sure to cover entire surface. Smooth potatoes with back of spoon, then use tines of fork to make ridges over surface. Place skillet on rimmed baking sheet and broil until potatoes are golden brown and crusty and filling is bubbly, 10 to 15 minutes. Let cool for 10 minutes before serving.

POTATO AND CHORIZO TACOS

Serves 4   Total time: 50 minutes

WHY THIS RECIPE WORKS *Tender potatoes and highly seasoned fresh Mexican chorizo are the keys to these classic tacos. We started by toasting ancho chile powder, paprika, and other spices in oil to intensify their flavors, and then we mixed ground pork into the spiced oil. We added parboiled diced potatoes to absorb all that flavor as they finished cooking. Mashing some of the potatoes and mixing them into the filling made it more cohesive. A bright yet creamy puree of tomatillos, avocado, cilantro, and jalapeños complemented the richness of the filling. If you can purchase good-quality Mexican-style chorizo, skip step 2 and cook the chorizo as directed in*

Potato and Chorizo Tacos

step 3. *The sharp, crunchy raw onion is an excellent counterpoint to the soft, rich taco filling, so we do not recommend omitting it. For a spicier sauce, use two jalapeño chiles. You will need a 12-inch nonstick skillet with a tight-fitting lid for this recipe.*

FILLING

- 1 pound Yukon Gold potatoes, peeled and cut into ½-inch pieces
  Salt and pepper
- 3 tablespoons vegetable oil
- 1 tablespoon ancho chile powder
- 1 tablespoon paprika
- 1½ teaspoons ground coriander
- 1½ teaspoons dried oregano
- ¼ teaspoon ground cinnamon
  Pinch cayenne pepper
  Pinch ground allspice
- 3 tablespoons cider vinegar
- 1½ teaspoons sugar
- 1 garlic clove, minced
- 8 ounces ground pork

SAUCE

- 8 ounces tomatillos, husks and stems removed, rinsed well, dried, and cut into 1-inch pieces
- 1 avocado, halved, pitted, and cut into 1-inch pieces
- 1–2 jalapeño chiles, stemmed, seeded, and chopped
- ¼ cup chopped fresh cilantro leaves and stems
- 1 tablespoon lime juice
- 1 garlic clove, minced
- ¾ teaspoon salt

TACOS

- 12 (6-inch) corn tortillas, warmed
  Finely chopped white onion
  Fresh cilantro leaves
  Lime wedges

1. For the filling Bring 1 quart water to boil in 12-inch nonstick skillet over high heat. Add potatoes and 1 teaspoon salt. Reduce heat to medium, cover, and cook until potatoes are just tender and paring knife can be slipped in and out of potatoes with little resistance, 3 to 5 minutes. Drain potatoes and set aside. Wipe skillet clean with paper towels.

2. Combine oil, chile powder, paprika, coriander, oregano, cinnamon, cayenne, allspice, ¾ teaspoon salt, and ½ teaspoon pepper in now-empty skillet. Cook over medium heat, stirring constantly, until mixture is bubbling and fragrant. Off heat, carefully stir in vinegar, sugar, and garlic (mixture will sputter). Let sit until steam subsides and skillet cools slightly, about 5 minutes. Add pork to skillet. Mash and mix with rubber spatula until spice mixture is evenly incorporated into pork.

3. Return skillet to medium-high heat and cook, mashing and stirring until pork has broken into fine crumbles and juices are bubbling, about 3 minutes.

4. Stir in potatoes, cover, and reduce heat to low. Cook until potatoes are fully softened and have soaked up most of pork juices, 6 to 8 minutes, stirring halfway through cooking. Off heat, using spatula, mash approximately one-eighth of potatoes. Stir mixture until mashed potatoes are evenly distributed. Cover and keep warm.

5. For the sauce Process all ingredients in food processor until smooth, about 1 minute, scraping down sides of bowl as needed. Transfer to serving bowl.

6. For the tacos Spoon filling into center of each tortilla and serve, passing sauce, onion, cilantro, and lime wedges separately.

LEMON-HERB COD FILLETS WITH CRISPY GARLIC POTATOES

Serves 4   Total time: 40 minutes
WHY THIS RECIPE WORKS *Who isn't looking for more simple, crowd-pleasing meals that are perfect for any night of the week during any time of the year? This ingenious recipe delivers perfectly roasted fillets and potatoes all in one sheet pan. We roasted the cod fillets atop beds of shingled sliced spuds to give the quick-cooking fish some insulation. Slicing and microwaving starchy russets with garlic and oil before roasting jump-started their cooking so that the potatoes and fish finished at the same time. To infuse the mild cod with flavor, we topped each fillet with butter, thyme sprigs,* *and slices of lemon, allowing the three components to gently baste and season the cod as it roasted. In the end, we were met with four elegant portions of rich, tender cod and fragrant, crisp potatoes. You can substitute haddock or halibut for the cod.*

- 3 tablespoons extra-virgin olive oil
- 1½ pounds russet potatoes, unpeeled, sliced into ¼-inch-thick rounds
- 3 garlic cloves, minced
  Salt and pepper
- 4 (6- to 8-ounce) skinless cod fillets, 1 to 1½ inches thick
- 3 tablespoons unsalted butter, cut into ¼-inch pieces
- 4 sprigs fresh thyme
- 1 lemon, sliced thin

1. Adjust oven rack to lower-middle position and heat oven to 425 degrees. Brush rimmed baking sheet with 1 tablespoon oil. Combine potatoes, garlic, and remaining 2 tablespoons oil in bowl and season with salt and pepper. Microwave, uncovered, until potatoes are just tender, 12 to 14 minutes.

2. Shingle potatoes into 4 rectangular piles that measure roughly 4 by 6 inches on prepared sheet. Pat cod dry with paper towels, season with salt and pepper, and lay on top of potatoes skinned side down. Place butter, thyme sprigs, and lemon slices on top of cod.

3. Roast until cod flakes apart when gently prodded with paring knife and registers 140 degrees, 15 to 18 minutes. Slide spatula underneath potatoes and cod, gently transfer to plates, and serve.

POTATO DINNER ROLLS

Makes 12 rolls   Total time: 1 hour 30 minutes (plus 1 hour rising time)
WHY THIS RECIPE WORKS *While the decadently buttery white dinner rolls associated with holiday dinners are delicious, sometimes we crave something similarly soft and tender but a little leaner. Old-fashioned potato rolls, with their light, moist crumb, fit the bill. Potato roll recipes abound, but almost none specify what type of potato to use, and some turn out rather leaden rolls. We wanted to nail down a*

foolproof recipe for airy, light, and tender potato rolls. We learned in the test kitchen that more starch is better, so we chose high-starch russet potatoes. Potato starch granules are about five times larger than wheat granules, so they can absorb at least five times as much water, resulting in a moister crumb. As we made batch after batch of rolls with different amounts of mashed russets, we discovered something interesting: The more potato we used, the less time the dough needed to rise. As it turns out, the potassium in potatoes activates yeast; the more of it there is, the quicker and more vigorous the rise. This led us to consider the cooking water. When potatoes are boiled, they leach almost half of their potassium into the water, which helped explain why so many recipes called for adding the cooking water to the dough. We found that when we switched from using 5 tablespoons of milk to using the same amount of potato cooking water, the rising times dropped still more. These rolls weren't just light, moist, and satisfying; they also needed significantly less rising time than many standard dinner rolls. Don't salt the water in which you boil the potato.

- 1 **large russet potato (10 ounces), peeled and cut into 1-inch pieces**
- 2 **tablespoons unsalted butter, cut into 4 pieces**
- 2¼ **cups (12⅓ ounces) bread flour**
- 2 **teaspoons instant or rapid-rise yeast**
- 1 **teaspoon salt**
- 2 **large eggs (1 room temperature and 1 lightly beaten with 1 tablespoon water and pinch salt)**
- 1 **tablespoon sugar**

1. Place potato in medium saucepan and add water to cover by 1 inch. Bring to boil over high heat, then reduce to simmer and cook until potato is just tender (paring knife can be slipped in and out of potato with little resistance), 8 to 10 minutes.

2. Transfer 5 tablespoons (2½ ounces) potato cooking water to 4-cup liquid measuring cup and let cool completely. Drain potato pieces, return to now-empty saucepan, and place over low heat. Cook, shaking saucepan occasionally, until any surface moisture has evaporated,

about 30 seconds. Off heat, process potato through ricer or food mill or mash well with potato masher. Measure 1 cup very firmly packed potato (8 ounces) and transfer to separate bowl. Stir in butter until melted and let mixture cool completely before using. Save remaining mashed potato for another use.

3. Whisk flour, yeast, and salt together in bowl of stand mixer. Whisk egg and sugar into potato cooking water until sugar has dissolved. Add potato mixture to flour mixture and mix with your hands until combined (some large lumps are OK). Using dough hook on low speed, slowly add cooking water mixture and mix until cohesive dough starts to form and no dry flour remains, about 2 minutes, scraping down bowl as needed. Increase speed to medium-low and knead until dough is smooth and elastic and clears sides of bowl but sticks to bottom, about 8 minutes.

4. Transfer dough to lightly floured counter and knead by hand to form smooth, round ball, about 30 seconds. Place dough seam side down in lightly greased large bowl or container, cover tightly with plastic wrap, and let rise until doubled in size, 30 minutes to 1 hour.

5. Line rimmed baking sheet with parchment paper. Press down on dough to deflate. Transfer dough to clean counter and stretch into even 12-inch log. Cut log into 12 equal pieces (about 2 ounces each) and cover loosely with greased plastic.

6. Working with 1 piece of dough at a time (keep remaining pieces covered), form into rough ball by stretching dough around your thumbs and pinching edges together so that top is smooth. Place ball seam side down on clean counter and, using your cupped hand, drag in small circles until dough feels taut and round.

7. Arrange dough balls seam side down on prepared sheet, spaced about 1½ inches apart. Cover loosely with greased plastic and let rise until nearly doubled in size and dough springs back minimally when poked gently with your knuckle, 30 minutes to 1 hour.

8. Adjust oven rack to upper-middle position and heat oven to 425 degrees. Gently brush rolls with beaten egg mixture and bake until golden brown, 12 to 14 minutes, rotating sheet halfway through baking. Transfer rolls to wire rack and let cool for 15 minutes. Serve warm or at room temperature.

RADISHES

The seemingly pedestrian radish is well-traveled. First cultivated in China, radishes spread to Europe by the 15th century and traveled to America in the 1620s. They belong to the large Brassica family, which includes cabbage, broccoli, and kale, and their strong flavor comes from the same compound that gives mustard and horseradish their pungency.

Peppery-hot and juicy, raw radishes are a welcome addition to salads, crudité platters, and the like. We especially enjoy them with sweeter flavor counterpoints, as in our Radish and Carrot Slaw with Sesame and Scallions and our Southwestern Radish and Apple Salad. They work well with creamy flavors, too: Our updated version of a venerable rustic French recipe—Baguette with Radishes, Butter, and Herbs—was instantaneously devoured in the test kitchen every single time it was prepared.

For many people, a little bit of pungent raw radish goes a long way. Start cooking radishes, though, and you will find that the possibilities expand exponentially. If you've only had them raw, cooked radishes will come as a delicious surprise. The heat of cooking changes them completely, as their characteristic pungency disappears, to be replaced by a milder, almost turnip-like sweetness.

We like to braise them in a small amount of broth with shallots and chives, or with garlic and thyme. We also love sautéing them in a bit of butter with chili and lime, or with curry and almonds. Like most root vegetables, radishes take well to roasting, emerging from the hot oven mellowed and creamy-textured. Unlike most root vegetables, radishes roast to tenderness superfast. Our Roasted Radishes with Yogurt-Tahini Sauce uses them from tip to tail in a modern, revelatory way.

shopping and storage

Most varieties of radishes are available year-round, though their best seasons are typically spring and fall.

Try to buy radishes with their greens attached. If they are healthy and crisp, this is a sign that the radishes will be fresh and crisp. If the radishes are sold without their greens (as they often are sold in plastic bags in supermarkets), make sure they are firm and their skin is smooth and not cracked. Avoid very large radishes, which can have a woody texture.

Store radishes wrapped in paper towels in a loosely closed plastic produce bag in the refrigerator for about a week. Remove and store greens separately, wrapped in paper towels in a plastic produce bag.

radish varieties

ROUND Red is the most commonly seen color, but they also appear in shades of white, pink, and purple. The different colors are sometimes sold in a bunch and labeled as "Easter egg radishes." Their flavor is sharp and bright and they have a juicy crunch.

FRENCH BREAKFAST These red-and-white radishes are an elongated version of regular round radishes. They are harvested primarily in the springtime and tend to have the mildest flavor of the various varieties.

WATERMELON These magical-looking radishes have a pale green skin and a bright watermelon-pink interior, with a mildly spicy-sweet flavor. They are gorgeous raw—it's a waste to cook these, since their striking coloring will fade.

DAIKON Long and white, this is the most commonly available large radish variety (they can grow to more than a foot in length!). Daikon are more typically served cooked, but they can be eaten raw and have a mildly peppery flavor. If you find them with their greens attached, buy them, since these freshly harvested daikon will have a more mellow flavor, and the greens are edible.

BLACK Also called Spanish radishes, this winter radish has a thick, black, bumpy skin and a snow-white interior that's drier in texture than other radish varieties, with the sharpest flavor of the various varieties. It's a stalwart of Eastern European cooking because it's so hardy.

WHITE ICICLE This heirloom variety is long and slender, like its namesake, and has a sinus-clearing peppery quality and slow-burning heat.

vegetable prep

Two Ways to Slice Radishes Thin

To make it easier to slice radishes thin, as for our Quick-Pickled Radishes, leave root tail attached to use as a handle while slicing; trim off when finished.

Or, try using a vegetable peeler; the sharp blade makes it easier to cut wafer-thin radish slices.

Peeling Daikon Radish

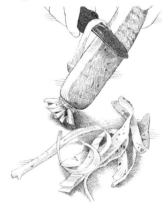

Daikon radish has a thicker skin that is best removed with a vegetable peeler before cooking or serving raw.

SAUTÉED RADISHES

Serves 4 to 6   Total time: 20 minutes

WHY THIS RECIPE WORKS *Here's a simple introduction to the mellow, sweet flavor of cooked radishes. Heat concentrates the natural sugars in radishes while downplaying many of the compounds responsible for radishes' pungent, peppery flavor. Here we started by cooking quartered radishes in butter over moderate heat. The butter provided substantial browning and lent subtle, nutty notes to the radishes. And since radishes contain relatively little water, within 10 minutes they were golden brown all over and perfectly tender, with a slight bite. To provide some textural variety and color, we cooked the greens at the end, so that they retained a slight crispness that complemented the heartier radish pieces. We've provided two variations, but feel free to try this with any number of spice mixes. If you can't find radishes with their greens, you can substitute baby arugula or watercress, or skip step 2.*

- 3 tablespoons unsalted butter, cut into 3 pieces
- 1½ pounds radishes with their greens, radishes trimmed and quartered, 8 cups greens reserved
  Salt and pepper
- 1 garlic clove, minced
  Lemon wedges

1. Melt 2 tablespoons butter in 12-inch skillet over medium-high heat. Add radishes, ¼ teaspoon salt, and ⅛ teaspoon pepper and cook, stirring occasionally, until radishes are lightly browned and crisp-tender, 10 to 12 minutes. Stir in garlic and cook until fragrant, about 30 seconds; transfer to bowl.

2. Melt remaining 1 tablespoon butter in now-empty skillet over medium heat. Add radish greens, ⅛ teaspoon salt, and ⅛ teaspoon pepper and cook, stirring frequently, until wilted, about 1 minute. Off heat, stir in radishes and season with salt and pepper to taste. Serve with lemon wedges.

VARIATIONS

Sautéed Radishes with Chili and Lime
Stir 1 teaspoon paprika and ½ teaspoon chili powder into radishes with garlic. Substitute lime wedges for lemon.

Sautéed Radishes with Vadouvan Curry and Almonds
We prefer the flavor of vadouvan curry here, but any variety will work.
Omit lemon wedges. Substitute 1½ teaspoons vadouvan curry for garlic. Sprinkle with 2 tablespoons coarsely chopped toasted almonds before serving.

ROASTED RADISHES WITH YOGURT-TAHINI SAUCE

Serves 4 to 6   Total time: 30 minutes

WHY THIS RECIPE WORKS *While they're great raw or in salads, radishes are a worthy candidate for roasting. Their crisp texture holds up well to high heat, yielding a tender but meaty interior. Roasting also mellows the spiciness of radishes, concentrating their natural sugars for a nutty, slightly sweet flavor. We started by roasting halved radishes cut side down in oil. These radishes were mild and slightly sweet, but also too bland for a finished dish and lacking any golden-brown color— a bit anemic. To facilitate browning and to complement the nuttiness of the radishes, we tossed them in a mixture of melted butter and white miso, then roasted them on the bottom rack of the oven. The butter produced superior browning on the cut side, while the miso added a pleasing savory quality. To make the most of our radishes, we used the mild, peppery green tops in a simple salad, pairing them both with a tangy yogurt-tahini sauce and a sprinkling of pistachios and sesame seeds. This is a simple but elegant dish, with bold and complementary flavors that bring out the unexpectedly sweeter side of radishes. If you can't find radishes with their greens, you can substitute baby arugula or watercress.*

- ½ cup plain whole-milk yogurt
- 2 tablespoons tahini
- 1 teaspoon grated lemon zest plus 4 teaspoons juice
- 1 garlic clove, minced
  Salt and pepper
- 2 tablespoons chopped toasted pistachios or almonds
- 1½ teaspoons toasted sesame seeds
- ⅛ teaspoon ground cumin
- 3 tablespoons unsalted butter, melted

- 5½ teaspoons white miso (optional)
- 1½ teaspoons honey
- 2 pounds radishes with their greens, root ends of radishes trimmed, radishes halved lengthwise, 8 cups greens reserved
- 1 teaspoon extra-virgin olive oil

1. Adjust oven rack to lowest position and heat oven to 500 degrees. Whisk yogurt, tahini, lemon zest and 1 tablespoon juice, garlic, ¼ teaspoon salt, and ⅛ teaspoon pepper together in bowl; set aside for serving. Combine pistachios, sesame seeds, cumin, and ⅛ teaspoon salt in small bowl; set aside for serving.

2. Line rimmed baking sheet with aluminum foil. Whisk melted butter; 5 teaspoons miso, if using; 1 teaspoon honey; and ¼ teaspoon salt in large bowl until smooth. Add radishes and toss to coat. Arrange radishes cut side down on prepared sheet and roast until tender and well browned on cut side, 10 to 15 minutes.

3. Whisk oil; remaining 1 teaspoon lemon juice; remaining ½ teaspoon miso, if using; remaining ½ teaspoon honey; ¼ teaspoon salt; and ⅛ teaspoon pepper in clean large bowl until smooth. Add radish greens and toss to coat. Season with salt and pepper to taste.

4. To serve, spread portion of yogurt-tahini sauce over bottom of individual serving plates. Top with roasted radishes and radish greens, then sprinkle with pistachio mixture.

BRAISED RADISHES

Serves 4   Total time: 20 minutes

WHY THIS RECIPE WORKS *When developing this speedy recipe for stovetop-braised radishes, we discovered that sautéing the radishes briefly in butter before braising helped to coax out their natural flavor. For the braising liquid, broth proved to be the best choice: Wine made the radishes taste too harsh and acidic, while water rendered them bland. The sweet oniony flavor of the chives worked well with the radishes, which themselves were surprisingly sweet when braised.*

ROASTED RADISHES WITH YOGURT-TAHINI SAUCE

We use the entire radish—greens and roots—in this elegant salad that can be either a side dish or, with some fresh crusty baguette alongside, a light meal. The mildly spicy radish greens perfectly complement the sweetness that roasting brings to the radishes, and the simple savory sauce and nutty topping lift this salad to a sophisticated plane.

1. Trim the root ends of the radishes and cut them in half lengthwise. Reserve their leaves for the salad.

2. Whisk together the yogurt, tahini, lemon zest and juice, garlic, and salt and pepper for the yogurt sauce and set the bowl aside for serving. Combine the pistachios, sesame seeds, cumin, and salt for the nut-and-seed topping and set it aside for serving.

3. Toss the cut radishes in a large bowl with the flavorful mixture of butter, miso, honey, and salt.

4. Arrange the radishes cut side down on a lined baking sheet and roast on the lowest rack of the oven at 500 degrees for 10 minutes. Check the cut side to make sure they are nicely browned.

5. Meanwhile, whisk together the lemon juice, miso, honey, olive oil, salt, and pepper in a large bowl to make the dressing. Add the radish greens and toss to coat them evenly.

6. Spread a portion of the yogurt-tahini sauce on each serving plate. Top with the roasted radishes and their greens, then sprinkle the pistachio mixture over the top.

1 tablespoon unsalted butter
1 shallot, minced
Salt and pepper
1 pound radishes, trimmed and halved if small or quartered if large
⅓ cup chicken or vegetable broth
2 teaspoons minced fresh chives

1. Melt butter in 12-inch skillet over medium-high heat. Add shallot and ¼ teaspoon salt, and cook until softened, 2 to 3 minutes. Add radishes and broth, cover, and cook until radishes are tender, about 10 minutes, stirring halfway through cooking.

2. Uncover and continue to cook until liquid thickens slightly, about 1 minute. Stir in chives and season with salt and pepper to taste. Serve.

VARIATION
Creamy Braised Radishes with Garlic and Thyme
Omit chives. Substitute 3 minced garlic cloves for shallot and cook until fragrant, about 30 seconds. Reduce broth to ¼ cup and add 2 tablespoons heavy cream and 1 teaspoon minced fresh thyme to skillet with radishes.

～

QUICK PICKLED RADISHES
Makes 1 cup   Total time: 25 minutes
WHY THIS RECIPE WORKS *With their distinctive lime aroma and clean, fresh bite, quick-pickled radishes are a delicious staple in many Mexican kitchens, used to add a layer of crunch and liveliness to countless dishes. Cutting our radishes into thin slices gave us delicate, elegant pickles and exposed a generous amount of surface area to absorb the flavorful brine. Some sugar and a touch of salt were all we needed to balance the bright, aromatic acidity of the lime juice. Thin slices of shallot added a touch of sweetness and character. To enable our radish mixture to move beyond a salad-like consistency and take on true pickle-like flavor and texture, we allowed it to sit at room temperature for 15 minutes—any less and the pickles seemed too raw, any longer and the vegetables became too soft. After draining, the radishes can be served immediately or held in the refrigerator for up to 1 hour. Avoid*

pickling the radishes for longer than 1 hour; they will begin to turn limp, gray, and bitter. Choose radishes that are firm and heavy for their size.

¼ cup lime juice (2 limes)
1 teaspoon sugar
½ teaspoon kosher salt
6 large radishes, trimmed and sliced thin
1 shallot, sliced thin

Whisk lime juice, sugar, and salt in medium bowl until sugar and salt have dissolved. Stir in radishes and shallot and let sit for 15 minutes for flavors to blend (or refrigerate for up to 1 hour). Drain vegetables and serve.

VARIATIONS
Quick Spicy Pickled Radishes
Add 1 jalapeño chile, trimmed and sliced thin, to bowl with radishes.

Quick Lemon-Tarragon Pickled Radishes
Substitute 2 thinly sliced scallions for shallot and lemon juice for lime juice. Add 1 tablespoon chopped fresh tarragon to drained pickles before serving.

～

BAGUETTE WITH RADISHES, BUTTER, AND HERBS
Serves 8 to 12   Total time: 20 minutes
WHY THIS RECIPE WORKS *Leave it to the French to come up with one of the most indulgent, rustic-chic snacks of all time. Crusty baguette, radishes, and butter are a time-tested combination. But often the radishes play second fiddle. Here we wanted to really highlight the vegetable. We started by halving our loaf lengthwise and laying down just enough butter on top to coat both halves. Leaving the baguette whole allowed us to place more radishes on the bread, and made for an impressive presentation. (Easter egg and watermelon radishes are especially pretty.) We shingled thinly sliced radishes all over in a fish-scale pattern, ensuring that each bite was packed with radish flavor. To coax even more flavor out of this dish, we made a simple compound butter with chives and cultured butter. And to complement the*

pepperiness of the radishes, we topped the baguette with a parsley salad for visual contrast and welcome brightness. Of course, this snack wouldn't be complete without a generous sprinkle of sea salt. The success of this recipe depends on high-quality ingredients, including European-style butter, fresh baguette, and in-season radishes.

10 tablespoons European-style unsalted butter, softened
6 tablespoons minced fresh chives
Salt and pepper
1 teaspoon lemon juice
1 teaspoon extra-virgin olive oil
1 cup coarsely chopped fresh parsley
1 (18-inch) baguette, halved lengthwise
8 ounces radishes, trimmed and sliced thin
Flake sea salt

1. Combine butter, ¼ cup chives, ¼ teaspoon salt, and ¼ teaspoon pepper in bowl. Whisk remaining 2 tablespoons chives, lemon juice, and oil in medium bowl. Add parsley and toss to coat. Season with salt and pepper to taste.

2. Spread butter mixture over cut sides of baguette. Shingle radishes evenly over butter and top with parsley salad. Sprinkle with sea salt to taste. Cut baguette crosswise into 12 pieces. Serve.

～

SOUTHWESTERN RADISH AND APPLE SALAD
Serves 4   Total time: 25 minutes
WHY THIS RECIPE WORKS *Peppery radishes, sweet-tart Granny Smith apples, and sharp red onion form the basis of this satisfying but light salad with plenty of crunch. It's a lovely side dish for barbecued chicken but is also substantial enough to stand alone as a refreshing summertime meal. We added avocado and cotija cheese for creamy richness, and a generous amount of cilantro contributed a bright, grassy note. A dressing spiked with cumin and lime continued the southwestern theme, and a sprinkling of toasted pepitas before serving added a final crunchy burst of flavor. If you can't find cotija cheese, use farmer's cheese or a mild feta instead.*

Baguette with Radishes, Butter, and Herbs

Southwestern Radish and Apple Salad

¼ cup extra-virgin olive oil

2 tablespoons lime juice

1 tablespoon rice vinegar

1 tablespoon honey

1 teaspoon ground cumin

1 garlic clove, minced

Salt and pepper

12 ounces radishes, trimmed, each cut into 6 wedges

1 Granny Smith apple, cored and cut into 2-inch-long matchsticks

½ cup thinly sliced red onion

2 avocados, halved, pitted, and cut into ¾-inch pieces

1 cup fresh cilantro leaves

4 ounces cotija cheese, crumbled (1 cup)

⅓ cup pepitas, toasted

Whisk oil, lime juice, vinegar, honey, cumin, garlic, ¾ teaspoon salt, and ¼ teaspoon pepper in large bowl until combined. Add radishes, apple, and onion and toss to coat. Gently fold in avocados, cilantro, and cotija. Season with salt and pepper to taste. Sprinkle with pepitas and serve.

RADISH AND CARROT SLAW WITH SESAME AND SCALLIONS

Serves 6 to 8   Total time: 30 minutes

WHY THIS RECIPE WORKS *Raw radishes have a peppery, mustard-like flavor and crisp texture that makes them ideal for slaw-type salads. But use too many and the resulting sulfurous flavor can be a little overwhelming. Here we wanted to highlight radishes by tempering that pepperiness in a nontraditional slaw. We initially started with a mix of globe radishes, carrots, and Asian pear. Pretreating the carrots with salt and sugar softened them slightly and drew out excess moisture, and this added sugar provided enough sweetness to balance the pungent radishes. But tasters thought that the pear provided a little too much sweetness, so we substituted daikon radish for the pear. Its milder flavor and crisper texture gave the salad lift and a more tempered sweetness. A bright Dijon-based sesame vinaigrette brought plenty of bold flavor, and a handful of scallions contributed welcome savory hits of allium to the slaw.*

1 pound carrots, peeled and grated

¼ cup sugar

Salt and pepper

½ cup vegetable oil

3 tablespoons rice vinegar, plus extra for seasoning

2 tablespoons Dijon mustard

1 tablespoon toasted sesame oil

1 pound radishes, trimmed, halved, and sliced thin

4 ounces daikon radish, peeled and cut into matchsticks

10 scallions, green parts only, sliced thin on bias

1. Toss carrots with sugar and 1 teaspoon salt in colander set over large bowl and let sit until partially wilted and reduced in volume by one-third, about 15 minutes. Press, but do not squeeze, to drain, then blot dry with paper towels.

2. Whisk oil, vinegar, mustard, sesame oil, ½ teaspoon salt, and ½ teaspoon pepper in separate large bowl until combined. Add carrots, radishes, daikon radish, and scallions and toss to combine. Season with salt, pepper, and extra vinegar to taste. Serve immediately.

SESAME NOODLES WITH RADISHES, CUCUMBER, AND CARROT

Serves 4 to 6   Total time: 30 minutes

WHY THIS RECIPE WORKS *Served at room temperature or chilled, sesame noodles with crunchy vegetables make an ideal light warm-weather meal. Our choice of radishes, scallions, cucumber, and carrots both bulked up the noodles and provided peppery, oniony, sweet vegetable flavors and crunchy, juicy texture. We relied on everyday pantry staples to achieve the requisite sweet, nutty, addictive flavor of authentic-tasting sesame noodles. Chunky peanut butter and toasted sesame seeds, ground together in the blender, made the perfect stand-in for hard-to-find Asian sesame paste. Garlic, ginger, soy sauce, rice vinegar, hot sauce, and brown sugar rounded out the flavors of the sauce, and thinning it with hot water achieved the best texture for coating the noodles without being gloppy. To avoid the pitfalls of most sesame noodle*

recipes—gummy noodles and bland, pasty sauce—we rinsed the cooked noodles to rid them of excess starch. Tossing them with sesame oil separately, before adding the sauce, also helped keep the noodles from absorbing too much sauce and becoming pasty. We like conventional chunky peanut butter here; it tends to be sweeter than natural or old-fashioned versions. If you cannot find fresh Chinese egg noodles, substitute 12 ounces dried spaghetti or linguine.

SAUCE

5 tablespoons soy sauce

¼ cup chunky peanut butter

3 tablespoons sesame seeds, toasted

2 tablespoons rice vinegar

2 tablespoons packed light brown sugar

1 tablespoon grated fresh ginger

2 garlic cloves, minced

1 teaspoon hot sauce

½ cup hot water

NOODLES AND VEGETABLES

1 pound fresh Chinese noodles

2 tablespoons toasted sesame oil

5 radishes, trimmed, halved, and sliced thin

4 scallions, sliced thin on bias

1 English cucumber, halved lengthwise and sliced thin

1 carrot, peeled and grated

1 tablespoon chopped fresh cilantro

1 tablespoon toasted sesame seeds

1. **For the sauce** Process all ingredients except water in blender until smooth, about 30 seconds. With blender running, add hot water, 1 tablespoon at a time, until sauce has consistency of heavy cream (you may not need all of water).

2. **For the noodles and vegetables** Meanwhile, bring 4 quarts water to boil in large pot. Add noodles and cook, stirring often, until tender. Drain noodles, rinse with cold water, and drain again, leaving noodles slightly wet.

3. Transfer noodles to large bowl and toss with oil. Add radishes, scallions, cucumber, carrot, cilantro, and sauce and toss to combine. Sprinkle individual portions with sesame seeds before serving.

ROASTED CHICKEN WITH RADISHES, SPINACH, AND BACON

Serves 4   Total time: 50 minutes

WHY THIS RECIPE WORKS *The spicy crunch of radishes and earthy softness of spinach complement chicken that has been luxuriously cooked in bacon fat in this rustic chicken-and-veg weeknight dinner. We first browned the chicken pieces in rendered bacon fat on the stovetop, and then transferred the skillet to the oven to finish cooking. Cooking the chicken in the bacon fat ensured both crisp, crackly skin and a subtle smoky flavor. After it came out of the oven, we removed the chicken from the skillet and then quickly cooked the radishes and spinach in the fat left in the skillet. To ensure crispy chicken skin, resist the urge to move the chicken while browning it in step 2.*

- 2 slices bacon, chopped fine
- 3 pounds bone-in chicken pieces (split breasts cut in half, drumsticks, and/or thighs), trimmed
  Salt and pepper
- 10 ounces radishes, trimmed and quartered
- 2 garlic cloves, minced
- 10 ounces (10 cups) baby spinach
- 2 teaspoons lemon juice, plus lemon wedges for serving

1. Adjust oven rack to middle position and heat oven to 450 degrees. Cook bacon in 12-inch oven-safe skillet over medium-high heat until crisp, about 5 minutes. Using slotted spoon, transfer bacon to paper towel–lined plate; set aside for serving.

2. Pat chicken dry with paper towels and season with salt and pepper. Heat fat left in skillet over medium-high heat until just smoking. Brown chicken skin side down, about 5 minutes. Flip chicken, transfer skillet to oven, and roast until breasts register 160 degrees and drumsticks/thighs register 175 degrees, about 15 minutes.

3. Using pot holder, remove skillet from oven. Being careful of hot skillet handle, transfer chicken skin side up to serving platter and let rest while preparing vegetables.

4. Pour off all but 1 tablespoon fat from skillet. Add radishes and ½ teaspoon salt and cook over medium-high heat until tender, about 2 minutes. Stir in garlic and cook until fragrant, about 30 seconds. Stir in spinach, 1 handful at a time, and cook until wilted, about 2 minutes. Off heat, stir in reserved bacon and lemon juice. Serve chicken with vegetables and lemon wedges.

VIETNAMESE PORK BANH MI

Serves 4   Total time: 50 minutes
(plus 30 minutes chilling time)

WHY THIS RECIPE WORKS *Banh mi is an iconic Vietnamese street food, consisting of a soft-style Vietnamese baguette split in half and loaded with all kinds of meats and vegetables. Variations abound, but in all of them, the true star is the pickled daikon radish and carrots. We set out to develop a recipe with the perfect balance of sugar, salt, tang, and depth—and with the perfect crunch. We tried rice vinegar, but most tasters found this too sweet. For a fresher approach, we tried lime juice with a touch of sugar; we loved this flavor. A splash of fish sauce provided a savory note. We paired the pickles with lightly charred, marinated pork and decadent chicken liver pâté. A simple sriracha mayo plus plenty of cucumbers, jalapeño, and cilantro completed a rich, satisfying flavor profile. You can find pâté in the gourmet cheese section of most well-stocked supermarkets. Be sure to use a smooth-textured pâté, not a coarse country pâté. Avoid pickling the radishes and carrots for longer than 1 hour; the radishes will begin to turn limp, gray, and bitter.*

PICKLES

- 1½ teaspoons fish sauce
- 1½ teaspoons packed dark brown sugar
- ½ teaspoon grated lime zest plus ¼ cup lime juice (2 limes)
- ¼ teaspoon salt
- 8 ounces daikon radish, peeled and cut into 2-inch-long matchsticks
- 1 small carrot, peeled and cut into 2-inch-long matchsticks

BANH MI

- 1 (12-ounce) pork tenderloin, trimmed and halved crosswise
- 3 tablespoons fish sauce
- 1 teaspoon grated lime zest plus 2 tablespoons lime juice
- 2 tablespoons packed dark brown sugar
- ½ teaspoon red pepper flakes
- 1 tablespoon vegetable oil
- ⅓ cup mayonnaise
- 4 teaspoons sriracha sauce
- 6 ounces chicken or duck liver pâté
- 1 (18-inch) baguette, ends trimmed, cut crosswise into 4 equal lengths, and halved lengthwise
- ½ English cucumber, halved lengthwise and sliced thin
- 1 jalapeño chile, stemmed and sliced thin
- 1 cup fresh cilantro leaves and stems, trimmed and cut into 2-inch lengths

1. For the pickles Whisk fish sauce, sugar, lime zest and juice, and salt in medium bowl until sugar and salt have dissolved. Stir in radish and carrot and refrigerate for at least 15 minutes or up to 1 hour. Drain vegetables and set aside for serving.

2. For the banh mi Meanwhile, place pork pieces between 2 layers of plastic wrap and pound to ¼ inch thickness. Whisk fish sauce, lime juice, sugar, and pepper flakes in large bowl until sugar has dissolved. Add pork and toss to coat. Cover and refrigerate for at least 30 minutes or up to 1 hour.

3. Remove pork from marinade and pat dry with paper towels. Heat oil in 12-inch nonstick skillet over medium-high heat until shimmering. Add pork, reduce heat to medium, and cook until pork is well-browned and registers 140 degrees, about 4 minutes per side. Transfer pork to cutting board and let rest for 5 to 10 minutes.

4. Whisk mayonnaise, sriracha, and lime zest together in small bowl. Slice pork ¼ inch thick. Spread pâté evenly over cut sides of baguette, followed by mayonnaise mixture. Layer pickled vegetables, pork, cucumber, jalapeño, and cilantro evenly over bottom halves. Top with baguette tops and serve.

Vietnamese Pork Banh Mi

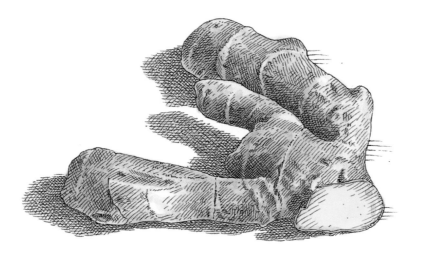

R H I Z O M E S

Reading this, you might be asking yourself: What kind of vegetable is a rhizome? A rhizome, unlike a root vegetable, is simply a modified plant stem that grows underground, from which new plants can emerge.

GINGER is the rhizome of a flowering plant in the same family as turmeric and cardamom (you can actually grow a ginger plant from the rhizomes found in grocery stores). Native to southeast Asia, ginger has been used for medicinal and culinary purposes for thousands of years. It stars in our sweet-spicy Ginger Lemonade and homemade Pickled Ginger, and it's an indispensable ingredient in Tandoori Chicken with Raita and Spicy Citrus-Ginger Grilled Pork Tenderloin Steaks.

HORSERADISH has been around since 1500 BC and is often considered the world's first condiment. This rhizome has been praised throughout history and even into modern times for its medicinal purposes. We simply think it tastes delicious. Among our favorite ways to use it are in Fresh Horseradish Bloody Mary and our Shrimp Cocktail with Horseradish Cocktail Sauce. For a showstopping dish featuring a horseradish trifecta, see our Horseradish-Crusted Beef Tenderloin.

SUNCHOKES, also called Jerusalem artichokes, are neither from Jerusalem nor are they artichokes. These knobby-looking North American natives are part of the sunflower genus and were quite popular during the colonial era. In modern times, farmers' markets have brought attention back to this neglected rhizome. They have a tender, creamy texture and sweet, vegetal taste like a cross between potatoes and artichokes. Our Fried Sunchokes are a delicious way to introduce yourself to them, and their deep, nutty qualities are highlighted in our sumptuous Sunchoke Chowder.

GINGER Fresh ginger is available year-round. For short-term storage of a couple of weeks or so, we've found the best method is to simply store it in the refrigerator unwrapped.

There are two good methods we've discovered for storing ginger for several weeks or longer. The first method is to peel it, cut it into chunks, and store it in the freezer in a zipper-lock bag, removing chunks as needed (you can grate it directly from the freezer). The second method is to peel it, cut it into chunks, and store it submerged in vodka in the refrigerator. The alcohol inhibits the natural enzymes that cause ginger's texture to break down over time.

HORSERADISH You can purchase either fresh horseradish root in the vegetable aisle or prepared horseradish in the refrigerated section or condiment aisle. We learned in the test kitchen that prepared horseradishes can taste strikingly different. We prefer refrigerated varieties, particularly those with finely shredded textures and sinus-clearing heat; look for labels that list simply horseradish, vinegar, and salt. The shelf-stable products found in the condiment aisle are full of additives and have a weaker flavor and mushier texture than refrigerated horseradish. Bottled horseradish will keep for three to four months in the refrigerator, though its potency will decline sooner. Fresh horseradish root will keep unwrapped in the refrigerator for a few weeks.

SUNCHOKES Sunchokes are available from fall through spring. When shopping for them, look for those with tan or light yellow skin, with no soft or green spots or signs of sprouting or blemishes. Choose those that are to clean and peel. Although they look sturdy and potato-like, they actually bruise fairly easily. Sunchokes will keep wrapped in paper towels in a plastic produce bag in the refrigerator for about one week.

Peeling and Grating Ginger

1. Remove peel by scraping with spoon.

2. Grate using either rasp-style grater or box grater, holding ginger so fibers run perpendicularly across teeth. (Since fibers in ginger run from top to bottom of root, positioning cut end of ginger perpendicular to grater's surface so that fibers meet teeth of grater straight on will result in clogged teeth.)

Cleaning Sunchokes

1. Since sunchokes are tubers, they will be dirty. Be sure to wash and scrub sunchokes of all dirt.

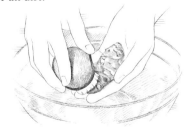

2. We also recommend peeling sunchokes before cooking to remove their fibrous skin. Dry sunchokes thoroughly before cooking.

Peeling Horseradish

Peel horseradish root, then grate it using rasp-style grater.

Fresh Horseradish Bloody Mary

GINGER LEMONADE

Serves 6 to 8   Total time: 20 minutes (plus 1 hour chilling time)

WHY THIS RECIPE WORKS *From-scratch lemonade is a wonderful thirst-quencher all by itself, but incorporating some pungent, sweetly spicy ginger takes this beverage to another level entirely. To get there, we simply mashed (or muddled) lemon slices and grated fresh ginger with granulated sugar to extract the oils contained in the peel and pulp and punch up their flavor. We then whisked in some water and freshly squeezed lemon juice—no simple syrup needed. A bit more whisking was all that was needed to dissolve the sugar. Before serving, we strained the mixture and chilled it for an hour. When purchasing lemons, choose large ones that give to gentle pressure; hard lemons have thicker skin and yield less juice. Lemons are commonly waxed to prevent moisture loss, increase shelf life, and protect them from bruising during shipping. Scrub them with a vegetable brush under running water to remove wax, or buy organic lemons. Don't worry about the seeds in the extracted juice; the entire juice mixture is strained at the end of the recipe. Serve poured over ice, if desired.*

13 lemons (2 scrubbed and sliced thin, 11 juiced to yield 2 cups)
1½ cups sugar
3 tablespoons grated fresh ginger
Pinch salt (optional)
7 cups cold water

Using potato masher, mash half of lemon slices, sugar, ginger, and salt, if using, in large bowl until sugar is completely wet. Whisk in water and lemon juice until sugar has completely dissolved. Strain mixture through fine-mesh strainer set over large bowl or pitcher, pressing on solids to extract as much juice as possible; discard solids. Add remaining lemon slices to strained lemonade and chill for at least 1 hour before serving.

FRESH HORSERADISH BLOODY MARY

Makes 6 cocktails   Total time: 15 minutes

WHY THIS RECIPE WORKS *Most bloody Marys have plenty of capsaicin burn from hot sauce but fall flat when it comes to the clean, sinus-clearing heat we get from horseradish. We remedied that problem by replacing timid jarred prepared horseradish with the Chuck Norris roundhouse kick of freshly grated horseradish. Horseradish heat dissipates fairly quickly once grated, so the prepared stuff can simply never compete with fresh. To add another layer of heady heat, we included dry mustard, as both mustard and horseradish (along with wasabi) get their eye-watering sting from the same natural compound. But this drink isn't all bite—it's also an umami bomb with fish sauce, Worcestershire sauce, and Old Bay in the mix. Lemon juice brings everything into balance with some fresh acidity. In addition to lemon wedges and celery ribs, we often like to garnish these cocktails with skewered olives, cocktail onions, and cornichons.*

BLOODY MARY BASE

3¾ cups tomato juice, chilled
¼ cup lemon juice
¼ cup finely grated fresh horseradish root
2 tablespoons Worcestershire sauce
1 tablespoon fish sauce
1 tablespoon dry mustard
1 tablespoon Old Bay seasoning

COCKTAILS

Ice
1 cup plus 2 tablespoons vodka
1 lemon, cut into 6 wedges
6 celery ribs

1. For the bloody Mary base Whisk all ingredients together in large bowl or pitcher. (Base can be refrigerated for up to 24 hours.)

2. For each cocktail Fill tall glass with ice. Combine ¾ cup bloody Mary base, 3 tablespoons vodka, and ¼ cup ice in cocktail shaker and vigorously shake for 30 seconds. Strain cocktail into prepared glass and garnish with lemon wedge and celery rib. Serve immediately.

PREPARED HORSERADISH

Makes two 1-cup jars   Total time: 15 minutes

WHY THIS RECIPE WORKS *Homemade horseradish has a bright, spicy flavor that blows any store-bought alternative out of the water. Not only does making your own result in a fresher horseradish, but the signature heat of the homemade version also packs even more of a punch. We set out to create our own recipe for this piquant condiment and found the process to be surprisingly simple. Unlike store-bought brands, many of which contain a long list of ingredients, our recipe calls for only three: horseradish root, vinegar, and salt. We peeled the horseradish root and chopped it into pieces small enough to be pulsed in a food processor and then processed to a pulpy consistency. Vinegar balances the spicy bite of fresh horseradish root. Throughout our testing, tasters preferred cider vinegar, due to its sweet tang. We simply drizzled the vinegar into the food processor while blending the horseradish. A teaspoon of salt helped balance the acidity and intensified the spicy, earthy flavor of the horseradish.*

10 ounces fresh horseradish root, peeled and chopped coarse (2 cups)
1 teaspoon kosher salt
1 cup cider vinegar

1. Pulse horseradish and salt in food processor until coarsely chopped, about 15 pulses, scraping down bowl as needed. With processor running, slowly add vinegar until incorporated and mixture has pulp-like consistency, about 1 minute, scraping down bowl as necessary.

2. Portion horseradish into two 1-cup jars. (Horseradish can be refrigerated for up to 3 weeks.)

VARIATIONS

Creamy Horseradish
Serve this with all types of smoked fish.
Lightly squeeze excess liquid from ½ cup prepared horseradish, then transfer to small bowl. Stir in ¼ cup mayonnaise, ¼ teaspoon pepper, and ⅛ teaspoon salt. Serve. (Makes ½ cup. Sauce can be refrigerated for up to 3 days.)

Creamy Horseradish-Mustard Sauce
Whisk 6 tablespoons mayonnaise, 2 tablespoons prepared horseradish, 1 tablespoon whole-grain mustard, 1 minced garlic clove, ⅛ teaspoon salt, ⅛ teaspoon pepper, and dash hot sauce together. Serve. (Makes ½ cup. Sauce can be refrigerated for up to 3 days.)

PICKLED GINGER

**Makes 1 cup   Total time: 30 minutes
(plus 4 days refrigeration time)**

WHY THIS RECIPE WORKS *Pickling zesty ginger and serving it alongside sushi is a classic presentation for this healthful rhizome. Traditionally, pickled young ginger is eaten between bites of sushi, as a natural palate cleanser. Because young ginger isn't easily found in common grocery stores all year long, we wanted to develop this recipe using the readily available mature ginger root. On our first try, our thin strips of pickled mature ginger were tough and fibrous. So then we sliced the root thin against the grain into small coins to eliminate the tougher texture and added sugar to our recipe to balance the pungency of the mature ginger and tang of the vinegar. We also found that a brief 40-second boil helped to soften our ginger and mellow its flavor. The ginger needs to be refrigerated for four days to allow the brine to fully penetrate and pickle the vegetable. Your pickled ginger may turn a blush pink; this is due to pigments called anthocyanins, which turn pink when in contact with acid. Slicing the ginger paper-thin is essential to the success of the recipe; we recommend using a mandoline or V-slicer to do this. If using a glass storage container, be sure to fill it with hot water to warm, then drain it before packing it with the ginger.*

- 7 ounces fresh ginger, peeled and sliced paper-thin against grain
- ½ cup rice vinegar
- 3 tablespoons sugar
- 1½ teaspoons kosher salt

1. Bring 2 quarts water to boil in medium saucepan over high heat. Add ginger and boil until slightly darker and softened, about 40 seconds. Drain ginger and pat dry with paper towels. Transfer to airtight container, leaving ½ inch of headspace.

2. Bring vinegar, sugar, and salt to boil in now-empty saucepan over medium-high heat, stirring occasionally to dissolve sugar. Pour hot brine over ginger and let cool to room temperature. Cover and refrigerate for at least 4 days before serving. (Pickled ginger can be refrigerated for at least 6 months; ginger flavor will mellow over time.)

SHRIMP COCKTAIL WITH HORSERADISH COCKTAIL SAUCE

**Serves 6   Total time: 35 minutes
(plus 1 hour chilling time)**

WHY THIS RECIPE WORKS *Our take on this party staple boasts perfectly tender, sweet shrimp and a lively, horseradish-forward cocktail sauce. Rather than simply boiling the shrimp in water, we cooked them more gently in a simple mixture of water and bold seasonings to infuse the shrimp with as much flavor as possible. Old Bay seasoning contributed a perceptible depth of flavor to the shrimp. To avoid overcooking, we brought the water and aromatics to a boil, took the pot off the heat, and then added the shrimp, leaving them to poach for 7 minutes. This method delivered perfectly tender, not rubbery, shrimp every time. We prefer our Prepared Horseradish (page 377); if you purchase prepared horseradish, buy the refrigerated kind, not the shelf-stable kind, which contains preservatives and additives.*

SHRIMP
- 2 teaspoons lemon juice
- 2 bay leaves
- 1 teaspoon salt
- 1 teaspoon black peppercorns
- 1 teaspoon Old Bay seasoning
- 1 pound extra-large shrimp (21 to 25 per pound), peeled and deveined

HORSERADISH COCKTAIL SAUCE
- 1 cup ketchup
- 2 tablespoons lemon juice
- 2 tablespoons prepared horseradish, plus extra for seasoning
- 2 teaspoons hot sauce, plus extra for seasoning
- ⅛ teaspoon salt
- ⅛ teaspoon pepper

1. **For the shrimp** Bring lemon juice, bay leaves, salt, peppercorns, Old Bay, and 1 quart water to boil in medium saucepan for 2 minutes. Remove pan from heat and add shrimp. Cover and steep off heat until shrimp are firm and pink, about 7 minutes.

2. Meanwhile, fill large bowl with ice water. Drain shrimp, plunge immediately into ice water to stop cooking, and let sit until cool, about 2 minutes. Drain shrimp and transfer to bowl. Cover and refrigerate until thoroughly chilled, at least 1 hour.

3. **For the cocktail sauce** Stir all ingredients together in small bowl and season with additional horseradish and hot sauce as desired. (Cocktail sauce can be refrigerated for up to 24 hours.) Arrange shrimp and sauce on serving platter and serve.

FRIED SUNCHOKES

Serves 4 to 6   Total time: 1 hour

WHY THIS RECIPE WORKS *Though they may look like knobby potatoes, sunchokes do not contain any starch. Instead, these rhizomes are rich in inulin, a soluble fiber that is mostly indigestible. Inulin is also what gives sunchokes their earthy, sweet flavor. Since—like potatoes—sunchokes fry up really well, we wanted to achieve supercrispy sunchokes with a creamy, tender interior. Initially we tried oven-roasting the sunchokes until they were soft and finishing them in a hotter oven. Unfortunately, they turned leathery and burnt, because we weren't driving off enough moisture quickly enough to get those desirable crispy edges. So we turned to deep frying: First we fried the sunchokes whole to get rid of some moisture and cook the interiors, and then we increased the temperature to crisp them up. These sunchokes were much crisper and had a deep golden-brown color. But our tasters wanted an even higher ratio of crispy edges to creamy interior, so we took a page out of our potato playbook and smashed them after the initial frying. This vastly increased the number of crags, edges, nooks, and crannies in each sunchoke, and resulted in ultracrispy, crunchy fried sunchokes. These bites are great on their own*

Shrimp Cocktail with
Horseradish Cocktail Sauce

with a squeeze of lemon, but we like to jazz them up with Old Bay or even a spicy chili oil once they're out of the fryer. Use a Dutch oven that holds 6 quarts or more for this recipe.

2 quarts peanut or vegetable oil
2 pounds sunchokes, unpeeled
Salt and pepper

1. Add oil to large Dutch oven until it measures 1½ inches deep and heat over medium-high heat to 250 degrees. Carefully add sunchokes to oil and cook, stirring occasionally, until tender and knife slips easily in and out of flesh, 30 to 35 minutes.

2. Using wire skimmer or slotted spoon, transfer sunchokes to rimmed baking sheet and let cool slightly, about 10 minutes. Space sunchokes evenly over sheet and place second baking sheet on top. Press down firmly on top sheet until sunchokes are flattened to ½-inch thickness.

3. Meanwhile, heat oil to 375 degrees. Set wire rack in top sheet and line with triple layer of paper towels. Carefully return sunchokes to oil and fry, stirring occasionally, until deep golden brown and crispy, 5 to 7 minutes. Adjust burner, if necessary, to maintain oil temperature between 350 and 375 degrees. Transfer sunchokes to prepared rack and season with salt and pepper to taste. Serve.

VARIATIONS

Fried Sunchokes with Old Bay and Lemon
Toss fried sunchokes with 2 teaspoons Old Bay seasoning and 1 teaspoon grated lemon zest before seasoning with salt and pepper. Serve with lemon wedges.

Fried Sunchokes with Mexican Chile Oil
Microwave 2 tablespoons vegetable oil, 1 teaspoon sesame seeds, ½ teaspoon cayenne pepper, ½ teaspoon ground chipotle chile powder, ¼ teaspoon garlic powder, ⅛ teaspoon cocoa powder, ⅛ teaspoon salt, pinch cinnamon, and pinch cumin in large bowl, stirring occasionally, until fragrant and bubbling, 1 to 3 minutes. Toss fried sunchokes with oil mixture before seasoning with salt and pepper. Serve with lime wedges.

SUNCHOKE CHOWDER

Serves 6 to 8   Total time: 1 hour

WHY THIS RECIPE WORKS *Sunchokes have an earthy, sweet, nutty flavor that makes them ideal for hearty soups. Here we wanted to highlight that flavor in a rich, wintery chowder. Since sunchokes do not contain any starch, they blend up well into purees and soups without developing a gummy or gluey texture. We started by cooking sunchokes in an aromatic base of butter, onions, and water and blending this mixture with some cream. Tasters enjoyed the richness of the chowder, but wanted more depth and sweetness. So, to bring more robust flavor, we tried caramelizing the sunchokes in butter before adding the aromatics, which produced a deep brown fond in the pot. We deglazed the mixture with white ale, which added sweetness and malty notes. Our team loved this combination, and found the finished chowder deeply satisfying. For some textural contrast, we reserved some caramelized sunchokes to stir in at the end, and sprinkled on some toasted almonds for crunch. We prefer to use a mild white ale in this recipe, but you can substitute a mild lager, such as Budweiser, if desired.*

4 tablespoons unsalted butter
1½ pounds sunchokes, unpeeled, cut into ½-inch pieces
2 onions, chopped
Salt
1 garlic clove, minced
2½ cups water, plus extra as needed
1 cup white ale
1 cup heavy cream
¼ cup sliced almonds, toasted
2 tablespoons minced fresh chives
3 tablespoons crème fraîche

1. Melt butter in Dutch oven over medium heat. Add sunchokes and cook, stirring occasionally, until browned and tender (paring knife should slip easily in and out of sunchokes), 15 to 20 minutes. Measure out 1 cup cooked sunchokes and set aside.

2. Stir onions and 1½ teaspoons salt into pot with remaining sunchokes and cook over medium heat until softened, about 5 minutes. Stir in garlic and cook until fragrant, about 30 seconds. Stir in water and ale, scraping up any browned bits, and bring to simmer. Cover,

reduce heat to medium-low, and cook until sunchokes are very tender and easily break apart when poked with paring knife, 20 to 25 minutes. Stir in cream.

3. Working in batches, process soup in blender until smooth, about 1 minute. Strain soup through fine-mesh strainer set over now-empty pot, pressing on solids to extract as much liquid as possible. Stir in reserved sunchokes and bring to brief simmer over medium-low heat. Adjust consistency with extra hot water as needed. Season with salt to taste. Sprinkle individual portions with almonds and chives and dollop with crème fraîche before serving.

GINGERY CHICKEN TERIYAKI

Serves 4   Total time: 35 minutes

WHY THIS RECIPE WORKS *Too many chicken teriyaki recipes are lackluster, with overmarinated chicken chunks shellacked in a one-dimensional corn-syrupy sauce. They're a long way from the sweet-salty recipe promised in the name (in Japanese, teri means "shine"—referring to the sauce—and yaki means "broiling"). We wanted a straightforward, authentic recipe for crisp, moist chicken with a strong gingery punch. To stand up to the bold sauce, we chose bone-in, skin-on chicken thighs. We set a weight on top of the chicken as it cooked (we used a heavy Dutch oven), which helped to brown a greater surface area of the chicken evenly, as well as to aid in pressing out most of the fat. Our quick mixture of soy sauce, sugar, mirin, ginger, and garlic made an incredible sauce that far surpassed anything from a bottle. A splatter screen (or an inverted large strainer) helps control the splatter that occurs when the second side of the chicken browns. Mirin can be found in the international section of most major supermarkets and in most Asian markets. If you cannot find it, substitute 2 tablespoons of white wine and 1 teaspoon of sugar.*

8 (5- to 7-ounce) bone-in chicken thighs, trimmed
Pepper
2 teaspoons vegetable oil
½ cup soy sauce

SUNCHOKE CHOWDER

This unusual chowder is truly soul-satisfying, homey yet elegant all at once. Since sunchokes don't contain starch, they transform nicely into soups and purees without becoming pasty or gummy. We caramelized the sunchokes in butter before adding the aromatics, which produced a deep brown fond. Pureeing most of the sunchokes into the chowder and adding some whole pieces to the finished soup ensured textural variety.

1. Scrub the sunchokes clean, but do not peel them. Cut the sunchokes into ½-inch pieces.

2. Melt the butter in the Dutch oven and cook the sunchokes until browned and tender, 15 to 20 minutes. Remove and reserve 1 cup of the cooked sunchokes to stir in at the end.

3. After stirring in and cooking the onions and garlic, add the water and ale to the pot, scrape up any browned bits, bring to a simmer, and cook over medium-low heat until the sunchokes are very tender, 20 to 25 minutes. Stir in the cream.

4. Working in batches as needed, transfer the hot soup to a blender and blend until smooth, about 1 minute for each batch.

5. Strain the soup through a fine-mesh strainer back into the now-empty pot, pressing on the solids to extract as much liquid as possible. Stir in the reserved sunchokes and bring back to a simmer to reheat.

6. Sprinkle individual portions with almonds and chives, and dollop with the crème fraîche.

½ cup sugar

2 tablespoons mirin

2 teaspoons grated fresh ginger

1 garlic clove, minced

½ teaspoon cornstarch

2 scallions, sliced thin on bias

1. Pat chicken thighs dry with paper towels and season with pepper. Heat oil in 12-inch nonstick skillet over medium-high heat until just smoking. Carefully lay chicken skin side down in skillet. Place weighted Dutch oven on top of chicken and cook until skin is deep mahogany brown and very crisp, 15 to 20 minutes. (Chicken should be moderately brown after 10 minutes. If it is very brown, reduce heat; if it is still pale, increase heat.)

2. Remove weighted pot and flip chicken. Reduce heat to medium and continue to cook, without weight, until chicken is lightly browned on second side and registers 175 degrees, about 2 minutes; transfer to serving platter.

3. Whisk soy sauce, sugar, mirin, ginger, garlic, and cornstarch together in bowl. Pour off fat from skillet, then add soy sauce mixture and bring to simmer over medium heat. Cook, stirring occasionally, until sauce is thick and glossy, about 2 minutes. Stir in any accumulated chicken juices. Return chicken to skillet and turn to coat with sauce. Return chicken to serving platter, sprinkle with scallions, and serve, passing remaining sauce separately.

TANDOORI CHICKEN WITH RAITA

Serves 4   Total time: 1 hour 15 minutes

WHY THIS RECIPE WORKS *Traditional tandoori chicken is marinated in yogurt and a blend of spices and roasted in a superhot tandoor oven to produce tender meat beneath beautifully charred skin. The spice mix can vary, but fresh ginger is an integral component. To make an authentic-tasting version at home, we started by peeling the skin off of bone-in chicken parts and slashing the surface of the meat so the flavors could penetrate deeply. We built a fragrant paste, blooming ginger and garlic in oil before adding garam masala, cumin, and chili powder*

and binding everything together with lime juice. We used this paste twice, applying some directly to the exposed meat and stirring the rest into whole-milk yogurt. The spices imparted plenty of flavor and the yogurt marinade gave our chicken tang. Arranged on a wire rack placed in a rimmed baking sheet, our chicken roasted gently and evenly in a moderate oven, and a final few minutes under the broiler delivered the charred finish we wanted. A cool, creamy raita sauce offered the perfect complement to our flavorful tandoori-style chicken. If using large chicken breasts (about 1 pound each), cut each breast into three pieces.

RAITA

1 cup plain whole-milk yogurt

2 tablespoons minced fresh cilantro

1 garlic clove, minced

Salt

Cayenne pepper

CHICKEN

2 tablespoons vegetable oil

6 garlic cloves, minced

2 tablespoons grated fresh ginger

1 tablespoon garam masala

2 teaspoons ground cumin

2 teaspoons chili powder

1 cup plain whole-milk yogurt

¼ cup lime juice (2 limes), plus lime wedges for serving

2 teaspoons salt

3 pounds bone-in chicken pieces (split breasts cut in half, drumsticks, and/or thighs), skin removed, trimmed

1. For the raita Combine yogurt, cilantro, and garlic in bowl and season with salt and cayenne to taste. Refrigerate until ready to serve. (Raita can be refrigerated for up to 24 hours.)

2. For the chicken Heat oil in 10-inch skillet over medium heat until shimmering. Add garlic and ginger and cook until fragrant, about 30 seconds. Stir in garam masala, cumin, and chili powder and continue to cook until fragrant, about 30 seconds. Transfer half of garlic mixture to medium bowl, stir in yogurt and 2 tablespoons lime juice, and set aside. In large bowl, combine remaining garlic mixture, remaining 2 tablespoons lime juice, and salt.

3. Using sharp knife, make 2 or 3 short slashes into each piece of chicken. Transfer chicken to bowl with garlic–lime juice mixture and rub until all pieces are evenly coated. Let sit at room temperature for 30 minutes.

4. Adjust oven rack to upper-middle position and heat oven to 325 degrees. Set wire rack in aluminum foil–lined rimmed baking sheet. Pour yogurt mixture over chicken and toss until chicken is evenly coated with thick layer. Arrange chicken pieces, scored side down, on prepared rack. Discard excess yogurt mixture. Roast chicken until breast pieces register 125 degrees and thighs and/or drumsticks register 130 degrees, 15 to 25 minutes. (Smaller pieces may cook faster than larger pieces. Remove pieces from oven as they reach correct temperature.)

5. Adjust oven rack 6 inches from broiler element and heat broiler. Return chicken to wire rack, scored side up, and broil until chicken is lightly charred in spots and breast pieces register 160 degrees and thighs and/or drumsticks register 175 degrees, 8 to 15 minutes. Transfer chicken to serving dish and let rest for 10 minutes. Serve with raita and lime wedges.

HORSERADISH-CRUSTED BEEF TENDERLOIN

Serves 6   Total time: 1 hour 45 minutes (plus 1 hour sitting time and 20 minutes resting time)

WHY THIS RECIPE WORKS *A crisp, pungent horseradish crust is a classic and elegant flavor pairing with mild beef tenderloin, but with many recipes, when carving time comes around, the crust falls right off the meat in patches. Not so with our tenderloin, which features a golden crust that stays put when serving. It also has a triple whammy of horseradish flavor: first, a paste that's rubbed on the tenderloin; second, a coating blend of bread crumbs, homemade potato chips, and horseradish; and third, a creamy horseradish sauce for serving. The potato chips may seem unusual, but they kept their crunch and contributed lots of flavor, especially since we made our own by frying shredded potato in oil until crispy. For the beef, we chose a center-cut roast for its uniform shape. To* make the crust adhere to the meat after being sliced, we used gelatin. Because both meat and gelatin are made up of linear proteins that form tight bonds with each other, the gelatin mixture bound the coating firmly to the meat, yet yielded slightly as we cut it. And to prevent the crust from turning soggy from meat juices released during cooking, we seared the meat in a hot skillet and let it rest so that its juices could drain off before applying the paste and the crumbs. Then we coated only the top and sides of the tenderloin, leaving an "opening" on the bottom for meat juices to escape as it roasted. Center-cut beef tenderloin roasts are sometimes sold as Châteaubriand. We prefer our Prepared Horseradish (page 377); if you purchase prepared horseradish, buy the refrigerated kind, not the shelf-stable kind, which contains preservatives and additives. If using table salt, reduce the amount in step 1 to 1½ teaspoons. Add the gelatin to the horseradish paste at the last moment or the mixture will become unspreadable.

ROAST

- 1 (2-pound) center-cut beef tenderloin roast, trimmed
  Kosher salt and pepper
- 3 tablespoons panko bread crumbs
- 1 cup plus 2 teaspoons vegetable oil
- 1 small russet potato (about 6 ounces), peeled and grated
- ¼ cup prepared horseradish, drained
- 1½ teaspoons mayonnaise
- 1½ teaspoons Dijon mustard
- ½ teaspoon powdered gelatin
- 1 small shallot, minced
- 2 garlic cloves, minced
- 2 tablespoons minced fresh parsley
- ½ teaspoon minced fresh thyme

HORSERADISH CREAM SAUCE

- ½ cup heavy cream
- ½ cup prepared horseradish
- 1 teaspoon salt
- ⅛ teaspoon pepper

1. For the roast Sprinkle roast with 1 tablespoon salt, cover with plastic wrap, and let sit at room temperature for 1 hour or refrigerate for up to 24 hours. (If refrigerating, let roast sit at room temperature for 1 hour before cooking.)

2. Adjust oven rack to middle position and heat oven to 400 degrees. Combine bread crumbs, 2 teaspoons oil, ¼ teaspoon salt, and ¼ teaspoon pepper in 12-inch nonstick skillet. Cook over medium heat, stirring frequently, until deep golden brown, 3 to 5 minutes. Transfer to rimmed baking sheet and let cool to room temperature, about 15 minutes.

3. Wipe skillet clean with paper towels. Rinse grated potato in colander under cold water, then squeeze dry in kitchen towel. Transfer potato and remaining 1 cup oil to now-empty skillet. Cook over high heat, stirring frequently, until potato is golden brown and crisp, 6 to 8 minutes.

4. Using slotted spoon, transfer potato to paper towel–lined plate and season lightly with salt. Reserve 1 tablespoon oil from skillet and discard remainder. Let potato cool for 5 minutes, then crush until coarsely ground. Transfer ground potato to sheet with bread-crumb mixture and toss to combine. (Bread crumb–potato mixture can be stored at room temperature for up to 1 day.)

5. Pat roast dry with paper towels and sprinkle with 1 teaspoon pepper. Heat reserved 1 tablespoon oil in again-empty skillet over medium-high heat until just smoking. Brown roast on all sides, 8 to 10 minutes. Transfer to wire rack set in second rimmed baking sheet and let rest for 10 minutes.

6. Just before coating tenderloin, combine 2 tablespoons horseradish, mayonnaise, mustard, and gelatin in small bowl. Toss bread crumb–potato mixture with shallot, garlic, parsley, thyme, and remaining 2 tablespoons horseradish. Spread horseradish paste on top and sides of roast, leaving bottom and ends bare. Roll coated sides of roast in bread-crumb mixture, pressing gently so crumbs adhere in even layer that just covers horseradish paste; pat off any excess.

7. Return tenderloin to rack and roast until it registers 120 to 125 degrees (for medium-rare), 25 to 30 minutes.

8. For the horseradish cream sauce Meanwhile, whisk cream in medium bowl until thickened but not yet holding soft peaks,

1 to 2 minutes. Gently fold in horseradish, salt, and pepper. Cover and refrigerate for at least 30 minutes or up to 1 hour.

9. Transfer roast to carving board and let rest for 20 minutes. Slice roast ½ inch thick and serve with sauce.

SPICY CITRUS-GINGER GRILLED PORK TENDERLOIN STEAKS

Serves 4 to 6   Total time: 40 minutes (plus 45 minutes marinating time)

WHY THIS RECIPE WORKS *A gingery, garlicky, citrusy marinade is the key flavor component in this quick and easy rendition of grilled pork tenderloins. One of the most common ways to grill pork tenderloin is to turn it into medallions, but this treatment requires you to pay constant attention to the slices lest they overcook or, worse, slip through the grate. Since tenderloin is a mild cut, it does makes sense to cut the roast into smaller pieces to expose more surface area and build up as much flavor as possible on the exterior. To get these benefits without dealing with fussy medallions, we turned our tenderloins into smaller, flatter "steaks" with almost 30 percent more surface area than the tenderloins for a greatly improved ratio of browned exterior to tender interior. We also cut thin slashes in the steaks to promote better penetration of our deeply flavorful marinade. Finally, we left excess marinade on the steaks to help keep their exteriors from drying out on the grill and then thickened some reserved marinade with mayonnaise for a bold finishing sauce. Since marinating is a key step in this recipe, we don't recommend using enhanced pork.*

- 2 (1-pound) pork tenderloins, trimmed
- 1½ teaspoons grated orange zest plus 2 tablespoons juice
- 1½ teaspoons grated lime zest plus 2 tablespoons juice
- 4 garlic cloves, minced
- 4 teaspoons honey
- 2 teaspoons fish sauce
- 2 teaspoons grated fresh ginger
- ¾ teaspoon salt
- ½ teaspoon pepper
- ¼ teaspoon cayenne pepper

Bold and Spicy Gingerbread Bundt Cake

½ cup vegetable oil
4 teaspoons mayonnaise
1 tablespoon chopped fresh cilantro
Flake sea salt (optional)

1. Slice each tenderloin in half crosswise to create 4 steaks total. Pound each half to ¾-inch thickness. Using sharp knife, cut ⅛-inch-deep slits spaced ½ inch apart in crosshatch pattern on both sides of steaks.

2. Whisk orange zest and juice, lime zest and juice, garlic, honey, fish sauce, ginger, salt, pepper, and cayenne together in large bowl. Whisking constantly, slowly drizzle oil into orange mixture until smooth and slightly thickened. Transfer ½ cup orange mixture to small bowl and whisk in mayonnaise; set aside sauce. Add steaks to bowl with remaining marinade and toss thoroughly to coat; transfer steaks and marinade to 1-gallon zipper-lock bag, press out as much air as possible, and seal bag. Let steaks sit at room temperature for 45 minutes.

3a. For a charcoal grill Open bottom vent completely. Light large chimney starter filled with charcoal briquettes (6 quarts). When top coals are partially covered with ash, pour evenly over half of grill. Set cooking grate in place, cover, and open lid vent completely. Heat grill until hot, about 5 minutes.

3b. For a gas grill Turn all burners to high, cover, and heat grill until hot, about 15 minutes. Leave primary burner on high and turn off other burner(s).

4. Clean and oil cooking grate. Remove steaks from marinade (do not pat dry) and place over hotter part of grill. Cook, uncovered, until well browned on first side, 3 to 4 minutes. Flip steaks and cook until well browned on second side, 3 to 4 minutes. Transfer steaks to cooler part of grill, with wider end of each steak facing hotter part of grill. Cover and cook until meat registers 145 degrees, 3 to 8 minutes (remove steaks as they come to temperature). Transfer steaks to carving board and let rest for 5 minutes.

5. While steaks rest, microwave reserved sauce until warm, 15 to 30 seconds; stir in cilantro. Slice steaks against grain into ½-inch-thick slices. Drizzle with half of sauce; sprinkle with sea salt, if using; and serve, passing remaining sauce separately.

BOLD AND SPICY GINGERBREAD BUNDT CAKE

Serves 12   Total time: 1 hour 15 minutes (plus 2 hours 20 minutes cooling time)

WHY THIS RECIPE WORKS *In our opinion, gingerbread is only worth eating if its flavor is unmistakably bold and gingery. For this cake, we employed a quadruple ginger punch. We used robust molasses instead of mild, and stout beer instead of water, giving the cake a malty tang that tasters loved. Ground ginger provided the first spicy kick, and cinnamon and allspice contributed warm notes. Blooming the spices in melted butter (a technique the test kitchen uses for savory spiced dishes) intensified their flavor, but tasters still wanted more ginger. Grated fresh ginger brought a second layer of heat that the dried spice alone couldn't muster. Another traditionally savory ingredient, black pepper, added a mild bite that further enhanced the ginger flavor. We used the glaze as an additional opportunity to turn up the ginger dial by mixing ground ginger with confectioners' sugar and adding a few tablespoons of ginger ale to thin the glaze to just the right consistency. Be sure to use finely ground black pepper here. Do not use blackstrap molasses in this recipe.*

CAKE
2½ cups (12½ ounces) all-purpose flour
2 teaspoons baking powder
¾ teaspoon baking soda
¾ teaspoon salt
16 tablespoons unsalted butter
2 tablespoons ground ginger
2 teaspoons ground cinnamon
1 teaspoon ground allspice
¼ teaspoon pepper
4 large eggs, room temperature
1½ cups (10½ ounces) granulated sugar
4 teaspoons grated fresh ginger
¾ cup robust or full molasses
¾ cup stout beer

GLAZE
1¾ cups (7 ounces) confectioners' sugar
3 tablespoons ginger ale
1 teaspoon ground ginger

1. For the cake Adjust oven rack to middle position and heat oven to 375 degrees. Spray 12-cup nonstick Bundt pan with baking spray with flour. Whisk flour, baking powder, baking soda, and salt together in bowl.

2. Melt butter in medium saucepan over medium heat. Stir in ground ginger, cinnamon, allspice, and pepper and cook until fragrant, about 30 seconds. Remove from heat and set aside to cool slightly.

3. Whisk eggs, sugar, and fresh ginger together in large bowl until light and frothy. Whisk in cooled melted butter mixture, molasses, and beer until incorporated. Add flour mixture to egg mixture and whisk until no lumps remain.

4. Transfer batter to prepared pan and smooth top with rubber spatula. Gently tap pan on counter to release air bubbles. Bake until skewer inserted in center comes out clean, about 45 minutes, rotating pan halfway through baking. Let cake cool in pan on wire rack set in rimmed baking sheet for 20 minutes. Invert cake onto rack, remove pan, and let cool completely, about 2 hours.

5. For the glaze Whisk sugar, ginger ale, and ginger together in bowl until smooth. Drizzle glaze over cooled cake and let set, about 15 minutes, before serving. (Cake can stored at room temperature for up to 2 days.)

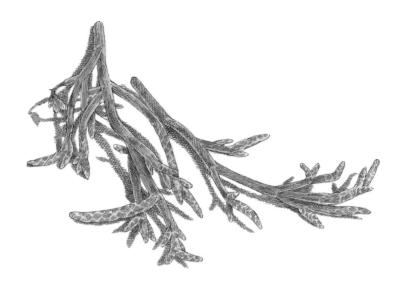

SEA VEGETABLES

Sea vegetables are the plants formerly known as seaweed. Americans have been slow to embrace them, but they have long been integral to Asian cuisines. Historically they were also part of the traditional diet in coastal areas of Great Britain, Norway, Iceland, and New Zealand. Unlike land plants, sea vegetables do not have true roots, stems, or leaves. There are dozens of edible varieties; in this chapter, we focus on the most popular.

NORI is the most widely recognizable and readily available sea vegetable. You probably know nori from its use in sushi rolls, but it also makes a crispy snacking chip and is superversatile ground into a powder and mixed with popcorn, worked into pasta dough, and in our Nori-Crusted Salmon.

Mild and almost mushroomy in flavor, with its dark shreds resembling loose black tea, dark brown or black **HIJIKI** seems to be more about the land than the sea. This unique quality makes it a wonderfully contrasting flavor addition to our Seaweed Salad.

KOMBU, a type of kelp, is a mainstay in Japanese cooking. It's often used to make soups, including dashi (the broth for miso soup), and hot pots, like our Vegetable Shabu-Shabu with Sesame Sauce.

Bright green and succulent, **SEA BEANS** grow wild all over coastal North America, Europe, and Asia. They shine in summer salads, such as our Black Rice and Sea Bean Salad. Our Pickled Sea Beans make a brilliant topping for seafood burgers.

WAKAME is the leafy green seaweed found in miso soup and often in seaweed salads. We have developed a foolproof recipe in our test kitchen for Miso Soup with Wakame and Tofu, a healthful and delicious classic Japanese dish.

shopping and storage

Sea vegetables are typically sold dried, in packages, with the exception of sea beans, which are sold fresh. You can readily find most varieties of dried sea vegetables year-round in the international aisle of well-stocked supermarkets, in Asian and natural foods markets, and online. Look for sea beans at farmers' markets and in well-stocked supermarkets and natural foods stores.

A note about kombu: When purchasing it, take note of the chalky, white powder on the exterior. This is an indication of the glutamic acid content and translates to increased flavor.

Store dried seaweed at room temperature in an airtight container to prevent it from picking up moisture from the kitchen environment. It will keep for many months.

Sea beans can be found in the late spring and summer months. They should be small sprigs that are firm and bright green; avoid any sprigs that are limp or slimy. As the weather turns colder, sea beans will turn red, a sign that they have developed woody stems and have become too salty to enjoy eating. Store sea beans wrapped in a damp paper towel inside a plastic produce bag for up to a week.

all about sea vegetables

NORI Nori is usually sold dried, in pliable sheets; it is often emerald green but can be dark purple. The fresh nori is shredded, pressed into thin sheets, and then dried. *Nori* is actually the Japanese word for "seaweed" and is the only variety used for *maki* (rolled sushi). It is also crumbled and used as a garnish for rice and noodles. Nori is available plain; seasoned with a mixture of soy sauce, sugar, and spices; or seasoned with sesame oil and salt (Korean-style). It is often toasted before being added to a dish to release its flavor and to make it more pliable for rolling sushi.

HIJIKI Hijiki resembles loose black tea, since it is sold in twig-like shreds or in small "buds." Once rehydrated and cooked, the shreds swell to three or four times their dried size. Hijiki is very popular among home cooks in Japan because of its ease of preparation. It is extremely high in iron, containing more than is found in chicken liver!

KOMBU Kombu is dried kelp, dark purple in color and rich in flavor-enhancing glutamic acid, and is used extensively in Japanese cooking. It is sold in dried sheets or strips that are quite thick—several to a package—and the sheets are naturally dusted with a desirable whitish powder that adds flavor. Kombu is a key ingredient in dashi, a broth essential to Japanese cuisine. It is often simmered in soups or broths to impart flavor, and the softened kombu can then be eaten as part of the meal. It generally needs to simmer for a while to become tender and expands quite a bit in volume as it soaks up water.

SEA BEANS Sea beans, also known as salicornia, samphire, glasswort, or sea asparagus, tend to grow along the shoreline, so they can be found on the beach and in salt marshes and springs. If you live in a coastal area, you can forage for them, and you can even grow sea beans in your garden, though they will lose much of their salinity if grown in soil away from the ocean.

WAKAME Wakame is quite popular in Japan, where it is a traditional component in miso soup and many salads. It is available dried in thin sheets, shreds (or flakes), or fresh-salted. Its color is dark grayish or brownish green, and it is the most tender of the sea vegetables, with a briny, slightly sweet flavor. Both dried and fresh varieties are used to flavor soups and can be made into salads. Dried wakame must be rehydrated in water before using, while fresh wakame should be rinsed briefly to remove the excess salt and then soaked in water for a couple of minutes.

vegetable prep

 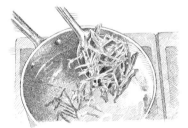

Most dried sea vegetables must be soaked in water to rehydrate and soften them before cooking; nori is the exception to this rule. Individual recipes provide direction for how long to soak the sea vegetables.

Fresh sea vegetables such as sea beans are sometimes blanched before use in order to tame their natural saltiness. Individual recipes will instruct you if this is necessary.

SESAME NORI CHIPS

Makes 60 chips   Total time: 30 minutes

WHY THIS RECIPE WORKS *Our nori chips boast a light, crisp texture and fresh-from-the-sea flavor. To create a great chip, we focused on a few simple elements. First, we tested various oven temperatures and times and found that a moderately hot oven (350 degrees) produced the best chips. Neither a low oven temperature (275 degrees) nor a high temperature (400 degrees) yielded successful results within a varied time range. The low temperature gave us floppy chips, while the high temperature produced chips with an unpleasant burnt taste. Further testing revealed that our initial 15-minute cook time could be shortened to a mere 8 minutes. In order to preserve the clean nori flavor, we added only sesame seeds, which toasted nicely while the chips baked, and a little kosher salt. Vegetable oil brushed on the chips pulled double duty, helping the sesame seeds to adhere while helping to further crisp up the chips. For a sturdier chip with even better crunch, we folded the nori sheets to double their thickness; water brushed between the folded sheets kept them together. Finally, we cut each sheet into uniform strips. After a few minutes in the oven, these toasty dark green treats were ready to enjoy. You can use either toasted or untoasted nori sheets for this recipe. Leftover chips can be stored in a paper towel–lined airtight container for up to seven days.*

    10 sheets nori
  1¼ teaspoons vegetable oil
     5 teaspoons sesame seeds
         Kosher salt

1. Adjust oven racks to upper-middle and lower-middle positions and heat oven to 350 degrees. Line 2 rimmed baking sheets with parchment paper. Working with 1 nori sheet at a time, brush bottom half liberally with water. Fold top half toward you and press firmly until sealed. Brush top of folded nori with ⅛ teaspoon oil, sprinkle with ½ teaspoon sesame seeds, and season with salt to taste. Cut nori into 1-inch strips.

2. Arrange nori strips in single layer, spaced evenly apart on prepared baking sheets. Bake until nori is very crisp and sesame seeds are golden, about 8 minutes, switching and rotating sheets halfway through baking (nori strips should be dark and shriveled slightly). Let cool completely on sheets, 8 to 10 minutes. Serve.

POPCORN WITH NORI BUTTER

Serves 6 to 8   Total time: 10 minutes

WHY THIS RECIPE WORKS *A well-seasoned version of homemade popcorn should be a mainstay at any casual gathering, and this unique recipe will have your guests asking about the secret ingredient. Nori powder brings a deeply savory umami flavor element to the light, fluffy popcorn. The key to this recipe was making the popcorn in a large, heavy-bottomed Dutch oven. The Dutch oven did the best job of heating the oil evenly, which ensured that the kernels heated and popped at the same rate, leaving us with few unpopped kernels and less risk of burning. Once we had the technique down, it was easy to come up with variations, but this was our favorite. You'll want a good-size Dutch oven to make the popcorn—at least 5 or 6 quarts. Be sure to shake the pot vigorously when cooking to prevent the popcorn from scorching.*

     3 tablespoons unsalted butter
     1 teaspoon Nori Powder (recipe follows)
     2 tablespoons vegetable oil
    ½ cup popcorn kernels
         Salt

Microwave butter and nori powder in bowl at 50 percent power until just melted, 1 to 3 minutes. Combine oil and popcorn in large Dutch oven. Cover and place over medium-high heat, shaking occasionally, until first few kernels begin to pop. Continue to cook, shaking pot vigorously, until popping has mostly stopped. Transfer to large bowl, toss with melted butter, and season with salt to taste. Serve.

NORI POWDER

Makes ½ cup   Total time: 40 minutes

WHY THIS RECIPE WORKS *A staple pantry item in some restaurants is nori powder, which is just toasted nori sheets ground to a fine powder in a spice grinder or blender. The powder stores well for weeks and can be used in any number of ways to bring a subtle sea-flavored umami quality to both savory and sweet dishes. It can be blended into butter or worked into pasta dough, and it's quite tasty sprinkled over popcorn, potato chips, or other salty snacks. So grab a package of nori sheets, get your grind on, and open up some new possibilities in your kitchen. It's a great way to tap into the versatility of seaweed and add a supersimple "chef-y" item to your pantry. A spice grinder produces the finest nori powder and is our preferred tool for the job. A blender can also be used, but the resulting powder will be coarser. You can use either toasted or untoasted nori sheets for this recipe. Either type should be toasted in step 1.*

    10 sheets nori

1. Adjust oven racks to upper-middle and lower-middle positions and heat oven to 275 degrees. Spread nori evenly in single layer on 2 rimmed baking sheets. Bake until nori is aromatic and shrinks slightly, 20 to 25 minutes, flipping nori and also switching and rotating baking sheets halfway through toasting. Tear nori sheets into rough 1½-inch pieces.

2. Loosely pack spice grinder chamber three-quarters full with nori pieces and grind to fine powder, about 30 seconds. Without emptying spice grinder, add more nori pieces until grinding chamber is three-quarters full and grind to fine powder, about 30 seconds. Transfer nori powder to airtight container. Repeat grinding process twice with remaining nori pieces.

Popcorn with Nori Butter

PICKLED SEA BEANS

Makes one 1-pint jar   Total time: 45 minutes (plus 24 hours refrigeration time)

WHY THIS RECIPE WORKS *Rather than employing the usual suspects, like cucumbers or onions, for this quick pickle, we happily settled on the unique sea bean. In just a few easy steps, we transformed a handful of sea beans into pickles perfect for an antipasto platter or sandwich topping—crunchy, tangy, a bit sweet, and loaded with fresh oceany flavor. Some pickling recipes call for seasoned rice vinegar, which already contains vinegar, sugar, and salt, but favoring control over convenience, we opted for the unseasoned variety. This allowed the sea beans to contribute all the natural salinity that our pickling solution required, while still letting us regulate the amount of sweetness. We gave these pickles a classic flavor profile, with a hint of warm spice from black peppercorns, mustard seeds, and turmeric and a hit of garlic. Fresh dill sprigs added a mild anise flavor, similar to a hamburger pickle. Unlike classic pickles, however, after bringing the brine to a boil, we let the liquid cool completely before pouring it over the beans. This cooling step helped ensure a crisp texture and vibrant color even after the required one-day pickling time.*

1½ cups unseasoned rice vinegar
¼ cup water
1 tablespoon sugar
1 garlic clove, peeled and halved
¼ teaspoon ground turmeric
⅛ teaspoon black peppercorns
⅛ teaspoon yellow mustard seeds
4 ounces sea beans, trimmed
2 sprigs fresh dill

1. Bring vinegar, water, sugar, garlic, turmeric, peppercorns, and mustard seeds to boil in medium saucepan over medium-high heat; remove from heat and let cool to room temperature, about 30 minutes.

2. Tightly pack sea beans and dill sprigs into jar. Using funnel and ladle, pour cooled brine over sea beans to cover. Cover jar with lid and refrigerate for 24 hours before serving. (Pickled sea beans can be refrigerated for up to 1 week; sea beans will become soft and darken significantly after 1 week.)

SEAWEED SALAD

Serves 4   Total time: 35 minutes

WHY THIS RECIPE WORKS *The commercial seaweed salad in many grocery stores and restaurants is often uninspired, typically consisting of just one type of seaweed, with additives and preservatives, and tossed with a dressing so sweet it could practically be mistaken for dessert. For our version, the bar was much higher: a salad with textural contrast, a flavorful but balanced dressing, and a fresh, sweet-briny finish. To showcase variety, we chose three types of dried seaweed. Wakame is most recognizable as the leafy green seaweed in miso soup. Kombu is a type of kelp and one of the two primary ingredients used to make traditional dashi broth. Finally, we included hijiki, which is milder than kombu and wakame and adds an understated vegetal sea flavor without being briny. Rehydrating in warm water for about 15 minutes gave the seaweed just the right texture. We also sliced the kombu thin, to make its firmer, leathery consistency more palatable for a salad. For the dressing, we used vegetable oil, rice wine vinegar, sesame oil, soy sauce, and fresh ginger. A little brown sugar provided just the right amount of sweetness, while sesame seeds added a toasty note and fresh scallions offset the slightly sweet vinaigrette perfectly.*

6 tablespoons (½ ounce) wakame
1½ tablespoons (⅛ ounce) hijiki
¼ ounce kombu
¼ cup vegetable oil
3 tablespoons unseasoned rice vinegar
2 tablespoons packed brown sugar
1½ tablespoons soy sauce
1½ teaspoons toasted sesame oil
¼ teaspoon grated fresh ginger
1 tablespoon toasted sesame seeds
2 scallions, sliced thin on bias

1. Place wakame and hijiki in large bowl and add warm water to cover completely. In warm water. Let seaweed sit until softened (wakame should double in size and kombu should be pliable), about 15 minutes, stirring occasionally.

2. Drain wakame and hijiki in fine-mesh strainer, pressing firmly on seaweed to extract as much water as possible. Transfer wakame and hijiki to paper towel–lined plate and pat dry. Set aside.

3. Drain kombu, rinse well, and pat dry with paper towels. Place kombu on cutting board with long side facing you. Roll kombu away from you into tight cylinder, then slice thin crosswise.

4. Whisk vegetable oil, vinegar, sugar, soy sauce, sesame oil, and ginger together in large bowl. Add sesame seeds, wakame, hijiki, and kombu, and toss to combine. Transfer to individual serving bowls and sprinkle with scallions. Serve.

BLACK RICE AND SEA BEAN SALAD

Serves 4 to 6   Total time: 1 hour

WHY THIS RECIPE WORKS *A grain-and-vegetable salad should present a satisfying mix of contrasting flavors, textures, and colors. The best can also be the simplest, as is the case here. Black rice, also known as forbidden rice, is an ancient grain that was once reserved for the emperors of China. It has a delicious roasted, nutty taste that works extremely well in many dishes, especially salads. We thought it would be a successful pairing with crunchy sea beans, which develop their strong, briny flavor from the salty water and air in the marshes where they typically grow. One hurdle was tempering the saltiness of the sea beans. Tasters found the beans overwhelming when simply added to the salad raw. Blanching them first helped to tame their saltiness and gave them a vibrant green color, creating a gorgeous contrast when tossed with the black rice. Since it's easy to overcook black rice, that was our other concern in developing this recipe. We discovered that the best way to cook it evenly was to cook it like pasta (in the water we used for blanching the sea beans), giving it space to move around. After we drained it, we let it cool completely on a baking sheet. This ensured perfectly cooked grains that had the expected chew of black rice without any mushiness. Grapefruit segments offered a sweet-tart component that helped balance the salinity of the sea beans, and a simple vinaigrette (white wine vinegar, shallot, garlic, and honey) tied the whole salad together.*

    5 ounces sea beans, trimmed and
        cut into 2-inch lengths
 1½ cups black rice

 1 grapefruit
¼ cup white wine vinegar
 1 shallot, chopped fine
 1 garlic clove, minced
 1 teaspoon honey
 6 tablespoons extra-virgin olive oil
 2 tablespoons chopped fresh mint

1. Bring 4 quarts water to boil in large pot. Fill large bowl halfway with ice and water. Add sea beans to boiling water and cook until crisp-tender, about 1 minute. Using slotted spoon, transfer sea beans to ice water and let sit until cool, about 5 minutes.

2. Transfer sea beans to triple layer of paper towels and dry well. Return water in pot to boil, add rice, and cook until rice is tender, 20 to 25 minutes. Drain rice, spread on rimmed baking sheet, and let sit until cooled, about 15 minutes.

3. Cut away peel and pith from grapefruit. Quarter grapefruit, then slice crosswise into ¼-inch-thick pieces. Whisk vinegar, shallot, garlic, and honey together in large serving bowl. While whisking constantly, slowly drizzle in oil until combined. Add rice, sea beans, grapefruit, and mint to vinaigrette in bowl and toss to coat. Serve.

MISO SOUP WITH WAKAME AND TOFU

Serves 8 to 10   Total time: 30 minutes

WHY THIS RECIPE WORKS *Often served as a starter, miso soup is a Japanese restaurant standard. Though there are several types of miso available, white miso is traditionally used for this soup, and two types of sea vegetables are integral ingredients: wakame and kombu. Miso soup is common in Japanese homes, too, where it's considered a comfort food, akin to our chicken soup. When it is served in a restaurant, miso soup is rarely judged, but it doesn't take a connoisseur to appreciate its subtleties and finer points. Bad miso soup is immediately identifiable as overly salty, with a one-dimensional flavor that is sometimes compensated for with the addition of monosodium glutamate. Our miso soup is alive with complex layers of sweet, smoky, briny, and earthy flavors, and it is a pleasure to sip. Just as chicken soup has a base of chicken stock, miso soup has a base called dashi, which means "broth" in Japanese. We made our basic dashi from a simple combination of water, kombu (kelp), and dried bonito flakes (bonito is a type of fish). But unlike chicken stock, we made our dashi in less than 20 minutes. We then added the miso to the strained dashi, and with the addition of wakame and tofu, plus a sprinkling of scallions, our soup was complete.*

DASHI
    8 cups water
 ¼ ounce kombu
    2 cups bonito flakes

SOUP
    1 tablespoon wakame
    1 cup white miso
    8 ounces silken tofu, cut into
        ½-inch pieces
    3 scallions, sliced thin

1. **For the dashi** Bring water and kombu to rapid simmer in large saucepan over medium heat. When water reaches rapid simmer, discard kombu and turn off heat. Stir in bonito flakes and let sit for 3 to 5 minutes. Strain dashi through fine-mesh strainer into large bowl. Reserve 1 cup dashi and return remaining dashi to saucepan.

2. **For the soup** Soak wakame in cold water until softened, about 15 minutes. Drain and reserve. Whisk miso and reserved 1 cup dashi in small bowl until combined. Bring dashi in saucepan to simmer over medium-high heat, then stir in miso mixture. Return to brief simmer and immediately remove saucepan from heat.

3. Meanwhile, while soup is heating, divide tofu and wakame evenly among individual serving bowls. Ladle soup into bowls, sprinkle with scallions, and serve immediately.

NORI PAPPARDELLE WITH BLISTERED CHERRY TOMATOES

When you see green fresh pasta, you are likely to think it is flavored (or more likely merely colored) with spinach. This fresh pasta is made using our homemade nori powder, which makes it deeply flavorful and incredibly satisfying. We pair it with a simple skillet sauce based on charred cherry tomatoes, olive oil, vinegar, and fish sauce, for a uniquely savory and umami-rich meal.

1. Combine the dough ingredients in the bowl of a stand mixer fitted with the dough hook. Mix the dough on low speed until it comes together, 2 to 4 minutes, adding more water if needed. Increase the speed to medium and knead until the dough is smooth and shiny, 7 to 10 minutes.

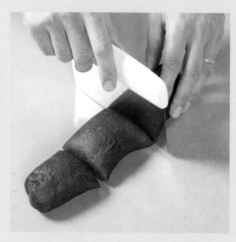

2. Transfer the dough to a counter and form it into a 9-inch log. Wrap the log tightly in plastic wrap and let sit at room temperature for at least 30 minutes. Unroll the dough, cut it into three equal pieces, and cover with plastic wrap.

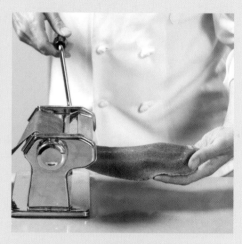

3. Using a pasta machine with the rollers set to the widest position, feed a dough piece through the rollers twice. Narrow the rollers to the next setting; feed the dough through the rollers twice. Progressively narrow the rollers, feeding the dough through each setting twice, until it is 1/16 inch thick.

4. Cut the dough sheet crosswise into 12-inch lengths. Layer the sections on top of each other, dusting with flour between the layers to prevent sticking. Cover the dough loosely with plastic and set aside. Repeat the rolling and cutting with the remaining two dough pieces.

5. Stack two lengths of dough. With the short side facing you, fold the dough into thirds from top to bottom (like a letter). Cut the dough into 1-inch strips, then gently unfurl the noodles. Dust the noodles with flour and form them into nests.

6. Cook the noodles in boiling water, then add to the skillet with the blistered tomatoes. Stir in the cooking water, vinegar, and fish sauce, and toss to combine. Sprinkle individual servings with Pecorino and chives.

VEGETABLE SHABU-SHABU WITH SESAME SAUCE

Serves 6 to 8   Total time: 40 minutes

WHY THIS RECIPE WORKS Shabu-shabu *is a Japanese hot-pot dish in which beef, vegetables, and tofu are simmered in broth and served with chewy udon noodles and dipping sauces. We wanted to develop a version without the meat (or the hot pot). Since the traditional dashi broth is made from glutamate-rich kombu seaweed and bonito (tuna) flakes, we needed to find a way to replicate the bonito's fishy flavor. After a good deal of trial and error, we found that adding a second variety of seaweed (wakame), plenty of fish sauce, rice wine, and sugar replicated the depth of the bonito. Shabu-shabu typically includes carrots, napa cabbage or bok choy, enoki or shiitake mushrooms, tofu, and chrysanthemum leaves. Luckily, the hard-to-find chrysanthemum leaves were not missed when omitted. We preferred bok choy to cabbage and the fuller flavor of shiitake mushrooms to enoki. A dollop of a sesame sauce made with mayonnaise, miso, garlic, and lemon juice was the perfect garnish. We prefer the flavor of red miso here, but white miso can be substituted; do not substitute "light" miso, as its flavor is too mild.*

SESAME SAUCE

- ¼   cup sesame seeds, toasted
- 2   tablespoons mayonnaise
- 1   tablespoon red miso
- 2   teaspoons lemon juice
- 2   teaspoons sugar
- 1   garlic clove, minced
- ½   teaspoon water

SOUP

- 8   ounces dried udon noodles
- Salt
- 9   cups water
- ½   ounce kombu
- 6   tablespoons (½ ounce) wakame
- ½   cup mirin
- ¼   cup fish sauce
- 1½   teaspoons sugar
- 3   heads baby bok choy (4 ounces each), sliced ⅛ inch thick
- 3   carrots, peeled and sliced ⅛ inch thick
- 14   ounces soft tofu, cut into ½-inch pieces
- 8   ounces shiitake mushrooms, stemmed and sliced thin

1. For the sesame sauce Stir all ingredients in bowl until well-combined.

2. For the soup Bring 2 quarts water to boil in large pot. Add noodles and 1½ teaspoons salt and cook, stirring often, until tender; drain and set aside.

3. Meanwhile, bring water, kombu, and wakame to brief boil in large pot over medium heat. Remove from heat and discard seaweed.

4. Stir in mirin, fish sauce, and sugar and bring to simmer over medium heat. Stir in bok choy and carrots and simmer until crisp-tender, 2 to 4 minutes. Stir in tofu, mushrooms, and cooked noodles and cook until warmed through, about 1 minute. Serve with sesame sauce.

NORI PAPPARDELLE WITH BLISTERED CHERRY TOMATOES

Serves 4   Total time: 1 hour (plus 30 minutes resting time)

WHY THIS RECIPE WORKS *A fitting description for this nori-infused pasta would be "umami bomb." Seaweed is rich in naturally occurring glutamic acid, the amino acid that makes some of our favorite foods incredibly savory. We wanted to turn up the umami factor to 11, so we looked to other ingredients that are also high in glutamic acid: tomatoes, fish sauce, and aged cheese. We balanced these heavy hitters with extra-virgin olive oil, sherry vinegar, and smoked paprika to make a simple but intensely savory and satisfying sauce that came together quickly. Cutting the flour in this recipe with powdered nori reduces the amount of potential gluten in the pasta, and gluten is what gives pasta its satisfying chew. So, to compensate for the lower proportion of flour, we switched to higher-protein bread flour in place of*
all-purpose. King Arthur bread flour is the highest-protein bread flour available at the supermarket and produces pasta with an especially nice bite. It is our preferred flour for this recipe, but other bread flours will also work well. Fish sauce may seem like a strange addition to a pasta dish, but minced anchovies are a common ingredient in Italian pasta sauces. Like them, the fish sauce adds deep meatiness without tasting fishy.*

- 1½   cups (8¼ ounces) bread flour, plus extra for dusting
- 1   recipe Nori Powder (page 388)
- Salt
- 3   large eggs plus 2 large yolks
- ¼   cup plus 1 teaspoon extra-virgin olive oil
- 12   ounces cherry tomatoes
- ½   teaspoon smoked paprika
- 2   teaspoons sherry vinegar
- 1   teaspoon fish sauce
- 1   ounce Pecorino Romano cheese, grated (½ cup)
- ¼   cup minced fresh chives

1. Whisk flour, nori powder, and ¼ teaspoon salt together in bowl of stand mixer. Whisk eggs and yolks and 1 teaspoon oil together in small bowl. Make well in center of flour mixture and pour in egg mixture. Fit stand mixer with dough hook and mix on low speed until dough comes together, 2 to 4 minutes. (If dough doesn't become cohesive, add up to 2 tablespoons extra water, 1 teaspoon at a time, until it just comes together.) Increase speed to medium and knead until dough is smooth and shiny, 7 to 10 minutes. Transfer dough to counter and form dough into 9-inch log. Wrap tightly in plastic wrap and let sit at room temperature for at least 30 minutes.

2. Transfer dough to clean counter, cut into 3 equal pieces, and cover with plastic. Flatten 1 piece of dough into ½-inch-thick disk. Using pasta machine with rollers set to widest position, feed dough through rollers twice. Narrow rollers to next setting; feed dough through rollers twice. Progressively narrow rollers, feeding through each setting twice, until dough is ¹⁄₁₆ inch thick. If dough gets dry or cracks during rolling, lightly spray with water or dip fingers in water and rub over surface of dough. Cut dough sheet crosswise into 12-inch lengths. Layer sections on top of each other, dusting with flour between layers to prevent sticking. Cover loosely with plastic and set aside. Repeat with remaining 2 pieces of dough.

3. Stack 2 sheets of dough. With short side facing you, fold dough into thirds from top to bottom (like a letter). Cut dough into 1-inch strips, then gently unfurl noodles. Dust noodles with flour, form into nests, and set aside. Repeat with remaining dough.

4. Bring 4 quarts water to boil in large pot. Meanwhile, cook tomatoes in 12-inch skillet over high heat until skins blister and tomatoes are well charred, 4 to 6 minutes. Let cool off heat for 5 minutes, then stir in remaining ¼ cup oil, paprika, and ¼ teaspoon salt.

5. Add pasta and 1 tablespoon salt to boiling water and cook, stirring often, until tender, 1 to 2 minutes. Reserve ½ cup cooking water, then drain pasta and transfer it to skillet with tomatoes. Return skillet to high heat, add ¼ cup reserved cooking water, vinegar, and fish sauce and toss to thoroughly combine. Season with salt to taste. Adjust consistency with remaining reserved cooking water as needed. Divide pasta among individual serving bowls and sprinkle with Pecorino and chives. Serve.

NORI-CRUSTED SALMON
Serves 4   Total time: 30 minutes
WHY THIS RECIPE WORKS *Our homemade nori powder becomes a deeply flavorful crust for rich salmon fillets, creating a simple seafood dish that tastes like the essence of the ocean. We set the bar high: a flavorful rub, a deeply seared—but not burnt—crust, a perfectly medium-rare center, and crispy skin. We rubbed the nori–sesame seed crust mixture only on the flesh side of the fish, allowing the skin to cook more slowly without fear of burning the nori crust. For even more great nori flavor and textural contrast, we sprinkled a little furikake (a Japanese seasoning comprised of crumbled nori, red pepper flakes, sugar, and salt) over the salmon as a finishing touch. You can use either toasted or untoasted nori sheets for this recipe. Both types should be toasted in step 1. Skin-on salmon fillets hold together best during cooking, and the skin helps keep the fish moist. To ensure uniform pieces of fish that cook at the same rate, we find it best to buy a whole center-cut fillet and cut it into four pieces ourselves. If using wild salmon, which contains less fat than farmed salmon, cook the fillets until they register 120 degrees (for medium-rare).*

- 2   teaspoons vegetable oil
- 1   sheet nori
- 3   tablespoons sesame seeds
  Kosher salt and pepper
- ¼   teaspoon red pepper flakes
- ⅛   teaspoon sugar
- ¼   cup Nori Powder (page 388)
- 1   (2-pound) skin-on salmon fillet, 1½ inches thick
- 2   scallions, sliced thin on bias

1. Heat 1 teaspoon oil in 12-inch nonstick skillet over medium heat until just shimmering. Using paper towels, wipe out oil, leaving thin film in pan. Place nori sheet in skillet and cook until fragrant and shrunken slightly, about 3 minutes, flipping every 30 seconds; remove and let cool slightly.

2. Crumble nori sheet into rough ¼-inch flakes in small bowl. Add 1 tablespoon sesame seeds, ¼ teaspoon salt, pepper flakes, and sugar; set aside for serving.

3. Combine remaining 2 tablespoons sesame seeds and nori powder in shallow dish. Cut salmon crosswise into 4 fillets. Using sharp knife, make 3 or 4 shallow slashes about 1 inch apart on skin side of each fillet, being careful not to cut into flesh. Pat salmon dry with paper towels and season with salt and pepper. Dredge top flesh side of fillets in nori powder mixture, pressing to adhere, and transfer, skin side down, to large plate.

4. Heat remaining 1 teaspoon oil in now-empty skillet over medium heat until shimmering. Place salmon flesh side down in skillet and cook until nori powder is dark green and sesame seeds are well toasted, about 3 minutes. Using 2 spatulas, gently flip salmon skin side down, reduce heat to medium-low, and cook until center is still translucent when checked with tip of paring knife and registers 125 degrees (for medium-rare), 9 to 12 minutes longer. Transfer skin side down to serving platter and sprinkle with flaked nori mixture and scallions. Serve.

Nori-Crusted Salmon

S P I N A C H

Spinach is the original healthful leafy green, achieving that exalted status long before the trendiness of kale, arugula, and the like. Spinach doesn't go in and out of style like some other greens; spinach abides. And with good reason: It's a nutritional powerhouse, chock-full of vitamins and minerals, with some of the highest levels for iron and potassium among plants. Its dark green color is thanks to high levels of chlorophyll and carotenoids (including beta carotene), which promote good eyesight. But besides all of that healthful goodness, it's also delicious, easy to prep and cook, and versatile in the kitchen.

Spinach is a native of Persia; from there, it traveled to China and then to Europe in the seventh century. It didn't reach America until the 19th century, and in fact the United States is the number two producer of spinach, far behind China, where it is still called "the Persian green."

All varieties are vibrant green, with an earthy, mineral flavor. Curly-leaf spinach has pretty ruffled leaves that are chewy, with thick, fibrous stems. We think it's ideal in cooked preparations, including our Saag Paneer and Spanakopita, and in baked casseroles, like our Spinach Lasagna. We also love it with a warm dressing poured over it to wilt it, as in our Lemon, Feta, and Pistachio Wilted Spinach Salad (with two variations).

Flat-leaf spinach has spade-shaped leaves that are more tender than the curly-leaf variety, with thinner stems. Baby spinach is a miniature flat-leaf variety with very tender leaves that are ideal for using raw in salads. We also enjoy this more delicate type of spinach cooked very quickly, as in our Sautéed Baby Spinach with Almonds and Golden Raisins, our Fusilli with Spinach and Ricotta, and our classic Chicken Florentine.

shopping and storage

Spinach is available year-round. In the market, you may see mature curly-leaf spinach, often prewashed in bags, which is good steamed and sautéed. Choose tender flat-leaf or baby spinach for salads or very quick cooking. Baby spinach is sometimes sold loose and sometimes sold in bags or plastic containers. Regardless of which variety you are purchasing, be sure to turn over the bags and inspect the greens as closely as you can, to make sure there are no signs of moisture in the bags or blackened edges on the leaves. The leaves should be deep green and smooth, with no hint of yellowing.

Spinach is highly perishable and should be used within a few days of bringing it home. Store leftover spinach either in its original bag with the open end folded over and taped shut, or in its original plastic container, as long as it has holes that allow air to pass through. These specially designed breathable bags and containers keep the spinach fresh as long as possible; if you transfer the spinach to a sealed airtight bag or container, it will spoil prematurely. If you purchase loose spinach, wrap it in paper towels and store in an open plastic produce bag in the refrigerator.

frozen is a-ok

While frozen spinach obviously is not appropriate for making a salad, it can be an excellent option for other dishes, including our Herbed Spinach Dip and our Breakfast Strata with Spinach and Gruyère. It is available in both "bricks" andas loose frozen leaves in bags. Make sure to thaw and squeeze excess water from frozen spinach before cooking.

all about spinach

CURLY-LEAF SPINACH It used to be that this type of spinach, also called savoy spinach, was the only one you would find in supermarkets: thick cellophane bags of sturdy, crinkly, dark green spinach leaves with thick stems that needed to be removed and lots of sandy grit that needed to be rinsed away. Semi-savoy spinach is a variety of curly-leaf that has the same crinkly leaves and similar crisp texture, but it's not as difficult to clean as regular savoy. Curly-leaf spinach has the crispest texture of all the varieties and a stronger, slightly more bitter flavor than flat-leaf spinach. It is at its best when used in cooked preparations; even though it's getting a little harder to find these days, we often favor it in cooked dishes over the other varieties because of its good flavor and texture.

FLAT-LEAF SPINACH Sold in bunches, flat-leaf has become the most popular and widely available variety sold in America nowadays. It has less grit and thus is easier to clean than curly-leaf spinach. Flat-leaf spinach has smooth, spade-shaped leaves, a sweet flavor, and a tender texture, which makes it delicious whether raw or cooked. When cooked, however, it needs to be treated properly to remove excess moisture, or else it will become a wilted, waterlogged mess.

BABY SPINACH Baby spinach is most typically sold loose, and sometimes it's available in bags. Baby spinach is simply a variety of flat-leaf spinach that has been picked early, when it's particularly sweet and tender; the leaves are more oval-shaped and haven't developed the spade shape of mature flat-leaf spinach. Baby spinach is perfect for using raw, as in spinach salads.

vegetable prep

Stemming Spinach

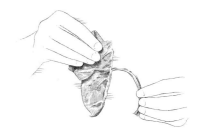

Curly-leaf spinach must be stemmed before cooking. Holding leaf with your hand, use your other hand to pull down and remove stem.

Squeezing Spinach Dry

To rid blanched (or thawed) spinach of excess water before adding to recipes, wrap in clean dish towel or cheesecloth and squeeze firmly.

the popeye effect

Whenever the cartoon hero Popeye the Sailor Man needed some strength to fight the bad guys, he would down an entire tin of spinach. And indeed, spinach is extremely high in iron and other minerals, as well as vitamins A, C, and K. It's also loaded with natural anti-inflammatory and antioxidant compounds. Spinach is also a good natural source of calcium, and cooking the spinach actually increases the amount of calcium available to your body. This is because the oxalic acid present in spinach (which inhibits absorption of minerals) breaks down during the cooking process. So while your muscles might not double in size instantaneously from eating spinach, it sure does your body good.

SAUTÉED BABY SPINACH WITH ALMONDS AND GOLDEN RAISINS

Serves 4   Total time: 20 minutes

WHY THIS RECIPE WORKS *Baby spinach is undeniably convenient—no tough stems to remove or sandy grit to rinse out—but cooking often turns these very tender greens into a watery, mushy mess. We were determined to find a method for cooking baby spinach that would give us a worthwhile side dish. Parcooking the spinach in the microwave turned out to be the best way to help the vegetable release plenty of liquid. We pressed the microwaved spinach against a colander to eliminate more water, coarsely chopped it, and pressed it again. Then all we had to do was quickly sauté it. We then combined the spinach with a few complementary flavors and appealing textures to finish the dish. If you don't have a bowl large enough to accommodate the entire amount of spinach, cook it in a smaller bowl in two batches. Reduce the water to 2 tablespoons per batch and cook the spinach for about 1½ minutes.*

- 18 ounces (18 cups) baby spinach
- ¼ cup water
- 2 tablespoons plus 2 teaspoons extra-virgin olive oil
- 4 garlic cloves, sliced thin crosswise
- ¼ teaspoon red pepper flakes
- ½ cup golden raisins
     Salt
- 2 teaspoons sherry vinegar
- ⅓ cup slivered almonds, toasted

1. Microwave spinach and water in covered bowl until spinach is wilted and decreased in volume by half, 3 to 4 minutes. Remove bowl from microwave and keep covered for 1 minute. Carefully transfer spinach to colander and, using back of rubber spatula, gently press spinach against colander to release excess liquid. Transfer spinach to cutting board and chop coarse. Return spinach to colander and press again.

2. Cook 2 tablespoons oil, garlic, pepper flakes, and raisins in 10-inch skillet over medium-high heat, stirring constantly, until garlic is light golden brown and beginning to sizzle, 3 to 6 minutes. Stir in spinach and ¼ teaspoon salt and cook until uniformly wilted and glossy green, about 2 minutes. Stir in vinegar and almonds. Drizzle with remaining 2 teaspoons oil and season with salt to taste. Serve immediately.

VARIATIONS

Sautéed Baby Spinach with Pecans and Feta
Omit pepper flakes and raisins. Substitute 4 thinly sliced shallots for garlic. Cook shallots until golden brown, 3 to 5 minutes, in step 2. Substitute red wine vinegar for sherry vinegar and toasted and chopped pecans for almonds. Sprinkle spinach with ⅓ cup crumbled feta cheese before serving.

Sautéed Baby Spinach with Chickpeas and Sun-Dried Tomatoes
Omit pepper flakes, raisins, and sherry vinegar. Add ¾ cup rinsed canned chickpeas and ½ cup drained and thinly sliced oil-packed sun-dried tomatoes to skillet with spinach in step 2. Substitute 2 tablespoons grated Parmesan cheese for almonds. Sprinkle spinach with 6 tablespoons grated Parmesan cheese before serving.

HERBED SPINACH DIP

Serves 8   Total time: 15 minutes (plus 1 hour refrigeration time)

WHY THIS RECIPE WORKS *Spinach dip can often feel like the healthy choice on a table of finger foods or appetizers, but it should still be flavor-packed. For a spinach dip that pleased everyone, we opted for the convenience of frozen spinach and ramped up the flavor with fragrant fresh herbs, sweet red bell pepper, scallions, garlic, and some hot sauce for a little kick. To combine these disparate ingredients with ease, we used the food processor to help distribute the spinach evenly throughout the dip. This method also made it easy to add other flavors to the dip for a couple of creative variations. The garlic must be minced before going into the food processor or else the finished dip will contain large chunks of garlic. Serve with crudités or crackers.*

- 10 ounces frozen chopped spinach, thawed and squeezed dry
- ½ red bell pepper, chopped fine
- ½ cup sour cream
- ½ cup mayonnaise
- ½ cup fresh parsley leaves
- 3 scallions, sliced thin

1 tablespoon chopped fresh dill or
   1 teaspoon dried
1 garlic clove, minced
¼ teaspoon hot sauce
   Salt and pepper

Process all ingredients with ½ teaspoon salt and ¼ teaspoon pepper in food processor until well combined, about 1 minute. Transfer to serving bowl, cover, and refrigerate until flavors have blended, at least 1 hour or up to 24 hours. Season with salt and pepper to taste before serving.

VARIATIONS

Spinach Dip with Blue Cheese and Bacon
Omit bell pepper, dill, hot sauce, and salt. Add ⅓ cup crumbled blue cheese to food processor with spinach. Sprinkle with 2 slices cooked, crumbled bacon before serving.

Cilantro-Lime Spinach Dip
Omit bell pepper, dill, and hot sauce. Add ¼ cup fresh cilantro leaves, 1 tablespoon chopped canned chipotle chile in adobo sauce, ½ teaspoon grated lime zest, 1 tablespoon lime juice, ½ teaspoon light brown sugar, and ⅛ teaspoon ground cumin to food processor with spinach.

SPANAKOPITA

Serves 10 to 12   Total time: 1 hour
WHY THIS RECIPE WORKS *The roots of spanakopita, a savory spinach and feta pie with trademark layers of flaky, crisp phyllo, run deep in Greek culture, yet most American versions are just soggy layers of phyllo with a sparse, bland filling. We wanted to create a casserole-style pie with a perfect balance of zesty spinach filling and shatteringly crisp phyllo—and we didn't want to spend all day in the kitchen. Among the spinach options—baby, frozen, mature curly-leaf— tasters favored the bold flavor of fresh curly-leaf spinach. Crumbling the feta into fine pieces ensured salty tang in every bite, and Greek yogurt buffered the feta's assertiveness. Pecorino Romano (a good stand-in for a traditional Greek hard sheep's-milk cheese) added complexity and, when sprinkled between the phyllo sheets, helped the flaky layers hold together. Using a baking*

sheet rather than a dish allowed excess moisture to evaporate, ensuring a crisp crust. Two pounds of flat-leaf spinach can be substituted for the curly-leaf spinach, but do not use baby spinach. Phyllo dough is also available in 18 by 14-inch sheets; if using those, cut them to make 14 by 9-inch sheets. Thaw the phyllo in the refrigerator overnight or on the counter for 4 to 5 hours; do not microwave it. While working with it, cover the sheets with plastic wrap, then a damp kitchen towel to prevent drying.

FILLING
20 ounces curly-leaf spinach, stemmed
 8 ounces feta cheese, crumbled (2 cups)
 ¾ cup whole-milk Greek yogurt
 4 scallions, sliced thin
 2 large eggs, lightly beaten
 ¼ cup minced fresh mint
 2 tablespoons minced fresh dill
 3 garlic cloves, minced
 1 teaspoon grated lemon zest plus
   1 tablespoon juice
 1 teaspoon ground nutmeg
 ½ teaspoon pepper
 ¼ teaspoon salt
 ⅛ teaspoon cayenne pepper

PHYLLO LAYERS
 7 tablespoons extra-virgin olive oil
 8 ounces (14 by 9-inch) phyllo, thawed
1½ ounces Pecorino Romano cheese, grated (¾ cup)
 2 teaspoons sesame seeds (optional)

1. For the filling Microwave spinach and ¼ cup water in bowl until spinach is shrunk by half, about 5 minutes. Remove bowl from microwave and set aside, covered, for 1 minute. Transfer spinach to colander to drain and let cool slightly. Once cool enough to handle, transfer spinach to clean dish towel, wrap towel tightly around spinach to form ball, and wring until dry. Chop spinach, then mix spinach, feta, yogurt, scallions, eggs, mint, dill, garlic, zest and juice, nutmeg, pepper, salt, and cayenne in bowl until thoroughly combined.

2. For the phyllo layers Adjust oven rack to lower-middle position and heat oven to 425 degrees. Line rimmed baking sheet with parchment paper. Using pastry brush, lightly

brush 14 by 9-inch rectangle in center of parchment with oil. Lay 1 phyllo sheet on oiled parchment and brush thoroughly with oil. Repeat with 9 more phyllo sheets, brushing each with oil (you should have total of 10 layers of phyllo).

3. Spread spinach mixture evenly over phyllo, leaving ¼-inch border on all sides. Cover spinach with 6 more phyllo sheets, brushing each with oil and sprinkling each with 2 tablespoons Pecorino. Lay 2 more phyllo sheets on top, brushing each with oil (do not sprinkle these top layers with Pecorino).

4. Working from center outward, use palms of your hands to compress layers and press out any air pockets. Using sharp knife, score spanakopita through top 3 layers of phyllo into 24 equal pieces. Sprinkle with sesame seeds, if using. Bake until phyllo is golden and crisp, 20 to 25 minutes. Let spanakopita cool on sheet for at least 10 minutes or up to 2 hours. Slide spanakopita, still on parchment, to cutting board. Cut into squares and serve.

WILTED SPINACH SALAD WITH WARM BACON-PECAN VINAIGRETTE

Serves 4 to 6   Total time: 25 minutes
WHY THIS RECIPE WORKS *A perfect wilted spinach salad is a thing of beauty—but it is a careful balancing act. The spinach leaves (here, tender baby spinach) should be just gently wilted by the warm vinaigrette dressing. If you use too much dressing, or if the dressing is too hot, the spinach will end up overwilted and lifeless. But if you don't use enough dressing, or if you allow the dressing to cool too much, the spinach will remain chewy and raw and less pleasant to eat. An easy trick for ensuring a properly wilted spinach salad is to have everything at the ready before you begin—tongs and all— and then toss your spinach and serve your salad the moment the vinaigrette is at the right temperature. We chose particularly sweet, fragrant, and crisp apple varieties to emphasize and offset the bacon-pecan dressing's smoky, salty, nutty richness.*

Wilted Spinach Salad with Warm
Bacon-Pecan Vinaigrette

5 tablespoons white wine vinegar
1 tablespoon whole-grain mustard
1 teaspoon sugar
1 shallot, halved through root end and sliced thin crosswise
6 slices bacon, cut into ½-inch pieces
⅓ cup pecans, chopped
12 ounces (12 cups) baby spinach
1 Fuji or Honeycrisp apple, cored, halved, and sliced thin
   Salt and pepper

1. Whisk vinegar, mustard, sugar, and ¼ teaspoon salt together in small bowl. Add shallot, cover tightly with plastic wrap, and microwave until steaming, 30 to 60 seconds. Stir briefly to submerge shallot. Let cool to room temperature, about 15 minutes.

2. Cook bacon and pecans in 12-inch skillet over medium heat, stirring frequently, until bacon is crisp and pecans are toasted and fragrant, 8 to 10 minutes. Off heat, stir in shallot mixture and let sit until heated through, about 30 seconds.

3. Gently toss spinach with warm vinaigrette in large bowl until evenly coated and wilted slightly. Add apple and toss to combine. Season with salt and pepper to taste. Serve.

LEMON, FETA, AND PISTACHIO WILTED SPINACH SALAD

Serves 6   Total time: 25 minutes

WHY THIS RECIPE WORKS *We love adding a fruity element to our wilted spinach salads. In the previous recipe, we used baby spinach and introduced apple to the traditional dressing of bacon, vinegar, and mustard. For this version, we chose hardier curly-leaf spinach, replaced the bacon fat with fruity extra-virgin olive oil, and dropped the vinegar in favor of fresh lemon juice and zest, for brighter but softer flavor. Adding strips of lemon zest to the hot oil was the perfect way to infuse the dressing with more citrus flavor. We wanted to add bulk to these salads, but not so much as to weigh down the spinach. Adding cheese and nuts seemed like a good combination, so we came up with a few variations on that theme. Quickly freezing the cheeses before adding them to the salad prevented them from melting in the heat of the dressing. The crunchy nuts added a welcome textural contrast. Be sure to cook the spinach just until it begins to wilt; any longer and the leaves will overcook and clump. Use curly-leaf spinach here; do not substitute flat-leaf or baby spinach.*

1½ ounces feta cheese, crumbled (⅓ cup)
3 tablespoons extra-virgin olive oil
1 (2-inch) strip lemon zest plus 1½ tablespoons juice
1 shallot, minced
2 teaspoons sugar
10 ounces curly-leaf spinach, stemmed and torn into bite-size pieces
6 radishes, trimmed and sliced thin
3 tablespoons chopped toasted pistachios
   Salt and pepper

1. Place feta on plate and freeze until slightly firm, about 15 minutes.

2. Cook oil, lemon zest, shallot, and sugar in Dutch oven over medium-low heat until shallot is softened, about 5 minutes. Off heat, discard zest and stir in lemon juice. Add spinach, cover, and let steam off heat until spinach just begins to wilt, about 30 seconds.

3. Transfer spinach mixture and liquid left in pot to large bowl. Add radishes, pistachios, and chilled feta and toss to combine. Season with salt and pepper to taste. Serve.

VARIATIONS

Strawberry, Goat Cheese, and Almond Wilted Spinach Salad
Substitute goat cheese for feta, grapefruit zest and juice for lemon, 6 thinly sliced strawberries for radishes, and almonds for pistachios.

Lime, Mango, and Peanut Wilted Spinach Salad
Omit feta. Substitute lime zest and juice for lemon, ½ chopped mango for radishes, and chopped dry-roasted peanuts for pistachios. Sprinkle with 1 tablespoon finely chopped fresh cilantro before serving.

FUSILLI WITH SPINACH AND RICOTTA

Serves 4 to 6   Total time: 35 minutes

WHY THIS RECIPE WORKS *Pastas like manicotti and tortellini are often stuffed with a creamy mixture of fresh spinach and ricotta. The combination is irresistible, but making fresh stuffed pasta is labor-intensive. We decided to turn this dish inside out for a quick weeknight meal that would highlight the spinach and not let it be overpowered by the rich cheese. We also needed to prevent the ricotta from curdling, which would result in a grainy, chalky sauce. To keep the spinach bright and green (and eliminate the tedious task of blanching and squeezing it dry), we cooked it very briefly in the pot along with the pasta. To keep the ricotta texture and flavor distinct, we opted to add most of the cheese in large dollops over the finished dish rather than fold it into the sauce. And to provide the sauce with both complexity and balance, we added lots of minced garlic, along with cayenne pepper, nutmeg, lemon juice and zest, and Parmesan cheese. We like corkscrew-shaped fusilli for this recipe since it traps the sauce well, but penne or campanelle also works.*

1 pound fusilli
   Salt and pepper
1 pound (16 cups) baby spinach, chopped
3 tablespoons extra-virgin olive oil
4 garlic cloves, minced
¼ teaspoon ground nutmeg
⅛ teaspoon cayenne pepper
11 ounces (1⅓ cups) whole-milk ricotta cheese
¼ cup heavy cream
1 teaspoon grated lemon zest plus 2 teaspoons juice
1 ounce Parmesan cheese, grated (½ cup), plus extra for serving

1. Bring 4 quarts water to boil in large pot. Add pasta and 1 tablespoon salt and cook, stirring often, until al dente. Stir spinach into pot with pasta and cook for 30 seconds. Reserve 1 cup cooking water, then drain pasta-spinach mixture and return it to pot.

2. Meanwhile, heat 2 tablespoons oil, garlic, nutmeg, and cayenne in small saucepan over medium heat until fragrant, about 1 minute.

Off heat, whisk in ⅓ cup ricotta, cream, lemon zest and juice, and ¾ teaspoon salt until smooth. In bowl, whisk remaining 1 cup ricotta, remaining 1 tablespoon oil, ¼ teaspoon pepper, and ⅛ teaspoon salt until smooth; set aside for serving.

3. Add cooked ricotta-cream mixture and Parmesan to pasta and toss to combine. Let pasta rest, tossing frequently, until sauce has thickened slightly and coats pasta, 2 to 4 minutes. Adjust consistency with reserved cooking water as needed. Transfer pasta to serving bowl and dot evenly with reserved seasoned ricotta mixture. Serve, passing extra Parmesan separately.

SPINACH LASAGNA

Serves 8 to 10   Total time: 1 hour 45 minutes

WHY THIS RECIPE WORKS *Fresh, emerald-green spinach highlighted by a delicate, savory white sauce; tender noodles; and mild, creamy cheese makes this spinach lasagna a spectacular success. We preferred cottage cheese to ricotta in this recipe, for the extra tang and creaminess it lent to the dish. We found certain other components useful as well: no-boil noodles that we soaked in hot water for 5 minutes to soften and blanched spinach from which we wrung out all excess water. Be sure to use Italian fontina rather than bland and rubbery Danish or American fontina. If it is not available, substitute whole-milk mozzarella. To make the cheese easier to shred, freeze it for 30 minutes to firm it up. If your baking dish is not broiler-safe, brown the lasagna at 500 degrees for about 10 minutes. Two pounds of flat-leaf spinach can be substituted for the curly-leaf spinach, but do not use baby spinach because it is much too delicate. Be sure to set up the ice water bath before cooking the spinach, as plunging it into the cold water immediately after blanching retains its bright green color and ensures that it doesn't overcook.*

SAUCE

1¼ pounds curly-leaf spinach, stemmed
    Salt and pepper
  5 tablespoons unsalted butter

  6 shallots, minced
  4 garlic cloves, minced
  ¼ cup all-purpose flour
3½ cups whole milk
  2 bay leaves
  ½ teaspoon ground nutmeg
  3 ounces Parmesan cheese, grated
     (1½ cups)

CHEESE FILLING

  8 ounces (1 cup) whole-milk cottage cheese
  1 large egg
  ¼ teaspoon salt

 12 no-boil lasagna noodles
  8 ounces Italian fontina cheese, shredded (2 cups)

1. **For the sauce** Bring 4 quarts water to boil in large pot. Fill large bowl halfway with ice and water. Add spinach and 1 tablespoon salt to boiling water and cook until just wilted, about 5 seconds. Using slotted spoon, transfer spinach to ice water, and let sit until cool, about 1 minute. Drain spinach and transfer to clean dish towel. Wrap towel tightly around spinach to form ball and wring until dry. Chop spinach and set aside.

2. Melt butter in medium saucepan over medium heat. Stir in shallots and garlic and cook until softened, about 4 minutes. Add flour and cook, stirring constantly, until thoroughly combined, about 1½ minutes (mixture should not brown). Gradually whisk in milk, scraping up any browned bits and smoothing out any lumps. Bring to boil, whisking often, then stir in bay leaves, nutmeg, ½ teaspoon salt, and ¼ teaspoon pepper. Reduce heat to low and simmer, whisking occasionally, for 10 minutes. Discard bay leaves, then whisk in ½ cup Parmesan until completely melted. Reserve ½ cup sauce in small bowl, then press plastic wrap directly against surface; set aside. Transfer remaining sauce to second bowl and stir in spinach, mixing well to break up any clumps, then press plastic directly against surface; set aside.

3. **For the cheese filling** Process cottage cheese, egg, and salt in food processor until very smooth, about 30 seconds; set aside.

4. Adjust oven rack to middle position and heat oven to 425 degrees. Pour 2 inches boiling water into 13 by 9-inch broiler-safe baking dish. Slip noodles into water, one at a time, and soak until pliable, about 5 minutes, separating noodles with tip of paring knife to prevent sticking. Remove noodles from water and place in single layer on clean dish towels, discarding water. Dry and grease dish.

5. Spread reserved sauce evenly over bottom of prepared dish. Arrange 3 noodles in single layer on top of sauce. Spread 1 cup spinach mixture evenly over noodles, sprinkle remaining 1 cup Parmesan over spinach mixture, and top cheese with 3 noodles. Spread 1 cup spinach mixture evenly over noodles, sprinkle 1 cup fontina over spinach mixture, and top with 3 noodles. Spread 1 cup spinach mixture evenly over noodles, followed by cheese filling. For final layer, arrange remaining 3 noodles over cheese filling, then cover noodles with remaining spinach mixture. Sprinkle remaining 1 cup fontina over spinach mixture.

6. Cover dish tightly with greased aluminum foil and bake until edges are just bubbling, about 20 minutes, rotating dish halfway through baking. Remove dish from oven and discard foil. Adjust oven rack 6 inches from broiler element and heat broiler. Broil lasagna until spotty brown, 4 to 6 minutes. Let lasagna cool for 15 minutes before serving.

SAAG PANEER

Serves 4 to 6   Total time: 1 hour 15 minutes

WHY THIS RECIPE WORKS *Saag paneer, a spicy pureed spinach mixture with soft cubes of creamy fresh cheese, is an Indian restaurant classic. We found that re-creating this dish at home wasn't as difficult as we expected. We made our own cheese by heating whole milk and buttermilk, squeezing the curds of excess moisture, then weighting the cheese down until it was firm enough to slice. For the spinach sauce, instead of cooking the spinach in batches on the stovetop, we simply wilted it all in the microwave. Adding the mustard greens lent additional complexity that worked well with the warm*

spices. *Leaving some water clinging to the spinach and mustard green leaves after rinsing helped encourage steam when cooking. Canned diced tomatoes brightened the dish, and buttery cashews—both pureed and chopped—gave our dish a subtle nutty richness. To ensure that the cheese is firm, wring it tightly in step 2 and use two plates that nestle together snugly. Fifteen ounces of flat-leaf spinach can be substituted for the curly-leaf spinach, but do not use baby spinach because it is much too delicate.*

CHEESE
- 3 quarts whole milk
- 3 cups buttermilk
- 1 tablespoon salt

SPINACH SAUCE
- 10 ounces curly-leaf spinach, stemmed
- 12 ounces mustard greens, stemmed
- 3 tablespoons unsalted butter
- 1 teaspoon cumin seeds
- 1 teaspoon ground coriander
- 1 teaspoon paprika
- ½ teaspoon ground cardamom
- ¼ teaspoon ground cinnamon
- 1 onion, chopped fine
    Salt and pepper
- 3 garlic cloves, minced
- 1 tablespoon grated fresh ginger

- 1 jalapeño chile, stemmed, seeded, and minced
- 1 (14.5-ounce) can diced tomatoes, drained and chopped
- ½ cup cashews, toasted and chopped
- 1 cup water
- 1 cup buttermilk
- 3 tablespoons minced fresh cilantro

1. For the cheese Line colander with triple layer of cheesecloth and set in sink. Bring milk to boil in Dutch oven. Off heat, whisk in buttermilk and salt and let sit for 1 minute. Pour milk mixture through cheesecloth and let curds drain for 15 minutes.

2. Pull edges of cheesecloth together to form pouch. Twist edges of cheesecloth together, firmly squeezing out as much liquid as possible. Place taut, twisted cheese pouch between 2 large plates and weight down with heavy Dutch oven. Set aside at room temperature until cheese is firm and set, about 45 minutes, then remove cheesecloth. Cut cheese into ½-inch pieces; set aside.

3. For the spinach sauce Microwave spinach in covered bowl until wilted, about 3 minutes. Let cool slightly, then chop enough spinach to measure ⅓ cup. Transfer remaining spinach to blender. Microwave mustard

greens in covered bowl until wilted, about 4 minutes. Let cool slightly, then chop enough mustard greens to measure ⅓ cup, and combine with chopped spinach; set aside. Transfer remaining mustard greens to blender with remaining spinach; set aside.

4. Melt butter in 12-inch skillet over medium-high heat. Add cumin seeds, coriander, paprika, cardamom, and cinnamon and cook until fragrant, about 30 seconds. Add onion and ¾ teaspoon salt and cook until softened, about 3 minutes. Stir in garlic, ginger, and jalapeño and cook until lightly browned and just beginning to stick to pan, 2 to 3 minutes. Stir in tomatoes and cook until pan is dry and tomatoes are beginning to brown, 3 to 4 minutes. Remove skillet from heat.

5. Transfer half of onion mixture, ¼ cup cashews, and water to blender with greens and process until smooth, about 1 minute. Stir puree, chopped greens, and buttermilk into skillet with remaining onion mixture and bring to simmer over medium-high heat. Reduce heat to low, cover, and cook until flavors have blended, 5 minutes. Season with salt and pepper to taste. Gently fold in cheese cubes and cook until just heated through, 1 to 2 minutes. Transfer to serving platter, sprinkle with remaining ¼ cup cashews and cilantro, and serve.

CHICKEN FLORENTINE
Serves 4   Total time: 50 minutes
WHY THIS RECIPE WORKS *Legend has it that in the 16th century, Catherine de' Medici, of the influential Medici family of Florence, brought a cadre of Florentine cooks to France with her when she married King Henry II. It is also said that spinach was her favorite vegetable, and the dishes that her cooks created for her in France were the origins of the culinary term "Florentine" or "à la Florentine" in relation to dishes featuring spinach. So, to honor this history and restore chicken Florentine to its elegant roots, we started with fresh spinach. To prevent the water from the spinach from washing out the other flavors in the dish, we drained excess liquid from the cooked spinach by pressing the leaves with the back*

of a spoon in a colander. For flavor, we seared the chicken breasts first and then poached them in the sauce before broiling. We used cream to make the sauce silky and built volume with equal amounts of chicken broth and water. We also added a squeeze of lemon juice and a hit of zest, along with Parmesan cheese for its nutty, savory punch. You will need a broiler-safe dish for this recipe.

 2 tablespoons vegetable oil
12 ounces (12 cups) baby spinach
 4 (6- to 8-ounce) boneless, skinless
     chicken breasts, trimmed
     Salt and pepper
 1 shallot, minced
 2 garlic cloves, minced
1¼ cups chicken broth
1¼ cups water
 1 cup heavy cream
 6 tablespoons grated Parmesan cheese
 1 teaspoon grated lemon zest plus
     1 teaspoon juice

1. Adjust oven rack to upper-middle position and heat broiler. Heat 1 tablespoon oil in 12-inch skillet over medium-high heat until shimmering. Add spinach and cook, stirring occasionally, until wilted, 1 to 2 minutes. Transfer spinach to colander to drain and let cool slightly. Once cool enough to handle, transfer spinach to clean dish towel, wrap towel tightly around spinach to form ball, and wring until dry; set aside.

2. Pat chicken dry with paper towels and season with salt and pepper. Wipe skillet dry with paper towels. Heat remaining 1 tablespoon oil in now-empty skillet over medium-high heat until just smoking. Add chicken and cook until golden, 2 to 3 minutes per side. Add shallot and garlic to skillet and cook until fragrant, about 30 seconds. Stir in broth, water, and cream and bring to boil.

3. Reduce heat to medium-low and simmer until chicken registers 160 degrees, about 10 minutes. Transfer chicken to plate and tent with aluminum foil. Continue to simmer sauce until reduced to 1 cup, about 10 minutes. Off heat, stir in ¼ cup Parmesan and lemon zest and juice.

4. Slice chicken crosswise ½ inch thick and arrange in broiler-safe dish. Scatter spinach over chicken and pour sauce over spinach. Sprinkle with remaining 2 tablespoons Parmesan and broil until golden brown, 3 to 5 minutes. Serve.

BREAKFAST STRATA WITH SPINACH AND GRUYÈRE
Serves 4 to 6   Total time: 2 hours 15 minutes (plus 1 hour refrigeration time)
WHY THIS RECIPE WORKS *Earthy spinach and nutty cheese star in this brunch-worthy strata. Ideally, this savory make-ahead bread pudding should be rich enough to satisfy without being overindulgent. And, since strata is such a great make-ahead dish, it should also be straightforward to put together. Unfortunately, too many recipes for strata are soggy and laden with excessive custard and filling ingredients. Looking to create a go-to breakfast or brunch casserole, we first considered the bread. Whole dried bread slices had the best texture and appearance, and buttering them added richness. Spinach, shallot, and Gruyère complemented each other perfectly for the filling, and we sautéed the vegetables to remove excess moisture and prevent the casserole from becoming waterlogged. Weighting down the assembled strata overnight improved its texture; we found that two 1-pound boxes of brown or confectioners' sugar, laid side by side over the plastic wrap, made ideal weights. One hour is minimum, but you could do it overnight to bake the strata the following morning. The recipe can be doubled and assembled in a greased 13 by 9-inch baking dish; increase the baking time to 1 hour and 20 minutes. Substitute any semisoft melting cheese, such as Havarti, sharp cheddar, or Colby, for the Gruyère.*

8–10 (½-inch-thick) slices French or
       Italian bread
   4 tablespoons unsalted butter,
       softened
   4 shallots, minced
       Salt and pepper
  10 ounces frozen chopped spinach,
       thawed and squeezed dry
   ½ cup dry white wine
   6 ounces Gruyère cheese,
       shredded (1½ cups)
   6 large eggs
1¾ cups half-and-half

1. Adjust oven rack to middle position and heat oven to 225 degrees. Arrange bread in single layer on rimmed baking sheet and bake until dry and crisp, about 40 minutes, flipping slices halfway through baking. Let bread cool slightly, then spread 2 tablespoons butter evenly over 1 side of bread slices.

2. Meanwhile, melt remaining 2 tablespoons butter in 10-inch nonstick skillet over medium heat. Add shallots and pinch salt and cook until softened, about 3 minutes. Stir in spinach and cook until warmed through, about 2 minutes; transfer to bowl. Add wine to now-empty skillet and simmer over medium-high heat until reduced to ¼ cup, about 3 minutes; set aside to cool.

3. Grease 8-inch square baking dish. Arrange half of bread slices, buttered side up, in single layer in dish. Sprinkle half of spinach mixture and ½ cup Gruyère over top. Repeat with remaining bread, remaining spinach mixture, and ½ cup Gruyère to make second layer.

4. Whisk eggs, reduced wine, half-and-half, 1 teaspoon salt, and pinch pepper together in bowl, then pour evenly over top of bread and cheese in dish. Cover dish tightly with plastic wrap, pressing it flush to surface. Weight down strata and refrigerate for at least 1 hour.

5. Adjust oven rack to middle position and heat oven to 325 degrees. Meanwhile, let strata sit at room temperature for 20 minutes. Unwrap strata and top with remaining ½ cup Gruyère. Bake until edges and center are puffed and edges have pulled away slightly from sides of dish, 50 to 55 minutes. Let casserole cool for 5 minutes before serving.

Breakfast Strata with Spinach and Gruyère

SWEET PEPPERS

The world of sweet peppers is smaller than the world of chile peppers, although in most kitchens sweet peppers get a lot more use. **BELL PEPPERS** are the most important category of sweet peppers and the ones we most typically cook and serve as a vegetable dish. In addition to the ubiquitous bell peppers, this chapter includes **PIMENTOS**, which are primarily available bottled rather than fresh, and **CUBANELLE** peppers—also called Italian frying peppers—the light yellowish-green long, skinny peppers, known for their thin walls and mildly sweet flavor.

Like tomatoes, sweet peppers are technically a fruit, because they are produced from flowering plants and contain seeds. But we treat peppers like a vegetable. Sweet peppers, like all peppers, are members of the capsicum genus; bell peppers are the only variety that doesn't produce capsaicin, the compound that gives chile peppers their heat.

In our cooking, we tend to gravitate toward the sunshiny sweetness of red peppers, showcasing them in the sweet-tart-smoky Middle Eastern dip Muhammara and in the Red Bell Pepper Chutney that we pair with our Slow-Roasted Pork Shoulder. They also serve as a counterpoint to more savory ingredients, as in our Quinoa Salad with Red Bell Pepper and Cilantro. Then there are times when the less sweet, slightly bitter flavor of green bell peppers is desired, as in our Cuban-Style Black Beans and Rice, where their vegetal quality cuts through the richness of the salt pork.

The most famous use for pimentos may be to stuff green olives, but we favor them in the classic and beloved Southern cheddar cheese spread. AndxCubanelle peppers bring their delicate flavor and texture to the richly spiced Basque dish of Eggs Pipérade.

shopping and storage

Sweet peppers are available year-round, though their traditional season is late summer and into the fall. Select firm, crisp peppers that feel heavy for their size and are glossy-looking and vibrant in color; avoid any with shriveled, wrinkled, or soft spots. Store sweet peppers in an open plastic produce bag in the refrigerator for one week or longer.

taste the rainbow

Sweet peppers come in a veritable rainbow of colors: green, orange, yellow, red, even purple, brown, and multicolored. These various colors don't taste the same, nor do they have the same nutritional profile.

All sweet peppers start out green. The bell pepper is a dark green, and the Cubanelle is a light green. As they mature, bell peppers change to either yellow or orange, and then most peppers change to red, their most ripened state (some bell pepper varieties stay yellow or orange at their most ripened state). Cubanelle peppers will turn orange-red or bright red if allowed to ripen on the plant.

Green peppers are less expensive than other colors because they are harvested sooner; this is also why they are less sweet than other colors, and they have fewer vitamins overall. Purple peppers have green flesh and are similar to green peppers in flavor; they turn green when cooked.

Orange and yellow peppers are mildly sweet. Red peppers have been left on the plant the longest, and they are much sweeter than other peppers, with significantly more vitamin C and beta-carotene. Because they are the ripest sweet peppers, they also have the shortest shelf life.

not all bell peppers are the same

There are two basic types of sweet bell peppers that are readily available: boxy, identical-looking, thick-walled hothouse bell peppers and slightly elongated, more irregularly shaped, thinner-walled field bell peppers. They won't be labeled as "hothouse" or "field" in the market, but they're easy enough to distinguish by sight.

HOTHOUSE BELL PEPPERS Hothouse bell peppers are thicker-walled, more watery, and a bit less crunchy; these are the supermarket standard and tend to be more expensive because of their growing conditions. They are valued for their uniform size and shape, and so are excellent for making crudités or stuffed peppers, or for use in dishes where this consistency is important.

FIELD BELL PEPPERS Field bell peppers were simply grown in a field rather than in a greenhouse. They are a bit more irregularly shaped and have thinner walls, which gives them more surface area per ounce. This means they become very flavorful when roasted or grilled (since the surface area is where the sweet, smoky flavor compounds develop). Field peppers work well in dishes where they are chopped or pureed.

what is a pimento?

The pimento is a sweet pepper, but it's not a bell pepper. Though they look a lot like jarred roasted red peppers, jarred pimentos are made from a heart-shaped variety of red pepper that is slightly sweeter than a red bell pepper. In addition to being available jarred or canned in an acidic brine (they are occasionally available fresh), pimentos are stuffed into pitted green olives or dried and finely ground to make paprika.

vegetable prep

Coring and Cutting Peppers

1. Slice off thin slice from top of pepper (and bottom, if recipe directs). Remove stem from top.

2. Cut around core, then use your fingers to remove core from pepper.

3. Slice down through side of pepper.

4. Lay pepper flat on cutting board, cut away any remaining ribs, then cut pepper into pieces as directed in recipe.

ROASTED BELL PEPPERS

Makes 1½ cups   Total time: 30 minutes

WHY THIS RECIPE WORKS *The simple process of roasting bell peppers transforms them into soft, succulent sweetness. Incredibly versatile, they can be used to top pizzas and sandwiches; in pasta sauces, frittatas or omelets, and chicken or tuna salads; or as a simple side on their own alongside steak or chicken. For roasted bell peppers that boasted plenty of sweet flavor and were properly softened but not mushy, we turned to the broiler. Cutting the bell peppers into three pieces each so that they would lie flat helped them cook evenly. Broiling the pieces until the skin was well charred ensured maximum flavor in the flesh beneath. Steaming the bell pepper pieces in a pouch fashioned from the aluminum foil on which they were cooked expedited both peeling and cleanup. Cooking times will vary depending on the broiler and the thickness of the bell pepper walls, so watch the bell peppers carefully as they cook. Use any color of peppers here, but since green bell peppers retain some bitterness even when roasted, we think they are best used as a complement to sweeter red, yellow, and orange bell peppers.*

   3 large bell peppers

1. Line rimmed baking sheet with aluminum foil and spray with vegetable oil spray. Slice ½ inch from top and bottom of each bell pepper. Gently remove stems from tops. Twist and pull out each core, using knife to loosen at edges if necessary. Cut slit down 1 side of each bell pepper.

2. Turn each bell pepper skin side down and gently press so it opens to create long strip. Slide knife along insides of bell peppers to remove remaining ribs and seeds.

3. Arrange bell pepper strips, tops, and bottoms skin side up on prepared sheet and flatten all pieces with your hand. Adjust oven rack 3 to 4 inches from broiler element and heat broiler. Broil until skin is puffed and most of surface is well charred, 10 to 13 minutes, rotating sheet halfway through broiling.

4. Using tongs, pile bell peppers in center of foil. Gather foil over bell peppers and crimp to form pouch. Let steam for 10 minutes.

Open foil packet carefully and spread out bell peppers. When cool enough to handle, peel bell peppers and discard skins. Serve.

GRILL-ROASTED PEPPERS WITH SHERRY VINAIGRETTE

Serves 4   Total time: 55 minutes

WHY THIS RECIPE WORKS *Grill roasting is a great, simple way to add deep, smoky flavor to sweet red bell peppers, making forxan unexpectedly luscious side dish for all manner of grilled meats, poultry, or seafood. To infuse the peppers with even more flavor and ensure that they were perfectly tender, we started by steaming them in a disposable pan with a mixture of olive oil, garlic, salt, and pepper. We then transferred the softened peppers to the grate to char and blacken. After the peppers were done grilling, we used the remaining oil mixture from the pan—now boosted with pepper juices and a hit of sherry vinegar— as a tangy vinaigrette for the tender peeled peppers. Take care not to overroast the peppers—when the skin of the pepper puffs up and turns black, it has reached the point at which the flavor is maximized and the texture of the flesh is soft but not mushy.*

  ¼ cup extra-virgin olive oil
  3 garlic cloves, peeled and smashed
      Salt and pepper
  1 (13 by 9-inch) disposable aluminum pan
  6 red bell peppers
  1 tablespoon sherry vinegar

1. Combine oil, garlic, ½ teaspoon salt, and ¼ teaspoon pepper in disposable pan. Using paring knife, cut around stems of peppers and remove cores and seeds. Place peppers in pan and turn to coat with oil. Cover pan tightly with aluminum foil.

2a. For a charcoal grill Open bottom vent completely. Light large chimney starter filled with charcoal briquettes (6 quarts). When top coals are partially covered with ash, pour evenly over half of grill. Set cooking grate in place, cover, and open lid vent completely. Heat grill until hot, about 5 minutes.

2b. For a gas grill Turn all burners to high, cover, and heat grill until hot, about 15 minutes. Turn all burners to medium-high.

3. Clean and oil cooking grate. Place pan on grill (hotter side if using charcoal) and cook, covered, until peppers are just tender and skins begin to blister, 10 to 15 minutes, rotating and shaking pan halfway through cooking.

4. Remove pan from heat and carefully remove foil (reserve foil to use later). Using tongs, remove peppers from pan, allowing juices to drip back into pan, and place on grill (hotter side if using charcoal). Grill peppers, covered, turning every few minutes until skins are blackened, 10 to 15 minutes.

5. Transfer juices and garlic in pan to medium bowl and whisk in vinegar. Remove peppers from grill, return to now-empty pan, and cover tightly with foil. Let peppers steam for 5 minutes. Using spoon, scrape blackened skin off each pepper. Quarter peppers lengthwise, add to vinaigrette in bowl, and toss to combine. Season with salt and pepper to taste, and serve.

VARIATION

Grill-Roasted Peppers with Rosemary
Add 1 rosemary sprig to oil mixture in step 1 (discard after grilling). Substitute red wine vinegar for sherry vinegar.

PIMENTO CHEESE SPREAD

Serves 8   Total time: 15 minutes

WHY THIS RECIPE WORKS *This deconstructed cheese ball is a popular Southern spread that can be slathered on anything from crackers and sandwiches to crudités. Drained jarred sweet red pimento peppers are what give the cheesy spread its name and trademark color. You can buy it premade at the grocery store, but homemade spreads are infinitely better and quick to make. Most recipes use a combination of extra-sharp cheddar cheese and a milder cheddar or Monterey Jack, but we found that batches made with all extra-sharp cheese tasted more complex and satisfying. To give our spread a well-rounded flavor and a little kick, we also*

GRILL-ROASTED PEPPERS WITH SHERRY VINAIGRETTE

Our grill-roasting technique adds a new depth of smoky savoriness to the sweetness of roasted red bell peppers. After cooking on the grill in a covered grill pan to soften, the peppers then go right onto the grill grate to blacken and absorb the smoky flavors and aromas from the live fire. Making a bright vinaigrette right in the grill pan with the juices from cooking the peppers ensures that every bit of sweet pepper flavor goes into this dish.

1. Combine the oil, garlic, salt, and pepper in a 13 by 9-inch disposable aluminum pan. Place the cored, seeded peppers in the pan and turn to coat them with the oil. Cover the pan tightly with aluminum foil.

2. Cook the peppers on the grill until they are just tender and their skins begin to blister, 10 to 15 minutes, rotating and shaking the pan halfway through the cooking process.

3. Remove the pan from the grill, remove the foil, and, using tongs, transfer the peppers from the pan directly to the grill grate. Grill the peppers, turning them as needed, until their skins are blackened, 10 to 15 minutes.

4. Meanwhile, transfer the juices and garlic from the pan to a bowl and whisk in the vinegar. Return the peppers to the empty pan, cover again with foil, and let the peppers steam in the pan for 5 minutes.

5. Using a spoon, scrape the blackened skin off each pepper. Quarter the peppers lengthwise.

6. Add the grill-roasted peppers to the vinaigrette and toss to combine.

added some Worcestershire sauce, minced garlic, and a dash or two of hot sauce. Finally, we mixed in just enough mayonnaise to bind everything together. Both white and orange extra-sharp cheddar work well here. Don't substitute store-bought preshredded cheese; it doesn't blend well and produces a dry spread. If you can't find jarred pimentos, an equal amount of roasted red peppers may be substituted.

½ cup jarred pimentos, drained
  and patted dry
6 tablespoons mayonnaise
2 garlic cloves, minced
1½ teaspoons Worcestershire sauce
1 teaspoon hot sauce, plus extra to taste
1 pound extra-sharp cheddar cheese,
  shredded (4 cups)
  Salt and pepper

Process pimentos, mayonnaise, garlic, Worcestershire, and hot sauce in food processor until smooth, about 20 seconds. Add cheese and pulse until uniformly blended, with fine bits of cheese throughout, about 20 pulses. Season with salt, pepper, and extra hot sauce to taste, and serve.

~

MUHAMMARA

Makes about 1½ cups
Total time: 15 minutes
WHY THIS RECIPE WORKS *Our quick version of this traditional Middle Eastern red pepper dip is simple to make and bursting with authentic sweet, smoky, savory flavors. We started with home-roasted red peppers, which gave our muhammara a sweet, smoky depth and velvety texture, and spiced things up with paprika, cumin, and cayenne. Toasted walnuts added a creamy richness, which was offset by the tartness of the pomegranate molasses and lemon juice. Cracker crumbs absorbed extra juices, so the finished dip wasn't runny. We whirred everything in the food processor for ease of preparation and a smooth consistency. We prefer our home-made roasted red bell peppers here (page 408), but you can substitute store-bought jarred roasted red bell peppers. Any type of lean cracker may be used for the crumbs.*

Crush the crackers in a zipper-lock bag with a rolling pin. Serve muhammara with pita bread or crudités, or use as a sandwich spread.

1 cup roasted red bell peppers, chopped
½ cup walnuts, toasted
⅓ cup cracker crumbs
3 scallions, chopped
¼ cup extra-virgin olive oil
1½ tablespoons pomegranate molasses
4 teaspoons lemon juice
1½ teaspoons paprika
1 teaspoon ground cumin
½ teaspoon salt
⅛ teaspoon cayenne pepper

Process all ingredients in food processor until uniform coarse puree forms, about 15 seconds, scraping down sides of bowl halfway through processing. Transfer to bowl and serve. (Dip can be refrigerated for up to 3 days.)

~

QUINOA SALAD WITH RED BELL PEPPER AND CILANTRO

Serves 4 Total time: 1 hour
WHY THIS RECIPE WORKS *Bell peppers work especially well in room-temperature grain salads, lending a burst of crunchy, juicy sweetness. Here we chose red bell pepper, along with jalapeño and red onion for a spicy counterpoint, and fresh cilantro for a bright herbal note. All these ingredients both tasted and looked great paired with the hearty, chewy quinoa (which happens to be high in protein). Before serving, we tossed the salad mixture with a bright dressing flavored with lime juice, mustard, garlic, and cumin. Rinse the quinoa in a fine-mesh strainer, drain it, and then spread it on a rimmed baking sheet lined with a dish towel and let dry for 15 minutes before proceeding with the recipe. To make this dish spicier, add the chile seeds.*

1 cup prewashed white quinoa,
  rinsed and dried
1½ cups water
  Salt and pepper
½ red bell pepper, chopped fine
½ jalapeño chile, minced

2 tablespoons finely chopped red onion
1 tablespoon minced fresh cilantro
2 tablespoons fresh lime juice
1 tablespoon extra-virgin olive oil
2 teaspoons Dijon mustard
1 garlic clove, minced
½ teaspoon ground cumin

1. Toast quinoa in large saucepan over medium heat, stirring frequently, until quinoa is lightly toasted and aromatic, about 5 minutes. Stir in water and ¼ teaspoon salt and bring to simmer. Cover, reduce heat to low, and cook until water is mostly absorbed and quinoa is nearly tender, about 12 minutes. Spread quinoa out over rimmed baking sheet and set aside until tender and cool, about 20 minutes.

2. Transfer cooled quinoa to large bowl. Stir in bell pepper, jalapeño, onion, and cilantro. In separate bowl, whisk lime juice, oil, mustard, garlic, and cumin together, then pour over quinoa mixture and toss to coat. Season with salt and pepper to taste, and serve.

~

ROASTED RED PEPPER SOUP WITH PAPRIKA AND CILANTRO CREAM

Serves 6 to 8 Total time: 1 hour 15 minutes
WHY THIS RECIPE WORKS *We wanted to concentrate the smoky, rich flavor of roasted red peppers in a silky pureed soup. We started by broiling the peppers until they were charred and puffed. Next, we built an aromatic base for our soup with garlic, red onion, cumin, and smoked paprika. Sautéing some tomato paste and flour gave the soup umami flavor and a velvety thickness. Finally, we whisked in broth, added the peppers, and simmered them until tender before blending the soup until smooth. For a garnish, we whisked up a bright cilantro-lime yogurt. The flavor of this soup depends on homemade roasted red peppers; do not substitute jarred. The broiling time for the peppers in step 2 may vary depending on the intensity of your broiler. Sweet paprika can be substituted for the smoked paprika. We prefer the rich flavor of whole-milk yogurt here; however, low-fat yogurt will also work. Do not use nonfat.*

Roasted Red Pepper Soup with Paprika
and Cilantro Cream

½ cup whole-milk yogurt

3 tablespoons minced fresh cilantro

1 teaspoon lime juice

Salt and pepper

8 red bell peppers, cored and flattened

1 tablespoon extra-virgin olive oil

2 garlic cloves, minced

1 red onion, chopped

½ teaspoon ground cumin

½ teaspoon smoked paprika

2 tablespoons tomato paste

1 tablespoon all-purpose flour

4 cups chicken or vegetable broth, plus extra as needed

1 bay leaf

½ cup half-and-half

2 tablespoons dry sherry

1. Whisk yogurt, 1 tablespoon cilantro, and lime juice together in bowl. Season with salt and pepper to taste. Cover and refrigerate until ready to serve.

2. Adjust oven rack 3 inches from broiler element and heat broiler. Spread half of peppers skin side up on aluminum foil–lined baking sheet. Broil until skin is charred and puffed but flesh is still firm, 8 to 10 minutes, rotating sheet halfway through broiling. Transfer broiled peppers to bowl, cover with plastic wrap or foil, and let steam until skins peel off easily, 10 to 15 minutes. Repeat with remaining peppers. Peel broiled peppers, discarding skins, and chop coarse.

3. Cook oil and garlic together in Dutch oven over low heat, stirring constantly, until garlic is foamy, sticky, and straw-colored, 6 to 8 minutes. Stir in onion and ¼ teaspoon salt, increase heat to medium, and cook until softened, about 5 minutes.

4. Stir in cumin and paprika and cook until fragrant, about 30 seconds. Stir in tomato paste and flour and cook for 1 minute. Slowly whisk in broth, scraping up any browned bits and smoothing out any lumps. Stir in bay leaf and chopped peppers, bring to simmer, and cook until peppers are very tender, 5 to 7 minutes.

5. Discard bay leaf. Working in batches, process soup in blender until smooth, about 2 minutes. Return soup to clean pot and stir

in half-and-half and sherry. Heat soup gently over low heat until hot (do not boil) and adjust consistency with extra hot broth as needed. Stir in remaining 2 tablespoons cilantro and season with salt and pepper to taste. Serve, drizzling individual portions with yogurt mixture.

EGGS PIPÉRADE

Serves 6 to 8   Total time: 50 minutes

WHY THIS RECIPE WORKS *The sweet pepper and tomato sauté known as* pipérade *is a classic Basque accompaniment to scrambled eggs. Pipérade delivers richness, acidity, and tempered heat from a combination of fresh sweet peppers, tomatoes, and fragrant spices like paprika. Since we had already perfected our scrambled egg technique, we focused our attention on achieving a great pipérade. Tasters liked a combination of red bell peppers and Italian Cubanelle peppers for their sweetness and delicate fresh flavor. By using canned peeled tomatoes, we avoided chewy bits of tomato skin; draining the tomatoes of most of their juice kept the dish from being watery. Onion, garlic, bay leaf, and thyme offered aromatic complexity; a bit of sherry vinegar brought the flavors*

into focus. While in many pipérade recipes the eggs are scrambled with the vegetable mixture, we found that the liquid from the produce caused the eggs to cook up stringy and wet rather than fluffy and creamy. We opted to cook the eggs separately and then plate the two elements alongside one another to preserve the clean yellow color of the eggs. We prefer to make this dish with Cubanelle peppers, which are chartreuse in color and look similar to banana peppers; if you can't find them, you can substitute green bell peppers. You will need a 12-inch nonstick skillet with a tight-fitting lid for this recipe.

5 tablespoons extra-virgin olive oil

1 large onion, chopped

1 bay leaf

Salt and pepper

4 garlic cloves, minced

2 teaspoons paprika

1 teaspoon minced fresh thyme or ¼ teaspoon dried

¾ teaspoon red pepper flakes

3 red bell peppers, stemmed, seeded, and cut into ½-inch-wide strips

3 Cubanelle peppers, stemmed, seeded, and cut into ½-inch-wide strips

1 (14-ounce) can whole peeled tomatoes, drained with ¼ cup juice reserved, chopped
3 tablespoons minced fresh parsley
2 teaspoons sherry vinegar
12 large eggs
2 tablespoons water

1. Heat 3 tablespoons oil in 12-inch nonstick skillet over medium heat until shimmering. Add onion, bay leaf, and ½ teaspoon salt and cook until onion is softened and lightly browned, 5 to 7 minutes. Stir in garlic, paprika, thyme, and pepper flakes and cook until fragrant, about 1 minute. Add bell peppers, Cubanelle peppers, and 1 teaspoon salt, cover, and cook, stirring occasionally, until peppers begin to soften, about 10 minutes.

2. Reduce heat to medium-low. Uncover, add tomatoes and reserved juice, and cook, stirring occasionally, until mixture appears dry and peppers are tender but not mushy, 10 to 12 minutes. Off heat, discard bay leaf. Stir in 2 tablespoons parsley and vinegar and season with salt and pepper to taste. Transfer to bowl and cover to keep warm.

3. Beat eggs, water, ½ teaspoon salt, and ¼ teaspoon pepper with fork in bowl until thoroughly combined and mixture is pure yellow; do not overbeat.

4. Wipe skillet clean with paper towels. Heat remaining 2 tablespoons oil in now-empty skillet over medium heat until shimmering. Add egg mixture and, using heat-resistant rubber spatula, constantly and firmly scrape along bottom and sides of skillet until eggs begin to clump and spatula leaves trail on bottom of skillet, 1½ to 2 minutes.

5. Reduce heat to low and gently but constantly fold eggs until clumped and slightly wet, 30 to 60 seconds. Off heat, sprinkle with remaining 1 tablespoon parsley and serve immediately with pepper mixture.

CUBAN-STYLE BLACK BEANS AND RICE

Serves 6 to 8   Total time: 2 hours (plus 8 hours soaking time)

WHY THIS RECIPE WORKS *Beans and rice in some configuration is a familiar dish the world over, but Cuban black beans and rice is unique in that the rice is cooked in the inky concentrated liquid left over from cooking the beans, which renders the rice just as flavorful. For our own superlative version, we also wanted to enhance the flavors of the bell peppers and onions in the traditional* sofrito. *So we reserved a portion of the sofrito ingredients and simmered them with our beans to infuse them with pepper-and-onion flavor. Then, instead of dumping that flavorful bean-cooking liquid, we used it again to cook our rice and beans together. Lightly browning the remaining peppers, onions, and garlic with rendered salt pork added complex flavor, and baking the dish in the oven eliminated the crusty bottom that can form when it's cooked on the stove. It is important to use lean salt pork. If you can't find it, substitute six slices of bacon, decreasing the cooking time in step 4 to 8 minutes. If you are pressed for time, you can "quick-brine" your beans. In step 1, combine the salt, water, and beans in a large Dutch oven and bring to a boil over high heat. Remove the pot from the heat, cover, and let stand for 1 hour. Drain and rinse the beans and proceed with the recipe.*

Salt
1 cup dried black beans, picked over and rinsed
2 cups chicken broth
2 large green bell peppers, halved, stemmed, and seeded
1 large onion, halved crosswise and peeled, root end left intact
1 garlic head, 5 cloves minced, rest of head halved crosswise with skin left intact
2 bay leaves
1½ cups long-grain white rice
2 tablespoons extra-virgin olive oil
6 ounces lean salt pork, cut into ¼-inch pieces
4 teaspoons ground cumin
1 tablespoon minced fresh oregano
2 tablespoons red wine vinegar
2 scallions, sliced thin
Lime wedges

1. Dissolve 1½ tablespoons salt in 2 quarts cold water in large bowl or container. Add beans and soak at room temperature for at least 8 hours or up to 24 hours. Drain and rinse well.

2. Bring beans, 2 cups water, broth, 1 bell pepper half, 1 onion half (with root end), halved garlic head, bay leaves, and 1 teaspoon salt to simmer in Dutch oven over medium-high heat. Cover, reduce heat to low, and cook until beans are just soft, 30 to 35 minutes. Using tongs, discard bell pepper, onion, garlic, and bay leaves. Drain beans in colander set over large bowl, reserving 2½ cups bean cooking liquid. (If you don't have enough bean cooking liquid, add water to equal 2½ cups.) Do not clean pot.

3. Adjust oven rack to middle position and heat oven to 350 degrees. Place rice in large fine-mesh strainer and rinse under cold running water until water runs clear, about 1½ minutes. Shake strainer vigorously to remove all excess water; set rice aside. Cut remaining bell peppers and remaining onion half into 2-inch pieces and pulse in food processor until broken into rough ¼-inch pieces, about 8 pulses, scraping down sides of bowl as needed; set vegetables aside.

4. Heat 1 tablespoon oil and salt pork in now-empty pot over medium-low heat and cook, stirring frequently, until lightly browned and rendered, 15 to 20 minutes. Stir in remaining 1 tablespoon oil, chopped bell peppers and onion, cumin, and oregano. Increase heat to medium and cook, stirring frequently, until vegetables are softened and beginning to brown, 10 to 15 minutes. Add minced garlic and cook, stirring constantly, until fragrant, about 1 minute. Add rice and stir to coat, about 30 seconds.

5. Stir in beans, reserved bean cooking liquid, vinegar, and ½ teaspoon salt. Increase heat to medium-high and bring to simmer. Cover and transfer pot to oven. Cook until liquid is absorbed and rice is tender, about 30 minutes. Fluff with fork and let rest, uncovered, for 5 minutes. Serve, passing scallions and lime wedges separately.

CHICKEN PAPRIKASH

Serves 4   Total time: 2 hours

WHY THIS RECIPE WORKS *Chicken paprikash should be an aromatic, warmly flavored braise with succulent chicken, tender vegetables, and a rich, flavorful sour cream sauce with paprika at center stage. To achieve this goal for the home kitchen, we pared down the usual mile-long ingredient list and simplified the preparation. After browning chicken thighs, we ditched the skin so the sauce wouldn't become greasy. Sautéing red and green bell peppers and onion in the fond led to a rich base for our sauce, which we enhanced with paprika twice: once while sautéing the vegetables to let its flavor bloom, and then again after adding sour cream to finish the dish and instill it with spicy richness. Serve with buttered egg noodles; rice or mashed potatoes are also good options.*

8 (5- to 7-ounce) bone-in chicken thighs, trimmed
  Salt and pepper
1 teaspoon vegetable oil
1 large onion, halved and sliced thin
1 large red bell pepper, stemmed, seeded, halved widthwise, and cut into thin strips
1 large green bell pepper, stemmed, seeded, halved widthwise, and cut into thin strips
3½ tablespoons paprika
1 tablespoon all-purpose flour
¼ teaspoon dried marjoram
½ cup dry white wine
1 (14.5-ounce) can diced tomatoes, drained
⅓ cup sour cream
2 tablespoons minced fresh parsley

1. Adjust oven rack to lower-middle position and heat oven to 300 degrees. Pat chicken dry with paper towels and season with salt and pepper. Heat oil in Dutch oven over medium-high heat until shimmering. Add 4 chicken thighs, skin side down, and cook without moving them until skin is crisp and well browned, about 5 minutes. Using tongs, flip chicken and brown on second side, about 5 minutes; transfer to large plate. Repeat with remaining 4 chicken thighs; transfer to plate. When cool enough to handle, discard skin.

2. Pour off all but 1 tablespoon fat from pot, add onion, and cook over medium heat until softened, about 5 minutes. Stir in bell peppers and cook until onions are browned and peppers are softened, about 3 minutes. Stir in 3 tablespoons paprika, flour, and marjoram and cook, stirring constantly, until fragrant, about 1 minute. Stir in wine, tomatoes, and 1 teaspoon salt, scraping up any brown bits, and bring to simmer.

3. Nestle chicken into pot along with any accumulated juices. Cover, transfer pot to oven, and cook until chicken offers no resistance when poked with tip of paring knife but still clings to bone, about 1¼ hours.

4. Combine sour cream and remaining ½ tablespoon paprika in small bowl. Remove pot from oven and transfer chicken to individual serving bowls. Stir few tablespoons of hot sauce into sour cream to temper, then stir mixture back into remaining peppers and sauce. Ladle peppers and sauce over chicken, sprinkle with parsley, and serve.

STUFFED PEPPERS WITH CHICKPEAS, GOAT CHEESE, AND HERBS

Serves 6   Total time: 1 hour 15 minutes

WHY THIS RECIPE WORKS *Stuffed bell peppers are most typically prepared with a simple meat-and-rice filling, but we like to let our imagination wander further afield when thinking of creative stuffing mixtures. Here we decided on a flavorful vegetarian filling made up of coarsely mashed chickpeas combined with chunks of crispy toasted bread, garlic, scallions, parsley, and capers. Creamy goat cheese added richness and helped to bind the other stuffing ingredients together, and lemon zest and juice contributed a fresh brightness. Roasting the bell peppers until they were slightly blistered before stuffing them intensified their flavors, ensuring the peppers kept the center stage and were far more than just a vehicle for the stuffing. Altogether, this makes for a wonderful side dish or light main course. You can use any color of bell pepper in this recipe.*

½ cup extra-virgin olive oil, plus extra for drizzling
6 (7- to 8-ounce) bell peppers
  Salt and pepper
1 (15-ounce) can chickpeas, rinsed
7 ounces baguette, cut into ½-inch pieces (4 cups)
8 garlic cloves, minced
¼ teaspoon red pepper flakes
8 scallions, sliced
¼ cup minced fresh parsley
¼ cup minced fresh basil
3 tablespoons capers, chopped
1 tablespoon grated lemon zest plus 1 tablespoon juice
6 ounces goat cheese, crumbled (1½ cups)

1. Adjust oven rack to upper-middle position and heat oven to 475 degrees. Grease 13 by 9-inch baking pan with 1 tablespoon oil. Cut off top ½ inch of bell peppers and reserve; discard stems and seeds. Arrange bell peppers and their tops cut side down in prepared pan. Brush bell peppers and tops with 1 tablespoon oil, then season with salt and pepper.

2. Roast until bell peppers are softened and beginning to blister, about 20 minutes. Flip bell peppers cut side up and let sit until cool enough to handle, about 5 minutes. Season insides with salt and pepper. Reduce oven temperature to 350 degrees.

3. Using potato masher, coarsely mash chickpeas in large bowl. Chop bell pepper tops into ¼-inch pieces and add to bowl with chickpeas.

4. Heat ¼ cup oil in 12-inch nonstick skillet over medium heat until shimmering. Add bread and cook, stirring occasionally, until light golden brown and crispy, 5 to 7 minutes. Push bread to 1 side of skillet and add remaining 2 tablespoons oil to empty spot. Add garlic and pepper flakes to oil and cook until fragrant, about 30 seconds. Stir garlic mixture and ½ teaspoon salt into bread to combine. Transfer to bowl with chickpea mixture; let cool completely, about 10 minutes.

5. Stir scallions, parsley, basil, capers, lemon zest and juice, 1 teaspoon salt, and 1 teaspoon pepper into chickpea mixture. Gently fold in goat cheese until combined.

6. Divide filling evenly among bell peppers, mounding slightly. Bake until filling registers between 100 and 120 degrees and begins to brown on top, 15 to 20 minutes. Drizzle with extra oil before serving.

SLOW-ROASTED PORK SHOULDER WITH RED BELL PEPPER CHUTNEY

Serves 8 to 12   Total time: 6 hours 15 minutes (plus 12 hours refrigeration time)

WHY THIS RECIPE WORKS *Pork has a natural affinity to being served with sweet vegetable or fruit flavors. We decided to elevate this classic flavor pairing by using our Red Bell Pepper Chutney, which is sweet from bell peppers and a bit of sugar; spicy from ginger, mustard seeds, and garlic; and savory from red onion. While lean pork loin is common (and has its merits), this old-fashioned pork butt roast has much more flavor than most other cuts of pork; plus, it boasts a thick fat cap that renders to a bronze, bacon-like crust in the oven. We started by rubbing the roast's exterior with brown sugar and salt, and left it to rest in the refrigerator overnight. The sugar boosted browning and offered a subtle sweetness that was nicely echoed by the aromatic chutney. Elevating the pork shoulder on a V-rack and pouring water into the roasting pan kept the pork's drippings from burning as the meat slowly roasted. Pork butt roast is often labeled Boston butt in the supermarket. Add more water to the roasting pan as necessary to prevent the fond from burning in step 3. Avoid adding the parsley to the chutney before it is fully cooled, or the parsley will wilt.*

PORK
- 1 (6- to 8-pound) **bone-in pork butt roast**
- ⅓ cup **kosher salt**
- ⅓ cup **packed light brown sugar**
  Pepper

RED BELL PEPPER CHUTNEY
- 1 tablespoon **extra-virgin olive oil**
- 1 **red onion, chopped fine**
- 4 **red bell peppers, stemmed, seeded, and cut into ½-inch pieces**
- 1 cup **white wine vinegar**
- ½ cup plus 2 tablespoons **sugar**
- 2 **garlic cloves, peeled and smashed**
- 1 (1-inch) piece **ginger, peeled, sliced into thin coins, and smashed**
- 1 teaspoon **yellow mustard seeds**
- ½ teaspoon **kosher salt**
- ½ teaspoon **red pepper flakes**
- ¼ cup **minced fresh parsley**

1. For the pork Using sharp knife, cut slits 1 inch apart in crosshatch pattern in fat cap of roast, being careful not to cut into meat. Combine salt and sugar in bowl. Rub salt mixture over entire pork shoulder and into slits. Wrap roast tightly in double layer of plastic wrap, place on rimmed baking sheet, and refrigerate for at least 12 hours or up to 24 hours.

2. Adjust oven rack to lowest position and heat oven to 325 degrees. Unwrap roast and brush any excess salt mixture from surface. Season roast with pepper. Spray V-rack with vegetable oil spray, set rack in large roasting pan, and place roast on rack. Add 1 quart water to roasting pan.

3. Roast pork, basting twice during cooking, until meat is extremely tender and meat near bone registers 190 degrees, 5 to 6 hours. Transfer roast to carving board, tent with aluminum foil, and let rest for 1 hour.

4. For the bell pepper chutney Meanwhile, heat oil in large saucepan over medium heat until shimmering. Add onion and cook until softened, about 5 minutes. Stir in bell peppers, vinegar, sugar, garlic, ginger, mustard seeds, salt, and pepper flakes. Bring to simmer and cook until thickened and measures about 2 cups, about 40 minutes. Transfer to bowl and let cool to room temperature, about 2 hours. Discard garlic and ginger, then stir in parsley. (Chutney can be refrigerated for up to 1 week; bring to room temperature before serving.)

5. Using sharp paring knife, cut around inverted T-shaped bone until it can be pulled free from roast (use clean dish towel to grasp bone). Using slicing knife, slice roast into ¼-inch-thick-slices. Serve with chutney.

SWEET POTATOES

This may come as a surprise, but sweet potatoes are not related to potatoes. They are actually members of the morning glory family, whereas potatoes belong to the nightshade family. And sweet potatoes are emphatically not the same vegetable as yams. (See "Sweet Potatoes and Yams.") Many of us would be surprised at what a true yam looks like: blackish-brown, bark-like skin covering a tuber that can be 5 feet long! The rusty-skinned, orange-fleshed, and sweet-tasting root vegetable traditionally found next to the potatoes is always a variety of sweet potato.

There's a world of sweet potatoes that extends far beyond the orange confines of American markets. Ninety percent of the world's sweet potatoes are grown in Asia, where they are most often white-fleshed and neither as sweet nor as soft as the traditional orange-fleshed varieties we know in the United States.

But we love our sweet orange spuds, and thankfully the days of looking for them primarily in the canned-foods aisle have mostly passed. They are nearly as versatile in the kitchen as regular potatoes and can be cooked in many of the same preparations, though the techniques need to be adjusted to account for the higher sugar and lower starch content of sweet potatoes.

In these pages, we mash, roast, and spiralize them and give them different flavor profiles. We've reinvented classic Sweet Potato Casserole for a new generation, putting the vegetable in the spotlight. Their inherent sweetness makes them perfect in spicier dishes, such as our Sweet Potato, Poblano, and Black Bean Tacos and our Sweet Potato Vindaloo. And, of course, we've developed an easy, foolproof technique for perfectly crispy Thick-Cut Sweet Potato Fries.

shopping and storage

Sweet potatoes are available year-round, though their best season is in the fall. Look for firm potatoes that feel heavy for their size, with skin that shows no signs of wrinkling or sprouting. Sweet potatoes with a greenish tinge beneath the skin have had too much exposure to light, causing a natural toxin to develop, and they should also be avoided. Sweet potatoes come in a wide range of sizes. For even cooking, buy potatoes that are uniform in size and avoid potatoes larger than 1½ pounds; they require a longer roasting time and tend to cook unevenly.

Stored in a dark, cool, well-ventilated spot, sweet potatoes will keep for about one month; stored at room temperature, they will keep for a week or two. Do not store them in a plastic bag, which will hasten spoilage. Refrigeration is also a no-no for sweet potatoes, as it will cause their cores to change texture and become distressingly similar to a damp cork.

sweet potatoes and yams

You often hear the terms "yam" and "sweet potato" used interchangeably, but these vegetables belong to completely different botanical families. In the kitchen, they cannot be substituted for one another. Yams, generally sold in Latin and Asian markets, are often sold in chunks (they can grow to be several feet long) and can be found in dozens of varieties, with flesh ranging from white to light yellow to pink, and skin from off-white to brown. They all have very starchy, dry flesh. Sweet potatoes are also found in several varieties and can have firm or soft flesh, but it's the soft varieties that have in the past been mislabeled as "yams," and the confusion continues to this day. In an attempt to remedy this, the U.S. Department of Agriculture now requires labels listing the term "yam" to also list the term "sweet potato" when appropriate.

sweet potato varieties

Many varieties of sweet potatoes are available, and they can differ quite a bit in color, texture, and flavor. Often the conventional orange varieties found in supermarkets are not labeled as being particular varieties, which is usually fine since these sweet potatoes are fairly interchangeable in recipes. If we think a specific variety works best in a particular recipe, we've made a note of that.

BEAUREGARD Beauregard (most often sold as the conventional sweet potato) has dusky red skin and is sweet, moist, and buttery. Its versatility makes it our favorite variety.

JEWEL Jewel, with copper skin and tender, moist orange flesh, is also frequently found in supermarkets and is another favorite of ours.

RED GARNET Red Garnet is named for its red-purple skin; it has orange flesh that is more savory and less dense than Beauregard or Jewel.

WHITE White sweet potatoes, like the Japanese White and White Sweet, tend to be less moist and starchier than the orange-fleshed varieties.

PURPLE Purple sweet potatoes, like the Stokes Purple, have a dry, dense texture and the highest level of antioxidants of all the sweet potato varieties.

vegetable science

You Say Po-tay-to, I Say Po-tah-to

The familiar sweet potato varieties in American supermarkets contain far less starch and more sugar than regular white potatoes. As a result, they cook very differently. To illustrate this, consider the simple baked potato.

Baking a russet potato in a 450-degree oven for about 45 minutes produced an ideally fluffy interior. But the same approach using a sweet potato resulted in a leaden, watery interior. In the test kitchen, we discovered that baking sweet spuds in a 275-degree oven for about 3 hours produced tender, plush interiors with highly concentrated, caramelized flavors. This is because when a sweet potato's internal temperature hovers at 200 degrees, the pectin that gives its cell walls structure begins to break down so that the flesh softens and allows moisture to escape. At the same time, starch granules within the cell walls take up water and gelatinize, which makes the potato smooth and creamy.

To make these results useful for the home cook, we developed a method to jump-start the cooking process in the microwave. This hybrid cooking method turned russets gluey. But it sure did the trick with sweet potatoes, making them creamy, sweet, and complex.

vegetable prep

Cutting Sweet Potatoes into Wedges

1. Halve scrubbed potatoes and cut halves lengthwise into 1½-inch-thick wedges.

2. Cut thick wedges into ¾-inch-thick wedges, if recipe directs.

MASHED SWEET POTATOES

Serves 4   Total time: 45 minutes

WHY THIS RECIPE WORKS *Mashed sweet potatoes often appear on the table overdressed with seasonings and toppings. But these candied concoctions don't hold a candle to an honest sweet potato mash in terms of flavor. With a deep, natural sweetness that doesn't require much assistance, the humble sweet potato, we thought, would taste far better if prepared using only a modicum of ingredients. So we created this straightforward recipe to honor the sweet potato. We tried it with whole milk and with half-and-half, but a small amount of heavy cream, in combination with the butter, stole the show. For seasonings, we used just a little sugar, salt, and pepper; the various baking spices often added to mashed sweet potatoes were simply distracting. This is a silky puree with enough body to hold its shape while sitting on a fork, and it pushes this root vegetable's deep, earthy flavor to the forefront, where it should be.*

- 2 pounds sweet potatoes, peeled, quartered lengthwise, and sliced crosswise ¼ inch thick
- 4 tablespoons unsalted butter, cut into 4 pieces
- 2 tablespoons heavy cream
- 1 teaspoon sugar
  Salt and pepper

1. Cook potatoes, butter, cream, sugar, and ½ teaspoon salt in large saucepan, covered, over low heat, stirring occasionally, until potatoes fall apart when poked with fork, 35 to 45 minutes.

2. Off heat, mash potatoes in saucepan with potato masher until smooth. Season with salt and pepper to taste, and serve.

VARIATIONS

Mashed Sweet Potatoes with Garlic and Coconut

Substitute ½ cup coconut milk for butter and cream, and add 1 small minced garlic clove and ¼ teaspoon red pepper flakes to pot with potatoes. Stir in 1 tablespoon minced fresh cilantro just before serving.

Indian-Spiced Mashed Sweet Potatoes with Raisins and Cashews

Substitute dark brown sugar for granulated sugar and add ¾ teaspoon garam masala to saucepan along with sweet potatoes in step 1. Stir ¼ cup golden raisins and ¼ cup roasted unsalted cashews, chopped, into mashed sweet potatoes just before serving.

SLOW-COOKER MASHED SWEET POTATOES

Serves 6 to 8   Total time: 5 to 6 hours on low or 3 to 4 hours on high

WHY THIS RECIPE WORKS *Smooth and velvety with a buttery finish, these mashed sweets will keep you coming back for more. They're a great alternative to traditional mashed sweet potatoes at holiday time, since they free the stovetop for other dishes. Pressing a piece of parchment on top of the sweet potatoes resulted in even cooking, without any dry edges. For an accurate measurement of the boiling water, bring a full kettle of water to a boil and then measure out the desired amount. You will need a 5- to 7-quart slow cooker for this recipe. This recipe can be easily doubled in a 7-quart slow cooker; you will need to increase the cooking time range by 1 hour.*

- 3 pounds sweet potatoes, peeled and sliced ¼ inch thick
- ½ cup boiling water
- 1 teaspoon sugar
  Salt and pepper
- 6 tablespoons half-and-half, warmed
- 3 tablespoons unsalted butter, melted

1. Combine potatoes, boiling water, sugar, and ¾ teaspoon salt in slow cooker. Cut parchment paper into rectangular piece measuring 16 by 12 inches and press it firmly onto potatoes, folding down edges as needed. Cover and cook until potatoes are tender, 5 to 6 hours on low or 3 to 4 hours on high.

2. Discard parchment. Mash potatoes with potato masher until smooth. Stir in warm half-and-half and melted butter, and season with salt and pepper to taste. Serve.

BEST BAKED SWEET POTATOES WITH GARLIC AND CHIVE SOUR CREAM

Serves 4   Total time: 1 hour 15 minutes

WHY THIS RECIPE WORKS *The goal when baking sweet potatoes is entirely different than when baking russets: creamy—rather than fluffy—flesh with deeply complex flavor. Sweet potatoes bake differently than russets due to their lower starch level and higher sugar content. We learned that to bake a whole sweet potato to the point where its exterior was nicely tanned and its interior was silky and sweetly caramelized, the potatoes needed to reach 200 degrees and stay there for an hour, long enough for the starches to gelatinize and the moisture to evaporate for concentrated flavor. To keep our recipe efficient, we microwaved the potatoes until they hit 200 degrees and then transferred them to a hot oven to linger. Putting them on a wire rack set in a rimmed baking sheet allowed air to circulate around the potatoes and also caught any sugar that oozed from the potatoes as they roasted. A quick garlic-chive sour cream topping provided a cool, creamy finishing touch.*

GARLIC AND CHIVE SOUR CREAM
- ½ cup sour cream
- 1 tablespoon minced fresh chives
- 1 garlic clove, minced
- ⅛ teaspoon salt

POTATOES
- 4 small sweet potatoes (8 ounces each), unpeeled, each lightly pricked with fork in 3 places
  Salt and pepper

1. For the garlic and chive sour cream Combine all ingredients in small bowl. Refrigerate until ready to serve.

2. For the potatoes Adjust oven rack to middle position and heat oven to 425 degrees. Place potatoes on large plate and microwave until potatoes yield to gentle pressure and register 200 degrees, 6 to 9 minutes, flipping potatoes every 3 minutes.

3. Place wire rack in aluminum foil–lined rimmed baking sheet and spray rack with vegetable oil spray. Transfer potatoes to

prepared rack and bake for 1 hour (exteriors of potatoes will be lightly browned and potatoes will feel very soft when squeezed).

4. Slit each potato lengthwise. Using clean dish towel, hold ends and squeeze slightly to push flesh up and out. Transfer potatoes to serving platter. Season with salt and pepper to taste. Serve with sour cream topping.

VARIATION
Best Baked Sweet Potatoes with Garam Masala Yogurt
Omit garlic and chive sour cream. Combine ½ cup plain yogurt, 2 teaspoons lemon juice, ½ teaspoon garam masala, and ⅛ teaspoon salt in small bowl, and serve with potatoes.

ROASTED SWEET POTATOES

Serves 6 to 8   Total time: 1 hour 15 minutes
WHY THIS RECIPE WORKS *Too often, roasted sweet potatoes turn out starchy and wan. We wanted a method that gave us potatoes with a nicely caramelized exterior, a smooth, creamy interior, and an earthy sweetness. Cutting them into ¾-inch-thick rounds and laying them flat on a baking sheet ensured even cooking. A few experiments proved that a lower roasting temperature resulted in a sweeter potato, so we started the sliced potatoes in a cold (versus preheated) oven and covered them with aluminum foil, which allowed plenty of time for their starches to convert to sugars. We removed the foil after 30 minutes and continued to roast the potatoes until their edges were crisp. Choose potatoes that are as even in width as possible; trimming the small ends prevents them from burning. If you prefer not to peel the potatoes, just scrub them well before cutting.*

- 3 pounds sweet potatoes, peeled, ends squared off, sliced into ¾-inch-thick rounds
- 2 tablespoons extra-virgin olive oil
  Salt and pepper

1. Line rimmed baking sheet with parchment paper and spray with vegetable oil spray. Toss potatoes, oil, 1 teaspoon salt, and ¼ teaspoon pepper together in bowl. Arrange potatoes in single layer on prepared sheet and cover tightly with aluminum foil.

2. Adjust oven rack to middle position and place potatoes in cold oven. Turn oven to 425 degrees and cook potatoes for 30 minutes.

3. Remove baking sheet from oven and discard foil. Return potatoes to oven and cook until bottom edges of potatoes are golden brown, 15 to 25 minutes.

4. Remove baking sheet from oven and, using thin metal spatula, flip slices over. Continue to roast until bottom edges of potatoes are golden brown, 18 to 22 minutes. Let potatoes cool for 5 to 10 minutes, then transfer to serving platter. Serve.

VARIATIONS
Roasted Sweet Potatoes with Maple-Thyme Glaze
Whisk ¼ cup maple syrup, 2 tablespoons melted unsalted butter, and 2 teaspoons minced fresh thyme together in bowl. Brush mixture over both sides of partially cooked potatoes when flipping in step 4, then continue to roast potatoes as directed.

Roasted Sweet Potatoes with Spiced Brown Sugar Glaze
Cook ¼ cup packed light brown sugar, 2 tablespoons apple juice, 2 tablespoons unsalted butter, ¼ teaspoon ground cinnamon, ¼ teaspoon ground ginger, and ⅛ teaspoon ground nutmeg in small saucepan over medium heat until butter has melted and sugar is dissolved, 2 to 4 minutes. Brush mixture over both sides of partially cooked potatoes when flipping in step 4, then continue to roast potatoes as directed.

ROASTED SPIRALIZED SWEET POTATOES WITH WALNUTS AND FETA

Serves 4 to 6   Total time: 30 minutes
WHY THIS RECIPE WORKS *Roasted quickly in a hot oven, spiralized sweet potatoes make a fun, crowd-pleasing alternative to regular roasted white potatoes. We decided to use a spiralizer to cut the potatoes into beautiful ⅛-inch-thick noodles that would cook quickly. We found that simply roasting the potatoes in a hot oven, uncovered, for about 12 minutes gave us the result we were after: sweet potatoes that were tender but not mushy, with just a bit of caramelization.*

ROASTED SPIRALIZED SWEET POTATOES WITH WALNUTS AND FETA

Spiralizing offers a fun and easy way to fill your plate with the bounty of vegetables, and sweet potatoes are a heartier choice than most of the usual suspects. Though spiralized vegetable noodles are often served steamed, sautéed, or raw, roasting them caramelizes them slightly, concentrating and enhancing their flavor. The rich, slightly bitter walnuts and creamy-tangy feta provide the perfect counterpoint to the natural sweetness of the potatoes.

1. Peel the sweet potatoes and trim both ends of each sweet potato to square them off.

2. Using a spiralizer, cut the sweet potatoes into ⅛-inch-thick noodles.

3. Cut the potato noodles into 12-inch lengths.

4. Gently toss the potato noodles, olive oil, salt, and pepper together in a bowl.

5. Spread the noodles on a rimmed baking sheet and roast until tender, 12 to 14 minutes, stirring once halfway through roasting.

6. Season the sweet potatoes with salt and pepper to taste, and transfer them to a serving platter. Sprinkle the walnuts, feta, and parsley over the top, then drizzle with extra olive oil to taste.

To finish the dish, we sprinkled on ¼ cup each of tangy feta and rich toasted walnuts, plus a generous sprinkle of fresh parsley. Sweet potato noodles are quite delicate; be careful when tossing them with the oil and seasonings in step 2, and again when transferring them to the serving platter before serving. If you do not have a spiralizer, you can use a mandoline or V-slicer fitted with a ⅛-inch julienne attachment. Make sure to position the vegetables on the mandoline so that the resulting noodles are as long as possible. We do not recommend cutting vegetable noodles by hand.

- 2 pounds sweet potatoes, peeled and ends squared off
- 1 tablespoon extra-virgin olive oil, plus extra for serving
  Salt and pepper
- ¼ cup walnuts, toasted and chopped
- 1 ounce feta cheese, crumbled (¼ cup)
- 2 tablespoons chopped fresh parsley

1. Adjust oven rack to middle position and heat oven to 450 degrees. Using spiralizer, cut sweet potatoes into ⅛-inch-thick noodles, then cut noodles into 12-inch lengths.

2. Toss potato noodles, oil, ¼ teaspoon salt, and ⅛ teaspoon pepper together in bowl, then spread on rimmed baking sheet. Roast until just tender, 12 to 14 minutes, stirring once halfway through roasting.

3. Season potatoes with salt and pepper to taste, and transfer to serving platter. Sprinkle walnuts, feta, and parsley over top, then drizzle with extra oil to taste. Serve.

THICK-CUT SWEET POTATO FRIES

Serves 6 to 8   Total time: 45 minutes
WHY THIS RECIPE WORKS Sweet potatoes cook very differently than white potatoes—a fact that is nowhere more apparent than when making fries. It's very hard to make sweet potato fries that rival classic French fries made from russets. Sweet potato fries are typically either soggy or burnt—and

often they hit both marks at once. Occasionally a restaurant manages to deliver crispy sweet potato fries, but they never taste much like the tuber. These fries are usually not even house-made: They're frozen fries purchased from a food-processing plant. Furthermore, they're frequently cut too thin for our liking, offering little in the way of a supercreamy, sweet-tasting interior—which is, in our opinion, the biggest selling point of this vegetable. Fueled by a serious hunger for good thick-cut sweet potato fries, we ordered 50 pounds of the orange spuds and got to work. The secret is the cornstarch, which creates a thin coating that ensures a crisp exterior for the sweet potato fries. If your sweet potatoes are shorter than 4 inches in length, do not cut the wedges crosswise.

SPICY FRY SAUCE (OPTIONAL)
- 6 tablespoons mayonnaise
- 1 tablespoon Asian chili-garlic sauce
- 2 teaspoons white vinegar

FRIES
- ½ cup cornstarch
  Kosher salt
- 1 teaspoon baking soda
- 3 pounds sweet potatoes, peeled, cut lengthwise into ¾-inch-thick wedges, wedges halved crosswise
- 3 cups peanut or vegetable oil

1. For the spicy fry sauce Combine all ingredients in a small bowl and set aside for serving.

2. For the fries Adjust oven rack to middle position and heat oven to 200 degrees. Set wire rack in rimmed baking sheet. Whisk cornstarch and ½ cup cold water together in large bowl; set aside.

3. Bring 2 quarts water, ¼ cup salt, and baking soda to boil in Dutch oven. Add potatoes and return to boil. Reduce heat to simmer and cook until exteriors turn slightly mushy (centers will remain firm), 3 to 5 minutes. Whisk cornstarch slurry to recombine. Using slotted spoon, transfer potatoes to bowl with slurry.

4. Using rubber spatula, fold potatoes with slurry until slurry turns light orange, thickens to paste, and clings to potatoes.

5. Heat oil in 12-inch nonstick skillet over high heat to 325 degrees. Using tongs, carefully add one-third of potatoes to oil, making sure that potatoes aren't touching one another. Fry until crispy and lightly browned, 7 to 10 minutes, using tongs to flip potatoes halfway through frying (adjust heat as necessary to maintain oil temperature between 280 and 300 degrees). Using slotted spoon, transfer fries to prepared rack (fries that stick together can be separated). Season with salt to taste, and transfer to oven to keep warm. Return oil to 325 degrees and repeat in 2 more batches with remaining potatoes. Serve immediately, with the sauce, if desired.

SWEET POTATO CASSEROLE

Serves 10 to 12   Total time: 2 hours 30 minutes
WHY THIS RECIPE WORKS Without fail, every Thanksgiving millions of cooks across the country prepare the butter-laden, over-spiced, marshmallow-topped casserole we all know. It's as much a side of nostalgia as it is a side dish, but with all that fat, sugar, and spice, the sweet potatoes get lost. Here is our potato-focused version of this home-style classic. For precooking the potatoes, we found that, although baking took longer than microwaving or boiling, it produced a rich, intense sweetness that was worth every minute. Baking intensified their flavor to the point that the excessive amounts of sugar traditionally added became superfluous. The next question to resolve was texture. We wanted the best of both worlds—chunky and smooth—so we tried a mix of potato chunks and smooth puree, gently folding in the chunks just before baking. Bites of dense potato were thus suspended throughout the puree. This varied texture paired perfectly with the crunchy streusel topping, which stole the show in the test kitchen, with its crisp texture and nutty, bittersweet flavor that held the filling's richness at bay. Nobody even missed the marshmallows.

POTATOES

   7 pounds sweet potatoes, unpeeled, each
      lightly pricked with fork in 6 places

STREUSEL

   ½ cup (2½ ounces) all-purpose flour
   ½ cup packed (3½ ounces) dark brown
      sugar
   ¼ teaspoon salt
   5 tablespoons unsalted butter, cut
      into 5 pieces and softened
   1 cup pecans

FILLING

   5 tablespoons unsalted butter, melted
   4 teaspoons lemon juice
   1 tablespoon vanilla extract
   2 teaspoons salt
   ½ teaspoon ground nutmeg
   ½ teaspoon pepper
      Granulated sugar
   4 large egg yolks
  1½ cups half-and-half

1. For the potatoes Adjust oven rack to lower-middle position and heat oven to 400 degrees. Evenly space potatoes on aluminum foil–lined rimmed baking sheet. Bake potatoes, turning once, until very tender and easy to squeeze with tongs, 1 to 1½ hours. Cut potatoes in half lengthwise and let cool for at least 10 minutes. Reduce oven temperature to 375 degrees.

2. For the streusel Grease 13 by 9-inch baking dish. Pulse flour, sugar, and salt in food processor until combined, about 4 pulses. Sprinkle butter over flour mixture and pulse until crumbly mass forms, 6 to 8 pulses. Sprinkle pecans over top and pulse until combined but some large pecan pieces remain, 4 to 6 pulses. Transfer streusel to bowl.

3. Once potatoes have cooled slightly, use soupspoon to scoop flesh into large bowl (you should have about 8 cups). Transfer half of potato flesh to now-empty food processor. Using rubber spatula, break remaining potato flesh in bowl into coarse 1-inch pieces.

4. For the filling Add melted butter, lemon juice, vanilla, salt, nutmeg, and pepper to processor and process until smooth, about 20 seconds. Season with up to 4 tablespoons

sugar to taste. Add egg yolks. With processor running, slowly add half-and-half until incorporated, about 20 seconds. Add to bowl with potato pieces and stir to combine.

5. Spread potato mixture in prepared dish. Sprinkle with streusel, breaking up any large pieces with your fingers. Bake until topping is well browned and filling is slightly puffy around edges, 40 to 45 minutes. Let cool for at least 10 minutes before serving.

SWEET POTATO AND SWISS CHARD GRATIN

Serves 4 to 6   Total time: 1 hour 45 minutes

WHY THIS RECIPE WORKS *For a new twist on a classic potato gratin, we created a decidedly savory and elegant sweet potato version. To mitigate some of the potatoes' natural sweetness, we turned to earthy, slightly bitter Swiss chard, which we sautéed in butter with shallot, garlic, and thyme. We shingled half the sliced potatoes along the bottom of the gratin dish, topped them with the chard, and then layered on the remaining potatoes. Pouring a combination of water, wine, and cream over the vegetables encouraged the potatoes to cook evenly and imparted a welcome richness. Covering the gratin dish for the first half of baking ensured that the potatoes cooked through. We then uncovered the dish so that the excess liquid could evaporate and the cheesy topping could brown. Slicing the potatoes ⅛ inch thick is crucial for the success of this dish; use a mandoline, a V-slicer, or a food processor fitted with a ⅛-inch-thick slicing blade.*

   2 tablespoons unsalted butter
   2 shallots, minced
      Salt
   2 pounds Swiss chard, stemmed and
      cut into ½-inch-wide strips
   3 garlic cloves, minced
   2 teaspoons minced fresh thyme
   ¾ teaspoon pepper
   ⅓ cup heavy cream
   ⅓ cup water
   ⅓ cup dry white wine
   3 pounds sweet potatoes, peeled and
      sliced ⅛ inch thick
   2 ounces Parmesan cheese, grated (1 cup)

1. Adjust oven rack to middle position and heat oven to 350 degrees. Melt butter in Dutch oven over medium-high heat. Add shallots and 1 teaspoon salt and cook until shallots are softened, about 2 minutes. Stir in chard and cook until wilted, about 2 minutes. Stir in garlic, thyme, and pepper and cook until fragrant, about 30 seconds; transfer to bowl.

2. Add cream, water, wine, and 1 teaspoon salt to now-empty pot and bring to simmer over medium-high heat. Remove pot from heat and cover to keep warm.

3. Shingle half of potatoes evenly into 3-quart gratin dish (or 13 by 9-inch baking dish). Spread wilted chard mixture evenly over potatoes, then shingle remaining potatoes over top. Pour cream mixture evenly over top and sprinkle with Parmesan.

4. Cover dish with aluminum foil and bake for 20 minutes. Uncover and continue to bake until gratin is golden and feels tender when poked with paring knife, 40 to 50 minutes. Let cool for 10 minutes before serving.

GRILLED SWEET POTATO SALAD

Serves 4 to 6   Total time: 1 hour

WHY THIS RECIPE WORKS *To bring together two favorite summer traditions— potato salad and grilling—we used the grill to both steam and char sweet potatoes, so all the cooking was done outside. We first tossed the potatoes with a spiced vinaigrette in a disposable aluminum pan; the vinaigrette generated steam and helped cook the potatoes through while also seasoning them. Once the potatoes were steamed, we transferred them from the pan to the hot cooking grate to give them some flavorful char. Threading toothpicks through the onion rounds kept them intact and prevented them from falling through the grate during cooking. We sprinkled feta, scallions, and cilantro over the grilled salad to finish it off. We recommend using medium potatoes, 2 to 3 inches in diameter, because they'll fit neatly in the disposable aluminum pan.*

Grilled Sweet Potato Salad

1 small red onion, sliced into
    ½-inch-thick rounds
3 tablespoons lime juice (2 limes),
    plus lime wedges for serving
2 tablespoons honey
1 teaspoon minced canned chipotle
    chile in adobo sauce
½ teaspoon ground cumin
    Salt and pepper
⅓ cup vegetable oil
2½ pounds sweet potatoes, peeled and
    cut into ½-inch-thick rounds
1 (13 by 9-inch) disposable aluminum
    pan
2 ounces feta cheese, crumbled (½ cup)
3 scallions, sliced thin on bias
¼ cup chopped fresh cilantro

1. Thread 1 toothpick horizontally through
each onion round. Whisk lime juice, honey,
chipotle, cumin, ½ teaspoon salt, and
¼ teaspoon pepper together in large bowl.
While whisking constantly, slowly drizzle
in oil until combined; set aside.

2. Toss potatoes, onion rounds, ¼ cup vinaigrette, ½ teaspoon salt, and ½ teaspoon
pepper together in separate bowl. Place
onion rounds in bottom of disposable pan,
layer potatoes over top, then pour in any
remaining liquid from bowl. Cover disposable pan tightly with aluminum foil.

3a. For a charcoal grill Open bottom vent
completely. Light large chimney starter filled
with charcoal briquettes (6 quarts). When
top coals are partially covered with ash,
pour evenly over grill. Set cooking grate in
place, cover, and open lid vent completely.
Heat grill until hot, about 5 minutes.

3b. For a gas grill Turn all burners to high,
cover, and heat grill until hot, about 15 minutes. Turn all burners to medium. Adjust
burners as needed to maintain grill temperature around 400 degrees.

4. Clean and oil cooking grate. Place disposable pan on grill. Cover grill and cook until
vegetables are tender, 20 to 25 minutes, shaking disposable pan halfway through cooking
to redistribute potatoes. Remove disposable
pan from grill.

5. Place vegetables on cooking grate. Cook
(covered if using gas) until lightly charred
and tender, 2 to 4 minutes per side. Transfer
vegetables to bowl with remaining vinaigrette, discarding toothpicks from onion
rounds and separating rings. Toss vegetables to coat, then transfer to serving platter.
Sprinkle feta, scallions, and cilantro over
top. Serve with lime wedges.

～

SWEET POTATO SOUP
Serves 4 to 6   Total time: 50 minutes
WHY THIS RECIPE WORKS *What's the
secret to our creamy sweet potato soup's
deep, earthy-sweet flavor? Keeping the
skins in play. Before simmering and pureeing
the peeled potatoes, we coaxed out more
natural sweetness by soaking them in hot
water, allowing their starches to turn into
pure sugar. Pureeing some of the skins along
with the softened potatoes added depth to
the otherwise sweet soup, a contrast we reinforced with some brown sugar and a touch of
cider vinegar. The simple maple–sour cream
topping adds some sweet-tangy coolness
when serving the soup, and a sprinkling of
minced chives adds a pop of color and delicate oniony flavor.*

MAPLE SOUR CREAM
⅓ cup sour cream
1 tablespoon maple syrup

SOUP
4 tablespoons unsalted butter
1 shallot, sliced thin
4 sprigs fresh thyme
4¼ cups water
2 pounds sweet potatoes, peeled, halved
    lengthwise, and sliced ¼ inch thick,
    ¼ of peels reserved
1 tablespoon packed brown sugar
½ teaspoon cider vinegar
    Salt and pepper
2 tablespoons minced fresh chives

1. For the maple sour cream Combine
ingredients in small bowl and refrigerate
until ready to serve.

2. For the soup Melt butter in large saucepan over medium-low heat. Add shallot and
thyme sprigs and cook until shallot is softened but not browned, about 5 minutes. Stir
in water and bring to simmer over high heat.
Off heat, add sweet potatoes and reserved
peels, and let stand uncovered for 20 minutes.

3. Stir in sugar, vinegar, 1½ teaspoons salt,
and ¼ teaspoon pepper. Bring to simmer
over high heat. Reduce heat to medium-low,
cover, and cook until potatoes are very soft,
about 10 minutes.

4. Discard thyme sprigs. Working in batches,
process soup in blender until smooth, about
1 minute. Return soup to clean pot. Return
to simmer, adjusting consistency if desired.
Season with salt and pepper to taste. Serve,
topping each portion with sprinkle of chives
and drizzle of maple sour cream.

～

HEARTY BEEF AND SWEET
POTATO CHILI
Serves 6 to 8   Total time: 3 hours
WHY THIS RECIPE WORKS *Sweet potatoes
do double duty in this beef-and-veggie chili.
We added some early in the cooking process
so that they would break down and thicken
the chili and then added the rest later, along
with tomatoes, bell peppers, and scallions.
For the beef, we chose well-marbled,
inexpensive beef chuck-eye for its ability to
become meltingly tender. We browned it for
rich flavor and then stewed it long enough
to make it fork-tender. An aromatic base
of garlic, cumin, chipotle, and chili powder
gave our stew real depth of flavor and some
heat. The heat balanced out the sweetness
of the sweet potatoes and bell pepper, and
mild beer added further complexity. Once
our meat was tender, we added the rest of
the sweet potatoes and bell pepper, cooking
them just long enough to have toothsome
chunks in our stew. Light-bodied American
lagers, such as Budweiser, work best in
this recipe. Serve with lime wedges, sliced
avocado, cilantro leaves, sour cream, and
shredded Monterey Jack or cheddar cheese.*

Hearty Beef and Sweet Potato Chili

3½ pounds boneless beef chuck-eye roast, pulled apart at seams, trimmed, and cut into 1-inch pieces
   Salt and pepper
3 tablespoons vegetable oil
1 onion, chopped
1½ pounds sweet potatoes, peeled and cut into ½-inch pieces
3 garlic cloves, minced
1 tablespoon ground cumin
1 tablespoon minced canned chipotle chile in adobo sauce
2 teaspoons chili powder
1 (28-ounce) can diced tomatoes
1½ cups beer
2 (15-ounce) cans black beans, rinsed
1 red bell pepper, stemmed, seeded, and cut into ½-inch pieces
4 scallions, sliced thin

1. Adjust oven rack to middle position and heat oven to 300 degrees. Pat beef dry with paper towels and season with salt and pepper. Heat 1 tablespoon oil in Dutch oven over medium heat until shimmering. Add half of beef and brown on all sides, 6 to 8 minutes; transfer to large bowl. Repeat with 1 tablespoon oil and remaining beef.

2. Add remaining 1 tablespoon oil to now-empty pot and heat until shimmering. Add onion and ¾ cup sweet potatoes and cook until just beginning to brown, 5 to 7 minutes. Stir in garlic, cumin, chipotle, chili powder, and 1 teaspoon salt and cook until fragrant, about 30 seconds. Stir in tomatoes and their juice, beer, beans, and browned beef along with any accumulated juices, scraping up any browned bits.

3. Bring chili to simmer. Cover, transfer pot to oven, and cook, stirring occasionally, until sweet potatoes are broken down and beef is just tender, about 1 hour 40 minutes.

4. Remove pot from oven and stir in bell pepper and remaining sweet potatoes. Return to oven and continue to cook until meat and sweet potatoes are tender, about 20 minutes.

5. Remove pot from oven, uncover, and let chili stand until thickened slightly, about 15 minutes. Season with salt and pepper to taste, and sprinkle with scallions before serving.

SWEET POTATO VINDALOO

Serves 4 to 6   Total time: 55 minutes

WHY THIS RECIPE WORKS *Vindaloo is a complex dish that blends Portuguese and Indian cuisines in a potent braise featuring warm spices, chiles, wine vinegar, tomatoes, onions, garlic, and mustard seeds. It's often made with pork, lamb, or chicken as the main ingredient, but here we translated its comfort-food appeal into a hearty vegetarian stew. Centering our dish on a combination of sweet potatoes and red potatoes proved just right, since the low-and-slow cooking developed complex flavors. However, after 45 minutes of simmering, the potatoes weren't fully cooked. A second look at our ingredients showed us why: The acidic environment created by the tomatoes and vinegar was preventing our potatoes from becoming tender. To test our theory, we whipped up another batch, this time leaving out the tomatoes and vinegar until the end, cooking them just enough to mellow their flavors. Sure enough, after just 15 minutes, our potatoes were perfectly tender. To give our vindaloo exceptionally deep flavor, we used a mix of Indian spices, along with bay leaves and mustard seeds, and simmered the spices along with the potatoes. We finished the dish with a cooling dollop of yogurt.*

2 tablespoons vegetable oil
2 onions, chopped fine
1 pound sweet potatoes, peeled and cut into ½-inch pieces
1 pound red potatoes, unpeeled, cut into ½-inch pieces
   Salt and pepper
10 garlic cloves, minced
4 teaspoons paprika
1 teaspoon ground cumin
¾ teaspoon ground cardamom
½ teaspoon cayenne pepper
¼ teaspoon ground cloves
2½ cups water
2 bay leaves
1 tablespoon mustard seeds
1 (28-ounce) can diced tomatoes
2½ tablespoons red wine vinegar
¼ cup minced fresh cilantro

1. Heat oil in Dutch oven over medium heat until shimmering. Add onions, sweet potatoes, red potatoes, and ½ teaspoon salt and cook, stirring occasionally, until onions are softened and potatoes begin to soften at edges, 10 to 12 minutes.

2. Stir in garlic, paprika, cumin, cardamom, cayenne, and cloves and cook until fragrant and vegetables are well coated, about 2 minutes. Gradually stir in water, scraping up any browned bits. Stir in bay leaves, mustard seeds, and 1 teaspoon salt and bring to simmer. Cover, reduce heat to medium-low, and cook until potatoes are tender, 15 to 20 minutes.

3. Stir in tomatoes and their juice and vinegar and continue to simmer, uncovered, until flavors are blended and sauce has thickened slightly, about 15 minutes. Discard bay leaves, stir in cilantro, and season with salt and pepper to taste. Serve.

SWEET POTATO, POBLANO, AND BLACK BEAN TACOS

Serves 4 to 6   Total time: 1 hour

WHY THIS RECIPE WORKS *To make a great vegetarian taco, we experimented with lots of different ingredient and flavor combinations. One of our favorites turned out to be sweet potatoes and poblano chiles, which we seasoned with fragrant garlic, cumin, coriander, and oregano. Roasting the potatoes and chiles produced caramelized exteriors and tender interiors. Adding black beans to the filling made the filling even heartier and also contributed protein. Instead of topping the tacos with queso fresco or sour cream, we made a quick and delicious avocado crema. For a tangy, spicy, perfect finish, we sprinkled the tacos with our Quick Sweet and Spicy Pickled Red Onions.*

3 tablespoons extra-virgin olive oil
3 garlic cloves, minced
1½ teaspoons ground cumin
1½ teaspoons ground coriander
1 teaspoon minced fresh oregano or ¼ teaspoon dried
   Salt and pepper
1 pound sweet potatoes, peeled and cut into ½-inch pieces
4 poblano chiles, stemmed, seeded, and cut into ½-inch strips

1 large onion, halved and sliced ½ inch thick
1 (15-ounce) can black beans, rinsed
¼ cup chopped fresh cilantro
12 (6-inch) corn tortillas, warmed
1 recipe Quick Sweet and Spicy Pickled Red Onions (page 314)

1. Adjust oven racks to upper-middle and lower-middle positions and heat oven to 450 degrees. Whisk oil, garlic, cumin, coriander, oregano, 1 teaspoon salt, and ½ teaspoon pepper together in large bowl. Add potatoes, poblanos, and onion to oil mixture and toss to coat.

2. Spread vegetable mixture in even layer over 2 aluminum foil–lined rimmed baking sheets. Roast vegetables until tender and golden brown, about 30 minutes, stirring vegetables and switching and rotating sheets halfway through baking.

3. Return vegetables to now-empty bowl, add black beans and cilantro, and gently toss to combine. Divide vegetable fillings evenly among tortillas and top with pickled onions. Serve.

SWEET POTATO BISCUITS

Makes 16 biscuits   Total time: 1 hour 30 minutes

WHY THIS RECIPE WORKS *It was only a matter of time before sweet potato–loving Southern cooks combined the fluffy texture and pleasant tang of biscuits with the earthy sweetness of this popular tuber. To add this potato's natural sweetness to biscuits without weighing down the dough, we microwaved the sweet potatoes, which eliminated their moisture while concentrating their flavor. After mashing the flesh, we stirred in cider vinegar to mimic buttermilk's tang and to create greater lift once combined with the dough's baking powder and baking soda. We maximized the biscuits' tender texture with low-protein cake flour and opted for the deep, molasses-like sweetness of brown sugar to complement the sweet potatoes. The dough took on a pretty orange color, and, once baked, the biscuits emerged tender and subtly sweet, perfectly ready for a smear of butter or jam, or to be sliced and stuffed with ham and mustard. If you can find them, Beauregard sweet potatoes are the best variety for these biscuits. The biscuits can be stored in airtight container for up to two days.*

2½ pounds sweet potatoes, unpeeled, lightly pricked all over with fork
2 tablespoons cider vinegar
3¼ cups (13 ounces) cake flour
¼ cup packed (1¾ ounces) dark brown sugar
5 teaspoons baking powder
½ teaspoon baking soda
1½ teaspoons salt
8 tablespoons unsalted butter, cut into ½-inch pieces and chilled, plus 2 tablespoons melted
4 tablespoons vegetable shortening, cut into ½-inch pieces and chilled

1. Microwave potatoes on plate until very soft and surfaces are wet, 15 to 20 minutes, flipping every 5 minutes. Immediately cut potatoes in half. When potatoes are cool enough to handle, scoop flesh into large bowl and, using potato masher, mash until smooth. (You should have 2 cups. Reserve any extra for another use.) Stir in vinegar and refrigerate until cool, about 15 minutes.

2. Adjust oven rack to middle position and heat oven to 425 degrees. Line rimmed baking sheet with parchment paper. Process flour, sugar, baking powder, baking soda, and salt in food processor until combined. Scatter chilled butter and shortening over top and pulse until mixture resembles coarse meal, about 15 pulses. Transfer flour mixture to bowl with cooled potatoes and fold with rubber spatula until incorporated.

3. Turn out dough onto floured counter and knead until smooth, 8 to 10 times. Pat dough into 9-inch circle, about 1 inch thick. Using floured 2¼-inch round cutter, stamp out biscuits and arrange on prepared sheet. Gently pat dough scraps into 1-inch-thick circle and stamp out remaining biscuits. (You should have 16 biscuits total.)

4. Brush tops of biscuits with melted butter and bake until golden brown, 18 to 22 minutes. Let biscuits cool on sheet for 15 minutes before serving.

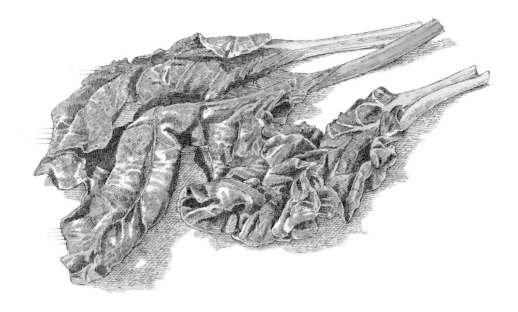

SWISS CHARD

Despite its name (the origins of which are uncertain), Swiss chard actually originated in the Mediterranean region, where it was cooked by the ancient Greeks. It's in the beet family, and, similar to beets, you could think of chard as two vegetables in one: the dark green, ruffled leaves, which can be treated like spinach or any similar tender green, and the thick white or colored stems, which have a sturdier texture that's more akin to celery.

For a long time, there were only two varieties seen in the market: chard with white stems and white veins running through the leaves, and chard with red stems and red veins. Now rainbow chard is everywhere, with its festive orange, yellow, crimson, and pink stems and veins. The colored varieties are slightly sweeter in flavor than the traditional green-and-white chard, but you should use whatever variety you prefer in any of these recipes.

Like spinach and beet greens, Swiss chard is tender and rich in moisture. Its leaves are a bit sturdier than spinach, but its flavor is a little more mellow and delicate. Chard cooks much more quickly than hearty greens such as kale or collards. It takes especially well to quick sautéing, which turns the leaves tender before they have a chance to get soggy. We offer you our favorite ways to take advantage of that quick-cooking quality, including our couldn't-be-simpler Garlicky Swiss Chard, which includes three flavor variations, and our Pasta with Beans, Swiss Chard, and Rosemary.

Silkiness emerges when chard is cooked slowly, as in our Pomegranate Roasted Salmon with Swiss Chard and Lentils. We love it in soups, especially our Super Greens Soup with Lemon-Tarragon Cream. And it's a superstar in Swiss Chard Pie, a flaky, savory chard-packed pie with pancetta and Parmesan that is a beloved dish from central Italy.

shopping and storage

Swiss chard is available year-round, though it's best and most abundant from the end of summer through the winter. Swiss chard should have deep green, crisp leaves and stems. The stems should be brightly colored, whether they are white, red, or rainbow. Avoid bunches with raggedy leaves, leaves with holes and rips, and leaves that are yellowing or turning brown at the edges. Store chard wrapped in paper towels in a loosely closed plastic produce bag for several days, changing the paper towels as needed (the drier the chard is, the longer it will keep).

swiss chard varieties

Fordhook Giant is the classic white-stemmed, white-veined variety with dark green leaves that for so long was the only type available in grocery stores. It is sometimes called "green chard" or "white chard."

Ruby Red, or Rhubarb, chard is the next most commonly seen variety, with deep red stems and red veins running through the green leaves.

The now frequently seen "rainbow chard" is a type called Bright Lights, featuring multicolored stems in shades of pink, yellow, orange, and crimson.

There are many other varieties, but when it comes to cooking, the variety and color matter less than the maturity of the chard. If it is young, with very thin stems, you can just leave those tender stems attached to the leaves and chop everything up together, trimming only the very thick bottom stem parts. But most chard is mature, with stems as thick as a pencil. In that case, the stems should be removed and treated separately from the leaves.

stems and leaves

Swiss chard has an undeniable advantage over other hearty greens, such as kale or collards, in that the stems are entirely edible. And delicious: The crisp, succulent stems taste even more strongly of the vegetable's elemental flavor than do the leaves. Combine the two and you have a one-two punch of satisfying flavor and textural appeal.

There's one catch, however. Swiss chard is a bit like the chicken of the vegetable world, in that the stems and leaves cook at two very different rates, with the stems taking longer to become tender. As a result, most recipes either separate the leaves and stems into different dishes entirely or cook them independently of one another before combining the two at the finish.

Dealing with both parts of the vegetable in that way can be something of a hassle—maybe that's why many cooks simply discard the stems. Rather than miss out on the great flavor and texture that the stems provide, many of our recipes call for cutting the stems into small enough pieces so that they can be part of an easy, one-pan chard-cooking process.

vegetable prep

Preparing Chard for Cooking

1. Cut away leafy green portion from either side of stem using chef's knife.

2. Stack a few stems together and slice into thin pieces.

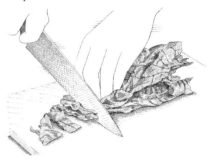

3. Stack several leaves on top of one another and slice crosswise into strips.

Cleaning Chard

Swiss shard can be gritty and should be washed in a sink or large bowl full of water.

Garlicky Swiss Chard with Golden
Raisins and Goat Cheese

GARLICKY SWISS CHARD

Serves 4 to 6   Total time: 15 minutes

WHY THIS RECIPE WORKS *This quick one-pot approach to cooking Swiss chard results in a hearty, flavorful, and versatile side dish. To avoid watery, overcooked chard, we started cooking the greens in a covered pot just until they wilted down. Then we uncovered the pot and continued to cook the greens until all the liquid evaporated. Cutting the tough stems smaller than the tender leaves meant that we could throw both in the pot at the same time and still get evenly cooked results. Sautéing plenty of garlic in olive oil before adding the chard gave this simple side a big hit of flavor, while a splash of mild white wine vinegar and red pepper flakes added brightness and subtle heat.*

    3 tablespoons extra-virgin olive oil
    6 garlic cloves, minced
    2 pounds Swiss chard, stems
       chopped fine, leaves sliced into
       ½-inch-wide strips
       Salt and pepper
    ⅛ teaspoon red pepper flakes
    1 teaspoon white wine vinegar

1. Cook 2 tablespoons oil and garlic in Dutch oven over medium-low heat, stirring occasionally, until garlic is light golden and fragrant, about 3 minutes. Stir in chard, ¼ teaspoon salt, and pepper flakes. Increase heat to high, cover, and cook, stirring occasionally, until chard is wilted but still bright green, 2 to 4 minutes.

2. Uncover and continue to cook, stirring often, until liquid evaporates, 4 to 6 minutes. Stir in vinegar and remaining 1 tablespoon oil. Season with salt and pepper to taste. Serve.

VARIATIONS

Garlicky Swiss Chard with Walnuts and Feta
Sprinkle chard with ⅓ cup crumbled feta cheese and ¼ cup chopped, toasted walnuts before serving.

Garlicky Swiss Chard with Golden Raisins and Goat Cheese
Add ¼ cup golden raisins to pot with chard. Sprinkle chard with ⅓ cup crumbled goat cheese and ¼ cup chopped, toasted hazelnuts before serving.

Asian-Style Swiss Chard
Add 1 tablespoon grated fresh ginger to pot with chard. In step 2, substitute 1 tablespoon toasted sesame oil for olive oil and substitute 4 teaspoons soy sauce for vinegar. Sprinkle chard with 3 tablespoons sliced scallion and ¼ cup chopped, salted, dry-roasted peanuts before serving.

SUPER GREENS SOUP WITH LEMON-TARRAGON CREAM

Serves 4 to 6   Total time: 1 hour 30 minutes

WHY THIS RECIPE WORKS *There's a big dose of healthy, hearty greens in this deceptively delicious, silky-smooth soup. First, we built a flavorful foundation of sweet caramelized onions and earthy sautéed mushrooms. We added broth, water, and lots of leafy greens (we liked a mix of Swiss chard, kale, arugula, and parsley), and simmered the greens until tender before blending them until smooth. We were happy with the soup's depth of flavor, but it was still watery and too thin. Many recipes we found used potatoes as a thickener, but they lent an overwhelmingly earthy flavor. Instead, we tried using Arborio rice. The rice's high starch content thickened the soup to a velvety, lush consistency without clouding its bright, vegetal flavors. For a vibrant finish—and a touch of decadence— we whisked together heavy cream, sour cream, lemon zest, lemon juice, and tarragon and drizzled it over the top.*

    ¼ cup heavy cream
    3 tablespoons sour cream
    ¼ teaspoon grated lemon zest plus
       ½ teaspoon juice
    ½ teaspoon minced fresh tarragon
       Salt and pepper
    2 tablespoons extra-virgin olive oil
    1 onion, halved and sliced thin
    ¾ teaspoon light brown sugar
    3 ounces white mushrooms,
       trimmed and sliced thin
    2 garlic cloves, minced
       Pinch cayenne pepper
    3 cups water
    3 cups vegetable broth
    ⅓ cup Arborio rice
    12 ounces Swiss chard, stemmed and
       chopped
    9 ounces kale, stemmed and chopped
    ¼ cup fresh parsley leaves
    2 ounces (2 cups) baby arugula

1. Combine cream, sour cream, lemon zest and juice, tarragon, and ¼ teaspoon salt in bowl. Cover and refrigerate until ready to serve.

2. Heat oil in Dutch oven over medium-high heat until shimmering. Add onion, sugar, and 1 teaspoon salt and cook, stirring occasionally, until onion releases some moisture, about 5 minutes. Reduce heat to low and continue to cook, stirring often and scraping up any browned bits, until onion is deeply browned and slightly sticky, about 30 minutes. (If onion is sizzling or scorching, reduce heat. If onion is not browning after 15 to 20 minutes, increase heat.)

3. Stir in mushrooms and cook until they have released their moisture, about 5 minutes. Stir in garlic and cayenne and cook until fragrant, about 30 seconds. Stir in water, broth, and rice, scraping up any browned bits, and bring to simmer. Reduce heat to low, cover, and cook for 15 minutes.

4. Stir in chard, kale, and parsley, 1 handful at a time, until wilted. Return to simmer, cover, and cook until greens are tender, about 10 minutes.

5. Off heat, stir in arugula until wilted. Working in batches, process soup in blender until smooth, about 1 minute. Return soup to clean pot and bring to brief simmer over medium-low heat. Season with salt and pepper to taste. Drizzle individual portions with lemon-tarragon cream before serving.

MOROCCAN LENTIL AND SWISS CHARD SOUP

Serves 6 to 8   Total time: 1 hour

WHY THIS RECIPE WORKS *There are countless adaptations of the traditional Moroccan soup called* harira, *depending on the region or even the family. They all share the use of tomatoes, legumes, dried spices, and fresh herbs. Often lamb or chicken is included, but our version is vegetarian. Many versions include fresh greens, and we particularly love to stir in a generous amount of tender, earthy-sweet Swiss chard at the end of cooking. As for the rest, we streamlined the ingredients and technique for this classic dish to deliver bold North African flavors in just a fraction of the time. Using canned chickpeas rather than dried saved about 2 hours of cooking time. Paring down the number of spices and fresh herbs made for more efficient prep. Finishing the dish with lemon juice helped focus all the flavors. We like to garnish this soup with a small amount of harissa, a fiery North African chili paste, which is available at most well-stocked supermarkets. We prefer brown or green lentils for this recipe, but it will work with any type of lentil except red or yellow (note that cooking times will vary depending on the type used).*

- ⅓ cup extra-virgin olive oil
- 1 large onion, chopped fine
- 2 celery ribs, chopped fine
- 5 garlic cloves, minced
- 1 tablespoon grated fresh ginger
- 2 teaspoons ground coriander
- 2 teaspoons smoked paprika
- 1 teaspoon ground cumin
- ½ teaspoon ground cinnamon
- ⅛ teaspoon red pepper flakes
- ¾ cup minced fresh cilantro
- ½ cup minced fresh parsley
- 4 cups chicken or vegetable broth
- 4 cups water
- 1 (15-ounce) can chickpeas, rinsed
- 1 cup brown lentils, picked over and rinsed
- 1 (28-ounce) can crushed tomatoes
- ½ cup orzo
- 4 ounces Swiss chard, stemmed and cut into ½-inch pieces
- 2 tablespoons lemon juice, plus lemon wedges for serving
  Salt and pepper
- ½ cup harissa (optional)

1. Heat oil in Dutch oven over medium heat until shimmering. Add onion and celery and cook, stirring frequently, until softened and lightly browned, about 8 minutes. Stir in garlic and ginger and cook until fragrant, 1 minute. Stir in coriander, paprika, cumin, cinnamon, and pepper flakes and cook for 1 minute. Stir in ½ cup cilantro and ¼ cup parsley and cook for 1 minute.

2. Stir in broth, water, chickpeas, and lentils, scraping up any browned bits, and bring to simmer. Reduce heat to medium-low, partially cover, and gently simmer until lentils are just tender, about 20 minutes.

3. Stir in tomatoes and pasta and return to simmer. Partially cover and cook, stirring occasionally, for 7 minutes. Stir in chard and cook until pasta is tender, about 5 minutes. Off heat, stir in lemon juice, remaining ¼ cup cilantro, and remaining ¼ cup parsley. Season with salt and pepper to taste. Serve, drizzling individual portions with harissa, if using, and passing lemon wedges separately.

FRIED EGGS WITH GARLICKY SWISS CHARD AND BELL PEPPER

Serves 4   Total time: 25 minutes

WHY THIS RECIPE WORKS *Garlicky greens topped with fried eggs are a surprising and immensely satisfying way to start the day right. And, of course, this dish makes for a great speedy weeknight dinner as well. The hearty Swiss chard leaves made an ideal partner for a fried egg (a welcome change from toast at breakfast time), especially when the rich, drippy yolk broke and mingled with the earthy, nutritious greens. To keep our breakfast quick, we simply bloomed minced garlic in olive oil, then wilted handfuls of chard before adding red bell pepper for sweetness and a pinch of red pepper flakes to perk everything up. The greens became tender and vibrant in 5 minutes. We then drained our vegetables to banish excess liquid before portioning them out and used the same skillet to quickly fry four eggs before sliding them atop our greens. A complementary spritz from a lemon wedge added pleasant brightness. You will need a 12-inch nonstick skillet with a tight-fitting lid for this recipe.*

- 2 tablespoons extra-virgin olive oil, plus extra for drizzling
- 5 garlic cloves, minced
- 2 pounds Swiss chard, stemmed, 1 cup stems chopped fine, leaves sliced into ½-inch-wide strips
- 1 small red bell pepper, stemmed, seeded, and cut into ¼-inch pieces
  Salt and pepper
- ⅛ teaspoon red pepper flakes
- 4 large eggs
  Lemon wedges

1. Cook 1 tablespoon oil and garlic in 12-inch nonstick skillet over medium-low heat, stirring occasionally, until garlic is light golden and fragrant, about 3 minutes. Increase heat to high, add chopped chard stems, then chard leaves, 1 handful at a time, and cook until wilted, about 2 minutes. Add bell pepper, ¼ teaspoon salt, and pepper flakes and cook, stirring often, until chard is tender and peppers are softened, about 3 minutes. Off heat, season with salt and pepper to taste. Transfer to colander set in bowl; wipe skillet clean with paper towels.

2. Crack 2 eggs into small bowl and season with salt and pepper. Repeat with remaining 2 eggs in second bowl. Heat remaining 1 tablespoon oil in now-empty skillet over medium-high heat until shimmering, and quickly swirl to coat skillet. Working quickly, pour 1 bowl of eggs in 1 side of pan and second bowl of eggs in other side. Cover and cook for 1 minute.

3. Remove skillet from heat and let sit, covered, 15 to 45 seconds for runny yolks (white around edge of yolk will be barely opaque), 45 to 60 seconds for soft-set yolks, or about 2 minutes for medium-set yolks.

4. Divide chard mixture evenly among serving plates, top each with 1 egg, and drizzle with extra oil to taste. Serve immediately with lemon wedges.

Fried Eggs with Garlicky Swiss Chard
and Bell Pepper

2. Heat 2 teaspoons oil in 8-inch nonstick skillet over medium-high heat until shimmering. Add ½ cup batter to skillet, tilting pan to coat bottom evenly. Reduce heat to medium and cook until crisp at edges and golden brown on bottom, 3 to 5 minutes. Flip socca and continue to cook until second side is browned, 2 to 3 minutes. Transfer to prepared rack and keep warm in oven. Repeat with remaining oil and batter.

3. **For the topping** Heat oil in 12-inch nonstick skillet over medium heat until shimmering. Add onion and cook until softened, about 5 minutes. Stir in garlic, cumin, ¼ teaspoon salt, and allspice and cook until fragrant, about 30 seconds. Stir in Swiss chard and apricots and cook until chard is wilted, 4 to 6 minutes. Off heat, stir in pistachios and vinegar and season with salt and pepper to taste. Top each cooked socca with ⅓ cup chard mixture, slice, and serve.

SOCCA WITH SWISS CHARD, APRICOTS, AND PISTACHIOS

Makes 5 flatbreads, serves 4
Total time: 45 minutes

WHY THIS RECIPE WORKS *Socca is a savory flatbread made with chickpea flour that is popular in southern France, where it is served as an appetizer or a street-food snack. Often it's served plain, but we decided to create a flavorful topping of Swiss chard, dried apricots, and toasted pistachios, tied together with the warm spiciness of cumin and allspice. The loose, pancake-like batter for the socca came together in less than a minute. Traditionally the batter is poured into a cast-iron skillet and baked in a wood-burning oven to make a large socca with a blistered top and a smoky flavor. But in a home oven, this technique produced socca that was dry and limp. So we ditched the oven for the higher heat of the stovetop, which gave us crispy, golden-brown socca. But flipping the skillet-size socca wasn't as easy as we'd hoped. We solved this problem by making several smaller flatbreads instead. As an added bonus, the smaller flatbreads had a higher ratio of crunchy crust to tender interior. Chickpea flour is also sold as garbanzo bean flour and is available in most well-stocked supermarkets.*

BATTER
- 1½ cups (6¾ ounces) chickpea flour
- ½ teaspoon salt
- ½ teaspoon pepper
- ½ teaspoon turmeric
- 1½ cups water
- 6 tablespoons plus 1 teaspoon extra-virgin olive oil

TOPPING
- 1 tablespoon extra-virgin olive oil
- 1 onion, chopped fine
- 2 garlic cloves, minced
- ¾ teaspoon ground cumin
  Salt and pepper
- ⅛ teaspoon allspice
- 12 ounces Swiss chard, stemmed and chopped
- 3 tablespoons finely chopped dried apricots
- 2 tablespoons finely chopped toasted pistachios
- 1 teaspoon white wine vinegar

1. **For the batter** Set wire rack in rimmed baking sheet. Adjust oven rack to middle position, place prepared sheet in oven, and heat oven to 200 degrees. Whisk flour, salt, pepper, and turmeric together in bowl. Slowly whisk in water and 3 tablespoons oil until combined and smooth.

PASTA WITH BEANS, SWISS CHARD, AND ROSEMARY

Serves 6 Total time: 45 minutes

WHY THIS RECIPE WORKS *Pasta, beans, and greens provide a great combination of flavors and textures for this one-dish meal. In addition to the usual creamy cannellini beans, we added pinto beans for meatiness, while Swiss chard made an appealing twofer for the greens component. We sautéed the chopped chard stems at the outset of cooking but waited until the end to sprinkle the tender leaves on top, and then we covered the pot and let the leaves steam gently off the heat. A small amount of pancetta provided a meaty background, and two additions of rosemary gave the dish a subtle but pervasive herbal flavor. Instead of draining and rinsing the canned beans, we mixed the starchy liquid with water and a handful of grated Parmesan to produce a creamy, stew-like sauce to bring it all together. We cooked the pasta separately until just shy of al dente and then finished cooking it in the broth so that it could soak up some of the broth's meaty flavor. If fusilli is unavailable, farfalle or campanelle are good substitutes. A rasp-style grater makes easy work of mincing the garlic to a paste. The sauce will thicken as it cools.*

2 tablespoons extra-virgin olive oil
3 ounces pancetta, chopped fine
1 onion, chopped fine
10 ounces Swiss chard, stems chopped fine, leaves cut into 1-inch pieces
2 teaspoons minced fresh rosemary
1 garlic clove, minced to paste
¼ teaspoon red pepper flakes
1 (15-ounce) can cannellini beans
1 (15-ounce) can pinto beans
1 Parmesan cheese rind (optional), plus 1 ounce Parmesan, grated (½ cup), plus extra for serving
8 ounces (2½ cups) fusilli
Salt
1 tablespoon red wine vinegar

1. Heat oil in Dutch oven over medium-high heat until just smoking. Add pancetta and cook, stirring occasionally, until pancetta begins to brown, 2 to 3 minutes. Add onion and chard stems and cook, stirring occasionally, until slightly softened, about 3 minutes. Stir in 1 teaspoon rosemary, garlic, and pepper flakes and cook until fragrant, about 1 minute. Stir in beans and their liquid, 1½ cups water, and Parmesan rind, if using, and bring to simmer. Reduce heat to medium-low and cook for 10 minutes.

2. Meanwhile, bring 2 quarts water to boil in large saucepan. Add pasta and 1½ teaspoons salt and cook until pasta is just shy of al dente. Drain pasta, then stir into beans. Spread chard leaves on top, cover, and remove pot from heat. Let sit until pasta is fully cooked and chard leaves are wilted, 5 to 7 minutes. Discard Parmesan rind, if using. Stir in remaining 1 teaspoon rosemary, ½ cup Parmesan, and vinegar. Season with salt to taste. Serve, passing extra Parmesan separately.

SWISS CHARD AND PINTO BEAN ENCHILADAS
Serves 4 to 6   Total time: 1 hour 30 minutes
WHY THIS RECIPE WORKS *Cheesy, meaty fillings are common and typical for enchiladas, but this hearty, delicious version uses neither, while still delivering tons of flavor. We kept things green by wilting flavorsome Swiss chard and crisp, slightly bitter green peppers with garlic and onions. To add*

creamy cohesiveness and heft, we mashed half a can of pinto beans and mixed in our greens; we stirred in the rest of the beans whole for contrasting texture. This clean-tasting filling needed a robust sauce to round out the flavors; a quick simmer of canned tomato sauce with aromatics and spices did the trick. Traditional recipes call for frying the tortillas one at a time, but we found that brushing them with oil and microwaving worked just as well—and without the mess. A topping of a crema-like cilantro sauce and chopped avocado was ideal: tangy, creamy, fresh-tasting, and rich.

CILANTRO SAUCE
¼ cup mayonnaise
¼ cup sour cream
3 tablespoons water
3 tablespoons minced fresh cilantro
¼ teaspoon salt

ENCHILADAS
¼ cup vegetable oil
2 onions, chopped fine
   Salt and pepper
3 tablespoons chili powder
2 teaspoons ground cumin
2 teaspoons sugar
6 garlic cloves, minced
2 (8-ounce) cans tomato sauce
½ cup water
1 pound Swiss chard, stemmed and sliced into ½-inch-wide strips
2 green bell peppers, stemmed, seeded, and cut into ½-inch pieces
1 (15-ounce) can pinto beans, rinsed
12 (6-inch) corn tortillas
1 avocado, halved, pitted, and cut into ½-inch pieces
¼ cup fresh cilantro leaves
   Lime wedges

1. **For the cilantro sauce** Whisk all ingredients together in bowl. Cover and refrigerate until ready to serve.

2. **For the enchiladas** Adjust oven rack to middle position and heat oven to 450 degrees. Heat 1 tablespoon oil in large saucepan over medium heat until shimmering. Add half of onions and ½ teaspoon salt and cook until softened, about 5 minutes. Stir in chili powder, cumin, sugar, and half of garlic and cook until fragrant, about 30 seconds. Stir in

tomato sauce and water, bring to simmer, and cook until slightly thickened, about 7 minutes. Season with salt and pepper to taste; set aside.

3. Heat 1 tablespoon oil in Dutch oven over medium heat until shimmering. Add remaining onions and ¼ teaspoon salt and cook until softened and lightly browned, 5 to 7 minutes. Add remaining garlic and cook until fragrant, about 30 seconds. Add chard and bell peppers, cover, and cook until chard is tender, 6 to 8 minutes. Using potato masher, coarsely mash half of beans in large bowl. Stir in chard-pepper mixture, ¼ cup sauce, and remaining whole beans.

4. Grease 13 by 9-inch baking dish. Spread ½ cup sauce over bottom of prepared dish. Brush both sides of tortillas with remaining 2 tablespoons oil. Stack tortillas, wrap in damp dish towel, and place on plate. Microwave until warm and pliable, about 1 minute. Working with 1 warm tortilla at a time, spread ¼ cup chard filling across center. Roll tortilla tightly around filling and place seam side down in dish, arranging enchiladas in 2 columns across width of dish. Cover completely with remaining sauce.

5. Cover dish tightly with greased aluminum foil and bake until enchiladas are heated through, 15 to 20 minutes. Let enchiladas cool for 10 minutes. Drizzle with cilantro sauce and sprinkle with avocado and cilantro. Serve with lime wedges.

SWISS CHARD PIE
Serves 12   Total time: 2 hours 30 minutes (plus 2 hours chilling time)
WHY THIS RECIPE WORKS *Hailing from central Italy, this greens-packed savory pie, locally called* erbazzone, *makes a satisfying snack, appetizer, or light lunch. Although different greens may be used, Swiss chard is the most typical. The greens are cooked down, flavored with pancetta and plenty of Parmigiano-Reggiano cheese, and wrapped in a flaky crust. Variations abound—some call for egg in the filling, and some are shaped into rectangles while others are shaped into circles—but the one controversial ingredient is ricotta. Many recipes don't include it, while*

some sources claim it's not erbazzone without it. We liked the cleaner, earthier taste of the erbazzone without the ricotta, but if you prefer a cheesier filling we've provided the option. This dough will be moister than most pie doughs; as the dough chills, it will absorb any excess moisture, leaving it supple and workable. You must chill the dough for at least 2 hours or up to two days before using.

CRUST

 20 tablespoons (2½ sticks) unsalted butter, chilled
 2½ cups (12½ ounces) all-purpose flour
  1 teaspoon salt
  ½ cup ice water

FILLING

  1 tablespoon extra-virgin olive oil
  3 ounces pancetta, chopped fine
  1 onion, chopped fine
  4 garlic cloves, minced
  3 pounds Swiss chard, stemmed and cut into 1-inch pieces
  4 ounces Parmesan cheese, grated (2 cups)
  6 ounces (¾ cup) whole-milk ricotta cheese (optional)
  1 large egg, lightly beaten

1. For the crust Grate half stick butter using coarse holes on box grater and place in freezer. Cut remaining 2 sticks butter into ½-inch pieces.

2. Pulse 1½ cups flour and salt in food processor until combined, about 4 pulses. Add butter pieces and process until homogenous dough forms, about 30 seconds. Using your hands, carefully break dough into 2-inch pieces and redistribute evenly around processor blade. Add remaining 1 cup flour and pulse until mixture is broken into pieces no larger than 1 inch (most pieces will be much smaller), 4 or 5 pulses. Empty mixture into medium bowl. Add grated butter and toss until butter pieces are separated and coated with flour.

3. Sprinkle ¼ cup ice water over mixture. Toss with rubber spatula until mixture is evenly moistened. Sprinkle remaining ¼ cup ice water over mixture and toss to combine.

Press dough with spatula until dough sticks together. Divide dough in half and transfer to sheets of plastic wrap. Draw edges of plastic wrap over first dough half and press firmly on sides and top to form compact fissure-free mass. Flatten to form 5-inch square. Repeat with second dough half. Refrigerate for at least 2 hours or up to 2 days. Let chilled dough sit on counter to soften slightly, about 10 minutes, before rolling.

4. For the filling Adjust oven rack to lower-middle position and heat oven to 400 degrees. Cook oil and ⅓ cup pancetta in Dutch oven over medium-low heat until pancetta is browned and fat is rendered, 5 to 7 minutes. Using slotted spoon, transfer pancetta to bowl. Pour off all but 1 tablespoon fat from pot.

5. Add onion to fat left in pot and cook over medium heat until softened, about 5 minutes. Stir in garlic and cook until fragrant, about 30 seconds. Increase heat to high. Add chard, 1 handful at a time, and cook until beginning to wilt, about 1 minute. Cover and continue to cook, stirring occasionally, until chard is wilted but still bright green, 2 to 4 minutes. Uncover and continue to cook until liquid evaporates, about 5 minutes. Transfer chard to large bowl and let cool to room temperature, about 30 minutes.

6. Grease rimmed baking sheet. Stir Parmesan; ricotta, if using; and cooked pancetta into chard. Roll 1 dough square into 14 by 10-inch rectangle on well-floured counter. Loosely roll dough around rolling pin and unroll it onto prepared sheet. Spread chard mixture evenly over crust, leaving 1-inch border around edges. Brush edges of crust with egg.

7. Roll remaining dough square into 14 by 10-inch rectangle on lightly floured counter. Loosely roll dough around rolling pin and unroll it over filling. Press edges of crusts together to seal. Roll edges inward and use your fingers to crimp. Using sharp knife, cut through top crust into 12 equal squares (do not cut through filling). Brush with remaining egg and sprinkle with remaining pancetta.

8. Bake until pie is golden brown and pancetta is crisp, 30 to 35 minutes, rotating sheet halfway through baking. Transfer sheet to wire rack and let pie cool completely, about 30 minutes. Transfer pie to cutting board, cut into squares, and serve.

TURKEY CUTLETS WITH SWISS CHARD AND BARLEY

Serves 4 Total time: 1 hour

WHY THIS RECIPE WORKS *Hearty Swiss chard and rustic, chewy barley are paired with quick-cooking turkey cutlets for a great weeknight meal. Since the cutlets cook so quickly, we prepared our barley first, simmering it with aromatics and the chard stems before folding in the Swiss chard leaves. To give the turkey bright flavor, we employed a simple trick: We caramelized lemon halves in the cooking oil, infusing it (and thus the cutlets) with flavor. A hint of lemon zest in the barley complemented the lemony oil. A half a cup of Parmesan added a salty richness, tying the whole dish together. Do not substitute hulled, hull-less, quick-cooking, or presteamed barley (read the ingredient list on the package carefully to determine this) in this recipe.*

  3 tablespoons extra-virgin olive oil
  ¼ cup finely chopped onion
 12 ounces Swiss chard, stemmed, 1 cup stems chopped fine, leaves cut into 1-inch pieces
 1½ cups pearl barley, rinsed
  2 garlic cloves, minced
 2½ cups chicken broth
  1 teaspoon grated lemon zest, plus 1 lemon, halved and seeded
  1 ounce Parmesan cheese, grated (½ cup)
   Salt and pepper
  6 (4-ounce) turkey cutlets, trimmed

1. Heat 2 tablespoons oil in large saucepan over medium-high heat until shimmering. Add onion and chard stems and cook until softened, about 5 minutes. Stir in barley and garlic and cook until barley is lightly toasted and fragrant, about 3 minutes. Stir in broth and bring to simmer. Reduce heat to low, cover, and cook until barley is tender and broth is absorbed, 20 to 40 minutes.

2. Fold chard leaves and lemon zest into barley, increase heat to medium-high, and cook, uncovered, stirring gently, until chard is wilted, about 2 minutes. Off heat, stir in ¼ cup Parmesan and season with salt and pepper to taste. Cover to keep warm.

3. Pat cutlets dry with paper towels and season with salt and pepper. Heat 1 teaspoon oil in 12-inch nonstick skillet over medium-high heat until shimmering. Add lemon halves, cut side down, and cook until browned, about 2 minutes; set aside. Heat remaining 2 teaspoons oil in now-empty skillet until shimmering. Add cutlets to skillet and cook until well browned and tender, about 2 minutes per side. Off heat, squeeze lemon halves over cutlets. Serve with barley mixture, sprinkling individual portions with remaining ¼ cup Parmesan.

POMEGRANATE ROASTED SALMON WITH SWISS CHARD AND LENTILS

Serves 4   Total time: 1 hour 15 minutes

WHY THIS RECIPE WORKS *Rich salmon and an earthy Swiss chard–lentil combo are brightened by sweet-tart pomegranate molasses and seeds in this satisfying and creative meal. Chard stems have great flavor, so we softened them with aromatics before simmering with the lentils, stirring in the chard leaves near the end of cooking. We painted the salmon with pomegranate molasses, and fresh pomegranate seeds stirred in at the end tied the dish together. To ensure uniform pieces of fish that cooked at the same rate, we found it best to buy a whole center-cut fillet and cut it ourselves. Be sure to purchase skin-on salmon; it helps the salmon hold together during cooking. If using wild salmon, which contains less fat than farmed, cook the fillets until they are 120 degrees. Pomegranate molasses can be found in the international aisle of well-stocked supermarkets; if you can't find it, substitute 1 tablespoon lemon juice plus 1 tablespoon mild molasses. We prefer* lentilles du Puy, *also called French green lentils, for this recipe, but it will work with any type of lentil except red or yellow (note that cooking times will vary).*

2 tablespoons plus 1 teaspoon extra-virgin olive oil
12 ounces Swiss chard, stemmed, ½ cup stems chopped fine, leaves cut into 2-inch pieces
1 small onion, chopped fine
    Salt and pepper
2 garlic cloves, minced
4 sprigs fresh thyme
2 cups chicken broth
1 cup lentilles du Puy, picked over and rinsed
1 (1½-pound) skin-on salmon fillet, 1 inch thick
2 tablespoons pomegranate molasses
½ cup pomegranate seeds

1. Heat 1 tablespoon oil in large saucepan over medium-high heat until shimmering. Add chard stems, onion, and ¼ teaspoon salt and cook until softened, about 5 minutes. Stir in garlic and thyme sprigs and cook until fragrant, about 30 seconds. Stir in broth and lentils and bring to simmer. Reduce heat to low, cover, and cook, stirring occasionally, until lentils are mostly tender, 45 to 50 minutes.

2. Adjust oven rack to lowest position, place aluminum foil–lined rimmed baking sheet on rack, and heat oven to 500 degrees. Uncover lentils and stir in chard leaves. Increase heat to medium-low and cook until chard leaves are tender, about 4 minutes. Off heat, discard thyme sprigs. Stir in 1 tablespoon oil and season with salt and pepper to taste; cover to keep warm.

3. Cut salmon crosswise into 4 fillets. Pat salmon dry with paper towels. Brush with remaining 1 teaspoon oil, then brush with 1 tablespoon pomegranate molasses and season with salt and pepper. Once oven reaches 500 degrees, reduce oven temperature to 275 degrees. Carefully place salmon skin-side down on hot sheet and roast until center is still translucent when checked with tip of paring knife and registers 125 degrees (for medium-rare), 4 to 6 minutes.

4. Remove sheet from oven and brush salmon with remaining 1 tablespoon pomegranate molasses. Slide fish spatula along underside of fillets and transfer to serving platter, discarding skin. Stir pomegranate seeds into lentil mixture and serve with salmon.

TOMATILLOS AND CAPE GOOSEBERRIES

Small, spherical, and a lovely shade of pale green, **TOMATILLOS** removed from their husks resemble miniature green tomatoes. In fact, they are called *tomates verdes* in Mexico, where they originated; alternate names are Mexican husk tomatoes and Mexican ground cherries.

Part of the nightshade family, tomatillos were first cultivated thousands of years ago by the Aztecs. They continue to be a staple of Mexican cuisine today and are beloved both raw and cooked in a wide variety of dishes. In this chapter, we offer our Roasted Tomatillo Salsa, which is as delicious with tortilla chips as it is when used as a topping for steak or chicken. We also include a grilled version of tomatillo salsa to serve with grilled pork tenderloin. Along with green chiles, tomatillos are a hallmark ingredient in Enchiladas Verdes, and our bright, fresh, tangy version of this authentic Mexican classic is memorably delicious.

Another dark-horse member of the nightshade family is the **CAPE GOOSEBERRY**, which was first cultivated in the Andes and also goes by the names husk cherry, Peruvian ground cherry, golden berry, and Inca berry. These small golden fruits are encased in delicate, paper lantern–shaped husks. They have a unique flavor, with hints of pineapple, tomato, and green grapes. Famed naturalist and wild-foods proponent Euell Gibbons once said that the flavor of the Cape gooseberry is "so good it doesn't have to resemble something else."

Cape gooseberries are delicious raw or cooked, in both savory and sweet dishes. They make a great addition to a summer salad, as in our Cape Gooseberry Salad with Ginger-Lime Dressing, and they're ethereally wonderful in our Cape Gooseberry–Rose Preserves.

shopping and storage

Tomatillos are in season in the summer and fall. When shopping for tomatillos, choose those of a similar size so they will cook evenly. Look for firm specimens that boast bright green skin—a yellow color indicates that the flesh is overripe and will taste sweet, not tangy. A light green, flexible, unblemished husk is also desirable; a brown hue and a dry, papery texture indicate overripeness. Finally, the tomatillo should completely fill out its husk (the husk should not balloon away from the fruit). Don't remove the husks or rinse off the sticky coating (which protects the fruit from bugs) until you are ready to cook the tomatillos. Store tomatillos in an open plastic produce bag in the refrigerator for a couple of weeks. Canned tomatillos are a reasonable substitute for fresh in a pinch, though they won't contribute the same depth of flavor.

Cape gooseberries are not widely cultivated commercially, making them a wonderful height-of-summer find at your local farmers' market or specialty supermarket. As they ripen, they turn from green to golden or pale orange, and from tart to sweet. Try them at all stages of ripeness to see how you like their flavor. Cape gooseberries are more perishable than tomatillos; store them in an open plastic produce bag in the refrigerator for up to one week.

tomatillos versus tomatoes

Tomatillos may look like small green tomatoes, but they are emphatically not the same thing. Both are technically fruits that we treat in the kitchen like vegetables. They are two different species in the same family of nightshades, which also includes potatoes, eggplant, bell peppers, and Cape gooseberries.

So if a tomatillo is not like a tomato, then what is it like? Tomatillos are much firmer than tomatoes. They have a tangier, more citrusy flavor than green tomatoes, without even a hint of sweetness. Typically they are too acidic and coarse-textured to eat "straight up" in slices, as we do with tomatoes. They can be used raw to delicious effect, as in our Shrimp Ceviche with Tomatillos, Jícama, and Avocado, but most often they are roasted or grilled.

about cape gooseberries

Cape gooseberries are closely related to tomatillos and are entirely different from American gooseberries (which are fruits in the currant family). There is no consensus on how Cape gooseberries got their name. Some stories claim it's because they were grown on the Cape of Good Hope, in South Africa, at the turn of the 19th century. Other stories say they are called that because of the cape-like husk that covers the berries. Although they are still little known in the United States, these diminutive berries are world travelers. They are most widely cultivated today in South America, South Africa, Australia, and New Zealand.

vegetable prep

Preparing Tomatillos for Cooking

1. Remove stems and peel away inedible husks.

2. Rinse well to remove slightly sticky coating and drain in colander.

Preparing Cape Gooseberries for Cooking

Remove outer lantern-shaped husks and stems, and rinse well.

Roasted Tomatillo Salsa

ROASTED TOMATILLO SALSA

Makes about 2 cups   Total time: 1 hour

WHY THIS RECIPE WORKS *Salsa verde ("green sauce") is even more common than tomato-based salsa on the Mexican table. We wanted a tangy salsa that highlighted the green, citrusy notes of tomatillos. While some recipes use raw tomatillos, most call for cooking them by either boiling or roasting. Cooking softens the fruit, which can be quite firm, and mellows its acidity. We found that charring half of the tomatillos under the broiler and leaving the other half raw produced a salsa with clean, fresh flavor and subtle, smoky nuances. We combined the tomatillos with traditional salsa seasonings (jalapeño, onion, garlic, cilantro, lime juice, and salt) in the bowl of a food processor, and pulsed the salsa to a chunky consistency. Serve with tortilla chips or dolloped on steaks, chicken, or fish.*

1 pound tomatillos, husks and stems removed, rinsed well and dried
1 teaspoon vegetable oil
1 small white onion, chopped
1 jalapeño chile, stemmed, halved, and seeded
½ cup fresh cilantro leaves
2 tablespoons lime juice
1 garlic clove, minced
  Salt
2 teaspoons extra-virgin olive oil
  Sugar

1. Adjust oven rack 6 inches from broiler element and heat broiler. Line rimmed baking sheet with aluminum foil. Toss half of tomatillos with vegetable oil and transfer to prepared sheet. Broil until tomatillos are spotty brown and skins begin to burst, 7 to 10 minutes. Transfer tomatillos to food processor and let cool completely.

2. Halve remaining tomatillos and add to food processor with broiled tomatillos. Add onion, jalapeño, cilantro, lime juice, garlic, and ¼ teaspoon salt. Pulse until slightly chunky, 16 to 18 pulses. Transfer salsa to serving bowl, cover, and let sit at room temperature for at least 30 minutes. Stir in olive oil and season with salt and sugar to taste before serving. (Salsa can be refrigerated for up to 2 days.)

TOMATILLO AND PINTO BEAN NACHOS

Serves 4 to 6   Total time: 45 minutes

WHY THIS RECIPE WORKS *These vegetarian nachos are not just a pile of chips, cheese, and beans. They deliver big flavor thanks to mouth-puckering fresh tomatillos and bold seasonings including garlic, oregano, and coriander. We chopped the tomatillos and sautéed them with corn (frozen kernels were ideal for year-round nacho convenience). To avoid soggy chips, we cooked the tomatillo mixture until all the moisture had evaporated, and we also sprinkled the cheese on the chips first, so it would act as a protective layer. We especially liked the flavor of spicy pepper Jack here. We wanted to add a bean component to these nachos, but refried beans added too much moisture. We opted for whole canned pinto beans instead, sprinkling them between each layer of filling. Fresh jalapeños added another layer of flavor and texture to our nachos. Once everything was layered, it took just 10 minutes in the oven to melt the cheese—any longer and the chips became soggy. Once the nachos came out of the oven, we added sliced radishes for fresh, cooling crunch. Our homemade tomato salsa and guacamole are key for making this recipe stand out, but if you are short on time you can use your favorite store-bought varieties.*

1 tablespoon vegetable oil
1 onion, chopped fine
3 garlic cloves, minced
2 teaspoons minced fresh oregano or ½ teaspoon dried
1 teaspoon ground coriander
1 teaspoon salt
12 ounces tomatillos, husks and stems removed, rinsed well and dried, cut into ½-inch pieces
1 cup frozen corn, thawed
8 ounces tortilla chips
12 ounces pepper Jack cheese, shredded (3 cups)
1 (15-ounce) can pinto beans, rinsed
2 jalapeño chiles, stemmed and sliced thin
3 radishes, trimmed and sliced thin
1½ cups Super Guacamole (page 24)
1 cup Fresh Tomato Salsa (page 452)
½ cup sour cream
  Lime wedges

1. Adjust oven rack to middle position and heat oven to 400 degrees. Heat oil in 12-inch nonstick skillet over medium heat until shimmering. Add onion and cook until softened, about 5 minutes. Stir in garlic, oregano, coriander, and salt and cook until fragrant, about 30 seconds. Add tomatillos and corn, reduce heat to medium-low, and cook until tomatillos have released all their moisture and mixture is nearly dry, about 10 minutes. Let cool slightly.

2. Spread half of tortilla chips evenly into 13 by 9-inch baking dish. Sprinkle 1½ cups pepper Jack evenly over chips, then top evenly with half of tomatillo mixture, followed by half of beans and, finally, half of jalapeños. Repeat layering with remaining chips, pepper Jack, tomatillo mixture, beans, and jalapeños. Bake until cheese is melted and just beginning to brown, 7 to 10 minutes.

3. Let nachos cool for 2 minutes, then sprinkle with radishes. Drop scoops of guacamole, salsa, and sour cream around edges of nachos. Serve immediately, passing lime wedges separately.

SHRIMP CEVICHE WITH TOMATILLOS, JÍCAMA, AND AVOCADO

Serves 4 to 6 as a main dish or 6 to 8 as an appetizer   Total time: 1 hour

WHY THIS RECIPE WORKS *Tomatillos do double-duty in this ceviche: Pureed, they help to marinate the shrimp; and diced, they provide citrusy-tart flavor and crunchy texture to the finished dish. Because shrimp "cook" much more slowly in acid as compared with fish and scallops, we first poached our shrimp in seasoned water and then cut them into bite-size pieces. To create a flavorful yet balanced marinade for our ceviche, we made what's known as a* leche de tigre *by blending lime juice, tomatillos, jalapeño, garlic, and extra-virgin olive oil along with a small amount of shrimp. Once strained, the liquid was an intensely flavorful and silky-textured emulsion. We marinated the poached shrimp in the leche for just 30 minutes to allow the flavors to penetrate and the shrimp to firm slightly. To complete the dish, we added diced tomatillos, crunchy jícama, Vidalia onion,* creamy avocado, and chopped cilantro. We served the ceviche with corn nuts and popcorn, which provided salty crunch. Shrimp of other sizes may be used in this recipe; just be sure to adjust the cooking time accordingly. If Vidalia onions are unavailable, substitute another sweet onion or ¼ cup chopped red onion. Serving the corn nuts and popcorn separately allows diners to customize their ceviche to suit their taste.

5 sprigs fresh cilantro, plus ¼ cup coarsely chopped
4 garlic cloves, lightly crushed and peeled
  Salt and pepper
1 pound large shrimp (26–30 per pound), peeled, deveined, and tails removed
12 ounces tomatillos, husks and stems removed, rinsed well and dried
½ cup lime juice (4 limes)
1 jalapeño chile, stemmed and seeded
3 tablespoons extra-virgin olive oil
8 ounces jícama, peeled and cut into ¼-inch pieces (1 cup)
½ cup chopped Vidalia or Walla Walla onion
1 avocado, halved, pitted, and cut into ½-inch pieces
1 cup corn nuts
1 cup lightly salted popcorn

1. Bring 2 cups water, cilantro sprigs, 2 garlic cloves, and ½ teaspoon salt to boil in large saucepan over high heat. Add shrimp, cover, and let sit off heat, stirring occasionally, until shrimp are just opaque, 1 to 2 minutes. Meanwhile, fill large bowl halfway with ice and water. Drain shrimp well, transfer to ice water, and let sit until just cool, about 2 minutes. Transfer shrimp to triple layer of paper towels and dry well. Cut shrimp in half lengthwise and then cut each half into ½-inch pieces. Transfer ⅓ cup shrimp pieces to blender jar. Refrigerate remaining shrimp.

2. Cut 8 ounces tomatillos into ¼-inch pieces and set aside. Cut remaining tomatillos into quarters and add to blender jar with shrimp. Add lime juice, jalapeño, 2 tablespoons oil, remaining 2 garlic cloves, and 1 teaspoon salt and process until mixture is smooth, 30 to 60 seconds, scraping down sides of blender jar as needed. Strain liquid

through fine-mesh strainer set over large bowl, pressing on solids to extract as much liquid as possible; discard solids. (Sauce can be made up to 24 hours in advance and refrigerated. It will separate slightly; whisk to recombine before proceeding with recipe.)

3. Add chopped shrimp, reserved diced tomatillo, and jícama to bowl with sauce and toss to combine. Refrigerate for 30 minutes.

4. Add onion and chopped cilantro to bowl with ceviche and toss to combine. Portion ceviche into individual bowls, garnish with avocado, and drizzle with remaining 1 tablespoon oil. Serve, passing corn nuts and popcorn separately.

~

CAPE GOOSEBERRY SALAD WITH GINGER-LIME DRESSING

Serves 4   Total time: 20 minutes
WHY THIS RECIPE WORKS *Lightly sweet Cape gooseberries are balanced by a bold dressing and creamy, tangy goat cheese in this light summertime salad. The simple vinaigrette, made with lime juice, fresh ginger, Dijon mustard, and cayenne pepper, added exciting bright freshness without overpowering the mild flavor of the gooseberries. Simply whisking the dressing together in the salad bowl before tossing in the remaining ingredients made the salad easy to prepare. Bibb lettuce added bulk and a delicate buttery bite to accompany the gooseberries. Mint offered a refreshing twist to the vinaigrette and complemented the lime juice and ginger. The addition of goat cheese made for a nice creamy counterpoint to the zesty dressing and sweet gooseberries, and a final sprinkle of pistachios added a crunchy bite. Adjust the amount of lime juice depending on the sweetness level of your Cape gooseberries.*

2–3 teaspoons lime juice
1 teaspoon grated fresh ginger
½ teaspoon Dijon mustard
  Pinch cayenne pepper
  Salt and pepper
¼ cup extra-virgin olive oil

1 head Bibb lettuce (8 ounces), leaves separated and torn into 2-inch pieces
8 ounces Cape gooseberries, husks and stems removed, rinsed well and dried, halved
¼ cup chopped fresh mint
1½ ounces goat cheese, crumbled (⅓ cup)
2 tablespoons chopped toasted pistachios

Whisk lime juice, ginger, mustard, cayenne, and ¼ teaspoon salt together in large bowl. Whisking constantly, slowly drizzle in oil until well combined. Add lettuce, gooseberries, and mint and gently toss to coat. Season with salt and pepper to taste. Transfer to serving platter and sprinkle with goat cheese and pistachios. Serve.

~

SALAD WITH PICKLED TOMATILLOS, SUN-DRIED TOMATOES, AND GOAT CHEESE

Serves 4 to 6   Total time: 45 minutes
WHY THIS RECIPE WORKS *While tomatillos are Mexican in origin and are often used in Mexican dishes, we wanted to create a tomatillo salad with a different and unexpected flavor profile. So we started by pickling our tomatillos. They're a great fit for pickling, since their crunchy skin holds up well to the pickling process and their tart flavor is enhanced by a balanced sweet and vinegary brine. We boiled the tomatillo wedges in a simple brine of cider vinegar, sugar, water, and salt for just 1 minute to infuse flavor before transferring the mixture to a bowl to cool to room temperature. While the tomatillo pickles were cooling, we built our salad. Oil-packed sun-dried tomatoes were an unexpected flavor complement, their assertively bright flavor pairing perfectly with the pickled tomatillos. Refreshing leaf lettuce made a sturdy base for our salad. For a zippy, punchy dressing, we used the sun-dried tomato packing oil and the tomatillo pickle brine. To finish the salad, creamy goat cheese balanced the acidity of the tomatillos and dressing, and toasted walnuts added a crunchy final touch.*

SALAD WITH PICKLED TOMATILLOS, SUN-DRIED TOMATOES, AND GOAT CHEESE

Tomatillos are most typically used in Mexican and southwestern-style dishes, but here we created a refreshing salad using more of a Mediterranean flavor profile. Crunchy, sweet-tart pickled tomatillos and unctuous oil-packed sun-dried tomatoes are the green and red jewels nestling into the leaf lettuce, complemented by tangy goat cheese and rich toasted walnuts for a stunner of a salad.

1. Remove the husks and stems from the tomatillos, rinse them well, dry them, and cut them into eighths.

2. Bring the vinegar, sugar, water, and salt to a boil in a medium saucepan and boil the tomatillos in the pickling liquid for 1 minute.

3. Transfer the tomatillos and pickling liquid to a bowl and let cool for 30 minutes. Drain the tomatillos over a bowl and reserve 2 tablespoons of the liquid.

4. Whisk the reserved pickling liquid, sun-dried tomato oil, basil, garlic, pepper flakes, and salt together in a large serving bowl.

5. Add the pickled tomatillos, lettuce, and sun-dried tomatoes and toss to combine.

6. Sprinkle the salad with the goat cheese and toasted walnuts.

½ cup cider vinegar

¼ cup sugar
  Salt and pepper

12 ounces tomatillos, husks and stems removed, rinsed well and dried, and cut into eighths

⅓ cup oil-packed sun-dried tomatoes, patted dry and sliced thin, plus 2 tablespoons packing oil

¼ cup chopped fresh basil

1 garlic clove, minced

¼ teaspoon red pepper flakes

1 head red or green leaf lettuce (8 ounces), torn into bite-size pieces

2 ounces goat cheese, crumbled (½ cup)

¼ cup walnuts, toasted and chopped

1. Bring vinegar, sugar, 2 tablespoons water, and 2 teaspoons salt to boil in medium saucepan over medium-high heat. Add tomatillos and boil for 1 minute. Transfer mixture to bowl and let cool to room temperature, about 30 minutes. Drain tomatillos, reserving 2 tablespoons brine.

2. Whisk reserved brine, sun-dried tomato oil, basil, garlic, pepper flakes, and ¼ teaspoon salt together in large serving bowl. Add pickled tomatillos, red leaf lettuce, and sun-dried tomatoes and toss to combine. Season with salt and pepper to taste. Sprinkle with goat cheese and walnuts. Serve.

CHICKEN POSOLE VERDE

Serves 6 to 8   Total time: 2 hours

WHY THIS RECIPE WORKS *Posole is the Mexican name for both hominy (dried field corn kernels treated with lime and boiled until tender but still chewy) and the full-flavored stew made with it. We decided to create a green chicken posole—a style with a trademark tanginess that comes from tomatillos, jalapeños, and cilantro. Using whole bone-in chicken thighs resulted in easy-to-shred meat, giving our stew a pleasant, rustic texture. We quickly browned the chicken and then sautéed our aromatics after we removed the chicken from the pot, allowing us to incorporate the flavorful browned bits into our broth. When we returned the partially cooked chicken to the pot, we moved the cooking*

from the stove to the more even, gentle heat of the oven. Adding the tomatillo puree late in the cooking process allowed the flavors to meld without dulling the puree's bright freshness. Finally, we returned the shredded chicken to the pot to warm briefly before serving the posole. Serve with lime wedges, diced avocado, and/or sliced radishes.

4 pounds bone-in chicken thighs, trimmed
  Salt and pepper

2 tablespoons vegetable oil

1 onion, chopped fine

3 garlic cloves, minced

1 tablespoon chopped fresh oregano or 1 teaspoon dried

4½ cups chicken broth

12 ounces tomatillos, husks and stems removed, rinsed well and dried, quartered

2½ cups fresh cilantro leaves and stems, trimmed (2 bunches)

2 jalapeño chiles, stemmed, halved, and seeded

2 (15-ounce) cans white or yellow hominy, rinsed

1. Adjust oven rack to lower-middle position and heat oven to 300 degrees. Pat chicken dry with paper towels and season with salt and pepper. Heat 1 tablespoon oil in Dutch oven over medium-high heat until just smoking. Brown half of chicken, about 5 minutes per side; transfer to plate. Repeat with remaining 1 tablespoon oil and remaining chicken; transfer to plate. Let chicken cool slightly, then discard skin.

2. Pour off all but 1 tablespoon fat from pot. Add onion and ¼ teaspoon salt and cook over medium heat until softened, about 5 minutes. Stir in garlic and oregano and cook until fragrant, about 30 seconds. Stir in 4 cups broth, scraping up any browned bits, and bring to simmer. Nestle chicken into pot along with any accumulated juices. Cover, transfer pot to oven, and cook until chicken is tender, about 1 hour.

3. Remove pot from oven. Transfer chicken to cutting board, let cool slightly, then shred into bite-size pieces using 2 forks; discard bones.

4. Meanwhile, process tomatillos, cilantro, jalapeños, and remaining ½ cup broth in blender until smooth, about 30 seconds. Stir tomatillo mixture and hominy into stew, bring to simmer over medium heat, and cook until flavors meld, 10 to 15 minutes. Stir in chicken and cook until heated through, about 2 minutes. Season with salt and pepper to taste. Serve.

ENCHILADAS VERDES

Serves 4 to 6   Total time: 1 hour 30 minutes

WHY THIS RECIPE WORKS *The green tomatillo-based sauce used in enchiladas verdes cooks much more quickly than the red enchilada sauce variety, making these a great choice for a weeknight meal. We love the combination of rustic-textured, vibrant green sauce, tender chicken, soft corn tortillas, and gooey cheese topping. To keep this recipe easy while still mimicking traditional recipes, which call for dry-roasting whole tomatillos and poblanos on the stovetop until charred, we broiled the vegetables. The pepper Jack cheese has a mildly spicy kick that complements the poblanos. To increase spiciness, reserve some of the chiles' ribs and seeds and add them to the food processor in step 4. To avoid soggy enchiladas, be sure to cool the chicken filling before filling the tortillas.*

3 tablespoons vegetable oil

1 onion, chopped

½ teaspoon ground cumin

3 garlic cloves, minced

1½ cups chicken broth

1 pound boneless, skinless chicken breasts, trimmed

1½ pounds tomatillos, husks and stems removed, rinsed well and dried

3 poblano chiles, stemmed, halved, and seeded

1–2½ teaspoons sugar
  Salt and pepper

8 ounces pepper Jack or Monterey Jack cheese, shredded (2 cups)

½ cup chopped fresh cilantro

12 (6-inch) corn tortillas

2 scallions, sliced thin
  Thinly sliced radishes
  Sour cream

1. Adjust 1 oven rack to middle position and second rack 6 inches from broiler element; heat broiler. Heat 2 teaspoons oil in medium saucepan over medium heat until shimmering. Add onion and cook until softened and lightly browned, 5 to 7 minutes. Stir in cumin and two-thirds of garlic and cook until fragrant, about 30 seconds. Stir in broth and bring to simmer.

2. Add chicken and reduce heat to medium-low. Cover and simmer until chicken registers 160 degrees, 15 to 20 minutes, flipping chicken halfway through cooking. Transfer chicken to cutting board and let cool slightly.

3. While chicken cools, measure out ½ cup liquid and set aside; discard remaining liquid. Toss tomatillos and poblanos with 1 teaspoon oil. Arrange tomatillos cut side down and poblanos skin side up on aluminum foil–lined rimmed baking sheet. Broil on upper rack until vegetables blacken and start to soften, 5 to 10 minutes, rotating sheet halfway through broiling. Let tomatillos and poblanos cool slightly, then remove skins from poblanos (leave tomatillo skins intact). Heat oven to 450 degrees.

4. Transfer vegetables, along with any accumulated juices, to food processor. Add 1 teaspoon sugar, 1 teaspoon salt, remaining garlic, and reserved cooking liquid to food processor and pulse until sauce is somewhat chunky, about 8 pulses. Season with salt and pepper to taste, and adjust tartness by stirring in remaining sugar, ½ teaspoon at a time; set aside.

5. When chicken is cool, use 2 forks to shred into bite-size pieces. Combine chicken with 1½ cups pepper Jack and cilantro; season with salt to taste.

6. Grease 13 by 9-inch baking dish. Brush both sides of tortillas with remaining 2 tablespoons oil. Stack tortillas, wrap in damp dish towel, and place on plate. Microwave until warm and pliable, about 1 minute. Working with 1 warm tortilla at a time, spread ⅓ cup chicken filling across center. Roll tortilla tightly around filling and place seam side down in dish, arranging enchiladas in 2 columns across width of

dish. Cover completely with remaining sauce. Sprinkle with remaining ½ cup pepper Jack.

7. Cover dish tightly with greased aluminum foil and bake until enchiladas are heated through, 15 to 20 minutes. Let enchiladas cool for 10 minutes. Sprinkle with scallions, and serve, passing radishes and sour cream separately.

GRILLED PORK TENDERLOINS WITH GRILLED TOMATILLO SALSA

Serves 4 to 6   Total time: 1 hour

WHY THIS RECIPE WORKS *A grilled green salsa adds loads of bright flavor to pork. We grilled tomatillos, scallions, and garlic right alongside the tenderloins and then, while the meat rested, combined them in a food processor with cilantro, serrano chiles, lime juice, and spices to make the piquant salsa. For a rich crust and a tender, juicy interior on our pork, we seared it on the hotter side of the grill to develop flavorful browning. Then we moved the meat to the cooler side of the grill to finish cooking. Seasoning it with a mixture of salt, cumin, and chipotle chile powder added smoky, savory flavor, and a touch of sugar encouraged browning. We prefer unenhanced pork in this recipe, but enhanced pork (injected with a salt solution) can be used.*

PORK
1½   teaspoons kosher salt
1½   teaspoons sugar
½   teaspoon ground cumin
½   teaspoon chipotle chile powder
2   (12- to 16-ounce) pork tenderloins, trimmed

SALSA
1   pound tomatillos, husks and stems removed, rinsed well and dried
9   scallions
6   garlic cloves, peeled and threaded onto wooden skewer
2   tablespoons plus 1 teaspoon extra-virgin olive oil
¾   cup minced fresh cilantro

2   serrano chiles, stemmed, seeded, and minced
3   tablespoons lime juice, plus extra for seasoning (2 limes)
Salt

1. For the pork Combine salt, sugar, cumin, and chile powder in small bowl. Reserve ½ teaspoon spice mixture. Rub remaining spice mixture evenly over surface of both tenderloins. Transfer to large plate and refrigerate while preparing grill.

2a. For a charcoal grill Open bottom vent completely. Light large chimney starter filled with charcoal briquettes (6 quarts). When top coals are partially covered with ash, pour evenly over half of grill. Set cooking grate in place, cover, and open lid vent completely. Heat grill until hot, about 5 minutes.

2b. For a gas grill Turn all burners to high, cover, and heat grill until hot, about 15 minutes. Leave primary burner on high and turn off other burner(s).

3. Clean and oil cooking grate. Place tenderloins on hotter side of grill. Cover and cook, turning tenderloins every 2 minutes, until well browned on all sides, about 8 minutes.

4. For the salsa Brush tomatillos, scallions, and garlic with 1 teaspoon oil. Move tenderloins to cooler side of grill (6 to 8 inches from heat source) and place tomatillos, scallions, and garlic on hotter side of grill. Cover and cook until tomatillos, scallions, and garlic are charred on both sides and softened, 8 to 10 minutes, and until pork registers 140 degrees, 12 to 17 minutes, turning tenderloins every 5 minutes. As vegetables and tenderloins reach desired level of doneness, transfer vegetables to plate and transfer tenderloins to carving board. Tent tenderloins with aluminum foil and let rest for 10 minutes.

5. While tenderloins rest, chop scallions coarse. Pulse scallions, tomatillos, garlic, cilantro, serranos, lime juice, reserved spice mixture, and remaining 2 tablespoons oil in food processor until mixture is coarsely chopped, 4 to 6 pulses. Transfer to bowl and season with salt and extra lime juice to taste. Slice tenderloins crosswise ½ inch thick. Serve with salsa.

PAN-ROASTED COD WITH AMARILLO SAUCE

Serves 4   Total time: 45 minutes

WHY THIS RECIPE WORKS *A light rust orange in color, classic amarillo sauce is a mole-style sauce from Oaxaca that includes chiles, tomatillos, and masa harina as a thickener. We wanted to create a lively, tangy, slightly spicy version of this sauce to dress up mild white fish. Through typically aji amarillo chiles are used, most modern recipes use guajillos, which we found gave the mole a pleasant, mild heat. We complemented that chile flavor with some warm spices. Our aromatic base benefited from the addition of clam broth, which provided a subtle seafood backbone. We cooked the tomatillos only briefly, to preserve their bright, tart flavor, before pureeing the sauce in the blender. We cooked the cod fillets simply, sprinkling them with just a bit of sugar to accelerate browning. This shortened the cooking time and ensured that the fish didn't dry out. Halibut, sea bass, and red snapper are good substitutes for the cod. Because most fish fillets differ in thickness, some pieces may finish cooking before others—be sure to immediately remove any fillet that reaches 140 degrees. You will need a 12-inch ovensafe nonstick skillet for this recipe.*

3 guajillo chiles, stemmed, seeded, and torn into ½-inch pieces (6 tablespoons)
2 tablespoons vegetable oil
1 onion, chopped
4 garlic cloves, peeled
½ teaspoon dried oregano
¼ teaspoon whole cumin seeds
⅛ teaspoon ground cloves
⅛ teaspoon ground allspice
3 tablespoons masa harina
1 (8-ounce) bottle clam juice
8 ounces tomatillos, husks and stems removed, rinsed well and dried, cut into ½-inch pieces
6 sprigs cilantro
Salt and pepper
4 (6- to 8-ounce) skinless cod fillets, 1 to 1½ inches thick
½ teaspoon sugar

1. Toast guajillos in medium saucepan over medium heat, stirring frequently, until fragrant, 2 to 6 minutes; transfer to bowl. Heat 1 tablespoon oil in now-empty saucepan over medium heat until shimmering. Add onion and cook until softened, about 5 minutes. Stir in garlic, oregano, cumin seeds, cloves, and allspice and cook until fragrant, about 30 seconds. Stir in masa harina and cook for 1 minute. Slowly whisk in clam juice, scraping up any browned bits and smoothing out any lumps.

2. Stir in tomatillos, cilantro sprigs, guajillos, ½ teaspoon salt, and ¼ teaspoon pepper. Bring to simmer and cook until tomatillos begin to soften, about 3 minutes. Carefully transfer mixture to blender and process until smooth, 1 to 2 minutes. Return to clean pot and cover to keep warm.

3. Adjust oven rack to middle position and heat oven to 425 degrees. Pat cod dry with paper towels, season with salt and pepper, and sprinkle sugar lightly over 1 side of each fillet.

4. Heat remaining 1 tablespoon oil in 12-inch ovensafe nonstick skillet over high heat until just smoking. Lay fillets, sugared side down, in skillet and press lightly to ensure even contact with skillet. Cook until browned, 1 to 1½ minutes.

5. Turn fillets over using 2 spatulas and transfer skillet to oven. Roast cod until fish flakes apart when gently prodded with paring knife and registers 140 degrees, 7 to 10 minutes. Serve with sauce.

～～～

CAPE GOOSEBERRY–ROSE PRESERVES

Makes two 1-cup jars

Total time: 45 minutes (plus 12 hours refrigeration time)

WHY THIS RECIPE WORKS *When cooked into preserves, the flavors of Cape gooseberries intensify, and their natural juices give the preserves a dense, velvety texture without having to add any pectin. To balance the sweetness of our preserves, we added lemon juice, and to highlight the gentle floral tones of the fruit, we stirred in a small amount of rose water just before portioning our preserves into jars. Cape gooseberries turn from green to golden, and tart to sweet, as they ripen. Look for fruits that are mostly golden (some underripe fruit will add a bit of tartness, if you like), with dry, clean husks. You will need two 1-cup mason jars with tight-fitting lids for this recipe. You must chill the preserves for at least 12 hours before using.*

1¼ pounds Cape gooseberries, husks and stems removed, rinsed well and dried
1½ cups sugar
3 tablespoons lemon juice
2 teaspoons rose water

1. Place 2 small plates in freezer to chill. In large saucepan, bring gooseberries, sugar, and lemon juice to boil, stirring often, over medium-high heat. Once sugar has completely dissolved, remove pot from heat and use potato masher to crush fruit coarse, leaving some berries intact.

2. Return mixture to boil over medium-high heat and cook, stirring and adjusting heat as needed, until mixture registers 217 to 220 degrees, 12 to 15 minutes. Remove pot from heat.

3. To test consistency, place 1 teaspoon preserves on chilled plate and freeze for 2 minutes. Drag your finger through preserves on plate. Preserves have correct consistency when your finger leaves distinct trail. If runny, return pot to heat and simmer for 1 to 3 minutes before retesting. Skim any foam from surface of preserves using spoon and stir in rose water.

4. Meanwhile, place two 1-cup jars in bowl and place under hot running water until heated through, 1 to 2 minutes, then shake dry.

5. Using funnel and ladle, portion hot preserves into hot jars. Let cool to room temperature, cover, and refrigerate until preserves are set, 12 to 24 hours. (Preserves can be refrigerated for up to 2 months.)

Cape Gooseberry–Rose Preserves

TOMATOES

Tomatoes are a bit like peaches: When you get a mealy one, it goes right into the trash, but when you get a perfectly ripe one, it's a truly transcendent food experience. (And yes, like the peach, the tomato is a fruit.) Who among us hasn't eaten such a luscious tomato right over the kitchen sink to catch its dripping juices?

And what's the best way to ensure that you get that juicy, flavorful tomato? Buy a locally grown one from a small farmer. This is because, first, the shorter the distance the tomato has to travel, the riper it can be when it's picked. Second, commercial high-yield production can strain the plants, resulting in tomatoes without enough sugars and other flavor compounds to make them tasty. Third, commercial varieties are bred to be sturdier, with thick walls that withstand the rigors of machine harvesting and long-distance transport.

The best-tasting tomatoes have thin walls, leaving more room for the jelly that surrounds the seeds; this jelly is flavor central, with three times more savory flavor compounds known as glutamates than the tomato flesh. Some of the most delicious tomatoes you'll find are heirloom tomatoes. This is a term that gets bandied about freely, but any variety not associated with large-scale commercial production may be labeled as heirloom. Most have been grown for decades from naturally pollinated plants and seeds that haven't been hybridized for productivity, unlike commercial varieties.

In this chapter, you'll find recipes for tomato salads, sauces, salsa, jam, relish, and pesto. Don't miss our elegant Best Summer Tomato Gratin or Creamy Gazpacho Andaluz. And, when tomato season draws to a close, console yourself with Fried Green Tomatoes.

shopping and storage

High quality control for commercially grown grape tomatoes and cherry tomatoes, plus their ubiquity in the supermarket, make these two varieties reasonable year-round choices. We've also found vine-ripened tomatoes to be juicy and flavorful supermarket options. However, for getting the juiciest, most flavorful fruit, nothing comes close to buying locally field-grown, vine-ripened tomatoes at the height of summer. Always choose tomatoes that smell fruity and feel heavy for their size. Commercial tomatoes have been bred to be perfectly symmetrical and uniformly attractive. When shopping at farmers' markets, you will see plenty of oddly shaped tomatoes, which are completely fine to purchase. Even cracked skin, which you see often on heirloom varieties, is OK. Just avoid tomatoes that are bruised, overly soft, or leaking juice.

go ahead and refrigerate ripe tomatoes

Standard wisdom dictates that tomatoes should never be refrigerated, supposedly because cold kills their flavor-producing enzymes and ruins their texture by causing cells to rupture. We decided to test this. Over two summers, we acquired heirloom and farmers' market tomatoes that had never been refrigerated (most supermarket tomatoes are refrigerated during storage and/or transport). Once they were ripe, we left some tomatoes whole and halved others. We then refrigerated one set and left the second set at room temperature, storing them until they started to degrade. We stored the whole tomatoes loose and the cut tomatoes in airtight containers to protect from off flavors. We then sampled all the tomatoes at room temperature. Shelf life for the refrigerated whole tomatoes was prolonged by five days. The cut tomatoes held up well for two days in the refrigerator. Best of all? Their flavor was unaffected. So feel free to refrigerate both whole and cut ripe tomatoes to prolong their life.

canned tomato products

Canned tomatoes, which are processed at the height of freshness, deliver more flavor than off-season fresh tomatoes. But with all the options lining supermarket shelves, it's not always clear what to buy. We tested a variety of canned tomato products.

WHOLE TOMATOES Peeled whole tomatoes are packed in either their own juice or puree. They are quite soft and break down quickly when cooked. They're best when fresh tomato flavor is a must. We prefer Muir Glen Organic Whole Peeled Tomatoes.

DICED TOMATOES Tomatoes are peeled, machine-diced, and packed in either their own juice or puree. Diced tomatoes are best for rustic tomato sauces with a chunky texture, and in long-cooked stews and soups in which you want the tomatoes to hold their shape. We favor diced tomatoes packed in juice, rather than puree, because they have a fresher flavor. Our winning brand is Hunt's Diced Tomatoes.

CRUSHED TOMATOES Whole tomatoes are ground very fine and then enriched with tomato puree. They work well in smoother sauces, and their thicker consistency makes them ideal when you want to make a sauce quickly. You can make your own by pulsing canned diced tomatoes in a food processor. We prefer SMT Crushed Tomatoes.

TOMATO PUREE Made from cooked tomatoes that are strained to remove their seeds and skins, tomato puree works well in long-simmered, smooth, thick sauces with a deep, hearty flavor. Our winning brand is Muir Glen Organic Tomato Puree.

TOMATO PASTE Tomato paste is tomato puree that has been cooked to remove almost all moisture. Because it's so concentrated, tomato paste brings out subtle deep savory notes. We use it in a variety of recipes, including both long-simmered sauces and quicker-cooking dishes, to lend a complex, rounded tomato flavor and color. Our winning brand is Goya Tomato Paste.

vegetable prep

Coring and Chopping or Dicing Tomatoes

1. Cut around core of tomato with paring knife and remove core.

2. Slice cored tomato crosswise into even slices and stack a couple of slices. Cut stacked slices first crosswise and then widthwise into pieces of desired size.

Stuffing Tomatoes

1. Cut top ½ inch off stem and set aside.

2. Using melon baller, scoop out tomato pulp into fine-mesh strainer set over bowl.

FRESH TOMATO SAUCE

Makes 4 cups; enough for 1 pound pasta
Total time: 20 minutes
WHY THIS RECIPE WORKS *The best tomato sauce recipes are pure, quick, and simple, consisting of nothing more than tomatoes, olive oil, garlic, herbs, salt, a bit of sugar, and pepper. With that philosophy in mind, we set out to develop a fresh tomato sauce recipe that capitalized on this list of ingredients. We found that cooking the garlic in the oil for a minute or two prevented it from burning. The tomatoes, which we cooked for just 10 minutes, broke down readily and thickened slightly, just enough to ably coat the pasta. The success of this recipe depends on using ripe, in-season tomatoes. If you're using exceptionally sweet tomatoes, omit the sugar.*

 3 tablespoons extra-virgin olive oil
 2 garlic cloves, minced
 2 pounds ripe plum tomatoes, cored and cut into ½-inch pieces
   Salt and pepper
 ½ teaspoon sugar (optional)
 2 tablespoons chopped fresh basil

Cook oil and garlic in large saucepan over medium heat until garlic is fragrant but not browned, 1 to 2 minutes. Stir in tomatoes, ¾ teaspoon salt, ½ teaspoon pepper, and sugar, if using. Increase heat to medium-high and cook until tomatoes are broken down and sauce is slightly thickened, about 10 minutes. Stir in basil and season with salt and pepper to taste. Serve.

~

ROASTED TOMATOES

Makes about 1½ cups
Total time: 2 hours 15 minutes
WHY THIS RECIPE WORKS *If you've never roasted tomatoes, you should. It's a largely hands-off technique that yields the ultimate condiment: bright, concentrated, savory-sweet tomatoes that are soft but retain their shape. There are so many ways to use them, including as a topping for crostini and pizza, in sandwiches, tossed into pasta, or added*

to a quiche or frittata. The flavorful tomato oil is great in salad dressings or drizzled over roasted meat, fish, or vegetables. For intensely flavored tomatoes, we started by cutting the tomatoes into thick slices and arranging them on a foil-lined rimmed baking sheet. Drizzling on plenty of extra-virgin olive oil helped the tomatoes roast faster. Adding smashed garlic cloves lent flavor and fragrance to the tomatoes and oil. Avoid using tomatoes smaller than 3 inches in diameter, which have a smaller ratio of flavorful jelly to skin than larger tomatoes. To double the recipe, use two baking sheets, increase the roasting time in step 2 to 40 minutes, and rotate and switch the sheets halfway through baking. In step 3, increase the roasting time to 1½ to 2½ hours.

 3 pounds large tomatoes, cored, bottom ⅛ inch trimmed, and sliced ¾ inch thick
 2 garlic cloves, peeled and smashed
 ¼ teaspoon dried oregano
   Kosher salt and pepper
 ¾ cup extra-virgin olive oil

1. Adjust oven rack to middle position and heat oven to 425 degrees. Line rimmed baking sheet with aluminum foil. Arrange tomatoes in even layer on prepared sheet, with larger slices around edge and smaller slices in center. Place garlic cloves on tomatoes. Sprinkle with oregano and ¼ teaspoon salt and season with pepper. Drizzle oil evenly over tomatoes.

2. Roast for 30 minutes, rotating sheet halfway through roasting. Remove sheet from oven. Reduce oven temperature to 300 degrees and prop open door with wooden spoon to cool oven. Using thin spatula, flip tomatoes.

3. Return tomatoes to oven and cook until spotty brown, skins are blistered, and tomatoes have collapsed to ¼ to ½ inch thick, 1 to 2 hours. Remove from oven and let cool completely, about 30 minutes. Discard garlic and serve. (Tomatoes and oil can be refrigerated in airtight container for up to 5 days or frozen for up to 2 months.)

SLOW-COOKER TOMATOES WITH OLIVE OIL

Serves 4 to 6   Total time: 5 to 6 hours on low or 3 to 4 hours on high
WHY THIS RECIPE WORKS *If you're lucky enough to have an overabundance of freshly picked August tomatoes, or you're just looking for a way to improve average supermarket specimens, this "slow-roasted" method for melt-in-your-mouth tomatoes is a great way to go. They are amazing alongside roasted meat or fish with plenty of crusty bread for dipping into the extra cooking liquid. To start, we cored the tomatoes, then halved them lengthwise through the stem end. We gently tossed them with just enough extra-virgin olive oil to infuse them with bright, fruity flavor as they released their juices into the slow cooker, creating a flavorful cooking liquid. The addition of smashed garlic cloves, which mellowed and softened during the long cooking time, lent a rich, nutty flavor to the oil and paired well with the fresh thyme that we used. Aside from a little salt and pepper, no other seasoning was needed for this uncomplicated dish. You will need a 5- to 7-quart slow cooker for this recipe.*

 6 tomatoes, cored and halved
 ½ cup extra-virgin olive oil
 6 garlic cloves, peeled and smashed
 2 teaspoons minced fresh thyme or ¾ teaspoon dried
   Salt and pepper

1. Combine tomatoes, oil, garlic, thyme, ¾ teaspoon salt, and ¼ teaspoon pepper in slow cooker. Cover and cook until tomatoes are tender and slightly shriveled around edges, 5 to 6 hours on low or 3 to 4 hours on high.

2. Let tomatoes cool in liquid for at least 15 minutes or up to 4 hours. Season with salt and pepper to taste. Serve. (Tomatoes and liquid can be refrigerated in airtight container for up to 5 days or frozen for up to 2 months.)

Slow-Cooker Tomatoes with Olive Oil

FRIED GREEN TOMATOES

Serves 4 to 6   Total time: 45 minutes

WHY THIS RECIPE WORKS *Southern cooks have long made the most of an unripe tomato crop by dunking sliced green tomatoes in breading and frying them to a golden crust. For a crisp, stay-put coating, we first drained tomato slices on paper towels. Once dry, the tomatoes were ready for breading. We found that processing some of the cornmeal to a fine crumb minimized its grittiness. We then dunked the slices in egg and buttermilk and dredged them through our cornmeal blend before frying. The acid in the buttermilk helped the starchy coating absorb moisture, making it especially crisp when fried. After just a few minutes, these sweet-tart tomatoes developed a golden-brown crust that was so good, we found ourselves looking forward to the first frost and its bonanza of never-to-ripen green tomatoes.*

1½   pounds green tomatoes, cored and sliced ¼ inch thick
⅔   cup cornmeal
⅓   cup all-purpose flour
1½   teaspoons salt
½   teaspoon pepper
⅛   teaspoon cayenne pepper
⅔   cup buttermilk
1   large egg
2   cups peanut or vegetable oil

1. Place tomatoes on paper towel–lined rimmed baking sheet. Cover with more paper towels, let sit for 20 minutes, and pat dry. Meanwhile, process ⅓ cup cornmeal in blender until very finely ground, about 1 minute. Combine processed cornmeal, remaining ⅓ cup cornmeal, flour, salt, pepper, and cayenne in shallow dish. Whisk buttermilk and egg together in second shallow dish.

2. Working with 1 tomato slice at a time, dip in buttermilk mixture, then dredge in cornmeal mixture, pressing firmly to adhere; transfer to clean baking sheet.

3. Set wire rack in rimmed baking sheet. Heat oil in 12-inch skillet over medium-high heat to 350 degrees. Fry 4 tomato slices until golden brown on both sides, 4 to 6 minutes. Drain on prepared wire rack. Return oil to 350 degrees and repeat with remaining tomato slices in batches. Serve.

SPICY TOMATO JAM

Makes 2 cups   Total time: 1 hour 15 minutes (plus 1 hour cooling time)

WHY THIS RECIPE WORKS *Ruby-red tomato jam is a flavorful way to transform your tomatoes into a unique topping for sandwiches or a base for dips; or dollop it onto a cheese plate. It's a cinch to make: Just combine everything in a large pot and cook it down to a deliciously sweet and spicy jam. Leaving the peels on the tomatoes gave our chunky jam a good texture. In our attempts to achieve the right amount of heat, we started by adding three jalapeños, seeds included. The jam barely had a kick to stand up to the sweet tomato flavors but instead had a prominent grassy flavor. So, we swapped the jalapeños for a single seeded habanero. This chile packed the heat we were looking for as well as a complementary fruity flavor. For an even spicier tomato jam, include the habanero seeds.*

2½   pounds tomatoes, cored and chopped
1   cup red wine vinegar
¾   cup sugar
7   garlic cloves, minced
1   habanero chile, stemmed, seeded, and minced
½   teaspoon ground cumin
½   teaspoon salt

Bring all ingredients to simmer in large saucepan over medium-high heat and cook, stirring often, until mixture has thickened and darkened in color and measures slightly more than 2 cups, 1 to 1¼ hours. Let jam cool completely, about 1 hour, before serving. (Jam can be refrigerated for at least 4 months; flavor will become milder over time.)

FRESH TOMATO SALSA

Makes about 3 cups   Total time: 40 minutes

WHY THIS RECIPE WORKS *Tomato-based salsa fresca (or salsa cruda) accompanies a wide variety of Mexican dishes; it's treated more like a relish than a sauce or a dip and can be served with chicken, seafood, burritos, and more. We set out to create our own version of this versatile, chunky, brightly flavored salsa. We first drained diced tomatoes in a colander. We layered the other ingredients on top of the tomatoes while they drained and then simply stirred everything together in a bowl. We finished the salsa with lime juice (which tasted more authentic than lemon juice), salt, and sugar.*

1½ pounds tomatoes, cored and
cut into ½-inch pieces

½ cup finely chopped red onion

¼ cup chopped fresh cilantro

1 large jalapeño chile, stemmed,
seeds reserved, and minced

1 small garlic clove, minced

2 teaspoons lime juice, plus extra
for seasoning
Salt and pepper
Sugar

Place tomatoes in colander and let drain for
30 minutes. As tomatoes drain, layer onion,
cilantro, jalapeño, and garlic on top. Shake
colander to drain excess juice, then transfer
vegetables to serving bowl. Stir in lime juice.
Add reserved jalapeño seeds to increase heat
as desired. Season with salt, pepper, sugar,
and extra lime juice to taste before serving.

SIMPLE TOMATO SALAD

Serves 4 to 6   Total time: 15 minutes

WHY THIS RECIPE WORKS *A simple,
made-in-minutes tomato salad is one of
the elemental joys of summer. This recipe
starts with the ripest tomatoes you can
find, either at the farmers' market or at the
grocery store. Because tomatoes are already
fairly acidic, we found that a dressing made
with the typical 3:1 ratio of oil to acid was
too sharp here. Adjusting the amount of
lemon juice to minimize the acidity perfectly balanced the salad. A minced shallot
added just a bit of sweetness, toasted pine
nuts added a buttery nuttiness, and both
contributed crunch. Torn basil leaves
completed the salad with a fresh herbal
note. The success of this recipe depends
on using ripe, in-season tomatoes. Serve
with crusty bread to sop up the dressing.*

1½ pounds mixed ripe tomatoes,
cored and sliced ¼ inch thick

3 tablespoons extra-virgin olive oil

1 tablespoon minced shallot

1 teaspoon lemon juice

½ teaspoon salt

¼ teaspoon pepper

2 tablespoons pine nuts, toasted

1 tablespoon torn fresh basil leaves

Arrange tomatoes on large, shallow platter.
Whisk oil, shallot, lemon juice, salt, and
pepper together in bowl. Spoon dressing
over tomatoes. Sprinkle with pine nuts and
basil. Serve immediately.

VARIATIONS

Simple Tomato Salad with Capers
and Parsley

Omit pine nuts. Add 1 tablespoon rinsed
capers, 1 rinsed and minced anchovy fillet,
and ⅛ teaspoon red pepper flakes to dressing.
Substitute chopped fresh parsley for basil.

Simple Tomato Salad with Pecorino
Romano and Oregano

Add ½ teaspoon grated lemon zest and
⅛ teaspoon red pepper flakes to dressing.
Substitute 1 ounce shaved Pecorino Romano
cheese for pine nuts and 2 teaspoons chopped
fresh oregano for basil.

CHERRY TOMATO
SALAD WITH BASIL AND
FRESH MOZZARELLA

Serves 4 to 6   Total time: 50 minutes

WHY THIS RECIPE WORKS *Cherry tomatoes
make a delicious all-season salad, but the
liquid they exude can make a soggy mess. To
get rid of some of their juice without also
draining away flavor, we salted them, then
used a salad spinner to separate the tomato
liquid from the flesh. We reduced this liquid
to a flavorful concentrate (adding shallot,
olive oil, and vinegar) and reunited it with
the tomatoes. Some fresh mozzarella and
chopped basil filled out this great salad. If
you don't have a salad spinner, wrap the
bowl tightly with plastic wrap after the
salted tomatoes have sat for 30 minutes
and gently shake to remove seeds and excess
liquid. Strain the liquid and proceed with
the recipe as directed. If you have less than
½ cup of juice after spinning, proceed with
the recipe using the entire amount of juice
you do have and reduce it to 3 tablespoons
as directed (the cooking time will be shorter).*

1½ pounds cherry tomatoes, quartered

½ teaspoon sugar
Salt and pepper

8 ounces fresh mozzarella, cut into
½-inch pieces and patted dry with
paper towels

1½ cups lightly packed fresh basil leaves,
roughly torn

1 shallot, minced

1 tablespoon balsamic vinegar

2 tablespoons extra-virgin olive oil

1. Toss tomatoes with sugar and ¼ teaspoon
salt in bowl and let sit for 30 minutes. Transfer tomatoes to salad spinner and spin until
seeds and excess liquid have been removed,
45 to 60 seconds, stopping to redistribute
tomatoes several times during spinning. Add
tomatoes, mozzarella, and basil leaves to
large bowl; set aside.

2. Strain ½ cup tomato liquid through
fine-mesh strainer into liquid measuring
cup; discard remaining liquid. Bring tomato
liquid, shallot, and vinegar to simmer in
small saucepan over medium heat and cook
until reduced to 3 tablespoons, 6 to 8 minutes. Transfer to small bowl and let cool to
room temperature, about 5 minutes. Whisking constantly, slowly drizzle in oil. Drizzle
dressing over salad and gently toss to coat.
Season with salt and pepper to taste. Serve.

VARIATIONS

Cherry Tomato Salad with Tarragon and
Blue Cheese

Substitute ½ cup crumbled blue cheese for
mozzarella and 1½ tablespoons chopped
fresh tarragon for basil. Add ½ cup toasted
and chopped pecans to bowl with drained
tomatoes. Substitute cider vinegar for
balsamic vinegar and add 4 teaspoons honey
and 2 teaspoons Dijon mustard to saucepan
with tomato liquid before cooking.

Cherry Tomato Salad with Mango and
Lime-Curry Vinaigrette

Substitute 1 mango, cut into ½-inch pieces,
for mozzarella and 3 tablespoons chopped
fresh cilantro for basil. Add ½ cup toasted
slivered almonds to bowl with drained
tomatoes. Substitute 4 teaspoons lime juice
for balsamic vinegar and add ¼ teaspoon
curry powder to saucepan with tomato
liquid before cooking.

TOMATO AND BURRATA SALAD WITH PANGRATTATO AND BASIL

Caprese salad is a faithful Italian standby, but we wanted to up the ante to create a luxe modern reimagined showstopper. To intensify the flavor of the tomatoes, we salted and drained them and dressed them with a white balsamic vinaigrette. Decadent burrata stepped in for the regular mozzarella. And our pangrattato—crispy, garlicky bread crumbs made from a rustic, crusty loaf—brought this salad firmly into the 21st century.

1. Toss the tomato pieces and the cherry tomato halves with the salt and let them drain in a colander for 30 minutes.

2. To make the pangrattato, pulse the bread pieces in a food processor into large crumbs ⅛ to ¼ inch thick.

3. Cook the crumbs in the seasoned oil in a skillet until crisp and golden, about 10 minutes. Clear the center of the skillet, add the garlic, and cook until fragrant, about 30 seconds, then stir the garlic into the toasted bread crumbs.

4. To make the vinaigrette, whisk together the shallot, vinegar, and salt in a large bowl. Drizzle in the olive oil while whisking constantly.

5. Add the drained tomatoes and the basil and gently toss with the vinaigrette.

6. Arrange the tomatoes on a serving platter. Arrange the burrata over the tomatoes, drizzle with the creamy liquid, and sprinkle with the bread crumbs.

TOMATO AND BURRATA SALAD WITH PANGRATTATO AND BASIL

Serves 4 to 6   Total time: 40 minutes

WHY THIS RECIPE WORKS *Burrata is a deluxe version of fresh mozzarella in which supple cheese is bound around a filling of cream and bits of cheese. We wanted to create a Caprese-inspired salad in which summer's best tomatoes could star alongside this decadent cheese. We quickly realized that just tomatoes, basil, and good olive oil weren't enough to bring out the best in the rich burrata. To concentrate the tomato flavor, we used a combination of standard tomatoes and cherry tomatoes, and we found that salting them for 30 minutes helped draw out their watery juices. Blending the olive oil with a little minced shallot and mild white balsamic vinegar gave us a bold vinaigrette. Finally, adding a topping of Italian pangrattato (rustic garlicky bread crumbs) brought the dish together, soaking up both the tomato juices and the burrata cream. The success of this dish depends on using ripe, in-season tomatoes and very fresh, high-quality burrata.*

- 1½ pounds ripe tomatoes, cored and cut into 1-inch pieces
- 8 ounces ripe cherry tomatoes, halved
  Salt and pepper
- 3 ounces rustic Italian bread, cut into 1-inch pieces (1 cup)
- 6 tablespoons extra-virgin olive oil
- 1 garlic clove, minced
- 1 shallot, halved and sliced thin
- 1½ tablespoons white balsamic vinegar
- ½ cup chopped fresh basil
- 8 ounces burrata cheese, room temperature

1. Toss tomatoes with ¼ teaspoon salt and let drain in colander for 30 minutes.

2. Pulse bread in food processor into large crumbs measuring between ⅛ and ¼ inch, about 10 pulses. Combine crumbs, 2 tablespoons oil, pinch salt, and pinch pepper in 12-inch nonstick skillet. Cook over medium heat, stirring often, until crumbs are crisp and golden, about 10 minutes. Clear center of skillet, add garlic, and cook, mashing it

into skillet, until fragrant, about 30 seconds. Stir garlic into crumbs. Transfer to plate and let cool slightly.

3. Whisk shallot, vinegar, and ¼ teaspoon salt together in large bowl. Whisking constantly, slowly drizzle in remaining ¼ cup oil. Add tomatoes and basil and gently toss to combine. Season with salt and pepper to taste, and arrange on serving platter. Cut burrata into 1-inch pieces, collecting creamy liquid. Sprinkle burrata over tomatoes and drizzle with creamy liquid. Sprinkle with bread crumbs and serve immediately.

FRESH TOMATO SOUP WITH BASIL

Serves 4 to 6   Total time: 2 hours

WHY THIS RECIPE WORKS *We thought we knew tomato soup: velvety smooth, creamy, and comforting—perfect for a cold winter day. But there's another kind of tomato soup: made without cream and bursting with fresh tomato essence. Usually flavored with onions, garlic, and basil, it's the perfect way to use a surplus of ripe summer tomatoes. We concentrated the tomato flavor and evaporated excess moisture by roasting the tomatoes, then pureed them in a blender. We salted our reserved chopped tomatoes to soften their texture and added them at the end of cooking, boosting the fresh tomato flavor. The success of this recipe depends on using ripe, in-season tomatoes.*

- 6 pounds ripe tomatoes, cored (5 pounds quartered, 1 pound cut into ½-inch pieces)
- 2 onions, chopped
- 9 garlic cloves, peeled (8 whole, 1 minced)
- 3 tablespoons extra-virgin olive oil
  Salt
  Sugar
- 1 cup chopped fresh basil

1. Adjust oven rack to upper-middle position and heat oven to 450 degrees. Combine quartered tomatoes, onions, whole garlic cloves, oil, ½ teaspoon salt, and ¼ teaspoon sugar in large roasting pan. Roast until tomatoes are brown in spots, about 1½ hours, stirring halfway through roasting. Let tomato mixture cool slightly.

2. Meanwhile, combine diced tomatoes, minced garlic, basil, and ¼ teaspoon salt in bowl and let sit for 30 minutes. Working in batches, process roasted tomato mixture in food processor until smooth; transfer to large saucepan. Stir in diced tomato mixture and bring to simmer over medium heat. Cook until diced tomatoes are slightly softened, about 5 minutes. Season with salt and sugar to taste. Serve.

CREAMY GAZPACHO ANDALUZ

Serves 4 to 6   Total time: 30 minutes (plus 1 hour draining time and 2 hours chilling time)

WHY THIS RECIPE WORKS *Open nearly any refrigerator in Spain in the summertime and you'll find a pitcher of refreshing gazpacho. The key to fresh tomato flavor in our gazpacho Andaluz recipe was salting the tomatoes and letting them sit to concentrate flavor. We did the same with the cucumber, bell pepper, and red onion and soaked the bread, which we used to thicken the soup, in the exuded vegetable juices. A final dash of olive oil and sherry vinegar further brightened the flavors, and a diced-vegetable garnish made our gazpacho Andaluz look as fresh as it tasted. The success of this recipe depends on using ripe, in-season tomatoes. For fullest flavor, refrigerate the gazpacho overnight before serving. Red wine vinegar can be substituted for the sherry vinegar.*

- 3 pounds ripe tomatoes, cored
- 1 small cucumber, peeled, halved lengthwise, and seeded
- 1 green bell pepper, stemmed, halved, and seeded
- 1 small red onion, peeled and halved
- 2 garlic cloves, peeled and quartered
- 1 small serrano chile, stemmed and halved lengthwise
  Salt and pepper
- 1 slice hearty white sandwich bread, crust removed, torn into 1-inch pieces
- ½ cup extra-virgin olive oil, plus extra for serving
- 2 tablespoons sherry vinegar, plus extra for serving
- 2 tablespoons minced fresh parsley, chives, or basil

1. Coarsely chop 2 pounds tomatoes, half of cucumber, half of bell pepper, and half of onion and place in large bowl. Add garlic, serrano, and ¾ teaspoon salt and toss to combine.

2. Cut remaining tomatoes, cucumber, and bell pepper into ¼-inch pieces and place in medium bowl. Finely chop remaining onion and add to vegetables. Toss with ¼ teaspoon salt and transfer to fine-mesh strainer set over medium bowl. Let drain for 1 hour. Transfer drained vegetables to second medium bowl and set aside, reserving liquid (you should have about ¼ cup liquid. Discard any extra liquid).

3. Add bread to reserved liquid and soak for 1 minute. Add soaked bread and any remaining liquid to coarsely chopped vegetables and toss thoroughly to combine.

4. Transfer half of vegetable-bread mixture to blender and process for 30 seconds. With blender running, slowly drizzle in ¼ cup oil in steady stream and continue to process until completely smooth, about 2 minutes. Strain soup through fine-mesh strainer into large bowl, using back of ladle or rubber spatula to press soup through strainer; discard remaining solids. Repeat with remaining vegetable-bread mixture and remaining ¼ cup oil.

5. Stir vinegar, parsley, and half of drained vegetables into soup and season with salt and pepper to taste. Cover and refrigerate until chilled and flavors meld, about 2 hours. Serve, passing remaining drained vegetables, extra oil, extra vinegar, and pepper separately.

PASTA WITH TOMATO AND ALMOND PESTO

Serves 4 to 6   Total time: 35 minutes

WHY THIS RECIPE WORKS *There's a very different kind of pesto found in the western Sicilian village of Trapani. Almonds replace pine nuts, but the big difference is the appearance of fresh tomatoes—not as the main ingredient, but as a fruity, sweet accent. We wanted a recipe for a clean, bright version of this sauce, not a chunky tomato salsa or thin, watery slush. For this uncooked sauce,*

fresh tomatoes were best. Cherry and grape tomatoes proved equal contenders, sharing a similar brightness and juiciness that were far more reliable than those of their larger cousins. We processed the tomatoes with a handful of basil, garlic, and toasted almonds. The almonds contributed body and thickened the sauce while retaining just enough crunch to offset the tomatoes' pulpiness; using blanched, slivered almonds avoided the muddy flavor often contributed by the nuts' papery skins. We added a scant amount of hot vinegar peppers for zing, then drizzled in olive oil in a slow, steady stream to emulsify the pesto. Stirred-in Parmesan was the finishing touch to this light, bright, and texturally satisfying pesto. While we prefer linguini or spaghetti, any pasta shape will work here. You can substitute ½ teaspoon of red wine vinegar and ¼ teaspoon of red pepper flakes for the pepperoncini.

1 pound linguini or spaghetti
  Salt
12 ounces cherry or grape tomatoes
½ cup fresh basil leaves
¼ cup slivered almonds, toasted
1 small jarred pepperoncini, stemmed, seeded, and minced
1 garlic clove, minced
  Pinch red pepper flakes (optional)
⅓ cup extra-virgin olive oil
1 ounce Parmesan cheese, grated (½ cup), plus extra for serving

1. Bring 4 quarts water to boil in large pot. Add pasta and 1 tablespoon salt and cook, stirring often, until al dente. Reserve ½ cup cooking water, then drain pasta and return it to pot.

2. Meanwhile, process tomatoes, basil, almonds, pepperoncini, garlic, 1 teaspoon salt, and pepper flakes, if using, in food processor until smooth, about 1 minute, scraping down sides of bowl as needed. With processor running, slowly drizzle in oil until incorporated, about 30 seconds.

3. Add pesto and Parmesan to pasta and toss to combine. Adjust consistency with reserved cooking water as needed. Serve immediately, passing extra Parmesan separately.

FRITTATA WITH SUN-DRIED TOMATOES, MOZZARELLA, AND BASIL

Serves 4   Total time: 20 minutes

WHY THIS RECIPE WORKS *The intensely potent, sweet-tart flavor of sun-dried tomatoes in oil infuses this frittata, which makes a great anytime meal. Easy-to-make frittatas are the Italian version of the filled omelet. Whereas an omelet should be soft, delicate, and slightly runny, a frittata should be tender but firm throughout. And whereas an omelet usually encases its filling, a frittata incorporates it evenly throughout, like an egg pie. Our testing found that starting the frittata on the stovetop and finishing it in the oven set it evenly while ensuring that it didn't burn or dry out. Conventional skillets required so much oil to prevent sticking that frittatas cooked in them were likely to be greasy, so we used a nonstick pan for a clean release without using too much oil. You will need a 10-inch ovensafe nonstick skillet for this recipe.*

6 large eggs
¼ teaspoon salt
¼ teaspoon pepper
2 ounces mozzarella cheese, shredded (½ cup)
¼ cup oil-packed sun-dried tomatoes, patted dry and chopped fine
2 tablespoons chopped fresh basil
1 tablespoon extra-virgin olive oil
½ onion, chopped fine

1. Adjust oven rack to upper-middle position and heat oven to 350 degrees. Whisk eggs, salt, and pepper in large bowl until thoroughly combined. Stir in mozzarella, tomatoes, and basil.

2. Heat oil in 10-inch ovensafe nonstick skillet over medium heat until shimmering. Add onion and cook until softened, about 4 minutes. Add egg mixture and stir gently until eggs on bottom are set and firm, about 30 seconds.

3. Using spatula, gently pull cooked eggs back from edge of skillet and tilt pan, allowing any uncooked egg to run to cleared edge of skillet. Repeat this process, working your way around skillet, until egg on top is mostly set but still moist, 1 to 2 minutes.

4. Transfer skillet to oven and bake until frittata top is set and dry to touch, about 3 minutes. Run spatula around skillet edge to loosen frittata, then carefully slide it out onto serving platter. Serve.

STUFFED TOMATOES

Serves 6   Total time: 1 hour 15 minutes

WHY THIS RECIPE WORKS *Stuffed tomatoes always sound elegant and delicious, but too often you end up with tasteless, mushy tomatoes and a lackluster stuffing that falls out in a wet clump. To concentrate flavor and get rid of excess moisture, we seasoned hollowed-out tomato shells with salt and sugar and let them drain. Couscous proved the best base for the filling, combined with baby spinach and Gruyère cheese. We rehydrated the couscous with the reserved tomato juice, ensuring plenty of the savory flavor we craved. A topping of panko bread crumbs—pretoasted for proper browning—mixed with more cheese added crunch and richness, and a drizzle of the cooking liquid mixed with red wine vinegar provided a piquant final touch. Look for large tomatoes, about 3 inches in diameter.*

  6 large tomatoes (8 to 10 ounces each)
  1 tablespoon sugar
      Kosher salt and pepper
4½ tablespoons extra-virgin olive oil
  ¼ cup panko bread crumbs
  3 ounces Gruyère cheese, shredded
      (¾ cup)
  1 onion, halved and sliced thin
  2 garlic cloves, minced
  ⅛ teaspoon red pepper flakes
  8 ounces (8 cups) baby spinach, chopped
  1 cup couscous
  ½ teaspoon grated lemon zest
  1 tablespoon red wine vinegar

1. Adjust oven rack to middle position and heat oven to 375 degrees. Cut top ½ inch off stem end of tomatoes and set aside. Using melon baller, scoop out tomato pulp into fine-mesh strainer set over bowl. Press on pulp with wooden spoon to extract juice, setting aside juice and discarding pulp. (You should have about ⅔ cup tomato juice. If not, add water as needed to equal ⅔ cup.)

2. Combine sugar and 1 tablespoon salt in bowl. Sprinkle each tomato cavity with 1 teaspoon sugar mixture, then turn tomatoes upside down on plate to drain for 30 minutes.

3. Combine 1½ teaspoons oil and panko in 10-inch skillet and toast over medium-high heat, stirring frequently, until golden brown, about 3 minutes. Transfer to bowl and let cool for 10 minutes. Stir in ¼ cup Gruyère.

4. Heat 2 tablespoons oil in now-empty skillet over medium heat until shimmering. Add onion and ½ teaspoon salt and cook until softened, 5 to 7 minutes. Stir in garlic and pepper flakes and cook until fragrant, about 30 seconds. Add spinach, 1 handful at a time, and cook until wilted, about 3 minutes. Stir in couscous, lemon zest, and reserved tomato juice. Off heat, cover, and let sit until couscous has absorbed liquid, about 7 minutes. Transfer couscous mixture to bowl and stir in remaining ½ cup Gruyère. Season with salt and pepper to taste.

5. Coat bottom of 13 by 9-inch baking dish with remaining 2 tablespoons oil. Blot tomato cavities dry with paper towels and season

with salt and pepper. Pack each tomato with couscous mixture, about ½ cup per tomato, mounding excess. Top stuffed tomatoes with 1 heaping tablespoon panko mixture. Place tomatoes in prepared dish. Season reserved tops with salt and pepper and place in empty spaces in dish.

6. Bake, uncovered, until tomatoes have softened but still hold their shape, about 20 minutes. Using slotted spoon, transfer to serving platter. Whisk vinegar into oil remaining in dish, then drizzle over tomatoes. Place tops on tomatoes and serve.

VARIATIONS

Stuffed Tomatoes with Currants and Pistachios
Substitute crumbled feta for Gruyère. Stir 2 tablespoons currants and 2 tablespoons chopped pistachios into cooked couscous mixture with feta.

Stuffed Tomatoes with Olives and Orange
Substitute shredded Manchego for Gruyère. Substitute ¼ teaspoon grated orange zest for lemon zest. Stir ¼ cup pitted kalamata olives, chopped, into cooked couscous mixture with Manchego.

BEST SUMMER TOMATO GRATIN

Serves 6 to 8   Total time: 1 hour 15 minutes

WHY THIS RECIPE WORKS *A summer tomato gratin should burst with concentrated, bright tomato flavor and contrasting firm texture from the bread, but most recipes lead to mushy results. Starting our gratin on the stovetop initiated the breakdown of the tomatoes, drove off some moisture that would otherwise have sogged out the bread, and shortened the overall cooking time. We finished the dish in the dry, even heat of the oven. Toasting large cubes of a crusty artisan-style baguette ensured that the bread didn't get too soggy once combined with the tomatoes. After toasting the bread, we added the coarsely chopped tomatoes as well as garlic, a small amount of sugar, and salt and pepper. Just before moving the skillet to the oven, we folded in most of the toasted bread and scattered the remainder over the top along with some Parmesan to create a crusty, savory topping that contrasted with the custardy interior. A scattering of fresh basil provided color and bright flavor. The success of this recipe depends on using ripe, in-season tomatoes. Do not use plum tomatoes, which contain less juice than regular round tomatoes and will result in a dry gratin. You can serve the gratin hot, warm, or at room temperature. You will need a 12-inch ovensafe skillet for this recipe.*

- 6 tablespoons extra-virgin olive oil
- 6 ounces crusty baguette, cut into ¾-inch pieces (4 cups)
- 3 garlic cloves, sliced thin
- 3 pounds ripe tomatoes, cored and cut into ¾-inch pieces
- 2 teaspoons sugar
- 1 teaspoon salt
- 1 teaspoon pepper
- 1½ ounces Parmesan cheese, grated (¾ cup)
- 2 tablespoons chopped fresh basil

1. Adjust oven rack to middle position and heat oven to 350 degrees. Heat ¼ cup oil in 12-inch oven-safe skillet over medium-low heat until shimmering. Add bread and stir to coat. Cook, stirring constantly, until bread is browned and toasted, about 5 minutes; transfer to bowl.

2. Cook remaining 2 tablespoons oil and garlic in now-empty skillet over low heat, stirring constantly, until garlic is golden at edges, 30 to 60 seconds. Stir in tomatoes, sugar, salt, and pepper. Increase heat to medium-high and cook, stirring occasionally, until tomatoes have started to break down and have released enough juice to be mostly submerged, 8 to 10 minutes.

3. Off heat, gently stir in 3 cups bread until completely moistened and evenly distributed. Using spatula, press down on bread until completely submerged. Arrange remaining 1 cup bread evenly over surface, pressing to partially submerge. Sprinkle evenly with Parmesan.

4. Transfer skillet to oven and bake until top of gratin is deeply browned, tomatoes are bubbling, and juice has reduced, 40 to 45 minutes. After 30 minutes, run spatula around edge of skillet to loosen crust and release any juice underneath. (Gratin will appear loose and jiggle around outer edges but will thicken as it cools.)

5. Remove skillet from oven and let sit for 15 minutes. Sprinkle with basil and serve.

GRILLED PORK SKEWERS WITH GRILLED TOMATO RELISH

Serves 4 to 6   Total time: 50 minutes (plus 30 minutes marinating time)

WHY THIS RECIPE WORKS *Grill-charred tomatoes, scallions, and lemons make a quick relish that explodes with pungent, sweet-tart flavors. Best of all, these items cook on the grill right alongside the pork skewers. Compared with beef and chicken, pork skewers get little love from grillers. Without the right ingredients and techniques, both the texture and the flavor of the meat tend to be unsatisfactory. For moist, flavorful pork, we turned to boneless country-style ribs, which are quick-cooking and tender yet have enough fat to keep them from drying out. A flavorful spice rub of garlic, coriander, cumin, nutmeg, cinnamon, and lemon did triple duty: first in a marinade, later in a basting sauce, and again as part of the* tomato relish. *These skewers offer an easy, flavorful addition to your grilling options for any night of the week. You will need seven 12-inch metal skewers for this recipe.*

- ¼ cup vegetable oil
- 2 lemons (1 grated to yield 1 teaspoon zest), halved
- 5 garlic cloves, minced
- 1 tablespoon ground coriander
- 2 teaspoons ground cumin
- Salt and pepper
- ½ teaspoon ground nutmeg
- ½ teaspoon ground cinnamon
- 2 pounds boneless country-style pork ribs, trimmed and cut into 1-inch pieces
- 12 ounces cherry tomatoes
- 2 tablespoons honey
- 2 tablespoons unsalted butter
- 6 scallions

1. Whisk oil, lemon zest, garlic, coriander, cumin, 1½ teaspoons salt, ½ teaspoon pepper, nutmeg, and cinnamon together in large bowl. Measure out and reserve 2 tablespoons marinade. Add pork to remaining marinade and toss to coat; refrigerate for at least 30 minutes or up to 24 hours.

2. Remove pork from marinade and thread onto four 12-inch metal skewers so pieces are touching; discard any remaining used marinade. Thread tomatoes onto three 12-inch metal skewers.

3. Combine honey, butter, and reserved marinade in small saucepan and cook over medium heat, whisking constantly, until butter is melted and mixture is fragrant, about 1 minute. Divide honey mixture evenly between 2 bowls. (Use 1 bowl for grilling pork in step 5 and second bowl for sauce in step 6.)

4a. For a charcoal grill Open bottom vent completely. Light large chimney starter filled with charcoal briquettes (6 quarts). When top coals are partially covered with ash, pour evenly over grill. Set cooking grate in place, cover, and open lid vent completely. Heat grill until hot, about 5 minutes.

Best Summer Tomato Gratin

Thin-Crust Pizza

4b. For a gas grill Turn all burners to high, cover, and heat grill until hot, about 15 minutes. Turn all burners to medium.

5. Clean and oil cooking grate. Place scallions, pork skewers, tomato skewers, and lemon halves, cut side down, on grill. Cook pork (covered if using gas), turning every 2 minutes and basting with honey mixture reserved for grilling, until pork registers 145 degrees, 12 to 15 minutes. Cook tomatoes, scallions, and lemon halves until charred, turning scallions and tomatoes as needed to brown evenly, 5 to 10 minutes. Transfer items to serving platter as they finish grilling.

6. Tent pork with aluminum foil and let rest while preparing tomato relish. Slide tomatoes from skewers into large bowl. Chop scallions and add to tomatoes along with honey mixture reserved for sauce; squeeze lemon halves into tomato mixture. Using potato masher, coarsely mash tomato mixture. Add any accumulated pork juices. Season with salt and pepper to taste. Serve tomato relish with pork.

THIN-CRUST PIZZA
Makes two 13-inch pizzas
Total time: 1 hour 15 minutes (plus 24 hours refrigeration time and 1 hour resting time)
WHY THIS RECIPE WORKS *New York pizza parlor–style pizza is truly a thing of beauty: marinara-style tomato sauce and a mozz-Parm topping blanketing a thin, crisp crust that's spottily charred on the exterior and tender and chewy within. But with ovens that reach only 500 degrees and dough that's impossible to stretch thin, even the savviest home cooks can struggle to produce parlor-quality pizza. We were determined to make it happen. High-protein bread flour gave us a chewy crust, and the right ratio of flour to water to yeast gave us dough that was easy to stretch. We kneaded the dough quickly in a food processor and let it proof for a few hours. After we shaped and topped the pizza, it went onto a blazing-hot baking stone. Placing the stone near the top of the oven was a revelation, allowing the top of the pizza to brown as well as the bottom. In minutes we had a pizza with everything in sync: a crisp, browned crust*

with a slightly chewy texture, just like a good parlor slice. Our favorite bread flour is from King Arthur. Some baking stones can crack under the intense heat of the broiler; be sure to check the manufacturer's website. It is important to use ice water in the dough to prevent it from overheating in the food processor. Don't top the second pizza until right before you bake it. If you add more toppings, keep them light or they may weigh down the thin crust. This recipe yields extra sauce; the remaining sauce can be refrigerated for up to one week or frozen for up to one month.

DOUGH
- 3 cups (16½ ounces) bread flour
- 2 tablespoons sugar
- ½ teaspoon instant or rapid-rise yeast
- 1⅓ cups ice water
- 1 tablespoon vegetable oil
- 1½ teaspoons salt

SAUCE
- 1 (28-ounce) can whole peeled tomatoes, drained
- 1 tablespoon extra-virgin olive oil
- 1 teaspoon red wine vinegar
- 2 garlic cloves, minced
- 1 teaspoon salt
- 1 teaspoon dried oregano
- ¼ teaspoon pepper

- 1 ounce Parmesan cheese, grated fine (½ cup)
- 8 ounces whole-milk mozzarella, shredded (2 cups)

1. **For the dough** Pulse flour, sugar, and yeast in food processor until combined, about 5 pulses. With processor running, slowly add ice water and process until dough is just combined and no dry flour remains, about 10 seconds. Let dough rest for 10 minutes.

2. Add oil and salt to dough and process until dough forms satiny, sticky ball that clears sides of bowl, 30 to 60 seconds. Transfer dough to lightly oiled counter and knead by hand to form smooth, round ball, about 30 seconds. Place dough seam side down in lightly greased large bowl or container, cover tightly with plastic wrap, and refrigerate for at least 24 hours or up to 3 days.

3. **For the sauce** Process all ingredients in food processor until smooth, about 30 seconds. Transfer to bowl and refrigerate until ready to use.

4. **To bake the pizza** Press down on dough to deflate. Transfer dough to clean counter, divide in half, and cover loosely with greased plastic. Pat 1 piece of dough into 4-inch round (keep remaining piece covered). Working around circumference of dough, fold edges toward center until ball forms.

5. Flip ball seam side down and, using your cupped hands, drag in small circles on counter until dough feels taut and round and all seams are secured on underside. (If dough sticks to your hands, lightly dust top of dough with flour.) Repeat with remaining piece of dough. Space dough balls 3 inches apart, cover loosely with greased plastic, and let rest for 1 hour. Meanwhile, adjust oven rack 4 inches from broiler element, set baking stone on rack, and heat oven to 500 degrees for 1 hour.

6. When ready to bake, heat broiler for 10 minutes. Meanwhile, coat 1 dough ball generously with flour and place on well-floured counter. Using your fingertips, gently flatten into 8-inch round, leaving 1 inch of outer edge slightly thicker than center. Using your hands, gently stretch dough into 12-inch round, working along edge and giving disk quarter turns.

7. Transfer dough to well-floured pizza peel and stretch into 13-inch round. Using back of spoon or ladle, spread ½ cup tomato sauce in even layer over surface of dough, leaving ¼-inch border around edge. Sprinkle ¼ cup Parmesan evenly over sauce, followed by 1 cup mozzarella.

8. Slide pizza carefully onto baking stone and return oven to 500 degrees. Bake until crust is well browned and cheese is bubbly and partially browned, 8 to 10 minutes, rotating pizza halfway through baking. Transfer pizza to wire rack and let cool for 5 minutes before slicing and serving. Heat broiler for 10 minutes. Repeat with remaining dough, sauce, and toppings, returning oven to 500 degrees when each pizza is placed on stone.

WINTER SQUASH

Along with corn and beans, squash was historically one of the three primary crops of the Americas known by the Iroquois as the "three sisters." Not only did these foodstuffs grow together symbiotically, but together they provided a complete balance of carbohydrates, protein, and vitamins. Native Americans of all tribes were eating winter squash for centuries before Europeans arrived; the word "squash" derives from the Narragansett word *askutasquash*.

Winter squashes vary greatly in size, color, and shape but often can be substituted for each other in recipes. For a primer on the most common types found in markets, see the opposite page. In this chapter, we focus on four test-kitchen favorites.

The mild, earthy taste of **ACORN SQUASH** lends itself to bold flavorings, which we provide in spades in our Stuffed Acorn Squash with raisins, onions,

and spinach. Versatile **BUTTERNUT SQUASH** can be turned into a puree or a soup, roasted in chunks with all sorts of flavor combinations, and even transformed into pillow-like, pasta-free dumplings called *gnudi*.

Somewhat resembling its summer cousins in appearance, **DELICATA SQUASH** tastes like a happy cross between fresh corn and pumpkin pie. Drizzling roasted half-moons with a fresh herb sauce makes for a simple but elegant presentation.

Looking at the yellow, oblong **SPAGHETTI SQUASH**, you would never know that nestled inside are hundreds of noodle-like strands that resemble spaghetti. Only the name gives it away. It does make an excellent stand-in for pasta in recipes both hot and cold, as we prove in our Spaghetti Squash with Garlic and Parmesan and our Spaghetti Squash Salad with Tomatoes and Pecorino.

shopping and storage

Fall is the usual harvest time for winter squash. But because it keeps so well, winter squash is typically available year-round. No matter the variety, winter squash should feel very hard; any soft spots are an indication that the squash has been mishandled. Squash should also feel heavy for its size, a sign that the flesh inside is moist and ripe. Store winter squash at cool room temperature, away from light, for up to a month.

is packaged squash acceptable?

Cutting, peeling, and seeding winter squash is time-consuming and even intimidating. We wondered if we could use convenient packages of peeled cut squash in dishes like our Butternut Squash Puree with Sage and Toasted Almonds and our Barley Risotto with Roasted Butternut Squash. In a word, no. Prepared packaged squash is usually dried out, woody, and lacking in flavor. Whole squash that you peel yourself has far superior texture and taste.

all about winter squash

ACORN SQUASH Acorn squash is one of the most ubiquitous winter squashes found in supermarkets. The orange flesh of this dark green acorn-shaped squash has a dense texture and mild flavor.

BUTTERCUP SQUASH A flattened rounded green squash with pale green stripes and a circular ridge on the bottom, buttercup squash has flesh that is on the drier side and very mild in flavor.

BUTTERNUT SQUASH Butternut squash is immediately recognizable by its bell shape. Beneath the tan skin lies moist, bright orange flesh with a sweet taste.

DELICATA SQUASH Oblong and pale yellow with green stripes, delicata has thin, edible skin and creamy flesh is more earthy than sweet in flavor.

HUBBARD SQUASH Typically huge and bumpy and precut into chunks, these gray-blue squashes are increasingly available whole in more manageable sizes. They have lightly sweet and moist orange flesh. Red kuri is a small orange-skinned variety.

KABOCHA SQUASH Kabocha is somewhat similar in size and shape to buttercup. The green variety is slightly sweet in flavor, with nutty, earthy notes. The red variety is noticeably sweeter than the green.

SPAGHETTI SQUASH Spaghetti squash has pale, translucent flesh that scrapes into noodle-like strands when cooked. It has a delicate, grassy, flavor that's fresher than that of other winter squashes.

SUGAR PUMPKINS More than just Halloween decorations, these small, squat squashes have thick-textured orange flesh that's packed with classic pumpkin flavor.

SWEET DUMPLING SQUASH This small squash has edible yellowish white skin with green stripes. Its flesh is similar in texture and flavor to sweet potato.

vegetable prep

Cutting Squash Safely

Winter squashes have tough skins and can therefore be difficult to cut through. To cut squash safely, set squash on damp dish towel, position knife on rind of squash, and strike back of knife with rubber mallet to drive knife into squash. Continue to hit until knife halves squash.

Prepping Butternut Squash

1. Lop ends off squash, peel away skin and fibrous white flesh with vegetable peeler, and use chef's knife to cut it into 2 pieces where bulb meets neck.

2. Halve bulb end, then scoop out and discard seeds and pulp. Chop as recipe directs.

Shredding Spaghetti Squash

Holding roasted squash half with clean dish towel over large bowl, use fork to scrape squash flesh from skin, shredding flesh into fine pieces.

MAPLE-GLAZED ACORN SQUASH

Serves 6 to 8   Total time: 1 hour

WHY THIS RECIPE WORKS *The earthy flavor of acorn squash is beautifully highlighted by a sweet maple glaze. But most recipes for maple-glazed squash just halve the squash, pour on some syrup, top with a pat of butter, and roast, which results in a thin pool of buttery syrup at the bottom of each half. We wanted every bite of our roasted squash to be coated with a deeply flavored maple glaze. So we started by cutting the squash into eighths, so that the increased surface area would provide room for ample amounts of glaze. While this was more efficient, it also meant the squash cooked so quickly that it was barely browning. To remedy this, we tossed the squash wedges with vegetable oil and a small amount of granulated sugar before roasting them in a hot oven, then flipped them before glazing so that both sides had time to brown. This approach boosted caramelization, achieving the desired deep brown color and rich flavor. We reduced the maple syrup only slightly and then painted both sides with the glaze. We recommend using real maple syrup in this recipe.*

- 2 acorn squashes (1½ pounds each), halved pole to pole and seeded
- 2 tablespoons vegetable oil
- 2 teaspoons sugar
- ¾ teaspoon salt
- ½ teaspoon pepper
- 5 tablespoons maple syrup
- 4 tablespoons unsalted butter
- ⅛ teaspoon cayenne pepper

1. Adjust oven rack to middle position and heat oven to 475 degrees. Cut each squash half into 4 wedges. Toss squash, oil, sugar, salt, and pepper in large bowl to coat, then arrange cut side down in single layer on rimmed baking sheet. Bake until bottoms of squash are deep golden brown, about 25 minutes.

2. Meanwhile, bring maple syrup to boil in small saucepan over medium-high heat. Reduce heat to medium-low and simmer until slightly thickened, about 3 minutes. Off heat, whisk in butter and cayenne until smooth. Cover and keep warm.

3. When bottoms of squash are deep golden, remove from oven. Flip and brush with 6 tablespoons glaze. Return to oven and bake until squash is tender and deep golden all over, about 15 minutes. Flip and brush with remaining glaze. Serve.

STUFFED ACORN SQUASH

Serves 4   Total time: 30 minutes

WHY THIS RECIPE WORKS *Stuffing and roasting an acorn squash the traditional way can take hours, but our impressive version is ready in a fraction of the time without compromising on either flavor or texture. Our solution was to microwave the squash, which takes about 15 minutes, and make our filling in the meantime. While couscous cooked off the heat, we sautéed garlic and onion, then cooked baby spinach until it wilted, folding this mixture into the couscous along with pine nuts and Pecorino Romano cheese. Golden raisins brought a touch of sweetness that complemented the squash. To finish, we just needed a sprinkle of additional cheese and a few minutes under the broiler. Be sure to look for similar-size squash (1½ pounds each) to ensure even cooking. For an accurate measurement of boiling water, bring a full kettle of water to a boil, then measure out the desired amount.*

- 2 acorn squashes (1½ pounds each), halved pole to pole and seeded
- 3 tablespoons vegetable oil
- 1 cup couscous
- ½ cup golden raisins
  Salt and pepper
- 1 cup boiling water
- 1 onion, chopped fine
- 4 garlic cloves, minced
- 6 ounces (6 cups) baby spinach
- ½ cup pine nuts, toasted
- 1½ ounces Pecorino Romano cheese, grated (¾ cup)

1. Brush cut side of squash with 1 tablespoon oil and place, cut side down, on large plate. Microwave, covered, until tender and soft, 12 to 16 minutes.

2. Meanwhile, combine couscous, raisins, 1 teaspoon salt, and 1 tablespoon oil in medium bowl. Stir in boiling water, cover

tightly, and let sit until liquid is absorbed and couscous is tender, about 5 minutes. Fluff couscous with fork.

3. Heat remaining 1 tablespoon oil in 12-inch skillet over medium heat until shimmering. Add onion and cook until softened, about 5 minutes. Stir in garlic and cook until fragrant, about 30 seconds. Stir in spinach and cook until wilted and most of liquid has evaporated, about 2 minutes. Off heat, stir in couscous mixture, pine nuts, and ½ cup Pecorino. Season with salt and pepper to taste.

4. Adjust oven rack 8 inches from broiler element and heat broiler. Transfer squash, cut side up, to rimmed baking sheet and season with salt and pepper. Mound couscous mixture into squash, pack lightly with back of spoon, and sprinkle with remaining ¼ cup Pecorino.

5. Broil until lightly browned, 4 to 5 minutes. Serve.

ROASTED DELICATA SQUASH

Serves 6 to 8   Total time: 50 minutes

WHY THIS RECIPE WORKS *Delicata is the easiest winter squash to cook because its prettily striated skin is so thin that it doesn't need to be peeled before cooking and eating. Roasting intensifies delicata squash's mildly sweet and earthy flavors, so here we simply sliced the squash into half-moons and roasted the pieces on a baking sheet with a combination of olive oil and butter until tender and golden brown. A bright sauce made with fresh herbs, garlic, and sherry vinegar lent a bold, contrasting flavor punch without overshadowing our star vegetable. To ensure even cooking, choose squashes that are similar in size and shape.*

HERB SAUCE

- ¼ cup minced fresh parsley or chives
- ¼ cup extra-virgin olive oil
- 2 tablespoons sherry vinegar
- 2 garlic cloves, minced
- 1 teaspoon smoked paprika
- ¼ teaspoon salt

Roasted Delicata Squash

SQUASH

  3 delicata squashes (12 to 16 ounces
    each), ends trimmed, halved
    lengthwise, seeded, and sliced
    crosswise ½-inch thick
  4 teaspoons extra-virgin olive oil
  ½ teaspoon salt
  2 tablespoons unsalted butter,
    cut into 8 pieces

1. For the sauce Stir all ingredients together
in bowl; set aside for serving.

2. For the squash Adjust oven rack to
lowest position and heat oven to 425 degrees.
Toss squash, oil, and salt in bowl to coat.
Arrange squash in single layer on rimmed
baking sheet. Cover tightly with aluminum
foil and bake until squash is tender when
pierced with tip of paring knife, 18 to
20 minutes.

2. Uncover and continue to bake until side
touching baking sheet is golden brown, 8 to
11 minutes. Remove squash from oven and
using thin metal spatula, flip slices over.
Scatter butter pieces over squash. Return to
oven and continue to bake until side touching
baking sheet is golden brown, 8 to 11 minutes. Transfer squash to serving platter and
drizzle with herb sauce. Serve.

～～

SPAGHETTI SQUASH WITH
GARLIC AND PARMESAN

Serves 4 to 6   Total time: 50 minutes
WHY THIS RECIPE WORKS *The delicate
flavor and noodle-y texture of spaghetti
squash make it a great addition to any meal,
but many recipes bury the squash underneath
a heavy sauce with too many competing flavors. We kept our recipe simple so that the
unique flavor and texture of the squash would
shine through. Brushing the squash halves
with oil, seasoning them with salt and pepper,
and roasting them cut side down brought out
the sweetness of the flesh. Once the squash
was cooked, shredding it was as simple as
holding the halves over a bowl and scraping
them with a fork. After draining the excess
liquid, we dressed the squash with Parmesan,
fresh basil, lemon juice, and garlic for an easy,
flavorful side dish that tasted like summer.*

  1 (2½ pound) spaghetti squash,
    halved lengthwise and seeded
  2 tablespoons extra-virgin olive oil
    Salt and pepper
  ¼ cup grated Parmesan cheese
  1 tablespoon chopped fresh basil
  1 teaspoon lemon juice
  1 garlic clove, minced

1. Adjust oven rack to middle position and
heat oven to 450 degrees. Brush cut sides
of squash with 1 tablespoon oil and season
with salt and pepper. Place squash, cut side
down, on rimmed baking sheet. Roast until
squash is tender when pierced with tip of
paring knife, 25 to 30 minutes.

2. Flip squash over and let cool slightly.
Holding squash with clean dish towel over
large bowl, use fork to scrape squash flesh
from skin while shredding it into fine pieces,
discarding skin.

3. Drain excess liquid from bowl, then gently
stir in Parmesan, basil, lemon juice, garlic,
and remaining 1 tablespoon oil. Season with
salt and pepper to taste, and serve.

VARIATION

Spaghetti Squash with Asian Flavors
Omit Parmesan, basil, lemon juice, garlic,
and remaining 1 tablespoon oil in step 3. Toss
shredded squash with 2 thinly sliced scallions,
1 tablespoon soy sauce, 2½ teaspoons vegetable oil, 1 teaspoon rice vinegar, ½ teaspoon
toasted sesame oil, and ½ teaspoon toasted
sesame seeds before serving.

～～

BUTTERNUT SQUASH
PUREE WITH SAGE AND
TOASTED ALMONDS

Serves 8 to 10   Total time: 30 minutes
WHY THIS RECIPE WORKS *With its silky
texture and earthy, lightly sweet flavor, pureed
butternut squash is a crowd-pleasing cool-
weather side dish. Most recipes for pureed
squash are similar in that they call for cooking
the squash until tender and then pureeing
it with some butter and/or heavy cream in
a food processor. We pitted four butternut
squash cooking methods against one another:
roasting, steaming, braising, and microwaving.*

*Roasting took more than an hour, while
steaming and braising washed away some of
the distinct squash flavor. Microwaving, in
addition to being one of the easiest and fastest cooking methods, won tasters over for
producing a clean, sweet squash flavor. We
found that microwaving peeled chunks, rather
than halves or whole squash, resulted in even
cooking. Squash cooked this way needed only
a small amount of dairy to add some complexity. We found the ideal additions to be
butter and half-and-half; the combination
added richness without overpowering the
squash flavor. Infusing the butter with sage
and topping the puree with toasted almonds
elevated this side dish. You can substitute
delicata squash for the butternut squash; for
a smoother puree, peel the delicata squash.*

  4 pounds butternut squash, peeled,
    seeded, and cut into 1½-inch
    pieces (10 cups)
  4 tablespoons unsalted butter
  1 teaspoon minced fresh sage
  ¼ cup half-and-half
  2 tablespoons packed brown sugar,
    plus extra for seasoning
    Salt and pepper
  ½ cup sliced almonds, toasted

1. Place squash in large bowl. Microwave,
covered, until tender and easily pierced with
tip of paring knife, 15 to 20 minutes, stirring
halfway through microwaving.

2. Meanwhile, melt butter in 8-inch skillet
over medium-low heat. Add sage and cook
until fragrant, about 2 minutes; set aside.

3. Uncover squash, being careful of steam,
and drain in colander. Process drained squash,
sage butter, half-and-half, sugar, and 1 teaspoon salt in food processor until smooth,
about 20 seconds, scraping down sides of
bowl as needed. Season with salt, pepper, and
extra sugar to taste. Sprinkle with almonds
and serve.

VARIATION

Butternut Squash Puree with Orange
Omit sage and almonds. Skip step 2. Add
2 tablespoons orange marmalade to food
processor with butter in step 3.

SLOW-COOKER BUTTERNUT SQUASH PUREE

Serves 6 to 8   Total time: 5 to 6 hours on low or 3 to 4 hours on high

WHY THIS RECIPE WORKS *Especially at holiday time, having a foolproof slow-cooker method for squash can be a lifesaver. Since the flavor of butternut squash is delicate, our goal was to bump it up so it would taste great even after hours in the slow cooker. First we tried cooking the squash in water to cover, but this left us with a bland, watery puree. Since the squash exuded a lot of moisture during cooking, we thought we could take down the amount of water dramatically. In the end, it took only a bare minimum—½ cup—to properly braise the squash. Even this small amount of water, however, seemed to be diluting the squash flavor significantly. We considered alternative braising liquids and settled on apple cider, which accented the squash's inherent sweetness and added a brightness that tasters loved. A small amount of heavy cream and some butter added richness to round out the flavors. This recipe can easily be doubled in a 7-quart slow cooker; you will need to increase the cooking time range by 1 hour.*

- 3 pounds butternut squash, peeled, seeded, and cut into 1-inch pieces (8 cups)
- ½ cup apple cider, plus extra as needed
    Salt and pepper
- 4 tablespoons unsalted butter, melted
- 2 tablespoons heavy cream, warmed
- 2 tablespoons packed brown sugar, plus extra for seasoning

1. Combine squash, cider, and ½ teaspoon salt in slow cooker. Press 16 by 12-inch sheet of parchment paper firmly onto squash, folding down edges as needed. Cover and cook until squash is tender, 5 to 6 hours on low or 3 to 4 hours on high.

2. Discard parchment. Using potato masher, mash squash until smooth. Stir in melted butter, cream, and sugar. Season with salt, pepper, and extra sugar to taste. Serve. (Squash can be held on warm or low setting for up to 2 hours. Adjust consistency with extra hot cider as needed before serving.)

ROASTED BUTTERNUT SQUASH WITH BROWNED BUTTER AND HAZELNUTS

Serves 4 to 6   Total time: 1 hour

WHY THIS RECIPE WORKS *You may not immediately recognize this dish and its variations as the familiar roasted butternut squash, but actually, that's the point. A recipe in London-based chef Yotam Ottolenghi's book Plenty introduced us to an alternative squash universe. He roasts thin skin-on half-moons of squash and then tosses them with savory ingredients, from chiles and lime to toasted nuts and spiced yogurt, which serve as a surprisingly successful foil to the squash's natural sweetness. We decided to bring this approach into the test kitchen and put our own spin on it. Tasters were equally smitten with Ottolenghi's approach, but they also had a few suggestions. So our first move was to lose both the skin and the white layer of flesh underneath, both of which tasters found unappealing. (We could have bought prepeeled squash, but we've found that the flavor of whole squash that you peel yourself is superior.) To achieve deeper caramelization on the squash slices, we positioned the baking sheet on the lowest oven rack, where it would absorb more heat from the main heating element on the oven's floor. We then flipped the squash (and rotated the baking sheet) partway through roasting so that both sides could caramelize. Melted butter produced better browning than olive oil, thanks to its milk proteins that undergo the Maillard reaction, leading to more complex flavors and aromas. These slices emerged perfectly caramelized, wonderfully sweet, and tender. The crowning touch was to come up with a few toppings that provided a mix of contrasting textures and bold flavors.*

SQUASH

- 1 large (2½- to 3-pound) butternut squash, peeled, seeded, and sliced crosswise ½ inch thick
- 3 tablespoons unsalted butter, melted
- ½ teaspoon salt
- ½ teaspoon pepper

TOPPING

- 3 tablespoons unsalted butter, cut into 3 pieces
- ⅓ cup hazelnuts, toasted, skinned, and chopped
- 1 tablespoon water
- 1 tablespoon lemon juice
    Pinch salt
- 1 tablespoon minced fresh chives

Spaghetti Squash Salad with
Chickpeas and Feta

1. For the squash Adjust oven rack to lowest position and heat oven to 425 degrees. Toss squash with melted butter, salt, and pepper in bowl to coat. Arrange squash in single layer on rimmed baking sheet. Roast squash until side touching sheet toward back of oven is well browned, 25 to 30 minutes. Rotate sheet and continue to bake until side touching sheet toward back of oven is well browned, 6 to 10 minutes. Remove squash from oven and use metal spatula to flip each piece. Return to oven and roast until squash is very tender and side touching sheet is browned, 10 to 15 minutes.

2. For the topping While squash roasts, melt butter with hazelnuts in 8-inch skillet over medium-low heat. Cook, stirring frequently, until butter and hazelnuts are brown and fragrant, about 2 minutes. Immediately remove skillet from heat and stir in water (butter will foam and sizzle). Let cool for 1 minute. Stir in lemon juice and salt.

3. Transfer squash to large serving platter. Drizzle butter mixture evenly over squash. Sprinkle with chives. Serve warm or at room temperature.

VARIATIONS

Roasted Butternut Squash with Radicchio and Parmesan

Omit topping. Whisk 1 tablespoon sherry vinegar, ½ teaspoon mayonnaise, and pinch salt together in small bowl. While whisking constantly, slowly drizzle in 2 tablespoons extra-virgin olive oil until combined. Before serving, drizzle vinaigrette over squash and sprinkle with ½ cup coarsely shredded radicchio, ½ ounce Parmesan cheese, shaved into thin strips, and 3 tablespoons toasted pine nuts.

Roasted Butternut Squash with Tahini and Feta

Omit topping. Whisk 1 tablespoon tahini, 1 tablespoon extra-virgin olive oil, 1½ teaspoons lemon juice, 1 teaspoon honey, and pinch salt together in small bowl. Before serving, drizzle tahini mixture over squash and sprinkle with ¼ cup finely crumbled feta cheese, ¼ cup shelled pistachios, toasted and chopped fine, and 2 tablespoons chopped fresh mint.

Roasted Butternut Squash with Yogurt and Sesame Seeds

Omit topping. Whisk 3 tablespoons plain Greek yogurt, 4 teaspoons extra-virgin olive oil, 4 teaspoons water, and pinch salt together in small bowl. Combine 1 teaspoon toasted sesame seeds, 1 teaspoon toasted and crushed coriander seeds, ¼ teaspoon dried thyme, and pinch salt in second small bowl. Before serving, drizzle yogurt mixture over squash, sprinkle with sesame seed mixture and ¼ cup fresh cilantro leaves.

SPAGHETTI SQUASH SALAD WITH TOMATOES AND PECORINO

Serves 4 to 6   Total time: 1 hour (plus 1 hour cooling time)

WHY THIS RECIPE WORKS *Too often, spaghetti squash is positioned as a vegetable alternative to pasta and treated in a way that obscures its flavor. We wanted to meet this squash on its own merits and create an unexpected, fresh-tasting, room-temperature salad that would highlight its grassy, nutty sweetness. With this direction in mind, we zeroed in on roasting as the best cooking method. We cut the squash in half lengthwise, removed the seeds, positioned it cut side down on a baking sheet (to maximize browning), and roasted it in a 375-degree oven. This resulted in soft, non-soggy strings of squash with just a hint of caramelization. The strands were tender but firm enough to hold their shape, and the delicate but distinct nutty, squashy flavor stood out, all of which made for a fine base with which to build a salad. We tossed our cooked squash with a bright lemony vinaigrette, halved grape tomatoes, fresh basil, and Pecorino Romano cheese, and liked the results so much that we came up with two variations to take advantage of this way to prepare spaghetti squash.*

1   (2½-pound) spaghetti squash, halved lengthwise and seeded
6   tablespoons extra-virgin olive oil, plus extra for drizzling
      Salt and pepper
2   teaspoons grated lemon zest plus 7 teaspoons juice

3   ounces grape tomatoes, halved
1   ounce Pecorino Romano cheese, grated (½ cup)
¼   cup torn fresh basil leaves
1   shallot, sliced thin
2   tablespoons pine nuts, toasted

1. Adjust oven rack to middle position and heat oven to 375 degrees. Brush cut sides of squash with 2 tablespoons oil and season with salt and pepper. Place squash, cut side down, on rimmed baking sheet. Roast until squash is tender when pierced with tip of paring knife, 40 to 45 minutes. Transfer squash to wire rack, cut side up, and let cool completely, about 1 hour.

2. Combine lemon zest and juice, remaining ¼ cup oil, ½ teaspoon salt, and ½ teaspoon pepper in large bowl. Holding squash over bowl, use fork to scrape flesh from skin into strands, discarding skin.

3. Add tomatoes to bowl with squash and toss gently to coat. Transfer to serving platter and sprinkle with Pecorino, basil, shallot, and pine nuts. Drizzle with extra oil before serving.

VARIATIONS

Spaghetti Squash Salad with Chickpeas and Feta

Substitute 1 can rinsed chickpeas for tomatoes. Substitute ½ cup crumbled feta for Pecorino. Substitute ½ cup coarsely chopped parsley for basil. Substitute 4 thinly sliced scallions for shallot. Substitute 2 tablespoons toasted and chopped pistachios for pine nuts.

Spaghetti Squash Salad with Radishes and Queso Fresco

Substitute 4 halved and thinly sliced radishes for tomatoes. Substitute ½ cup crumbled queso fresco for Pecorino. Substitute ½ cup fresh cilantro leaves for basil. Substitute ¼ cup thinly sliced red onion for shallot. Substitute 2 tablespoons pepitas for pine nuts.

Butternut Squash and White Bean
Soup with Sage Pesto

BUTTERNUT SQUASH AND WHITE BEAN SOUP WITH SAGE PESTO

Serves 6 to 8   Total time: 1 hour

WHY THIS RECIPE WORKS *This hearty version of butternut squash soup can stand on its own as a meal. Instead of the usual creamy, rich pureed style of butternut squash soup, we opted to feature chunks of squash paired with creamy cannellini beans to give our soup some heft. Because the bulb portion of the squash is difficult to cut into cubes that will cook evenly, and because it naturally cooks faster than the dense neck portion, we cut the bulb into wedges, cooked them in the broth until they were soft, and then mashed them to make a "squash stock" that gave our soup base body and flavor. We then cooked the neck portion, cut into chunks, in this stock. Adding butter to the stock at the start of its simmering time allowed it to fully emulsify, giving the soup base richness and a more velvety texture. A swirl of sage pesto, which we quickly made in the food processor, lent just the right bright, fresh finish.*

PESTO
- ½ cup walnuts, toasted
- 2 garlic cloves, minced
- 1 cup fresh parsley leaves
- ½ cup fresh sage leaves
- ¾ cup extra-virgin olive oil
- 1 ounce Parmesan cheese, grated (½ cup), plus extra for serving
  Salt and pepper

SOUP
- 1 (2- to 2½-pound) butternut squash, peeled
- 4 cups chicken or vegetable broth
- 3 cups water
- 4 tablespoons unsalted butter
- 1 tablespoon soy sauce
- 1 tablespoon vegetable oil
- 1 pound leeks, white and light green parts only, halved lengthwise, sliced thin, and washed thoroughly
- 1 tablespoon tomato paste

- 2 garlic cloves, minced
  Salt and pepper
- 3 (15-ounce) cans cannellini beans
- 1 teaspoon white wine vinegar

1. For the pesto Pulse walnuts and garlic in food processor until coarsely chopped, about 5 pulses. Add parsley and sage. With processor running, slowly add oil until incorporated. Transfer to bowl, stir in Parmesan, and season with salt and pepper to taste; set aside.

2. For the soup Cut round bulb section off squash and cut in half lengthwise. Discard seeds, then cut each half into 4 wedges.

3. Bring squash wedges, broth, water, butter, and soy sauce to boil in medium saucepan over high heat. Reduce heat to medium, partially cover, and simmer vigorously until squash is very tender and starting to fall apart, about 20 minutes. Remove pot from heat and use potato masher to mash squash, still in broth, until completely broken down. Cover to keep warm; set aside.

4. While broth cooks, cut neck of squash into ½-inch pieces. Heat oil in Dutch oven over medium heat until shimmering. Add leeks and tomato paste and cook, stirring occasionally, until leeks are softened and tomato paste is darkened, about 5 minutes. Add garlic and cook until fragrant, about 30 seconds. Add squash pieces, ¾ teaspoon salt, and ¼ teaspoon pepper and cook, stirring occasionally, for 5 minutes. Add squash broth and bring to simmer. Partially cover and cook for 10 minutes.

5. Add beans and their liquid, partially cover, and cook, stirring occasionally, until squash is just tender, 15 to 20 minutes. Stir in vinegar and season with salt and pepper to taste. Serve, passing pesto and extra Parmesan separately.

BARLEY RISOTTO WITH ROASTED BUTTERNUT SQUASH

Serves 8   Total time: 2 hours

WHY THIS RECIPE WORKS *In this hearty cold-weather side dish or main course, sweet roasted butternut squash is paired with nutty, chewy barley, sage, and Parmesan. Barley is sold in several forms, but in the test kitchen we prefer pearl barley, which has been hulled and polished. With the bran removed, the texture of the cooked grain is pleasantly springy. Also, the grain's starchy interior is exposed, which creates a supple, velvety sauce when simmered. Barley requires more liquid and more time to cook than the usual Arborio rice, but we have found that barley takes well to a modified version of our risotto method. We started traditionally by sautéing aromatics, toasting the grain, and simmering the mixture with wine. We then bucked the tradition of adding hot liquid in small intervals and poured in 3 cups of it at once, allowing the barley to simmer and only giving it the occasional stir. The simmering action agitated the barley enough that it released its starch, making constant stirring unnecessary. Once the barley had absorbed the broth, we added 2 more cups of liquid and continued to simmer. After the grains absorbed that liquid, we gradually added more, stirring constantly, until the barley cooked through. We added half of our squash to the simmering barley to break down and thicken, and then stirred in the remaining squash pieces right before serving.*

- 1½ cups pearl barley
- 2 pounds butternut squash, peeled, seeded, and cut into ½-inch pieces (6 cups)
- 1 tablespoon extra-virgin olive oil
  Salt and pepper
- 4 cups chicken or vegetable broth
- 4 cups water
- 1 onion, chopped fine
- 2 garlic cloves, minced
- 1 cup dry white wine
- 1½ ounces Parmesan cheese, grated (¾ cup)
- 1 tablespoon unsalted butter
- 1 teaspoon minced fresh sage
- ⅛ teaspoon ground nutmeg

1. Adjust oven rack to upper-middle position and heat oven to 450 degrees. Rinse barley in fine-mesh strainer under cold running water until water runs clear. Drain briefly. Spread grains on rimmed baking sheet lined with clean dish towel. Let dry for 15 minutes.

2. Line second rimmed baking sheet with parchment paper. Toss squash with 2 teaspoons oil, ¼ teaspoon salt, and ⅛ teaspoon pepper in bowl to coat. Spread squash over prepared sheet. Roast until tender and golden brown, about 30 minutes; set aside.

3. Meanwhile, bring broth and water to simmer in medium saucepan. Reduce heat to lowest possible setting and cover to keep warm.

4. Cook remaining 1 teaspoon oil and onion, covered, in large saucepan over medium-low heat, stirring occasionally, until onion is softened, 8 to 10 minutes. Stir in garlic and cook until fragrant, about 30 seconds. Stir in barley and increase heat to medium. Cook, stirring often, until lightly toasted and aromatic, about 4 minutes. Stir in wine and continue to cook, stirring often, until wine has been completely absorbed, about 2 minutes.

5. Stir in 3 cups warm broth mixture and half of roasted squash. Simmer, stirring occasionally, until liquid is absorbed and bottom of pan is dry, 22 to 25 minutes. Stir in 2 cups warm broth mixture and continue to simmer, stirring occasionally, until liquid is absorbed and bottom of pan is dry, 15 to 18 minutes. Continue to cook, stirring often and adding remaining broth, ½ cup at a time, as needed to keep pan bottom from becoming dry (about every 4 minutes). Continue to add broth until barley is cooked through and still somewhat firm in center, 15 to 20 minutes.

6. Off heat, stir in Parmesan, butter, sage, nutmeg, and remaining squash. Season with salt and pepper to taste, and serve.

BUTTERNUT SQUASH GNUDI WITH KALE, PARMESAN, AND PEPITAS

Serves 4   Total time: 2 hours (plus 1 hour chilling time)

WHY THIS RECIPE WORKS Gnudi *are gnocchi-like dumplings that are traditionally made with strained ricotta and nothing more than a light dusting of semolina flour— essentially a ravioli filling minus the pasta. The result is something much more cloud-like and ethereal than gnocchi. In this version, we used butternut squash instead of ricotta to create the ultimate fall dish, with wilted kale, Parmesan, and pumpkin seeds. The challenge in trying to make these dumplings was getting them to hold together without diluting the squash flavor with large quantities of binders such as flour and eggs. So we used a little tapioca starch and egg white powder to effectively bind water and form a stable but supertender gel. The dough was too delicate to knead and roll out, so instead we baked it in a water bath and then cut the gnudi by hand. Do not substitute raw egg whites for the egg white powder, as the extra water will ruin the texture of the gnudi. You will need a 12-inch nonstick skillet with a tight-fitting lid for this recipe. It may seem strange, but the dish towel raises the baking pan off the bottom of the roasting pan, preventing the gnudi from overcooking on the bottom, and also provides traction for the baking pan so it doesn't slip when removing the roasting pan from the oven. A few gnudi will not be a perfect 1 by ¾-inch size. If you prefer, trim the whole block into a 6-inch square and then cut into 48 even pieces.*

GNUDI
- 2½ pounds butternut squash, peeled, halved, seeded, and cut into 1½-inch pieces
- 1½ ounces Parmesan cheese, grated fine (¾ cup)
- 3 tablespoons plus 1 teaspoon egg white powder
- 3 tablespoons unsalted butter, cut into 4 pieces
- 2 tablespoons plus 2 teaspoons tapioca starch
- ½ teaspoon salt

KALE
- 2 tablespoons extra-virgin olive oil, plus extra for drizzling
- 1 pound kale, stemmed and chopped
- 2 tablespoons water
- 5 tablespoons unsalted butter
- 2 garlic cloves, minced
- 1 teaspoon sherry vinegar
  Salt and pepper
- 2 tablespoons minced fresh sage
- 2 tablespoons roasted, salted pepitas
  Finely grated lemon zest
  Parmesan cheese, shaved

1. For the gnudi Microwave squash in large bowl, covered, until tender when pierced with tip of paring knife, 15 to 20 minutes, stirring halfway through microwaving. Uncover squash, being careful of steam, and transfer to colander to drain; set aside to cool slightly.

2. Meanwhile, adjust oven rack to middle position and heat oven to 300 degrees. Line bottom of large roasting pan with dish towel, folding towel to fit smoothly; set aside. Spray 8-inch square baking pan with vegetable oil spray and line with plastic wrap, smoothing bottom.

3. Measure out 3 cups cooked squash and place in bowl of food processor, reserving remaining squash for another use. Process squash in food processor until smooth, about 1 minute, scraping down sides of bowl as needed. Add Parmesan, egg white powder, butter, tapioca starch, and salt and process until well combined, about 30 seconds, scraping down sides of bowl as needed. Transfer mixture to prepared baking pan, smooth top with spatula, and tap pan on counter to release air bubbles.

4. Cover pan tightly with aluminum foil and place in center of prepared roasting pan. Place roasting pan in oven and carefully pour boiling water into roasting pan to come halfway up sides of baking pan. Bake until center of mixture is set, no longer sticks to your fingers when gently pressed, and registers 170 to 180 degrees, 1 hour to 1 hour 10 minutes. Remove baking pan from water bath, discard foil, and let cool slightly, about 10 minutes. Refrigerate gnudi in pan until firm, about 1 hour. Carefully unmold gnudi onto cutting board, discarding plastic.

BUTTERNUT SQUASH GNUDI WITH KALE, PARMESAN, AND PEPITAS

Gnudi *means "naked" in Italian, and these pillowy little dumplings are so named because they resemble ravioli without their pasta jackets. Traditionally gnudi are made with ricotta cheese, but we reimagined them made with butternut squash instead. With a wilted kale sauté serving as the bed for our gnudi, we think we've created an outstanding fall dish that's far superior to anything pumpkin-spiced.*

1. Microwave the squash in a large bowl, covered, until it's tender when pierced with the tip of a paring knife, 15 to 20 minutes, stirring halfway through microwaving. Uncover the squash and transfer it to a colander to drain; let cool slightly.

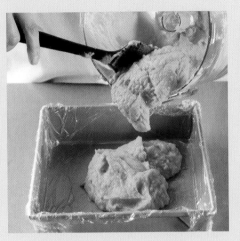

2. After processing the squash and adding the Parmesan, egg white powder, butter, tapioca starch, and salt, transfer the mixture to the prepared pan, smooth the top with a spatula, and tap the pan on the counter to release air bubbles.

3. Cover the pan with aluminum foil and place in the center of the prepared roasting pan. Place the setup in the oven and carefully pour the boiling water into the roasting pan. Bake until the center of the mixture is set and registers 170 to 180 degrees, 1 hour to 1 hour 10 minutes.

4. Remove the baking pan from the water bath, discard the foil, let cool, and refrigerate until firm. Carefully unmold the gnudi onto a cutting board. Dip a sharp knife in hot water, wipe dry, and cut the gnudi into 1 by ¾-inch rectangular pieces, rewetting and wiping the knife clean between cuts.

5. Cook the kale in the oil until slightly wilted, 1 to 2 minutes. Add the water, butter, garlic, and vinegar and cook, stirring occasionally, until wilted and fragrant, 1 to 2 minutes. Season with salt and pepper and divide among individual serving bowls.

6. Cook half of the gnudi and sage in the remaining butter in a 12-inch nonstick skillet over medium heat until browned on one side, 2 to 4 minutes. Divide the gnudi evenly among the serving bowls. Repeat, and then sprinkle the gnudi with the pepitas, lemon zest, and Parmesan and drizzle with oil.

Dip sharp knife in very hot water, wipe dry, and cut gnudi into 1 by ¾-inch rectangular pieces, rewetting and wiping knife clean between cuts. (You will have 50 to 60 pieces.)

5. For the kale Heat oil in large saucepan over medium-high heat until shimmering. Add kale and cook until slightly wilted, 1 to 2 minutes. Add water, 2 tablespoons butter, garlic, and vinegar and cook, stirring occasionally, until wilted and fragrant, 1 to 2 minutes. Season with salt and pepper to taste and divide among individual serving bowls.

6. Meanwhile, melt remaining 3 tablespoons butter in 12-inch nonstick skillet over medium heat. Add half of gnudi and 1 tablespoon sage, cover, and cook until browned on one side, 2 to 4 minutes. Season with salt and pepper to taste, and divide gnudi evenly between 2 serving bowls. Repeat with remaining gnudi and remaining 1 tablespoon sage. Sprinkle with pepitas, lemon zest, and Parmesan and drizzle with oil. Serve.

BUTTERNUT SQUASH GALETTE WITH GRUYÈRE

Serves 4 to 6   Total time: 1 hour 45 minutes (plus 1 hour 30 minutes chilling time)

WHY THIS RECIPE WORKS *This savory, flaky, rustic tart starring butternut squash and baby spinach is bound to be a favorite on any fall or winter table. In developing this recipe, we were looking for a filling that was robust and flavorful and a crust that was extra-sturdy while still being tender, moist, and flaky. To achieve that goal with a dough using whole-wheat flour, we decided to take a hands-off approach to mixing and let the flour absorb the water on its own. We thought this might allow the water to migrate to drier parts and produce pastry that was workable—but not overworked. So we gave it a shot, just barely mixing the dry and wet ingredients and then chilling the dough. After an hour, most of the dry flour*

had disappeared; even better, the dough was remarkably supple. To get the long, striated layers of puff pastry we were after, we dumped the rested shaggy mass onto the counter, rolled it into a rectangle, and folded it into thirds, like a business letter. We repeated the process just twice more. The result? A wonderfully flaky crust that was less apt to shatter when cut. Working with a sturdy crust, however, didn't mean that we could throw in the vegetables—spinach and butternut squash—raw: They'd still leach far too much moisture and render the crust soggy. Fortunately, parcooking the spinach and squash separately in the microwave took only a few minutes. To introduce rich, complex flavor and not too much moisture, we added sautéed onion, a dollop of crème fraîche, Gruyère, and a splash of sherry vinegar to the vegetables just before baking. An equal amount of rye flour can be substituted for the whole-wheat flour. Cutting a few small holes in the dough prevents it from lifting off the pan as it bakes. A pizza stone helps to crisp the crust but is not essential.

DOUGH
- 1¼ cups (6¼ ounces) all-purpose flour
- ½ cup (2¾ ounces) whole-wheat flour
- 1 tablespoon sugar
- ¾ teaspoon salt
- 10 tablespoons unsalted butter, cut into ½-inch pieces and chilled
- 7 tablespoons ice water
- 1 teaspoon distilled white vinegar

FILLING
- 6 ounces (6 cups) baby spinach
- 1¼ pounds butternut squash, peeled and cut into ½-inch pieces (3½ cups)
- 5 teaspoons extra-virgin olive oil
- 1 red onion, sliced thin
- ½ teaspoon minced fresh oregano
- 3 ounces Gruyère cheese, shredded (¾ cup)
- 2 tablespoons crème fraîche
- 1 teaspoon sherry vinegar
   Salt and pepper
- 1 large egg, lightly beaten
- 2 tablespoons minced fresh parsley

1. **For the dough** Process all-purpose flour, whole-wheat flour, sugar, and salt in food processor until combined. Scatter chilled butter over top and pulse until butter is pea-sized, about 10 pulses; transfer to medium bowl.

2. Sprinkle ice water and vinegar over flour mixture. Using rubber spatula, fold mixture until loose, shaggy mass forms with some dry flour remaining (do not overwork). Transfer to center of large sheet of plastic wrap, press gently into rough 4-inch square, and wrap tightly. Refrigerate for 45 minutes.

3. Transfer dough to lightly floured counter and roll into 11 by 8-inch rectangle with short side parallel to edge of counter. Using bench scraper, fold bottom third of dough away from you, then fold upper third toward you like business letter into 8 by 4-inch rectangle. Turn dough 90 degrees counterclockwise. Repeat rolling dough into 11 by 8-inch rectangle and folding into thirds. Turn dough 90 degrees counterclockwise and repeat rolling and folding into thirds. After last set of folds, fold dough in half to create 4-inch square. Press top of dough gently to seal. Wrap with plastic and refrigerate for at least 45 minutes or up to 2 days.

4. **For the filling** Microwave spinach and ¼ cup water in large bowl, covered, until spinach is shrunk by half, 3 to 4 minutes. Remove bowl from microwave and set aside, covered, for 1 minute. Transfer spinach to colander to drain. Using back of rubber spatula, gently press spinach to release excess liquid. Transfer spinach to cutting board and chop coarse. Return spinach to colander and press again with rubber spatula; set aside. Add squash to now-empty bowl and microwave, covered, until just tender, about 8 minutes; set aside.

5. Meanwhile, heat 1 tablespoon oil in 12-inch skillet over medium heat until shimmering. Add onion and oregano, cover, and cook, stirring frequently, until onion is tender and beginning to brown, 5 to 7 minutes. Off heat, add onion mixture to bowl with squash along with spinach, Gruyère, crème fraîche, and vinegar and stir gently to combine. Season with salt and pepper to taste and set aside.

6. Adjust oven rack to lower-middle position, place pizza stone on rack, and heat oven to 400 degrees. Line rimmed baking sheet with parchment paper. Remove dough from refrigerator and let stand at room temperature for 15 to 20 minutes. Roll dough into 14-inch circle about ⅛ inch thick on well-floured counter. (Trim edges as needed to form rough circle). Transfer dough to prepared sheet. Using straw or tip of paring knife, cut five ¼-inch circles in dough (one at center and four evenly spaced halfway from center to edge of dough). Brush top of dough with 1 teaspoon oil.

7. Spread filling evenly over dough, leaving 2-inch border around edge. Drizzle remaining 1 teaspoon oil over filling. Grasp 1 edge of dough and fold outer 2 inches over filling. Repeat around circumference of tart, overlapping dough every 2 to 3 inches; gently pinch pleated dough to secure but do not press dough into filling. Brush dough with egg wash.

8. Reduce oven temperature to 375 degrees. Set sheet on stone and bake until crust is deep golden brown and filling is beginning to brown, 35 to 45 minutes. Let tart cool on sheet on wire rack for 10 minutes. Using offset or wide metal spatula, loosen tart from parchment and carefully slide tart onto cutting board. Sprinkle parsley over filling and cut tart into wedges. Serve.

folding galette dough

1. Place dough on lightly floured counter and roll into 11 by 8-inch rectangle with short side parallel to edge of counter.

2. Using bench scraper, fold bottom third of dough away from you.

3. Using bench scraper, fold upper third of dough toward you into 8 by 4-inch rectangle.

4. Turn dough 90 degrees counterclockwise. Repeat steps 1 to 3. Turn dough 90 degrees and repeat steps 1 to 3 again.

5. After third roll-and-fold, fold dough rectangle in half to create 4-inch square, pressing gently to seal.

ZUCCHINI AND SUMMER SQUASH

I n the height of summer, you can't escape zucchini and summer squash. The little green and yellow squashes (and some not so little) are piled high at seemingly every farmers' market and supermarket. Gardeners know that these squashes are very easy to grow, thriving in many different climates and soil conditions. They're so easy to grow, in fact, that come midsummer, home horticulturists across the nation are faced with a surfeit of zucchini. Even if you aren't growing it in your own backyard, you've probably got a neighbor trying to unload extra zukes as a "gift."

According to *The Old Farmer's Almanac*, August 8 is National Sneak Some Zucchini onto Your Neighbor's Porch Day. As the writer explains, "To celebrate it, you simply wait until the dead of night and quietly creep up to your neighbors' front door, leaving plenty of zucchini for them to enjoy."

Unlike corn or tomatoes, all this bounty doesn't take well to either freezing or canning. But luckily for the home cook, zucchini and summer squash are remarkably versatile. We like to braise them with cherry tomatoes for an in-a-flash stovetop side; grill them with red onion and a citrus-herb vinaigrette for a cookout-perfect accompaniment; batter and fry them and serve with a spicy aïoli for a great snack; and create ribbons for an elegant raw salad with fresh mint and Parmesan.

Adorable little pattypan squash, which somewhat resembles a flying saucer, roasts up perfectly and looks so pretty. Don't miss our chile and lime flavor variation of simply roasted baby pattypans. And to round out our recipe collection, we offer a classic version of an ephemeral summer delicacy: Fried Stuffed Zucchini Blossoms.

shopping and storage

These days, summer squashes are available in supermarkets all year round, but of course their traditional season is summer. Choose zucchini and other summer squashes that are firm and without soft spots. Smaller, younger squashes have thinner skins and more concentrated flavor and are less watery than larger specimens; they also have fewer seeds. Look for zucchini and yellow squash no heavier than 8 ounces, and preferably just 6 ounces. The skins should be free of blemishes and have a vibrant green or yellow color. Zucchini and yellow squash are fairly perishable; store them in the refrigerator in a partially sealed zipper-lock bag for up to five days.

Pattypan squash should be vibrant yellow with green ends; if they are all green, they are not ripe. Choose pattypans that are 2 to 4 inches in size; they can grow up to 7 inches in size, but those larger specimens will be tough and woody.

And keep an eye out for squash blossoms, particularly at farmers' markets and specialty food stores. They are pricey and rare but deliciously edible. They should be vibrant yellow and soft but not wilted, drying, or turning brown. Squash blossoms are extremely perishable and should be used within a day or two.

about zucchini and summer squash

Despite their name, these squashes are actually more closely related to other members of the curcubit family, including cucumbers and watermelon, than to winter squash. Inhabitants of Central and South America have been eating zucchini for thousands of years, but the variety we know and love in the United States today is a type of squash that was developed in Italy in the 19th century. As with broccoli, seeds were brought to America and cultivated commercially in the 20th century. Zucchini has only really been popular in a mainstream way in American kitchens since the 1970s.

Yellow summer squash encompasses several varieties of yellow squash, all of which share similar characteristics and flavor. Yellow squash has a fat bottom and a tapered neck, unlike zucchini, which is more uniform along its length. Yellow squashes can either be straight or have a curved neck (these are called crooknecks). There is also a yellow variety of zucchini, with a golden skin.

Small, squat, and round pattypan squash shares many of the same qualities as its ubiquitous relatives: It's crisp and bright when raw and silky and buttery when cooked.

vegetable prep

Cutting Zucchini into Ribbons

Using vegetable peeler or mandoline, slice zucchini lengthwise into thin ribbons, stopping when you reach the seedy core.

Shredding Zucchini

1. Shred zucchini on large holes of box grater.

2. Squeeze shredded zucchini in clean dish towel or several layers of paper towels until dry.

Preparing Zucchini for Stuffing

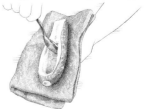

Trim ends if recipe directs; halve squash lengthwise and then use spoon or melon baller to scoop out seeds.

about squash blossoms

Many flowers are edible, including nasturtiums, pansies, hibiscus, and chive blossoms. Often these types of flowers are used simply as an attractive garnish. But large, sunshiny squash blossoms (most commonly from the zucchini plant) are easily treated like a full-fledged vegetable in the kitchen. These ephemeral treats have been described as having a flavor like "squash perfume." Although the flowers are delicate, they are actually quite easy to work with. A classic Italian preparation is to stuff them with a mild cheese, dip them in a light batter, and flash-fry them, to be eaten à la minute. Zucchini blossoms also make a wonderful topping for a white pizza or a filling ingredient for frittatas. In Mexico, they are used in quesadillas. Or simply eat them raw, tossed into a green salad.

Roasted Baby Pattypan Squash with
Lemon and Basil

ROASTED BABY PATTYPAN SQUASH

Serves 4 to 6   Total time: 30 minutes

WHY THIS RECIPE WORKS *Beautiful yellow-and-green pattypans come in a variety of sizes; here we chose baby ones for their tender skin and vibrant flavor (some say the squash loses flavor as it matures) and, quite frankly, because they are so adorable. We wanted to create a recipe where the squash would retain its beautiful shape and color while getting good browning. Roasting was the fastest and easiest way to get a decent amount of squash done in one batch, and we knew a couple of tricks to help things along. First, we cut the squash in half horizontally, creating flower-shaped slabs. Then we cranked the oven to 500 degrees and preheated a sheet pan, for maximum searing. Tossing the squash in butter and honey both complemented the squash's own sweet and creamy profile and promoted browning. We didn't even have to flip the squash—they were beautifully browned on the cut side, retained their bright color on top, and were fully cooked through. Use baby pattypan squashes between 1½ and 2 inches in diameter.*

3   tablespoons unsalted butter, melted
1   teaspoon honey
    Salt and pepper
1½ pounds baby pattypan squash, halved horizontally

Adjust oven rack to lowest position, place rimmed baking sheet on rack, and heat oven to 500 degrees. Whisk melted butter, honey, ¼ teaspoon salt, and ⅛ teaspoon pepper in large bowl until honey has fully dissolved. Add squash and toss to coat. Working quickly, arrange squash cut side down on hot sheet. Roast until cut side is browned and squash is tender, 15 to 18 minutes. Transfer to serving platter and season with salt and pepper to taste. Serve.

VARIATIONS

Roasted Baby Pattypan Squash with Lemon and Basil
Whisk ½ teaspoon lemon zest and 1 tablespoon lemon juice into butter mixture. Sprinkle squash with 2 tablespoons chopped fresh basil before serving.

Roasted Baby Pattypan Squash with Chile and Lime
Omit pepper. Whisk 1 minced Thai chile pepper, ½ teaspoon lime zest, and 1 tablespoon lime juice into butter mixture. Sprinkle squash with 2 tablespoons chopped fresh mint before serving.

SAUTÉED ZUCCHINI

Serves 4 to 6   Total time: 50 minutes

WHY THIS RECIPE WORKS *Because zucchini and summer squash are quite watery, they often cook up soggy and bland. We wanted to find a way to make sautéed zucchini or summer squash with concentrated flavor and an appealing texture. The key was to remove water before cooking by salting and draining the squash for 30 minutes and then patting it dry. We sautéed an onion first for some depth of flavor and added the squash, along with some lemon zest, to the hot skillet, where the squash became tender and lightly browned with minimal stirring. Lemon juice and basil, stirred in off the heat, lent bright flavors. Do not add more salt when cooking or the dish will be too salty.*

1½ pounds zucchini or yellow summer squash, trimmed and sliced ¼ inch thick
    Kosher salt and pepper
3   tablespoons extra-virgin olive oil
1   small onion, chopped fine
1   teaspoon grated lemon zest plus 1 tablespoon juice
1   tablespoon minced fresh basil, mint, or parsley

1. Toss zucchini with 1 tablespoon salt in colander set over bowl and let drain until roughly ⅓ cup liquid drains from zucchini, about 30 minutes; discard liquid. Pat zucchini dry with paper towels and carefully wipe away any residual salt.

2. Heat oil in 12-inch nonstick skillet over medium heat until shimmering. Add onion and cook until almost softened, about 3 minutes. Increase heat to medium-high, add zucchini and lemon zest, and cook until zucchini is golden brown, about 10 minutes. Off heat, stir in lemon juice and basil and season with pepper to taste. Serve.

BRAISED ZUCCHINI

Serves 6 to 8   Total time: 20 minutes

WHY THIS RECIPE WORKS *Braising is a speedy and convenient stovetop way to prepare a simple zucchini side dish. But since the vegetable naturally contains a lot of water, it's easy to end up with water-logged zucchini. To avoid this, we brought the zucchini pieces to a boil in a skillet, in a flavorful mixture of oil, water, basil, garlic, and pepper flakes. We then covered the skillet and let it simmer for 8 minutes, just until the pieces were fork-tender. Stirring it every 2 minutes ensured even tenderness throughout. We added cherry tomatoes and finished cooking the veggies uncovered to drive off excess moisture. Once reduced, the flavorful liquid ably coated the vegetables. If possible, use smaller, in-season zucchini, which have thinner skins and fewer seeds. You will need a 12-inch skillet with a tight-fitting lid for this recipe.*

4   zucchini (8 ounces each), trimmed, quartered lengthwise, and cut into 2-inch lengths
¼   cup extra-virgin olive oil
¼   cup water
2   sprigs fresh basil
2   garlic cloves, sliced thin
    Salt and pepper
¼   teaspoon red pepper flakes
3   ounces cherry tomatoes, halved
    Lemon wedges

1. Bring zucchini, oil, water, basil sprigs, garlic, 1 teaspoon salt, ¼ teaspoon pepper, and pepper flakes to boil in 12-inch nonstick skillet over medium-high heat. Cover, reduce heat to medium, and simmer until zucchini is fork-tender, about 8 minutes, stirring with rubber spatula every 2 minutes.

2. Gently stir in tomatoes and cook, uncovered, until tomatoes are just softened, about 2 minutes. Discard basil sprigs. Serve with lemon wedges.

GREEK STEWED ZUCCHINI

Zucchini, tomatoes, kalamata olives, and fresh mint might make us first think of a fresh summery salad, raw or lightly cooked, but in Greece these ingredients are beloved when melded together in a deeply savory vegetable stew. For our version, we browned our zucchini until golden to bring out its sweetness, and then we cooked our summery stew in a low oven until meltingly tender and deeply concentrated in flavor.

1. Trim the zucchini, quarter them lengthwise, cut away the seeds, and cut the zucchini into 2-inch lengths.

2. Puree the whole peeled tomatoes in the food processor until they are completely smooth in texture.

3. Heat the oil in a Dutch oven over medium-high heat and, working in batches, brown the zucchini on both sides, about 3 minutes per side. Transfer the zucchini to a bowl.

4. In the now-empty Dutch oven, cook the onion until golden brown, 9 to 11 minutes. Add the garlic, oregano, and pepper flakes and cook for about 30 seconds. Stir in the olives and tomatoes and simmer until the sauce has thickened, about 30 minutes.

5. Stir in the zucchini and any accumulated juices from the bowl. Transfer the Dutch oven to the oven and bake until the zucchini is very tender, 30 to 40 minutes.

6. Stir in the mint, season with salt and pepper to taste, and serve.

GREEK STEWED ZUCCHINI

Serves 6 to 8   Total time: 1 hour 30 minutes

WHY THIS RECIPE WORKS *Stewed vegetable dishes are popular across Greece and vary widely from region to region, both as to how many vegetables they include and what cooking method they employ. We wanted to develop a version in which our vegetables retained their individual character while still coming together in a deeply flavored, cohesive stew. After testing a variety of recipes, we landed on a combination of zucchini and tomatoes. We started by browning seeded zucchini on the stovetop (in batches to ensure thorough, even browning), then set it aside while we built our savory tomato sauce. Tasters found canned diced tomatoes mealy, canned crushed tomatoes sludgy and cloying, and fresh tomatoes inconsistent in quality. Canned whole peeled tomatoes, processed until smooth, gave the dish the right balance of tomato flavor and silky texture. A smattering of olives complemented the sauce. Once our sauce had simmered and thickened, we stirred in the browned zucchini and transferred the pot to the oven to allow it to gently finish cooking and develop deep, concentrated flavor. A traditional garnish of shredded fresh mint, stirred in at the end, added brightness. If possible, use smaller, in-season zucchini, which have thinner skins and fewer seeds.*

- 1 (28-ounce) can whole peeled tomatoes
- 3 tablespoons extra-virgin olive oil
- 5 zucchini (8 ounces each), trimmed, quartered lengthwise, seeded, and cut into 2-inch lengths
- 1 onion, chopped fine
  Salt and pepper
- 3 garlic cloves, minced
- 1 teaspoon minced fresh oregano or ¼ teaspoon dried
- ¼ teaspoon red pepper flakes
- 2 tablespoons chopped pitted kalamata olives
- 2 tablespoons shredded fresh mint

1. Adjust oven rack to lower-middle position and heat oven to 325 degrees. Process tomatoes and their juice in food processor until completely smooth, about 1 minute; set aside.

2. Heat 2 teaspoons oil in Dutch oven over medium-high heat until just smoking. Brown one-third of zucchini, about 3 minutes per side; transfer to bowl. Repeat with 4 teaspoons oil and remaining zucchini in 2 batches; transfer to bowl.

3. Add remaining 1 tablespoon oil, onion, and ¾ teaspoon salt to now-empty pot and cook, stirring occasionally, over medium-low heat until onion is very soft and golden brown, 9 to 11 minutes. Stir in garlic, oregano, and pepper flakes and cook until fragrant, about 30 seconds. Stir in olives and tomatoes, bring to simmer, and cook, stirring occasionally, until sauce has thickened, about 30 minutes.

4. Stir in zucchini and any accumulated juices, cover, and transfer pot to oven. Bake until zucchini is very tender, 30 to 40 minutes. Stir in mint and adjust sauce consistency with hot water as needed. Season with salt and pepper to taste. Serve.

GRILLED ZUCCHINI AND RED ONION WITH LEMON VINAIGRETTE

Serves 4 to 6   Total time: 45 minutes

WHY THIS RECIPE WORKS *For this summery side dish, perfect for any cookout, we paired zucchini planks with sweet red onion rings, cutting the vegetables into similar-size pieces so that we could grill them in sync over a medium-hot fire. After about 5 minutes, faint grill marks began to appear on the undersides of the vegetables; we adjusted their position on the grill or the heat level as needed to brown both sides. Our zucchini and onions reached tender, charred perfection in only about 20 minutes. To unify and boost their flavors further, we whisked up a quick lemony vinaigrette with a touch of Dijon mustard to drizzle over the vegetables after they came off the grill, and for a finishing touch, we sprinkled everything with chopped fresh basil. You will need two 12-inch metal skewers for this recipe. The vegetables can be served hot, warm, or at room temperature.*

- 1 red onion, sliced into ½-inch-thick rounds
- 1 pound zucchini, trimmed and sliced lengthwise into ¾-inch-thick planks
- 6 tablespoons extra-virgin olive oil
  Salt and pepper
- 1 teaspoon grated lemon zest plus 1 tablespoon juice
- 1 garlic clove, minced
- ¼ teaspoon Dijon mustard
- 1 tablespoon chopped fresh basil

1. Thread onion rounds, from side to side, onto 2 metal skewers. Brush onion and zucchini with ¼ cup oil, sprinkle with 1 teaspoon salt, and season with pepper. Whisk lemon zest and juice, garlic, mustard, remaining 2 tablespoons oil, and ¼ teaspoon salt together in bowl.

2a. For a charcoal grill Open bottom vent completely. Light large chimney starter half filled with charcoal briquettes (3 quarts). When top coals are partially covered with ash, pour evenly over grill. Set cooking grate in place, cover, and open lid vent completely. Heat grill until hot, about 5 minutes.

2b. For a gas grill Turn all burners to high, cover, and heat grill until hot, about 15 minutes. Turn all burners to medium.

3. Clean and oil cooking grate. Place onion and zucchini on grill. Cook (covered if using gas), turning as needed, until tender and caramelized, 18 to 22 minutes. Transfer vegetables to serving platter as they finish cooking. Remove onion from skewers and discard any charred outer rings. Whisk dressing to recombine and drizzle over vegetables. Sprinkle with basil and serve.

FRIED ZUCCHINI STICKS WITH SPICY AÏOLI

Serves 4 to 6   Total time: 30 minutes

WHY THIS RECIPE WORKS *Fried zucchini sticks with a dipping sauce are a delicious pub-style snack or fun side dish. Since zucchini has a high water content, working quickly when frying to prevent moisture from leaching from the zucchini is key. We cut the zucchini into spears and removed the watery*

inner seed pulp. Then we floured the spears, shook off the excess, and coated the zucchini in a light beer batter seasoned with garlic powder and cayenne. To keep the spears crisp, we fried them quickly in hot (375-degree) oil, drained them briefly, and served them right away with a mayonnaise-based dipping sauce flavored with garlic, lemon juice, and a bit of hot sauce. Use a Dutch oven that holds 6 quarts or more for this recipe. Dredge the zucchini just before frying for the best texture. This recipe can easily be doubled.

AÏOLI

½ cup mayonnaise
1½ teaspoons lemon juice
1 teaspoon hot sauce
1 garlic clove, minced
Salt and pepper

ZUCCHINI

2 zucchini, trimmed
¾ cup plus 1 tablespoon all-purpose flour
¼ cup cornstarch
1 teaspoon baking powder
1 teaspoon garlic powder
Salt and pepper
¾ teaspoon cayenne pepper
¾ cup lager, such as Budweiser
2 quarts peanut or vegetable oil

1. For the aïoli Combine all ingredients in bowl. Refrigerate until ready to serve. Season with salt and pepper to taste. (Aïoli can be refrigerated for up to 1 day.)

2. For the zucchini Quarter zucchini lengthwise. Using vegetable peeler, shave seeds from inner portion of each quarter. Halve each quarter lengthwise, then cut in half crosswise. (You should have 32 pieces total.)

3. Whisk flour, cornstarch, baking powder, garlic powder, 1 teaspoon salt, ¾ teaspoon pepper, and cayenne together in large bowl. Reserve ½ cup flour mixture. Slowly whisk beer into remaining flour mixture until consistency of pancake batter (you may have leftover beer).

4. Set wire rack in rimmed baking sheet and line with triple layer of paper towels. Add oil to large Dutch oven until it measures about 1½ inches deep and heat over medium-high heat to 375 degrees.

5. Toss half of zucchini in bowl with reserved flour mixture until evenly coated. Set fine-mesh strainer over second large bowl and transfer zucchini and flour mixture to strainer. Shake to remove all excess flour mixture from zucchini (catching excess in second bowl).

6. Transfer zucchini to batter and stir to coat. Using tongs, drop each spear into hot oil and stir quickly to prevent pieces from clumping together. Cook until light golden brown, about 4 minutes. Adjust burner, if necessary, to maintain oil temperature between 350 and 375 degrees.

7. Transfer spears to prepared rack and season with salt. Return oil to 375 degrees and repeat with remaining zucchini spears, flour mixture, and batter. Serve.

FRIED STUFFED ZUCCHINI BLOSSOMS

Serves 4 to 6   Total time: 30 minutes
WHY THIS RECIPE WORKS *Delicately crisp, fried zucchini blossoms capture the essence of summer and make for a special seasonal treat as an alfresco appetizer or snack. We took our inspiration for this recipe from Italy, stuffing them with a ricotta filling and dipping them into a light batter that enhanced their flavor and texture. Using a twirling motion (like winding a watch) when dipping the blossoms in the batter encourages the petals to twist closed around the filling. Do not omit the vodka; it is critical for a crisp coating. Use zucchini blossoms that measure 3 to 4½ inches in length from base to tip. Use a Dutch oven that holds 6 quarts or more for this recipe. Be sure to begin mixing the batter when the oil reaches 325 degrees.*

1 cup whole-milk ricotta cheese
1 ounce Pecorino Romano cheese, grated (½ cup)
2 large eggs
1 tablespoon minced fresh mint
1 teaspoon grated lemon zest
Salt and pepper
16 zucchini blossoms

2 quarts peanut or vegetable oil
1½ cups all-purpose flour
½ cup cornstarch
1 cup vodka
1 cup seltzer water

1. Line 2 rimmed baking sheets with triple layer of paper towels. Combine ricotta, Pecorino, 1 egg, mint, zest, ⅛ teaspoon salt, and ⅛ teaspoon pepper together in bowl; set aside. Trim zucchini blossom stems to 1 inch and remove spiny leaves at base of flower. Gently peel open petals as needed to remove pistil and brush away any dirt. Rinse exterior of blossoms, gently shake off excess water, and transfer to one prepared sheet. Pat dry with paper towels.

2. Transfer cheese mixture to zipper-lock bag and snip off 1 corner to create ½-inch opening. Working with 1 blossom at a time, pipe enough filling into blossom to fill green base, stopping just before orange petals begin. Gently twist petals to seal and return to sheet. Repeat with remaining blossoms. Refrigerate until ready to fry.

3. Add oil to large Dutch oven until it measures about 1½ inches deep and heat over medium-high heat to 350 degrees. While oil heats, whisk flour and cornstarch together in large bowl. In separate bowl, whisk remaining 1 egg, vodka, and seltzer together. Once oil reaches 325 degrees, gently whisk seltzer mixture into flour mixture until just combined (it is OK if small lumps remain).

4. Once oil reaches 350 degrees, working with 1 blossom at a time, hold by stem and twirl through batter to coat. Lift blossom, allowing excess batter to drip back into bowl, then gently lower into oil. Working quickly but carefully, repeat with 7 more blossoms. Fry until crisp and lightly golden, about 2 minutes. Adjust burner, if necessary, to maintain oil temperature between 325 and 350 degrees.

5. Using slotted spoon, transfer blossoms to second prepared sheet and season with salt to taste. Return oil to 350 degrees and repeat with remaining blossoms. Serve immediately.

ZUCCHINI RIBBON SALAD WITH SHAVED PARMESAN

Serves 4 to 6   Total time: 15 minutes

WHY THIS RECIPE WORKS *This elegant alternative to a traditional green salad is also a unique way to serve zucchini without softening its crunchy texture or altering its fresh flavor by cooking. Slicing the zucchini lengthwise into thin ribbons maximized its surface area for dressing to cling to and was more visually appealing than cutting the zucchini into rounds. A vegetable peeler or mandoline made quick work of this step. Then we dressed the zucchini simply with extra-virgin olive oil, lemon juice, mint, and shaved Parmesan cheese. Using in-season zucchini, good olive oil, and high-quality Parmesan is crucial in this simple side dish. If possible, use smaller zucchini, which have thinner skins and fewer seeds. Be ready to serve this dish shortly after it is assembled.*

3 zucchini (8 ounces each), trimmed
  Salt and pepper
½ cup extra-virgin olive oil
¼ cup lemon juice (2 lemons)
2 tablespoons minced fresh mint
6 ounces Parmesan cheese, shaved

Using vegetable peeler, slice zucchini lengthwise into very thin ribbons. Gently toss zucchini ribbons in bowl with salt and pepper to taste, then arrange attractively on serving platter. Drizzle with oil and lemon juice, sprinkle with mint and Parmesan, and serve.

ZUCCHINI NOODLE SALAD WITH TAHINI-GINGER DRESSING

Serves 4   Total time: 30 minutes

WHY THIS RECIPE WORKS *There's a reason zucchini noodles are so popular: The squash is easy to work with and produces long, satisfying noodles with a pleasant texture and neutral flavor. We took advantage of that ease and neutrality to create a boldly flavored, Asian-inspired salad with zucchini noodles as the base. We tried both boiling the noodles and stir-frying them to cook them, but in the end, we realized that leaving the zucchini noodles raw gave us the best texture and flavor. We added red bell pepper, shredded carrot, and sautéed broccoli and replaced the usual peanut sauce with tahini, a nutty, buttery paste made from ground sesame seeds. Soy sauce, ginger, rice vinegar, and garlic rounded out the Asian-inspired dressing. If possible, use smaller, in-season zucchini, which have thinner skins and fewer seeds. We prefer to spiralize our zucchini at home for the best flavor, but you can use store-bought zucchini noodles. You'll need 2½ pounds of noodles.*

½ cup tahini
5 tablespoons soy sauce
2 tablespoons rice vinegar
4 teaspoons grated fresh ginger
1 tablespoon honey
2 teaspoons hot sauce
1 garlic clove, minced
  Salt and pepper
2 tablespoons toasted sesame oil
12 ounces broccoli florets, cut into
   ½-inch pieces
3 pounds zucchini, trimmed
1 red bell pepper, stemmed, seeded,
   and cut into ¼-inch-wide strips
1 carrot, peeled and shredded
4 scallions, sliced thin on bias
1 tablespoon sesame seeds, toasted

1. Process tahini, soy sauce, vinegar, ginger, honey, hot sauce, garlic, and ½ teaspoon salt in blender until smooth, about 30 seconds. Transfer to large serving bowl.

2. Heat oil in 12-inch nonstick skillet over medium-high heat until shimmering. Add broccoli and cook until softened and spotty brown, about 5 minutes. Transfer to plate and let cool slightly.

3. Using spiralizer, cut zucchini into ⅛-inch-thick noodles, cutting noodles into 12-inch lengths with kitchen shears as you spiralize (every 4 or 5 revolutions). Add zucchini, bell pepper, carrot, scallions, and broccoli to bowl with dressing and toss to combine. Sprinkle with sesame seeds. Serve.

ZUCCHINI NOODLES WITH ROASTED TOMATOES AND CREAM SAUCE

Serves 4 Total time: 50 minutes

WHY THIS RECIPE WORKS *Spiralized veggie noodles provide all the comfort-food appeal of pasta, but in a lighter, healthier way. This dish coats zucchini noodles with a rich, creamy sauce and sweet, garlicky roasted tomatoes. Roasting the noodles rids them of excess moisture and ensures that the sauce won't get washed out. If possible, use smaller, in-season zucchini, which have thinner skins and fewer seeds. We prefer to spiralize our zucchini at home, but you can use store-bought zucchini noodles. You'll need 2½ pounds of noodles. A toasted loaf of ciabatta bread makes the perfect vehicle for wiping up every drop of cheesy sauce and roasted tomatoes.*

- 3 pounds zucchini or yellow summer squash, trimmed
- 1 pound cherry tomatoes
- 1 shallot, sliced thin
- 3 tablespoons extra-virgin olive oil
- 5 garlic cloves, minced
- 1 tablespoon tomato paste
- 1 teaspoon dried oregano
- ¼ teaspoon red pepper flakes
  Salt and pepper
- 1 cup heavy cream
- 2 tablespoons unsalted butter
- 1½ ounces Parmesan cheese, grated (¾ cup)
- ¼ cup fresh basil leaves, torn into bite-size pieces

1. Adjust oven racks to upper-middle and lower-middle positions and heat oven to 375 degrees. Line 2 rimmed baking sheets with aluminum foil; set aside. Using spiralizer, cut zucchini into ⅛-inch-thick noodles, cutting noodles into 12-inch lengths with kitchen shears as you spiralize (every 4 or 5 revolutions).

2. Toss tomatoes, shallot, 2 tablespoons oil, garlic, tomato paste, oregano, pepper flakes, ½ teaspoon salt, and ¼ teaspoon pepper together in bowl. Spread tomato mixture on 1 prepared sheet and place on lower rack. Roast, without stirring, until tomatoes are softened and skins begin to shrivel, about 25 minutes.

3. Meanwhile, toss zucchini with remaining 1 tablespoon oil, ½ teaspoon salt, and ¼ teaspoon pepper, spread on second prepared sheet, and roast on upper rack until tender, 20 to 25 minutes. Transfer roasted zucchini to colander and shake to remove any excess liquid.

4. While vegetables are roasting, bring cream and butter to simmer in large saucepan over medium heat. Reduce heat to low and simmer gently until mixture measures ⅔ cup, 12 to 15 minutes. Stir in Parmesan, ½ teaspoon salt, and ¼ teaspoon pepper and cook over low heat, stirring often, until Parmesan is melted. Add zucchini and gently toss to combine. Season with salt and pepper to taste. Transfer to serving platter, top with roasted tomatoes, and sprinkle with basil. Serve immediately.

ZUCCHINI AND ORZO TIAN

Serves 4 Total time: 1 hour

WHY THIS RECIPE WORKS *For a Mediterranean-inspired vegetable casserole pairing the summery flavors (and striking colors) of green zucchini, yellow summer squash, and red tomatoes with orzo, we sought out a relatively hands-off approach. The challenge was getting the pasta and vegetables to finish cooking simultaneously without sacrificing the taste or texture of either. While most recipes first cook the orzo separately in a pot, we were able to skip that step by tightly shingling the vegetables on the orzo's surface, trapping the moisture within the confines of the casserole dish. Using broth as our cooking liquid boosted the vegetables' flavor, and shallots and garlic provided aromatic depth and sweetness. Stirring in some Parmesan gave the orzo a creamy texture, and oregano and red pepper flakes contributed floral, spicy notes. To our delight, the pasta and vegetables were close to perfection after 20 minutes in a hot oven. More Parmesan cheese sprinkled on top of the vegetables before a few minutes under the broiler made for an appealing presentation, and chopped basil gave our tian a fresh, bright finish. When shopping, look for squash, zucchini, and tomatoes with similar-size circumferences so that they are easy to shingle into the dish.*

- 3 ounces Parmesan cheese, grated (1½ cups)
- 1 cup orzo
- 2 shallots, minced
- 3 tablespoons minced fresh oregano or 1 teaspoon dried
- 3 garlic cloves, minced
- ⅛ teaspoon red pepper flakes
  Salt and pepper
- 1 zucchini, trimmed and sliced ¼ inch thick
- 1 yellow summer squash, trimmed and sliced ¼ inch thick
- 1 pound plum tomatoes, cored and sliced ¼ inch thick
- 1¾ cups chicken or vegetable broth
- 1 tablespoon extra-virgin olive oil
- 2 tablespoons chopped fresh basil

1. Adjust oven rack to middle position and heat oven to 425 degrees. Combine ½ cup Parmesan, orzo, shallots, oregano, garlic, pepper flakes, and ¼ teaspoon salt in bowl. Spread mixture evenly into broiler-safe 13 by 9-inch baking dish. Alternately shingle zucchini, squash, and tomatoes in tidy rows on top of orzo. Carefully pour broth over top of vegetables. Bake until orzo is just tender and most of broth is absorbed, about 20 minutes.

2. Remove dish from oven, adjust oven rack 9 inches from broiler element, and heat broiler. Drizzle vegetables with oil, season with salt and pepper, and sprinkle with remaining 1 cup Parmesan. Broil until browned and bubbling around edges, about 5 minutes. Let rest for 10 minutes, then sprinkle with basil and serve.

MEDITERRANEAN STUFFED ZUCCHINI

Serves 4   Total time: 1 hour 15 minutes

WHY THIS RECIPE WORKS *Zucchini is a perfect shape for hollowing out and stuffing, and the possibilities for fillings are endlessly versatile. We wanted a recipe for perfectly baked zucchini boats filled with a rich, gently spiced lamb stuffing. We took several steps to avoid overcooked and flavorless zucchini: We scooped out the seeds to reduce moisture; we roasted the unstuffed zucchini cut side down to achieve a flavorful sear and give the vegetable a head start on cooking; and we returned the zucchini to the hot oven—packed with our robust filling—for a final burst of heat before serving. To balance the distinct flavor of the lamb, we decided on a trio of elements popular in Moroccan cuisine: sweet dried apricots, buttery pine nuts, and aromatic ras el hanout, the North African spice blend that includes coriander, cardamom, cinnamon, and more. After browning the lamb, we poured off all but a small amount of the fat to keep our filling from tasting too greasy; to offset the filling's meaty texture and add a mild, wheaty chew, we incorporated a small amount of bulgur. It's important to use smaller, in-season zucchini, which have thinner skins and fewer seeds. You can find ras el hanout in the spice aisle of most well-stocked supermarkets.*

- 4 zucchini (8 ounces each), trimmed, halved lengthwise, and seeded
- 2 tablespoons plus 1 teaspoon extra-virgin olive oil
  Salt and pepper
- 8 ounces ground lamb
- 1 onion, chopped fine
- 4 garlic cloves, minced
- 2 teaspoons ras el hanout
- ⅔ cup chicken broth
- ½ cup medium-grind bulgur, rinsed
- ¼ cup dried apricots, chopped fine
- 2 tablespoons pine nuts, toasted
- 2 tablespoons minced fresh parsley

1. Adjust oven racks to upper-middle and lowest positions, place rimmed baking sheet on lower rack, and heat oven to 400 degrees. Brush cut sides of zucchini with 2 tablespoons oil and season with salt and pepper.

Lay zucchini cut side down in hot sheet and roast until slightly softened and skins are wrinkled, 8 to 10 minutes. Remove zucchini from oven and flip cut side up on sheet; set aside.

2. Meanwhile, heat remaining 1 teaspoon oil in large saucepan over medium-high heat until just smoking. Add lamb, ½ teaspoon salt, and ¼ teaspoon pepper and cook, breaking up meat with wooden spoon, until browned, 3 to 5 minutes. Using slotted spoon, transfer lamb to paper towel–lined plate.

3. Pour off all but 1 tablespoon fat from saucepan. Add onion to fat left in saucepan and cook over medium heat until softened, about 5 minutes. Stir in garlic and ras el hanout and cook until fragrant, about 30 seconds. Stir in broth, bulgur, and apricots and bring to simmer. Reduce heat to low, cover, and simmer gently until bulgur is tender, 16 to 18 minutes.

4. Off heat, lay clean dish towel underneath lid and let pilaf sit for 10 minutes. Add pine nuts and parsley to pilaf and gently fluff with fork to combine. Season with salt and pepper to taste.

5. Pack each zucchini half with bulgur mixture, about ½ cup per zucchini half, mounding excess. Place baking sheet on upper rack and bake zucchini until heated through, about 6 minutes. Serve.

HALIBUT IN FOIL WITH ZUCCHINI AND TOMATOES

Serves 4   Total time: 1 hour

WHY THIS RECIPE WORKS *Cooking fish and vegetables en papillote—baking them in a tightly sealed package to steam in their own juices—is a quick, surefire way to an elegant but easy, sophisticated but satisfying meal. Here, zucchini slices both complement the mild flavor of the halibut and cook in the same amount of time. We salted the zucchini first, to remove excess moisture. To give our packets plenty of flavor without overpowering the halibut and zucchini, we made a tomato "salsa," which added just the right kick. A splash of white wine boosted the flavor even more. Using aluminum foil rather than parchment made packet construction simple. The sealed packets needed only 15 to 20 minutes in the oven to steam and baste the fish and* soften the vegetables. A final garnish of chopped basil and lemon wedges made the perfect finish. Cod, haddock, red snapper, and sea bass also work well in this recipe, as long as the fillets are 1 to 1½ inches thick. Be sure to open each packet promptly after baking to prevent overcooking, being careful to avoid the hot steam.

    1 pound zucchini, trimmed and
       sliced ¼ inch thick
       Kosher salt and pepper
    2 plum tomatoes, cored, seeded,
       and chopped
    2 tablespoons extra-virgin olive oil
    2 garlic cloves, minced
    1 teaspoon minced fresh oregano
       or ¼ teaspoon dried
    ⅛ teaspoon red pepper flakes
    ¼ cup dry white wine
    4 (6- to 8-ounce) skinless halibut fillets,
       1 to 1½ inches thick
    ¼ cup chopped fresh basil
       Lemon wedges

1. Toss zucchini with 1 teaspoon salt in colander and let drain for 30 minutes. Pat zucchini dry with paper towels and carefully wipe away any residual salt. Meanwhile, combine tomatoes, oil, garlic, oregano, pepper flakes, ¼ teaspoon salt, and ⅛ teaspoon pepper in bowl.

2. Adjust oven rack to lower-middle position and heat oven to 450 degrees. Cut eight 12-inch-square sheets of aluminum foil. Arrange 4 foil squares on counter. Shingle zucchini in center of sheets and sprinkle with wine. Pat halibut dry with paper towels, season with salt and pepper, and place on top of zucchini. Spread tomato mixture evenly over halibut.

3. Place second foil square on top of each piece of halibut. Press edges of foil together and fold over several times until packet is well sealed and measures about 7 inches square. Place packets on rimmed baking sheet, overlapping as needed.

4. Bake until halibut registers 140 degrees, 15 to 20 minutes. (To check temperature, poke thermometer through foil of 1 packet and into halibut.) Transfer halibut packets to individual serving plates, open carefully (steam will escape), and slide contents onto plates. Sprinkle with basil and serve with lemon wedges.

~

ZUCCHINI BREAD

Makes 1 loaf   Total time: 1 hour
30 minutes (plus 30 minutes cooling time)
WHY THIS RECIPE WORKS *Baked goods are a great way to use up an abundance of zucchini, and we like our zucchini bread to be bursting with the flavor of the vegetable. Zucchini naturally produces a moist loaf or cake thanks to its high moisture content. However, if not used correctly, zucchini can impart too much moisture, leaving baked goods extremely wet and gummy. By removing a majority of the liquid from the zucchini, along with most other sources of moisture, and lowering the fat, we were able to up our zucchini content from 12 ounces to 1½ pounds, getting more zucchini flavor without sacrificing a properly moist and tender crumb. Use the large holes of a box grater to shred the zucchini. The test kitchen's preferred loaf pan measures 8½ by 4½ inches; if you use a 9 by 5-inch loaf pan, start checking for doneness 5 minutes early.*

  1½ pounds zucchini, trimmed and
      shredded
  1¼ cups packed (8¾ ounces) brown sugar
   ¼ cup vegetable oil
    2 large eggs
    1 teaspoon vanilla extract
  1½ cups (7½ ounces) all-purpose flour
   ½ cup (2¾ ounces) whole-wheat flour
    1 tablespoon ground cinnamon
  1½ teaspoons salt
    1 teaspoon baking powder
    1 teaspoon baking soda
   ½ teaspoon ground nutmeg
   ¾ cup walnuts, toasted and chopped
      (optional)
    1 tablespoon granulated sugar

1. Adjust oven rack to middle position and heat oven to 325 degrees. Grease 8½ by 4½-inch loaf pan.

2. Wrap zucchini in clean dish towel and squeeze out excess liquid (½ to ⅔ cup). Whisk brown sugar, oil, eggs, and vanilla together in medium bowl. Fold in zucchini.

3. Whisk all-purpose flour, whole-wheat flour, cinnamon, salt, baking powder, baking soda, and nutmeg together in large bowl. Fold in zucchini mixture until just incorporated. Fold in walnuts, if using. Pour batter into prepared pan and sprinkle with granulated sugar.

4. Bake until top bounces back when gently pressed and toothpick inserted in center comes out with few moist crumbs attached, 1 hour 5 minutes to 1¼ hours. Let bread cool in pan on wire rack for 30 minutes. Remove bread from pan and let cool completely on rack. Serve.

VARIATIONS
Zucchini Bread with Pistachios and Orange
Substitute 1 teaspoon grated orange zest for cinnamon. Add ½ teaspoon ground cardamom in with nutmeg. Substitute pistachios for walnuts.

Zucchini Bread with Walnuts and Cherries
Substitute cocoa powder for cinnamon and ground cloves for nutmeg. Prepare bread with walnuts and add ¾ cup dried cherries, chopped, to batter with walnuts.

Zucchini Bread with
Pistachios and Orange

Nutritional Information for Our Recipes

To calculate the nutritional values of our recipes per serving, we used The Food Processor SQL by ESHA Research. When using this program, we entered all the ingredients, using weights for important ingredients such as most vegetables. We also used our preferred brands in these analyses. When the recipe called for seasoning with an unspecified amount of salt and pepper, we added ½ teaspoon of salt and ¼ teaspoon of pepper to the analysis. We did not include additional salt or pepper for food that's "seasoned to taste." If there is a range in the serving size, we used the highest number of servings to calculate the nutritional values.

	CALORIES	TOTAL FAT (G)	SAT FAT (G)	CHOL (MG)	SODIUM (MG)	TOTAL CARBS (G)	FIBER (G)	SUGAR (G)	PROTEIN (G)
ARTICHOKES									
Roasted Artichokes with Lemon Vinaigrette	330	32	4.5	0	830	10	5	1	3
Roman-Style Stuffed Braised Artichokes	320	28	4	0	550	15	6	2	4
Braised Artichokes with Tomatoes and Thyme	160	7	1	0	730	16	6	4	5
Slow-Cooker Braised Artichokes with Garlic Butter	230	20	11	45	230	11	5	1	3
Grilled Artichokes with Lemon Butter	260	24	12	45	520	11	5	1	3
Jewish-Style Fried Artichokes	140	12	1.5	0	55	6	3	1	2
Roasted Artichoke Dip	290	25	6	30	440	12	4	2	4
Marinated Artichokes	70	3.5	0.5	0	360	8	4	1	2
Bruschetta with Artichoke Hearts and Parmesan	190	8	1.5	5	370	24	1	1	7
Artichoke Soup à la Barigoule	210	11	3.5	10	900	19	3	5	7
Tagliatelle with Artichokes and Parmesan	520	18	3	5	740	70	5	3	16
ASPARAGUS									
Pan-Roasted Asparagus	40	2.5	0	0	0	4	2	2	3
Roasted Asparagus with Mint-Orange Gremolata	80	6	1	0	190	5	2	2	3
Parmesan-Crusted Asparagus	140	6	3	15	580	13	2	3	11
Braised Asparagus, Peas, and Radishes with Tarragon	140	9	1.5	0	400	11	4	4	4
Grilled Asparagus	100	8	5	25	0	5	2	2	3
Asparagus Salad with Radishes, Pecorino Romano, and Croutons	330	29	7	20	560	13	4	4	8
Tortellini Salad with Asparagus and Fresh Basil Dressing	310	18	4	30	690	30	4	4	9
Creamy Asparagus Soup	150	10	6	25	520	11	3	5	7
Asparagus–Goat Cheese Tart	420	31	13	15	500	32	3	2	11
Stir-Fried Asparagus with Shiitake Mushrooms	80	4.5	0	0	230	7	2	5	3
AVOCADOS									
Power Smoothie	270	12	1.5	0	160	40	7	16	6
Super Guacamole	120	11	1.5	0	160	7	5	1	2
Bean and Beef Taquitos with Avocado Sauce	280	18	3	35	290	23	6	3	8
Avocado Salad with Tomatoes and Radishes	280	25	5	15	550	13	8	3	5
Cobb Salad with Creamy Avocado Dressing	390	26	8	225	590	7	4	3	31
Shrimp Salad with Avocado and Orange	210	15	2.5	110	290	8	3	4	13
Crispy Skillet Turkey Burgers with Charred Avocado Relish	760	47	11	65	950	48	9	5	41

	CALORIES	TOTAL FAT (G)	SAT FAT (G)	CHOL (MG)	SODIUM (MG)	TOTAL CARBS (G)	FIBER (G)	SUGAR (G)	PROTEIN (G)
AVOCADOS (continued)									
Tuna Poke with Avocado	360	24	3.5	35	1010	15	9	4	25
Avocado Toast	330	23	3	0	390	28	8	2	5
California Barley Bowls with Avocado, Snow Peas, and Lemon-Mint Yogurt Sauce	670	44	7	10	770	61	19	7	15
BEETS									
Sautéed Beet Greens with Raisins and Almonds	250	18	2.5	0	390	20	8	11	6
Roasted Beets	100	7	1	0	60	7	2	5	1
Braised Beets with Lemon and Almonds	120	6	0.5	0	360	13	4	8	4
Pickled Beets	30	0	0	0	55	6	2	5	1
Beet Muhammara	160	13	1.5	0	320	9	2	5	3
Beet Chips	70	0	0	0	700	15	4	10	2
Marinated Beet Salad with Oranges and Pecorino	290	21	4.5	15	560	19	5	12	9
Charred Beet Salad	180	13	6	20	830	10	2	7	6
Beet and Carrot Noodle Salad	190	11	2	0	300	20	5	11	6
Beet and Wheat Berry Soup with Dill Cream	240	11	2	10	1690	32	6	7	5
Pinto Bean–Beet Burgers	440	20	2	0	870	54	6	6	12
Beet and Barley Risotto	320	7	1.5	5	800	49	10	5	8
Red Flannel Hash	390	24	8	395	520	29	4	8	16
BROCCOLI									
Steamed Broccoli with Lime-Cumin Dressing	140	11	1.5	0	40	8	3	2	3
Pan-Roasted Broccoli with Lemon Browned Butter	140	12	5	20	220	6	2	2	2
Roasted Broccoli	90	7	1	0	220	6	2	2	2
Grilled Broccoli with Lemon and Parmesan	100	8	1.5	0	290	5	2	1	3
Pan-Steamed Broccolini with Shallot	80	6	3.5	15	330	4	3	1	4
Broccolini with Pancetta and Parmesan	180	14	4	20	580	5	3	1	11
Sautéed Broccoli Rabe with Roasted Red Peppers	80	6	1	0	260	4	3	1	4
Broiled Broccoli Rabe	120	11	1.5	0	250	4	3	0	4
Broccoli Rabe and Spicy Tomato Sauce	100	3.5	1	5	500	12	5	5	7
Broccoli Rabe with White Beans	140	10	1.5	0	360	10	4	1	6
Broccoli Salad with Raisins and Walnuts	260	20	2.5	5	340	18	3	12	4
Broccoli-Cheese Soup	130	8	5	25	650	7	2	2	8
Parmesan Polenta with Broccoli Rabe, Sun-Dried Tomatoes, and Pine Nuts	520	33	10	40	1870	40	7	1	23
Farro and Broccoli Rabe Gratin	390	13	3.5	15	780	51	9	4	22
Thai-Style Stir-Fried Noodles with Chicken and Broccolini	560	21	2.5	200	1590	59	3	8	32
Beef and Chinese Broccoli Stir-Fry	470	26	7	115	1350	16	3	5	41
Philadelphia Roast Pork Sandwiches with Broccoli Rabe	900	41	12	105	1670	82	7	7	51
Orecchiette with Broccoli Rabe and Sausage	420	12	3.5	20	570	59	5	2	21
Roasted Salmon and Broccoli Rabe with Pistachio Gremolata	630	44	9	125	610	6	4	1	52
Cheesy Broccoli Calzones	640	26	13	105	1070	67	4	3	32

	CALORIES	TOTAL FAT (G)	SAT FAT (G)	CHOL (MG)	SODIUM (MG)	TOTAL CARBS (G)	FIBER (G)	SUGAR (G)	PROTEIN (G)
BRUSSELS SPROUTS									
Sautéed Sliced Brussels Sprouts	70	2.5	0	0	410	9	4	2	4
Pan-Roasted Brussels Sprouts with Lemon and Pecorino Romano	210	19	3	0	220	10	4	2	4
Roasted Brussels Sprouts	100	6	1	0	250	10	4	3	4
Braised Brussels Sprouts with Mustard-Herb Butter	150	11	7	30	410	9	4	2	3
Maple-Glazed Brussels Sprouts	110	6	3.5	15	60	13	4	5	4
Fried Brussels Sprouts with Lemon-Chive Dipping Sauce	260	24	2.5	5	140	10	4	2	4
Brussels Sprout Salad with Pecorino and Pine Nuts	240	20	3.5	5	410	11	4	3	8
Brussels Sprout and Kale Slaw with Herbs and Peanuts	150	8	1	0	220	16	4	9	5
Skillet Bratwurst with Brussels Sprouts and Apples	1100	81	16	175	2480	58	9	37	33
Seared Trout with Brussels Sprouts and Bacon	520	34	7	115	960	10	4	2	42
Whole-Wheat Rotini with Brussels Sprouts	600	33	12	50	570	59	12	6	20
Brussels Sprout and Potato Hash	420	23	6	380	940	35	8	7	19
Brussels Sprout Gratin	300	23	13	65	460	16	5	4	10
CABBAGES									
Sautéed Baby Bok Choy with Miso Sauce	90	5	0	0	290	9	1	6	2
Stir-Fried Bok Choy with Soy Sauce and Ginger	60	5	0	0	370	3	1	2	2
Braised Bok Choy with Garlic	60	5	0	0	115	3	1	1	2
Sautéed Cabbage with Parsley and Lemon	80	4.5	0	0	320	8	3	4	1
Pan-Roasted Cabbage	160	12	5	20	420	9	4	5	2
Simple Cream-Braised Cabbage	90	5	3.5	15	30	9	3	5	2
Braised Red Cabbage	140	4.5	2.5	10	390	20	3	14	2
Grilled Cabbage	140	11	1.5	0	190	9	3	6	1
Sauerkraut	15	0	0	0	200	3	1	2	1
Creamy Buttermilk Coleslaw	120	7	1.5	10	560	11	3	7	3
Honey-Mustard Coleslaw	110	2.5	0	0	720	16	3	13	1
Memphis Chopped Coleslaw	150	7	1.5	5	440	21	3	16	2
Napa Cabbage Slaw with Carrots and Sesame	80	4.5	0.5	0	210	7	2	4	2
Chinese Chicken Salad	520	28	4	110	780	25	6	16	44
Kimchi Beef and Tofu Soup	270	14	3.5	50	870	10	2	7	21
Savoy Cabbage "Soup" with Ham, Rye Bread, and Fontina	310	17	6	30	1050	28	5	4	14
Stir-Fried Chicken with Bok Choy and Crispy Noodle Cake	650	34	3.5	85	1940	46	3	8	36
Stuffed Cabbage Rolls	740	43	14	125	2420	53	10	32	35
CARROTS									
Boiled Carrots with Cumin, Lime, and Cilantro	70	4	0.5	0	360	10	3	5	1
Roasted Carrots and Shallots with Chermoula	300	23	6	15	690	23	6	11	3
Roasted Carrot Noodles	100	5	0.5	0	290	14	4	7	1
Braised Carrots with Apple	110	4.5	2.5	10	620	17	4	11	2
Whole Carrots with Red Pepper and Almond Relish	150	9	2	5	450	16	5	8	2
Glazed Carrots with Orange and Cranberries	130	3	2	10	390	26	3	20	1

	CALORIES	TOTAL FAT (G)	SAT FAT (G)	CHOL (MG)	SODIUM (MG)	TOTAL CARBS (G)	FIBER (G)	SUGAR (G)	PROTEIN (G)
CARROTS (continued)									
Brined Grilled Carrots with Cilantro-Yogurt Sauce	160	8	3.5	5	300	18	5	9	6
Carrot-Habanero Dip	80	5	0.5	0	180	8	2	4	1
Chopped Carrot Salad with Mint, Pistachios, and Pomegranate Seeds	240	18	2	1	460	18	5	10	4
Brown Rice Bowls with Roasted Carrots, Kale, and Fried Eggs	460	26	4.5	185	1030	49	7	6	12
Bulgur Salad with Carrots and Almonds	300	17	2	0	330	35	7	3	7
Chickpea Salad with Carrots, Arugula, and Olives	190	12	1.5	0	620	17	5	2	5
Carrot-Ginger Soup	290	13	6	25	1090	40	6	17	4
One-Pan Chicken with Couscous and Carrots	510	10	2	160	1310	58	9	6	44
Carrot Layer Cake	600	38	13	90	360	58	3	43	6
CAULIFLOWER									
Pan-Roasted Cauliflower with Garlic and Lemon	170	12	2	0	480	12	3	3	4
Roasted Cauliflower	120	10	1.5	0	45	8	3	3	3
Braised Cauliflower with Garlic and White Wine	120	8	1.5	0	170	8	3	3	3
Whole Pot-Roasted Cauliflower with Tomatoes and Olives	190	7	1.5	5	1060	25	6	14	9
Whole Romanesco with Berbere and Yogurt-Tahini Sauce	300	25	12	50	230	16	5	6	7
Grilled Cauliflower	80	5	1	0	95	8	3	3	3
Cauliflower Rice	60	3	0.5	0	380	8	3	3	3
Cauliflower Buffalo Bites	510	45	13	25	950	25	2	4	3
North African Cauliflower Salad with Chermoula	240	16	2.5	0	370	24	5	15	4
Cauliflower Soup	190	15	10	40	640	11	4	4	3
Cauliflower Steaks with Salsa Verde	320	29	4.5	0	500	14	6	5	5
Thai Red Curry with Cauliflower	380	30	19	0	800	27	8	10	10
Indian-Style Mixed Vegetable Curry	270	12	4.5	0	450	33	9	7	9
Vegan Fettuccine Alfredo	520	23	12	0	810	66	5	5	15
Campanelle with Roasted Cauliflower, Garlic, and Walnuts	500	21	3	5	710	67	6	5	16
Lavash Pizzas with Cauliflower, Fennel, and Coriander	270	16	5	20	410	21	3	4	10
Baja-Style Cauliflower Tacos	420	27	17	10	530	44	8	9	7
Cauliflower Cakes	350	24	8	70	830	22	5	7	15
Modern Cauliflower Gratin	170	11	7	30	630	12	4	4	6
Roast Chicken with Cauliflower and Tomatoes	650	44	10	205	860	22	7	9	43
CELERY									
Braised Celery with Vermouth-Butter Glaze	90	6	3.5	15	310	4	2	3	1
Sage–Brown Butter Celery Root Puree	190	12	7	30	520	19	4	3	3
Roasted Celery Root with Yogurt and Sesame Seeds	110	6	1	0	310	12	2	2	2
Roasted Celery Root Bites with Chimichurri	250	22	4.5	10	470	11	2	2	2
Shaved Celery Salad with Pomegranate-Honey Vinaigrette	200	13	2.5	5	280	17	4	9	5
Rhubarb, Celery, and Radish Salad with Feta and Cilantro	130	12	3	10	270	4	1	1	2

	CALORIES	TOTAL FAT (G)	SAT FAT (G)	CHOL (MG)	SODIUM (MG)	TOTAL CARBS (G)	FIBER (G)	SUGAR (G)	PROTEIN (G)
CELERY (continued)									
Celery Root Salad with Apple and Parsley	170	13	2	5	520	14	2	6	2
Celery Root, Celery, and Apple Slaw	270	19	2.5	0	640	22	4	12	2
Cream of Celery Soup	200	11	7	30	630	20	2	7	3
Celery Root, Fennel, and Apple Chowder	200	8	4.5	20	700	27	4	8	3
Celery Root and Potato Roesti with Lemon-Parsley Créme Fraîche	380	23	14	55	620	41	4	4	6
Shrimp Salad with Celery and Shallot	170	11	1.5	110	370	6	0	4	12
Salmon en Cocotte with Celery and Orange	650	43	11	140	520	15	2	8	48
CHICORIES									
Braised Belgian Endive	100	8	5	25	180	4	2	1	1
Utica Greens	200	14	3.5	20	920	12	6	2	9
Sesame-Hoisin Braised Escarole	180	13	1.5	0	410	12	7	3	4
Braised Radicchio with Apple and Cream	230	17	10	50	40	18	3	11	3
Lemony Roasted Radicchio, Fennel, and Root Vegetables	210	8	1	0	360	33	7	9	5
Grilled Radicchio with Garlic- and Rosemary-Infused Oil	160	14	2	0	125	6	1	1	2
Wheat Berry and Endive Salad with Blueberries and Goat Cheese	450	28	5	10	350	43	9	4	11
Endive, Beet, and Pear Slaw	260	19	2.5	0	570	22	5	15	2
Escarole and Orange Salad with Green Olive Vinaigrette	220	19	2	0	180	13	5	6	4
Bistro Salad	420	38	11	225	680	4	2	2	14
Bitter Greens Salad	120	10	2.5	10	480	5	3	1	2
Radicchio Salad with Apple, Arugula, and Parmesan	360	26	5	10	880	25	3	18	9
Citrus-Radicchio Salad with Dates and Smoked Almonds	240	13	1.5	0	280	31	5	25	4
Orzo Salad with Radicchio, Chickpeas, and Pecorino	350	18	3.5	5	560	38	3	5	10
Lentil-Escarole Soup	260	11	1.5	0	760	32	9	5	11
Tuscan White Bean and Escarole Soup	370	19	2.5	35	1270	39	8	8	11
Whole-Wheat Pasta with Lentils, Escarole, and Pancetta	510	17	3.5	15	770	67	15	4	21
CHILES									
Blistered Shishito Peppers	50	4.5	0	0	0	2	1	1	0
Pickled Jalapeños	10	0	0	0	55	2	0	2	0
Habanero and Peach Chutney	40	1.5	0	0	0	6	1	6	0
Stuffed Jalapeños	250	21	11	80	630	4	0	2	10
Spicy Pinto Bean Soup	250	8	0.5	0	1180	33	11	5	11
Pork Posole Rojo	480	26	8	105	1130	26	5	7	34
Best Ground Beef Chili	330	17	6	60	710	21	6	3	22
Three-Chile White Bean Chili	300	9	0.5	0	650	46	12	10	14
Ultimate Vegetarian Chili	440	13	1	0	1120	67	16	10	19
Maccheroni di Fuoco	360	17	2	0	190	46	2	1	8
Chiles Rellenos	460	18	8	35	1160	54	4	6	14
Thai Green Curry with Chicken, Broccoli, and Mushrooms	780	54	39	125	1060	27	6	11	47
Jerk Chicken	710	48	11	230	2010	13	4	4	55

	CALORIES	TOTAL FAT (G)	SAT FAT (G)	CHOL (MG)	SODIUM (MG)	TOTAL CARBS (G)	FIBER (G)	SUGAR (G)	PROTEIN (G)
CHILES (continued)									
Chicken Mole Poblano	630	42	10	155	1020	24	6	10	41
Stir-Fried Thai-Style Beef with Chiles and Shallots	540	31	8	155	830	16	2	7	52
Ground Beef and Cheese Enchiladas	570	35	11	85	630	38	7	6	30
Shredded Beef Tacos with Cabbage-Carrot Slaw	410	14	5	50	900	49	10	10	22
Tacos al Pastor	530	24	7	105	780	46	6	11	35
Carne Adovada	580	34	12	165	950	17	5	5	49
CORN									
Foolproof Boiled Corn with Chili-Lime Salt	100	3	0	0	1170	19	3	5	4
Garden-Fresh Corn with Zucchini and Herbs	160	7	0	0	10	27	3	9	6
Creamed Corn	140	7	2.5	10	440	21	2	6	5
Husk-Grilled Corn	190	14	7	30	190	18	2	5	4
Mexican-Style Grilled Corn	220	16	3	10	270	19	2	5	6
Corn Relish	45	0.5	0	0	380	9	1	5	1
Fresh Corn Salsa with Tomato	30	1.5	0	0	110	4	1	2	1
Corn Fritters with Chipotle-Maple Mayonnaise	200	18	2	20	160	8	1	2	2
Fresh Corn Salad	140	8	1	0	490	17	2	5	4
Roasted Corn and Poblano Chowder	290	14	3	10	1230	37	5	8	9
Crispy Pork Chops with Succotash	860	42	8	130	1390	71	7	11	50
South Carolina Shrimp Boil	350	15	4.5	165	940	27	3	5	31
Creamy Corn Bucatini with Ricotta and Basil	400	8	3	15	350	69	4	7	17
Fresh Corn Cornbread	290	12	6	95	540	40	3	6	8
Sweet Corn Spoonbread	260	15	8	125	470	26	2	8	10
CUCUMBERS									
Smashed Sichuan Cucumbers	50	2.5	0	0	650	5	2	3	3
Quick Pickle Chips	5	0	0	0	0	1	0	0	0
Bread-and-Butter Pickles	60	0	0	0	440	14	0	13	0
Parsley-Cucumber Salad with Feta, Walnuts, and Pomegranate	280	24	5	15	290	11	3	6	7
Creamy Cucumber Salad with Radishes, Lemon, and Mint	50	3.5	1.5	10	200	5	1	3	1
Country-Style Greek Salad	190	15	4	15	430	9	2	6	4
Pita Bread Salad with Tomatoes and Cucumber (Fattoush)	360	26	3.5	0	280	27	5.19	5	7
Orzo Salad with Cucumber, Red Onion, and Mint	290	17	3.5	10	380	30	1.98	3	7
Chilled Cucumber and Yogurt Soup	150	9	7	15	620	9	2.12	7	8
Greek-Style Lamb Pita Sandwiches with Tzatziki Sauce	630	36	15	105	910	44	5.61	7	32
Grilled Thai Beef Salad with Cucumbers	230	10	4	75	300	10	2.11	3	26
EGGPLANT									
Broiled Eggplant with Basil	90	7	1	0	290	7	3	4	1
Grilled Eggplant with Cherry Tomatoes and Cilantro Vinaigrette	230	21	3	0	100	9	4	5	2
Sicilian Eggplant Relish (Caponata)	90	4.5	0.5	0	190	11	3	8	2
Walkaway Ratatouille	210	12	1.5	0	530	24	7	12	4
Baba Ghanoush	80	6	1	0	220	8	3	4	2
Crispy Thai Eggplant Salad	560	38	4	0	1330	52	12	31	12
Hasselback Eggplant with Garlic-Yogurt Sauce	640	45	10	10	1600	49	8	22	13

	CALORIES	TOTAL FAT (G)	SAT FAT (G)	CHOL (MG)	SODIUM (MG)	TOTAL CARBS (G)	FIBER (G)	SUGAR (G)	PROTEIN (G)
EGGPLANT (continued)									
Roasted Eggplant and Tomato Soup	230	15	2	0	910	21	6	12	3
Stuffed Eggplant	340	25	5	10	790	26	10	13	9
Eggplant Involtini	320	21	5	20	860	23	8	11	11
Eggplant Parmesan	330	24	7	20	480	23	9	12	11
Pasta alla Norma	470	14	3.5	15	790	71	8	9	15
Stir-Fried Japanese Eggplant	140	7	0.5	0	330	13	3	6	3
Charred Sichuan-Style Eggplant	620	42	3	0	740	37	8	20	10
FENNEL									
Braised Fennel with Radicchio and Parmesan	240	14	7	30	400	21	7	11	4
Slow-Cooker Braised Fennel with Orange-Tarragon Dressing	70	5	0.5	0	240	6	3	3	1
Roasted Fennel with Rye Crumble	180	13	8	35	700	13	4	4	4
Fennel Confit	280	28	4	0	120	7	3	4	1
Quick Pickled Fennel	10	0	0	0	15	2	1	1	0
Fennel Salad	220	13	1.5	0	580	22	5	16	3
Algerian-Style Fennel Salad with Oranges and Olives	160	10	1.5	0	180	17	5	12	2
Fennel, Olive, and Goat Cheese Tarts	540	38	17	25	570	38	4	5	16
Whole-Wheat Pasta with Italian Sausage and Fennel	480	22	3	10	720	53	10	4	18
Spice-Rubbed Pork Tenderloin with Fennel, Tomatoes, Artichokes, and Olives	390	16	3	110	730	22	8	10	41
Steamed Mussels with Fennel, White Wine, and Tarragon	760	33	16	185	2000	39	3	3	58
Cod Baked in Foil with Fennel and Shallots	330	12	7	105	280	18	5	11	33
FORAGED GREENS									
Horta	110	8	1	0	160	10	4	1	3
Fried Fiddleheads with Lemon-Chive Dipping Sauce	380	32	3	5	500	22	1	1	5
Grilled Ramps	45	3.5	0.5	0	5	3	1	1	1
Pickled Ramps	5	0	0	0	20	1	0	1	0
Nettle Soup	230	16	9	35	490	14	2	2	7
Purslane and Watermelon Salad	170	12	4.5	20	220	11	1	8	6
Fiddlehead Panzanella	290	21	4	5	360	17	1	1	8
Smashed Potatoes with Sorrel-Almond Sauce	250	19	2.5	0	240	19	2	2	3
Orecchiette with Baby Dandelion Greens in Lemony Cream Sauce	550	28	14	65	640	61	4	3	17
Nettle and Mushroom Galette	490	33	16	90	660	36	3	3	11
Crispy Pan-Seared Sea Bass with Ramp Pesto	370	23	4	70	1270	4	1	2	34
FRESH LEGUMES									
Boiled Peanuts	160	14	2	0	300	5	2	1	7
Peanut Granola	300	17	3	5	220	32	4	9	7
Gingery Stir-Fried Edamame	130	7	0.5	0	240	8	4	3	11
Fava Bean Crostini with Manchego and Pine Nuts	210	10	2	5	290	22	6	8	9
Fava Bean and Radish Salad	250	11	1.5	0	320	28	10	14	13

	CALORIES	TOTAL FAT (G)	SAT FAT (G)	CHOL (MG)	SODIUM (MG)	TOTAL CARBS (G)	FIBER (G)	SUGAR (G)	PROTEIN (G)
FRESH LEGUMES (continued)									
Edamame Salad	320	20	2	0	600	19	8	10	18
Butternut Squash and Peanut Chili with Quinoa	580	38	15	0	660	55	11	10	13
Edamame and Spicy Peanut Noodle Bowls	480	23	2.5	0	410	57	5	6	13
Fried Rice with Bean Sprouts and Peas	350	9	1	60	780	55	2	2	11
Almost Hands-Free Risotto with Fava Beans, Peas, and Arugula	460	12	6	25	960	67	8	10	19
Sizzling Saigon Crêpes	300	11	3	0	960	44	4	8	6
Kung Pao Shrimp	350	23	3	105	630	16	3	4	19
GARLIC									
Roasted Garlic	35	1	0	0	75	5	0	0	1
Roasted Garlic Vinaigrette	80	7	1	0	120	2	0	1	0
Roasted Garlic Hummus	150	11	1.5	0	290	10	2	0	4
Garlic-Potato Soup	320	16	9	40	890	38	3	4	6
Garlicky Spaghetti with Lemon and Pine Nuts	680	30	4	5	420	87	5	3	20
Spanish Tortilla with Garlic Aïoli	590	51	7	310	650	22	2	2	12
Chicken with 40 Cloves of Garlic	730	53	18	270	610	14	1	2	43
Garlic Fried Chicken	1270	88	27	290	1450	51	3	0	64
Teriyaki Stir-Fried Garlic Scapes with Chicken	340	18	2.5	85	690	14	2	4	29
Sunday Best Garlic Roast Beef	430	23	5	155	630	3	0	0	54
Garlicky Broiled Shrimp with Parsley and Anise	240	18	6	165	270	2	0	0	16
Garlic Bread	260	13	7	30	460	29	2	2	5
Garlic Knots	140	6	3.5	15	280	18	1	0	3
GREEN BEANS									
Blanched Green Beans with Bistro Mustard Vinaigrette	170	14	2	0	240	8	3	3	2
Sautéed Green Beans with Garlic and Herbs	100	8	2.5	10	150	8	3	3	2
Green Beans Amandine	120	8	4	15	200	10	3.77	4	3
Roasted Green Beans with Goat Cheese and Hazelnuts	220	20	3.5	5	260	9	3.4	4	5
Mediterranean Braised Green Beans	160	12	1.5	0	630	12	4.06	6	3
Green Bean Salad with Cilantro Sauce	190	16	2	0	150	9	3.49	4	3
Tarragon-Mustard Bean Salad	110	7	1	0	190	10	3.1	6	2
Three-Bean Salad	140	7	1	0	320	17	4.41	7	4
Extra-Crunchy Green Bean Casserole	410	31	16	65	680	25	3.64	7	7
One-Pan Pork Tenderloin with Green Beans and Potatoes	580	25	10	140	1080	48	7.23	11	41
Stir-Fried Sichuan Green Beans	200	15	3.5	20	610	12	3.51	6	8
Stir-Fried Shrimp and Long Beans	320	19	3	145	830	18	4.71	6	21
HEARTY GREENS									
Quick Collard Greens	100	8	1	0	115	6	4	1	3
Collard Greens with Raisins and Almonds	240	17	2.5	0	640	18	5	11	5
Southern Braised Collard Greens	130	8	2.5	10	810	8	4	2	6
Black-Eyed Peas and Collard Greens	180	9	3	15	940	17	5	3	8
Garlicky Braised Kale	130	8	1	0	160	13	5	4	6
Slow-Cooker Braised Kale with Garlic and Chorizo	250	18	6	35	750	11	4	3	14
Kale Chips	60	4	0.5	0	160	5	2	1	3

	CALORIES	TOTAL FAT (G)	SAT FAT (G)	CHOL (MG)	SODIUM (MG)	TOTAL CARBS (G)	FIBER (G)	SUGAR (G)	PROTEIN (G)
HEARTY GREENS (continued)									
Kale Salad with Sweet Potatoes and Pomegranate Vinaigrette	240	16	2	0	200	22	4	10	3
Easy Chickpea and Kale Soup	190	9	1	0	1100	21	7	5	7
Caldo Verde	360	24	7	35	1190	22	3	1	14
Udon Noodles with Mustard Greens and Shiitake-Ginger Sauce	360	5	0	0	980	59	7	6	17
Salmon Tacos with Collard Slaw	490	27	5	85	510	28	5	1	34
Sausage and White Beans with Mustard Greens	350	17	4	25	1040	26	6	5	21
Smoked Trout Hash with Eggs	340	16	3.5	220	540	28	7	4	25
Whole-Wheat Pizza with Kale and Sunflower Seed Pesto	490	25	4.5	5	1000	54	7	3	15
HERBS									
Herb-Garlic Compound Butter	50	6	3.5	15	35	0	0	0	0
Classic Pesto	220	23	3	0	45	2	1	0	2
Parsley and Pecan Pesto	140	14	2	0	20	2	1	0	1
Oregano, Lemon, and Feta Pesto	210	21	3.5	5	45	3	0	1	2
Cilantro-Mint Chutney	10	0	0	0	35	1	0	1	0
Green Goddess Dip	200	21	4.5	20	200	2	0	1	1
Tabbouleh	190	14	2	0	210	14	3	2	3
Herbed Roast Chicken	670	51	18	215	470	3	1	1	47
Thai-Style Chicken with Basil	260	10	1	85	570	10	1	5	28
Grilled Argentine Steaks with Chimichurri Sauce	450	26	6	120	860	3	1	0	53
Rack of Lamb with Mint-Almond Relish	350	20	5	95	1270	6	1	4	36
Gravlax	110	6	1.5	25	700	4	0	4	9
Almost Hands-Free Risotto with Herbs and Parmesan	400	12	6	25	940	56	3	4	13
Summer Rolls with Basil and Spicy Almond Butter Sauce	290	10	1	0	640	37	6	9	14
Rosemary and Parmesan Drop Biscuits	190	10	6	30	350	19	1	1	5
Classic Bread Stuffing with Sage and Thyme	280	10	4.5	55	630	37	2	6	7
KOHLRABI, RUTABAGAS, AND TURNIPS									
Roasted Kohlrabi with Crunchy Seeds	100	8	1	0	310	7	4	3	2
Spicy Turnips with Chickpeas	170	6	0.5	0	550	25	6	8	6
Pink Pickled Turnips	10	0	0	0	200	2	1	2	0
Kohlrabi, Radicchio, and Apple Slaw	240	19	2.5	0	520	16	3	12	2
Creamy Kohlrabi Soup	190	15	6	25	560	13	6	7	5
Irish Stew with Turnips and Carrots	510	24	8	135	920	27	5	11	44
Vegetable Pot Pie	470	29	15	85	840	42	4	8	9
Root Vegetable Gratin	290	13	8	35	630	34	3	4	7
Simple Glazed Pork Tenderloins with Creamy Turnip Puree	850	48	27	220	1650	71	4	4	32
Cornish Pasties	450	20	10	115	440	34	4	23	26
LETTUCES AND LEAFY GREENS									
Simplest Salad	15	0	0	0	0	0	0	0	0
Bibb Lettuce, Orange, and Jícama Salad with Honey-Mustard Vinaigrette	150	10	1.5	0	260	14	4	8	2

	CALORIES	TOTAL FAT (G)	SAT FAT (G)	CHOL (MG)	SODIUM (MG)	TOTAL CARBS (G)	FIBER (G)	SUGAR (G)	PROTEIN (G)
LETTUCES AND LEAFY GREENS (continued)									
Wedge Salad	290	25	9	40	470	9	3	6	9
Killed Salad	230	17	6	30	880	13	1	11	6
Grilled Caesar Salad	360	32	5	10	600	13	2	2	5
Roast Chicken and Warm Bread Salad with Arugula	690	47	11	150	1050	23	2	4	42
Chinese Chicken Lettuce Wraps	300	17	2.5	105	940	10	2	3	26
Arugula Salad with Steak Tips and Gorgonzola	570	46	16	115	1130	8	2	4	35
Salmon, Avocado, Grapefruit, and Watercress Salad	780	55	10	125	620	23	11	11	50
Spaghetti al Vino Bianco	570	19	6	30	840	61	3	3	17
MUSHROOMS									
Sautéed Mushrooms with Shallot and Thyme	120	7	2	10	105	9	0	7	3
Roasted King Trumpet Mushrooms	140	11	7	30	300	7	0	5	3
Roasted Mushrooms with Parmesan and Pine Nuts	230	18	6	20	290	10	0	7	9
Marinated Mushrooms	80	7	1	0	135	3	0	2	1
Brioche Toasts with Mushroom Conserva and Ricotta	310	20	7	45	350	23	2	5	9
Shaved Mushroom and Celery Salad	140	12	2.5	5	290	4	1	2	5
Wild Rice and Mushroom Soup	260	12	7	30	890	29	2	4	7
Stir-Fried Portobellos with Soy-Maple Sauce	290	14	1.5	0	810	33	6	23	9
Grilled Portobello Burgers	700	58	12	35	1370	34	3	9	11
Mushroom Ragu	180	6	3.5	15	550	20	4	10	7
Mushroom Bolognese	470	10	5	25	810	73	5	11	15
Mushroom Bourguignon	320	15	2	0	600	20	4	10	11
Chicken Marsala	560	23	6	110	1510	30	2	15	35
OKRA									
Sautéed Okra	110	8	1	0	5	8	3	1	2
Roasted Okra with Fennel and Oregano	100	7	1	0	105	8	4	1	2
Greek Stewed Okra with Tomatoes	200	14	2	0	600	16	5	6	3
Charred Sichuan-Style Okra	360	28	2	0	770	18	4	6	3
Deep-Fried Okra	480	39	3	35	630	30	3	2	5
Cajun Pickled Okra	25	0	0	0	880	6	2	2	1
Caribbean Okra Pepper Pot	260	8	1	80	680	28	7	8	21
Gumbo	470	24	4	230	1130	19	2	3	43
Red Beans and Rice with Okra and Tomatoes	480	7	3	15	910	81	12	5	22
Madras Okra Curry	260	22	8	0	320	14	4	4	5
ONIONS									
Caramelized Onions	50	2	0	0	120	8	1	4	1
Glazed Pearl Onions	140	6	2	10	95	21	0	9	1
Balsamic Glazed Cipollini Onions	140	4	2.5	10	240	23	0	11	1
Braised Leeks	190	14	2	0	330	15	2	4	2
Slow-Cooker Braised Leeks	240	18	10	45	450	16	2	5	3
Grilled Onions with Balsamic Vinaigrette	360	28	4	0	880	25	4	13	3
Quick Sweet and Spicy Pickled Red Onions	10	0	0	0	35	3	0	2	0

	CALORIES	TOTAL FAT (G)	SAT FAT (G)	CHOL (MG)	SODIUM (MG)	TOTAL CARBS (G)	FIBER (G)	SUGAR (G)	PROTEIN (G)
ONIONS (continued)									
Beer-Battered Onion Rings	280	12	1	0	470	32	1	2	2
Caramelized Onion Dip	45	3	1.5	10	115	3	0	2	1
Roasted Cipollini and Escarole Salad	290	19	4.5	20	880	21	3	5	10
Creamy Leek and Potato Soup	160	8	4.5	20	620	20	2	4	3
Best French Onion Soup	390	19	11	55	1460	36	5	13	18
Mujaddara	470	14	2	5	810	73	10	10	15
Leek and Goat Cheese Quiche	410	29	16	175	370	24	1	5	11
Roasted Chicken Thighs with Creamed Shallots and Bacon	880	66	22	290	690	10	2	5	45
Oklahoma Fried Onion Cheeseburgers	440	25	11	85	1230	26	1	5	27
Southern-Style Smothered Pork Chops	590	37	5	85	1560	29	2	2	35
Braised Halibut with Leeks and Mustard	370	19	11	130	740	8	1	2	32
Pissaladière	470	13	2	5	900	73	5	8	14
Smoked Salmon and Leek Tart	290	18	10	90	470	22	1	3	9
PARSNIPS									
Sautéed Parsnips with Ginger, Maple, and Fennel Seeds	210	9	0.5	0	480	32	7	11	3
Pan-Roasted Parsnips	100	4	0	0	230	17	5	5	1
Simple Pureed Parsnips	150	4.5	2.5	10	15	26	7	7	2
Braised Parsnips with Cranberries	220	6	3.5	15	760	40	7	21	2
Glazed Parsnips and Celery	170	9	5	25	450	22	5	8	2
Parsnip Hummus	140	10	1.5	0	230	11	3	2	2
Creamy Root Vegetable Soup	230	15	9	45	630	21	3	5	3
Roasted Chicken with Honey-Glazed Parsnips	650	29	7	145	450	48	10	21	50
Red Wine–Braised Short Ribs with Bacon, Parsnips, and Pearl Onions	660	31	12	130	1140	29	5	10	43
PEAS									
Quick Buttered Peas	150	6	3.5	15	0	19	5	8	7
Smashed Minty Peas	130	7	4.5	20	50	11	4	4	5
Sautéed Snow Peas with Lemon and Parsley	70	3.5	0	0	150	7	2	4	2
Sugar Snap Peas with Pine Nuts, Fennel, and Lemon Zest	100	7	0.5	0	140	8	3	3	3
Ricotta Crostini with Peas and Mint	360	10	2	5	620	54	3	3	13
Pea Green Salad with Warm Apricot-Pistachio Vinaigrette	180	10	1	0	150	18	6	10	5
Black Rice Salad with Sugar Snap Peas and Ginger-Sesame Vinaigrette	280	13	1.5	0	250	39	4	4	5
Creamy Pea Soup	130	4.5	3	15	440	15	4	6	6
Risi e Bisi	280	12	2.5	10	610	32	3	3	13
Tagliatelle with Prosciutto and Peas	550	24	13	80	1180	62	4	4	24
Easy Sichuan-Style Orange Beef with Sugar Snap Peas	410	21	7	115	1020	13	2	9	40
Pan-Seared Scallops with Sugar Snap Pea Slaw	310	18	2.5	45	520	13	2	4	23

	CALORIES	TOTAL FAT (G)	SAT FAT (G)	CHOL (MG)	SODIUM (MG)	TOTAL CARBS (G)	FIBER (G)	SUGAR (G)	PROTEIN (G)
POTATOES									
Buttermilk Mashed Potatoes	340	17	11	50	410	37	2	3	7
French-Style Mashed Potatoes (Pommes Purée)	350	29	18	80	170	19	1	2	4
Slow-Cooker Mashed Potatoes	240	13	8	35	400	29	2	1	4
Braised Red Potatoes with Lemon and Chives	130	6	3.5	15	310	19	2	2	2
Best Baked Potatoes	210	3.5	0	0	85	41	3	1	5
Twice-Baked Potatoes with Bacon, Cheddar, and Scallions	340	23	12	60	240	24	2	2	10
Roasted Smashed Potatoes	350	21	3	0	330	36	4	3	4
Crisp Roasted Fingerling Potatoes	160	4.5	0.5	0	300	27	4	1	3
Salt-Crusted Fingerling Potatoes	120	0	0	0	400	27	4	1	3
Slow-Cooker Lemon-Herb Fingerling Potatoes	160	4.5	0.5	0	400	28	4	1	3
Potato Galette	180	7	4.5	20	300	26	2	0	3
Classic Potato Gratin	230	11	7	35	550	28	2	5	6
Kettle Chips	170	14	1	0	0	10	1	0	1
Thick-Cut Oven Fries	200	7	0.5	0	200	30	2	0	4
Easier French Fries	260	12	1	0	200	33	2	0	4
Patatas Bravas	320	22	2	5	630	29	2	2	4
Crispy Potato Latkes	140	7	1	35	250	17	1	1	3
Better Hash Browns	220	9	0.5	0	200	28	2	0	4
All-American Potato Salad	270	17	3.5	75	670	25	2	1	6
French Potato Salad with Dijon and Fines Herbes	190	10	1.5	0	260	25	3	2	3
Potato Gnocchi with Sage Brown Butter	370	12	7	75	900	56	3	1	9
Skillet-Roasted Chicken and Potatoes	710	36	8	165	1620	35	3	0	56
Shepherd's Pie	460	19	9	125	1030	41	4	6	30
Potato and Chorizo Tacos	630	33	6	40	1160	66	11	5	18
Lemon-Herb Cod Fillets with Crispy Garlic Potatoes	450	20	7	95	470	32	2	1	34
Potato Dinner Rolls	150	2.5	1.5	20	200	27	1	1	5
RADISHES									
Sautéed Radishes	80	6	3.5	15	200	6	3	3	2
Roasted Radishes with Yogurt-Tahini Sauce	160	12	4.5	20	420	12	4	6	4
Braised Radishes	50	3	2	10	240	5	2	3	1
Quick Pickled Radishes	5	0	0	0	25	1	0	0	0
Baguette with Radishes, Butter, and Herbs	120	11	6	25	90	6	1	1	1
Southwestern Radish and Apple Salad	510	43	10	30	880	27	10	12	12
Radish and Carrot Slaw with Sesame and Scallions	200	16	1.5	0	590	14	3	10	1
Sesame Noodles with Radishes, Cucumber, and Carrot	390	14	2	10	1220	55	4	8	14
Roasted Chicken with Radishes, Spinach, and Bacon	640	42	12	240	960	6	3	2	56
Vietnamese Pork Banh Mi	480	25	4.5	230	1320	35	2	12	29

	CALORIES	TOTAL FAT (G)	SAT FAT (G)	CHOL (MG)	SODIUM (MG)	TOTAL CARBS (G)	FIBER (G)	SUGAR (G)	PROTEIN (G)
RHIZOMES									
Ginger Lemonade	160	0	0	0	5	42	0	39	0
Fresh Horseradish Bloody Mary	130	1	0	0	960	14	4	7	3
Prepared Horseradish	10	0	0	0	35	2	1	1	0
Pickled Ginger	10	0	0	0	20	2	0	0	0
Shrimp Cocktail with Horseradish Cocktail Sauce	100	0.5	0	70	630	15	0	11	8
Fried Sunchokes	220	16	1	0	0	18	2	10	2
Sunchoke Chowder	260	20	12	55	460	16	2	9	3
Gingery Chicken Teriyaki	690	42	11	235	2040	29	0	28	44
Tandoori Chicken with Raita	400	18	4	190	520	9	1	5	49
Horseradish-Crusted Beef Tenderloin	480	31	9	120	1200	13	2	2	36
Spicy Citrus-Ginger Grilled Pork Tenderloin Steaks	380	24	3	100	470	6	0	4	32
Bold and Spicy Gingerbread Bundt Cake	490	16	10	100	330	80	1	57	5
SEA VEGETABLES									
Sesame Nori Chips	30	1.5	0	0	65	2	1	0	2
Popcorn with Nori Butter	110	8	3	10	0	8	2	0	1
Nori Powder	15	0	0	0	65	1	1	0	1
Pickled Sea Beans	10	0	0	0	125	2	0	1	0
Seaweed Salad	200	17	1.5	0	650	10	3	7	2
Black Rice and Sea Bean Salad	320	16	2	0	210	43	5	5	5
Miso Soup with Wakame and Tofu	70	1	0	0	790	10	1	5	5
Vegetable Shabu-Shabu with Sesame Sauce	270	8	0.5	0	1050	35	5	12	12
Nori Pappardelle with Blistered Cherry Tomatoes	500	23	5	235	920	50	4	2	19
Nori-Crusted Salmon	550	36	7	125	430	3	2	0	49
SPINACH									
Sautéed Baby Spinach with Almonds and Golden Raisins	240	14	1.5	0	250	23	5	15	6
Herbed Spinach Dip	130	13	2.5	10	310	3	1	1	2
Spanakopita	240	17	6	55	420	14	2	2	9
Wilted Spinach Salad with Warm Bacon-Pecan Vinaigrette	200	15	4	20	390	9	3	5	6
Lemon, Feta, and Pistachio Wilted Spinach Salad	130	10	2.5	5	105	6	2	3	3
Fusilli with Spinach and Ricotta	490	19	8	35	670	59	5	2	20
Spinach Lasagna	380	20	11	80	740	29	3	7	20
Saag Paneer	540	29	15	75	1640	46	5	35	27
Chicken Florentine	530	35	16	195	710	7	2	3	46
Breakfast Strata with Spinach and Gruyère	440	229	16	260	910	18	2	6	20
SWEET PEPPERS									
Roasted Bell Peppers	20	0	0	0	0	4	1	2	1
Grill-Roasted Peppers with Sherry Vinaigrette	190	15	2	0	300	12	4	7	2
Pimento Cheese Spread	300	26	13	65	470	3	0	0	14

	CALORIES	TOTAL FAT (G)	SAT FAT (G)	CHOL (MG)	SODIUM (MG)	TOTAL CARBS (G)	FIBER (G)	SUGAR (G)	PROTEIN (G)
SWEET PEPPERS (continued)									
Muhammara	190	16	2	0	350	10	1	5	2
Quinoa Salad with Red Bell Pepper and Cilantro	200	6	1	0	230	30	3	2	6
Roasted Red Pepper Soup with Paprika and Cilantro Cream	100	4.5	1.5	5	410	12	3	8	3
Eggs Pipérade	240	16	3.5	280	770	11	3	6	11
Cuban-Style Black Beans and Rice	430	21	7	20	940	50	4	5	10
Chicken Paprikash	700	45	13	245	1250	23	6	9	44
Stuffed Peppers with Chickpeas, Goat Cheese, and Herbs	450	27	7	15	1260	39	7	8	14
Slow-Roasted Pork Shoulder with Red Bell Pepper Chutney	300	11	3.5	95	1650	20	1	18	28
SWEET POTATOES									
Mashed Sweet Potatoes	280	14	9	40	400	35	6	12	3
Slow-Cooker Mashed Sweet Potatoes	160	5	3.5	15	300	27	4	9	3
Best Baked Sweet Potatoes with Garlic and Chive Sour Cream	220	4.5	2.5	15	200	42	7	13	4
Roasted Sweet Potatoes	140	3.5	0	0	370	26	4	8	2
Roasted Spiralized Sweet Potatoes with Walnuts and Feta	160	6	1.5	5	210	24	4	7	3
Thick-Cut Sweet Potato Fries	260	14	1	0	260	33	4	8	2
Sweet Potato Casserole	420	20	9	95	580	55	8	22	7
Sweet Potato and Swiss Chard Gratin	320	11	7	30	1350	42	9	13	10
Grilled Sweet Potato Salad	290	15	2.5	10	560	37	6	15	4
Sweet Potato Soup	210	9	6	25	660	30	4	12	3
Hearty Beef and Sweet Potato Chili	710	43	15	175	1100	34	9	8	45
Sweet Potato Vindaloo	210	5	0	0	960	38	7	10	5
Sweet Potato, Poblano, and Black Bean Tacos	350	9	1	0	680	60	10	15	7
Sweet Potato Biscuits	210	9	4.5	15	430	29	2	3	3
SWISS CHARD									
Garlicky Swiss Chard	90	7	1	0	390	6	2	2	3
Super Greens Soup with Lemon-Tarragon Cream	180	10	3.5	15	1010	19	3	4	5
Moroccan Lentil and Swiss Chard Soup	300	12	1.5	0	620	42	9	8	12
Fried Eggs with Garlicky Swiss Chard and Bell Pepper	190	12	2.5	185	810	11	4	3	10
Socca with Swiss Chard, Apricots, and Pistachios	480	31	4	0	630	40	11	10	13
Pasta with Beans, Swiss Chard, and Rosemary	400	11	3	15	910	56	10	3	20
Swiss Chard and Pinto Bean Enchiladas	460	25	3.5	10	1340	52	12	8	10
Swiss Chard Pie	380	25	14	75	730	27	3	2	11
Turkey Cutlets with Swiss Chard and Barley	600	15	2.5	75	1090	63	13	2	55
Pomegranate Roasted Salmon with Swiss Chard and Lentils	660	33	6	95	1000	45	10	13	48

	CALORIES	TOTAL FAT (G)	SAT FAT (G)	CHOL (MG)	SODIUM (MG)	TOTAL CARBS (G)	FIBER (G)	SUGAR (G)	PROTEIN (G)
TOMATILLOS AND CAPE GOOSEBERRIES									
Roasted Tomatillo Salsa	40	2.5	0	0	90	5	1	3	1
Tomatillo and Pinto Bean Nachos	710	46	15	60	1260	56	11	7	24
Shrimp Ceviche with Tomatillos, Jícama, and Avocado	200	12	1.5	55	470	19	5	3	8
Cape Gooseberry Salad with Ginger-Lime Dressing	220	19	4	5	210	9	3	1	5
Salad with Pickled Tomatillos, Sun-Dried Tomatoes, and Goat Cheese	100	7	2	5	260	7	2	3	4
Chicken Posole Verde	540	37	9	190	960	16	3	4	34
Enchiladas Verdes	500	25	8	90	840	40	8	11	32
Grilled Pork Tenderloins with Grilled Tomatillo Salsa	210	9	1.5	70	340	9	2	5	24
Pan-Roasted Cod with Amarillo Sauce	300	9	1	75	800	18	2	4	34
Cape Gooseberry–Rose Preserves	90	0	0	0	0	23	1	19	1
TOMATOES									
Fresh Tomato Sauce	90	7	1	0	300	6	2	4	1
Roasted Tomatoes	150	14	2	0	30	4	1	3	1
Slow-Cooker Tomatoes with Olive Oil	200	19	2.5	0	300	6	2	3	1
Fried Green Tomatoes	280	20	2	35	640	21	2	5	5
Spicy Tomato Jam	50	0	0	0	80	12	1	11	1
Fresh Tomato Salsa	15	0	0	0	0	3	1	2	1
Simple Tomato Salad	100	9	1	0	200	5	1	3	1
Cherry Tomato Salad with Basil and Fresh Mozzarella	180	13	6	25	210	7	2	5	8
Tomato and Burrata Salad with Pangrattato and Basil	300	24	7	25	400	15	2	6	10
Fresh Tomato Soup with Basil	160	8	1	0	310	21	6	13	5
Creamy Gazpacho Andaluz	240	19	2.5	0	420	14	4	7	3
Pasta with Tomato and Almond Pesto	440	18	2.5	5	590	58	4	3	13
Frittata with Sun-Dried Tomatoes, Mozzarella, and Basil	200	15	5	290	370	4	1	1	13
Stuffed Tomatoes	340	16	4.5	15	900	38	5	9	11
Best Summer Tomato Gratin	210	13	2.5	5	460	19	2	5	6
Grilled Pork Skewers with Grilled Tomato Relish	380	22	6	120	500	11	2	7	33
Thin-Crust Pizza	370	11	5	25	1120	50	2	6	16
WINTER SQUASH									
Maple-Glazed Acorn Squash	170	9	4	15	220	23	2	11	1
Stuffed Acorn Squash	600	26	3.5	5	930	84	9	22	15
Roasted Delicata Squash	150	12	3	10	220	11	2	2	1
Spaghetti Squash with Garlic and Parmesan	100	6	1	0	260	10	2	4	2
Butternut Squash Puree with Sage and Toasted Almonds	150	7	3.5	15	240	22	4	6	3

	CALORIES	TOTAL FAT (G)	SAT FAT (G)	CHOL (MG)	SODIUM (MG)	TOTAL CARBS (G)	FIBER (G)	SUGAR (G)	PROTEIN (G)
WINTER SQUASH (continued)									
Slow-Cooker Butternut Squash Puree	150	7	4.5	20	150	22	3	8	2
Roasted Butternut Squash with Browned Butter and Hazelnuts	210	15	7	30	200	20	4	4	3
Spaghetti Squash Salad with Tomatoes and Pecorino	210	18	3	5	480	12	3	5	3
Butternut Squash and White Bean Soup with Sage Pesto	520	34	8	20	1130	42	11	7	15
Barley Risotto with Roasted Butternut Squash	270	6	2	10	430	43	8	3	9
Butternut Squash Gnudi with Kale, Parmesan, and Pepitas	520	35	17	70	600	41	8	7	16
Butternut Squash Galette with Gruyère	500	30	16	100	430	45	5	5	12
ZUCCHINI AND SUMMER SQUASH									
Roasted Baby Pattypan Squash	70	6	3.5	15	95	5	1	4	1
Sautéed Zucchini	90	7	1	0	35	5	1	3	1
Braised Zucchini	80	7	1	0	300	4	1	3	1
Greek Stewed Zucchini	100	6	1	0	420	10	2	6	3
Grilled Zucchini and Red Onion with Lemon Vinaigrette	150	14	2	0	500	4	1	2	1
Fried Zucchini Sticks with Spicy Aïoli	390	32	3.5	5	720	20	1	2	3
Fried Stuffed Zucchini Blossoms	500	26	6	80	200	31	1	0	12
Zucchini Ribbon Salad with Shaved Parmesan	310	27	7	20	520	4	1	3	14
Zucchini Noodle Salad with Tahini-Ginger Dressing	380	26	3.5	0	1610	31	8	15	15
Zucchini Noodles with Roasted Tomatoes and Cream Sauce	490	42	21	90	1140	20	5	13	12
Zucchini and Orzo Tian	340	11	4	15	940	43	4	9	18
Mediterranean Stuffed Zucchini	390	24	7	40	740	30	6	11	16
Halibut in Foil with Zucchini and Tomatoes	260	10	1.5	85	370	6	1	3	33
Zucchini Bread	230	6	0.5	30	450	41	2	22	4

Conversions and Equivalents

Some say cooking is a science and an art. We would say geography has a hand in it, too. Flours and sugars manufactured in the United Kingdom and elsewhere will feel and taste different from those manufactured in the United States. So we cannot promise that a loaf of bread you bake in Canada or England will taste the same as a loaf baked in the States, but we can offer guidelines for converting weights and measures. We also recommend that you rely on your instincts when making our recipes. Refer to the visual cues provided. If the dough hasn't come together as described, you may need to add more flour—even if the recipe doesn't tell you to. You be the judge.

The recipes in this book were developed using standard U.S. measures following U.S. government guidelines. The charts below offer equivalents for U.S. and metric measures. All conversions are approximate and have been rounded up or down to the nearest whole number.

EXAMPLE:
1 teaspoon = 4.9292 milliliters, rounded up to 5 milliliters
1 ounce = 28.3495 grams, rounded down to 28 grams

VOLUME CONVERSIONS	
U.S.	**METRIC**
1 teaspoon	5 milliliters
2 teaspoons	10 milliliters
1 tablespoon	15 milliliters
2 tablespoons	30 milliliters
¼ cup	59 milliliters
⅓ cup	79 milliliters
½ cup	118 milliliters
¾ cup	177 milliliters
1 cup	237 milliliters
1¼ cups	296 milliliters
1½ cups	355 milliliters
2 cups (1 pint)	473 milliliters
2½ cups	591 milliliters
3 cups	710 milliliters
4 cups (1 quart)	0.946 liter
1.06 quarts	1 liter
4 quarts (1 gallon)	3.8 liters

WEIGHT CONVERSIONS	
OUNCES	**GRAMS**
½	14
¾	21
1	28
1½	43
2	57
2½	71
3	85
3½	99
4	113
4½	128
5	142
6	170
7	198
8	227
9	255
10	283
12	340
16 (1 pound)	454

CONVERSIONS FOR INGREDIENTS COMMONLY USED IN BAKING

Baking is an exacting science. Because measuring by weight is far more accurate than measuring by volume, and thus more likely to achieve reliable results, in our recipes we provide ounce measures in addition to cup measures for many ingredients. Refer to the chart below to convert these measures into grams.

INGREDIENT	OUNCES	GRAMS
Flour		
1 cup all-purpose flour*	5	142
1 cup whole-wheat flour	5½	156
Sugar		
1 cup granulated (white) sugar	7	198
1 cup packed brown sugar (light or dark)	7	198
1 cup confectioners' sugar	4	113
Butter†		
4 tablespoons (½ stick, or ¼ cup)	2	57
8 tablespoons (1 stick, or ½ cup)	4	113
16 tablespoons (2 sticks, or 1 cup)	8	227

* U.S. all-purpose flour, the most frequently used flour in this book, does not contain leaveners, as some European flours do. These leavened flours are called self-rising or self-raising. If you are using self-rising flour, take this into consideration before adding leavening to a recipe.

† In the United States, butter is sold both salted and unsalted. We generally recommend unsalted butter. If you are using salted butter, take this into consideration before adding salt to a recipe.

OVEN TEMPERATURES

FAHRENHEIT	CELSIUS	GAS MARK
225	105	¼
250	120	½
275	135	1
300	150	2
325	165	3
350	180	4
375	190	5
400	200	6
425	220	7
450	230	8
475	245	9

CONVERTING FAHRENHEIT TO CELSIUS

We include doneness temperatures in many of the recipes in this book. We recommend an instant-read thermometer for the job. Refer to the above table to convert Fahrenheit degrees to Celsius. Or, for temperatures not represented in the chart, use this simple formula:

Subtract 32 degrees from the Fahrenheit reading, then divide the result by 1.8 to find the Celsius reading.

EXAMPLE:
"Roast chicken until thighs register 175 degrees."
To convert:
$175°F - 32 = 143°$
$143° \div 1.8 = 79.44°C$, rounded down to 79°C

Index

Note: Page references in *italics* indicate photographs.

A

Aïoli, Spicy, 482
Algerian-Style Fennel Salad with Oranges and Olives, 198
All-American Potato Salad, 356–57
Allium family, 311
Almond Butter Sauce, Spicy, Summer Rolls with Basil and, 267–69
Almond(s)
  and Carrots, Bulgur Salad with, 94
  Coriander, and Orange Zest, Sugar Snap Peas with, 337
  Goat Cheese, and Grapes, Asparagus Salad with, 18
  and Golden Raisins, Sautéed Baby Spinach with, 398
  Green Beans Amandine, 238–39
  and Green Olives, Garlicky Spaghetti with, 228
  and Lemon, Braised Beets with, 36, *37*
  -Mint Relish, 266
  Raisin and Caper Relish, 105
  and Raisins, Collard Greens with, 248
  and Raisins, Sautéed Beet Greens with, 34
  and Red Pepper Relish, Whole Carrots with, *88*, 89–90
  Smoked, and Dates, Citrus-Radicchio Salad with, 134, *135*
  -Sorrel Sauce, Smashed Potatoes with, *209*, 209–10
  Toasted, and Sage, Butternut Squash Puree with, 466
  and Tomato Pesto, Pasta with, 456
  and Vadouvan Curry, Sautéed Radishes with, 366
Almost Hands-Free Risotto with Fava Beans, Peas, and Arugula, 221
Almost Hands-Free Risotto with Herbs and Parmesan, 267
Anaheim chiles, about, 140
Ancho chiles, about, 140
Anchovy(ies)
  and Capers, Braised Cauliflower with, 102
  -Garlic Butter, Grilled Broccoli with, 48
  Pissaladière, 323–25
Anise seeds, about, 193
Apple(s)
  Arugula, and Parmesan, Radicchio Salad with, 133
  Braised Carrots with, 89
  Braised Red Cabbage, 75
  and Brussels Sprouts, Skillet Bratwurst with, 66–67
  Celery Root, and Celery Slaw, 123
  Celery Root, and Fennel Chowder, 123–24
  Cheddar, and Hazelnuts, Brussels Sprout Salad with, 66

Apple(s) *(cont.)*
  and Cream, Braised Radicchio with, 129
  Kohlrabi, and Radicchio Slaw, 275
  and Parsley, Celery Root Salad with, *122*, 122–23
  and Radish Salad, Southwestern, 368–71, *370*
  and Walnuts, Napa Cabbage Slaw with, 79
Apricot(s)
  Mediterranean Stuffed Zucchini, 485, *485*
  -Pistachio Vinaigrette, Warm, Pea Green Salad with, 338, *339*
  Swiss Chard, and Pistachios, Socca with, 434, *434*
Artichoke(s), 2–11
  anatomy of, 3
  Braised, with Tomatoes and Thyme, 6
  cut, preventing browning of, 3
  Fennel, Tomatoes, and Olives, Spice-Rubbed Pork Tenderloin with, 200
  fresh, preparing, 3
  Grilled, with Lemon Butter, 6–8, *7*
  Hearts and Parmesan, Bruschetta with, 10
  Jewish-Style Fried, 8, *9*
  Marinated, 10
  and Parmesan, Tagliatelle with, 11
  Roasted, Dip, 8–10
  Roasted, with Lemon Vinaigrette, *4*, 5
  Roman-Style Stuffed Braised, 5
  shopping and storage, 3
  Slow-Cooker Braised, with Garlic Butter, 6
  Soup à la Barigoule, 11
Arugula
  about, 281
  Apple, and Parmesan, Radicchio Salad with, 133
  Carrots, and Olives, Chickpea Salad with, 94
  Edamame Salad, 219
  Fava Beans, and Peas, Almost Hands-Free Risotto with, 221
  and Feta Guacamole, 24
  -Goat Cheese Fresh Corn Salad, 164
  Marinated Beet Salad with Oranges and Pecorino, 39
  Marinated Beet Salad with Pear and Feta, 39
  Marinated Beet Salad with Raspberries and Blue Cheese, 39
  Roast Chicken and Warm Bread Salad with, 285
  Salad with Steak Tips and Gorgonzola, 286
  Spaghetti al Vino Bianco, 287, *287*
  Super Greens Soup with Lemon-Tarragon Cream, 431
Asian-Style Swiss Chard, 431
Asparagus, 12–21
  cutting on bias, 13
  and Fresh Basil Dressing, Tortellini Salad with, 18–19

Asparagus *(cont.)*
  -Goat Cheese Tart, 20, *21*
  Grilled, 17–18
  Grilled, with Chili-Lime Butter, 18
  Grilled, with Orange-Thyme Butter, 18
  Pan-Roasted, 14
  Pan-Roasted, with Cherry Tomatoes and Kalamata Olives, 14
  Pan-Roasted, with Red Onion and Bacon, 14
  Parmesan-Crusted, *16*, 17
  Peas, and Radishes, Braised, with Tarragon, 17
  Roasted, with Cilantro-Lime Gremolata, 14
  Roasted, with Mint-Orange Gremolata, 14, *15*
  Roasted, with Tarragon-Lemon Gremolata, 14
  Salad with Grapes, Goat Cheese, and Almonds, 18
  Salad with Oranges, Feta, and Hazelnuts, 18
  Salad with Radishes, Pecorino Romano, and Croutons, 18
  shopping and storage, 13
  Soup, Creamy, *19*, 19–20
  Stir-Fried, with Red Bell Pepper, 20
  Stir-Fried, with Shiitake Mushrooms, 20
  trimming and peeling, 13
  varieties and colors, 13
Avocado(s), 22–31
  Charred, Relish, Crispy Skillet Turkey Burgers with, *28*, 29
  Chipotle and Pepita Guacamole, 24
  Crema, 254
  cut, storing, 23
  determining ripeness, 23
  dicing, 23
  Dressing, Creamy, Cobb Salad with, 26–27
  Feta and Arugula Guacamole, 24
  Habanero and Mango Guacamole, 24
  and Orange, Shrimp Salad with, 27
  pitting, 23
  Power Smoothie, 24
  Salad with Mangos and Jícama, 26
  Salad with Oranges and Fennel, 26
  Salad with Tomatoes and Radishes, 26
  Salmon, Grapefruit, and Watercress Salad, 286–87
  Sauce, Bean and Beef Taquitos with, 24–26
  shopping and storage, 23
  Snow Peas, and Lemon-Yogurt Sauce, California Barley Bowls with, 30
  Super Guacamole, 24, *25*
  Toast, 30, *31*
  and Toasted Cumin, Fresh Corn Salsa with, 162
  Toast with Fried Eggs, 30
  Tomatillos, and Jícama, Shrimp Ceviche with, 441–42
  Tuna Poke with, 29–30
  varieties of, 22

J

Jalapeño chiles, about, 140
Jam, Spicy Tomato, 452, *452*
Jerk Chicken, 148–50, *149*
Jewish-Style Fried Artichokes, 8, *9*
Jícama
  Bibb Lettuce, and Orange Salad with
    Honey-Mustard Vinaigrette, 282
  and Mangos, Avocado Salad with, 26
  and Pepitas, Napa Cabbage Slaw with, 79
  and Pineapple, Fresh Corn Salsa with, 162
  Salmon Tacos with Collard Slaw, 254
  Tomatillos, and Avocado, Shrimp Ceviche with,
    441–42

K

Kale
  about, 246, 247
  and Brussels Sprouts Slaw with Herbs
    and Peanuts, 66
  and Chickpea Soup, Easy, 253
  Chips, 251, *251*
  Chips, Ranch-Style, 251
  Chips, Spicy Sesame-Ginger, 251
  curly, about, 247
  Garlicky Braised, 250
  Garlicky Braised, with Bacon and Onion,
    250
  Garlicky Braised, with Coconut and Curry,
    250
  Lacinato, about, 247
  Parmesan, and Pepitas, Butternut Squash
    Gnudi with, 472–74, *473*
  Power Smoothie, 24
  Roasted, Carrots, and Fried Eggs, Brown Rice
    Bowls with, 93–94
  Salad with Sweet Potatoes and Pomegranate
    Vinaigrette, 251–53, *252*
  shopping and storage, 247
  Slow-Cooker Braised, with Garlic and
    Chorizo, 250–51
  and Sunflower Seed Pesto, Whole-Wheat
    Pizza with, *256*, 257
  Super Greens Soup with Lemon-Tarragon
    Cream, 431
Kettle Chips, 353, *353*
Killed Salad, 283
Kimchi Beef and Tofu Soup, *80*, 81
Kohlrabi
  about, 270
  peeling, 271
  Radicchio, and Apple Slaw, 275
  Roasted, with Crunchy Seeds, 272
  shopping and storage, 271
  slicing, 271
  Soup, Creamy, *274*, 275
Kombu
  about, 386, 387
  Dashi, 391
  Seaweed Salad, *390*, 390–91
  shopping for, 387

Kombu *(cont.)*
  Vegetable Shabu-Shabu with Sesame
    Sauce, 393
Kung Pao Shrimp, 222, *223*

L

Lamb
  Irish Stew with Turnips and Carrots, 275–76
  Mediterranean Stuffed Zucchini, 485, *485*
  Pita Sandwiches, Greek-Style, with Tzatziki
    Sauce, *176*, 176–77
  Rack of, with Mint-Almond Relish, 266
Lasagna, Spinach, 402
Latkes, Crispy Potato, 355–56
Lavash Pizzas with Cauliflower, Fennel, and
    Coriander, 112
Leafy greens, 280–87
  drying, for salads, 281
  pairing with vinaigrettes, 281
  shopping and storage, 281
  types of, 280, 281
  see also specific types of greens
Leek(s)
  about, 311
  Braised, 313, *313*
  Braised, Slow-Cooker, 313–14
  and Chives, Buttermilk Mashed Potatoes
    with, 346
  and Goat Cheese Quiche, 320
  and Mustard, Braised Halibut with,
    322–23, *323*
  and Potato Soup, Creamy, 317
  shopping and storage, 311
  and Smoked Salmon Tart, *324*, 325
Legumes, fresh
  types of, 214, 215
  see also Bean Sprouts; Edamame; Fava
    Bean(s); Peanut(s)
Lemon
  –Brown Butter Vinaigrette, 290
  Browned Butter, Pan-Roasted Broccoli
    with, 46
  Butter, Grilled Artichokes with, 6–8, *7*
  -Chive Dipping Sauce, Fried Brussels Sprouts
    with, 65–66
  -Chive Dipping Sauce, Fried Fiddleheads
    with, 204, *205*
  Feta, and Pistachio Wilted Spinach Salad, 401
  Ginger Lemonade, 377
  -Herb Cod Fillets with Crispy Garlic
    Potatoes, 362
  and Parmesan, Grilled Broccoli with, 48, *49*
  and Parsley, Sautéed Cabbage with, 74
  and Pecorino Romano, Pan-Roasted Brussels
    Sprouts with, 62
  and Pine Nuts, Garlicky Spaghetti with,
    227, 227–28
  -Tarragon Gremolata, Roasted Asparagus
    with, 14
  and Thyme, Honey-Glazed Carrots with, 91
  Vinaigrette, Roasted Artichokes with, *4*, 5
Lemony Roasted Radicchio, Fennel, and
    Root Vegetables, 129–31

Lentil(s)
  Escarole, and Pancetta, Whole-Wheat
    Pasta with, 137
  -Escarole Soup, 134
  Mujaddara, 319–20
  and Swiss Chard, Pomegranate Roasted
    Salmon with, 437, *437*
  and Swiss Chard Soup, Moroccan, 432
Lettuce, 280–87
  bibb, about, 281
  Bibb, Orange, and Jícama Salad with
    Honey-Mustard Vinaigrette, 282
  Bistro Salad, 132–33
  Boston, about, 281
  Cape Gooseberry Salad with Ginger-Lime
    Dressing, 442
  Chinese Chicken Salad, 79–81
  Cobb Salad with Creamy Avocado
    Dressing, 26–27
  Grilled Caesar Salad, *283*, 283–85
  iceberg, about, 281
  Killed Salad, 283
  loose-leaf, about, 281
  mâche, about, 281
  mesclun, about, 281
  romaine, about, 281
  Salad with Pickled Tomatillos, Sun-Dried
    Tomatoes, and Goat Cheese, 442–44, *443*
  shopping and storage, 281
  Simplest Salad, 282
  Smashed Minty Peas, 336
  Wedge Salad, 282
  Wraps, Chinese Chicken, *284*, 285–86
Lime
  -Chili Butter, Grilled Asparagus with, 18
  -Chili Salt, Foolproof Boiled Corn with,
    158, 159
  and Cilantro, Garlicky Broiled Shrimp with,
    232, 234
  -Cilantro Butter, Husk-Grilled Corn with, 160
  -Cilantro Gremolata, Roasted Asparagus
    with, 14
  Cumin, and Cilantro, Boiled Carrots with, 86
  -Cumin Dressing, Steamed Broccoli with, 46
  Mango, and Peanut Wilted Spinach Salad, 401
  and Pepitas, Braised Beets with, 36

M

Maccheroni di Fuoco, 146
Mâche, about, 281
Madras Okra Curry, 309, *309*
Mango(s)
  Baja-Style Cauliflower Tacos, 112
  and Habanero Guacamole, 24
  and Jícama, Avocado Salad with, 26
  Lime, and Peanut Wilted Spinach Salad, 401
  and Lime-Curry Vinaigrette, Cherry Tomato
    Salad with, 453
Maple
  -Chipotle Mayonnaise, Corn Fritters with, 162
  -Glazed Acorn Squash, 464
  -Glazed Brussels Sprouts, 65
  Sour Cream, 424